TEACH
Instructor Resource Manual

for

Basic Pharmacology for Nurses

15th Edition

Bruce Clayton
Yvonne Stock
Sandra Cooper

Prepared by:
Michelle Willihnganz, RN, MS

ELSEVIER
MOSBY

3251 Riverport Lane
St. Louis, Missouri 63043

TEACH Instructor Resource Manual
for BASIC PHARMACOLOGY FOR NURSES

ISBN: 978-0-323-06780-5

Notices

Knowledge and best practice in this field are constantly changing. As new research and experience broaden our understanding, changes in research methods, professional practices, or medical treatment may become necessary.

Practitioners and researchers must always rely on their own experience and knowledge in evaluating and using any information, methods, compounds, or experiments described herein. In using such information or methods, they should be mindful of their own safety and the safety of others, including parties for whom they have a professional responsibility.

With respect to any drug or pharmaceutical products identified, readers are advised to check the most current information provided (i) on procedures featured or (ii) by the manufacturer of each product to be administered, to verify the recommended dose or formula, the method and duration of administration, and contraindications. It is the responsibility of practitioners, relying on their own experience and knowledge of their patients, to make diagnoses, to determine dosages and the best treatment for each individual patient, and to take all appropriate safety precautions.

To the fullest extent of the law, neither the Publisher nor the authors, contributors, or editors, assume any liability for any injury and/or damage to persons or property as a matter of products liability, negligence or otherwise, or from any use or operation of any methods, products, instructions, or ideas contained in the material herein.

International Standard Book Number: 978-0-323-06780-5

Senior Editor: Lee Henderson
Senior Developmental Editor: Rae Robertson
Publishing Services Manager: Anne Altepeter
Senior Project Manager: Doug Turner

Transferred to Digital Printing 2009

How to Use This Instructor Resource Manual

Welcome to TEACH, your Total Curriculum Solution!

This Instructor Resource Manual is designed to help you prepare for classes using ***Basic Pharmacology for Nurses,*** 15th Edition, by Bruce Clayton, Yvonne Stock, and Sandra Cooper. We hope it will reduce your lesson preparation time, give you new and creative ideas to promote student learning, and help you make full use of the rich array of resources in the Clayton teaching package.

The lesson plans are designed to promote active student learning and get students involved in class discussions and activities. They include assessment tools to help you gauge your students' understanding of the course material and adapt lessons to their needs.

Each textbook chapter is divided into 50-minute lessons—building blocks that can be sequenced to fit your class schedule. The lesson plans are available in electronic format so that you can customize them to fit the requirements of your course.

Every lesson includes a wide variety of teaching resources. In many cases, our subject matter experts have provided more resources and activities than can be covered in a 50-minute lesson. We encourage you to choose activities that match the needs of your students and your curriculum, as well as the materials and resources available at your school.

Lesson plans can be a valuable tool for documenting how your curriculum covers learning objectives in compliance with accrediting organizations. Some accrediting organizations require that learning resources be integrated into a program's curriculum to enhance students' learning experiences. The activities in this Instructor Resource Manual will help your students use resources such as the library and the Internet to complement their textbook.

Instructor Resource Manual Format

The Instructor Resource Manual is available on Evolve online at http://evolve.elsevier.com/Clayton. Access codes are available from your sales representative.

Instructor Resource Manual Organization

TEACH lesson plans complement Elsevier textbooks; there is a lesson plan chapter for each book chapter. Each lesson plan chapter includes the following three sections:

1. **Preparation:** checklists to help you prepare classes based on the chapter
2. **Lessons:** each chapter divided into 50-minute lessons, providing you with the building blocks for your curriculum
3. **Lecture Outlines:** also divided into 50-minute lessons

Preparation

The Preparation section ensures that you are well prepared for class and includes the following checklists:

- *Teaching Focus*—identifies key student learning goals for the chapter
- *Materials and Resources*—lists materials needed for each lesson within the chapter
- *Lesson Checklist*—includes instructor preparation suggestions
- *Key Terms*—provides page references for each key term in the chapter
- *Additional Resources*—lists instructor resources available for this chapter

Lessons

Each chapter includes the following sections:

Background Assessment. The first lesson in each chapter includes two Background Assessment questions designed to help you gauge your students' readiness for the lesson. Depending on students' responses, you may wish to modify your lesson. Students who are comfortable with the topic may need more challenging activities. Students who have difficulty with the topic may need to start by addressing more fundamental concepts.

Critical Thinking Question. Every lesson includes a Critical Thinking Question to motivate students by demonstrating real-world applications of the lesson content.

Lesson Roadmap. The heart of the TEACH lesson plan is the three-column roadmap that links Objectives and Content from ***Basic Pharmacology for Nurses*** with its Teaching Resources. Teaching Resources reference all the elements of the ancillary package and include additional teaching tips such as Class Activities, discussion topics, and much more. This section correlates your textbook and its ancillary materials with the objectives on which your course is based.

Homework/Assignments and *Instructor's Notes/Student Feedback.* These sections are provided for you to add your own assignments, record student feedback, and write other notes relating to the lesson.

Lecture Outlines

The Lecture Outlines include PowerPoint slides to provide a compelling visual presentation and summary of the main chapter points. Lecture notes for each slide highlight key topics and provide questions for discussion to help create an interactive classroom environment.

We encourage you to select material from the Instructor Resource Manual that meets your students' needs, to integrate TEACH into your existing lesson plans, and to put your own teaching approach into the plans. We hope that TEACH will be an invaluable tool in your classroom.

Table of Contents

Basic Pharmacology for Nurses

LESSON PLANS AND LECTURE OUTLINES

UNIT I FOUNDATIONS OF PHARMACOLOGY

UNIT II ILLUSTRATED ATLAS OF MEDICATION ADMINISTRATION AND MATH REVIEW

UNIT III DRUGS AFFECTING THE AUTONOMIC AND CENTRAL NERVOUS SYSTEMS

UNIT IV DRUGS AFFECTING THE CARDIOVASCULAR SYSTEM

1 Lesson Plan
Definitions, Names, Standards, and Information Sources

TEACHING FOCUS

In this chapter, the student will learn foundation topics related to pharmacology, including drug names, standards, and reference sources. The student has the opportunity to differentiate between chemical drug names, generic drug names, official drug names, and brand names. Additionally, the chapter presents the various references available, which health professionals use to validate drug names, usage, doses, interactions, and side effects. The student has the opportunity to become acquainted with the drug development process and the federal regulations that govern prescription medications.

MATERIALS AND RESOURCES

- ☐ computer and PowerPoint projector (all Lessons)
- ☐ drug reference (Lesson 1.1)
- ☐ *Physicians' Desk Reference* (PDR) (Lesson 1.1)
- ☐ Internet access (Lesson 1.2)

LESSON CHECKLIST

Preparations for this lesson include:

- lecture
- guest speakers: registered nurse, U.S. Food and Drug Administration (FDA) representative
- evaluation of student comprehension and skills needed for entry-level activities related to patient care, including:
  - drug names
  - effects of drugs on the body
  - drug interactions
  - reviewing and locating drugs in reference guides

KEY TERMS

American Drug Index (p. 3)
American Hospital Formulary Service, Drug Information (p. 3)
birth defect (p. 11)
brand name (p. 2)
chemical name (p. 1)
clinical research (p. 9)
Compendium of Pharmaceuticals and Specialties (CPS) (p. 12)
Compendium of Self-Care Products (CSCP) (p. 13)
Controlled Drugs and Substances Act, 1997 (p. 14)
Controlled Substances Act (p. 7)
Drug Facts and Comparisons (p. 4)
Drug Interaction Facts (p. 4)
drugs (p. 1)
European Pharmacopoeia (p. 12)
Federal Food, Drug, and Cosmetic Act (p. 7)
Food and Drug Regulations (p. 12)
Food and Drug Regulations, 1953, 1954, 1979 (p. 14)
Food and Drugs Act, 1927 (p. 14)
generic name (p. 1)
Handbook of Nonprescription Drugs: An Interactive Approach to Self-Care (p. 4)
Handbook on Injectable Drugs (p. 4)
Health on the Net Foundation (HON) (p. 7)
health orphans (p. 10)
illegal drugs (p. 2)
Martindale—The Complete Drug Reference (p. 5)
medicines (p. 1)
Natural Medicines Comprehensive Database (p. 5)
New Drug Application (p. 10)
nonprescription drugs (p. 15)
official name (p. 2)
over-the-counter (OTC) drugs (p. 2)
Patient Self-Care: Helping Patients Make Therapeutic Choices (p. 13)
pharmacology (p. 1)
Physicians' Desk Reference (PDR) (p. 5)
postmarketing surveillance (p. 10)
preclinical research (p. 9)
proprietary names (p. 2)
schedules (p. 7)
teratogens (p. 11)
The United States Pharmacopeia (USP)/National Formulary (NF) (p. 2)
Therapeutic Choices (p. 14)
therapeutic methods (p. 1)
trademark (p. 2)

ELSEVIER

ADDITIONAL RESOURCES

PowerPoint slides (IER): 1-18

Legend

ARQ	PPT	TB	CTQ	SG	INRQ
Audience Response Questions	PowerPoint Slides	Test Bank	Critical Thinking Questions	Study Guide	Interactive NCLEX Review Questions

Class Activities are indicated in ***bold italic.***

LESSON 1.1

BACKGROUND ASSESSMENT

Question: What is the primary focus of the FDA?
Answer: The primary focus of the FDA is to protect the public from risks associated with the manufacture and sale of drugs.

Question: What is a "scheduled" drug?
Answer: The term *scheduled drug* was initiated by the Controlled Substance Act in 1970 to classify drugs according to their potential for abuse. There are five classifications ranging from a high potential to a low potential for abuse. Examples: schedule I, LSD; schedule II, morphine; schedule III, Tylenol with codeine; schedule IV, diazepam; schedule V, diphenoxylate. Schedule V drugs may not require a prescription.

CRITICAL THINKING QUESTION

The physician wrote an order for metoclopramide (Reglan), 10 mg IV, for a patient who is currently receiving potassium chloride IV. The nurse is unfamiliar with the drug metoclopramide; she has not given this drug in the past. What are the sources of information the nurse can use to learn more about the drug?
Guidelines: Many drug references provide extensive monographs containing vital information about drug administration. Three other useful sources of information for drugs are the PDR, *Drug Facts and Comparisons*, and the *Handbook on Injectable Drugs*. The PDR offers general information and includes reprints of drug package inserts. *Drug Facts and Comparisons* is particularly useful for drug interaction information, and the *Handbook on Injectable Drugs* is an authoritative source of information about injectable drug compatibilities.

OBJECTIVES	CONTENT	TEACHING RESOURCES
State the origin and definition of pharmacology.	■ Definitions (p. 1) □ Pharmacology (p. 1) Review the definition of pharmacology and differentiate from therapeutic methods.	PPT 5 SG Review Sheet question 1 (p. 1) SG Learning Activities questions 1, 4-5, 17 (p. 3) ▸ *Discuss the history and evolution of pharmacology as a critical role in the nursing profession.* ▸ *Discuss the importance of understanding pharmacology and how the knowledge impacts patient care.*

OBJECTIVES	CONTENT	TEACHING RESOURCES
		Class Activity ***Give students the following list of terms and have them identify the two that combined provide the meaning of the word pharmacology:*** – ***Study*** – ***Science*** – ***Medications*** – ***Herbs*** – ***Drugs*** – ***Collection*** – ***Therapeutic*** Class Activity ***Divide the class into four groups and have each group take one of the following topics to discuss in class: drug therapy, diet therapy, physiotherapy, and psychological therapy.***
Explain the meaning of therapeutic methods.	□ Therapeutic methods (p. 1) □ Drugs (p. 1)	PPT 5 TB Multiple Response question 1 INRQ 1 SG Practice Question for the NCLEX Examination (p. 4) ▸ Discuss the terms *drugs* and *medications* as they are appropriately used in the clinical practice. Class Activity ***Lead a discussion in which students identify conditions that may require a combination of therapeutic methods for treatment. What are some examples of therapeutic methods? Explain why these illnesses are not effectively managed with one therapeutic method. What role do drugs play?***
Describe the process used to name drugs.	■ Drug names (United States) (p. 1) Discuss how drugs are named and how to tell the difference between generic and brand names.	PPT 7 TB Multiple Choice question 1 INRQ 2 SG Learning Activities question 2 (p. 3) Review Question for the NCLEX Examination 5 (p. 15) ▸ Discuss incidents in which medication errors occurred as a result of failure to administer the correct prescribed drug. ▸ Discuss incidents in which spelling errors or poor penmanship jeopardized patient health. Class Activity ***Divide the class into groups, and assign each group one of the following types of drug names: chemical, generic, official, and trade. Ask each group to explain what the terms mean and to provide an example of the four names for the same drug. Then give***

ELSEVIER

OBJECTIVES	CONTENT	TEACHING RESOURCES
		groups the drug names listed below and have them give the additional three names for each. Students may use a drug reference book. – ***acetazolamide*** – ***pantoprazole*** – ***metronidazole***
Differentiate among the chemical, generic, official, and brand names of medicines.	□ Chemical name (p. 1) □ Generic name (nonproprietary name) (p. 1) □ Official name (p. 2) □ Trademark (brand name) (p. 2) □ Drug classifications (p. 2)	PPT 6-7 INRQ 4 ARQ 1 CTQ 1, 2 SG Review Sheet questions 4-7 (p. 1) SG Learning Activities question 2 (p. 3) SG Practice Question for the NCLEX Examination (p. 4) Review Question for the NCLEX Examination 1 (p. 15) Figure 1-1 (p. 2): Ampicillin, an antibiotic. ▸ Discuss how and why chemical, generic, and brand names developed. ▸ Discuss which drug name is best to use when performing patient medication teaching. *Class Activity* ***Have students match the following list of terms with the appropriate definitions:*** ***Terms:*** ***1. Chemical name*** ***2. Brand name*** ***3. Generic name*** ***4. Official name*** ***Definitions:*** ***a. FDA name of the drug*** ***b. Simple chemical name of a drug*** ***c. Chemical constitution of the drug*** ***d. Name restricted to the owner of the drug***
List official sources of American drug standards.	■ Sources of drug standards (United States) (p. 2) □ *USP/NF* (p. 2) □ *USP Dictionary of USAN and International Drug Names* (p. 3) Review the resources used in the United States for drug information	PPT 8 ARQ 2 TB Multiple Choice question 2 SG Review Sheet question 8 (p. 1) *Class Activity* ***After reviewing the sources listed in the book for drug information, divide the class in half to play a memory game. Have students match the name of the resource with a***

OBJECTIVES	CONTENT	TEACHING RESOURCES
	related to drug interactions and drug incompatibilities.	***brief description of the contents. Review the results with the class.***
List and describe literature resources for researching prescription and nonprescription medications.	■ Sources of drug information (United States) (p. 3) □ *American Drug Index* (p. 3) □ *American Hospital Formulary Service* (p. 3) □ *Drug Interaction Facts* (p. 4) □ *Drug Facts and Comparisons* (p. 4) □ *Handbook on Injectable Drugs* (p. 4) □ *Handbook of Nonprescription Drugs: An Interactive Approach to Self Care* (p. 4) □ *Martindale—The Complete Drug Reference* (p. 5)	PPT 8 TB Multiple Choice questions 9, 10 TB Multiple Response question 2 CTQ 3, 4 SG Review Sheet question 8 (p. 1) ▸ Discuss the importance of using drug information resources in the health care setting. ▸ Discuss the types of resources used in the hospital, extended care facility, ambulatory care setting, and the physician's office. Class Activity ***Divide the class into groups, and ask each to locate and examine three different drug resource publications: one for prescription drugs, one for nonprescription drugs, and one for herbal and/or natural supplements. Have each group prepare a brief report. The report should identify the main focus of each resource, the type of information contained, and for whom the resource is best suited (i.e., health professionals or consumers). As a class, compare and contrast the resources based on student reports. Which are most useful for nurses? For patient education? Have students use the resources listed in the text. (For students to prepare for this activity, see Homework/ Assignments 1.1)***
List and describe literature resources for researching drug interactions and drug incompatibilities.	□ *Natural Medicines Comprehensive Database* (p. 5) □ *Physicians' Desk Reference* (p. 5) □ Package inserts (p. 6) □ Nursing journals (p. 6) □ Electronic databases (p. 6)	PPT 8 TB Multiple Choice questions 3, 4 INRQ 10 Review Question for the NCLEX Examination 2 (p. 15) ▸ Discuss the importance of reading up to date articles about drug information. ▸ Discuss resources a nurse can use to validate the accuracy of drug information. Class Activity ***Invite a registered nurse to speak to the class about the nurse's role in assessing and monitoring patient response to drug therapy. What should the nurse look for? What information does the nurse need to be aware of regarding drug reactions, interactions, compatibilities, effects, and side effects for each patient and each drug? What resources***

OBJECTIVES	CONTENT	TEACHING RESOURCES
		are most useful in practice if the nurse needs more information? Ask students to prepare questions in advance. Class Activity ***Divide students into group of three. Assign each group one of the drugs listed below. Have each group use the PDR to locate where the manufacturer of the drug is located; brand and generic name index; what category the drug product is listed under; the product information guide for the drug; product information section; and diagnostic product information. Assign one of the following drugs to each group: ampicillin, morphine sulfate, Darvocet-N 100, Nexium, Lipitor, tamoxifen, and Dilantin.***
Cite a resource that helps ensure credibility to medical and patient information sites on the Internet.	Review the resources used in patient education regarding drugs: *United States Pharmacopeia Dispensing Information* (USPDI) and *Therapeutic Choices*.	PPT 8 TB Multiple Choice question 5

1.1 Homework/Assignments:
1. Divide the class into groups and ask each to examine three different drug resources: one for prescription drugs, one for nonprescription drugs, and one for herbal and/or natural supplements. Each group should prepare a brief report. The report should identify the main focus of each resource, the type of information contained, and for whom the resource is best suited (i.e., health professionals or consumers). Which are most useful for nurses? For patient education? As a class, compare and contrast the resources based on student reports. Students should use the resources listed in the text.

1.1 Instructor's Notes/Student Feedback:

LESSON 1.2

CRITICAL THINKING QUESTION

A patient asks about using saw palmetto to alleviate the symptoms of benign prostatic hypertrophy. What are three sources of information the nurse can use to learn about this and other natural supplements? What is a particular distinguishing characteristic of each source? Which would be appropriate for health professionals? Which is better for patients? What general information could the nurse give the patient regarding the use of herbal preparations and other natural supplements?

Guidelines: Sources of information about herbal and/or natural supplements are *Martindale—The Complete Drug Reference*, and *Natural Medicines Comprehensive Database*. *Martindale* has worldwide listings of both drugs and herbal preparations, whereas *Natural Medicines Comprehensive Database* includes

information on clinically tested herbal medicines and dietary preparations. Because the *Natural Medicines* database has evidence-based information, it is the most appropriate source for the health professional. If the patient asks about herbal and/or natural supplements, the nurse should respond in a nonjudgmental manner. The nurse should inform the patient that the FDA does not test or regulate these products and that few of these products have had scientifically substantiated research performed. Therefore, there is no assurance regarding quality, dosage, or efficacy.

OBJECTIVES	CONTENT	TEACHING RESOURCES
List legislative acts controlling drug use and abuse.	■ Drug legislation (United States) (p. 7) □ Federal Food, Drug, and Cosmetic Act, June 25, 1938 (amended 1952, 1962) (p. 7)	PPT 11 ARQ 3 TB Multiple Choice question 6 INRQ 6, 9 Review Questions for the NCLEX Examination 7, 8 (p. 16) ▸ Discuss the potential of drug use and abuse in the general population and in health care settings. Class Activity ***Divide the class into groups, and assign each group one of the following:*** – ***Federal Food, Drug, and Cosmetic Act*** – ***Controlled Drugs and Substances Act*** – ***Food and Drugs Act and Food and Drug Regulations*** ***Ask students to describe the purpose of each act and how it affects nursing practice. Then have groups make brief reports to the class for feedback and discussion.***
Differentiate among schedule I, II, III, IV, and V medications, and describe nursing responsibilities associated with the administration of each type.	□ Controlled Substances Act, 1970 (p. 7) □ Possession of controlled substances (p. 8)	PPT 11 ARQ 4 TB Multiple Choice questions 7, 11 INRQ 5 SG Review Sheet question 9 (p. 1) SG Learning Activities questions 3, 6-16, 18-19 (p. 3) SG Practice Questions for the NCLEX Examination 4, 6 (p. 4) Review Question for the NCLEX Examination 3 (p. 15) ▸ Discuss examples of each level of scheduled medications. ▸ Discuss how drugs are determined and categorized as schedule I, II, II, IV, or V medications.

ELSEVIER

OBJECTIVES	CONTENT	TEACHING RESOURCES
		Class Activity ***Ask the class to describe each category of scheduled drugs, I through V. Then lead a discussion in which students describe the nursing responsibilities involved for patients when each drug category is administered. What patient education is indicated?***
Describe the procedure outlined by the FDA to develop and market new medicines.	■ New drug development (p. 8) □ Preclinical research and development stage (p. 9) □ Clinical research and development stage (p. 9) □ New drug application review (p. 10) □ Postmarketing surveillance (p. 10) □ Rare diseases and orphan drugs (p. 10)	PPT 12 ARQ 5 TB Multiple Choice question 8 INRQ 7, 8 CTQ 5 SG Review Sheet question 10 (p. 1) SG Practice Questions for the NCLEX Examination 1, 2 (p. 3) Figure 1-2 (p. 9): New drug review process. ▸ Discuss how a company creates and submits an application for a new drug approval. ▸ Discuss what is meant by rare disease and orphan drugs and why finding remedies for them is more challenging. What has the government done to facilitate research and development? Class Activity ***Divide the class into small groups, and give them this scenario. A group has discovered a medicinal drug that it believes will cure the common cold. What steps would the group take to bring the new product to the consumer market? Ask volunteer groups to make a presentation to the class for feedback and discussion.*** Class Activity ***Ask students to complete a search on the FDA website (www.fda.gov) outside of class. Ask each student to identify a drug that has been approved within the past year. Allow class time for discussion of findings.***
List the definitions of the use-in-pregnancy categories A, B, C, D, and X	Review the pregnancy categories for medications: A, B, C, D, and X	PPT 13 INRQ 7 Review Questions for the NCLEX Examination 4, 6 (pp. 15-16)

1.2 Homework/Assignments:

1.2 Instructor's Notes/Student Feedback:

LESSON 1.3

CRITICAL THINKING QUESTION

A patient is prescribed morphine for pain upon discharge from the hospital. According to the drug schedule, what education is appropriate for this patient? What would be a good source to consult to outline patient education for this drug?

Guidelines: The nurse should advise the patient that morphine is a schedule II drug, which means it has a high potential for physical and psychological dependence. Therefore, the patient must be instructed to avoid stopping the drug suddenly or changing the dosage without consulting the physician because withdrawal symptoms could occur. For patient education, many health care institutions have placed materials and resources for use online on an intranet (e.g., Micromedex), which help health professionals review teaching points regarding specific medications with the patient.

OBJECTIVES	CONTENT	TEACHING RESOURCES
List official sources of Canadian drug standards.	■ Sources of drug standards (Canada) (p. 12) Review the drug information sources used in Canada, such as the *Compendium of Pharmaceuticals and Specialties* and the *Compendium of Self-Care Products*, and what they contain.	PPT 13 Class Activity ***Have students call out official sources of Canadian drug standards. Then as a class, discuss the purpose and focus of each standard. Why is the USP/NF an accepted source of drug standards in Canada?*** Class Activity ***Locate several of the resources listed in the book for drug information used in Canada and bring them to class. Pass them around and have several students identify one different aspect of each. Discuss the findings with the class.***
Describe the organization of the *Compendium of Pharmaceuticals and Specialties* and the information contained in each colored section.	■ Sources of drug information (Canada) (p. 12) □ *Compendium of Pharmaceuticals and Specialties* (p. 12)	PPT 14 ▸ Discuss the rationale for the various sections compiled in the *Compendium of Pharmaceuticals and Specialties.* ▸ Discuss the similarities and differences between Canadian and U.S. drug references. Class Activity ***Lead a discussion in which students identify and describe the contents of each section of the*** **Compendium of**

OBJECTIVES	CONTENT	TEACHING RESOURCES
		Pharmaceuticals and Specialties ***used in Canada.*** ***Then give students the following scenarios and ask them to identify in which section the nurse would look to find more information:*** – ***A nurse working in the emergency department finds pills in an unlabeled bottle in the purse of an unconscious patient.*** – ***A patient says he is allergic to gluten.*** – ***A new mother discharged home says she needs more of the stool softener they prescribed after delivery but cannot remember the name.***
Describe the organization of the *Compendium of Self Care Products.*	□ *Patient Self-Care: Helping Patients Make Therapeutic Choices* (p. 13) □ *Compendium of Self-Care Products* (p. 13)	PPT 15 ▸ Discuss the role of the Canadian Pharmacists Association in patient care in the health care industry. ▸ Discuss the similarities and differences among the Canadian and U.S. pharmacy associations. Class Activity ***Lead a class discussion in which students identify sources of information, such as the*** **Compendium of Pharmaceuticals and Specialties,** ***electronic resources, such as*** **Medline,** ***the*** **Compendium of Self-Care Products,** ***and*** **Patient Self-Care: Helping Patients Make Therapeutic Choices.** ***Have students compare and contrast significant characteristics, such as content and organization, for each one. Under what circumstances might a nurse find these resources useful for patient education?*** Class Activity ***Divide the class into small groups. Ask each group to develop a brief teaching plan for a patient who has arthritis, using the resources listed in the previous activity. The teaching plan should include pathophysiology, symptoms, drug options, prescription drugs, OTC remedies, and nonpharmacologic treatment options. Have groups identify which resource is best suited for each part of the teaching plan. Then have groups share their findings with the class for feedback and discussion.***
Cite a literature resource for reviewing information to be	Review the resources used in patient education regarding drugs: ▪ *Therapeutic Choices*	PPT 17 ▸ Discuss the role of the pharmacist in patient care.

OBJECTIVES	CONTENT	TEACHING RESOURCES
given to the patient concerning a prescribed medication.		▸ Discuss the role of herbal medicines in treating illness. ▸ Discuss hospitals that have incorporated herbal medicine options for patients. Class Activity *Lead a discussion in which students identify sources of information that the nurse can consult when providing patients with information about prescription medications. Students should consider the following:* **PDR, Martindale—The Complete Drug Reference, Compendium of Pharmaceuticals and Specialties,** *and* **Natural Medicines Comprehensive Database.** ▪ *Discuss several sources available to health care workers that can be useful in providing patient information. Bring package inserts to class and discuss what must be reviewed as important information for the patient to understand.*
List legislative acts controlling drug use and abuse.	□ Controlled Drugs and Substance Act, 1997 (p. 14) □ Nonprescription drugs (p. 15) Discuss the legislative acts in the United States designed to prevent drug abuse, and differentiate how drugs are categorized into schedules.	PPT 18 ▸ Discuss the classifications of nonprescription medication. ▸ Discuss the resources a nurse professional can use to obtain information about nonprescription drugs. Class Activity *Ask students to identify the legislative act in Canada that controls drug use and abuse. Have students compare the drug schedules used in Canada with those used in the United States. Why is it important for nurses to be familiar with the categories used in both countries?* Class Activity *Invite a representative from the FDA to speak to the class about the effect and effectiveness of drug legislation. How widespread is drug abuse among the general population and in the health care industry? How does legislation affect the nurse in practice? What key issues must the nurse be aware of, and what is the nurse's role?*
Differentiate between Schedule F and Controlled Drugs, and describe nursing responsibilities with each.	■ Drug legislation (Canada) (p. 14) □ Food and Drugs Act, 1927; Food and Drug Regulations, 1953 and 1954, revised 1979, and periodic amendments (p. 14)	PPT 18 ▸ Discuss how Canada's scheduled medications may differ from the U.S. schedule I, II, III, IV, and V classifications. ▸ Discuss the FDA's role in the regulation of controlled substances.

ELSEVIER

OBJECTIVES	CONTENT	TEACHING RESOURCES
		Class Activity ***Lead a discussion in which students differentiate between schedule F and controlled drugs. Would morphine and ampicillin be included in both schedule F and controlled drugs categories? Why? Ask students to compare and contrast the nursing responsibilities associated with administering drugs from these two categories.***
Performance evaluation		Test Bank SG Learning Activities (p. 3) SG Practice Questions for the NCLEX Examination (p. 4) Critical Thinking Questions

1.3 Homework/Assignments:
1. SG Learning Activities (p. 3)

1.3 Instructor's Notes/Student Feedback:

Lecture Outline

Definitions, Names, Standards, and Information Sources

Slide 1

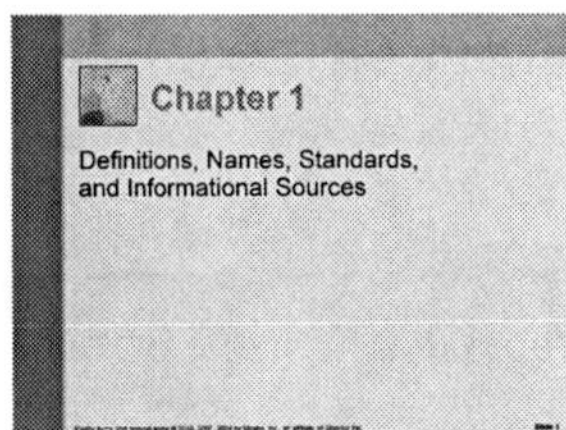
Chapter 1
Definitions, Names, Standards, and Informational Sources

Slide 2

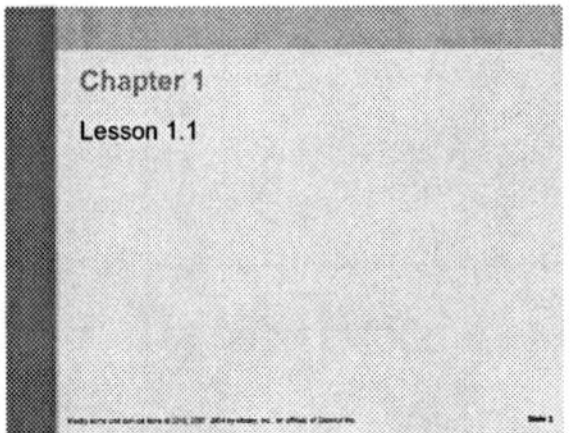
Chapter 1
Lesson 1.1

Slide 3

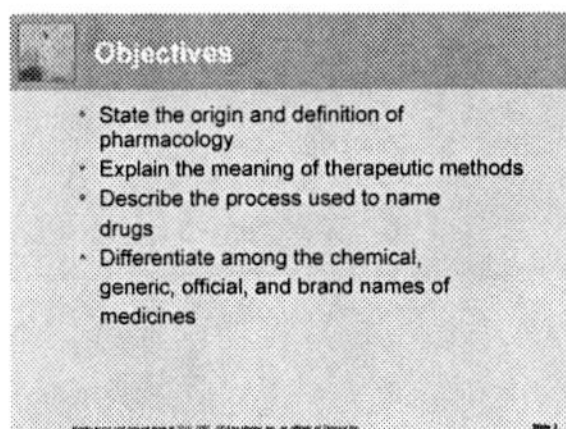
Objectives
State the origin and definition of pharmacology
Explain the meaning of therapeutic methods
Describe the process used to name drugs
Differentiate among the chemical, generic, official, and brand names of medicines

---

Slide 4

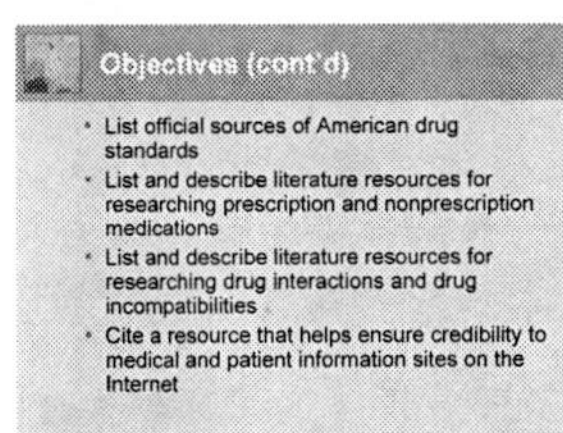
Objectives (cont'd)
List official sources of American drug standards
List and describe literature resources for researching prescription and nonprescription medications
List and describe literature resources for researching drug interactions and drug incompatibilities
Cite a resource that helps ensure credibility to medical and patient information sites on the Internet

---

Slide 5

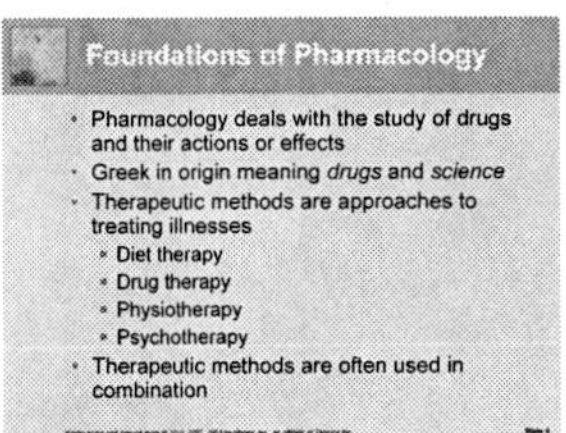
Foundations of Pharmacology
Pharmacology deals with the study of drugs and their actions or effects
Greek in origin meaning drugs and science
Therapeutic methods are approaches to treating illnesses
Diet therapy
Drug therapy
Physiotherapy
Psychotherapy
Therapeutic methods are often used in combination

- *Pharmakon* is Greek for drugs and *logos* is Greek for science: the origin of pharmacology.
- Physiotherapy uses water, light, and heat.
- Psychotherapy identifies stressors and methods used to reduce them.

Slide 6

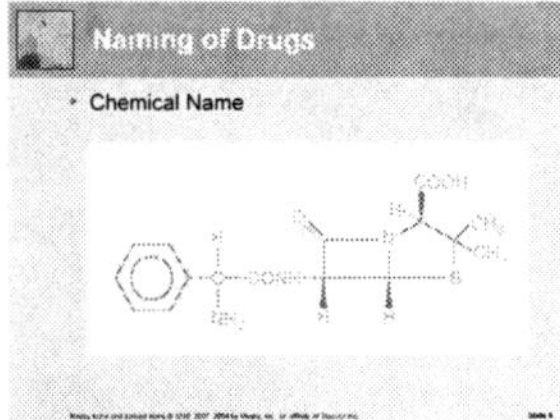
Naming of Drugs
Chemical Name

- The figure shows how a chemist views the chemical structure for the drug ampicillin, an antibiotic.

Slide 7

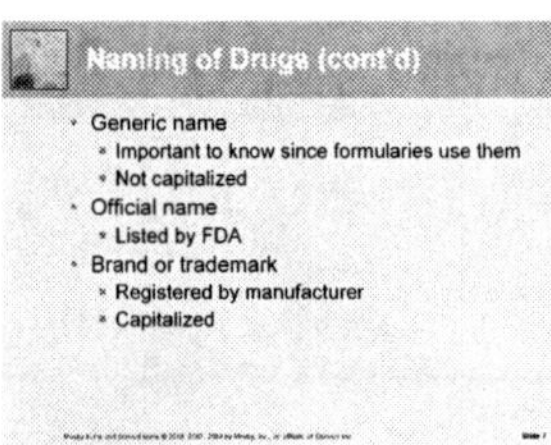
Naming of Drugs (cont'd)
Generic name
Important to know since formularies use them
Not capitalized
Official name
Listed by FDA
Brand or trademark
Registered by manufacturer
Capitalized

- Example: Glucotrol XL is an antidiabetic drug. Generic name is glipizide. Brand name is Glucotrol XL.

Slide 8

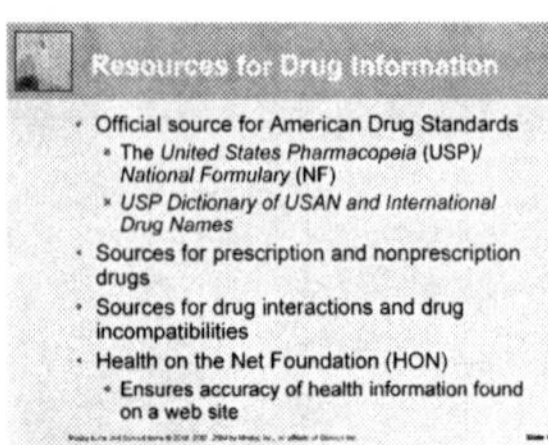
Resources for Drug Information
Official source for American Drug Standards
The United States Pharmacopeia (USP)/ National Formulary (NF)
USP Dictionary of USAN and International Drug Names
Sources for prescription and nonprescription drugs
Sources for drug interactions and drug incompatibilities
Health on the Net Foundation (HON)
Ensures accuracy of health information found on a web site

- USP/NF sets standards of purity for drugs and lab tests used to determine the purity.
- USAN contains more than 10,000 drug names.

Slide 9

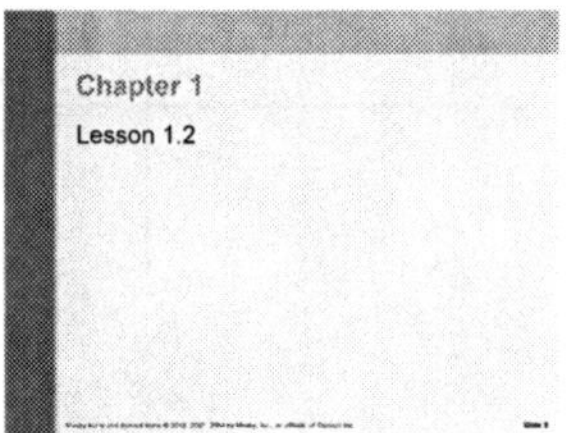
Chapter 1
Lesson 1.2

Slide 10

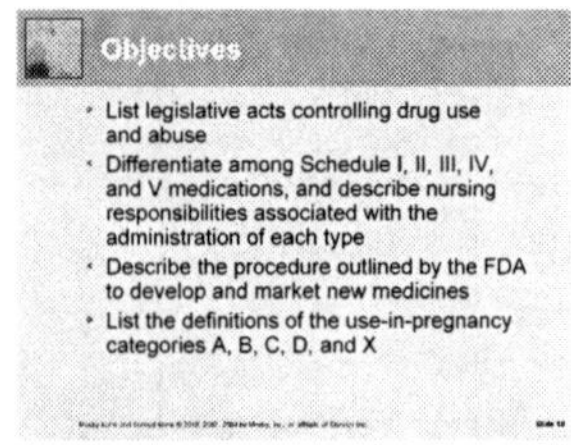
Objectives
List legislative acts controlling drug use and abuse
Differentiate among Schedule I, II, III, IV, and V medications, and describe nursing responsibilities associated with the administration of each type
Describe the procedure outlined by the FDA to develop and market new medicines
List the definitions of the use-in-pregnancy categories A, B, C, D, and X

Slide 11

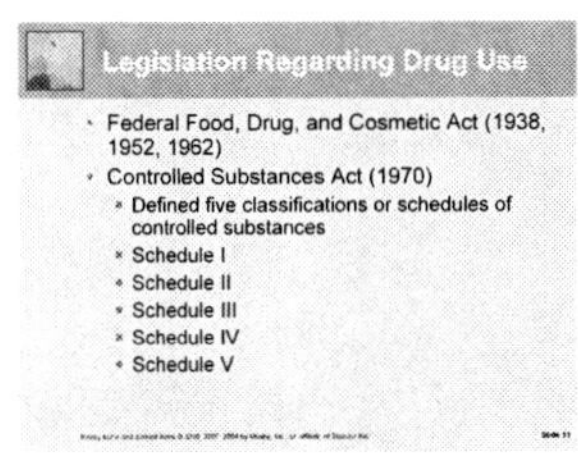
Legislation Regarding Drug Use
Federal Food, Drug, and Cosmetic Act (1938, 1952, 1962)
Controlled Substances Act (1970)
Defined five classifications or schedules of controlled substances
Schedule I
Schedule II
Schedule III
Schedule IV
Schedule V

- Schedule I – high abuse potential; no medical use (e.g., heroin)
- Schedule II – high abuse potential; some medical use (e.g., pentobarbital)
- Schedule III – high abuse potential; some medical use (e.g., codeine)
- Schedule IV – low abuse potential; some medical use (e.g., diazepam)
- Schedule V – low abuse potential; prescription not needed (e.g., Robitussin)

Slide 12

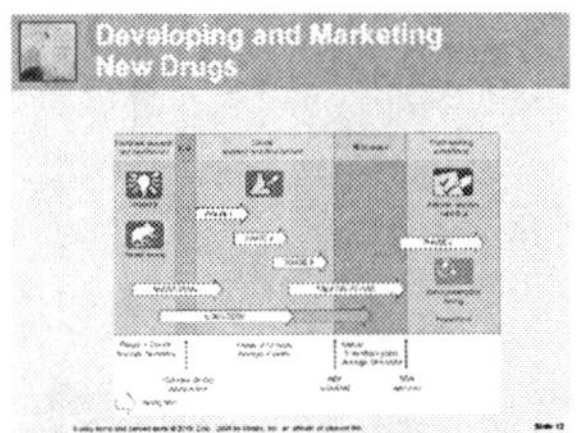
Developing and Marketing New Drugs

Slide 13

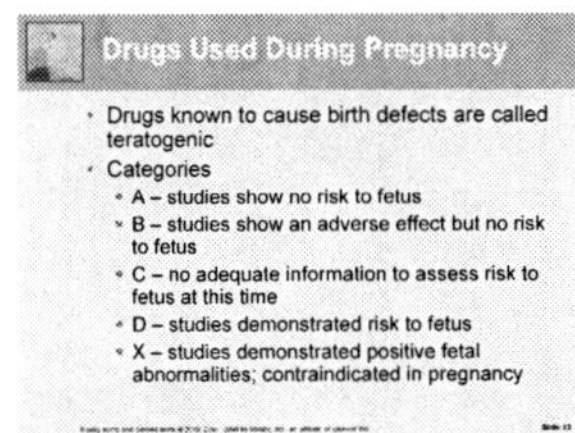
Drugs Used During Pregnancy
Drugs known to cause birth defects are called teratogenic
Categories
A – studies show no risk to fetus
B – studies show an adverse effect but no risk to fetus
C – no adequate information to assess risk to fetus at this time
D – studies demonstrated risk to fetus
X – studies demonstrated positive fetal abnormalities; contraindicated in pregnancy

---

Slide 14

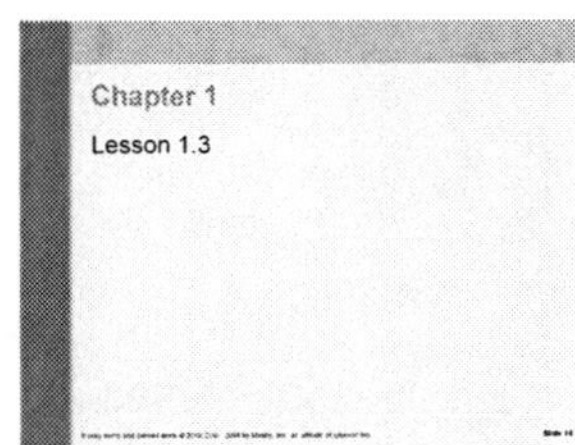
Chapter 1
Lesson 1.3

Slide 15

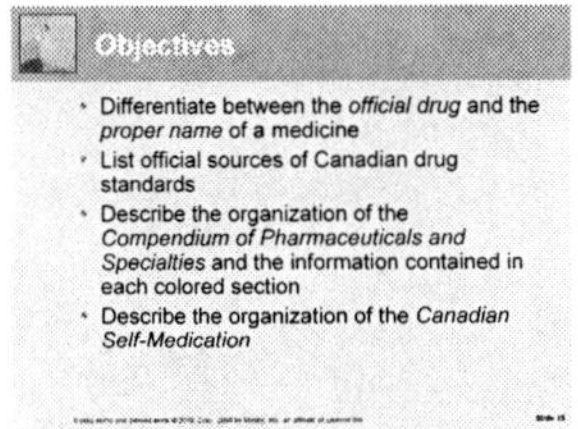
Objectives
Differentiate between the official drug and the proper name of a medicine
List official sources of Canadian drug standards
Describe the organization of the Compendium of Pharmaceuticals and Specialties and the information contained in each colored section
Describe the organization of the Canadian Self-Medication

Slide 16

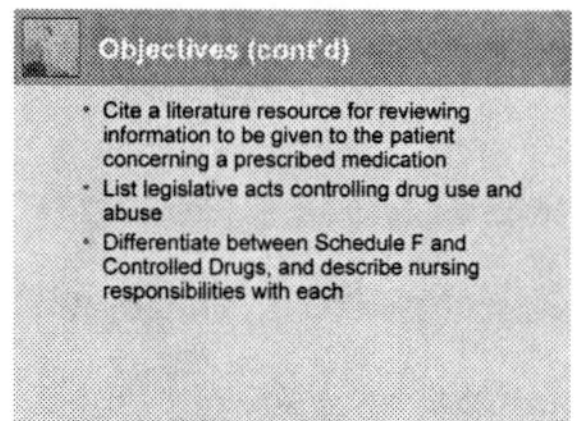
Objectives (cont'd)
Cite a literature resource for reviewing information to be given to the patient concerning a prescribed medication
List legislative acts controlling drug use and abuse
Differentiate between Schedule F and Controlled Drugs, and describe nursing responsibilities with each

---

Slide 17

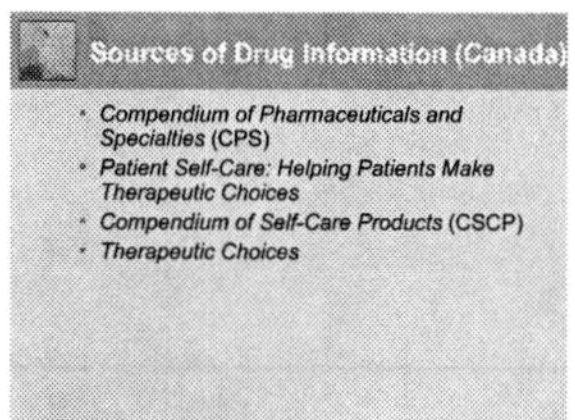
Sources of Drug Information (Canada)
Compendium of Pharmaceuticals and Specialties (CPS)
Patient Self-Care: Helping Patients Make Therapeutic Choices
Compendium of Self-Care Products (CSCP)
Therapeutic Choices

Slide 18

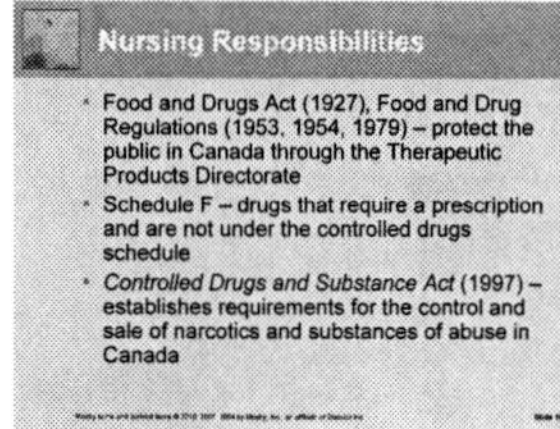
Nursing Responsibilities
Food and Drugs Act (1927), Food and Drug Regulations (1953, 1954, 1979) – protect the public in Canada through the Therapeutic Products Directorate
Schedule F – drugs that require a prescription and are not under the controlled drugs schedule
Controlled Drugs and Substance Act (1997) – establishes requirements for the control and sale of narcotics and substances of abuse in Canada

2 Lesson Plan
Principles of Drug Action and Drug Interactions

TEACHING FOCUS

This chapter introduces students to the principles of drug action and drug interactions, including an overview of basic human anatomy and physiology relating to drug absorption, distribution, metabolism, and excretion. Additionally, the student has the opportunity to learn the types of drug actions and how to identify drug reactions in a patient.

MATERIALS AND RESOURCES

- ☐ computer and PowerPoint projector (all Lessons)
- ☐ copy of Figure 2-2 (p. 19) with right side covered (Lesson 2.1)
- ☐ drug reference book (all Lessons)

LESSON CHECKLIST

Preparations for this lesson include:

- lecture
- evaluation of student knowledge and skills needed to perform all entry-level activities related to principles of drug action and drug interactions, including:
    - evaluation of patient condition
    - routes for drug administration
    - patient evaluation after administering medication
    - drug reactions
    - safety procedures

KEY TERMS

absorption (p. 18)
additive effect (p. 24)
ADME (p. 17)
adverse effects (p. 21)
agonists (p. 17)
allergic reactions (p. 21)
antagonistic effect (p. 24)
antagonists (p. 17)
biotransformation (p. 19)
carcinogenicity (p. 22)
desired action (p. 21)
displacement (p. 24)
distribution (p. 18)
drug accumulation (p. 23)
drug blood level (p. 19)
drug dependence (p. 23)
drug interaction (p. 23)
duration of action (p. 20)
enteral (p. 18)
excretion (p. 19)
half-life (p. 20)
hives (p. 21)
idiosyncratic reaction (p. 21)
incompatibility (p. 25)
interference (p. 24)
metabolism (p. 19)
nocebo effect (p. 23)
onset of action (p. 20)
parameters (p. 21)
parenteral (p. 18)
partial agonists (p. 17)
peak action (p. 20)
percutaneous (p. 18)
pharmacodynamics (p. 17)
pharmacokinetics (p. 17)
placebo (p. 23)
placebo effect (p. 23)
receptors (p. 17)
side effects (p. 21)
synergistic effect (p. 24)
teratogen (p. 22)
tolerance (p. 23)
toxicity (p. 21)
unbound drug (p. 24)
urticaria (p. 21)

ELSEVIER

ADDITIONAL RESOURCES

PowerPoint slides: 1-12

Legend

ARQ	PPT	TB	CTQ	SG	INRQ
Audience Response Questions	PowerPoint Slides	Test Bank	Critical Thinking Questions	Study Guide	Interactive NCLEX Review Questions

Class Activities are indicated in ***bold italic.***

LESSON 2.1

BACKGROUND ASSESSMENT

Question: What are the four stages a drug goes through after it is administered? Describe each stage. What is one factor that affects each of these stages in the enteral route?
Answer: A drug goes through the four stages of absorption, distribution, metabolism, and excretion. Absorption occurs when the drug enters the circulation, through the intestines (enteral route), through the skin, or directly into the circulation. Distribution occurs when the drug is transported to body tissue. Metabolism is the process of inactivating the drug. Excretion is the elimination of drug metabolites or active drug. For the enteral route, the presence of food or the acidity of the stomach can affect absorption. The amount of body fat can influence distribution, and the presence or absence of enzyme systems can alter metabolism. Hepatic and renal functions can alter drug metabolism and excretion.

Question: What is the definition of an adverse drug reaction? What are some common signs and symptoms? What drugs commonly cause adverse reactions?
Answer: An adverse drug reaction is a noxious, unintended, and undesired effect of a drug that occurs in doses used for humans for the purpose of prophylaxis, diagnosis, or therapy. Common signs and symptoms are rash, nausea, vomiting, diarrhea, itching, thrombocytopenia, and hyperglycemia. Drugs that commonly cause allergic reactions are antibiotics, cardiovascular medications, cancer chemotherapy agents, analgesics, and antiinflammatory agents.

CRITICAL THINKING QUESTION

The nurse is caring for two patients who are both receiving gentamicin, IV, for a wound infection. The physician has ordered serum peak and trough levels. The nurse notes that although the patients are each receiving the same dose, one patient's trough level is much higher than the other's. Why is this? What can be done? What should the nurse do?
Guidelines: The high trough level of one patient may be due to impaired hepatic function, which decreases the metabolism of the drug, or to impaired renal function, which decreases the excretion of the drug. The patients' ages and metabolic rates also may be factors. The doses can be adjusted by the physician to attain a normal, therapeutic trough level. The nurse should notify the physician of the patients' peak and trough serum levels.

OBJECTIVES	CONTENT	TEACHING RESOURCES
Identify five basic principles of drug action.	■ Basic principles (p. 17) 1. Drugs alter existing physiologic responses. 2. Drugs interact in the body at specific sites called receptors.	PPT 3, 5-6 TB Multiple Response questions 5-6 CTQ 1, 2, 4 SG Review Sheet questions 1-7 (p. 5)

OBJECTIVES	CONTENT	TEACHING RESOURCES
	3. The intensity of the drug response is related in part to the fit of the receptor site and the number of sites occupied by the drug. 4. Drugs can stimulate a receptor, *agonist*, block a receptor, *antagonist*, or stimulate one response from a receptor and block another, *partial agonist.* 5. Drugs go through five stages after administration (ADME).	SG Learning Activities questions 1-3, 12 (p. 8) SG Practice Questions for the NCLEX Examination 4, 7 (p. 10) Figure 2-1 (p. 18): Drugs act by forming a chemical bond with specific receptor sites, similar to a key and lock. ▸ Discuss the effect of drugs on the human body. ▸ Explain the terms *agonist*, *antagonist*, and *partial agonist*. ▸ Review the five stages of pharmacokinetics: liberation, absorption, distribution, metabolism, and excretion. Class Activity ***A 65-year-old man is prescribed propranolol for his blood pressure. Ask students to determine how they will know if the drug is effective.***
Explain nursing assessments necessary to evaluate potential problems associated with the absorption of medications.	□ Absorption (p. 18) Absorption depends on the route of administration. • Nursing assessments to enhance drug absorption: determine correct route and dosage; know the various forms of packaged drugs (e.g., capsules, solutions, suspensions); understand the effect of warming, cooling, or massaging an injection area; discuss absorption rate in infants versus older adults.	PPT 4, 6 TB Multiple Choice question 9 SG Review Sheet question 8 (p. 5) ▸ Discuss the role of absorption and the successful outcome of medication usage. Class Activity ***Divide the class into three groups. Assign each group one of the following routes of drug administration: enteral, parenteral, and dermal. Ask each group to identify two assessments the nurse should make for its assigned route to evaluate potential problems with absorption. Then reconvene the class and have groups share their assessments and their rationales. Make a comprehensive descriptive list for each route of drug administration.***
Describe nursing interventions that can enhance drug absorption.	□ Absorption (p. 18) Nursing interventions include: • Enteral (oral drugs): provide adequate water, determine hydration status. • Parenteral drugs: subcutaneous, IM, IV; deposit in correct tissue and determine adequate blood flow. • Percutaneous: topical, sublingual, inhalation; identify correct surface for	PPT 4, 6 ARQ 2 TB Multiple Response question 3 SG Learning Activities questions 11, 22 (pp. 8-9) ▸ Discuss factors that affect drug solubility. Class Activity ***Assign groups of three to four students to a different drug and have them determine all the routes that can be used for their drug, as well as interventions that can enhance its absorption. Have each group present their findings to the class.***

OBJECTIVES	CONTENT	TEACHING RESOURCES
	application and length of contact as well as age, which will affect skin turgor.	
List three categories of drug administration and state the routes of administration for each category.	□ Absorption (p. 18) Categories of drug dministration: 1. Enteral: oral, via nasogastric tubes or other small bowel tubes, rectal 2. Parenteral: injections, whether subcutaneous, intramuscular, or intravenous 3. Percutaneous: topical, inhaled, sublingual	PPT 3, 6 SG Review Sheet questions 9-11 (p. 5) SG Learning Activities questions 15-16, 19, 22 (pp. 8-9) Review Question for the NCLEX Examination 6 (p. 25) ▸ Discuss types of medications that are administered through enteral, parenteral, and percutaneous routes. ▸ Discuss the routes of medication for each of the three categories of drug administration. Class Activity ***Have students match the three categories of drug administration with the routes of administration for each category.*** ***Categories of drug administration:*** ***1. Enteral*** ***2. Parenteral*** ***3. Percutaneous*** ***Routes of administration:*** ***1. IV, IM, and subcutaneous*** ***2. Inhalation, topical, and sublingual*** ***3. Oral, rectal, and nasogastric*** ***What are the differences between the three categories of drug administration? What are the differences between the various routes of each category?***
Differentiate between general and selective types of drug distribution mechanisms.	□ Distribution (pp. 18-19) • Distribution depends on circulation. • General or selective types of drugs depend on whether they can cross barriers. • Discuss lipid solubility and protein binding, which affect distribution.	PPT 3, 6 TB Multiple Choice questions 6-7 INRQ 7 SG Review Sheet question 12 (p. 5) SG Learning Activities question 24 (p. 9) SG Practice Question for the NCLEX Examination 2 (p. 10) Review Question for the NCLEX Examination 2 (p. 25) ▸ Discuss the process of medication distribution within the body. ▸ Discuss the outcome of a drug once it leaves the bloodstream.

OBJECTIVES	CONTENT	TEACHING RESOURCES
		Class Activity ***Divide the class into small groups. Ask each group member to determine the evaluation that is done after administration of medications and how nurses determine drug reactions. Have students present their findings in class. (For students to prepare for this activity, see Homework/Assignment 1.)***
Name the process that inactivates drugs.	□ Metabolism (p. 19) □ Excretion (p. 19) • Metabolism depends on enzyme systems primarily in the liver, concurrent use of other drugs, environmental pollutants, disease processes, and age. • Excretion depends on organ system function . • Two primary routes are GI tract and urine. • Know other routes of excretion (e.g., skin and lungs).	PPT 4, 6 TB Multiple Choice questions 8, 13 TB Multiple Response questions 1-2 INRQ 3, 6, 11 SG Review Sheet questions 14-15 (p. 6) SG Learning Activities questions 23, 25-26 (p. 9) SG Practice Questions for the NCLEX Examination 1, 10 (pp. 10-11) Review Question for the NCLEX Examination 3 (p. 25) Figure 2-2 (p. 19): Factors modifying the quantity of drug reaching a site of action after a single oral dose. ▸ Discuss the process of drug metabolism in the body. ▸ Discuss the primary routes for drug excretion from the body. Class Activity ***Lead a discussion in which students summarize the process whereby a drug becomes inactive before reaching the site of intended action. Then show students a copy of Figure 2-2 (p. 19) with the right side covered up. Have students complete the right side by describing how some of the drug is lost at each stage in the process.***
Identify the meaning and significance to the nurse of the term *half-life* when used in relation to drug therapy.	□ Half-life (p. 20) • Defined as the measure of time needed to eliminate 50% of the drug from the body • Each drug has this determined; important for dosing and understanding drug effects	PPT 7 ARQ 3 TB Multiple Choice question 10 TB Multiple Response question 4 INRQ 5 CTQ 3 SG Review Sheet questions 16-17 (p. 6)

OBJECTIVES	CONTENT	TEACHING RESOURCES
		SG Learning Activities question 27 (p. 9) SG Practice Questions for the NCLEX Examination 6, 12-13 (pp. 10-11) Review Question for the NCLEX Examination 1 (p. 25) ▸ Discuss and practice the calculation of a drug's half-life. ▸ Discuss how the health care practitioner determines the half-life of a drug. Class Activity ***Divide the class into pairs, and ask each pair to determine how much of a 1-gram dose of a drug would be left after 24 hours if the drug has a half-life of 6 hours. Ask students what the findings mean in terms of therapeutic effect and administration. Have students share their findings with the class and determine the correct answer. What are two ways in which the patient's capability to metabolize drugs should be monitored?***

2.1 Homework/Assignments:
1. Ask each group member to pick a drug from a list you provide and describe how nurse evalute the effectiveness of the drug after administration, as well as how nurses determine drug reactions. Have student present their finding in class.

2.1 Instructor's Notes/Student Feedback:

LESSON 2.2

CRITICAL THINKING QUESTION

Several minutes after starting the infusion of a patient's first dose of ampicillin IV, the patient's skin becomes flushed, and he says his heart is racing. Red raised bumps appear on his skin, and he reports feeling itchy. What should the nurse suspect? What are the risks to the patient? What should the nurse do?

Guidelines: The patient is most likely experiencing an allergic reaction to the ampicillin. His body has formed antibodies against the ampicillin, producing the allergic symptoms. These reactions can sometimes develop into anaphylaxis, a life-threatening allergic reaction. The nurse should stop the infusion of the medicine and notify the physician immediately. The patient should be monitored closely for worsening or further reactions.

ELSEVIER

OBJECTIVES	CONTENT	TEACHING RESOURCES
Compare and contrast the following terms used in relationship to medications: desired action, side effects, adverse effects, allergic reactions, and idiosyncratic reactions.	■ Drug action (p. 20) • Review the various drug actions within the body: desired effects, side effects, adverse effects, and allergic reactions. • Remind students that all drug actions are predictable and must be monitored.	PPT 9, 12 ARQ 4, 5 TB Multiple Choice questions 1-2, 12 INRQ 4, 8, 10 CTQ 5-6 SG Review Sheet questions 18-25 (p. 6) SG Learning Activities questions 4-5, 13 (p. 8) SG Practice Question for the NCLEX Examination 7 (p. 10) Review Question for the NCLEX Examination 4 (p. 25) ▸ Discuss approaches that a nurse can use to educate a patient regarding how to determine an allergic reaction to a prescribed drug. ▸ Discuss ways that extended-care facilities can prevent drug-related injuries to patients. ▸ Review Figure 2-3 (p. 21), A time-response curve, to discuss how drug concentrations are calculated. Class Activity ***Create a worksheet with these headings: medications, desired action, side effects, adverse effects, allergic reactions. Select medications from various classifications and have groups of two or three students present one medication from each group. Repeat as many times as needed.*** Class Activity ***Divide the class into small groups and present this clinical situation:*** ***A patient receives tobramycin IV for cellulitis. After the first dose, the area of cellulitis decreases in size, but the patient experiences redness and itching. After the second dose, the patient becomes diaphoretic, has palpitations, and begins to wheeze.*** ***What should the nurse suspect? What are appropriate nursing interventions?***
State the mechanisms whereby drug interactions may occur.	■ Drug interactions (p. 23) • Review the various factors that affect drug effectiveness in each patient such as age, body	PPT 9, 11 TB Multiple Choice questions 3-4 CTQ 7-8 SG Review Sheet questions 25-28 (pp. 6-7)

OBJECTIVES	CONTENT	TEACHING RESOURCES
	weight, metabolic rate, and illness. • Discuss the psychological effects such as placebo effect, nocebo effect, drug tolerance, and drug dependence that influence how drugs work.	SG Learning Activities question 14 (p. 8) SG Practice Questions for the NCLEX Examination 8-9 (p. 10) ▸ Discuss the process of how a drug interaction occurs. ▸ Discuss the impact of drug interactions in a patient whose illness requires the treatment for successful management of his or her condition. Class Activity ***Hand out cards with the terms*** **placebo effect, nocebo effect, placebo, tolerance,** ***and*** **drug dependence.** ***Have students play a word guessing game where one student attempts to explain the word without using the word in the definition, and the other students guess the word.***
Differentiate among the following terms used in relationship to medications: additive effect, synergistic effect, antagonistic effect, displacement, interference, and incompatibility.	■ Drug interactions (p. 23) • Review the types of drug interactions that can occur: additive, synergistic, and antagonistic. • Discuss the way drugs are considered active and inactive depending on whether they are bound to a protein.	PPT 10 TB Multiple Choice question 5 INRQ 12 SG Review Sheet questions 29-36 (p. 7) SG Learning Activities questions 6-10, 18, 20-21 (p. 8-9) SG Practice Questions for the NCLEX Examination 3, 5 (p. 10) Review Question for the NCLEX Examination 5 (p. 25) ▸ Discuss why certain age-groups tolerate adverse effects better than others. ▸ Discuss resources the nurse can use to identify drug reactions when suspected. Class Activity ***Assign pairs of students to demonstrate how the terms*** **additive effect, synergistic effect, antagonistic effect,** ***and*** **unbound drug** ***would look if one student (or more) was the drug and the other student was the cell membrane.***
Performance evaluation		Test Bank SG Learning Activities (pp. 8-9) SG Practice Questions for the NCLEX Examination (pp. 10-11) Critical Thinking Questions

2.2 Homework/Assignments:
Have students play the role of a patient researching a medication on the Internet. Student should access at least two different websites that contain drug infomration and compare the two sites. What information is presented in table format? How well did each site include appropriate patient information? Have student present their findings to the class.

2.2 Instructor's Notes/Student Feedback:

Lecture Outline

2 Principles of Drug Action and Drug Interactions

Slide 1

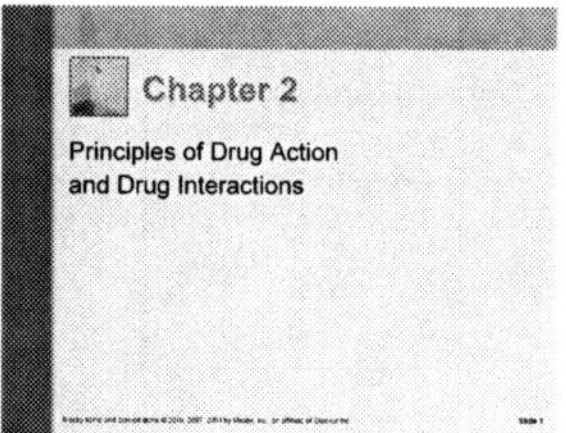
Chapter 2
Principles of Drug Action
and Drug Interactions

Slide 2

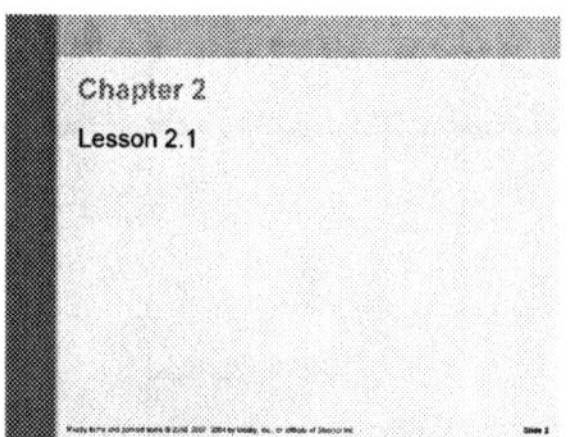
Chapter 2
Lesson 2.1

Slide 3

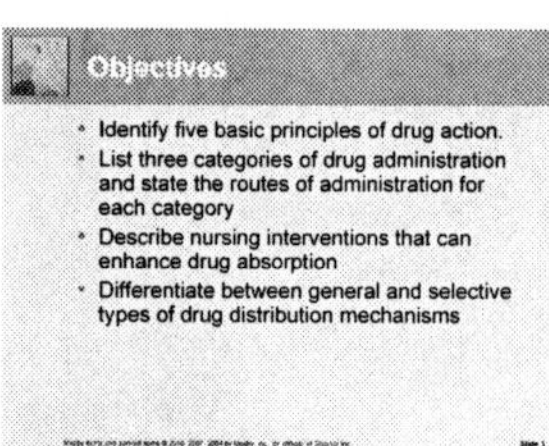
Objectives
Identify five basic principles of drug action.
List three categories of drug administration and state the routes of administration for each category
Describe nursing interventions that can enhance drug absorption
Differentiate between general and selective types of drug distribution mechanisms

- Five basic principles of drug action have to do with pharmacodynamics.
- What are the three categories of drug administration? *enteral, parenteral, and percutaneous*
- List the parenteral routes in order of fastest to slowest absorption. *IV, IM, subcutaneous, intradermal*

Slide 4

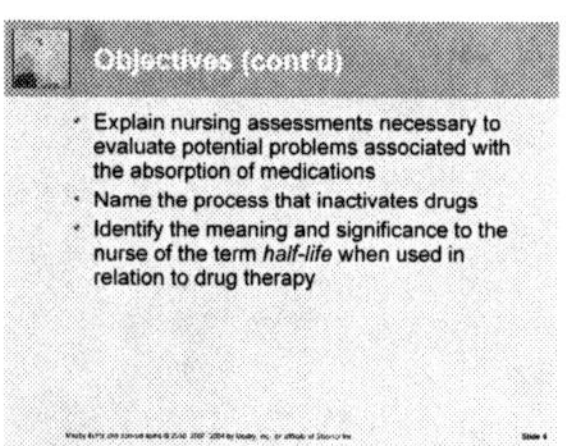
Objectives (cont'd)
Explain nursing assessments necessary to evaluate potential problems associated with the absorption of medications
Name the process that inactivates drugs
Identify the meaning and significance to the nurse of the term half-life when used in relation to drug therapy

- The process that inactivates drugs is called *biotransformation.*
- The term *half-life* refers to the amount of time required for 50% of the drug to be eliminated from the body: a patient receiving 1 g of a medication that has a half-life of 4 hours would have 1/8 of a gram left after 24 hours.

Slide 5

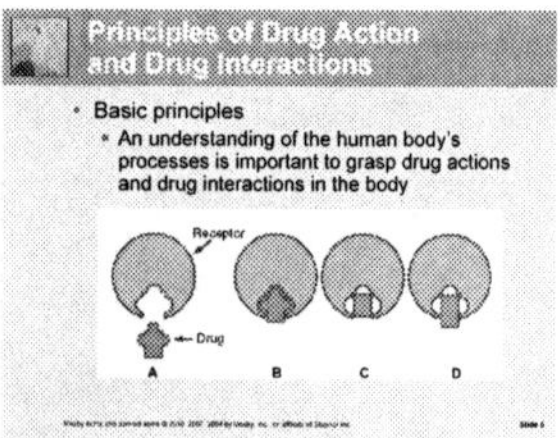
Principles of Drug Action and Drug Interactions
Basic principles
An understanding of the human body's processes is important to grasp drug actions and drug interactions in the body
Receptor
Drug
A
B
C
D

- A – Drugs act by forming a chemical bond with specific receptor sites, similar to a key and lock.
- B – The better the "fit," the better the response are called *agonists.*
- C – Drugs that attach but do not elicit a response are called *antagonists.*
- D – Drugs that attach and elicit a small response, but also block other responses, are called *partial agonists.*

Slide 6

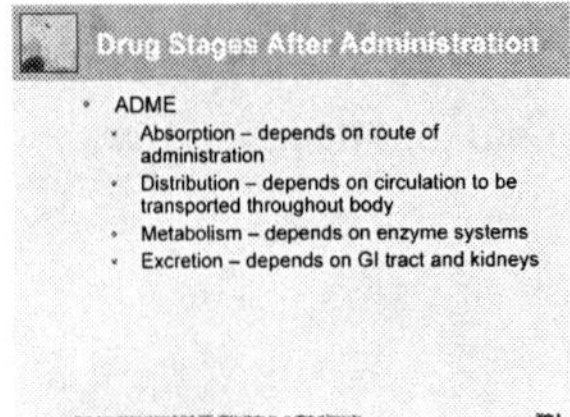
Drug Stages After Administration
ADME
Absorption – depends on route of administration
Distribution – depends on circulation to be transported throughout body
Metabolism – depends on enzyme systems
Excretion – depends on GI tract and kidneys

- Briefly describe *absorption* focusing on how the administration route effects rate and solubility (i.e., oral drugs won't take effect as quickly as IVs).
- Briefly describe *distribution* focusing on how the blood and lymph systems effect drug transport.
- Briefly describe *metabolism* focusing on how concurrent use of other drugs, environmental pollutants, disease processes, and age effect this process.
- Briefly describe *excretion.* Discuss other excretion routes besides the GI tract and kidneys (i.e., skin and lungs).

Slide 7

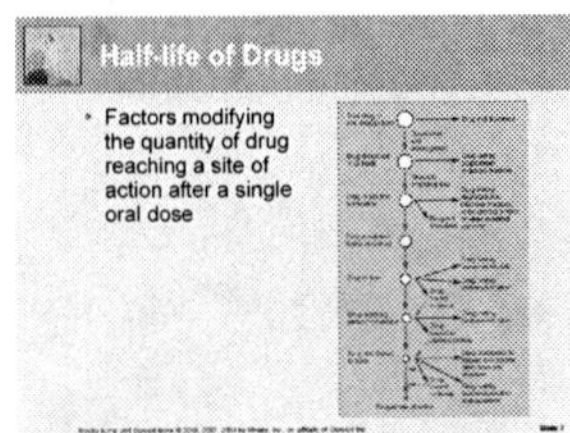
Half-life of Drugs
Factors modifying the quantity of drug reaching a site of action after a single oral dose

- When the half-life of a drug is known, dosages and frequency of administration can be calculated.
- Drugs with long half-lives (digoxin is 36 hours) need to be administered once daily.

Slide 8

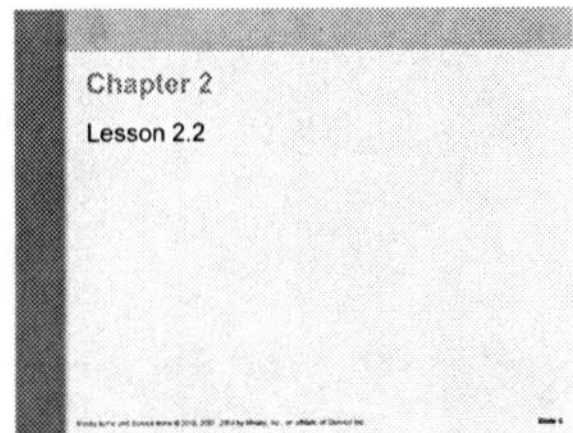
Chapter 2
Lesson 2.2

Slide 9

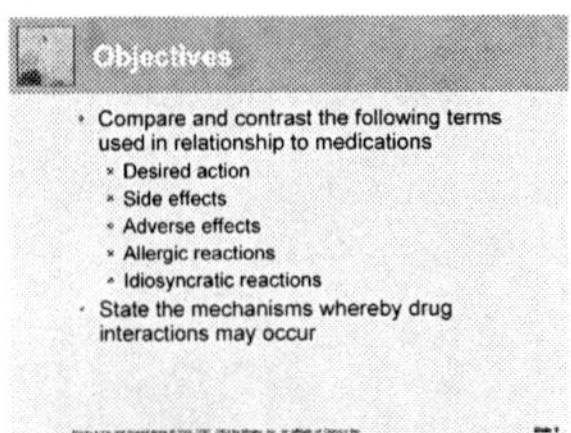
Objectives
Compare and contrast the following terms used in relationship to medications
Desired action
Side effects
Adverse effects
Allergic reactions
Idiosyncratic reactions
State the mechanisms whereby drug interactions may occur

- Drug interactions can occur in two ways:
  1. When combined, the two drugs will increase in their actions.
  2. When combined, the two drugs will decrease in their actions.
- Drug interactions represent 3% to 6% of preventable in-hospital adverse drug reaction cases.
- Drug interactions are a major component of the number of hospital emergency department visits and admissions.

Slide 10

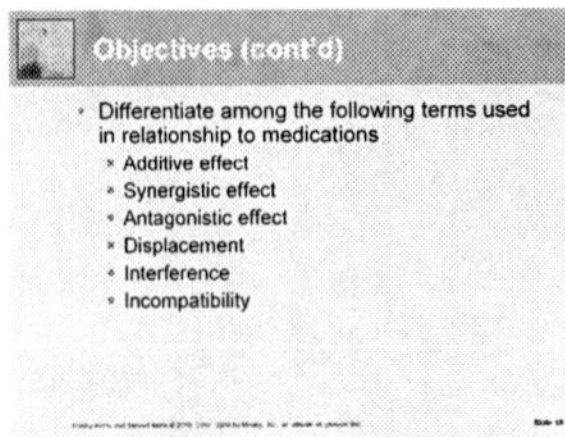
Objectives (cont'd)
Differentiate among the following terms used in relationship to medications
Additive effect
Synergistic effect
Antagonistic effect
Displacement
Interference
Incompatibility

Slide 11

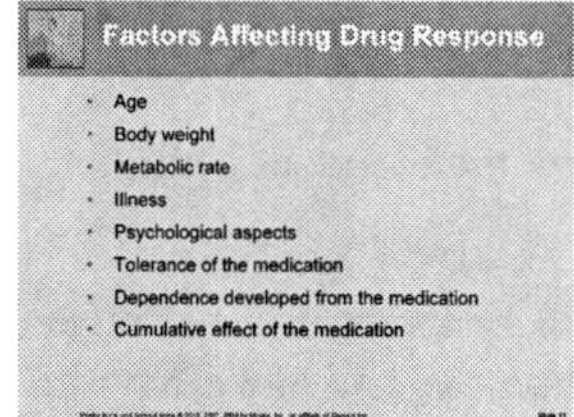
Factors Affecting Drug Response
Age
Body weight
Metabolic rate
Illness
Psychological aspects
Tolerance of the medication
Dependence developed from the medication
Cumulative effect of the medication

- Aging changes body composition and organ function.
- Smoking enhances the metabolism of some drugs.
- Psychological aspects include the placebo effect and nocebo effect.

Slide 12

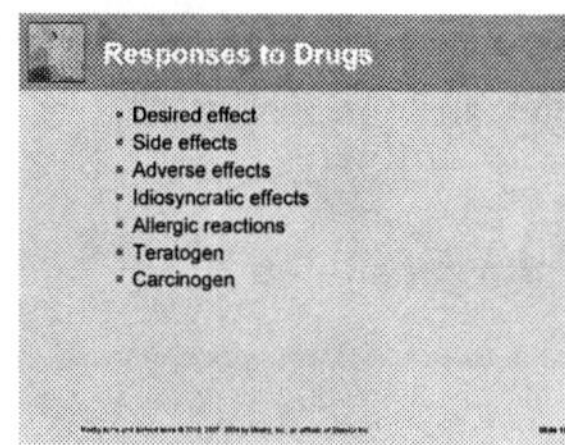
Responses to Drugs
Desired effect
Side effects
Adverse effects
Idiosyncratic effects
Allergic reactions
Teratogen
Carcinogen

- The nurse is expected to know the desired effect and side effects of drugs administered, as well as recognize adverse effects and allergic reactions.
- Allergic reactions occur because of a previous exposure to an antigen (the drug) that results in the development of antibodies against the drug.

3 Lesson Plan

Drug Action Across the Life Span

TEACHING FOCUS

This chapter provides students with the opportunity to learn how age and gender affect drug therapy. The chapter explores the developing science of gender-specific medicine and describes the special considerations that pediatric and geriatric patients require. Drug absorption, drug distribution, drug metabolism, and drug excretion at various stages of life are also discussed. In addition, the chapter introduces students to the use of monitoring parameters in pediatric and geriatric patients, and in pregnant women and nursing mothers.

MATERIALS AND RESOURCES

- ☐ computer and PowerPoint projector (all Lessons)

LESSON CHECKLIST

Preparations for this lesson include:

- lecture
- demonstration
- guest speakers: nurses specializing in women's health, older adults, and infants
- evaluation of student knowledge and skills needed to perform all entry-level nursing activities related to drug action across the life span, including:
  - how drugs are absorbed, metabolized, excreted, and distributed differently in pediatric and geriatric patients
  - ways in which men and women can respond differently to medications
  - methods of therapeutic drug monitoring for all patients, including pregnant and nursing mothers

KEY TERMS

drug metabolism (p. 29)
gender-specific medicine (p. 27)
genetics (p. 26)
genome (p. 26)
hydrolysis (p. 28)
intestinal transit (p. 28)
metabolites (p. 30)
passive diffusion (p. 28)
pharmacogenetics (p. 26)
polymorphisms (p. 26)
polypharmacy (p. 33)
protein binding (p. 29)
therapeutic drug monitoring (p. 30)

ADDITIONAL RESOURCES

PowerPoint slides: 1-21

Legend

ARQ	**PPT**	**TB**	**CTQ**	**SG**	**INRQ**
Audience Response Questions	PowerPoint Slides	Test Bank	Critical Thinking Questions	Study Guide	Interactive NCLEX Review Questions

Class Activities are indicated in ***bold italic.***

LESSON 3.1

BACKGROUND ASSESSMENT

Question: What are four factors that influence drug action on the body? What are some additional factors that affect drug action?
Answer: Absorption, distribution, metabolism, and excretion (ADME) influence how a drug affects the body. Hepatic and renal function, body weight, and the route of administration also affect drug action, depending on a person's age and gender. For example, age can affect excretion because renal function diminishes as a person ages. Reduced hepatic function in older patients can influence how a drug is metabolized. The route of administration influences drug absorption, whereas gender can influence the distribution of fat-soluble drugs.

Question: How do age and gender affect the gastrointestinal absorption of medications? What are some examples relative to older adults and to infants?
Answer: Gender can affect the oral absorption of medications because women have a slower gastric emptying time and because their stomachs have a lower level of alcohol dehydrogenase than men. The older patient has a higher gastric pH, a slower gastric emptying time, and a decreased blood flow to the small intestine, which affect the absorption of medications. In infants, the gastric pH is higher, whereas the intestinal transit time and gastric emptying time are slower than in adults, which influence the oral absorption of drugs. Infants and older adults may lack enough teeth for chewable medicines.

CRITICAL THINKING QUESTION

The nurse is caring for a 77-year-old woman who has been prescribed IV tobramycin for cellulitis, ketoprofen for pain, and lorazepam for anxiety. What are the four basic parameters that the nurse must always consider when administering these medications? What specific nursing interventions related to absorption, distribution, metabolism, and excretion would be important when a patient receives these drugs?
Guidelines: The nurse must always be aware of the intended therapeutic effect, the common adverse effects, the reportable adverse effects, and possible drug interactions. For tobramycin, the patient's temperature and pulse must be monitored to observe for a therapeutic effect, such as the eradication of an infection. The nurse must make sure that peak and trough drug levels are drawn at the appropriate time and must check the results before administering doses. For the NSAID, the nurse must monitor the patient's response in terms of pain relief. The nurse should also be aware that women are more susceptible than men to the gastric irritation these drugs can produce. The nurse should make sure that the patient takes the drug with food and is instructed to report any abdominal pain. For the benzodiazepine, the nurse must be aware that the effects of these drugs may be prolonged in female patients because of their higher proportion of body fat. The nurse should monitor the patient for excessive sedation and institute safety measures to prevent falls.

OBJECTIVES	CONTENT	TEACHING RESOURCES
Discuss the effects of patient age on drug action.	■ Changing drug action across the life span (p. 27)	PPT 3-4 ARQ 2 INRQ 11 CTQ 6 SG Review Sheet questions 1, 3, 8-9, 10-12 (pp. 13-14) SG Learning Activities question 11 (p. 16) SG Practice Question for the NCLEX Examination 6 (p. 19) ▸ Discuss the different age ranges and the titles of the stages of different populations.

ELSEVIER

OBJECTIVES	CONTENT	TEACHING RESOURCES
		▸ Discuss the developing science of gender-specific medicine and U.S. Food and Drug Administration (FDA) guidelines that mandate the evaluation of drug effects on both genders. Class Activity ***Lead an open discussion in which students review the factors—ADME—that affect drug action in the body. (Students may refer to Chapter 2.) How does a person's age contribute to the effects of a drug on the body?***
Discuss the role of genetics and its influence on drug action.	□ Genetics and drug metabolism (p. 26) Discuss research applications that now focus on Hispanic Americans and why it has become important.	PPT 1-2 Review Question for the NCLEX Examination 5 (p. 36) ▸ Discuss the concept of pharmacogenetics, the Human Genome Project, and genotyping use to tailor drug selection to individual genetic makeup. ▸ Discuss monoclonal antibodies designed to attack cancer cells. Class Activity ***Have students look up the genomic biomarkers from the website identified in the text and compile a list. Discuss findings with the class and the significance of the biomarkers.***
Cite major factors associated with drug absorption, distribution, metabolism, and excretion in the pediatric and geriatric populations.	□ Drug absorption (p. 27) – Age considerations (p. 27) Review what are considered age-related issues for drug absorption: drug routes, gastric pH, presence of enzymes, and intestinal transit times.	PPT 9-12 ARQ 2 TB Multiple Choice question 10 TB Multiple Response questions 1-2 INRQ 2 CTQ 3-4 SG Review Sheet questions 14, 17 (p. 14) SG Learning Activities question 12 (p. 16) Review Questions for the NCLEX Examination 1-3 (p. 36) ▸ Discuss special considerations for administering topical medications to an infant and to an older adult. ▸ Discuss how gastrointestinal absorption of medicine differs in newborns and geriatric patients. How does this affect the dosage of oral medications compared with older children and adults?

ELSEVIER

OBJECTIVES	CONTENT	TEACHING RESOURCES
		Class Activity ***Divide the class into small groups. Assign each group one of the following methods of drug administration:*** – ***Intramuscular*** – ***Intravenous*** – ***Oral*** – ***Topical*** ***Ask each group to discuss how its assigned method of administration affects the action of medications in infants, children, adults, and older adults. What are some examples of specific drugs? Have each group make a presentation to the class for feedback and discussion.*** Class Activity ***Discuss how gastrointestinal factors (pH, emptying time, motility, enzymatic activity, blood flow of the mucous lining, and permeability and maturation of mucosal membrane) and concurrent disease processes affect the absorption of a drug. What is passive diffusion? Hydrolysis? How does a person's age affect the factors previously listed?***
Cite major factors associated with drug absorption, distribution, metabolism, and excretion in men and women.	– Gender considerations (p. 28) Discuss how gender affects drug absorption, such as slower transit time and gastric pH differences in women compared with men.	PPT 14 CTQ 2, 5 SG Review Sheet questions 2, 20 (pp. 13, 15) SG Learning Activities questions 1, 8 (p. 16) Class Activity ***Ask the class to list three ways in which drug absorption differs for women and men. Provide this clinical scenario:*** ***A man and a woman, both tennis players, each sprain an ankle. Each is prescribed ibuprofen, 800 mg q6h. They each decide to have a glass of wine to help them relax and cope with the pain.*** ***Ask the class how the absorption of the ibuprofen and wine will differ in the man and woman and the clinical implications of the difference. Discuss combining a drug with alcohol and its effect on the liver as it relates to drug metabolism.***
Cite major factors associated with drug absorption, distribution, metabolism, and excretion in the pediatric	□ Drug distribution (p. 28) – Age and gender considerations (p. 28) Identify the ways that drugs are transported by the circulating body fluids to the sites of action, and	PPT 15-16 ARQ 1, 5 TB Multiple Choice questions 8-9 TB Multiple Response questions 3-4 INRQ 5

OBJECTIVES	CONTENT	TEACHING RESOURCES
and geriatric populations.	how they depend on blood volume, body mass, tissue fat, and blood flow to various organs. Discuss the aging process and the resulting decrease in total body water and lean body mass while total fat increases, thus affecting drug distribution. Discuss decreased albumin levels that occur with aging, affecting the protein binding effect.	SG Review Sheet questions 4-6, 18, 21-23 (pp. 13-15) SG Learning Activities questions 2-3, 6-7, 13-18, 20-22, 25 (pp. 16-17) SG Practice Questions for the NCLEX Examination 1-3 (p. 18) Review Question for the NCLEX Examination 4 (p. 36) Table 3-1: Proportions of Body Water (p. 29) ▸ Discuss the ways in which drugs are transported throughout the body. On which six factors does distribution depend? Class Activity ***Divide the class into small groups. Assign each group one of the following body factors on which drug distribution depends:*** – ***Body water concentration*** – ***Presence and quantity of fat tissue*** – ***Protein binding*** ***Ask each group to discuss how the assigned factor affects drug distribution differently in infants, children, adults, and older adults. Have the groups come up with examples of specific medications. Then have groups present their findings to the class for feedback and questions.***
Cite major factors associated with drug absorption, distribution, metabolism, and excretion in men and women.	– Gender considerations (p. 29) Discuss how gender affects drug distribution, such as women's greater proportion of fat compared with men.	SG Learning Activities questions 24, 26 (p. 17) ▸ Discuss the levels of albumin protein and globulin proteins in men and women and why this is important in drug distribution. Class Activity ***Describe to the class how the composition of body proteins changes as an individual ages. How does this affect the distribution of medications in men's bodies and women's bodies? How might dosage levels of drugs change?***
Cite major factors associated with drug absorption, distribution, metabolism, and excretion in the pediatric and geriatric populations.	□ Drug metabolism (p. 29) – Age considerations (p. 29) Review the hepatic system and its role in inactivating medications; thus, drug metabolism occurs via enzyme action in the liver. Identify those factors that affect liver function, including the	PPT 17 CTQ 3, 4, 5, 6 SG Review Sheet question 24 (p. 15) SG Learning Activities question 10 (p. 16) Table 3-2: Medications that Require Hepatic Monitoring (p. 30) ▸ Discuss the definition of drug metabolism and factors such as genes, diet, age, and

OBJECTIVES	CONTENT	TEACHING RESOURCES
	presence of liver disease and heart failure, in relation to age.	maturity of enzyme systems that control drug metabolism. Class Activity ***Have the class discuss drug metabolism as it relates to age. Ask the class to list three factors that affect drug metabolism. The class should note how these factors are influenced by age in the pediatric and geriatric populations. Have the class list three drugs whose metabolism would be affected by age and explain why. This list could include the following:*** ***1. Propranolol: This drug is extensively metabolized by the liver. Older adults are likely to have decreased hepatic function compared with children.*** ***2. Ampicillin: This drug is destroyed by stomach acids. Older adults have a higher gastric pH than children, so in equal doses the drug would be less effective.*** ***3. Diazepam: This drug is stored in fat. Older adults have a higher body fat concentration than children, so the drug is more extensively stored and will have a longer duration of action.***
Cite major factors associated with drug absorption, distribution, metabolism, and excretion in men and women.	– Gender considerations (p. 29) Discuss how gender affects drug metabolism; women and men differ in enzyme activity, with the cytochrome P-450 system being 40% more active in women.	Class Activity ***Have students identify how males and females differ in the concentrations of certain enzymes. Which drugs are metabolized faster in women than in men? What are the implications for dosage and monitoring?*** Class Activity ***Invite a nurse who specializes in women's health to speak to the class about how the ADME factors influence drug action differently in men and women. What are some examples of health conditions and associated pharmacologic remedies? What nursing assessments, interventions, and monitoring are typically practiced for men and women? Have students prepare questions in advance.***
Cite major factors associated with drug absorption, distribution, metabolism, and excretion in the pediatric and geriatric populations.	□ Drug excretion (p. 30) – Age considerations (p. 30) Review the renal system and how the renal tubules eventually excrete drugs from the body. Discuss the alternative routes of excretion, including the GI system.	PPT 18 ARQ 4 CTQ 6 SG Review Sheet question 25 (p. 15) SG Learning Activities questions 4, 19 (pp. 16-17) Table 3-3, Selected Medications that Require Dosage Adjustment in Renal Failure (p. 31) ▸ Discuss the routes through which drug metabolites are excreted from the body.

OBJECTIVES	CONTENT	TEACHING RESOURCES
	Review how monitoring of drug concentrations is done by drawing blood levels 30 minutes before the next dose of medication to see the lowest blood level (trough), and then 20 minutes after the next dose is given to get the highest blood level (peak).	Class Activity ***Provide students with clinical situations in which penicillin is prescribed for these three patients:*** – ***A full-term newborn infant*** – ***A woman*** – ***An older man*** ***Then lead a discussion in which students identify the criteria used to determine appropriate dosages for each patient. What factors are considered as a patient ages? What information does renal function provide? What is the value of knowing the blood urea nitrogen (BUN) concentration in determining drug dosage?*** Class Activity ***Distribute a list of drugs to students and ask them to identify the drugs for which excretion would be affected by age. The list will include penicillin, verapamil, diltiazem, tobramycin, gentamycin, and isoniazid. Ask the students to explain how age affects the excretion of these drugs, and identify the limitations of using serum BUN and creatinine for assessing renal function. Also, ask the students to identify two nursing interventions related to the effect of age on drug excretion.*** Class Activity ***Invite two nurses, one experienced in care of older adults and one experienced in care of infants and children, to discuss practical applications for nurses involved in drug administration and monitoring. The speakers should address absorption, distribution, metabolism, and excretion of drugs for their age-group. How do these ADME factors affect drug action differently from each other and from adults? What nursing assessments, practices, and interventions are appropriate for each age-group? Ask students to prepare questions in advance.***

ELSEVIER

3.1 Homework/Assignments:

3.1 Instructor's Notes/Student Feedback:

LESSON 3.2

CRITICAL THINKING QUESTION

A nurse is caring for a 2-year-old child with cancer. The patient receives hydromorphone (Dilaudid) orally for pain and metoclopramide by IV for nausea. How should the nurse help the child accept and take the medications? Also, the child's parents ask why medications are dosed differently for a child. What should the nurse tell them?

Guidelines: Children younger than 5 years have difficulty swallowing tablets so, if possible, the medication should be crushed and mixed with a small bit of food. The nurse should allow the child to choose the order in which the medications are taken, and she should make sure to explain the medication regimen in terms appropriate for a 2-year-old child. The nurse should explain to the parents that there are four phases of drug administration, and each one is affected by the patient's age. The nurse should tell the parents that the organs and body systems of a child may not be fully developed, and this can alter the way in which medications affect children. Finally the nurse should advise the parents that because of the child's small body size and inability to verbalize, therapeutic drug monitoring is very important. It is important for the nurse to focus on family-centered care when caring for children. Children may be unable to verbalize accurately, and the parents may partner with the nurse in validating medication effectiveness based on the child's typical behavioral patterns.

OBJECTIVES	CONTENT	TEACHING RESOURCES
Discuss the effects of patient age on drug action.	□ Therapeutic drug monitoring (p. 30) Discuss age considerations with regard to physiologic changes in the kidneys, from the very young how the filtration rate increases during infancy to the effects of decreased renal blood flow in the older adult and the loss of kidney function. Drug monitoring to measure the drugs concentration is generally done with blood assay tests, but saliva samples can also be used.	PPT 4 TB Multiple Choice questions 5, 11 INRQ 3, 8 CTQ 1 Appendix C: Commonly Used Laboratory Tests and Drug Values (CD/Evolve) SG Review Sheet question 13 (p. 14) SG Learning Activities questions 5, 9, 28 (pp. 16-17) ▸ Discuss therapeutic drug monitoring and why it is important. What medications require monitoring? What are the methods used to assess therapeutic levels?

OBJECTIVES	CONTENT	TEACHING RESOURCES
		Class Activity ***Have students identify types of patients for whom drug monitoring is especially important. Ask students to consider age, gender, certain medical conditions, and the possibility of drug abuse. Why is therapeutic drug monitoring critical for neonates, infants, and children?*** Class Activity ***Divide the class into small groups and give each group the following list of therapeutic drugs: digoxin, phenytoin, carbamazepine, acetaminophen, gentamycin, lidocaine, and diazepam. Have the groups identify for which medical conditions and for which age-groups therapeutic drug monitoring is routine or especially important. Have students explain how age affects drug action and the rationale for their conclusions. Have groups make a report to the class and compare their findings.***
	■ Nursing implications when monitoring drug therapy (p. 31) □ Use of monitoring parameters (p. 31) Discuss the nursing implications of monitoring drug therapy that the nurse must know, such as the expected therapeutic actions, common and serious adverse effects, and any probable drug interactions. Monitoring parameters include vital signs, urine output, renal function test. Review the Beers Criteria for medication that are considered safe to give in nursing homes.	PPT 5 TB Multiple Choice questions 1-2, 4, 12 SG Learning Activities question 27 (p. 17) SG Practice Question for the NCLEX Examination 8 (p. 19) ▸ Discuss the high-risk populations (pediatric, older adult, pregnant women, nursing mothers) for whom nursing actions relative to pharmacology are especially important. Class Activity ***Ask students to describe what is meant by each of the following drug parameters:*** – ***Expected therapeutic actions*** – ***Common adverse effects*** – ***Serious adverse effects*** – ***Probable drug interactions*** ***Then have students identify the monitoring parameters (such as vital signs, urine output, and renal function) that are used to plan dosages and monitor drug action. Why must the normal values for these parameters and laboratory tests be related to the age of the patient? Why is patient education important, and what role does the nurse play?***
	– Pediatric patients (p. 32) Discuss the different ways to administer drugs to children.	PPT 6 ARQ 3 SG Review Sheet questions 15, 19 (p. 14)

OBJECTIVES	CONTENT	TEACHING RESOURCES
	Review growth and development to assist in understanding the difference between use of liquids for infants and how older children can take chewable drugs. Discuss general principles about pediatric patients that the nurse must recognize, such as higher total water content, weight variations, growth spurts, and adjustment of dosages. Know the symptoms of an allergic reaction; the first symptoms may be intense anxiety, weakness, sweating, and shortness of breath, with other symptoms of hypotension, shock laryngeal edema, and nausea. Know what to do in case of a suspected allergic reaction.	SG Learning Activities questions 23, 29 (p. 17) Table 3-4: Selected Guidelines for Administration of Oral Medicine to Pediatric Patients (p. 33) ▸ Discuss why principles of drug therapy can not be transferred to infants and children and altered on the basis of size. Why are infants and children at greater risk for complications? ▸ Discuss symptoms of an allergic drug reaction and nursing interventions appropriate to this condition. Class Activity ***Divide the class into small groups, and have each group develop two role plays, as follows:*** ***1. A nurse explains to parents general principles relative to drug administration to follow when caring for infants and children*** ***2. A nurse explains how to administer oral medications to infants, toddlers, and preschoolers*** ***Ask volunteer groups to present their role plays and invite the class to assist the groups with accurate and complete information by filling in any omitted items.***
	– Geriatric patients (p. 32) Identify the need to do a thorough drug history for older adult patients and review multidrug regimens Review nutritional status and renal and hepatic functioning for older adults.	PPT 7-8 SG Review Sheet questions 16, 24, 26-29 (pp. 14-15) Table 3-5: Potentially Inappropriate Medications for Older Adult Patients (p. 34) ▸ Discuss factors that place an older adult at greater risk for drug interactions or toxicity. What special steps should a nurse take when initiating drug therapy for a geriatric patient? Class Activity ***Have students describe the following areas and why they are of particular concern when administering medications to geriatric populations:*** – ***Renal and hepatic function*** – ***Nutritional status*** – ***Multiple medication*** – ***Accurate medication history*** ***Then divide the class into small groups, and ask them to identify appropriate nursing interventions for the areas of concern listed above. Have groups present their findings to the class for discussion and feedback.***

ELSEVIER

OBJECTIVES	CONTENT	TEACHING RESOURCES
	– Pregnant patients (p. 34) – Breast-feeding infants (p. 35) Pregnant patients should avoid taking drugs because of the risk for injury to the developing fetus. Few medications are considered safe to take during pregnancy. Review teratogenic drugs. Breast-feeding patients should be aware that drugs may pass through the breast milk and have an effect on the infant. Review the list of medications that are known to have an effect on nursing infants.	PPT 19-21 TB Multiple Choice Questions 3, 6-7 SG Review Sheet question 30 (p. 15) SG Learning Activities question 30 (p. 17) SG Practice Questions for the NCLEX Examination 4-5, 7 (pp. 18-19) Table 3-6: Drugs Known to be Teratogens (p. 35) Table 3-7: Drugs and Nursing Infants (p. 35) ▶ Discuss why it is important for pregnant women and nursing mothers to minimize ingestion of prescription medicines and nonprescription self-care remedies. *Class Activity* ***Divide the class into small groups. Ask each group to describe key points the nurse should follow when caring for a pregnant or nursing patient. Have groups include a plan for patient education. Ask volunteer groups to present their conclusions for discussion and feedback. As a class, develop an optimal plan.***
Performance evaluation		Test Bank SG Learning Activities (pp. 16-17) SG Practice Questions for the NCLEX Examination (pp. 18-19) Critical Thinking Questions

3.2 Homework/Assignments:

3.2 Instructor's Notes/Student Feedback:

3 Lecture Outline
Drug Action Across the Life Span

Slide 1

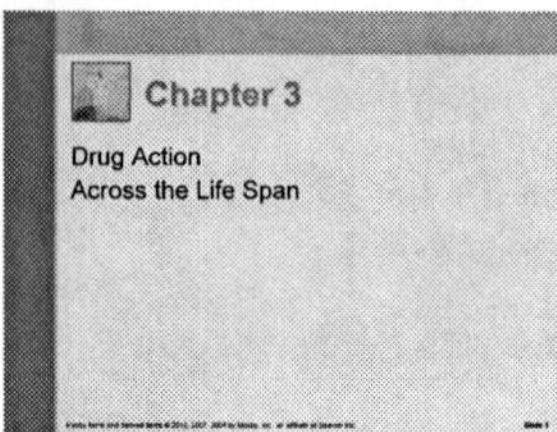
Chapter 3
Drug Action
Across the Life Span

Slide 2

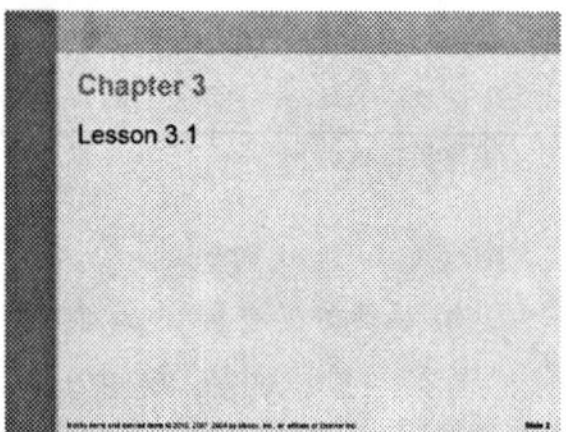
Chapter 3
Lesson 3.1

Slide 3

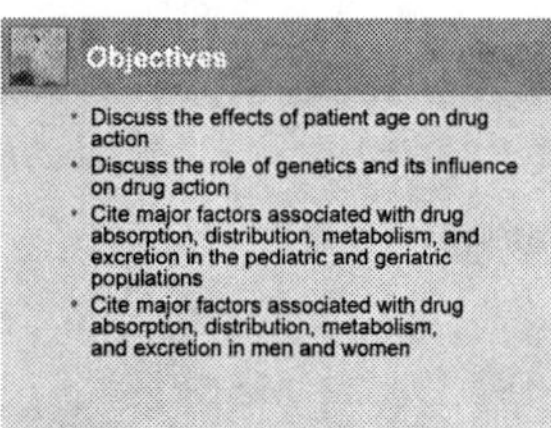
Objectives
Discuss the effects of patient age on drug action
Discuss the role of genetics and its influence on drug action
Cite major factors associated with drug absorption, distribution, metabolism, and excretion in the pediatric and geriatric populations
Cite major factors associated with drug absorption, distribution, metabolism, and excretion in men and women

- Gender-specific medicine is a developing science that looks at how men and women perceive and experience disease, as well as how pharmacokinetics affect each gender.

Slide 4

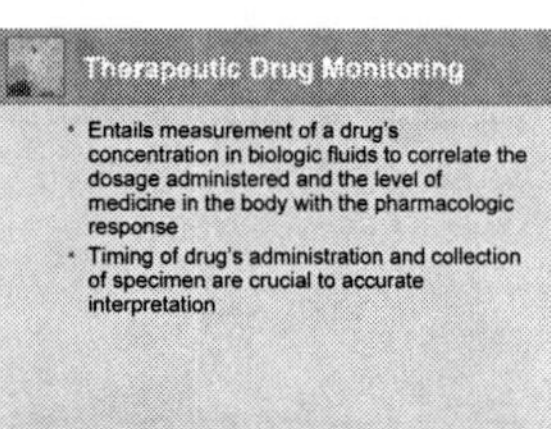
Therapeutic Drug Monitoring
Entails measurement of a drug's concentration in biologic fluids to correlate the dosage administered and the level of medicine in the body with the pharmacologic response
Timing of drug's administration and collection of specimen are crucial to accurate interpretation

- Essential in neonates, infants, and children, given the major physiologic changes that affect drug ADME.

Slide 5

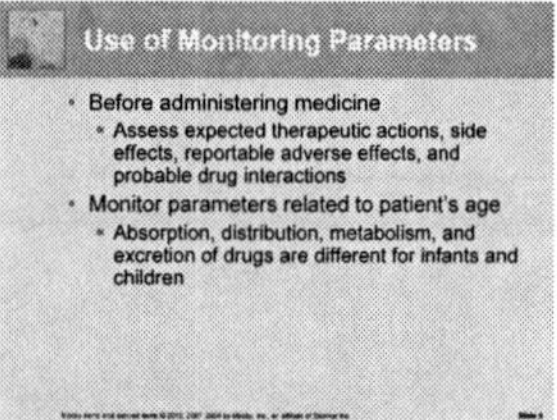
Use of Monitoring Parameters
Before administering medicine
Assess expected therapeutic actions, side effects, reportable adverse effects, and probable drug interactions
Monitor parameters related to patient's age
Absorption, distribution, metabolism, and excretion of drugs are different for infants and children

- These parameters often change; therapeutic drug monitoring is very important for pediatric patients.

ELSEVIER

Slide 6

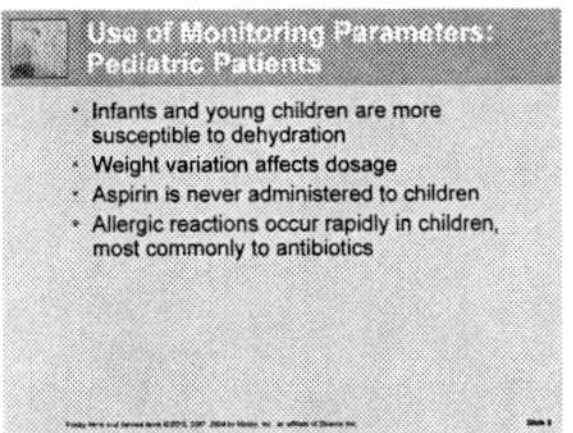
Use of Monitoring Parameters:
Pediatric Patients
Infants and young children are more susceptible to dehydration
Weight variation affects dosage
Aspirin is never administered to children
Allergic reactions occur rapidly in children, most commonly to antibiotics

- Why should aspirin not be given to children? *(Reye's syndrome)*
- What two common drugs are appropriate analgesics and antipyretics for children? *(Ibuprofen and acetaminophen)*
- What is it called when a medication is prescribed for a child but there is no FDA-approved use for children? *(Off-label use)*
- What symptoms may be indicative of an allergic reaction? *(Urticaria, difficulty breathing, swelling in the oropharynx)*
- If the patient is exhibiting signs of a severe allergic reaction, what is the appropriate nursing intervention?

Slide 7

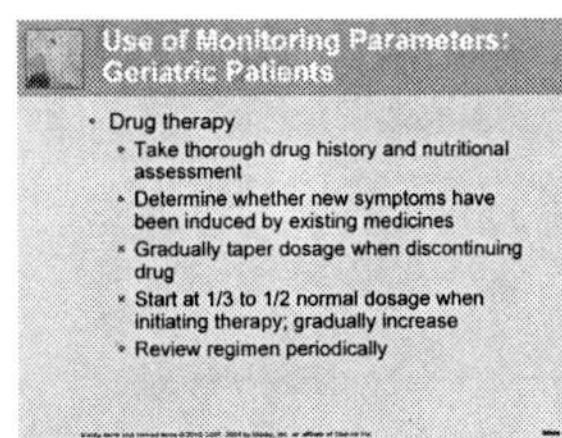
Use of Monitoring Parameters:
Geriatric Patients
Drug therapy
Take thorough drug history and nutritional assessment
Determine whether new symptoms have been induced by existing medicines
Gradually taper dosage when discontinuing drug
Start at 1/3 to 1/2 normal dosage when initiating therapy; gradually increase
Review regimen periodically

- Use calendars or pill boxes to avoid confusion with multidrug regimens.
- Offer assistance in destroying old medicines.

Slide 8

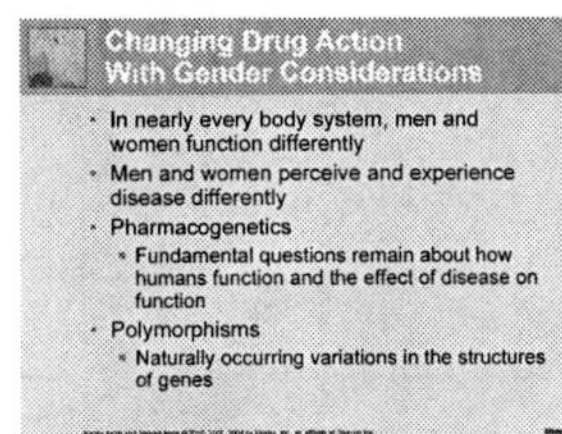
Changing Drug Action
With Gender Considerations
In nearly every body system, men and women function differently
Men and women perceive and experience disease differently
Pharmacogenetics
Fundamental questions remain about how humans function and the effect of disease on function
Polymorphisms
Naturally occurring variations in the structures of genes

- Having parameters or guidelines for both men and women is one of the goals of this research.
- Women's studies need to include the different phases of the menstrual cycle, as well as pre- and post-menopausal women.

Slide 9

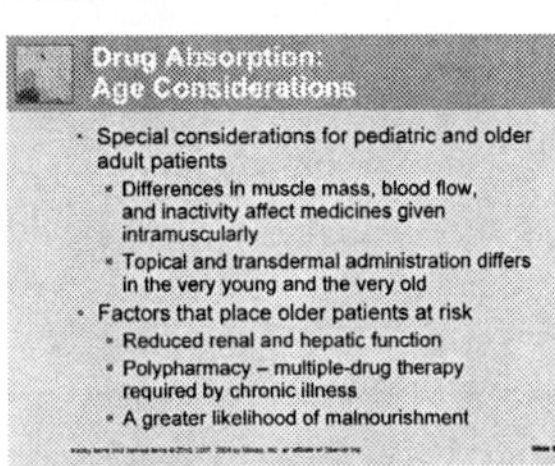
Drug Absorption:
Age Considerations
Special considerations for pediatric and older adult patients
Differences in muscle mass, blood flow, and inactivity affect medicines given intramuscularly
Topical and transdermal administration differs in the very young and the very old
Factors that place older patients at risk
Reduced renal and hepatic function
Polypharmacy – multiple-drug therapy required by chronic illness
A greater likelihood of malnourishment

- Discuss why the amount of muscle mass and blood flow affect the absorption of IM drugs.
- Describe why IM drugs may be absorbed differently in older adults compared with younger adults.
- Explain why topical and transdermal medications may be absorbed differently in children and older adults.

Slide 10

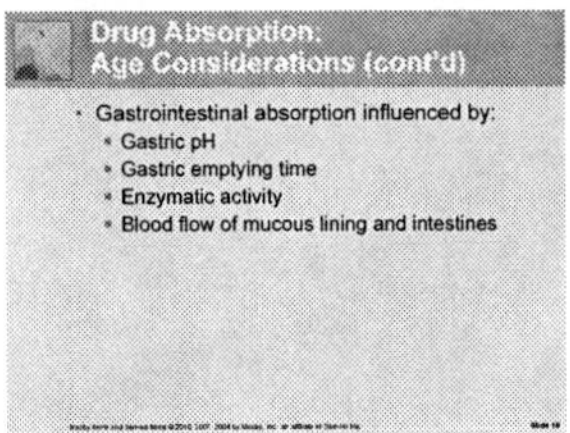
Drug Absorption:
Age Considerations (cont'd)
Gastrointestinal absorption influenced by:
Gastric pH
Gastric emptying time
Enzymatic activity
Blood flow of mucous lining and intestines

- Discuss why intestinal blood flow influences drug absorption.

ELSEVIER

Slide 11

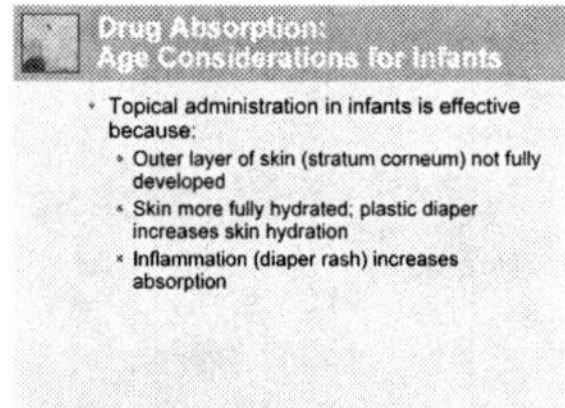
Drug Absorption:
Age Considerations for Infants
Topical administration in infants is effective because:
Outer layer of skin (stratum corneum) not fully developed
Skin more fully hydrated; plastic diaper increases skin hydration
Inflammation (diaper rash) increases absorption

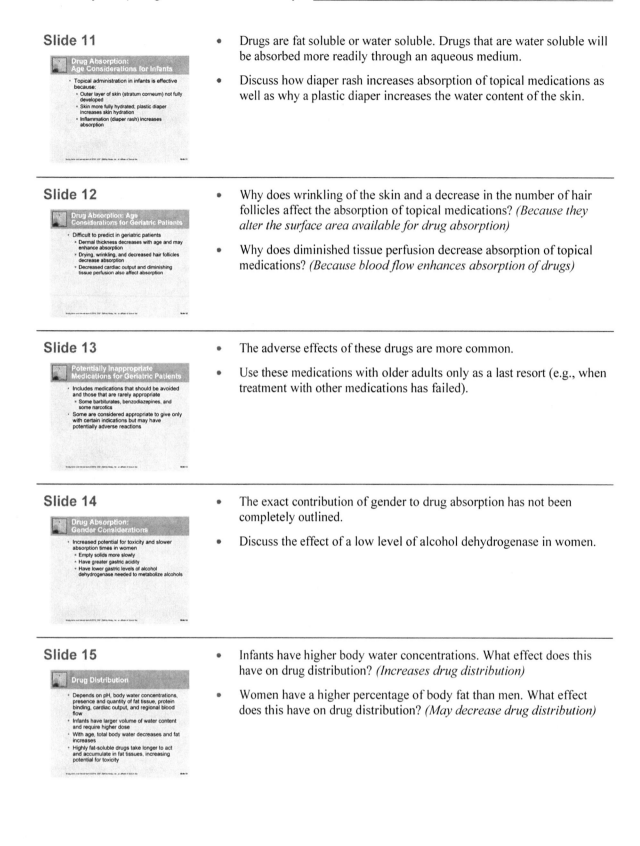

- Drugs are fat soluble or water soluble. Drugs that are water soluble will be absorbed more readily through an aqueous medium.
- Discuss how diaper rash increases absorption of topical medications as well as why a plastic diaper increases the water content of the skin.

Slide 12

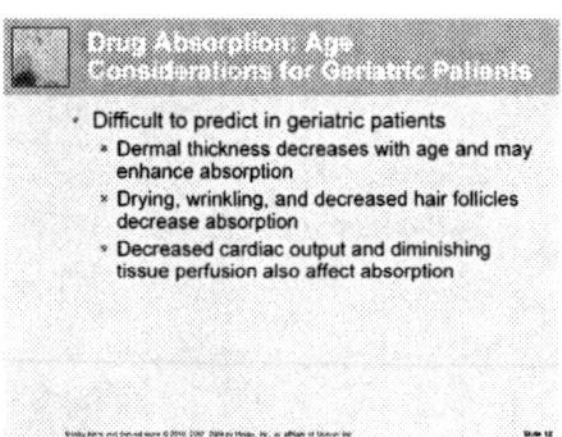
Drug Absorption: Age Considerations for Geriatric Patients
Difficult to predict in geriatric patients
Dermal thickness decreases with age and may enhance absorption
Drying, wrinkling, and decreased hair follicles decrease absorption
Decreased cardiac output and diminishing tissue perfusion also affect absorption

- Why does wrinkling of the skin and a decrease in the number of hair follicles affect the absorption of topical medications? *(Because they alter the surface area available for drug absorption)*
- Why does diminished tissue perfusion decrease absorption of topical medications? *(Because blood flow enhances absorption of drugs)*

Slide 13

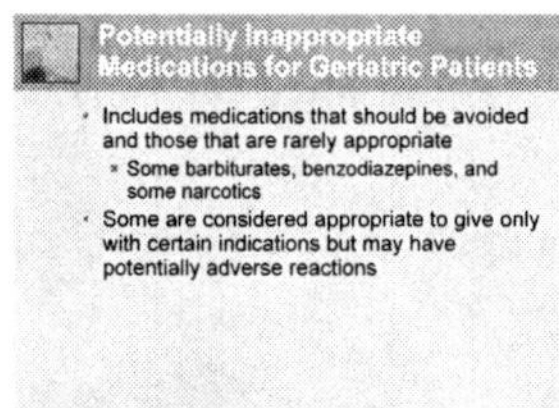
Potentially Inappropriate Medications for Geriatric Patients
Includes medications that should be avoided and those that are rarely appropriate
Some barbiturates, benzodiazepines, and some narcotics
Some are considered appropriate to give only with certain indications but may have potentially adverse reactions

- The adverse effects of these drugs are more common.
- Use these medications with older adults only as a last resort (e.g., when treatment with other medications has failed).

Slide 14

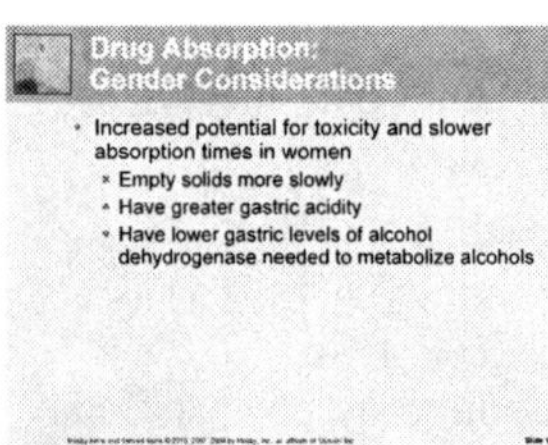
Drug Absorption:
Gender Considerations
Increased potential for toxicity and slower absorption times in women
Empty solids more slowly
Have greater gastric acidity
Have lower gastric levels of alcohol dehydrogenase needed to metabolize alcohols

- The exact contribution of gender to drug absorption has not been completely outlined.
- Discuss the effect of a low level of alcohol dehydrogenase in women.

Slide 15

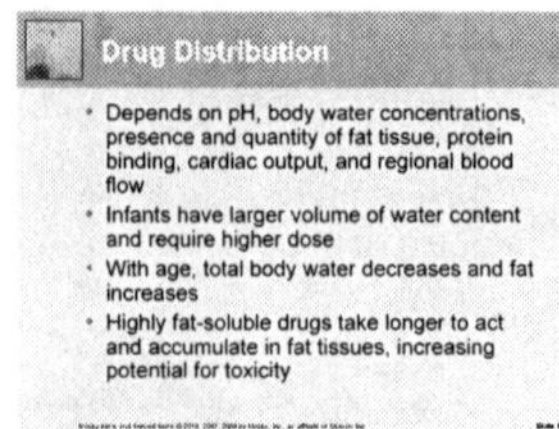
Drug Distribution
Depends on pH, body water concentrations, presence and quantity of fat tissue, protein binding, cardiac output, and regional blood flow
Infants have larger volume of water content and require higher dose
With age, total body water decreases and fat increases
Highly fat-soluble drugs take longer to act and accumulate in fat tissues, increasing potential for toxicity

- Infants have higher body water concentrations. What effect does this have on drug distribution? *(Increases drug distribution)*
- Women have a higher percentage of body fat than men. What effect does this have on drug distribution? *(May decrease drug distribution)*

ELSEVIER

Slide 16

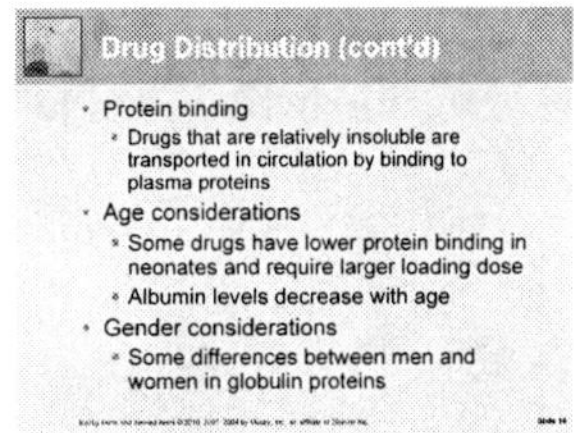
Drug Distribution (cont'd)
Protein binding
Drugs that are relatively insoluble are transported in circulation by binding to plasma proteins
Age considerations
Some drugs have lower protein binding in neonates and require larger loading dose
Albumin levels decrease with age
Gender considerations
Some differences between men and women in globulin proteins

- Drugs that are highly fat soluble include antidepressants, phenothiazines, benzodiazepines, and calcium channel blockers.
- Lower protein binding may lead to greater immediate pharmacologic effect.

Slide 17

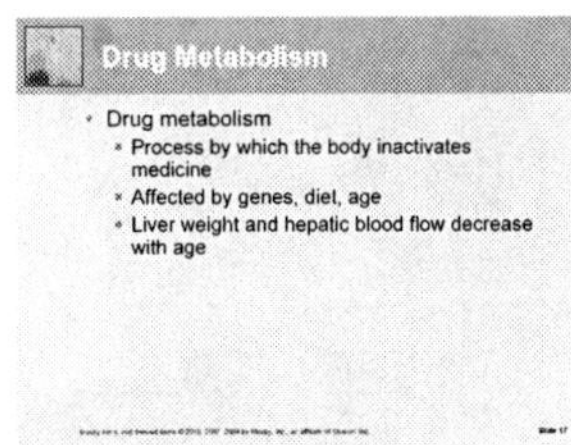
Drug Metabolism
Drug metabolism
Process by which the body inactivates medicine
Affected by genes, diet, age
Liver weight and hepatic blood flow decrease with age

- Explain why a decrease in liver weight and hepatic blood flow affect drug metabolism. *(Because it may cause a decline in the liver's ability to metabolize a drug)*
- Discuss the effect liver disease has on drug metabolism and why. *(It will affect the patient's ability to metabolize a drug, increasing the risk for drug toxicity)*

Slide 18

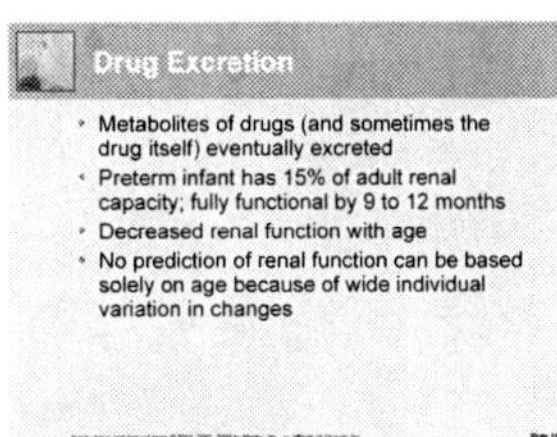
Drug Excretion
Metabolites of drugs (and sometimes the drug itself) eventually excreted
Preterm infant has 15% of adult renal capacity; fully functional by 9 to 12 months
Decreased renal function with age
No prediction of renal function can be based solely on age because of wide individual variation in changes

- Occasionally drug metabolites can be pharmacologically active.
- Why is it important to know that the renal capacity of an infant is less than that of an adult? *(Because it will affect excretion of drugs)*
- What are the two common blood tests that measure renal function? *(Blood urea nitrogen [BUN] and creatinine [Cr])*

Slide 19

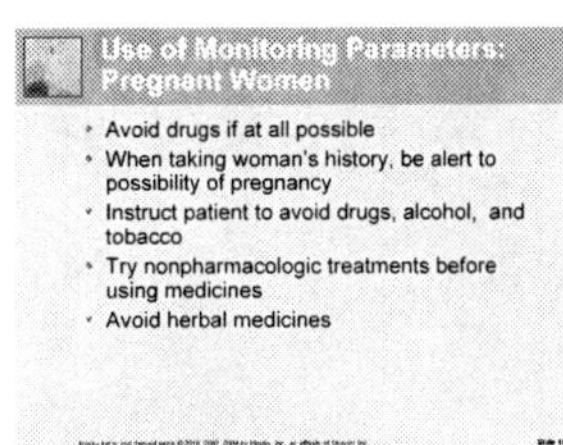
Use of Monitoring Parameters: Pregnant Women
Avoid drugs if at all possible
When taking woman's history, be alert to possibility of pregnancy
Instruct patient to avoid drugs, alcohol, and tobacco
Try nonpharmacologic treatments before using medicines
Avoid herbal medicines

- Alcohol and tobacco are not essential nutrients, and have been proven to have detrimental effects on the fetus.
- Herbal medications are not regulated by the FDA and pose a risk to the pregnant patient, including miscarriage.

Slide 20

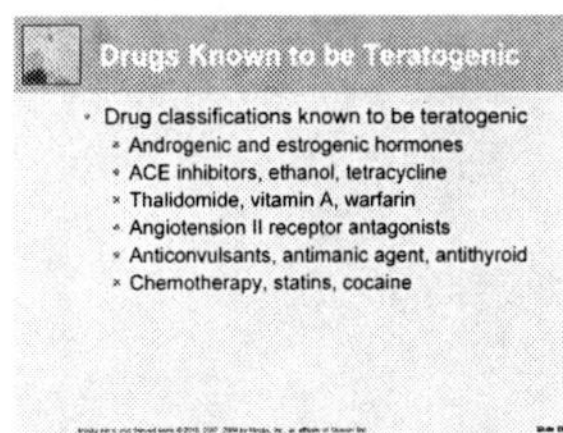
Drugs Known to be Teratogenic
Drug classifications known to be teratogenic
Androgenic and estrogenic hormones
ACE inhibitors, ethanol, tetracycline
Thalidomide, vitamin A, warfarin
Angiotension II receptor antagonists
Anticonvulsants, antimanic agent, antithyroid
Chemotherapy, statins, cocaine

- Discuss teratogenic drugs or any substances that cause birth defects.

Slide 21

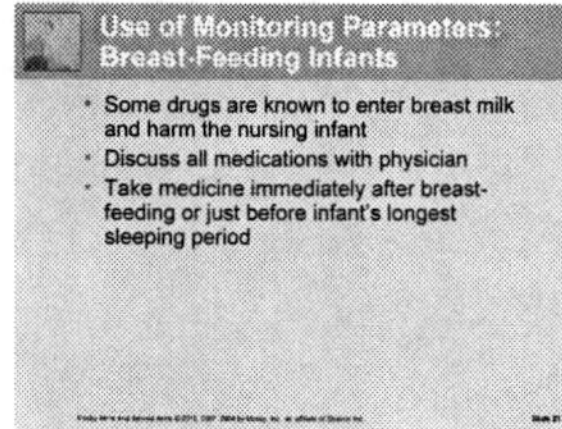
Use of Monitoring Parameters: Breast-Feeding Infants
Some drugs are known to enter breast milk and harm the nursing infant
Discuss all medications with physician
Take medicine immediately after breast-feeding or just before infant's longest sleeping period

- For many drugs that are excreted in breast milk, no one knows with certainty what effect they will have on the infant.
- Medications include prescription, nonprescription, and herbal products.

4 Lesson Plan

The Nursing Process and Pharmacology

TEACHING FOCUS

In this chapter, students have the opportunity to learn the five steps in the nursing process and how to apply them as a method of problem solving in nursing practice. Students will learn about the process of assessment and discuss when and how to make a nursing diagnosis. Identifying the steps in the planning of nursing care; comparing the types of nursing functions in intervention, implementation, and the evaluation process will also be discussed. Students will also have the opportunity to learn how this process relates to pharmacology and the procedure for evaluating therapeutic outcomes from prescribed drug therapy.

MATERIALS AND RESOURCES

- ☐ computer and PowerPoint projector (all Lessons)
- ☐ drug monographs for propranolol, warfarin, and metformin (Lesson 4.2)

LESSON CHECKLIST

Preparations for this lesson include:

- lecture
- evaluation of student knowledge and skills needed to perform all entry-level activities related to the nursing process and pharmacology, including:
  - the components of the assessment process
  - nursing diagnoses and the wording used in diagnosis statements
  - steps involved in planning nursing care and prioritizing individual patient needs
  - comparing dependent, interdependent, and independent nursing functions
  - evaluating and recording therapeutic outcomes from prescribed medication therapy

KEY TERMS

actual nursing diagnosis (p. 40)
adverse effects (p. 48)
anticipated therapeutic and expected outcome statements (p. 47)
assessment (p. 39)
collaborative problem (p. 42)
common adverse effects (p. 49)
critical care pathway (p. 44)
defining characteristics (p. 40)
dependent actions (p. 46)
drug history (p. 48)
drug monographs (p. 48)
evidence-based practice (p. 45)
focused assessment (p. 44)
health promotion and wellness nursing diagnosis (p. 40)
independent actions (p. 47)
interdependent actions (p. 46)
measurable goal statement (p. 45)
medical diagnosis (p. 42)
multidisciplinary team (p. 37)
nursing actions (p. 46)
nursing care plan (p. 44)
nursing classification systems (p. 37)
nursing diagnosis (p. 40)
nursing intervention or implementation (p. 46)
nursing orders (p. 47)
nursing process (p. 37)
objective data (p. 48)
patient goals (p. 46)
primary source (p. 48)
priority setting (p. 45)
risk/high-risk nursing diagnosis (p. 40)
secondary sources (p. 48)
serious adverse effects (p. 49)
subjective data (p. 48)
syndrome nursing diagnosis (p. 40)
tertiary sources (p. 48)
therapeutic intent (p. 49)

ADDITIONAL RESOURCES

PowerPoint slides: 1-26

ELSEVIER

Legend

ARQ	PPT	TB	CTQ	SG	INRQ
Audience Response Questions	PowerPoint Slides	Test Bank	Critical Thinking Questions	Study Guide	Interactive NCLEX Review Questions

Class Activities are indicated in ***bold italic.***

LESSON 4.1

BACKGROUND ASSESSMENT

Question: A patient with postoperative discomfort has a standing order for morphine sulfate. Which parts of the nursing process might apply to this patient?
Answer: The nurse should assess the patient for pain by measuring and recording vital signs and asking him or her to describe the level of pain. If the patient is experiencing pain, a nursing diagnosis of "pain, acute" would be made, followed by a plan of care related to the diagnosis. The nurse would then implement the plan of care using dependent and independent measures and evaluate the plan of care by again asking the patient to describe the level of pain and measuring and recording vital signs.

Question: What sources of information are used to assess a patient's medication status?
Answer: There are three sources used to develop a medication information base. The primary source is the patient. Subjective and objective data are gathered from the patient whenever the patient is able to provide reliable information. Secondary sources of information are the patient's family, significant others, other medical professionals, nursing notes, and medical records. These sources are interpreted by someone other than the patient. Tertiary sources include published literature, such as textbooks and medical journals.

CRITICAL THINKING QUESTION

A 59-year-old woman recently had a stroke and is now paraplegic and unable to feed herself. What is the nursing process as it relates to this patient's self-care deficit? How do the different parts of the nursing process overlap and build on one another?
Guidelines: The assessment process would begin by determining the patient's physical ability and assessing the patient's inability to feed herself. This finding will determine the diagnosis. The diagnosis will determine the plan of care (e.g., ensuring that the patient is fed in an upright position and maintaining an upright position for 30 minutes after each meal, making sure that the food is of a size and texture that can be swallowed safely, and ensuring that the patient consumes adequate amounts of food). Implementing the plan of care will entail using the dietary department and the nursing staff and educating the patient's family about her limitations and care measures. Evaluating the success of the interventions will determine the need for further monitoring and education.

OBJECTIVES	CONTENT	TEACHING RESOURCES
Explain the purpose of the nursing process and methodology used to apply to the study of pharmacology.	■ The nursing process (p. 37) Review the five components of the nursing process, with an emphasis on pharmacology	PPT 8 ARQ 4 SG Review Sheet questions 1-3 (p. 21) SG Learning Activities 12, 14 (pp. 24-25)

OBJECTIVES	CONTENT	TEACHING RESOURCES
		▸ Discuss the five-step process in relation to the administration of medication. Class Activity ***Lead a class discussion about the nursing process. Ask students to identify ways that it applies to the study of pharmacology. Record student responses on the board for comparison.***
State the five steps in the nursing process and describe them in terms of a problem-solving method used in nursing practice.	■ The nursing process (p. 37) Review the five steps of the nursing process as they relate to the problem-solving method: 1. Assessment 2. Diagnosis 3. Planning 4. Implementation 5. Evaluation Discuss how the holistic approach to nursing is important to help identify patient needs.	PPT 8-9 INRQ 1 SG Learning Activities question 15 (p. 25) SG Practice Questions for the NCLEX Examination 1-2 (p. 26) Table 4-1: Principles of the Nursing Process (p. 38) Figure 4-1 (p. 39): The nursing process and the holistic needs of the patient. ▸ Discuss how the nursing process is ongoing and cyclical in nature. Class Activity ***Divide the class into groups. Have each group identify the five steps of the nursing process, briefly discuss each step, and identify two actions or activities associated with each. Have each group present its findings to the class and discuss how each successive step depends on the one that precedes it.***
Describe the components of the assessment process.	□ Assessment (p. 39) Describe the information gathered by nurses during the assessment phase of the nursing process.	PPT 10 ARQ 2 TB Multiple Choice questions 13-14, 16 CTQ 2 SG Review Sheet question 4 (p. 21) SG Learning Activities questions 4-5 (p. 24) ▸ Discuss the importance of taking a health history. What sources should the nurse rely upon? ▸ Discuss some possible risk factors to look for when assessing a patient. Review Box 4-1 (p. 40) during discussion. Class Activity ***Present the following scenario to the class:*** ***A 76-year-old woman who has been diagnosed with congestive heart failure has just been transferred to your floor.***

OBJECTIVES	CONTENT	TEACHING RESOURCES
		The patient takes digoxin and furosemide. ***Divide the class into groups and have each group list and describe the components of the assessment process as it relates to this patient, and present its findings to the class.***
Compare current methods used to collect, organize, and analyze information about the health care needs of patients and their significant others.	□ Assessment (p. 39)	PPT 10 Box 4-1: Gordon's Functional Health Patterns Model (p. 40) ▸ Discuss different models for assessment. Which elements are likely to be omitted from a body systems approach? Class Activity ***Present the following scenario to the class and have students list three methods used to collect, organize, and analyze information about the health care needs of the patient.*** ***A 42-year-old woman has just been diagnosed with breast cancer.*** ***Then have students apply the methods that were identified for this patient and discuss the unique findings gathered when each method is used.***
Define the term *nursing diagnosis*, and discuss the wording used in formulating nursing diagnosis statements.	□ Nursing diagnosis (p. 40) Review the five types of nursing diagnoses: 1. Actual 2. Risk/high-risk 3. Possible 4. Health promotion and wellness 5. Syndrome nursing	PPT 11 ARQ 5 TB Multiple Choice questions 2, 4, 6 CTQ 1 SG Review Sheet questions 5, 9 (pp. 21-22) SG Learning Activities questions 1, 2, 11, 16 (pp. 24-25) SG Practice Question for the NCLEX Examination 7 (p. 27) Review Questions for the NLCEX Examination 1-2 (p. 52) Figure 4-2 (p. 41): Decision tree. Box 4-2: Nursing Diagnoses Approved by NANDA International (2009-2011) (pp. 43-44) ▸ Discuss the five types of nursing diagnoses. Class Activity ***Present the following scenario to the class:*** ***A 67-year-old man with chronic obstructive pulmonary disease (COPD)***

OBJECTIVES	CONTENT	TEACHING RESOURCES
		becomes short of breath when walking to the bathroom. ***Divide the class into groups and have each group define the term* nursing diagnosis. *Then have groups define the terms that are in the definition of nursing diagnosis as they pertain to the scenario. Have each group present its findings to the class.***
Define the term *collaborative problem.*	– Collaborative problems (p. 42) Collaborative problems are different from nursing diagnoses when the intervention used is to prevent or treat a problem, and they are worded with "potential complication" in the diagnosis.	PPT 13 Figure 4-3 (p. 42): Differentiation of nursing diagnosis from collaborative problems. ▶ Discuss how diagnosing collaborative problems might prevent potential complications. *Class Activity* ***Lead a class discussion about collaborative problems. Ask students to identify how to differentiate between a problem requiring a nursing diagnosis and a potential complication. Record student responses on the board for comparison.***
Differentiate between a nursing diagnosis and a medical diagnosis.	□ Nursing diagnosis (p. 40) Medical diagnosis is concerned with alterations in structure and function of the patient that results in disease. Nursing diagnosis is concerned with the ability to function in activities of daily living in relation to the impairment.	PPT 11 ARQ 1 TB Multiple Response question 2 INRQ 10 SG Review Sheet question 6 (p. 21) ▶ Discuss why a nursing diagnosis may vary depending on the patient's state of recovery. What is meant by ADL? *Class Activity* ***Draw a Venn diagram on the board and label one circle "Nursing Diagnosis" and the other "Medical Diagnosis." Have students compare and contrast the two diagnoses and ask student volunteers to fill in the diagram on the board.***
Differentiate between problems that require formulation of a nursing diagnosis and those categorized as collaborative problems, which may not require nursing diagnosis statements.	– Collaborative problems (p. 42) – Focused assessment (p. 44)	CTQ 2 SG Review Sheet question 8 (p. 21) ▶ Discuss the decision-making process for differentiating between a problem requiring a nursing diagnosis and a collaborative problem. ▶ Discuss how collaborative problem statements are worded. *Class Activity* ***Present the following scenarios to the class and have students identify which ones***

OBJECTIVES	CONTENT	TEACHING RESOURCES
		contain a collaborative problem and which require the formulation of a nursing diagnosis: *1.* ***An 81-year-old woman with congestive heart failure who takes digoxin and furosemide*** *2.* ***A 37-year-old man with type 1 diabetes mellitus*** *3.* ***A 77-year-old man with Alzheimer's disease who is not fully oriented to his surroundings***
Identify the steps in the planning of nursing care.	□ Planning (p. 44) Discuss the four phases of planning: 1. Priority setting 2. Development of measurable goal outcome statements 3. Formulation of nursing interventions 4. Formulation of anticipated therapeutic outcomes that can be used to evaluate patients	PPT 14-15 TB Multiple Choice question 17 SG Review Sheet question 11 (p. 22) SG Practice Question for the NCLEX Examination 6 (p. 26) ▸ Discuss the four phases that planning encompasses. What is a nursing care plan? ▸ Discuss the importance of including both the patient and the patient's significant others in the planning of nursing care. Class Activity ***Present the following terms to the class and have students identify which terms are steps in the planning of nursing care:*** – ***Evaluation*** – ***Assessment*** – ***Networking*** – ***Symptom list*** – ***Planning*** – ***Medication history*** – ***Intervention*** – ***Physical assessment*** – ***Nursing diagnosis*** – ***Intervention*** – ***Assessing social needs***
Explain the process of prioritizing individual patient needs using Maslow's hierarchy of needs.	□ Planning (p. 44) Discuss how using Maslow's hierarchy of needs helps the nurse prioritize patient needs. Review with the class the categories in Maslow's hierarchy of needs: ▪ Physiologic ▪ Safety ▪ Belonging ▪ Self-esteem ▪ Self-actualization	TB Other question 1 INRQ 3 SG Review Sheet question 12 (p. 22) Box 4-3: Priority Ranking of Maslow's Subcategories of Human Needs (p. 45) ▸ Discuss Maslow's hierarchy of needs. How does this relate to a patient's involvement in establishing a goal and/or outcome statement? ▸ Discuss priority setting and how Maslow's model can assist in organizing how to best meet a patient's needs.

OBJECTIVES	CONTENT	TEACHING RESOURCES
		Class Activity: ***Using Maslow's hierarchy of needs, have students identify under which category each of the following patient situations falls:*** ***1. Patient with fatigue*** ***2. Patient with shortness of breath*** ***3. Patient with recent loss of spouse*** ***4. Patient with chronic diarrhea***
Formulate measurable goal statements for assigned patients in the clinical practice setting.	□ Planning (p. 44) Review the process that nurses use to generate outcome statements and measurable goals in planning for patient care.	SG Learning Activities question 17 (p. 25) Class Activity ***Present the following scenario to the class:*** ***A 67-year-old woman has just had a below-the-knee amputation. Her husband died 2 months ago, and upon discharge she will be living alone.*** ***Divide the class into groups. Have each group generate one measurable goal statement and present its findings to the class. Compare results.***
State the behavioral responses around which goal statements revolve when the discharge of a patient is planned.	– Measurable goal and outcome statements (p. 45) Discuss goal statements in terms of patient goals, not nursing goals for the patient.	TB Multiple Choice questions 7, 13 SG Review Sheet question 25 (p. 23) ▸ Discuss patient education and goal statements. What things are important for a patient to understand about his or her disease and the treatment plan? ▸ Discuss long-term goals for a discharged patient. Class Activity ***Lead a class discussion about goal statements. Have students apply the six behavioral responses surrounding goal statements to the following patient, a 67-year-old woman with cellulitis on both legs. Record student responses on the board for comparison.***
Identify the purposes and uses of a patient care plan.	□ Planning (p. 44) Review the use of short-term goals as a bridge to meet long-term goals, and how referral agencies can help meet these goals.	▸ Discuss the team members involved in developing a patient care plan. ▸ Discuss the importance of setting short-term and long-term goals in a patient care plan. Class Activity ***Divide the class into groups and have each group discuss the components, purposes, and uses of a care plan for a 74-year-old man who has just been diagnosed with angina pectoris. Have each group present its findings to the class for discussion.***

OBJECTIVES	CONTENT	TEACHING RESOURCES
Integrate outcome and classification system(s) and critical pathways into care plans.	□ Planning (p. 44) Discuss critical care pathways and CareMaps as a method of documenting patient progress toward established outcomes.	TB Multiple Choice questions 12, 15 TB Multiple Response question 1 INRQ 11 SG Review Sheet question 10 (p. 22) SG Learning Activities questions 3, 13 (p. 24) ▸ Discuss the role of electronic medical records and standardized care plans. ▸ Discuss the effect of information systems on nursing diagnoses and interventions and ultimately on patients' outcomes. Class Activity ***Divide the class into groups and have each group discuss how an outcome classification system and a critical pathway could be integrated into the care plan for the following patient, a 72-year-old man who has just been diagnosed with colon cancer and who will need to have a colostomy performed. Have each group present its findings to the class for discussion.***
Discuss the use of evidence-based practice in planning for nursing care.	□ Planning (p. 44) Discuss the need for nurses to recognize evidence-based practice changes in planning patient care.	PPT 13 INRQ 7 ▸ Give a brief overview of the ways nurses participate in evidence-based practice. • Evidence-based practice allows nurses to incorporate from research the clinical expertise and patient preference discussed in the study into decisions about health care for patients. Class Activity ***Divide the class into groups and have each group identify one example of an evidence-based practice change. Review each group's findings with the class.***
Differentiate between nursing interventions and therapeutic outcomes.	– Nursing actions or nursing interventions (p. 47) – Anticipated therapeutic and expected outcome statements (p. 47) Using preprinted care plans, have students verbalize how they would implement the plan of care for a patient with fatigue, shortness of breath, and chronic diarrhea.	PPT 17 ▸ Discuss the difference between a nursing intervention and anticipated therapeutic outcomes. What is a nursing action and a nursing order? ▸ Discuss how drug classifications are used to identify the anticipated outcomes of medications. Class Activity ***Lead a class discussion about nursing interventions and therapeutic outcomes. Have students outline two nursing diagnoses, two nursing interventions, and two***

OBJECTIVES	CONTENT	TEACHING RESOURCES
		therapeutic outcomes for the following patient, a 44-year-old woman recently diagnosed with breast cancer.
Compare the types of nursing functions classified as dependent, interdependent, and independent, and give examples of each.	□ Nursing intervention or implementation (p. 46) Describe the three types of nursing actions—dependent, independent, and interdependent—with an emphasis on what is involved with patient interventions.	PPT 16 ARQ 3 TB Multiple Choice question 8 INRQ 2 SG Review Sheet questions 13-14 (p. 22) Review Question for the NCLEX Examination 4 (p. 52) ▸ Discuss when and why interdependent actions may be most beneficial to a patient. When should other health care professionals be involved? ▸ Discuss which actions are dependent and when the nursing care plan may call for an independent action. Class Activity ***Divide the class into groups. Present the following scenario to the class and have each group identify a dependent, independent, and interdependent nursing function for the patient, a 65-year-old woman with COPD. Have each group present its findings to the class for discussion.***
Describe the evaluation process used to establish whether patient behaviors are consistent with the identified short-term or long-term goals.	□ Evaluating and recording therapeutic and expected outcomes (p. 47) Identify the nurse's role in determining short- and long-term goal attainment for patient care plans.	PPT 17 TB Multiple Choice questions 10, 15 INRQ 3 CTQ 3-4 SG Review Sheet question 15 (p. 22) SG Learning Activities questions 9, 18 (pp. 24-25) ▸ Discuss the evaluation process used to establish if patient behaviors are consistent with short-term or long-term goals. ▸ Discuss the role of family members and significant others in the evaluation process. Which nonmedical factors should be taken into consideration? Class Activity ***Using the scenario from the previous class activity, have students discuss how nursing diagnoses are formed. Then have***

ELSEVIER

OBJECTIVES	CONTENT	TEACHING RESOURCES
		students describe the three parts of the nursing process used to decide if the goals of the nursing diagnosis have been met.

4.1 Homework/Assignments:
1. Have students look up an article on the Internet that describes an example of an evidence-based practice change that has affected how nurses administer medications.

4.1 Instructor's Notes/Student Feedback:

LESSON 4.2

CRITICAL THINKING QUESTION

A 67-year-old man has developed a fever of 103.6° F after returning from the recovery room following a carotid endarterectomy. What is the nursing process as it applies to this situation? What are specific medication-related issues?

Guidelines: The nurse should first assess the patient by taking and recording vital signs and assessing for a possible source of infection (pulmonary, wound, urinary tract, or thrombophlebitis). Based on the assessment, a diagnosis would then be made (hyperthermia). A plan of care involving medications might include nursing interventions, such as hydration with IV fluids, use of antipyretics, and administering antibiotics. The desired outcome would be a decrease in body temperature to normal levels. Implementing these nursing interventions will include following the health care provider's orders and using safe medication practices. Evaluating would involve measuring the patient's temperature regularly.

OBJECTIVES	CONTENT	TEACHING RESOURCES
State the information that should be obtained as a part of a medication history.	■ Relating the nursing process to pharmacology (p. 47) □ Assessment (p. 47) Review the importance of obtaining a complete and thorough drug history.	PPT 22 SG Review Sheet question 17 (p. 22) SG Learning Activities question 6 (p. 24) SG Practice Questions for the NCLEX Examination 4-5 (p. 26) ▸ Discuss risk factors that should be considered when taking a drug history. Class Activity ***Have two students role play a nurse interviewing a patient on admission asking for a complete drug history. Review with the class important aspects to include in the interview.***

OBJECTIVES	CONTENT	TEACHING RESOURCES
Identify primary, secondary, and tertiary sources of information used to build a patient information base.	□ Assessment (p. 47) Review the different sources of information that a nurse can access to gain a clear picture of patient information: 1. Primary 2. Secondary 3. Tertiary sources	PPT 22 TB Multiple Choice question 9 Review Question for the NCLEX Examination 3 (p. 52) ▸ Discuss the difference between subjective data and objective data taken from a primary source. ▸ Discuss the benefits of obtaining information from a secondary source. Class Activity ***Divide the class into groups and have each group identify two sources for primary, secondary, and tertiary information about patient medications. Have groups share their findings with the class for discussion.***
Define the problem.	□ Nursing diagnoses (p. 48) Review the five categories of etiologic and contributing factors: 1. Pathophysiologic 2. Treatment related 3. Personal 4. Environmental 5. Maturational	PPT 22-23 TB Multiple Choice question 11 ▸ Discuss what etiologic and contributing factors must be recognized to deal effectively with identified problems. Class Activity ***Divide the class into groups and assign each group one of the following situational categories that affect diagnoses: pathophysiologic, treatment-related, personal, environmental, and maturational. Have each group give five examples of how its assigned situation can cause or influence a problem and identify a nursing intervention for each. Have each group present its findings to the class for discussion.***
Describe the process used to identify factors that could result in patient problems when medications are prescribed.	□ Nursing diagnoses (p. 48) Review the two nursing diagnoses that are to be included with all drug education.	CTQ 4 ▸ Discuss the process used to identify factors that could result in patient problems when medications are prescribed. ▸ Discuss the importance of reviewing drug monographs. What diagnoses might result from some types of drug therapy? Class Activity ***Present the following scenario to the class and have students identify and discuss the five factors that can result in medication problems: a 16-year-old boy with primary hypertension has been prescribed propranolol. Record student responses on the board for comparison.***

OBJECTIVES	CONTENT	TEACHING RESOURCES
Review the content of several drug monographs to identify information that may result in patient problems from the medication therapy.	□ Nursing diagnoses (p. 48)	CTQ 3 SG Review Sheet question 18 (p. 23) SG Learning Activities question 7 (p. 24) ▸ Discuss Table 4-2 (p. 51). What drug levels should be routinely monitored, and why? ▸ Discuss adverse effects that may be alleviated through patient education. Why is cooperative planning for modifications important? Class Activity ***Provide students with drug monographs for propranolol, warfarin, and metformin. Then divide the class into groups and have students identify three potential problems that could arise from the use of each drug. Have groups share and discuss their findings with the class.***
Identify steps used to plan nursing care in relation to a medication regimen prescribed for a patient.	□ Planning (p. 49)	PPT 23-24 ▸ Discuss the eight steps used to plan nursing care in relation to medication. ▸ Discuss the importance of teaching a patient to keep written records. How can a nurse help the patient to keep accurate records of both medication administration and responses? Class Activity ***Present the following scenario to the class:*** ***A 55-year-old man who has been diagnosed with type 2 diabetes mellitus has been prescribed glipizide.*** ***In groups have students list the steps used to plan a medication regimen for this patient and present their findings to the class.***
Describe an acceptable method of organizing, implementing, and evaluating the patient education delivered.	□ Planning (p. 49)	PPT 24 ▸ Discuss what should be considered when developing a patient education plan around medication. ▸ Discuss the importance of doing patient education in increments. How can the nurse be sure of the patient's level of understanding? Class Activity ***Present the following scenario to the class:*** ***A 55-year-old man with type 2 diabetes mellitus and hypertension has been prescribed glipizide and alprazolam.***

OBJECTIVES	CONTENT	TEACHING RESOURCES
		Divide the class into groups. Have each group discuss patient education, list the four factors that must be considered when doing medication teaching, and give specific examples that would apply to this patient. Have each group present its findings to the class for discussion.
Practice developing short- and long-term patient education objectives, and have them critiqued by the instructor.	□ Planning (p. 49)	PPT 24 ▸ Discuss the importance of re-evaluating the patient's ability to manage a medication regimen. Class Activity ***Divide the class into groups and have each group develop two short-term and two long-term patient education objectives for the following patient:*** ***A 65-year-old woman who has just been diagnosed with atrial fibrillation has been prescribed warfarin.*** ***Have each group share and discuss its findings with the class.***
Differentiate among dependent, interdependent, and independent nursing actions and give an example of each.	□ Nursing intervention or implementation (p. 50) – Dependent nursing actions (p. 50) – Interdependent nursing actions (p. 50) – Independent nursing actions (p. 50)	PPT 25 TB Multiple Choice question 13 SG Learning Activities question 8 (p. 24) ▸ Discuss the differences between dependent, independent, and interdependent nursing actions. Class Activity ***Divide the class into groups and have students identify two dependent, interdependent, and independent nursing actions for the following patient: a 29-year-old woman with type 1 diabetes mellitus. Have each group share and discuss its findings with the class.***
Describe the procedure for evaluating the therapeutic outcomes obtained from prescribed therapy.	□ Evaluating and recording therapeutic and expected outcomes (p. 47) Discuss important evaluation components to include when evaluating therapeutic outcomes of drugs.	PPT 26 TB Multiple Choice question 10 SG Review Sheet question 19 (p. 23) SG Practice Question for the NCLEX Examination 9 (p. 27) Table 4-2, The Nursing Process Applied to the Patient's Pharmacologic Needs (p. 51) ▸ Discuss the evaluation process for drug therapy. What factors must be considered?

OBJECTIVES	CONTENT	TEACHING RESOURCES
		▸ Discuss Table 4-2 (p. 51). Name some routinely prescribed drug therapies and discuss the procedure used to evaluate their outcomes. Class Activity ***Present the following scenario to the class:*** ***A 66-year-old man has been diagnosed with atrial fibrillation and congestive heart failure. The physician has prescribed digoxin, 0.125 mg, PO, daily; and warfarin, 5 mg, PO, daily.*** ***Have students outline the procedure for evaluating the therapeutic outcomes of this patient's drug therapy. Record student responses on the board for comparison.***
Performance evaluation		Test Bank SG Learning Activities (pp. 24-25) SG Practice Questions for the NCLEX Examination (pp. 26-27) Critical Thinking Questions

4.2 Homework/Assignments:

4.2 Instructor's Notes/Student Feedback:

ELSEVIER

4

Lecture Outline

The Nursing Process and Pharmacology

Slide 1

Chapter 4
The Nursing Process
and Pharmacology

Slide 2

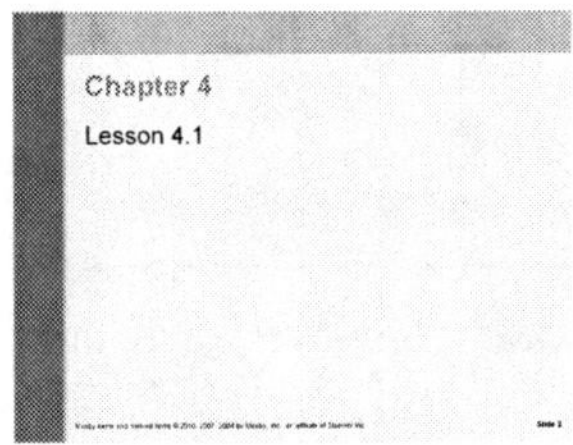

Chapter 4
Lesson 4.1

Slide 3

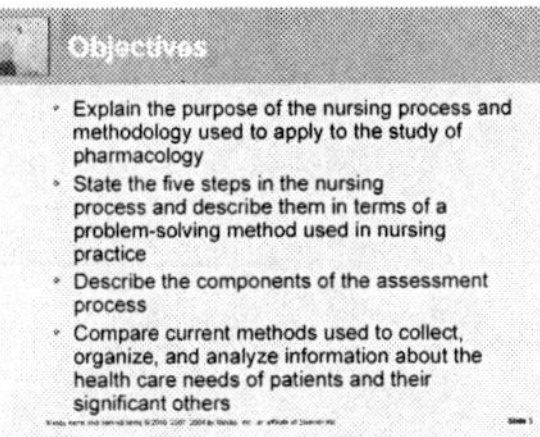

Objectives
Explain the purpose of the nursing process and methodology used to apply to the study of pharmacology
State the five steps in the nursing process and describe them in terms of a problem-solving method used in nursing practice
Describe the components of the assessment process
Compare current methods used to collect, organize, and analyze information about the health care needs of patients and their significant others

Slide 4

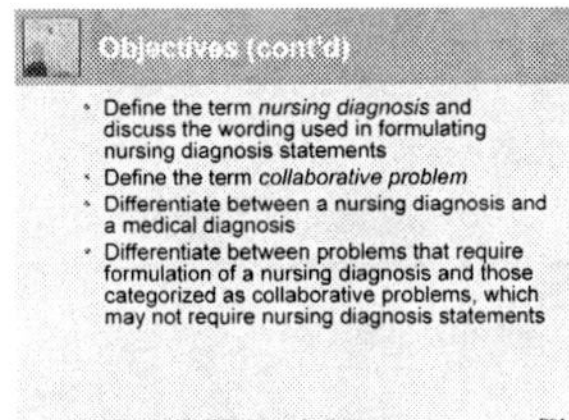

Objectives (cont'd)
Define the term nursing diagnosis and discuss the wording used in formulating nursing diagnosis statements
Define the term collaborative problem
Differentiate between a nursing diagnosis and a medical diagnosis
Differentiate between problems that require formulation of a nursing diagnosis and those categorized as collaborative problems, which may not require nursing diagnosis statements

Slide 5

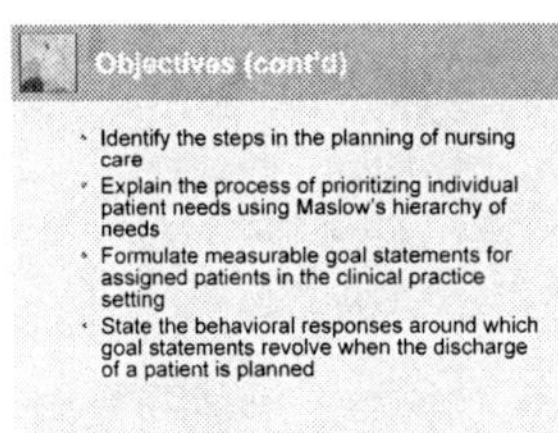

Objectives (cont'd)
Identify the steps in the planning of nursing care
Explain the process of prioritizing individual patient needs using Maslow's hierarchy of needs
Formulate measurable goal statements for assigned patients in the clinical practice setting
State the behavioral responses around which goal statements revolve when the discharge of a patient is planned

Slide 6

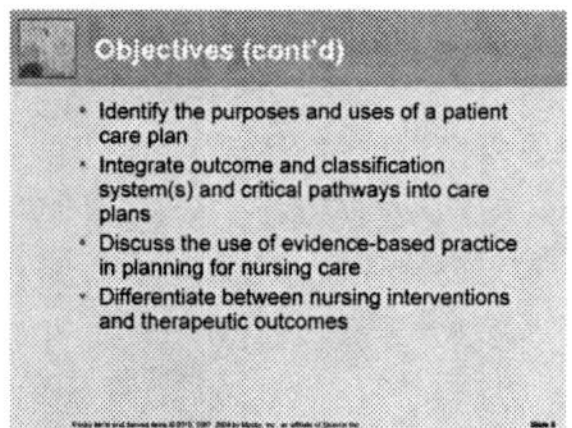
Objectives (cont'd)
Identify the purposes and uses of a patient care plan
Integrate outcome and classification system(s) and critical pathways into care plans
Discuss the use of evidence-based practice in planning for nursing care
Differentiate between nursing interventions and therapeutic outcomes

Slide 7

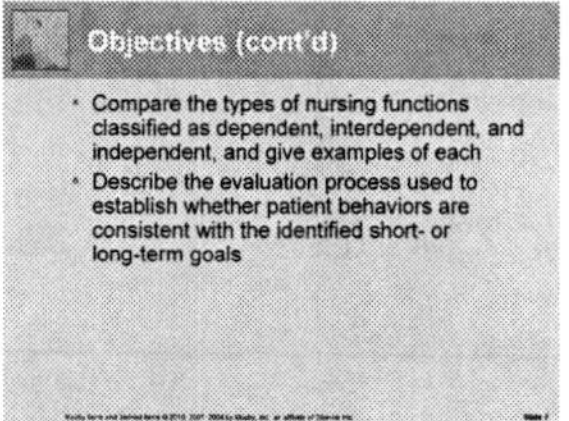
Objectives (cont'd)
Compare the types of nursing functions classified as dependent, interdependent, and independent, and give examples of each
Describe the evaluation process used to establish whether patient behaviors are consistent with the identified short- or long-term goals

Slide 8

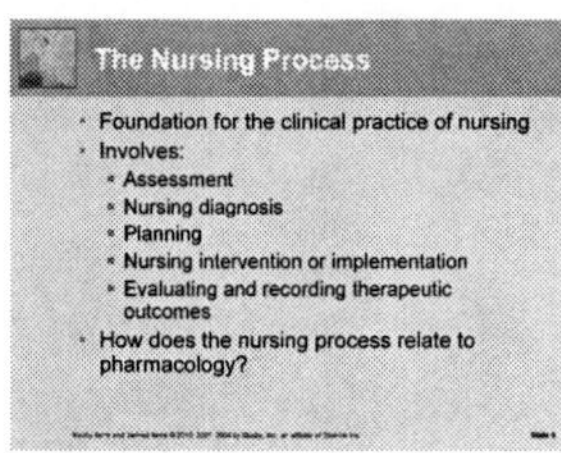
The Nursing Process
Foundation for the clinical practice of nursing
Involves:
Assessment
Nursing diagnosis
Planning
Nursing intervention or implementation
Evaluating and recording therapeutic outcomes
How does the nursing process relate to pharmacology?

- Many institutions use a five-step nursing process; however, there are other models.
- The five steps are an overlapping process; each step builds on the one that precedes it.

Slide 9

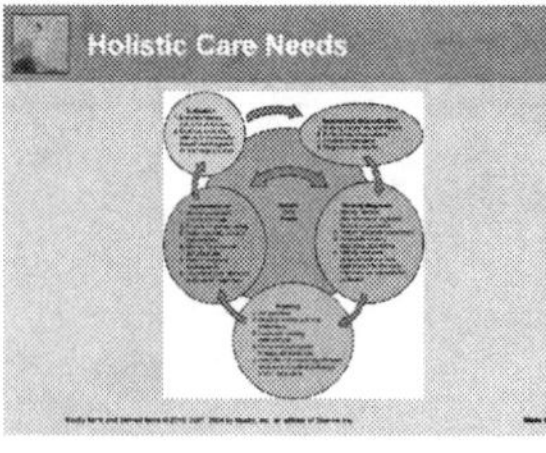
Holistic Care Needs

- The nursing process assists the nurse in responding to the changing needs of the patient.

Slide 10

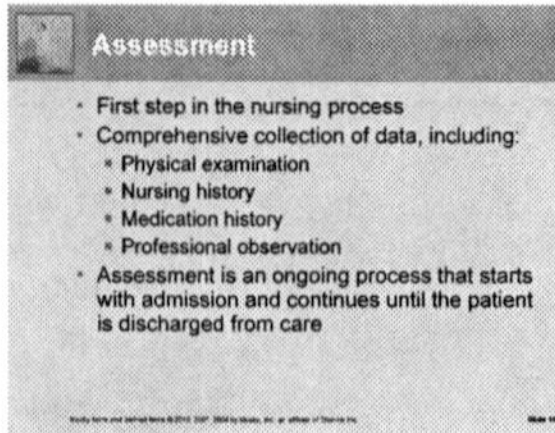
Assessment
First step in the nursing process
Comprehensive collection of data, including:
Physical examination
Nursing history
Medication history
Professional observation
Assessment is an ongoing process that starts with admission and continues until the patient is discharged from care

ELSEVIER

Slide 11

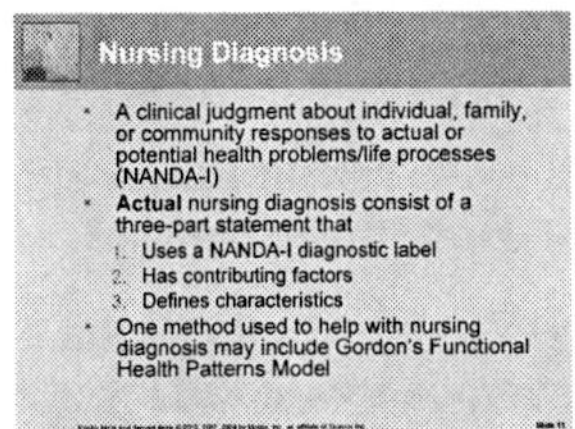
Nursing Diagnosis
A clinical judgment about individual, family, or community responses to actual or potential health problems/life processes (NANDA-I)
Actual nursing diagnosis consist of a three-part statement that
1. Uses a NANDA-I diagnostic label
2. Has contributing factors
3. Defines characteristics
One method used to help with nursing diagnosis may include Gordon's Functional Health Patterns Model

- The nursing diagnosis differs from the medical diagnosis because the nursing diagnosis indicates a human response pattern that the nurse is licensed to treat; the medical diagnosis indicates a medical condition.

Slide 12

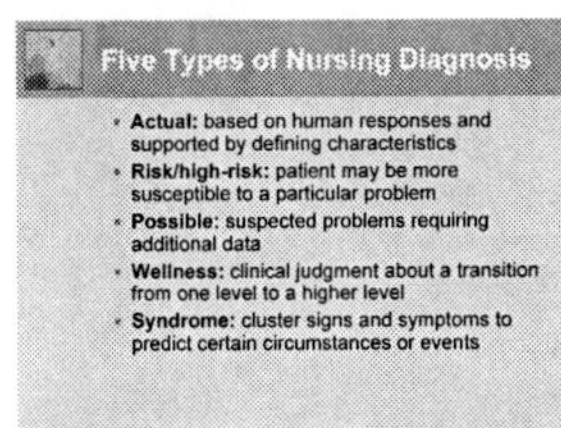
Five Types of Nursing Diagnosis
Actual: based on human responses and supported by defining characteristics
Risk/high-risk: patient may be more susceptible to a particular problem
Possible: suspected problems requiring additional data
Wellness: clinical judgment about a transition from one level to a higher level
Syndrome: cluster signs and symptoms to predict certain circumstances or events

- The nursing diagnosis determines what the nursing interventions will be based on defining characteristics gathered from the assessment.
- Defining characteristics support an actual nursing diagnosis with signs and symptoms that indicate the diagnosis.

Slide 13

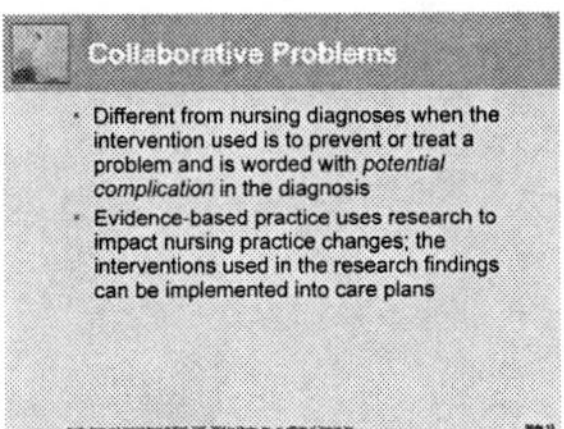
Collaborative Problems
Different from nursing diagnoses when the intervention used is to prevent or treat a problem and is worded with potential complication in the diagnosis
Evidence-based practice uses research to impact nursing practice changes; the interventions used in the research findings can be implemented into care plans

---

Slide 14

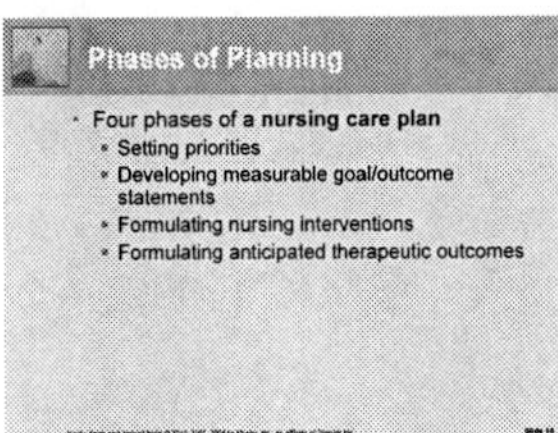
Phases of Planning
Four phases of a nursing care plan
Setting priorities
Developing measurable goal/outcome statements
Formulating nursing interventions
Formulating anticipated therapeutic outcomes

Slide 15

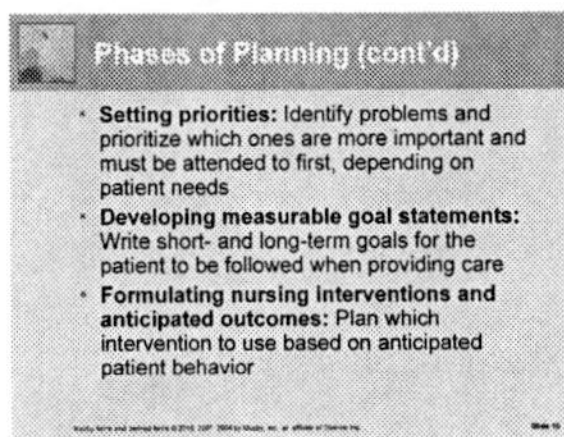
Phases of Planning (cont'd)
Setting priorities: Identify problems and prioritize which ones are more important and must be attended to first, depending on patient needs
Developing measurable goal statements: Write short- and long-term goals for the patient to be followed when providing care
Formulating nursing interventions and anticipated outcomes: Plan which intervention to use based on anticipated patient behavior

- One system for prioritizing problems is Maslow's hierarchy of needs.
- Problems can be prioritized based on how they affect homeostasis.
- The Nursing Outcome Classification (NOC) system provides standardized outcomes and specific indicators to assess the effectiveness of nursing interventions.
- The Nursing Interventions Classification (NIC) system provides scientifically validated nursing interventions to treat a diagnosis.

Slide 16

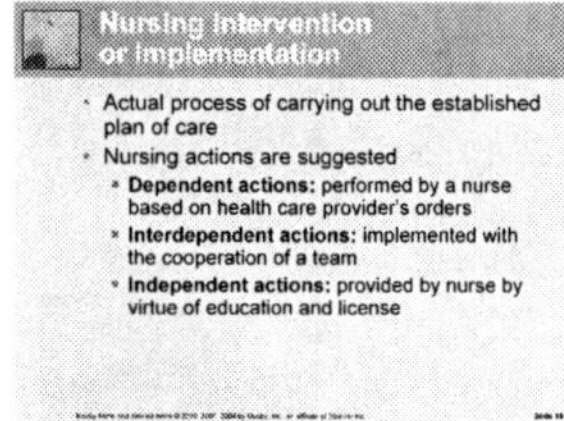
Nursing Intervention
or Implementation
Actual process of carrying out the established plan of care
Nursing actions are suggested
Dependent actions: performed by a nurse based on health care provider's orders
Interdependent actions: implemented with the cooperation of a team
Independent actions: provided by nurse by virtue of education and license

- Example of a dependent action: administering an antibiotic every 6 hours as ordered (but can still require the nurse's professional judgment).
- Example of an interdependent action: monitoring a patient's heart rate and rhythm while the patient is receiving antidysrhythmic therapy.
- Example of an independent action: listening to a patient's lung sounds after a respiratory treatment and monitoring laboratory values.

Slide 17

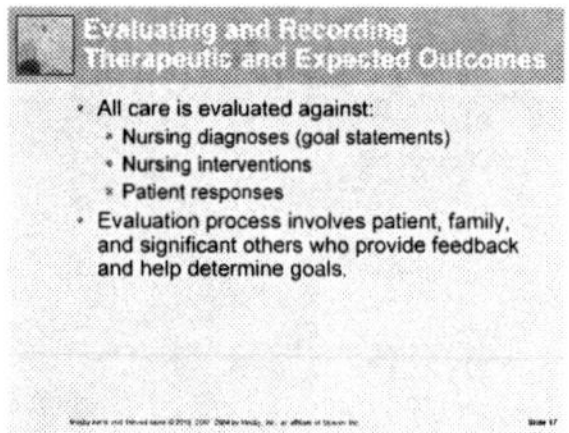
Evaluating and Recording
Therapeutic and Expected Outcomes
All care is evaluated against:
Nursing diagnoses (goal statements)
Nursing interventions
Patient responses
Evaluation process involves patient, family, and significant others who provide feedback and help determine goals.

Slide 18

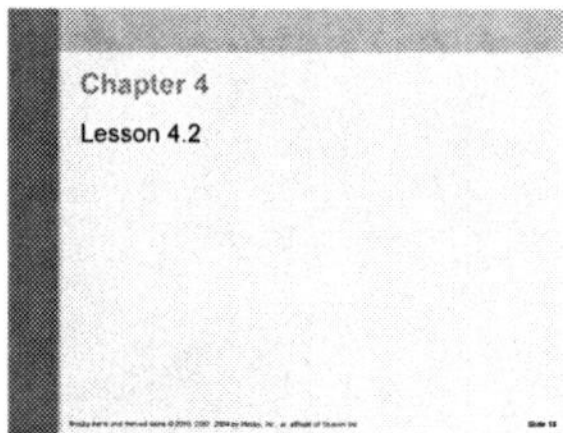
Chapter 4
Lesson 4.2

Slide 19

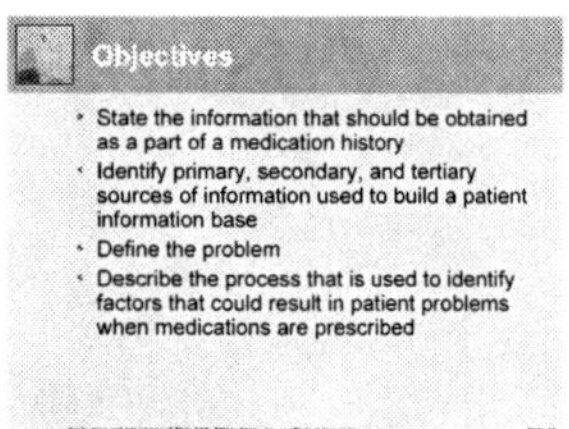
Objectives
State the information that should be obtained as a part of a medication history
Identify primary, secondary, and tertiary sources of information used to build a patient information base
Define the problem
Describe the process that is used to identify factors that could result in patient problems when medications are prescribed

---

Slide 20

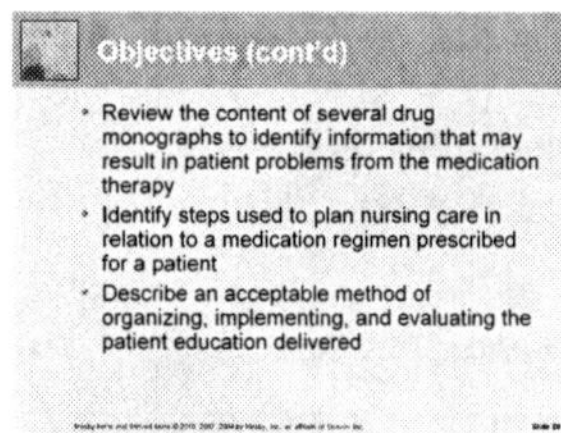
Objectives (cont'd)
Review the content of several drug monographs to identify information that may result in patient problems from the medication therapy
Identify steps used to plan nursing care in relation to a medication regimen prescribed for a patient
Describe an acceptable method of organizing, implementing, and evaluating the patient education delivered

Slide 21

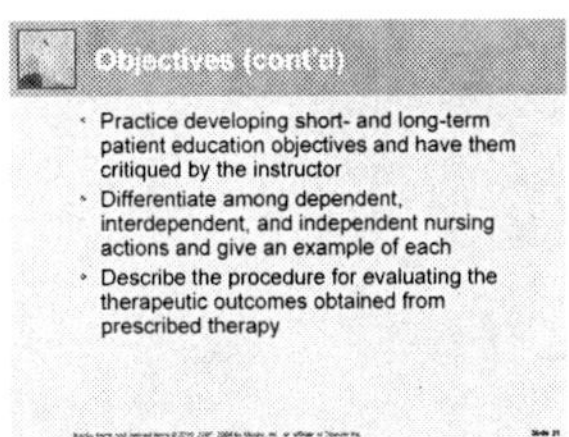
Objectives (cont'd)
Practice developing short- and long-term patient education objectives and have them critiqued by the instructor
Differentiate among dependent, interdependent, and independent nursing actions and give an example of each
Describe the procedure for evaluating the therapeutic outcomes obtained from prescribed therapy

Slide 22

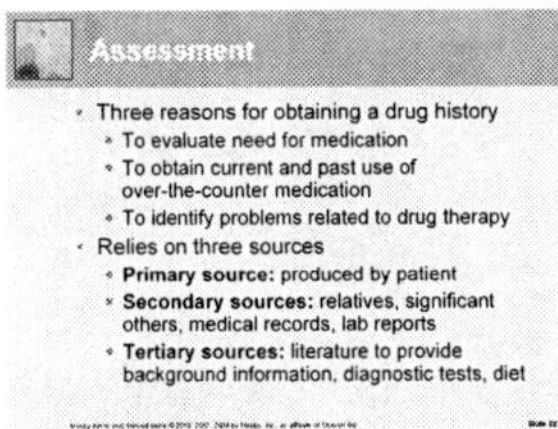
Assessment
Three reasons for obtaining a drug history
To evaluate need for medication
To obtain current and past use of over-the-counter medication
To identify problems related to drug therapy
Relies on three sources
Primary source: produced by patient
Secondary sources: relatives, significant others, medical records, lab reports
Tertiary sources: literature to provide background information, diagnostic tests, diet

- Primary patient information may be unreliable or patients may be poor historians.
- Tertiary source information may not apply to all patients' needs.

Slide 23

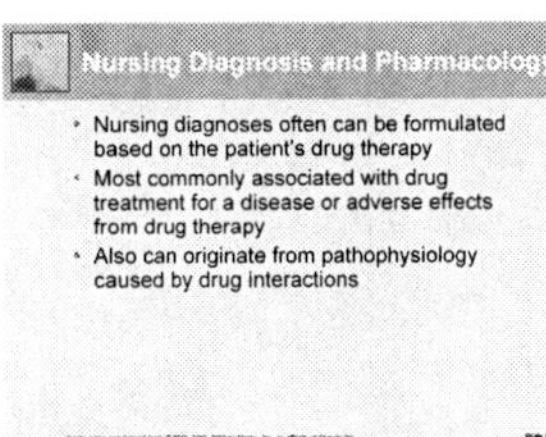
Nursing Diagnosis and Pharmacology
Nursing diagnoses often can be formulated based on the patient's drug therapy
Most commonly associated with drug treatment for a disease or adverse effects from drug therapy
Also can originate from pathophysiology caused by drug interactions

- Other factors influencing nursing diagnosis are a patient's personal and environmental situations and maturation.

Slide 24

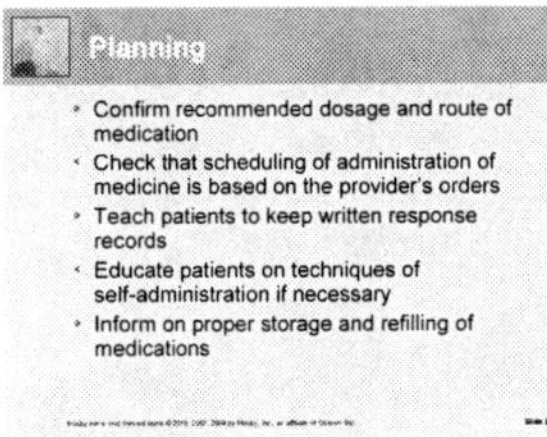
Planning
Confirm recommended dosage and route of medication
Check that scheduling of administration of medicine is based on the provider's orders
Teach patients to keep written response records
Educate patients on techniques of self-administration if necessary
Inform on proper storage and refilling of medications

- The following should be included in a patient response record: drug name, dosage, route, time of administration, all adverse effects, dosages missed, and reason.

Slide 25

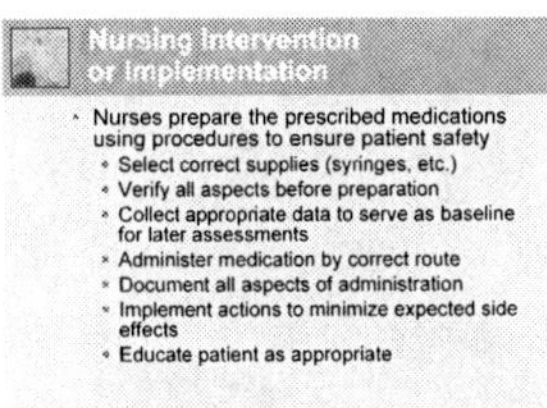
Nursing Intervention or Implementation
Nurses prepare the prescribed medications using procedures to ensure patient safety
Select correct supplies (syringes, etc.)
Verify all aspects before preparation
Collect appropriate data to serve as baseline for later assessments
Administer medication by correct route
Document all aspects of administration
Implement actions to minimize expected side effects
Educate patient as appropriate

- The nurse must remember the six rights of drug administration.

ELSEVIER

Slide 26

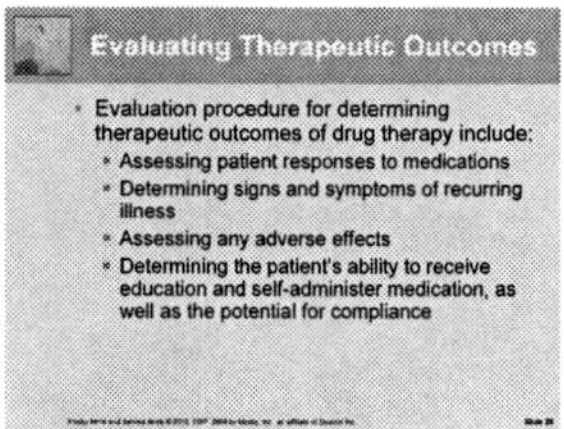
Evaluating Therapeutic Outcomes
Evaluation procedure for determining therapeutic outcomes of drug therapy include:
Assessing patient responses to medications
Determining signs and symptoms of recurring illness
Assessing any adverse effects
Determining the patient's ability to receive education and self-administer medication, as well as the potential for compliance

5 Lesson Plan

Patient Education and Health Promotion

TEACHING FOCUS

In this chapter, the student will be introduced to basic learning concepts and principles of learning. Students will have the opportunity to learn about the factors that affect a person's ability to learn, such as learning styles, readiness to learn, motivational factors, educational level, and cultural diversity. A major focus of this chapter is patient education associated with medication therapy. Students will have the opportunity to learn about the importance of explaining medical therapy in sufficient detail and involving the patient in the execution and evaluation of medical therapy.

MATERIALS AND RESOURCES

- ☐ computer and PowerPoint projector (all Lessons)

LESSON CHECKLIST

Preparations for this lesson include:

- lecture
- guest speaker: nurse educator
- evaluation of student knowledge and skills needed to perform all entry-level nursing activities related to patient education and health promotion, including:
  - identification of the three domains of learning
  - the principles of learning
  - common beliefs about health and illness
  - ethnic and cultural influences on health beliefs
  - patient education associated with medication therapy

KEY TERMS

affective domain (p. 53)
cognitive domain (p. 53)
ethnocentrism (p. 56)
ethnography (p. 58)
health teaching (p. 58)
objectives (p. 54)
psychomotor domain (p. 53)

ADDITIONAL RESOURCES

PowerPoint slides: 1-17

Legend

ARQ	PPT	TB	CTQ	SG	INRQ
Audience Response Questions	PowerPoint Slides	Test Bank	Critical Thinking Questions	Study Guide	Interactive NCLEX Review Questions

Class Activities are indicated in ***bold italic.***

LESSON 5.1

BACKGROUND ASSESSMENT

Question: The patient underwent repair of a hip fracture 2 days ago. She is in pain and is requesting pain medicine. The nurse says "I will go get your pain medication while an occupational therapist explains to you how to fall proof your home after you are discharged." What can the nurse do differently?

Answer: Before making an attempt to teach the patient new skills or delivering new information, the nurse should determine if the patient is ready to learn. If the patient is in pain, it is unlikely that she will be able to

absorb and retain new information effectively. She may also want to learn how to perform more important activities, such as ambulation, first. The nurse should administer the pain medication first and assess the patient for the degree of pain relief. Then she may ask the patient if she is ready to have the occupational therapist present the information on rearranging the patient's home to prevent falls.

Question: The nurse is teaching a patient about his newly prescribed blood pressure medication. After a while, the patient says "I cannot remember a word you said this morning about my new medicine. Can you tell me again why I am taking it?" How can the nurse help the patient retain the information?
Answer: The nurse can start by assessing the patient's learning style. If the patient is not readily retaining spoken information, she can provide him with a video, a pamphlet, or written instructions. For many patients, a combination of teaching methods works best. The nurse should determine the patient's understanding of the new information by asking him to repeat back to her what he has learned or answer her questions. When the nurse makes sure that the patient has understood the information correctly, she should still provide him with written instructions that he can refer to. The nurse can help the patient make a written schedule of when he is supposed to take the medication and give him a pillbox, where he can arrange his pills by the day and time they need to be taken. The nurse can also involve the family in the teaching and ask them to remind the patient to take the medication.

CRITICAL THINKING QUESTION

The patient is newly diagnosed with diabetes. When the nurse attempts to teach him about blood glucose monitoring, he says "I don't really care how to take my blood sugar. I am not planning to do that at home. I have lived without doing it for 55 years, and I was doing fine." What should the nurse do?
Guidelines: The nurse should determine why the patient is unwilling to learn. He may be overwhelmed by the diagnosis and trying to adjust to the new situation psychologically. He may be in denial about the seriousness of his condition and not willing to learn for that reason. He may not comprehend the consequences of having diabetes. He may be facing other challenges, such as altered family processes and lack of support. He may be unable to pay for blood testing supplies. Or, he may think that making lifestyle changes is not worth the trouble. Once the nurse determines the cause of the lack of motivation, she can address the issues. She can stress the positive in the changes the patient needs to make, such as not feeling fatigued as a result of low blood sugar, not feeling excessively thirsty, and not having to use the bathroom all the time.

OBJECTIVES	CONTENT	TEACHING RESOURCES
Differentiate among cognitive, affective, and psychomotor learning domains.	■ The three domains of learning (p. 53) □ Cognitive domain (p. 53) □ Affective domain (p. 53) □ Psychomotor domain (p. 53) Review the three domains of learning: cognitive, affective, and psychomotor.	PPT 4 ARQ 1 TB Multiple Choice questions 1, 4, 6 TB Multiple Response questions 1, 6 INRQ 7 SG Review Sheet questions 1-3, 5 (p. 29) SG Learning Activities questions 1-2, 4, 6 (p. 31) SG Practice Questions for the NCLEX Examination 1, 3 (p. 32) ▸ Discuss how previous experiences with health and illness influence a person's ability to learn new things. ▸ Discuss how the affective domain influences learning.

OBJECTIVES	CONTENT	TEACHING RESOURCES
		Class Activity ***Divide the class into three groups. Assign each group a learning domain: cognitive, affective, or psychomotor. Have each group identify the features of the domain they have been assigned. Then have the groups present their findings to the class and compare the domains.*** Class Activity ***As a class, discuss how to address the psychomotor domain when teaching a patient a new skill, such as self-injection of insulin.***
Identify the main principles of learning applied when teaching a patient, family, or group.	■ Principles of learning (p. 53) □ Focusing the learning (p. 53) □ Learning styles (p. 54) □ Organization fosters learning (p. 54) □ Motivating the individual to learn (p. 54) □ Readiness to learn (p. 54) □ Spacing the content (p. 55) □ Repetition enhances learning (p. 55) □ Education level (p. 55) □ Culture and ethnic diversity (p. 56) □ Internet (p. 57) □ Adherence (p. 57) Discuss the importance of determining a patient's readiness to learn, ways that can be used to motivate patients to learn, and understanding learning styles.	PPT 5-8 ARQ 2-3 TB Multiple Choice questions 3, 5, 7-8 TB Multiple Response question 2 INRQ 5-6, 8, 11-12 CTQ 2 SG Review Sheet questions 4, 6-8 (pp. 29-30) SG Learning Activities questions 3, 5, 7-8, 10, 13 (p. 31) SG Practice Questions for the NCLEX Examination 2, 4-6 (p. 32) Review Questions for the NCLEX Examination 3 (p. 60) ▸ Discuss how to foster the most conducive environment for learning. Why might it be best to address a patient's questions first before presenting all the information on a topic? ▸ Discuss the various ways in which people learn. What modalities are available to address each of these learning styles? ▸ Discuss how patient education materials can be standardized and what advantage this would provide. ▸ Discuss considerations and adjustments that must be made when teaching children or persons whose native language is not English. What changes in the style of teaching or teaching plan must be made when caring for older adults? ▸ Discuss how different ethnic groups may differ in their health behaviors and willingness to provide health-related information.

ELSEVIER

OBJECTIVES	CONTENT	TEACHING RESOURCES
		▸ Discuss the role of costs and other factors that may impact the patient at discharge. Class Activity ***Divide the class into small groups. Have students in each group describe their learning styles and the methods by which they prefer to acquire new skills and information. Have each group share its findings. Which learning style is most prevalent in the class?***
Apply the principles of learning to the content taught in pharmacology.	■ Patient education associated with medication therapy (p. 58) □ Health teaching (p. 58) – Nursing process (p. 58) □ Communication and responsibility (p. 58) □ Expectations of therapy (p. 60) □ Changes in expectations (p. 60) □ Changes in therapy through cooperative goal setting (p. 60) □ At discharge (p. 60) Discuss how the nursing process can be used in developing a plan of care for teaching about medication therapies.	PPT 9-11 INRQ 2, 9 SG Practice Question for the NCLEX Examination 7 (p. 33) Review Question for the NCLEX Examination 2 (p. 60) Box 5-1: Sample Teaching Plan for a Patient with Diabetes Mellitus Taking One Type of Insulin (p. 59) ▸ Discuss under which conditions a translator would be useful and ways to optimize use of a translator. ▸ Discuss how to facilitate patient compliance with any follow-up visits or tests. Class Activity ***Divide the class into small groups. Have each group discuss the following situations and describe the possible teaching approaches:*** ***– A patient with Alzheimer's disease is prescribed a new medication.*** ***– A 5-year-old child is going to have sutures placed.*** ***– A patient with schizophrenia who is experiencing hallucinations is prescribed a new antipsychotic medication.*** ***– A patient newly diagnosed with cancer needs chemotherapy.*** ***Then have each group share its approaches with the class.*** Class Activity ***Invite a nurse educator to class to talk about her role in patient and staff education. What are some challenging aspects of his or her work? Have the students write a brief report based on the presentation.***

5.1 Homework/Assignments:

5.1 Instructor's Notes/Student Feedback:

LESSON 5.2

CRITICAL THINKING QUESTION

The home health nurse has instructed a patient with hyperemesis gravidarum how to infuse her hydration IV fluids in the home. The patient confirmed her understanding verbally, and the nurse left. When the nurse returns the following morning, she sees that the patient has not infused any of the IV fluids, her peripheral IV is pulled out, and the patient is crying. How should the nurse resolve this situation?

Guidelines: The nurse should assess the reasons for the patient's noncompliance. The patient appears overwhelmed and possibly frustrated by the experience. It is also possible that she does not understand the importance of IV fluid infusion for hydration. The nurse should determine the patient's learning style, understanding of her condition, and support systems. The nurse needs to make sure that the patient understands how to perform the procedure. The nurse should leave written instructions with the patient and some phone numbers where the patient can get professional support by means of telephone triage. The nurse should ask the patient to practice connecting herself to the IV in the nurse's presence until she feels comfortable with the procedure.

OBJECTIVES	CONTENT	TEACHING RESOURCES
Describe essential elements of patient education in relation to the prescribed medications.	■ Patient education associated with medication therapy (p. 58) □ Health teaching (p. 58) – Nursing process (p. 58) □ Communication and responsibility (p. 58) □ Expectations of therapy (p. 60) □ Changes in expectations (p. 60) □ Changes in therapy through cooperative goal setting (p. 60) □ At discharge (p. 60)	PPT 15 ARQ 4 TB Multiple Response question 3 SG Learning Activities question 11 (p. 31) ▸ Discuss the importance of patient education with regard to medical therapy. ▸ Discuss possible legal implications of inadequate patient education with regard to prescribed medications. ▸ Discuss how to explain the need for finishing an entire regimen of antibiotic and for not abruptly stopping certain medications. Class Activity ***Have students identify several factors that affect the patient's readiness to learn, and write the factors on the board. Then divide the class into small groups, and have***

ELSEVIER

OBJECTIVES	CONTENT	TEACHING RESOURCES
		each group outline nursing interventions to promote the patient's readiness to learn for each factor.
Describe the nurse's role in fostering patient responsibility for maintaining well-being and adhering to the therapeutic regimen.	□ Health teaching (p. 58) – Nursing process (p. 58) □ Communication and responsibility (p. 58) □ Expectations of therapy (p. 60) □ Changes in expectations (p. 60) □ Changes in therapy through cooperative goal setting (p. 60) □ At discharge (p. 60)	PPT 16 TB Multiple Response questions 4-5 Review Question for the NCLEX Examination 1 (p. 60) Box 5-1: Sample Teaching Plan for a Patient With Diabetes Mellitus Taking One Type of Insulin (p. 59) ▸ Discuss how to involve the patient in providing feedback about the efficacy of prescribed medications. ▸ Discuss how to adapt the teaching plan to the patient's needs at every step of the instruction. Class Activity ***Have students work individually to create educational materials for the nursing staff of a local hospital about how to use interpreter services. How should the staff communicate with a non–English-speaking patient? When should they call an interpreter? Have the students present their educational materials to the class.*** Class Activity ***Divide the class into small groups. Have each group identify barriers to learning and compliance in the following situations and develop patient teaching materials to improve learning and compliance.*** ***– A homeless patient with diabetes*** ***– A Mexican seasonal laborer with chest pain*** ***– A 24-year-old woman diagnosed with breast cancer, whose mother died of breast cancer 2 years ago*** ***Then have the groups share their materials with the class.***
Identify the types of information that should be discussed with the patient or significant others to establish reasonable expectations for the prescribed therapy.	□ Expectations of therapy (p. 60) □ Changes in expectations (p. 60) □ Changes in therapy through cooperative goal setting (p. 60) □ At discharge (p. 60)	PPT 17 CTQ 1, 5 SG Review Sheet question 9 (p. 30) ▸ Discuss why expectations may change throughout the course of therapy. ▸ Discuss why it is important to explain what responses the patient might have from each medication he is taking.

OBJECTIVES	CONTENT	TEACHING RESOURCES
		▸ Discuss how patient expectations might differ with acute versus chronic illnesses. Class Activity ***Divide the class into small groups. Have each group discuss how to apply the health teaching process to the following situations:*** – ***A patient with diabetes who is noncompliant with his oral hypoglycemic medications*** – ***An older retired patient on Medicare who has to start taking a new, expensive medication for blood pressure control*** – ***A Chinese patient who believes that her pneumonia is the result of an evil eye*** – ***A Korean woman who refuses to breast-feed because she believes that formula is more healthy than breast milk*** ***Then have each group discuss its solutions with the class.***
Discuss specific techniques used in the practice setting to document the patient education performed and degree of achievement attained.	□ Changes in therapy through cooperative goal setting (p. 60) □ At discharge (p. 60)	TB Multiple Choice question 2 SG Learning Activities questions 9, 12 (p. 31) ▸ Discuss ways in which the patient can be motivated to keep records of data important to the evaluation of efficacy of a therapy. ▸ Discuss how to foster a health care alliance with the patient. ▸ Discuss which items are necessary to document on the patient's discharge notes. Class Activity ***Have student pairs take turns teaching each other about the use of medications and about health conditions. Then have the students document their teaching appropriately, and present their documentation to the class.***
Performance evaluation		Test Bank SG Learning Activities (p. 31) SG Practice Questions for the NCLEX Examination (pp. 32-33) Critical Thinking Questions

5.2 Homework/Assignments:

5.2 Instructor's Notes/Student Feedback:

5

Lecture Outline

Patient Education and Health Promotion

Slide 1

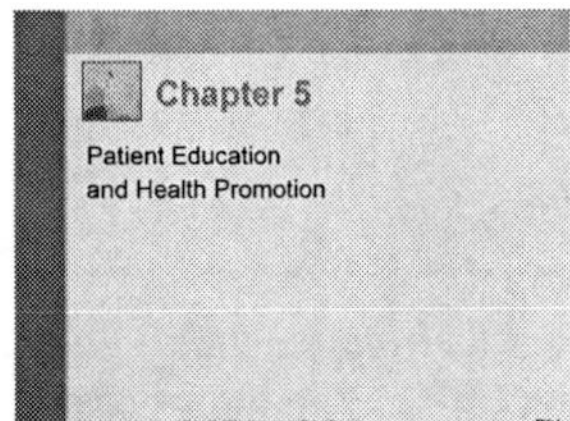
Chapter 5
Patient Education
and Health Promotion

Slide 2

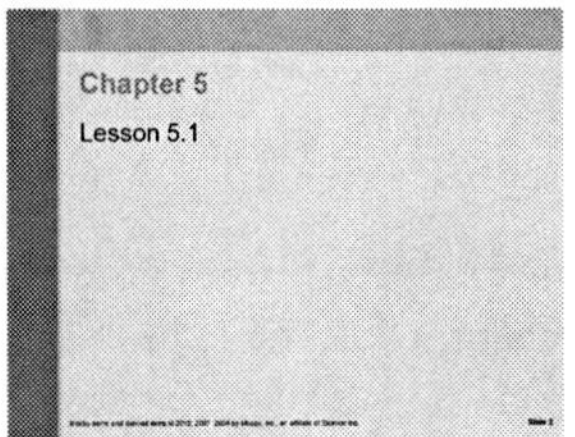
Chapter 5
Lesson 5.1

Slide 3

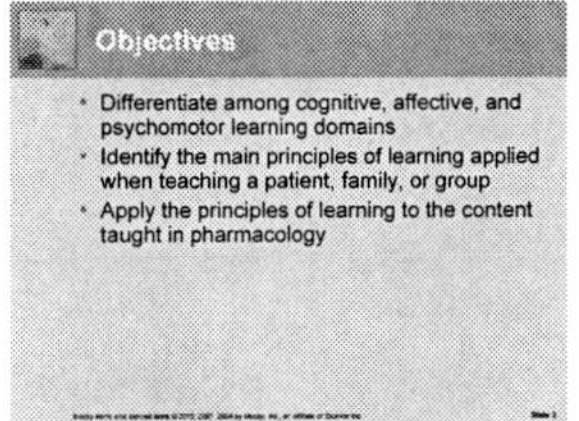
Objectives
Differentiate among cognitive, affective, and psychomotor learning domains
Identify the main principles of learning applied when teaching a patient, family, or group
Apply the principles of learning to the content taught in pharmacology

Slide 4

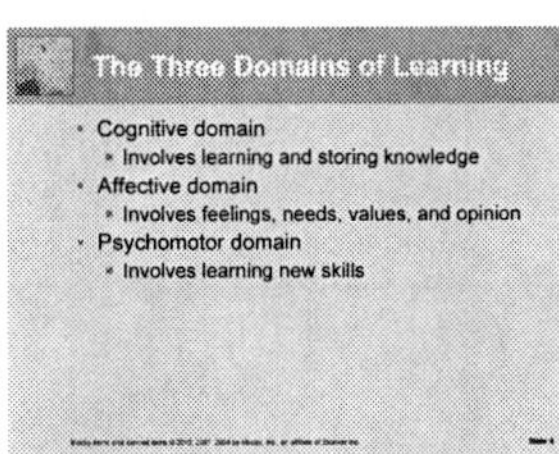
The Three Domains of Learning
Cognitive domain
Involves learning and storing knowledge
Affective domain
Involves feelings, needs, values, and opinion
Psychomotor domain
Involves learning new skills

- The affective domain is involved when the patient develops trust and confidence in the health care provider.
- The psychomotor domain is involved when patients demonstrate a procedure or skill to validate learning.

Slide 5

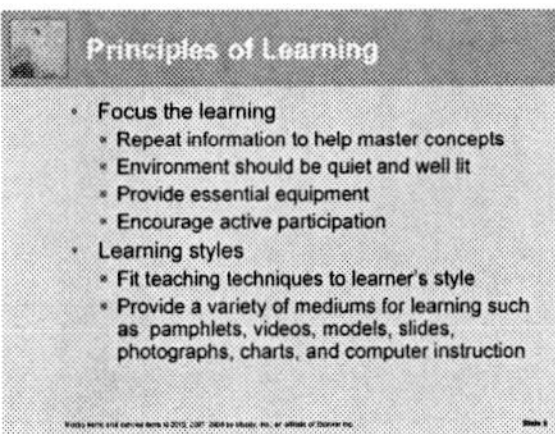
Principles of Learning
Focus the learning
Repeat information to help master concepts
Environment should be quiet and well lit
Provide essential equipment
Encourage active participation
Learning styles
Fit teaching techniques to learner's style
Provide a variety of mediums for learning such as pamphlets, videos, models, slides, photographs, charts, and computer instruction

- Begin teaching patients by answering any questions the patient may have.

Slide 6

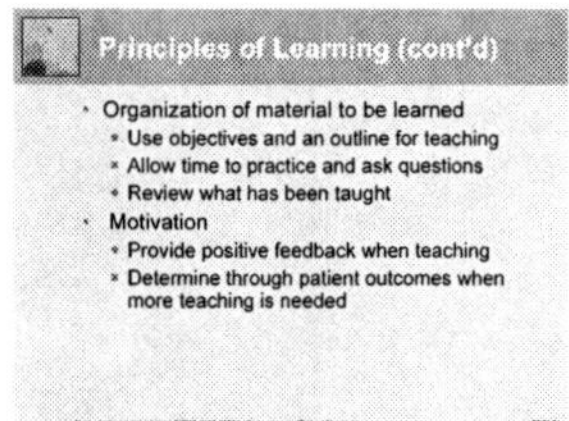
Principles of Learning (cont'd)
Organization of material to be learned
Use objectives and an outline for teaching
Allow time to practice and ask questions
Review what has been taught
Motivation
Provide positive feedback when teaching
Determine through patient outcomes when more teaching is needed

---

Slide 7

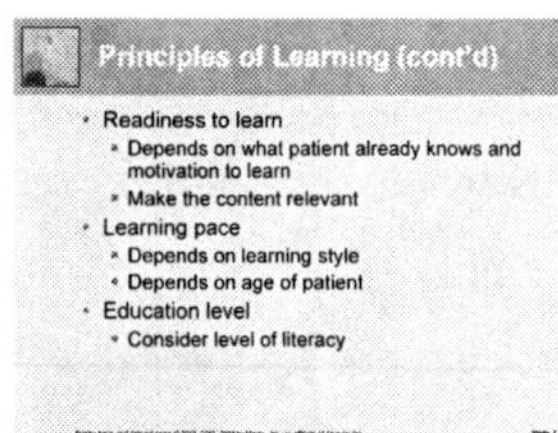
Principles of Learning (cont'd)
Readiness to learn
Depends on what patient already knows and motivation to learn
Make the content relevant
Learning pace
Depends on learning style
Depends on age of patient
Education level
Consider level of literacy

- Determine if the patient is well enough to benefit from teaching; pain will interfere with learning. Health care beliefs should be incorporated into the overall plan.
- Older adults need assessments of vision, hearing, short- and long-term memory, and financial ability.

Slide 8

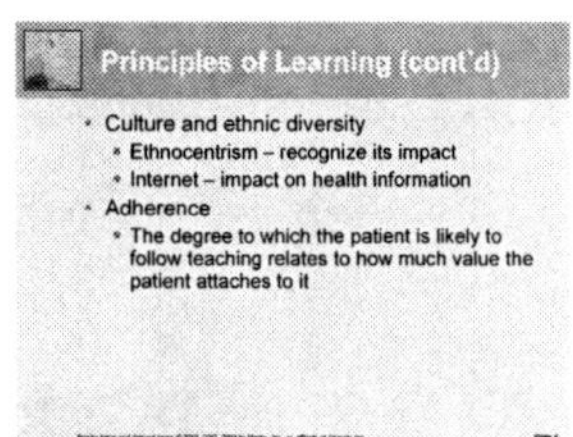
Principles of Learning (cont'd)
Culture and ethnic diversity
Ethnocentrism – recognize its impact
Internet – impact on health information
Adherence
The degree to which the patient is likely to follow teaching relates to how much value the patient attaches to it

- Perform a cultural assessment to determine factors that relate to the beliefs of the patient.
- Understand that each nurse brings beliefs about health practices that affect relationships with patients.

Slide 9

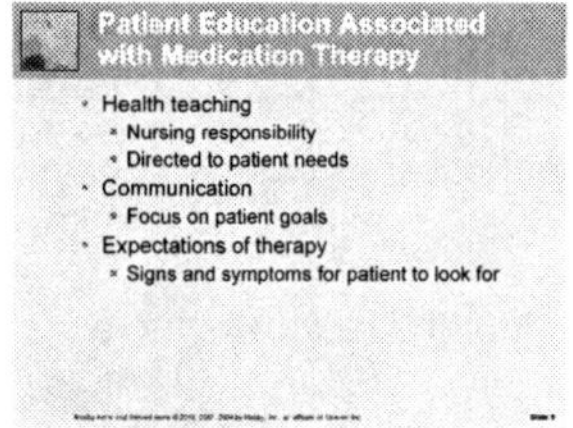
Patient Education Associated with Medication Therapy
Health teaching
Nursing responsibility
Directed to patient needs
Communication
Focus on patient goals
Expectations of therapy
Signs and symptoms for patient to look for

Slide 10

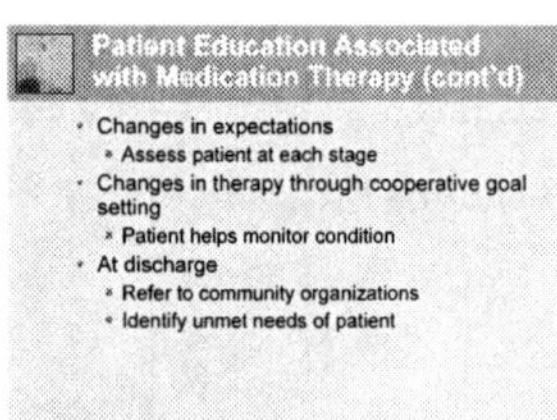
Patient Education Associated with Medication Therapy (cont'd)
Changes in expectations
Assess patient at each stage
Changes in therapy through cooperative goal setting
Patient helps monitor condition
At discharge
Refer to community organizations
Identify unmet needs of patient

- Discuss cooperative goal setting.

ELSEVIER

Slide 11

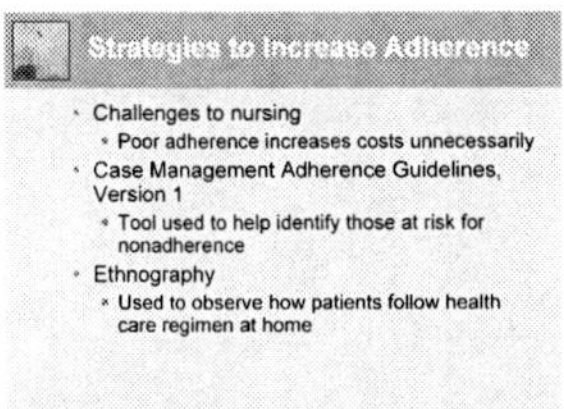
Strategies to Increase Adherence
Challenges to nursing
Poor adherence increases costs unnecessarily
Case Management Adherence Guidelines, Version 1
Tool used to help identify those at risk for nonadherence
Ethnography
Used to observe how patients follow health care regimen at home

- Areas assessed through the Case Management Adherence Guidelines include the patient's motivation and knowledge level of prescribed medications. It also assesses social support systems.

Slide 12

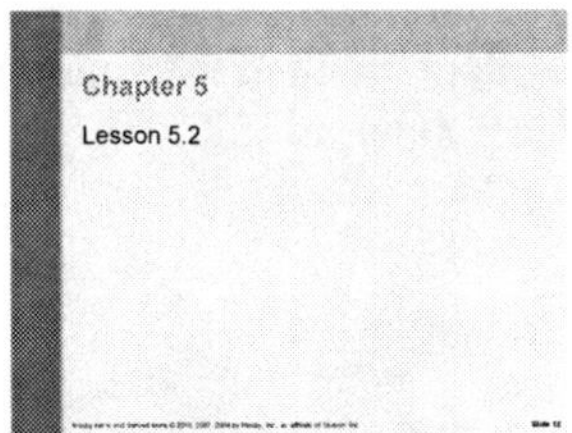
Chapter 5
Lesson 5.2

Slide 13

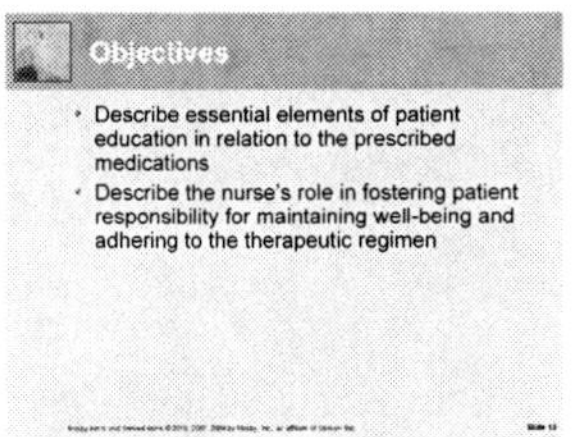
Objectives
Describe essential elements of patient education in relation to the prescribed medications
Describe the nurse's role in fostering patient responsibility for maintaining well-being and adhering to the therapeutic regimen

Slide 14

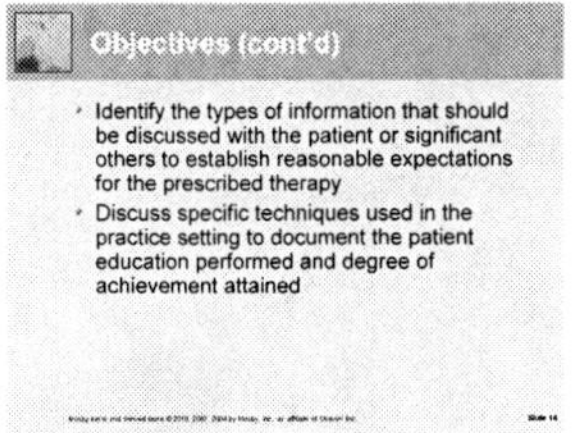
Objectives (cont'd)
Identify the types of information that should be discussed with the patient or significant others to establish reasonable expectations for the prescribed therapy
Discuss specific techniques used in the practice setting to document the patient education performed and degree of achievement attained

Slide 15

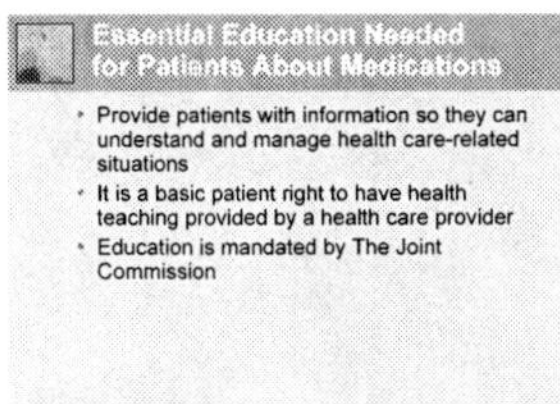
Essential Education Needed for Patients About Medications
Provide patients with information so they can understand and manage health care-related situations
It is a basic patient right to have health teaching provided by a health care provider
Education is mandated by The Joint Commission

- Make sure that patients know the reason for the medication and its adverse effects.

ELSEVIER

Slide 16

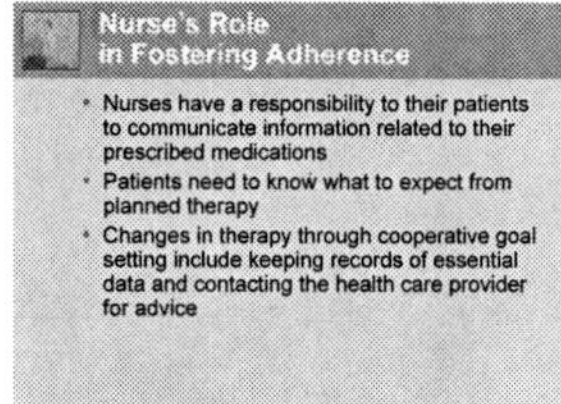
Nurse's Role
in Fostering Adherence
Nurses have a responsibility to their patients to communicate information related to their prescribed medications
Patients need to know what to expect from planned therapy
Changes in therapy through cooperative goal setting include keeping records of essential data and contacting the health care provider for advice

- Teach patients about any changes that may occur, and what to do in cases of unexpected circumstances.

Slide 17

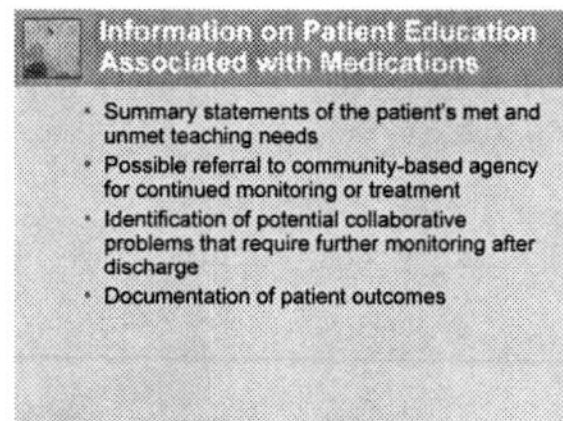
Information on Patient Education
Associated with Medications
Summary statements of the patient's met and unmet teaching needs
Possible referral to community-based agency for continued monitoring or treatment
Identification of potential collaborative problems that require further monitoring after discharge
Documentation of patient outcomes

- Patient education is started in the hospital setting; decreased lengths of stay make it a challenge to get all the education done before discharge. When education in-hospital is not adequately done, written information to take home is always provided, along with a number to call with questions.

ELSEVIER

6 Lesson Plan
A Review of Arithmetic

TEACHING FOCUS

This chapter provides a review of important arithmetic operations used in the dosing of drugs. Operations with fractions and decimal fractions and multiplying and dividing decimals are reviewed. Percentages, ratios, and proportions are also covered. Various systems of weights and measures are discussed, and conversion factors between the systems are given. Students are also given examples for calculation of oral and IV administration. Finally, temperature measurement is presented in Fahrenheit and centigrade, and conversion between the two systems is demonstrated.

MATERIALS AND RESOURCES

- ☐ calculator (all Lessons)
- ☐ computer and PowerPoint projector (all Lessons)
- ☐ Fahrenheit and centigrade thermometers (Lesson 6.3)
- ☐ household measuring cups and spoons (Lesson 6.2)
- ☐ three different household spoons (Lesson 6.2)
- ☐ macrodrip and microdrip chambers (Lesson 6.2)
- ☐ medication error reports (Lesson 6.2)
- ☐ metric graduated cylinders (Lesson 6.2)
- ☐ metric weighing scale (Lesson 6.3)

LESSON CHECKLIST

Preparations for this lesson include:

- lecture
- demonstration
- guest speaker: nurse
- evaluation of student knowledge and skills needed to perform all entry-level activities related to calculating and administering prescribed medication doses, including:
  - operations involving fractions
  - operations involving decimals
  - operations involving percents
  - conversion between the various numeric representations
  - systems of weights and measures and conversion between the systems
  - calculation of IV and medication administration rates
  - Fahrenheit and centigrade temperatures and conversions between them

KEY TERMS

administration sets (p. 76)
apothecary system (p. 71)
Celsius (p. 78)
centigrade (p. 78)
denominator (p. 62)
drip chamber (p. 76)
drop factor (DF) (p. 76)
Fahrenheit (p. 78)
gram (p. 71)
household measurements (p. 70)
kilograms (p. 73)
liter (p. 71)
macrodrip (p. 76)
meter (p. 71)
metric system (p. 71)
microdrip (p. 76)
milligrams (p. 72)
numerator (p. 62)
round (p. 76)

ELSEVIER

ADDITIONAL RESOURCES

PowerPoint slides: 1-16

Legend

ARQ	**PPT**	**TB**	**CTQ**	**SG**	**INRQ**
Audience Response Questions	PowerPoint Slides	Test Bank	Critical Thinking Questions	Study Guide	Interactive NCLEX Review Questions

Class Activities are indicated in ***bold italic.***

LESSON 6.1

BACKGROUND ASSESSMENT

Question: What does a common fraction consist of?
Answer: The common fraction is considered part of a whole number. The number above the line is called the numerator (dividend). The numerator identifies how many parts of the whole are used. The number below the line is called the denominator (divisor). A line separating the numerator and denominator indicates a division.

Question: How does the use of measurement abbreviations affect the number of medication errors, and how can the situation be improved?
Answer: The use of medical measurement abbreviations makes medication errors likely. Different providers may use different measurement systems (apothecary versus metric) and different or excessive abbreviations. The medication order can be difficult to read if the provider writing the order has poor handwriting. Pediatric medication errors can also occur if a decimal point is misplaced in a medication dose or if there is an incorrect conversion in the child's weight from pounds to kilograms. To reduce the risk of an error, prescribers should print all orders for medications and include the purpose for each drug on all prescriptions. Both the milligram dose and the microgram conversion should be listed in all applicable situations (e.g., Synthroid 0.1 mg (100 mcg). Prescribers should always write a leading zero for doses that are less than 1 mg to prevent misinterpreting a dose. They should never include trailing zeros (Synthroid 25.0 mcg) because the order may be misread (Synthroid 250 mcg). Patients can also help prevent errors by verifying the appearance and dosage of their medication orders.

CRITICAL THINKING QUESTION

A nurse administered a 1000-part solution that has 40 parts of medication. What percentage of the solution is medication?
Guidelines: To determine the percentage of the total solution, divide 40 by 1000. The result is 0.04. Next, multiply 0.04 by 100. The answer is 4, or 4%. This means that the nurse administered a 1000-part solution that has 4% medication to the patient.

OBJECTIVES	CONTENT	TEACHING RESOURCES
Read and write selected numerical values using Roman numerals.	■ Roman numerals (p. 61) Review the way Roman numerals are read and written.	PPT 5-6 ARQ 1 TB Completion questions 1-6, 8-14 SG Learning Activities Part 2 questions 1, 3-6 (p. 36)

OBJECTIVES	CONTENT	TEACHING RESOURCES
		▸ Discuss and list the most common Roman numerals associated with medication administration. Class Activity ***Present the following numbers to the class, and have students convert them to Roman numerals:*** – ***17*** – ***153*** – ***1204*** – ***86*** – ***697*** Class Activity ***Have students get into pairs and quiz each other on Roman numerals. Review with the class common forms of Roman numerals found in drug calculations.***
Demonstrate proficiency in mathematic problems using addition, subtraction, multiplication, and division of fractions.	■ Fractions (p. 61) □ Common fractions (p. 62) □ Types of common fractions (p. 62) □ Working with fractions (p. 62) – Reducing to lowest terms (p. 62) – Addition (p. 63) – Subtraction (p. 64) – Multiplication (p. 65) – Division (p. 66) – Fractions as decimals (p. 66) – Using cancellation to speed your work (p. 66) Discuss the importance of fractions and when they would be used in drug calculations.	PPT 7 ARQ 2 TB Completion questions 15-30 SG Learning Activities Part 2 questions 7-51 (pp. 36-37) ▸ Discuss why, with a common numerator, the smaller the denominator, the larger the fraction really is. ▸ Discuss how using cancellation can speed your work with fractions. Class Activity ***Divide the class into groups, and assign each group one of the types of fractions: simple, complex, proper, improper, or decimal. Have each group outline how to perform calculations with the assigned fraction type, and identify two situations in which it might be used.*** Class Activity ***Choose student volunteers to explain to the class how to perform each of the following functions with fractions: reducing to the lowest terms, adding, subtracting, dividing, and multiplying. After each presenter has finished, have the rest of the class evaluate the instructions for completeness and accuracy.***
Demonstrate proficiency in calculating mathematic problems using addition, subtraction, multiplication,	■ Decimal fractions (p. 66) □ Multiplying decimals (p. 67) – Multiplying whole numbers and decimals (p. 67) – Multiplying a decimal by a decimal (p. 67)	PPT 8 TB Completion questions 31-46 SG Learning Activities Part 2 questions 52-57, 66-71 (p. 37) Class Activity ***Divide the class into groups. Have each group identify three tricks or teaching tips***

OBJECTIVES	CONTENT	TEACHING RESOURCES
and division of decimals.	– Multiplying numbers with zero (p. 67) □ Dividing decimals (p. 68) Review the principles of converting decimals to fractions and vice versa as well as calculating math problems in decimals.	***to help with multiplying and dividing decimals. Have each group share its tips with the class for discussion.***
Convert decimals to fractions and fractions to decimals.	□ Changing decimals to common fractions (p. 68) □ Changing common fractions to decimal fractions (p. 68)	PPT 8 TB Completion questions 47-54 SG Learning Activities Part 2 questions 66-71 (p. 37) *Class Activity* ***Lead a class discussion about converting between fractions and decimals. Have students explain how performing mathematic operations with decimals differs from fractions. When might a nurse need to use these skills? Record student responses on the board for comparison.***

6.1 Homework/Assignments:

6.1 Instructor's Notes/Student Feedback:

LESSON 6.2

CRITICAL THINKING QUESTION

A physician prescribes 120 milliliters (mL) of medication to be taken once a day. The nurse must convert the order from milliliters to ounces (oz). How many ounces should the nurse tell the patient to take per day?

Guidelines: Thirty milliliters (30 mL) equals one ounce (1 oz). The nurse should divide 120 mL by 30. The order of 120 mL is equal to 4 oz. The nurse should instruct the patient to take 4 oz of medication per day.

ELSEVIER

OBJECTIVES	CONTENT	TEACHING RESOURCES
Demonstrate proficiency in calculating mathematic problems using percentages.	■ Percents (p. 68) □ Determining percent that one number is of another (p. 68) Discuss the conversion of decimals to percents and why this is a necessary skill to master.	PPT 12 Class Activity ***Ask the class to calculate the following:*** ***A 10,000-part solution is one part drug. What percent of the solution is drug?*** Class Activity ***Have students practice in groups reading percents and converting them to fractions. Convert percents to decimals and fractions to percents to gain practice. Discuss the importance of understanding how to convert percents to fractions for drug calculation.***
Convert percents to fractions, percents to decimals, decimal fractions to percents, and common fractions to percents.	□ Changing percents to fractions (p. 68) □ Changing percents to decimal fractions (p. 68) □ Changing common fractions to percents (p. 69) □ Changing decimal fractions to percents (p. 69) □ Points to remember in reading decimals (p. 69)	TB Completion questions 55-58 SG Learning Activities Part 2 questions 58-65 (p. 37) ▸ Discuss why 1 and 1.0 represent the same number. ▸ Discuss whether or not 0.01 and .01 represent the same number. Class Activity ***Divide the class into four groups, and assign each group one of the following operations: changing percents to fractions, changing percents to decimal fractions, changing common fractions to percents, and changing decimal fractions to percents. Have each group outline the steps involved in its procedure and choose a representative to present the conversion to the class.***
Demonstrate proficiency in converting ratios to percentages and percentages to ratios, in simplifying ratios, and in use of the proportion method for solving problems.	■ Ratios (p. 69) □ Changing ratio to percent (p. 69) □ Changing percent to ratio (p.69) □ Simplifying ratios (p. 70) □ Proportions (p. 70) Review how to calculate ratios and their percentages.	PPT 13 TB Completion questions 77-79 SG Learning Activities Part 2 questions 72-74 (p. 37) Class Activity ***Lead a class discussion about ratios. Have students discuss the definition of ratios, and identify situations in nursing where ratios might be used. Record student responses on the board for comparison.***
Memorize the basic equivalents of the household and metric systems.	■ Systems of weights and measures (p. 70) □ Household measurements (p. 70) □ Metric system (p. 71) – Other prefixes (p. 71)	PPT 14 TB Multiple Choice questions 1, 3 TB Completion questions 59-70, 80-84 SG Learning Activities Part 1 questions 1-9 (p. 35)

OBJECTIVES	CONTENT	TEACHING RESOURCES
		Figure 6-1 (p. 71): A graduated cylinder is used to measure the volume of liquids. ▸ Discuss the volume differences in the imperial system of measurement. ▸ Discuss the basic units of length, volume, and weight in the metric system. ▸ Use three different household spoons and fill with water. Measure the amounts each spoon holds to illustrate that household measures are the most inaccurate of all systems. Class Activity ***Have students research the history of apothecary measurements, and present their findings to the class. (For students to prepare for this activity, see Homework/Assignments 1.)*** Class Activity ***Divide the class into groups and present the following scenarios:*** ***1. A 6-year-old is prescribed ear drops.*** ***2. A 3-year-old is prescribed cough syrup.*** ***3. A patient is prescribed digoxin daily.*** ***4. A patient is prescribed normal saline infused at a set rate per hour.*** ***Have each group identify which measurement system is most likely to be used in each scenario and share its findings with the class.***
Demonstrate proficiency in performing conversion of medication problems using the household and metric systems.	□ Conversion of metric units (p. 72) – Converting milligrams (metric) to grams (metric) (p. 72) – Solid dosage for oral administration (p. 72) – Conversion problems (p. 73) – Converting weight to kilograms (p. 73) □ Calculating dosage ranges for mg/kg/day (p. 74) □ Calculations with other forms of measure that do not require conversions (p. 74) – Sliding scale insulin dosage (p. 75) Review the measures of the household and metric systems. Discuss how to convert from one system to the other.	PPT 14 ARQ 3 TB Completion questions 71-73 INRQ 3, 4, 8-10 CTQ 1 SG Learning Activities Part 2 questions 75-82 (p. 37) SG Practice Questions for the NCLEX Examination 1-5, 8-9 (p. 38) ▸ Discuss which measurements are the least accurate and which are preferred: household, apothecary, or metric. Why? ▸ Discuss whether or not it would be advisable to give dosages to a parent in household measurements. Class Activity ***Divide the class into groups, and have students create a conversion table showing how to convert between the metric and***

OBJECTIVES	CONTENT	TEACHING RESOURCES
		apothecary systems. Then have students practice making conversions with the help of the table.

6.2 Homework/Assignments:

6.2 Instructor's Notes/Student Feedback:

LESSON 6.3

CRITICAL THINKING QUESTION

A physician writes an order to mix 20,000 units of heparin in 1000 mL of dextrose to infuse at a rate of 120 units/hr. At what flow rate does the physician want the solution to be infused?

Guidelines: 1000 mL:20,000 units as *x* mL:120 units. Multiply the means:20,000 units *(x)* = 20,000 units(*x*). Multiply the extremes: 1000 mL × 120 units/hr = 120,000 mL units/hr. Next, divide both sides of the equation by the number with *x*. (20,000 units)(*x*)/20,000 units = (120,000 mL units/hr)/20,000 units. Reduce: *x* = 6 mL/hr. The nurse should set the infusion pump to 6 mL/hr.

OBJECTIVES	CONTENT	TEACHING RESOURCES
Use formulas to calculate intravenous fluid and medicine administration rates.	■ Calculation of intravenous fluid and medication administration rates (p. 75) □ Intravenous fluid orders, drip rates, pumps, and rounding (p. 76) □ Rounding (p. 76) □ Volumetric and nonvolumetric pumps (p. 76) □ Calculation of flow rates (p. 76) – Milliliters per hour (mL/hr) (p. 76) – Calculating rates of infusion for other than 1 hour (p. 77) – Drops per minute (gtt/min) (p. 77)	PPT 15 ARQ 4 TB Multiple Choice question 2 TB Completion questions 74-76 INRQ 5, 11 CTQ 2 SG Practice Questions for the NCLEX Examination 6-7 (p. 38) Figure 6-2 (p. 76): **A,** Macrodrip chamber. **B,** Microdrip chamber. ▸ Discuss methods for rounding. ▸ Discuss how the type of infusion pump affects the choice of flow rate.

ELSEVIER

OBJECTIVES	CONTENT	TEACHING RESOURCES
	□ Drugs ordered in units per hour or milligrams per hour (p. 77) Review the formula used to calculate intravenous fluid rates.	Class Activity ***Divide the class into groups, and present the following scenarios:*** ***1. A patient states that he believes his pump is delivering too much medication per hour.*** ***2. IV fluids are drawn in by gravity.*** ***3. IV fluids are administered on a pump.*** ***4. A patient states that the pump administered the medication over 5 hours, but it was supposed to be administered over 3 hours.*** ***Have each group identify which administration rate or drop rate calculation will be most appropriate for each scenario and share its findings with the class for discussion.***
Demonstrate proficiency in performing conversions between the centigrade and Fahrenheit systems of temperature measurement.	■ Fahrenheit and centigrade (Celsius) temperatures (p. 78) □ Formula for converting Fahrenheit temperature to centigrade temperature (p. 79) □ Formula for converting centigrade temperature to Fahrenheit temperature (p. 79) Discuss how to convert temperatures from Fahrenheit to Celsius.	PPT 16 ARQ 5 CTQ 3 SG Practice Question for the NCLEX Examination 10 (p. 38) Figure 6-3 (p. 79): Clinical thermometers. ▸ Discuss differences and similarities between centigrade and Fahrenheit thermometers. ▸ Discuss normal body temperatures as expressed in the centigrade and Fahrenheit systems. Class Activity ***Divide the class into groups, and have each group make a conversion table that explains how to convert between Celsius and Fahrenheit. Then have students practice converting between the two temperature scales, first using the table and then using the formula.***
Performance evaluation		Test Bank SG Learning Activities (pp. 35-37) SG Practice Questions for the NCLEX Examination (p. 38) Critical Thinking Questions

6.3 Homework/Assignments:

6.3 Instructor's Notes/Student Feedback:

6 Lecture Outline

A Review of Arithmetic

Slide 1

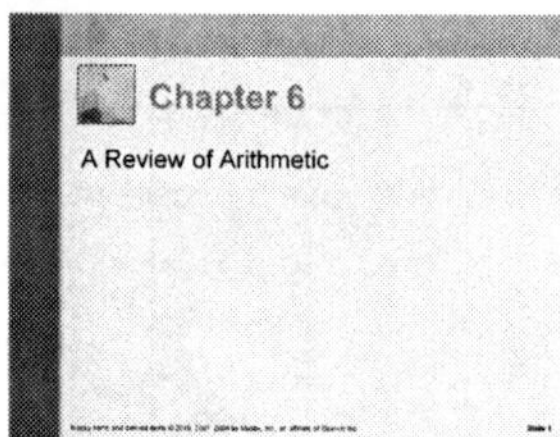
Chapter 6
A Review of Arithmetic

Slide 2

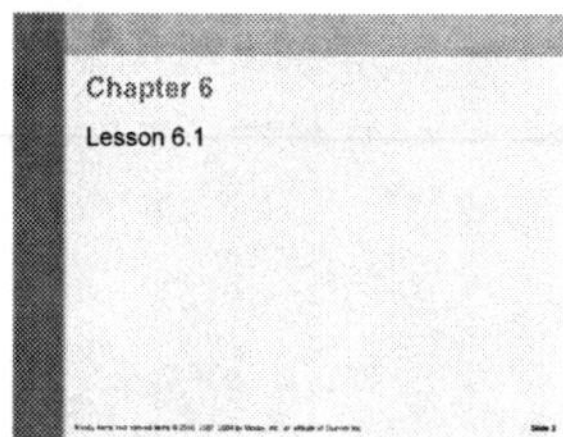
Chapter 6
Lesson 6.1

Slide 3

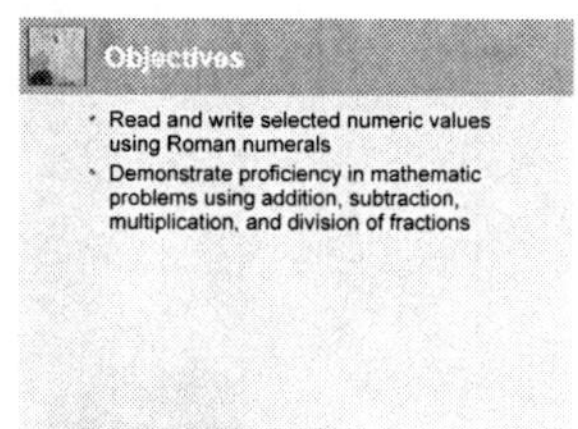
Objectives
Read and write selected numeric values using Roman numerals
Demonstrate proficiency in mathematic problems using addition, subtraction, multiplication, and division of fractions

Slide 4

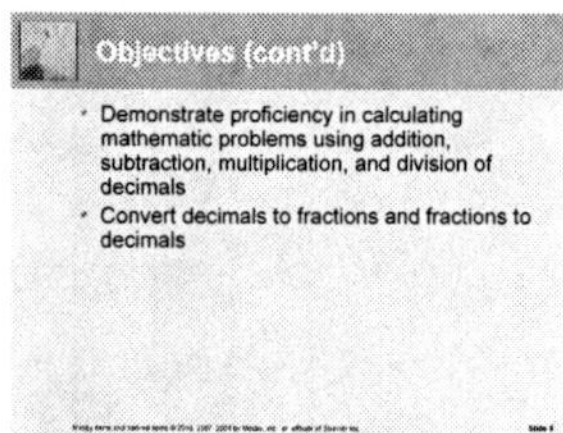
Objectives (cont'd)
Demonstrate proficiency in calculating mathematic problems using addition, subtraction, multiplication, and division of decimals
Convert decimals to fractions and fractions to decimals

Slide 5

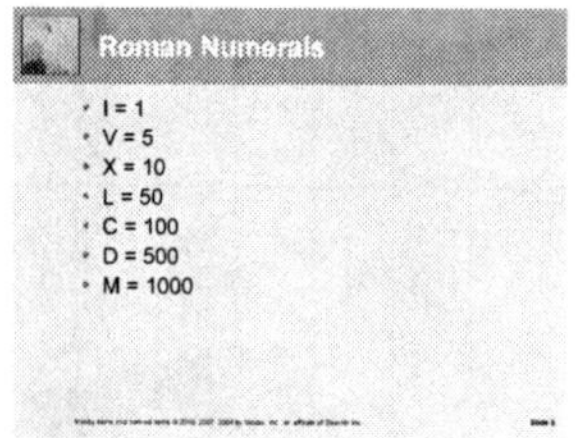
Roman Numerals
I = 1
V = 5
X = 10
L = 50
C = 100
D = 500
M = 1000

- Roman numerals are not often used in medicine.
- Practice converting Arabic numerals to Roman and back.
- Write the year in Roman numerals.

ELSEVIER

Slide 6

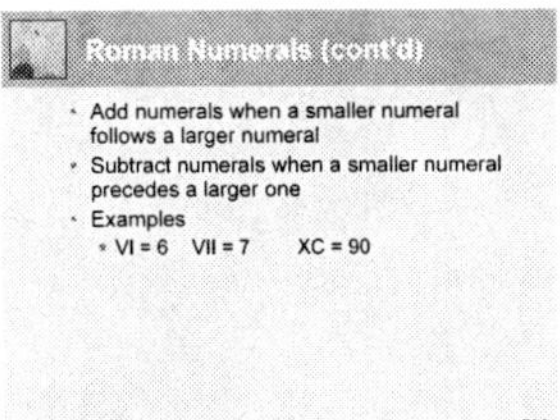
Roman Numerals (cont'd)
Add numerals when a smaller numeral follows a larger numeral
Subtract numerals when a smaller numeral precedes a larger one
Examples
VI = 6 VII = 7 XC = 90

Slide 7

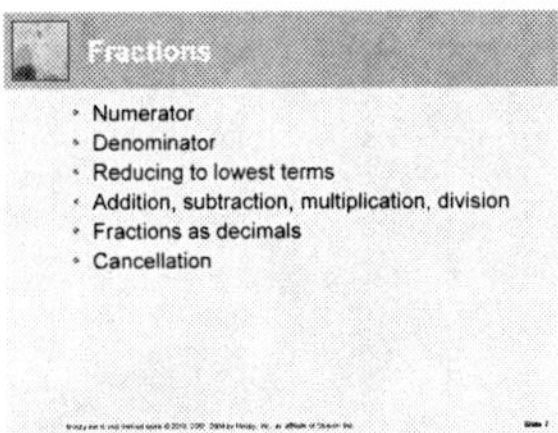
Fractions
Numerator
Denominator
Reducing to lowest terms
Addition, subtraction, multiplication, division
Fractions as decimals
Cancellation

- Fractions are not used in prescriptions very often, except for decimal fractions.
- Practice working mathematical problems using fractions.

Slide 8

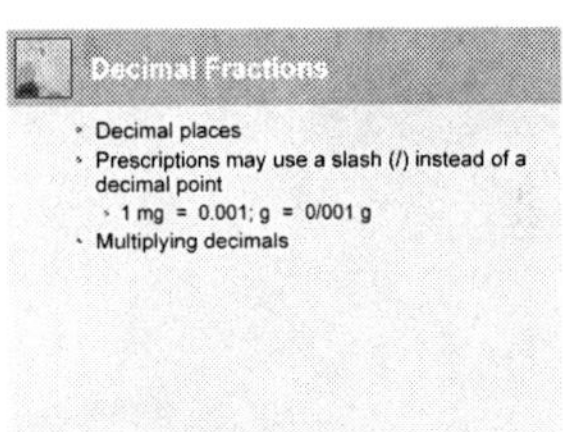
Decimal Fractions
Decimal places
Prescriptions may use a slash (/) instead of a decimal point
1 mg = 0.001; g = 0/001 g
Multiplying decimals

- Write a leading zero for doses less than 1 mg to avoid misinterpreting a dose: .25 mg versus 0.25 mg.
- Never include trailing zeroes because the order may be misread: 25.0 mcg versus 250 mcg.

Slide 9

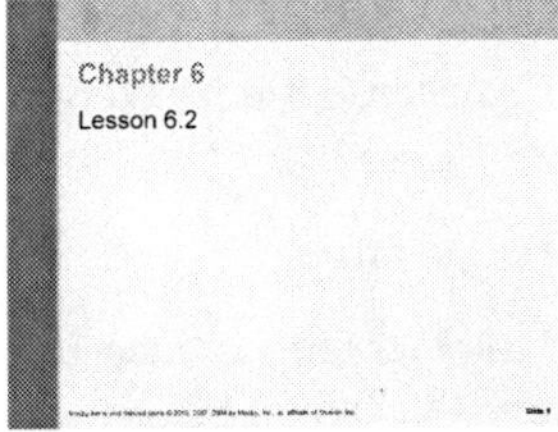
Chapter 6
Lesson 6.2

Slide 10

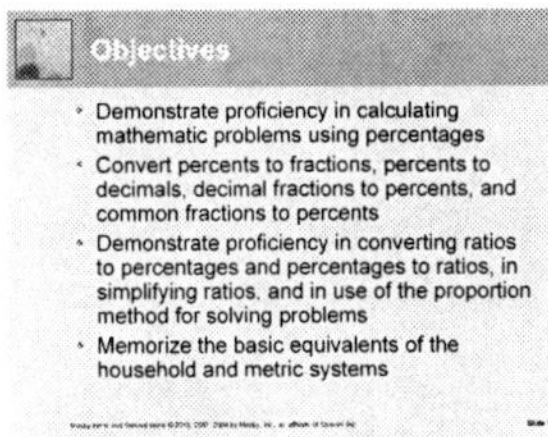
Objectives
Demonstrate proficiency in calculating mathematic problems using percentages
Convert percents to fractions, percents to decimals, decimal fractions to percents, and common fractions to percents
Demonstrate proficiency in converting ratios to percentages and percentages to ratios, in simplifying ratios, and in use of the proportion method for solving problems
Memorize the basic equivalents of the household and metric systems

ELSEVIER

Slide 11

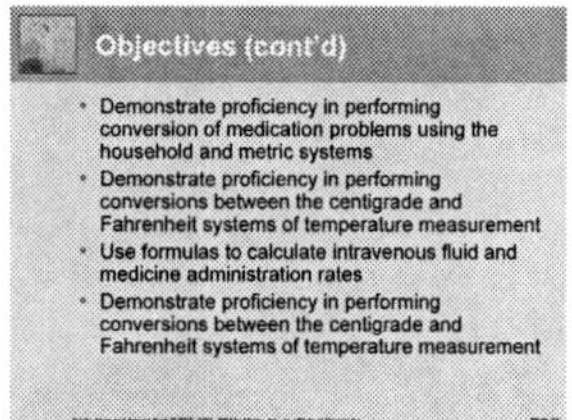
Objectives (cont'd)
Demonstrate proficiency in performing conversion of medication problems using the household and metric systems
Demonstrate proficiency in performing conversions between the centigrade and Fahrenheit systems of temperature measurement
Use formulas to calculate intravenous fluid and medicine administration rates
Demonstrate proficiency in performing conversions between the centigrade and Fahrenheit systems of temperature measurement

Slide 12

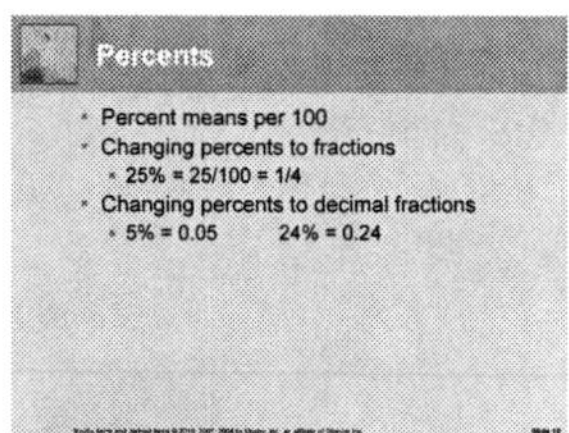
Percents
Percent means per 100
Changing percents to fractions
25% = 25/100 = 1/4
Changing percents to decimal fractions
5% = 0.05 24% = 0.24

- Common percentage mistake: converting oral therapy to IV doses in the hospital.

Slide 13

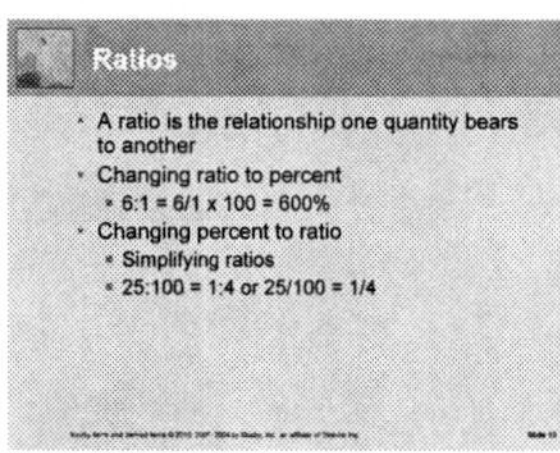
Ratios
A ratio is the relationship one quantity bears to another
Changing ratio to percent
6:1 = 6/1 x 100 = 600%
Changing percent to ratio
Simplifying ratios
25:100 = 1:4 or 25/100 = 1/4

- A few drugs (e.g., epinephrine, lidocaine) have concentrations expressed as a dilution ratio or percentage. These expressions are error-prone.

Slide 14

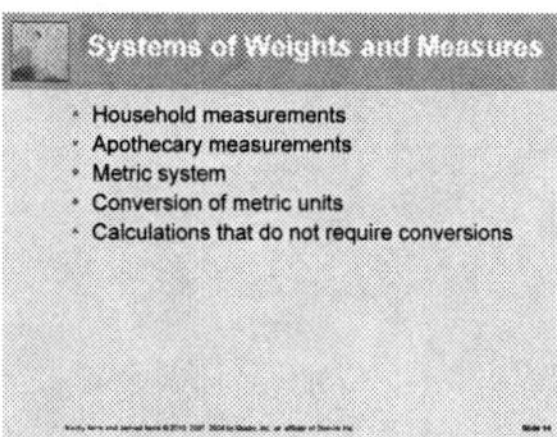
Systems of Weights and Measures
Household measurements
Apothecary measurements
Metric system
Conversion of metric units
Calculations that do not require conversions

- The FDA urges prescribers to abandon archaic household (most inaccurate) and apothecary (easy to misinterpret) measurements.
- The metric system is simpler and easier to use because it is based on factors of 10.
- Conversions between any two systems can lead to errors.
- Milliequivalents (mEq) cannot be converted to other units of measure, and "units" used for insulin, heparin, and penicillin cannot be converted to any other measurement.

Slide 15

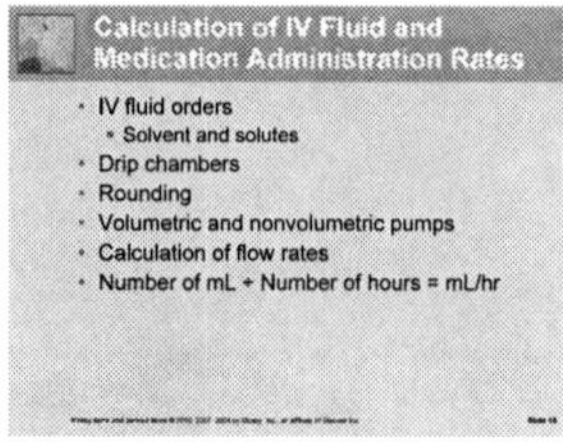
Calculation of IV Fluid and Medication Administration Rates
IV fluid orders
Solvent and solutes
Drip chambers
Rounding
Volumetric and nonvolumetric pumps
Calculation of flow rates
Number of mL ÷ Number of hours = mL/hr

- The drop factor is the standardized drops per milliliter an administration set delivers. Know the difference between macrodrip and microdrip (used for pediatrics).
- When rounding, if the number is 0.5 or greater, increase the answer to the next whole number; if the answer is less than 0.5, leave the number at the current value.
- Volumetric pumps measure the volume of medication being infused in milliliters per hour, whereas nonvolumetric pumps are set in drops per minute.

Slide 16

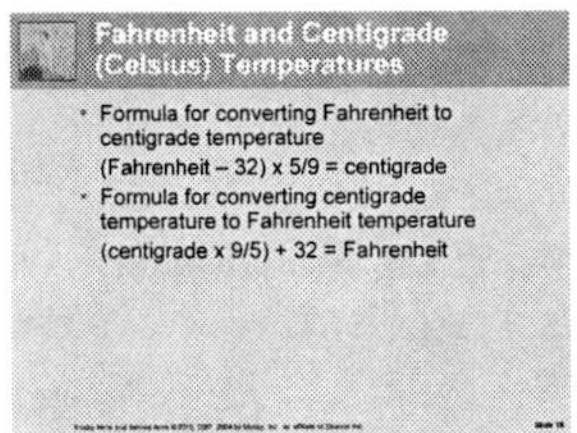
Fahrenheit and Centigrade (Celsius) Temperatures
Formula for converting Fahrenheit to centigrade temperature
(Fahrenheit – 32) x 5/9 = centigrade
Formula for converting centigrade temperature to Fahrenheit temperature
(centigrade x 9/5) + 32 = Fahrenheit

- The centigrade scale uses the point at which water freezes as 0° C; the Fahrenheit scale uses the point at which water freezes as 32° F.
- Practice converting temperature problems.

7 Lesson Plan

Principles of Medication Administration and Medication Safety

TEACHING FOCUS

In this chapter, students will be introduced to topics related to medication administration. Students will become acquainted with legal and ethical considerations, patient medical records, drug distribution systems, the medication order, medication errors, and the six rights of drug administration.

MATERIALS AND RESOURCES

- ☐ computer and PowerPoint projector (all Lessons)
- ☐ copies of your state's nurse practice act (Lesson 7.1)
- ☐ Kardex card (Lesson 7.1)
- ☐ sample drug administration policies (Lesson 7.1)
- ☐ sample patient chart (Lesson 7.1)
- ☐ sample controlled substance sheet (Lesson 7.2)

LESSON CHECKLIST

Preparations for this lesson include:

- lecture
- evaluation of student knowledge and skills needed to perform all entry-level activities related to principles of medication administration, including:
  - patient charts
  - drug distribution systems
  - types of medication orders and the nurse's responsibilities in preventing medication errors
  - six rights of drug administration
  - guest speaker: informatics nurse

KEY TERMS

adverse drug events (ADEs) (p. 100)
bar codes (p. 92)
case management (p. 89)
clinical decision-making support systems (CDSSs) (p. 101)
computer-controlled dispensing system (p. 92)
computerized prescriber order entry (CPOE) (p. 101)
consent form (p. 82)
consultation reports (p. 87)
core measures (p. 84)
critical pathways (p. 84)
disposal of unused medicines (p. 99)
evidence-based medicine or practice (p. 84)
floor or ward stock system (p. 91)
flow sheets (p. 87)
graphic record (p. 86)
handoffs (p. 101)
high-alert medications (p. 101)
history and physical examination form (p. 84)
individual prescription order system (p. 91)
Kardex (p. 89)
laboratory tests record (p. 85)
long-term care unit dose system (p. 96)
medication administration record (MAR) (p. 87)
medication errors (p. 100)
medication profile (p. 87)
medication reconciliation (p. 101)
medication safety (p. 100)
narcotic control systems (p. 97)
nurse practice act (p. 81)
nurses' notes (p. 84)
nursing care plan (p. 84)
nursing history (p. 84)
other diagnostic reports (p. 87)
patient education record (p. 89)
physician's order form (p. 82)
PRN (p. 88)
PRN order (p. 100)
progress notes (p. 84)
renewal order (p. 100)
single order (p. 99)
standards of care (p. 81)
standing order (p. 100)
stat order (p. 99)
summary sheet (p. 82)
transcription (p. 102)
unit dose drug distribution systems (p. 94)
unscheduled medication orders (p. 89)
variance (p. 102)
verification (p. 102)

ELSEVIER

ADDITIONAL RESOURCES

PowerPoint slides: 1-22

Legend

ARQ	PPT	TB	CTQ	SG	INRQ
Audience Response Questions	PowerPoint Slides	Test Bank	Critical Thinking Questions	Study Guide	Interactive NCLEX Review Questions

Class Activities are indicated in ***bold italic.***

LESSON 7.1

BACKGROUND ASSESSMENT

Question: What are the types of medication orders?
Answer: The different types of drugs orders are stat, single, PRN, standing, and verbal. Stat indicates that a drug will be given one time only and that it is to be given immediately. It is generally used in emergencies. A single order indicates that the drug will be given one time only and at a certain time. A PRN order indicates that the drug can be given if the patient needs it and if the nurse feels it is appropriate. A standing order indicates that a drug is to be given until the health care provider orders it to be discontinued or for a specified number of doses.

Question: What are the nursing responsibilities regarding taking and verifying drug orders?
Answer: When taking a drug order, the nurse must make sure that it contains the patient's name, the date, the name of the drug, the dose, the route of administration, and the duration of therapy. Orders should be signed by the health care provider, but verbal orders can be taken. When verifying the order, it is the nurse's responsibility to ensure that the drug is appropriate for the patient, the dose and the route are correct, and the patient is not allergic to the drug. It is also the nurse's responsibility to clarify any part of the order that is unclear before administering the medication.

CRITICAL THINKING QUESTION

A patient has type 1 diabetes mellitus. What general guidelines must be met before this patient can receive insulin? What specific responsibilities does the nurse have when administering insulin, and who develops the standards of care that results in these guidelines?
Guidelines: Before any patient can receive medication, there must be an order for the drug by a practitioner who has prescriptive privileges, and the nurse must have a valid state license. There also must be a policy in place at the health care facility that permits the nurse to administer insulin. Specific responsibilities of the nurse when administering the insulin include giving the right drug to the right patient, at the right time, via the right route, at the right dose, and using the right documentation. The nurse should also understand the basic action of the drug, make sure the drug is appropriate for the patient's clinical condition, be aware of the patient's recent blood glucose level, and monitor for therapeutic and adverse effects. The standards of care that generate these guidelines come from the institution, the nurse practice act of each state, and professional nursing organizations.

ELSEVIER

OBJECTIVES	CONTENT	TEACHING RESOURCES
Identify the limitations relating to medication administration placed on licensed practical nurses, vocational nurses, registered nurses, and nurse clinicians by the nurse practice act in the state where you will be practicing.	■ Legal and ethical considerations (p. 81) Review the nurse practice act specific to your state, and policies and procedures that govern the administration of medications by nurses.	PPT 5 TB Multiple Response questions 1-2 INRQ 7, 11 CTQ 1 SG Review Sheet questions 1-5, 11 (pp. 39-40) ▸ Discuss the standards of care in your state and list the organizations that define them. ▸ Discuss the three elements that must be present before a nurse can administer a medication. Class Activity ***Divide the class into groups, and provide students with copies of your state's nurse practice act. Have each group identify two limitations of medication administration defined in the nurse practice act for licensed practical/vocational nurses, registered nurses, and advanced practice nurses. Then have each group present its findings to the class.***
Study the policies and procedures of the practice setting to identify specific regulations concerning medication administration by licensed practical nurses, vocational nurses, registered nurses, and nurse clinicians.	■ Legal and ethical considerations (p. 81)	ARQ 1 TB Multiple Choice question 10 SG Review Sheet question 19 (p. 40) ▸ Discuss the aspects of the patient and the medication that must be understood by the nurse before administering the medication. Class Activity ***Divide the class into groups. Assign the students to get copies of the drug administration policies from one or more health care organizations. Then have each group present its findings to the class for discussion. Encourage students to compare their findings. (To prepare students for this activity, refer to Homework/Assignments 1.)***
Identify the basic categories of information available in a patient's chart.	■ Patient charts (p. 82) □ Contents of patient charts (p. 82) Discuss the different aspects that are included in the patient's chart, as well as the Kardex and its purpose.	PPT 6-7 TB Multiple Choice questions 1, 6 CTQ 3 SG Review Sheet question 8-9 (pp. 39-40) SG Learning Activities questions 1-3, 7-8, 12 (pp. 41-42) SG Practice Questions for the NCLEX Examination 19, 23 (p. 45) Review Questions for the NCLEX Examination 3, 8 (p.107)

OBJECTIVES	CONTENT	TEACHING RESOURCES
		Figure 7-1 (p. 83): Physician's order form and progress record. Figure 7-2 (p. 85): First 3 days of 9-day CareMap for sepsis with neutropenia. Figure 7-3 (p. 87): Standard care plan on Risk for Infection. Figure 7-4 (p. 89): Laboratory test reports Figure 7-5 (p. 90): **A,** Manual vital signs record. **B,** Electronic charting of vital signs and intake and output. Figure 7-6 (p. 92) Pain flow sheet. Figure 7-7 (p. 93): **A,** Example of medication administration record (MAR). **B,** Electronically generated medication sheet. Figure 7-8 (p. 95): Example of medication administration record used in long-term care setting. ▸ Discuss the purposes of the different forms that may be found in a patient' medical record. ▸ Discuss how a nurse might use and contribute to an MAR in actual clinical practice. Class Activity ***Hand out the different forms available on a patient's chart—the summary sheet, consent forms, physicians' order forms, H&P forms, nurse's notes, laboratory test record, flow sheets, and Kardex. Have students explain what is on these forms and where to find them. Review with the class the importance of these forms.***
Cite the information contained in a Kardex, and describe the purpose of this file.	□ Kardex records (p. 89)	PPT 7 SG Learning Activities question 10 (p. 41) Figure 7-9 (p. 96): Transcription of a medication order. ▸ Discuss why Kardex cards are destroyed on patient discharge. Why are Kardex cards not considered legal documents? Class Activity ***Lead a class discussion about Kardex records. Using a sample Kardex, have students identify various components and ask students to explain why Kardex cards are primarily used by nurses. Record student responses on the board for comparison.***

OBJECTIVES	CONTENT	TEACHING RESOURCES
Study patient charts at different practice settings to identify the various formats used to chart patient data.	□ Evolving charting methodologies (p. 89)	SG Practice Question for the NCLEX Examination 21 (p. 45) ▸ Discuss how the content of progress notes, nurses' notes, and critical pathways varies among institutions and health care settings. Class Activity ***Lead a class discussion about charting methodologies. Ask students to identify different formats used to chart patient data, and discuss the advantages and disadvantages of each. Discuss The Joint Commission standards. Record student responses on the board. Have students access The Joint Commission at www.jointcommission.org outside of class time and complete a search for standards of charting appropriate to health care facilities. Allow time in class for discussion.***

7.1 Homework/Assignments:
1. Have each group contact local hospitals or other health care settings to learn about regulations concerning medication administration by licensed practical nurses, vocational nurses, registered nurses, and nurse clinicians. Have students request the institution's drug administration policy.

7.1 Instructor's Notes/Student Feedback:

LESSON 7.2

CRITICAL THINKING QUESTION

The health care provider has given a verbal order for acetaminophen, 500 mg PO q6h PRN, for headache. What does this order mean and how soon must the health care provider cosign the order? Which medication system—the unit dose system or the floor stock system—is less likely to result in an error?

Guidelines: The order indicates that the patient can receive acetaminophen, 500 mg, by mouth, every 6 hours as needed for headache. The health care provider must cosign the order within 24 hours. The unit dose system is less likely to result in an error because the medication is in a medication drawer specific to that patient. Also, the drug, the dosage, the route, and the time of administration have been checked by both the pharmacist and the nurse to ensure accuracy. With the floor stock system, the nurse is the only person responsible for accuracy.

ELSEVIER

OBJECTIVES	CONTENT	TEACHING RESOURCES
Cite the advantages and disadvantages of the ward stock system, computer-controlled ordering and dispensing systems, individual prescription order system, and unit dose system.	■ Drug distribution systems (p. 90) Review the advantages and disadvantages of the different types of drug distribution systems.	PPT 11 ARQ 3-4 TB Multiple Choice question 7 TB Multiple Response question 3 INRQ 2 CTQ 4 SG Review Sheet question 10 (p. 40) SG Learning Activities question 4 (p. 41) SG Practice Questions for the NCLEX Examination 18, 22 (pp. 44-45) Figure 7-10 (p. 96): Electronic dispensing system—the Pyxis system. Figure 7-11 (p. 96): Unit dose cabinet. ▸ Discuss the computer-controlled dispensing system. Are there any disadvantages to this system? Class Activity ***Lead a class discussion about the unit dose drug distribution system. Ask students to respond to the argument that nurses should never administer anything that they have not prepared themselves. Do the benefits of the unit dose system outweigh that argument? What are the disadvantages of this system? Record student responses on the board for comparison.***
Study the narcotic control system used at your assigned clinical practice setting and compare it with the requirements of the Controlled Substances Act of 1970.	□ Narcotic control systems (p. 97)	PPT 12 TB Multiple Choice question 2 INRQ 5 CTQ 5 SG Review Sheet questions 13-14 (p. 40) SG Practice Questions for the NCLEX Examination 8, 10, 14 (p. 44) Figure 7-12 (p. 98): Controlled substances inventory form. ▸ Discuss the nursing procedure when a controlled substance is ordered for a patient. Class Activity ***Divide the class into groups, and have each group list controlled substances that may be dispensed by nurses. Then have each group share its list with the class for***

OBJECTIVES	CONTENT	TEACHING RESOURCES
		discussion. Bring in a blank controlled substance sheet for student viewing; circulate in class.
Define the four categories of medication orders used.	■ The drug order (p. 99) Review the four categories of medication orders and the procedure used when taking verbal orders.	PPT 14 ARQ 2, 5 TB Multiple Choice question 3 TB Multiple Response questions 4-5 INRQ 1, 3, 6 SG Review Sheet questions 6, 11, 15-16 (pp. 39-40) SG Learning Activities questions 5, 9, 13-14 (pp. 41-42) SG Practice Questions for the NCLEX Examination 9, 11, 20 (pp. 44-45) Review Question for the NCLEX Examination 4 (p. 107) Figure 7-13 (p. 98): A prescription example. ▸ Discuss the four categories of medication orders and when each is typically used. ▸ Discuss the nurse's responsibilities when a PRN order is given. Class Activity ***Present the following items to the class, and have students identify which items are standard categories of medication orders:*** – ***PRN*** – ***Stat*** – ***Single*** – ***Every day*** – ***As the patient requests*** – ***Standing*** – ***By an RN only***
Describe the procedure used in the assigned clinical setting for taking, recording, transcribing, and verifying verbal medication orders.	□ Types of medication orders (p. 99)	SG Review Sheet question 15, 17 (p. 40) SG Practice Questions for the NCLEX Examination 12-13 (p. 44) Review Question for the NCLEX Examination 6 (p. 107) ▸ Discuss the nurse's responsibilities when a verbal order is given. ▸ Discuss electronic transmission of patient orders. Emphasize that fax transmissions must have an original signature within a given time frame, usually 24 hours.

OBJECTIVES	CONTENT	TEACHING RESOURCES
		Class Activity ***Present the following scenario to the class:*** ***The health care provider has verbally ordered regular insulin, 20 units, Subcut, qAM; do not administer until results of the morning blood glucose have been obtained.*** ***Have students describe the process they would use for taking this order, including what information they should obtain, where they would record it, and how they would verify it.*** Class Activity ***Have two students role-play a nurse receiving a verbal order from a health care provider. Review the verification, transcription, and correct documentation that is necessary when taking verbal orders. Discuss when it is acceptable to take a verbal order and when it is not.***
Identify common types of drug errors and actions for their prevention.	■ Medication safety (p. 100) □ Nurse's responsibilities (p. 102) Discuss common medication errors and how to prevent them.	PPT 15-16 INRQ 9 SG Review Sheet question 12 (p. 40) SG Learning Activities question 15 (p. 42) SG Practice Questions for the NCLEX Examination 2-4 (p. 43) Review Question for the NCLEX Examination 7 (p. 107) Box 7-1: Examples of Medication Errors (p. 100) ▸ Discuss the types of potential medication errors and technologies that can help reduce their occurrence. ▸ Discuss the nurse's responsibilities in verifying the safety of the drug order. Class Activity ***Present the following types of medication errors to the class: prescribing, transcription, dispensing, administration, and monitoring. Divide the class into groups and have each group identify two ways that each of these errors could occur and two ways they could be prevented. Then have each group present its findings to the class for discussion.***

ELSEVIER

7.2 Homework/Assignments:

7.2 Instructor's Notes/Student Feedback:

LESSON 7.3

CRITICAL THINKING QUESTION

A 76-year-old woman is receiving digoxin, 0.125 mg PO qAM, for atrial fibrillation; furosemide, 40 mg PO qAM for congestive heart failure; and supplemental potassium, 40 mEq PO qAM. The patient also has a history of renal failure. How can the nurse ensure that the six rights of medication administration are followed? What special precautions should be taken before administering the digoxin and the potassium?

Guidelines: To ensure that the medications are given to the right person, the nurse should ask the patient his or her name and check the hospital identification band. To ensure that the right drug is administered by the right route and at the right time, the nurse should check the original order in the patient's chart and the MAR. The nurse should also make sure that the drug is appropriate for the patient's clinical condition. To make sure the proper documentation is done, the dose, route, date, and time of administration should be recorded. Special precautions for these medications include checking the apical pulse before giving the digoxin. If it is below 60, do not give the drug and call the health care provider. Before giving the patient the potassium, check her serum blood urea nitrogen and creatinine levels. Potassium and digoxin are excreted through the kidneys, and the levels of the drugs may be elevated if kidney function is compromised.

OBJECTIVES	CONTENT	TEACHING RESOURCES
Identify specific precautions needed to ensure that the right drug is prepared for the patient.	■ The six rights of drug administration (p. 102) □ Right drug (p. 103)	PPT 20 TB Multiple Choice question 11 SG Review Sheet question 18 (p. 40) Clinical Landmine (p. 103) ▸ Discuss the three times when drug labels should be read to confirm that the right drug has been selected. Class Activity ***Divide the class into groups, and have each group list the precautions necessary to ensure that the right drug is prepared for the patient. Then have each group present its list to the class for discussion.***

OBJECTIVES	CONTENT	TEACHING RESOURCES
		Class Activity ***Invite an informatics nurse to serve as a guest speaker, and discuss the role of computerized drug administration systems in reducing medication errors in a health care facility.***
Memorize and recite standard abbreviations associated with the scheduling of medications.	□ Right time (p. 103)	PPT 20 SG Review Sheet question 22 (p. 40) SG Practice Questions for the NCLEX Examination 1, 6-7, 17 (pp. 43-44) ▸ Discuss factors to be considered in scheduling drug administration. ▸ Discuss PRN medications. Emphasize that patient charts should be checked before administration of PRN medications and explain why. Class Activity ***Present the following abbreviations to the class, and have students identify their meanings:*** – ***bid*** – ***PRN*** – ***STAT*** – ***qid*** – ***q6h*** – ***tid*** ***Then review the Institute for Safe Medication Practices' list and The Joint Commission's list of prohibited abbreviations.***
Identify data found in the patient's chart used to determine if the patient has abnormal renal or hepatic function.	□ Right dose (p. 103)	PPT 21 TB Multiple Response question 6 SG Review Sheet question 20 (p. 40) ▸ Discuss the laboratory tests used to monitor liver and kidney function. Class Activity ***Lead a class discussion about drug dosing, and have students explain how abnormal hepatic or renal function can affect drug dosing. Record student responses on the board for comparison.***
Describe specific safety precautions that the nurse should follow to ensure that correct drug calculations are made.	□ Right dose (p. 103)	PPT 21 TB Multiple Choice question 4 SG Practice Questions for the NCLEX Examination 5, 16 (pp. 43-44) Clinical Landmine (p. 104)

OBJECTIVES	CONTENT	TEACHING RESOURCES
		▸ Discuss the methodology used to establish drug doses for pediatric and geriatric patients. ▸ Discuss appropriate steps for drug administration in the case of the patient with nausea and/or vomiting. Class Activity ***Present the following scenario to the class:*** ***The health care provider has ordered the patient to receive digoxin, 0.125 mg IV and regular insulin, 10 units subcutaneously.*** ***Divide the class into groups, and have students list specific safety precautions to ensure that the correct calculations are made. Then have groups share their findings with the class.***
Review the policies and procedures of the practice setting to identify drugs for which doses must be checked by two qualified people.	□ Right patient (p. 104)	PPT 21 Review Question for the NCLEX Examination 5 (p. 107) Clinical Landmine (p. 104) ▸ Discuss how to ensure that the right patient is getting the right drug when using the medication card system and the unit dose system. ▸ Discuss how to ensure that the right patient is getting the right drug when treating pediatric patients and geriatric patients. Class Activity ***Lead a class discussion about drug doses. Ask students to identify common drugs that must be checked by two qualified persons before they can be administered. Record student responses on the board for comparison.***
Describe the methods that should be used to ensure that the correct patient receives the correct medication, by the correct route, in the correct amount, and at the correct time.	□ Right route (p. 104) Review the six rights of drug administration—right drug, right dose, right route, right patient, right time, and right documentation. Discuss safety checks that are used to prevent errors.	PPT 22 TB Multiple Choice questions 5, 8 SG Review Sheet question 21 (p. 40) Clinical Landmine (p. 105) ▸ Discuss the differences in drug absorption among the IV route, the intramuscular route, the subcutaneous route, and the oral route. Class Activity ***Have a student demonstrate how to give a medication properly. Have the class critique the demonstration and discuss if the six rights were done correctly.***

OBJECTIVES	CONTENT	TEACHING RESOURCES
Identify appropriate nursing actions to document the administration and therapeutic effectiveness of each medication administered.	□ Right documentation (p. 105)	PPT 22 Review Questions for the NCLEX Examination 1-2 (pp. 106-107) ▸ Discuss information that should always be included in the chart with regard to medications. ▸ Discuss appropriate documentation by a nurse when a patient refuses medication. Class Activity ***Present the following scenario to the class, and have students identify the appropriate nursing documentation:*** ***A nurse must administer morphine sulfate, 10 mg, IM to a patient.***
Compare each safety measure described to ensure safe preparation and administration of medications with those procedures used in the clinical practice setting.	■ The six rights of drug administration (p. 102) □ Right drug (p.103) □ Right time (p. 103) □ Right dose (p. 103) □ Right patient (p. 104) □ Right route (p. 104) □ Right documentation (p. 105)	CTQ 2 ▸ Discuss the six rights of drug administration. Review a sample drug administration policy and highlight safety measures that ensure the six rights of drug administration. Class Activity ***Lead a class discussion about the six rights of drug administration. Ask students to identify three nursing responsibilities for each. Record student responses on the board for comparison.***
Performance evaluation		Test Bank SG Learning Activities (pp. 41-42) SG Practice Questions for the NCLEX Examination (pp. 43-45) Critical Thinking Questions

7.3 Homework/Assignments:

7.3 Instructor's Notes/Student Feedback:

ELSEVIER

7

Lecture Outline

Principles of Medication Administration and Medication Safety

Slide 1

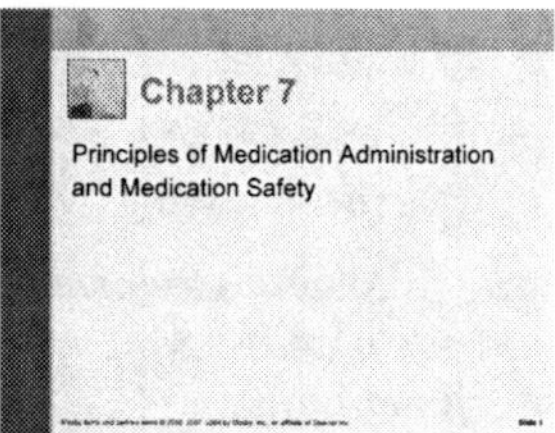
Chapter 7
Principles of Medication Administration and Medication Safety

---

Slide 2

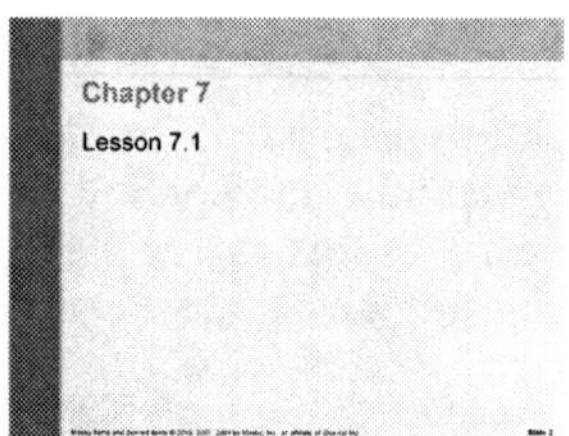
Chapter 7
Lesson 7.1

Slide 3

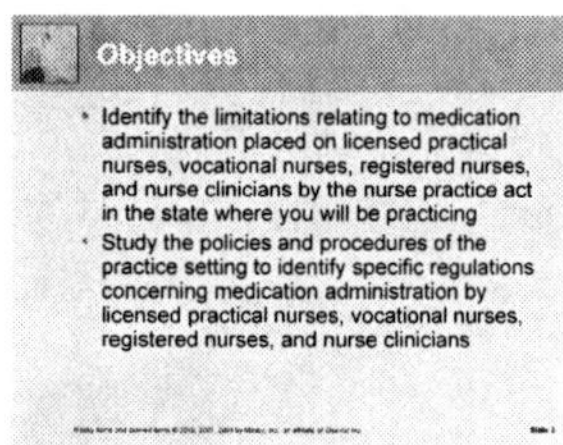
Objectives
Identify the limitations relating to medication administration placed on licensed practical nurses, vocational nurses, registered nurses, and nurse clinicians by the nurse practice act in the state where you will be practicing
Study the policies and procedures of the practice setting to identify specific regulations concerning medication administration by licensed practical nurses, vocational nurses, registered nurses, and nurse clinicians

---

Slide 4

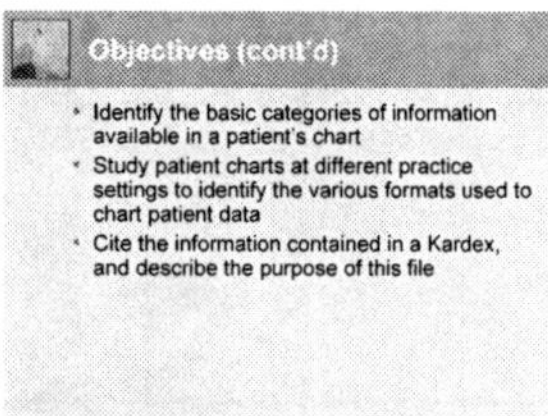
Objectives (cont'd)
Identify the basic categories of information available in a patient's chart
Study patient charts at different practice settings to identify the various formats used to chart patient data
Cite the information contained in a Kardex, and describe the purpose of this file

ELSEVIER

Slide 5

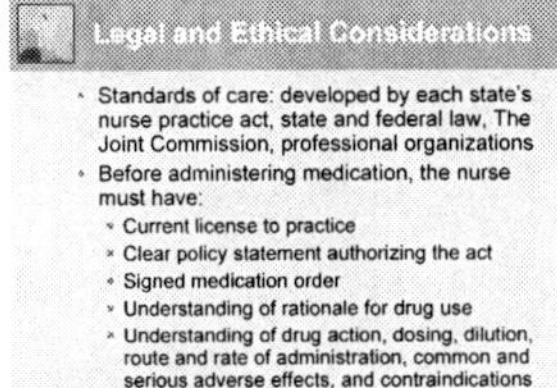
Legal and Ethical Considerations
Standards of care: developed by each state's nurse practice act, state and federal law, The Joint Commission, professional organizations
Before administering medication, the nurse must have:
Current license to practice
Clear policy statement authorizing the act
Signed medication order
Understanding of rationale for drug use
Understanding of drug action, dosing, dilution, route and rate of administration, common and serious adverse effects, and contraindications

- Nurses must be familiar with the nurse practice act in their state; claiming unfamiliarity with its contents is considered negligence.
- Each state has limitations imposed on medication administration.
- Each agency that employs nurses has procedures and policies specific to the administration of medication.

Slide 6

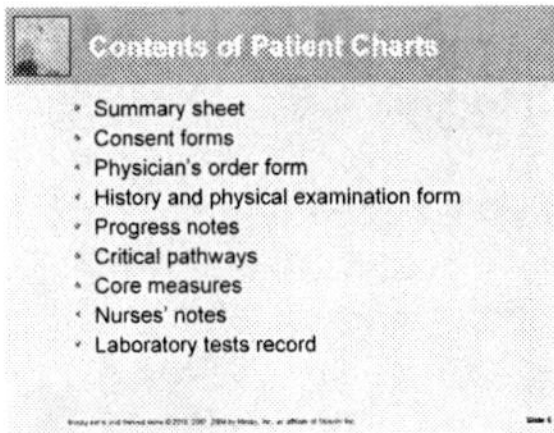
Contents of Patient Charts
Summary sheet
Consent forms
Physician's order form
History and physical examination form
Progress notes
Critical pathways
Core measures
Nurses' notes
Laboratory tests record

- Patient charts are legal documents.
- Many health care providers have transitioned to the electronic medical record (EMR). In essence, many of these same forms are included within the computerized record.

Slide 7

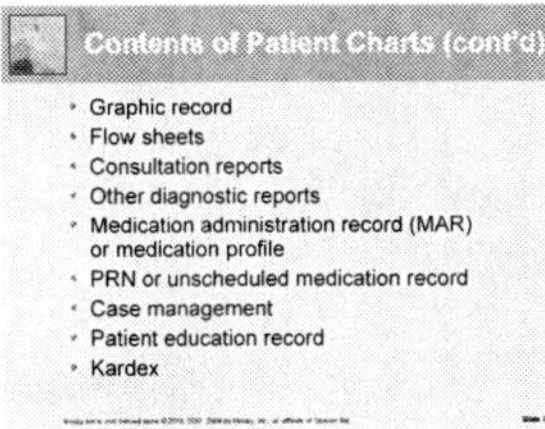
Contents of Patient Charts (cont'd)
Graphic record
Flow sheets
Consultation reports
Other diagnostic reports
Medication administration record (MAR) or medication profile
PRN or unscheduled medication record
Case management
Patient education record
Kardex

Slide 8

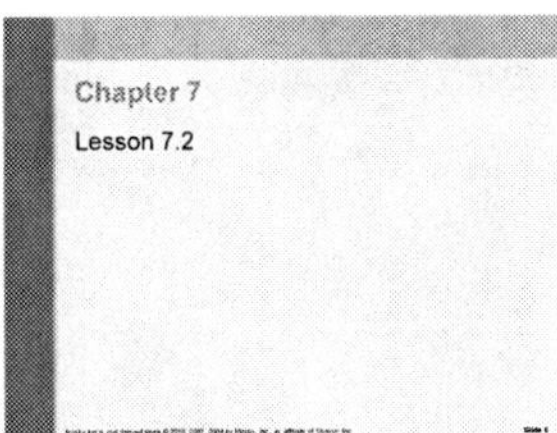
Chapter 7
Lesson 7.2

Slide 9

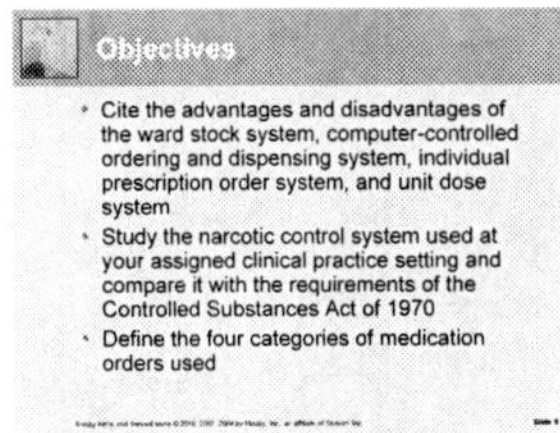
Objectives
Cite the advantages and disadvantages of the ward stock system, computer-controlled ordering and dispensing system, individual prescription order system, and unit dose system
Study the narcotic control system used at your assigned clinical practice setting and compare it with the requirements of the Controlled Substances Act of 1970
Define the four categories of medication orders used

Slide 10

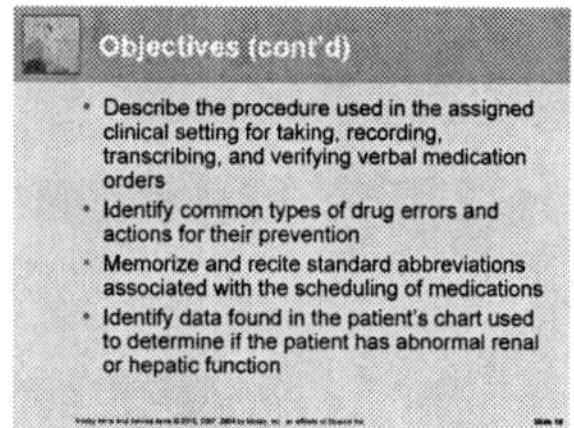
Objectives (cont'd)
Describe the procedure used in the assigned clinical setting for taking, recording, transcribing, and verifying verbal medication orders
Identify common types of drug errors and actions for their prevention
Memorize and recite standard abbreviations associated with the scheduling of medications
Identify data found in the patient's chart used to determine if the patient has abnormal renal or hepatic function

Slide 11

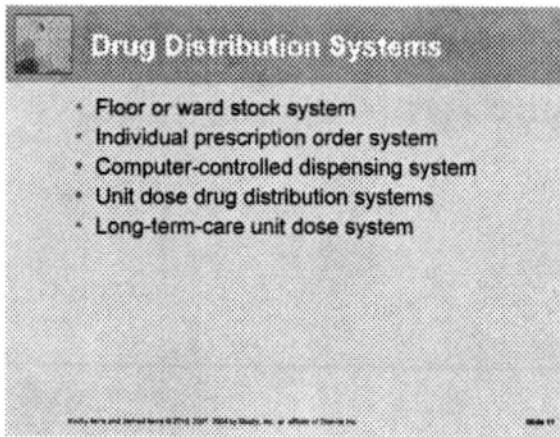
Drug Distribution Systems
Floor or ward stock system
Individual prescription order system
Computer-controlled dispensing system
Unit dose drug distribution systems
Long-term-care unit dose system

- Floor or ward stock system is used primarily in small hospitals.
- Computer-controlled dispensing system is the safest and most economical method of drug distribution used today.
- Preventing medication errors has been the primary goal of computerized drug distribution systems.

Slide 12

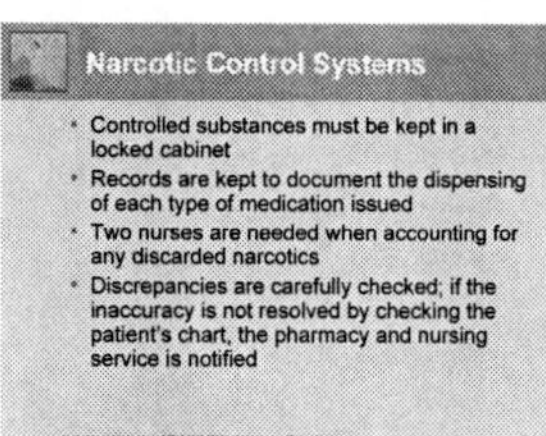
Narcotic Control Systems
Controlled substances must be kept in a locked cabinet
Records are kept to document the dispensing of each type of medication issued
Two nurses are needed when accounting for any discarded narcotics
Discrepancies are carefully checked; if the inaccuracy is not resolved by checking the patient's chart, the pharmacy and nursing service is notified

- For any unresolved discrepancies, a reconciliation sheet must be completed to account for inaccuracies in the count of any narcotics.

Slide 13

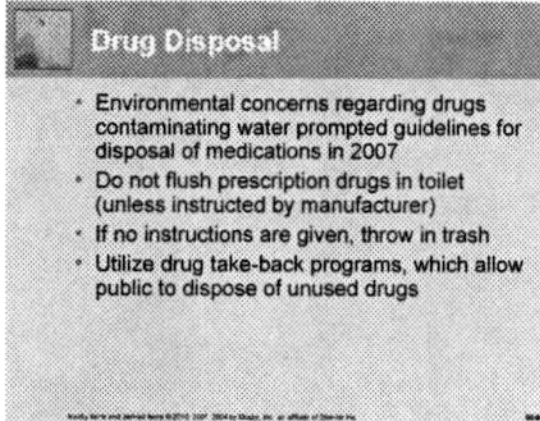
Drug Disposal
Environmental concerns regarding drugs contaminating water prompted guidelines for disposal of medications in 2007
Do not flush prescription drugs in toilet (unless instructed by manufacturer)
If no instructions are given, throw in trash
Utilize drug take-back programs, which allow public to dispose of unused drugs

- Nurses must be aware of the proper disposal recommended by the drug manufacturer, as well as agency policy for the proper disposal of medications. Chemotherapy medications, as well as narcotics, have specific requirements.

Slide 14

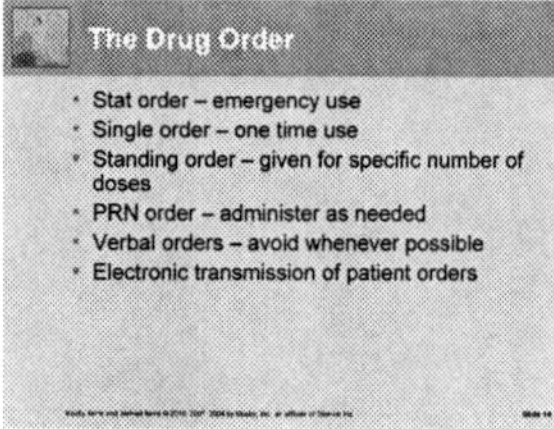
The Drug Order
Stat order – emergency use
Single order – one time use
Standing order – given for specific number of doses
PRN order – administer as needed
Verbal orders – avoid whenever possible
Electronic transmission of patient orders

ELSEVIER

Slide 15

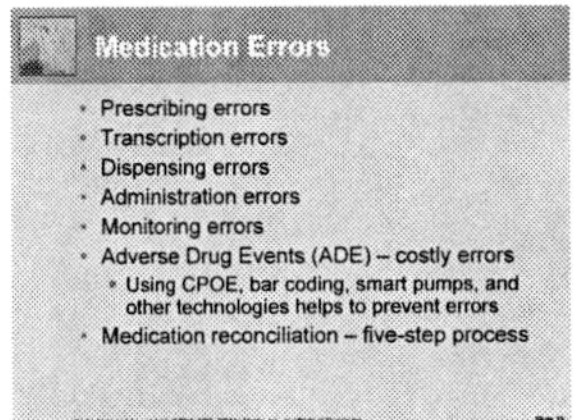
Medication Errors
Prescribing errors
Transcription errors
Dispensing errors
Administration errors
Monitoring errors
Adverse Drug Events (ADE) – costly errors
Using CPOE, bar coding, smart pumps, and other technologies helps to prevent errors
Medication reconciliation – five-step process

- Adverse drug events result from medication errors.
- Computerized health records are critical for reducing medication errors.

Slide 16

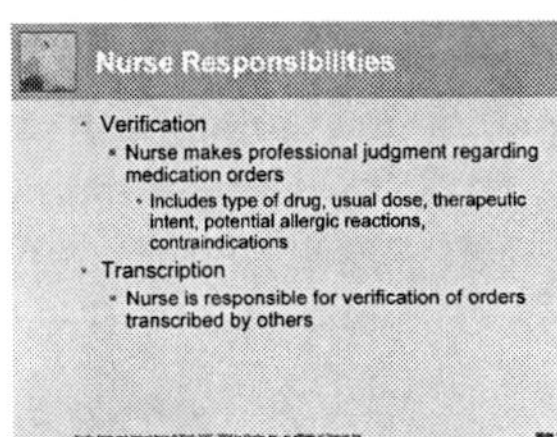
Nurse Responsibilities
Verification
Nurse makes professional judgment regarding medication orders
Includes type of drug, usual dose, therapeutic intent, potential allergic reactions, contraindications
Transcription
Nurse is responsible for verification of orders transcribed by others

- Patient safety is of primary importance, and the verification process is an important nursing responsibility.

Slide 17

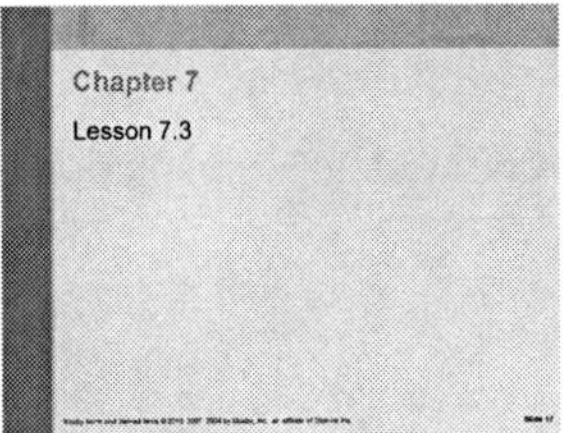
Chapter 7
Lesson 7.3

Slide 18

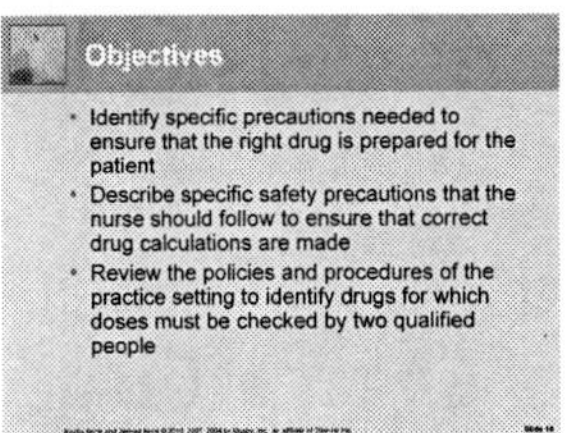
Objectives
Identify specific precautions needed to ensure that the right drug is prepared for the patient
Describe specific safety precautions that the nurse should follow to ensure that correct drug calculations are made
Review the policies and procedures of the practice setting to identify drugs for which doses must be checked by two qualified people

Slide 19

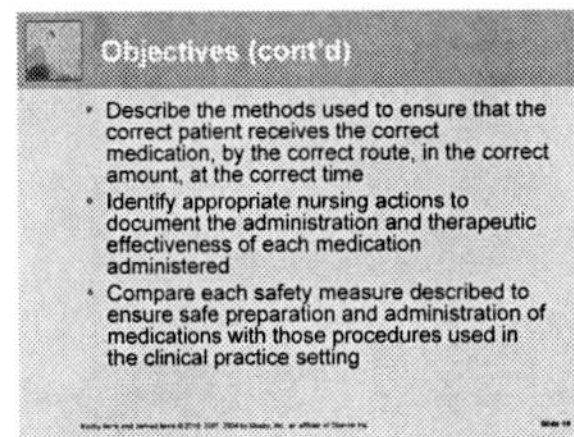
Objectives (cont'd)
Describe the methods used to ensure that the correct patient receives the correct medication, by the correct route, in the correct amount, at the correct time
Identify appropriate nursing actions to document the administration and therapeutic effectiveness of each medication administered
Compare each safety measure described to ensure safe preparation and administration of medications with those procedures used in the clinical practice setting

- If in doubt, check calculations with another nurse. Also, when the calculation is complete, is the dose within the prescribed range for the drug?
- The use of some abbreviations should be avoided in the health care setting to avoid misinterpretation and medication errors (i.e., SC, qhs, U, hs)

ELSEVIER

Slide 20

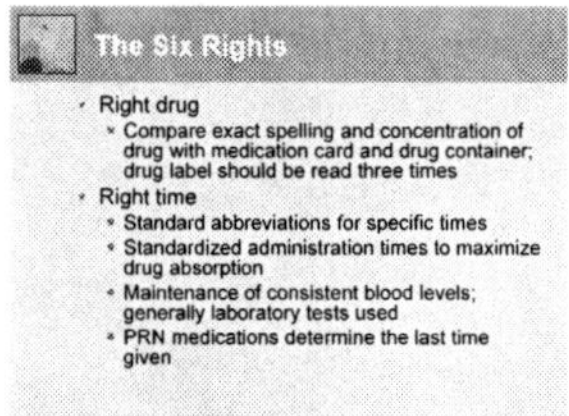
The Six Rights
Right drug
Compare exact spelling and concentration of drug with medication card and drug container; drug label should be read three times
Right time
Standard abbreviations for specific times
Standardized administration times to maximize drug absorption
Maintenance of consistent blood levels; generally laboratory tests used
PRN medications determine the last time given

Slide 21

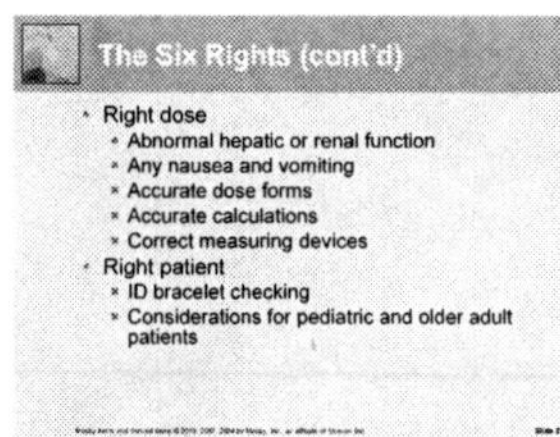
The Six Rights (cont'd)
Right dose
Abnormal hepatic or renal function
Any nausea and vomiting
Accurate dose forms
Accurate calculations
Correct measuring devices
Right patient
ID bracelet checking
Considerations for pediatric and older adult patients

- Oral medications are not be to given when patients are nauseated or vomiting; another route is generally required.
- Nurse must use reliable sources of information for determining correct drug doses. Most agencies require two nurses to check doses of certain drugs like insulin, heparin, and IV digitalis before administration.

Slide 22

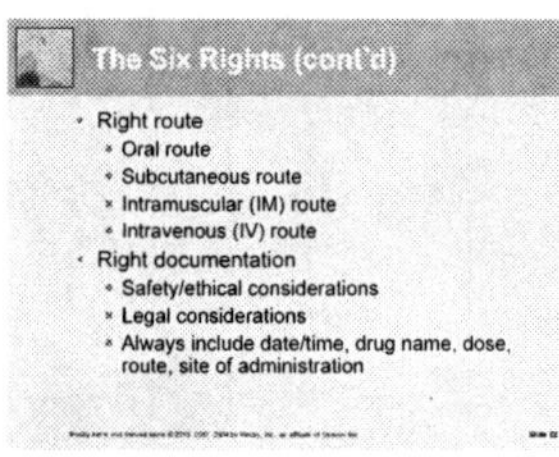
The Six Rights (cont'd)
Right route
Oral route
Subcutaneous route
Intramuscular (IM) route
Intravenous (IV) route
Right documentation
Safety/ethical considerations
Legal considerations
Always include date/time, drug name, dose, route, site of administration

- There is great variation in the absorption rate of a medication between different routes of administration. The route should never be changed without a medication order.
- Medications not administered must be recorded with the explanation of why they were not given.

8

Lesson Plan

Percutaneous Administration

TEACHING FOCUS

In this chapter, students will be introduced to topics related to percutaneous administration. Students will become acquainted with administration of various medications delivered percutaneously, including creams, lotions, and ointments; nitroglycerin ointment; transdermal drug delivery systems; topical powders; and medications applied to mucous membranes. Students will also be introduced to patch testing for allergens.

MATERIALS AND RESOURCES

- ☐ computer and PowerPoint projector (all Lessons)
- ☐ cotton-tipped applicators (Lesson 8.1)
- ☐ creams, lotions, and ointments (Lesson 8.1)
- ☐ ear drops (Lesson 8.2)
- ☐ gauze sponges (Lesson 8.1)
- ☐ gloves (Lesson 8.1)
- ☐ nasal drops, spray, nebulizer, metered-dose inhaler, dry powder inhaler (Lesson 8.2)
- ☐ talcum powder (Lesson 8.1)
- ☐ tongue blade (Lesson 8.1)
- ☐ transdermal patches (Lesson 8.1)
- ☐ vaginal applicator and douche tip (Lesson 8.2)

LESSON CHECKLIST

Preparations for this lesson include:

- lecture
- evaluation of student knowledge and skills needed to perform all entry-level activities related to percutaneous administration of medications, including:
  - creams, lotions, ointments, and topical powders
  - patch testing for allergens
  - nitroglycerin ointment
  - transdermal drug delivery systems
  - medications applied to mucous membranes

KEY TERMS

aerosols (p. 120)
allergens (p. 110)
antigens (p. 110)
buccal (p. 116)
creams (p. 108)
dressings (p. 108)
dry powder inhaler (DPI) (p. 122)
lotions (p. 108)
metered-dose inhaler (MDI) (p. 121)
nebulae (p. 120)
ointments (p. 108)
ophthalmic (p. 116)
otic (p. 118)
patch testing (p. 110)
transdermal disk (p. 113)

ADDITIONAL RESOURCES

PowerPoint slides: 1-22

Legend

ARQ	**PPT**	**TB**	**CTQ**	**SG**	**INRQ**
Audience Response Questions	PowerPoint Slides	Test Bank	Critical Thinking Questions	Study Guide	Interactive NCLEX Review Questions

Class Activities are indicated in ***bold italic.***

LESSON 8.1

BACKGROUND ASSESSMENT

Question: What are the advantages and disadvantages of percutaneous administration, and what are the different uses of topical preparations?
Answer: The main advantage of percutaneous administration is that the drug's action is concentrated at the site of administration, which reduces adverse effects. Disadvantages are that the drugs are difficult to apply, are messy, have a short duration, and must be reapplied frequently. Topical medications are used to rehydrate the skin, provide a protective barrier, reduce inflammation, cleanse and débride a wound, relieve localized symptoms, and reduce thickening of the skin.

Question: What basic principles must be observed when administering medications across mucous membranes?
Answer: Medications can be delivered across the mucous membranes by the ophthalmic route, the otic route, intranasally, via inhalation, sublingually, and vaginally. The nurse must give the right medication to the right patient, in the right dose, at the right time, by the right route, and using the right documentation. For the ophthalmic route, the medications must be warmed to room temperature, there should be a separate bottle and/or tube for each patient, exudates should be removed before application, and the eye should not be touched. For the otic route, the medication must be warmed to room temperature, there should be a separate bottle for each patient, the ear canal should be assessed for wax, and the patient should remain on one side for a few minutes after instillation. Do not touch the ear canal with the medicine dropper. For the nasal route, warm the medication, have the patient gently blow his or her nose, visually inspect the nares, and have the patient stay in the application position for a few minutes after instillation. For the sublingual route, place the tablet under the tongue or between the cheek and gum; do not administer water. For the inhalation route, place the patient in a sitting position. Have the patient exhale and then inhale while activating the inhaler and/or nebulizer. Then have the patient exhale through pursed lips. For the vaginal route, have the patient void and place her in the lithotomy position. Insert the suppository or the applicator with the cream and then apply a perineal pad to prevent leakage.

CRITICAL THINKING QUESTION

A transdermal nitroglycerin patch has been ordered for a patient. What teaching points should the nurse review with the patient before discharge?
Guidelines: The patient should be shown how to apply the patch and told for what length of time it should be worn. Nitroglycerin patches are usually worn for 10 to 14 hours and followed by a drug-free period of 10 to 12 hours. The nurse should also explain to the patient that the old patch must always be removed before the new one is applied, and the skin should be cleansed before applying a new patch. Some patients may forget where they applied a patch; it is important to look for the patch and remove it before applying the new one. When applying the patch, the patient should not touch the exposed adhesive. The patient should select a dry hairless site on or near the torso. After pressing the patch onto the skin with the palm, the outside

edge of the patch should be circled with the fingers to ensure adherence. If the patch starts to fall off, it should be completely removed before a new one is applied. The patient should also be instructed not to apply a new patch for a sudden onset of chest pain. If this occurs, the health care provider should be contacted immediately.

OBJECTIVES	CONTENT	TEACHING RESOURCES
Describe the topical forms of medications used on the skin.	■ Administration of creams, lotions, and ointments (p. 108) □ Dose forms (p. 108) □ Dressings (p. 108) Review the different types of topical forms of medications and the steps used to apply each one.	PPT 8 TB Multiple Choice questions 1, 6 TB Multiple Response questions 1, 3 SG Review Sheet questions 1-3 (p. 47) SG Learning Activities questions 1, 6 (p. 49) ▸ Discuss the factors that can influence absorption when applying topical medications to the skin. ▸ Discuss administration of creams, lotions, and ointments and describe different types of dressings used to treat wounds. Class Activity ***Bring samples of creams, lotions, and ointments to class and pass them around. Have students describe each one in terms of consistency, and demonstrate the application of one type of topical medication.*** Class Activity ***Divide the class into groups and assign each group one of the following types of topical medications: ointment, cream, powder, or lotion. Have each identify a product or medication in that category and determine what the medications are used to treat. Then have each group present its findings to the class for discussion.***
Cite the equipment needed and techniques used to apply each of the topical forms of medications to the skin surface.	□ Equipment (p. 109) □ Sites (p. 109) □ Techniques (p. 109) □ Patient teaching (p. 109) □ Documentation (p. 109)	PPT 6, 9 TB Multiple Choice questions 12, 16 TB Multiple Response question 2 Drug Administration Performance Checklist 8-1 SG Review Sheet questions 4, 9 (p. 47) SG Practice Question for the NCLEX Examination 1 (p. 50) ▸ Discuss techniques to apply topical medications. Class Activity ***Choose several student volunteers to demonstrate proper and improper application and dressing of topical medication for the class. Have the rest of the class identify and correct the mistakes.***

OBJECTIVES	CONTENT	TEACHING RESOURCES
Describe the procedure used and purpose of performing patch testing.	■ Patch testing for allergens (p. 110) □ Equipment (p. 110) □ Sites (p. 110) □ Technique (p. 110) Discuss the need for patch testing and the procedure used, as well as the patient education needed.	PPT 10-11 INRQ 4, 6 Drug Administration Performance Checklist 8-2 SG Review Sheet questions 5-7 (p. 47) SG Learning Activities question 7 (p. 49) ▸ Discuss patient teaching for allergy testing. Why is it important for patients not to bathe until patches are read? Class Activity ***Demonstrate with a chart how patch testing would look on a patient. Have two students role-play the instructions that a nurse would give to a patient undergoing allergy patch testing.***
Describe specific charting methods used with allergy testing.	□ Patient teaching (p. 112) □ Documentation (p. 112)	TB Multiple Choice question 10 Figure 8-1 (p. 111): Patch test for contact dermatitis. ▸ Discuss the importance of accurate documentation of allergy testing. What are some ways to prevent documentation errors, and what can be done if errors are made? Class Activity ***Lead a class discussion about the purpose and procedure for allergy testing. Ask students to identify common allergies, and discuss how the allergens to be tested are chosen. Why is it necessary to have emergency equipment nearby when testing for allergies? What are the symptoms of a serious reaction? What is the procedure to follow if an emergency arises?***
Identify the equipment needed, sites and techniques used, and patient education required when nitroglycerin ointment is prescribed.	■ Administration of nitroglycerin ointment (p. 112) □ Dose form (p.112) □ Equipment (p. 112) □ Sites (p. 112) □ Techniques (p. 112) □ Patient teaching (p. 113) Review the proper technique used for application of nitroglycerin ointment and the patient education needed.	PPT 6-7 ARQ 3 TB Multiple Choice questions 2, 7, 11 INRQ 7 CTQ 1 Drug Administration Performance Checklist 8-3 SG Review Sheet question 8 (p. 47) SG Learning Activities question 8 (p. 49) SG Practice Questions for the NCLEX Examination 3, 10 (pp. 50-51) Review Question for the NCLEX Examination 1 (p. 125)

OBJECTIVES	CONTENT	TEACHING RESOURCES
		Figure 8-2 (p. 112): Sites for nitroglycerin application. Lifespan Considerations: Applying Nitroglycerin (p. 113) Figure 8-3 (p. 113): Administering nitroglycerin topical ointment. ▸ Discuss the timing of nitroglycerin ointment application. Class Activity ***Describe a scenario where a nurse must instruct a patient going home how to apply nitroglycerin ointment; include how to measure out the dose, using plastic wrap to protect clothes, and washing hands after application.*** Class Activity ***Lead a class discussion about nitroglycerin medication, and have students compare and contrast the procedures for applying nitroglycerin ointment and prepared patches. Why is it important to wear gloves during application? What should be done if medication gets on the skin? How should old patches be disposed of?***
Describe specific documentation methods used to record the therapeutic effectiveness of nitroglycerin ointment therapy.	□ Documentation (p. 113)	▸ Discuss the elements to document and emphasize the importance of recording ongoing assessment data, including signs of adverse drug effects. Class Activity ***Present the following scenario to the class for discussion:*** ***A patient has been prescribed nitroglycerin ointment four times per day, with a drug-free period every 24 hours.*** ***Have students discuss in groups how this information should be documented, and explain ways to assess and record the medication's therapeutic effectiveness. Then have each group share its findings with the class for discussion.***
Identify the equipment needed, sites and techniques used, and patient education required when transdermal	■ Administration of transdermal drug delivery systems (p. 113) □ Dose form (p. 113) □ Equipment (p. 114) □ Sites (p. 114) □ Techniques (p. 114) □ Patient teaching (p. 114)	ARQ 2 Drug Administration Performance Checklist 8-4 SG Review Sheet questions 4, 9-12 (pp. 47-48) Review Question for the NCLEX Examination 2 (p. 125)

OBJECTIVES	CONTENT	TEACHING RESOURCES
medication systems are prescribed.	Review the different types of medications that are available in the transdermal form and the proper patient education needed.	Figure 8-4 (p. 114): Administering a nitroglycerin topical patch. ▸ Discuss the care of transdermal patches. How should one bathe while wearing a patch, and what should be done if the patch falls off? Class Activity ***Divide the class into pairs, and have students practice applying transdermal patches on one another. Have each pair come up with two teaching tips or suggestions for applying the medication and share their findings with the class.*** Class Activity ***List on a worksheet several medications that are available in transdermal disk form. Instruct students to describe the types of medications that are available in this form and the patient education necessary.***
Describe specific documentation methods used to record the therapeutic effectiveness of medications administered using a transdermal delivery system.	□ Documentation (p. 115)	▸ Discuss important elements to include in patient teaching about transdermal patches. Class Activity ***Present the following list to the class, and have students identify which items should be documented for a patient receiving transdermal medications and why:*** – ***Pain and/or pain relief*** – ***Tissue turgor*** – ***Presence of a wheal*** – ***Pulse*** – ***Adverse effects*** – ***Urinary frequency*** – ***Patient's emotional state*** – ***Date and time*** – ***Dosage*** ***Then have students identify other information that should be included in documentation.***
Describe the dose form, sites used, and techniques used to administer medications in topical powder form.	■ Administration of topical powders (p. 115) □ Dose form (p. 115) □ Equipment (p. 115) □ Site (p. 115) □ Technique (p. 115) □ Patient teaching (p. 115) □ Documentation (p. 115) Review the proper administration of topical powders and their uses.	Drug Administration Performance Checklist 8-5 ▸ Discuss techniques. Emphasize the need to clean the skin appropriately before application. ▸ Discuss patient teaching. Emphasize the need to tell the patient to avoid inhaling the powder during application. Class Activity ***Bring samples of powders to class and have students explain to the class how they are used, and the patient education that is needed.***

OBJECTIVES	CONTENT	TEACHING RESOURCES
		Class Activity ***Choose two student volunteers to demonstrate both proper and improper administration of powder medications to the class. Have the class identify which methods are incorrect and discuss ways to apply the medication properly.***

8.1 Homework/Assignments:

8.1 Instructor's Notes/Student Feedback:

LESSON 8.2

CRITICAL THINKING QUESTION

The health care provider has ordered otic drops to be administered twice daily for a 7-year-old patient with an ear infection. What instructions should be given to the patient's mother regarding proper instillation of the medication?

Guidelines: Before instilling the medication, the mother should assess the ear canal for wax accumulation and, when the wax is clear, she should position the child with the affected ear facing upward. The medication should be allowed to warm to room temperature, shaken, and then drawn into the dropper. When administering the medication, the mother should pull the patient's earlobe upward and back and instill the proper number of drops. It is important that the medicine dropper not touch any part of the child's ear. After instilling the drops, the patient should continue to lie on his side for a few minutes. It is also helpful to massage the tragus in front of the ear gently to propel the medication inward.

OBJECTIVES	CONTENT	TEACHING RESOURCES
Describe the dose forms, sites, equipment used, and techniques for administration of medications to the mucous membranes.	■ Administration of medications to mucous membranes (p. 115) □ Administration of sublingual and buccal tablets (p. 116) – Dose forms (p. 116) – Equipment (p. 116) – Site (p. 116) – Technique (p. 116) – Patient teaching (p. 116)	PPT 17-22 TB Multiple Choice questions 3-4, 9 INRQ 8 Drug Administration Performance Checklist 8-6 SG Review Sheet questions 13-14 (p. 48) SG Learning Activities question 2 (p. 49)

OBJECTIVES	CONTENT	TEACHING RESOURCES
	– Documentation (p. 116) Discuss the different types of medications that are applied to mucous membranes; include sublingual tablets, nasal sprays, eye drops, ear drops, inhalers, and vaginal suppositories.	Review Question for the NCLEX Examination 3 (p. 125) Figure 8-5 (p. 116): Placing medications in the mouth. ▸ Discuss the difference between sublingual administration and administration to the buccal pouch. ▸ Discuss the need to explain the exact placement of the medication and to list potential adverse effects. Class Activity ***Ask volunteers to describe the administration of sublingual and buccal medications. Why is this form of medication used? What are examples of this medication? How should the nurse instruct a patient to take it? Have the rest of the class discuss the volunteers' responses.*** Class Activity ***Lead a class discussion about the administration of medications to mucous membranes, and have students identify how applying medication to mucous membranes differs from applying topical or transdermal medications.***
Identify the dose forms safe for administration to the eye.	□ Administration of eye drops and ointment (p. 116) – Dose form (p. 116) – Equipment (p. 116) – Site (p. 117) – Technique (p. 117)	PPT 18 SG Review Sheet question 15 (p. 48) SG Learning Activities question 3 (p. 49) SG Practice Questions for the NCLEX Examination 4, 6 (pp. 50-51) ▸ Discuss the different dose forms of ophthalmic medications. Class Activity ***Divide the class into groups, and assign each group one of the following types of ophthalmic medications: drops, ointment, or disk. Have students from each group identify and research three medications related to the assigned topic and explain what they are used to treat and how they are administered. Have each group present its findings to the class. (For students to prepare for this activity, see Homework/Assignments 1.)***
Describe patient education necessary for patients requiring ophthalmic medications.	– Patient teaching (p. 117) – Documentation (p. 118) □ Administration of eye drops and ointment (p. 116) – Dose form (p. 116) – Equipment (p. 116)	PPT 18 ARQ 4 TB Multiple Choice questions 5, 8, 13 INRQ 1 CTQ 2

OBJECTIVES	CONTENT	TEACHING RESOURCES
	– Site (p. 117) – Technique (p. 117)	Drug Administration Performance Checklist 8-7 Review Question for the NCLEX Examination 5 (p. 125) Figure 8-6 (p. 117), Administering ophthalmic drops Figure 8-7 (p. 118), Administering ophthalmic ointment ▸ Discuss the advantages and disadvantages of using ophthalmic medications. ▸ Discuss the importance of follow-up care for eye disorders. Class Activity ***Lead a class discussion about ophthalmic medications, and have students compare and contrast the uses and application of each form. Record student responses on the board for comparison.*** Class Activity ***Divide the class into groups. Have the groups identify three nursing interventions and three areas of patient education for a patient receiving ophthalmic medications. Have each group share its findings with the class for discussion.***
Compare the techniques used to administer ear drops in patients younger than 3 years with those older than 3 years.	□ Administration of ear drops (p. 118) – Dose form (p. 118) – Equipment (p. 118) – Site (p.118) – Techniques (p. 118) – Patient teaching (p. 119) – Documentation (p. 119)	PPT 19 ARQ 1 CTQ 3 Drug Administration Performance Checklist 8-8 SG Review Sheet question 16 (p. 48) SG Learning Activities question 4 (p. 49) SG Practice Questions for the NCLEX Examination 7-8 (p. 51) Figure 8-8 (p. 118): Administering ear drops. ▸ Discuss the administration of ear drops. Class Activity ***Lead a class discussion about otic medications. Have students identify the different techniques used to administer ear drops to toddlers and adults and discuss the physiologic reasons for the different techniques.*** Class Activity ***Ask student volunteers to demonstrate how to administer otic medications to a child younger than 3 years and to an adult.***

ELSEVIER

OBJECTIVES	CONTENT	TEACHING RESOURCES
Describe the purpose, precautions necessary, and patient education required for those requiring medications by inhalation.	□ Administration of nose drops (p. 119) – Equipment (p. 119) – Site (p. 119) – Technique (p. 119) – Patient teaching (p. 120) – Documentation (p. 120) □ Administration of nasal spray (p. 120) – Equipment (p. 120) – Site (p. 120) – Techniques (p. 120) – Patient teaching (p. 120) – Documentation (p. 120) □ Administration of medications by inhalation (p. 120) – Equipment (p. 121) – Site (p. 121) – Techniques (p. 121) – Patient teaching (p. 121) – Documentation (p. 121) □ Administration of medications by oral inhalation (p. 121) – Dose forms (p. 121) – Equipment (p. 121) – Site (p. 121) – Technique (p. 121) – Aerosolized metered-dose inhaler (p. 121) – Dry powder inhaler (p. 121) – Patient teaching (p. 122) – Documentation (p. 122)	PPT 20-21 ARQ 5 TB Multiple Choice question 14 INRQ 5, 9 Drug Administration Performance Checklists 8-9, 8-10, 8-11, 8-12 SG Review Sheet questions 17-21 (p. 48) SG Learning Activities questions 5, 9 (p. 49) SG Practice Question for the NCLEX Examination 5 (p. 51) Review Question for the NCLEX Examination 4 (p. 125) Figure 8-9 (p. 119): Administering nose drops. Figure 8-10 (p. 121): Administering nasal spray. Figure 8-11 (p. 122): **A,** Metered-dose inhaler (MDI). **B,** Automated MDI. **C,** Dry powder inhaler (DPI). Figure 8-12 (p. 122): Metered-dose inhaler with an extender or spacer. Life Span Considerations: Medicines Administered by Inhalation (p. 123) ▸ Discuss assessments of the patient's ability to manipulate the nebulizer or metered-dose inhaler. ▸ Discuss the use of spacer devices for pediatric and older patients. How can the nurse ensure that older adults have the strength and dexterity to use aerosol therapy? ▸ Discuss the "rebound effect" that can occur with overuse of nasal medications. Class Activity ***Divide the class into groups, and assign each group one of the following types of nasal medications: drops, spray, nebulizer, metered-dose inhaler, or dry powder inhaler. Have each group identify what its assigned medication is used to treat, name common medications in this group, and explain the advantages and disadvantages of its type of medication. Then have each group present its findings to the class for discussion.***

OBJECTIVES	CONTENT	TEACHING RESOURCES
		Class Activity ***Choose two student volunteers to role-play a nurse administering the different types of nasal medications to a patient. Have the rest of the class identify which type of medication is being administered and discuss techniques for administering each.*** Class Activity ***Divide the class into small groups, and ask each group to draw a diagram illustrating how medication is inhaled and the path it takes. Have each group present its diagram to the class and explain how to use the inhaler. Ask the class for feedback.***
Describe the dose forms available for vaginal administration of medications.	□ Administration of vaginal medications (p. 123)	PPT 22 Figure 8-13 (p. 124): Applying vaginal medication. ▸ Discuss vaginal medications. List the various forms of vaginal medications. ▸ Discuss techniques. Describe the different techniques for administering creams, foams, jellies, and suppositories. ▸ Discuss patient teaching. Emphasize proper hygiene and the need to wash the applicator in warm soapy water after each use. Class Activity ***Ask the class to name different medications that can be administered vaginally. How are these medications absorbed?***
Identify the equipment needed, site, and specific techniques required to administer vaginal medications or douches.	□ Administration of vaginal medications (p. 123) – Equipment (p. 123) – Site (p. 123) – Techniques (p. 123) – Patient teaching (p. 124) – Documentation (p. 124) □ Administration of a vaginal douche (p. 124) – Equipment (p. 124) – Site (p. 124) – Techniques (p. 124) – Patient teaching (p. 125) – Documentation (p. 125)	PPT 22 TB Multiple Choice question 3 INRQ 3 Drug Administration Performance Checklists 8-13, 8-14 SG Review Sheet question 22 (p. 48) SG Learning Activities question 10 (p. 49) ▸ Discuss techniques for administering the different vaginal medications. Class Activity ***Lead a class discussion about vaginal medications. Have students compare and contrast the different types of medications, including creams, jellies, tablets, foams, and suppositories. Write student comments on the board for comparison.***

OBJECTIVES	CONTENT	TEACHING RESOURCES
State the rationale and procedure used for cleansing vaginal applicators or douche tips following use.	□ Administration of vaginal medications (p. 123)	▸ Discuss the importance of cleansing all equipment thoroughly after use. Class Activity ***Using a vaginal applicator and a douche tip, have a student volunteer describe to the class the procedure used for cleansing these items following use.***
Develop a plan for patient education of people taking medications via percutaneous routes.	All chapter content addresses this objective.	▸ Discuss placement and dosage of topical medications to the skin. ▸ Discuss placement and dosage of sublingual and buccal medications. ▸ Discuss placement and dosage of eye drops and ointment. ▸ Discuss placement and dosage of ear drops. ▸ Discuss placement and dosage of inhaled medications. ▸ Discuss placement and dosage of vaginal medications. Class Activity ***Divide the class into groups. Have each group identify medication routes that are considered percutaneous and explain how drugs are administered via these routes. What patient teaching is required for each route? Have groups present their findings to the class for discussion.***
Performance evaluation		Test Bank SG Learning Activities (p. 49) SG Practice Questions for the NCLEX Examination (pp. 50-51) Drug Administration Performance Checklists Critical Thinking Questions

8.2 Homework/Assignments:
1. Divide the class into groups and assign each group one of the following types of ophthalmic medications: drops or ointment. Have students from each group identify and research three medications related to the assigned topic and explain what they are used to treat and how they are administered.

8.2 Instructor's Notes/Student Feedback:

8

Lecture Outline

Percutaneous Administration

Slide 1

Chapter 8
Percutaneous Administration

Slide 2

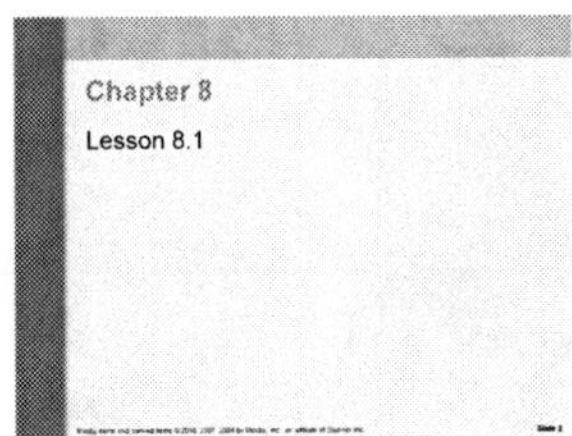
Chapter 8
Lesson 8.1

Slide 3

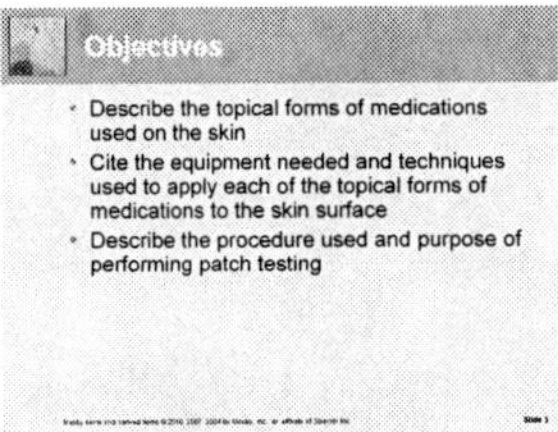
Objectives
Describe the topical forms of medications used on the skin
Cite the equipment needed and techniques used to apply each of the topical forms of medications to the skin surface
Describe the procedure used and purpose of performing patch testing

Slide 4

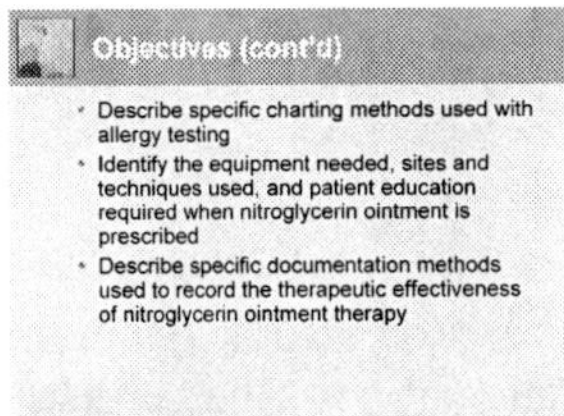
Objectives (cont'd)
Describe specific charting methods used with allergy testing
Identify the equipment needed, sites and techniques used, and patient education required when nitroglycerin ointment is prescribed
Describe specific documentation methods used to record the therapeutic effectiveness of nitroglycerin ointment therapy

Slide 5

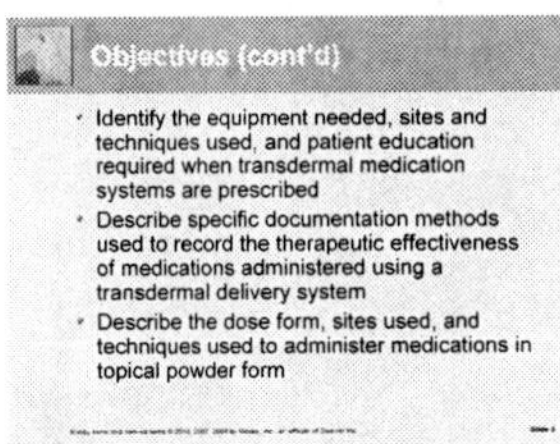
Objectives (cont'd)
Identify the equipment needed, sites and techniques used, and patient education required when transdermal medication systems are prescribed
Describe specific documentation methods used to record the therapeutic effectiveness of medications administered using a transdermal delivery system
Describe the dose form, sites used, and techniques used to administer medications in topical powder form

ELSEVIER

Slide 6

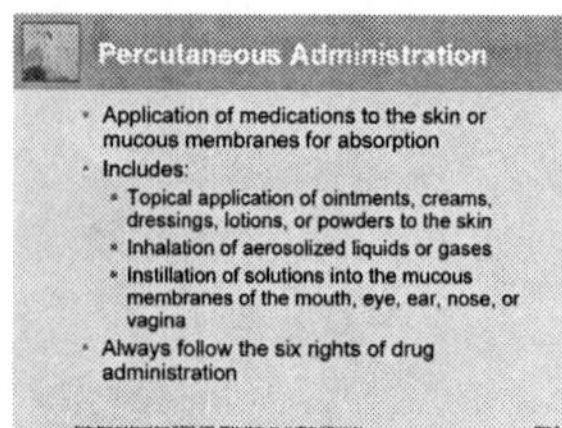
Percutaneous Administration
Application of medications to the skin or mucous membranes for absorption
Includes:
Topical application of ointments, creams, dressings, lotions, or powders to the skin
Inhalation of aerosolized liquids or gases
Instillation of solutions into the mucous membranes of the mouth, eye, ear, nose, or vagina
Always follow the six rights of drug administration

- Percutaneous medications are affected by the amount of drug used, how long the medication is in contact with the skin or mucous membranes, the size of the area in contact, thickness of the skin, hydration status, and any areas of disruption, such as broken skin.

Slide 7

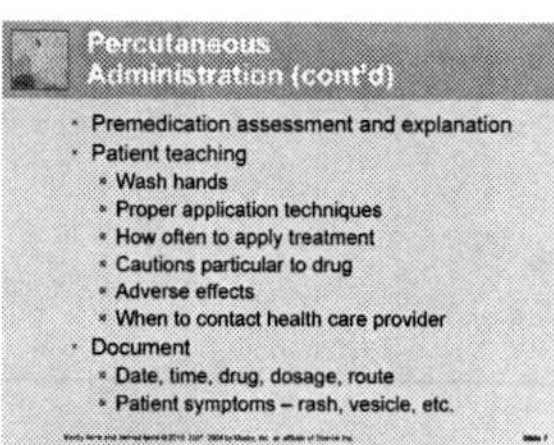
Percutaneous Administration (cont'd)
Premedication assessment and explanation
Patient teaching
Wash hands
Proper application techniques
How often to apply treatment
Cautions particular to drug
Adverse effects
When to contact health care provider
Document
Date, time, drug, dosage, route
Patient symptoms – rash, vesicle, etc.

- Percutaneous medications are used to cleanse wounds, rehydrate the skin, reduce inflammation, relieve localized symptoms, provide a protective barrier, and reduce thickening of the skin.
- Educate patients on procedure protocol (as detailed in next slides).

Slide 8

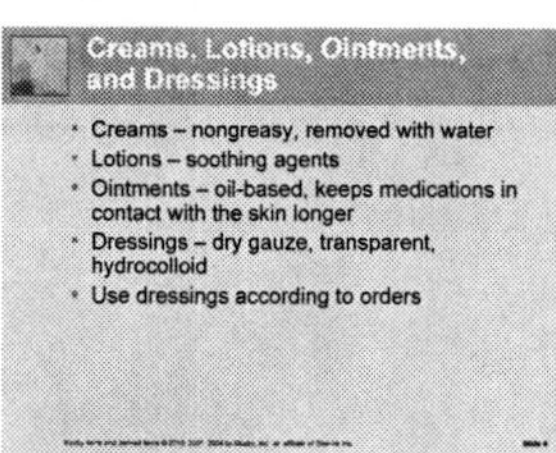
Creams, Lotions, Ointments, and Dressings
Creams – nongreasy, removed with water
Lotions – soothing agents
Ointments – oil-based, keeps medications in contact with the skin longer
Dressings – dry gauze, transparent, hydrocolloid
Use dressings according to orders

- What are the differences between creams, lotions, and ointments? Why is each used?

Slide 9

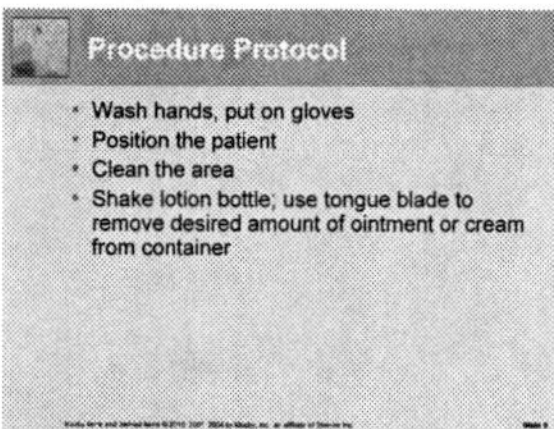
Procedure Protocol
Wash hands, put on gloves
Position the patient
Clean the area
Shake lotion bottle; use tongue blade to remove desired amount of ointment or cream from container

Slide 10

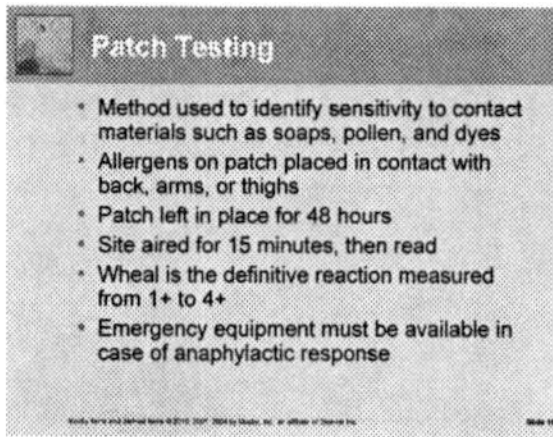
Patch Testing
Method used to identify sensitivity to contact materials such as soaps, pollen, and dyes
Allergens on patch placed in contact with back, arms, or thighs
Patch left in place for 48 hours
Site aired for 15 minutes, then read
Wheal is the definitive reaction measured from 1+ to 4+
Emergency equipment must be available in case of anaphylactic response

- The signs and symptoms of an anaphylactic reaction include tightness and/or itching in the throat, difficulty breathing, drop in blood pressure, hoarseness, and unconsciousness.

ELSEVIER

Slide 11

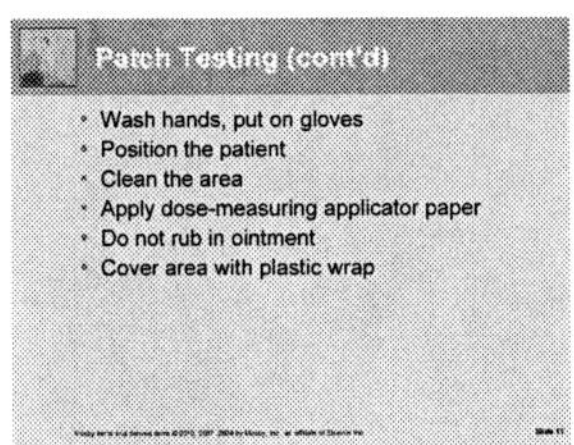
Patch Testing (cont'd)
Wash hands, put on gloves
Position the patient
Clean the area
Apply dose-measuring applicator paper
Do not rub in ointment
Cover area with plastic wrap

- Hair is shaved from the test site to keep the antigen in close contact with the skin surface.
- The patient should be positioned so that the surface where the test will be applied is horizontal.
- Patch testing also may be read in 3 days and 7 days to detect delayed reactions.

Slide 12

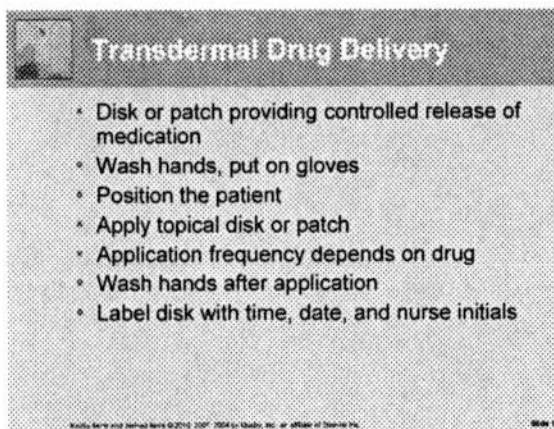
Transdermal Drug Delivery
Disk or patch providing controlled release of medication
Wash hands, put on gloves
Position the patient
Apply topical disk or patch
Application frequency depends on drug
Wash hands after application
Label disk with time, date, and nurse initials

- Always remove the old patch before applying the new one.

Slide 13

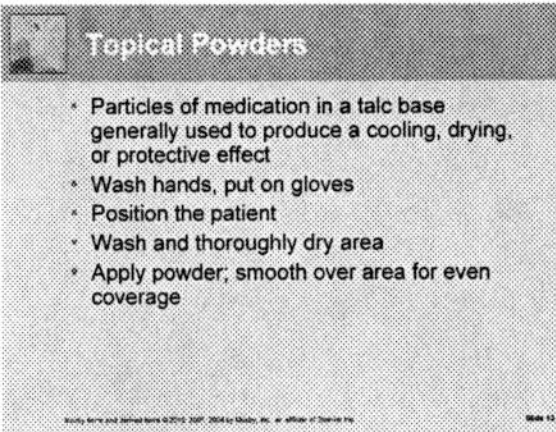
Topical Powders
Particles of medication in a talc base generally used to produce a cooling, drying, or protective effect
Wash hands, put on gloves
Position the patient
Wash and thoroughly dry area
Apply powder; smooth over area for even coverage

- Avoid inhaling the powder during application.

Slide 14

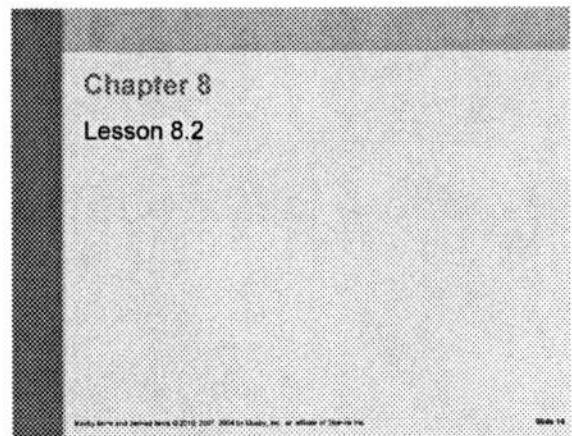
Chapter 8
Lesson 8.2

Slide 15

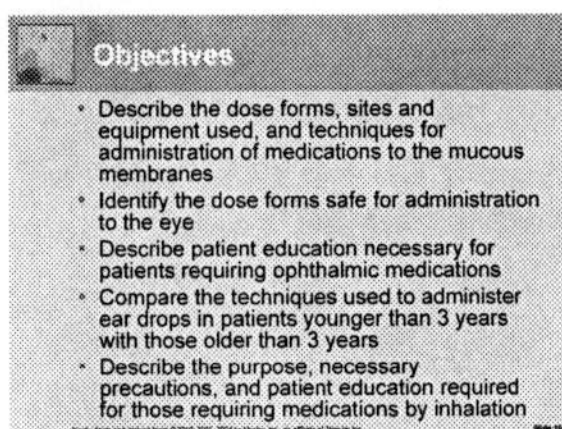
Objectives
Describe the dose forms, sites and equipment used, and techniques for administration of medications to the mucous membranes
Identify the dose forms safe for administration to the eye
Describe patient education necessary for patients requiring ophthalmic medications
Compare the techniques used to administer ear drops in patients younger than 3 years with those older than 3 years
Describe the purpose, necessary precautions, and patient education required for those requiring medications by inhalation

ELSEVIER

Slide 16

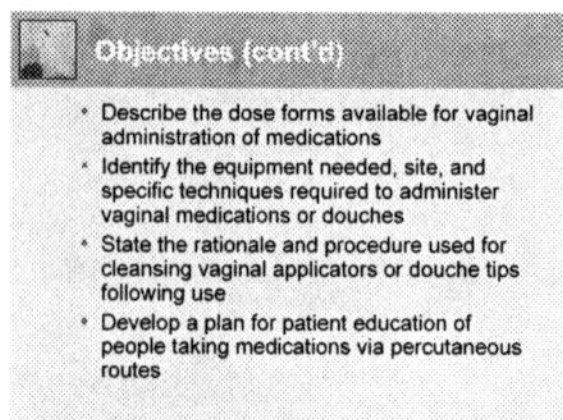
Objectives (cont'd)
Describe the dose forms available for vaginal administration of medications
Identify the equipment needed, site, and specific techniques required to administer vaginal medications or douches
State the rationale and procedure used for cleansing vaginal applicators or douche tips following use
Develop a plan for patient education of people taking medications via percutaneous routes

Slide 17

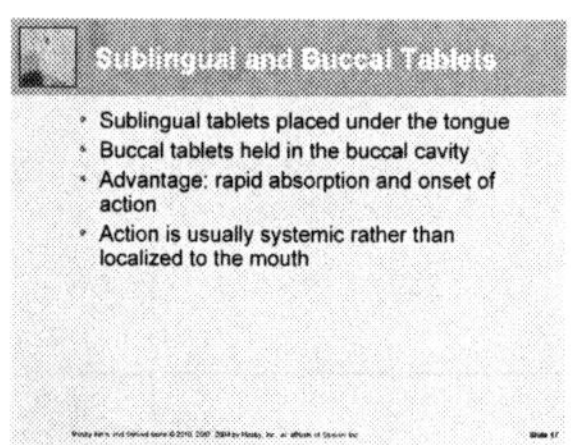
Sublingual and Buccal Tablets
Sublingual tablets placed under the tongue
Buccal tablets held in the buccal cavity
Advantage: rapid absorption and onset of action
Action is usually systemic rather than localized to the mouth

- Do not use water with these types of medications.

Slide 18

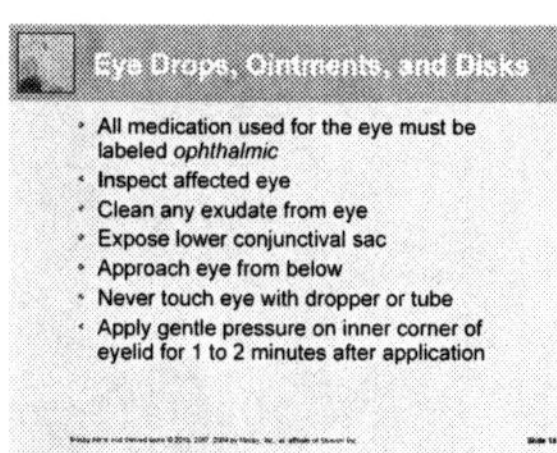
Eye Drops, Ointments, and Disks
All medication used for the eye must be labeled ophthalmic
Inspect affected eye
Clean any exudate from eye
Expose lower conjunctival sac
Approach eye from below
Never touch eye with dropper or tube
Apply gentle pressure on inner corner of eyelid for 1 to 2 minutes after application

- Wash hands and position patient so the back of the head is supported and the face is directed toward the ceiling.
- Never share ophthalmic drops or ointments between patients.

Slide 19

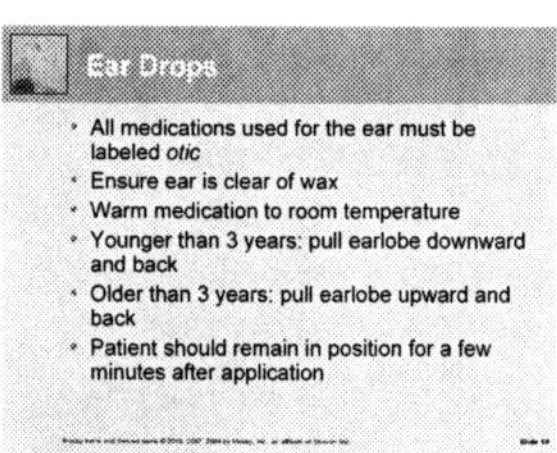
Ear Drops
All medications used for the ear must be labeled otic
Ensure ear is clear of wax
Warm medication to room temperature
Younger than 3 years: pull earlobe downward and back
Older than 3 years: pull earlobe upward and back
Patient should remain in position for a few minutes after application

- Ear drops are used for treatment of localized infection or inflammation of the ear.
- Instilling cold ear drops can be painful to the patient.
- The ear can also be gently massaged after the medication is applied to increase absorption.

Slide 20

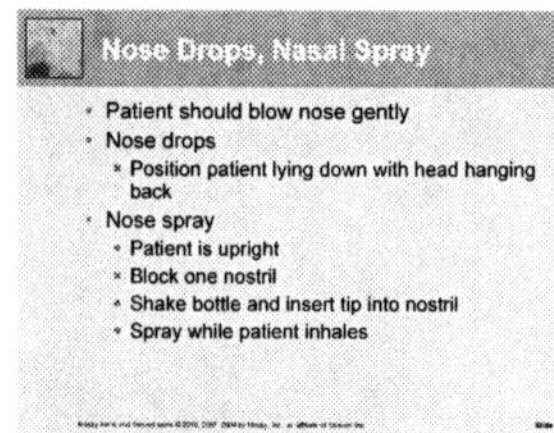
Nose Drops, Nasal Spray
Patient should blow nose gently
Nose drops
Position patient lying down with head hanging back
Nose spray
Patient is upright
Block one nostril
Shake bottle and insert tip into nostril
Spray while patient inhales

- Nasal solutions are used to treat temporary disorders of the nasal membranes.
- Advantage of nasal spray over drops is less waste of medication.
- Patient should remain in position for 2 to 3 minutes after administration.

ELSEVIER

Slide 21

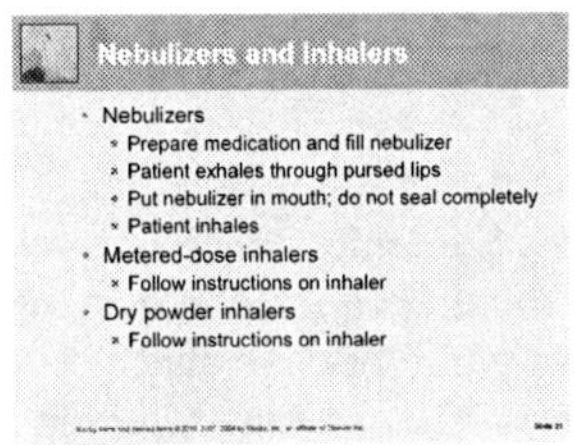
Nebulizers and Inhalers
Nebulizers
Prepare medication and fill nebulizer
Patient exhales through pursed lips
Put nebulizer in mouth; do not seal completely
Patient inhales
Metered-dose inhalers
Follow instructions on inhaler
Dry powder inhalers
Follow instructions on inhaler

- As the patient inhales, activate the nebulizer or inhaler; have the patient hold the breath for 10 seconds before exhaling.
- The use of a spacer is recommended to ensure that the medication inhaled gets to the lungs and not just the back of the throat.
- Never share inhalers or nebulizers between patients.

Slide 22

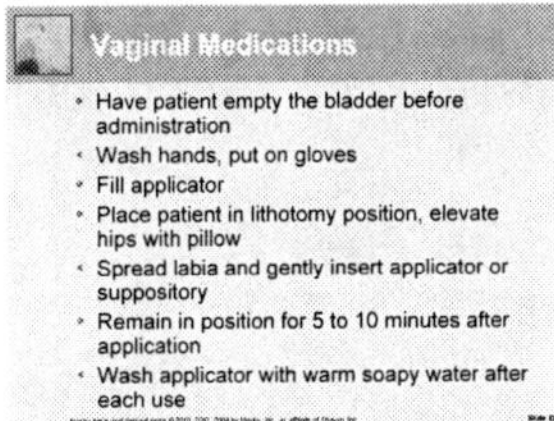
Vaginal Medications
Have patient empty the bladder before administration
Wash hands, put on gloves
Fill applicator
Place patient in lithotomy position, elevate hips with pillow
Spread labia and gently insert applicator or suppository
Remain in position for 5 to 10 minutes after application
Wash applicator with warm soapy water after each use

- Applicators are used to administer creams, foams, tablets, and jellies. Suppositories are inserted with a gloved finger.

9 Lesson Plan
Enteral Administration

TEACHING FOCUS

In this chapter, students will have the opportunity to define and identify oral dose forms of medications correctly and to identify common receptacles used to administer oral medications. Students will also have the opportunity to describe the general principles of solid form medications and the different techniques of distribution, including use of a medication card, computer-controlled distribution, and unit dose distribution. Students will be able to compare techniques used to administer liquid forms of oral medications using the medication card and unit dose systems of distribution. They will also have the opportunity to cite the equipment needed, techniques used, and precautions necessary when administering medications via a nasogastric (NG) tube. Students will have the opportunity to learn about a person's basic metabolic requirements and how to provide adequate nutritional intake through the use of enteral nutrition support. The equipment needed and techniques used to administer rectal suppositories and disposable enemas will also be discussed.

MATERIALS AND RESOURCES

- ☐ common receptacles used to administer oral medications, such as a soufflé cup (Lesson 9.1)
- ☐ computer and PowerPoint projector (all Lessons)

LESSON CHECKLIST

Preparations for this lesson include:

- lecture
- evaluation of student knowledge and skills needed to perform all entry-level activities related to the enteral administration of medications, including administration of:
  - oral medication
  - medications via NG tube
  - enteral feedings via gastrostomy or jejunostomy tube
  - rectal suppositories and disposable enemas

KEY TERMS

bar code (p. 128)
capsules (p. 126)
elixirs (p. 127)
emulsions (p. 128)
lozenges (p. 127)
medicine cup (p. 128)
medicine dropper (p. 129)
nasogastric tube (p. 134)
oral syringe (p. 129)
orally disintegrating tablet (p. 127)
soufflé cup (p. 128)
suspensions (p. 128)
syrups (p. 128)
tablets (p. 127)
unit dose packaging (p. 128)

ADDITIONAL RESOURCES

PowerPoint slides: 1-19

Legend

ARQ	PPT	TB	CTQ	SG	INRQ
Audience Response Questions	PowerPoint Slides	Test Bank	Critical Thinking Questions	Study Guide	Interactive NCLEX Review Questions

Class Activities are indicated in ***bold italic.***

ELSEVIER

LESSON 9.1

BACKGROUND ASSESSMENT

Question: An oral antibiotic is ordered for a 2-month-old baby who has been diagnosed with pneumonia. How will this medication be administered?
Answer: The medication will come in a liquid form and can be administered with a medicine dropper. Pediatric doses vary from adult doses and using an appropriate dropper allows for dosage accuracy and ease in administration. The nurse should tell the parent that because there is great variation in the size of a drop, it is important to use the correct medicine dropper for the medication.

Question: The nurse is preparing to administer a patient's morning medications. After checking the label on the unit dose package against the patient's medication administration record, what should the nurse do next?
Answer: The nurse should ensure that she has the (1) right patient, (2) right drug, (3) right route of administration, (4) right dose, (5) right time of administration and, after administration, (6) the right documentation. Consistently checking these points every time helps decrease medication errors and improves patient safety.

CRITICAL THINKING QUESTION

A postoperative patient recovering from gallbladder surgery is ordered both an oral medication for nausea and a rectal suppository. She says to the nurse, "My nausea has increased so I need the nausea pill now." As the nurse is leaving the patient's room, she notices that the patient has begun vomiting. Why is the medication ordered in two forms, and what should the nurse do?
Guidelines: Medications come in a variety of forms to serve the needs of changing patient conditions. In this situation, because nausea can be an anticipated postoperatively, an antiemetic has been ordered in two forms. The nurse should administer the antiemetic in the form of a rectal suppository because if the patient is vomiting, the medication may not stay in the stomach long enough for absorption and therefore may not provide effective relief.

OBJECTIVES	CONTENT	TEACHING RESOURCES
Correctly define and identify oral dose forms of medications.	■ Administration of oral medications (p. 126) □ Dose forms (p. 126) – Capsules (p. 126) – Timed-release capsules (p. 126) – Lozenges or troches (p. 127) – Pills (p. 127) – Tablets (p.127) – Elixirs (p.127) – Emulsions (p.128) – Suspensions (p.128) – Syrups (p. 128) Review the route of oral medications, including advantages and disadvantages.	PPT 4-5 TB Multiple Choice questions 4-5 TB Multiple Response question 2 INRQ 6-7, 12 CTQ 2, 6 SG Review Sheet question 3 (p. 53) SG Learning Activities 2-3, 6-7, 11-12 (p. 55) Figure 9-1 (p. 127): Various sizes and numbers of gelatin capsules. Figure 9-2 (p. 127): Timed-release capsule. Clinical Landmine: Timed-Release Capsules (p. 127) Figure 9-3 (p. 127): Tablets. Clinical Landmine: Enteric-Coated Tablets (p. 127) ▸ Discuss the importance of patients swallowing timed-release capsules and enteric-coated tablets intact.

OBJECTIVES	CONTENT	TEACHING RESOURCES
		Class Activity ***Divide the class into three groups. Assign one of the following sets of terms to each group. Have the groups define the terms and present them to the class.*** – ***Capsules, lozenges, tablets, elixirs*** – ***Emulsions, suspensions, syrups, bar code*** – ***Unit dose packaging, soufflé cup, medicine cup, medicine dropper, oral syringe*** Class Activity ***Using the six rights of medication administration, have several students role play giving oral medications to a patient, including patient education.***
Identify common delivery systems used to administer oral medications.	□ Equipment (p. 128) – Unit dose or single dose (p.128) – Soufflé cup (p.128) – Medicine cup (p.128) – Medicine dropper (p. 129) – Teaspoon (p. 129) – Oral syringe (p.129) – Nipple (p.129)	ARQ 3 TB Multiple Response question 3 INRQ 3 SG Review Sheet questions 4-5 (p. 53) SG Learning Activities questions 4, 8-9, 15 (p. 55) SG Practice Question for the NCLEX Examination 1 (p. 57) Figure 9-4 (p. 128): Unit dose packages. Figure 9-5 (p. 128): Bar code. Figure 9-6 (p. 128): Medicine cup and soufflé cup. Figure 9-7 (p. 128): Measures on a medicine cup. Figure 9-8 (p. 129): Medicine dropper. Figure 9-9 (p. 129): Measuring teaspoon. Table 9-1: Commonly Used Measurement Equivalents (p. 128) Figure 9-10 (p. 129): Plastic oral syringe. Figure 9-11 (p. 129): Nipple. ▸ Discuss the drawbacks of certain receptacles, such as medicine droppers and teaspoons, as shown in Figures 9-8 and 9-9. Emphasize the importance of noting the precise calibration of whatever receptacle is being used. Class Activity ***Have students identify the correct receptacle for the following types of oral medications.***

ELSEVIER

OBJECTIVES	CONTENT	TEACHING RESOURCES
		– *A capsule* – *Eye drops* – *An elixir* – *A liquid pediatric medication* ***Next have students identify the importance of the receptacle to medication administration.*** Class Activity ***Bring to the class receptacles commonly used to administer oral medications, such as a soufflé cup or medicine dropper. Have the students examine each receptacle, and practice drawing up liquid or placing items in cups.***
Describe general principles of administering solid forms of medications and the different techniques used with a medication card, computer-controlled, and unit dose distribution systems.	■ Administration of solid form oral medications (p.129) □ Medication card system (p. 129) – Procedure protocol (p. 129) – Equipment (p. 130) – Technique (p. 130) □ Unit dose system (p. 130) – Equipment (p. 130) – Technique (p. 130) □ Electronic control system (p. 130) – Equipment (p. 130) – Technique (p. 130) □ General principles of solid form medication administration (p. 131) – Documentation (p. 131)	PPT 6-8 ARQ 2 TB Multiple Choice question 7 TB Multiple Response questions 1, 4 CTQ 1 Drug Administration Performance Checklists 9-1, 9-2, 9-3 SG Review Sheet questions 6-7 (p. 53) SG Learning Activities questions 1, 10 (p. 55) Review Questions for the NCLEX Examination 1, 3 (p. 140) ▸ Discuss the different techniques used to administer solid form oral medications, comparing and contrasting the techniques used with the three different distribution systems, citing common aspects, and emphasizing the differences. Class Activity ***Using a student volunteer to write the answers on the board, have students determine the similarities and differences among the processes for the various administration systems.***
Compare techniques used to administer liquid forms of oral medication using medication card and unit dose systems of distribution.	■ Administration of liquid form oral medications (p. 131) □ Medication card system (p. 131) – Equipment (p. 131) – Technique (p. 131) □ Unit dose system (p. 133) – Equipment (p. 133) – Technique (p. 133)	PPT 9-11 ARQ 4 INRQ 4 Drug Administration Performance Checklists 9-4, 9-5 SG Practice Question for the NCLEX Examination 6 (p. 57)

OBJECTIVES	CONTENT	TEACHING RESOURCES
	□ General principles of liquid form oral medication administration (p. 133) – For an adult or child (p. 133) – For an infant (p. 133) – Documentation (p. 134)	Figure 9-12 (p. 131): Tablet crusher. Figure 9-13 (p. 132): Reading meniscus. Figure 9-14 (p. 132): Tray for medication card system. Figure 9-15 (p. 132): Removing medication directly from a bottle. Figure 9-16 (p. 133): Filling a syringe directly from a medicine cup. Figure 9-17 (p. 134): Positioning the infant. ▸ Discuss the importance of reading a meniscus. Ask students to offer examples of the consequences of misreading a liquid form medication. Class Activity ***Have students discuss safety issues related to administration of liquid medications with the medication card system versus the unit dose system.*** Class Activity ***Divide the class into three groups. Have each group analyze the following scenarios to determine whether the right documentation has been completed. If correct, state why, and if incomplete, state what information is missing.*** – ***A nurse charts the date, time, and drug name after administering a medication.*** – ***An hour after pain medication is given, the nurse charts that the patient is quiet and sleeping.*** – ***The nurse notices that a patient has developed a rash after she has given him an antibiotic. He is scratching his arms and says, "I don't understand how I got this rash." The nurse responds by saying, "Maybe you have an allergy to the bed sheets."***

9.1 Homework/Assignments:

9.1 Instructor's Notes/Student Feedback:

LESSON 9.2

CRITICAL THINKING QUESTION

The physician inserted an NG tube into a patient who has become comatose. The patient's daughter asks the nurse, "Why does my mother have that tube, how will she eat, and how will she take her medications? How do you know the tube is in the right place?" How can the nurse help the daughter understand the use and management of the NG tube?

Guidelines: The nurse can begin by explaining that the NG tube is used in patients who are unable to swallow, as in the case of a comatose patient. Both nutrition and medications can be administered through the tube. Medications are ordered when possible in a liquid form for easier administration through the tube. However, if the patient's medication is not available in a liquid form, a tablet or capsule can be crushed or opened and mixed with an appropriate amount of water for administration through the NG tube. The nurse can also explain the safety precautions that are taken to ensure proper placement of the tube in the stomach, including an x-ray to confirm the location after the tube is initially inserted. In addition, the placement of the NG tube is checked before administration of each medication and before any nutritional supplement. If the patient resumes a conscious state, the NG tube can be removed and the patient can revert back to the oral administration of medications and nutrition.

OBJECTIVES	CONTENT	TEACHING RESOURCES
Cite the equipment needed, techniques used, and precautions necessary when administering medications via a nasogastric tube.	■ Administration of medications by nasogastric tube (p. 134) □ Equipment (p. 134) □ Technique (p. 134) □ Documentation (p. 135)	PPT 14-15 ARQ 1 TB Multiple Response questions 5, 7 INRQ 9, 11, 14 CTQ 3 Drug Administration Performance Checklist 9-6 SG Review Sheet questions 1, 8-12 (pp. 53-54) SG Learning Activities questions 16-20, 23-26 (pp. 55-56) SG Practice Questions for the NCLEX Examination 2-4, 7 (pp. 57-58) Review Question for the NCLEX Examination 4 (p. 140) Figure 9-18 (p. 135): Checking the location of the nasogastric (NG) tube. Figure 9-19 (p. 136): Administering medication via nasogastric (NG) tube. ▸ Discuss the principles of administering medications in solid form, liquid form, and via NG tube, emphasizing both the commonalities in the procedures and the differences. ▸ Discuss the methods used to administer medication via an NG tube. Highlight the important differences in the methods. Class Activity ***Divide the class into three groups. Assign each group one of the following items***

OBJECTIVES	CONTENT	TEACHING RESOURCES
		related to administration of medications via an NG tube. Have the groups outline or list the necessary items for their assignment and provide the rationale. – ***Equipment needed*** – ***Technique*** – ***Precautions*** ***Have each group present its findings to the class.*** Class Activity ***Bring an example of a nasogastric tube to class and have students push water through the two ports using a catheter tip and Luer lock syringe. Discuss the difference between the two ports.***
Meet the person's basic metabolic requirements and provide adequate nutritional intake through the use of enteral nutrition support.	■ Administration of enteral feedings via gastrostomy or jejunostomy tube (p. 135) □ Dose form (p. 135) □ Equipment (p. 136) □ Technique (p. 136) □ Documentation (p. 138)	PPT 16-17 TB Multiple Choice question 1 INRQ 8 CTQ 4-5 Drug Administration Performance Checklist 9-7 Review Questions for the NCLEX Examination 2, 4 (p. 140) Clinical Landmine (p. 137) ▸ Discuss the most important cautions that apply to enteral formula administration. Focus the discussion on proper use and timely disposal of unused formula. Class Activity ***Bring examples of various tube feedings to class and discuss the proper procedure to follow when administering the feeding. Review gravity feedings and feedings via a pump.*** Class Activity ***Have students evaluate the following statements to determine whether they are appropriate and correct. If not, have them provide a rationale.*** – ***It is unnecessary to check the date and time of preparation for mixed formulas that come from the pharmacy.*** – ***Before use, store all prepared formula in the refrigerator.*** – ***Tube placement can be verified by looking at the rise and fall of the chest.*** – ***The patient may be placed in a supine position immediately after an intermittent tube feeding***

ELSEVIER

OBJECTIVES	CONTENT	TEACHING RESOURCES
Cite the equipment needed and technique required to administer rectal suppositories.	■ Administration of rectal suppositories (p. 138) □ Dose form (p. 138) □ Equipment (p. 138) □ Technique (p. 138) □ Documentation (p. 139) Review the correct sequence to follow when administering rectal suppositories.	PPT 18 TB Multiple Choice questions 2-3, 6 INRQ 2 Drug Administration Performance Checklist 9-8 SG Review Sheet questions 2, 13 (pp. 53-54) SG Learning Activities questions 5, 13, 21 (pp. 55-56) Figure 9-20 (p. 138): Rectal suppositories. Figure 9-21 (p. 138): Administering a rectal suppository. Class Activity ***Ask the class to discuss and review the following elements of administration of a rectal suppository:*** – ***Proper position*** – ***Storage*** – ***Proper type of lubricant to use*** Class Activity ***Have students review in class the correct steps to follow when giving a rectal suppository. Include needed equipment: gloves, water-soluble lubricant, and the suppository. Discuss when suppositories are contraindicated.***
Cite the equipment needed and technique used to administer a disposable enema.	■ Administration of a disposable enema (p. 139) □ Dose Form (p. 139) □ Equipment (p. 139) □ Technique (p. 139) □ Documentation (p. 140) Discuss the proper procedure to follow for administration of a disposable enema, as well as patient education.	PPT 19 ARQ 5 TB Multiple Response question 6 Drug Administration Performance Checklist 9-9 SG Review Sheet question 14 (p. 54) SG Learning Activities question 14, 22 (pp. 55-56) SG Practice Question for the NCLEX Examination 5 (p. 57) Figure 9-22 (p. 139); Administering a disposable enema. ▸ Discuss problems that might be encountered when administering a disposable enema and possible solutions. Class ***Activity Ask students as a class to review and list the equipment and procedure for administering an enema.*** Class Activity ***Have students review in class the steps to follow in preparation for giving a***

OBJECTIVES	CONTENT	TEACHING RESOURCES
		disposable enema. Discuss the need for privacy, proper positioning, and the need to encourage the patient to hold the solution for about 30 minutes, if possible.
Performance evaluation		Test Bank SG Learning Activities (pp. 55-56) SG Practice Questions for the NCLEX Examination (pp. 57-58) Drug Administration Performance Checklists Critical Thinking Questions

9.2 Homework/Assignments:

9.2 Instructor's Notes/Student Feedback:

ELSEVIER

9 Lecture Outline
Enteral Administration

Slide 1

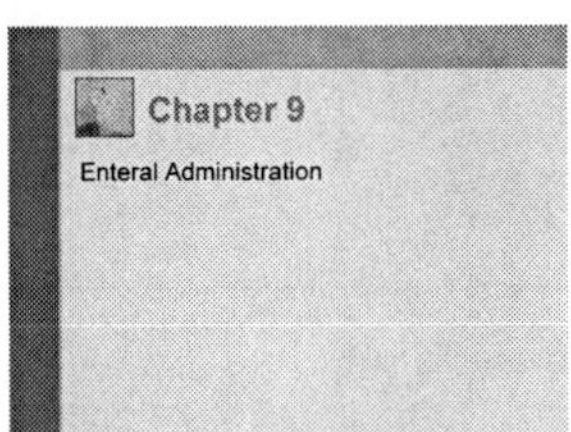

Chapter 9
Enteral Administration

Slide 2

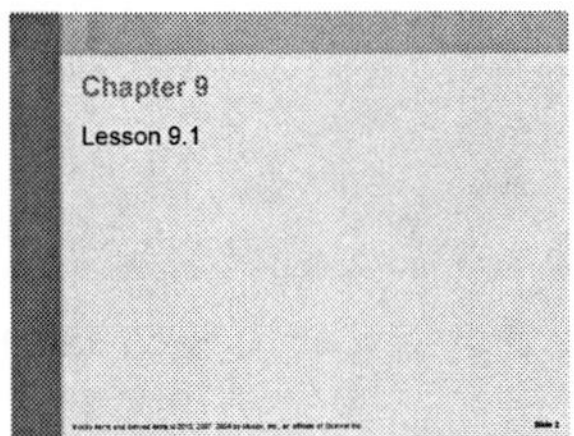

Chapter 9
Lesson 9.1

Slide 3

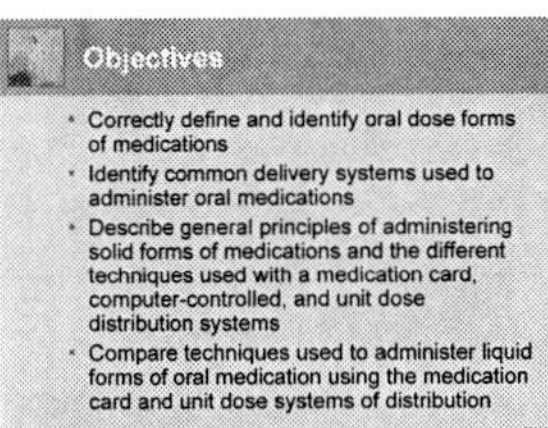

Objectives
Correctly define and identify oral dose forms of medications
Identify common delivery systems used to administer oral medications
Describe general principles of administering solid forms of medications and the different techniques used with a medication card, computer-controlled, and unit dose distribution systems
Compare techniques used to administer liquid forms of oral medication using the medication card and unit dose systems of distribution

Slide 4

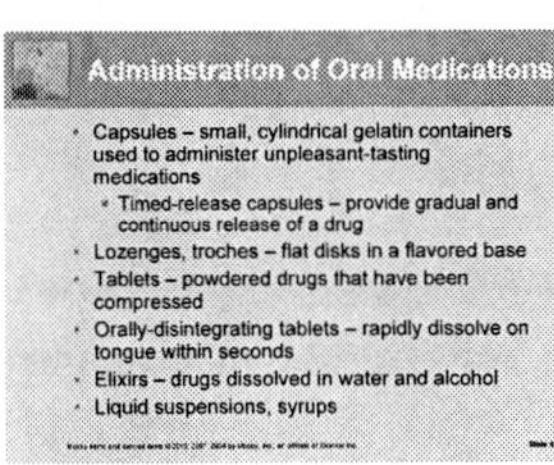

Administration of Oral Medications
Capsules – small, cylindrical gelatin containers used to administer unpleasant-tasting medications
Timed-release capsules – provide gradual and continuous release of a drug
Lozenges, troches – flat disks in a flavored base
Tablets – powdered drugs that have been compressed
Orally-disintegrating tablets – rapidly dissolve on tongue within seconds
Elixirs – drugs dissolved in water and alcohol
Liquid suspensions, syrups

- Oral doses are safe, convenient, and economical.
- Time-released capsules should never be broken apart because this can affect the absorption rate.
- Elixirs are used primarily when a drug will not dissolve in water.

Slide 5

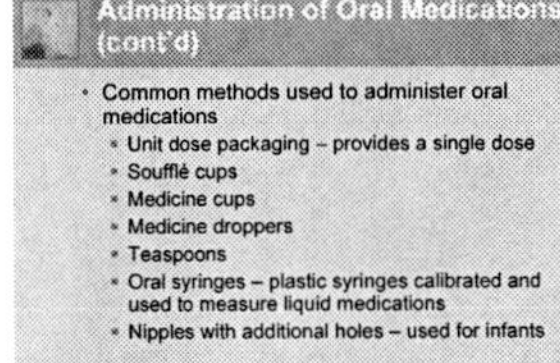

Administration of Oral Medications (cont'd)
Common methods used to administer oral medications
Unit dose packaging – provides a single dose
Soufflé cups
Medicine cups
Medicine droppers
Teaspoons
Oral syringes – plastic syringes calibrated and used to measure liquid medications
Nipples with additional holes – used for infants

- Unit dose provides a bar code for electronic charting and inventory control.
- Within the metric system, 1 teaspoon is equal to 5 mL.
- The size of the home teaspoon varies; use of a measuring teaspoon used in baking is recommended when taking liquid medications at home.

ELSEVIER

Slide 6

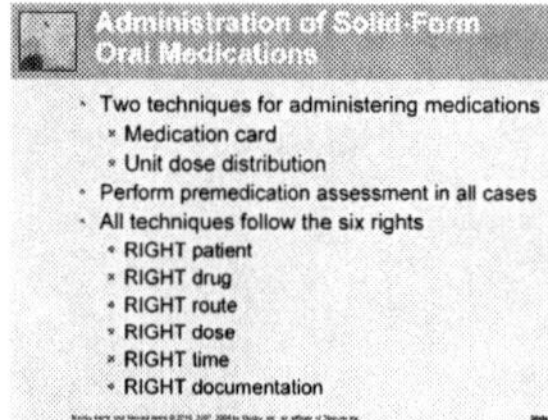
Administration of Solid-Form Oral Medications
Two techniques for administering medications
Medication card
Unit dose distribution
Perform premedication assessment in all cases
All techniques follow the six rights
RIGHT patient
RIGHT drug
RIGHT route
RIGHT dose
RIGHT time
RIGHT documentation

- The six rights help decrease medication errors and promote patient safety.
- Other assessments that must be checked before medication administration may include patient parameters such as apical pulses, respiratory rates, blood pressure, and laboratory values.

Slide 7

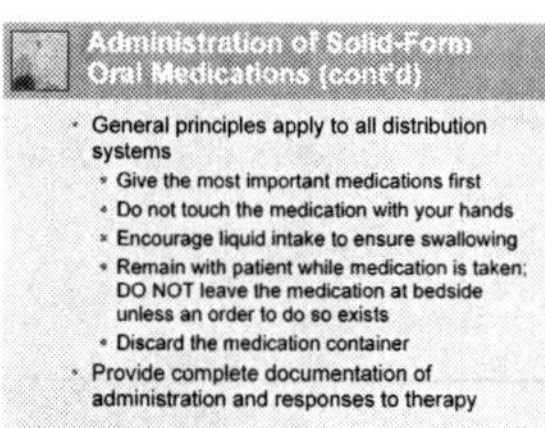
Administration of Solid-Form Oral Medications (cont'd)
General principles apply to all distribution systems
Give the most important medications first
Do not touch the medication with your hands
Encourage liquid intake to ensure swallowing
Remain with patient while medication is taken; DO NOT leave the medication at bedside unless an order to do so exists
Discard the medication container
Provide complete documentation of administration and responses to therapy

- Never dilute a medication without specific instructions.

Slide 8

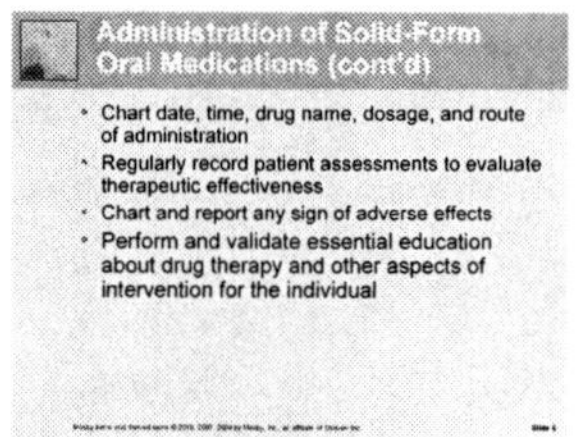
Administration of Solid-Form Oral Medications (cont'd)
Chart date, time, drug name, dosage, and route of administration
Regularly record patient assessments to evaluate therapeutic effectiveness
Chart and report any sign of adverse effects
Perform and validate essential education about drug therapy and other aspects of intervention for the individual

- Documentation ensures that medications are provided as ordered and prevents duplication of drugs.
- It is especially important to observe for adverse events during administration of the first few doses of a new medication.
- Nurses must verify that the patient understands the reasons for his or her medications at the time of administration.

Slide 9

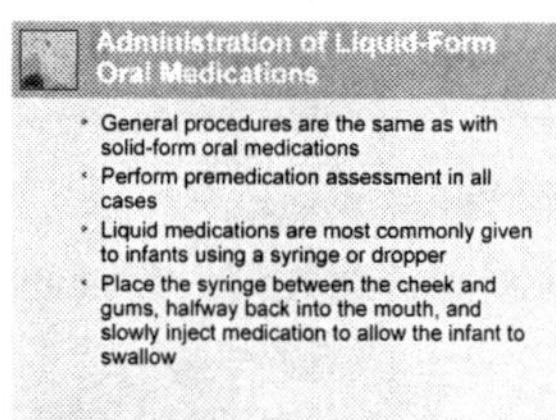
Administration of Liquid-Form Oral Medications
General procedures are the same as with solid-form oral medications
Perform premedication assessment in all cases
Liquid medications are most commonly given to infants using a syringe or dropper
Place the syringe between the cheek and gums, halfway back into the mouth, and slowly inject medication to allow the infant to swallow

- Accuracy is imperative in pouring liquid medications.
- Read at the level of the lowest point of the meniscus curve.

Slide 10

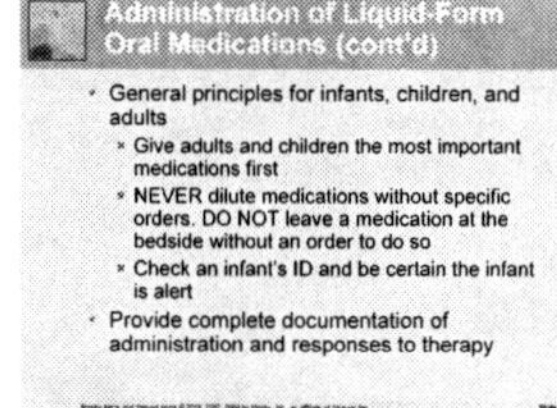
Administration of Liquid-Form Oral Medications (cont'd)
General principles for infants, children, and adults
Give adults and children the most important medications first
NEVER dilute medications without specific orders. DO NOT leave a medication at the bedside without an order to do so
Check an infant's ID and be certain the infant is alert
Provide complete documentation of administration and responses to therapy

- For an infant, slightly elevate the head and administer the medication with oral syringe, dropper, or nipple.

ELSEVIER

Slide 11

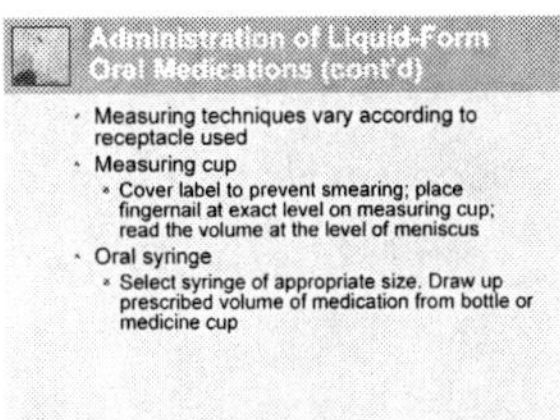
Administration of Liquid-Form Oral Medications (cont'd)
Measuring techniques vary according to receptacle used
Measuring cup
Cover label to prevent smearing; place fingernail at exact level on measuring cup; read the volume at the level of meniscus
Oral syringe
Select syringe of appropriate size. Draw up prescribed volume of medication from bottle or medicine cup

- Clean hands before drawing up medications to avoid contaminating the medication in the bottle. Try not to drip liquid medication on the bottle; it obstructs the ability to read the label.
- A large-bore needle can be used to draw up liquid medication if necessary.

Slide 12

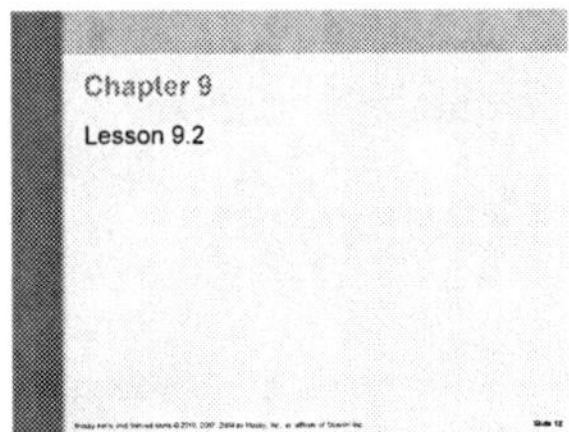
Chapter 9
Lesson 9.2

Slide 13

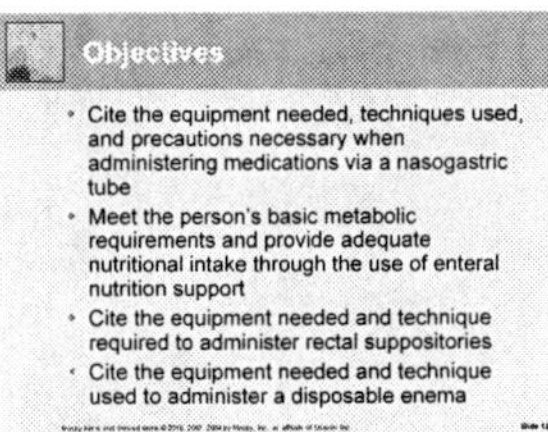
Objectives
Cite the equipment needed, techniques used, and precautions necessary when administering medications via a nasogastric tube
Meet the person's basic metabolic requirements and provide adequate nutritional intake through the use of enteral nutrition support
Cite the equipment needed and technique required to administer rectal suppositories
Cite the equipment needed and technique used to administer a disposable enema

Slide 14

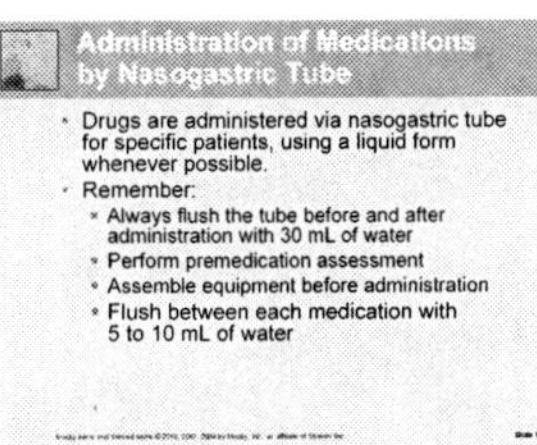
Administration of Medications by Nasogastric Tube
Drugs are administered via nasogastric tube for specific patients, using a liquid form whenever possible.
Remember:
Always flush the tube before and after administration with 30 mL of water
Perform premedication assessment
Assemble equipment before administration
Flush between each medication with 5 to 10 mL of water

- If solid forms of medications are required, then crush the tablets or open the capsules and dissolve in 30 mL of water. NEVER crush enteric-coated tablets or timed-release capsules.
- Equipment to assemble may include water, syringe with catheter tip, pH tape, and gloves.

Slide 15

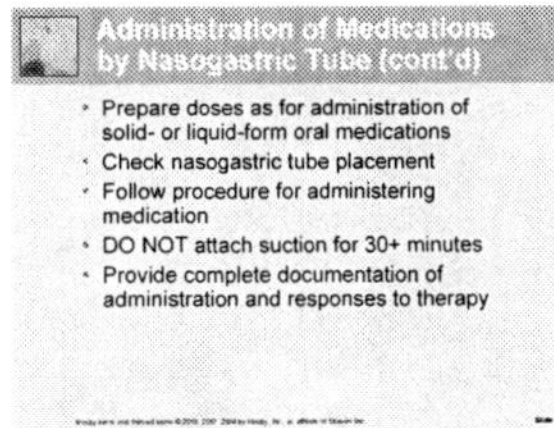
Administration of Medications by Nasogastric Tube (cont'd)
Prepare doses as for administration of solid- or liquid-form oral medications
Check nasogastric tube placement
Follow procedure for administering medication
DO NOT attach suction for 30+ minutes
Provide complete documentation of administration and responses to therapy

- It is important to determine that the nasogastric tube is in the stomach to prevent aspiration pneumonia.

Slide 16

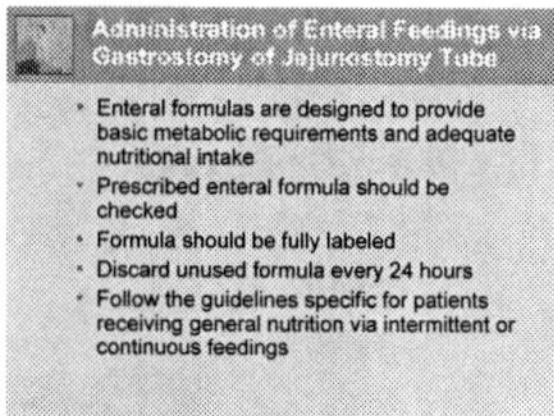
Administration of Enteral Feedings via Gastrostomy of Jejunostomy Tube
Enteral formulas are designed to provide basic metabolic requirements and adequate nutritional intake
Prescribed enteral formula should be checked
Formula should be fully labeled
Discard unused formula every 24 hours
Follow the guidelines specific for patients receiving general nutrition via intermittent or continuous feedings

- The type of formula ordered is selected by the health care provider to meet the patient's requirements to maintain proper function and repair tissues.
- During initiation of enteral feedings, blood glucose levels may be checked.

Slide 17

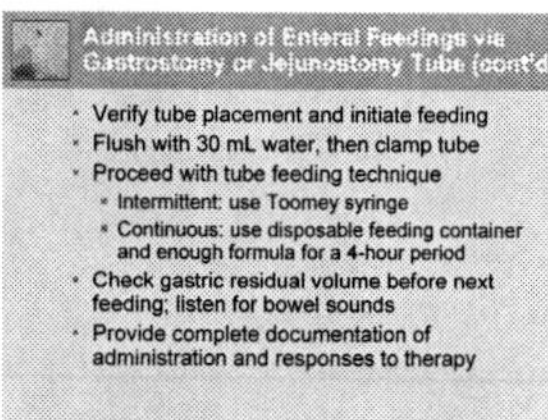
Administration of Enteral Feedings via Gastrostomy or Jejunostomy Tube (cont'd)
Verify tube placement and initiate feeding
Flush with 30 mL water, then clamp tube
Proceed with tube feeding technique
Intermittent: use Toomey syringe
Continuous: use disposable feeding container and enough formula for a 4-hour period
Check gastric residual volume before next feeding; listen for bowel sounds
Provide complete documentation of administration and responses to therapy

- The procedure for checking placement of a gastrostomy or jejunostomy tube differs slightly.
- Formula should be at room temperature at the time of initiation.

Slide 18

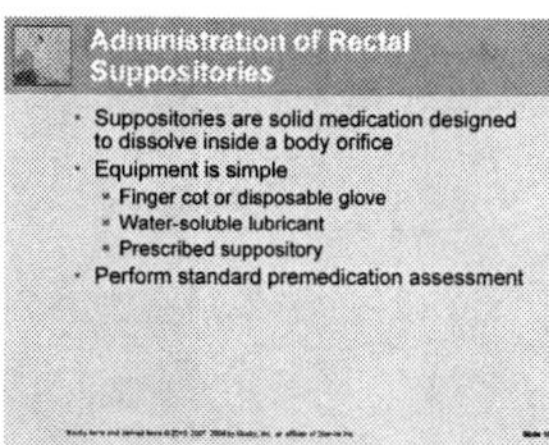
Administration of Rectal Suppositories
Suppositories are solid medication designed to dissolve inside a body orifice
Equipment is simple
Finger cot or disposable glove
Water-soluble lubricant
Prescribed suppository
Perform standard premedication assessment

- Suppositories are absorbed through mucous membranes.
- Lubricants such as petroleum jelly are NOT to be used; use water-soluble lubricant.

Slide 19

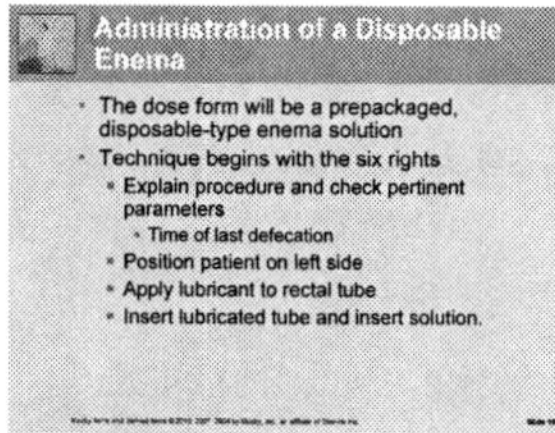
Administration of a Disposable Enema
The dose form will be a prepackaged, disposable-type enema solution
Technique begins with the six rights
Explain procedure and check pertinent parameters
Time of last defecation
Position patient on left side
Apply lubricant to rectal tube
Insert lubricated tube and insert solution.

- Provide privacy during the procedure, and keep the patient draped to avoid unnecessary exposure.
- If the patient takes a deep breath on insertion, it is easier to advance the rectal tube.
- The patient should hold the solution for 30 minutes and should NOT flush the toilet until you see the results of the enema.
- Provide complete documentation of administration and responses to therapy.

ELSEVIER

Lesson Plan

10 Parenteral Administration: Safe Preparation of Parenteral Medications

TEACHING FOCUS

In this chapter, students will have the opportunity to identify the parts of a syringe, the calibrations on different types of syringes, and where to read medication volume on a glass or a plastic syringe. The students will also have the opportunity to identify the volumes of medication that can be measured in a tuberculin syringe versus a larger volume syringe and the advantages and disadvantages of using prefilled syringes. They will also have the opportunity to explain the system of measurement used to define the inside diameter of a syringe, identify the parts of a needle, and explain how the gauge of a needle is determined.

MATERIALS AND RESOURCES

- ☐ computer and PowerPoint projector (all Lessons)
- ☐ examples of the various types of syringes and needle lengths (all Lessons)
- ☐ examples of ampules, vials, and Mix-O-Vials (all Lessons)

LESSON CHECKLIST

Preparations for this lesson include:

- lecture
- guest speaker: registered nurse
- evaluation of student knowledge and skills needed to perform all entry-level activities related to preparing parenteral medications for administration, including:
  - differentiating ampules, vials, and Mix-O-Vials
  - listing equipment needed to prepare parenteral medications
  - preparing two different drugs in one syringe
  - preparing various doses of medication for parenteral administration
  - selecting the correct syringe and needle
  - types and calibration of syringes and needles

KEY TERMS

ampules (p. 149)
barrel (p. 142)
insulin pen (p. 145)
insulin syringe (p. 144)
milliliter scale (p. 143)
minim scale (p. 143)
Mix-O-Vials (p. 149)
needle gauge (p. 145)
plunger (p. 142)
prefilled syringe (p. 144)
safety devices (p. 147)
tip (p. 142)
tuberculin syringe (p. 143)
vials (p. 149)

ADDITIONAL RESOURCES

PowerPoint slides: 1-20

Legend

ARQ	**PPT**	**TB**	**CTQ**	**SG**	**INRQ**
Audience Response Questions	PowerPoint Slides	Test Bank	Critical Thinking Questions	Study Guide	Interactive NCLEX Review Questions

Class Activities are indicated in ***bold italic.***

ELSEVIER

LESSON 10.1

BACKGROUND ASSESSMENT

Question: What does the term *parenteral* mean? Describe the term *parenteral route* and the medical abbreviations for each.
Answer: The term *parenteral* means administration of medication by any route other than enteral, or gastrointestinal tract. The parenteral route refers to intradermal, subcutaneous, intramuscular (IM), or intravenous (IV) injection.

Question: What are the essential roles of the nurse when preparing and administering medications to a patient?
Answer: The nurse must have a basic knowledge of the specific drug being ordered and how it is prepared and administered. The nurse also has to know the symptoms for which the medication is prescribed and expected outcomes to continually assess the patient for any adverse reactions. Finally, the nurse must use his or her clinical judgment in the start of new medications, missed doses of medications, or changes in the patient's condition that warrant a modification in medication dosage.

CRITICAL THINKING QUESTION

A nurse is ordered to administer an IM medication. The nurse obtains the medication, syringe, alcohol prep, and needle. The needle gauge selected is a 22-gauge needle. What is the importance of selecting a proper needle gauge and length in parenteral administration of medication?
Guidelines: The needle gauge represents the diameter of the hole through the needle. The larger the gauge, the smaller the hole. Proper needle gauge selection is based on the thickness of the solution being injected and the correct needle length for effective delivery of the medication. A thicker solution requires a larger diameter hole in the needle, so a lower gauge number should be chosen. To select the proper needle length, the nurse must assess the amount of adipose tissue. The thicker the layer of adipose tissue present and the larger the muscle mass, the longer the needle required.

OBJECTIVES	CONTENT	TEACHING RESOURCES
Name the three parts of a syringe.	■ Safe preparation, administration, and disposal of parenteral medications and supplies (p. 141) ■ Equipment used in parenteral administration (p. 142) □ Syringes (p. 142)	PPT 7 TB Multiple Choice question 1 TB Multiple Response question 2 SG Review Sheet questions 1-4 (p. 59) SG Learning Activities questions 2, 10, 26-27 (pp. 61, 63) Figure 10-1 (p. 142): Parts of a syringe. ▸ Discuss standardization of syringe tips, using Figures 10-3 and 10-4 as a starting point (p. 143). ▸ Discuss the parts of a syringe, using Figure 10-3 to include a discussion of the Luer system and Tru-lock technology (p. 143). Class Activity ***Display different types of syringes for the class. Have the students identify the parts of a syringe and practice placing and locking the connectors on the syringes.***

OBJECTIVES	CONTENT	TEACHING RESOURCES
Read the calibrations of the minim and cubic centimeter or milliliter scale on different types of syringes.	– Glass syringe (p. 142) – Plastic syringe (p. 142) – Syringe calibration (p. 143) – Reading the calibration of the syringe (p. 143)	PPT 7 CTQ 1 SG Review Sheet questions 5, 8 (p. 59) SG Learning Activities questions 11-21 (pp. 61-62) Figure 10-2 (p. 142): Reading the calibrations of a 3-mL syringe. Figure 10-3 (p. 143): The Luer system. Figure 10-4 (p. 143): Luer slip and lock. Lifespan Considerations: Tuberculin Syringe (p. 144) ▸ Discuss the different syringe volume indications, using Figures 10-5, 10-6, 10-7, and 10-8 to prompt discussion (pp. 143-144). ▸ Discuss different syringe calibrations, comparing the scales depicted in Figures 10-5 and 10-8 (pp. 143-144). Class Activity ***Divide the class into small groups, and provide each group with various types of syringes. Have each group practice reading the calibrations on the syringes. Then, as a class, discuss the differences in calibrations of the syringes.***
Identify the sites where the volume of medication is read on a glass syringe and a plastic syringe.	– Reading the calibration of the syringe (p. 143)	PPT 10 SG Practice Questions for the NCLEX Examination 8-9 (p. 65) Figure 10-6 (p. 144): Reading measured amount of medication in a glass syringe. Figure 10-7 (p. 144): Reading measured amount of medication in a plastic syringe. Figure 10-8 (p. 144): Calibration of insulin syringes. ▸ Discuss the accurate calibration points of different syringes using Figures 10-6 and 10-7 to prompt discussion (p. 144). ▸ Discuss the differences in volume measurements in glass and plastic syringes, using Figures 10-6 and 10-7 as examples (p. 144). Class Activity ***Divide the class into small groups and provide each group with glass and plastic syringes. Have each group practice measuring and reading dose amounts.***

ELSEVIER

OBJECTIVES	CONTENT	TEACHING RESOURCES
Give examples of volumes of medications that can be measured in a tuberculin syringe rather than a larger volume syringe.	– Reading the calibration of the syringe (p. 143)	Figure 10-5 (p. 143); Tuberculin syringe calibration. Lifespan Considerations: Tuberculin Syringe (p. 144) ▸ Discuss comparative volumes of syringes, using Figures 10-5 and 10-8 as guides for the discussion, emphasizing the greater accuracy of a tuberculin syringe (pp.143-144). ▸ Discuss the likely uses of a tuberculin syringe and why its greater precision is important in those applications. *Class Activity* ***Demonstrate and review with the class the specifics of tuberculin syringe markings for doses. Provide each student with a tuberculin syringe, and practice various doses of measurements. Go around the room to verify accuracy on measurements.***
State the advantages and disadvantages of using prefilled syringes.	– Prefilled syringes (p. 144)	PPT 10 TB Multiple Choice question 11 Figure 10-9 (p. 145): Carpuject syringe and prefilled sterile cartridge with needle. Figure 10-10 (p. 145): Elements of the insulin pen. Figure 10-11 (p. 145): Prefilled syringe and needle containing epinephrine for use in emergencies. ▸ Discuss the most common uses of prefilled syringes and the different types of prefilled syringes that are now available. ▸ Discuss the risk of contamination when administering medications through syringes and needles, using the prefilled syringes depicted in Figures 10-9, 10-10, and 10-11 as a starting point (p. 145). *Class Activity* ***Divide the class into two groups. Have one group identify the medications that are commonly dispensed in prefilled syringes. Have the other group list the advantages and disadvantages of using prefilled syringes.***
Explain the system of measurement used to define the inside diameter of a syringe.	– Reading the calibration of the syringe (p. 143)	▸ Discuss the different syringe volumes, using Figures 10-2, 10-5, and 10-8 for comparative purposes (pp. 142-144). *Class Activity* ***As a class, discuss the importance of understanding differences in the interior volume measurements of syringes, using***

OBJECTIVES	CONTENT	TEACHING RESOURCES
		Figures 10-6 and 10-7 (p. 144) as a basis for comparison.
Identify the parts of a needle.	□ The needle (p. 145)	PPT 8 SG Learning Activities questions 3, 22 (pp. 61-62) Figure 10-12 (p. 146); Parts of a needle. ▸ Discuss the purpose of a beveled tip on a needle in the context of the three parts of a needle. ▸ Discuss the consequences of needles becoming lodged in a patient's arm and what nursing personnel should do if a needle breaks. Class Activity ***Display several needles with their packaging in various lengths and gauges. Have the students identify the various parts of the needles.***
Explain how the gauge of a needle is determined.	□ The needle (p. 145)	ARQ 2, 4 SG Review Sheet questions 12-13 (pp. 59-60) SG Learning Activities question 4 (p. 61) Figure 10-13 (p. 146): Needle length and gauge. ▸ Discuss the relationship between needle length and needle gauge, using Figure 10-13 as a basis for the discussion (p. 146). ▸ Discuss the ramifications of a patient requiring repeated IV medications and the impact that needle gauge can have on patient comfort. Class Activity ***Using the display from the previous demonstration, review with the class the designation of gauge on the packaging and on the hub of the needle. As a class, discuss the meaning of the numbers in relationship to the size of the hole. Have each student see each needle and hole.***
Compare the usual volume of medication that can be administered at one site when giving a medication by intradermal, subcutaneous, or IM route.	□ Selection of the syringe and needle (p. 145)	PPT 11 TB Multiple Choice questions 3, 7 INRQ 7-8 SG Review Sheet question 6 (p. 59) SG Learning Activities questions 6-9 (p. 61) SG Practice Question for the NCLEX Examination 7 (p. 65)

OBJECTIVES	CONTENT	TEACHING RESOURCES
		Figure 10-14 (p. 147): Clinical example: selection of needle length for IM administration. ▸ Discuss the relationship between medication volume and needle gauge, using Table 10-1 to make comparisons (p. 147). ▸ Discuss medication volumes in conjunction with the depth of an injection, using Figure 10-14 for reference (p. 147). Class Activity ***Divide the class into small groups, and have each group prepare nursing education materials on the amount of medication and the appropriate syringe and needle for the various routes. Then have each group present its materials to the class.***
State the criteria used for the selection of the correct needle gauge and length.	□ Selection of the syringe and needle (p. 145) Review the different parenteral routes. Discuss the differences between intradermal, subcutaneous, intramuscular, and intravenous routes using doses, needle size, and desired drug effect.	TB Multiple Choice questions 2, 9-10 INRQ 1, 10 SG Learning Activities question 5 (p. 61) SG Practice Questions for the NCLEX Examination 5-6 (pp. 64-65) Table 10-1: Selection of Syringe and Needle (p. 147) ▸ Discuss hypothetical patients and appropriate needle gauges and lengths, using Figure 10-14 as a starting point for the discussion (p. 147). ▸ Discuss the differences in subcutaneous tissue in different patients, as shown in Figure 10-14, to explain the drawbacks, both physical and psychological, of presenting with a long needle for a juvenile patient (p. 147). Class Activity ***Have the class work in pairs. Assign each pair two different clinical descriptions of patients needing injections by various routes. Have each pair present their findings to the class.***
Identify examples of the safety-type syringes and needles.	□ Packaging of syringes and needles (p. 146)	PPT 12 ARQ 1 TB Multiple Choice question 8 INRQ 2, 4 CTQ 3 SG Review Sheet questions 7, 14-18 (pp. 59-60) SG Learning Activities question 1 (p. 61)

OBJECTIVES	CONTENT	TEACHING RESOURCES
		Review Question for the NCLEX Examination 1 (p. 156) Figure 10-15 (p. 147): Needleless access devices. Figure 10-16 (p. 148): Example of a safety syringe that uses a full protective sheath. Figures 10-17 and 10-18 (p. 148): Examples of a safety syringe that uses a shielding mechanism. Figure 10-19 (p. 149): Needle disposal container. ▸ Discuss the various safety type of syringes and needles, using Figures 10-16, 10-17, and 10-18 as a basis for comparison (p. 148). ▸ Discuss the relative practical use of the minim scale versus the millimeter scale on syringes. Also, compare these systems of calibration with the cubic centimeter scale. Compare the calibration systems, discuss which is most accurate, and discuss which scale should be the choice whenever possible. Class Activity ***Divide the class into two groups. Have one group research information on the Needlestick Safety and Prevention Act of 2000 and the incidence of needlesticks in health care workers. Have the other group present and demonstrate the various types of safety needles and syringes. (For students to prepare for this activity, see Homework/Assignments 1.)***

10.1 Homework/Assignments:
1. Have one group research information on the Needlestick Safety and Prevention Act of 2000 and the incidence of needlesticks in health care workers.

10.1 Instructor's Notes/Student Feedback:

LESSON 10.2

CRITICAL THINKING QUESTION

Nurse A hands Nurse B a nonprefilled syringe and tells Nurse B to please give this injection to the patient in room 1 because the health care provider just called her to assist with a procedure. How should Nurse B handle this situation?

Answer: Nurse B knows that she should never give an injection to anyone if she did not draw up the medication herself. Some of the steps that Nurse B could take are to tell her coworker that she will assist the health care provider with the procedure and the coworker can give the injection, or check the chart for the injection order, draw it up herself, and give the injection to the patient. Afterward, Nurse B should talk with her coworker about safe medication administration practices.

OBJECTIVES	CONTENT	TEACHING RESOURCES
Differentiate among ampules, vials, and Mix-O-Vials.	■ Parenteral dose forms (p. 149) □ Ampules (p. 149) □ Vials (p. 149) □ Mix-O-Vials (p. 149) Review the differences among an ampule, vial, and Mix-O-Vial, and an expectation of what the nurse must know for each.	PPT 15 ARQ 3 TB Multiple Choice question 12 SG Review Sheet question 19 (p. 60) SG Learning Activities questions 23-25, 30 (pp. 62-63) Review Question for the NCLEX Examination 2 (p. 156) Figure 10-20 (p. 149): Scored and ringed ampules. Figure 10-21 (p. 149): Metal lid and rubber diaphragm vials. Figure 10-22 (p. 150): Mix-O-Vial. ▸ Discuss the different methods of preparing parenteral medications, using Figures 10-20, 10-21, and 10-22 for comparisons (pp. 149-150). Class Activity ***Bring the different types of parenteral dose forms to class—an ampule, a vial, and a Mix-O-Vial—and have a student demonstrate how each is used. Discuss the use of a filtered needle (or a filter straw) with an ampule.*** Class Activity ***Divide the class into small groups, and provide each group with ampules, vials, and Mix-O-Vials. Have each group prepare a list of the advantages and disadvantages of each. Then have the groups present their findings to the class.***
List the equipment needed for the preparation of	■ Preparation of parenteral medication (p. 150) □ Equipment (p. 150)	PPT 16 Class Activity ***Divide the class into small groups, and provide each group with ampules.***

OBJECTIVES	CONTENT	TEACHING RESOURCES
parenteral medications.		***Have each group practice the procedure for removing a drug from an ampule.***
Describe, practice, and perfect the preparation of medications using the various dose forms for parenteral administration.	□ Technique (p. 150) □ Guidelines for preparing medications (p. 150) – Preparing a medication from an ampule (p. 150) – Preparing a medication from a vial (p. 151) – Preparing a drug from a Mix-O-Vial (p. 151)	PPT 17-20 TB Multiple Choice questions 4-5 Drug Administration Performance Checklists 10-1, 10-2, 10-3, 10-4 SG Review Sheet question 20 (p. 60) SG Practice Questions for the NCLEX Examination 1-3 (p. 61) Figure 10-23 (pp. 151-152): Withdrawing from an ampule and changing needle. Figure 10-24 (p. 153): Removal of a volume of liquid from a vial; reconstitution of a powder. Figure 10-25 (p. 153): Mix-O-Vial. ▶ Discuss the different techniques for preparing medications in syringes, using the discussion to review the differences among syringes. ▶ Discuss the process of correctly preparing medications under duress, such as in an emergency situation, using Figures 10-23 and 10-24 to spur discussion (pp. 151-153). *Class Activity* ***First, describe and demonstrate to the class all steps in the process of parenteral administrations. Supply the class with adequate supplies to practice. Have the class work in pairs to practice and critique one another.***
Describe, practice, and perfect the technique of preparing two different drugs in one syringe, such as insulin or preoperative medications.	– Preparing two medications in one syringe (p. 152) – Preparing medications for use in the sterile field during a surgical procedure (p. 155) Review the type of medications that can be mixed together: preoperative medications and insulin. Review the procedure used to mix two medications in one syringe.	ARQ 5 TB Multiple Choice question 6 TB Multiple Response question 1 CTQ 2 Drug Administration Performance Checklists 10-5, 10-6 SG Learning Activities questions 28-29 (p. 63) SG Practice Questions for the NCLEX Examination 4, 8 (pp. 64-65) Review Question for the NCLEX Examination 3 (p. 156) Figure 10-26 (p. 154): Preparing two drugs in one syringe. Figure 10-27 (p. 155): Preparing a medication in the operating room.

ELSEVIER

OBJECTIVES	CONTENT	TEACHING RESOURCES
		▸ Discuss the differences between preparing medication in the clinic and in the operating room, emphasizing the importance of teamwork in the operating room. ▸ Discuss possible contamination of medication when withdrawing it from ampules, vials, and Mix-O-Vials. Ask for opinions on which of the three containers seems to have the most and least possibilities for contamination. Discuss techniques for preventing contamination. Class Activity ***First, describe and demonstrate to the class all steps in the process of preparing two different medications in one syringe. Discuss the various medications that can be mixed in one syringe, such as different insulins. Supply the class with adequate supplies for practice. Have the class work in pairs to practice and critique each other. Present each pair with clinical situations and medications to work on.***
Performance evaluation		Test Bank SG Learning Activities (pp. 61-63) SG Practice Questions for the NCLEX Examination (pp. 64-65) Drug Administration Performance Checklists Critical Thinking Questions

10.2 Homework/Assignments:

10.2 Instructor's Notes/Student Feedback:

Lecture Outline

10 Parenteral Administration: Safe Preparation of Parenteral Medications

Slide 1

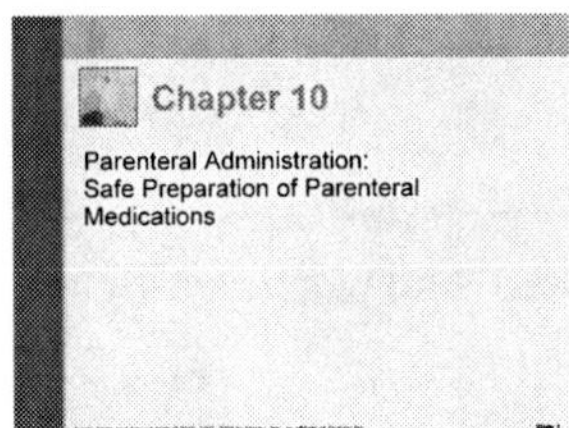
Chapter 10
Parenteral Administration:
Safe Preparation of Parenteral
Medications

Slide 2

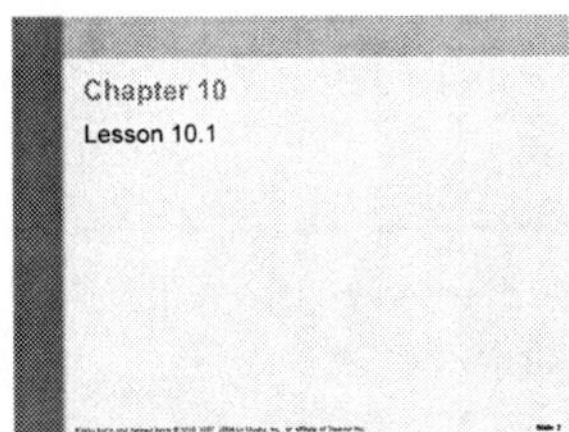
Chapter 10
Lesson 10.1

Slide 3

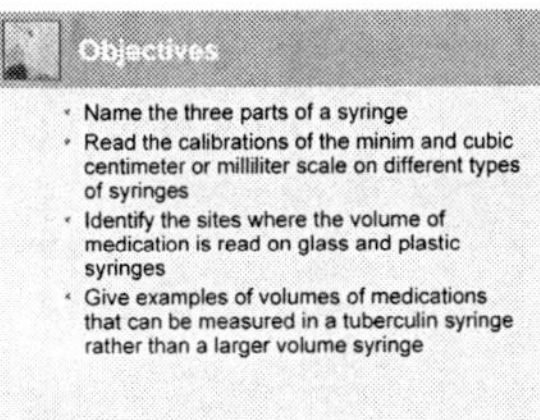
Objectives
Name the three parts of a syringe
Read the calibrations of the minim and cubic centimeter or milliliter scale on different types of syringes
Identify the sites where the volume of medication is read on glass and plastic syringes
Give examples of volumes of medications that can be measured in a tuberculin syringe rather than a larger volume syringe

Slide 4

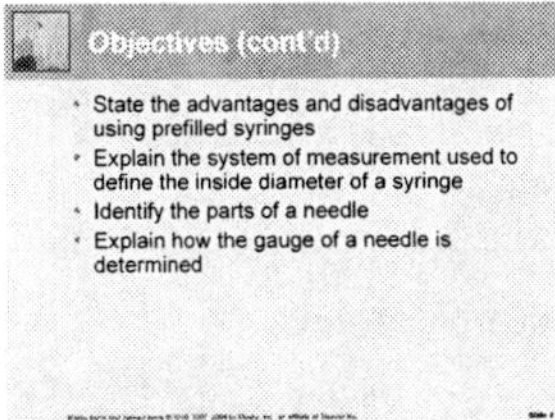
Objectives (cont'd)
State the advantages and disadvantages of using prefilled syringes
Explain the system of measurement used to define the inside diameter of a syringe
Identify the parts of a needle
Explain how the gauge of a needle is determined

Slide 5

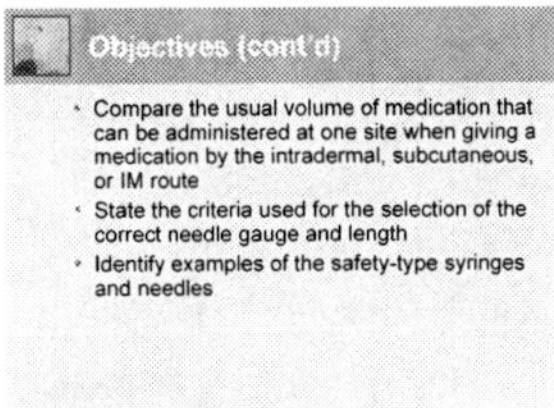
Objectives (cont'd)
Compare the usual volume of medication that can be administered at one site when giving a medication by the intradermal, subcutaneous, or IM route
State the criteria used for the selection of the correct needle gauge and length
Identify examples of the safety-type syringes and needles

ELSEVIER

Slide 6

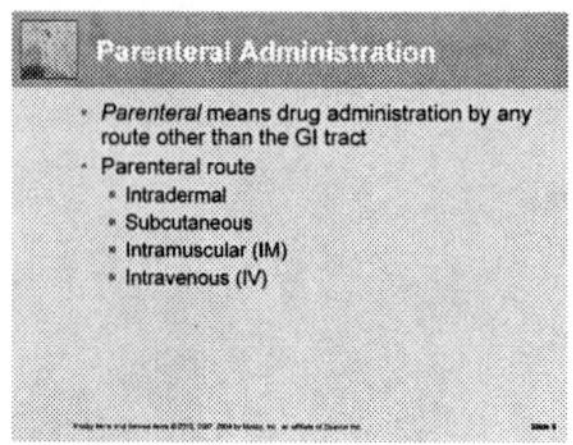
Parenteral Administration
Parenteral means drug administration by any route other than the GI tract
Parenteral route
Intradermal
Subcutaneous
Intramuscular (IM)
Intravenous (IV)

- Onset of drug action with parenteral administration is faster but of shorter duration.
- Dose is often smaller, but the cost is greater.

Slide 7

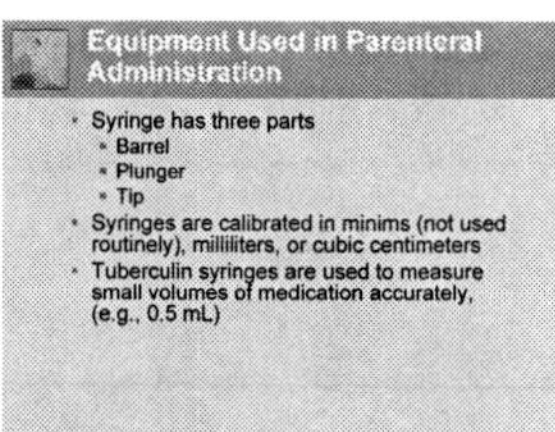
Equipment Used in Parenteral Administration
Syringe has three parts
Barrel
Plunger
Tip
Syringes are calibrated in minims (not used routinely), milliliters, or cubic centimeters
Tuberculin syringes are used to measure small volumes of medication accurately, (e.g., 0.5 mL)

- Reading the dose differs on glass (seldom used) and plastic syringes.

Slide 8

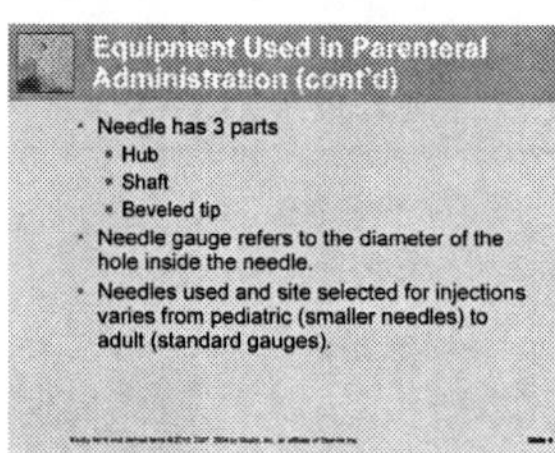
Equipment Used in Parenteral Administration (cont'd)
Needle has 3 parts
Hub
Shaft
Beveled tip
Needle gauge refers to the diameter of the hole inside the needle.
Needles used and site selected for injections varies from pediatric (smaller needles) to adult (standard gauges).

- The larger the gauge number, the smaller the diameter; 18-gauge needles are larger in diameter than 22-gauge needles.

Slide 9

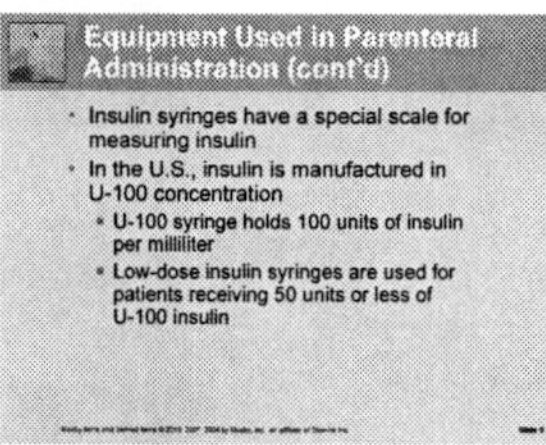
Equipment Used in Parenteral Administration (cont'd)
Insulin syringes have a special scale for measuring insulin
In the U.S., insulin is manufactured in U-100 concentration
U-100 syringe holds 100 units of insulin per milliliter
Low-dose insulin syringes are used for patients receiving 50 units or less of U-100 insulin

- Insulin also is available in prefilled syringes known as insulin pens.

Slide 10

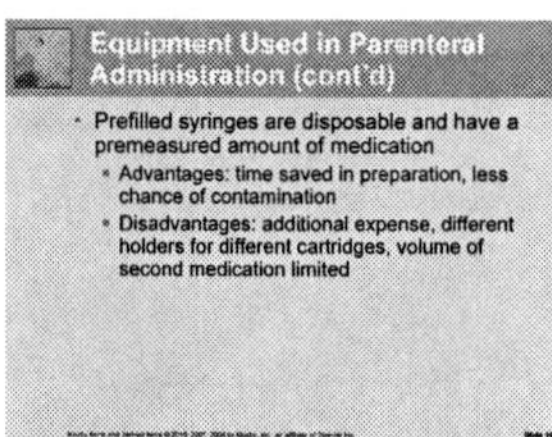
Equipment Used in Parenteral Administration (cont'd)
Prefilled syringes are disposable and have a premeasured amount of medication
Advantages: time saved in preparation, less chance of contamination
Disadvantages: additional expense, different holders for different cartridges, volume of second medication limited

- Referred to by brand names such as Tubex and Carpuject.
- EpiPen is a syringe prefilled with epinephrine; used in emergencies involving allergic reactions.

ELSEVIER

Slide 11

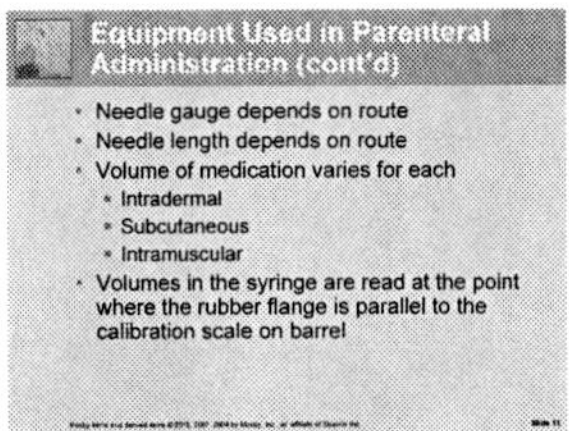
Equipment Used in Parenteral Administration (cont'd)
Needle gauge depends on route
Needle length depends on route
Volume of medication varies for each
Intradermal
Subcutaneous
Intramuscular
Volumes in the syringe are read at the point where the rubber flange is parallel to the calibration scale on barrel

Slide 12

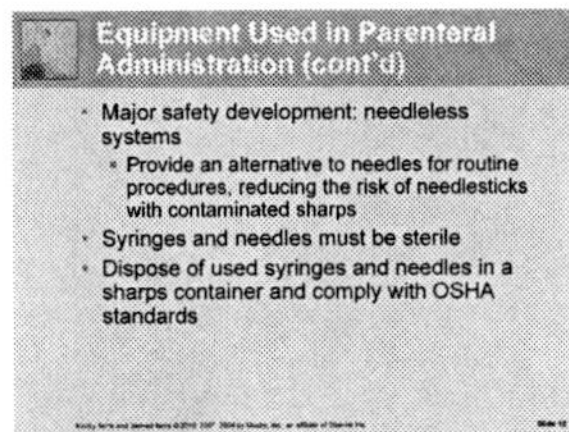
Equipment Used in Parenteral Administration (cont'd)
Major safety development: needleless systems
Provide an alternative to needles for routine procedures, reducing the risk of needlesticks with contaminated sharps
Syringes and needles must be sterile
Dispose of used syringes and needles in a sharps container and comply with OSHA standards

- Patients who must use needles at home can get "sharps by mail disposal systems" for home use.

Slide 13

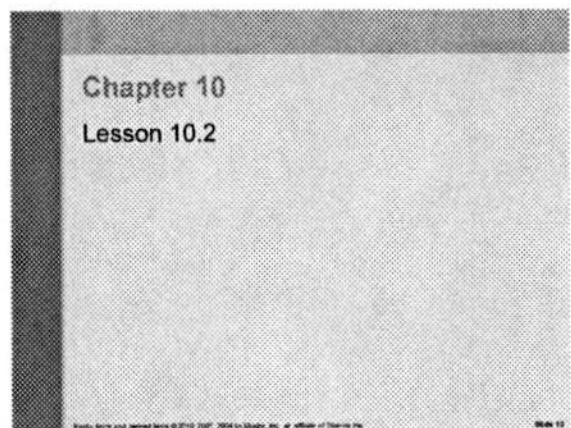
Chapter 10
Lesson 10.2

Slide 14

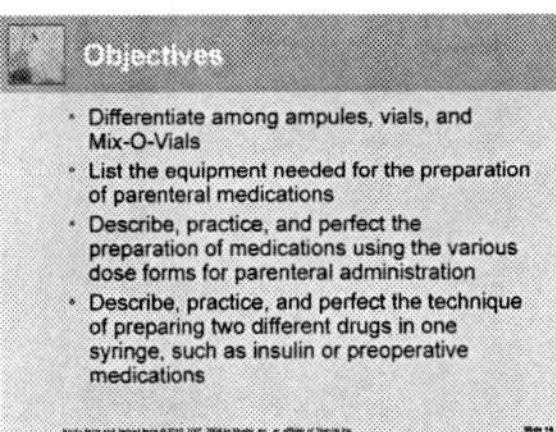
Objectives
Differentiate among ampules, vials, and Mix-O-Vials
List the equipment needed for the preparation of parenteral medications
Describe, practice, and perfect the preparation of medications using the various dose forms for parenteral administration
Describe, practice, and perfect the technique of preparing two different drugs in one syringe, such as insulin or preoperative medications

Slide 15

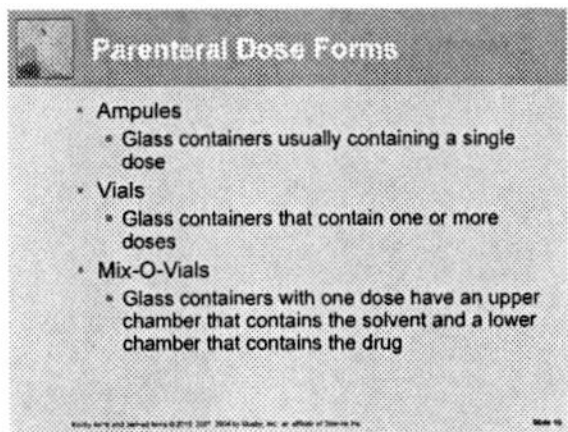
Parenteral Dose Forms
Ampules
Glass containers usually containing a single dose
Vials
Glass containers that contain one or more doses
Mix-O-Vials
Glass containers with one dose have an upper chamber that contains the solvent and a lower chamber that contains the drug

- A filter needle or filter straw must be used to filter out any potential glass particles after an ampule is opened.

ELSEVIER

Slide 16

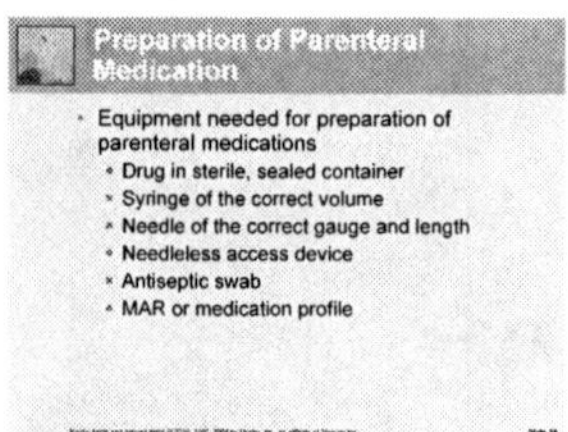
Preparation of Parenteral Medication
Equipment needed for preparation of parenteral medications
Drug in sterile, sealed container
Syringe of the correct volume
Needle of the correct gauge and length
Needleless access device
Antiseptic swab
MAR or medication profile

- Wash hands before preparing any medication or handling any supplies.
- Prepare the drug in a clean, well-lighted area, using aseptic technique.
- Concentrate: ensure accuracy in preparation.

Slide 17

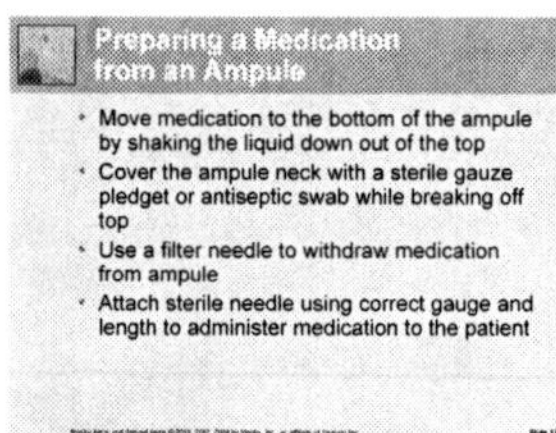
Preparing a Medication from an Ampule
Move medication to the bottom of the ampule by shaking the liquid down out of the top
Cover the ampule neck with a sterile gauze pledget or antiseptic swab while breaking off top
Use a filter needle to withdraw medication from ampule
Attach sterile needle using correct gauge and length to administer medication to the patient

- Check medication calculations.
- Know the hospital policy regarding limitations on the types of medications to be administered by nursing personnel.

Slide 18

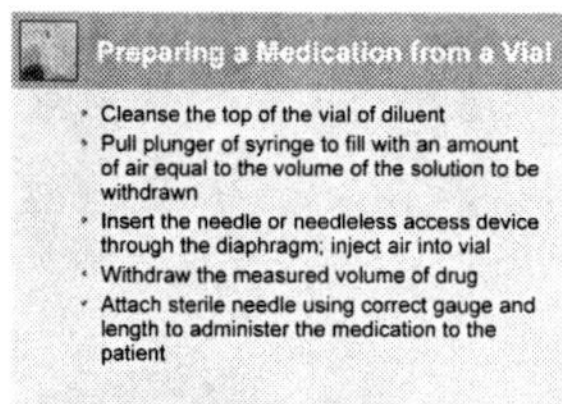
Preparing a Medication from a Vial
Cleanse the top of the vial of diluent
Pull plunger of syringe to fill with an amount of air equal to the volume of the solution to be withdrawn
Insert the needle or needleless access device through the diaphragm; inject air into vial
Withdraw the measured volume of drug
Attach sterile needle using correct gauge and length to administer the medication to the patient

- Follow specific instructions for reconstituting.
- Check expiration date on medication container.

Slide 19

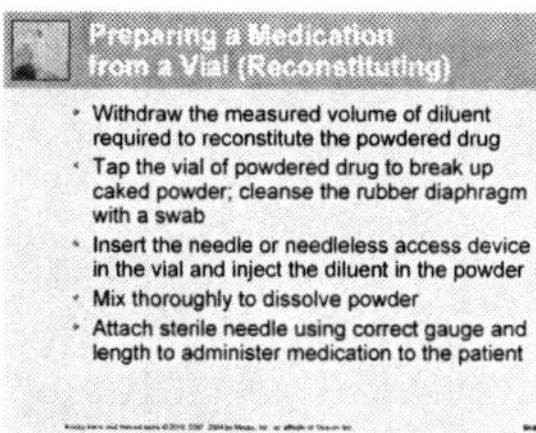
Preparing a Medication from a Vial (Reconstituting)
Withdraw the measured volume of diluent required to reconstitute the powdered drug
Tap the vial of powdered drug to break up caked powder; cleanse the rubber diaphragm with a swab
Insert the needle or needleless access device in the vial and inject the diluent in the powder
Mix thoroughly to dissolve powder
Attach sterile needle using correct gauge and length to administer medication to the patient

- Recheck the type and volume of diluent.
- Label the reconstituted medication.

Slide 20

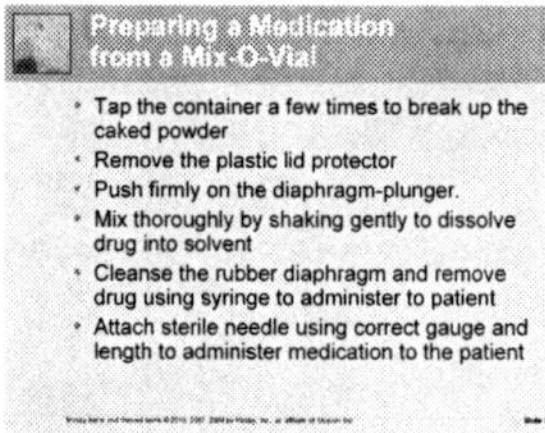
Preparing a Medication from a Mix-O-Vial
Tap the container a few times to break up the caked powder
Remove the plastic lid protector
Push firmly on the diaphragm-plunger.
Mix thoroughly by shaking gently to dissolve drug into solvent
Cleanse the rubber diaphragm and remove drug using syringe to administer to patient
Attach sterile needle using correct gauge and length to administer medication to the patient

11 Lesson Plan

Parenteral Administration: Intradermal, Subcutaneous, and Intramuscular Routes

TEACHING FOCUS

In this chapter, the student is introduced to parenteral administration of drugs by intradermal, subcutaneous, and intramuscular routes. The student has the opportunity to learn about equipment used, proper techniques, common sites, safety precautions, and proper documentation for parenteral administration of medication.

MATERIALS AND RESOURCES

- ☐ ampule (all Lessons)
- ☐ antiseptic pledget (all Lessons)
- ☐ computer and PowerPoint projector (all Lessons)
- ☐ gloves (all Lessons)
- ☐ medication cartridge and holder (all Lessons)
- ☐ mannequin(s) (all Lessons)
- ☐ Mix-O-Vial (all Lessons)
- ☐ puncture-resistant container (all Lessons)
- ☐ syringe and needle (all Lessons)
- ☐ overhead projector and overhead materials

LESSON CHECKLIST

Preparations for this lesson include:

- demonstration
- lecture
- evaluation of student knowledge and skills needed to perform all entry-level activities related to parental administration, including:
  - medication administration through the intradermal, subcutaneous, and intramuscular routes
  - skills for reading intradermal testing
  - documentation
  - patient teaching

KEY TERMS

anergic (p. 159)
deltoid muscle (p. 163)
dorsogluteal area (p. 163)
erythema (p. 159)
intradermal (p. 157)
intramuscular (p. 161)
rectus femoris (p. 162)
subcutaneous (p. 159)
vastus lateralis (p. 162)
ventrogluteal area (p. 163)
Z-track method (p. 166)

ADDITIONAL RESOURCES

PowerPoint slides: 1-10

Legend

ARQ	**PPT**	**TB**	**CTQ**	**SG**	**INRQ**
Audience Response Questions	PowerPoint Slides	Test Bank	Critical Thinking Questions	Study Guide	Interactive NCLEX Review Questions

Class Activities are indicated in ***bold italic.***

ELSEVIER

LESSON 11.1

BACKGROUND ASSESSMENT

Question: How does the Z-track method of intramuscular administration technique differ from the ordinary intramuscular injection technique?
Answer: The Z-track method is used for medications that can irritate or stain, therefore requiring a deeper muscle site, such as the dorsogluteal muscle. The skin is stretched to one side approximately 1 inch. After injecting the medication, the nurse should wait 10 seconds before removing the needle. After removing the needle, the nurse should allow the skin to return to the normal position. The nurse should not massage the site. For an ordinary intramuscular injection, the skin at the site is not pulled to one side, and gentle pressure is applied after administration.

Question: What standard safety precautions should the nurse take when administering parenteral injections?
Answer: The nurse should wash her hands before preparing the medication for administration, before giving the medication, and after administration. Gloves should be worn for all injections to prevent the possibility of contamination from body fluid, specifically blood. Needles should never be recapped to prevent a stick to the nurse. Needles and syringes should be disposed of immediately in a puncture-resistant container marked with biohazard signs, according to facility policy. Gloves should be discarded in the appropriate receptacle and hands washed after administration. The nurse should check bed linen and the patient's clothing for any blood contamination and treat the contamination according to facility policy.

CRITICAL THINKING QUESTION

A 30-year-old patient is undergoing allergy testing, which consists of intradermal injections of an allergen. The nurse has completed the intradermal injections and is preparing to document the procedure. What should the nurse include in the documentation?
Guidelines: The nurse should provide the correct documentation of the medication administration and responses. The documentation should include the following:

1. Chart the date, time, drug name, dosage, and site of administration.
2. Perform a reading of the site after each administration.
3. Chart and report any signs of adverse drug effects.
4. Perform and document essential patient education about the drug therapy and other essential aspects of intervention.

OBJECTIVES	CONTENT	TEACHING RESOURCES
Describe the technique used to administer a medication via the intradermal route.	■ Administration of medication by the intradermal route (p. 157) □ Equipment (p. 157) □ Sites (p. 157) □ Technique (p. 157) □ Patient teaching (p. 159) □ Documentation (p. 159)	PPT 5 ARQ 1 TB Multiple Choice questions 7, 12-13 TB Multiple Response question 1 INRQ 3, 8, 9 Drug Administration Performance Checklist 11-1 SG Review Sheet questions 1-3, 5-8 (p. 67) SG Learning Activities questions 7, 17 (pp. 68, 70) SG Practice Questions for the NCLEX Examination 1, 7, 10 (pp. 71-72) Review Questions for the NCLEX Examination 1-2 (p. 167)

OBJECTIVES	CONTENT	TEACHING RESOURCES
		Figure 11-1 (p. 157), Intradermal injection technique Figure 11-2 (p. 158), Intradermal sites ▸ Discuss all aspects of intradermal injections, including appropriate equipment, site selection, and absorption medications, and explain the rationale for each. ▸ Divide the class into two groups. Have one group research nursing assessments relevant to allergy testing. Have the other group complete a teaching plan for the patient undergoing allergy testing. Allow class time for presentation and discussion. Class Activity ***Bring hotdogs to class and intradermal needles. Have students practice making a bleb under the skin of the hotdog.***
Identify the equipment needed and describe the technique used to administer a medication via the subcutaneous route.	■ Administration of medication by the subcutaneous route (p 159) □ Equipment (p. 159) □ Sites (p. 160) □ Technique (p. 160) □ Patient teaching (p. 161) □ Documentation (p. 161) Review the proper technique to use when giving a subcutaneous injection, sites used, and rotation plan.	PPT 6 ARQ 2 TB Multiple Choice questions 1-2, 10 INRQ 2, 4, 10 CTQ 2, 5 Drug Administration Performance Checklist 11-2 SG Review Sheet question 9 (p. 67) SG Learning Activities questions 5-6, 15, 18-19 (pp. 68-70) SG Practice Questions for the NCLEX Examination 4-5, 8 (p. 71) Review Question for the NCLEX Examination 3 (p. 167) Figure 11-3 (p. 159), Subcutaneous injection technique Figure 11-4 (p. 160), Subcutaneous injection sites and rotation plan ▸ Discuss all aspects of subcutaneous injections, including appropriate equipment, site selection, absorption, and medications, including the rationale for each. Class Activity ***Demonstrate on a mannequin how to prepare and administer an injection using the subcutaneous route. Then have the students practice on mannequins.***

OBJECTIVES	CONTENT	TEACHING RESOURCES
		Class Activity ***Divide the class into pairs, and have them develop a patient teaching plan to educate diabetic patients on self-administration of insulin. Have each pair share its plan with the group. Formulate a complete teaching plan to be used.*** Class Activity ***Divide the class into pairs. Have each student identify subcutaneous sites on their partner.***

11.1 Homework/Assignments:

11.1 Instructor's Notes/Student Feedback:

LESSON 11.2

CRITICAL THINKING QUESTION

The nurse is preparing an intramuscular injection for an infant of normal weight. What site should the nurse select? As the nurse aspirates before injecting the medication, blood returns into the syringe. What should the nurse do?

Guidelines: The nurse should select the infant's vastus lateralis muscle because it has the largest muscle mass for that age-group. It is located one handbreadth above the knee and one handbreadth below the greater trochanter. If blood returns into the syringe upon aspiration, the nurse should place an antiseptic pledget over the injection site, withdraw the needle, and dispose of this medication. Otherwise the medication would have been injected into a blood vessel and absorbed more quickly than intended. A new injection needs to be prepared with all new equipment.

OBJECTIVES	CONTENT	TEACHING RESOURCES
Identify suitable sites for intramuscular administration of medication in an infant, a child, an adult, and an older adult.	■ Administration of medication by the intramuscular route (p. 161) □ Equipment (p. 161) Review the proper technique to use when giving an intramuscular injection. Discuss the different sites that are used for intramuscular injections	PPT 7-8 ARQ 3, 5 TB Multiple Choice questions 3-6, 11 INRQ 5, 7 CTQ 1 SG Review Sheet question 11 (p. 67)

ELSEVIER

OBJECTIVES	CONTENT	TEACHING RESOURCES
		SG Learning Activities questions 1-2, 4, 8, 16, 20-21 (pp. 68-70) Review Question for the NCLEX Examination 4 (p. 167) Figure 11-5 (p. 161), Intramuscular injection technique ▸ Discuss all aspects of intramuscular injections, including appropriate equipment, site selection, absorption, medications, and the rationale. Include specifics for each age-group. Class Activity ***Divide the class into four groups. Give each group an age category and have them identify the sites for their assigned age. Why would they use that site with that age-group? Why are other sites contraindicated? Have groups share their conclusions with the class for questions and feedback.***
Describe the technique used to administer medications in the vastus lateralis muscle, rectus femoris muscle, ventrogluteal area, dorsogluteal area, or the deltoid muscle.	□ Sites (p. 161) – Vastus lateralis muscle (p. 162) – Rectus femoris muscle (p. 162) – Gluteal area (p. 162) – Deltoid muscle (p. 163)	ARQ 4 TB Multiple Choice question 8 TB Multiple Response question 3 INRQ 6, 11-12 CTQ 3, 4 Drug Administration Performance Checklist 11-3 Lifespan Considerations: Injection Sites (p. 162) SG Review Sheet question 10 (p. 67) SG Practice Questions for the NCLEX Examination 2-3, 6 (p. 71) Figure 11-6 (p. 162), Vastus lateralis muscle Figure 11-7 (p. 162), Rectus femoris muscle Figure 11-8 (p. 163), Ventrogluteal site Figure 11-9 (p. 163), Prone position Figure 11-10 (p. 163), Patient lying on side Figure 11-11 (p. 164), Dorsogluteal site Figure 11-12 (p. 164), Deltoid muscle site Class Activity ***Demonstrate how to inject medication into the vastus lateralis muscle, the rectus femoris muscle, the ventrogluteal area, the dorsogluteal area, or the deltoid muscle.***

ELSEVIER

OBJECTIVES	CONTENT	TEACHING RESOURCES
		Identify each location, and point out important factors relative to each site that the nurse should know. Then have students practice giving injections at each site on a mannequin. Ask students to share what they learned when practicing injection techniques.
For each anatomic site studied, describe the landmarks used to identify the site before medication is administered.	□ Site rotation (p. 163) □ Technique (p. 164) □ Patient teaching (p. 165) □ Documentation (p. 165) □ Z-track method (p. 166)	PPT 9 TB Multiple Choice question 9 TB Multiple Response question 2 INRQ 1 Drug Administration Performance Checklist 11-4 SG Review Sheet questions 4, 12-13 (p. 67) SG Learning Activities question 3 (p. 68) Review Question for the NCLEX Examination 5 (p. 167) Figure 11-13 (p. 165), Intramuscular master rotation plan Figure 11-14 (p. 166), Z-track method ▸ Discuss all aspects of the Z-track method of administration. ▸ Place an overhead up with other parenteral sites (intravenous, intramuscular, intra-arterial, intraperitoneal, intrathecal, intracardiac, and intrasternal). Discuss locations in the body and provide clinical examples when each of these routes would be used for drug administration. *Class Activity* ***Divide the class into small groups, and assign each group one of the five body muscles or areas from the previous activity. Have each group determine the landmarks for identifying its injection site and point out the position on a mannequin for the class.***
Performance evaluation		Test Bank SG Learning Activities (pp. 68-70) SG Practice Questions for the NCLEX Examination (pp. 71-72) Drug Administration Performance Checklists Critical Thinking Questions

11.2 Homework/Assignments:

11.2 Instructor's Notes/Student Feedback:

Lecture Outline

11 Parenteral Administration: Intradermal, Subcutaneous, and Intramuscular Routes

Slide 1

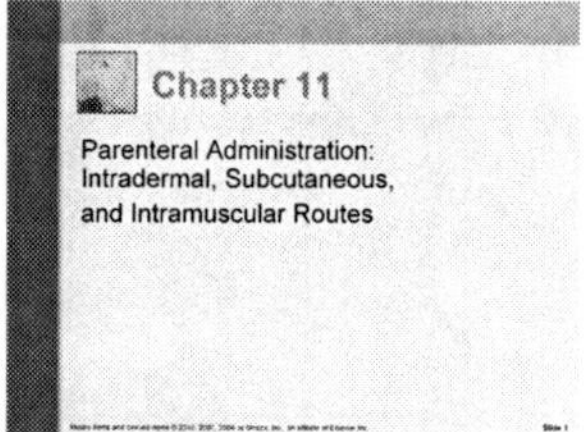
Chapter 11
Parenteral Administration:
Intradermal, Subcutaneous,
and Intramuscular Routes

Slide 2

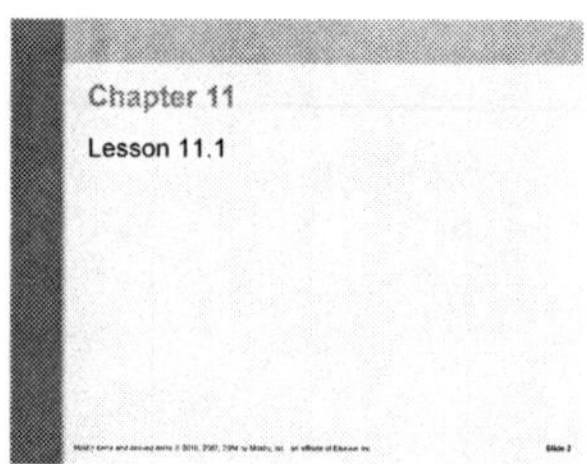
Chapter 11
Lesson 11.1

Slide 3

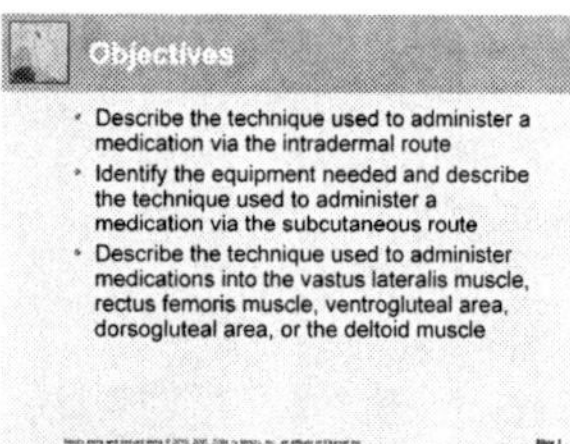
Objectives
Describe the technique used to administer a medication via the intradermal route
Identify the equipment needed and describe the technique used to administer a medication via the subcutaneous route
Describe the technique used to administer medications into the vastus lateralis muscle, rectus femoris muscle, ventrogluteal area, dorsogluteal area, or the deltoid muscle

Slide 4

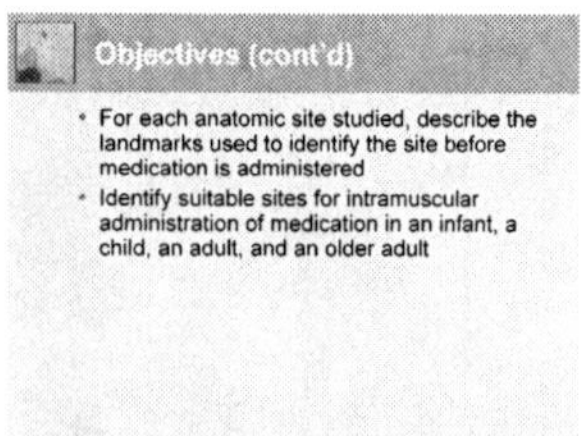
Objectives (cont'd)
For each anatomic site studied, describe the landmarks used to identify the site before medication is administered
Identify suitable sites for intramuscular administration of medication in an infant, a child, an adult, and an older adult

Slide 5

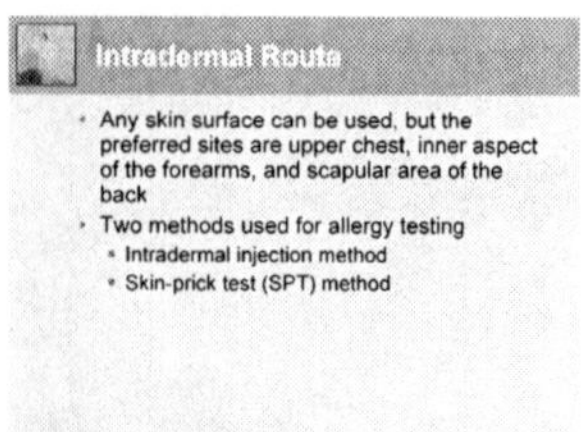
Intradermal Route
Any skin surface can be used, but the preferred sites are upper chest, inner aspect of the forearms, and scapular area of the back
Two methods used for allergy testing
Intradermal injection method
Skin-prick test (SPT) method

- Measure reaction in millimeters – wheal and erythema, no reaction is referred to as *anergic*.

ELSEVIER

Slide 6

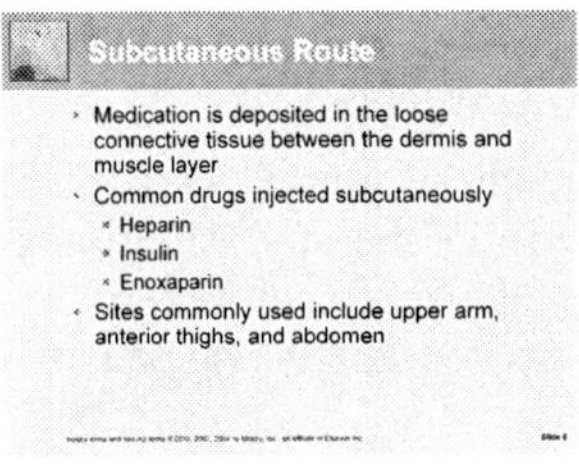
Subcutaneous Route
Medication is deposited in the loose connective tissue between the dermis and muscle layer
Common drugs injected subcutaneously
Heparin
Insulin
Enoxaparin
Sites commonly used include upper arm, anterior thighs, and abdomen

- The usual amount of fluid administered with this type of injection is 1 mL or less.
- Rate of absorption is slow and drug action is generally longer with this route than IM or IV injections.
- It is important to rotate injection sites to enhance absorption and prevent atrophy of the subcutaneous tissue.
- Injections can be given at 45- or 90-degree angles, depending on the amount of tissue present.

Slide 7

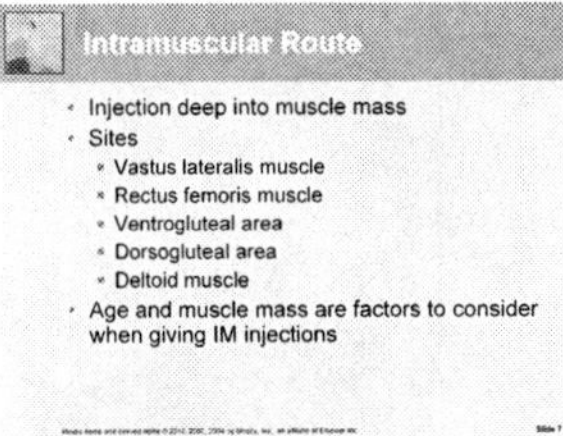
Intramuscular Route
Injection deep into muscle mass
Sites
Vastus lateralis muscle
Rectus femoris muscle
Ventrogluteal area
Dorsogluteal area
Deltoid muscle
Age and muscle mass are factors to consider when giving IM injections

- The drug volume differs for each of the sites according to muscle size.

Slide 8

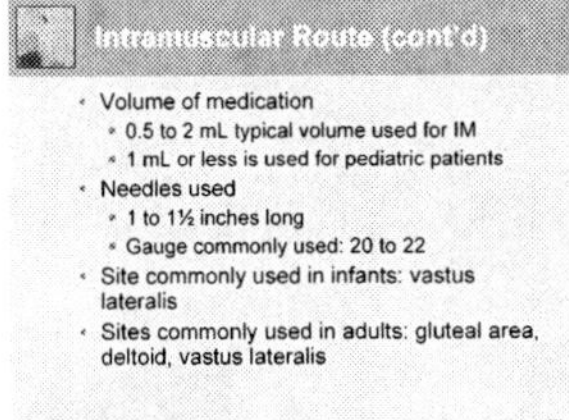
Intramuscular Route (cont'd)
Volume of medication
0.5 to 2 mL typical volume used for IM
1 mL or less is used for pediatric patients
Needles used
1 to 1½ inches long
Gauge commonly used: 20 to 22
Site commonly used in infants: vastus lateralis
Sites commonly used in adults: gluteal area, deltoid, vastus lateralis

Slide 9

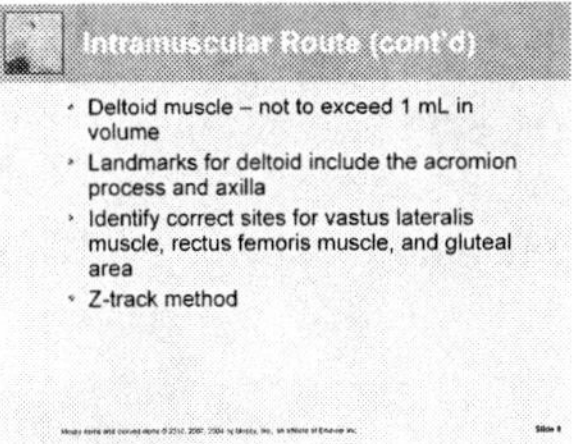
Intramuscular Route (cont'd)
Deltoid muscle – not to exceed 1 mL in volume
Landmarks for deltoid include the acromion process and axilla
Identify correct sites for vastus lateralis muscle, rectus femoris muscle, and gluteal area
Z-track method

Slide 10

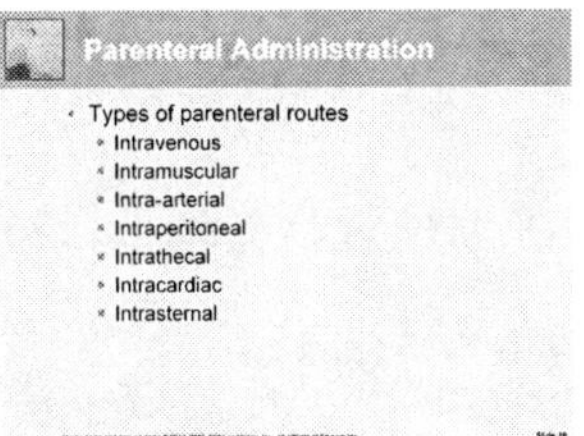
Parenteral Administration
Types of parenteral routes
Intravenous
Intramuscular
Intra-arterial
Intraperitoneal
Intrathecal
Intracardiac
Intrasternal

- Know where each of these routes is located in the body.

ELSEVIER

12 Lesson Plan

Parenteral Administration: Intravenous Route

TEACHING FOCUS

In this chapter, the student will be introduced to parenteral administration by the intravenous (IV) route. The student will have the opportunity to learn the concept and requirements to perform IV therapy. Additionally the student will have the opportunity to learn the equipment used for IV therapy, the administration of medications by way of the IV route, guidelines that govern the IV therapy, and approaches the nurse uses to monitor and document IV therapy.

MATERIALS AND RESOURCES

- ☐ administration set (all Lessons)
- ☐ antiseptic solution (all Lessons)
- ☐ antiseptic swabs (all Lessons)
- ☐ armboard (all Lessons)
- ☐ computer and PowerPoint projector (all Lessons)
- ☐ gloves (all Lessons)
- ☐ peripheral and central IV access devices (all Lessons)
- ☐ standard IV pole or rod (all Lessons)
- ☐ solutions and tubing for IV administration (all Lessons)
- ☐ tape (all Lessons)
- ☐ tourniquet (all Lessons)

LESSON CHECKLIST

Preparations for this lesson include:

- lecture
- demonstration
- student performance evaluation of all entry-level skills required for comprehension and application of patient care, including:
  - knowledge of IV administration equipment
  - proper skills for IV equipment setup
  - proper techniques in performing a venipuncture
  - monitoring and documentation

KEY TERMS

air embolism (p. 196)
central devices (p. 171)
electrolytes (p. 174)
extravasation (p. 195)
hypertonic (p. 174)
hypotonic (p. 174)
implantable infusion ports (p. 173)
implantable venous infusion ports (p. 171)
infiltration (p. 195)
infiltration scale (p. 195)
Infusion Nurses Society (p. 168)
in-the-needle catheters (p. 172)
intravascular compartment (p. 174)
intravenous (p. 168)
intravenous (IV) solutions (p. 174)
isotonic (p. 174)
IV administration set (p. 169)
midline catheters (p. 171)
nonvolumetric IV controllers (p. 169)
over-the-needle catheters (p. 171)
peripheral devices (p. 171)
peripherally inserted central venous catheters (PICCs) (p. 172)
phlebitis (p. 194)
pulmonary edema (p. 196)
pulmonary embolism (p. 196)
saline, heparin, or medlock (p. 171)
SASH guideline (p. 178)
septicemia (p. 195)
"speed shock" (p. 197)
syringe pumps (p. 170)
tandem setup, piggyback (IVPB), or IV rider (p. 176)
thrombophlebitis (p. 194)
tunneled central venous catheters (p. 172)
volumetric IV controllers (p. 170)
winged, butterfly, or scalp needles (p. 171)

ELSEVIER

ADDITIONAL RESOURCES

PowerPoint slides: 1-24

Legend

ARQ	PPT	TB	CTQ	SG	INRQ
Audience Response Questions	PowerPoint Slides	Test Bank	Critical Thinking Questions	Study Guide	Interactive NCLEX Review Questions

Class Activities are indicated in ***bold italic.***

LESSON 12.1

BACKGROUND ASSESSMENT

Question: In some states, LPNs and/or LVNs are not allowed to start IV therapy without special training. Even so, if a patient is receiving IV therapy, it is still the LPN's and/or LVN's responsibility to know the signs and symptoms of infiltration. What are those signs, and how should the nurse assess the patient?
Answer: The nurse should inspect the IV site at regular intervals. Signs of infiltration include redness, warmth, coolness and blanching of the skin, swelling, and a dull ache at the site. The nurse should observe the site extremity and compare it with the opposite extremity for any of the previously listed changes. If signs of infiltration are present, the nurse should apply a tourniquet proximal to the infusion site to constrict the flow. If flow continues, infiltration is confirmed. The nurse should stop the infusion immediately, check capillary refill, and check pulses proximal and distal to the area of infiltration. The nurse should apply cold or moist heat to the site, depending on the type of medication that has infiltrated. The nurse should notify the nurse in charge.

Question: There are various types of IV controllers to use when administering an IV line. Those which are electronic are classified as non-volumetric and volumetric. What is the difference between these two types of controllers?
Answer: The non-volumetric IV controllers monitor only the gravity infusion rate by counting the drops that drip through the chamber. Nonvolumetric IV controllers protect the patient by sounding an alarm if the clamp slips and results in an inadvertent gravity free flow. Nonvolumetric IV controllers sound an alarm if the number of drops per minute slows down or stops as a result of patient position, air in the tubing, or low solution volume. In contrast, volumetric IV controllers are actually pumps that apply external pressure to the administration set tubing to squeeze the solution through the tubing at a specific rate. Volumetric IV controllers can be programmed for a specific volume over time and are much more accurate than nonvolumetric. Volumetric IV controllers have alarm systems that sound if there is resistance in the IV line caused by a developing occlusion from thrombus formation or by a kink in the line.

CRITICAL THINKING QUESTION

A patient is admitted to the emergency department with a large amount of blood loss following an automobile accident. The nurse has been asked to start an IV line. What type of needle and infusion set and site should the nurse use to treat the patient most effectively?
Guidelines: Because of the amount of blood loss, the patient is at risk for hypovolemic shock and may later need large amounts of fluid replacement and possibly a blood transfusion. Therefore a large bore needle or PICC line placed in a large vein, such as the cephalic or basilic vein, would be the best choice. The infusion set initially would be a roller and clamp controller because the flow will need to be adjusted as the patient stabilizes.

ELSEVIER

OBJECTIVES	CONTENT	TEACHING RESOURCES
Define intravenous (IV) therapy.	■ Intravenous therapy (p. 168) Review advantages and disadvantages of delivering medications via the IV route.	PPT 6-8 SG Review Sheet questions 1-3 (p. 73) ▸ Discuss why the IV route is a faster route for drug absorption. ▸ Discuss the reasons the nurse should understand IV access systems when performing infusion therapy to patients. ▸ Discuss why a plastic catheter is used most often during infusion therapy. ▸ Discuss the difference between macrodrip chambers and microdrip chambers used as part of an IV administration set. Class Activity ***Lead a discussion in which students describe IV therapy. What are the advantages and disadvantages compared with other ways of administering medications? Show the class macrodrip and microdrip chambers and explain the difference.***
Describe the processes used to establish guidelines for nurses to perform infusion therapy.	■ Intravenous therapy (p. 168)	SG Learning Activities question 16 (p. 76) Class Activity ***Have students research state regulations for LPN and/or LVN administration of IV therapy. What are the LPN's and/or LVN's responsibilities? Have students present their findings to the class. (For students to prepare for this activity, see Homework/Assignments #1.)***
Describe equipment used to perform IV therapy (e.g., winged or butterfly needle, over-the-needle catheter, administration sets, and IV access devices).	■ Equipment used for intravenous therapy (p. 169) □ Intravenous administration sets (p. 169) □ Types of infusion control devices (p. 169) □ Intravenous access devices (p. 171)	PPT 9-10 ARQ 2 TB Multiple Choice questions 10, 13 TB Multiple Response question 1 CTQ 1, 4-5 SG Review Sheet questions 4-6 (p. 73) SG Learning Activities questions 1, 7-12, 17-18 (pp. 76-77) SG Practice Questions for the NCLEX Examination 6-8 (p. 79) Figure 12-1 *(A, B)* (p. 170), different types of IV administration sets using a macrodrip chamber; *(C)* An administration set using a microdrip chamber Figure 12-2 (p. 171), Control clamps for IV administration sets

OBJECTIVES	CONTENT	TEACHING RESOURCES
		Figure 12-3 (p. 171), Winged needle with female Luer adapter Figure 12-4 *(A)* (p. 172), Over-the-needle catheter; (B) In-the-needle catheters Figure 12-5 *(A)* (p. 173), Hickman catheter; *(B)* Broviac catheter; *(C)* Groshong catheter Figure 12-6 (p. 173), Silicone venous catheter with infusion ports Class Activity ***Divide the class into small groups, and assign commonly used pieces of equipment to each group, providing samples if available. Have each group explain and demonstrate how the equipment is used, for which type of treatment, and on what type of patient. As a class, compare features and benefits of related pieces of equipment.***
Differentiate among peripheral, midline, central venous, and implantable access devices used for IV therapy.	□ Intravenous access devices (p. 171) Review the different types of equipment used for IV therapy. Discuss the various access devices used: peripheral, midline, central venous, and implantable.	PPT 11 TB Multiple Choice questions 1, 7 INRQ 1 CTQ 3 SG Review Sheet questions 7, 10 (p. 73) SG Practice Questions for the NCLEX Examination 1-2 (p. 78) Figure 12-5 *(A)* (p. 173), Hickman catheter; *(B)* Broviac catheter; *(C)* Groshong catheter Figure 12-6 (p. 173), Silicone venous catheter with infusion ports Class Activity ***Bring IV equipment to class: various peripheral IV types, PICC, tunneled central venous catheters, and central line catheters. Pass them around and review with the class how to differentiate them and the purpose of each.***

12.1 Homework/Assignments:
1. Have students research state regulations for LPN and/or LVN administration of IV therapy. What are the LPN's and/or LVN's responsibilities? Have students present their findings to the class.

12.1 Instructor's Notes/Student Feedback:

LESSON 12.2

CRITICAL THINKING QUESTION

A patient receiving an IV infusion exhibits dyspnea, cough, anxiety, rales, rhonchi, thready pulse, frothy sputum, and high blood pressure. What complication is this, and what nursing interventions are appropriate?

Guidelines: The patient is exhibiting signs of pulmonary edema, possibly related to fluid overload from the infusion. The nurse should immediately slow the IV line to a "keep open" rate and notify the health care provider. The nurse should place the patient in high Fowler's position and start oxygen, as ordered. The nurse should also anticipate an order for an IV diuretic and morphine sulfate to help eliminate the extra fluid. The patient should be reassured and monitored closely.

OBJECTIVES	CONTENT	TEACHING RESOURCES
Differentiate among isotonic, hypotonic, and hypertonic intravenous solutions.	■ Intravenous dose forms (p. 174) □ Types of intravenous solutions (p. 174) Review the different IV solutions available (isotonic, hypotonic, and hypertonic) and their uses.	PPT 12-14 ARQ 1 TB Multiple Choice question 3 SG Review Sheet questions 11-13 (p. 73) SG Learning Activities questions 2, 14-15 (p. 76) Table 12-1 Types of Intravenous Solutions (p. 175) ▶ Discuss disease states in which a patient may require IV therapy. Identify the types of IV solutions to be used and why. Class Activity ***Bring the different types of IV solutions to class, and have students determine which one of the classifications (isotonic, hypotonic, and hypertonic) each belongs to. Review with the class the uses of each type.***

OBJECTIVES	CONTENT	TEACHING RESOURCES
Explain the usual circumstances for administering isotonic, hypotonic, and hypertonic IV solutions.	■ Intravenous dose forms (p. 174)	TB Multiple Choice questions 4, 11 INRQ 2-3, 9 SG Learning Activities question 6 (p. 76) SG Practice Question for the NCLEX Examination 3 (p. 78) ▸ Discuss reasons a nurse should change a patient's IV solution bag or bottles every 24 hours. ▸ Discuss the importance of *not* using a marking pen directly on the IV solution bag or bottles. Class Activity ***Ask the groups from the previous Class Activity to provide examples of illnesses in which their assigned solutions would be used and why.***
Describe the three intravascular compartments and the distribution of body water in them.	■ Intravenous dose forms (p. 174)	PPT 5 SG Learning Activities question 13 (p. 76) Figure 12-7 (p. 175), Fluid compartments of the body Table 12-2 Intravenous Solutions, Electrolyte Concentrations, and Osmolality (p. 176) Class Activity ***Lead a discussion in which students identify the intravascular compartments and how body water is distributed through them. What are intracellular compartments? What are interstitial compartments? Ask volunteers to diagram the compartments on the board, as directed by the class. Why is it important for nurses to understand the physiology of body water?***
Describe the different types of large-volume solution containers.	□ Large-volume solution containers (p. 176) □ Small-volume solution containers (p. 176)	ARQ 3 SG Review Sheet question 14 (p. 73) Figure 12-8 (p. 176), Tandem, secondary, or piggyback intermittent administration setup ▸ Discuss the differences between and uses of the large-volume solution containers and the small-volume solution containers. Class Activity ***Show the class examples of large- and small-volume solution containers and invite students to examine them. Ask students which important administration techniques the nurse should know when piggybacking into an existing line. What medications are likely to be infused by***

OBJECTIVES	CONTENT	TEACHING RESOURCES
		piggybacking? What should the nurse do when the piggybacking infusion is completed?
Identify the dose forms available, the type of sites of administration, and general principles of administering medications via the IV route.	■ Administration of medications by the intravenous route (p. 176) □ Dose forms (p. 176) □ Equipment (p. 176) □ Sites (p. 176) □ General principles of intravenous medication administration (p. 176)	PPT 19 TB Multiple Choice question 6 SG Review Sheet questions 23, 25-26 (p. 74) SG Learning Activities question 19 (p. 77) Class Activity ***Present students the following problems associated with IV administration and ask for solutions:*** ***1. How should the nurse check to make sure he or she has the correct IV solution?*** ***2. How does the nurse determine if the medication is specifically for IV use?*** ***3. What should the nurse do if the container does not say "For IV use"?***
List criteria used for the selection of an IV access site.	□ Sites (p. 177) □ General principles of intravenous medication administration (p. 177)	SG Review Sheet questions 15-18 (p. 74) SG Learning Activities question 3 (p. 76) Review Questions for the NCLEX Examinations 4 (p. 198) Figure 12-9 (p. 177), IV sites on the hand Clinical Landmine (p. 179) Figure 12-10 (p. 178), Veins in the forearm used as IV sites Figure 12-11 (p. 179), Veins in infants and children used as IV sites Lifespan Considerations: Intravenous Sites (p. 179) ▸ Discuss reasons an IV line should not be started in a patient's artery. ▸ Discuss key points for the selection of an IV site. Review the anatomy or the location. ▸ Discuss the appropriate time frame to use topical antibiotic ointment on the insertion site of a patient. Class Activity ***Divide the class into groups, and assign each group an IV site, either peripheral or central. Have the groups determine where the sites may be located and under what circumstances each is appropriate. What equipment typically is chosen? After infusion has begun, what site care is important? Identify appropriate nursing interventions in the care of a patient receiving an IV.***

12.2 Homework/Assignments:

12.2 Instructor's Notes/Student Feedback:

LESSON 12.3

CRITICAL THINKING QUESTION

A 40-year-old woman has an IV line established after being admitted to the hospital for Crohn's disease. The nurse observes that the IV line is flowing correctly and prepares to educate the patient about the IV line. What should the nurse teach the patient?

Guidelines: The nurse should explain the importance of the IV therapy, including the set rate of infusion that needs to be maintained. The nurse should ask the patient to watch for and immediately report any redness, swelling, or discomfort in the IV site. The patient should be educated on the importance of keeping the IV site and dressing clean and dry. The nurse should also answer any questions the patient or family may have.

OBJECTIVES	CONTENT	TEACHING RESOURCES
Describe the recommended guidelines and procedures for IV catheter care, including proper maintenance of patency of IV lines and implanted access devices, IV line dressing changes, and peripheral and central venous IV needle or catheter changes.	□ Preparing an IV solution for infusion (p. 179) □ Intravenous fluid monitoring (p. 180) Review the principles of administering medications via the IV route. Discuss how to correctly use the different types of equipment and review catheter care for all types of devices.	PPT 20 ARQ 5 TB Multiple Choice questions 5, 12 INRQ 7 CTQ 2 Drug Administration Performance Checklist 12-1 Lifespan Considerations: Intravenous Fluid Monitoring (p. 180) SG Review Sheet questions 8-9, 20 (pp. 73-74) SG Learning Activities questions 4, 20-21 (pp. 76-77) SG Practice Question for the NCLEX Examination 4 (p. 78) Review Question for the NCLEX Examination 7 (p. 198) ▸ Discuss the procedure for performing a venipuncture for the purpose of parenteral administration.

ELSEVIER

OBJECTIVES	CONTENT	TEACHING RESOURCES
		Class Activity ***Divide the class into two groups. Assign one group procedures for IV catheter care and assign the other group IV line dressing changes. Ask each group to discuss and recommend guidelines for its assigned topic. Have groups share their guidelines for feedback and discussion.*** Class Activity ***Demonstrate techniques for IV catheter care, IV line dressing changes, and for peripheral and central venous IV needle or catheter changes. Then have students practice the techniques with various access devices.***
Describe the correct techniques for administering medications by means of an established peripheral or central IV line, a heparin lock, an IV bag, a bottle or volume control device, or a secondary piggyback set.	■ Basic guidelines of intravenous administration of medicines (p. 180) □ Venipuncture (p. 181) – Selection of the catheter or butterfly needle (p. 182) □ Administration of medication by a heparin-saline-medlock (p. 184) □ Administration of medications into an established intravenous line (IV bolus) (p. 185) □ Administration of medication through an implanted venous access device (p. 186) □ Adding a medication to an intravenous bag, bottle, or volume control (p. 187) □ Adding a medication with a piggyback set (p. 187) □ Changing to the next container of intravenous solution (p. 188) □ Care of peripheral sites, central venous catheters, and implanted ports (p. 189) □ Flushing of peripheral catheters (p. 189) □ Peripheral site dressing changes (p. 189) □ Flushing of central venous catheters (p. 190) □ Dressing changes for central lines (p. 190) □ Care of venous ports (p. 191) □ Discontinuing an intravenous infusion (p. 192)	PPT 21-22 INRQ 10, 12 Drug Administration Performance Checklists 12-2 through 12-13 SG Review Sheet questions 19, 21-22 (p. 74) SG Practice Questions for the NCLEX Examination 5, 9-10 (p. 79) Review Question for the NCLEX Examination 5 (p. 198) Lifespan Considerations: Benzyl Alcohol Preservative (p. 185) Figure 12-12 (p. 183), Venipuncture steps Figure 12-13 (p. 184), Heparin-saline-medlock Figure 12-14 (p. 185), Syringe with blunt access cannula Figure 12-15 (p. 186), The Baxter Clearlink Access System Figure 12-16 (p. 188), The ADD-Vantage during delivery system Figure 12-17 (p. 188), A male Luer lock with an Interlink Leverlock cannula Clinical Landmine (pp. 189, 192) Class Activity ***Using samples of IV equipment, including solutions, tubing, access devices, piggyback, heparin lock, etc., demonstrate the procedures to follow in administering medications. Then divide the class into groups, and have students practice the various procedures with the equipment available.***

ELSEVIER

OBJECTIVES	CONTENT	TEACHING RESOURCES
Discuss the proper baseline patient assessments needed to evaluate the IV therapy.	■ Monitoring intravenous therapy (p. 193)	PPT 23 ARQ 4 TB Multiple Choice question 2 SG Review Sheet questions 24, 27-28 (pp. 74-75) Review Question for the NCLEX Examination 3 (p. 198) Class Activity ***Present the assessments listed below to the class, and ask whether each is used to evaluate IV therapy. Ask students to explain their rationales.*** – ***Checking the flow rate*** – ***Checking for infiltration*** – ***Checking for reactive pupils*** – ***Checking for mechanical bowel obstruction*** ***Then lead a discussion in which students identify and describe the proper baseline assessments required to evaluate IV therapy.***
Explain the signs, symptoms, and treatment of complications associated with IV therapy (e.g., phlebitis, thrombophlebitis, localized infection, septicemia, infiltration, extravasation, air in tubing, pulmonary edema, catheter embolism, and "speed shock").	□ Complications associated with intravenous therapy (p. 194) – Phlebitis, thrombophlebitis, and local infection (p. 194) – Septicemia (p. 195) – Infiltration and extravasation (p. 195) – Air in tubing or air embolus (p. 196) – Circulatory overload and pulmonary edema (p. 196) – Pulmonary embolism (p. 196) – "Speed shock" (p. 197) Review the phlebitis scale and the complications associated with IV therapy	PPT 24 TB Multiple Choice questions 8-9, 14-15 TB Multiple Response question 2 INRQ 5 SG Review Sheet questions 29-31 (p. 75) SG Learning Activities questions 22-23 (p. 77) Review Questions for the NCLEX Examination 1-2, 6 (p. 198) Figure 12-18 (p. 195), Assessing the severity of phlebitis Figure 12-19 (p. 195), Infiltration scale Class Activity ***As a class, list complications associated with IV therapy on the board. Divide the class into four groups, and assign each group two complications from the list on the board. Ask each group to:*** ***1. Describe its assigned complication.*** ***2. Identify the signs and symptoms.*** ***3. Profile patents at greatest risk.*** ***4. Identify treatment options.*** ***5. Describe nursing interventions.*** ***Ask each group to present its findings to the class for feedback and discussion. Record information on the board.***

OBJECTIVES	CONTENT	TEACHING RESOURCES
Performance evaluation		Test Bank SG Learning Activities (pp. 76-77) SG Practice Questions for the NCLEX Examination (pp. 78-79) Drug Administration Performance Checklists Critical Thinking Questions

12.3 Homework/Assignments:

12.3 Instructor's Notes/Student Feedback:

12 Lecture Outline
Parenteral Administration: Intravenous Route

Slide 1

Chapter 12
Parental Administration:
Intravenous Route

Slide 2

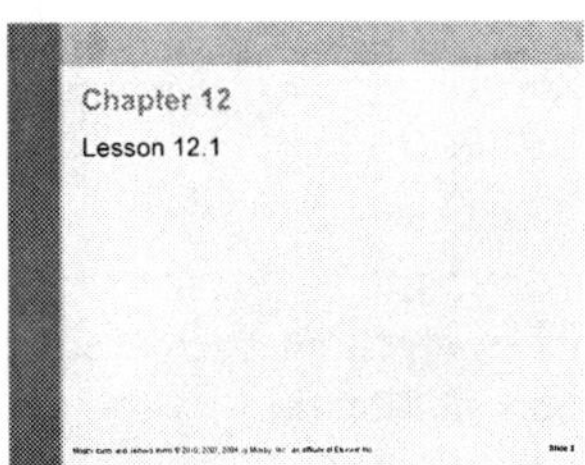
Chapter 12
Lesson 12.1

Slide 3

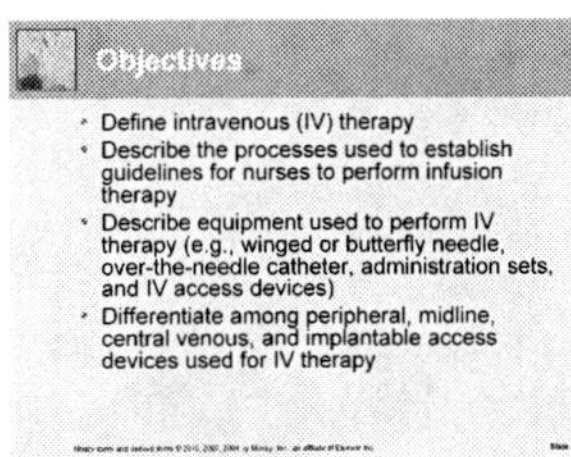
Objectives
Define intravenous (IV) therapy
Describe the processes used to establish guidelines for nurses to perform infusion therapy
Describe equipment used to perform IV therapy (e.g., winged or butterfly needle, over-the-needle catheter, administration sets, and IV access devices)
Differentiate among peripheral, midline, central venous, and implantable access devices used for IV therapy

Slide 4

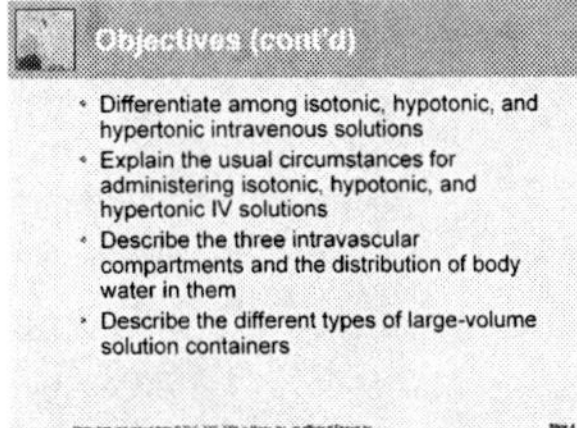
Objectives (cont'd)
Differentiate among isotonic, hypotonic, and hypertonic intravenous solutions
Explain the usual circumstances for administering isotonic, hypotonic, and hypertonic IV solutions
Describe the three intravascular compartments and the distribution of body water in them
Describe the different types of large-volume solution containers

Slide 5

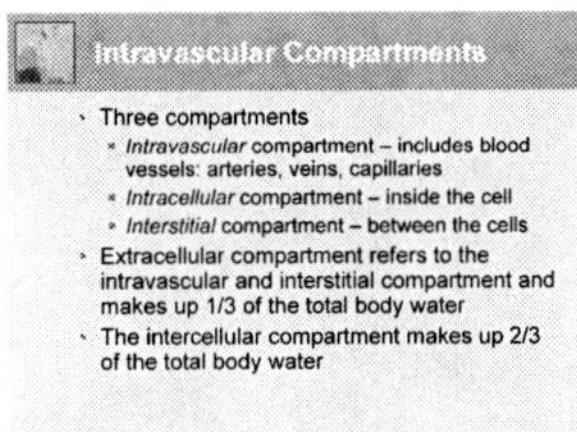
Intravascular Compartments
Three compartments
Intravascular compartment – includes blood vessels: arteries, veins, capillaries
Intracellular compartment – inside the cell
Interstitial compartment – between the cells
Extracellular compartment refers to the intravascular and interstitial compartment and makes up 1/3 of the total body water
The intercellular compartment makes up 2/3 of the total body water

ELSEVIER

Slide 6

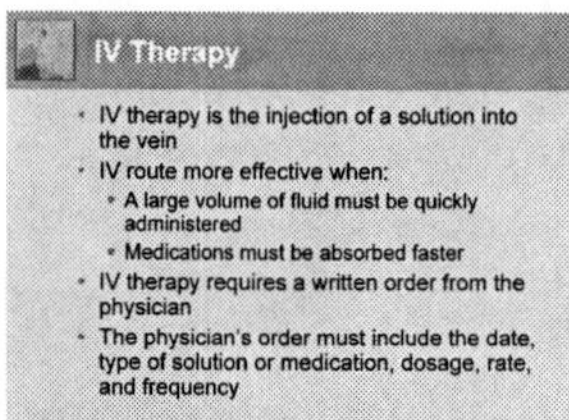
IV Therapy
IV therapy is the injection of a solution into the vein
IV route more effective when:
A large volume of fluid must be quickly administered
Medications must be absorbed faster
IV therapy requires a written order from the physician
The physician's order must include the date, type of solution or medication, dosage, rate, and frequency

- Guidelines for IV therapy are delineated in the scope of practice for each state, by the state board of nursing, and by the institutional agency policy. In general, LPN responsibilities do not include IV administration of medication, blood products, or neoplastic agents.

Slide 7

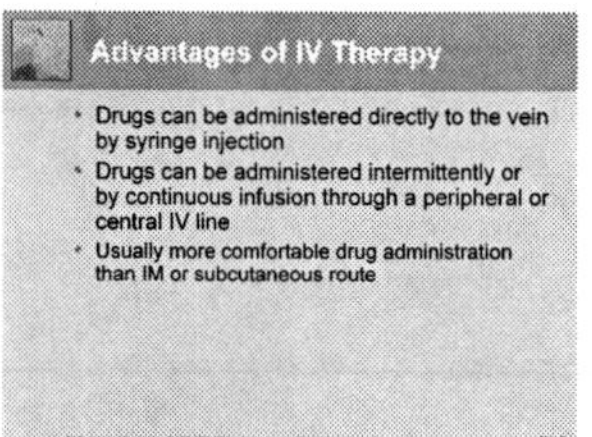
Advantages of IV Therapy
Drugs can be administered directly to the vein by syringe injection
Drugs can be administered intermittently or by continuous infusion through a peripheral or central IV line
Usually more comfortable drug administration than IM or subcutaneous route

Slide 8

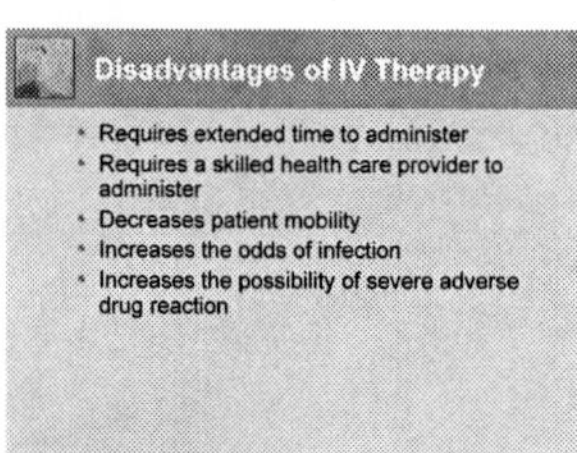
Disadvantages of IV Therapy
Requires extended time to administer
Requires a skilled health care provider to administer
Decreases patient mobility
Increases the odds of infection
Increases the possibility of severe adverse drug reaction

- Signs of infection at the IV site include redness, swelling, increased tenderness, as well as any signs and symptoms of infection.
- An adverse reaction may be immediate or it may occur after a few doses, depending on the infusion.

Slide 9

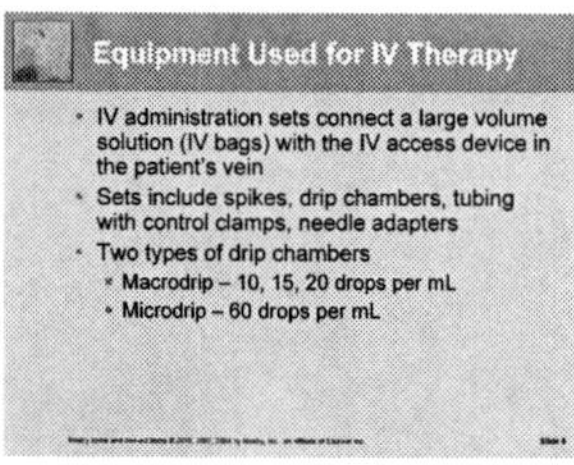
Equipment Used for IV Therapy
IV administration sets connect a large volume solution (IV bags) with the IV access device in the patient's vein
Sets include spikes, drip chambers, tubing with control clamps, needle adapters
Two types of drip chambers
Macrodrip – 10, 15, 20 drops per mL
Microdrip – 60 drops per mL

- The type of system a particular hospital uses is based on agreements established with medical suppliers through central supply.

Slide 10

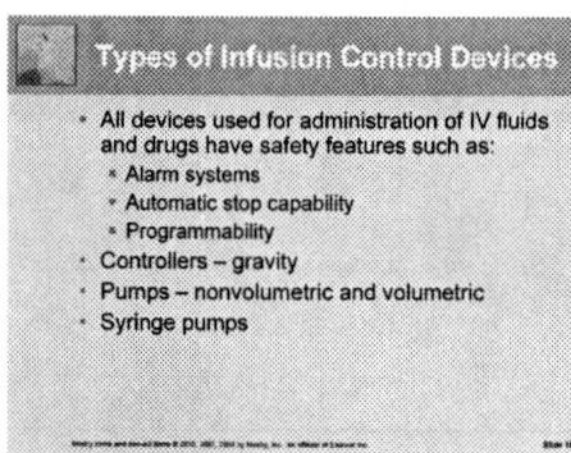
Types of Infusion Control Devices
All devices used for administration of IV fluids and drugs have safety features such as:
Alarm systems
Automatic stop capability
Programmability
Controllers – gravity
Pumps – nonvolumetric and volumetric
Syringe pumps

- Gravity controllers allow the nurse to regulate the rate of the infusion using a roller clamp.
- Volumetric pumps are programmed for a specific volume to be infused.

Slide 11

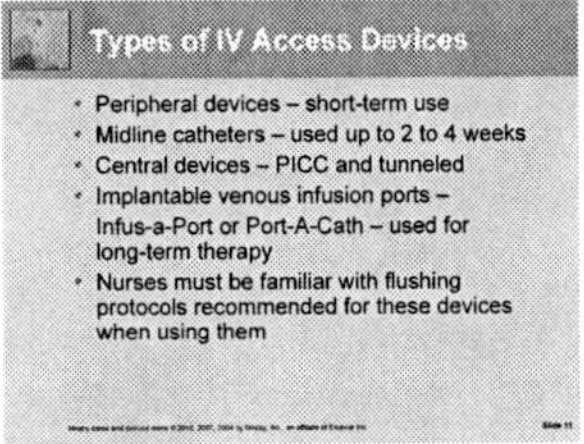
Types of IV Access Devices
Peripheral devices – short-term use
Midline catheters – used up to 2 to 4 weeks
Central devices – PICC and tunneled
Implantable venous infusion ports – Infus-a-Port or Port-A-Cath – used for long-term therapy
Nurses must be familiar with flushing protocols recommended for these devices when using them

- Peripheral devices commonly use veins in the hand or forearm.
- Midline catheters can be inserted into cephalic or basilic veins and advanced to the superior vena cava.
- Central venous sites used are commonly the subclavian and jugular veins.

Slide 12

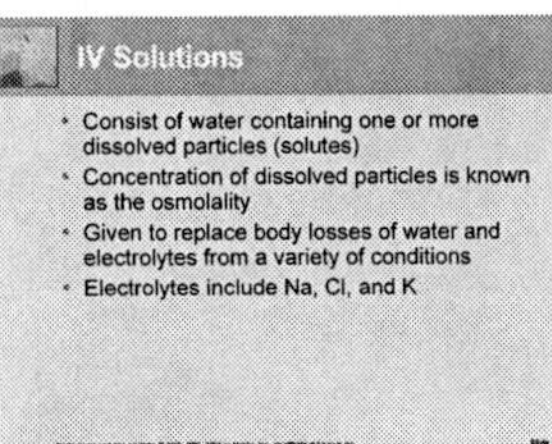
IV Solutions
Consist of water containing one or more dissolved particles (solutes)
Concentration of dissolved particles is known as the osmolality
Given to replace body losses of water and electrolytes from a variety of conditions
Electrolytes include Na, Cl, and K

- Electrolytes are solutes that dissolve in water and dissociate into ion particles.

Slide 13

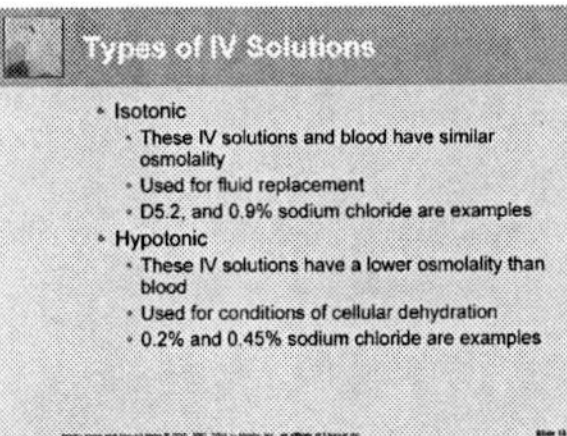
Types of IV Solutions
Isotonic
These IV solutions and blood have similar osmolality
Used for fluid replacement
D5.2, and 0.9% sodium chloride are examples
Hypotonic
These IV solutions have a lower osmolality than blood
Used for conditions of cellular dehydration
0.2% and 0.45% sodium chloride are examples

Slide 14

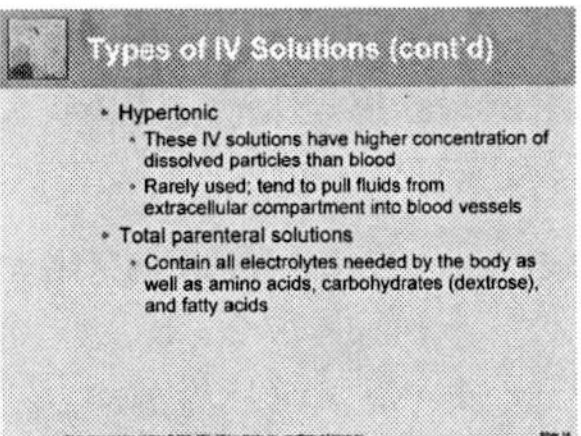
Types of IV Solutions (cont'd)
Hypertonic
These IV solutions have higher concentration of dissolved particles than blood
Rarely used; tend to pull fluids from extracellular compartment into blood vessels
Total parenteral solutions
Contain all electrolytes needed by the body as well as amino acids, carbohydrates (dextrose), and fatty acids

Slide 15

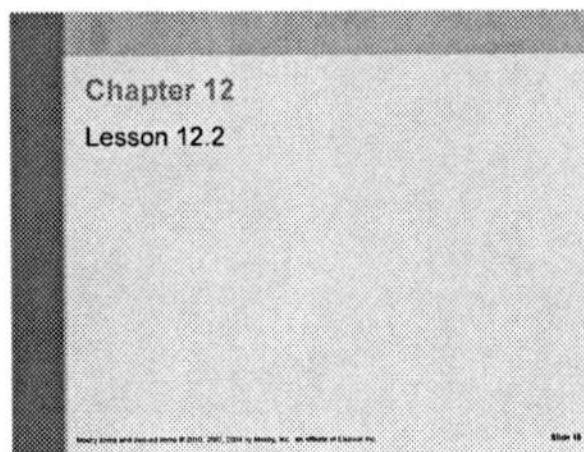
Chapter 12
Lesson 12.2

Slide 16

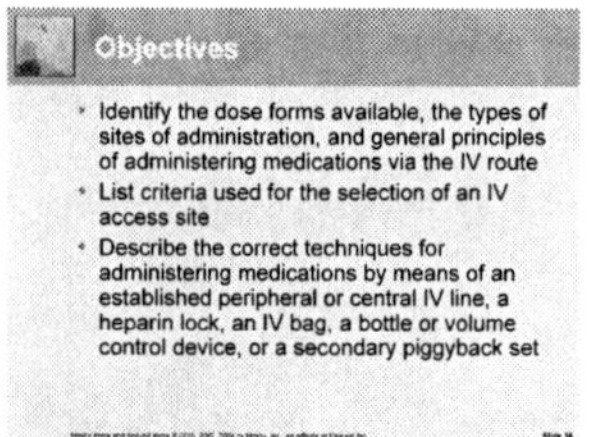
Objectives
Identify the dose forms available, the types of sites of administration, and general principles of administering medications via the IV route
List criteria used for the selection of an IV access site
Describe the correct techniques for administering medications by means of an established peripheral or central IV line, a heparin lock, an IV bag, a bottle or volume control device, or a secondary piggyback set

Slide 17

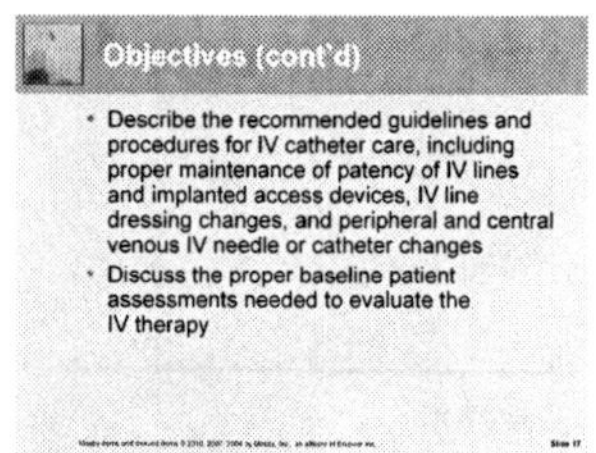
Objectives (cont'd)
Describe the recommended guidelines and procedures for IV catheter care, including proper maintenance of patency of IV lines and implanted access devices, IV line dressing changes, and peripheral and central venous IV needle or catheter changes
Discuss the proper baseline patient assessments needed to evaluate the IV therapy

Slide 18

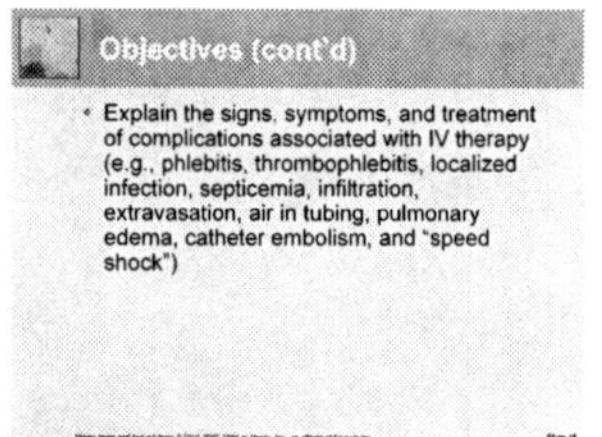
Objectives (cont'd)
Explain the signs, symptoms, and treatment of complications associated with IV therapy (e.g., phlebitis, thrombophlebitis, localized infection, septicemia, infiltration, extravasation, air in tubing, pulmonary edema, catheter embolism, and "speed shock")

Slide 19

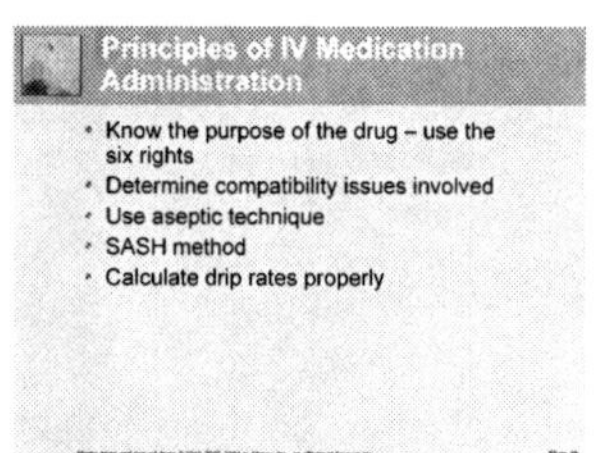
Principles of IV Medication Administration
Know the purpose of the drug – use the six rights
Determine compatibility issues involved
Use aseptic technique
SASH method
Calculate drip rates properly

- Review equipment necessary for administering IV medications via peripheral and central routes.
- IV sites are chosen depending on the intended use: long term, short term, type of drug, etc.
- SASH method is used for catheters that need heparin instilled in them to keep them patent.

Slide 20

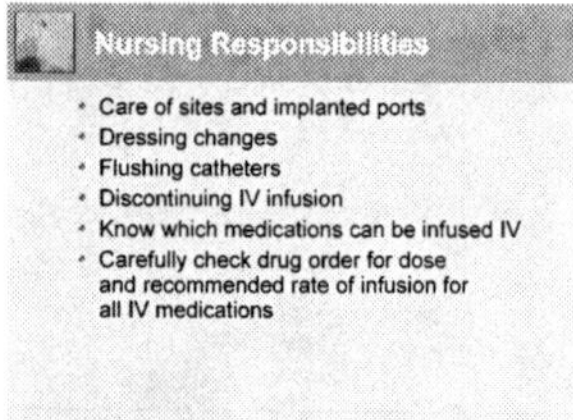
Nursing Responsibilities
Care of sites and implanted ports
Dressing changes
Flushing catheters
Discontinuing IV infusion
Know which medications can be infused IV
Carefully check drug order for dose and recommended rate of infusion for all IV medications

- Venipuncture site dressings should be changed when they become damp, loose, or soiled, and according to the recommendations from the company that manufactures them.

ELSEVIER

Slide 21

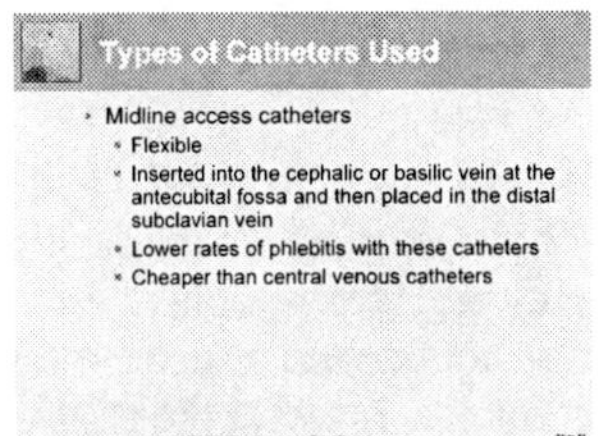
Types of Catheters Used
Midline access catheters
Flexible
Inserted into the cephalic or basilic vein at the antecubital fossa and then placed in the distal subclavian vein
Lower rates of phlebitis with these catheters
Cheaper than central venous catheters

Slide 22

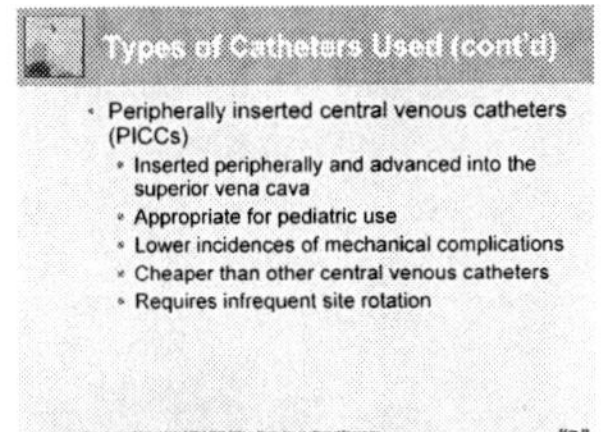
Types of Catheters Used (cont'd)
Peripherally inserted central venous catheters (PICCs)
Inserted peripherally and advanced into the superior vena cava
Appropriate for pediatric use
Lower incidences of mechanical complications
Cheaper than other central venous catheters
Requires infrequent site rotation

Slide 23

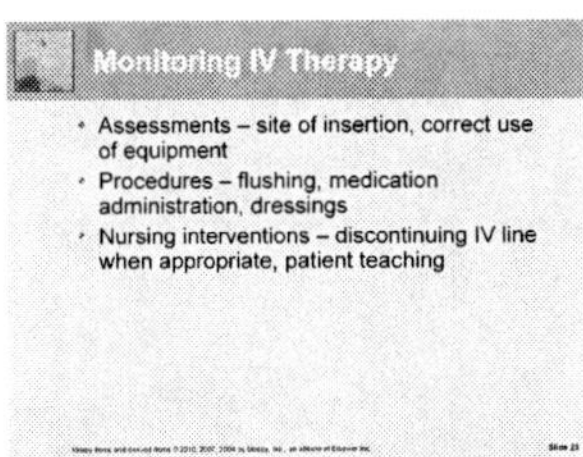
Monitoring IV Therapy
Assessments – site of insertion, correct use of equipment
Procedures – flushing, medication administration, dressings
Nursing interventions – discontinuing IV line when appropriate, patient teaching

- Assessments include watching for signs and symptoms of infection: elevated temperature, redness, swelling, drainage.
- Interventions include using the proper flushing protocol, checking the condition of the insertion site, checking when tubing needs to be changed, and checking dressings according to policy.
- Patient teaching includes learning the signs and symptoms of infection.

Slide 24

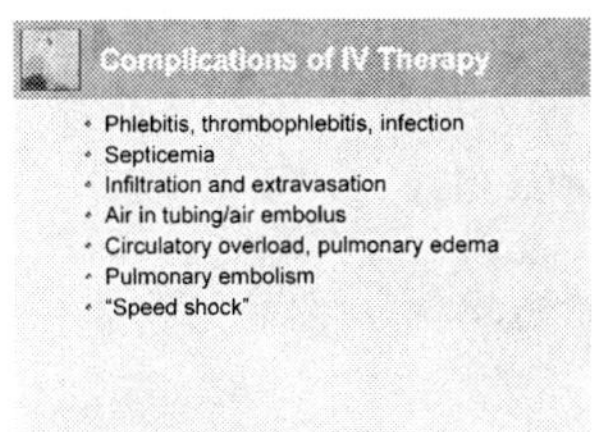
Complications of IV Therapy
Phlebitis, thrombophlebitis, infection
Septicemia
Infiltration and extravasation
Air in tubing/air embolus
Circulatory overload, pulmonary edema
Pulmonary embolism
"Speed shock"

13 Lesson Plan
Drugs Affecting the Autonomic Nervous System

TEACHING FOCUS

In this chapter, students will have an opportunity to learn about the autonomic nervous system (ANS) and the various drug classes that affect its function. Students will have the opportunity to learn about medications that mimic the actions produced by the autonomic nerve system (adrenergic agents and cholinergic agents) and those that block or prohibit these actions (alpha- and beta-adrenergic blocking agents and anticholinergic agents). In addition to explaining the actions and uses of these medications, this chapter reviews the nursing process for assessing, planning, implementing, and evaluating the administration of drugs that affect the ANS. Finally, common and serious adverse effects will also be discussed.

MATERIALS AND RESOURCES

- ☐ computer and PowerPoint projector (all Lessons)
- ☐ guest speaker: family nurse practitioner

LESSON CHECKLIST

Preparations for this lesson include:

- lecture
- evaluation of student knowledge and skills needed to perform all entry-level activities related to understanding the different classes of drugs that affect the ANS, including:
  - identifying receptors of the ANS
  - understanding the effect of adrenergic agents on the ANS
  - understanding how alpha- and beta-adrenergic blocking works on specific nerve receptors
  - understanding the effect of cholinergic agents on the ANS
  - understanding the effect of anticholinergic agents on the ANS
  - applying the nursing process of assessing, planning, implementing, and evaluating the use of these medications

KEY TERMS

acetylcholine (p. 200)
adrenergic agents (p. 200)
adrenergic blocking agents (p. 200)
adrenergic fibers (p. 200)
afferent nerves (p. 199)
alpha receptor (p. 200)
anticholinergic agents (p. 200)
autonomic nervous system (p. 200)
beta receptor (p. 200)
catecholamines (p. 200)
central nervous system (p. 199)
cholinergic agents (p. 200)
cholinergic fibers (p. 200)
dopaminergic receptors (p. 200)
efferent nerves (p. 199)
motor nervous system (p. 200)
neurons (p. 200)
neurotransmitters (p. 200)
norepinephrine (p. 200)
peripheral nervous system (p. 199)
synapse (p. 200)

ELSEVIER

ADDITIONAL RESOURCES

PowerPoint slides: 1-20
Flashcards, Decks 1 and 2

Legend

ARQ	PPT	TB	CTQ	SG	INRQ
Audience Response Questions	PowerPoint Slides	Test Bank	Critical Thinking Questions	Study Guide	Interactive NCLEX Review Questions

Class Activities are indicated in ***bold italic.***

LESSON 13.1

BACKGROUND ASSESSMENT

Question: What are the functions of the ANS? Why is it called the "involuntary" nervous system?
Answer: The ANS is a subdivision of the central nervous system (CNS), which controls body response by sending signals through efferent nerves, which carry impulses to other parts of the body. The efferent system is divided into two systems: the motor nervous system, which controls skeletal muscle contractions, and the ANS, which regulates body functions, such as heart rate, blood pressure, thermal control, light regulation of the eyes, gastrointestinal secretion and motility, urinary bladder function, and sweating. The system is known as "involuntary" because a person has little control over it. The body performs autonomic controls based on what the body tells the system that it needs.

Question: What are the four different drug classes for the ANS, and what are their specific functions?
Answer: The four different drug classes are adrenergic agents, alpha- and beta-adrenergic blocking agents, cholinergic agents, and anticholinergic agents. The adrenergic agents stimulate the sympathetic nervous system; they are used for their effects on the heart, blood vessels, and bronchi. The alpha- and beta-adrenergic blocking agents block the sympathetic nervous system receptors from the effects of catecholamines to produce a parasympathetic response. The cholinergic agents also stimulate the parasympathetic system, whereas the anticholinergic agents block the cholinergic receptors from the action of acetylcholine.

CRITICAL THINKING QUESTION

A new student is confused about the division of the nervous system and the location of the ANS. What information could a nurse provide to teach the student about the structure, functions, and divisions of the nervous system?
Guidelines: The nurse could explain to the student that the human nervous system is divided into the CNS and the peripheral nervous system (PNS). The PNS is further divided into afferent neurons, which bring impulses to the brain in the form of sensory messages, and efferent neurons, which take impulses away from the brain and spinal cord to the body in the form of motor messages. The efferent neurons are divided into the somatic nervous system and the ANS. The former is responsible for voluntary actions, such as moving an arm or leg, and the latter for involuntary actions, such as heart rate and digestion. The ANS is divided into the sympathetic nervous system and the parasympathetic nervous system.

ELSEVIER

OBJECTIVES	CONTENT	TEACHING RESOURCES
Differentiate between afferent and efferent nerve conduction in the central nervous system.	■ The central and autonomic nervous systems (p. 199) Review the nervous system functions, including afferent and efferent nerve endings and neurotransmitters.	PPT 5-7 ARQ 2 TB Multiple Response questions 2, 4 SG Review Sheet questions 1-4 (p. 81) SG Learning Activities questions 1, 19-20 (pp. 84-85) Table 13-1 Actions of Autonomic Nerve Impulses on Specific Tissues (p. 201) ▸ Discuss the types of body functions regulated by the ANS. Class Activity ***Divide the class into small groups, and have each group prepare an explanation of afferent and efferent nerves, along with body functions regulated by the ANS. Have volunteers from each group present its explanation to the class.***
Explain the role of neurotransmitters at synaptic junctions.	■ The central and autonomic nervous systems (p. 199)	PPT 8 Animation: Epinephrine SG Review Sheet question 2 (p. 81) SG Learning Activities questions 2, 21 (pp. 84-85) ▸ Discuss the difference between excitatory and inhibiting neurotransmitters. Class Activity ***Divide the class into small groups, and have each group make a drawing of two neurons connected by a synaptic junction. Students should label the parts of the neurons, including the receptors. Then each group should present an explanation of excitatory and inhibitory neurotransmitters to the class.***
Name the most common neurotransmitters known to affect central nervous system function.	■ The central and autonomic nervous systems (p. 199)	PPT 9-10 TB Multiple Response question 6 Figure 13-1 (p. 202), Receptors of the autonomic nervous system ▸ Discuss how control of neurotransmitters is a primary way to alleviate symptoms associated with disease. Give examples of possible drug treatments for diseases related to the CNS. Class Activity ***Ask students to identify the most common neurotransmitters of the ANS. Students should characterize each***

ELSEVIER

OBJECTIVES	CONTENT	TEACHING RESOURCES
		neurotransmitter as inhibitory or excitatory and describe how pharmacologic agents are used to regulate neurotransmitters.
Identify the two major neurotransmitters of the autonomic nervous system.	■ Autonomic nervous system (p. 200)	TB Multiple Choice question 9 SG Learning Activities questions 3-4 (p. 84) Figure 13-1 (p. 202), Receptors of the autonomic nervous system ▸ Discuss the meaning of the term "autonomic." Why is the ANS sometimes called the involuntary nervous system? Class Activity ***Ask students to characterize the effects of norepinephrine and acetylcholine and to list the similarities and differences between the two. What is the role of these neurotransmitters in the functioning of the ANS?***
Cite the names of nerve endings that liberate acetylcholine and those that liberate norepinephrine.	■ Autonomic nervous system (p. 200)	TB Multiple Choice question 8 SG Review Sheet questions 4-6 (p. 81) ▸ Discuss how organs react differently to adrenergic and cholinergic fibers. Class Activity ***As a class, discuss the cholinergic and adrenergic fibers and the organs they innervate. What are the effects of adrenergic and cholinergic agents on various organs? Discuss the role of the presynaptic membrane, synaptic cleft, and the postsynaptic receptors in the process of neural transmission.***
Explain the action of drugs that inhibit the actions of cholinergic and adrenergic fibers.	■ Autonomic nervous system (p. 200) Review the effects of cholinergic agents as similar to acetylcholine. Discuss the indirect-acting cholinergic agents that inhibit the metabolism of acetylcholine. Review the uses of these drugs; for example, in patients with glaucoma and urinary system diseases.	PPT 10 SG Review Sheet questions 7-10, 29 (pp. 81, 83) SG Learning Activities questions 9-10 (p. 84) Figure 13-1 (p. 202), Receptors of the autonomic nervous system ▸ Discuss the inhibitors in Figure 13-1. Class Activity ***Divide the class into small groups, and assign each group one of the adrenergic-receptor or cholinergic-receptor drug groups. Each group will discuss and identify the action that its particular group inhibits and then present its findings to the class.*** Class Activity ***Ask each student to write a cholinergic and adrenergic drug name on a***

OBJECTIVES	CONTENT	TEACHING RESOURCES
		card. Each student should then ask the class to identify the drug's action and group.
List the neurotransmitters responsible for cholinergic activity.	■ Autonomic nervous system (p. 200)	SG Review Sheet question 5 (p. 81) SG Learning Activities questions 8, 23 (pp. 84-85) ▸ Discuss the neurotransmitters responsible for cholinergic activity (see Figure 13-1). Class Activity ***Have students work in small groups, and ask each group to research the cholinergic activity of a different neurotransmitter. Have each group present its findings to the class. Discuss the similarities and differences among the various neurotransmitters.***
Identify two broad classes of drugs used to stimulate the adrenergic nervous system.	□ Drug class: adrenergic agents (p. 200) – Actions (p. 200) Review the alpha, beta, and dopaminergic receptors and their role in the autonomic nervous system	PPT 11-13 INRQ 7-8 Animation: Dopamine Release SG Review Sheet question 11 (p. 81) Drug Table 13-2 Adrenergic Agents (p. 203) ▸ Discuss which receptors cause vasoconstriction of blood vessels when stimulated. Which action would result in an increased heart rate? Class Activity ***Divide the class into small groups, and ask each group to create a chart that displays the three categories of the adrenergic system. Each category should include a description of the action created. Groups should present their findings to the class.*** Class Activity ***Discuss the nursing process for patients taking adrenergic agents, including appropriate premedication assessment, and evaluation of adverse effects. What drug interactions may increase the therapeutic or toxic effects of the adrenergic agent?***
Name the neurotransmitters that are called catecholamines.	□ Drug class: adrenergic agents (p. 200) – Actions (p. 200)	PPT 11-13 SG Learning Activities question 5 (p. 84) ▸ Discuss the difference between catecholamines and noncatecholamines. What are the body's naturally occurring catecholamines? Class Activity ***Divide the class into small groups. Ask the groups to discuss the role of***

OBJECTIVES	CONTENT	TEACHING RESOURCES
		catecholamines in the ANS. Students should identify the naturally occurring neurotransmitter catecholamines and indicate where they are secreted. *Class Activity* ***Call out the names of neurotransmitters, and ask students to identify which ones are catecholamines.***
Review the actions of adrenergic agents to identify conditions that would be affected favorably and unfavorably by these medications.	□ Drug class: adrenergic agents (p. 200) – Actions (p. 200) – Uses (p. 201) – Nursing process for adrenergic agents (p. 201)	INRQ 11 CTQ 1, 3 Animation: Dopamine Release SG Review Sheet questions 8-10, 12, 14-15, 29 (pp. 81-83) SG Learning Activities question 9 (p. 84) Drug Table 13-2 Adrenergic Agents (p. 203) ▸ Discuss which drugs act on more than one type of adrenergic receptor. *Class Activity* ***Call out a condition (e.g., emphysema, preterm labor, hypertension, common cold), and ask students to respond by indicating whether the action of an adrenergic agent would favorably or unfavorably affect the condition.***

13.1 Homework/Assignments:

13.1 Instructor's Notes/Student Feedback:

LESSON 13.2

CRITICAL THINKING QUESTION

A 25-year-old female is diagnosed with myasthenia gravis. Her health care provider tells her that he will prescribe a cholinergic medication for her condition. How does the nurse answer if the patient asks what this means and what effect it will have on her?

Guidelines: The nurse should explain to the patient that the cholinergic medication would act on the PNS, stimulating effects similar to acetylcholine. The actions of the PNS are described as resting or vegetative functions, including digestion, excretion, and cardiac deceleration. The action of the medication will slow

heart rate, increase gastrointestinal motility and secretions, and increase contractions of the urinary bladder, so she may experience nausea and vomiting, diarrhea, abdominal cramping, dizziness, low blood pressure, and urinary frequency. The medication will probably be started gradually until the maximal benefit is obtained. The patient should be instructed not to take antihistamines with this new medication because they may antagonize the effects.

OBJECTIVES	CONTENT	TEACHING RESOURCES
Explain the rationale for use of adrenergic blocking agents for conditions that have vasoconstriction as part of the disease pathophysiology.	□ Drug class: alpha- and beta-adrenergic blocking agents (p. 204) – Actions (p. 204) – Uses (p. 204) – Nursing process for beta-adrenergic blocking agents (p. 204)	PPT 17 CTQ 4 Animation: Beta Blockers SG Review Sheet question 16 (p. 82) ▸ Discuss which blocking agents are used in patients with diseases associated with vasoconstriction. Give some examples of diseases and list the medications that might be prescribed for them. Class Activity ***One week before class, each student should research various diseases that have a pathophysiology of vasoconstriction, such as Raynaud's phenomenon. In small groups, ask students to discuss why adrenergic blocking agents would help the symptoms of a disease process characterized by vasoconstriction. (For students to prepare for this activity, see Homework/Assignments #1.)*** Class Activity ***Divide the class in half and have one half represent the alpha-blocking agents, and the other half represent the beta-blocking agents. List on the board adverse effects: palpitations, tachycardia, dizziness, tremors, flushing, hypotension, hypertension, chest pain, dysrhythmias. Have the groups explain if they would be responsible for causing these symptoms. Review the exercise with the class.***
Describe the benefits of using beta-adrenergic blocking agents for hypertension, angina pectoris, cardiac dysrhythmias, and hyperthyroidism.	□ Drug class: alpha- and beta-adrenergic blocking agents (p. 204) – Uses (p. 204) – Nursing process for beta-adrenergic blocking agents (p. 204)	PPT 17-18 INRQ 1-2, 4-5 CTQ 3 Animation: Beta Blockers SG Review Sheet questions 16, 29 (pp. 82-83) Review Questions for the NCLEX Examination 2, 5 (p. 209) Drug Table 13-3 Beta-adrenergic blocking agents (p. 205) ▸ Discuss potential adverse effects in patients using beta-adrenergic blocking agents. When should they be used with extreme caution?

OBJECTIVES	CONTENT	TEACHING RESOURCES
		Class Activity ***Have the students identify if the following are alpha or beta blocking agents:*** – ***Atenolol*** – ***Carvedilol*** – ***Prazosin*** – ***Phentolamine*** – ***Labetalol*** ***Then have the students identify the action of each drug. Do some drugs have both alpha- and beta-adrenergic properties? Next have the students discuss the adverse effects that can occur when beta-adrenergic blocking agents are used.*** Class Activity ***Divide the class into pairs. Have each pair develop a teaching plan for a patient who has been prescribed a beta-adrenergic drug. Allow class time for sharing.***
Identify disease conditions that preclude the use of beta-adrenergic blocking agents.	□ Drug class: alpha- and beta-adrenergic blocking agents (p. 204) – Uses (p. 204) – Nursing process for beta-adrenergic blocking agents (p. 204)	PPT 17-18 CTQ 1, 5 SG Review Sheet questions 16-17, 19 (p. 82) ▸ Discuss why you should use extreme caution when using beta-adrenergic blockers for patients with emphysema. Class Activity ***Write a list of disease conditions on the board, such as asthma, hypertension, heart failure, diabetes mellitus, angina pectoris, and bronchitis. Ask students to identify whether beta-adrenergic blocking agents can be given for each condition. Ask students to describe the rationale for avoiding use of a beta-adrenergic blocking agent for various conditions.*** Class Activity ***Invite a family nurse practitioner as a guest speaker to discuss treatment options and education for those patients with hypertension and heart disease.***
List the predictable adverse effects of cholinergic agents.	□ Drug class: cholinergic agents (p. 206) – Actions (p. 206) – Uses (p. 206) – Nursing process for cholinergic agents (p. 206)	PPT 19 SG Review Sheet questions 18, 29 (pp. 82-83) Drug Table 13-4 Cholinergic Agents (p. 207) ▸ Discuss how cholinergic agents are used for patients with disorders of the eye. ▸ Discuss some common uses of cholinergic agents. What are some adverse effects one might expect in patients taking cholinergic agents?

OBJECTIVES	CONTENT	TEACHING RESOURCES
		Class Activity ***List the known symptoms that are effects of cholinergic agents: nausea, vomiting, diarrhea, abdominal cramping, dizziness, hypotension, bronchospasm, wheezing, and bradycardia. Have the class determine which effects are common and which are serious. Discuss the importance of patient education with these drugs.***
Describe the clinical uses of anticholinergic agents.	□ Drug class: anticholinergic agents (p. 207) – Actions (p. 207) – Uses (p. 207) Review the actions of anticholinergic agents. Discuss their use in the treatment of GI disorders, ophthalmic disorders, preoperatively, and other reasons.	PPT 20 CTQ 2 Animation: Atropine Drug Table 13-5 Anticholinergic Agents (p. 208) ▸ Discuss how anticholinergic agents affect the ANS. What diseases might this be relevant to? Class Activity ***Have students identify the following drugs as cholinergic or anticholinergic agents and provide one clinical use for the drug:*** – ***Atropine*** – ***Physostigmine*** – ***Belladonna*** – ***Propantheline*** – ***Guanidine***
List the predictable adverse effects of anticholinergic agents.	– Nursing process for anticholinergic agents (p. 207)	INRQ 9-10 SG Review Sheet questions 23, 28 (pp. 82-83) Review Question for the NCLEX Examination 4 (p. 209) ▸ Discuss some common adverse effects a patient might experience when receiving an anticholinergic agent. Which ones should be reported immediately? Class Activity ***List the known symptoms that are effects of anticholinergic agents: blurred vision; constipation; urinary retention; dryness of the mouth, nose, and throat; confusion; depression; nightmares; hallucinations. Have the class determine which effects are common and which are serious. Discuss the importance of patient education with these drugs.***
Performance evaluation		Test Bank SG Learning Activities (pp. 84-85) SG Practice Questions for the NCLEX Examination (pp. 86-87) Critical Thinking Questions

13.2 Homework/Assignments:
1. One week before class, each student should research various diseases that have a pathophysiology of vasoconstriction.

13.2 Instructor's Notes/Student Feedback:

13 Lecture Outline
Drugs Affecting the Autonomic Nervous System

Slide 1

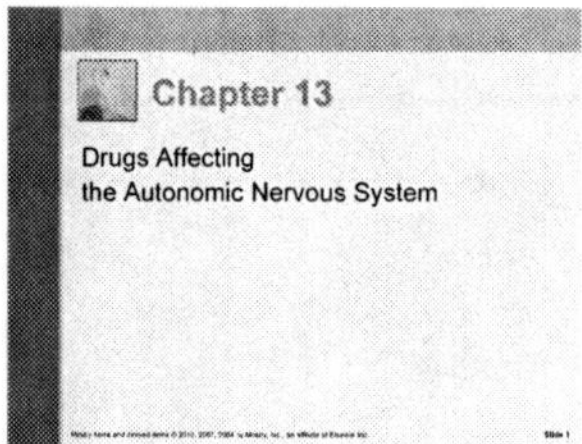
Chapter 13
Drugs Affecting
the Autonomic Nervous System

Slide 2

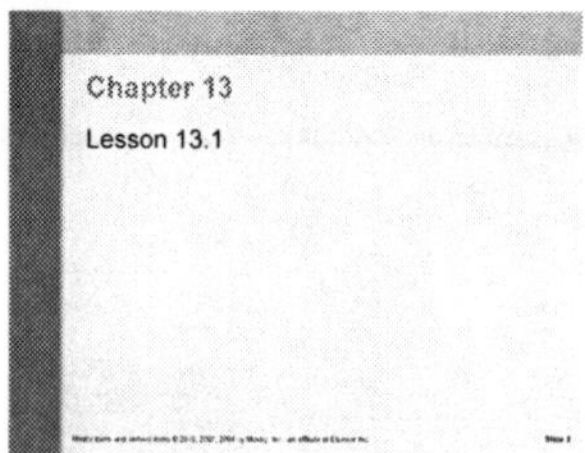
Chapter 13
Lesson 13.1

Slide 3

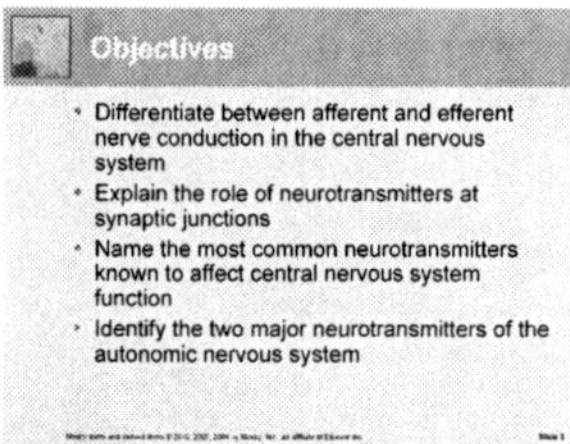
Objectives
Differentiate between afferent and efferent nerve conduction in the central nervous system
Explain the role of neurotransmitters at synaptic junctions
Name the most common neurotransmitters known to affect central nervous system function
Identify the two major neurotransmitters of the autonomic nervous system

Slide 4

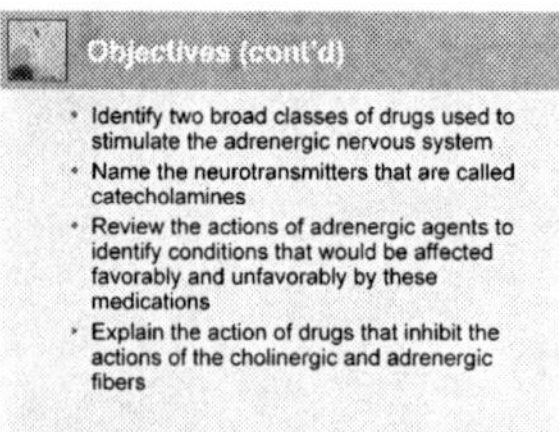
Objectives (cont'd)
Identify two broad classes of drugs used to stimulate the adrenergic nervous system
Name the neurotransmitters that are called catecholamines
Review the actions of adrenergic agents to identify conditions that would be affected favorably and unfavorably by these medications
Explain the action of drugs that inhibit the actions of the cholinergic and adrenergic fibers

Slide 5

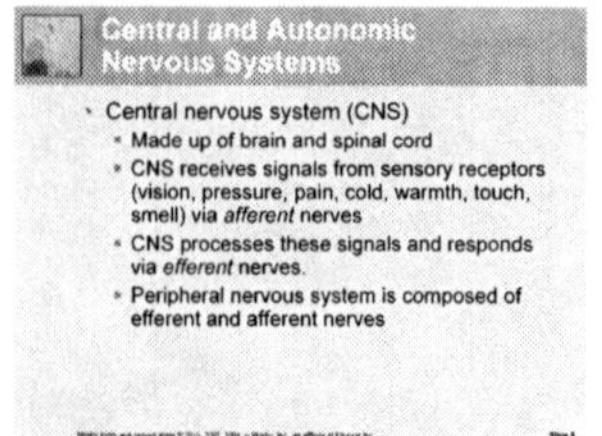
Central and Autonomic Nervous Systems
Central nervous system (CNS)
Made up of brain and spinal cord
CNS receives signals from sensory receptors (vision, pressure, pain, cold, warmth, touch, smell) via afferent nerves
CNS processes these signals and responds via efferent nerves.
Peripheral nervous system is composed of efferent and afferent nerves

- Think of how a person's world would be different if he or she were missing one of these signals, such as vision or pain.

Slide 6

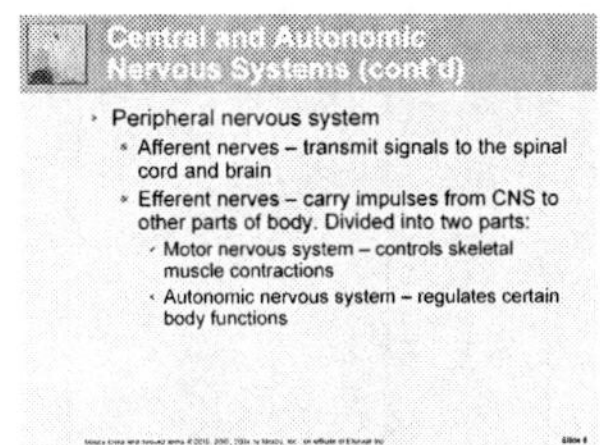
Central and Autonomic Nervous Systems (cont'd)
Peripheral nervous system
Afferent nerves – transmit signals to the spinal cord and brain
Efferent nerves – carry impulses from CNS to other parts of body. Divided into two parts:
Motor nervous system – controls skeletal muscle contractions
Autonomic nervous system – regulates certain body functions

- Name some of the body functions that the autonomic nervous system regulates. *(Heart rate, blood pressure, temperature, light regulation by the eyes)*

Slide 7

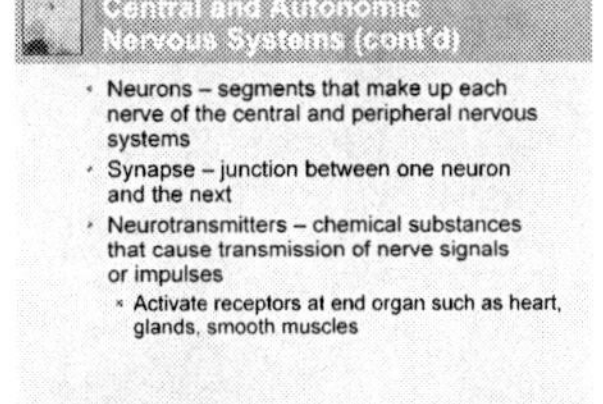
Central and Autonomic Nervous Systems (cont'd)
Neurons – segments that make up each nerve of the central and peripheral nervous systems
Synapse – junction between one neuron and the next
Neurotransmitters – chemical substances that cause transmission of nerve signals or impulses
Activate receptors at end organ such as heart, glands, smooth muscles

- For the neuron: hold out your arm and spread your fingers. Your hand represents the cell body (also called the soma); your fingers represent dendrites bringing information to the cell body; your arm represents the axon, taking information away from the cell body.
- The synapse is the space between your hand and another person's hand.

Slide 8

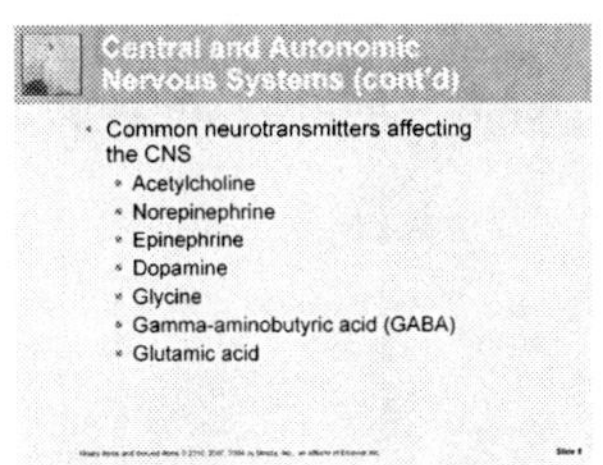
Central and Autonomic Nervous Systems (cont'd)
Common neurotransmitters affecting the CNS
Acetylcholine
Norepinephrine
Epinephrine
Dopamine
Glycine
Gamma-aminobutyric acid (GABA)
Glutamic acid

- Neurotransmitter regulation by pharmacologic agents is a major mechanism for controlling diseases caused by either an excess or deficiency neurotransmitters. There are at least 30 different types of neurotransmitters.
- Parkinson's disease is affected by neurotransmitter regulation.

Slide 9

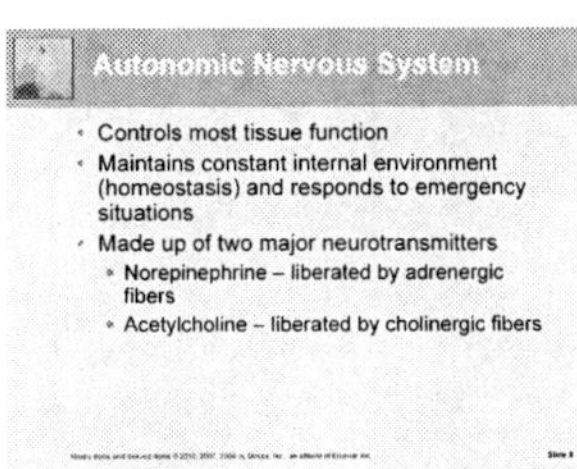
Autonomic Nervous System
Controls most tissue function
Maintains constant internal environment (homeostasis) and responds to emergency situations
Made up of two major neurotransmitters
Norepinephrine – liberated by adrenergic fibers
Acetylcholine – liberated by cholinergic fibers

- The two systems of the autonomic nervous system are sympathetic nervous system (SNS) and parasympathetic nervous system (PNS).
- Autonomic nervous system is sometimes referred to as the involuntary nervous system.

Slide 10

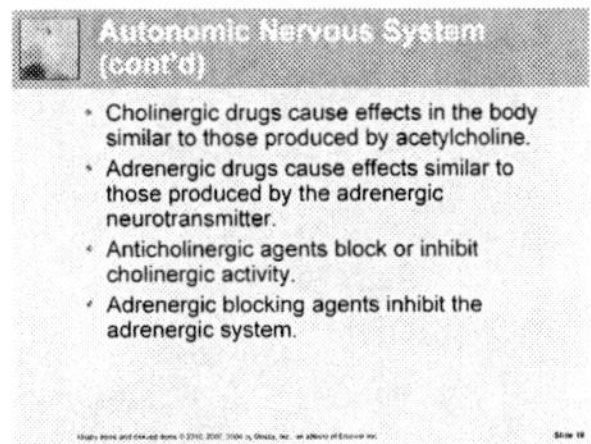
Autonomic Nervous System (cont'd)
Cholinergic drugs cause effects in the body similar to those produced by acetylcholine.
Adrenergic drugs cause effects similar to those produced by the adrenergic neurotransmitter.
Anticholinergic agents block or inhibit cholinergic activity.
Adrenergic blocking agents inhibit the adrenergic system.

- Medications that mimic the sympathetic system are known as adrenergic drugs.
- Medications that mimic the parasympathetic system are known as cholinergic drugs.
- The sympathetic system inhibits adrenergic blocking agents.
- The parasympathetic system inhibits anticholinergic agents.

Slide 11

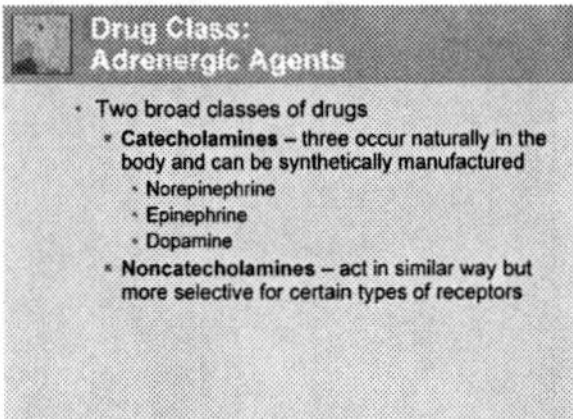
Drug Class:
Adrenergic Agents
Two broad classes of drugs
Catecholamines – three occur naturally in the body and can be synthetically manufactured
Norepinephrine
Epinephrine
Dopamine
Noncatecholamines – act in similar way but more selective for certain types of receptors

- Noncatecholamines do not work as quickly as catecholamines, are more selective for certain types of receptors, are not quite as long acting, and have a longer duration.

Slide 12

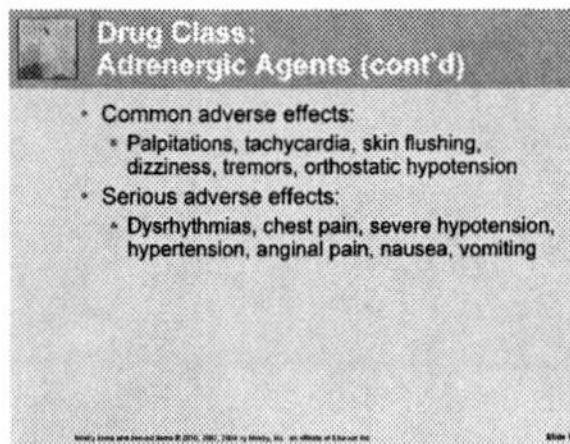
Drug Class:
Adrenergic Agents (cont'd)
Common adverse effects:
Palpitations, tachycardia, skin flushing, dizziness, tremors, orthostatic hypotension
Serious adverse effects:
Dysrhythmias, chest pain, severe hypotension, hypertension, anginal pain, nausea, vomiting

- Adverse effects are usually dose related and resolve when the drug is reduced or discontinued.

Slide 13

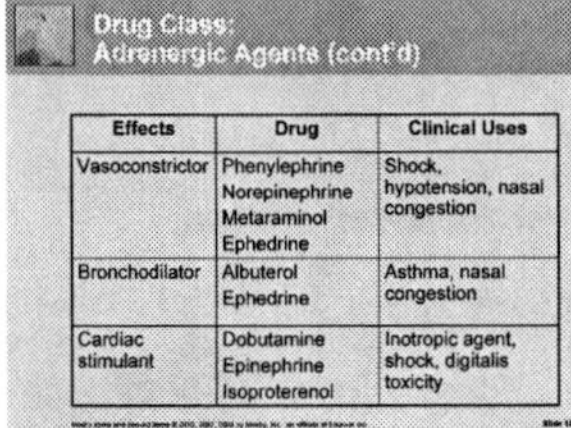
Drug Class:
Adrenergic Agents (cont'd)

Effects	Drug	Clinical Uses
Vasoconstrictor	Phenylephrine Norepinephrine Metaraminol Ephedrine	Shock, hypotension, nasal congestion
Bronchodilator	Albuterol Ephedrine	Asthma, nasal congestion
Cardiac stimulant	Dobutamine Epinephrine Isoproterenol	Inotropic agent, shock, digitalis toxicity

- For specific drug information, see Table 13-2.
- Some drugs have both effects of bronchodilator and vasoconstrictor; terbutaline is a uterine relaxant used in premature labor as well as a bronchodilator.

Slide 14

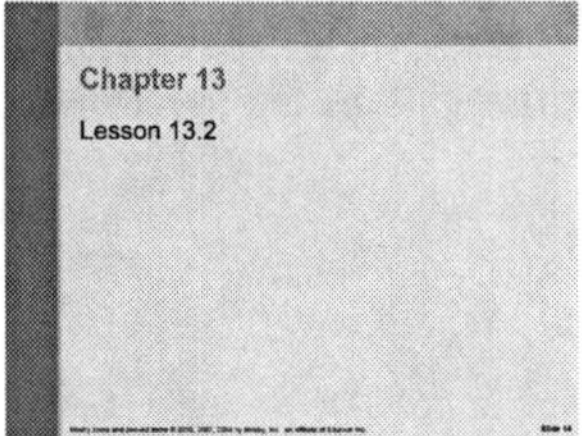
Chapter 13
Lesson 13.2

Slide 15

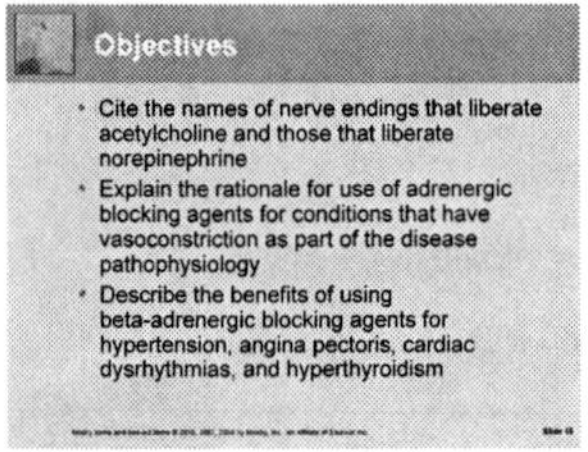
Objectives
Cite the names of nerve endings that liberate acetylcholine and those that liberate norepinephrine
Explain the rationale for use of adrenergic blocking agents for conditions that have vasoconstriction as part of the disease pathophysiology
Describe the benefits of using beta-adrenergic blocking agents for hypertension, angina pectoris, cardiac dysrhythmias, and hyperthyroidism

ELSEVIER

Slide 16

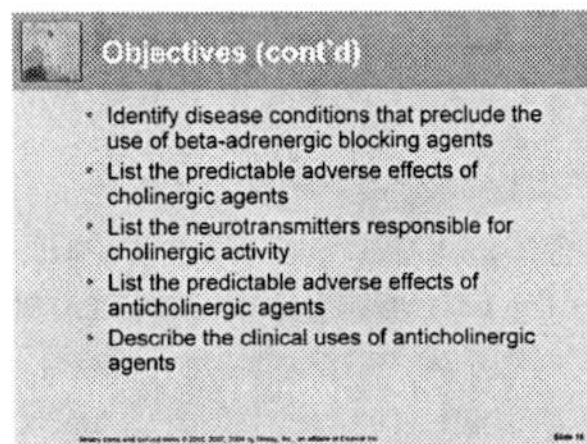
Objectives (cont'd)
Identify disease conditions that preclude the use of beta-adrenergic blocking agents
List the predictable adverse effects of cholinergic agents
List the neurotransmitters responsible for cholinergic activity
List the predictable adverse effects of anticholinergic agents
Describe the clinical uses of anticholinergic agents

Slide 17

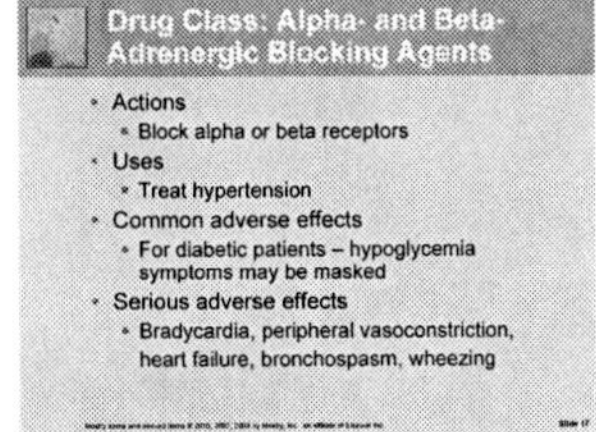
Drug Class: Alpha- and Beta-Adrenergic Blocking Agents
Actions
Block alpha or beta receptors
Uses
Treat hypertension
Common adverse effects
For diabetic patients – hypoglycemia symptoms may be masked
Serious adverse effects
Bradycardia, peripheral vasoconstriction, heart failure, bronchospasm, wheezing

- Stimulation of alpha-1 catecholamine receptors constricts blood vessels, thereby increasing blood pressure.
- Alpha blockers are used with diseases associated with vasoconstriction.
- Beta blockers are used extensively to treat hypertension.

Slide 18

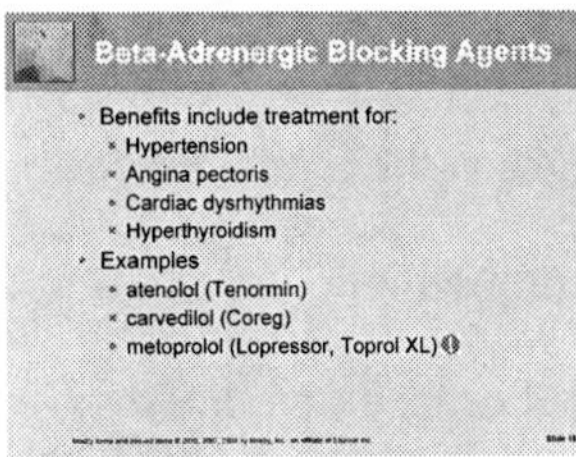
Beta-Adrenergic Blocking Agents
Benefits include treatment for:
Hypertension
Angina pectoris
Cardiac dysrhythmias
Hyperthyroidism
Examples
atenolol (Tenormin)
carvedilol (Coreg)
metoprolol (Lopressor, Toprol XL)

- For specific drug information, see Table 13-3.

Slide 19

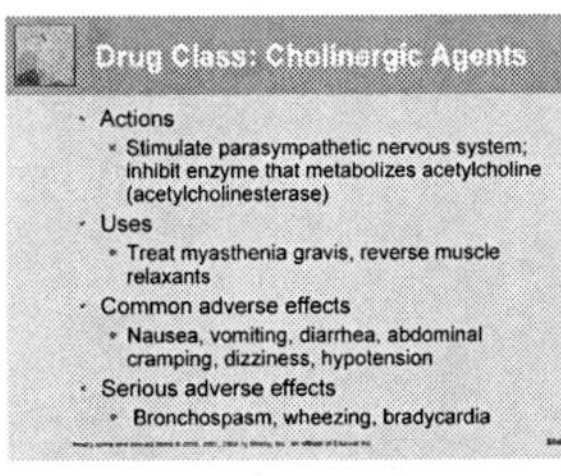
Drug Class: Cholinergic Agents
Actions
Stimulate parasympathetic nervous system; inhibit enzyme that metabolizes acetylcholine (acetylcholinesterase)
Uses
Treat myasthenia gravis, reverse muscle relaxants
Common adverse effects
Nausea, vomiting, diarrhea, abdominal cramping, dizziness, hypotension
Serious adverse effects
Bronchospasm, wheezing, bradycardia

- For specific drug information, see Table 13-4.
- Known as parasympathomimetic agents—produce effects similar to those of acetylcholine.
- Mnemonic for recalling the drug effects of cholinergics is SLUDGE: *S*alivation, *L*acrimation, *U*rinary incontinence, *D*iarrhea, *G*astrointestinal cramps, and *E*mesis.

Slide 20

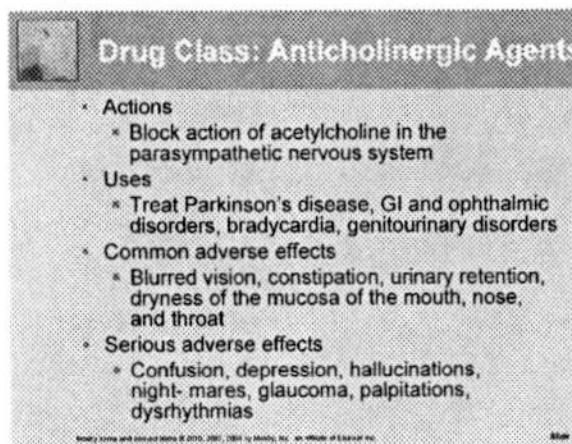
Drug Class: Anticholinergic Agents
Actions
Block action of acetylcholine in the parasympathetic nervous system
Uses
Treat Parkinson's disease, GI and ophthalmic disorders, bradycardia, genitourinary disorders
Common adverse effects
Blurred vision, constipation, urinary retention, dryness of the mucosa of the mouth, nose, and throat
Serious adverse effects
Confusion, depression, hallucinations, night- mares, glaucoma, palpitations, dysrhythmias

- For specific drug information, see Table 13-5.
- Known as cholinergic blocking agents or parasympatholytic agents.

14 Lesson Plan
Sedative-Hypnotics

TEACHING FOCUS

In this chapter, students will have the opportunity to learn about the most common sleep disturbance—insomnia—and how it can be treated. Nonpharmacologic treatments and the nursing processes that should be followed when using sedative-hypnotic therapy will be discussed. Students will be introduced to barbiturate and benzodiazepine drug therapies for sleep disturbance and also to nonbarbiturate, nonbenzodiazepine agents. In addition, students will have the opportunity to learn about patient education and health promotion and assessment, planning, implementation, and monitoring procedures.

MATERIALS AND RESOURCES

- ☐ computer and PowerPoint projector (all Lessons)
- ☐ copies of Patient Self-Assessment Form: Sleeping Medication (Lesson 14.1)
- ☐ index cards (Lesson 14.2)
- ☐ materials for students to create charts (Lesson 14.2)

LESSON CHECKLIST

Preparations for this lesson include:

- lecture
- guest speaker: sleep specialist (physician, nurse, or physiologist), or nurse anesthetist, cognitive relaxation therapist
- evaluation of student knowledge and skills needed to perform all entry-level activities related to sedative-hypnotic drug therapies, including:
  - identifying stages of sleep and sleep pattern disturbances
  - understanding effects of barbiturates, benzodiazepines, and other sleep aids on the central nervous system (CNS)
  - educating patients about alternatives to sedative-hypnotics for treatment of insomnia
  - learning nursing processes for each type of sedative-hypnotic agent
  - identifying laboratory tests that should be monitored for long-term users of benzodiazepines or barbiturates
  - educating patients who take sedative-hypnotics

KEY TERMS

hypnotic (p. 211)
insomnia (p. 211)
rebound sleep (p. 211)
REM sleep (p. 210)
sedative (p. 211)

ADDITIONAL RESOURCES

PowerPoint slides: 1-24
Flashcards, Decks 1 and 2

Legend

ARQ	PPT	TB	CTQ	SG	INRQ
Audience Response Questions	PowerPoint Slides	Test Bank	Critical Thinking Questions	Study Guide	Interactive NCLEX Review Questions

Class Activities are indicated in ***bold italic.***

ELSEVIER

LESSON 14.1

BACKGROUND ASSESSMENT

Question: What assessments should be performed for a healthy 32-year-old female patient who is prescribed a sedative-hypnotic for sleep?

Answer: The nurse should assess and record the patient's baseline vital signs while the patient is both sitting and lying down. The nurse also should assess the patient's baseline neurologic functions, including level of consciousness, orientation, speech, behavior, and gross motor function. The patient should be interviewed to determine whether there is any history of blood dyscrasias or hepatic disease and whether any medications or other drugs (e.g., alcohol or tobacco) the patient is taking might interact with the sedative-hypnotic agent. The patient should complete a self-assessment inventory to help the nurse identify any lifestyle or environmental variables that might contribute to the sleep disturbance. A pregnancy test should be administered because sedative-hypnotic agents are usually not appropriate during pregnancy. Finally the nurse should determine the patient's current method of contraception because some sedative-hypnotic agents will impair the effectiveness of oral contraceptives.

Question: What is a paradoxical response to a sedative-hypnotic? Who is more likely to experience this type of response?

Answer: A paradoxical response is one that is not expected, based on the properties of the substance being administered. Sedative-hypnotics are given to promote feelings of relaxation, rest, or sleep by depressing the CNS. In some cases, the results are unusual and contrary, or opposite to those intended. The patient might exhibit euphoria, restlessness, excitement, confusion, or agitation. A paradoxical reaction can occur in anyone, but is more commonly seen in older adults.

CRITICAL THINKING QUESTION

A 35-year-old male patient returns to the surgical unit at 5:00 PM following a procedure performed under conscious sedation. At 9:00 PM he is still drowsy. Should the nurse administer his scheduled dose of phenobarbital at bedtime? Why or why not?

Guidelines: Before administering phenobarbital, the nurse should assess the patient's vital signs, including the respiratory rate, depth, and rhythm. In addition, the nurse should assess neurologic function, including level of consciousness, orientation, speech, behavior, and gross motor function. If the patient is on long-term phenobarbital therapy for a seizure disorder, adequate drug levels should be maintained. If the patient's assessment reveals that his neurologic function or respiratory status is still compromised from the drugs given for conscious sedation, check with the health care provider before administering the phenobarbital.

OBJECTIVES	CONTENT	TEACHING RESOURCES
Differentiate among the terms *sedative* and *hypnotic*; *initial, intermittent,* and *terminal insomnia*; and *rebound sleep* and *paradoxical excitement.*	■ Sleep and sleep pattern disturbance (p. 210) Review the effects of sleep, the stages of sleep, effects of aging on sleep, and insomnia. Discuss the three types of insomnia: initial, intermittent, and terminal, as well as short-term and chronic insomnia and their effects.	PPT 4-7 ARQ 1-2 TB Multiple Choice questions 1-2, 6-7, 9, 11 CTQ 1 SG Review Sheet questions 1-3 (p. 89) SG Learning Activities questions 1-2, 5-10, 19, 21 (pp. 91-92) SG Practice Questions for the NCLEX Examination 5-7 (pp. 93-94) ▸ Discuss the stages of sleep and the effect of the type of insomnia (initial, intermittent, and terminal) on the sleep cycle.

OBJECTIVES	CONTENT	TEACHING RESOURCES
		Class Activity ***Divide the class into three groups, and assign each group one of the following scenarios:*** ***1. A 60-year-old female cannot fall asleep because she ruminates about her finances.*** ***2. A 43-year-old female wakes up at night with hot flashes and then can not fall back to sleep.*** ***3. A 72-year-old male has joint pain and wakes up several times throughout the night.*** ***Have each group identify the type of insomnia—initial, intermittent, or terminal—the patient is likely to have.*** Class Activity ***Have two students role-play an interview with a patient who is experiencing insomnia. Have the student playing the nurse ask the important questions that determine the type of insomnia and the timeline of symptoms. Review with the class the different types of insomnia and short-term versus chronic insomnia.***
Cite nursing interventions that can be implemented as an alternative to administering a sedative-hypnotic.	■ Sedative-hypnotic therapy (p. 211) – Nursing process for sedative-hypnotic therapy (p. 212) – Patient education and health promotion (p. 213) Review the difference between a sedative and a hypnotic. Discuss other uses for these medications, such as antidepressants, anticonvulsants, and antipsychotics. Review nursing considerations for the use of these drugs.	PPT 8-9 TB Multiple Choice questions 5, 10 INRQ 6, 14 CTQ 1, 3 SG Review Sheet questions 4-6, 8 (p. 89) SG Practice Question for the NCLEX Examination 10 (p. 94) ▸ Discuss the importance of patient education in creating long-term solutions to insomnia through the modification of environmental and lifestyle variables that affect the quality and quantity of sleep received. Class Activity ***Divide the class into groups, and have each group write down various nonpharmacologic methods for promoting sleep. How can the nurse help promote sleep in the hospitalized patient (such as avoiding waking the patient whenever possible)? Have each group present its list to the class.*** Class Activity ***Invite a cognitive relaxation therapist to speak to the class about various relaxation exercises that the nurse can use to help the patient sleep.***

OBJECTIVES	CONTENT	TEACHING RESOURCES
Develop a plan for patient education for a patient receiving a hypnotic.	– Patient education and health promotion (p. 213)	PPT 10-12 ARQ 4 INRQ 5, 11, 12 CTQ 3 Patient Self-Assessment Form: Sleeping Medication SG Review Sheet questions 11-12 (pp. 89-90) ▸ Discuss the importance of patient education when sedative-hypnotic agents are used and the need to focus patient attention on potential risks from their use. Class Activity *Ask the class to identify potential safety risks for a patient receiving a sedative-hypnotic agent in the hospital setting, in a long-term care facility, or at home. Ask class members to call out specific risks, and ask volunteers, one for each location, to list the risks on the board. Then have the class develop a nursing strategy or intervention to minimize each risk in each location.* Class Activity *Divide the class into small groups, and ask each group to develop a patient teaching plan for one of these scenarios: a 75-year-old male taking zolpidem (Ambien) to improve sleep; a 2-year-old child prescribed chloral hydrate administered by the mother before an outpatient CT scan of the head; a 25-year-old female taking phenobarbital to control seizures. Ask the groups to share their plans with the class for feedback and discussion.* Class Activity *Have students work in pairs to role-play a patient and nurse using the Patient Self-Assessment Form: Sleeping Medication (on the text Companion CD or the Evolve Resources) to evaluate the effects of three different sedative-hypnotic agents (one from each drug class) prescribed as a sleep aid. Patients should report symptoms of initial, intermittent, or terminal insomnia and the effects of each of the three agents. The interviews should include questions about specific adverse effects and contraindications. After the pairs have conducted their interviews, bring the class together, and ask students to summarize what they learned.*

14.1 Homework/Assignments:

14.1 Instructor's Notes/Student Feedback:

LESSON 14.2

CRITICAL THINKING QUESTION

A male weighing 100 kg will be undergoing surgery requiring an anesthetic. An intravenous line is established in the left hand for the delivery of midazolam. Before drug administration, a new graduate nurse has been asked by her nurse preceptor to explain why midazolam would be chosen as the anesthetic and to determine how much midazolam the patient should receive. How should the new graduate nurse respond?

Guidelines: The new graduate should explain that short-acting benzodiazepines, such as midazolam, are commonly used intravenously for induction of general anesthesia. The primary benefit of using midazolam is the short-acting amnesia effect it has on most patients. The new graduate nurse should also note that the onset of the medication is between 3 and 5 minutes when administered via an intravenous route and that the duration of the medication is between 2 and 6 hours. The patient should receive between 0.2 and 0.3 mg/kg of the anesthetic. The new nurse can determine the total amount of midazolam to administer by multiplying this dose guideline by the patient's weight in kilograms, namely 100 kg. The total amount of midazolam the patient should receive is between 20 to 30 mg.

OBJECTIVES	CONTENT	TEACHING RESOURCES
Compare the effects of barbiturates and benzodiazepines on the central nervous system.	■ Drug therapy for sleep disturbance (p. 213) □ Drug class: barbiturates (p. 213) – Nursing process for barbiturate therapy (p. 214) □ Drug class: benzodiazepines (p. 215) – Nursing process for benzodiazepines (p. 216) Review effects of barbiturates and their uses. Discuss common and serious adverse effects.	PPT 15-21 ARQ 3 TB Multiple Choice questions 3, 8 TB Multiple Response question 2 INRQ 2, 4 SG Review Sheet questions 7, 14-15, 18-20 (pp. 89-90) SG Learning Activities questions 3-4, 11-15, 20, 22-23 (pp. 91-92) SG Practice Questions for the NCLEX Examination 2, 4, 9 (pp. 93-94) Review Questions for the NCLEX Examination 1, 4-5 (pp. 221-222) Drug Table 14-1 Barbiturates (p. 214)

ELSEVIER

OBJECTIVES	CONTENT	TEACHING RESOURCES
		Drug Table 14-2 Benzodiazepines Used for Sedation-Hypnosis (p. 217) ▸ Discuss the adverse effects and contraindications for barbiturates and benzodiazepines in terms of their effects on the CNS. Consider both paradoxical excitement and rebound sleep as residual effects of these agents. Class Activity ***Have two students role-play a nurse giving patient education to a patient taking barbiturates. Have the class assist the "nurse" in determining what is important to discuss with the "patient." Review with the class therapeutic outcomes and common and serious adverse effects.*** Class Activity ***Ask small groups of students to outline patient assessment parameters for prescribing a sedative-hypnotic agent. Ask students to list variables they would assess before administration of (a) a barbiturate and (b) a benzodiazepine. Then have students list variables they would reassess after administration. Students should include the frequency of patient monitoring for each clinical variable and the rationale for the decision.*** Class Activity ***Divide the class in half, and assign one group the subject of barbiturates and the other group the subject of benzodiazepines. Ask groups to create a chart that lists the intended effects on the CNS and typical uses of various agents in their assigned drug class. Place the effects in the chart's first column, typical uses in the second, and the agents in the third, with appropriate column headings. Then bring students together and have them combine their charts into one. Review the final chart, and have students share what they learned in the process of making their charts.***
Explain the major benefits of administering benzodiazepines rather than barbiturates.	■ Drug therapy for sleep disturbance (p. 213) □ Drug class: barbiturates (p. 213) – Nursing process for barbiturate therapy (p. 214) □ Drug class: benzodiazepines (p. 215) – Nursing process for benzodiazepines (p. 216)	PPT 15-21 TB Multiple Response question 1 SG Review Sheet questions 16-17 (p. 90) ▸ Discuss the advantages of benzodiazepines, emphasizing their wider safety margin and fewer rebound effects when use of the drug is discontinued. Class Activity ***Compare and contrast the characteristics of benzodiazepines and***

OBJECTIVES	CONTENT	TEACHING RESOURCES
	Review effects of benzodiazepines and their uses. Discuss common and serious adverse effects.	***barbiturates. Use the board to draw a grid, and have the students fill in the grid with the correct information regarding the two classes of sedative-hypnotics. After all the data points have been completed, ask the students how the two drug classes are similar and how they differ.*** Class Activity ***Invite a nurse anesthetist to discuss how various sedative-hypnotic agents are used for patient sedation, conscious sedation, and anesthesia. Ask the speaker to describe specific situations, the preferred benzodiazepine agents, and the reasons for their use.***
Identify laboratory tests that should be monitored when benzodiazepines or barbiturates are administered over an extended period.	■ Drug therapy for sleep disturbance (p. 213) □ Drug class: barbiturates (p. 213) – Nursing process for barbiturate therapy (p. 214) □ Drug class: benzodiazepines (p. 215) – Nursing process for benzodiazepines (p. 216)	PPT 21 TB Multiple Choice question 4 INRQ 1 SG Review Sheet question 13 (p. 90) ▸ Discuss the potential long-term adverse effects of using sedative-hypnotic agents, and emphasize the importance of careful monitoring when these drugs must be used for extended periods (e.g., to treat a seizure disorder). ▸ Discuss lab tests for patient monitoring in long-term use of sedative-hypnotics. Identify a specific drug, ask students to determine which tests would be needed, and provide the rationale for the testing. Class Activity ***Divide the class into small discussion groups. Ask half the groups to summarize the laboratory tests, patient observations, and other measures that should be monitored when benzodiazepines are administered over an extended period, including how often each measure should be performed. The other half of the groups should do the same for barbiturates. Ask a volunteer member from each group to present results to the class. As a class, consolidate the group's findings, and ask a volunteer to write a compare-and-contrast summary for the two drug classes on the board.***
Identify the antidote drug used in the management of benzodiazepine overdose.	□ Drug class: benzodiazepines (p. 215) Uses (p. 216)	PPT 21 ▸ Discuss the antidote used for the management of intentional or accidental overdose of benzodiazepines - flumazenil

OBJECTIVES	CONTENT	TEACHING RESOURCES
Identify alterations found in the sleep pattern when hypnotics are discontinued.	■ Drug therapy for sleep disturbance (p. 213) □ Drug class: nonbarbiturate, nonbenzodiazepine sedative-hypnotic agents (p. 218) – Nursing process for miscellaneous sedative-hypnotic agents (p. 220) Review drug classifications of nonbarbiturate, nonbenzodiazepine agents, such as antihistamines and herbal medications. Discuss common and serious adverse effects and drug interactions with common medications.	PPT 22-24 ARQ 5 TB Multiple Choice question 12 TB Multiple Response question 3 INRQ 3 SG Review Sheet questions 9-10 (p. 89) SG Learning Activities questions 16-18 (p. 91) SG Practice Questions for the NCLEX Examination 1, 3, 8 (pp. 93-94) Review Questions for the NCLEX Examination 2-3, 6 (pp. 221-222) Drug Table 14-3 Miscellaneous Sedative-Hypnotic Agents (p. 219) ▸ Discuss the differences in rebound effects for benzodiazepines and barbiturates and the impact of the duration of treatment on the length and severity of rebound symptoms. Class Activity ***Invite a sleep specialist (physician, nurse, or physiologist) to present concepts of normal sleep patterns and common sleep disturbances. In particular, ask the specialist to discuss the effects on sleep patterns when hypnotics are discontinued and the rebound phenomenon that can occur. Invite students to prepare questions for the speaker before the presentation.*** Class Activity ***Assign groups of students to identify the rebound effects typical for each class of drugs (barbiturates, benzodiazepines, and nonbarbiturate, nonbenzodiazepines). Students should include the type of sleep disrupted and the severity of disruption. Have groups share their findings with the class.***
Performance evaluation		Test Bank SG Learning Activities (pp. 91-92) SG Practice Questions for the NCLEX Examination (pp. 93-94) Critical Thinking Questions

ELSEVIER

14.2 Homework/Assignments:

14.2 Instructor's Notes/Student Feedback:

14 Lecture Outline

Sedative-Hypnotics

Slide 1

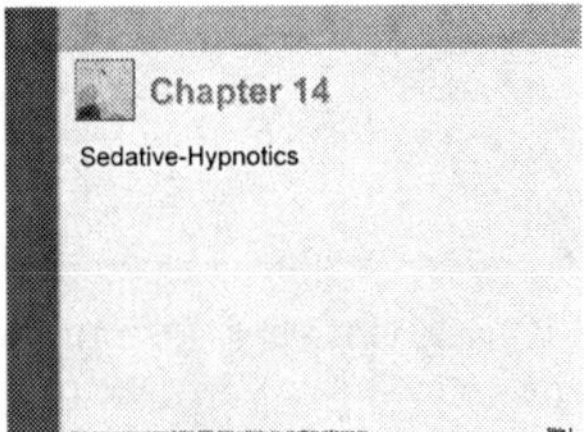
Chapter 14
Sedative-Hypnotics

Slide 2

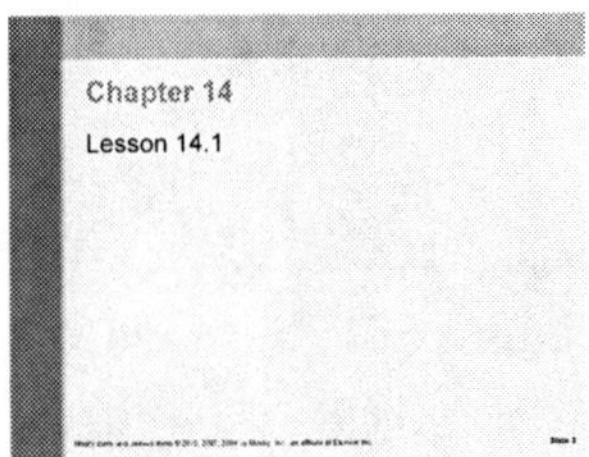
Chapter 14
Lesson 14.1

Slide 3

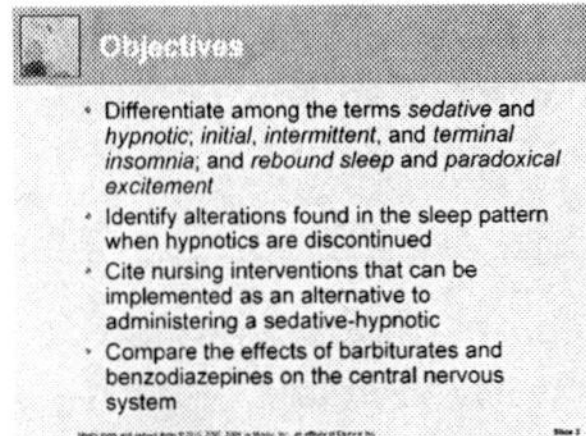
Objectives
Differentiate among the terms sedative and hypnotic; initial, intermittent, and terminal insomnia; and rebound sleep and paradoxical excitement
Identify alterations found in the sleep pattern when hypnotics are discontinued
Cite nursing interventions that can be implemented as an alternative to administering a sedative-hypnotic
Compare the effects of barbiturates and benzodiazepines on the central nervous system

Slide 4

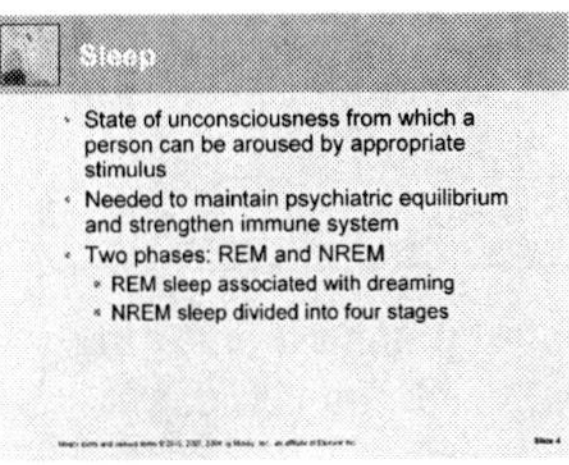
Sleep
State of unconsciousness from which a person can be aroused by appropriate stimulus
Needed to maintain psychiatric equilibrium and strengthen immune system
Two phases: REM and NREM
REM sleep associated with dreaming
NREM sleep divided into four stages

- Factors contributing to patterns of inadequate sleep: stress, anxiety, illness, change of environment, longer working hours, longer commute times, two-career families, alcohol and drug abuse, medication use, and caffeine.

Slide 5

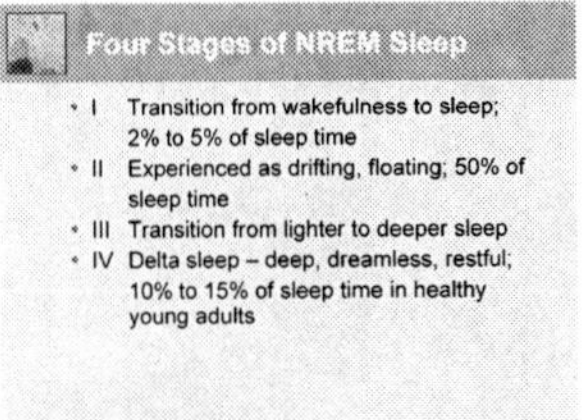
Four Stages of NREM Sleep
I Transition from wakefulness to sleep; 2% to 5% of sleep time
II Experienced as drifting, floating; 50% of sleep time
III Transition from lighter to deeper sleep
IV Delta sleep – deep, dreamless, restful; 10% to 15% of sleep time in healthy young adults

- The amount of time people sleep changes as they grow older. The pattern of sleep also changes throughout life.
- Typical sleep pattern of a 15-year-old compared with that of an 85-year-old – sleep cycles are longer and total sleep is greater in a 15-year-old.

ELSEVIER

Slide 6

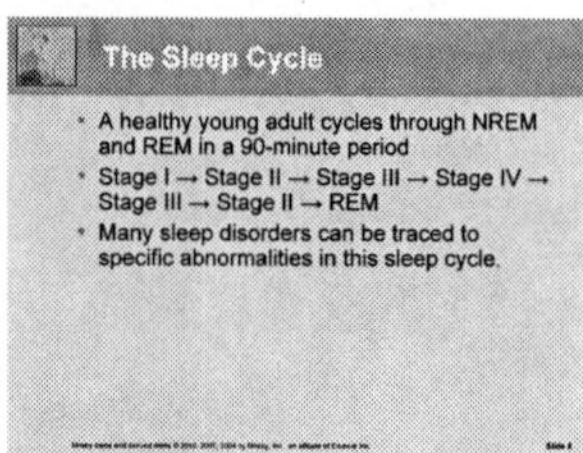
The Sleep Cycle
A healthy young adult cycles through NREM and REM in a 90-minute period
Stage I → Stage II → Stage III → Stage IV → Stage III → Stage II → REM
Many sleep disorders can be traced to specific abnormalities in this sleep cycle.

- If the amount of time in a particular stage is increased or decreased from normal averages, it upsets the overall balance.
- A sleep study involves scientific assessment of a person's sleep cycles and determines pattern abnormalities.

Slide 7

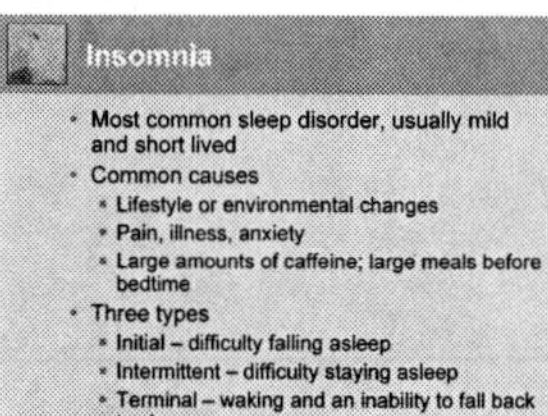
Insomnia
Most common sleep disorder, usually mild and short lived
Common causes
Lifestyle or environmental changes
Pain, illness, anxiety
Large amounts of caffeine; large meals before bedtime
Three types
Initial – difficulty falling asleep
Intermittent – difficulty staying asleep
Terminal – waking and an inability to fall back to sleep

- Up to 35% of adults experience insomnia in any given year. Insomnia is experienced by 95% of adults at some time.
- Some remedies people use to counter anxiety and stress – caffeine, alcohol, drugs – can disrupt sleep patterns even more.

Slide 8

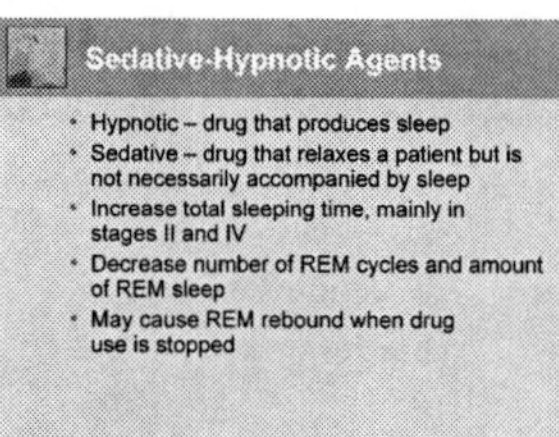
Sedative-Hypnotic Agents
Hypnotic – drug that produces sleep
Sedative – drug that relaxes a patient but is not necessarily accompanied by sleep
Increase total sleeping time, mainly in stages II and IV
Decrease number of REM cycles and amount of REM sleep
May cause REM rebound when drug use is stopped

- No single drug can produce all the desired effects of sedation and sleep induction without producing adverse effects.
- Most of these agents alter the sleep cycle in some manner and can be habit-forming.
- REM sleep restores mental and physiologic balance. If REM dreaming is cut short, balance is not restored, and REM rebound may occur.

Slide 9

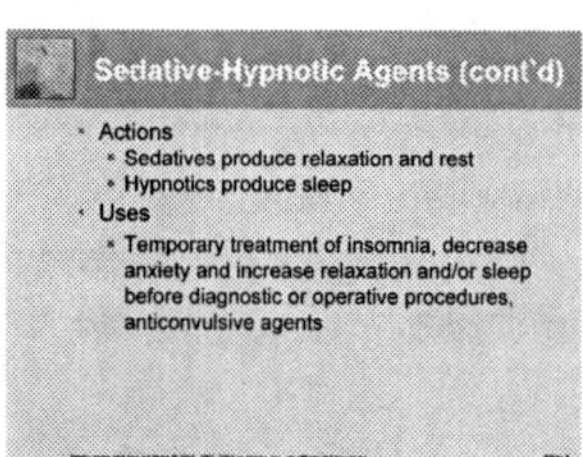
Sedative-Hypnotic Agents (cont'd)
Actions
Sedatives produce relaxation and rest
Hypnotics produce sleep
Uses
Temporary treatment of insomnia, decrease anxiety and increase relaxation and/or sleep before diagnostic or operative procedures, anticonvulsive agents

- A single sedative can produce different effects at different dosages; a small dose acts as sedative, a larger dose acts as hypnotic.
- Patient condition, baseline level of consciousness, and age also contribute to overall effects.

Slide 10

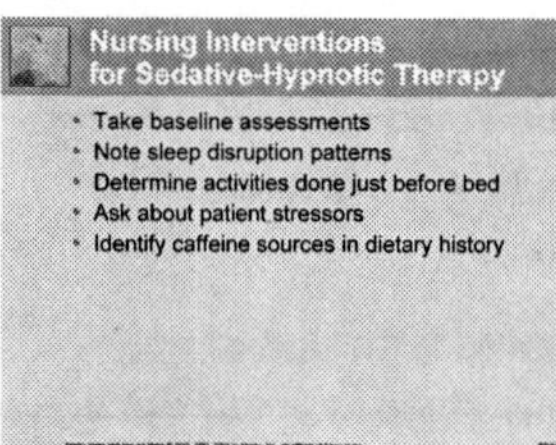
Nursing Interventions for Sedative-Hypnotic Therapy
Take baseline assessments
Note sleep disruption patterns
Determine activities done just before bed
Ask about patient stressors
Identify caffeine sources in dietary history

- Assessing CNS function is a key component of patient monitoring before and after any sedative-hypnotic agent is administered.
- Baseline level of consciousness and state of arousal should be recorded during assessment and then re-evaluated.
- Baseline sleep patterns may be difficult to measure in a health care setting because sleep patterns are usually disrupted by noise, interruptions, procedures, etc.

ELSEVIER

Slide 11

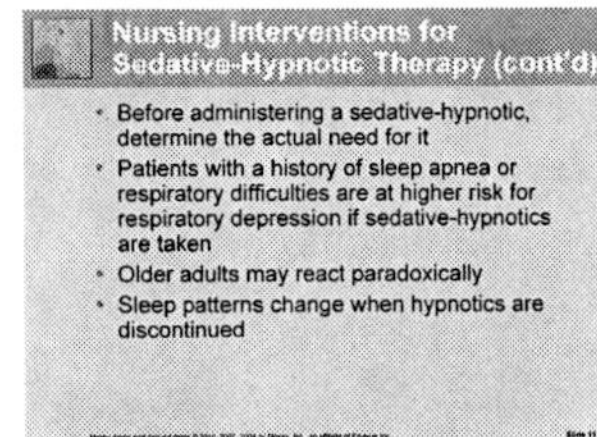
Nursing Interventions for Sedative-Hypnotic Therapy (cont'd)
Before administering a sedative-hypnotic, determine the actual need for it
Patients with a history of sleep apnea or respiratory difficulties are at higher risk for respiratory depression if sedative-hypnotics are taken
Older adults may react paradoxically
Sleep patterns change when hypnotics are discontinued

- Nonpharmacologic interventions include offering dairy products, dimming the lights, reducing noise level, increasing daytime activity, etc.

Slide 12

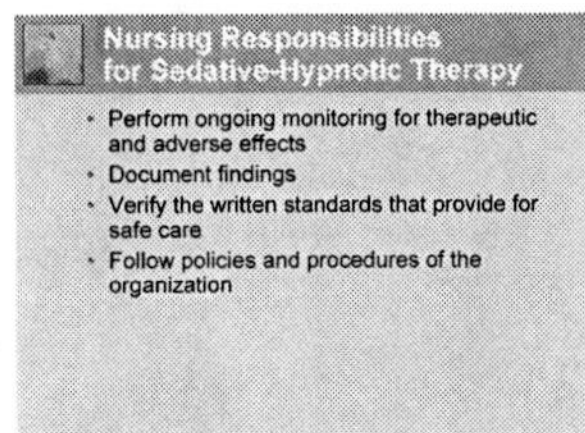
Nursing Responsibilities for Sedative-Hypnotic Therapy
Perform ongoing monitoring for therapeutic and adverse effects
Document findings
Verify the written standards that provide for safe care
Follow policies and procedures of the organization

- If the drug is ordered as part of a preoperative or preprocedure medication, it must be given at the correct time to ensure the peak effect will occur when it is needed.

Slide 13

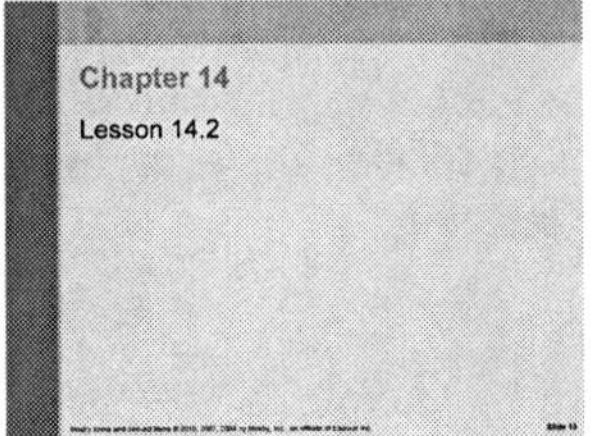
Chapter 14
Lesson 14.2

Slide 14

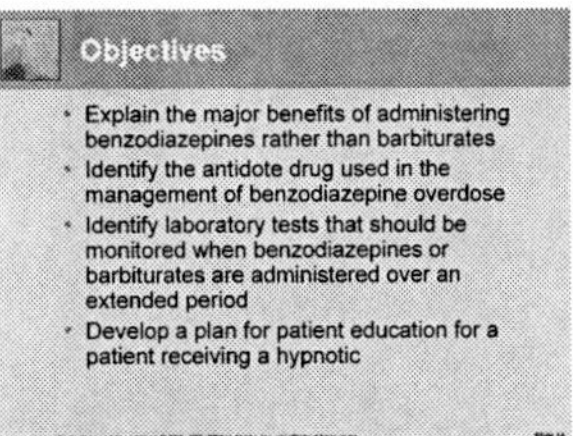
Objectives
Explain the major benefits of administering benzodiazepines rather than barbiturates
Identify the antidote drug used in the management of benzodiazepine overdose
Identify laboratory tests that should be monitored when benzodiazepines or barbiturates are administered over an extended period
Develop a plan for patient education for a patient receiving a hypnotic

---

Slide 15

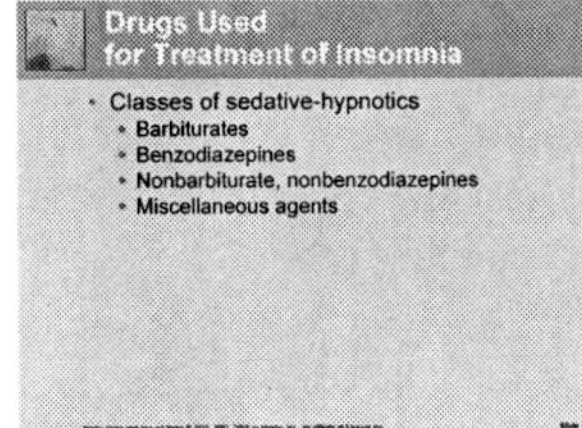
Drugs Used for Treatment of Insomnia
Classes of sedative-hypnotics
Barbiturates
Benzodiazepines
Nonbarbiturate, nonbenzodiazepines
Miscellaneous agents

Slide 16

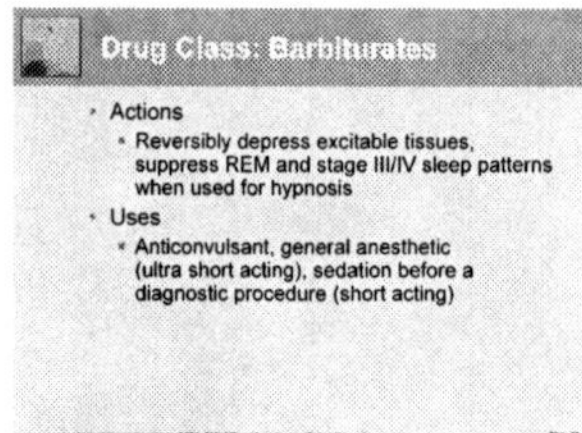
Drug Class: Barbiturates
Actions
Reversibly depress excitable tissues, suppress REM and stage III/IV sleep patterns when used for hypnosis
Uses
Anticonvulsant, general anesthetic (ultra short acting), sedation before a diagnostic procedure (short acting)

- For specific drug information, see Table 14-1.
- Barbiturates are so effective in reducing CNS activity that they are sometimes used to induce a coma-like state in cases of severe brain injury to reduce brain metabolism and preserve function.

Slide 17

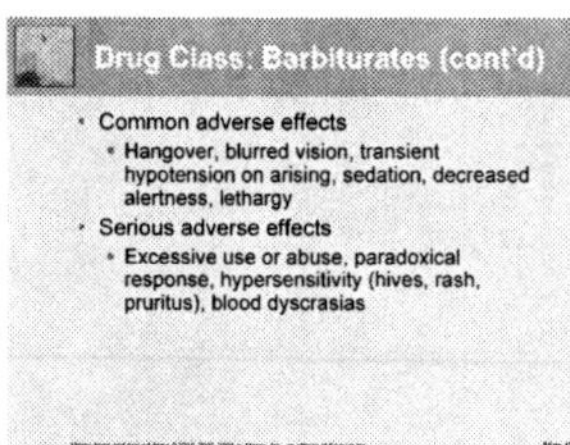
Drug Class: Barbiturates (cont'd)
Common adverse effects
Hangover, blurred vision, transient hypotension on arising, sedation, decreased alertness, lethargy
Serious adverse effects
Excessive use or abuse, paradoxical response, hypersensitivity (hives, rash, pruritus), blood dyscrasias

- Signs/symptoms of physiologic withdrawal can occur if drugs are stopped.

Slide 18

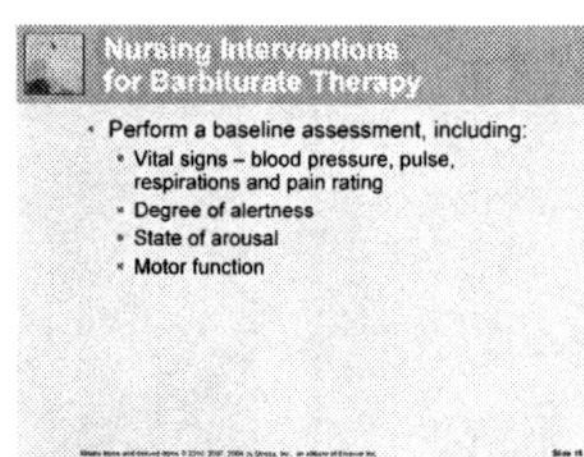
Nursing Interventions for Barbiturate Therapy
Perform a baseline assessment, including:
Vital signs – blood pressure, pulse, respirations and pain rating
Degree of alertness
State of arousal
Motor function

- The importance of a good baseline assessment before administering a sedative-hypnotic cannot be emphasized enough.
- The nurse can address patient safety concerns about paradoxical responses by providing additional supervision; considering restraining devices; helping patient channel energy by walking.

Slide 19

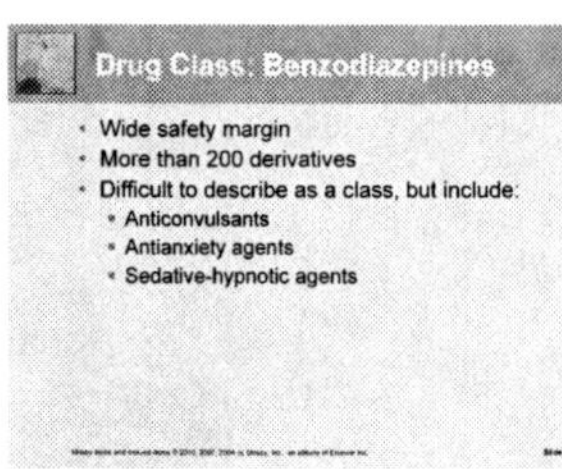
Drug Class: Benzodiazepines
Wide safety margin
More than 200 derivatives
Difficult to describe as a class, but include:
Anticonvulsants
Antianxiety agents
Sedative-hypnotic agents

- Overdoses can be better tolerated and are not fatal.
- Although there are many derivatives in this class, only a small subset is used clinically.

Slide 20

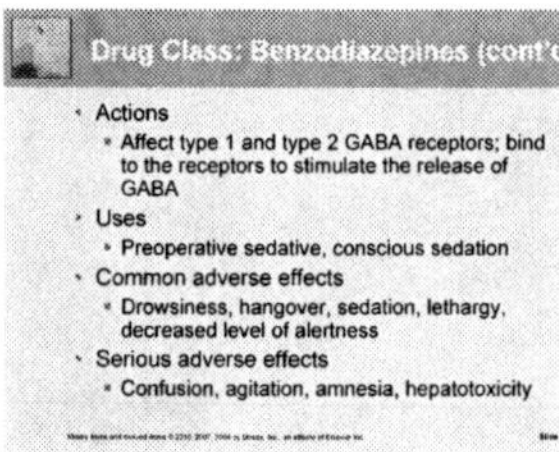
Drug Class: Benzodiazepines (cont'd)
Actions
Affect type 1 and type 2 GABA receptors; bind to the receptors to stimulate the release of GABA
Uses
Preoperative sedative, conscious sedation
Common adverse effects
Drowsiness, hangover, sedation, lethargy, decreased level of alertness
Serious adverse effects
Confusion, agitation, amnesia, hepatotoxicity

- For specific drug information, see Table 14-2.
- Most commonly used sedative-hypnotics.
- Individual drugs in this class are prescribed for different uses, such as sleep and anxiety, based on their site of action within the CNS. When they are stopped, a rebound effect can occur, causing rebound insomnia as well as bizarre dreams.

ELSEVIER

Slide 21

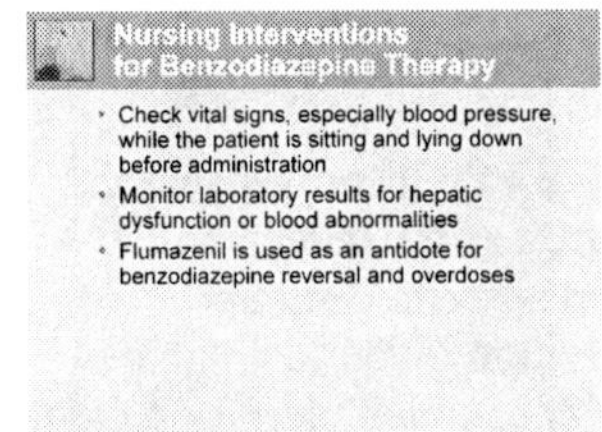
Nursing Interventions for Benzodiazepine Therapy
Check vital signs, especially blood pressure, while the patient is sitting and lying down before administration
Monitor laboratory results for hepatic dysfunction or blood abnormalities
Flumazenil is used as an antidote for benzodiazepine reversal and overdoses

Slide 22

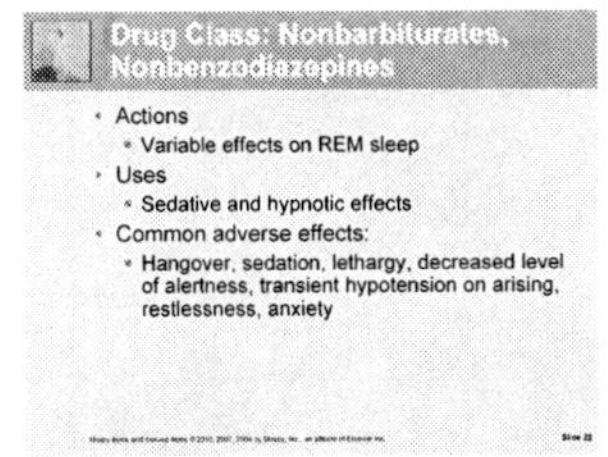
Drug Class: Nonbarbiturates, Nonbenzodiazepines
Actions
Variable effects on REM sleep
Uses
Sedative and hypnotic effects
Common adverse effects:
Hangover, sedation, lethargy, decreased level of alertness, transient hypotension on arising, restlessness, anxiety

- For specific drug information, see Table 14-3.
- Most recommended only for short-term use of 7 to 10 days, or for as long as 3 weeks with good evaluation.
- All cause CNS depression, but mechanisms of action differ.

Slide 23

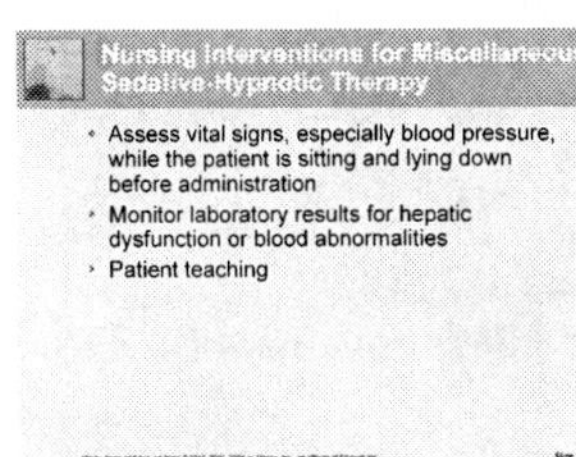
Nursing Interventions for Miscellaneous Sedative-Hypnotic Therapy
Assess vital signs, especially blood pressure, while the patient is sitting and lying down before administration
Monitor laboratory results for hepatic dysfunction or blood abnormalities
Patient teaching

- The patient must understand that habitual use can lead to physical dependency.
- Do not abruptly stop these drugs after long-term use because they can cause symptoms similar to alcohol withdrawal.

Slide 24

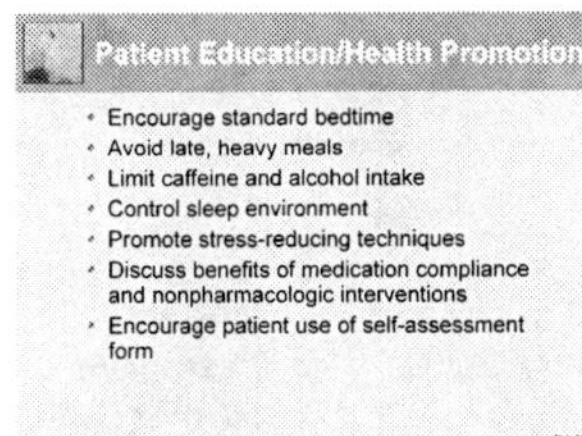
Patient Education/Health Promotion
Encourage standard bedtime
Avoid late, heavy meals
Limit caffeine and alcohol intake
Control sleep environment
Promote stress-reducing techniques
Discuss benefits of medication compliance and nonpharmacologic interventions
Encourage patient use of self-assessment form

ELSEVIER

15 Lesson Plan
Drugs Used for Parkinson's Disease

TEACHING FOCUS

This chapter introduces students to common therapeutic plans for the treatment of Parkinson's disease. A review of the disease mechanism is presented, along with drug therapy that addresses the defects involved in Parkinson's disease; signs and symptoms and methods of assessment are also presented. Common therapeutic agents from the various drug classes are discussed in detail with attention given to notable adverse effects. Students will have the opportunity to learn how to create a health teaching plan for patients being treated with the drug levodopa.

MATERIALS AND RESOURCES

☐ computer and PowerPoint projector (all Lessons)

LESSON CHECKLIST

Preparations for this lesson include:

- lecture
- demonstration
- evaluation of student knowledge and skills needed to perform all entry-level activities related to the drugs used to treat Parkinson's disease, including:
  - the signs and symptoms of Parkinson's disease
  - the basis of treatment for Parkinson's disease
  - common drugs used in the treatment of Parkinson's disease—their mode of action and adverse effects

KEY TERMS

acetylcholine (p. 223)
akinesia (p. 226)
anticholinergic agents (p. 225)
dopamine (p. 223)
dyskinesia (p. 226)
levodopa (p. 232)
neurotransmitter (p. 223)
Parkinson's disease (p. 223)
propulsive, uncontrolled movement (p. 226)
tremors (p. 226)

ADDITIONAL RESOURCES

PowerPoint slides: 1-17
Flashcards, Decks 1 and 2

Legend

ARQ	PPT	TB	CTQ	SG	INRQ
Audience Response Questions	PowerPoint Slides	Test Bank	Critical Thinking Questions	Study Guide	Interactive NCLEX Review Questions

Class Activities are indicated in ***bold italic.***

LESSON 15.1

BACKGROUND ASSESSMENT

Question: How is Parkinson's disease diagnosed and assessed?
Answer: There are no blood tests to diagnose Parkinson's disease. The diagnosis is based on patient reports and health care providers' observations. The best clinical predictors of a pathologic diagnosis of Parkinson's disease are asymmetry of movement, presence of resting tremor, and response to dopamine replacement

therapy. The cardinal signs of Parkinson's disease are resting tremor, rigidity, and bradykinesia. Postural instability is another cardinal sign, but it usually emerges late in the disease.

Question: What is levodopa, and why can it only be used for a few years?
Answer: Levodopa is a short-acting precursor to dopamine that can enter the brain, where it is subsequently converted into dopamine. Low-dose levodopa is commonly started when the patient experiences enough inconvenience or incapacity from the symptoms. Maximal results are obtained within the first few years on the medication, although most patients continue to benefit for many years. When levodopa first enters the brain and is converted into dopamine, Parkinson's symptoms diminish. In 3 to 5 years, however, they may begin to resurface. Scientists discovered that the cells that convert levodopa to dopamine deteriorate and eventually die off. Higher doses of levodopa can make up for the decreasing number of cells but may cause jerking movements of the limbs, trunk, and head (choreic movements), and hallucinations.

CRITICAL THINKING QUESTION

A patient was diagnosed with Parkinson's disease 7 years ago and has been taking Sinemet ever since. She tells the nurse that the medication worked for a while, but she now feels as if the medication wears off by midafternoon. What is the patient experiencing, and what can be done?
Guidelines: The patient is experiencing a common adverse effect of long-term use of levodopa, sometimes called the "wearing off effect." However, there are ways to counteract this effect. For example, the patient can switch to a different and more frequent dosing, or to a longer-lasting form of levodopa, such as Sinemet 25/250 or a sustained-release form. Also patients who start feeling the wearing off effects of levodopa may be prescribed a dopamine agonist. This class of medication includes pramipexole (Mirapex) and ropinirole hydrochloride (Requip). Dopamine agonists are intended to act as synthetic dopamine. They enter the central nervous system and, without any further transformation, stimulate dopamine receptors. The agents may be given by themselves or in combination with other antiparkinsonian agents. The nurse should encourage the patient to speak to the health care provider about her observations.

OBJECTIVES	CONTENT	TEACHING RESOURCES
Prepare a list of signs and symptoms of Parkinson's disease, and accurately define the vocabulary used for the pharmacologic agents prescribed and the disease state.	■ Key terms (p. 223) ■ Parkinson's disease (p. 223) Review the signs and symptoms of Parkinson's disease and the effects of the neurotransmitters dopamine and acetylcholine. Discuss the goal of nursing interventions for patients suffering from Parkinson's disease.	PPT 5-6 ARQ 1 TB Multiple Response question 1 INRQ 4 CTQ 1 SG Review Sheet questions 1, 4-6 (p. 95) SG Learning Activities questions 2-4, 13, 19 (pp. 97-98) SG Practice Questions for the NCLEX Examination 2, 5, 11-12 (pp. 99-100) Figure 15-1 (p. 224), Stages of parkinsonism Lifespan Considerations: Parkinson's Disease (p. 224) ▸ Discuss the initial symptoms of Parkinson's disease, the signs that you would expect to find during a physical examination, and the risks the patient with Parkinson's disease faces. ▸ Discuss the classes of pharmacologic agents used in the treatment of Parkinson's disease.

ELSEVIER

OBJECTIVES	CONTENT	TEACHING RESOURCES
		Class Activity ***List on the board the following terms: bradykinesia, extrapyramidal symptoms, primary and secondary parkinsonism, and dopamine antagonists. Divide the class into groups and have each group explain to the class what one of the terms means, and have them give examples of each. Discuss the outcome of the exercise.*** Class Activity ***Divide the class into groups, and assign each group one of the following topics: primary Parkinson's, secondary Parkinson's, or signs and symptoms. Have each group discuss its topic, including its progression, treatments, and pathologic conditions. Have each group present its findings to the class for discussion.***
Name the neurotransmitter that is found in excess and the neurotransmitter that is deficient in people with parkinsonism.	■ Parkinson's disease (p. 223)	INRQ 5 CTQ 2 Animation: Dopamine Release ▸ Discuss the relationship between dopamine and acetylcholine in the body. How does Parkinson's disease affect that relationship? ▸ Discuss the different types of parkinsonism. Class Activity ***Divide the class into groups, and have each group identify and discuss a nursing intervention for each of the following complications of Parkinson's disease:*** – ***Urinary urgency and frequency*** – ***Constipation*** – ***Orthostatic hypotension*** – ***Sexual dysfunction*** – ***Swallowing difficulty*** – ***Drooling*** – ***Insomnia*** – ***Sleep attacks*** ***Have each group share its findings with the class. Compile all the interventions into a comprehensive list on the board.*** Class Activity ***List on the board the following terms: tremors; dyskinesia; propulsive, uncontrolled movement; facial appearance; and akinesia. Have five students demonstrate each of the terms used to describe the symptoms of parkinsonism. Review with the class the scale used in patients with Parkinson's disease.***
Describe reasonable expectations of medications	■ Drug therapy for Parkinson's disease (p. 225)	PPT 7-8 ARQ 2-3 TB Multiple Choice question 8

OBJECTIVES	CONTENT	TEACHING RESOURCES
prescribed for treatment of Parkinson's disease.		INRQ 1, 10 SG Review Sheet questions 2, 8, 11, 19 (pp. 95-96) SG Learning Activities questions 20-25 (p. 98) SG Practice Questions for the NCLEX Examination 1, 5, 10 (pp. 99-100) Figure 15-2 (p. 226), Management of Parkinson's disease ▸ Discuss the available treatments for Parkinson's disease. What symptoms are usually targeted by drug therapy? ▸ Discuss patient education and health promotion measures that relate to the patient with Parkinson's disease. Class Activity ***Have two students role-play the part of a nurse interviewing a patient with Parkinson's disease and a patient with the symptoms. Have the student playing the nurse review all the important items to cover while taking a history (i.e., nutrition, motor function, stress management, self care, and safety needs). Discuss with the class the reasons why each item is necessary to be covered during a history.***
Identify the period necessary for a therapeutic response to be observable when drugs used to treat arkinsonism are initiated.	– Nursing process for Parkinson's disease therapy (p. 225) – Patient education and health promotion (p. 228) Review the stages of parkinsonism and the Unified Parkinson's Disease Rating Scale (UPDRS) used to monitor changes in symptoms that require medication adjustment.	PPT 7-8 TB Multiple Choice question 9 INRQ 8 CTQ 5, 7 SG Review Sheet questions 2-3, 15, 18 (pp. 95-96) SG Learning Activities question 7 (p. 97) SG Practice Questions for the NCLEX Examination 3-4, 6, 8 (p. 99) Patient Self-Assessment Form: Antiparkinson Agents ▸ Discuss why there is a delay in response to treatment with drugs for parkinsonism. ▸ Discuss the role of patient education in antiparkinsonian therapy. ▸ Discuss the various stages of Parkinson's disease and rating scales used in its assessment. Class Activity ***Present the following scenario to the class for discussion:***

OBJECTIVES	CONTENT	TEACHING RESOURCES
		A 62-year-old man reports tremors in both hands and increasing weakness. ***Have the class identify which stage of Parkinson's disease the patient is exhibiting, and discuss how the disease will likely progress.***
Name the action of carbidopa, levodopa, and apomorphine on neurotransmitters involved in Parkinson's disease.	□ Drug class: Dopamine agonists (p. 230) – Nursing process for apomorphine therapy (p. 230) – Nursing process for carbidopa-levodopa therapy (p. 232) – Nursing process for pramipexole therapy (p. 234) – Nursing process for ropinirole therapy (p. 235) Review the drug class dopamine agonists that are used to minimize the symptoms of Parkinson's disease. Discuss common and serious adverse effects along with drug interactions.	PPT 9-11 INRQ 2 CTQ 3 Animation: Dopamine Release SG Review Sheet questions 9-10, 11-13 (p. 96) SG Learning Activity questions 5, 14, 16 (p. 97) SG Practice Questions for the NCLEX Examination 9, 13, 15 (p. 100) Review Questions for the NCLEX Examination 1-3, 6 (p. 239) ▸ Discuss the on-off phenomenon that occurs with carbidopa-levodopa therapy. ▸ Discuss the actions of dopamine agonists on neurotransmitters in the body. ▸ Discuss the primary therapeutic outcomes of pramipexole and ropinirole therapy. ▸ Discuss the use of dopamine agonists in the therapy for Parkinson's, disease and explain why this class of drugs reduces symptoms associated with the disease. ▸ Discuss which drugs used for treatment of Parkinson's disease are dopamine agonists. Class Activity ***Divide the class into groups, and have each group identify 10 modifications or safety measures that can be made in a patient's home to ensure his or her safety as the disease progresses. Have each group present its findings to the class for discussion.***

15.1 Homework/Assignments:

15.1 Instructor's Notes/Student Feedback:

LESSON 15.2

CRITICAL THINKING QUESTION

A patient's spouse asks the nurse about alternative therapies for Parkinson's disease because his wife is already taking several medications. What other options are available?

Guidelines: The patient should not discontinue any medications without first consulting the health care provider. There are some nonpharmacologic therapies, however, that can be used. A variety of nonpharmacologic methods can be used to reduce the complications and comorbid symptoms of Parkinson's disease. For example, a bowel regimen can greatly reduce constipation. Increased fluid intake, a diet rich in vegetables and fruits, and increased dietary and/or supplemental fiber are some helpful interventions. The patient should try to maintain activity levels as much as possible. This will help with decreasing rigidity and bradykinesia, optimizing gait, and improving balance and motor coordination. The patient may be referred to physical therapy for some beneficial exercises and home and workplace modifications, improving accessibility and removing obstructions, and adaptation and simplification of utensils, such as toileting articles and beds. Other professionals, such as a dietitian and an occupational and speech therapist, can also be enlisted.

OBJECTIVES	CONTENT	TEACHING RESOURCES
Develop a health teaching plan for an individual being treated with levodopa.	– Nursing process for carbidopa-levodopa therapy (p. 232)	PPT 17 ARQ 5 TB Multiple Choice 6 question CTQ 4 SG Review Sheet questions 7, 14 (pp. 95-96) SG Learning Activities questions 4, 10-11 (p. 97) Review Question for the NCLEX Examination 7 (p. 239) ▸ Discuss how long it may take to achieve therapeutic benefits from levodopa therapy and how you would explain this to a patient. ▸ Discuss which adverse effects of levodopa therapy are serious and which are common.

OBJECTIVES	CONTENT	TEACHING RESOURCES
		Class Activity ***Divide the class into groups, and have each group identify and discuss the items that should be included in a health teaching plan for a patient being treated with levodopa. Have each group share its findings with the class for discussion.***
Name the action of entacapone and the monoamine oxidase inhibitors, selegiline and rasagiline, as it relates to treatment of Parkinson's disease.	□ Drug class: monoamine oxidase-B inhibitors (p. 228) – Nursing process for monoamine oxidase B inhibitor therapy (p. 229) □ Drug class: COMT inhibitor (p. 236) – Nursing process for entacapone therapy (p. 236)	PPT 14 TB Multiple Choice questions 1-2, 5, 7, 10-11 TB Multiple Response question 2 INRQ 6, 9, 13 SG Review Sheet question 8 (p. 96) SG Learning Activities question 12 (p. 97) SG Practice Questions for the NCLEX Examination 7, 10, 14 (pp. 99-100) Review Questions for the NCLEX Examination 4-5 (p. 239) Drug Table 15-1 Monoamine Oxidase B Inhibitors (p. 229) ▸ Discuss the role of entacapone and the monoamine inhibitors in the management of Parkinson's disease. Class Activity ***Divide the class into groups, and assign each group one of the following drug therapies:*** – ***Entacapone*** – ***Selegiline*** – ***Rasagiline*** ***Have each group outline the characteristics of its assigned drug, including how long the drug is beneficial for patients or how long it can safely be taken and nursing interventions for a patient taking the drug. Have each group present its findings to the class.***
List symptoms that can be attributed to the cholinergic activity of pharmacologic agents.	□ Drug class: anticholinergic agents (p. 237) – Nursing process for anticholinergic agent therapy (p. 237)	PPT 17-18 TB Multiple Choice question 4 CTQ 6 ▸ Discuss which pharmacologic agents have cholinergic activity. ▸ Discuss common symptoms associated with cholinergic activity. Class Activity ***Divide the class into groups, and have each group discuss the uses of anticholinergic agents in treating***

OBJECTIVES	CONTENT	TEACHING RESOURCES
		parkinsonism. How are they used in combination therapy and with what drugs? For which patients is this approach best suited? Have groups share their findings with the class.
Cite the specific symptoms that should show improvement when anticholinergic agents are administered to the patient with Parkinson's disease.	□ Drug class: anticholinergic agents (p. 237) – Nursing process for anticholinergic agent therapy (p. 237)	PPT 15-16 ARQ 4 TB Multiple Choice question 3 INRQ 3, 11-12, 14 SG Review Sheet questions 16-17 (p. 96) SG Learning Activities questions 6, 17-19 (pp. 97-98) SG Practice Questions for the NCLEX Examination 16-17 (p. 101) Drug Table 15-2 Anticholinergic Agents (p. 238) ▸ Discuss the therapeutic outcomes and effects of anticholinergic agents. Class Activity ***Lead a class discussion about anticholinergic agent therapy, and have students identify which Parkinson's symptoms it addresses and which symptoms it increases. How do its adverse effects compare with other drug therapies for Parkinson's?*** Class Activity ***Divide the class into groups, and assign each group a different antiparkinsonian drug. Have each group identify the dietary and lifestyle restrictions associated with its drug and develop a list of foods, activities, and so on that the drug prohibits or that are dangerous. Then have students identify safe and comparable alternatives. Have each group share its findings with the class for discussion.***
Performance evaluation		Test Bank SG Learning Activities (pp. 97-98) SG Practice Questions for the NCLEX Examination (pp. 99-101) Critical Thinking Questions

ELSEVIER

15.2 Homework/Assignments:

15.2 Instructor's Notes/Student Feedback:

15

Lecture Outline

Drugs Used for Parkinson's Disease

Slide 1

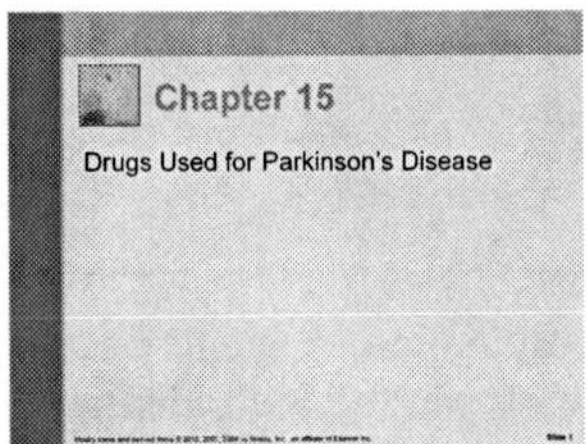
Chapter 15
Drugs Used for Parkinson's Disease

Slide 2

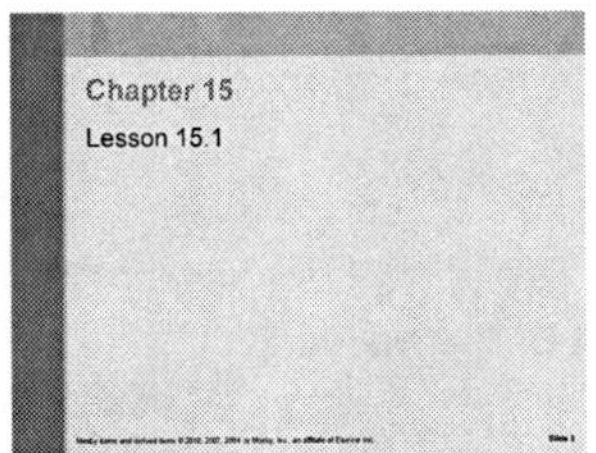
Chapter 15
Lesson 15.1

Slide 3

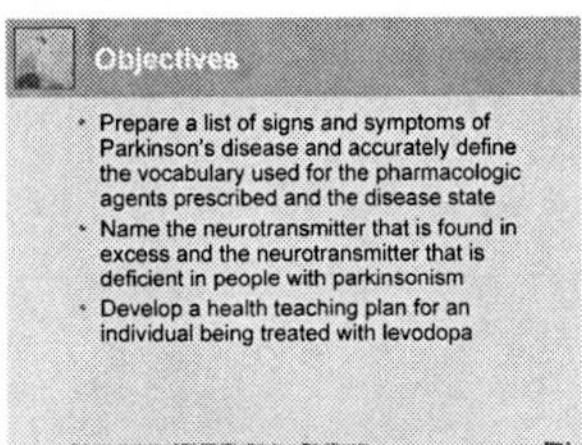
Objectives
Prepare a list of signs and symptoms of Parkinson's disease and accurately define the vocabulary used for the pharmacologic agents prescribed and the disease state
Name the neurotransmitter that is found in excess and the neurotransmitter that is deficient in people with parkinsonism
Develop a health teaching plan for an individual being treated with levodopa

Slide 4

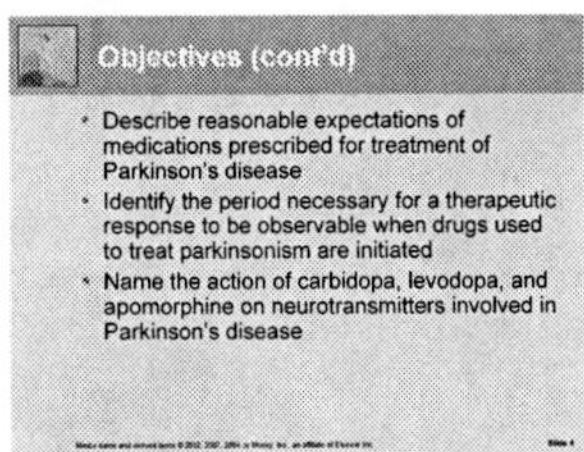
Objectives (cont'd)
Describe reasonable expectations of medications prescribed for treatment of Parkinson's disease
Identify the period necessary for a therapeutic response to be observable when drugs used to treat parkinsonism are initiated
Name the action of carbidopa, levodopa, and apomorphine on neurotransmitters involved in Parkinson's disease

Slide 5

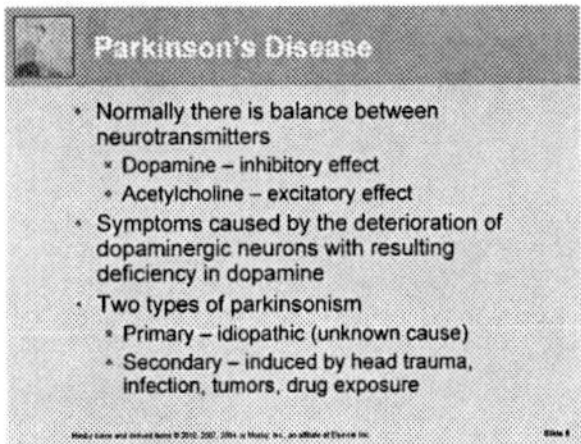
Parkinson's Disease
Normally there is balance between neurotransmitters
Dopamine – inhibitory effect
Acetylcholine – excitatory effect
Symptoms caused by the deterioration of dopaminergic neurons with resulting deficiency in dopamine
Two types of parkinsonism
Primary – idiopathic (unknown cause)
Secondary – induced by head trauma, infection, tumors, drug exposure

- Chronic progressive disorder of the CNS.
- Named after James Parkinson, the English physician who described the "shaking palsy" in 1817.

Slide 6

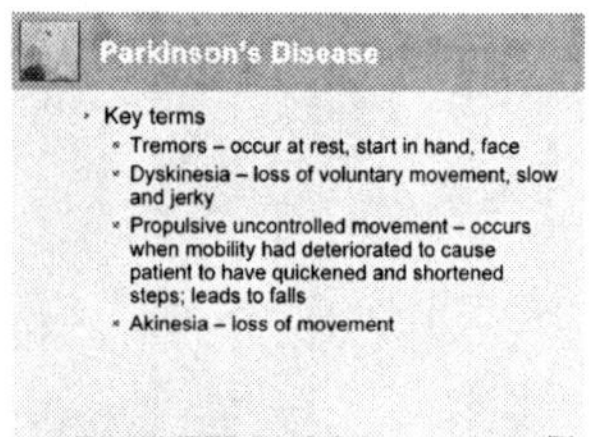
Parkinson's Disease
Key terms
Tremors – occur at rest, start in hand, face
Dyskinesia – loss of voluntary movement, slow and jerky
Propulsive uncontrolled movement – occurs when mobility had deteriorated to cause patient to have quickened and shortened steps; leads to falls
Akinesia – loss of movement

Slide 7

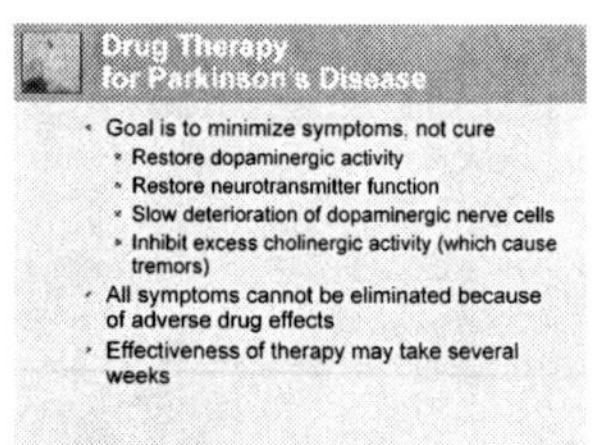
Drug Therapy for Parkinson's Disease
Goal is to minimize symptoms, not cure
Restore dopaminergic activity
Restore neurotransmitter function
Slow deterioration of dopaminergic nerve cells
Inhibit excess cholinergic activity (which cause tremors)
All symptoms cannot be eliminated because of adverse drug effects
Effectiveness of therapy may take several weeks

- Parkinson's is individualized and uses a combination of agents because symptoms and disease progression vary greatly among individuals.
- Therapy begins when symptoms interfere with the ability to function in daily life.

Slide 8

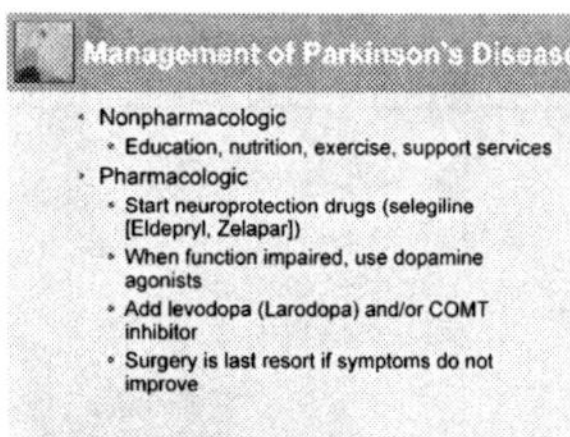
Management of Parkinson's Disease
Nonpharmacologic
Education, nutrition, exercise, support services
Pharmacologic
Start neuroprotection drugs (selegiline [Eldepryl, Zelapar])
When function impaired, use dopamine agonists
Add levodopa (Larodopa) and/or COMT inhibitor
Surgery is last resort if symptoms do not improve

- Stem cell research is ongoing for treatment of Parkinson's.

Slide 9

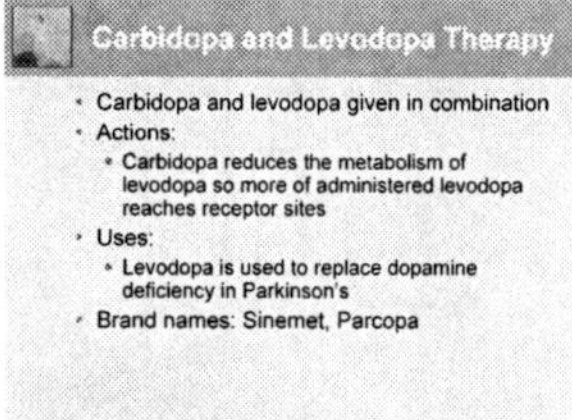
Carbidopa and Levodopa Therapy
Carbidopa and levodopa given in combination
Actions:
Carbidopa reduces the metabolism of levodopa so more of administered levodopa reaches receptor sites
Uses:
Levodopa is used to replace dopamine deficiency in Parkinson's
Brand names: Sinemet, Parcopa

Slide 10

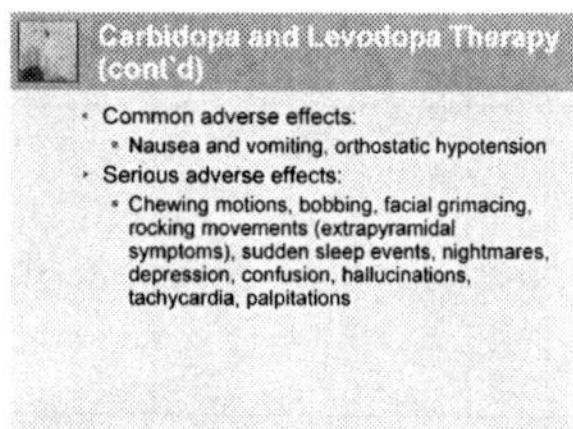
Carbidopa and Levodopa Therapy (cont'd)
Common adverse effects:
Nausea and vomiting, orthostatic hypotension
Serious adverse effects:
Chewing motions, bobbing, facial grimacing, rocking movements (extrapyramidal symptoms), sudden sleep events, nightmares, depression, confusion, hallucinations, tachycardia, palpitations

ELSEVIER

Slide 11

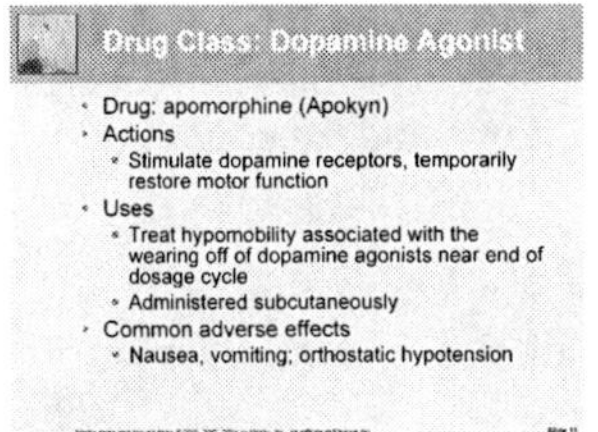
Drug Class: Dopamine Agonist
Drug: apomorphine (Apokyn)
Actions
Stimulate dopamine receptors, temporarily restore motor function
Uses
Treat hypomobility associated with the wearing off of dopamine agonists near end of dosage cycle
Administered subcutaneously
Common adverse effects
Nausea, vomiting; orthostatic hypotension

- Chemically related to morphine but has no opioid effect.
- Serious adverse effects: extrapyramidal symptoms; sudden sleep events, depression, confusion, hallucinations; tachycardia, palpitations, others.

Slide 12

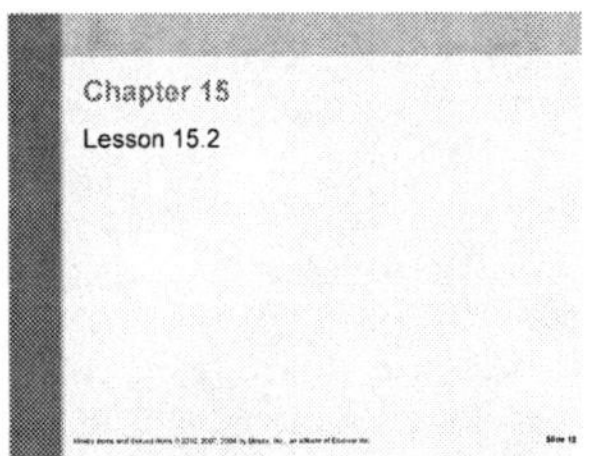
Chapter 15
Lesson 15.2

Slide 13

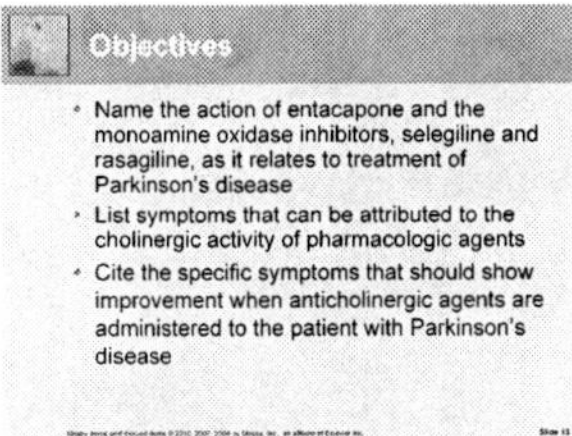
Objectives
Name the action of entacapone and the monoamine oxidase inhibitors, selegiline and rasagiline, as it relates to treatment of Parkinson's disease
List symptoms that can be attributed to the cholinergic activity of pharmacologic agents
Cite the specific symptoms that should show improvement when anticholinergic agents are administered to the patient with Parkinson's disease

Slide 14

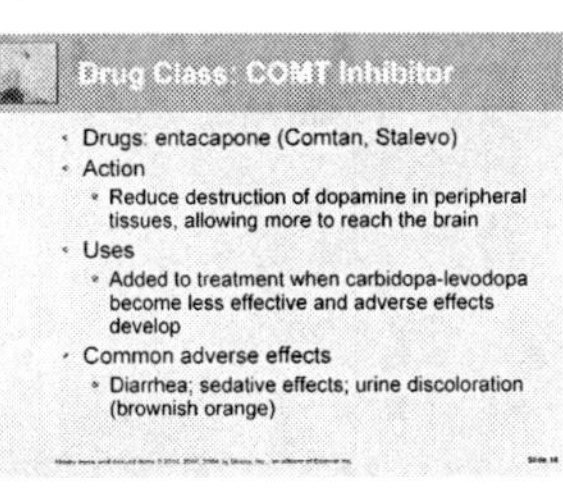
Drug Class: COMT Inhibitor
Drugs: entacapone (Comtan, Stalevo)
Action
Reduce destruction of dopamine in peripheral tissues, allowing more to reach the brain
Uses
Added to treatment when carbidopa-levodopa become less effective and adverse effects develop
Common adverse effects
Diarrhea; sedative effects; urine discoloration (brownish orange)

- Stalevo is a combination drug containing carbidopa, levodopa, and entacapone.
- Serious adverse effects: neurologic effects (chorea, confusion, hallucinations; orthostatic hypotension).

Slide 15

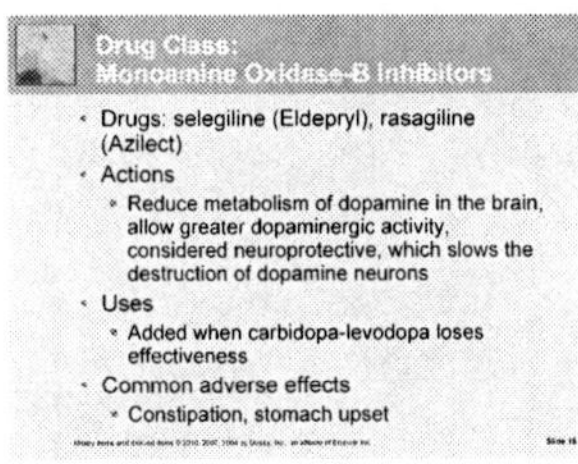
Drug Class: Monoamine Oxidase-B Inhibitors
Drugs: selegiline (Eldepryl), rasagiline (Azilect)
Actions
Reduce metabolism of dopamine in the brain, allow greater dopaminergic activity, considered neuroprotective, which slows the destruction of dopamine neurons
Uses
Added when carbidopa-levodopa loses effectiveness
Common adverse effects
Constipation, stomach upset

- Used to improve memory, motor speed, and may increase life expectancy.
- Serious adverse effects: neurologic effects (chorea, confusion, hallucinations; orthostatic hypotension).

Slide 16

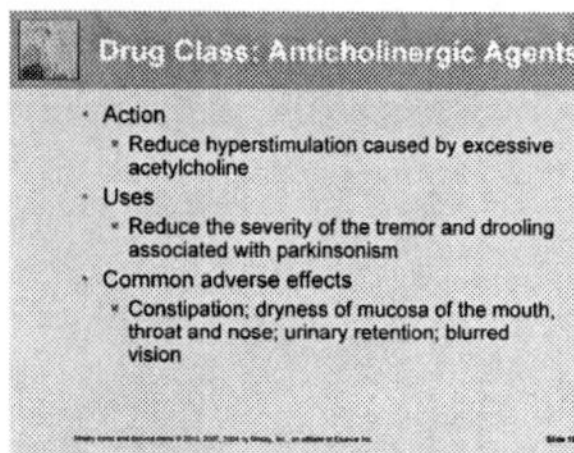
Drug Class: Anticholinergic Agents
Action
Reduce hyperstimulation caused by excessive acetylcholine
Uses
Reduce the severity of the tremor and drooling associated with parkinsonism
Common adverse effects
Constipation; dryness of mucosa of the mouth, throat and nose; urinary retention; blurred vision

- For specific drugs, see Table 15-2.
- Less effective for rigidity, bradykinesia, or postural abnormalities.
- More useful for patients with minimal symptoms and no cognitive impairment.
- Serious adverse effects: nightmares, depression, confusion, hallucinations; orthostatic hypotension, palpitations, dysrhythmias.

Slide 17

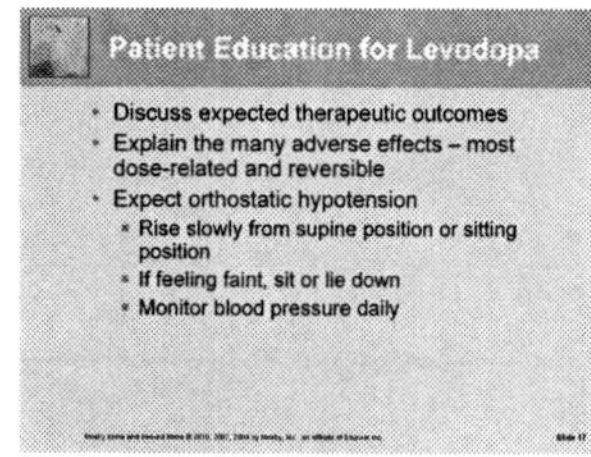
Patient Education for Levodopa
Discuss expected therapeutic outcomes
Explain the many adverse effects – most dose-related and reversible
Expect orthostatic hypotension
Rise slowly from supine position or sitting position
If feeling faint, sit or lie down
Monitor blood pressure daily

16 Lesson Plan

Drugs Used for Anxiety Disorders

TEACHING FOCUS

This chapter provides an introduction to various anxiety disorders and the drugs used in the treatment of such disorders. Several classes of drugs commonly used are explained in detail, including mode of action, indications, dosage, adverse effects, and drug interactions. Students will have an opportunity to learn about the primary therapeutic outcomes expected from treatment with these drugs, including psychological and physiologic drug dependence.

MATERIALS AND RESOURCES

☐ computer and PowerPoint projector (all Lessons)

LESSON CHECKLIST

Preparations for this lesson include:

- lecture
- demonstration
- guest speaker: mental health provider certified in the treatment of addictions
- evaluation of student knowledge and skills needed to perform all entry-level activities related to drugs used for anxiety disorders, including an understanding of:
  - types of anxiety disorders
  - drug therapy for anxiety disorders
  - various classes of drugs used in the treatment of anxiety disorders
  - the nursing process for antianxiety therapy
  - expected outcomes for antianxiety therapy

KEY TERMS

anxiety (p. 240)
anxiolytics (p. 241)
compulsion (p. 241)
generalized anxiety disorder (p. 240)
obsessive-compulsive disorder (p. 241)
panic disorder (p. 240)
phobias (p. 241)
tranquilizers (p. 241)

ADDITIONAL RESOURCES

PowerPoint slides: 1-16
Flashcards, Decks 1 and 2

Legend

ARQ	**PPT**	**TB**	**CTQ**	**SG**	**INRQ**
Audience Response Questions	PowerPoint Slides	Test Bank	Critical Thinking Questions	Study Guide	Interactive NCLEX Review Questions

Class Activities are indicated in ***bold italic.***

LESSON 16.1

BACKGROUND ASSESSMENT

Question: What are some reasons for patients to be noncompliant with pharmacotherapy for anxiety or discontinue it without medical advice? How can a nurse address these factors?
Answer: The main reason that patients discontinue the drug therapy is the adverse effects. The adverse effects of many antianxiety medications include dizziness, headache, and orthostatic hypotension. Other adverse effects, such as somnolence and drowsiness, prevent patients from maintaining normal functioning. If a person is abusing alcohol, the adverse effects of the medication may be exacerbated; patients should be educated on the importance of not using alcohol or other sedating drugs while taking antianxiety medication. Another reason patients may stop taking medication is because the medication may not have an immediate onset of action. When a patient is taking buspirone or selective serotonin reuptake inhibitors (SSRI)s, it may take 1 to 2 weeks for the symptoms of anxiety to decrease. If the patient does not notice immediate results, he or she may decide to discontinue the medication. The nurse can prevent this by advising the patient that the onset of action will be delayed. The nurse should also ensure that the patient is using adjunct psychotherapy with the pharmacologic therapy.

Question: The patient tells the nurse, "My health care provider prescribed Vistaril for my anxiety. I thought that Vistaril is used to relieve itching, not anxiety." How should the nurse respond?
Answer: Vistaril (hydroxyzine) is a first-generation antihistamine (H_1 blocker) used to relieve itching caused by allergic conditions. It is used as a mild tranquilizer in psychiatric conditions characterized by anxiety, tension, and agitation. It is possible that hydroxyzine is as effective as benzodiazepines in treating anxiety disorders. Histamine is a central nervous system neurotransmitter, and hydroxyzine works by blocking the H_1 receptors in the brain. By blocking the effects of histamine, hydroxyzine reduces anxiety, produces drowsiness, and, in high doses, impairs psychomotor performance of complex tasks. Mild tolerance to the sedative effects may occur with long-term use. The first-generation antihistamines have anticholinergic properties, which cause dry mouth, increased heart rate, and decreased gastrointestinal activity. Unlike other anxiolytic medications, such as benzodiazepines, antihistamines have no abuse or addiction potential.

CRITICAL THINKING QUESTION

The patient tells the nurse, "After taking Xanax for some time, I quit. I found that alcohol helps relieve my anxiety symptoms just as well, and it does not cost as much. Besides, it does not have any adverse effects. Why should I bother taking my medication?" How should the nurse respond?
Guidelines: Alcohol is a central nervous system depressant. Although it may help relieve anxiety symptoms, withdrawal from alcohol increases symptoms of anxiety. It is fairly common for patients with mental illness to self-medicate with alcohol and street drugs. The nurse can acknowledge that a part of the patient's observation is valid. However, alcohol has adverse effects as well. It can cause liver disease and subsequent cirrhosis, impaired functioning, and addiction. Alcohol consumption and dosage are not monitored by a health care provider. When a patient on medication receives the same dose each time, he or she will experience a consistent relief from anxiety. The nurse may mention to the patient that it is important not to use alcohol and antianxiety medications together because this can worsen adverse effects.

OBJECTIVES	CONTENT	TEACHING RESOURCES
Define key words associated with anxiety states.	■ Anxiety disorders (p. 240) Review the types of anxiety disorders and their associated symptoms. Discuss the use of drug therapy along with psychotherapy.	PPT 4 ARQ 1-2 INRQ 5-7 SG Review Sheet questions 1-4 (p. 103) SG Learning Activities questions 1-5, 10-11 (p. 105) SG Practice Question for the NCLEX Examination 5 (p. 106)

OBJECTIVES	CONTENT	TEACHING RESOURCES
		▸ Discuss the difference between mild anxiety and anxiety disorders. ▸ Discuss the distinguishing features of generalized anxiety disorder, panic disorder, phobias, and obsessive-compulsive disorder. Class Activity ***Divide the class into small groups. Assign each group an anxiety disorder, and have each group outline the symptoms and characteristics of the disorder. Have each group report its findings to the class.*** Class Activity ***List on the board the following terms: generalized anxiety disorder, panic disorder, phobias, and obsessive-compulsive disorder. Divide the class into four groups with each group taking a different disorder. Have each group explain the disorder by giving examples of symptoms exhibited by patients. Review the exercise with the class.***
Describe the essential components of a baseline assessment of a patient's mental status.	■ Drug therapy for anxiety disorders (p. 241) – Nursing process for antianxiety therapy (p. 242) Review the therapeutic outcome desired in treating patients with anxiety disorders. Discuss each disorder and its associated outcome.	PPT 5-9 ARQ 3 TB Multiple Choice question 8 TB Multiple Response question 4 INRQ 8 CTQ 1 Patient Self-Assessment Form: Antianxiety Medication SG Review Sheet questions 5-6, 10-11 (pp. 103-104) SG Learning Activities questions 6-9 (p. 105) ▸ Discuss the variety of pharmacologic agents that have been used to treat anxiety disorders. ▸ Discuss and name the four classes of drugs that the Food and Drug Administration (FDA) has approved for the treatment of anxiety disorders. ▸ Discuss the various patient parameters that are assessed at baseline and then reassessed throughout the course of therapy to ascertain outcome. ▸ Discuss why it is important to obtain an accurate assessment of the patient's mental status.

ELSEVIER

OBJECTIVES	CONTENT	TEACHING RESOURCES
		▸ Discuss ways in which the nurse can foster a supportive environment where the patient feels comfortable and therapeutic communication can take place. Class Activity ***Divide the class into small groups, and assign the following scenarios to the groups:*** – ***A 24-year-old woman who washes her hands 25 to 30 times a day because of a fear of germs*** – ***A 20-year-old woman with panic attacks*** – ***A 30-year-old man with a fear of public speaking*** – ***A 15-year-old who refuses to go to school because of a fear of being judged by others*** – ***A 70-year-old woman who lives in a house with 15 cats*** ***Have each group identify the disorder for each scenario and determine which medication would probably be prescribed for the disorder. Have groups share their findings with the class for discussion.*** Class Activity ***Have students research information related to antianxiety drugs on the FDA website. How are additional warnings added to the drug information? (For students to prepare for this activity, see Homework/ Assignments #1.)***
Develop a teaching plan for patient education of people taking antianxiety medications.	– Patient education and health promotion (p. 243)	PPT 10 ARQ 4 TB Multiple Choice questions 6-7, 9 CTQ 6 Patient Self-Assessment Form: Antianxiety Medication Review Question for the NCLEX Examination 6 (p. 249) ▸ Discuss what factors are important to consider when creating a teaching plan for patients taking antianxiety medications. ▸ Discuss the role of the patient self-assessment form. Class Activity ***Divide the class into pairs. Have students make drug cards for medications used for anxiety, including uses, mechanisms of action, adverse effects, classifications, and***

OBJECTIVES	CONTENT	TEACHING RESOURCES
		patient education information. Then have students take turns role-playing a nurse educating a patient about these medications. Class Activity ***Divide the class into small groups. Have each group identify reasons for patient noncompliance with psychotropic medications and the nursing interventions for this problem. Have each group present ideas to the class.***

16.1 Homework/Assignments:
1. Have students research information related to antianxiety drugs on the FDA website. How are additional warnings added to the drug information? Have students use the drug inserts from various anxiolytics and compare them with the FDA warnings.

16.1 Instructor's Notes/Student Feedback:

LESSON 16.2

CRITICAL THINKING QUESTION

The 76-year-old female patient's behavior changed after her husband died. Now she cannot leave the house without checking numerous times to see if the door is locked. When she does leave, she returns within minutes to check again. Her daughter accompanies her today and says, "We went shopping 2 days ago. I hadn't been driving for 5 minutes when Mom said that she needs to check to see whether she locked the door. I saw her lock it myself, so I told her I wasn't turning back. My mother became tearful, angry, and attempted to get out of the moving car." What assessment should the nurse perform?

Guidelines: The behaviors reported by the daughter may signify that the mother has an obsessive-compulsive disorder triggered by a stressful event—the death of her husband. The condition may also be exacerbated by depression, cognitive deficiencies, or a physiologic illness. The nurse should assess the patient for the presence of these comorbid conditions by completing a mental status exam and obtaining the patient and family history. Then the nurse should assess the patient for the frequency and severity of obsessive and compulsive behaviors and perform a psychiatric review of systems: mood and anxiety symptoms, somatoform disorders, eating disorders, impulse control disorders, and sleep patterns. The nurse should assess the impact of the compulsion on the person's life and then present the patient and her family with several treatment options.

OBJECTIVES	CONTENT	TEACHING RESOURCES
Describe signs and symptoms that the patient will display when a positive	□ Drug class: benzodiazepines (p. 244) – Nursing process for benzodiazepines (p. 245)	PPT 13-14 TB Multiple Choice questions 2-4, 10 TB Multiple Response question 1

OBJECTIVES	CONTENT	TEACHING RESOURCES
therapeutic outcome is being seen for the treatment of a high anxiety state.	□ Drug class: azapirones (p. 246) – Nursing process for buspirone therapy (p. 246) □ Drug class: selective serotonin reuptake inhibitors (p. 247) – Nursing process for fluvoxamine therapy (p. 247)	INRQ 1, 4, 10-11 CTQ 2-5 SG Review Sheet questions 7-9, 12, 15-17, 20 (pp. 103-104) SG Learning Activities questions 12-14 (p. 105) SG Practice Questions for the NCLEX Examination 1, 3-4, 8-9 (p. 106) Review Questions for the NCLEX Examination 3-5 (p. 249) Drug Table 16-1 Benzodiazepines Used to Treat Anxiety (p. 244) ▸ Discuss why benzodiazepines are the most commonly used anxiolytics. ▸ Discuss the seven benzodiazepine derivatives used as anxiolytics in terms of their dosage and route of administration. What are the common brand names? ▸ Discuss the proposed mode of action of azapirones. ▸ Discuss why SSRIs are used in the treatment of obsessive-compulsive disorders. Class Activity ***Have students research antianxiety drug classes and their high potential for abuse. Have students outline nursing interventions to prevent antianxiety drug abuse and share their findings with the class. (For students to prepare for this activity, see Homework/Assignments #1.)*** Class Activity ***Have students write patient education materials about azapirones. Then have pairs of students take turns role-playing a nurse teaching a patient about the method of action, indications, and adverse effects of azapirones.*** Class Activity ***Have students write patient education materials about SSRIs. Then have pairs of students take turns role-playing a nurse teaching a patient about the method of action, indications, and adverse effects of SSRIs.*** Class Activity ***Have one student role-play some expected behaviors of patients suffering from obsessive-compulsive disorders. Review recent movies that portrayed characters with this disorder (e.g., "As Good As It Gets").***

ELSEVIER

OBJECTIVES	CONTENT	TEACHING RESOURCES
Cite the adverse effects of hydroxyzine therapy, and identify those effects requiring close monitoring when used preoperatively.	□ Drug class: miscellaneous antianxiety agents (p. 247) – Nursing process for hydroxyzine therapy (p. 247) – Nursing process for meprobamate therapy (p. 248)	PPT 15-16 ARQ 5 TB Multiple Response questions 2-3 INRQ 3, 13 SG Review Sheet questions 13-14 (p. 104) SG Practice Questions for the NCLEX Examination 2, 7 (p. 106) Review Questions for the NCLEX Examination 1-2 (p. 249) ▸ Discuss why hydroxyzine is used preoperatively or postoperatively. ▸ Discuss common dosages for the various indications. Class Activity ***Have students write patient education materials about hydroxyzine. Then have them take turns role-playing a nurse teaching a patient about the method of action, indications, and adverse effects of hydroxyzine.***
Discuss psychological and physiologic drug dependence.	Discuss psychological and physiologic dependence.	TB Multiple Choice questions 1, 5 INRQ 2, 12 SG Practice Question for the NCLEX Examination 6 (p. 106) ▸ Discuss general principles to follow when discontinuing an anxiolytic. Why is it important to gradually withdraw the medication? ▸ Discuss which anxiolytic drugs are most likely to cause dependence. Class Activity ***Invite a mental health provider certified in the treatment of addictions to speak to the class about psychological and physiologic dependence.*** Class Activity ***Divide the class into small groups. Have them outline nursing interventions and medication-related patient teaching for the following patients:*** – ***A 30-year-old man taking alprazolam and drinking half of a bottle of whiskey a day*** – ***A 67-year-old man who is taking lorazepam PRN and just filled a sleeping pill prescription***

OBJECTIVES	CONTENT	TEACHING RESOURCES
		– ***A 40-year-old woman who has prescriptions for alprazolam, lorazepam, and diazepam from different health care providers*** – ***A 30-year-old woman who requests a benzodiazepine instead of an antihistamine for anxiety relief after trying the antihistamine for 2 days*** Class Activity ***Divide the class into groups. Using the scenarios from the previous Class Activity, have students identify nursing interventions to involve patients in the decision-making process of their treatment. Have groups share their findings with the class for discussion.***
Performance evaluation		Test Bank SG Learning Activities (p. 105) SG Practice Questions for the NCLEX Examination (p. 106) Critical Thinking Questions

16.2 Homework/Assignments:

16.2 Instructor's Notes/Student Feedback:

ELSEVIER

16 Lecture Outline
Drugs Used for Anxiety Disorders

Slide 1

Chapter 16
Drugs Used for Anxiety Disorders

Slide 2

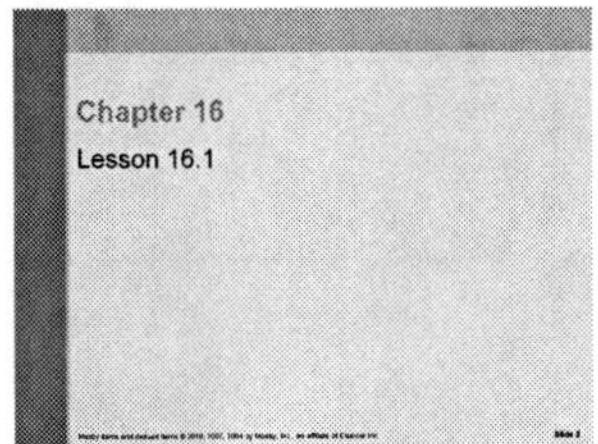
Chapter 16
Lesson 16.1

Slide 3

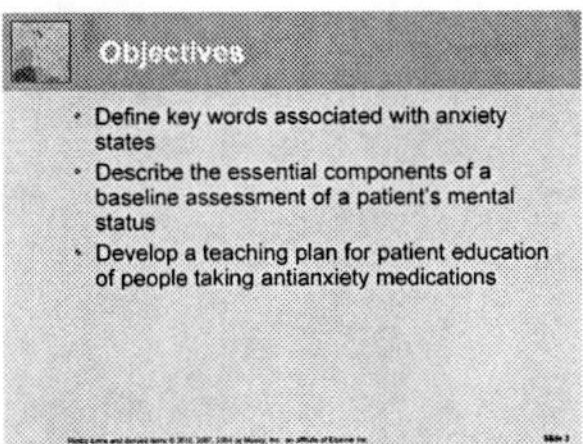
Objectives
Define key words associated with anxiety states
Describe the essential components of a baseline assessment of a patient's mental status
Develop a teaching plan for patient education of people taking antianxiety medications

Slide 4

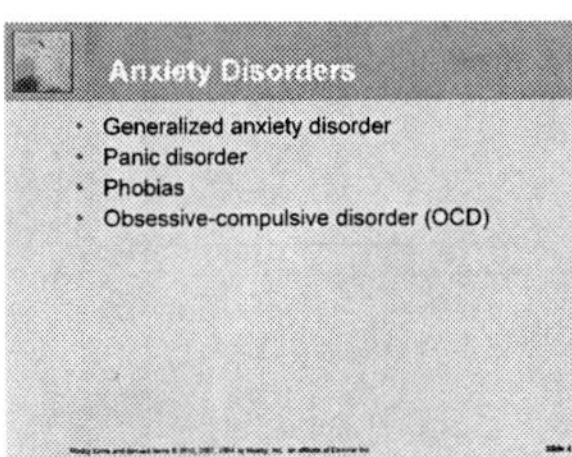
Anxiety Disorders
Generalized anxiety disorder
Panic disorder
Phobias
Obsessive-compulsive disorder (OCD)

- OCD is the most disabling of the anxiety disorders but responds to treatment.
- Major depressive disorder occurs frequently in individuals with panic disorder.

Slide 5

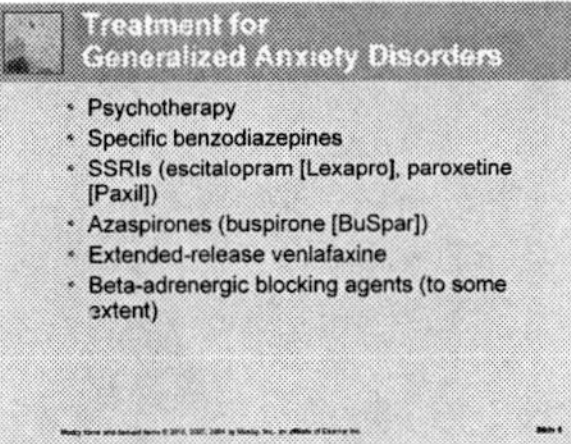
Treatment for Generalized Anxiety Disorders
Psychotherapy
Specific benzodiazepines
SSRIs (escitalopram [Lexapro], paroxetine [Paxil])
Azaspirones (buspirone [BuSpar])
Extended-release venlafaxine
Beta-adrenergic blocking agents (to some extent)

- SSRIs are preferred because their adverse effects are less prominent and they do not have the risk of cardiac dysrhythmias associated with tricyclic antidepressants.

ELSEVIER

Slide 6

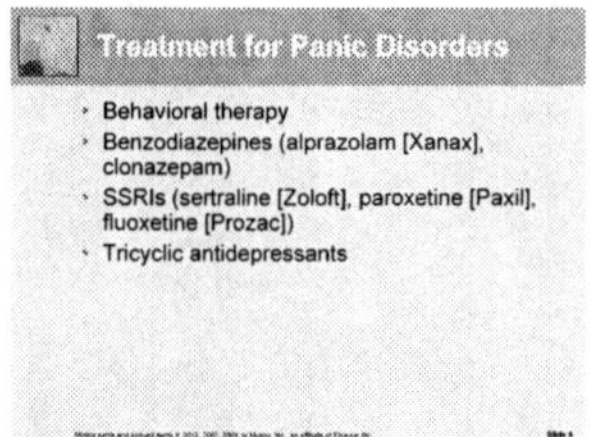
Treatment for Panic Disorders
Behavioral therapy
Benzodiazepines (alprazolam [Xanax], clonazepam)
SSRIs (sertraline [Zoloft], paroxetine [Paxil], fluoxetine [Prozac])
Tricyclic antidepressants

- SSRIs generally the drug of choice for long-term treatment.

Slide 7

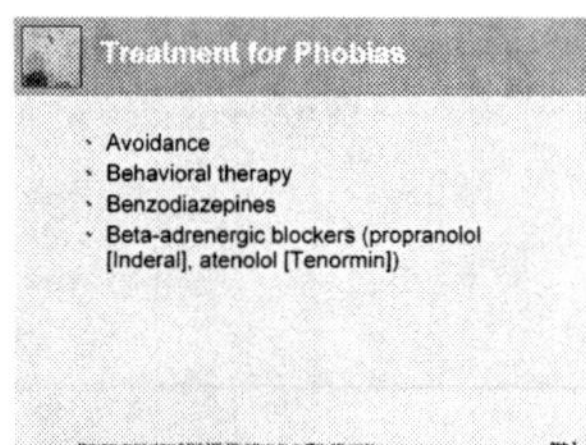
Treatment for Phobias
Avoidance
Behavioral therapy
Benzodiazepines
Beta-adrenergic blockers (propranolol [Inderal], atenolol [Tenormin])

Slide 8

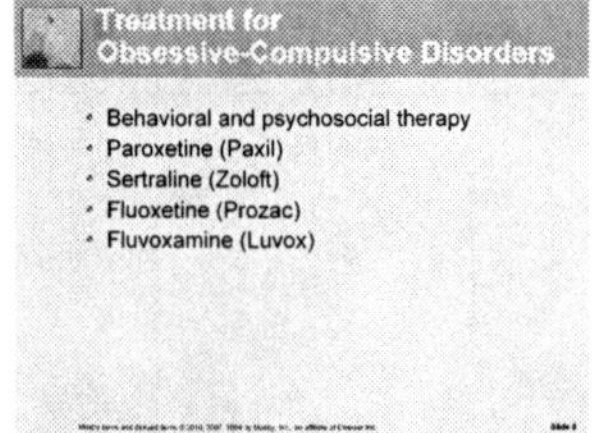
Treatment for Obsessive-Compulsive Disorders
Behavioral and psychosocial therapy
Paroxetine (Paxil)
Sertraline (Zoloft)
Fluoxetine (Prozac)
Fluvoxamine (Luvox)

Slide 9

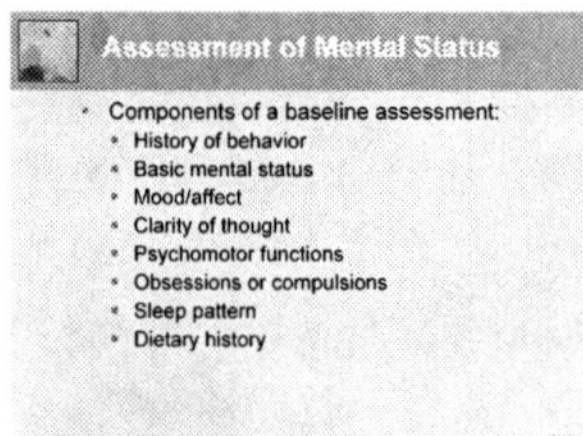
Assessment of Mental Status
Components of a baseline assessment:
History of behavior
Basic mental status
Mood/affect
Clarity of thought
Psychomotor functions
Obsessions or compulsions
Sleep pattern
Dietary history

Slide 10

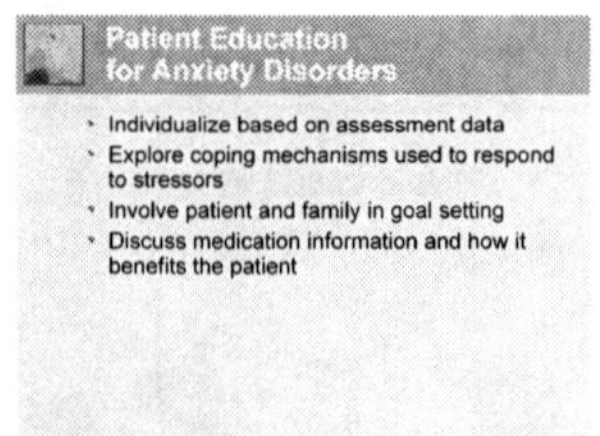
Patient Education for Anxiety Disorders
Individualize based on assessment data
Explore coping mechanisms used to respond to stressors
Involve patient and family in goal setting
Discuss medication information and how it benefits the patient

- Suddenly discontinuing a medication may cause withdrawal symptoms.

Slide 11

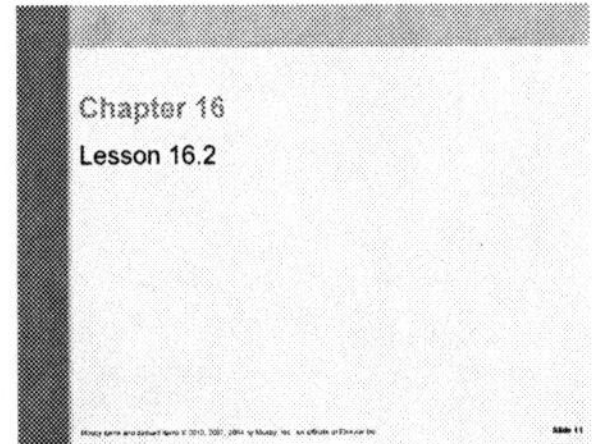
Chapter 16
Lesson 16.2

Slide 12

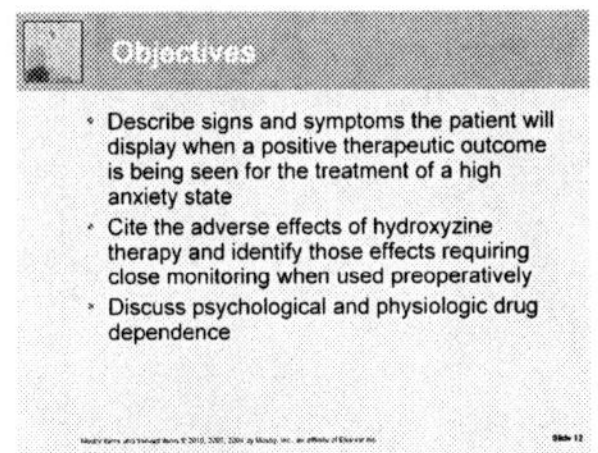
Objectives
Describe signs and symptoms the patient will display when a positive therapeutic outcome is being seen for the treatment of a high anxiety state
Cite the adverse effects of hydroxyzine therapy and identify those effects requiring close monitoring when used preoperatively
Discuss psychological and physiologic drug dependence

Slide 13

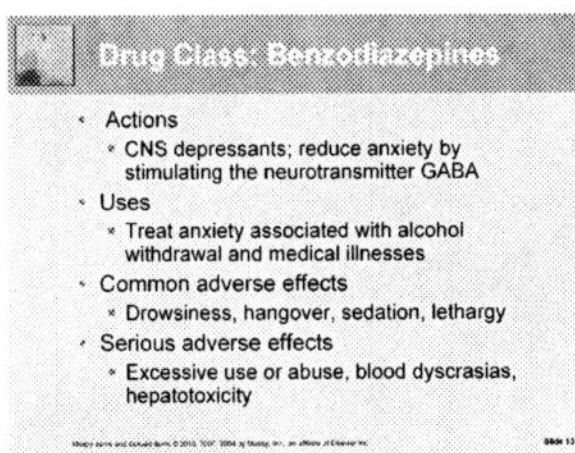
Drug Class: Benzodiazepines
Actions
CNS depressants; reduce anxiety by stimulating the neurotransmitter GABA
Uses
Treat anxiety associated with alcohol withdrawal and medical illnesses
Common adverse effects
Drowsiness, hangover, sedation, lethargy
Serious adverse effects
Excessive use or abuse, blood dyscrasias, hepatotoxicity

- For specific drugs, see Table 16-1.
- Drug of choice due to short half-life and high therapeutic index.

Slide 14

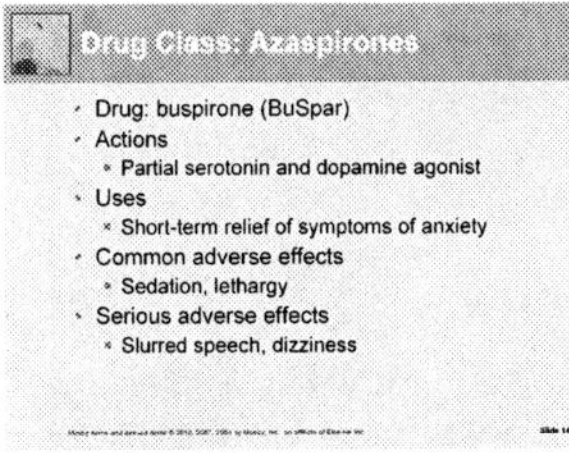
Drug Class: Azaspirones
Drug: buspirone (BuSpar)
Actions
Partial serotonin and dopamine agonist
Uses
Short-term relief of symptoms of anxiety
Common adverse effects
Sedation, lethargy
Serious adverse effects
Slurred speech, dizziness

- Azaspirones have no antipsychotic activity and should not be used in place of appropriate psychiatric treatment.

Slide 15

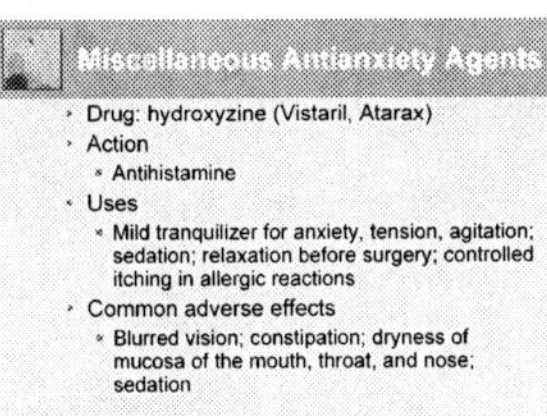
Miscellaneous Antianxiety Agents
Drug: hydroxyzine (Vistaril, Atarax)
Action
Antihistamine
Uses
Mild tranquilizer for anxiety, tension, agitation; sedation; relaxation before surgery; controlled itching in allergic reactions
Common adverse effects
Blurred vision; constipation; dryness of mucosa of the mouth, throat, and nose; sedation

- Used often for mild anxiety; not addictive.
- Serious adverse effects: slurred speech, dizziness.

ELSEVIER

Slide 16

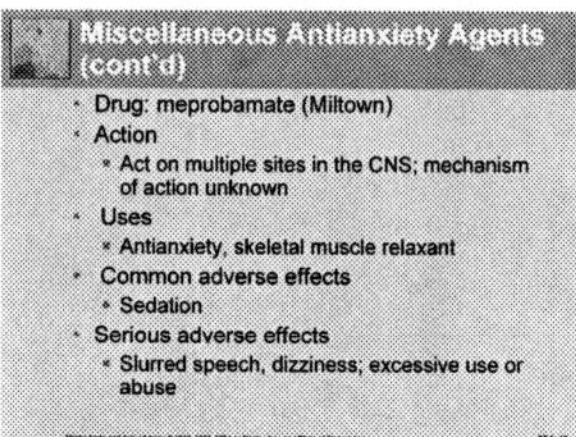
Miscellaneous Antianxiety Agents (cont'd)
Drug: meprobamate (Miltown)
Action
Act on multiple sites in the CNS; mechanism of action unknown
Uses
Antianxiety, skeletal muscle relaxant
Common adverse effects
Sedation
Serious adverse effects
Slurred speech, dizziness; excessive use or abuse

- Sedative-hypnotic; high potential for abuse.

17 Lesson Plan

Drugs Used for Mood Disorders

TEACHING FOCUS

In this chapter, students will be introduced to topics related to drugs used to treat mood disorders, including symptoms of mood disorders, such as depression and bipolar disorder. Nonpharmacologic and pharmacologic therapy will be discussed along with the nursing process for mood disorder therapy. Various drug therapies, including monoamine oxidase inhibitors (MAOIs), selective serotonin reuptake inhibitors (SSRIs), tricyclic antidepressants, and other agents, will also be discussed.

MATERIALS AND RESOURCES

☐ computer and PowerPoint projector (all Lessons)

LESSON CHECKLIST

Preparations for this lesson include:

- lecture
- guest speaker: psychiatric clinical nurse specialist
- evaluation of student knowledge and skills needed to perform all entry-level activities related to medical therapy for mood disorders, including:
  - cause, risk factors, and symptoms of mood disorders
  - nonpharmacologic treatment of mood disorders
  - the nursing process for MAOI therapy
  - the nursing process for SSRI therapy
  - the nursing process for tricyclic antidepressant therapy

KEY TERMS

antidepressants (p. 253)
bipolar disorder (p. 251)
cognitive symptoms (p. 251)
cyclothymia (p. 252)
depression (p. 251)
dysthymia (p. 251)
euphoria (p. 251)
grandiose delusions (p. 252)
labile mood (p. 251)
mania (p. 251)
mood (p. 250)
mood disorder (p. 250)
neurotransmitters (p. 250)
psychomotor symptoms (p. 251)
suicide (p. 252)

ADDITIONAL RESOURCES

PowerPoint slides: 1-24
Flashcards, Decks 1 and 2

Legend

ARQ	**PPT**	**TB**	**CTQ**	**SG**	**INRQ**
Audience Response Questions	PowerPoint Slides	Test Bank	Critical Thinking Questions	Study Guide	Interactive NCLEX Review Questions

Class Activities are indicated in ***bold italic.***

ELSEVIER

LESSON 17.1

BACKGROUND ASSESSMENT

Question: What are the symptoms of depression?
Answer: Depression is characterized by a persistent reduced ability or inability to derive pleasure from life's normal activities. Feelings of sadness and personality changes are common, and patients describe their moods as hopeless. Patients also often feel unrealistic guilt and exhibit symptoms of anxiety. The physical symptoms of depression are usually what motivate a person to seek treatment. These include chronic fatigue, disturbed sleep or insomnia, changes in appetite, inability to concentrate, confusion, slowed movements, and restlessness.

Question: What data should be collected before starting a patient on lithium therapy?
Answer: Laboratory tests should be done first for baseline information, including electrolytes, blood urea nitrogen, serum creatinine, creatinine clearance, urinalysis, and thyroid function tests. Baseline blood pressures should be taken in supine, sitting, and standing positions, and any significant hypotension should be recorded and reported before administering the drug. Daily weights, hydration, and urine specific gravity should also be recorded. Because lithium may deplete sodium and result in toxicity, signs of lithium toxicity should be reported before administering the medication. Signs of lithium toxicity include nausea, vomiting, abdominal pain, diarrhea, lethargy, speech difficulty, muscle twitching, and tremor.

CRITICAL THINKING QUESTION

A patient with a panic disorder has been prescribed an MAOI. He says that he is glad to be getting help and is looking forward to being cured once he starts his medication. How should the nurse respond?
Guidelines: MAOIs act by blocking the metabolic destruction of neurotransmitters by the enzyme monoamine oxidase in the presynaptic neurons of the brain. In preventing the degradation of these neurotransmitters, their concentration is increased. MAO inhibition will start within a few days of therapy. The antidepressant effects, however, require 2 to 4 weeks to become evident. The majority of clinical improvement will occur in the first 2 weeks, and the maximal improvement is usually attained within 4 weeks. It is also important to be aware of the common adverse effects, including orthostatic hypotension, drowsiness, restlessness and insomnia, blurred vision, constipation, and dry mouth. The patient should also be checked regularly for hypertension. He should be instructed about what foods to avoid to prevent a hypertensive crisis from occurring.

OBJECTIVES	CONTENT	TEACHING RESOURCES
Discuss the mood swings associated with bipolar disorder.	■ Mood disorders (p. 250) Review the definition of mood disorders and their relative frequency. Discuss depression and bipolar disorder and its prevalence in the population.	PPT 5-7 ARQ 1 TB Multiple Choice question 1 SG Review Sheet questions 1-6, 9-10, 13 (pp. 107-108) SG Learning Activities questions 1, 5 (p. 110) Lifespan Considerations: Depression (p. 251) ▸ Discuss the characteristics of a mood disorder. ▸ Discuss factors that appear to cause depressive disorders. Note that the underlying causes of mood disorders are unknown. Also discuss risk factors for depression, and describe cognitive and psychomotor symptoms. Class Activity ***Present the following scenarios to the class for students to discuss:***

OBJECTIVES	CONTENT	TEACHING RESOURCES
		1. A patient is sad all the time, has trouble sleeping, and never seems to be hungry. ***2. A patient is paranoid, agitated, and cannot stop moving or speaking.*** ***3. A patient experiences sudden mood swings, and is lethargic, suicidal, and feels needlessly guilty.*** ***Have students determine which mood disorder each patient is exhibiting and discuss appropriate nursing interventions for each.*** Class Activity ***Lead a class discussion about bipolar disorder, and have students identify the characteristics of each phase. How does the depressive phase differ from depression? What are the dangers of the manic phase?***
Differentiate between the physiologic and psychological therapeutic responses seen with antidepressant therapy.	■ Treatment of mood disorders (p. 252) ■ Drug therapy for mood disorders (p. 252) – Actions (p. 252) – Uses (p. 253)	PPT 8-10 ARQ 3, 5 TB Multiple Choice questions 5, 7 INRQ 5 CTQ 1-2, 7 SG Review Sheet questions 7-8, 14-16, 18, 22 (pp. 107-109) SG Learning Activities question 18 (p. 110) SG Practice Questions for the NCLEX Examination 1-2 (p. 111) ▸ Discuss treatment of mood disorders. Describe the three stages that patients pass through before achieving full functioning status. Class Activity ***Divide the class into two groups. Have one group discuss physiologic responses to antidepressant therapy, and have the other group discuss psychological responses. Have each group present its findings to the class.*** Class Activity ***Divide the class into four groups with each group taking one of the following topics: cognitive-behavioral therapy, psychodynamic therapy, interpersonal therapy, and pharmacologic treatment. Have each group discuss what these therapies entail and their goal in treating patients with mood disorders. Review the exercise with the class.***

ELSEVIER

OBJECTIVES	CONTENT	TEACHING RESOURCES
Compare drug therapy used during the treatment of the manic and depressive phases of bipolar disorder.	■ Treatment of mood disorders (p. 252) ■ Drug therapy for mood disorders (p. 252) – Actions (p. 252) – Uses (p. 253)	PPT 11 TB Multiple Choice question 4 TB Multiple Response question 2 CTQ 9-11 SG Practice Question for the NCLEX Examination 8 (p. 111) ▸ Discuss the use of electroconvulsive therapy and premedications used to prevent adverse effects. ▸ Discuss the physiologic manifestations and psychological symptoms of depression. Class Activity ***Invite a psychiatric clinical nurse specialist (CNS) to speak to the class about the treatment of mood disorders and related nursing considerations. Ask the CNS how therapy for bipolar disease differs during the manic and depressive phases of the disorder.***
Describe the essential components of a baseline assessment of a patient with depression or bipolar disorder.	– Nursing process for mood disorder therapy (p. 254)	PPT 12-13 ARQ 2, 4 TB Multiple Choice question 13 TB Multiple Response question 1 Patient Self-Assessment Form: Antidepressants SG Review Sheet questions 12, 15-16, 18 (p. 108) SG Learning Activities questions 15-17, 19 (p. 110) ▸ Discuss the assessment, planning, and implementation phases of the nursing process for mood disorder therapy. ▸ Discuss the implementation phase of the nursing process for mood disorder therapy. Class Activity ***Lead a class discussion about behavior common to mood disorders, and have students offer implementation strategies for handling manic, depressive, and manipulative behavior. What are some important communication strategies and behaviors for the nurse?***
Identify the premedication assessments necessary before the	– Patient education and health promotion (p. 256) ■ Drug therapy for depression (p. 257)	TB Multiple Choice questions 6, 8 TB Multiple Response questions 4-5 INRQ 1-2

ELSEVIER

OBJECTIVES	CONTENT	TEACHING RESOURCES
administration of MAOIs, SSRIs, SNRIs, tricyclic antidepressants, and antimanic agents.	□ Drug class: monoamine oxidase inhibitors (p. 257) – Actions (p. 257) – Uses (p. 257) – Therapeutic outcomes (p. 257) – Nursing process for MAOIs (p. 257)	CTQ 3, 5, 8 SG Review Sheet questions 11, 21 (pp. 107-108) SG Practice Questions for the NCLEX Examination 5-7 (p. 111) Review Question for the NCLEX Examination 7 (p. 271) Clinical Landmine (p. 257) Drug Table 17-1 Antidepressants (pp. 258-259) ▸ Discuss the action of MAOIs, and review under what patient circumstances they might be prescribed. ▸ Discuss MAOIs and special requirements for the diabetic patient. Class Activity ***Lead a class discussion about the importance of monitoring blood pressure while a patient is taking MAOIs. What are the symptoms of a hypertensive crisis, and how is a hypertensive crisis treated? What can happen if it goes untreated?*** Class Activity ***Using a game format, divide the class into groups that quiz each other on the MAOI common and serious adverse effects as well as the drug interactions to be alert for. Review the exercise with the class.***
Cite monitoring parameters used for patients taking monoamine oxidase inhibitors (MAOIs), selective serotonin reuptake inhibitors (SSRIs), serotonin-norepinephrine reuptake inhibitors (SNRIs), or tricyclic antidepressants.	□ Drug class: monoamine oxidase inhibitors (p. 257) – Nursing process for MAOIs (p. 257) □ Drug class: selective serotonin reuptake inhibitors (p. 260) – Nursing process for SSRI therapy (p. 261) □ Drug class: serotonin and norepinephrine reuptake inhibitors (p. 262) – Nursing process for SNRI therapy (p. 262) □ Drug class: tricyclic antidepressants (p. 262) – Nursing process for tricyclic antidepressants (p. 263)	PPT 13-15 TB Multiple Choice questions 2, 9 TB Multiple Response question 3 INRQ 3-4, 6 CTQ 4 SG Learning Activities questions 2, 6, 20 (p. 110) SG Practice Questions for the NCLEX Examination 3-4, 9-10 (pp. 111-112) ▸ Discuss SSRIs and list their advantages. Review the patient circumstances under which they might be prescribed.

17.1 Homework/Assignments:

17.1 Instructor's Notes/Student Feedback:

LESSON 17.2

CRITICAL THINKING QUESTION

A health care provider has ordered paroxetine (Paxil) for a patient. The patient is also taking phenytoin, furosemide, and warfarin. What should the nurse know before administering the paroxetine?

Guidelines: Phenytoin (Dilantin) enhances the metabolism of paroxetine, which requires a dosage increase in paroxetine for a therapeutic effect. Paroxetine increases the metabolism of phenytoin, which requires an increased dosage of phenytoin to maintain its therapeutic effect. Warfarin's (Coumadin) anticoagulant effects are enhanced by paroxetine. The patient must be observed for petechiae, ecchymosis, nosebleeds, bleeding gums, dark tarry stools, and bright red or "coffee ground" emesis. The prothrombin time must be monitored and the dose of warfarin reduced as prescribed. Confirm that the health care provider who wrote the order for paroxetine is aware that the patient is on warfarin and phenytoin.

OBJECTIVES	CONTENT	TEACHING RESOURCES
Compare the mechanism of action of SSRIs to that of other antidepressant agents.	□ Drug class: selective serotonin reuptake inhibitors (p. 260) – Actions (p. 260) – Uses (p. 260) – Therapeutic outcomes (p. 261) □ Drug class: serotonin and norepinephrine reuptake inhibitors (p. 262) – Nursing process for SNRI therapy (p. 262) □ Drug class: tricyclic antidepressants (p. 262) – Nursing process for tricyclic antidepressants (p. 263)	PPT 19-20 TB Multiple Response question 6 ▸ Discuss the mechanism of SSRIs on the brain. Class Activity ***Present the following scenario to the class for students to discuss: A patient taking fluoxetine (Prozac) reports insomnia, restlessness, and nausea. What nursing interventions could minimize adverse effects and encourage patient compliance?***
Cite the advantages of SSRIs over other antidepressant agents.	□ Drug class: selective serotonin reuptake inhibitors (p. 260) – Actions (p. 260) – Uses (p. 260)	PPT 19-20 TB Multiple Choice question 3 INRQ 5, 10-12

OBJECTIVES	CONTENT	TEACHING RESOURCES
	– Therapeutic outcomes (p. 262) – Nursing process for SSRI therapy (p. 261) □ Drug class: serotonin and norepinephrine reuptake inhibitors (p. 262) – Nursing process for SNRI therapy (p. 262) □ Drug class: tricyclic antidepressants (p. 262) – Nursing process for tricyclic antidepressants (p. 263)	CTQ 6 SG Practice Question for the NCLEX Examination 11 (p. 112) Review Questions for the NCLEX Examination 3-4, 6 (p. 271) ▸ Discuss SSRIs and list elements important for a premedication assessment, including gastrointestinal and central nervous system symptoms and hepatic function. Class Activity ***Lead a class discussion about the advantages of SSRIs over other antidepressants. Have students compare their adverse effects, uses, administration, and possible complications.*** Class Activity ***Draw two columns on the board. Write the heading "MAOIs" at the top of one column and "SSRIs" at the top of the other. Then have students explain how each drug acts on the body to reduce symptoms of depression and record responses in the appropriate column.***
Examine the drug monograph for SSRIs to identify significant drug interactions.	– Nursing process for SSRI therapy (p. 261)	TB Multiple Response question 7 INRQ 8 SG Practice Questions for the NCLEX Examination 12-13 (p. 112) ▸ Discuss how smoking affects the metabolism of fluvoxamine. Class Activity ***Divide the class into small groups. Have each group discuss the various drug interactions associated with SSRIs and identify methods of patient teaching to reduce the risk of dangerous interactions. Have groups share their findings with the class.***
Prepare a teaching plan for an individual receiving SSRIs.	□ Drug class: selective serotonin reuptake inhibitors (p. 260) – Actions (p. 260) – Uses (p. 260) – Therapeutic outcomes (p. 261) – Nursing process for SSRI therapy (p. 261)	PPT 24 TB Multiple Response question 8 INRQ 6-7, 9 SG Learning Activities questions 12, 14 (p. 110) ▸ Discuss SSRIs and identify the elements of a teaching plan for a patient receiving a tricyclic antidepressant. Class Activity ***Lead a class discussion about SSRIs, and have students identify and discuss the important elements of the premedication***

ELSEVIER

OBJECTIVES	CONTENT	TEACHING RESOURCES
		assessment. How does this premedication assessment differ from those for MAOIs and tricyclic antidepressants? What elements should be included in the evaluations? Class Activity ***Ask students to compare and contrast the adverse effects of MAOIs and SSRIs. Make a chart on the board, and have students discuss nursing interventions to help patients cope with the adverse effects.***
Identify the premedication assessments necessary before the administration of MAOIs, SSRIs, SNRIs, tricyclic antidepressants, and antimanic agents.	□ Drug class: miscellaneous agents (p. 264) – Nursing process for bupropion therapy (p. 265) – Nursing process for mirtazapine therapy (p. 266) – Nursing process for nefazodone therapy (p. 266) – Nursing process for trazodone therapy (p. 268) □ Drug class: antimanic agents (p. 268) – Nursing process for lithium therapy (p. 269)	PPT 22 TB Multiple Choice questions 10-12 SG Review Sheet questions 17, 19-20 (p. 108) SG Learning Activities questions 3-4, 7-14 (p. 110) SG Practice Questions for the NCLEX Examination 5-7, 15 (pp. 111-112) Review Questions for the NCLEX Examination 1-2, 5 (p. 271) Herbal Interactions: St. John's Wort (p. 267) ▸ Discuss the following drugs, including their actions, uses, therapeutic outcomes, premedication assessment, and planning, implementation, and evaluation elements important to the nursing process: bupropion, mirtazapine, nefazodone, trazodone, and venlafaxine. Class Activity ***Divide the class into groups, and assign each group one of the following drugs: bupropion, mirtazapine, nefazodone, trazodone, or venlafaxine. Have each group examine how the drug acts on the body and discuss its uses, assessments, adverse effects, interactions, and evaluation. Then have each group present its findings to the class.***
Performance evaluation		Test Bank SG Learning Activities (p. 110) SG Practice Questions for the NCLEX Examination (pp. 111-112) Critical Thinking Questions

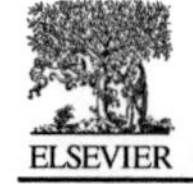

17.2 Homework/Assignments:

17.2 Instructor's Notes/Student Feedback:

17 Lecture Outline
Drugs Used for Mood Disorders

Slide 1

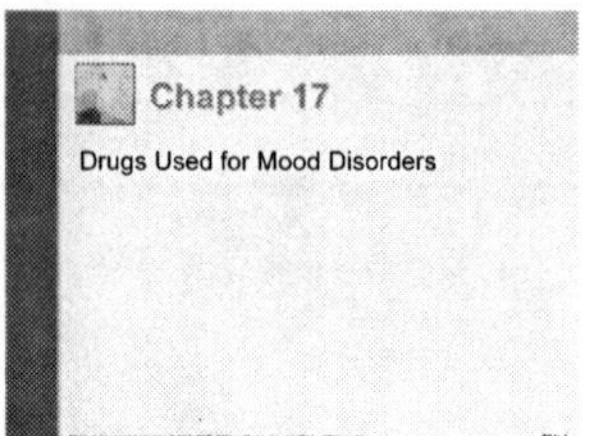
Chapter 17
Drugs Used for Mood Disorders

Slide 2

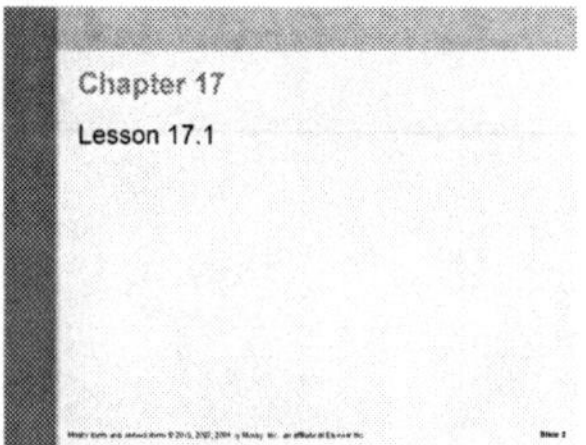
Chapter 17
Lesson 17.1

Slide 3

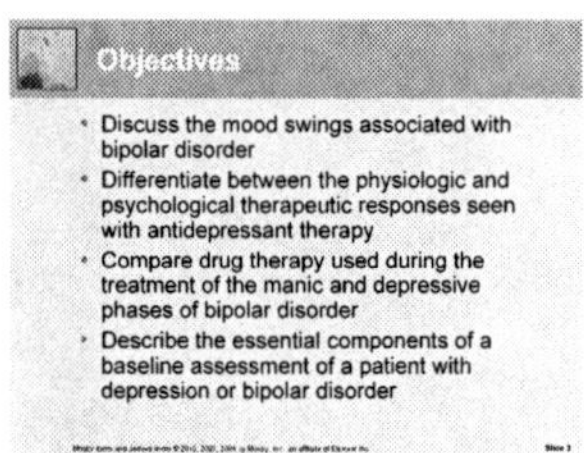
Objectives
Discuss the mood swings associated with bipolar disorder
Differentiate between the physiologic and psychological therapeutic responses seen with antidepressant therapy
Compare drug therapy used during the treatment of the manic and depressive phases of bipolar disorder
Describe the essential components of a baseline assessment of a patient with depression or bipolar disorder

Slide 4

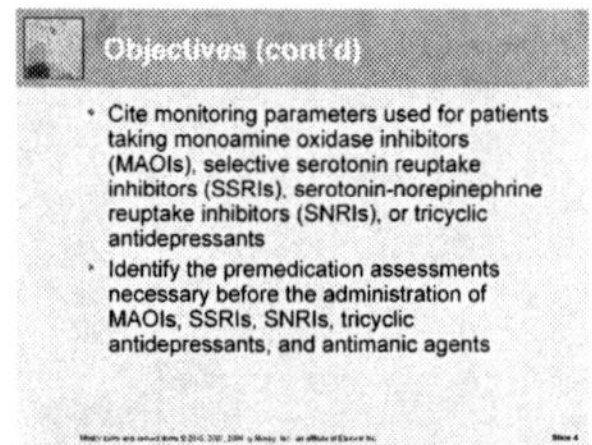
Objectives (cont'd)
Cite monitoring parameters used for patients taking monoamine oxidase inhibitors (MAOIs), selective serotonin reuptake inhibitors (SSRIs), serotonin-norepinephrine reuptake inhibitors (SNRIs), or tricyclic antidepressants
Identify the premedication assessments necessary before the administration of MAOIs, SSRIs, SNRIs, tricyclic antidepressants, and antimanic agents

Slide 5

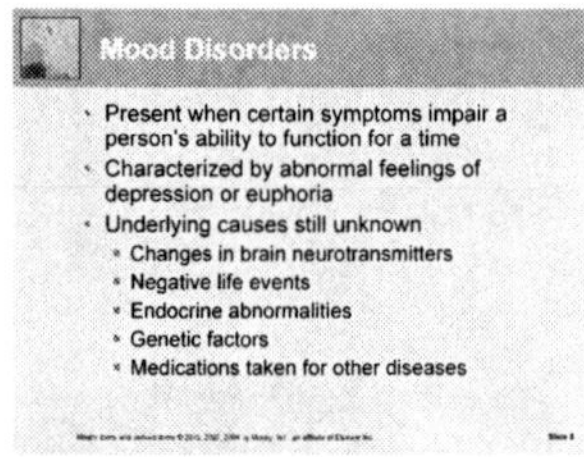
Mood Disorders
Present when certain symptoms impair a person's ability to function for a time
Characterized by abnormal feelings of depression or euphoria
Underlying causes still unknown
Changes in brain neurotransmitters
Negative life events
Endocrine abnormalities
Genetic factors
Medications taken for other diseases

- 15% to 20% of the U.S. population has a diagnosable mood disorder in their lifetime.
- Divided into four primary types: major depressive disorder, dysthymia, bipolar disorder, and cyclothymia.
- Patients have a high incidence of attempting suicide.

ELSEVIER

Slide 6

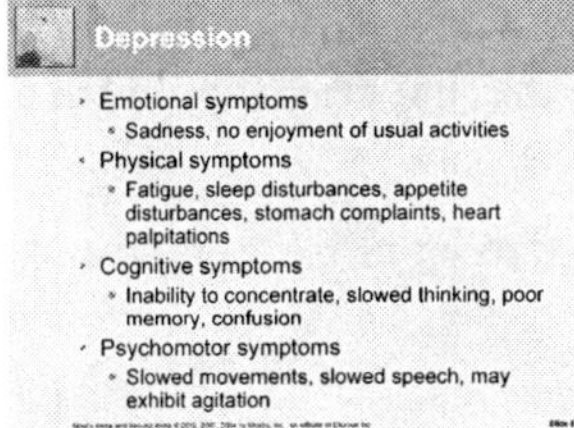
Depression
Emotional symptoms
Sadness, no enjoyment of usual activities
Physical symptoms
Fatigue, sleep disturbances, appetite disturbances, stomach complaints, heart palpitations
Cognitive symptoms
Inability to concentrate, slowed thinking, poor memory, confusion
Psychomotor symptoms
Slowed movements, slowed speech, may exhibit agitation

- Both the patient and family must understand the importance of taking medications.
- Most people go untreated because of social stigma, financial barriers, underrecognition by health care providers, and underappreciation by the public about the benefits of treatment.

Slide 7

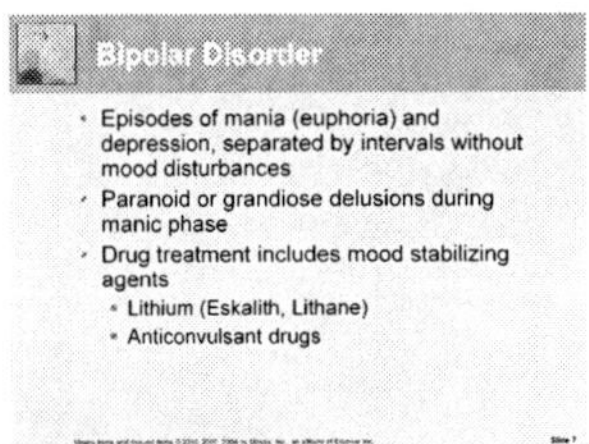
Bipolar Disorder
Episodes of mania (euphoria) and depression, separated by intervals without mood disturbances
Paranoid or grandiose delusions during manic phase
Drug treatment includes mood stabilizing agents
Lithium (Eskalith, Lithane)
Anticonvulsant drugs

- Formerly known as manic depression.
- Mood swings are what differentiates bipolar disorder from depression.

Slide 8

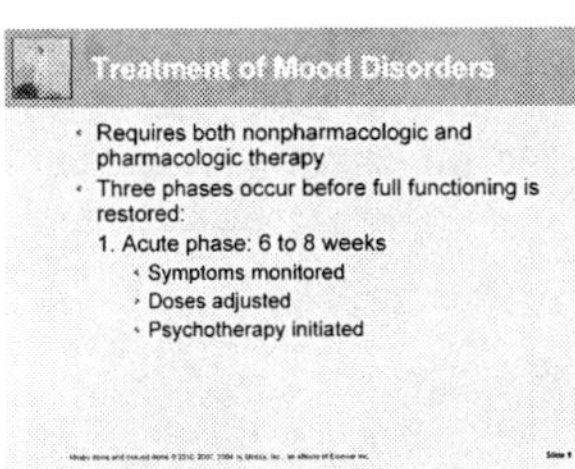
Treatment of Mood Disorders
Requires both nonpharmacologic and pharmacologic therapy
Three phases occur before full functioning is restored:
1. Acute phase: 6 to 8 weeks
Symptoms monitored
Doses adjusted
Psychotherapy initiated

- Cognitive-behavioral therapy, psychodynamic therapy, and interpersonal therapy are important treatments.
- Some patients become noncompliant during the acute phase.

Slide 9

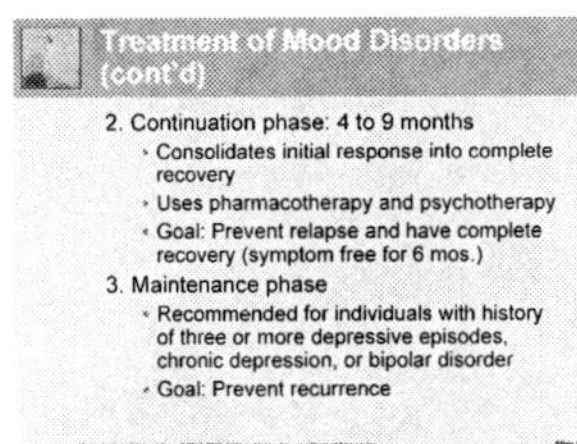
Treatment of Mood Disorders (cont'd)
2. Continuation phase: 4 to 9 months
Consolidates initial response into complete recovery
Uses pharmacotherapy and psychotherapy
Goal: Prevent relapse and have complete recovery (symptom free for 6 mos.)
3. Maintenance phase
Recommended for individuals with history of three or more depressive episodes, chronic depression, or bipolar disorder
Goal: Prevent recurrence

Slide 10

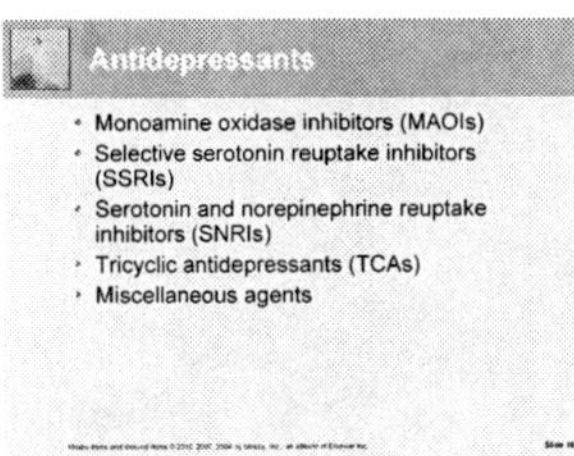
Antidepressants
Monoamine oxidase inhibitors (MAOIs)
Selective serotonin reuptake inhibitors (SSRIs)
Serotonin and norepinephrine reuptake inhibitors (SNRIs)
Tricyclic antidepressants (TCAs)
Miscellaneous agents

- Each antidepressant has varying degrees of effect.
- These drugs alter the availability of neurotransmitters within the brain.

Slide 11

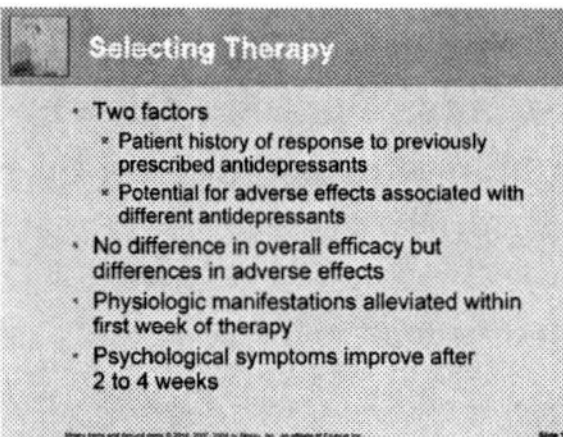
Selecting Therapy
Two factors
Patient history of response to previously prescribed antidepressants
Potential for adverse effects associated with different antidepressants
No difference in overall efficacy but differences in adverse effects
Physiologic manifestations alleviated within first week of therapy
Psychological symptoms improve after 2 to 4 weeks

- It is not possible to predict which drug will be most effective in a patient.
- Some patients do not show a response with the first drug chosen but do with the second.
- It may take 4 to 6 weeks to adjust the dosage to optimize therapy and minimize adverse effects.

Slide 12

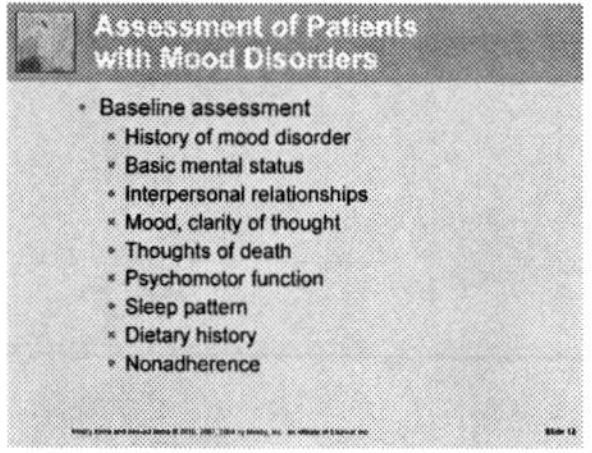
Assessment of Patients with Mood Disorders
Baseline assessment
History of mood disorder
Basic mental status
Interpersonal relationships
Mood, clarity of thought
Thoughts of death
Psychomotor function
Sleep pattern
Dietary history
Nonadherence

Slide 13

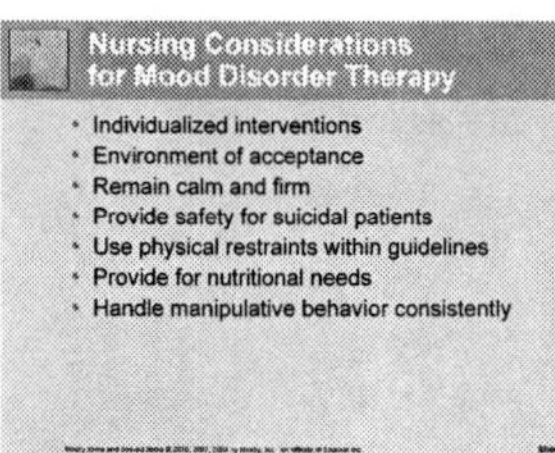
Nursing Considerations for Mood Disorder Therapy
Individualized interventions
Environment of acceptance
Remain calm and firm
Provide safety for suicidal patients
Use physical restraints within guidelines
Provide for nutritional needs
Handle manipulative behavior consistently

- Record observations; observing for suicidal ideation is a high priority.
- Administer PRN drugs when necessary.
- Use the least restrictive form of restraint; have sufficient staff available to control any situation.
- Provide positive reinforcement.
- Employ therapeutic communication techniques.

Slide 14

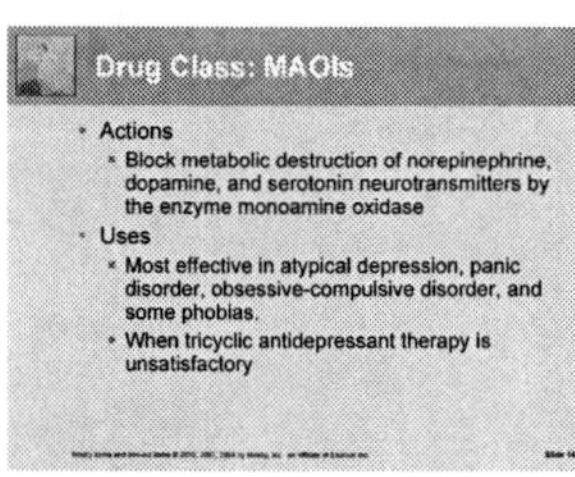
Drug Class: MAOIs
Actions
Block metabolic destruction of norepinephrine, dopamine, and serotonin neurotransmitters by the enzyme monoamine oxidase
Uses
Most effective in atypical depression, panic disorder, obsessive-compulsive disorder, and some phobias.
When tricyclic antidepressant therapy is unsatisfactory

- Neurotransmitters are increased in concentration with these medications.

Slide 15

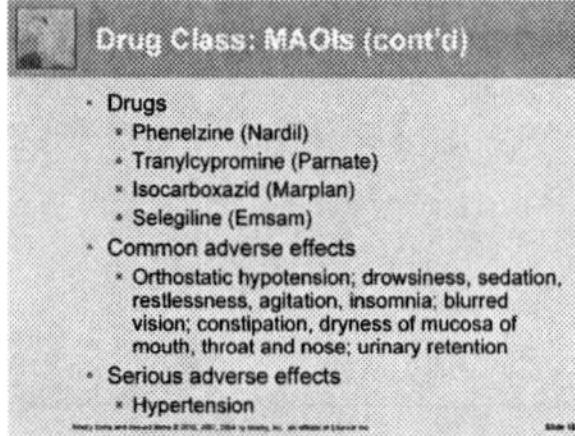
Drug Class: MAOIs (cont'd)
Drugs
Phenelzine (Nardil)
Tranylcypromine (Parnate)
Isocarboxazid (Marplan)
Selegiline (Emsam)
Common adverse effects
Orthostatic hypotension; drowsiness, sedation, restlessness, agitation, insomnia; blurred vision; constipation, dryness of mucosa of mouth, throat and nose; urinary retention
Serious adverse effects
Hypertension

ELSEVIER

Slide 16

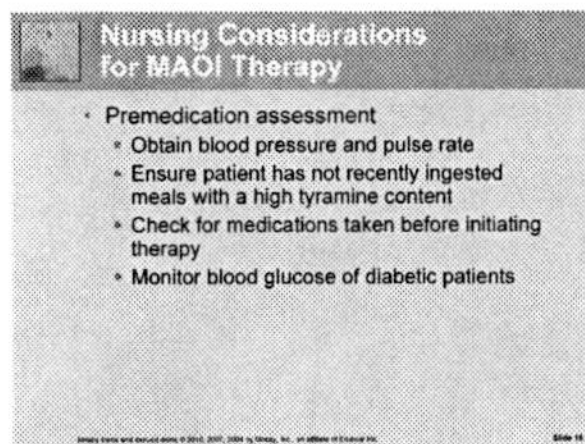
Nursing Considerations for MAOI Therapy
Premedication assessment
Obtain blood pressure and pulse rate
Ensure patient has not recently ingested meals with a high tyramine content
Check for medications taken before initiating therapy
Monitor blood glucose of diabetic patients

- Most common adverse effect is orthostatic hypotension.
- There is potential for hypertensive crisis.
- Provide patient education of dietary products to avoid.

Slide 17

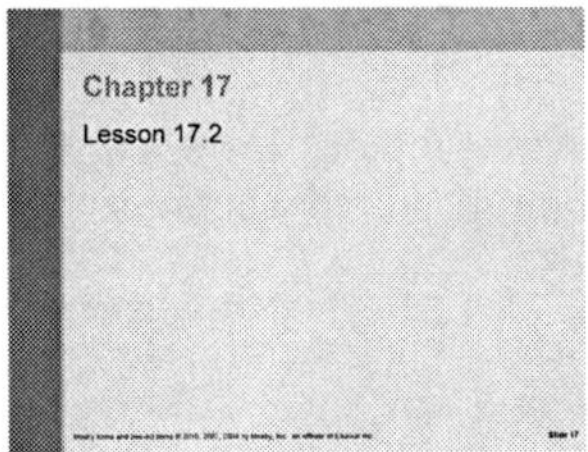
Chapter 17
Lesson 17.2

Slide 18

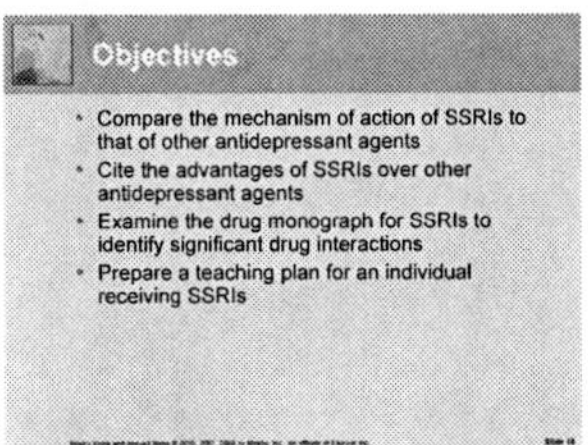
Objectives
Compare the mechanism of action of SSRIs to that of other antidepressant agents
Cite the advantages of SSRIs over other antidepressant agents
Examine the drug monograph for SSRIs to identify significant drug interactions
Prepare a teaching plan for an individual receiving SSRIs

Slide 19

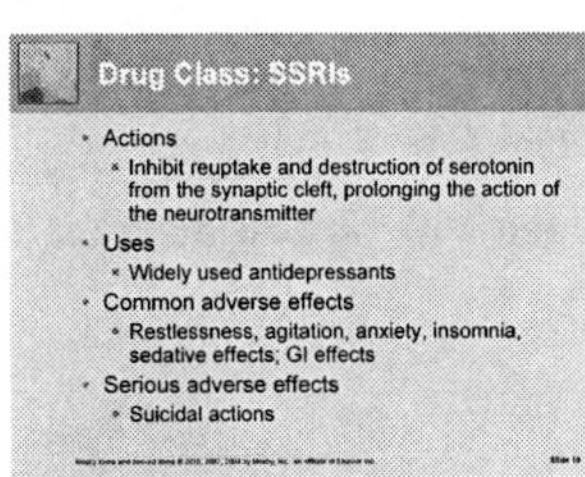
Drug Class: SSRIs
Actions
Inhibit reuptake and destruction of serotonin from the synaptic cleft, prolonging the action of the neurotransmitter
Uses
Widely used antidepressants
Common adverse effects
Restlessness, agitation, anxiety, insomnia, sedative effects; GI effects
Serious adverse effects
Suicidal actions

- For specific drugs, see Table 17-1.
- SSRIs do not have anticholinergic or cardiovascular adverse effects.
- Many drug interactions.
- Be alert for possible serotonin syndrome, which occurs with increased serotonin levels.

Slide 20

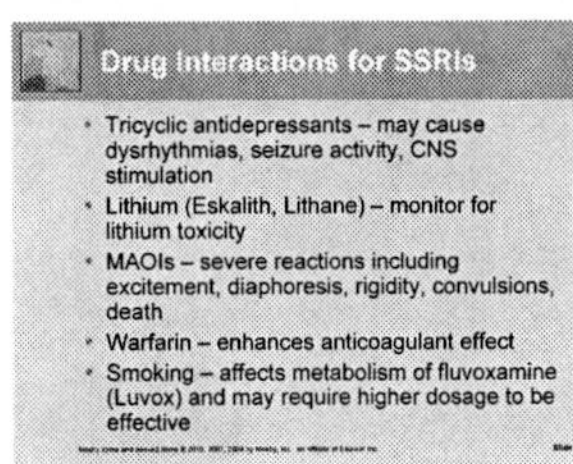
Drug Interactions for SSRIs
Tricyclic antidepressants – may cause dysrhythmias, seizure activity, CNS stimulation
Lithium (Eskalith, Lithane) – monitor for lithium toxicity
MAOIs – severe reactions including excitement, diaphoresis, rigidity, convulsions, death
Warfarin – enhances anticoagulant effect
Smoking – affects metabolism of fluvoxamine (Luvox) and may require higher dosage to be effective

- Potential for severe reactions with the concurrent use of MAOIs and SSRIs.
- Avoid bedtime doses to decrease insomnia.
- Advise patients and families of the sedative effects.

Slide 21

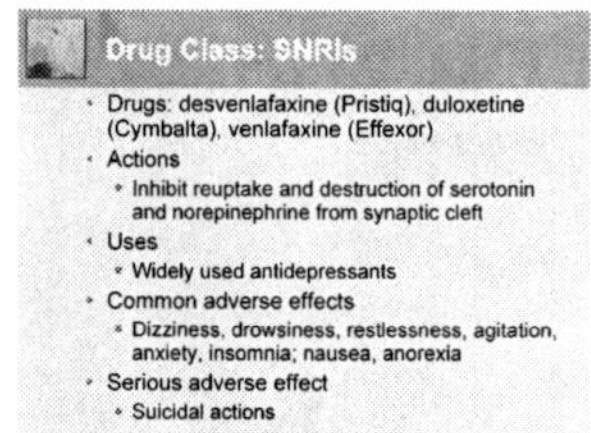
Drug Class: SNRIs
Drugs: desvenlafaxine (Pristiq), duloxetine (Cymbalta), venlafaxine (Effexor)
Actions
Inhibit reuptake and destruction of serotonin and norepinephrine from synaptic cleft
Uses
Widely used antidepressants
Common adverse effects
Dizziness, drowsiness, restlessness, agitation, anxiety, insomnia; nausea, anorexia
Serious adverse effect
Suicidal actions

Slide 22

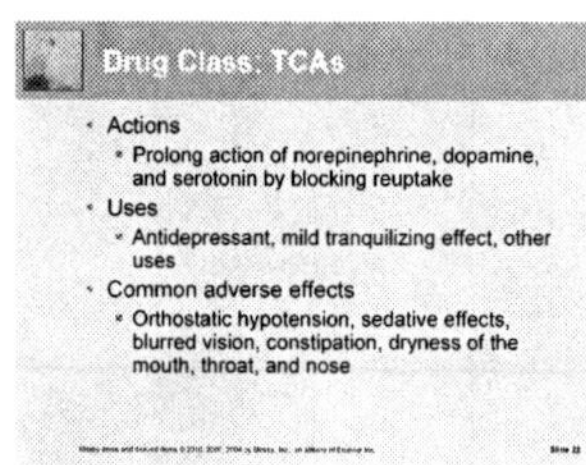
Drug Class: TCAs
Actions
Prolong action of norepinephrine, dopamine, and serotonin by blocking reuptake
Uses
Antidepressant, mild tranquilizing effect, other uses
Common adverse effects
Orthostatic hypotension, sedative effects, blurred vision, constipation, dryness of the mouth, throat, and nose

- For specific drugs, see Table 17-1.
- All have anticholinergic activity.
- Serious adverse effects: tremors, parkinsonian symptoms, seizure activity, dysrhythmias, tachycardia, heart failure, suicidal actions.

Slide 23

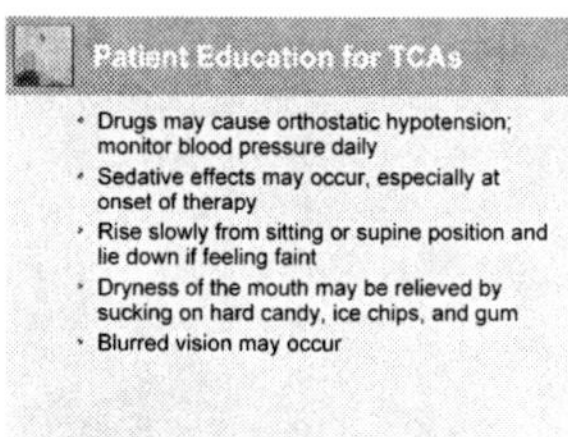
Patient Education for TCAs
Drugs may cause orthostatic hypotension; monitor blood pressure daily
Sedative effects may occur, especially at onset of therapy
Rise slowly from sitting or supine position and lie down if feeling faint
Dryness of the mouth may be relieved by sucking on hard candy, ice chips, and gum
Blurred vision may occur

Slide 24

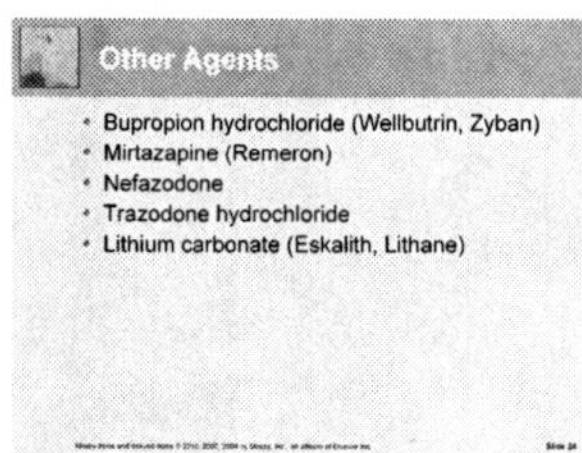
Other Agents
Bupropion hydrochloride (Wellbutrin, Zyban)
Mirtazapine (Remeron)
Nefazodone
Trazodone hydrochloride
Lithium carbonate (Eskalith, Lithane)

- Disadvantages of bupropion include seizure activity and multiple daily doses.
- Trazodone has a lower incidence of anticholinergic effects.
- Lithium is used to treat acute mania associated with bipolar disorder.

18 Lesson Plan
Drugs Used for Psychoses

TEACHING FOCUS

In this chapter, students will be introduced to topics related to the drugs used for psychoses. Students will become acquainted with the signs and symptoms of psychotic behavior, the major indications for the use of antipsychotic agents, and the common adverse effects observed with these agents. The development of teaching plans for patients taking haloperidol or clozapine will also be discussed.

MATERIALS AND RESOURCES

- □ computer and PowerPoint projector (Lessons 18.1)

LESSON CHECKLIST

Preparations for this lesson include:

- lecture
- evaluation of student knowledge and skills needed to perform all entry-level activities related to drugs used for psychoses, including:
  - signs and symptoms of psychotic behavior
  - major indications for the use of antipsychotic agents
  - common adverse effects observed with the use of antipsychotic agents
  - teaching plans for a patient taking haloperidol or clozapine

KEY TERMS

abnormal involuntary movement scale (p. 277)
akathisia (p. 276)
atypical (second-generation) antipsychotic agents (p. 273)
changes in affect (p. 273)
delusion (p. 272)
depot antipsychotic medicine (p. 277)
disorganized behavior (p. 273)
disorganized thinking (p. 273)
dyskinesia identification system: condensed user scale (p. 277)
dystonias (p. 276)
equipotent doses (p. 275)
extrapyramidal symptoms (EPS) (p. 276)
hallucinations (p. 272)
loosening of associations (p. 273)
neuroleptic malignant syndrome (p. 277)
pseudoparkinsonian symptoms (p. 276)
psychosis (p. 272)
tardive dyskinesia (p. 277)
target symptoms (p. 273)
typical (first-generation) antipsychotic agents (p. 273)

ADDITIONAL RESOURCES

PowerPoint slides: 1-17
Flashcards, Decks 1 and 2

Legend

ARQ	PPT	TB	CTQ	SG	INRQ
Audience Response Questions	PowerPoint Slides	Test Bank	Critical Thinking Questions	Study Guide	Interactive NCLEX Review Questions

Class Activities are indicated in ***bold italic.***

ELSEVIER

LESSON 18.1

BACKGROUND ASSESSMENT

Question: How do antipsychotic drugs work in the body?
Answer: Typical antipsychotic agents work by blocking dopamine receptors in the brain. The atypical antipsychotic agents block both dopamine receptors and serotonin receptors. Antipsychotic agents also stimulate or block cholinergic, histaminic, nicotinic, and alpha- and beta-adrenergic receptors, which account for many adverse effects of drug therapy. However, the mechanism by which these actions prevent psychotic symptoms is unknown.

Question: Why is the initial assessment important for a patient with acute psychosis?
Answer: A thorough initial assessment of a patient with acute psychosis is important to make an accurate diagnosis. A physical examination, mental status assessment, family and social history, and laboratory workup must be completed to exclude other possible causes of psychoses, such as drug abuse. It is also important to establish treatment goals and a baseline level of functioning and to identify target symptoms before starting therapy.

CRITICAL THINKING QUESTION

What is tardive dyskinesia, and how can it be prevented?
Guidelines: Tardive dyskinesia is an EPS associated with antipsychotic therapy. It is a drug-induced neurologic disorder that is characterized by orofacial movements, such as mild tongue movement in the beginning, and tongue thrusting, rolling, chewing, and lateral jaw movements as the condition progresses. Other facial symptoms include frequent blinking, grimacing, and brow arching. All antipsychotic drugs have the potential to produce the adverse effect of tardive dyskinesia, and the condition usually disappears after the medication has been reduced or discontinued. Because the signs of tardive dyskinesia may be irreversible, prevention is critical. Patients should be assessed regularly for early signs of the syndrome; several rating scales have been developed to aid in this assessment.

OBJECTIVES	CONTENT	TEACHING RESOURCES
Identify signs and symptoms of psychotic behavior.	■ Psychosis (p. 272) Review the term *psychosis* and its manifestations. Discuss common causes of psychosis (i.e., metabolic, infectious, or endocrine), as well as schizophrenia.	PPT 4-5 ARQ 2 TB Multiple Choice question 1 TB Multiple Response question 1 INRQ 5, 7-8 SG Review Sheet questions 1-3 (p. 113) SG Learning Activities questions 1-3, 6-7, 14-15 (p. 115) SG Practice Question for the NCLEX Examination 9 (p. 118) ▸ Discuss the symptoms of psychosis. Which are present in mood disorders, and how do they differ from psychosis? Class Activity ***Divide the class into groups, and have each group discuss the meaning of psychosis and develop a definition of the term. Then have each group identify the most common psychotic disorders and list some causes of psychosis. Have each group present its findings to the class for discussion.***

OBJECTIVES	CONTENT	TEACHING RESOURCES
		Class Activity ***As a class, ask volunteers to identify the psychotic symptoms exhibited in the following scenarios:*** – ***A male patient says that he is actually the king of a foreign country, but he does not want you to tell anyone.*** – ***As you interview a female patient, you ask her about her symptoms. She says she is anxious, starts talking about grocery shopping, talks about life when she was a child, and then continues to jump from one unrelated subject to another.*** – ***A female patient tells you that the voices in her head want her to steal her neighbor's dog.*** – ***A male patient is wearing mismatched clothes, looks disheveled, and has a pair of winter gloves on, although it is summer. As you are interviewing him, he does not make eye contact, sits, then stands, then walks in a circle, and then goes to the window.***
Describe major indications for the use of antipsychotic agents.	□ Treatment of psychosis (p. 273) □ Drug therapy for psychosis (p. 273) – Actions (p. 275) – Uses (p. 275) Review the treatment options currently available for patients suffering from acute psychosis. Discuss target symptoms and their importance. Review typical or first-generation antipsychotic agents and atypical or second-generation antipsychotic agents, and their effects and goals of therapy.	PPT 6 ARQ 4 TB Multiple Choice questions 2, 8 TB Multiple Response question 2 INRQ 4 SG Review Sheet questions 4-9 (p. 113) SG Learning Activities questions 4, 19 (pp. 115-116) SG Practice Questions for the NCLEX Examination 8, 12 (p. 118) Review Question for the NCLEX Examination 5 (p. 284) Clinical Landmine (p. 276) Drug Table 18-1 Antipsychotic Agents (pp. 274-275) ▸ Discuss the different classes of antipsychotic drugs. What are the indications for the use of each? ▸ Discuss initial goals of drug therapy, advantages of combined therapy, and timing of therapeutic effects of psychosis drug therapy.

ELSEVIER

OBJECTIVES	CONTENT	TEACHING RESOURCES
		Class Activity ***Divide the class into groups, and have students discuss the treatment goals of psychosis. Then have students explain the purpose of identifying target symptoms, discuss how target symptoms are chosen, and outline how they are assessed. Then have groups share their findings with the class.*** Class Activity ***Divide the class into groups, and assign each group one of the scales used to measure target symptoms of psychosis. Have each group research its rating scale, choose three or four symptoms, and make a class presentation that explains how the symptoms are measured. (For students to prepare for this activity, see Homework/Assignments #2.)***
Identify common adverse effects observed with antipsychotic medications.	□ Adverse effects of antipsychotic drug therapy (p. 276) – Extrapyramidal effects (p. 276) – Seizures (p. 277) – Weight gain (p. 277) – Hyperglycemia (p. 278) – Dyslipidemia (p. 278) – Dysrhythmias (p. 278) Review the many serious adverse effects of antipsychotic agents. Discuss the four categories of extrapyramidal symptoms: dystonic reaction, pseudoparkinsonism, akathisia, and tardive dyskinesia.	PPT 7 ARQ 1, 3, 5 TB Multiple Choice questions 3-4, 7, 9 TB Multiple Response questions 3-5 INRQ 1-2, 6, 9, 11-12 CTQ 1, 4 SG Review Sheet questions 10-15 (p. 114) SG Learning Activities questions 5, 8, 17-18, 20-22, 24 (pp. 115-116) SG Practice Questions for the NCLEX Examination 1-2, 4-7, 10-11, 13 (pp. 117-118) Review Questions for the NCLEX Examination 4, 6-7 (pp. 283-284) Box 18-1 Antipsychotic Medicines (p. 276) ▸ Discuss the prevention and treatment of other adverse effects of antipsychotic therapy, such as dry mouth, constipation, and skin pigmentation. Class Activity ***Divide the class into groups, and assign each group one of the following topics: dystonia, pseudoparkinsonian symptoms, akathisia, tardive dyskinesia, or NMS. Have each group outline how the adverse effect is produced, what its symptoms are, and how it is treated. Then have each group present its findings to the class for discussion.*** Class Activity ***Continuing from the previous Class Activity, have volunteers from the class identify the type of adverse effect that is exhibited in the following scenarios:***

OBJECTIVES	CONTENT	TEACHING RESOURCES
		– ***A 25-year-old man has neck torsion and tongue protrusion after taking antipsychotic medication for 3 days.*** – ***A 36-year-old man is brought to the ER for symptoms of fever, incontinence, mutism, and a blood pressure of 176/100 mm Hg. He was given an injection of antipsychotic medication 8 days ago.*** – ***A 75-year-old woman who has been on medication for 2 weeks is brought to the health care provider's office with symptoms of muscular rigidity and a shuffling gait.*** – ***A patient on antipsychotics for 5 months exhibits constant chewing motions, facial grimaces, and fly-catching movements.*** – ***A typically passive woman who has been taking antipsychotics became very aggressive and slapped her husband. She sits in a chair most of the day making constant rocking motions.***
Develop a teaching plan for a patient taking haloperidol and one receiving clozapine.	□ Other adverse effects (p. 278) – Nursing process for antipsychotic therapy (p. 278) – Patient education and health promotion (p. 280) □ Drug class: antipsychotic agents (p. 281) – Actions (p. 281) – Uses (p. 281) – Nursing process for antipsychotic agent therapy (p. 281)	PPT 8-13 TB Multiple Choice questions 5-6, 10 INRQ 3 CTQ 2-3 SG Review Sheet questions 16-17 (p. 114) SG Learning Activities questions 9-13, 23, 25 (pp. 115-116) SG Practice Questions for the NCLEX Examination 3, 14 (pp. 117-118) Review Questions for the NCLEX Examination 1-3 (p. 283) Herbal Interactions: St. John's Wort (p. 283) ▸ Discuss the physiologic causes of psychosis. What is the role of dopamine, serotonin, and other neurotransmitters in the development of psychotic symptoms? ▸ Discuss the adverse effects of antipsychotic drug therapy. How can the adverse effects be lessened or prevented? Class Activity ***Divide the class into groups, and assign each group one of the following topics: assessment, planning, implementation, evaluation. Have each group outline the important elements of its assigned topic***

ELSEVIER

OBJECTIVES	CONTENT	TEACHING RESOURCES
		regarding antipsychotic drug therapy and identify three appropriate nursing interventions. Then have each group share its findings with the class.
Performance evaluation		Test Bank SG Learning Activities (pp. 115-116) SG Practice Questions for the NCLEX Examination (pp. 117-118) Critical Thinking Questions

18.1 Homework/Assignments:

1. Divide the class into groups and assign each group one of the scales used to measure target symptoms of psychosis. Have each group research its rating scale, choose three or four symptoms, and make a class presentation that explains how the symptoms are measured.

18.1 Instructor's Notes/Student Feedback:

18 Lecture Outline

Drugs Used for Psychoses

Slide 1

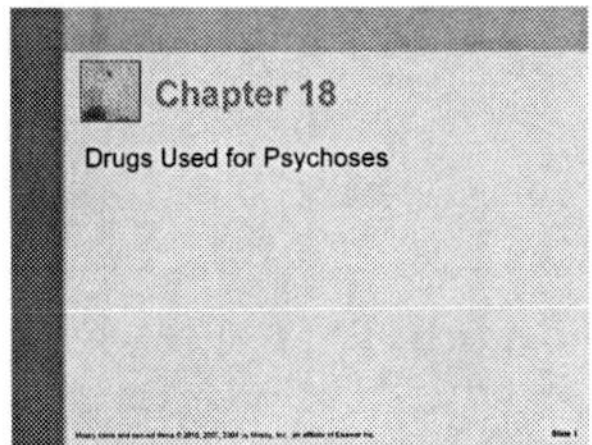
Chapter 18
Drugs Used for Psychoses

Slide 2

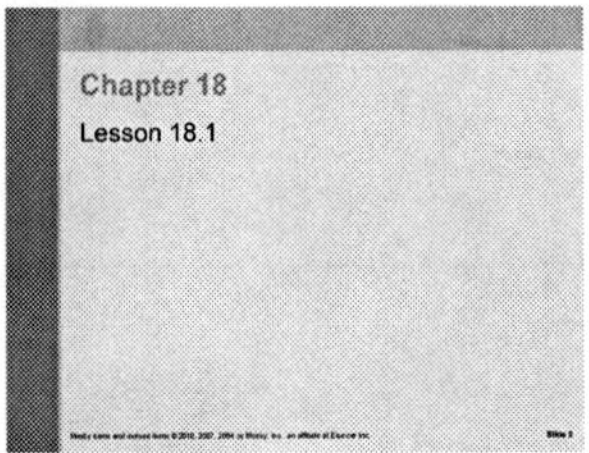
Chapter 18
Lesson 18.1

Slide 3

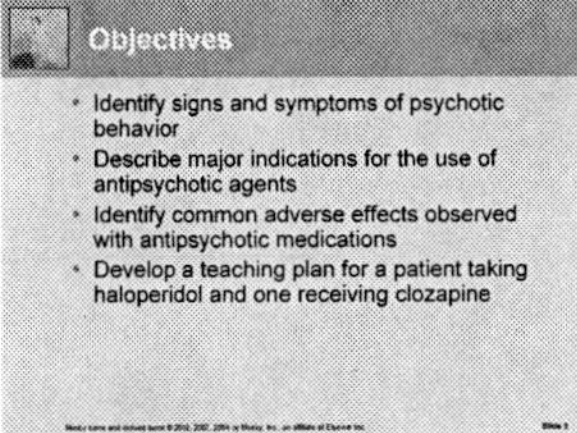
Objectives
Identify signs and symptoms of psychotic behavior
Describe major indications for the use of antipsychotic agents
Identify common adverse effects observed with antipsychotic medications
Develop a teaching plan for a patient taking haloperidol and one receiving clozapine

Slide 4

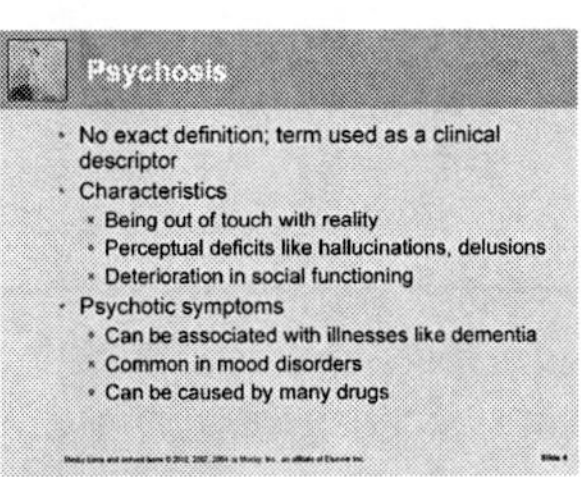
Psychosis
No exact definition; term used as a clinical descriptor
Characteristics
Being out of touch with reality
Perceptual deficits like hallucinations, delusions
Deterioration in social functioning
Psychotic symptoms
Can be associated with illnesses like dementia
Common in mood disorders
Can be caused by many drugs

- Schizophrenia is the most common psychotic disorder.
- Psychotic disorders are influenced by biologic, psychosocial, and environmental circumstances.
- May require several months of observation and testing before a final diagnosis is made.

Slide 5

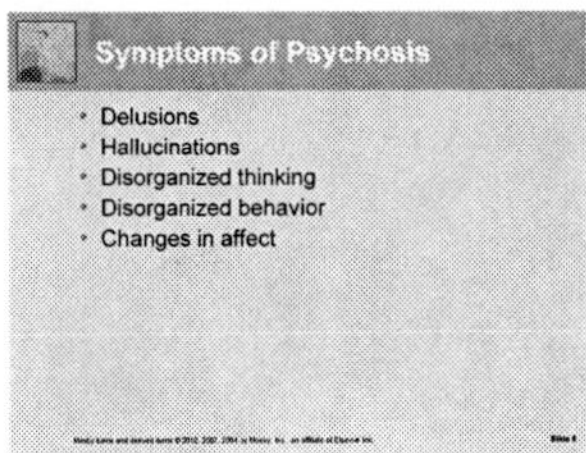
Symptoms of Psychosis
Delusions
Hallucinations
Disorganized thinking
Disorganized behavior
Changes in affect

Slide 6

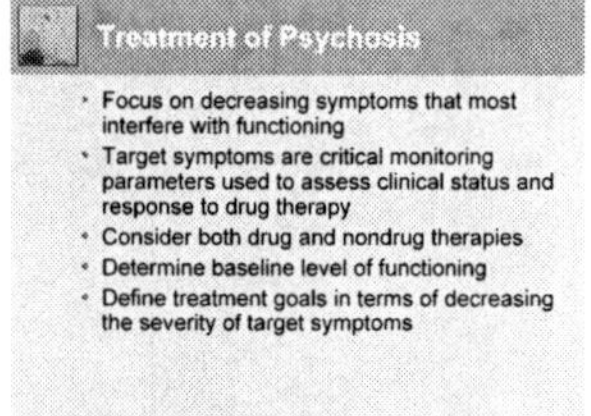
Treatment of Psychosis
Focus on decreasing symptoms that most interfere with functioning
Target symptoms are critical monitoring parameters used to assess clinical status and response to drug therapy
Consider both drug and nondrug therapies
Determine baseline level of functioning
Define treatment goals in terms of decreasing the severity of target symptoms

- Long-term outcome is much better with combination treatment.
- Most patients have recurring symptoms for most of their lives.

Slide 7

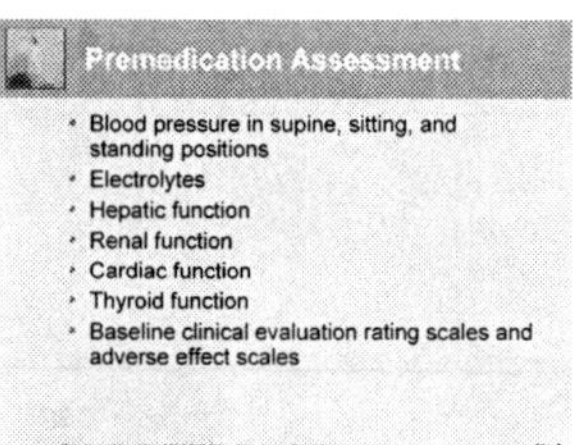
Premedication Assessment
Blood pressure in supine, sitting, and standing positions
Electrolytes
Hepatic function
Renal function
Cardiac function
Thyroid function
Baseline clinical evaluation rating scales and adverse effect scales

- Baseline clinical evaluation rating scales include BPRS, CGI, and PANSS.
- Adverse effect scales include GDS and TWSTRS (for dystonias), DISCUS (for type of tardive dyskinesia), and AIMS (for extrapyramidal symptoms).

Slide 8

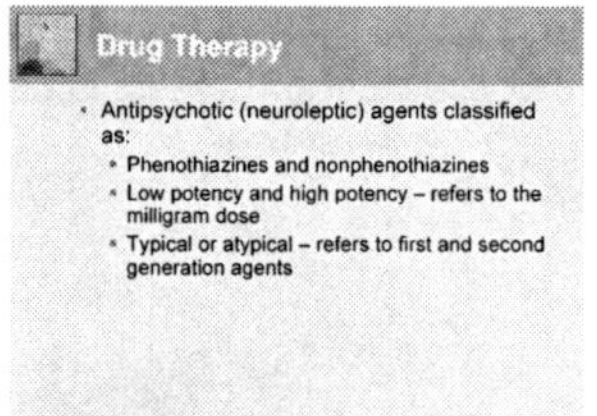
Drug Therapy
Antipsychotic (neuroleptic) agents classified as:
Phenothiazines and nonphenothiazines
Low potency and high potency – refers to the milligram dose
Typical or atypical – refers to first and second generation agents

---

Slide 9

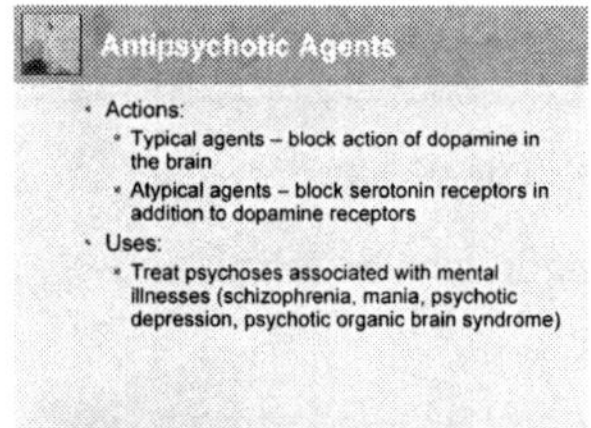
Antipsychotic Agents
Actions:
Typical agents – block action of dopamine in the brain
Atypical agents – block serotonin receptors in addition to dopamine receptors
Uses:
Treat psychoses associated with mental illnesses (schizophrenia, mania, psychotic depression, psychotic organic brain syndrome)

Slide 10

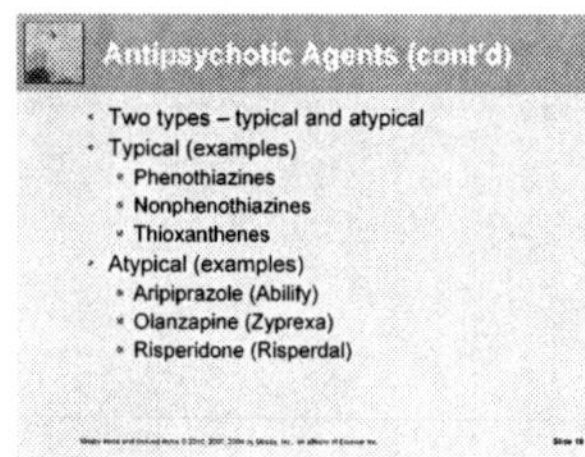
Antipsychotic Agents (cont'd)
Two types – typical and atypical
Typical (examples)
Phenothiazines
Nonphenothiazines
Thioxanthenes
Atypical (examples)
Aripiprazole (Abilify)
Olanzapine (Zyprexa)
Risperidone (Risperdal)

- Atypical agents block dopamine and serotonin receptors; are more effective and have fewer adverse effects than typical agents.
- For specific drugs, see Table 18-1.

ELSEVIER

Slide 11

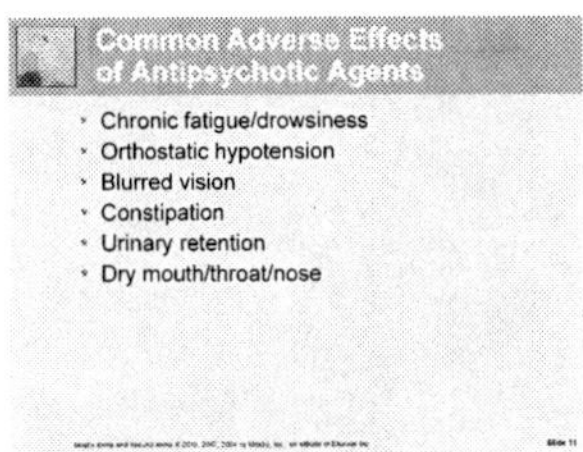
Common Adverse Effects of Antipsychotic Agents
Chronic fatigue/drowsiness
Orthostatic hypotension
Blurred vision
Constipation
Urinary retention
Dry mouth/throat/nose

- Sedative effects can be minimized by administering drugs at bedtime.
- Other adverse effects include weight gain, hyperglycemia, dyslipidemia, and dysrhythmias.

Slide 12

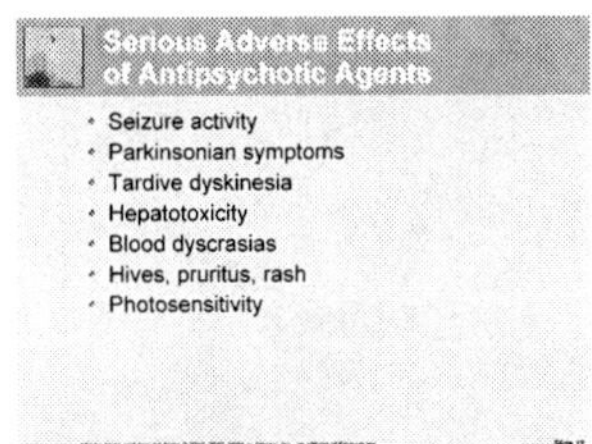
Serious Adverse Effects of Antipsychotic Agents
Seizure activity
Parkinsonian symptoms
Tardive dyskinesia
Hepatotoxicity
Blood dyscrasias
Hives, pruritus, rash
Photosensitivity

- Dosage adjustments may be necessary.

Slide 13

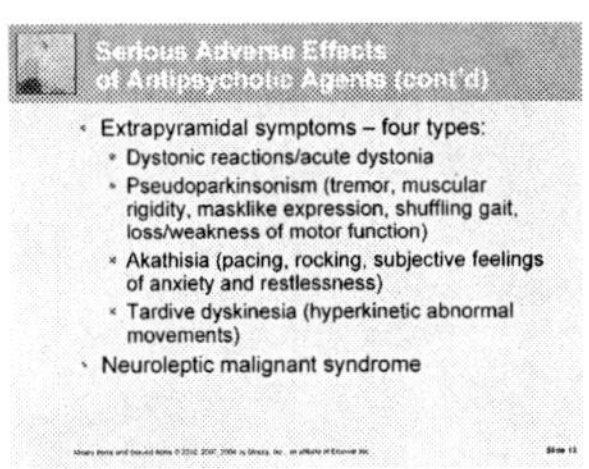
Serious Adverse Effects of Antipsychotic Agents (cont'd)
Extrapyramidal symptoms – four types:
Dystonic reactions/acute dystonia
Pseudoparkinsonism (tremor, muscular rigidity, masklike expression, shuffling gait, loss/weakness of motor function)
Akathisia (pacing, rocking, subjective feelings of anxiety and restlessness)
Tardive dyskinesia (hyperkinetic abnormal movements)
Neuroleptic malignant syndrome

- Extrapyramidal symptoms are the most common causes of antipsychotic therapy noncompliance.
- Neuroleptic malignant syndrome is potentially fatal.

Slide 14

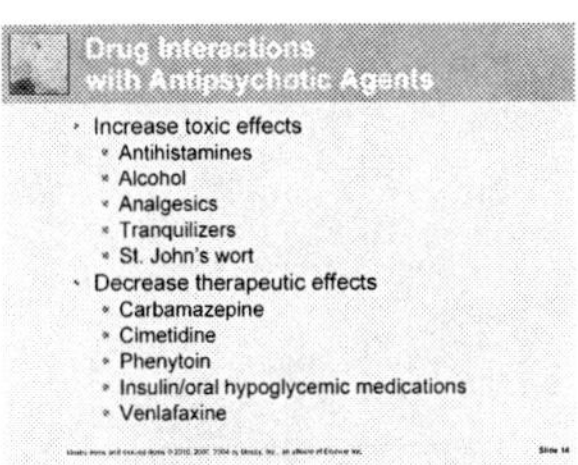
Drug Interactions with Antipsychotic Agents
Increase toxic effects
Antihistamines
Alcohol
Analgesics
Tranquilizers
St. John's wort
Decrease therapeutic effects
Carbamazepine
Cimetidine
Phenytoin
Insulin/oral hypoglycemic medications
Venlafaxine

- Diabetic patients must be monitored for hyperglycemia.
- Beta blockers enhance hypotensive effects of antipsychotics.

Slide 15

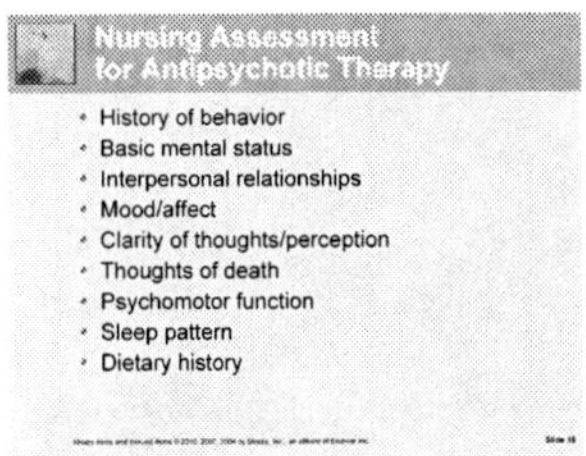
Nursing Assessment for Antipsychotic Therapy
History of behavior
Basic mental status
Interpersonal relationships
Mood/affect
Clarity of thoughts/perception
Thoughts of death
Psychomotor function
Sleep pattern
Dietary history

- Premedication assessment is used to rule out other causes of psychosis.
- Baseline assessment gathers information from the patient regarding onset, duration, and progression of symptoms.

ELSEVIER

Slide 16

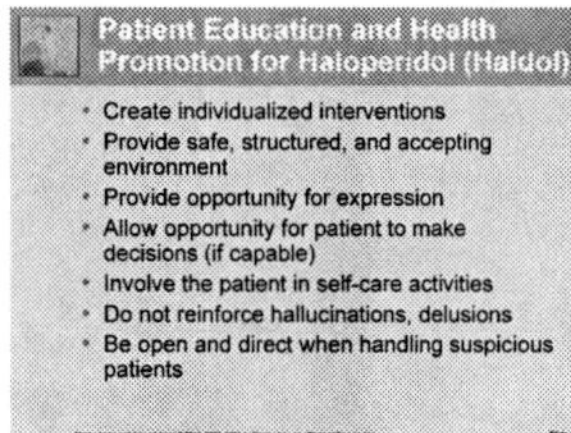
Patient Education and Health Promotion for Haloperidol (Haldol)
• Create individualized interventions
• Provide safe, structured, and accepting environment
• Provide opportunity for expression
• Allow opportunity for patient to make decisions (if capable)
• Involve the patient in self-care activities
• Do not reinforce hallucinations, delusions
• Be open and direct when handling suspicious patients

- Focus on patient's strengths.
- Use active listening and therapeutic communication techniques.
- Provide rewards for progress.

Slide 17

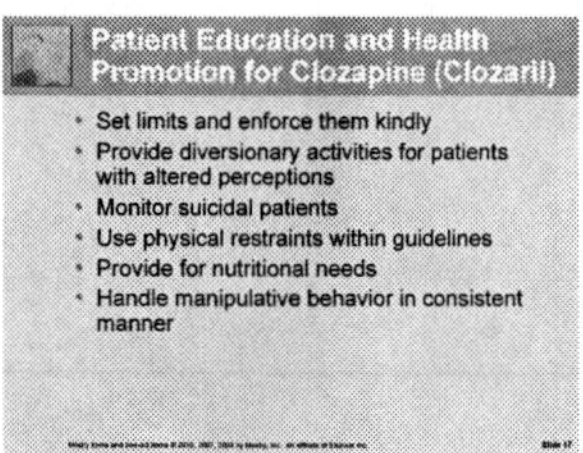
Patient Education and Health Promotion for Clozapine (Clozaril)
• Set limits and enforce them kindly
• Provide diversionary activities for patients with altered perceptions
• Monitor suicidal patients
• Use physical restraints within guidelines
• Provide for nutritional needs
• Handle manipulative behavior in consistent manner

- Thoughts of suicide should always be taken seriously.

19 Lesson Plan
Drugs Used for Seizure Disorders

TEACHING FOCUS

In this chapter, students will have the opportunity to learn about the basic classifications for epilepsy and the five classifications of drugs used to treat seizure disorders. Mechanisms of action thought to control seizure activity when anticonvulsants are administered and primary therapeutic outcomes will be discussed, along with nursing interventions and monitoring parameters for seizures. The students will also learn how to identify components of a teaching plan to educate patients diagnosed with seizure disorders.

MATERIALS AND RESOURCES

- ☐ computer and PowerPoint projector (Lesson 19.1)
- ☐ drug reference (Lesson 19.1)
- ☐ dry erase board and markers (Lesson 19.1)

LESSON CHECKLIST

Preparations for this lesson include:

- lecture
- guest speaker: nurse experienced in anticonvulsant therapy
- evaluation of student knowledge and skills needed to perform all entry-level nursing activities related to types of seizures and therapy used for seizure disorders, including:
  - knowledge of generalized and partial seizures
  - medications used to treat seizures
  - nursing interventions and monitoring parameters for seizures
  - desired therapeutic outcomes for drug therapy for seizure disorders

KEY TERMS

absence (petit mal) epilepsy (p. 286)
anticonvulsants (p. 286)
antiepileptic drug (AED) (p. 286)
atonic seizure (p. 286)
clonic phase (p. 286)
epilepsy (p. 285)
gamma-aminobutyric acid (GABA) (p. 287)
generalized seizures (p. 285)
gingival hyperplasia (p. 290)
myoclonic seizures (p. 286)
nystagmus (p. 293)
partial seizures (p. 285)
postictal state (p. 286)
seizure threshold (p. 287)
seizures (p. 285)
status epilepticus (p. 286)
tonic phase (p. 286)
treatment responsive (p. 287)
treatment resistant (p. 287)
urticaria (p. 297)

ADDITIONAL RESOURCES

PowerPoint slides: 1-28
Flashcards, Decks 1 and 2

Legend

ARQ	**PPT**	**TB**	**CTQ**	**SG**	**INRQ**
Audience Response Questions	PowerPoint Slides	Test Bank	Critical Thinking Questions	Study Guide	Interactive NCLEX Review Questions

Class Activities are indicated in ***bold italic.***

ELSEVIER

LESSON 19.1

BACKGROUND ASSESSMENT

Question: What is status epilepticus?
Answer: Status epilepticus is a rapidly recurring generalized seizure that does not allow the individual to regain normal function between seizures. It is a medical emergency requiring prompt treatment to minimize permanent nerve damage and prevent death.

Question: The nurse observes a patient having a seizure. Describe nursing management of this patient.
Answer: The nurse should assist the patient during a seizure by doing the following: protect the patient from further injury; place padding around or under the head; do not try to restrain. If the patient is in a standing position initially, the nurse should lower the patient to the floor. Once the patient enters into the relaxation stage, turn slightly onto the side to allow secretions to drain out of the mouth. Remain calm and quiet and give reassurance to the patient when the seizure is over. Suction the patient as needed and initiate ventilatory assistance if breathing does not return spontaneously. Provide a place for the patient to rest immediately after a seizure. Summon appropriate assistance so that the individual can get home. Initiate nursing interventions appropriate to the underlying disorder (head trauma, high fever, metabolic disorder, and drug and/or alcohol withdrawal). If the patient has another seizure within 4 minutes, immediately summon assistance; the patient may be going into status epilepticus. Observe all aspects of the seizure for detailed recording: aura (if present), time started and ended, body parts affected, order of progression of seizure action, autonomic signs (e.g., altered breathing, diaphoresis, incontinence, salivation, flushing, and pupil dilation), postictal period (vital signs. level of consciousness, speech pattern and/or disorder, muscle soreness, weakness, or paralysis), and note time each phase lasted.

CRITICAL THINKING QUESTION

A nurse administers 5 mg of diazepam intravenously to a 24-year-old patient with status epilepticus. The family informs the nurse that the patient has been a smoker for the past 8 years. They estimate that the patient smokes an average of two packs a day. How will smoking affect the administration of diazepam?
Guidelines: It is important for the nurse to receive an accurate patient history to properly treat the patient for status epilepticus. Smoking enhances the metabolism of benzodiazepines. Diazepam is part of the benzodiazepine class of medications. The patient will require larger doses of diazepam to maintain the effects of the medication. The maximum dose the patient can be safely administered is a total of 30 mg.

OBJECTIVES	CONTENT	TEACHING RESOURCES
Discuss the basic classification systems used for epilepsy.	■ Seizure disorders (p. 285) □ Descriptions of seizures (p. 286) – Generalized convulsive seizures (p. 286) – Generalized nonconvulsive seizures (p. 286) □ Anticonvulsant therapy (p. 286) – Actions (p. 287) – Uses (p. 288) – Nursing process for anticonvulsant therapy (p. 288) Review the classifications of seizures and the term *epilepsy*. Discuss causes and frequency of seizures in the general population.	PPT 5-6 ARQ 1 TB Multiple Response question 1 SG Review Sheet questions 1-8 (pp. 119-120) SG Learning Activities questions 1-4, 19-22 (pp. 124-125) SG Practice Question for the NCLEX Examination 9 (p. 127) Review Questions for the NCLEX Examination 5-7 (p. 306) ▸ Discuss characteristics of seizures, including symptoms and causes. ▸ Discuss the different classifications that have been used to categorize epilepsy.

OBJECTIVES	CONTENT	TEACHING RESOURCES
		Class Activity ***Invite a nurse experienced in anticonvulsant therapy to speak to the class about the different classifications of epilepsy. Have the nurse address the most common types of seizures encountered in his or her practice with the interventions taken and outcomes achieved.*** Class Activity ***List two broad categories of seizures: generalized seizures and partial seizures. Have students determine which of the following type of seizure is included under each category: tonic-clonic, atonic, myoclonic, simple motor, complex, and absence. Review the exercise with the class.***
Discuss nondrug treatment of seizures.	□ Anticonvulsant therapy (p. 286) – Actions (p. 287) Discuss nonpharmacologic therapies of refractory seizures: surgery, vagal nerve stimulators, ketogenic diet controls.	PPT 9
Develop a teaching plan for patient education for people diagnosed with a seizure disorder.	– Patient education and health promotion (p. 289)	PPT 7-8 ARQ 3 TB Multiple Choice questions 9, 13 CTQ 4 SG Review Sheet question 9 (p. 120) SG Practice Question for the NCLEX Examination 8 (p. 127) Patient Self-Assessment Form: Anticonvulsants Review Question for the NCLEX Examination 8 (p. 306) Lifespan Considerations: Anticonvulsant Therapy (p. 288) ▸ Discuss methods of educating patients about seizure disorders. Include a discussion of how to involve the patient's family. Talk about the nurse's ongoing role in education and monitoring of patients affected with seizure disorders. Class Activity ***Divide the class into small groups, and assign each a seizure disorder. Ask each group to develop a brief teaching plan for patients diagnosed with that disorder. Have thegroups include information regarding safety, exercise, oral hygiene, and medication***

OBJECTIVES	CONTENT	TEACHING RESOURCES
		considerations in their plans. Then ask the groups to share their teaching plans with the class.
Identify the mechanisms of action thought to control seizure activity when anticonvulsants are administered.	□ Drug therapy for seizure disorders (p. 290) □ Drug class: benzodiazepines (p. 290) – Nursing process for benzodiazepines (p. 290) □ Drug class: hydantoins (p. 292) – Nursing process for phenytoin (p. 292)	PPT 13-15 ARQ 2 TB Multiple Response question 3 CTQ 3 SG Review Sheet questions 10-13, 15-17, 22-23 (pp. 121-122) SG Learning Activities question 8 (p. 124) SG Practice Question for the NCLEX Examination 3 (pp. 126) Review Question for the NCLEX Examination 1 (p. 306) ▸ Discuss the actions that barbiturates, benzodiazepines, and hydantoins have on seizure activity. Talk about the uncertainties associated with the mechanisms of seizure activity. Class Activity ***Divide the class into three groups, and assign each group one of the following medications:*** ***1. Diazepam*** ***2. Phenytoin*** ***3. Phenobarbital*** ***Using a drug reference, have each group identify the specific drug class for the medication and the drug's mechanism of action. Then have the students develop a list of common adverse effects and three special considerations for their drug. Have the groups present their information to the class.***
Cite precautions needed when administering phenytoin or diazepam intravenously.	□ Drug class: benzodiazepines (p. 290) – Nursing process for benzodiazepines (p. 290) □ Drug class: hydantoins (p. 292) – Nursing process for phenytoin (p. 292)	TB Multiple Choice questions 3, 8, 10 TB Multiple Response question 2 INRQ 4 CTQ 1 SG Review Sheet questions 18-19 (pp. 121-122) SG Learning Activities questions 6, 9 (p. 124) SG Practice Question for the NCLEX Examination 1 (p. 126) Review Question for the NCLEX Examination 4 (p. 306)

ELSEVIER

OBJECTIVES	CONTENT	TEACHING RESOURCES
		Clinical Landmine (p. 292) ▸ Discuss the necessary guidelines for intravenous administration of phenytoin and diazepam. Include a discussion that cautions against mixing phenytoin and diazepam with other medications in the same syringe. Class Activity ***Ask the class to identify potential risks for a patient receiving phenytoin or diazepam intravenously. Ask students to call out specific risks as a volunteer lists them on the board. Then have the class offer a nursing strategy or intervention to minimize each risk.***
Describe the effects of the hydantoins on patients with diabetes and on people receiving oral contraceptives, theophylline, folic acid, or antacids.	□ Drug class: hydantoins (p. 292) – Nursing process for phenytoin (p. 292)	ARQ 5 TB Multiple Choice question 2 SG Review Sheet questions 14, 20 (pp. 121-122) SG Learning Activities question 25 (p. 125) ▸ Discuss common adverse effects and drug interactions to expect with hydantoin therapy. Class Activity ***Divide the class into five groups, and assign each group one of the following patient types receiving hydantoins:*** ***1. Patient with diabetes mellitus*** ***2. Patient receiving oral ontraceptives*** ***3. Patient receiving theophylline*** ***4. Patient receiving folic acid*** ***5. Patient receiving antacids*** ***Have each group determine what nursing action should be taken with that patient. Then have each group share its recommendations with the class.***
Explain the rationale for proper dental care for people receiving hydantoin therapy.	□ Drug class: hydantoins (p. 292) – Nursing process for phenytoin (p. 292)	TB Multiple choice questions 1, 11 INRQ 3, 6-7 SG Review Sheet question 21 (p. 122) SG Practice Question for the NCLEX Examination 2 (p. 126) ▸ Discuss the importance of patient education when hydantoin therapy is used and the need to focus patient attention on potential risks from hydantoin treatment. Class Activity ***Divide the class into small groups, and ask each group to discuss the components of a patient teaching plan for***

OBJECTIVES	CONTENT	TEACHING RESOURCES
		patients receiving hydantoin therapy. Make sure the plans include information about the role of gingival hyperplasia and why proper dental hygiene is key. Then ask the groups to share their plans with the class. Invite feedback and discussion.
Identify the mechanisms of action thought to control seizure activity when anticonvulsants are administered.	□ Drug class: succinimides (p. 294) – Nursing process for succinimides (p. 294) □ Drug class: miscellaneous anticonvulsants (p. 294) – Nursing process for carbamazepine (p. 295) – Nursing process for gabapentin (p. 296) – Nursing process for lamotrigine (p. 297) – Nursing process for levetiracetam (p. 298) – Nursing process for oxcarbazepine (p. 298) – Nursing process for pregabalin (p. 300) – Nursing process for primidone (p. 301) – Nursing process for tiagabine (p. 302) – Nursing process for topiramate (p. 302) – Nursing process for valproic acid (p. 304) – Nursing process for zonisamide (p. 304)	PPT 16-28 TB Multiple Choice questions 4-7, 12 INRQ 2, 5, 10 SG Review Sheet questions 24-26, 32-34 (pp. 122-123) SG Learning Activities questions 7, 10 (p. 124) SG Practice Questions for the NCLEX Examination 4-7 (p. 126) Review Questions for the NCLEX Examination 2-3 (p. 306) ▸ Discuss the actions that succinimides and the miscellaneous anticonvulsant drugs have on seizure activity. Talk about how little is known about the mechanisms of seizure activity. Class Activity ***Divide the class into four groups, and assign each group one medication used for seizure control. Ask each group to identify and discuss the mechanism of action for its assigned medication. Then have each group share its findings with the class.***
Cite the desired therapeutic outcomes for seizure disorders.	■ All content in this chapter supports this learning objective.	CTQ 2 ▸ Discuss how first-line agents are similar in their potential to prevent seizures, but vary in adverse effects. Include a discussion about the reason for which an agent is chosen, first based on its seizure control ability, then on its adverse effect profile. Class Activity ***Lead a class discussion on the expected therapeutic outcomes from the five anticonvulsant drug classes. What are the advantages and disadvantages associated with their use? What patient teaching can the nurse provide to patients undergoing seizure control treatment?***

OBJECTIVES	CONTENT	TEACHING RESOURCES
Prepare a chart to be used as a study guide that includes the following information: • Name of seizure type • Description of seizure • Medications used to treat each type of seizure • Nursing interventions and monitoring parameters for seizures	■ All content in this chapter supports this learning objective.	PPT 10 ARQ 4 SG Learning Activities questions 11-18 (p. 124) SG Practice Questions for the NCLEX Examination 10-12 (p. 127) Table 19-1 Antiepileptic Drugs of Choice Based on Type of Seizure (p. 287) Drug Table 19-2 Anticonvulsants (p. 291) ▸ Discuss the importance of the nurse's role in the accurate diagnosis of seizure disorders, proper medication selection, and monitoring response to anticonvulsant therapy. Class Activity ***Place an outline of a master chart on the board. Divide the class into four groups, and assign each group one of the following chart categories:*** ***1. Seizure type*** ***2. Description of seizure*** ***3. Medications used to treat each type of seizure*** ***4. Nursing interventions and monitoring parameters for seizures*** ***Have each group discuss its assignment. Then invite a representative from each group to write its information on the board. Discuss the information presented as a class, and make any corrections.***
Performance evaluation		Test Bank SG Learning Activities (pp. 124-125) SG Practice Questions for the NCLEX Examination (pp. 126-127) Critical Thinking Questions

19.1 Homework/Assignments:

19.1 Instructor's Notes/Student Feedback:

19 Lecture Outline

Drugs Used for Seizure Disorders

Slide 1

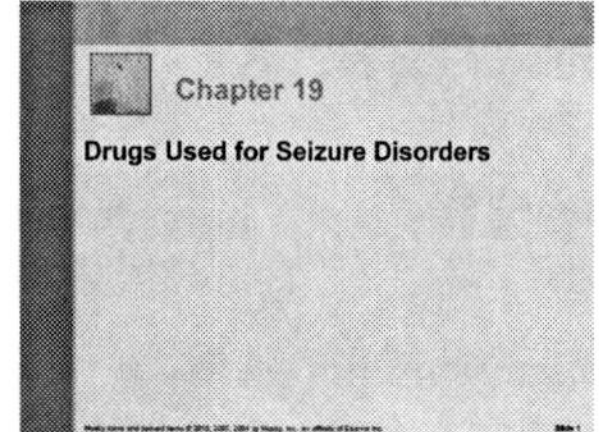

Chapter 19
Drugs Used for Seizure Disorders

Slide 2

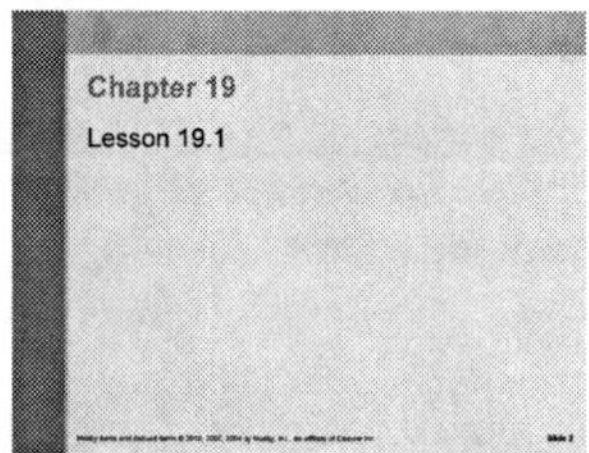

Chapter 19
Lesson 19.1

Slide 3

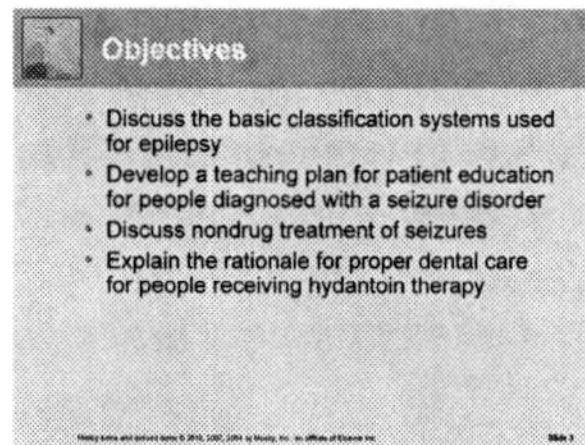

Objectives
Discuss the basic classification systems used for epilepsy
Develop a teaching plan for patient education for people diagnosed with a seizure disorder
Discuss nondrug treatment of seizures
Explain the rationale for proper dental care for people receiving hydantoin therapy

Slide 4

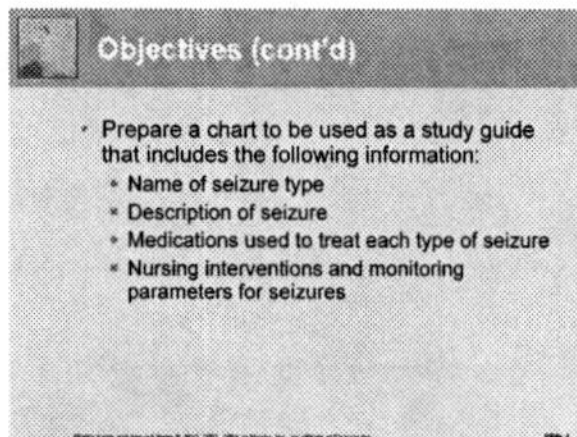

Objectives (cont'd)
Prepare a chart to be used as a study guide that includes the following information:
Name of seizure type
Description of seizure
Medications used to treat each type of seizure
Nursing interventions and monitoring parameters for seizures

Slide 5

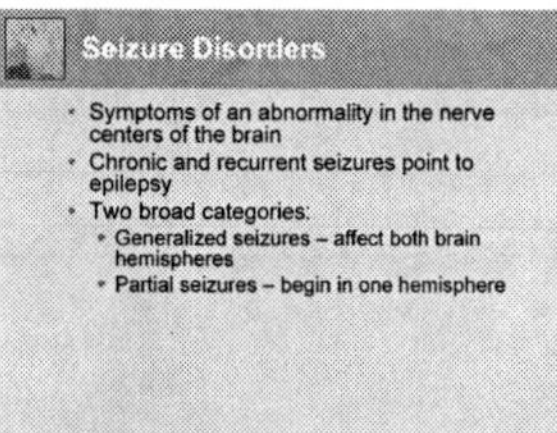

Seizure Disorders
Symptoms of an abnormality in the nerve centers of the brain
Chronic and recurrent seizures point to epilepsy
Two broad categories:
Generalized seizures – affect both brain hemispheres
Partial seizures – begin in one hemisphere

- Epilepsy is the most common of all neurologic disorders.
- Patients may report an aura prior to having a seizure.
- Sodium and calcium are ions that affect seizure activity within the brain.

Slide 6

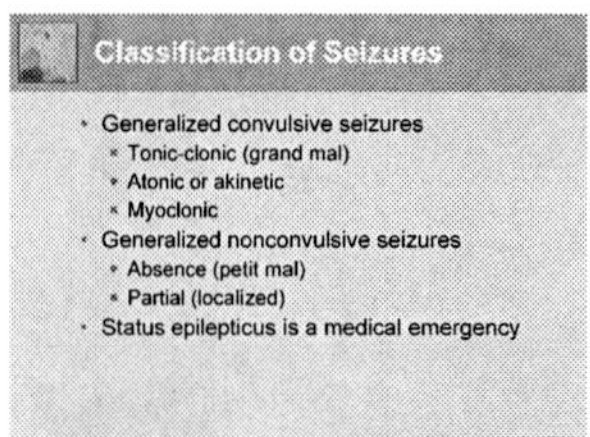
Classification of Seizures
Generalized convulsive seizures
Tonic-clonic (grand mal)
Atonic or akinetic
Myoclonic
Generalized nonconvulsive seizures
Absence (petit mal)
Partial (localized)
Status epilepticus is a medical emergency

Slide 7

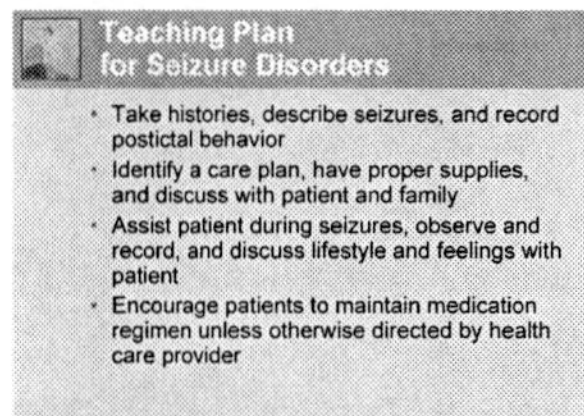
Teaching Plan for Seizure Disorders
Take histories, describe seizures, and record postictal behavior
Identify a care plan, have proper supplies, and discuss with patient and family
Assist patient during seizures, observe and record, and discuss lifestyle and feelings with patient
Encourage patients to maintain medication regimen unless otherwise directed by health care provider

- Long-term goals are to reduce the frequency of – and injury from – seizures while still having minimal adverse effects from therapy.

Slide 8

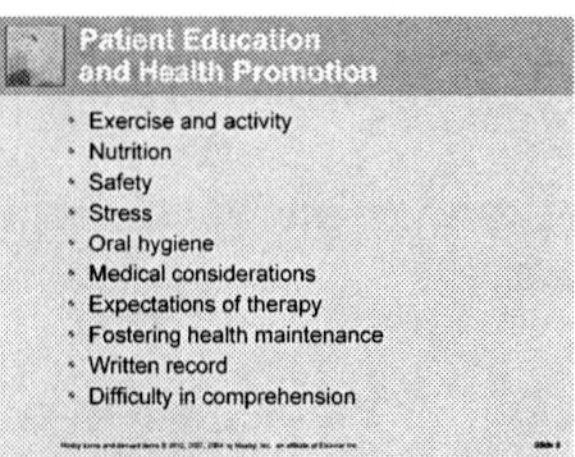
Patient Education and Health Promotion
Exercise and activity
Nutrition
Safety
Stress
Oral hygiene
Medical considerations
Expectations of therapy
Fostering health maintenance
Written record
Difficulty in comprehension

- Seizures are known to follow significant intake of alcoholic beverages.
- State laws may prohibit patients with seizures disorders from driving.
- Carry an identification card or bracelet.

Slide 9

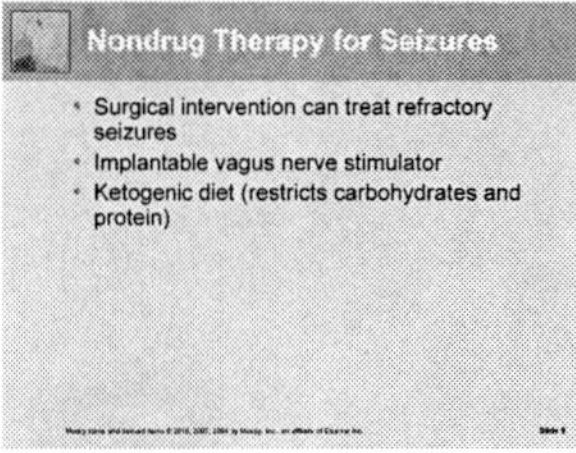
Nondrug Therapy for Seizures
Surgical intervention can treat refractory seizures
Implantable vagus nerve stimulator
Ketogenic diet (restricts carbohydrates and protein)

- A ketogenic diet has been shown to reduce refractory seizures in children who have not experienced effective control with drug therapy. Adverse effects include high lipid levels.

Slide 10

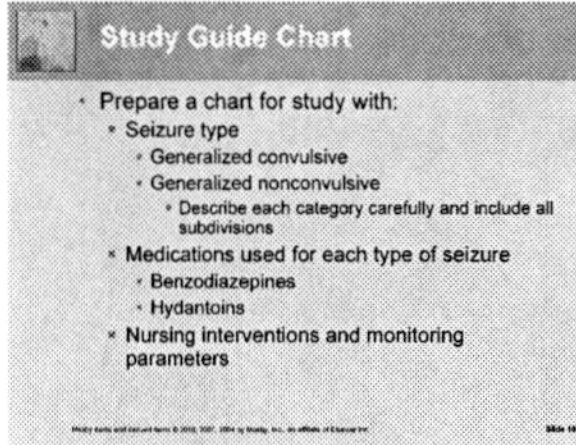
Study Guide Chart
Prepare a chart for study with:
Seizure type
Generalized convulsive
Generalized nonconvulsive
Describe each category carefully and include all subdivisions
Medications used for each type of seizure
Benzodiazepines
Hydantoins
Nursing interventions and monitoring parameters

Slide 11

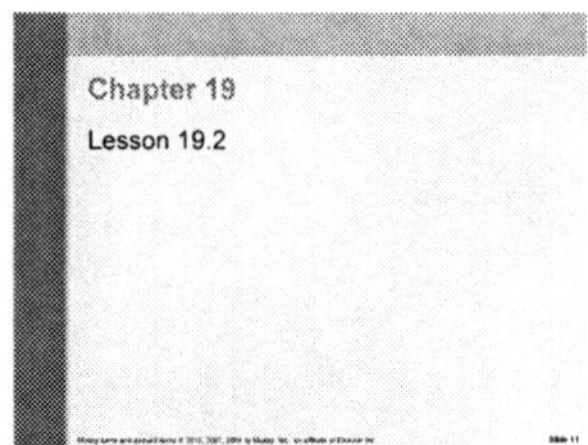
Chapter 19
Lesson 19.2

Slide 12

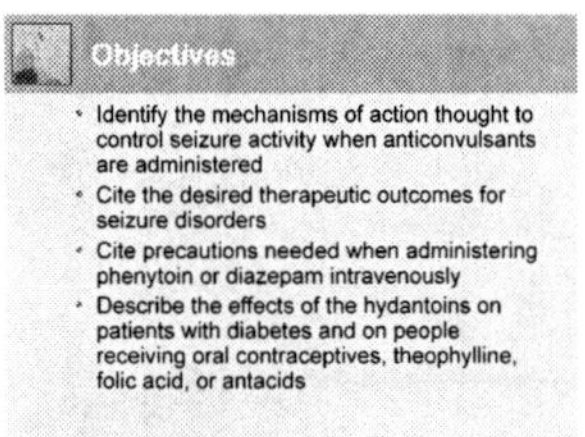
Objectives
Identify the mechanisms of action thought to control seizure activity when anticonvulsants are administered
Cite the desired therapeutic outcomes for seizure disorders
Cite precautions needed when administering phenytoin or diazepam intravenously
Describe the effects of the hydantoins on patients with diabetes and on people receiving oral contraceptives, theophylline, folic acid, or antacids

Slide 13

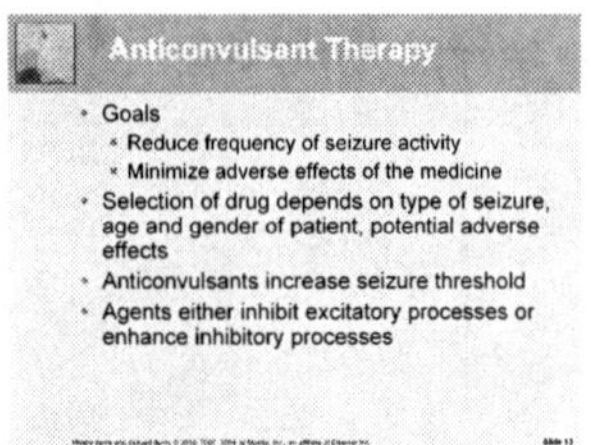
Anticonvulsant Therapy
Goals
Reduce frequency of seizure activity
Minimize adverse effects of the medicine
Selection of drug depends on type of seizure, age and gender of patient, potential adverse effects
Anticonvulsants increase seizure threshold
Agents either inhibit excitatory processes or enhance inhibitory processes

- *Anticonvulsant drugs* and *antiepileptic therapy* are used interchangeably.
- Prevent seizures from spreading to adjacent neurons.
- Can be either broad-spectrum or narrow-spectrum agents in relation to their efficacy against different types of seizures.

Slide 14

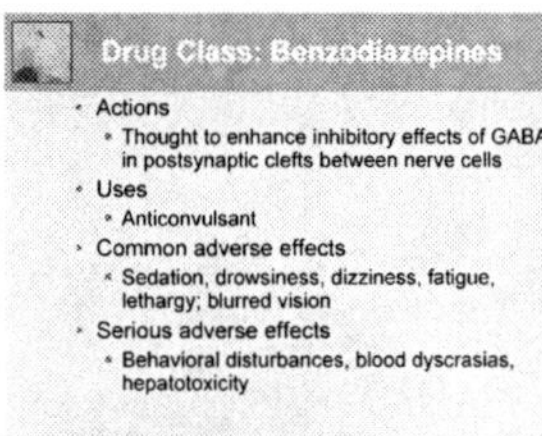
Drug Class: Benzodiazepines
Actions
Thought to enhance inhibitory effects of GABA in postsynaptic clefts between nerve cells
Uses
Anticonvulsant
Common adverse effects
Sedation, drowsiness, dizziness, fatigue, lethargy; blurred vision
Serious adverse effects
Behavioral disturbances, blood dyscrasias, hepatotoxicity

- For specific drugs, see Table 19-2.
- Therapeutic outcomes: reduced frequency of seizures, reduced injuries, minimal adverse effects from therapy.

Slide 15

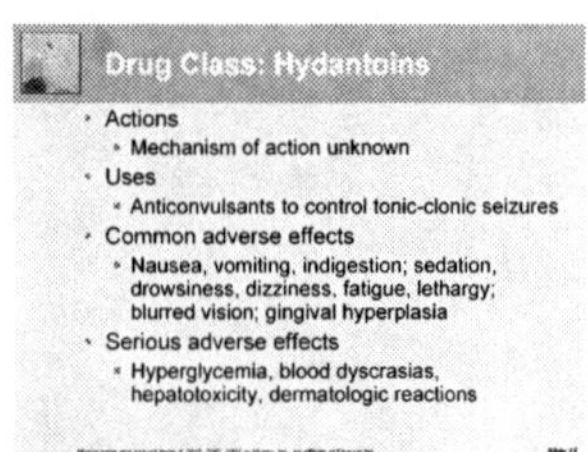
Drug Class: Hydantoins
Actions
Mechanism of action unknown
Uses
Anticonvulsants to control tonic-clonic seizures
Common adverse effects
Nausea, vomiting, indigestion; sedation, drowsiness, dizziness, fatigue, lethargy; blurred vision; gingival hyperplasia
Serious adverse effects
Hyperglycemia, blood dyscrasias, hepatotoxicity, dermatologic reactions

- For specific drugs, see Table 19-2.
- Phenytoin (Dilantin) is the most common hydantoin.
- Hydantoins are particularly effective with grand mal seizures.

ELSEVIER

Slide 16

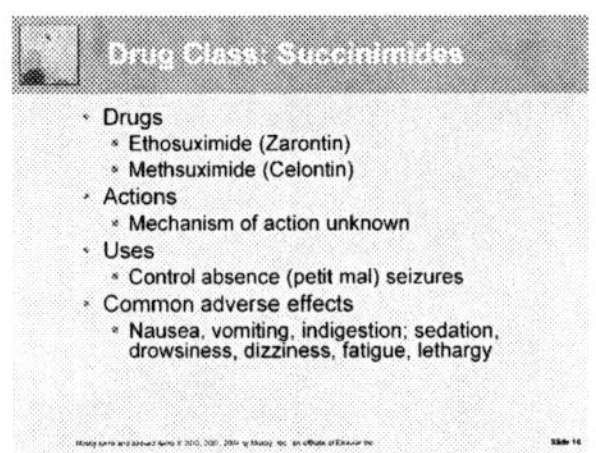
Drug Class: Succinimides
Drugs
Ethosuximide (Zarontin)
Methsuximide (Celontin)
Actions
Mechanism of action unknown
Uses
Control absence (petit mal) seizures
Common adverse effects
Nausea, vomiting, indigestion; sedation, drowsiness, dizziness, fatigue, lethargy

- Toxic effects can be enhanced by antihistamines, alcohol, analgesics, anesthetics, tranquilizers, other anticonvulsants, and sedative-hypnotics.
- Therapeutic outcomes: reduced frequency of seizures, reduced injuries; minimal adverse effects from therapy.

Slide 17

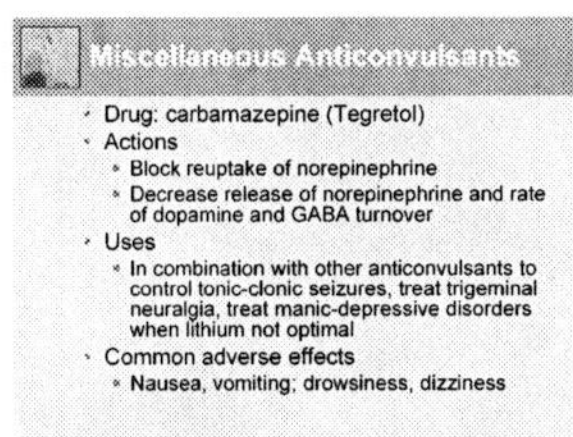
Miscellaneous Anticonvulsants
Drug: carbamazepine (Tegretol)
Actions
Block reuptake of norepinephrine
Decrease release of norepinephrine and rate of dopamine and GABA turnover
Uses
In combination with other anticonvulsants to control tonic-clonic seizures, treat trigeminal neuralgia, treat manic-depressive disorders when lithium not optimal
Common adverse effects
Nausea, vomiting; drowsiness, dizziness

- Not effective for myoclonic or absence seizures.
- Serious adverse effects: orthostatic hypotension, hypertension; dyspnea, edema; neurologic changes; nephrotoxicity; hepatotoxicity; blood dyscrasias; dermatologic reactions.

Slide 18

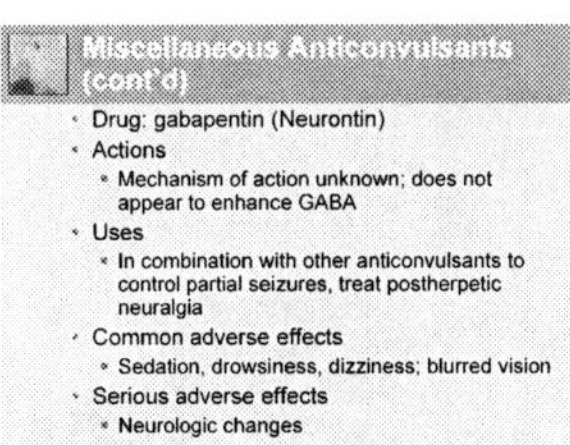
Miscellaneous Anticonvulsants (cont'd)
Drug: gabapentin (Neurontin)
Actions
Mechanism of action unknown; does not appear to enhance GABA
Uses
In combination with other anticonvulsants to control partial seizures, treat postherpetic neuralgia
Common adverse effects
Sedation, drowsiness, dizziness; blurred vision
Serious adverse effects
Neurologic changes

- Drugs enhancing its sedative effect include sleep aids, analgesics, tranquilizers, and alcohol.

Slide 19

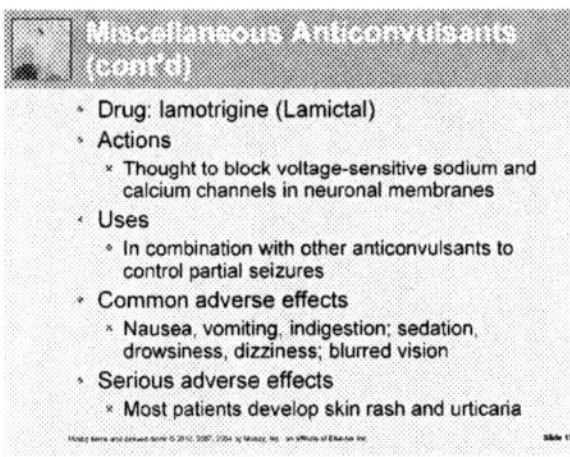
Miscellaneous Anticonvulsants (cont'd)
Drug: lamotrigine (Lamictal)
Actions
Thought to block voltage-sensitive sodium and calcium channels in neuronal membranes
Uses
In combination with other anticonvulsants to control partial seizures
Common adverse effects
Nausea, vomiting, indigestion; sedation, drowsiness, dizziness; blurred vision
Serious adverse effects
Most patients develop skin rash and urticaria

- Used to treat generalized seizures of Lennox-Gastaut syndrome in pediatric and adult patients.

Slide 20

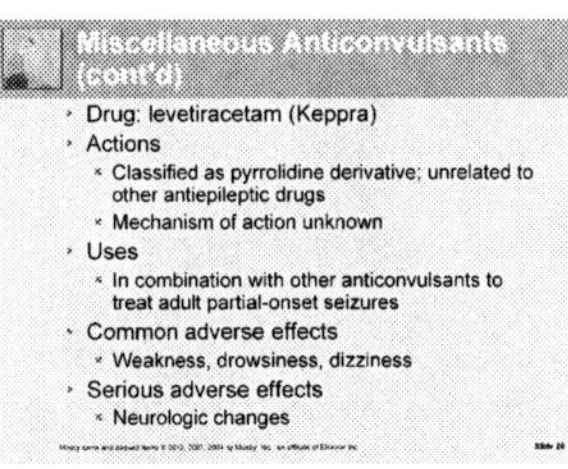
Miscellaneous Anticonvulsants (cont'd)
Drug: levetiracetam (Keppra)
Actions
Classified as pyrrolidine derivative; unrelated to other antiepileptic drugs
Mechanism of action unknown
Uses
In combination with other anticonvulsants to treat adult partial-onset seizures
Common adverse effects
Weakness, drowsiness, dizziness
Serious adverse effects
Neurologic changes

Slide 21

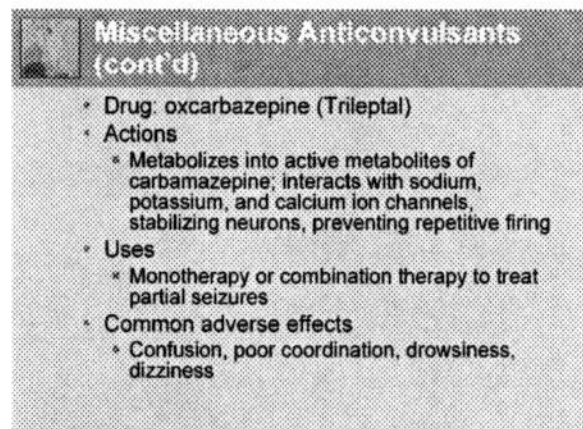
Miscellaneous Anticonvulsants (cont'd)
Drug: oxcarbazepine (Trileptal)
Actions
Metabolizes into active metabolites of carbamazepine; interacts with sodium, potassium, and calcium ion channels, stabilizing neurons, preventing repetitive firing
Uses
Monotherapy or combination therapy to treat partial seizures
Common adverse effects
Confusion, poor coordination, drowsiness, dizziness

- Used only as combination therapy in treating partial seizures in children 4 to 16 years of age.
- Serious adverse effects: nausea, headache, lethargy, confusion, obtundation, malaise; blood dyscrasias.

Slide 22

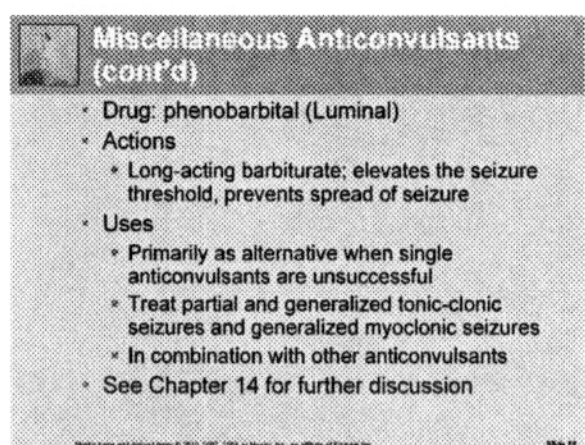
Miscellaneous Anticonvulsants (cont'd)
Drug: phenobarbital (Luminal)
Actions
Long-acting barbiturate; elevates the seizure threshold, prevents spread of seizure
Uses
Primarily as alternative when single anticonvulsants are unsuccessful
Treat partial and generalized tonic-clonic seizures and generalized myoclonic seizures
In combination with other anticonvulsants
See Chapter 14 for further discussion

Slide 23

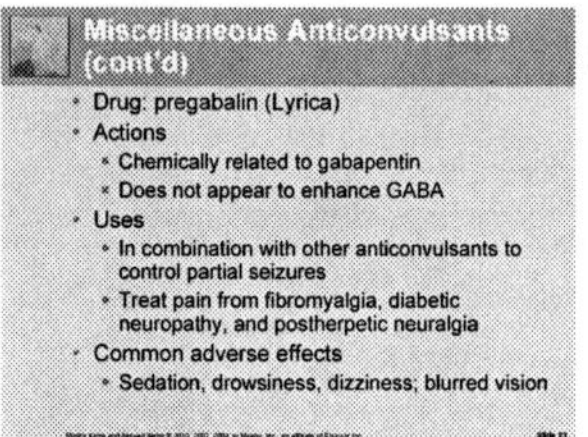
Miscellaneous Anticonvulsants (cont'd)
Drug: pregabalin (Lyrica)
Actions
Chemically related to gabapentin
Does not appear to enhance GABA
Uses
In combination with other anticonvulsants to control partial seizures
Treat pain from fibromyalgia, diabetic neuropathy, and postherpetic neuralgia
Common adverse effects
Sedation, drowsiness, dizziness; blurred vision

- Serious adverse effects: neurologic changes, excessive use or abuse.

Slide 24

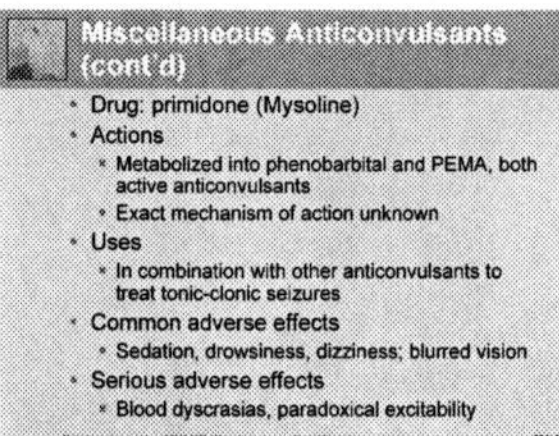
Miscellaneous Anticonvulsants (cont'd)
Drug: primidone (Mysoline)
Actions
Metabolized into phenobarbital and PEMA, both active anticonvulsants
Exact mechanism of action unknown
Uses
In combination with other anticonvulsants to treat tonic-clonic seizures
Common adverse effects
Sedation, drowsiness, dizziness; blurred vision
Serious adverse effects
Blood dyscrasias, paradoxical excitability

- Structurally related to barbiturates.

Slide 25

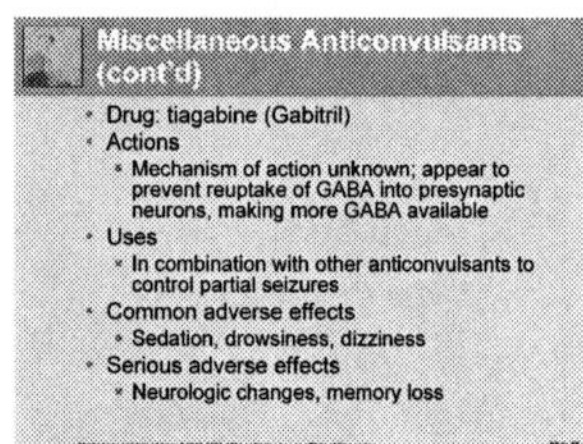
Miscellaneous Anticonvulsants (cont'd)
Drug: tiagabine (Gabitril)
Actions
Mechanism of action unknown; appear to prevent reuptake of GABA into presynaptic neurons, making more GABA available
Uses
In combination with other anticonvulsants to control partial seizures
Common adverse effects
Sedation, drowsiness, dizziness
Serious adverse effects
Neurologic changes, memory loss

ELSEVIER

Slide 26

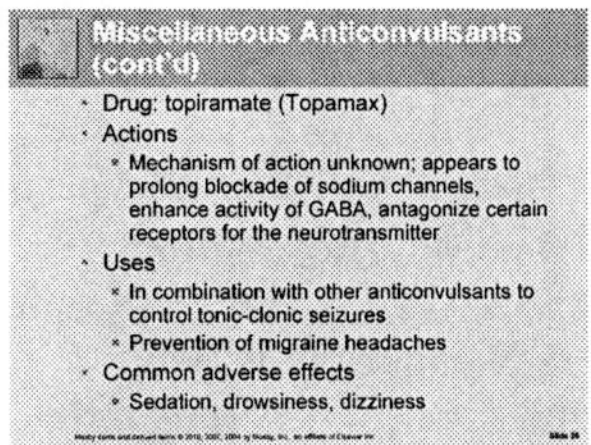
Miscellaneous Anticonvulsants (cont'd)
Drug: topiramate (Topamax)
Actions
Mechanism of action unknown; appears to prolong blockade of sodium channels, enhance activity of GABA, antagonize certain receptors for the neurotransmitter
Uses
In combination with other anticonvulsants to control tonic-clonic seizures
Prevention of migraine headaches
Common adverse effects
Sedation, drowsiness, dizziness

- Phenobarbital enhances the metabolism of topiramate.
- Serious adverse effects: neurologic changes, hydration status – decreased sweating and overheating have been reported.

Slide 27

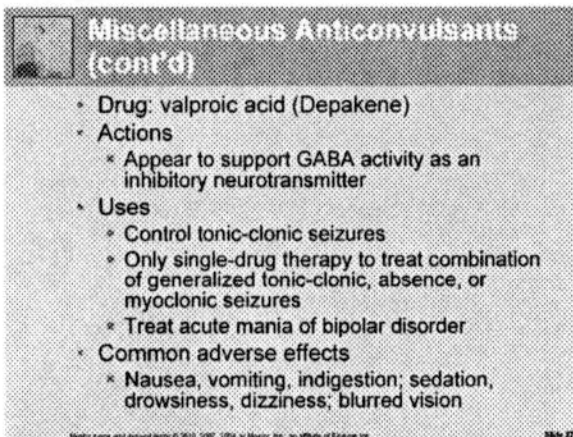
Miscellaneous Anticonvulsants (cont'd)
Drug: valproic acid (Depakene)
Actions
Appear to support GABA activity as an inhibitory neurotransmitter
Uses
Control tonic-clonic seizures
Only single-drug therapy to treat combination of generalized tonic-clonic, absence, or myoclonic seizures
Treat acute mania of bipolar disorder
Common adverse effects
Nausea, vomiting, indigestion; sedation, drowsiness, dizziness; blurred vision

- Serious adverse effects: blood dyscrasias, hepatotoxicity, pancreatitis.

Slide 28

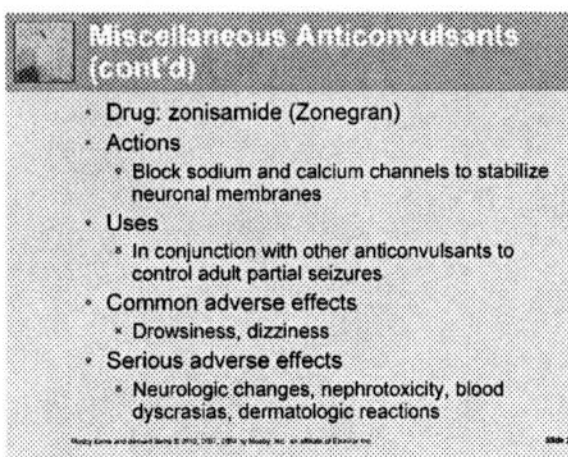
Miscellaneous Anticonvulsants (cont'd)
Drug: zonisamide (Zonegran)
Actions
Block sodium and calcium channels to stabilize neuronal membranes
Uses
In conjunction with other anticonvulsants to control adult partial seizures
Common adverse effects
Drowsiness, dizziness
Serious adverse effects
Neurologic changes, nephrotoxicity, blood dyscrasias, dermatologic reactions

- Classified as a sulfonamide.
- Phenobarbital enhances the metabolism of zonisamide.
- Determine if the patient has allergies to sulfonamides or a history of skin rashes.

ELSEVIER

20 Lesson Plan
Drugs Used for Pain Management

TEACHING FOCUS

This chapter introduces students to medications used to relieve pain, including opiate agonists, opiate partial agonists, and opiate antagonists. Students have the opportunity to learn about the monitoring parameters necessary for opiate agonists, the adverse effects of opiate agonists, and the analgesic effectiveness of opiate partial agonists used in conjunction with opiate agonists. The chapter also covers instances in which naloxone is effective against respiratory depression. In addition, students have the opportunity to examine therapeutic effects, adverse effects, and drug interactions of salicylates. The chapter examines the active ingredients in analgesics and compares the properties of different agents and presents reasons why synthetic nonopiate analgesics are not used for inflammatory disorders. Students also have the opportunity to prepare a patient education plan for patients who take analgesics.

MATERIALS AND RESOURCES

- ☐ computer and PowerPoint projector (all Lessons)
- ☐ index cards (Lesson 20.1)

LESSON CHECKLIST

Preparations for this lesson include:

- lecture
- evaluation of student knowledge and skills needed to perform all entry-level activities related to the understanding of prescription and over-the-counter analgesics, including:
  - opiate agonists
  - opiate partial agonists
  - opiate antagonists
  - salicylates
  - nonsteroidal anti-inflammatory drugs (NSAIDs)
  - other analgesics

KEY TERMS

acute pain (p. 307)
addiction (p. 318)
analgesics (p. 308)
ceiling effect (p. 322)
chronic pain (p. 308)
drug tolerance (p. 318)
idiopathic pain (p. 308)
neuropathic pain (p. 308)
nociception (p. 307)
nociceptive pain (p. 308)
nociceptors (p. 309)
nonsteroidal anti-inflammatory drugs (p. 309)
opiate agonists (p. 309)
opiate antagonists (p. 309)
opiate partial agonists (p. 309)
opiate receptors (p. 309)
pain experience (p. 307)
pain perception (p. 307)
pain threshold (p. 307)
pain tolerance (p. 307)
range orders (p. 316)
salicylates (p. 309)
somatic pain (p. 308)
visceral pain (p. 308)

ADDITIONAL RESOURCES

PowerPoint slides: 1-24
Flashcards, Decks 1 and 2

Legend

ARQ	PPT	TB	CTQ	SG	INRQ
Audience Response Questions	PowerPoint Slides	Test Bank	Critical Thinking Questions	Study Guide	Interactive NCLEX Review Questions

Class Activities are indicated in ***bold italic.***

LESSON 20.1

BACKGROUND ASSESSMENT

Question: What are the primary therapeutic outcomes the nurse can anticipate as a result of appropriate pain management?
Answer: The therapeutic outcomes are relief of pain intensity and duration of pain complaint, prevention of the conversion of persistent pain to chronic pain, prevention of suffering and disability associated with pain, prevention of psychological and socioeconomic consequences associated with inadequate pain management, control of adverse effects associated with pain management, and optimization of the ability to perform activities of daily living.

Question: What are the routes of administration of pain medication?
Answer: Patients may receive pain medication via the following routes: oral, rectal, intradermal, intravenous, intramuscular, subcutaneous, intraspinal, and epidural. The route depends on the patient's health profile and the course of the underlying disease or illness.

CRITICAL THINKING QUESTION

A 60-year-old patient is complaining of substernal chest pain that radiates down the left arm and up the left side of the neck. The patient is rating the pain an 8 on a scale of 1 to 10. An ECG is showing sinus tachycardia at a rate of 120 beats per minute. The health care team evaluating the patient suspects the patient is having an acute myocardial infarction (AMI). What type of salicylate should be administered to the patient? What opiate agonist should be considered if the pain is unrelieved?
Guidelines: The type of salicylate the patient should receive is aspirin because of the antiplatelet qualities. A suspected myocardial infarction patient should receive 324 mg. The health care provider is likely to order the opiate agonist morphine sulfate (MS) for this patient. MS can reduce the pain associated with a myocardial infarction and reduce the associated anxiety. The nurse can administer 2 mg of MS titrated until pain relief is achieved. The nurse should be assessing the patient, paying careful attention to the expected and anticipated adverse effects from MS.

OBJECTIVES	CONTENT	TEACHING RESOURCES
Differentiate among opiate agonists, opiate partial agonists, and opiate antagonists.	■ Pain (p. 307) □ Pain management (p. 308) Review the terms *opiate agonist* and *opiate partial agonist*. Discuss the therapeutic outcomes and	PPT 5-6 TB Multiple Choice questions 6-7, 14 SG Review Sheet questions 1-6 (p. 129) SG Learning Activities questions 1-3, 15-18 (p. 133)

OBJECTIVES	CONTENT	TEACHING RESOURCES
	assessments needed for patients taking opiate agonists, as well as the common and serious adverse effects. Review addiction and withdrawal signs.	SG Practice Questions for the NCLEX Examination 1-2, 9-10 (pp. 135-136) Figure 20-1 (p. 308), Nociceptive pain ▸ Discuss what is involved in the pain experience, including different components, descriptions, and classifications. Class Activity ***Lead a discussion in which students identify the main characteristics of these three drug classes: opiate agonists, opiate partial agonists, and opiate antagonists. Make a chart on the board with three columns headed with the name of each drug class. Then label four rows as follows: Action, Site, Uses, and Disease/Conditions. Compare and contrast the drug classes based on information in the rows.***
Describe monitoring parameters necessary for patients receiving opiate agonists.	□ Pain management (p. 308) – Nursing process for pain management (p. 310) Review the definitions of pain, pain experience, pain threshold, pain tolerance, and nociception. Discuss the difference between acute pain and chronic pain. Also discuss somatic pain, visceral pain, neuropathic pain, and idiopathic pain. Review the expectations of pain management and the classes of analgesics. Discuss the pain pathways and pain receptors to better understand the treatment of pain. Review the stepwise approach to pain management that the WHO recommends. Discuss the use of pain scales and the nursing process used for pain management.	TB Multiple Choice questions 1, 8, 15 TB Multiple Response question 1 INRQ 6 CTQ 4, 6 Animation: Opiate Intoxication SG Review Sheet questions 8-16, 19, 21 (pp. 129-130) SG Learning Activities questions 19, 25-26 (p. 134) SG Practice Question for the NCLEX Examination 5 (p. 135) Review Questions for the NCLEX Examination 7, 10-11 (p. 334) Box 20-1 Pain Care Bill of Rights (p. 311) Clinical Landmine (p. 310) Figure 20-2 (p. 310), WHO's pain relief ladder Figure 20-3 (p. 311), Wong-Baker pain rating scale Lifespan Considerations: Analgesics (p. 313) Figure 20-4 (p. 312), McGill-Melzack pain questionnaire Figure 20-5 (p. 313), Pain-rating scales Lifespan Considerations: Pain in the Older Adult Patient (p. 315)

ELSEVIER

<table>
<tr><th>OBJECTIVES</th><th>CONTENT</th><th>TEACHING RESOURCES</th></tr>
<tr><td></td><td></td><td>▸ Discuss the patient's right to adequate management of pain. What life span issues may be involved?

Class Activity As a class, outline the nursing process for a patient who is receiving an opiate agonist for pain. Include premedication assessment, planning, implementation, and evaluation. Then divide the class into small groups and assign each group one of the following parameters the nurse should monitor:
– Pain relief
– Tolerance
– Common adverse effects
– Serious adverse effects
– Vital signs
– Signs of overdose

Have each group report to the class about the signs and symptoms the nurse should watch for. What actions should the nurse take if the patient exhibits abnormal reactions?</td></tr>
<tr><td>Prepare a patient education plan for a person being discharged with a continuing prescription for an analgesic.</td><td>– Patient education and health promotion (p. 317)</td><td>TB Multiple Response question 2

ARQ 2

INRQ 5

Patient Self-Assessment Form: Analgesics

Review Question for the NCLEX Examination 11 (p. 334)

▸ Discuss the nursing processes described in the text as they pertain to ongoing pain management outside of a clinical setting.

Class Activity Divide the class into three groups. Ask each group to develop a teaching plan for discharged patients taking one of the following prescription analgesics:
– Oxycodone (OxyContin) controlled release tablets
– Oxaprozin (Daypro)
– Fiorinal with codeine
The teaching plan should include how to self-administer, changes in pain levels, signs and symptoms, serious adverse effects, how to keep a written record, and emphasis of the addictive nature of some drugs. Then ask members of each group to role-play a nurse teaching a patient key points. The role-play may include helping the patient complete the Patient Self-Assessment Form: Analgesics</td></tr>
</table>

OBJECTIVES	CONTENT	TEACHING RESOURCES
		(p. 327). Ask each group to present its teaching plan and role-play to the class, and then ask students what they learned.
Cite the common adverse effects when opiate agonists are administered.	□ Drug class: opiate agonists (p. 318) – Nursing process for opiate agonists (p. 320)	TB Multiple Choice questions 2, 9, 11, 13 TB Multiple Response question 3 ARQ 1 INRQ 2-4, 8 Animation: Opiate Intoxication SG Learning Activities questions 5, 20-23 (pp. 133-134) SG Practice Questions for the NCLEX Examination 3-4, 6, 11 (p. 135-136) Drug Table 20-1 Opiate Agonists (pp. 319-320) ▸ Discuss the adverse effects the nurse should be alert for in patients who receive opiate agonists. Class Activity ***Lead a discussion in which students describe the adverse effects that can occur when a patient receives an opiate agonist. What are common adverse effects, and what should the patient do? What adverse effects should the patient report? How should the nurse respond, or what actions should the nurse take?***
Differentiate among opiate agonists, opiate partial agonists, and opiate antagonists.	□ Drug class: opiate agonists (p. 318) – Nursing process for opiate agonists (p. 320) □ Drug class: opiate partial agonists (p. 322) – Nursing process for opiate partial agonists (p. 322) □ Drug class: opiate antagonists (p. 323) – Nursing process for naloxone (p. 324) – Nursing process for naltrexone (p. 325) Review the actions and uses of opiate partial agonist drugs. Discuss the effects of these drugs on a patient addicted to opiate agonists as well as the ceiling effect.	PPT 10-15 TB Multiple Choice question 2 INRQ 1 CTQ 2 SG Review Sheet questions 7, 17-18, 20-26 (pp. 129-130) SG Learning Activities questions 4, 9-13 (p. 133) SG Practice Question for the NCLEX Examination 15 (p. 136) Review Questions for the NCLEX Examination 3, 5 (pp. 333-334) Drug Table 20-2 Opiate Partial Agonists (p. 323) ▸ Discuss in what ways opiate agonists, partial agonists, and opiate antagonists are alike and different. What are their actions and intended uses?

ELSEVIER

OBJECTIVES	CONTENT	TEACHING RESOURCES
		Class Activity ***Have the students form pairs. Have one student prepare a flash card with the name of a drug that is an opiate agonist, opiate partial agonist, or an opiate antagonist. Then have the other student identify the drug class.***

20.1 Homework/Assignments:

20.1 Instructor's Notes/Student Feedback:

LESSON 20.2

CRITICAL THINKING QUESTION

A 30-year-old patient receives MS intravenously for a femur fracture. The nurse notes that the patient's respiratory rate is eight breaths per minute. What should the nurse suspect, and what action should the nurse take?

Guidelines: The nurse should suspect that the patient has received an overdose of morphine and is experiencing respiratory depression. The nurse should immediately report the respiratory rate to the charge nurse. To reverse the effects of MS on the respiratory system, the patient should receive naloxone, 2 mg every 2 to 3 minutes, as prescribed, until the desired response is achieved. The nurse should monitor the patient's response to the naloxone. If the patient does not improve within 10 minutes, the nurse should consider causes by a drug or disease process not responsive to naloxone.

OBJECTIVES	CONTENT	TEACHING RESOURCES
Compare the analgesic effectiveness of opiate partial agonists when administered before or after opiate agonists.	□ Drug class: opiate partial agonists (p. 322) – Nursing process for opiate partial agonists (p. 322) □ Drug class: opiate antagonists (p. 323) – Nursing process for naloxone (p. 324) – Nursing process for naltrexone (p. 325)	ARQ 3 SG Review Sheet question 25 (p. 130) Review Question for the NCLEX Examination 8 (p. 334) ▸ Discuss the purpose of administering opiate partial agonists before or after opiate agonists. Class Activity ***Present the class with this situation: A patient has been taking prescribed doses of morphine, but experiences less relief from pain than expected. If buprenorphine is prescribed, what are two possible effects? Why are these effects different?***

OBJECTIVES	CONTENT	TEACHING RESOURCES
Explain when naloxone can be used effectively to treat respiratory depression.	□ Drug class: opiate antagonists (p. 323) – Nursing process for naloxone (p. 324)	CTQ 5 SG Review Sheet questions 22-24 (p. 130) SG Learning Activities question 4 (p. 133) Review Questions for the NCLEX Examination 4, 6 (pp. 333-334) ▸ Discuss the drug action of naloxone and its therapeutic outcomes. Class Activity ***Have students role-play a nurse giving naloxone correctly to a patient with opiate overdose. Review what must be assessed and what adverse effects to expect after administration. Discuss the exercise with the class.*** Class Activity ***Present the following scenarios to the class:*** ***– A 21-year-old with respiratory depression from an overdose of morphine given for pain relief*** ***– A 40-year-old with difficulty breathing from pneumonia*** ***– A 30-year-old with respiratory depression for unknown reasons*** ***– A 55-year-old administered morphine for pain relief with no complaints or complications*** ***Which patient(s) would the health care provider most likely prescribe naloxone for? Why? What nursing actions should be taken?***
State the three pharmacologic effects of salicylates.	□ Drug class: salicylates (p. 325) – Nursing process for salicylates (p. 326) Review the three primary pharmacologic effects of salicylates. Discuss common uses of aspirin as well as common and adverse effects.	PPT 19-20 TB Multiple Response question 4 ARQ 4 SG Review Sheet questions 27-31 (p. 131) SG Learning Activities question 24 (p. 134) Review Question for the NCLEX Examination 1 (p. 333) ▸ Discuss the main drugs classed as salicylates, and explain their therapeutic outcomes. Class Activity ***Divide the class into groups. Assign each group one of the three pharmacologic effects of salicylates: antipyretic, anti-inflammatory, or analgesic. Have each group discuss and then present to the class***

OBJECTIVES	CONTENT	TEACHING RESOURCES
		relevant information about its assigned effect. What are common uses and dosages? What are some drugs typically prescribed? Class Activity ***List on the board the adverse effects of salicylates: gastric irritation, GI bleeding, salicylism, and drug interactions. Have students review what to look for and how to prevent each occurrence. Discuss the exercise with the class.***
Prepare a list of common and serious adverse effects and drug interactions associated with salicylates.	□ Drug class: salicylates (p. 325) – Nursing process for salicylates (p. 326) □ Drug class: nonsteroidal anti-inflammatory drugs (p. 330) – Nursing process for NSAIDs (p. 331)	PPT 19-22 TB Multiple Choice questions 3, 10 TB Multiple Response question 5 ARQ 5 CTQ 3 SG Review Sheet question 42 (p. 132) SG Learning Activities questions 6, 24 (pp. 133-134) SG Practice Question for the NCLEX Examination 7 (p. 135) Drug Table 20-3 Nonsteroidal and Anti-Inflammatory Drugs (pp. 327-329) ▸ Discuss ways in which the common and serious adverse effects and drug interactions associated with salicylates are alike and different. Class Activity ***Present the following scenarios to the class. Ask the class to identify whether each scenario represents a common adverse effect, a serious adverse effect, or a drug interaction associated with salicylate drugs. Ask students to state the reasons for their answers.*** – ***A 70-year-old patient with dark, tarry stool after taking aspirin for a week*** – ***A 50-year-old patient with "coffee ground" emesis after being administered corticosteroids while taking aspirin*** – ***A 30-year-old patient with abdominal discomfort after being given 324 mg of aspirin*** – ***A 65-year-old patient with ringing in the ears after taking a high-dose salicylate for 2 weeks***

OBJECTIVES	CONTENT	TEACHING RESOURCES
Explain why synthetic nonopiate analgesics are not used for inflammatory disorders.	□ Drug class: miscellaneous analgesics (p. 332) – Nursing process for acetaminophen (p. 332)	PPT 23 TB Multiple Choice questions 4-5 INRQ 9 SG Review Sheet questions 38-41 (pp. 131-132) SG Learning Activities questions 7-8 (p. 133) SG Practice Questions for the NCLEX Examination 12-14 (p. 136) Review Question for the NCLEX Examination 2 (p. 333) Drug Table 20-3 Nonsteroidal and Anti-inflammatory Drugs (pp. 327-329) ▸ Discuss the therapeutic outcomes of synthetic nonopiate analgesics. *Class Activity* ***Divide the class into two groups. Assign one group analgesics used for inflammatory disorders, and assign the other group synthetic nonopiate analgesics. Have each group discuss why its assigned topic is or is not used for inflammatory disorders. Then have each group share its findings with the class. Invite feedback and discussion.***
Examine Table 20-4 and identify the active ingredients in commonly prescribed analgesic combination products. Identify products containing aspirin, and compare the analgesic properties of agents available in different strengths.	□ Drug class: miscellaneous analgesics (p. 332) – Nursing process for acetaminophen (p. 332)	PPT 24 SG Review Sheet questions 38-40 (pp. 131-132) Review Question for the NCLEX Examination 9 (p. 334) Drug Table 20-4 Ingredients of Selected Analgesic Combination Products (p. 330) ▸ Discuss how the information in Table 20-4 (p. 330) about combination analgesic drugs affects the nursing process. *Class Activity* ***Divide the class into two groups. Have one group identify and discuss the active ingredients in prescribed analgesic combination products, and have the other group list and discuss products containing aspirin, comparing the analgesic properties of agents available in different strengths. Then have each group share its findings with the class. What products are most commonly used? What patient education is appropriate? What assessments and monitoring should the nurse perform?***

OBJECTIVES	CONTENT	TEACHING RESOURCES
Performance evaluation		Test Bank SG Learning Activities (pp. 133-134) SG Practice Questions for the NCLEX Examination (pp. 135-136) Critical Thinking Questions

20.2 Homework/Assignments:

20.2 Instructor's Notes/Student Feedback:

20 Lecture Outline
Drugs Used for Pain Management

Slide 1

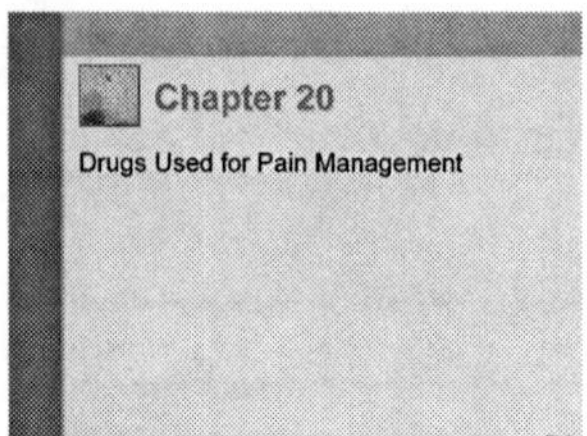
Chapter 20
Drugs Used for Pain Management

Slide 2

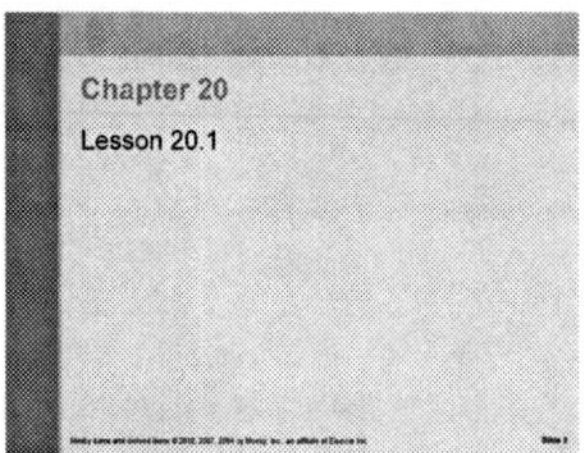
Chapter 20
Lesson 20.1

Slide 3

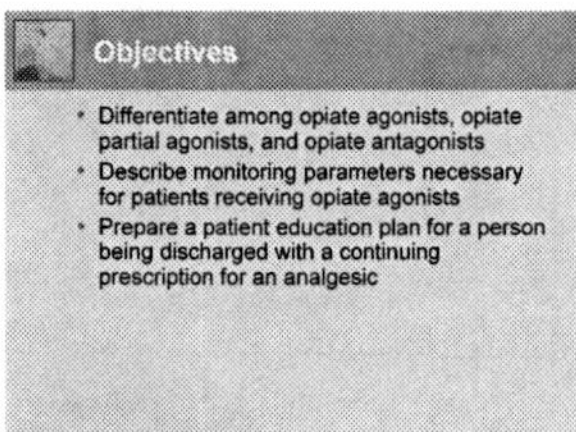
Objectives
Differentiate among opiate agonists, opiate partial agonists, and opiate antagonists
Describe monitoring parameters necessary for patients receiving opiate agonists
Prepare a patient education plan for a person being discharged with a continuing prescription for an analgesic

Slide 4

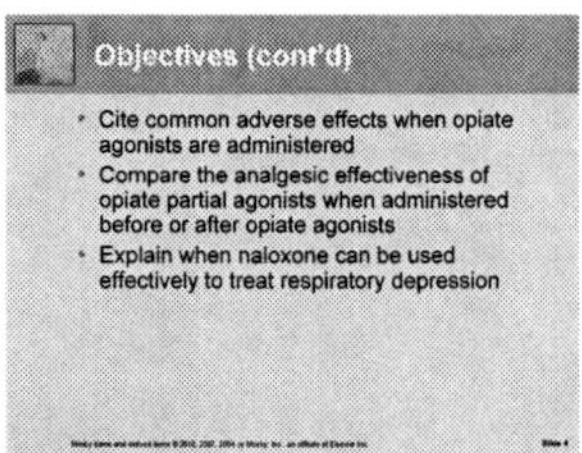
Objectives (cont'd)
Cite common adverse effects when opiate agonists are administered
Compare the analgesic effectiveness of opiate partial agonists when administered before or after opiate agonists
Explain when naloxone can be used effectively to treat respiratory depression

Slide 5

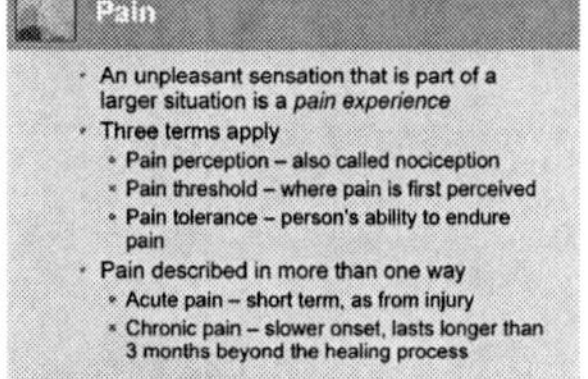
Pain
An unpleasant sensation that is part of a larger situation is a pain experience
Three terms apply
Pain perception – also called nociception
Pain threshold – where pain is first perceived
Pain tolerance – person's ability to endure pain
Pain described in more than one way
Acute pain – short term, as from injury
Chronic pain – slower onset, lasts longer than 3 months beyond the healing process

- Pain is highly subjective and can be influenced by behavioral, physiologic, sensory, emotional, and cultural factors.
- Chronic pain is subdivided into malignant (cancer) and nonmalignant.

Slide 6

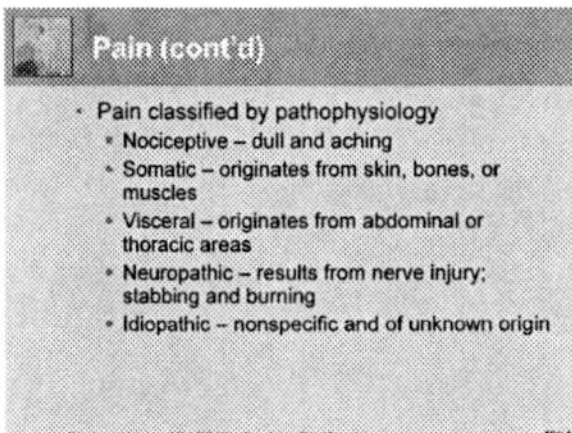
Pain (cont'd)
Pain classified by pathophysiology
Nociceptive – dull and aching
Somatic – originates from skin, bones, or muscles
Visceral – originates from abdominal or thoracic areas
Neuropathic – results from nerve injury; stabbing and burning
Idiopathic – nonspecific and of unknown origin

- Ask students to categorize the following reports of pain:
  - "These menstrual cramps are getting worse and worse." *(visceral)*
  - "I had a virus a couple months ago, but now everything just hurts." *(idiopathic)*
  - "I fell asleep in the back of my brother's car, and now my shoulder is killing me." *(somatic)*
  - "I have a stabbing, shooting pain that runs down my left leg." *(neuropathic)*

Slide 7

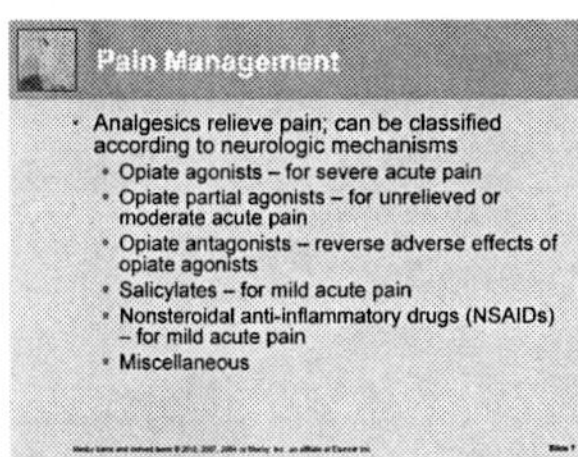
Pain Management
Analgesics relieve pain; can be classified according to neurologic mechanisms
Opiate agonists – for severe acute pain
Opiate partial agonists – for unrelieved or moderate acute pain
Opiate antagonists – reverse adverse effects of opiate agonists
Salicylates – for mild acute pain
Nonsteroidal anti-inflammatory drugs (NSAIDs) – for mild acute pain
Miscellaneous

- Analgesics relieve pain without producing loss of consciousness or reflex activity.
- Opiate receptors block pain when stimulated.
- Pain management must be potent enough to afford maximum relief of pain, not cause dependence, and have minimum adverse effects.

Slide 8

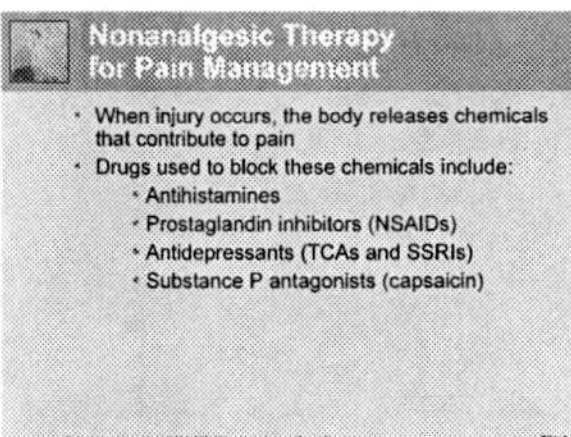
Nonanalgesic Therapy for Pain Management
When injury occurs, the body releases chemicals that contribute to pain
Drugs used to block these chemicals include:
Antihistamines
Prostaglandin inhibitors (NSAIDs)
Antidepressants (TCAs and SSRIs)
Substance P antagonists (capsaicin)

Slide 9

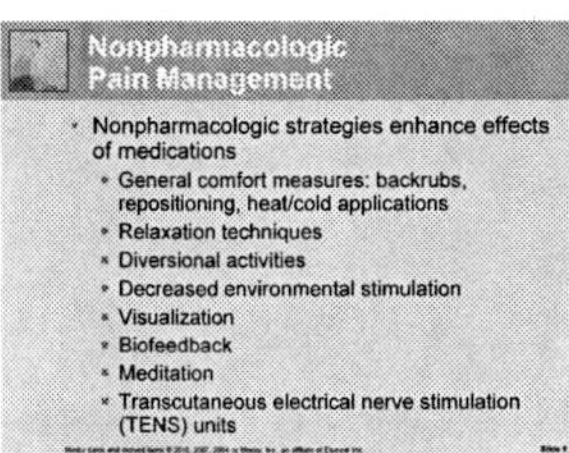
Nonpharmacologic Pain Management
Nonpharmacologic strategies enhance effects of medications
General comfort measures: backrubs, repositioning, heat/cold applications
Relaxation techniques
Diversional activities
Decreased environmental stimulation
Visualization
Biofeedback
Meditation
Transcutaneous electrical nerve stimulation (TENS) units

- Referral to a pain clinic for chronic pain is also an option.

Slide 10

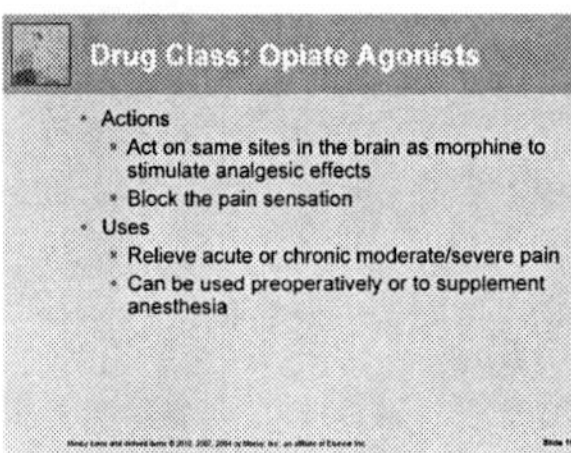
Drug Class: Opiate Agonists
Actions
Act on same sites in the brain as morphine to stimulate analgesic effects
Block the pain sensation
Uses
Relieve acute or chronic moderate/severe pain
Can be used preoperatively or to supplement anesthesia

- Prolonged use can produce drug tolerance or addiction (may develop after 3 to 6 weeks of use).

Slide 11

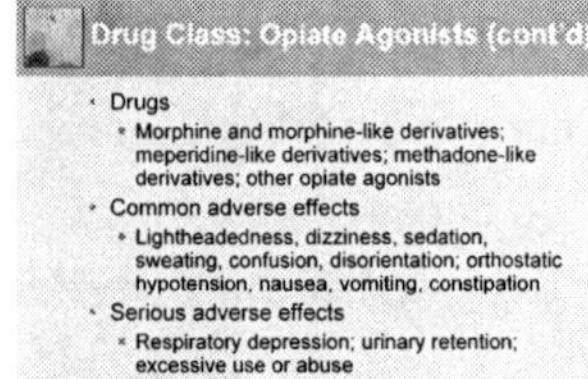
Drug Class: Opiate Agonists (cont'd)
Drugs
Morphine and morphine-like derivatives; meperidine-like derivatives; methadone-like derivatives; other opiate agonists
Common adverse effects
Lightheadedness, dizziness, sedation, sweating, confusion, disorientation; orthostatic hypotension, nausea, vomiting, constipation
Serious adverse effects
Respiratory depression; urinary retention; excessive use or abuse

- For specific drugs, see Table 20-1.
- Drug interactions: tranquilizers, tricyclic antidepressants, antihistamines, alcohol.

Slide 12

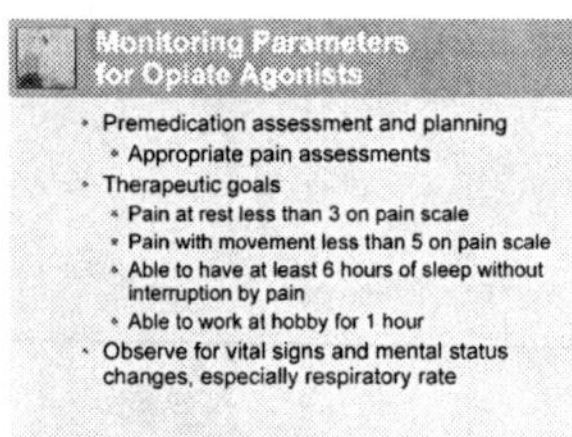
Monitoring Parameters for Opiate Agonists
Premedication assessment and planning
Appropriate pain assessments
Therapeutic goals
Pain at rest less than 3 on pain scale
Pain with movement less than 5 on pain scale
Able to have at least 6 hours of sleep without interruption by pain
Able to work at hobby for 1 hour
Observe for vital signs and mental status changes, especially respiratory rate

- Pain assessments include onset, location, depth, quality, duration and severity (using a scoring system). Pain scales use a rating of 0 to 10, with 10 being the worst possible pain.
- Administer smallest possible dose that allows for pain relief; determine effectiveness.

Slide 13

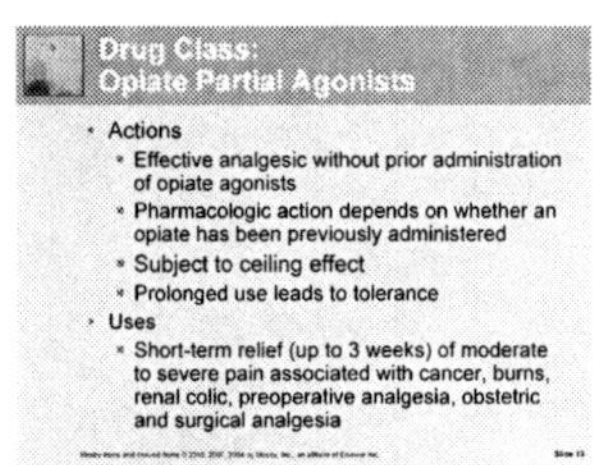
Drug Class: Opiate Partial Agonists
Actions
Effective analgesic without prior administration of opiate agonists
Pharmacologic action depends on whether an opiate has been previously administered
Subject to ceiling effect
Prolonged use leads to tolerance
Uses
Short-term relief (up to 3 weeks) of moderate to severe pain associated with cancer, burns, renal colic, preoperative analgesia, obstetric and surgical analgesia

- In the presence of opiate dependence, opiate partial agonists will induce withdrawal symptoms.

Slide 14

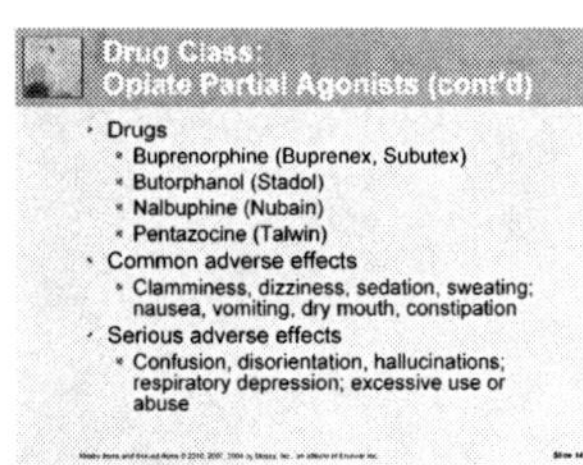
Drug Class: Opiate Partial Agonists (cont'd)
Drugs
Buprenorphine (Buprenex, Subutex)
Butorphanol (Stadol)
Nalbuphine (Nubain)
Pentazocine (Talwin)
Common adverse effects
Clamminess, dizziness, sedation, sweating; nausea, vomiting, dry mouth, constipation
Serious adverse effects
Confusion, disorientation, hallucinations; respiratory depression; excessive use or abuse

- Buprenorphine is also used to treat addictions to heroin, painkillers, and opiate products.
- Check for prior use of opiate agonists.

Slide 15

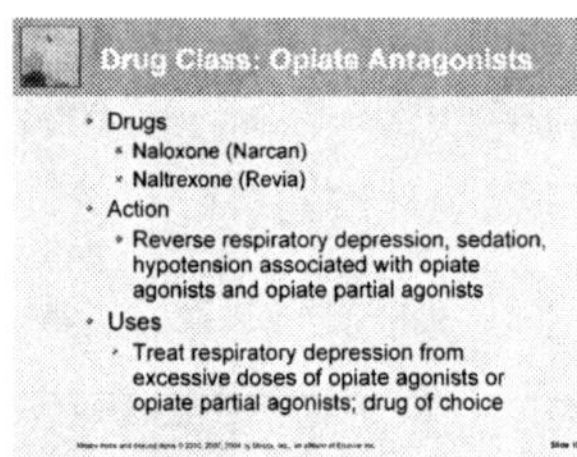
Drug Class: Opiate Antagonists
Drugs
Naloxone (Narcan)
Naltrexone (Revia)
Action
Reverse respiratory depression, sedation, hypotension associated with opiate agonists and opiate partial agonists
Uses
Treat respiratory depression from excessive doses of opiate agonists or opiate partial agonists; drug of choice

- Also approved to treat alcoholism.
- Not effective in CNS depression from tranquilizers or sedative-hypnotics.
- The most common adverse effects are rare: nausea, vomiting, chills, myalgia, dysphoria, abdominal cramps, joint pain, mental depression, apathy.

Slide 16

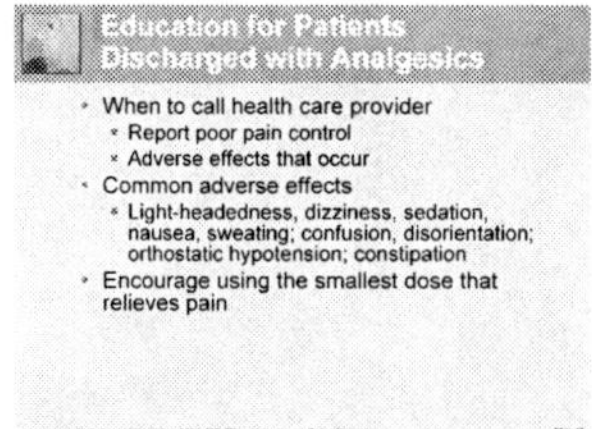
Education for Patients Discharged with Analgesics
When to call health care provider
Report poor pain control
Adverse effects that occur
Common adverse effects
Light-headedness, dizziness, sedation, nausea, sweating; confusion, disorientation; orthostatic hypotension; constipation
Encourage using the smallest dose that relieves pain

Slide 17

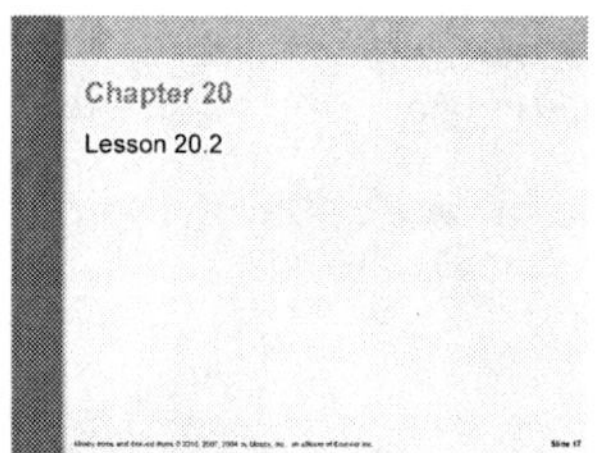
Chapter 20
Lesson 20.2

Slide 18

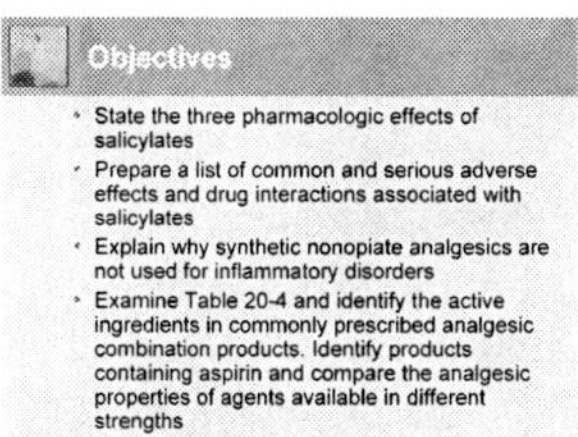
Objectives
State the three pharmacologic effects of salicylates
Prepare a list of common and serious adverse effects and drug interactions associated with salicylates
Explain why synthetic nonopiate analgesics are not used for inflammatory disorders
Examine Table 20-4 and identify the active ingredients in commonly prescribed analgesic combination products. Identify products containing aspirin and compare the analgesic properties of agents available in different strengths

Slide 19

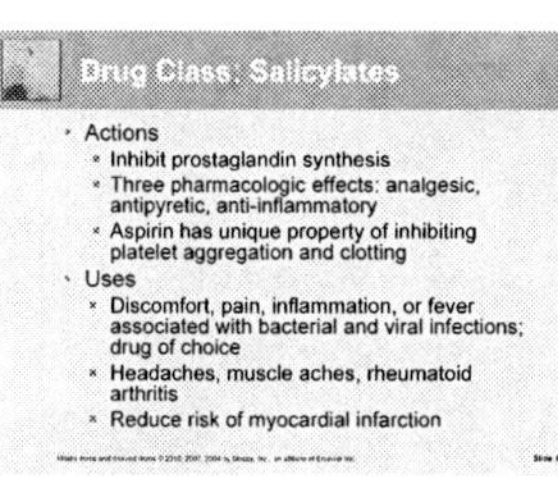
Drug Class: Salicylates
Actions
Inhibit prostaglandin synthesis
Three pharmacologic effects: analgesic, antipyretic, anti-inflammatory
Aspirin has unique property of inhibiting platelet aggregation and clotting
Uses
Discomfort, pain, inflammation, or fever associated with bacterial and viral infections; drug of choice
Headaches, muscle aches, rheumatoid arthritis
Reduce risk of myocardial infarction

- Not recommended for children due to the risk of Reye's syndrome.
- Consciousness level not dulled; no memory loss, mental sluggishness, hallucinations, euphoria, or sedation.

Slide 20

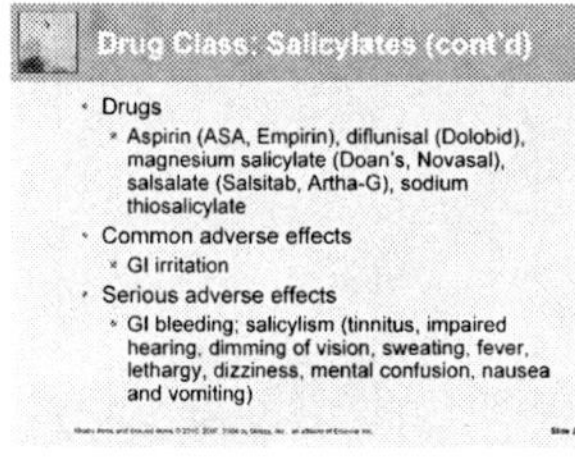
Drug Class: Salicylates (cont'd)
Drugs
Aspirin (ASA, Empirin), diflunisal (Dolobid), magnesium salicylate (Doan's, Novasal), salsalate (Salsitab, Artha-G), sodium thiosalicylate
Common adverse effects
GI irritation
Serious adverse effects
GI bleeding; salicylism (tinnitus, impaired hearing, dimming of vision, sweating, fever, lethargy, dizziness, mental confusion, nausea and vomiting)

- Increased risk of bleeding in older adults in the form of GI bleeding or a hemorrhagic stroke.
- No antidote exists for aspirin toxicity; discontinuing the drug is the only treatment and the condition is reversible.

Slide 21

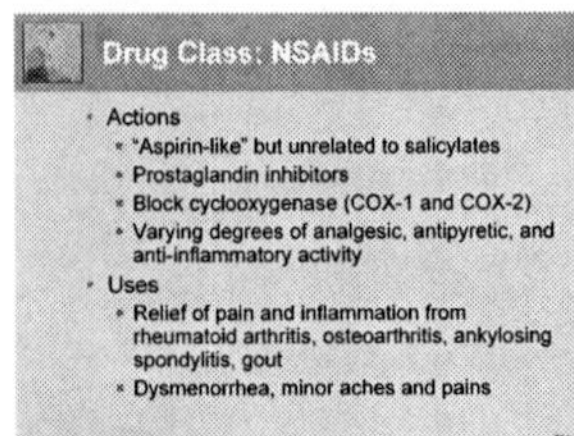
Drug Class: NSAIDs
Actions
"Aspirin-like" but unrelated to salicylates
Prostaglandin inhibitors
Block cyclooxygenase (COX-1 and COX-2)
Varying degrees of analgesic, antipyretic, and anti-inflammatory activity
Uses
Relief of pain and inflammation from rheumatoid arthritis, osteoarthritis, ankylosing spondylitis, gout
Dysmenorrhea, minor aches and pains

- None are superior to aspirin but are preferred options for patients who do not tolerate aspirin.

Slide 22

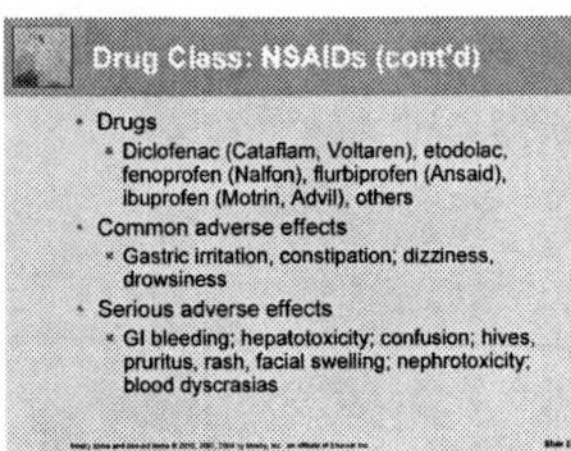
Drug Class: NSAIDs (cont'd)
Drugs
Diclofenac (Cataflam, Voltaren), etodolac, fenoprofen (Nalfon), flurbiprofen (Ansaid), ibuprofen (Motrin, Advil), others
Common adverse effects
Gastric irritation, constipation; dizziness, drowsiness
Serious adverse effects
GI bleeding; hepatotoxicity; confusion; hives, pruritus, rash, facial swelling; nephrotoxicity; blood dyscrasias

- For specific drugs, see Table 20-3.
- Increased risk of potentially fatal cardiovascular emergencies (heart attack, stroke) associated with long-term use.
- Drug interactions: warfarin, phenytoin, valproic acid, lithium, aspirin, furosemide, etc.

Slide 23

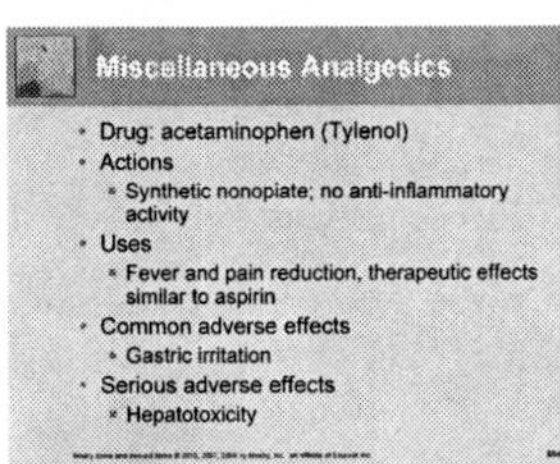
Miscellaneous Analgesics
Drug: acetaminophen (Tylenol)
Actions
Synthetic nonopiate; no anti-inflammatory activity
Uses
Fever and pain reduction, therapeutic effects similar to aspirin
Common adverse effects
Gastric irritation
Serious adverse effects
Hepatotoxicity

- Ineffective (other than as an analgesic) for the relief of symptoms of rheumatoid arthritis or other inflammation.

Slide 24

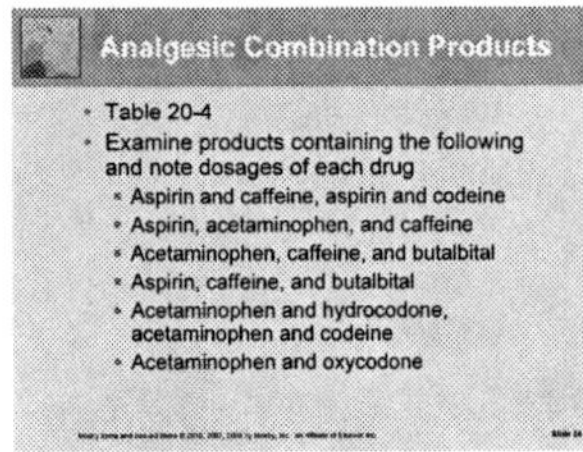
Analgesic Combination Products
Table 20-4
Examine products containing the following and note dosages of each drug
Aspirin and caffeine, aspirin and codeine
Aspirin, acetaminophen, and caffeine
Acetaminophen, caffeine, and butalbital
Aspirin, caffeine, and butalbital
Acetaminophen and hydrocodone, acetaminophen and codeine
Acetaminophen and oxycodone

ELSEVIER

Lesson Plan

21 Introduction to Cardiovascular Disease and Metabolic Syndrome

TEACHING FOCUS

In this chapter, students are introduced to various causes of coronary heart disease (CHD) and metabolic syndrome. Students also have the opportunity to learn about the treatment options and drug therapy for these disorders.

MATERIALS AND RESOURCES

- ☐ computer and PowerPoint projector (Lessons 21.1 and 21.2)
- ☐ guest speaker: nurse practitioner
- ☐ calculator

LESSON CHECKLIST

Preparations for this lesson include:

- lecture
- demonstration
- evaluation of student knowledge and skills of all entry-level activities related to metabolic syndrome and the drugs used to treat metabolic syndrome and cardiovascular disease, including those used to treat:
  - hypertension
  - dyslipidemia
  - type 2 diabetes mellitus

KEY TERMS

angina pectoris (p. 335)
body mass index (BMI) (p. 336)
cardiovascular disease (p. 335)
coronary artery disease (CAD) (p. 335)
dysrhythmias (p. 335)
heart failure (p. 335)
hypertension (p. 335)
insulin resistance syndrome (p. 336)
metabolic syndrome (p. 336)
myocardial infarction (MI) (p. 335)
peripheral arterial disease (p. 335)
peripheral vascular disease (p. 335)
stroke (p. 335)

ADDITIONAL RESOURCES

PowerPoint slides: 1-12

Legend

ARQ	**PPT**	**TB**	**CTQ**	**SG**	**INRQ**
Audience Response Questions	PowerPoint Slides	Test Bank	Critical Thinking Questions	Study Guide	Interactive NCLEX Review Questions

Class Activities are indicated in ***bold italic.***

LESSON 21.1

BACKGROUND ASSESSMENT

Question: What are the key characteristics of metabolic syndrome?
Answer: The key characteristics of metabolic syndrome are the presence of type 2 diabetes mellitus, abdominal obesity, hypertriglyceridemia, low high-density lipoproteins (HDLs), and hypertension.

Question: What is metabolic syndrome?
Answer: Metabolic syndrome is the term used to describe the cluster of risk factors that relate directly to excesses in lifestyle, which is the major contributor to hyperlipidemias. Metabolic syndrome is diagnosed if three or more of the following criteria are present: fasting blood glucose more than 110 mg/dL; blood pressure above 130/85 mm Hg; triglycerides greater than 150 mg/dL; waist circumference more than 40 inches in men and 36 inches in women; and HDL cholesterol less than 40 mg/dL in men and 50 mg/dL in women. The key characteristics of metabolic syndrome are type 2 diabetes mellitus, abdominal obesity, hypertriglyceridemia, low HDL cholesterol, and hypertension.

CRITICAL THINKING QUESTION

A 45-year-old man is obese, has a blood pressure of 160/96 mm Hg, smokes a half-pack of cigarettes per day, works long hours, has a poor diet, and engages in minimal physical exercise. What are the patient's risk factors for metabolic syndrome, and how could the patient benefit from modifying his lifestyle?
Guidelines: CHD is a major cause of death in the United States. The patient's risk factors for CHD are his high blood pressure and poor lifestyle choices, including cigarette smoking, sedentary lifestyle, and eating habits. Other causes are hypertension, atherosclerosis, and type 2 diabetes mellitus. The patient's several risk factors put him at risk not only for CHD but also for elevated cholesterol and triglyceride levels, hyperlipidemia, hypertriglyceridemia, and other serious medical conditions. There are several steps that the patient can take to modify his lifestyle and reduce these risk factors. These include reducing his weight, improving his diet by decreasing his fat and calorie intake, increasing his physical exercise, and decreasing or quitting smoking.

OBJECTIVES	CONTENT	TEACHING RESOURCES
Define metabolic syndrome.	■ Cardiovascular diseases (p. 335)	PPT 4 ARQ 1, 5 TB Multiple Choice question 5 TB Multiple Response questions 2, 4-5 SG Review Sheet questions 1-2 (p. 137) SG Learning Activities questions 1-2, 4 (p. 138) Box 21-1: Cardiovascular Disorders (p. 336) Class Activity ***Divide the class into groups of three, and assign one of the following to each group: coronary artery disease (CAD), angina pectoris, myocardial infarction (MI), stroke, hypertension, dysrhythmias, peripheral vascular disease or peripheral arterial disease, and venous disorders, such as acute deep vein thrombosis. Have each group discuss its assigned disorder, areas within the body affected, and the disorder's relationship to heart failure and eventual death.***

OBJECTIVES	CONTENT	TEACHING RESOURCES
List the major risk factors of metabolic syndrome.	■ Metabolic syndrome (p. 335) Review the disorders that can occur within the circulatory system: coronary artery disease, angina pectoris, myocardial infarction, stroke, hypertension, cardiac dysrhythmias, peripheral vascular disease (arterial and venous), and heart failure. Discuss risk factors that influence the development of these disorders.	PPT 5-6 ARQ 3 TB Multiple Choice question 3 INRQ 3 CTQ 2 SG Review Sheet questions 3-4 (p. 137) SG Learning Activities question 3 (p. 138) Table 21-1: Definitions and Characteristics of Metabolic Syndrome (p. 336) Table 21-2: Relationship Between Body Mass Index and Categories of Obesity (p. 336) ▸ Discuss risk factors. Class Activity ***Using the National Cholesterol Education Program (NCEP) diagnostic criteria for metabolic syndrome, have volunteer students place the following into "At Risk" or "Not at Risk" categories:*** – ***African American male with blood pressure of 135/85 mm Hg*** – ***Caucasian female with triglyceride level of 135*** – ***Mexican American woman with fasting glucose of 110*** – ***Adolescent male with HDL of 35*** ***Review with the class the importance of the exercise and compare the NCEP criteria with the International Diabetes Federation (IDF) criteria.***
List the diagnostic criteria for metabolic syndrome for men and women using the National Cholesterol Education Program guidelines.	■ Metabolic syndrome (p. 336) Review the key characteristics of metabolic syndrome: type 2 diabetes, abdominal obesity, hypertriglyceridemia, low high-density lipoproteins, and hypertension. Discuss the prevalence of obesity in the United States and efforts being made to fight the trend.	PPT 7 ARQ 2 TB Multiple Choice questions 1, 4 INRQ 7-8, 10 CTQ 3 Review Questions for the NCLEX Examination 5-7 (p. 340) ▸ Discuss 1998 National Heart, Lung, and Blood Institute (NHLBI) expert report, diagnostic criteria addressed in the NCEP guidelines, and formulas to calculate BMI.

OBJECTIVES	CONTENT	TEACHING RESOURCES
		Class Activity ***Ask students to calculate their individual BMI.*** Class Activity ***List on the board the following: type 2 diabetes, abdominal obesity, hypertriglyceridemia, low HDL, and hypertension. Divide the class into four groups, and have each group explain one of these characteristics and the effects of each of the disorders on the development of metabolic syndrome. Review the results with the class.***

21.1 Homework/Assignments:

21.1 Instructor's Notes/Student Feedback:

LESSON 21.2

CRITICAL THINKING QUESTION

You are a grade school nurse, and you are planning to develop student instruction on healthy lifestyles and prevention of metabolic syndrome. What areas will you include in the education?

Guidelines: The school nurse should educate students on the importance of making healthy lifestyle choices. This includes a diet low in saturated fats and simple sugars; regular physical activity appropriate to gender, age, and body height and weight; and avoiding unhealthy choices, such as smoking and excessive alcohol intake.

OBJECTIVES	CONTENT	TEACHING RESOURCES
State the importance of lifestyle modification in the treatment of metabolic syndrome.	□ Treatment of metabolic syndrome (p. 338) Review the focus of treatment options for metabolic syndrome. Lifestyle changes include weight loss and increased physical activity, changes in diet with reduced intake of fats, and maintaining normal blood pressure as well as normal lipid and glucose levels.	PPT 10-12 TB Multiple Choice questions 2, 6-7 TB Multiple Response question 1 INRQ 6, 11 SG Practice Question for the NCLEX Examination 4 (p. 139) Figure 21-1 (p. 337): Growth in overweight and obesity in the United States, 1990-2007.

ELSEVIER

OBJECTIVES	CONTENT	TEACHING RESOURCES
		Figure 21-2 (p. 338): Mechanisms of metabolic syndrome. ▸ Discuss lifestyle factors, including diet, physical activity, smoking, and alcohol use, and their relationship to metabolic syndrome. Class Activity ***Invite a guest speaker, such as a nurse practitioner, to discuss lifestyle education and motivation provided for the patient with metabolic syndrome.*** Class Activity ***Have two students role-play a nurse discussing the need to make lifestyle changes with an obese, sedentary, diabetic patient who is not concerned about his weight. Discuss important topics to cover that include diet, exercise, and weight control, and make a plan that can easily be followed with recommended periodic checkups.***
List the treatment goals for type 2 diabetes management, lipid management, and hypertension management.	□ Drug therapy for metabolic syndrome (p. 339) – Hypertension (p. 339) – Dyslipidemia (p. 339) – Type 2 diabetes mellitus (p. 339) Review the options for drug therapy that need to be individualized for the patient. Drugs should be used after lifestyle changes have not lowered risk for development of metabolic syndrome.	PPT 10-12 TB Multiple Response question 3 INRQ 1-2, 5 SG Review Sheet questions 5-11 (p. 137) SG Learning Activities questions 5-9 (p. 138) SG Practice questions for the NCLEX Examination 3, 5, 7-9 (pp. 139-140) Review Questions for the NCLEX Examination 1-4, 8 (pp. 339-340) ▸ Discuss conditions associated with metabolic syndrome requiring drug therapy: type 2 diabetes mellitus, hypertension, and dyslipidemia. Class Activity ***Divide the class into three groups, and assign each group one of the following: type 2 diabetes mellitus, hypertension, and dyslipidemia. Have each group research drug therapies listed in Chapter 21 to treat respective conditions. Have each group complete a drug card phototype of the various drugs listing common agents, dosages, adverse effects, and patient education for home management.*** Class Activity ***Bring descriptions of various diets to class: DASH diet, Atkins diet, South Beach diet, Mediterranean diet, and the American Diabetes Association (ADA) recommended diet.***

OBJECTIVES	CONTENT	TEACHING RESOURCES
		Have several students discuss which ones would be beneficial in promoting weight loss as well as which ones could be harmful. Review the exercise with the class.
State why long-term control and adherence to medications are important in managing metabolic syndrome.	□ Drug therapy for metabolic syndrome (p. 339) – Nursing process for metabolic syndrome (p. 339)	PPT 10-12 INRQ 4, 9, 12 CTQ 1, 4 SG Practice Questions for the NCLEX Examination 1-2, 6 (p. 139) Box 21-2: General Treatment Goals for Patients with Metabolic Syndrome (p. 338) ▸ Discuss general treatment goals for patients with metabolic syndrome (Box 21-2), including those for blood pressure, lipids, and blood glucose. *Class Activity* ***Divide the class into three groups, and assign each group one of the main categories listed in the chapter. Have each group research variables listed for each classification (e.g., proteinuria, hemoglobin A1C). Facilitate class discussion, and describe variables and their relationship to the diseases associated with metabolic syndrome.***
Performance evaluation		Test Bank SG Learning Activities (p. 138) SG Practice Questions for the NCLEX Examination (pp. 139-140) Critical Thinking Questions

21.2 Homework/Assignments:

21.2 Instructor's Notes/Student Feedback:

21 Lecture Outline
Introduction to Cardiovascular Disease and Metabolic Syndrome

Slide 1

Chapter 21
Introduction to Cardiovascular Disease and Metabolic Syndrome

Slide 2

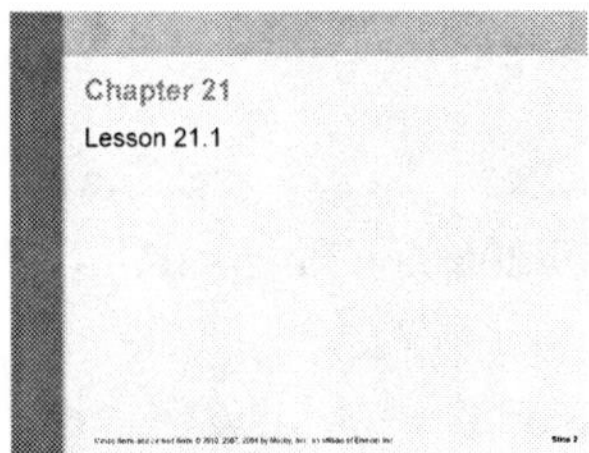
Chapter 21
Lesson 21.1

Slide 3

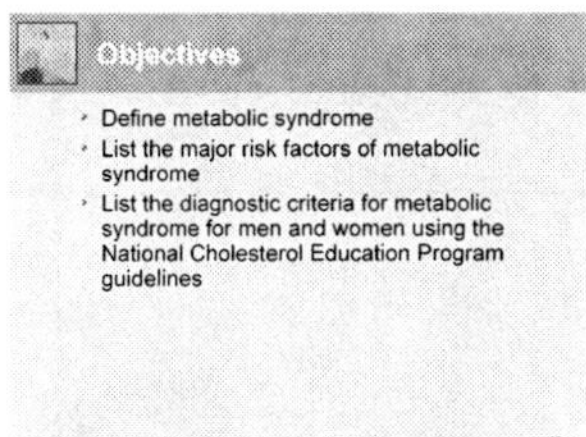
Objectives
Define metabolic syndrome
List the major risk factors of metabolic syndrome
List the diagnostic criteria for metabolic syndrome for men and women using the National Cholesterol Education Program guidelines

Slide 4

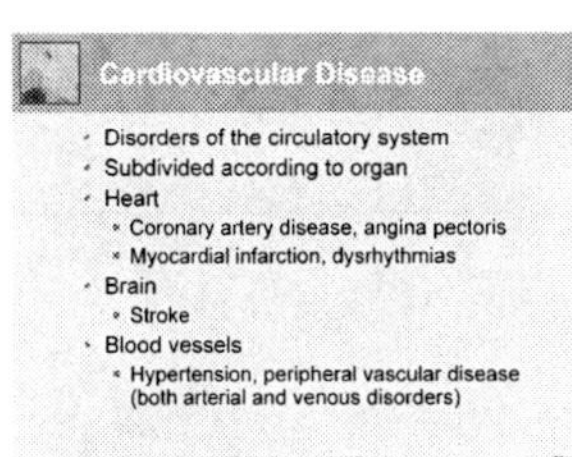
Cardiovascular Disease
Disorders of the circulatory system
Subdivided according to organ
Heart
Coronary artery disease, angina pectoris
Myocardial infarction, dysrhythmias
Brain
Stroke
Blood vessels
Hypertension, peripheral vascular disease (both arterial and venous disorders)

- Major cause of premature death in the United States.
- Long-term pathology of any one or combination of these diseases leads to heart failure.

Slide 5

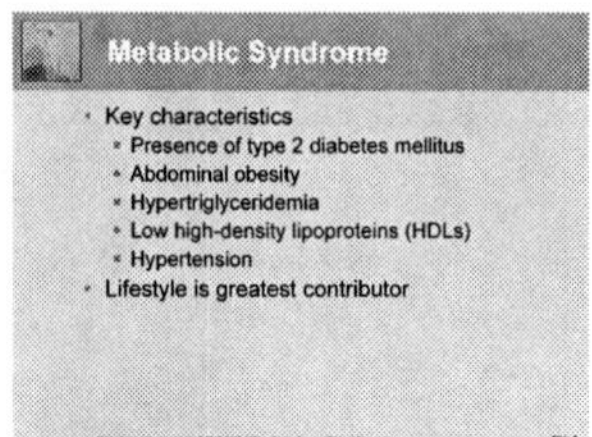
Metabolic Syndrome
Key characteristics
Presence of type 2 diabetes mellitus
Abdominal obesity
Hypertriglyceridemia
Low high-density lipoproteins (HDLs)
Hypertension
Lifestyle is greatest contributor

- Other terms include *diabesity* and *insulin resistance syndrome.*
- Insulin resistance leads to type 2 diabetes, which causes vascular damage and induces atherosclerosis.

Slide 6

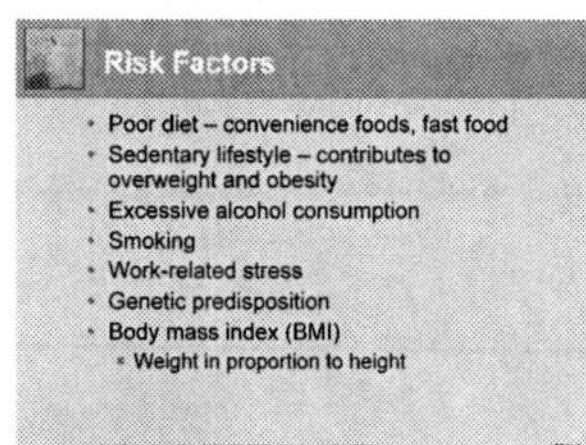
Risk Factors
Poor diet – convenience foods, fast food
Sedentary lifestyle – contributes to overweight and obesity
Excessive alcohol consumption
Smoking
Work-related stress
Genetic predisposition
Body mass index (BMI)
Weight in proportion to height

- BMI is measured by weight in kilograms divided by height in meters squared – OR – weight in pounds multiplied by 703 and divided by height in inches squared.

Slide 7

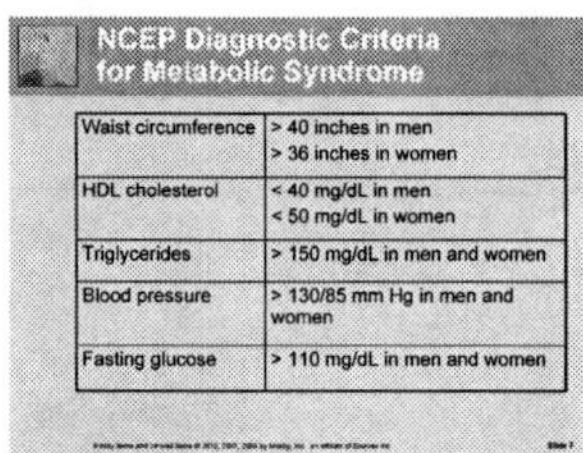
NCEP Diagnostic Criteria for Metabolic Syndrome

Waist circumference	> 40 inches in men > 36 inches in women
HDL cholesterol	< 40 mg/dL in men < 50 mg/dL in women
Triglycerides	> 150 mg/dL in men and women
Blood pressure	> 130/85 mm Hg in men and women
Fasting glucose	> 110 mg/dL in men and women

- Data according to the National Cholesterol Education Program (NCEP).
- People with central obesity and at least two of the remaining four factors are considered to have metabolic syndrome.

Slide 8

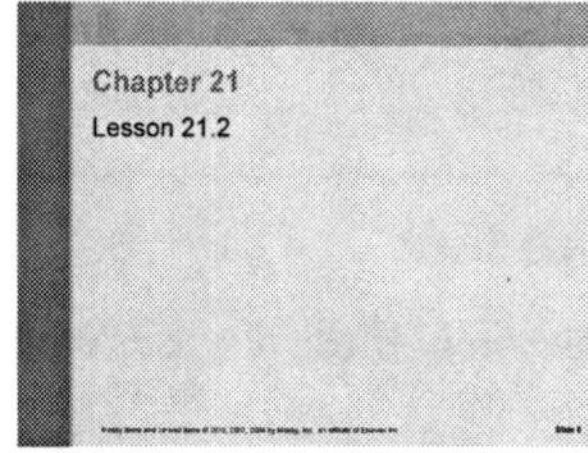
Chapter 21
Lesson 21.2

Slide 9

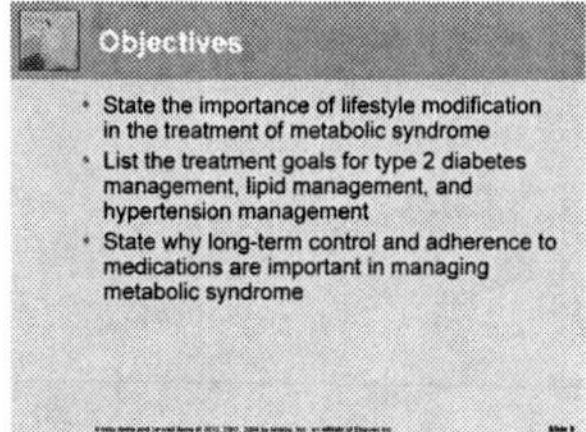
Objectives
State the importance of lifestyle modification in the treatment of metabolic syndrome
List the treatment goals for type 2 diabetes management, lipid management, and hypertension management
State why long-term control and adherence to medications are important in managing metabolic syndrome

ELSEVIER

Slide 10

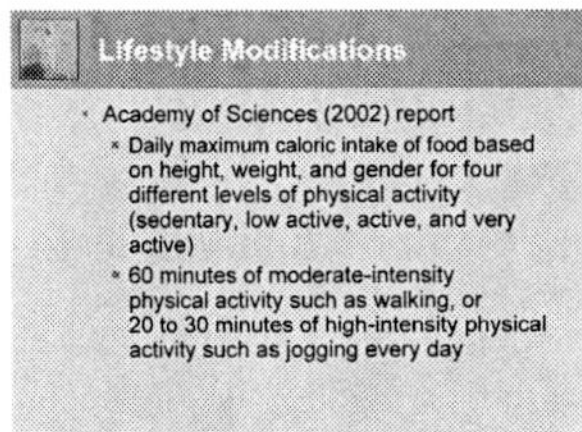
Lifestyle Modifications
Academy of Sciences (2002) report
Daily maximum caloric intake of food based on height, weight, and gender for four different levels of physical activity (sedentary, low active, active, and very active)
60 minutes of moderate-intensity physical activity such as walking, or 20 to 30 minutes of high-intensity physical activity such as jogging every day

- Most cost-effective treatments are smoking cessation, weight reduction, exercise, stress reduction, and dietary modification.

Slide 11

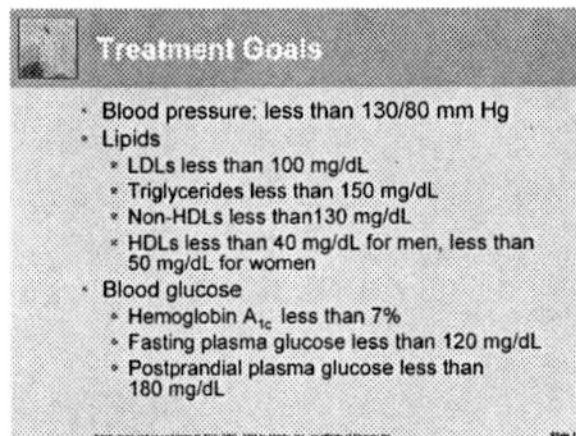
Treatment Goals
Blood pressure: less than 130/80 mm Hg
Lipids
LDLs less than 100 mg/dL
Triglycerides less than 150 mg/dL
Non-HDLs less than130 mg/dL
HDLs less than 40 mg/dL for men, less than 50 mg/dL for women
Blood glucose
Hemoglobin A_{1c} less than 7%
Fasting plasma glucose less than 120 mg/dL
Postprandial plasma glucose less than 180 mg/dL

Slide 12

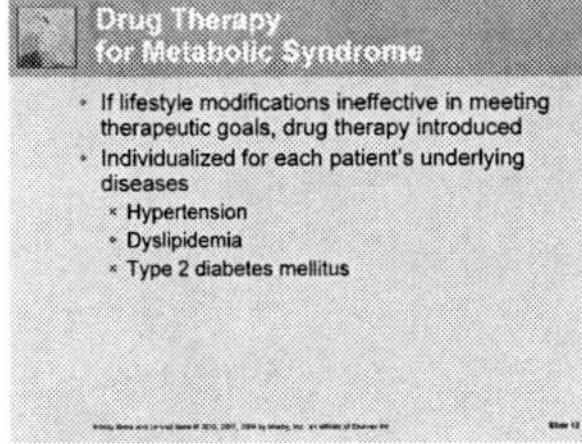
Drug Therapy for Metabolic Syndrome
If lifestyle modifications ineffective in meeting therapeutic goals, drug therapy introduced
Individualized for each patient's underlying diseases
Hypertension
Dyslipidemia
Type 2 diabetes mellitus

22 Lesson Plan
Drugs Used to Treat Dyslipidemias

TEACHING FOCUS

In this chapter, students will be introduced to various causes of coronary heart disease (CHD), such as atherosclerosis, hyperlipidemia, and metabolic syndrome. Students will also have the opportunity to learn about the treatment options and drug therapy for dyslipidemias.

MATERIALS AND RESOURCES

- ☐ computer and PowerPoint projector (Lesson 22.1)

LESSON CHECKLIST

Preparations for this lesson include:

- lecture
- demonstration
- evaluation of student knowledge and skills of all entry-level activities related to the drugs used to treat hyperlipidemias, including:
  - the major types of lipoproteins
  - treatment modalities for lipid disorders
  - oral administration instructions for antilipemic agents

KEY TERMS

atherosclerosis (p. 341)
chylomicrons (p. 341)
dyslipidemias (p. 341)
hyperlipidemia (p. 341)
lipoproteins (p. 341)
metabolic syndrome (p. 342)
triglycerides (p. 341)

ADDITIONAL RESOURCES

PowerPoint slides: 1-12
Flashcards, Decks 1 and 2

Legend

ARQ	**PPT**	**TB**	**CTQ**	**SG**	**INRQ**
Audience Response Questions	PowerPoint Slides	Test Bank	Critical Thinking Questions	Study Guide	Interactive NCLEX Review Questions

Class Activities are indicated in ***bold italic.***

LESSON 22.1

BACKGROUND ASSESSMENT

Question: What are the causes of dyslipidemias?
Answer: Genetic abnormalities, secondary causes, or both can bring about dyslipidemias. The secondary causes of dyslipidemias include lifestyle, poor dietary habits, medications, inadequate exercise, drugs, and underlying disease.

Question: What is metabolic syndrome?
Answer: *Metabolic syndrome* is the term used to describe the cluster of risk factors that relate directly to excesses in lifestyle, which is the major contributor to dyslipidemias. Metabolic syndrome is diagnosed

if three or more of the following criteria are present: fasting blood glucose more than 110 mg/dL, blood pressure above 130/85 mm Hg, triglycerides greater than 150 mg/dL, waist circumference more than 40 inches in men and 35 inches in women, and high-density lipoprotein (HDL) cholesterol less than 40 mg/dL in men and 50 mg/dL in women. The key characteristics of metabolic syndrome are type 2 diabetes mellitus, abdominal obesity, hypertriglyceridemia, low HDL cholesterol, and hypertension.

CRITICAL THINKING QUESTION

A 45-year-old man is obese, has a blood pressure of 160/96 mm Hg, smokes a half-pack of cigarettes per day, works long hours, has a poor diet, and engages in minimal physical exercise. What are the patient's risk factors for coronary artery disease (CAD), and how could the patient benefit from modifying his lifestyle?

Guidelines: CAD is a major cause of death in the United States. The patient's risk factors for CAD are his high blood pressure, cigarette smoking, and poor exercise and eating habits. Other causes are hypertension, atherosclerosis, and type 2 diabetes mellitus. The patient's several risk factors put him at risk not only for CAD but also for elevated cholesterol and triglyceride levels, hyperlipidemia, hypertriglyceridemia, and other serious medical conditions. There are several steps the patient can take to modify his lifestyle and reduce his risk of heart disease. These include reducing his weight, improving his diet by decreasing his fat and calorie intake, increasing his physical exercise, and decreasing or quitting smoking.

OBJECTIVES	CONTENT	TEACHING RESOURCES
Describe atherosclerosis and its effects on the cardiovascular system.	■ Atherosclerosis (p. 341) Review the definition and causes of atherosclerosis. Discuss the terms *hyperlipidemia* and *dyslipidemia.*	PPT 4 TB Multiple Choice question 13 SG Review Sheet question 1 (p. 141) SG Learning Activities questions 1-3, 18, 20, 26 (pp. 144-145) ▸ Discuss the role of low-density lipoprotein cholesterol (LDL-C) in the occurrence of a patient diagnosed with atherosclerosis. ▸ Discuss the significance of a patient who has low levels of high-density lipoprotein (HDL) and a patient who has high levels of HDL.
Identify the four major types of lipoproteins.	■ Atherosclerosis (p. 341)	PPT 4 ARQ 1 TB Multiple Choice questions 1, 6 SG Learning Activities question 24 (p. 145) ▸ Discuss other markers being tested to verify if they are better predictors of risk for impending heart disease. Table 22-1: Classification of Cholesterol and Triglyceride Levels Based on NCEP (National Cholesterol Education Program) Guidelines (p. 342) Class Activity ***As a class, discuss CAD and ask students to identify which conditions can lead to CAD. Can a person with one of these conditions make enough changes to prevent CAD from developing? What are possible treatments and nursing interventions?***

OBJECTIVES	CONTENT	TEACHING RESOURCES
		Class Activity ***List on the board the five categories of lipoproteins: chylomicrons, very low density lipoprotein (VLDL), intermediate-density lipoprotein (IDL), LDL, and HDL. Divide the class into five groups, and have each group discuss one of the different types of lipoproteins, their composition, and importance. Review the exercise with the class.***
Describe the primary treatment modalities for lipid disorders.	■ Treatment of hyperlipidemias (p. 342) Review the goals for the treatment of hyperlipidemia and the NCEP recommendations regarding therapeutic lifestyle changes.	PPT 5-7 ARQ 2 TB Multiple Choice questions 8, 13 TB Multiple Response question 3 INRQ 2, 13 Animation: Cholesterol-Lowering Drugs SG Review Sheet questions 3, 6 (p. 141) SG Learning Activities questions 19, 21- 23, 26 (p. 145) Table 22-2: Lipoprotein Disorders Treatable with Diet and Drug Therapy (p. 342) ▸ Discuss the therapeutic lifestyle changes (TLCs) primary to treatment of hyperlipidemia. ▸ Discuss the approaches a nurse can use to teach patients how to reduce their risk of hyperlipidemia. Class Activity ***Present the following scenario to the class for students to discuss:*** ***– A 51-year-old woman is overweight, has poor diet and exercise habits, and has a family history of CHD.*** ***Have the class identify appropriate nursing interventions for this patient and discuss possible treatment modalities. Is this patient likely to be prescribed an antilipemic agent?*** Class Activity ***Using a matching format, list the NCEP recommendations for lifestyle change, and have students match the goals for each category. Review the exercise with the class.***
State the oral administration instructions for antilipemic agents.	■ Drug therapy for hyperlipidemias (p. 342) – Nursing process for hyperlipidemia therapy (p. 343) – Patient education and health promotion (p. 344)	PPT 8-13 ARQ 3-5 TB Multiple Choice questions 2-5, 7, 9-12 TB Multiple Response questions 1-2, 4 INRQ 1, 3-12, 14

OBJECTIVES	CONTENT	TEACHING RESOURCES
	□ Drug class: Bile acid-binding resins (p. 344) – Nursing process for bile acid–binding resins (p. 345) □ Drug class: Niacin (p. 345) – Nursing process for niacin (p. 346) □ Drug class: HMG-CoA reductase inhibitors (p. 347) – Nursing process for HMG-CoA reductase inhibitors (p. 347) □ Drug class: Fibric acids (p. 349) – Nursing process for fibric acids (p. 349) □ Drug class: Miscellaneous antilipemic agents (p. 350) – Nursing process for ezetimibe (p. 350) – Nursing process for omega-3 fatty acids (p. 350)	CTQ 1-4 SG Review Sheet questions 4-5, 7-21 (pp. 141-143) SG Learning Activities questions 4-17, 25, 27-32 (pp. 144-145) SG Practice Questions for the NCLEX Examination 1-14 (pp. 146-147) Review Questions for the NCLEX Examination 1-10 (pp. 351-352) Drug Table 22-3: HMG-CoA Reductase Inhibitors (Statins) (p. 348) ▸ Discuss why a health care provider may initiate bile acid resins along with antilipemic therapy. ▸ Discuss the role and impact of vitamin K ingested with antilipemic medications. Class Activity ***Divide the class into four groups, and assign each group one of the following antilipemic drugs: bile acid–binding resins, niacin, HMG-CoA reductase inhibitors, and fibric acids. Using the chart that was compiled in the second class activity, have each group outline its assigned drug. Have students include the drug's classification, its action on cholesterol or triglyceride levels, uses, dosage, adverse effects, and patient teaching. Have each group present its findings to the class.***
Performance evaluation		Test Bank SG Learning Activities (pp. 144-145) SG Practice Questions for the NCLEX Examination (pp. 146-147) Critical Thinking Questions

22.1 Homework/Assignments:

22.1 Instructor's Notes/Student Feedback:

ELSEVIER

22 Lecture Outline
Drugs Used to Treat Dyslipidemias

Slide 1

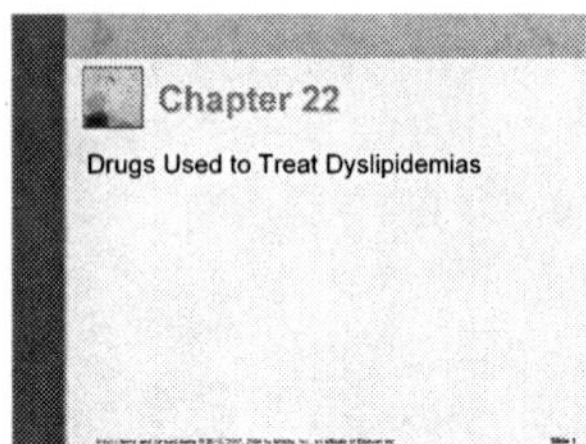
Chapter 22
Drugs Used to Treat Dyslipidemias

Slide 2

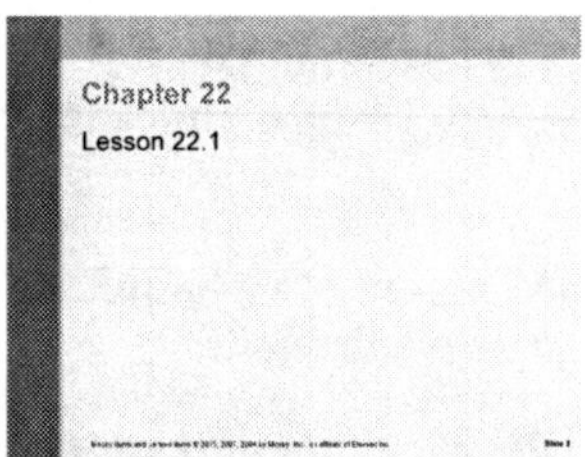
Chapter 22
Lesson 22.1

Slide 3

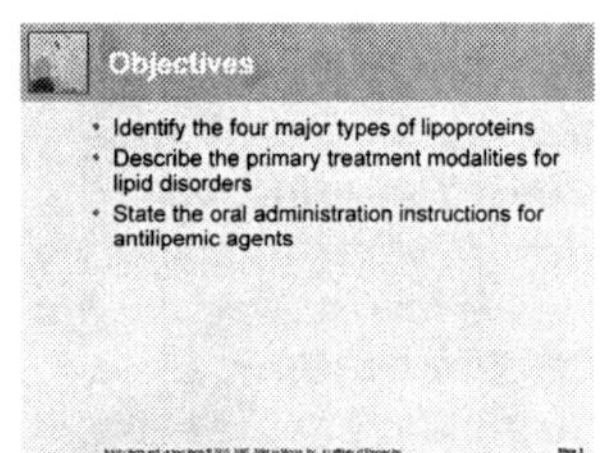
Objectives
Identify the four major types of lipoproteins
Describe the primary treatment modalities for lipid disorders
State the oral administration instructions for antilipemic agents

Slide 4

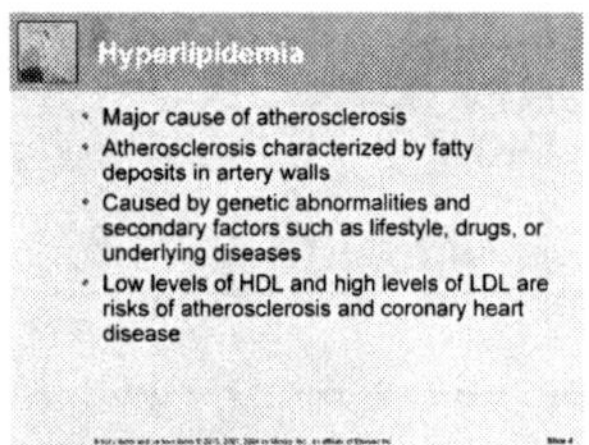
Hyperlipidemia
Major cause of atherosclerosis
Atherosclerosis characterized by fatty deposits in artery walls
Caused by genetic abnormalities and secondary factors such as lifestyle, drugs, or underlying diseases
Low levels of HDL and high levels of LDL are risks of atherosclerosis and coronary heart disease

- Hyperlipidemia – abnormal elevation of cholesterol and triglycerides.
- An estimated 105 million Americans have total cholesterol levels 200 mg/dL and greater, with about 37 million people with levels of 240 mg/dL and greater.

Slide 5

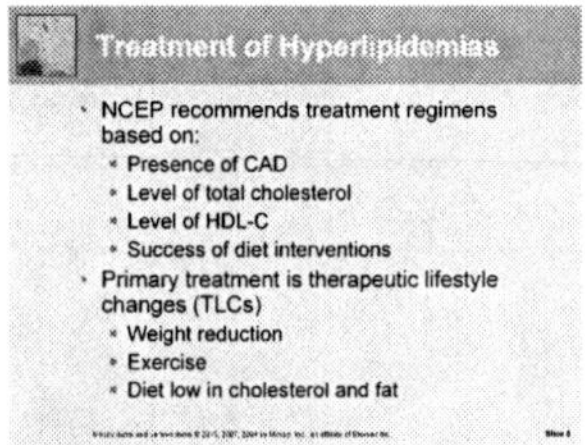
Treatment of Hyperlipidemias
NCEP recommends treatment regimens based on:
Presence of CAD
Level of total cholesterol
Level of HDL-C
Success of diet interventions
Primary treatment is therapeutic lifestyle changes (TLCs)
Weight reduction
Exercise
Diet low in cholesterol and fat

ELSEVIER

Slide 6

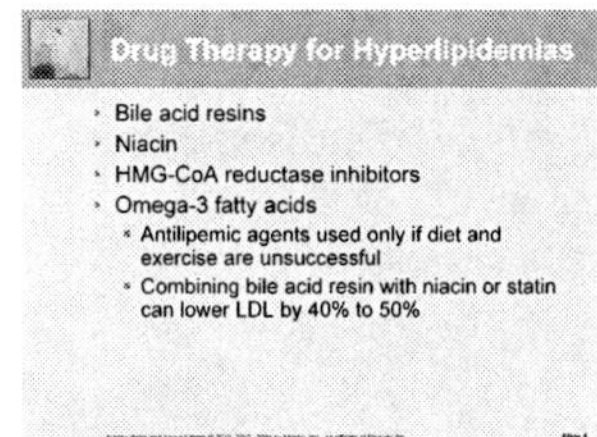
Drug Therapy for Hyperlipidemias
Bile acid resins
Niacin
HMG-CoA reductase inhibitors
Omega-3 fatty acids
Antilipemic agents used only if diet and exercise are unsuccessful
Combining bile acid resin with niacin or statin can lower LDL by 40% to 50%

- Omega-3 fatty acids were recently approved to treat adults with elevated triglyceride levels greater than 500 mg/dL.

Slide 7

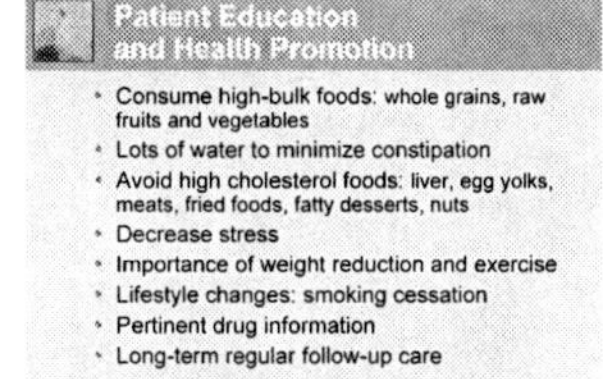
Patient Education and Health Promotion
Consume high-bulk foods: whole grains, raw fruits and vegetables
Lots of water to minimize constipation
Avoid high cholesterol foods: liver, egg yolks, meats, fried foods, fatty desserts, nuts
Decrease stress
Importance of weight reduction and exercise
Lifestyle changes: smoking cessation
Pertinent drug information
Long-term regular follow-up care

- 30 minutes of moderate daily exercise is recommended.
- A fasting lipoprotein profile (total cholesterol, LDL cholesterol, HDL cholesterol, and triglycerides) is recommended every 5 years for all adults older than 20 years of age.

Slide 8

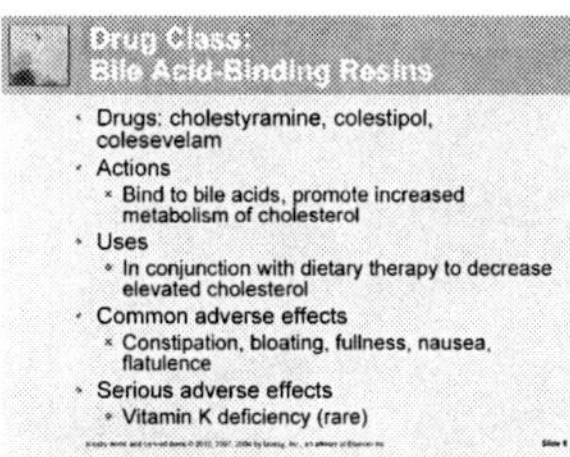
Drug Class: Bile Acid-Binding Resins
Drugs: cholestyramine, colestipol, colesevelam
Actions
Bind to bile acids, promote increased metabolism of cholesterol
Uses
In conjunction with dietary therapy to decrease elevated cholesterol
Common adverse effects
Constipation, bloating, fullness, nausea, flatulence
Serious adverse effects
Vitamin K deficiency (rare)

- Drug interactions: digoxin, warfarin, thyroid hormones, thiazide diuretics, phenobarital, NSAIDs, tetracycline, beta blockers, amiodarone, fat-soluble vitamins.

Slide 9

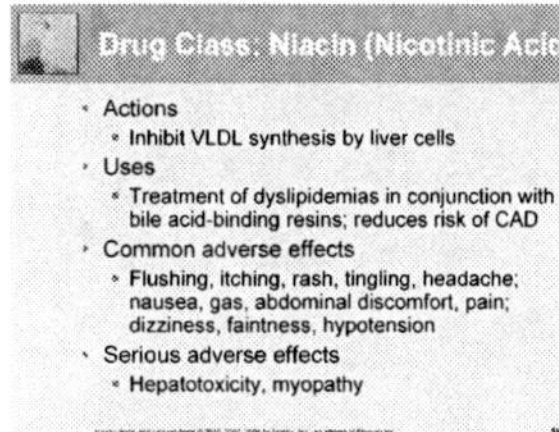
Drug Class: Niacin (Nicotinic Acid)
Actions
Inhibit VLDL synthesis by liver cells
Uses
Treatment of dyslipidemias in conjunction with bile acid-binding resins; reduces risk of CAD
Common adverse effects
Flushing, itching, rash, tingling, headache; nausea, gas, abdominal discomfort, pain; dizziness, faintness, hypotension
Serious adverse effects
Hepatotoxicity, myopathy

- Water-soluble B3 vitamin; only form of vitamin B3 approved by the FDA for treatment of dyslipidemias.
- Higher incidence of adverse effects with immediate-release products, and a greater possibility of hepatotoxicity with extended-release products.

Slide 10

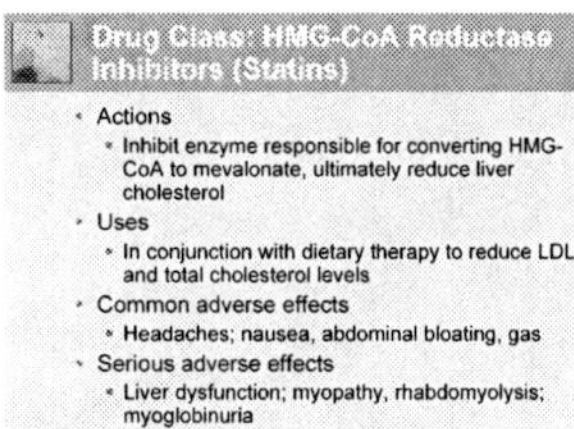
Drug Class: HMG-CoA Reductase Inhibitors (Statins)
Actions
Inhibit enzyme responsible for converting HMG-CoA to mevalonate, ultimately reduce liver cholesterol
Uses
In conjunction with dietary therapy to reduce LDL and total cholesterol levels
Common adverse effects
Headaches; nausea, abdominal bloating, gas
Serious adverse effects
Liver dysfunction; myopathy, rhabdomyolysis; myoglobinuria

- For specific drugs, see Table 22-3.
- Best administered at night because of peak cholesterol production at this time.
- Statins do not differ in effectiveness, but they do differ in potential drug interactions.
- Grapefruit juice inhibits the metabolism of several statins and should be avoided.

Slide 11

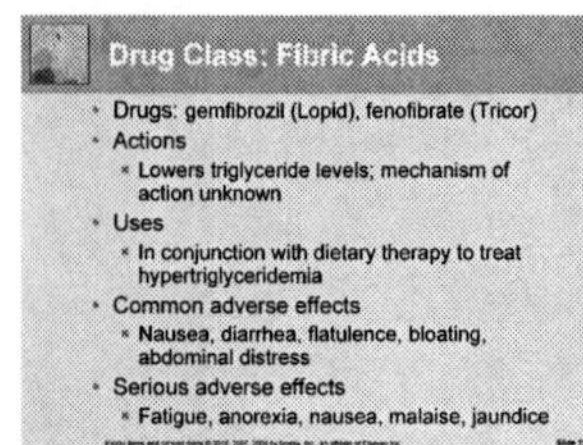
Drug Class: Fibric Acids
Drugs: gemfibrozil (Lopid), fenofibrate (Tricor)
Actions
Lowers triglyceride levels; mechanism of action unknown
Uses
In conjunction with dietary therapy to treat hypertriglyceridemia
Common adverse effects
Nausea, diarrhea, flatulence, bloating, abdominal distress
Serious adverse effects
Fatigue, anorexia, nausea, malaise, jaundice

- Most effective agents in lowering triglycerides.
- Myopathy may occur if used in conjunction with statins.
- Serious adverse effects: early symptoms of gallbladder disease and hepatotoxicity.

Slide 12

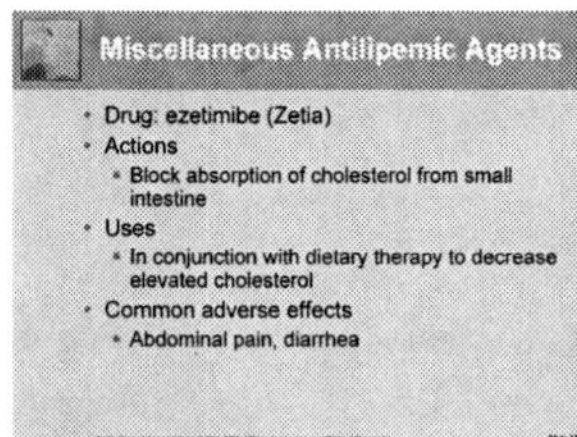
Miscellaneous Antilipemic Agents
Drug: ezetimibe (Zetia)
Actions
Block absorption of cholesterol from small intestine
Uses
In conjunction with dietary therapy to decrease elevated cholesterol
Common adverse effects
Abdominal pain, diarrhea

- Ezetimibe is the first drug in this class.
- Should not be used with fibric acid.

Slide 13

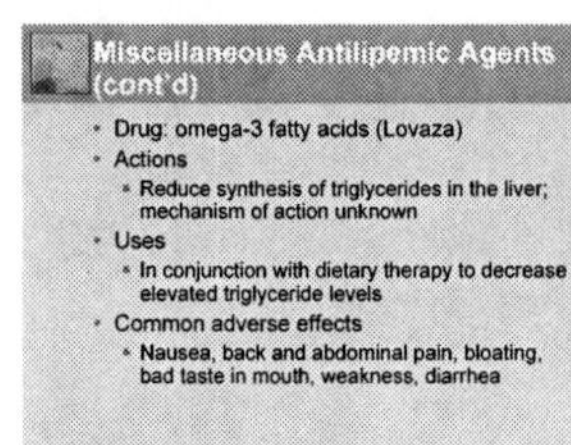
Miscellaneous Antilipemic Agents (cont'd)
Drug: omega-3 fatty acids (Lovaza)
Actions
Reduce synthesis of triglycerides in the liver; mechanism of action unknown
Uses
In conjunction with dietary therapy to decrease elevated triglyceride levels
Common adverse effects
Nausea, back and abdominal pain, bloating, bad taste in mouth, weakness, diarrhea

- New class of agents to reduce atherosclerosis.
- Often referred to as "fish oils"; use with caution in patients who are sensitive or allergic to fish.
- Their advantage over fibrates and niacin is that they do not cause myositis or rhabdomyolysis when combined with statins.

ELSEVIER

23 Lesson Plan

Drugs Used to Treat Hypertension

TEACHING FOCUS

In this chapter, students are introduced to hypertension, including its risk factors, causes, management, and the drugs used to treat hypertension. Students have the opportunity to learn the procedures to assess patients for hypertension. Additionally, students have the opportunity to develop teaching plans to inform patients about nutrition, stress management, and other lifestyle changes to help manage hypertension, once diagnosed.

MATERIALS AND RESOURCES

- ☐ computer and PowerPoint projector (all lessons)
- ☐ drug reference book (Lesson 23.2)

LESSON CHECKLIST

Preparations for this lesson include:

- lecture
- demonstration
- evaluation of student knowledge and skills needed to perform all entry-level activities related to drugs used to treat hypertension, including:
  - understanding the pathophysiology of hypertension, risk factors, and causes of hypertension
  - understanding drugs used to manage and treat hypertension
  - implementing a teaching plan to educate patients who have been diagnosed with hypertension regarding lifestyle and nutritional changes

KEY TERMS

arterial blood pressure (p. 353)
cardiac output (CO) (p. 353)
diastolic blood pressure (p. 353)
hypertension (p. 354)
mean arterial pressure (MAP) (p. 353)
primary hypertension (p. 354)
pulse pressure (p. 353)
secondary hypertension (p. 354)
systolic blood pressure (p. 353)
systolic hypertension (p. 354)

ADDITIONAL RESOURCES

PowerPoint slides: 1-22
Flashcards, Decks 1 and 2

Legend

ARQ	**PPT**	**TB**	**CTQ**	**SG**	**INRQ**
Audience Response Questions	PowerPoint Slides	Test Bank	Critical Thinking Questions	Study Guide	Interactive NCLEX Review Questions

Class Activities are indicated in ***bold italic.***

LESSON 23.1

BACKGROUND ASSESSMENT

Question: A neighbor asks a nurse about high blood pressure. The neighbor says that she knows many people with this problem, and they all seem to be on different medications. She wonders how this is possible. How can the nurse help her understand why this might be the case?
Answer: The nurse can explain that more than 50 million people in the United States have hypertension. The prevalence increases steadily with advancing age, and those over 55 years old have a 90% lifetime chance of developing this disease. The nurse can explain that there are several levels or classifications of high blood pressure, beginning with prehypertension and ending with stage 2 hypertension. When evaluating hypertension, many factors are taken into consideration to establish a treatment plan. Several types of medications are available for treatment, including diuretics, beta blockers, and angiotensin-converting enzyme (ACE) inhibitors. The health care provider decides the type of medication according to standard guidelines. These guidelines are based on the severity of the blood pressure elevation, patient age, coexisting diseases, and risk factors. Antihypertensive medication therapy is individualized to each patient and begins with altering risk factors to decrease the amount of medication necessary.

Question: A 60-year-old man is diagnosed with primary hypertension. He says, "I thought my blood pressure was fine. How does the doctor know I have high blood pressure? I feel okay. What do I need to do for it?" What should the nurse tell this patient?
Answer: The nurse should start by telling the patient that high blood pressure or hypertension does not always exhibit symptoms. She or he should educate the patient about hypertension by stating that it is a disease characterized by an elevation of the systolic or diastolic blood pressure. The cause of primary hypertension is unknown, and it affects more than 50 million people in the United States. At present, hypertension is incurable but controllable. Stage 1 hypertension is diagnosed based on two or more blood pressure readings between 140 to 159 mm Hg for systolic blood pressure or 90 to 99 mm Hg for diastolic blood pressure. Patients must have two or more elevated readings on two or more separate occasions after the initial screening to be classified as hypertensive. Control of hypertension includes medication and lifestyle changes, such as smoking cessation, weight loss, and increased physical activity.

CRITICAL THINKING QUESTION

A 76-year-old female patient with a history of hypertension, angina, gastric reflux disease, and arthritis is admitted to the hospital for excision of a large malignant tumor on her right leg. The nurse takes the patient's blood pressure and obtains a reading of 162/96 mm Hg. The patient states that she is taking propranolol, cimetidine, and nonsteroidal anti-inflammatory drugs (NSAIDs). She says the nurse will need to get the remainder of the information about her medications from her daughter. What should the nurse consider about the blood pressure medication, propranolol, as she or he admits the patient to the surgical unit?
Guidelines: First, the nurse needs to obtain a complete medical history and accurate information on the medications to complete the admission process. She or he needs to know the dose of the propranolol, because it is apparent that the patient's blood pressure is elevated. To evaluate the effectiveness of the medication, the nurse needs to know when the patient began taking the medication because it takes several days to several weeks to achieve optimal improvement. The nurse should be aware that the propranolol dose might need to be adjusted because the patient is taking both cimetidine and NSAIDs. Both these medications can affect the action of the drug. Cimetidine interferes with the metabolism of propranolol, and the NSAIDs inhibit antihypertensive activity; therefore, the health care provider may need to increase the dose of propranolol. In addition, because the patient has a history of angina, a beta blocker, such as propranolol, should not be withdrawn abruptly. Sudden withdrawal may exacerbate anginal symptoms. Finally the nurse should be aware that the administration of a local anesthetic, such as lidocaine, can cause arrhythmias and signs of heart failure when used with beta blockers.

ELSEVIER

OBJECTIVES	CONTENT	TEACHING RESOURCES
Discuss blood pressure and its measurement.	■ Hypertension (p. 353)	PPT 4 ▸ Discuss the difference between systolic blood pressure and diastolic blood pressure when assessing a patient's blood pressure. ▸ Discuss arterial blood pressure using cardiac output and vascular resistance. ▸ Discuss the role of the veins, arteries, and the heart in relation to hypertension. Class Activity ***Have a student volunteer describe the correct process for measuring blood pressure.*** Class Activity ***Present the following scenarios, and have students identify what should be done differently and provide the rationale:*** – ***A hurried patient runs into the health care provider's office, and the nurse immediately measures the patient's blood pressure while the patient is standing.*** – ***The nurse measures the blood pressure on an extremely obese patient using a standard cuff.***
Define hypertension.	■ Hypertension (p. 353) Review the definition of hypertension. Discuss systolic and diastolic blood pressure, mean arterial pressure, pulse pressure, and cardiac output.	PPT 4 ▸ Discuss normal blood pressure, prehypertension, stage 1, and stage 2 hypertension. Table 23-1: Classification and Management of Blood Pressure for Adults (p. 355) Class Activity ***Divide the class into pairs, and have each pair explain briefly the components of blood pressure and how to determine hypertension. Have as many definitions for students to explain as needed to cover the material. Review the exercise with the class.***
Differentiate between primary and secondary hypertension.	■ Hypertension (p. 353) Review the difference between primary and secondary hypertension, and the criteria used by the JNC 7 (Joint National Committee on Prevention, Detection, Evaluation, and Treatment of High Blood Pressure) for making a diagnosis of hypertension.	PPT 5 ▸ Discuss primary hypertension as having no discernable cause and secondary hypertension as being from some identifiable cause. Box 23-2: Identifiable Causes of Hypertension (p. 354)
Summarize nursing assessments and	■ Hypertension (p. 353)	PPT 7 ARQ 1-2

OBJECTIVES	CONTENT	TEACHING RESOURCES
interventions used for the treatment of hypertension.	Review major risk factors associated with hypertension and effects of hypertension on target organs. Discuss causes of hypertension.	TB Multiple Choice questions 2, 5, 7, 9-10 INRQ 3 CTQ 3, 5 SG Review Sheet questions 1-6, 9-11 (pp. 149-150) SG Learning Activities questions 1-2, 22-25, 31-32, 35-37, 40 (pp. 153-154) SG Practice Questions for the NCLEX Examination 1-2, 11 (pp. 155-156) ▸ Discuss approaches that are used to evaluate patients with a recent diagnosis of hypertension further, such as laboratory test and assessing any target organ damage or cardiovascular disease. Box 23-1: Major Risk Factors Associated with Hypertension and Target Organ Damage (p. 354) Class Activity ***Present the following scenario and ask the students to determine the reason hypertension is not diagnosed with one reading:*** – ***A nurse obtains an initial blood pressure of 152/88 mm Hg on a new patient who does not have a history of hypertension, and the nurse then says to the health care provider, "I think this patient needs to be treated for hypertension."***
State recommended lifestyle modifications for a diagnosis of hypertension.	■ Treatment of hypertension (p. 355) Review the primary goal for treatment of hypertension and the lifestyle modifications needed (e.g., proper diet, including moderation of alcohol, regular exercise, no smoking; weight control, stress reduction) before initiating drug therapy.	PPT 8 ARQ 3 TB Multiple Response questions 1-2 INRQ 13 CTQ 6 SG Learning Activities questions 3, 34 (pp. 153-154) Table 23-3: Lifestyle Modifications to Manage Hypertension (p. 356) ▸ Discuss approaches that a nurse can use to educate the patient regarding lifestyle changes associated with a diagnosis of hypertension. ▸ Discuss the emotional issues that may arise once a patient learns that he or she has been diagnosed with hypertension.

ELSEVIER

OBJECTIVES	CONTENT	TEACHING RESOURCES
		Class Activity ***Have two students role-play patient education on the lifestyle changes needed before the initiation of drug therapy for hypertension. Have the student playing the nurse to ask specifically for risk factors and then provide proper advice. Review the exercise with the class.***

23.1 Homework/Assignments:

23.1 Instructor's Notes/Student Feedback:

LESSON 23.2

CRITICAL THINKING QUESTION

A 71-year-old man is brought into the emergency room with a scalp laceration. His wife says that he fell after suddenly standing up from a chair. The nurse who is collecting data learns that the patient has been taking diuretics for high blood pressure and just st arted taking captopril (Capoten). What is the likely cause of the fall, and what should the nurse add to her physical assessment?

Guidelines: Because the patient was recently given a new antihypertensive medication, the fall was most likely caused by orthostatic hypotension. Captopril, an ACE inhibitor, is frequently used in combination with diuretics to manage hypertension. Although orthostatic changes are infrequent with this medication, they can occur in the older adult, especially when captopril is taken in conjunction with a diuretic. The nurse should assess orthostatic changes by checking and reporting blood pressures in both the supine and standing positions. When the nurse has the patient stand to check his blood pressure, an assistant should also be available to prevent another falling episode. In addition, the nurse should instruct the patient to rise slowly from a supine or sitting position and to sit or lie down if feeling dizzy or faint. The nurse can educate the patient and his wife on ways to minimize this type of adverse effect (e.g., changing positions slowly and moving the lower extremities before standing to minimize these effects).

OBJECTIVES	CONTENT	TEACHING RESOURCES
Identify specific factors that the hypertensive patient can use to assist in managing the disease.	■ Treatment of hypertension (p. 355)	PPT 11-12 ▸ Discuss approaches on how to deal with a patient who voluntarily discontinued antihypertensive medication. ▸ Discuss organizations that provide updated information regarding hypertension management options.

OBJECTIVES	CONTENT	TEACHING RESOURCES
		Class Activity ***Divide the class into four groups, and have the groups design simple, realistic plans to reduce the following risk factors for hypertension:*** – ***Overweight or obesity*** – ***Smoking*** – ***Inactivity*** – ***High-sodium diet*** ***Have each group share its plans with the class for discussion.*** Class Activity ***Outside of class time, have students search for websites to use as resources for patient education on lifestyle modifications. Allow class time for students to share the websites that were deemed most helpful.***
Identify 10 classes of drugs used to treat hypertension.	■ Drug therapy for hypertension (p. 356) Review the differences among the preferred agents, alternative agents, and adjunctive agents from the 10 drug classes used for the treatment of hypertension. Using the nursing process, discuss the important patient education and assessment criteria as well as baseline laboratory studies needed before hypertension therapy is initiated.	PPT 13-23 TB Multiple Choice question 8 INRQ 4-5 SG Review Sheet questions 8, 12 (p. 150) SG Learning Activities questions 4, 17-21, 33, 39 (pp. 153-154) SG Practice Questions for the NCLEX Examination 12, 14 (p. 156) Review Questions for the NCLEX Examination 8, 10 (p. 380) Figure 23-1 (p. 357): Sites of action of antihypertensive agents. ▸ Discuss the drugs that are commonly used to treat hypertension. Include a discussion of the adverse effects associated with each drug. Class Activity ***Divide the class into five groups, and assign each group two classes of drugs. Have each group list the following information: drug class, action, use, two specific drugs that fall under that category (generic and trade names), special considerations, and four adverse effects. Then have each group share its information with the class.*** Class Activity ***List the endings of common antihypertensives on the board: -lol, -pril, -dipine, -sartan, and -zosin. Next list the drug classes: beta-adrenergic blockers, calcium ion antagonists, ACE inhibitors, angiotensin II receptor blockers, and alpha-1 adrenergic blocking agents. Match the ending to the drug***

OBJECTIVES	CONTENT	TEACHING RESOURCES
		class. Review with students how to learn the endings of these drugs to recognize their class. Class Activity ***Divide the class into 10 groups. Have each group complete a phototype drug card for the 10 drug classifications to include drug names, clinical indications, action, dosage, adverse effects, nursing considerations, and patient education.***
Review Figure 23-2 to identify options and progression of treatment for hypertension.	■ Drug therapy for hypertension (p. 356) – Nursing process for hypertensive therapy (p. 358)	PPT 11 SG Review Sheet questions 7, 13 (pp. 149-150) SG Learning Activities questions 7-8 (p. 153) Review Questions for the NCLEX Examination 7, 9 (p. 380) Figure 23-2 (p. 358): Treatment algorithm for hypertension. Figure 23-3 (p. 359): Effects of antihypertensive agents. Drug Table 23-4: Combination Drugs for Hypertension (p. 360) Class Activity ***Display a blank algorithm for hypertension treatment on an overhead projector. Have students identify the appropriate parts of the algorithm, such as lifestyle modifications and prescribed medications, and provide a rationale for each component of the algorithm.*** Class Activity ***Have each student select one of the combination drugs for hypertension and use the drug reference book to provide a report on the drug for the class. (For students to prepare for this activity, see Homework/ Assignments 2.)***

23.2 Homework/Assignments:
1. Have each student select one of the combination drugs for hypertension and use a drug reference book to provide a report on the drug for the class.

23.2 Instructor's Notes/Student Feedback:

LESSON 23.3

CRITICAL THINKING QUESTION

A patient from a nursing home with type 2 diabetes mellitus and a history of myocardial infarction is admitted to the hospital with hyperglycemia and hypotension. Upon examining a list of the patient's medications, the nurse notices that the patient is taking verapamil for hypertension. Based on the patient's admitting diagnosis, what can the nurse surmise about the patient's condition in terms of the blood pressure medication? Why would the health care provider have ordered this particular antihypertensive medication for this patient?

Guidelines: The nurse should be aware that verapamil is classified as a calcium ion antagonist or calcium channel blocker that works by inhibiting the movement of calcium ions across the cell membrane. This action relaxes the smooth muscle of the blood vessels, resulting in vasodilation and a reduced blood pressure. Verapamil is typically used in patients with a cardiac history because it has less potential to cause arrhythmias than some of the other antihypertensive drugs. In addition, the nurse should be aware that calcium channel blockers can cause hypotension in the first week of treatment, which may require an adjustment in the dosage. Finally, the nurse should realize that this class of medication can interfere with the glucose metabolism of oral hypoglycemic agents, causing the increase in the patient's blood glucose.

OBJECTIVES	CONTENT	TEACHING RESOURCES
Develop patient education objectives for individuals with hypertension.	■ Patient education and health promotion (p. 361)	PPT 8 TB Multiple Choice questions 1, 6, 11-13, 16 INRQ 1-2, 8 CTQ 2 SG Review Sheet question 14 (p. 150) SG Learning Activities question 6 (p. 153) SG Practice Questions for the NCLEX Examination 3, 8-9, 13 (pp. 155-156) ▸ Discuss information that the nurse can provide to a patient who has been diagnosed with hypertension regarding symptoms that may occur when taking ACE inhibitors. ▸ Discuss important information that the nurse should communicate to pregnant women diagnosed with hypertension regarding their condition and the drugs they may be prescribed to treat the hypertension. Class Activity *Divide the class into three groups, and assign each group one of the following scenarios:* – *The blood pressure of a male patient taking antihypertensive medications is found to be 182/94 mm Hg. The nurse discusses the patient's medications with him and learns that he takes the medications whenever he "feels like it."* – *An obese patient who is being monitored for hypertension is at the clinic for a*

OBJECTIVES	CONTENT	TEACHING RESOURCES
		blood pressure checkup. The nurse notices that while the patient awaits her appointment, she is eating a lunch of French fries and drinking an extra large soft drink. – ***A sedentary, overweight, 40-year-old woman with a history of smoking is in the emergency room with a broken toe. Her blood pressure is 136/86 mm Hg. The health care provider schedules her to return the next day for a blood pressure check, stating that he wants to monitor her for prehypertension. The patient says to the nurse, "I really don't want to take any medication in the future."*** ***Have the groups develop educational objectives to improve the management of hypertension.***
Summarize the action of each drug class used to treat hypertension.	☐ Drug class: Diuretics (p. 363) – Nursing process for diuretic a`gents (p. 363) ☐ Drug class: Beta-adrenergic blocking agents (p. 363) – Nursing process for beta-adrenergic blocking agents (p. 363) ☐ Drug class: Angiotensin-converting enzyme inhibitors (p. 364) – Nursing process for angiotensin-converting enzyme inhibitors (p. 366) ☐ Drug class: Angiotensin-II receptor blockers (p. 368) – Nursing process for angiotensin-II receptor antagonists (p. 369) ☐ Drug class: Direct renin inhibitor (p. 370) – Nursing process for aliskiren (p. 370) ☐ Drug class: Aldosterone receptor antagonist (p. 371) – Nursing process for eplerenone (p. 371) ☐ Drug class: Calcium channel blockers (p. 373) – Nursing process for calcium channel blockers (p. 373)	PPT 13-23 ARQ 4-5 TB Multiple Choice questions 3-4, 14-15, 17-20 TB Multiple Response questions 3-4 INRQ 6, 9-12 CTQ 1, 4 Animation: Beta Blockers Animation: Calcium Channel Blockers Animation: Diuretics SG Review Sheet questions 16-36 (pp. 150-152) SG Learning Activities questions 5, 9-16, 26-29, 30, 38 (pp. 153-154) SG Practice Questions for the NCLEX Examination 4-7, 10, 15 (pp. 155-156) Review Questions for the NLCEX Examination 1-6, 11-12 (pp. 380-381) Lifespan Considerations: Antihypertensive Therapy (p. 367) Drug Table 23-5: Angiotensin-Converting Enzyme (ACE) Inhibitors (p. 365) Clinical Landmine: Hypotension with ACE Inhibitors (p. 367) Drug Table 23-6: Angiotensin-II Receptor Blockers (ARBs) (p. 368)

ELSEVIER

OBJECTIVES	CONTENT	TEACHING RESOURCES
	☐ Drug class: Alpha-1-drenergic blocking agents (p. 375) – Nursing process for alpha-1-adrenergic blocking agents (p. 375) ☐ Drug class: Central-acting alpha-2 agonists (p. 377) – Nursing process for central-acting alpha-2 agonists (p. 377) ☐ Drug class: Direct vasodilators (p. 378) – Nursing process for hydralazine (p. 379)	Drug Table 23-7: Calcium Channel Blockers Used to Treat Hypertension (pp. 374-375) Drug Table 23-8: Alpha-1-Adrenergic Blocking Agents (p. 376) Drug Table 23-9: Central-Acting Alpha-2 Agonists (p. 378) ▸ Discuss why the nurse should obtain blood pressure readings in supine or standing positions. Class Activity ***Have two students role-play a nurse teaching a patient about taking calcium ion antagonists (drugs ending in -dipine). Have the class assist the nurse in determining what is important to discuss with the patient. Review with the class therapeutic outcomes and adverse effects for calcium ion antagonists.***
Performance evaluation		Test Bank SG Learning Activities (pp. 153-154) SG Practice Questions for the NCLEX Examination (pp. 155-156) Critical Thinking Questions

23.3 Homework/Assignments:

23.3 Instructor's Notes/Student Feedback:

ELSEVIER

23 Lecture Outline
Drugs Used to Treat Hypertension

Slide 1

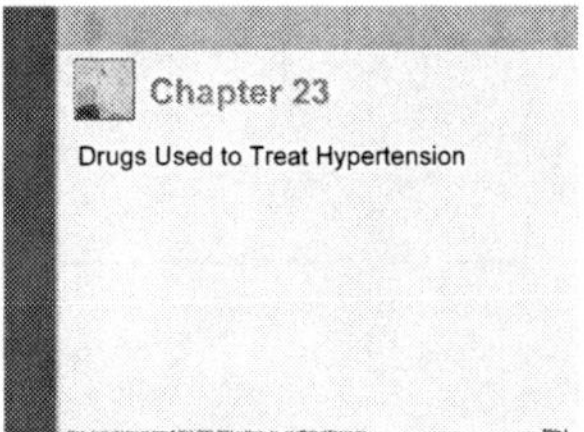
Chapter 23
Drugs Used to Treat Hypertension

Slide 2

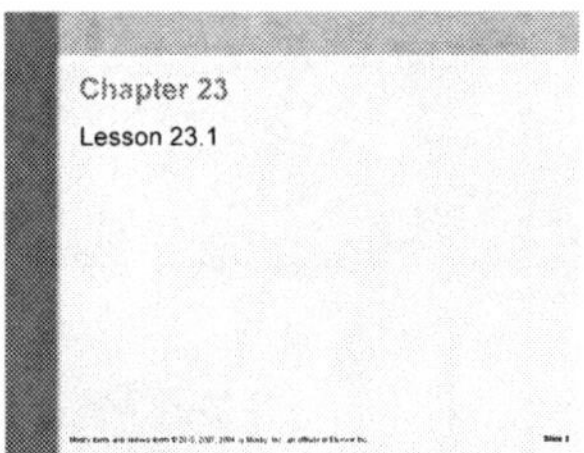
Chapter 23
Lesson 23.1

Slide 3

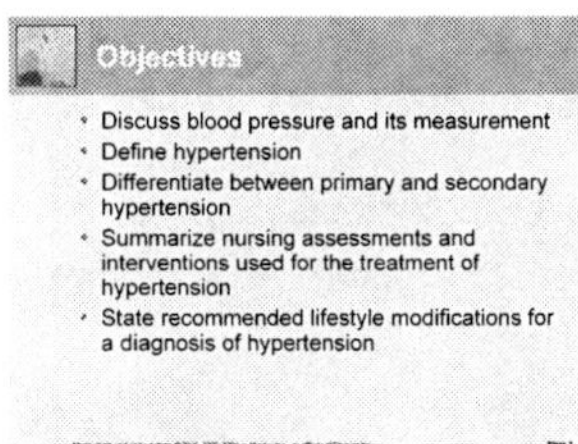
Objectives
Discuss blood pressure and its measurement
Define hypertension
Differentiate between primary and secondary hypertension
Summarize nursing assessments and interventions used for the treatment of hypertension
State recommended lifestyle modifications for a diagnosis of hypertension

Slide 4

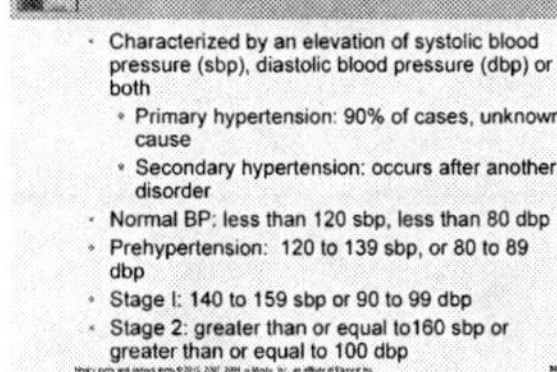
Hypertension
Characterized by an elevation of systolic blood pressure (sbp), diastolic blood pressure (dbp) or both
Primary hypertension: 90% of cases, unknown cause
Secondary hypertension: occurs after another disorder
Normal BP: less than 120 sbp, less than 80 dbp
Prehypertension: 120 to 139 sbp, or 80 to 89 dbp
Stage I: 140 to 159 sbp or 90 to 99 dbp
Stage 2: greater than or equal to160 sbp or greater than or equal to 100 dbp

- National High Blood Pressure Committee encourages practitioners to use systolic pressure as the determinant for diagnosis.
- Treatment is important because control of hypertension reduces the frequency of cardiovascular disease.
- More than 50 million people in the United States are affected.

Slide 5

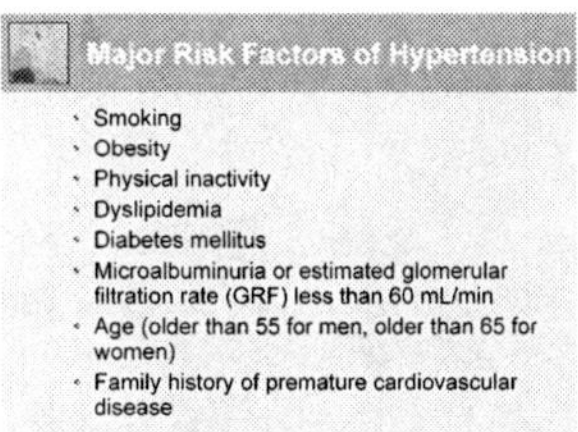
Major Risk Factors of Hypertension
Smoking
Obesity
Physical inactivity
Dyslipidemia
Diabetes mellitus
Microalbuminuria or estimated glomerular filtration rate (GRF) less than 60 mL/min
Age (older than 55 for men, older than 65 for women)
Family history of premature cardiovascular disease

- Increased circulation of cholesterol causes plaque formation within blood vessel walls, resulting in a narrowed lumen which increases vascular resistance.

ELSEVIER

Slide 6

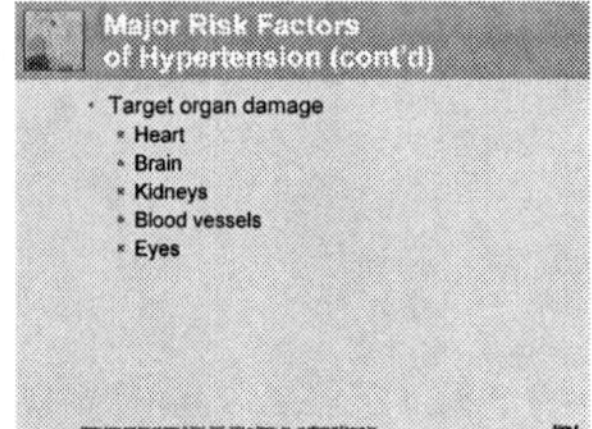
Major Risk Factors of Hypertension (cont'd)
Target organ damage
Heart
Brain
Kidneys
Blood vessels
Eyes

Slide 7

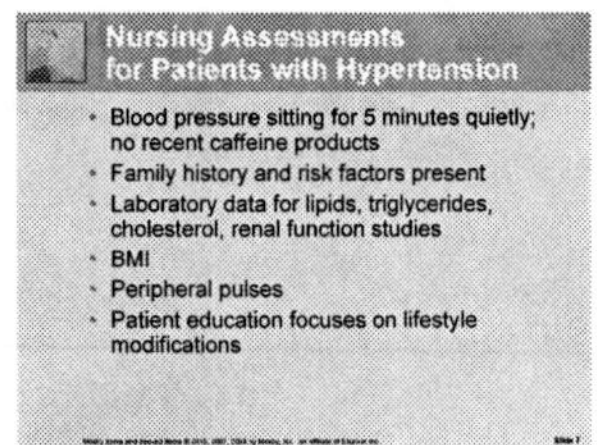
Nursing Assessments for Patients with Hypertension
Blood pressure sitting for 5 minutes quietly; no recent caffeine products
Family history and risk factors present
Laboratory data for lipids, triglycerides, cholesterol, renal function studies
BMI
Peripheral pulses
Patient education focuses on lifestyle modifications

Slide 8

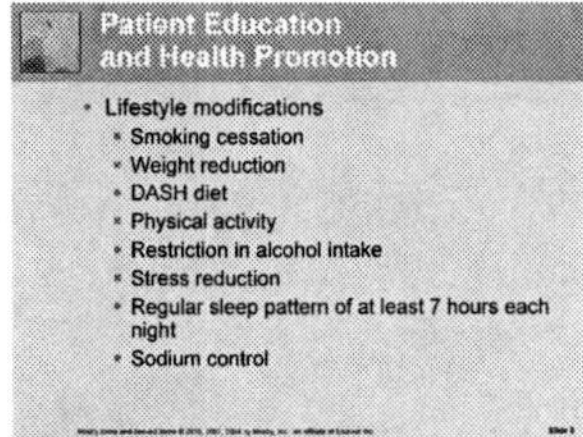
Patient Education and Health Promotion
Lifestyle modifications
Smoking cessation
Weight reduction
DASH diet
Physical activity
Restriction in alcohol intake
Stress reduction
Regular sleep pattern of at least 7 hours each night
Sodium control

Slide 9

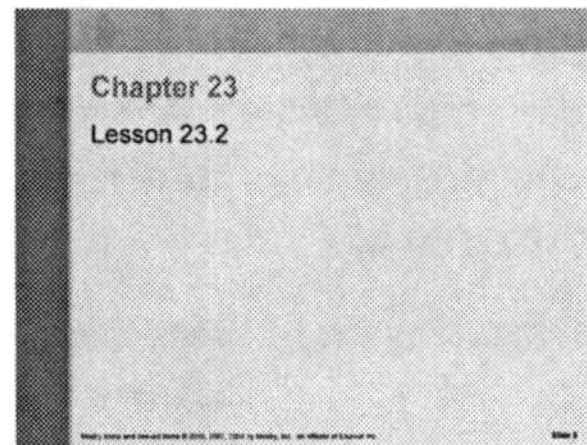
Chapter 23
Lesson 23.2

Slide 10

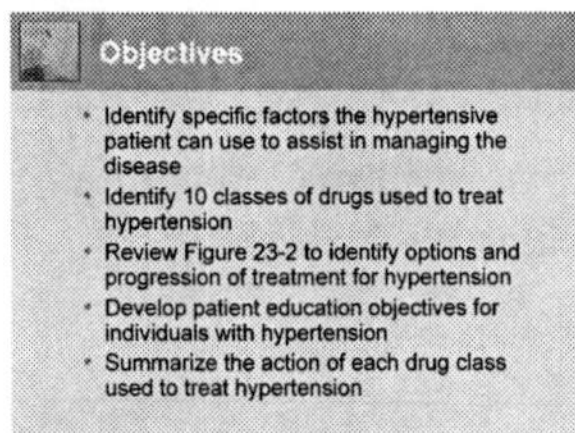
Objectives
Identify specific factors the hypertensive patient can use to assist in managing the disease
Identify 10 classes of drugs used to treat hypertension
Review Figure 23-2 to identify options and progression of treatment for hypertension
Develop patient education objectives for individuals with hypertension
Summarize the action of each drug class used to treat hypertension

ELSEVIER

Slide 11

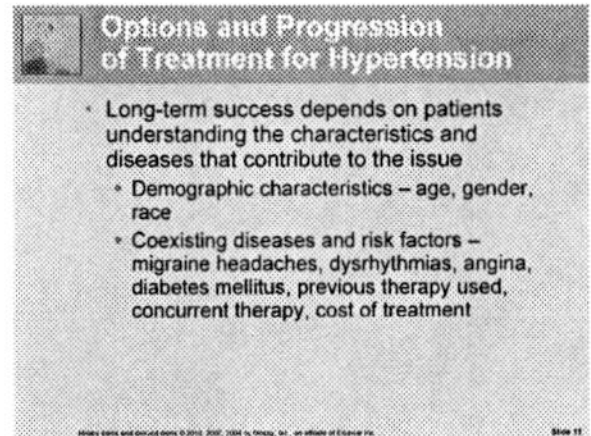
Options and Progression of Treatment for Hypertension
Long-term success depends on patients understanding the characteristics and diseases that contribute to the issue
Demographic characteristics – age, gender, race
Coexisting diseases and risk factors – migraine headaches, dysrhythmias, angina, diabetes mellitus, previous therapy used, concurrent therapy, cost of treatment

- The nurse must be willing to explore with the patient all aspects of therapy and the need for continual control of hypertension while avoiding potential adverse effects.

Slide 12

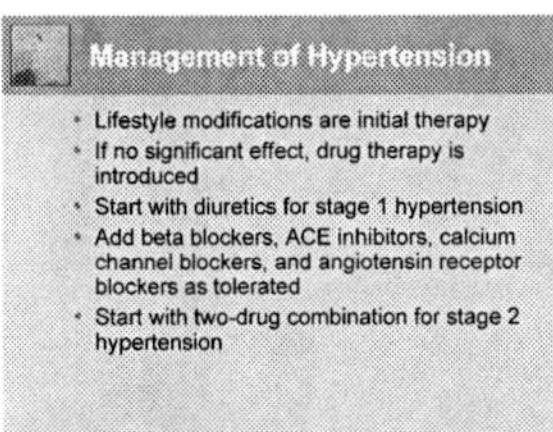
Management of Hypertension
Lifestyle modifications are initial therapy
If no significant effect, drug therapy is introduced
Start with diuretics for stage 1 hypertension
Add beta blockers, ACE inhibitors, calcium channel blockers, and angiotensin receptor blockers as tolerated
Start with two-drug combination for stage 2 hypertension

- Goal of blood pressure less than 140/90 mm Hg, or less than 130/80 mm Hg for patients with diabetes or chronic kidney disease.
- Additional drugs are added until goal blood pressure is achieved.

Slide 13

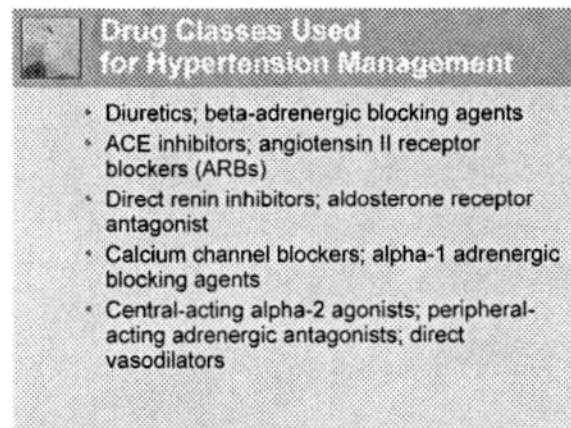
Drug Classes Used for Hypertension Management
Diuretics; beta-adrenergic blocking agents
ACE inhibitors; angiotensin II receptor blockers (ARBs)
Direct renin inhibitors; aldosterone receptor antagonist
Calcium channel blockers; alpha-1 adrenergic blocking agents
Central-acting alpha-2 agonists; peripheral-acting adrenergic antagonists; direct vasodilators

Slide 14

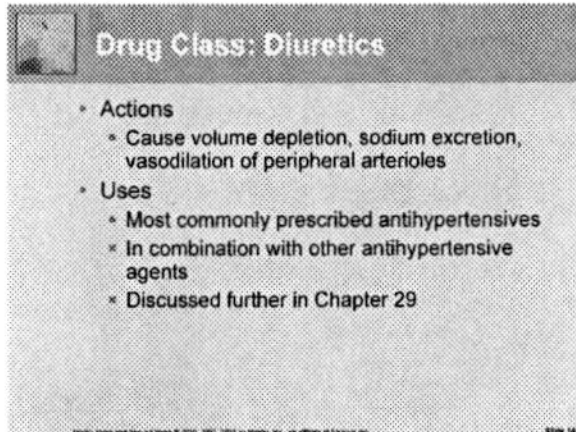
Drug Class: Diuretics
Actions
Cause volume depletion, sodium excretion, vasodilation of peripheral arterioles
Uses
Most commonly prescribed antihypertensives
In combination with other antihypertensive agents
Discussed further in Chapter 29

Slide 15

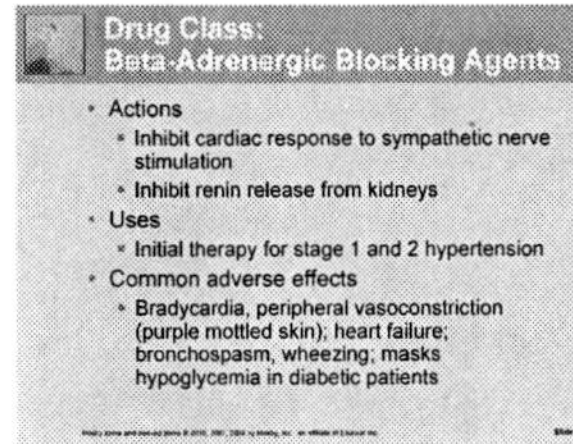
Drug Class: Beta-Adrenergic Blocking Agents
Actions
Inhibit cardiac response to sympathetic nerve stimulation
Inhibit renin release from kidneys
Uses
Initial therapy for stage 1 and 2 hypertension
Common adverse effects
Bradycardia, peripheral vasoconstriction (purple mottled skin); heart failure; bronchospasm, wheezing; masks hypoglycemia in diabetic patients

- Not effective for African Americans.
- Sudden discontinuation of therapy results in exacerbation of anginal symptoms.

ELSEVIER

Slide 16

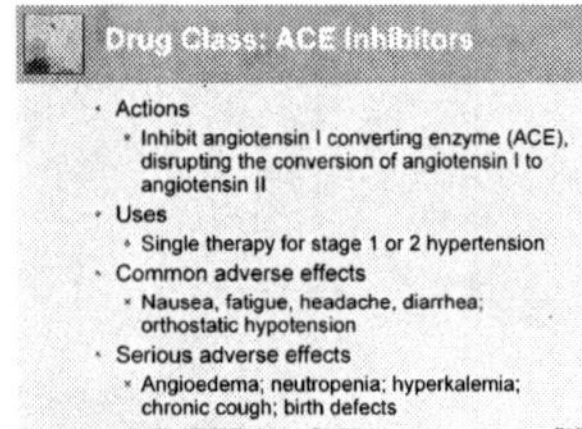
Drug Class: ACE Inhibitors
Actions
Inhibit angiotensin I converting enzyme (ACE), disrupting the conversion of angiotensin I to angiotensin II
Uses
Single therapy for stage 1 or 2 hypertension
Common adverse effects
Nausea, fatigue, headache, diarrhea; orthostatic hypotension
Serious adverse effects
Angioedema; neutropenia; hyperkalemia; chronic cough; birth defects

- For specific drugs, see Table 23-5.
- Understanding the renin-angiotensin-aldosterone system (RAAS) is critical to understanding the actions of most antihypertensives.

Slide 17

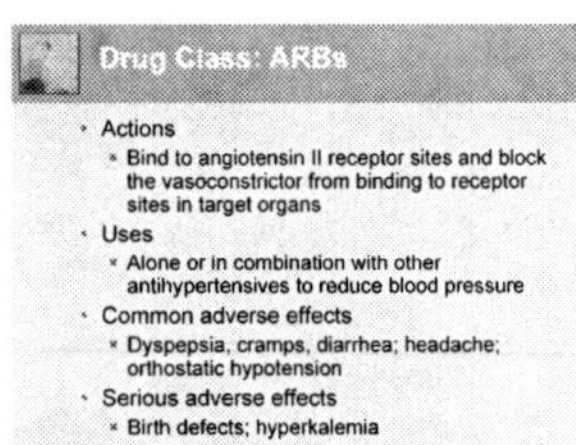
Drug Class: ARBs
Actions
Bind to angiotensin II receptor sites and block the vasoconstrictor from binding to receptor sites in target organs
Uses
Alone or in combination with other antihypertensives to reduce blood pressure
Common adverse effects
Dyspepsia, cramps, diarrhea; headache; orthostatic hypotension
Serious adverse effects
Birth defects; hyperkalemia

- For specific drugs, see Table 23-6.

Slide 18

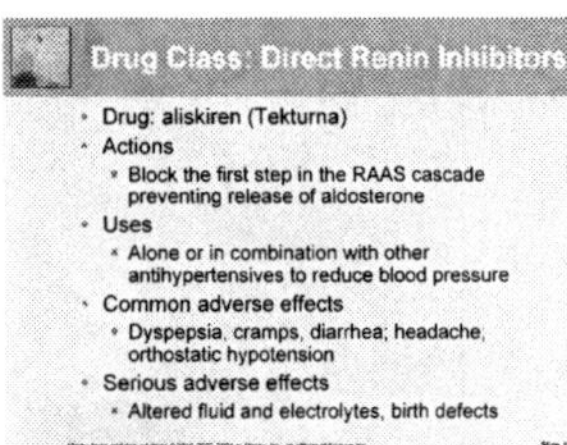
Drug Class: Direct Renin Inhibitors
Drug: aliskiren (Tekturna)
Actions
Block the first step in the RAAS cascade preventing release of aldosterone
Uses
Alone or in combination with other antihypertensives to reduce blood pressure
Common adverse effects
Dyspepsia, cramps, diarrhea; headache, orthostatic hypotension
Serious adverse effects
Altered fluid and electrolytes, birth defects

- Reserved for patients who do not respond to ACE inhibitors or ARBs.

Slide 19

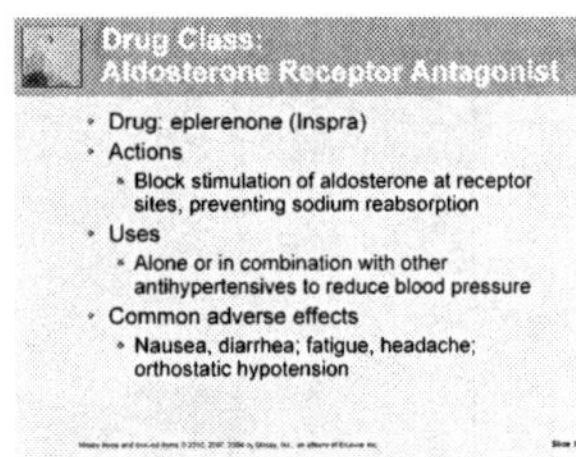
Drug Class: Aldosterone Receptor Antagonist
Drug: eplerenone (Inspra)
Actions
Block stimulation of aldosterone at receptor sites, preventing sodium reabsorption
Uses
Alone or in combination with other antihypertensives to reduce blood pressure
Common adverse effects
Nausea, diarrhea; fatigue, headache; orthostatic hypotension

- Serious adverse effects: hyperkalemia, hyperlipidemia, nephrotoxicity, hepatotoxicity, vaginal bleeding, gynecomastia.

Slide 20

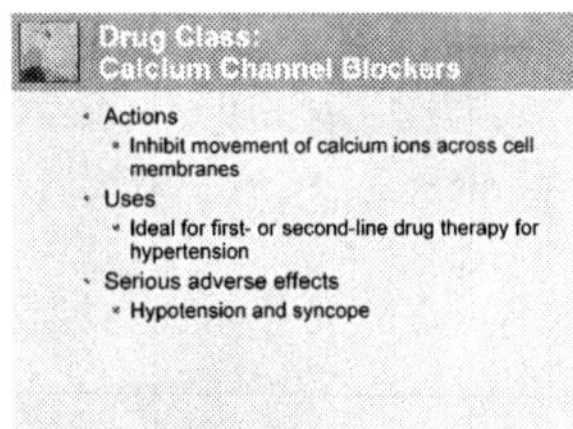
Drug Class: Calcium Channel Blockers
Actions
Inhibit movement of calcium ions across cell membranes
Uses
Ideal for first- or second-line drug therapy for hypertension
Serious adverse effects
Hypotension and syncope

- For specific drugs, see Table 23-7.
- Also used for heart rhythm disturbances and angina.
- Effective for African Americans and elderly patients.

ELSEVIER

Slide 21

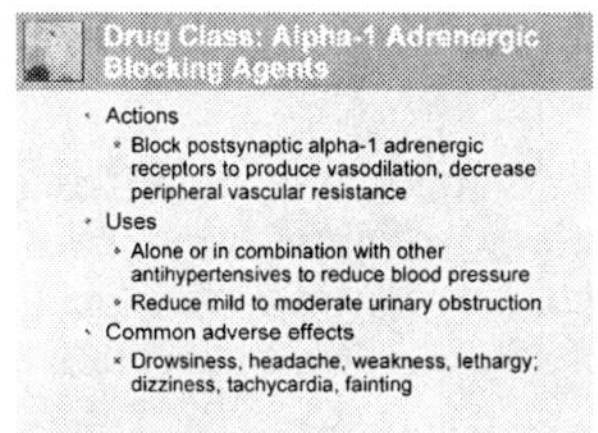
Drug Class: Alpha-1 Adrenergic Blocking Agents
Actions
Block postsynaptic alpha-1 adrenergic receptors to produce vasodilation, decrease peripheral vascular resistance
Uses
Alone or in combination with other antihypertensives to reduce blood pressure
Reduce mild to moderate urinary obstruction
Common adverse effects
Drowsiness, headache, weakness, lethargy; dizziness, tachycardia, fainting

- For specific drugs, see Table 23-8.

Slide 22

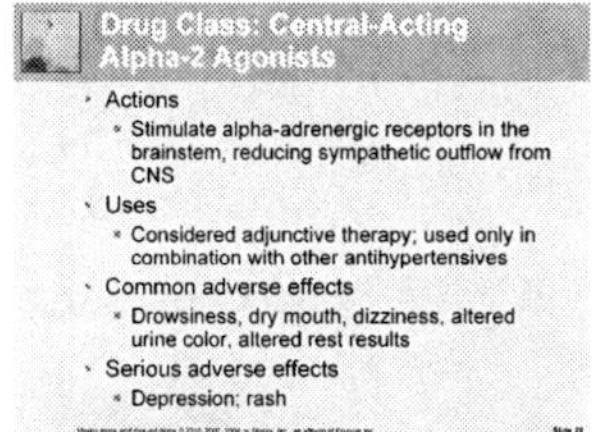
Drug Class: Central-Acting Alpha-2 Agonists
Actions
Stimulate alpha-adrenergic receptors in the brainstem, reducing sympathetic outflow from CNS
Uses
Considered adjunctive therapy; used only in combination with other antihypertensives
Common adverse effects
Drowsiness, dry mouth, dizziness, altered urine color, altered rest results
Serious adverse effects
Depression; rash

- For specific drugs, see Table 23-9.
- Adverse effects such as dry mouth and dizziness are self-limiting. Urine will darken on exposure to air and is not harmful. False-positive urine glucose tests may occur.
- Rash occurs with transdermal patch application of clonidine.

Slide 23

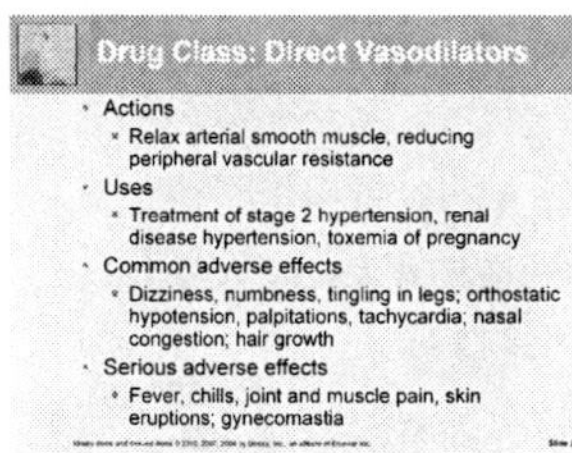
Drug Class: Direct Vasodilators
Actions
Relax arterial smooth muscle, reducing peripheral vascular resistance
Uses
Treatment of stage 2 hypertension, renal disease hypertension, toxemia of pregnancy
Common adverse effects
Dizziness, numbness, tingling in legs; orthostatic hypotension, palpitations, tachycardia; nasal congestion; hair growth
Serious adverse effects
Fever, chills, joint and muscle pain, skin eruptions; gynecomastia

- Drugs: hydralazine (Apresoline), minoxidil (Loniten), and nitroprusside sodium (Nitropress)
- Nitroprusside is used in severe hypertensive crisis and refractory heart failure.

24 Lesson Plan
Drugs Used to Treat Dysrhythmias

TEACHING FOCUS

In this chapter, students have the opportunity to learn about the treatment of dysrhythmias and the different types of drug therapies available. Students are introduced to the different drug classes of antidysrhythmic agents and review the process for assessing patient treatment. In addition, this chapter discusses therapeutic outcomes and adverse effects for antidysrhythmic agents and beta-adrenergic blockers. Patient education and health promotion are also discussed.

MATERIALS AND RESOURCES

- ☐ blank schematic diagram of the heart (Lesson 24.1)
- ☐ computer and PowerPoint projector (all lessons)

LESSON CHECKLIST

Preparations for this lesson include:

- lecture
- evaluation of student knowledge and skills required for entry-level applications with drugs used to treat dysrhythmias, including:
  - cause, signs, and symptoms of dysrhythmia
  - the therapeutic responses to antidysrhythmic drugs
  - common adverse effects and drug interactions that occur with beta-adrenergic blocking agents and other antidysrhythmic agents
  - baseline-nursing assessments

KEY TERMS

atrial fibrillation (p. 383)
atrial flutter (p. 383)
atrioventricular blocks (p. 383)
dysrhythmia (p. 382)
electrical system (p. 382)
paroxysmal supraventricular tachycardia (p. 383)
tinnitus (p. 388)

ADDITIONAL RESOURCES

PowerPoint slides: 1-18
Flashcards, Decks 1 and 2

Legend

ARQ	PPT	TB	CTQ	SG	INRQ
Audience Response Questions	PowerPoint Slides	Test Bank	Critical Thinking Questions	Study Guide	Interactive NCLEX Review Questions

Class Activities are indicated in ***bold italic.***

LESSON 24.1

BACKGROUND ASSESSMENT

Question: What are the most important clinical signs and symptoms of dysrhythmias?
Answer: A mild or infrequent dysrhythmia could be perceived as a palpitation or skipped heartbeat. More severe dysrhythmias may reflect some of the following manifestations: hypotension, bradycardia, tachycardia, irregular pulse, shortness of breath, dyspnea, cough, syncope, or mental confusion caused by oliguria or chest pain, angina, or myocardial infarction. Any of these conditions require further investigation.

ELSEVIER

Question: What are the differences between the supraventricular and ventricular dysrhythmias? What are examples of each?
Answer: Supraventricular dysrhythmias develop above the bundle of His. Examples are atrial flutter, atrial fibrillation, premature atrial contractions (PACs), sinus tachycardia, sinus bradycardia, and paroxysmal supraventricular tachycardia. Ventricular dysrhythmias develop below the bundle of His. Examples are premature ventricular contractions (PVCs), ventricular tachycardia, and ventricular fibrillation.

CRITICAL THINKING QUESTION

A 38-year-old male patient is admitted with a diagnosis of gastroenteritis and atrial fibrillation. What questions should the nurse ask the patient, and what nursing interventions should the nurse anticipate might be needed?
Guidelines: Questions the nurse should ask the patient include the following: Do you or your family have any history of cardiac dysrhythmias? Do you smoke? Do you drink a lot of caffeine? What medications are you taking? Are you under a lot of stress? The nurse should anticipate that the patient will be placed on telemetry monitoring and on a nothing-by-mouth (NPO) status, at least until the gastroenteritis has subsided and the health care provider does not request any further tests. Laboratory tests would be ordered for complete blood count (CBC), blood gases, electrolytes, chemistry profiles, and cardiac enzymes. Because the patient's fluid input and output will be tracked, the nurse should instruct the patient to use the urinal and, if vomiting does occur, the patient should try to use an emesis basin. The nurse should monitor vital statistics and vital signs, continually assess the patient for any further symptoms, and immediately notify the health care provider of any changes.

OBJECTIVES	CONTENT	TEACHING RESOURCES
Describe the anatomical structures and conduction systems of the heart.	■ Dysrhythmias (p. 382) Review the conduction system of the heart and how dysrhythmias can be atrial or ventricular. Discuss the types of supraventricular dysrhythmias as well as the ventricular dysrhythmias. Review atrioventricular blocks, and differentiate between slow conduction fibers and fast conduction fibers.	PPT 4-6 ARQ 1 INRQ 9-10 CTQ 1 SG Review Sheet questions 1-3, 7-8 (p. 157) Review Question for the NCLEX Examination 8 (p. 396) ▸ Discuss the sequence of the heart's conduction system. What are the causes of dysrhythmias? What areas of the conduction system are affected? Figure 24-1 (p. 383): Schematic diagram of the heart. Class Activity ***Provide the class with a blank schematic diagram of the heart. Have the students identify the anatomy and conduction system of the heart.***
Differentiate the common dysrhythmias.	■ Dysrhythmias (p. 382) Discuss common atrial and ventricular dysrhythmias.	PPT 7 CTQ 2 SG Review Sheet questions 4-6 (p. 157) Class Activity ***List on the board the following terms:*** **atrial fibrillation, atrial flutter, supraventricular tachycardia, ventricular**

OBJECTIVES	CONTENT	TEACHING RESOURCES
		tachycardia, ventricular fibrillation, ***and*** **atrioventricular blocks.** ***Provide rhythm strips for each type of dysrhythmia, and have the class attempt to match the strip to the correct dysrhythmia. Discuss the exercise in class, and differentiate between the supraventricular and ventricular dysrhythmias.***
Describe the therapeutic response that should be observable when an antidysrhythmic drug is administered.	■ Treatment for dysrhythmias (p. 383) ■ Drug therapy for dysrhythmias (p. 383) Review the goal for treatment of dysrhythmias to restore normal sinus rhythm, restore normal cardiac function, and prevent life-threatening dysrhythmias.	PPT 8 SG Review Sheet questions 9-10 (pp. 157-158) SG Learning Activities questions 12-13 (p. 160)
Identify baseline nursing assessments that should be implemented during the treatment of dysrhythmias.	– Nursing process for antidysrhythmic agents (p. 384) – Patient education and health promotion (p. 386)	PPT 8 TB Multiple Response question 1 INRQ 2 SG Review Sheet questions 11-15 (p. 158) SG Learning Activities question 5 (p. 160) ▸ Discuss the six cardinal signs of cardiovascular disease (pp. 384-385). What should the nurse look for in a patient's vital signs to assess whether the patient is at risk? Share with the class written documentation of a patient assessment. ▸ Discuss why it is important to assess a patient's mental status. Class Activity ***Divide the class into small groups. Each group should describe (as if on a nurse's notes) an assessment of a person experiencing all six cardinal signs of cardiovascular disease. Have the groups exchange their descriptions and then identify and discuss abnormal findings.***

ELSEVIER

24.1 Homework/Assignments:

24.1 Instructor's Notes/Student Feedback:

LESSON 24.2

CRITICAL THINKING QUESTION

The nurse is discharging a patient after a hospitalization for a dysrhythmia. The patient receives a prescription for amiodarone. What key points should the nurse include in her or his discharge teaching?

Guidelines: First, the nurse should make sure that the patient knows the name of the drug, how and when to take the drug, and possible adverse reactions to report. Amiodarone may cause yellow-brown pigmentation of the cornea and blue-gray pigmentation of the skin. The drug may need to be discontinued if these adverse reactions occur. The health care provider can minimize gastrointestinal adverse effects, such as nausea and vomiting, and neurologic adverse effects, such as tremors and ataxia, with a dosage adjustment. Because amiodarone can cause photosensitivity, the nurse should instruct the patient to avoid direct sunlight and use protective clothing and sunscreen. The patient should be instructed on the importance of follow-up care to detect and prevent serious complications of amiodarone therapy, such as pneumonitis and thyroid and liver problems. The patient should also be instructed not to take other medications without checking with the health care provider or pharmacist because of multiple potential drug interactions.

OBJECTIVES	CONTENT	TEACHING RESOURCES
Describe the therapeutic response that should be observable when an antidysrhythmic drug is administered.	■ Nursing process for antidysrhythmic agents (p. 384) Review the classification of antidysrhythmic agents and how they work to try to restore normal sinus rhythm. Discuss the six cardinal sign of cardiovascular disease: dyspnea, chest pain, fatigue, edema, syncope, and palpitations.	PPT 12-18 INRQ 11 Animation: Adenosine for Supraventricular Tachycardia Animation: Amiodarone Animation: Atropine for Sinus Bradycardia Animation: Beta Blockers Animation: Diltiazem for Atrial Fibrillation Animation: Epinephrine for Ventricular Fibrillation Animation: Heparin for Atrial Fibrillation SG Learning Activities question 12 (p. 160) Table 24-1: Classification of Antidysrhythmic Agents (p. 384)

ELSEVIER

OBJECTIVES	CONTENT	TEACHING RESOURCES
		Class Activity ***As a class, discuss the mechanism by which various antidysrhythmic drugs produce the therapeutic outcome of conversion of dysrhythmia to normal sinus rhythm. Provide the class with a list of these drugs, and ask the students to document desired outcomes for each.***
Cite common adverse effects that may be observed with the administration of amiodarone, sotalol, diltiazem, verapamil, lidocaine, and quinidine.	□ Drug class: Class 1a antidysrhythmic agents (p. 386) – Nursing process for disopyramide (p. 386) – Nursing process for procainamide (p. 387) – Nursing process for quinidine (p. 388) □ Drug class: Class 1b antidysrhythmic agents (p. 389) – Nursing process for lidocaine (p. 389) □ Drug class: Class 1c antidysrhythmic agents (p. 390) – Nursing process for flecainide (p. 390) – Nursing process for propafenone (p. 391) □ Drug class: Class II antidysrhythmics: Beta-adrenergic blocking agents (p. 392) – Nursing process for beta-adrenergic blocking agents (p. 392) □ Drug class: Class IV antidysrhythmic agents: Calcium channel blocking agents (p. 394) – Nursing process for calcium channel blocking agents (p. 394)	PPT 12-17 ARQ 2-4 TB Multiple Choice questions 1-3, 4, 6, 10-11 TB Multiple Response question 3 INRQ 8, 12-14 CTQ 4-7 SG Review Sheet questions 18-23 (pp. 158-159) SG Learning Activities questions 2, 4-10, 15, 17-20 (pp. 160-161) SG Practice Questions for the NCLEX Examination 1-7, 9-10 (pp. 162-163) Review Questions for the NCLEX Examination 1-2, 5-7 (pp. 395-396) ▸ Discuss some possible adverse effects and drug interactions that might be encountered when administering a sotalol beta-adrenergic blocking agent. ▸ Discuss some possible adverse effects and drug interactions that might be encountered when administering diltiazem or verapamil—calcium channel blocking agents. Class Activity ***Lead a discussion about the common adverse effects of selected beta-adrenergic blocking agents. Include appropriate nursing interventions and patient education.*** Class Activity ***Lead a discussion about the common adverse effects of selected calcium channel blocking agents. Include appropriate nursing interventions and patient education.***
List the dosage forms and precautions needed when preparing intravenous amiodarone for	□ Drug class: Class III antidysrhythmic agents (p. 392) – Nursing process for amiodarone (p. 392)	ARQ 5 TB Multiple Choice questions 5, 9 ▸ Discuss the difficulties surrounding the use of amiodarone. What premedication assessments must be made? How is the loading dose administered and monitored?

OBJECTIVES	CONTENT	TEACHING RESOURCES
the treatment of dysrhythmias.		Class Activity ***Divide the class into small groups. Each group will formulate a checklist of essential steps when preparing IV amiodarone. Have the groups switch lists and check to see if all information has been included. Then ask the groups to formulate an example of IV amiodarone administration, including each step in the process.***
Describe the therapeutic response that should be observable when an antidysrhythmic drug is administered.	□ Drug class: Miscellaneous antidysrhythmic agents (p. 394) – Nursing process for adenosine (p. 395) – Nursing process for digoxin (p. 395)	PPT 18-19 TB Multiple Choice question 8 TB Multiple Response question 2 INRQ 3 CTQ 3 SG Review Sheet questions 24-25 (p. 159) SG Learning Activities questions 1, 3, 11, 14, 16 (pp. 160-161) SG Practice Question for the NCLEX Examination 8 (p. 163) Review Questions for the NCLEX Examination 3-4 (p. 396)
Identify the potential effects of muscle relaxants used during surgical intervention when combined with antidysrhythmic drugs.	Review antidysrhythmic agents, such as procainamide, quinidine, and lidocaine, and their effects as muscle relaxants.	TB Multiple Choice question 7 SG Review Sheet question 17 (p. 158) ▸ Discuss which antidysrhythmic agents may prolong the effect of surgical muscle relaxants. What specifically should be monitored? Class Activity ***As a class, discuss the following agents that may prolong the effect of surgical muscle relaxants: procainamide, quinidine, and lidocaine. Identify which patient signs should be monitored. How do antidysrhythmic drugs affect the action and therapeutic outcome of muscle relaxants?***
Performance evaluation		Test Bank SG Learning Activities (pp. 160-161) SG Practice Questions for the NCLEX Examination (pp. 162-163) Critical Thinking Questions

ELSEVIER

24.2 Homework/Assignments:

24.2 Instructor's Notes/Student Feedback:

24 Lecture Outline

Drugs Used to Treat Dysrhythmias

Slide 1

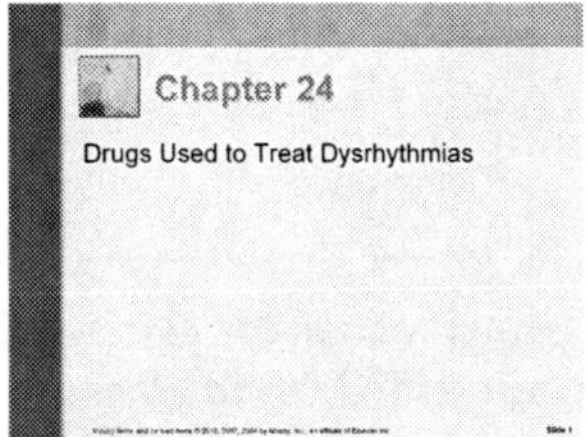
Chapter 24
Drugs Used to Treat Dysrhythmias

Slide 2

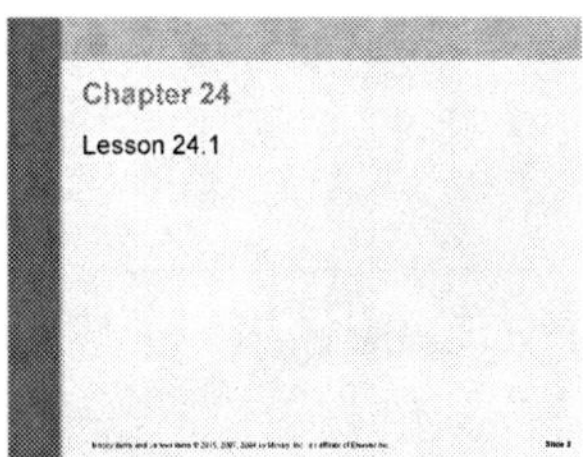
Chapter 24
Lesson 24.1

Slide 3

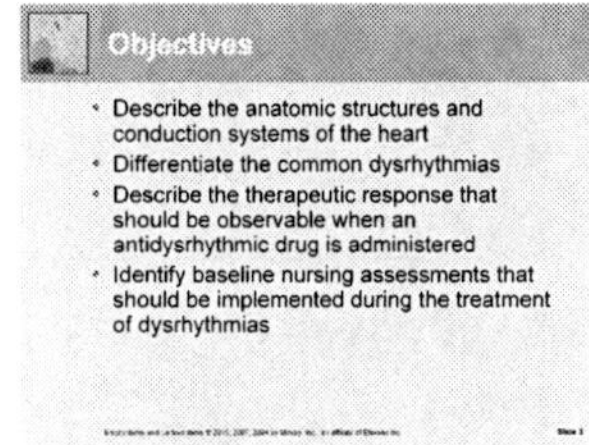
Objectives
Describe the anatomic structures and conduction systems of the heart
Differentiate the common dysrhythmias
Describe the therapeutic response that should be observable when an antidysrhythmic drug is administered
Identify baseline nursing assessments that should be implemented during the treatment of dysrhythmias

Slide 4

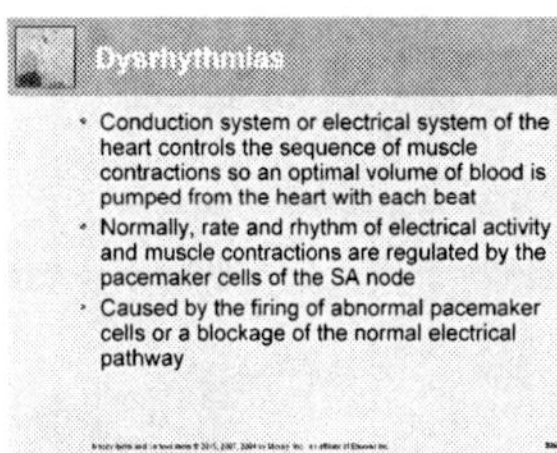
Dysrhythmias
Conduction system or electrical system of the heart controls the sequence of muscle contractions so an optimal volume of blood is pumped from the heart with each beat
Normally, rate and rhythm of electrical activity and muscle contractions are regulated by the pacemaker cells of the SA node
Caused by the firing of abnormal pacemaker cells or a blockage of the normal electrical pathway

- May be experienced as a flip-flop or racing heart.
- Cannot be diagnosed primarily on chest pain; a combination of physical examination, patient history, and ECG history is needed to diagnose.

Slide 5

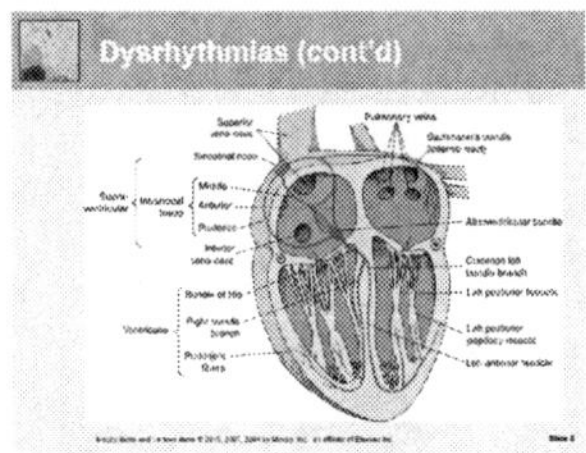
Dysrhythmias (cont'd)

ELSEVIER

Slide 6

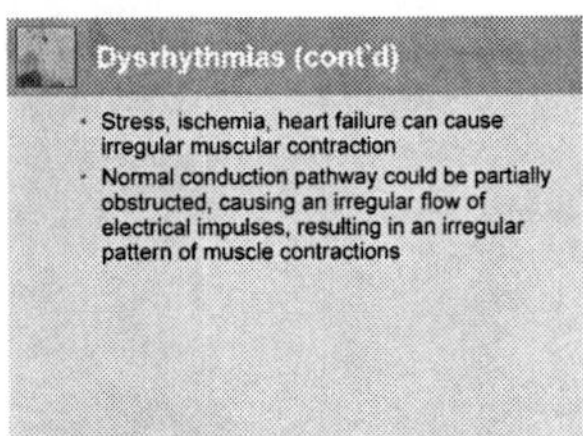
Dysrhythmias (cont'd)
Stress, ischemia, heart failure can cause irregular muscular contraction
Normal conduction pathway could be partially obstructed, causing an irregular flow of electrical impulses, resulting in an irregular pattern of muscle contractions

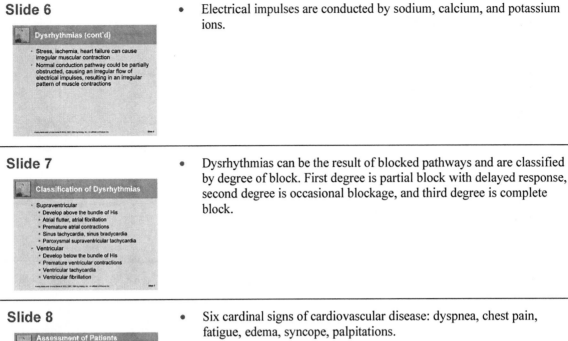

- Electrical impulses are conducted by sodium, calcium, and potassium ions.

Slide 7

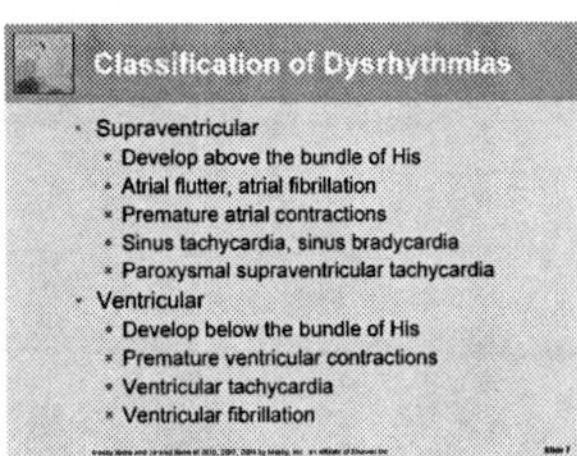
Classification of Dysrhythmias
Supraventricular
Develop above the bundle of His
Atrial flutter, atrial fibrillation
Premature atrial contractions
Sinus tachycardia, sinus bradycardia
Paroxysmal supraventricular tachycardia
Ventricular
Develop below the bundle of His
Premature ventricular contractions
Ventricular tachycardia
Ventricular fibrillation

- Dysrhythmias can be the result of blocked pathways and are classified by degree of block. First degree is partial block with delayed response, second degree is occasional blockage, and third degree is complete block.

Slide 8

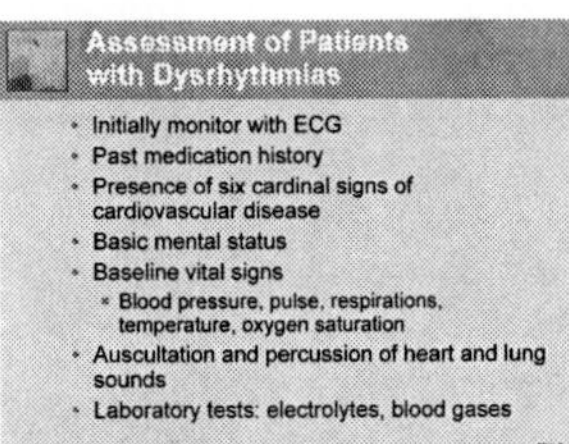
Assessment of Patients with Dysrhythmias
Initially monitor with ECG
Past medication history
Presence of six cardinal signs of cardiovascular disease
Basic mental status
Baseline vital signs
Blood pressure, pulse, respirations, temperature, oxygen saturation
Auscultation and percussion of heart and lung sounds
Laboratory tests: electrolytes, blood gases

- Six cardinal signs of cardiovascular disease: dyspnea, chest pain, fatigue, edema, syncope, palpitations.

Slide 9

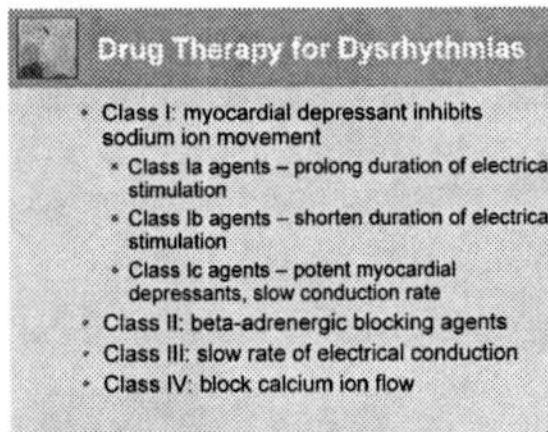
Drug Therapy for Dysrhythmias
Class I: myocardial depressant inhibits sodium ion movement
Class Ia agents – prolong duration of electrical stimulation
Class Ib agents – shorten duration of electrical stimulation
Class Ic agents – potent myocardial depressants, slow conduction rate
Class II: beta-adrenergic blocking agents
Class III: slow rate of electrical conduction
Class IV: block calcium ion flow

- Antidysrhythmic agents classified according to effects on the heart's electrical conduction system.

Slide 10

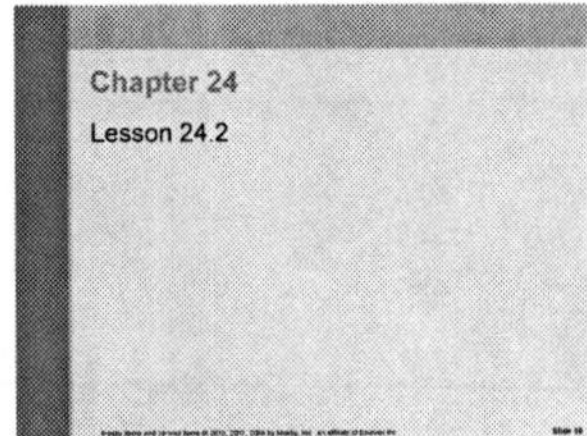
Chapter 24
Lesson 24.2

ELSEVIER

Slide 11

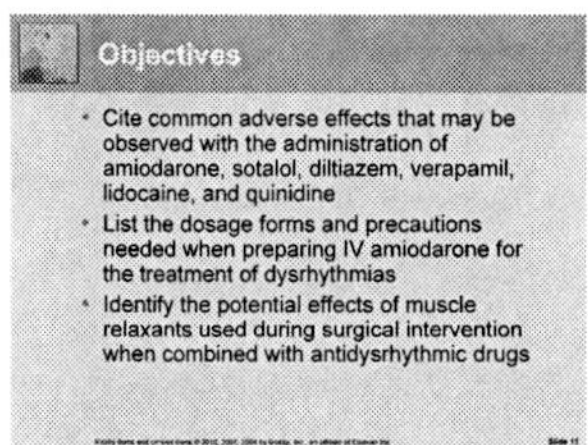
Objectives
Cite common adverse effects that may be observed with the administration of amiodarone, sotalol, diltiazem, verapamil, lidocaine, and quinidine
List the dosage forms and precautions needed when preparing IV amiodarone for the treatment of dysrhythmias
Identify the potential effects of muscle relaxants used during surgical intervention when combined with antidysrhythmic drugs

---

Slide 12

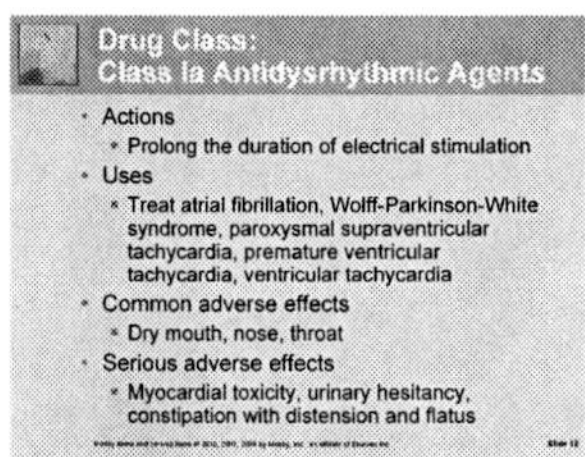
Drug Class: Class Ia Antidysrhythmic Agents
Actions
Prolong the duration of electrical stimulation
Uses
Treat atrial fibrillation, Wolff-Parkinson-White syndrome, paroxysmal supraventricular tachycardia, premature ventricular tachycardia, ventricular tachycardia
Common adverse effects
Dry mouth, nose, throat
Serious adverse effects
Myocardial toxicity, urinary hesitancy, constipation with distension and flatus

- For specific drugs, see Table 24-1.
- Therapeutic outcomes: conversion of dysrhythmia to normal sinus.

Slide 13

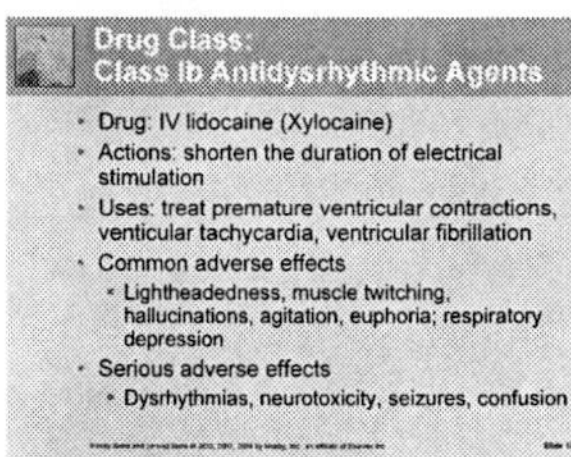
Drug Class: Class Ib Antidysrhythmic Agents
Drug: IV lidocaine (Xylocaine)
Actions: shorten the duration of electrical stimulation
Uses: treat premature ventricular contractions, venticular tachycardia, ventricular fibrillation
Common adverse effects
Lightheadedness, muscle twitching, hallucinations, agitation, euphoria; respiratory depression
Serious adverse effects
Dysrhythmias, neurotoxicity, seizures, confusion

- For specific drugs, see Table 24-1.
- *Lidocaine used for dysrhythmias is different from lidocaine used for local anesthesia; the label must read "Lidocaine for Dysrhythmia."*

Slide 14

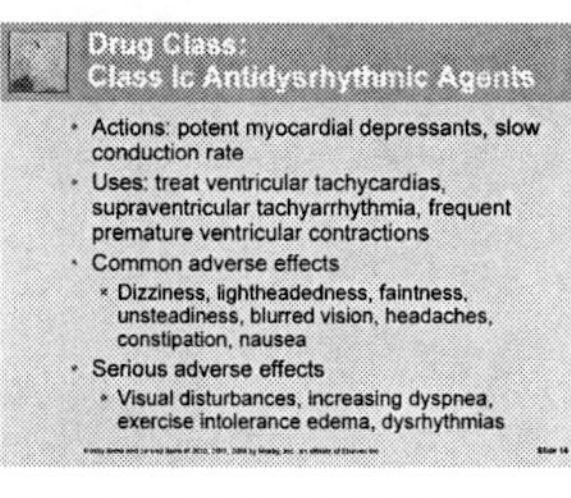
Drug Class: Class Ic Antidysrhythmic Agents
Actions: potent myocardial depressants, slow conduction rate
Uses: treat ventricular tachycardias, supraventricular tachyarrhythmia, frequent premature ventricular contractions
Common adverse effects
Dizziness, lightheadedness, faintness, unsteadiness, blurred vision, headaches, constipation, nausea
Serious adverse effects
Visual disturbances, increasing dyspnea, exercise intolerance edema, dysrhythmias

- For specific drugs, see Table 24-1.
- Propafenone recommended for treatment of paroxysmal atrial fibrillation and life-threatening ventricular dysrhythmias.

Slide 15

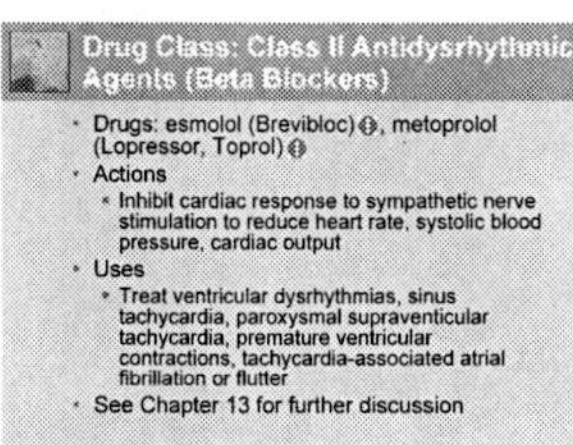
Drug Class: Class II Antidysrhythmic Agents (Beta Blockers)
Drugs: esmolol (Brevibloc), metoprolol (Lopressor, Toprol)
Actions
Inhibit cardiac response to sympathetic nerve stimulation to reduce heart rate, systolic blood pressure, cardiac output
Uses
Treat ventricular dysrhythmias, sinus tachycardia, paroxysmal supraventicular tachycardia, premature ventricular contractions, tachycardia-associated atrial fibrillation or flutter
See Chapter 13 for further discussion

- For specific drugs, see Table 24-1.

Slide 16

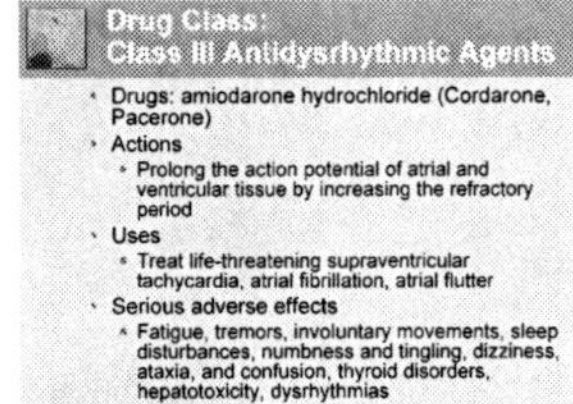
Drug Class:
Class III Antidysrhythmic Agents
Drugs: amiodarone hydrochloride (Cordarone, Pacerone)
Actions
Prolong the action potential of atrial and ventricular tissue by increasing the refractory period
Uses
Treat life-threatening supraventricular tachycardia, atrial fibrillation, atrial flutter
Serious adverse effects
Fatigue, tremors, involuntary movements, sleep disturbances, numbness and tingling, dizziness, ataxia, and confusion, thyroid disorders, hepatotoxicity, dysrhythmias

- For specific drugs, see Table 24-1.
- Successful in treating many dysrhythmias where other antidysrhythmics fail but have many adverse effects, some of which are severe and potentially fatal.

Slide 17

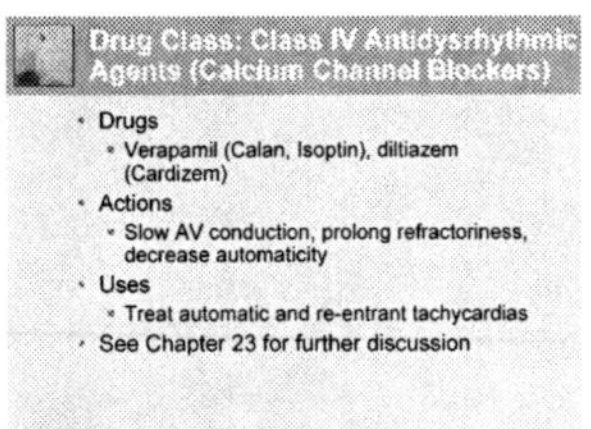
Drug Class: Class IV Antidysrhythmic Agents (Calcium Channel Blockers)
Drugs
Verapamil (Calan, Isoptin), diltiazem (Cardizem)
Actions
Slow AV conduction, prolong refractoriness, decrease automaticity
Uses
Treat automatic and re-entrant tachycardias
See Chapter 23 for further discussion

- Contraindicated in heart failure patients.

Slide 18

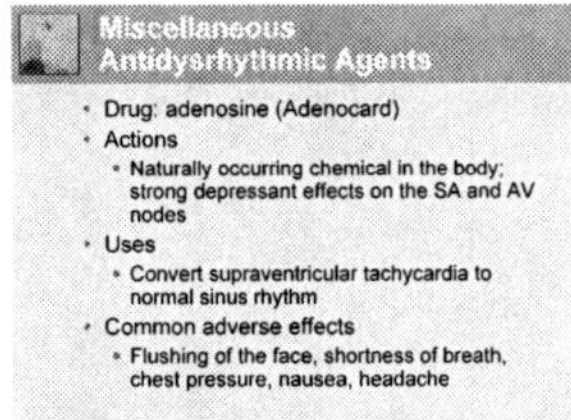
Miscellaneous Antidysrhythmic Agents
Drug: adenosine (Adenocard)
Actions
Naturally occurring chemical in the body; strong depressant effects on the SA and AV nodes
Uses
Convert supraventricular tachycardia to normal sinus rhythm
Common adverse effects
Flushing of the face, shortness of breath, chest pressure, nausea, headache

- Administered as a rapid IV bolus.
- Variety of physiologic effects: promotes prostaglandin release, inhibits platelet aggregation, has antiadrenergic effects, suppresses heart rate, and dilates coronary arteries.

Slide 19

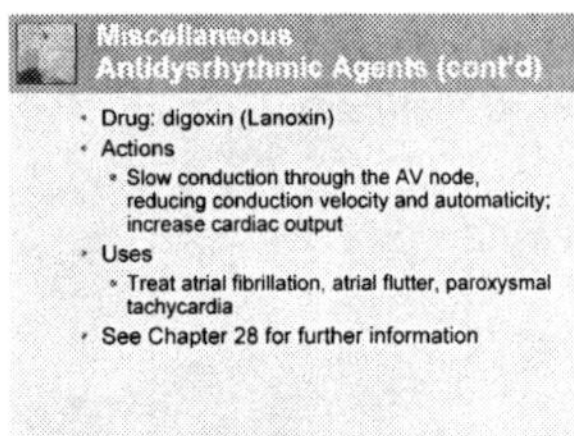
Miscellaneous Antidysrhythmic Agents (cont'd)
Drug: digoxin (Lanoxin)
Actions
Slow conduction through the AV node, reducing conduction velocity and automaticity; increase cardiac output
Uses
Treat atrial fibrillation, atrial flutter, paroxysmal tachycardia
See Chapter 28 for further information

ELSEVIER

25 Lesson Plan
Drugs Used to Treat Angina Pectoris

TEACHING FOCUS

This chapter focuses on angina pectoris and the drugs used to treat it. Students are introduced to the various types of angina and are given a brief introduction to its treatment and prevention. Students also have the opportunity to learn about detailed drug therapy for angina pectoris and the nursing considerations and responsibilities associated with its treatment.

MATERIALS AND RESOURCES

- ☐ computer and PowerPoint projector (Lesson 25.1)
- ☐ guest speaker: nurse practitioner who provides care to patients with angina pectoris

LESSON CHECKLIST

Preparations for this lesson include:

- lecture
- evaluation of student knowledge and skills needed to perform all entry-level activities related to drugs used to treat angina pectoris, including:
  - presentation of angina pectoris
  - types of angina pectoris, including detailed drug information for medications used
  - treatment of angina pectoris
  - nursing process for anginal therapy
  - drug classes used in the treatment of angina pectoris

KEY TERMS

angina pectoris (p. 397)
chronic stable angina (p. 397)
ischemic heart disease (p. 397)
unstable angina (p. 397)
variant angina (p. 397)

ADDITIONAL RESOURCES

PowerPoint slides: 1-15
Flashcards, Decks 1 and 2

Legend

ARQ	PPT	TB	CTQ	SG	INRQ
Audience Response Questions	PowerPoint Slides	Test Bank	Critical Thinking Questions	Study Guide	Interactive NCLEX Review Questions

Class Activities are indicated in ***bold italic.***

LESSON 25.1

BACKGROUND ASSESSMENT

Question: What is angina pectoris, and what are its precipitating factors?
Answer: Angina pectoris is a feeling of chest discomfort that arises because of a lack of oxygen to the heart muscle (myocardial) cells; it may be the first clinical symptom of underlying coronary artery disease. Anginal attacks are usually precipitated by factors or activities that require increased amounts of oxygen for the heart, such as climbing stairs or shoveling snow, cigarette smoking, eating heavy meals, drinking caffeinated beverages, emotional stress, sexual activity, and exposure to cold environments.

Question: What are the different classes of angina pectoris? What is the underlying pathophysiology, and what are the treatment options for each?
Answer: There are three classes of angina pectoris: chronic stable angina, variant angina, and unstable angina. In chronic stable angina, the attacks are usually preceded by physical activity or stress and are treated with rest or nitroglycerin. Chronic stable angina is primarily caused by fixed atherosclerotic obstruction in the coronary arteries. Variant anginal attacks occur when the patient is at rest or asleep. It is caused by coronary artery spasms, which restrict blood flow to the heart muscle. Variant angina is treated with two groups of drugs, calcium channel blockers and nitrates. Unstable angina changes in terms of onset, frequency, duration, and intensity. It is most likely caused by atherosclerotic narrowing, vasospasm, and thrombus formation. Treatment options for this condition can include antiplatelet therapy, nitrates, beta blockers, or calcium channel blockers.

CRITICAL THINKING QUESTION

A 59-year-old woman with a history of angina has recently gained 50 lb and smokes a pack of cigarettes per day. During the past 6 months, she has noticed shortness of breath and an increase in anginal symptoms when she gets angry. What educational information should the nurse provide for this woman?
Guidelines: The nurse should explain to the patient that weight loss, a healthy diet, and an exercise program are essential to managing the symptoms of heart disease. Under the direction of her health care provider, the patient should engage in regular, moderate exercise and modify her diet to lose weight, decrease her cholesterol level, and reduce overall fat and calorie intake. Smoking cessation is also imperative for patients with angina pectoris because smoking constricts blood vessels and contributes to anginal symptoms. The patient should be provided with brochures that explain angina pectoris, diet, exercise, and smoking cessation programs. The nurse should also encourage the patient to seek counseling to help her deal with her emotional stress if she feels that she cannot control the episodes of anger. It is important to empathize with the patient and to note that lifestyle changes are never easy but are necessary to control symptoms and prevent further disease.

OBJECTIVES	CONTENT	TEACHING RESOURCES
Define angina pectoris.	■ Angina pectoris (p. 397) Review the terms *angina pectoris*, *ischemic heart disease*, *chronic angina*, *unstable angina*, and *variant angina*. Discuss the physiology of angina and the various ways it may be presented.	PPT 5-6 TB Multiple Choice question 8 Lifespan Considerations: Anginal Attacks (p. 398) ▸ Discuss possible symptoms of angina pectoris. Class Activity ***Lead a group discussion identifying and describing the symptoms of angina.***
Define ischemic heart disease.	■ Angina pectoris (p. 397) Review the pathophysiology of ischemic heart disease, and discuss the role of drug therapy for patients with angina pectoris. Review the nursing process and how to apply it to be specific for patients with angina.	PPT 5-6 ▸ Discuss the physiologic factors that are responsible for the symptoms of angina pectoris.
Explain the rationale for the use of HMG-CoA reductase	■ Treatment of angina pectoris (p. 397) ■ Drug therapy for angina pectoris (p. 398)	PPT 8 TB Multiple Choice questions 1-2, 16 SG Review Sheet questions 1-5, 9 (p. 165)

OBJECTIVES	CONTENT	TEACHING RESOURCES
inhibitors (statins) in the treatment of cardiovascular disease.	Review the treatment goals for angina pectoris. Discuss risk factors to be aware of that must be controlled as well as lifestyle changes necessary for the treatment of angina pectoris.	SG Learning Activities questions 10, 15 (p. 167) Review Questions for the NCLEX Examination 8-9 (p. 408) ▸ Discuss the goals of treatment of angina pectoris. Class Activity ***Lead a group discussion defining the drug class "statins" and describing its actions.*** Class Activity ***Divide the class into four groups. Assign each group one of the following drug classifications: nitrates, beta-adrenergic blocking agents, calcium ion antagonists, and angiotensin-converting enzyme inhibitors. Have each group complete a drug card phototype for their assigned drug class that includes the following data: drug action, indications, dosage, routes, adverse effects, contraindications, nursing implications, and patient education. Allow class time for discussion.***
Identify assessment data needed to evaluate an anginal attack.	– Nursing process for anginal therapy (p. 398)	PPT 9 ARQ 2 TB Multiple Choice question 12 CTQ 1, 7 SG Review Sheet questions 6, 13, 15 (pp. 165-166) Review Question for the NCLEX Examination 4 (p. 407) ▸ Discuss which cardiovascular signs should be evaluated and recorded. ▸ Discuss the relevance of nutritional history on the care of the patient with angina pectoris. Class Activity ***Present the following scenario to the class, and have students identify the assessment data needed to evaluate the patient:*** ***A 52-year-old man experiences a squeezing and choking sensation after cutting the grass.*** ***Record student responses on the board for comparison.***
Implement medication therapy health teaching for an	– Patient education and health promotion (p. 400)	PPT 10 ARQ 3 TB Multiple Choice questions 3-5, 7, 10, 15

OBJECTIVES	CONTENT	TEACHING RESOURCES
anginal patient in the clinical setting.		TB Multiple Response questions 2-4 INRQ 2-5, 7-9 CTQ 4 SG Review Sheet question 10 (p. 166) SG Learning Activities questions 1, 16-17 (p. 167) SG Practice Questions for the NCLEX Examination 1-3, 8, 11 (pp. 168-169) Review Question for the NCLEX Examination 10 (p. 408) ▸ Discuss how you would implement a teaching plan for a patient taking nitrates. Consider such effects as hypotension and headache, and explain administration techniques and storage. Class Activity ***Divide the class into groups. Have students use the scenario from the previous class activity to list five areas of patient teaching for a patient with angina pectoris. Have each group present its findings to the class for discussion.*** Class Activity ***Outside of class time, have students access the website* www.heartinfo.com *and search the site for new updates and stories of patients with angina pectoris. Allow class time for discussion.***
Describe the actions of nitrates, beta-adrenergic blockers, calcium channel blockers, and angiotensin-converting enzyme inhibitors on the myocardial tissue of the heart.	□ Drug class: Nitrates (p. 401) – Nursing process for nitrates (p. 401) □ Drug class: Beta-adrenergic blocking agents (p. 404) – Nursing process for beta-adrenergic blocking agents (p. 404) □ Drug class: Calcium channel blockers (p. 404) – Nursing process for calcium channel blockers (p. 406) □ Drug class: Angiotensin-converting enzyme inhibitors (p. 406) – Nursing process for angiotensin-converting enzyme inhibitors (p. 406)	PPT 11-15 ARQ 1, 4-5 TB Multiple Choice questions 6, 9, 11, 13-14, 16 TB Multiple Response question 1 INRQ 1, 6, 10-12 CTQ 2-3, 5-6 Animation: Beta Blockers Animation: Calcium Channel Blockers SG Review Sheet questions 7-8, 11-12, 14, 16-20 (pp. 165-166) SG Learning Activities questions 2-9, 11-14 (p. 167)

OBJECTIVES	CONTENT	TEACHING RESOURCES
	□ Drug class: Fatty oxidase enzyme inhibitor (p. 406) – Nursing process for ranolazine (p. 407)	SG Practice Questions for the NCLEX Examination 4-7, 9-10, 12, 14 (pp. 168-169) Review Questions for the NCLEX Examination 1-3, 5-7 (pp. 407-408) Drug Table 25-1: Nitrates (p. 402) Drug Table 25-2: Calcium Channel Blockers Used to Treat Angina Pectoris (p. 405) ▸ Discuss the proper storage of nitrate compounds. ▸ Discuss why beta blocker therapy is used in addition to nitroglycerin use. ▸ Discuss the premedication assessment for patients for whom calcium channel blockers have been prescribed. Class Activity ***Have two students role-play the premedication assessment needed for patients starting on ACE inhibitors. Include the baseline blood pressure readings in the supine and standing positions and an apical pulse. The nurse should explain to the patient that blood pressure should be taken standing up. Include what laboratory values to check. The nurse should also ask if the patient has a cough. Review the exercise with the class.*** Class Activity ***Have students evaluate and comment on the following scenarios:*** – ***A patient with angina asks, "If one to two nitroglycerin tablets are good for relieving angina, can I take three to four for a bad attack?"*** – ***A patient with angina says that he likes to have his nitroglycerin with him at all times, so he puts a few tablets in a small bottle of Tylenol to take with him.*** – ***Invite a guest speaker, such as a nurse practitioner (NP), to discuss treatment options and considerations for patients with angina pectoris.***
Performance evaluation		Test Bank SG Learning Activities (p. 167) SG Practice Questions for the NCLEX Examination (pp. 168-169) Critical Thinking Questions

25.1 Homework/Assignments:

25.1 Instructor's Notes/Student Feedback:

Drugs Used to Treat Angina Pectoris

Slide 1

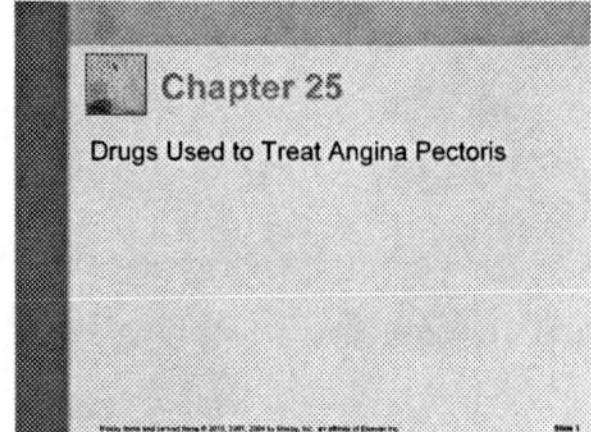
Chapter 25
Drugs Used to Treat Angina Pectoris

Slide 2

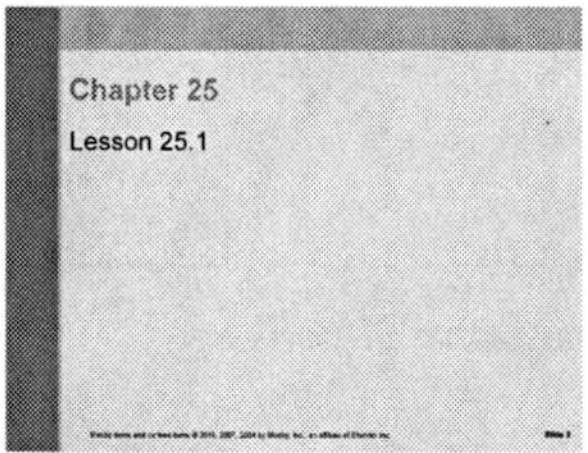
Chapter 25
Lesson 25.1

Slide 3

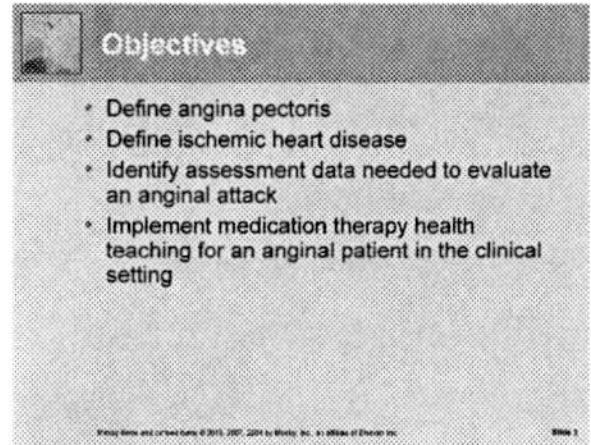
Objectives
Define angina pectoris
Define ischemic heart disease
Identify assessment data needed to evaluate an anginal attack
Implement medication therapy health teaching for an anginal patient in the clinical setting

Slide 4

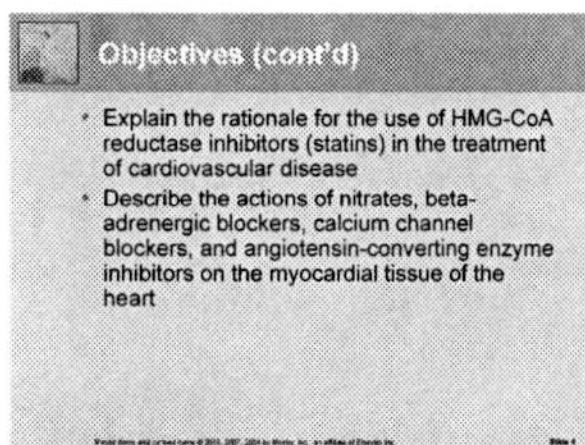
Objectives (cont'd)
Explain the rationale for the use of HMG-CoA reductase inhibitors (statins) in the treatment of cardiovascular disease
Describe the actions of nitrates, beta-adrenergic blockers, calcium channel blockers, and angiotensin-converting enzyme inhibitors on the myocardial tissue of the heart

Slide 5

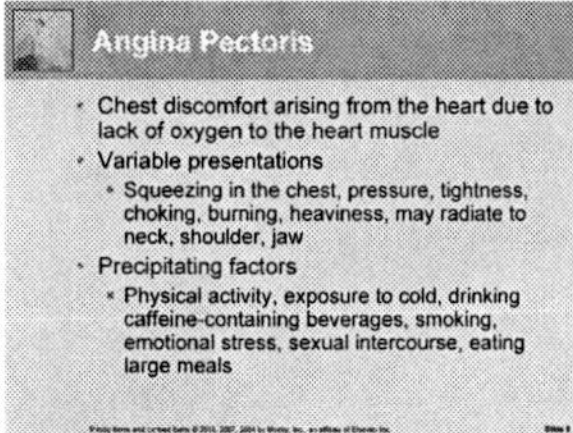
Angina Pectoris
Chest discomfort arising from the heart due to lack of oxygen to the heart muscle
Variable presentations
Squeezing in the chest, pressure, tightness, choking, burning, heaviness, may radiate to neck, shoulder, jaw
Precipitating factors
Physical activity, exposure to cold, drinking caffeine-containing beverages, smoking, emotional stress, sexual intercourse, eating large meals

- Symptom of coronary artery disease (CAD) caused by plaque buildup in blood vessels (atherosclerosis) or a spasm of the artery.
- Attacks may last from 30 seconds to 30 minutes and are often described as feeling like someone or something is sitting on the chest.

Slide 6

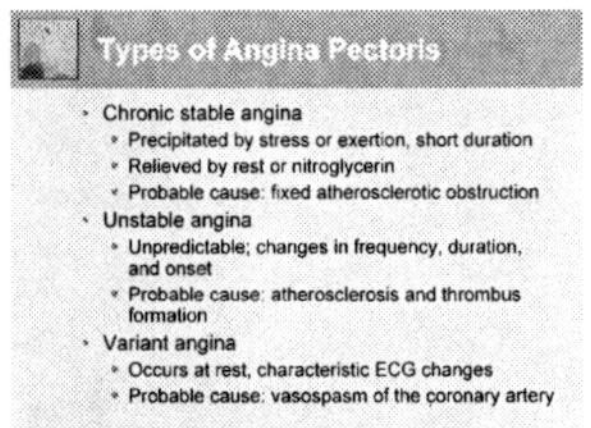
Types of Angina Pectoris
Chronic stable angina
Precipitated by stress or exertion, short duration
Relieved by rest or nitroglycerin
Probable cause: fixed atherosclerotic obstruction
Unstable angina
Unpredictable; changes in frequency, duration, and onset
Probable cause: atherosclerosis and thrombus formation
Variant angina
Occurs at rest, characteristic ECG changes
Probable cause: vasospasm of the coronary artery

Slide 7

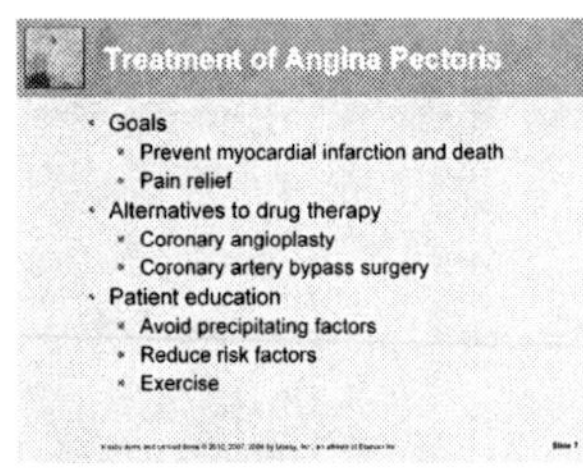
Treatment of Angina Pectoris
Goals
Prevent myocardial infarction and death
Pain relief
Alternatives to drug therapy
Coronary angioplasty
Coronary artery bypass surgery
Patient education
Avoid precipitating factors
Reduce risk factors
Exercise

- Symptoms must be caught early so quality of life can be improved and life can be prolonged.
- Risk factors include diabetes mellitus, hypertension, and dyslipidemia.

Slide 8

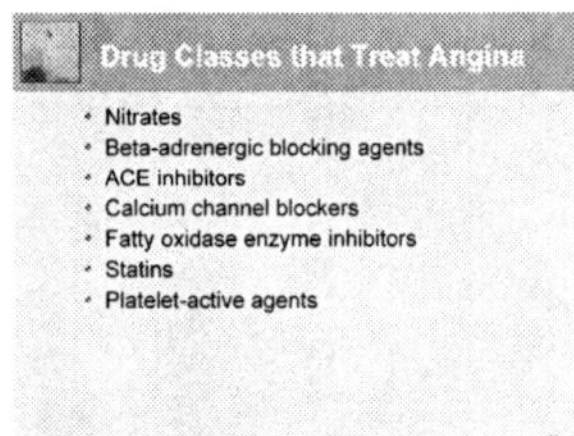
Drug Classes that Treat Angina
Nitrates
Beta-adrenergic blocking agents
ACE inhibitors
Calcium channel blockers
Fatty oxidase enzyme inhibitors
Statins
Platelet-active agents

- Nitrates are the oldest of all the drugs and are very effective.
- Combination therapy is beneficial for many patients.
- Statins have become a standard in drug therapy.

Slide 9

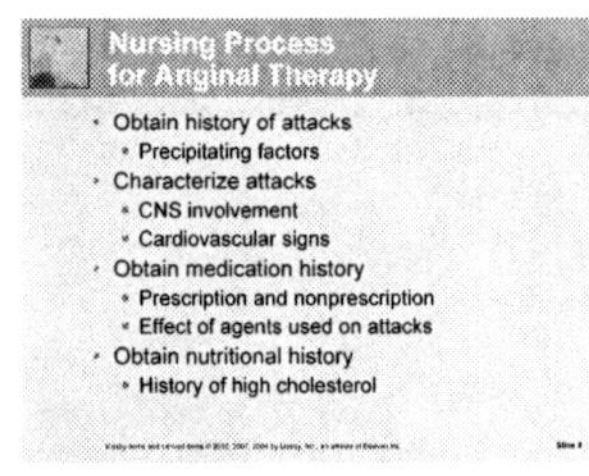
Nursing Process for Anginal Therapy
Obtain history of attacks
Precipitating factors
Characterize attacks
CNS involvement
Cardiovascular signs
Obtain medication history
Prescription and nonprescription
Effect of agents used on attacks
Obtain nutritional history
History of high cholesterol

- CNS involvement may be in the form of confusion, restlessness, or irritability, as well as syncope and anxiety.
- Cardiovascular signs include palpitations, peripheral pulses, and vital signs.

Slide 10

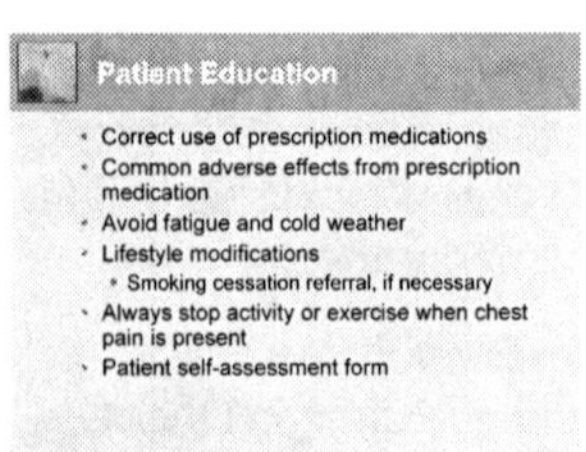
Patient Education
Correct use of prescription medications
Common adverse effects from prescription medication
Avoid fatigue and cold weather
Lifestyle modifications
Smoking cessation referral, if necessary
Always stop activity or exercise when chest pain is present
Patient self-assessment form

- It often helps patients to use a pill organizer.
- Rapid lifestyle adjustments can lead to feelings of depression. Allow patients and families to verbalize feelings.

ELSEVIER

Slide 11

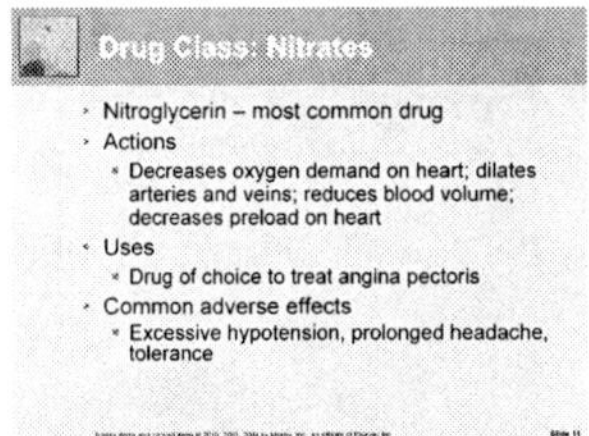
Drug Class: Nitrates
Nitroglycerin – most common drug
Actions
Decreases oxygen demand on heart; dilates arteries and veins; reduces blood volume; decreases preload on heart
Uses
Drug of choice to treat angina pectoris
Common adverse effects
Excessive hypotension, prolonged headache, tolerance

- For specific drugs, see Table 25-1.
- Patients can develop tolerance, especially when large doses are administered frequently. Nitrate-free periods are necessary.
- As patients become adjusted to therapy, headaches usually diminish.
- Drugs used for erectile dysfunction, such as sildenafil (Viagra), are contraindicated because a fatal drop in blood pressure may occur.

Slide 12

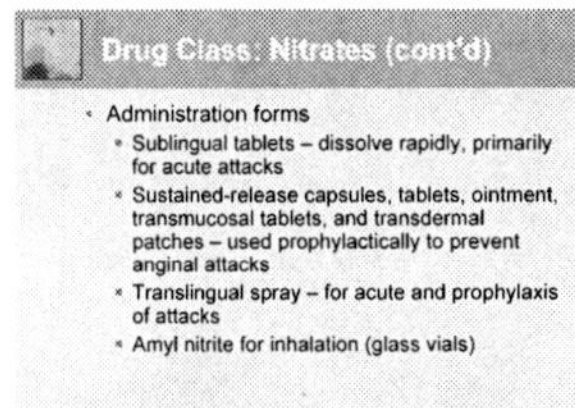
Drug Class: Nitrates (cont'd)
Administration forms
Sublingual tablets – dissolve rapidly, primarily for acute attacks
Sustained-release capsules, tablets, ointment, transmucosal tablets, and transdermal patches – used prophylactically to prevent anginal attacks
Translingual spray – for acute and prophylaxis of attacks
Amyl nitrite for inhalation (glass vials)

- Inform the patient of medication deterioration; every 3 months, nitroglycerin prescriptions should be refilled and a dark-colored glass container should be used for storage.

Slide 13

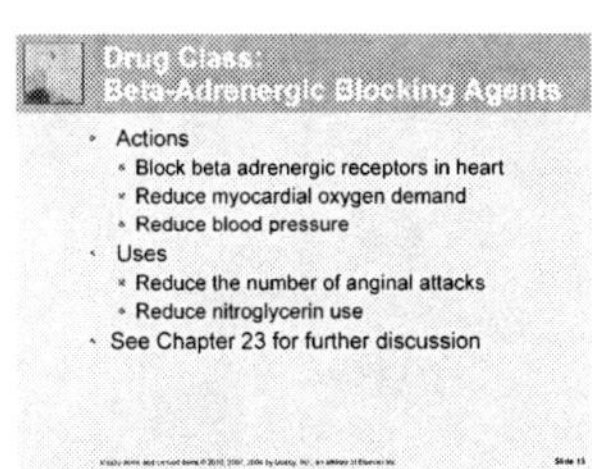
Drug Class: Beta-Adrenergic Blocking Agents
Actions
Block beta adrenergic receptors in heart
Reduce myocardial oxygen demand
Reduce blood pressure
Uses
Reduce the number of anginal attacks
Reduce nitroglycerin use
See Chapter 23 for further discussion

- For specific drugs, see Table 13-3.
- Therapy should start at low doses and work upward for patient tolerance.
- Combination therapy with nitrates is more effective than using either drug alone.

Slide 14

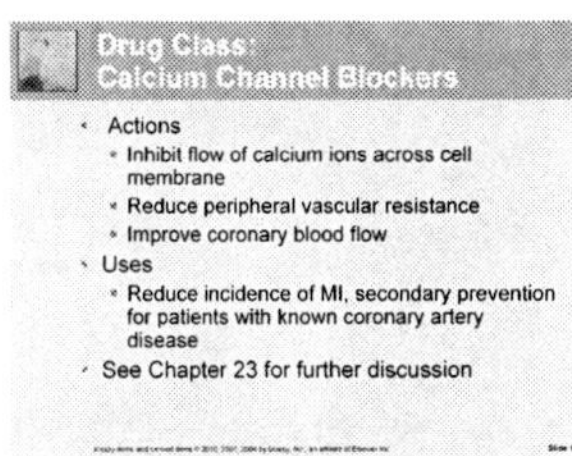
Drug Class: Calcium Channel Blockers
Actions
Inhibit flow of calcium ions across cell membrane
Reduce peripheral vascular resistance
Improve coronary blood flow
Uses
Reduce incidence of MI, secondary prevention for patients with known coronary artery disease
See Chapter 23 for further discussion

- For specific drugs, see Table 25-2.
- Potent vasodilators; have an overall effect on myocardial activity.
- Should be used with caution in patients who may be developing heart failure.

Slide 15

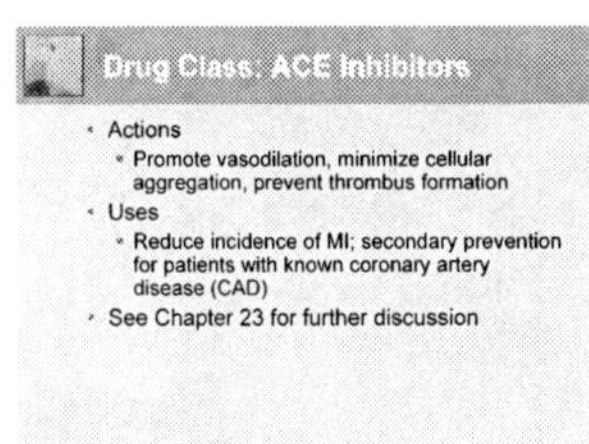
Drug Class: ACE Inhibitors
Actions
Promote vasodilation, minimize cellular aggregation, prevent thrombus formation
Uses
Reduce incidence of MI; secondary prevention for patients with known coronary artery disease (CAD)
See Chapter 23 for further discussion

- For specific drugs, see Table 23-5.
- Also recommended for patients with acute MI or heart failure with left systolic dysfunction.
- Adverse effects such as dizziness, tachycardia, and fainting may occur within 3 hours after the first several doses.

ELSEVIER

Slide 16

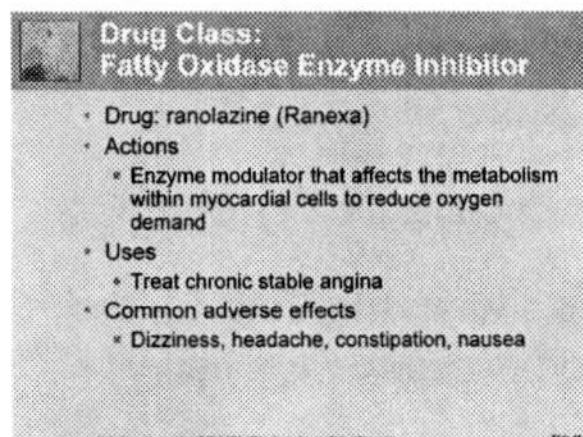
Drug Class:
Fatty Oxidase Enzyme Inhibitor
Drug: ranolazine (Ranexa)
Actions
Enzyme modulator that affects the metabolism within myocardial cells to reduce oxygen demand
Uses
Treat chronic stable angina
Common adverse effects
Dizziness, headache, constipation, nausea

- Used in combination with calcium channel blockers, beta-blockers, or nitrates.
- Does not affect blood pressure or heart rate. Prolongs Q-T interval; does not reduce symptoms of an acute attack.

Lesson Plan

26 Drugs Used to Treat Peripheral Vascular Disease

TEACHING FOCUS

In this chapter, students will have the opportunity to learn about a variety of illnesses classified as peripheral vascular disease (PVD) and the drugs used to treat them. These include several classifications, of which only two are approved by the U.S. Food and Drug Administration (FDA). Students will be presented with the opportunity to learn about the nursing assessment of patients with these illnesses, development of nursing diagnoses, treatment planning, and implementation of interventions. Various nonpharmacologic treatments, patient education, prevention, and health promotion will be discussed.

MATERIALS AND RESOURCES

- ☐ American Heart Association therapeutic lifestyle changes (TLC) diet (Lesson 26.1)
- ☐ chalkboard (Lessons 26.1 and 26.2)
- ☐ computer and PowerPoint projector (all Lessons)
- ☐ Doppler and supplies (Lesson 26.1)
- ☐ index cards (Lesson 26.1)

LESSON CHECKLIST

Preparations for this lesson include:

- lecture
- guest speaker: cardiovascular clinical nurse specialist
- Evaluation of student knowledge and skills needed to perform all entry-level nursing activities related to PVD and the drugs used to treat it, including:
    - classification and definition of PVD
    - nursing process for PVD therapy
    - nonpharmacologic and pharmacologic treatment of PVD
    - patient education topics relevant to treatment and health promotion of PVD

KEY TERMS

arteriosclerosis obliterans (p. 409)
intermittent claudication (p. 409)
paresthesias (p. 409)
Raynaud's disease (p. 409)
vasospasm (p. 410)

ADDITIONAL RESOURCES

PowerPoint slides: 1-16
Flashcards, Decks 1 and 2

Legend

ARQ	**PPT**	**TB**	**CTQ**	**SG**	**INRQ**
Audience Response Questions	PowerPoint Slides	Test Bank	Critical Thinking Questions	Study Guide	Interactive NCLEX Review Questions

Class Activities are indicated in ***bold italic.***

ELSEVIER

LESSON 26.1

BACKGROUND ASSESSMENT

Question: Define PVD. What are its two subdivisions?
Answer: PVD refers to a variety of illnesses that involve the blood vessels outside the heart—generally blood vessels of the arms and legs. The two subdivisions of PVD are peripheral arterial disease and venous disorders. The arterial disorders are subdivided further into those resulting from arterial narrowing and occlusion and those caused by spasm.

Question: What is the most common form of obstructive arterial disease? What does it result from? What are its risk factors and symptoms? What is the name of the PVD caused by arterial vasospasm? What does it result from? What other factors are associated with this condition, and what are the signs and symptoms?
Answer: The most common form of obstructive arterial disease is arteriosclerosis obliterans, which results from atherosclerotic plaque formation. This causes narrowing in the lower aorta and major arteries and provides circulation to the lower extremities. Risk factors include high low-density lipoprotein (LDL) levels, low high-density lipoprotein (HDL) levels, hypertension, smoking, and diabetes. As a result of the obstruction of blood flow through the arteries, there is also diminished blood supply to the surrounding tissues, resulting in ischemia. Intermittent claudication is the name of this condition, which has symptoms of pain in the lower extremities with exercise. The name of the PVD caused by arterial vasospasm is Raynaud's disease, which is usually characterized by numbness, tingling, and blanching of the hands and fingertips. The cause is unknown but is thought to be a result of vasoconstriction of blood vessels and subsequent ischemia of the arteries of the skin of the hands, fingers, and sometimes toes. Factors that trigger Raynaud's are exposure to cold temperatures, obstructive arterial disease, occupational trauma, and certain drugs.

CRITICAL THINKING QUESTION

A 60-year-old patient was diagnosed with PVD after he developed symptoms of intermittent claudication. The health care provider prescribed atorvastatin (Lipitor) and pentoxifylline (Trental) to help in the treatment of his illness. The health care provider asked the nurse to educate the patient on the disease, symptoms, medications and adverse effects, other treatments, and prevention. What should the nurse tell the patient?
Guidelines: The nurse should begin by educating the patient on the name and causes of his illness and the reasons for his symptoms. PVD is an illness associated with decreased blood supply to the arteries in the lower extremities caused by the formation of fatty plaques. This leads to narrowing of the blood vessels or spasms to these blood vessels, causing decreased oxygen to the tissues, resulting in pain, aching, or weakness with exercise. This is called intermittent claudication. Other contributing factors include increased cholesterol levels, hypertension, diabetes, and cigarette smoking. The nurse should educate the patient on the new medications prescribed, advising him that atorvastatin is to treat his elevated cholesterol levels and hopefully diminish plaque production in the blood vessels. Pentoxifylline is used to decrease the thickness of the blood, increasing blood flow and oxygen to the surrounding tissues and decreasing pain. Lifestyle changes should also be encouraged. The nurse should discuss with the patient the importance of weight loss, exercise, a low-fat and low-cholesterol diet, and smoking cessation to improve his health and well-being. The nurse should be supportive of the patient and offer suggestions about making these lifestyle changes.

OBJECTIVES	CONTENT	TEACHING RESOURCES
Discuss peripheral vascular disease	■ PVD (p. 409) Review the two types of peripheral vascular diseases, arterial and venous disorders. Discuss arteriosclerosis obliterans and the risk factors associated with it. Review intermittent claudication and paresthesias, their manifestations, and Raynaud's disease.	PPT 5-6 ARQ 1-2 SG Review Sheet question 1 (p. 171) SG Learning Activities questions 1-3, 9-10 (p. 173) Review Questions for the NCLEX Examination 6-7 (p. 416)

OBJECTIVES	CONTENT	TEACHING RESOURCES
		▸ Discuss and classify the various forms of PVD. ▸ Discuss the characteristics and possible causes of Raynaud's disease. Class Activity ***List on the board the following terms: intermittent claudication, paresthesias, Raynaud's disease, and peripheral vascular disease. Have students define the terms and state one symptom associated with each. Review the exercise with the class.***
Identify specific measures that the patient can use to improve peripheral circulation and prevent complications from peripheral vascular disease.	■ Treatment of peripheral vascular disease (p. 410)	PPT 7 TB Multiple Response question 2 SG Review Sheet question 6 (p. 171) SG Learning Activities questions 5, 12, 14 (p. 173) SG Practice Question for the NCLEX Examination 4 (p. 175) ▸ Discuss important lifestyle changes that the patient can take to reduce the effects of PVD. ▸ Discuss the effects of exercise on PVD. Class Activity ***Divide the class into groups, and then present them with the following scenario:*** ***A 59-year-old patient diagnosed with PVD has complaints of intermittent claudication. The patient, who has led an active life, is depressed and apathetic about the diagnosis. Have each group devise a teaching plan that includes treatment options and resources that a nurse could use to help the patient adjust to this diagnosis. Ask each group to present its plan to the class.*** Class Activity ***List on the board the following conditions: diabetes, hypertension, obesity, hypercholesterolemia, smoking, and high-fat diet. Have students take turns explaining how these conditions contribute to peripheral vascular disease and what must be controlled with each condition. Review the exercise with the class.***
State both pharmacologic and nonpharmaco-logic goals of treatment for PVD.	■ Treatment of peripheral vascular disease (p. 410) ■ Drug therapy for peripheral vascular disease (p. 410)	INRQ 8 CTQ 4 SG Review Sheet questions 2-5 (p. 171) SG Learning Activities questions 4, 6-8, 11, 15 (pp. 173-174)

OBJECTIVES	CONTENT	TEACHING RESOURCES
	Review the goals for treatment of patients with arteriosclerosis obliterans: improve blood flow, relieve pain, prevent skin ulcers, and reverse the progress of the atherosclerosis. Discuss the control and management of conditions, such as diabetes, which compound the problem.	▸ Discuss why nonpharmacologic measures are more significant in treating the underlying abnormalities of vascular disease than pharmacologic measures. ▸ Discuss what effect diet can have on PVD. ▸ Discuss the various classes of drugs used in the treatment of PVD, including their actions and degree of effectiveness. ▸ Discuss which drugs are FDA-approved for the treatment of intermittent claudication caused by chronic occlusive arterial disease. Class Activity ***List on the board the following conditions: diabetes, hypertension, obesity, hypercholesterolemia, smoking, and high-fat diet. Have students take turns explaining how these conditions contribute to peripheral vascular disease and what must be controlled with each condition. Review the exercise with the class.***
List the baseline assessments needed to evaluate a patient with peripheral vascular disease.	– Nursing process for peripheral vascular disease therapy (p. 411)	PPT 10 ARQ 3 TB Multiple Choice questions 1, 3 TB Multiple Response question 1 CTQ 1-2 SG Review Sheet questions 7, 10, 13 (pp. 171-172) SG Learning Activities question 13 (p. 173) Review Question for the NCLEX Examination 5 (p. 416) ▸ Discuss the relevance of family history of cardiovascular disease or hypertension to the patient with PVD. ▸ Demonstrate and discuss obtaining peripheral pulses. Demonstrate use of a Doppler in finding pulses difficult to palpate. Class Activity ***Divide the class into pairs, and ask each student to perform a five-point tissue assessment on his or her partner. The following should be assessed and recorded: oxygenation (note color, especially if cyanosis or redness), temperature (feel the temperature in each extremity), peripheral pulses (have students demonstrate proficiency using a Doppler and record pedal and radial pulses), edema***

OBJECTIVES	CONTENT	TEACHING RESOURCES
		(assess, record, and report edema), and extremity pain (assess details of onset and location). After the pairs have conducted their assessments, reconvene the class, and ask students to summarize their findings.
Develop measurable objectives for patient education of patients with peripheral vascular disease.	– Patient education and health promotion (p. 412)	PPT 11 TB Multiple Response question 3 CTQ 6 SG Review Sheet question 8 (p. 171) SG Learning Activities question 8 (p. 173) SG Practice Question for the NCLEX Examination 2 (p. 175) Review Questions for the NCLEX Examination 8-9 (p. 416) ▸ Discuss why drug therapy is not the most effective therapy for PVD. ▸ Discuss lifestyle changes that promote peripheral circulation. *Class Activity* ***In pairs, have students develop a teaching plan for promoting tissue perfusion in a patient with PVD.***

26.1 Homework/Assignments:

26.1 Instructor's Notes/Student Feedback

LESSON 26.2

CRITICAL THINKING QUESTION

The wife of a patient with PVD says, "I've heard that there are several types of medications available to treat my husband's problem, but what are they actually supposed to do?" How can the nurse explain the goal of medication in treating PVD?

Guidelines: The nurse can explain that there are several classes of medications available to treat PVD, including those that relax blood vessel walls, dilate the blood vessels, or decrease the viscosity of the blood.

The goals of all of these medications are essentially the same—to improve circulation to the tissues of the extremity, to provide oxygen to these tissues to reduce pain, to improve exercise tolerance, and to improve peripheral perfusion.

OBJECTIVES	CONTENT	TEACHING RESOURCES
State both pharmacologic and nonpharmacologic goals of treatment for peripheral vascular disease.	□ Drug class: Hemorrheologic agent (p. 413) – Nursing process for pentoxifylline (p. 413) Review the actions of drugs used for treatment of peripheral vascular disease. Discuss the effect of enhancing red blood cell flexibility.	PPT 14 ARQ 4 TB Multiple Choice questions 2, 6 TB Multiple Response question 4 INRQ 1, 9-10 CTQ 5 SG Review Sheet question 9 (p. 171) SG Learning Activities question 6, 10-11 (p. 173) SG Practice Questions for the NCLEX Examination 1, 5-6 (pp. 175-176) Review Questions for the NCLEX Examination 1, 4 (p. 416) ▸ Discuss the mode of action of pentoxifylline and why it is approved for this indication. ▸ Discuss common adverse effects of pentoxifylline and the patient teaching necessary for this class of drugs. *Class Activity* ***Present students with the following scenario:*** ***A 69-year-old patient who was diagnosed with PVD is prescribed pentoxifylline. Have student pairs take turns role-playing the nurse educating the patient on this medication to increase compliance. Then ask each pair to share highlights of its role play with the rest of the class.***
Identify the systemic effects to expect when peripheral vasodilating agents are administered.	□ Drug class: Vasodilators (p. 414) – Nursing process for papaverine (p. 414)	PPT 15 TB Multiple Choice questions 7 INRQ 2-4, 7 SG Review Sheet questions 10-12 (pp. 171-172) SG Learning Activities questions 16-17 (p. 174) SG Practice Questions for the NCLEX Examination 3, 8 (pp. 175-176) Review Question for the NCLEX Examination 2 (p. 416)

ELSEVIER

OBJECTIVES	CONTENT	TEACHING RESOURCES
		▸ Discuss why vasodilators are used in the treatment of PVD. ▸ Discuss what effects vasodilators can be expected to achieve that will relieve the symptoms of PVD. Class Activity ***Divide the class into groups, and have each group discuss how vasodilator agents treat peripheral vascular spasm, including actions, uses, adverse effects, and patient teaching information. Have groups share their information and record it on the board. Discuss the results as a class.*** Class Activity ***Have two students role-play the nurse educating a patient taking vasodilators. Have the class assist the "nurse" in determining what is important to discuss with the "patient." Review with the class therapeutic outcomes and adverse effects of vasodilators.***
Explain why hypotension and tachycardia occur frequently with the use of peripheral vasodilators.	□ Drug class: Vasodilators (p. 414) – Nursing process for papaverine (p. 414) Review the actions of drugs used for treatment of peripheral vascular disease. Discuss the effect of vasodilator therapy.	PPT 15 ARQ 5 TB Multiple Choice question 5 SG Review Sheet questions 11-12 (pp. 171-172) ▸ Discuss the effects of vasodilation on the smooth muscle walls of blood vessels and the subsequent impact on blood pressure. ▸ Discuss drugs that may interact with vasodilators and should be avoided. Include drugs that may enhance therapeutic effect and those that may reduce the therapeutic effect. Class Activity ***Discuss with the class why hypotension and tachycardia may occur with vasodilator use by creating an analogy. For example, before vasodilator use, the diameter of the vasculature may be the size of a straw and, after vasodilator use, it may be the size of a garden hose. Then using the student groups formed in the last class activity, have each group discuss nursing interventions and patient teaching for this class of drugs.***
State both pharmacologic and nonpharmaco-logic goals of treatment for peripheral vascular disease.	□ Drug class: Platelet aggregation inhibitor (p. 415) – Nursing process for cilostazol (p. 415) Review the drug cilostazol in the drug class platelet aggregation inhibitors. Discuss the action and	PPT 16 TB Multiple Choice questions 8-9 INRQ 5-6 CTQ 3 SG Practice Question for the NCLEX Examination 7 (p. 176)

OBJECTIVES	CONTENT	TEACHING RESOURCES
	use of the drug as well as common and serious adverse effects and drug interactions.	Review Question for the NCLEX Examination 3 (p. 416) ▸ Discuss why use of cilostazol should not be considered a replacement for smoking cessation, surgical bypass, weight loss, exercise, or surgical removal of obstruction. ▸ Discuss the drug cilostazol, including classification, action, contraindications, adverse effects, and patient teaching approaches. *Class Activity* ***Have student pairs take turns role-playing a nurse and patient discussing the adverse effects of cilostazol, particularly the serious adverse effects. The role play will allow students to practice imparting potentially frightening information to patients without causing them undue alarm. Have "patients" report techniques used by their partners that were especially effective. Then have students discuss what they learned from the exercise.***
Performance evaluation		Test Bank SG Learning Activities (pp. 173-174) SG Practice Questions for the NCLEX Examination (pp. 175-176) Critical Thinking Questions

26.2 Homework/Assignments:

26.2 Instructor's Notes/Student Feedback:

Drugs Used to Treat Peripheral Vascular Disease

Slide 1

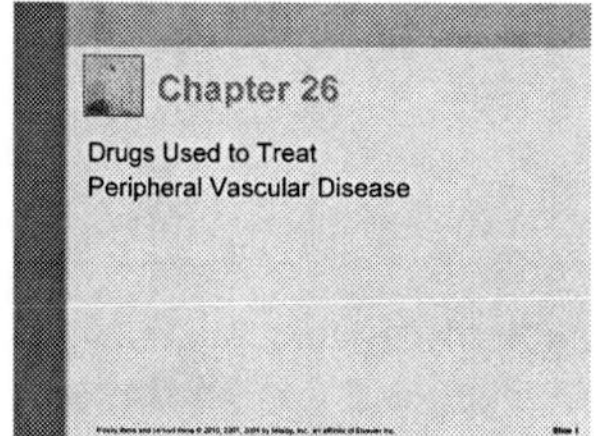
Chapter 26
Drugs Used to Treat
Peripheral Vascular Disease

Slide 2

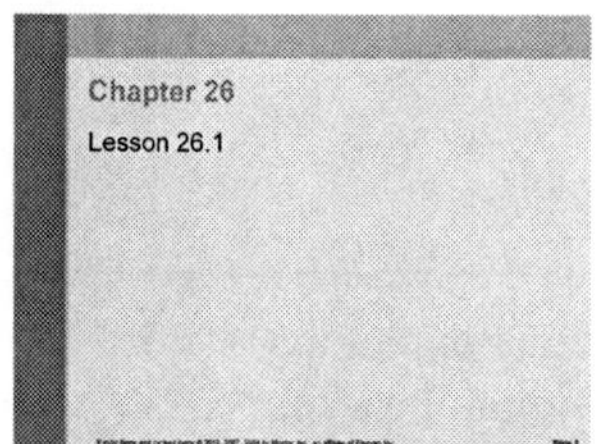
Chapter 26
Lesson 26.1

Slide 3

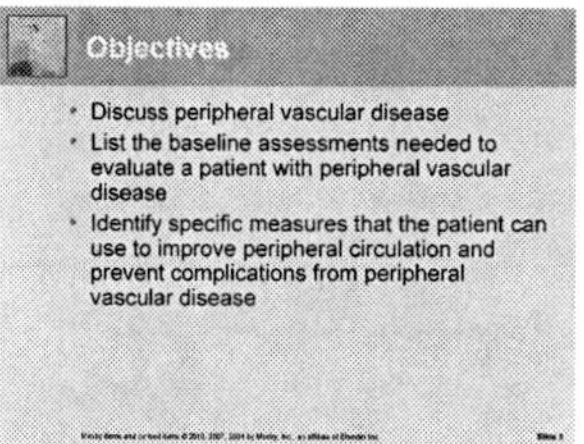
Objectives
Discuss peripheral vascular disease
List the baseline assessments needed to evaluate a patient with peripheral vascular disease
Identify specific measures that the patient can use to improve peripheral circulation and prevent complications from peripheral vascular disease

Slide 4

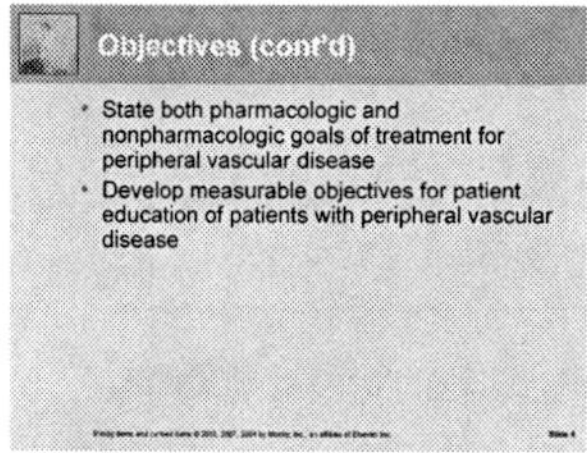
Objectives (cont'd)
State both pharmacologic and nonpharmacologic goals of treatment for peripheral vascular disease
Develop measurable objectives for patient education of patients with peripheral vascular disease

Slide 5

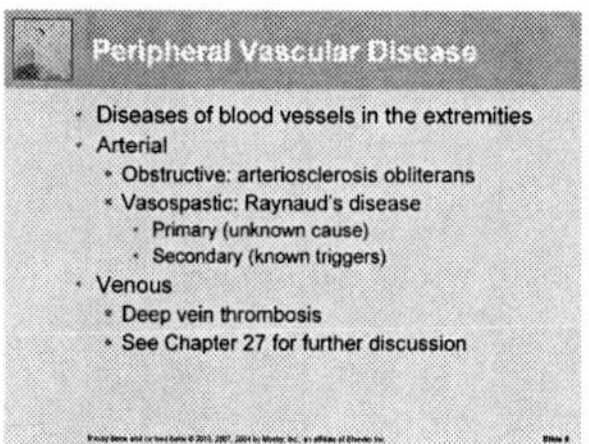
Peripheral Vascular Disease
Diseases of blood vessels in the extremities
Arterial
Obstructive: arteriosclerosis obliterans
Vasospastic: Raynaud's disease
Primary (unknown cause)
Secondary (known triggers)
Venous
Deep vein thrombosis
See Chapter 27 for further discussion

- Primary cause of arteriosclerosis obliterans is buildup of atherosclerotic plaque, resulting in narrowing of the lower aorta and the major arteries that provide circulation to the legs.

ELSEVIER

Slide 6

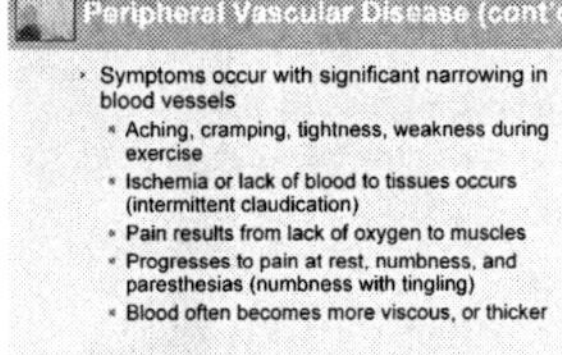
Peripheral Vascular Disease (cont'd)
Symptoms occur with significant narrowing in blood vessels
Aching, cramping, tightness, weakness during exercise
Ischemia or lack of blood to tissues occurs (intermittent claudication)
Pain results from lack of oxygen to muscles
Progresses to pain at rest, numbness, and paresthesias (numbness with tingling)
Blood often becomes more viscous, or thicker

- Patients tend to remain symptom-free until there is 75% to 90% occlusion in key locations of the major arteries and arterioles of the legs.

Slide 7

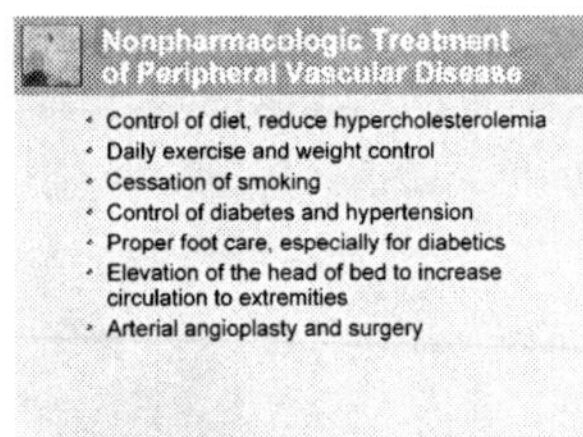
Nonpharmacologic Treatment of Peripheral Vascular Disease
Control of diet, reduce hypercholesterolemia
Daily exercise and weight control
Cessation of smoking
Control of diabetes and hypertension
Proper foot care, especially for diabetics
Elevation of the head of bed to increase circulation to extremities
Arterial angioplasty and surgery

- Raynaud's disease is best treated by avoidance of triggers, such as cold temperatures, emotional stress, and tobacco or other drugs known to induce attacks.

Slide 8

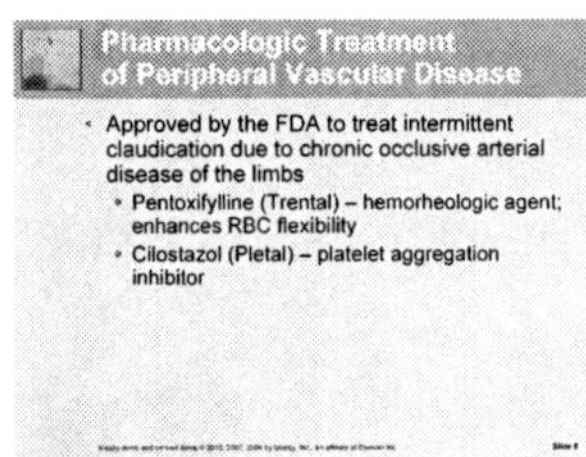
Pharmacologic Treatment of Peripheral Vascular Disease
Approved by the FDA to treat intermittent claudication due to chronic occlusive arterial disease of the limbs
Pentoxifylline (Trental) – hemorheologic agent; enhances RBC flexibility
Cilostazol (Pletal) – platelet aggregation inhibitor

- Even though pharmacologic therapy is added, nonpharmacologic measures must still be implemented for optimum benefit; nonpharmacologic treatment is more successful in treating the underlying disorder.

Slide 9

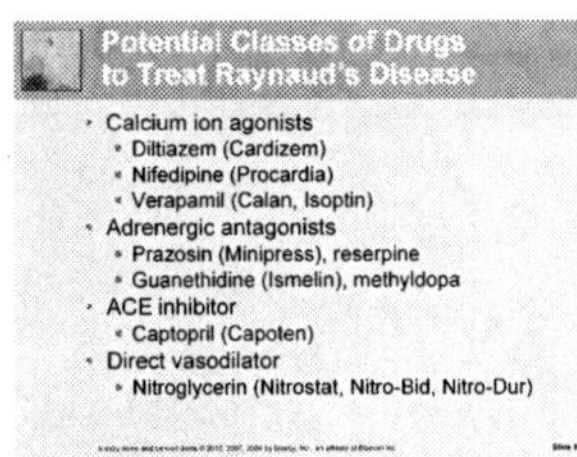
Potential Classes of Drugs to Treat Raynaud's Disease
Calcium ion agonists
Diltiazem (Cardizem)
Nifedipine (Procardia)
Verapamil (Calan, Isoptin)
Adrenergic antagonists
Prazosin (Minipress), reserpine
Guanethidine (Ismelin), methyldopa
ACE inhibitor
Captopril (Capoten)
Direct vasodilator
Nitroglycerin (Nitrostat, Nitro-Bid, Nitro-Dur)

- Nifedipine is the calcium ion agonist with the greatest success in reducing the occurrence of spasms.
- Captopril has been extensively studied and successful in reducing frequency and severity of attacks.
- Adrenergic antagonists have moderate success and many adverse effects.
- Nitroglycerin has adverse effects such as dizziness, headache, and hypotension.

Slide 10

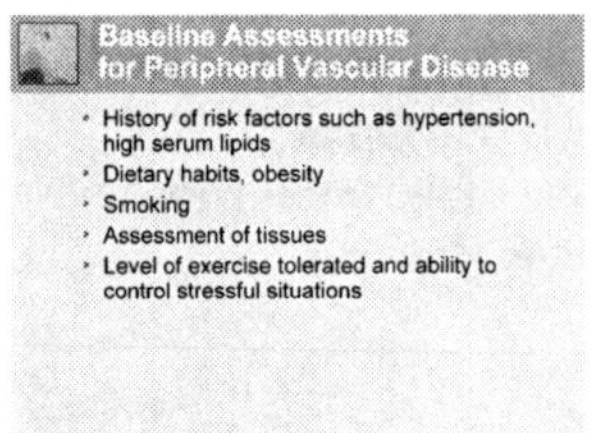
Baseline Assessments for Peripheral Vascular Disease
History of risk factors such as hypertension, high serum lipids
Dietary habits, obesity
Smoking
Assessment of tissues
Level of exercise tolerated and ability to control stressful situations

- Assessment of tissues includes oxygenation, temperature, edema, peripheral pulses, limb pain.

ELSEVIER

Slide 11

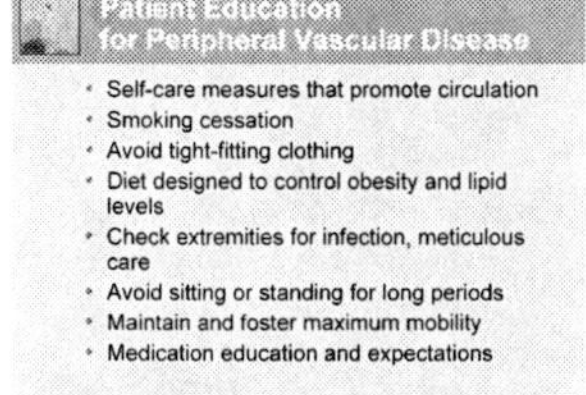
Patient Education for Peripheral Vascular Disease
Self-care measures that promote circulation
Smoking cessation
Avoid tight-fitting clothing
Diet designed to control obesity and lipid levels
Check extremities for infection, meticulous care
Avoid sitting or standing for long periods
Maintain and foster maximum mobility
Medication education and expectations

- Check with the health care provider before elevating extremities; it is contraindicated in patients with arterial insufficiency.
- Set short-term goals to control pain and symptoms.

Slide 12

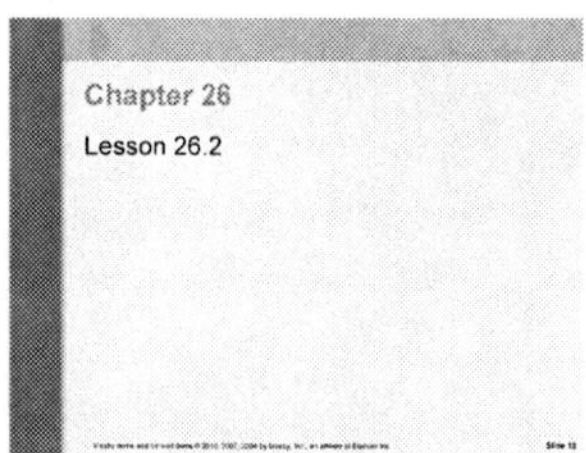
Chapter 26
Lesson 26.2

Slide 13

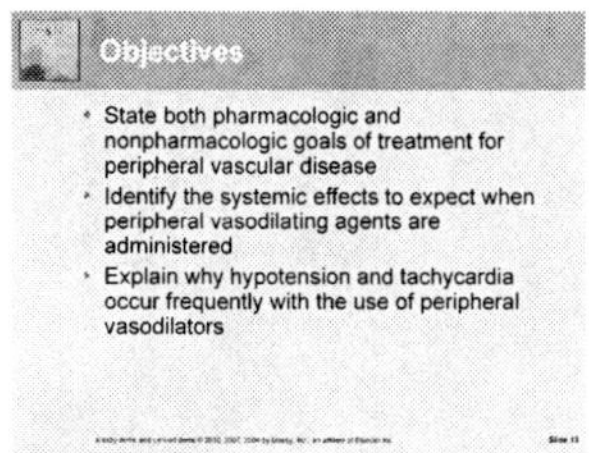
Objectives
State both pharmacologic and nonpharmacologic goals of treatment for peripheral vascular disease
Identify the systemic effects to expect when peripheral vasodilating agents are administered
Explain why hypotension and tachycardia occur frequently with the use of peripheral vasodilators

Slide 14

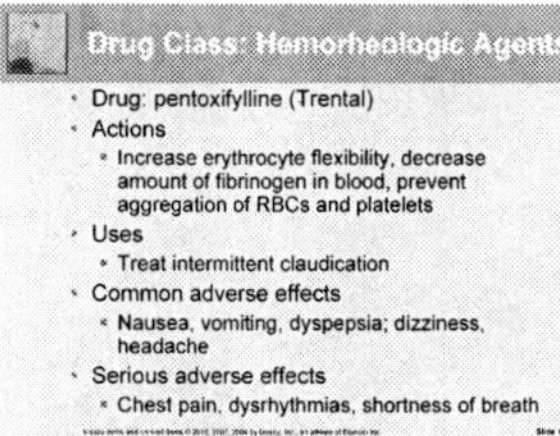
Drug Class: Hemorheologic Agents
Drug: pentoxifylline (Trental)
Actions
Increase erythrocyte flexibility, decrease amount of fibrinogen in blood, prevent aggregation of RBCs and platelets
Uses
Treat intermittent claudication
Common adverse effects
Nausea, vomiting, dyspepsia; dizziness, headache
Serious adverse effects
Chest pain, dysrhythmias, shortness of breath

- Decreases the viscosity of blood and improves tissue perfusion, which results in increased blood flow.

Slide 15

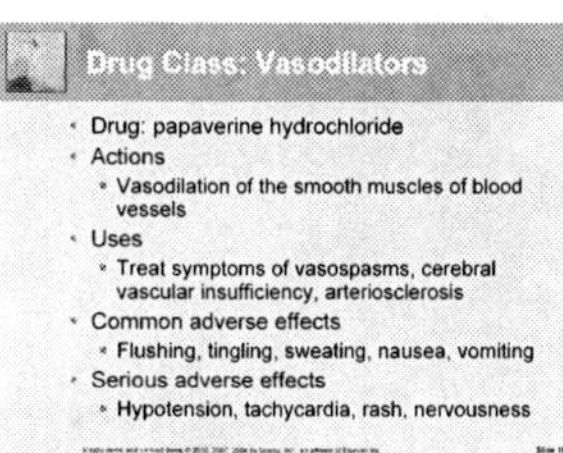
Drug Class: Vasodilators
Drug: papaverine hydrochloride
Actions
Vasodilation of the smooth muscles of blood vessels
Uses
Treat symptoms of vasospasms, cerebral vascular insufficiency, arteriosclerosis
Common adverse effects
Flushing, tingling, sweating, nausea, vomiting
Serious adverse effects
Hypotension, tachycardia, rash, nervousness

- Little objective evidence that papaverine has any therapeutic value.
- OTC cold and cough preparations may counteract its effect.

Slide 16

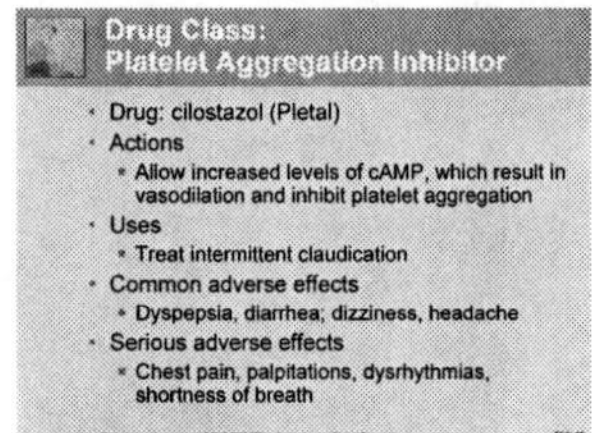
Drug Class:
Platelet Aggregation Inhibitor
Drug: cilostazol (Pletal)
Actions
Allow increased levels of cAMP, which result in vasodilation and inhibit platelet aggregation
Uses
Treat intermittent claudication
Common adverse effects
Dyspepsia, diarrhea; dizziness, headache
Serious adverse effects
Chest pain, palpitations, dysrhythmias, shortness of breath

- Therapeutic outcomes: improve tissue perfusion; reduce pain; improve tolerance of exercise; improve peripheral pulses.

27 Lesson Plan
Drugs Used to Treat Thromboembolic Disorders

TEACHING FOCUS

This chapter introduces the student to topics related to drugs used to treat thromboembolic disorders. Students will have the opportunity to become acquainted with thromboembolic diseases, appropriate drug therapy, and other treatments. Platelet inhibitors, anticoagulants, and fibrinolytic agents will be discussed. Students will also have the opportunity to become familiar with nursing care plans, including assessments, monitoring, administration, and patient education associated with anticoagulant therapies.

MATERIALS AND RESOURCES

- ☐ computer and PowerPoint projector (all Lessons)
- ☐ equipment for demonstration and student practice of medication administration (Lesson 27.2)

LESSON CHECKLIST

Preparations for this lesson include:

- lecture
- guest speaker: registered nurse
- evaluation of student knowledge and skills needed to perform all entry-level activities related to drugs used to treat thromboembolic disorders, including:
  - disease process associated with thromboembolic disorders
  - nursing process associated with anticoagulant therapy
  - mechanism of action, uses, and nursing process for platelet inhibitors, anticoagulants, and fibrinolytic agents

KEY TERMS

anticoagulants (p. 419)
embolus (p. 417)
extrinsic clotting pathway (p. 417)
intrinsic clotting pathway (p. 417)
platelet inhibitors (p. 419)
thromboembolic diseases (p. 417)
thrombolytic agents (p. 419)
thrombosis (p. 417)
thrombus (p. 417)

ADDITIONAL RESOURCES

PowerPoint slides: 1-20
Flashcards, Decks 1 and 2

Legend

ARQ	**PPT**	**TB**	**CTQ**	**SG**	**INRQ**
Audience Response Questions	PowerPoint Slides	Test Bank	Critical Thinking Questions	Study Guide	Interactive NCLEX Review Questions

Class Activities are indicated in ***bold italic.***

LESSON 27.1

BACKGROUND ASSESSMENT

Question: What is a thromboembolic disease? What are the main reasons that medications are given for thromboembolic disorders? What can occur if these medications are not administered?
Answer: Thromboembolic diseases are those associated with abnormal clotting within blood vessels. Medications are given for these disorders to prevent or manage the formation of blood clots that cause an obstruction to the blood flow. Clots can travel to the lungs, heart, and brain, resulting in serious illness or death if untreated.

Question: A patient on thrombolytic medication is being discharged from the hospital. What are some symptoms that the nurse should instruct the patient to watch for?
Answer: The nurse should instruct the patient to watch for nosebleeds, blood-tinged vomiting, excessive bruising, blood in the urine, cuts for which bleeding is difficult to control, and excessive menstrual flow. Because thrombolytic agents have a systemic effect, they can cause bleeding in other body systems. The symptoms mentioned here may indicate a need for a reduced dose of medication.

CRITICAL THINKING QUESTION

A 70-year-old woman is being discharged after treatment for a deep vein thrombosis of the left lower extremity. She states that she is worried and wants to know how she can prevent a recurrence. How should the nurse respond?
Guidelines: The nurse can tell the patient that although a recurrence cannot be predicted, she can take measures to reduce the risk. The nurse should encourage her to take regular walks and avoid sitting for long periods. For times when she cannot walk, the nurse should provide her with passive range-of-motion exercises to do several times a day. Suggest that she wear elastic stockings, called TEDS, to increase her lower extremity circulation. She should remove the stockings every 8 hours and check her skin for signs of breakdown. The nurse also can caution her to avoid activities that could cause trauma to the lower leg area (e.g., some types of yard work fall into this category). She also should drink at least eight glasses of water per day and avoid situations that impair circulation, such as wearing tight clothing, crossing her legs at the knees, or placing pillows under her knees when in bed. Suggest that if she travels by car, plane, or train to take walk breaks as often as possible. Describe the early signs and symptoms of deep vein thrombosis, and emphasize that she should call her health care provider immediately if she notices any changes.

OBJECTIVES	CONTENT	TEACHING RESOURCES
Describe conditions that place an individual at risk for developing blood clots.	■ Thromboembolic diseases (p. 417) Review the terms *thromboembolic diseases*, *embolus*, and *thrombosis*. Review the diseases caused by intravascular clotting: deep vein thrombosis, myocardial infarction, dysrhythmias with clot formation (atrial fibrillation), and coronary vasospasm.	PPT 5 SG Review Sheet questions 1-5 (p. 177) SG Learning Activities questions 1-2 (p. 179) ▸ Discuss thromboembolic diseases. List conditions that put an individual at risk for blood clots. Class Activity ***Lead a class discussion in which students identify health conditions that put individuals at risk for developing blood clots. Ask students these questions:*** – ***What happens in a clotting cascade?*** – ***How does each condition trigger a clotting cascade?*** – ***Differentiate between red thrombi and white thrombi.*** ***Allow class time to facilitate discussion on ways to prevent thromboembolic disease.***

OBJECTIVES	CONTENT	TEACHING RESOURCES
Analyze Figure 27-1 to identify the site of action of warfarin, heparin, and fibrinolytic agents.	■ Thromboembolic diseases (p. 417) ■ Treatment of thromboembolic diseases (p. 418) Describe the intrinsic and extrinsic clotting pathway as well as the coagulation cascade.	PPT 11 ARQ 1 TB Multiple Choice question 7 SG Learning Activities question 18 (p. 180) Figure 27-1 (p. 418): The clotting cascade. ▸ Discuss the treatment of thromboembolic diseases. Class Activity ***Divide the class into small groups, and ask each group to create a diagram showing intrinsic and extrinsic clotting pathways. Then ask each group to identify the sites of action for warfarin, heparin, and fibrinolytic agents.***
State the primary purposes of anticoagulant therapy.	■ Drug therapy for thromboembolic diseases (p. 419) Review the drug classes used to treat thromboembolic disease. Discuss the difference between drugs used to prevent formation of clots and drugs used to dissolve clots. Review the treatment goal when using these drugs. Discuss the techniques used to prevent clot formation and patient education to foster health maintenance.	PPT 7 TB Multiple Response question 2 SG Learning Activities question 19 ▸ Discuss the two main actions of thromboembolic drugs. Class Activity ***Present students with the following situations and ask (1) the purpose of anticoagulant therapy and (2) which class of drugs would most likely be prescribed:*** ***1. A 67-year-old man who has experienced myocardial infarction*** ***2. A 28-year-old woman with diabetes who has delivered a baby by cesarean section*** ***3. A 50-year-old obese man who has a broken hip*** ***4. A 35-year-old laborer who injured his leg on the job*** ***5. A 72-year-old man who has established peripheral artery disease***
Identify the effects of anticoagulant therapy on existing blood clots.	■ Drug therapy for thromboembolic diseases (p. 419)	TB Multiple Response question 3 SG Review Sheet question 7 (p. 177) Review Question for the NCLEX Examination 6 (p. 434) ▸ Discuss drug therapy for thromboembolic diseases. Describe the mechanism of action of platelet inhibitors, anticoagulants, and thrombolytic agents. Class Activity ***Have student pairs take turns role-playing a nurse and patient in the following scenario:***

OBJECTIVES	CONTENT	TEACHING RESOURCES
		A patient diagnosed with acute peripheral arterial embolism is prescribed heparin. The patient wants to know why he cannot just take aspirin for his condition. ***Have the nurse explain to the patient the expected therapeutic outcome of heparin and how it differs from aspirin. Ask volunteer pairs to present to the class for evaluation. Which approach was most informative? What did students learn?***
Explain laboratory data used to establish dosing of anticoagulant medications.	– Nursing process for anticoagulant therapy (p. 419) Review laboratory tests to assess the clotting process.	PPT 8 ARQ 4 TB Multiple Choice questions 3, 5 INRQ 2 CTQ 3 SG Review Sheet question 10 (p. 177) SG Learning Activities questions 9, 16-17 (p. 179) SG Practice Question for the NCLEX Examination 7 (p. 181) Review Question for the NCLEX Examination 5 (p. 433) ▶ Discuss laboratory data. Describe the purposes of white blood cell count (WBC), prothrombin time (PT), activated partial thromboplastin time (aPTT), and activated coagulation time. ▶ Discuss laboratory data. Note that the PT, reported as the international normalized ratio (INR), is commonly used to monitor warfarin therapy, and the aPTT is commonly used to monitor heparin therapy. Class Activity ***Divide the class into three groups, and assign each group one of the following diagnostic studies:*** – ***PT, aPTT, hematocrit, and platelet count*** – ***Doppler studies, exercise testing, and serum triglycerides*** – ***Arteriogram and cardiac enzyme studies*** ***Have students explain how the test is performed and how laboratory data is used to establish dosing of anticoagulant medications. What are the nurse's responsibilities? Have students make a brief report to the class. (For students to prepare for this activity, see Homework/Assignments 1.)***

OBJECTIVES	CONTENT	TEACHING RESOURCES
Describe procedures used to ensure that the correct dose of an anticoagulant is prepared and administered.	– Nursing process for anticoagulant therapy (p. 419)	PPT 9 CTQ 5 ▸ Discuss dosing and describe the use of the MAR. Emphasize that one-time dosages should be marked clearly. Emphasize that nurses should never administer an anticoagulant without first checking the chart for the most recent lab results. Class Activity ***Divide the class into three groups, and assign the groups one of the following drug classes. Have the group choose one specific drug from each class.*** ***– Platelet inhibitors (aspirin, dipyridamole, clopidogrel, ticlopidine)*** ***– Anticoagulants (dalteparin, enoxaparin, fondaparinux, heparin, tinzaparin, warfarin)*** ***– Fibrinolytic agents (streptokinase, urokinase, anistreplase, alteplase, reteplase, tenecteplase)*** ***Have each group outline a nursing care plan for administration of its chosen drug. For which conditions is this drug prescribed? How does the nursing care plan differ for different medical conditions? What measures are taken to ensure that the correct dose is prepared and administered? What is the nurse's role? Have students present to the class for feedback and discussion.***
Identify specific nursing interventions that can prevent clot formation.	– Nursing process for anticoagulant therapy (p. 419) Review nursing interventions intending to prevent clot formation	PPT 6 TB Multiple Choice question 9 SG Review Sheet questions 8-9 (p. 177) SG Learning Activities question 20 (p. 180) ▸ Discuss nursing interventions to prevent clot formation. List interventions, such as early ambulation after surgery, use of a turning schedule, and use of elastic hose. Class Activity ***Have small groups of students identify nursing interventions that can reduce the risk of clot formation in the following clinical situations:*** ***– Cardiac valve replacement*** ***– Stroke*** ***– Hip replacement surgery*** ***– Severe foot injury*** ***– Abdominal surgery***

OBJECTIVES	CONTENT	TEACHING RESOURCES
		Ask students to present to the class for feedback and discussion. Class Activity ***Divide the class into groups of five. Assign each group one of the five clinical conditions listed above. Have each group research the clinical indications of drug therapy and prepare an educational plan appropriate to that drug's therapy indicated for the prevention of clot formation for each condition.***
Develop objectives for patient education for patients receiving anticoagulant therapy.	– Patient education and health promotion (p. 420)	PPT 10 ARQ 3 TB Multiple Choice questions 10-11 TB Multiple Response question 3 INRQ 3, 8, 10 SG Review Sheet question 6 (p. 177) SG Learning Activities question 3 (p. 179) Review Questions for the NCLEX Examination 8, 10 (p. 434) ▸ Discuss patient education and health promotion. Emphasize diet limitations, adequate liquid intake, and level of exercise. ▸ Discuss patient education and health promotion, including dose, timing, common and serious adverse effects, drug interactions, and signs of internal bleeding. Class Activity ***Have pairs of students develop patient education objectives based on the following scenario:*** ***A 52-year-old woman who was diagnosed with a pulmonary embolism is being discharged on heparin therapy.*** ***Then have the students take turns role-playing a nurse explaining to the patient what she needs to know about the prescribed anticoagulant therapy. Select groups to present their objectives and role plays to the class for discussion. Ask students what they learned from the exercise.*** Class Activity ***As a class, develop a take-home informational brochure for patients who are receiving anticoagulant therapy. First, develop a list of teaching objectives that the brochure should achieve. Then draft key copy points. The copy points should include information***

OBJECTIVES	CONTENT	TEACHING RESOURCES
		about nutrition, exercise, activity, medication regimen, heath maintenance, and a written record for them to keep.

27.1 Homework/Assignments:
1. Divide the class into three groups, and assign each group one of the following diagnostic studies: (1) PT, aPTT, hematocrit, and platelet count; (2) Doppler studies, exercise testing, and serum triglycerides; and (3) arteriogram and cardiac enzyme studies. Have students explain how the test is performed and how laboratory data are used to establish dosing of anticoagulant medications. What are the nurse's responsibilities?

27.1 Instructor's Notes/Student Feedback:

LESSON 27.2

CRITICAL THINKING QUESTION

A 30-year-old man sustained a serious back injury from a motorcycle accident and is in traction. He is receiving 5000 units subcutaneous heparin twice daily, which he finds very uncomfortable. He asks why it is necessary and when it can be stopped. How should the nurse respond? How should the nurse administer the medication?

Guidelines: The nurse should explain that he is receiving a low dose of heparin prophylactically to prevent deep vein thrombosis, which is associated with prolonged immobility. When he is able to be out of bed and ambulating, the medication will be discontinued. Before administering the heparin, the nurse should check his last PTT laboratory value to make sure that it is within the prescribed range. If abnormal, the nurse should not administer the medication and report the value to the charge nurse and health care provider. The nurse should evaluate the technique for administering the injection. The nurse should select a 26- or 27-gauge, ½-inch needle to use for the injection. The nurse should confirm medication, amount, and needle size with another nurse, which is a routine safety practice at most hospitals. The nurse should cleanse an area 2 inches away from the umbilicus, grasp the area firmly, and insert the needle at a 90-degree angle. Aspiration and massage should not be performed; gentle pressure may be applied to control local bleeding after administration. The nurse should document the medication administration and the site used.

OBJECTIVES	CONTENT	TEACHING RESOURCES
State the nursing assessments needed to monitor therapeutic response and development of common and serious adverse effects from anticoagulant therapy.	□ Drug class: Platelet inhibitors (p. 421) – Nursing process for aspirin therapy (p. 421) – Nursing process for dipyridamole (p. 422) – Nursing process for clopidogrel (p. 422) – Nursing process for ticlopidine (p. 423)	PPT 15-18 TB Multiple Choice questions 4, 8 TB Multiple Response question 1 INRQ 4-5, 9 CTQ 1-2, 4 Patient Self-Assessment Form: Anticoagulants SG Review Sheet questions 11-15, 22 (p. 178)

OBJECTIVES	CONTENT	TEACHING RESOURCES
	□ Drug class: Anticoagulants (p. 424) – Nursing process for dalteparin (p. 424) – Nursing process for enoxaparin (p. 425) – Nursing process for fondaparinux (p. 426) – Nursing process for heparin (p. 428) Review the drugs in the anticoagulants drug class: dalteparin, enoxaparin, fondaparinux, heparin, tinzaparin, and warfarin. Discuss the actions, uses, and therapeutic outcomes of each drug as well as adverse effects and drug interactions for the drugs heparin and warfarin (Coumadin). Also, review their antidotes.	SG Learning Activities questions 4-5, 12-14, 21-25 (pp. 179-180) SG Practice Questions for the NCLEX Examination 1-3, 5, 9-11 (pp. 181-182) Review Questions for the NCLEX Examination 3, 9 (pp. 433-434) ▸ Discuss platelet inhibitors, including their actions, uses, and therapeutic outcomes. Review issues related to the premedication assessment, planning, and implementation. ▸ Discuss anticoagulants. Discuss actions, uses, and therapeutic outcomes. Review premedication assessment, planning, implementation, and evaluation. Class Activity ***Divide the class into groups, and assign each group one or two of the following anticoagulants: aspirin, dipyridamole, clopidogrel, ticlopidine, dalteparin, enoxaparin, and fondaparinux. Ask each group to prepare a brief report to the class for its assigned drug(s) regarding premedication assessment, planning, implementation, common and serious adverse effects, and drug interactions.*** Class Activity ***Ask volunteers to provide answers to the following:*** – ***Name three drugs used to prevent deep vein thrombosis after hip surgery.*** – ***Name a drug used to prevent thromboembolism after a cardiac valve replacement.*** – ***Name a drug that reduces the risk of additional atherosclerotic events in patients who have had a stroke.*** – ***Name a drug used to treat a pulmonary embolism.*** – ***Name a drug that works by inhibiting the action of vitamin K.***
Explain the specific procedures and techniques used to administer heparin subcutaneously via intermittent administration through a heparin lock and via intravenous (IV) infusion.	– Nursing process for heparin (p. 428)	PPT 17 ARQ 5 TB Multiple Choice question 2 TB Multiple Response question 4 INRQ 11-12, 14 Animation: Heparin for Acute Coronary Syndrome Animation: Heparin for Atrial Fibrillation

OBJECTIVES	CONTENT	TEACHING RESOURCES
		SG Learning Activities question 6 (p. 179) SG Practice Questions for the NCLEX Examination 4, 12-13 (pp. 181-182) Review Questions for the NCLEX Examination 1-2 (p. 433) Figure 27-2 (p. 428): Sites of heparin administration. ▸ Discuss procedures and techniques associated with the different routes of heparin administration. Class Activity ***Demonstrate how to draw up heparin and administer it using normal saline and an orange. Then have students practice the procedure. Have students look up laboratory values and follow proper safety procedures. Discuss the demonstration and practice as a class, and have students share what they learned and any problems they encountered.*** Class Activity ***Demonstrate how to administer heparin through a heparin lock and with a continuous IV infusion. Then divide the class into groups or pairs, and have them practice each procedure. Give each group a different amount to administer, and have students show their math calculations. Discuss as a class, and invite questions.***
Identify the purpose, dosing determination, and scheduling factors associated with the use of protamine sulfate.	– Nursing process for heparin (p. 428)	TB Multiple Choice question 1 INRQ 6 SG Review Sheet question 16 (p. 178) SG Learning Activities question 7 (p. 179) ▸ Discuss protamine sulfate and its judicious use in neutralizing heparin. Class Activity ***Lead a discussion in which students describe the intended use of protamine sulfate, how the dosage is determined, and when it is given. What are the nurse's responsibilities regarding assessment and monitoring? What are appropriate nursing interventions?***
State the nursing assessments needed to monitor therapeutic response and	– Nursing process for tinzaparin (p. 430) – Nursing process for warfarin (p. 431)	TB Multiple Choice question 12 SG Review Sheet questions 17-18 (p. 178) SG Learning Activities question 11 (p. 179)

OBJECTIVES	CONTENT	TEACHING RESOURCES
development of common and serious adverse effects from anticoagulant therapy.		SG Practice Questions for the NCLEX Examination 6, 14 (pp. 181-182) ▸ Discuss tinzaparin. Discuss its action, uses, and therapeutic outcomes. Review issues related to the premedication assessment, planning, and implementation. ▸ Discuss warfarin. Discuss its action, uses, and therapeutic outcomes. Review issues related to the premedication assessment, planning, and implementation. Class Activity ***Present students with the following groups of adverse effects, and have them identify which anticoagulant(s) are associated with each one. Then ask students what assessments the nurse should perform to monitor the intended therapeutic outcome and adverse effects. Which adverse effects should patients report? What patient education is appropriate?*** – ***Dizziness, abdominal distress*** – ***Neutropenia, agranulocytosis*** – ***Nausea, vomiting, anorexia, diarrhea*** – ***Bleeding*** – ***Hematoma, bleeding at injection site*** – ***Thrombocytopenia*** Class Activity ***Invite a nurse who has experience caring for patients who have received anticoagulant drug therapy to discuss practical aspects of nursing care. Ask the nurse to discuss the most common challenges faced by RNs and LPNs and/or LVNs. Where are there opportunities for error? How does nursing care in the hospital differ from home-based and office care? What patient education is most effective? Ask students to prepare questions in advance.***
Describe specific monitoring procedures to detect hemorrhage in the patient taking anticoagulants.	– Nursing process for warfarin (p. 431)	SG Learning Activities question 10 (p. 179) ▸ Discuss the therapeutic outcomes of warfarin. What is a risk? What is an antidote? Class Activity ***Lead a discussion in which students identify assessments and monitoring that the nurse should perform to determine if a patient taking warfarin is hemorrhaging. What body sites should be checked? What signs and symptoms should the nurse note? What interventions are appropriate?***

OBJECTIVES	CONTENT	TEACHING RESOURCES
State the nursing assessments needed to monitor therapeutic response and development of common and serious adverse effects from anticoagulant therapy.	□ Drug class: Glycoprotein IIb/IIIa inhibitors (p. 432) □ Drug class: Fibrinolytic agents (p. 432)	PPT 19-20 ARQ 2 TB Multiple Choice question 6 INRQ 1, 7 SG Review Sheet questions 19-20 (p. 178) SG Learning Activities question 8 (p. 179) SG Practice Question for the NCLEX Examination 8 (p. 182) Review Questions for the NCLEX Examination 4, 7 (pp. 433-434) ▸ Discuss fibrinolytic agents. Discuss their actions, uses, and therapeutic outcomes. List the six fibrinolytic agents. ▸ Discuss glycoprotein IIb/IIIa and its use during percutaneous coronary intervention procedures. Class Activity ***Have two students role-play the nurse educating the patient taking dalteparin. Have the class assist the "nurse" in teaching the "patient" about self-injections for dalteparin. Review with the class therapeutic outcomes and common and adverse effects for anticoagulants.***
Performance evaluation		Test Bank SG Learning Activities (pp. 179-180) SG Practice Questions for the NCLEX Examination (pp. 181-182) Critical Thinking Questions

27.2 Homework/Assignments:

27.2 Instructor's Notes/Student Feedback:

Lecture Outline

27 Drugs Used to Treat Thromboembolic Disorders

Slide 1

Chapter 27
Drugs Used to Treat
Thromboembolic Disorders

Slide 2

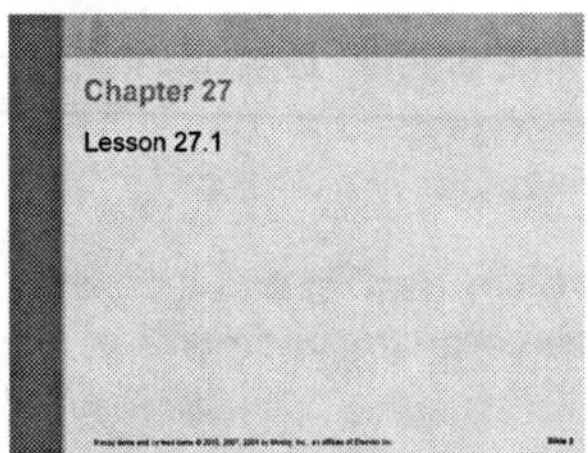
Chapter 27
Lesson 27.1

Slide 3

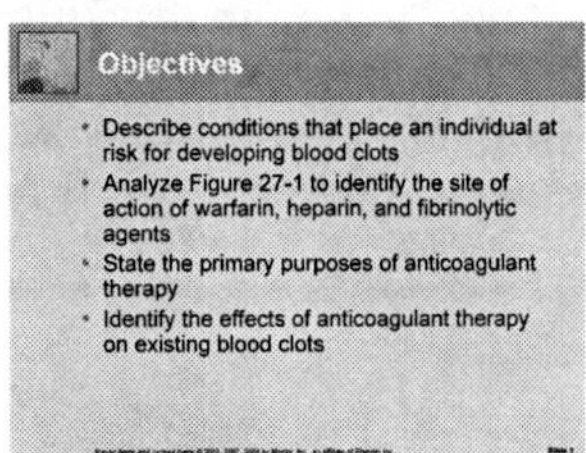
Objectives
Describe conditions that place an individual at risk for developing blood clots
Analyze Figure 27-1 to identify the site of action of warfarin, heparin, and fibrinolytic agents
State the primary purposes of anticoagulant therapy
Identify the effects of anticoagulant therapy on existing blood clots

Slide 4

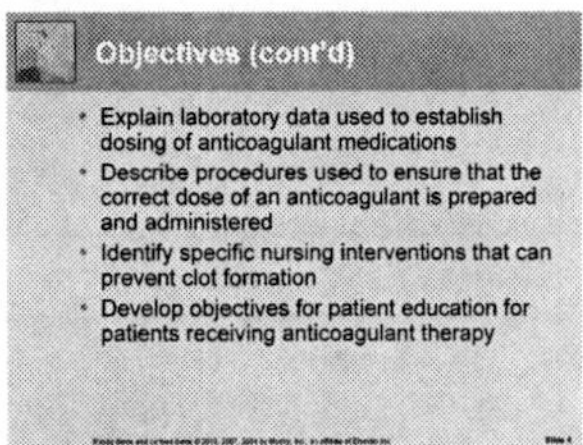
Objectives (cont'd)
Explain laboratory data used to establish dosing of anticoagulant medications
Describe procedures used to ensure that the correct dose of an anticoagulant is prepared and administered
Identify specific nursing interventions that can prevent clot formation
Develop objectives for patient education for patients receiving anticoagulant therapy

Slide 5

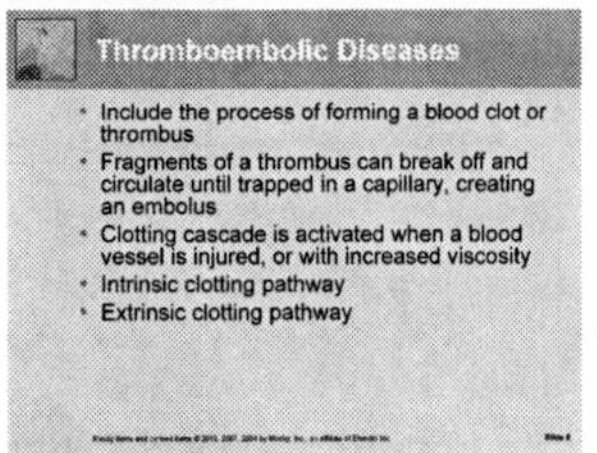
Thromboembolic Diseases
Include the process of forming a blood clot or thrombus
Fragments of a thrombus can break off and circulate until trapped in a capillary, creating an embolus
Clotting cascade is activated when a blood vessel is injured, or with increased viscosity
Intrinsic clotting pathway
Extrinsic clotting pathway

- Intrinsic clotting pathway is activated when there is damage to the blood vessel.
- Extrinsic clotting pathway is activated when there is damage outside of the blood vessels, usually to tissues.

ELSEVIER

Slide 6

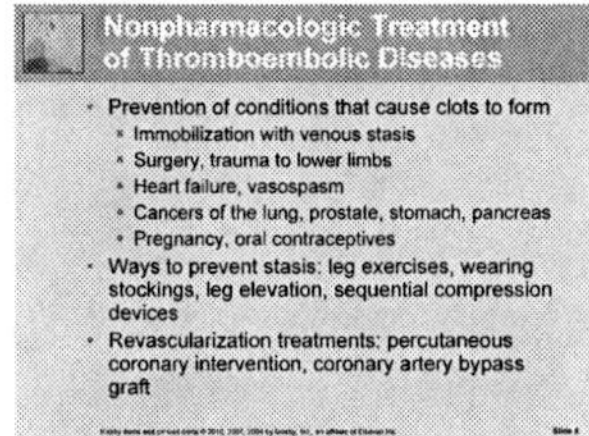
Nonpharmacologic Treatment of Thromboembolic Diseases
Prevention of conditions that cause clots to form
Immobilization with venous stasis
Surgery, trauma to lower limbs
Heart failure, vasospasm
Cancers of the lung, prostate, stomach, pancreas
Pregnancy, oral contraceptives
Ways to prevent stasis: leg exercises, wearing stockings, leg elevation, sequential compression devices
Revascularization treatments: percutaneous coronary intervention, coronary artery bypass graft

- Prevention is the best treatment.
- Patients need early, regular ambulation after surgery; develop and follow a turning schedule for patients on bed rest.

Slide 7

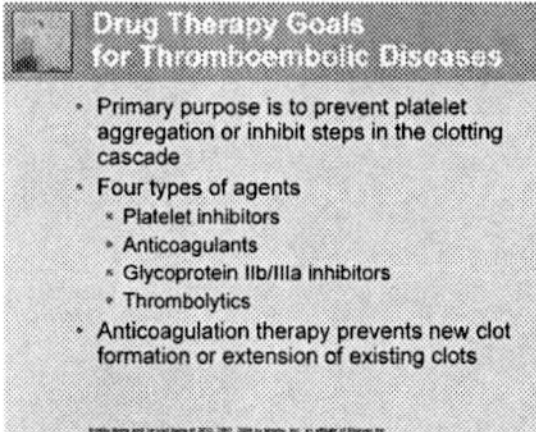
Drug Therapy Goals for Thromboembolic Diseases
Primary purpose is to prevent platelet aggregation or inhibit steps in the clotting cascade
Four types of agents
Platelet inhibitors
Anticoagulants
Glycoprotein IIb/IIIa inhibitors
Thrombolytics
Anticoagulation therapy prevents new clot formation or extension of existing clots

- Anticoagulants do not dissolve clots; only thrombolytics do this.
- Platelet inhibitors prevent platelet aggregation and can prevent stroke and heart attack.

Slide 8

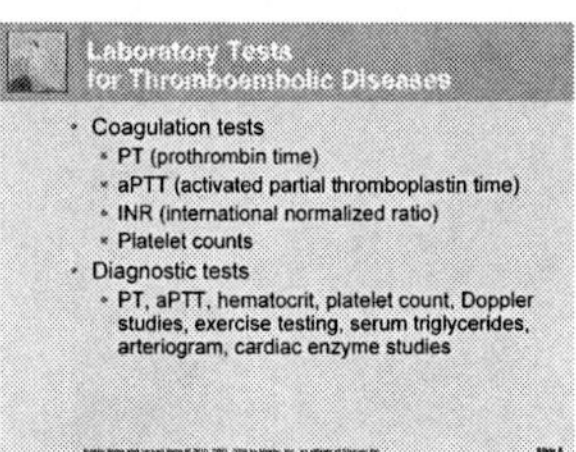
Laboratory Tests for Thromboembolic Diseases
Coagulation tests
PT (prothrombin time)
aPTT (activated partial thromboplastin time)
INR (international normalized ratio)
Platelet counts
Diagnostic tests
PT, aPTT, hematocrit, platelet count, Doppler studies, exercise testing, serum triglycerides, arteriogram, cardiac enzyme studies

- PT evaluates the adequacy of the extrinsic system.
- aPTT evaluates the intrinsic coagulation system.
- PT and INR determine the adequacy of warfarin doses.

Slide 9

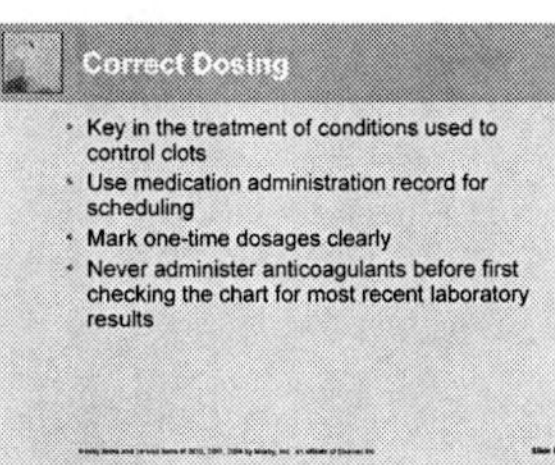
Correct Dosing
Key in the treatment of conditions used to control clots
Use medication administration record for scheduling
Mark one-time dosages clearly
Never administer anticoagulants before first checking the chart for most recent laboratory results

- Anticoagulants must be administered on schedule exactly as directed, and not in larger, more frequent doses for longer than the prescribed time. Taking too much medication can cause severe bleeding.

Slide 10

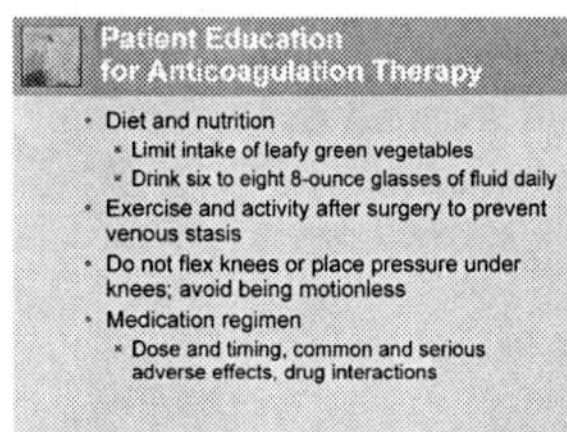
Patient Education for Anticoagulation Therapy
Diet and nutrition
Limit intake of leafy green vegetables
Drink six to eight 8-ounce glasses of fluid daily
Exercise and activity after surgery to prevent venous stasis
Do not flex knees or place pressure under knees; avoid being motionless
Medication regimen
Dose and timing, common and serious adverse effects, drug interactions

- High intake of leafy green vegetables may interfere with the effectiveness of anticoagulants; they contain vitamin K, which is used as an antidote for high doses of warfarin.

ELSEVIER

Slide 11

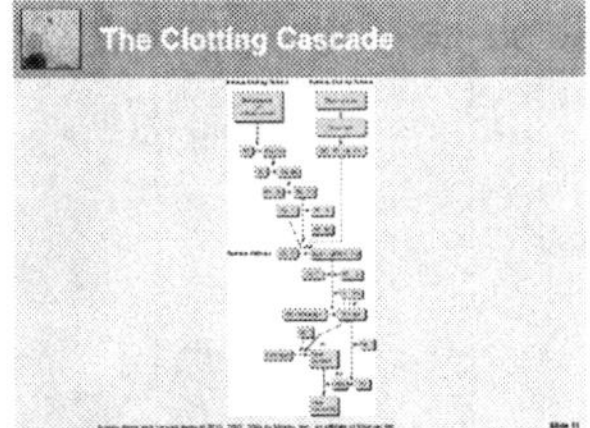
The Clotting Cascade

- Heparin prevents fibrin clots from becoming insoluble, but will not cause the clot to dissolve or be destroyed.
- Warfarin inhibits vitamin K activity, which activates clotting factors II, VII, IX, and X.
- Fibrinolytic agents stimulate the body to convert plasminogen to plasmin, which digests fibrin.

Slide 12

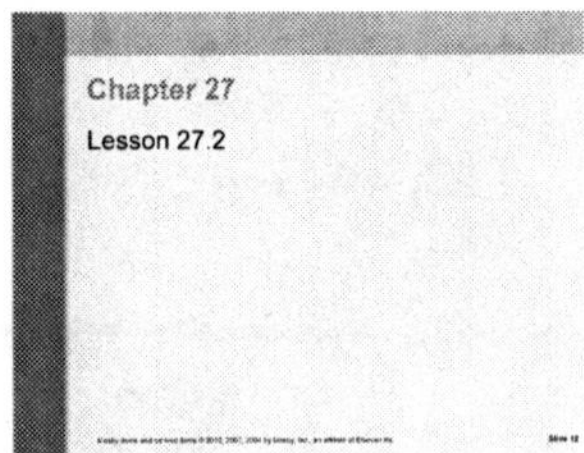
Chapter 27
Lesson 27.2

Slide 13

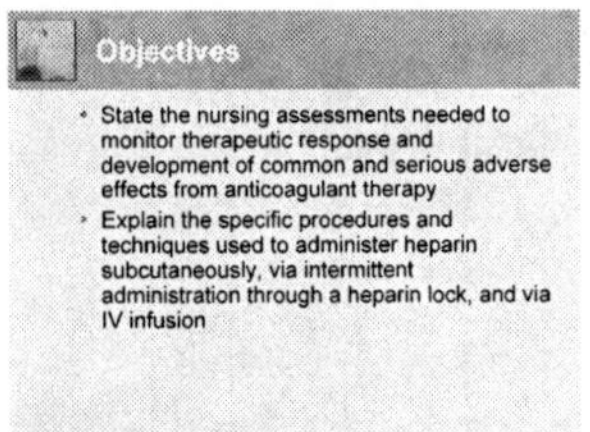
Objectives
State the nursing assessments needed to monitor therapeutic response and development of common and serious adverse effects from anticoagulant therapy
Explain the specific procedures and techniques used to administer heparin subcutaneously, via intermittent administration through a heparin lock, and via IV infusion

Slide 14

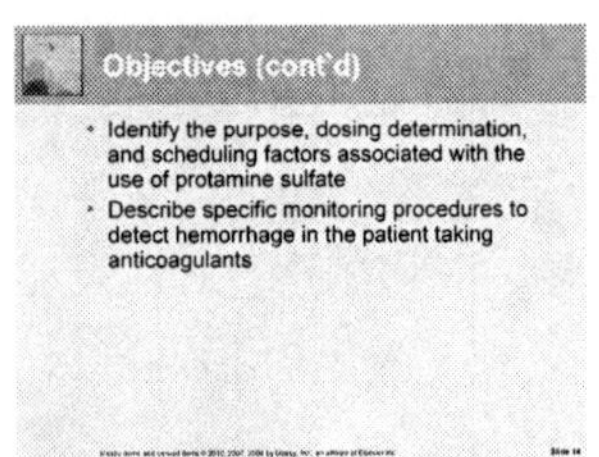
Objectives (cont'd)
Identify the purpose, dosing determination, and scheduling factors associated with the use of protamine sulfate
Describe specific monitoring procedures to detect hemorrhage in the patient taking anticoagulants

Slide 15

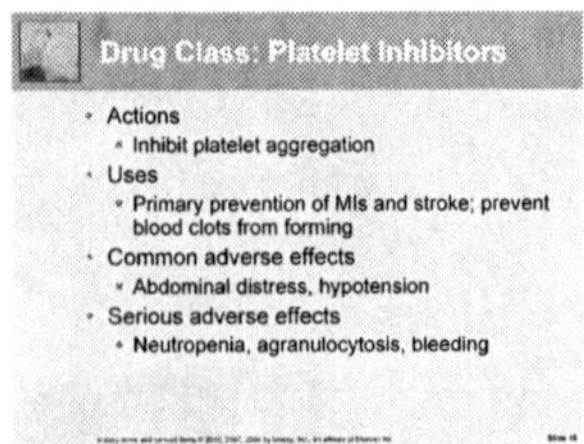
Drug Class: Platelet Inhibitors
Actions
Inhibit platelet aggregation
Uses
Primary prevention of MIs and stroke; prevent blood clots from forming
Common adverse effects
Abdominal distress, hypotension
Serious adverse effects
Neutropenia, agranulocytosis, bleeding

- Drugs: aspirin, dipyridamole (Persantine), clopidogrel (Plavix), ticlopidine (Ticlid).
- Recent research indicates aspirin is beneficial for men in preventing MI, and women taking aspirin have lower rates of stroke.

Slide 16

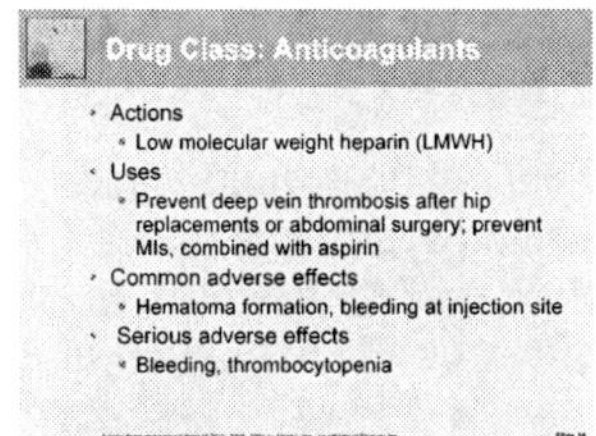
Drug Class: Anticoagulants
Actions
Low molecular weight heparin (LMWH)
Uses
Prevent deep vein thrombosis after hip replacements or abdominal surgery; prevent MIs, combined with aspirin
Common adverse effects
Hematoma formation, bleeding at injection site
Serious adverse effects
Bleeding, thrombocytopenia

- Drugs: dalteparin (Fragmin), enoxaparin (Lovenox), fondaparinux (Arixtra), tinzaparin (Innohep), warfarin (Coumadin)
- Administered subcutaneously only.
- Fondaparinux is a selective factor Xa inhibitor, not a LMWH.

Slide 17

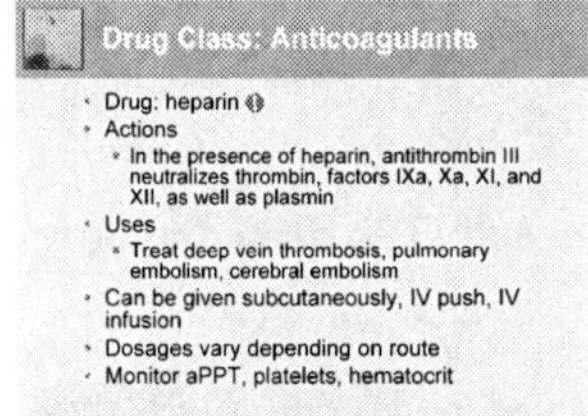
Drug Class: Anticoagulants
Drug: heparin
Actions
In the presence of heparin, antithrombin III neutralizes thrombin, factors IXa, Xa, XI, and XII, as well as plasmin
Uses
Treat deep vein thrombosis, pulmonary embolism, cerebral embolism
Can be given subcutaneously, IV push, IV infusion
Dosages vary depending on route
Monitor aPPT, platelets, hematocrit

- Common adverse effects: hematoma formation, bleeding at injection site
- Serious adverse effects: bleeding, thrombocytopenia
- Antidote for heparin is protamine sulfate.

Slide 18

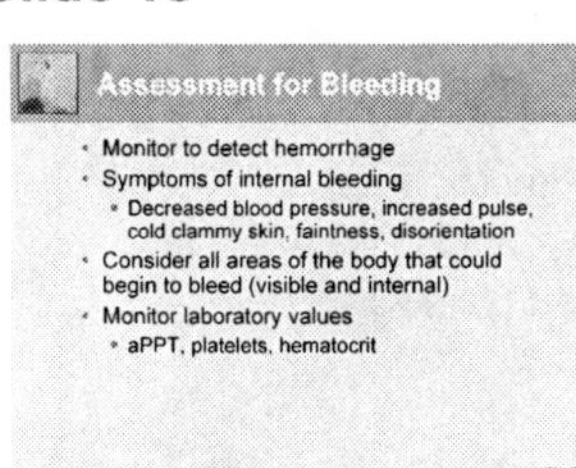
Assessment for Bleeding
Monitor to detect hemorrhage
Symptoms of internal bleeding
Decreased blood pressure, increased pulse, cold clammy skin, faintness, disorientation
Consider all areas of the body that could begin to bleed (visible and internal)
Monitor laboratory values
aPPT, platelets, hematocrit

- Areas of the body that may bleed: skin, mucous membranes, blood in urine, blood in stools (melena), menstrual flow, dressings and drainage tubes.

Slide 19

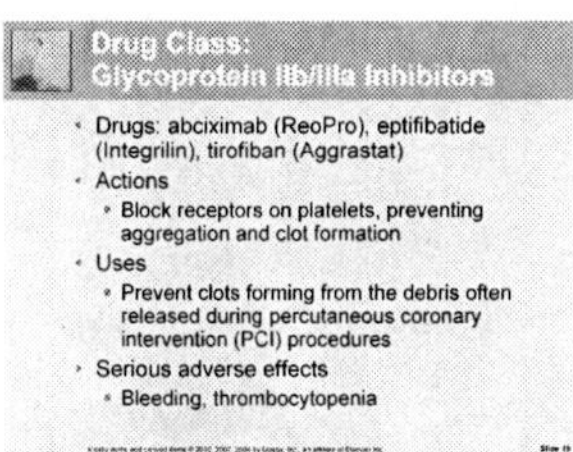
Drug Class:
Glycoprotein IIb/IIIa Inhibitors
Drugs: abciximab (ReoPro), eptifibatide (Integrilin), tirofiban (Aggrastat)
Actions
Block receptors on platelets, preventing aggregation and clot formation
Uses
Prevent clots forming from the debris often released during percutaneous coronary intervention (PCI) procedures
Serious adverse effects
Bleeding, thrombocytopenia

- Laboratory values to monitor: hematocrit, platelet counts, ACT.

Slide 20

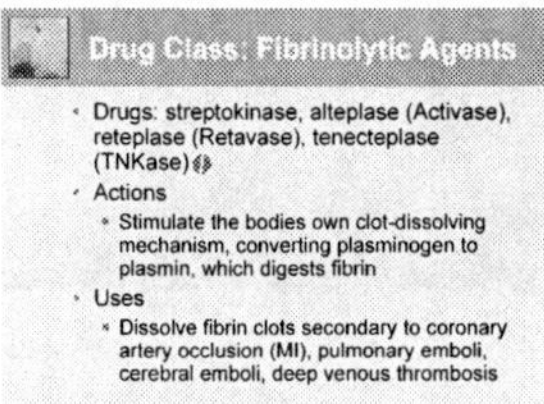
Drug Class: Fibrinolytic Agents
Drugs: streptokinase, alteplase (Activase), reteplase (Retavase), tenecteplase (TNKase)
Actions
Stimulate the bodies own clot-dissolving mechanism, converting plasminogen to plasmin, which digests fibrin
Uses
Dissolve fibrin clots secondary to coronary artery occlusion (MI), pulmonary emboli, cerebral emboli, deep venous thrombosis

- Streptokinase is still available but rarely used.
- Act during early phase of clot formation, limiting damage to surrounding tissues.
- Serious adverse effects: increased risk of bleeding, allergic reactions.

28 Lesson Plan

Drugs Used to Treat Heart Failure

TEACHING FOCUS

In this chapter, students will have the opportunity to learn the causes and treatments of heart failure and the different types of drug therapy available. Students will be introduced to signs and symptoms of heart disease and will review the process for assessing a patient for indications of altered cardiac function. In addition, this chapter will also discuss the four classes of drug therapy, their actions, and how to monitor the administration of these drugs. Patient education and health promotion will also be discussed.

MATERIALS AND RESOURCES

☐ computer and PowerPoint projector (all Lessons)

LESSON CHECKLIST

Preparations for this lesson include:

- lecture
- evaluation of student knowledge and skills required to perform all entry-level activities related to drugs used to treat heart failure, including:
  - causes, signs, and symptoms of congestive heart failure
  - the primary actions on the cardiac output of digoxin, ACE inhibitors, nitrates, and calcium channel blockers
  - essential assessment data and nursing interventions associated with heart failure
  - safety precautions and adverse effects associated with drugs used to treat heart failure

KEY TERMS

diastolic dysfunction (p. 435)
digitalis toxicity (p. 442)
digitalization (p. 443)
inotropic agents (p. 437)
negative chronotropy (p. 443)
positive inotropy (p. 443)
systolic dysfunction (p. 435)

ADDITIONAL RESOURCES

PowerPoint slides: 1-15
Flashcards, Decks 1 and 2

Legend

ARQ	PPT	TB	CTQ	SG	INRQ
Audience Response Questions	PowerPoint Slides	Test Bank	Critical Thinking Questions	Study Guide	Interactive NCLEX Review Questions

Class Activities are indicated in ***bold italic.***

LESSON 28.1

BACKGROUND ASSESSMENT

Question: What is systolic dysfunction, and what are the symptoms?
Answer: Systolic dysfunction is the most common cause of heart failure. Systolic heart failure occurs when the heart cannot pump enough blood to support the body's needs for oxygen and nutrients. Early symptoms of systolic dysfunction are decreased exercise tolerance and poor perfusion to the peripheral tissues, which may include symptoms such as weakness, confusion, and mottling of the extremities. Other signs and

ELSEVIER

symptoms can include weight gain, hypotension, tachycardia, dyspnea, orthopnea, and paroxysmal nocturnal dyspnea.

Question: What nursing interventions should be performed for a patient with heart failure?
Answer: For a patient with heart failure, nursing interventions should include administering medications safely and accurately, monitoring vital signs, and notifying the health care provider of hypotension. The nurse should monitor daily weights, urine output, and laboratory values, and assess the patient for dyspnea, chest pain, fatigue, edema, syncope, and palpitations. The nurse should also teach the patient how to use a high Fowler's position to maximize lung expansion and emphasize the dietary restrictions, such as sodium and salt substitutes (when potassium-sparing diuretics are given). Mental status and coping mechanisms in times of stress should also be assessed and discussed.

CRITICAL THINKING QUESTION

A man hospitalized for heart failure is being discharged to home. What instructions should the nurse provide for him and his family to monitor his condition?
Guidelines: The nurse should emphasize to the patient that his condition is lifelong and that he will need to be compliant in taking his medication and adhering to his diet and exercise regimens. Explain to the patient and his family that they need to be aware of the symptoms that will alert them to changes in his condition and that they should know when to notify the health care provider. Symptoms such as dyspnea, a productive cough, worsening fatigue, edema of the feet, weight gain of more than 2 pounds in 2 days, angina, palpitations, and confusion should be reviewed. The patient should also be encouraged to measure his blood pressure and weight daily and to assume the high Fowler's position if dyspnea does occur. The importance of good skin care, pacing his activities to prevent fatigue, and meeting with nutritionists for his diet plan should also be discussed.

OBJECTIVES	CONTENT	TEACHING RESOURCES
Summarize the pathophysiology of heart failure, including the body's compensatory mechanisms.	■ Heart failure (p. 435) Review the statistics associated with heart failure and the definitions of systolic and diastolic dysfunction. Discuss the pathophysiology of heart failure and the effects on other organ systems when perfusion of blood is inadequate.	PPT 4-5 ARQ 2, 4 TB Multiple Response question 4 Animation: Heart Failure and Pulmonary Edema SG Review Sheet questions 1-5 (p. 183) Review Question for the NCLEX Examination 4 (p. 448) Box 28-1: Clinical and Laboratory Presentation of Heart Failure (p. 437) Figure 28-1 (p. 436): Pathway for how heart failure develops. Figure 28-2 (p. 439): Stages in the development and treatment of heart failure. ▸ Discuss the symptoms of heart failure. What type of patient is most at risk? ▸ Discuss the role of the sympathetic nervous system in the body's compensatory mechanism. How does the body react to overcome inadequate heart output? Class Activity ***Divide the class into two groups. Have a diagram on the board of the circulatory system, and have students from each group***

OBJECTIVES	CONTENT	TEACHING RESOURCES
		take turns describing the circulation. Give points for correct answers. Then have the group with the most points describe several causes of heart failure, while the other group describes the effect of heart failure on the body. Review the exercise with the class. Class Activity ***Divide the class into groups. Assign each group one of the following causes of heart failure: systolic dysfunction or diastolic dysfunction. Have each group describe why the assigned dysfunction occurs, how it leads to heart failure, and what its signs and symptoms are. Have groups share their findings with the class.***
Identify the goals of treatment of heart failure.	■ Treatment of heart failure (p. 436) ■ Drug therapy for heart failure (p. 437) Review the terms *inotropy* and *chronotropy*. Discuss the New York Heart Association Functional Classification System used to determine the degree of heart failure (Table 28-1).	PPT 6-7 CTQ 4 SG Review Sheet questions 6-9, 11 (pp. 183-184) SG Learning Activities question 1 (p. 186) SG Practice Question for the NCLEX Examination 5 (p. 187) Table 28-1: New York Heart Association Functional Classification System (p. 438) ▸ Discuss the different classifications of patients with heart failure. What is the difference between functional capacity and objective assessment? Class Activity ***Divide the class into groups. Have each group outline the treatment options for heart failure, and identify the goals of each treatment. How do the goals differ for the different classes of patients? Have groups share their findings with the class, and encourage discussions regarding their rationale for findings and nursing care.***
Identify essential assessment data, nursing interventions, and health teaching needed for a patient with heart failure.	– Nursing process for heart failure therapy (p. 438) – Patient education and health promotion (p. 441) Review the treatment goals for inotropic agents used in heart failure. Discuss the six cardinal signs of heart disease. Review the indicators of altered cardiac function, including vital signs and	PPT 8 TB Multiple Choice questions 10-13 TB Multiple Response questions 1, 3 INRQ 4 Patient Self-Assessment Form: Cardiovascular Agents SG Review Sheet questions 12-13 (p. 184) SG Practice Questions for the NCLEX Examination 4, 6-7 (p. 187)

OBJECTIVES	CONTENT	TEACHING RESOURCES
	assessments as well as laboratory values. Discuss patient education and health promotion measures necessary to foster adherence to drug regimen.	Review Question for the NCLEX Examination 8 (p. 448) ▸ Discuss what you would tell a patient about intervention and lifestyle changes that may be needed to stabilize a patient's condition. ▸ Discuss the six cardinal signs of cardiovascular disease. What questions would you ask a patient when assessing the possibility of heart failure? Class Activity ***Lead a class discussion about heart failure therapy, and ask students to identify questions that the nurse should ask during the initial assessment. Record student responses on the board for comparison.*** Class Activity ***Divide the class into groups. Have each group develop a teaching plan that outlines the dietary and exercise guidelines for a patient with heart failure. Students should include foods and activities that are beneficial and those that are harmful. Have each group present its findings to the class for discussion.***

28.1 Homework/Assignments:

28.1 Instructor's Notes/Student Feedback:

LESSON 28.2

CRITICAL THINKING QUESTION

A 73-year-old woman who is taking 0.25 mg of digoxin and 20 mg of furosemide daily complains of nausea and asks if she can take an antacid to calm her upset stomach. How should the nurse respond?
Guidelines: Nausea is an early symptom of digoxin toxicity; this patient should be evaluated. The nurse should take her apical pulse for a full minute and check for dysrhythmias or bradycardia before administering digoxin. The nurse should also check the potassium level because toxicity is more likely if the patient is hypokalemic from the diuretic therapy. The nurse should explain to the patient that digoxin and antacids cannot be taken together because the antacids will reduce the digoxin's therapeutic effects. If the assessment data points to digoxin toxicity, the health care provider should be notified.

OBJECTIVES	CONTENT	TEACHING RESOURCES
State the primary actions on heart failure of digoxin, angiotensin-converting enzyme inhibitors, beta blockers, aldosterone antagonists, nitrates, and calcium channel blockers.	□ Drug class: Digitalis glycosides (p. 443)	PPT 11 ARQ 3 TB Multiple Choice question 7 INRQ 1, 5 CTQ 2-3 SG Review Sheet question 14 (p. 184) SG Learning Activities question 2 (p. 186) Review Questions for the NCLEX Examination 5-6, 9 (p. 448) Figure 28-3 (p. 440): Medicines that reduce preload and afterload to reduce heart failure. ▸ Discuss the net result of improved circulation in digoxin therapy. Class Activity ***Divide the class into small groups. Assign each group one of the following types of drugs:*** – ***Digoxin*** – ***ACE inhibitors*** – ***Beta blockers*** – ***Aldosterone antagonists*** – ***Nitrates*** – ***Calcium channel blockers*** ***Have groups explain how the drugs work to treat heart failure.***
Explain the process of digitalizing a patient, including the initial dosage, preparation, and administration of the medication, as well as the nursing assessments needed to monitor therapeutic response and digoxin toxicity.	– Nursing process for digoxin (p. 443) Review the action, use, and therapeutic outcome of digoxin. Discuss digitalization and digoxin toxicity as well as the antidote for digoxin toxicity. Review the premedication assessment of taking an apical pulse prior to administration.	TB Multiple Choice questions 1, 3, 5-6 INRQ 2, 7-8 CTQ 1 SG Review Sheet questions 15-16, 18, 20-21 (pp. 184-185) SG Learning Activities questions 3-4 (p. 186) SG Practice Questions for the NCLEX Examination 1-3, 8, 10-11 (pp. 187-188) Review Questions for the NCLEX Examination 1-3, 7, 10 (p. 448) Lifespan Considerations: Digoxin Toxicity (p. 443) ▸ Discuss what action a nurse would take before initiating drug therapy with digoxin. Why is it important to administer a loading dose?

OBJECTIVES	CONTENT	TEACHING RESOURCES
		Class Activity ***Have two students role-play a nurse instructing a patient with heart failure about home digoxin use. Have the class assist the "nurse" with correct instructions on how to take digoxin and the symptoms of digoxin toxicity. Review the exercise with the class.*** Class Activity ***Divide the class into groups. Have each group outline the signs and symptoms of digoxin toxicity, and identify the nursing interventions for each. Why are older adults prone to toxicity, and how are they affected? Have groups share their findings with the class for discussion.***
Describe safety precautions associated with the preparation and administration of digoxin.	– Nursing process for digoxin (p. 443)	ARQ 1 TB Multiple Choice questions 2, 4 TB Multiple Response question 2 INRQ 12 SG Review Sheet question 17 (p. 185) SG Learning Activities question 7 (p. 186) SG Practice Questions for the NCLEX Examination 12, 14-16 (p. 188) Lifespan Considerations: Digoxin Dosage (p. 444) ▸ Discuss the safety precautions for digoxin administration. Why is it important to always have someone else check calculations? Class Activity ***Divide the class into groups, and assign each group one of the following age-groups:*** ***– Age 1 to 24 months*** ***– Age 2 to 5 years*** ***– Age 5 to 10 years*** ***– Children older than 10 years*** ***– Adult*** ***Practice calculation exercises for administering digoxin to patients in these different age-groups with different body weights and body mass. Also include in the calculations the two primary administration routes of PO and IV.*** Class Activity ***Divide the class into groups, and have each group outline the process for obtaining serum digoxin levels in patients receiving digoxin. Why is it important to be consistent in the time that blood is drawn?***

OBJECTIVES	CONTENT	TEACHING RESOURCES
		Have each group determine the laboratory tests that would be essential for monitoring digoxin toxicity, and identify normal and abnormal laboratory values for its assigned age-group. Have each group present its findings to the class.
State the primary actions on heart failure of digoxin, angiotensin-converting enzyme inhibitors, beta blockers, aldosterone antagonists, nitrates, and calcium channel blockers.	□ Drug class: Phosphodiesterase inhibitors (p. 445) – Nursing process for inamrinone (p. 445) – Nursing process for milrinone (p. 446) □ Drug class: Angiotensin-converting enzyme inhibitors (p. 447) – Nursing process for angiotensin-converting enzyme inhibitors (p. 447) □ Drug class: Beta-adrenergic blocking agents (p. 447) – Nursing process for beta-adrenergic blocking agents (p. 447) □ Drug class: Natriuretic peptides (p. 447) Review the drugs inamrinone and milrinone in the drug class phosphodiesterase inhibitors. Discuss the actions, uses, and therapeutic outcomes of these two agents used for heart failure. Review the serious adverse effects and drug interactions. Review the drug class ACE inhibitors and their actions and therapeutic outcomes in treating patients with heart failure. Review the drug nesiritide in the drug class natriuretic peptides. Discuss the action, use, and therapeutic outcome of this drug for patients with heart failure.	PPT 12-15 ARQ 5 TB Multiple Choice questions 8-9 TB Multiple Response questions 5-6 INRQ 9-11 CTQ 5-6 Animation: Beta Blockers SG Review Sheet questions 10, 22-25 (pp. 184-185) SG Learning Activities questions 5-6, 9-12, 13-18 (p. 186) SG Practice Questions for the NCLEX Examination 9, 13 (pp. 187-188) ▸ Discuss how ACE inhibitors are used to treat heart failure. What medications are now recommended as the drugs of choice for the treatment of mild to moderate systolic dysfunction heart failure? ▸ Discuss when a phosphodiesterase inhibitor might be prescribed. What is the desired therapeutic outcome? ▸ Discuss the difference between inamrinone and milrinone. What adverse effects might you expect from each? What adverse effects would the nurse need to report? Class Activity ***Divide the class into small groups, and assign each group one of the following drugs used to treat heart failure: inamrinone, milrinone, or nesiritide. Have each group outline the actions, uses, adverse effects, and nursing interventions for its assigned drug and present its findings to the class. Discuss the rationale.*** Class Activity ***Have students research the use of ACE inhibitors to treat heart failure and share their findings with the class. (For students to***

OBJECTIVES	CONTENT	TEACHING RESOURCES
		prepare for this activity, see Homework/ Assignments 1.)
Performance evaluation		Test Bank SG Learning Activities (p. 186) SG Practice Questions for the NCLEX Examination (pp. 187-188) Critical Thinking Questions

28.2 Homework/Assignments:

1. Have students research the use of ACE inhibitors to treat heart failure and share their findings with the class.

28.2 Instructor's Notes/Student Feedback:

28 Lecture Outline
Drugs Used to Treat Heart Failure

Slide 1

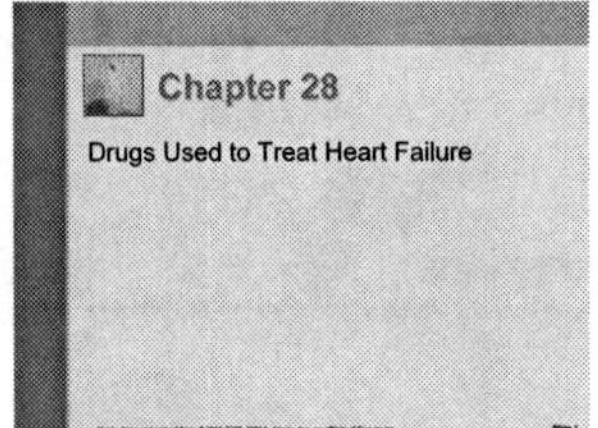

Chapter 28
Drugs Used to Treat Heart Failure

Slide 2

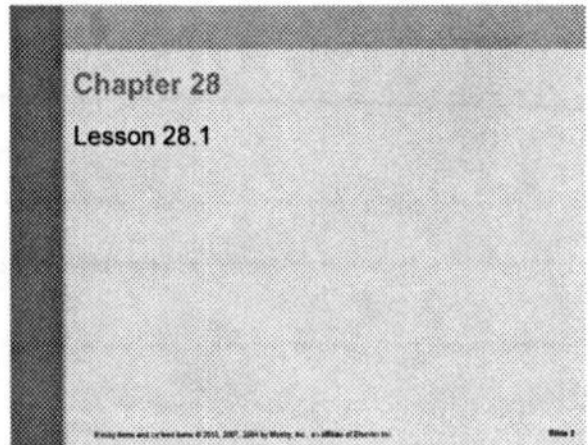

Chapter 28
Lesson 28.1

Slide 3

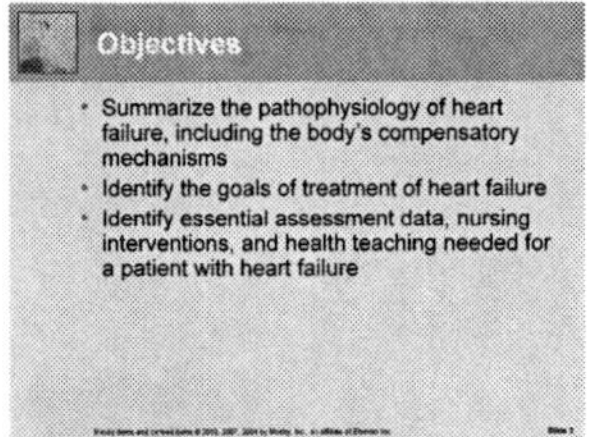

Objectives
Summarize the pathophysiology of heart failure, including the body's compensatory mechanisms
Identify the goals of treatment of heart failure
Identify essential assessment data, nursing interventions, and health teaching needed for a patient with heart failure

---

Slide 4

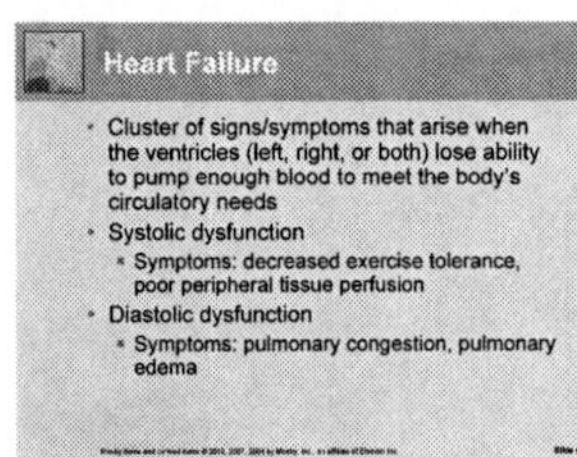

Heart Failure
Cluster of signs/symptoms that arise when the ventricles (left, right, or both) lose ability to pump enough blood to meet the body's circulatory needs
Systolic dysfunction
Symptoms: decreased exercise tolerance, poor peripheral tissue perfusion
Diastolic dysfunction
Symptoms: pulmonary congestion, pulmonary edema

- Affects an estimated 5 million Americans.
- The number of other conditions that complicate its treatment increases as people live longer.

Slide 5

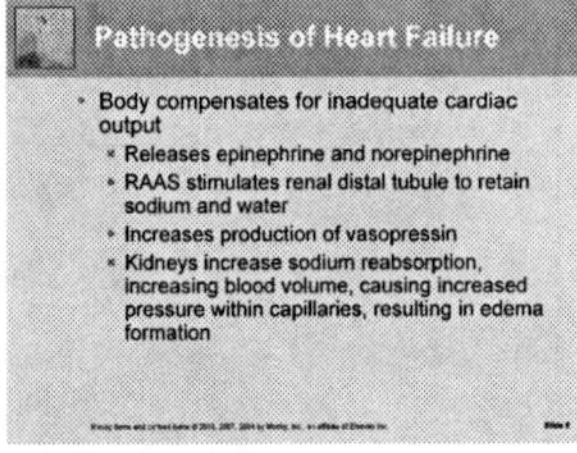

Pathogenesis of Heart Failure
Body compensates for inadequate cardiac output
Releases epinephrine and norepinephrine
RAAS stimulates renal distal tubule to retain sodium and water
Increases production of vasopressin
Kidneys increase sodium reabsorption, increasing blood volume, causing increased pressure within capillaries, resulting in edema formation

- Release of epinephrine and norepinephrine produces tachycardia and increases contractility and peripheral vasoconstriction, increasing afterload.
- RAAS increases load on the heart from water retention, which increases circulating blood volume, increasing preload.
- Vasopressin increases intravascular volume and preload.

ELSEVIER

Slide 6

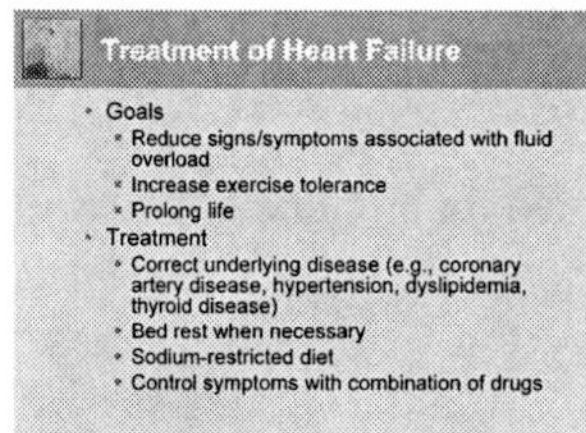
Treatment of Heart Failure
Goals
Reduce signs/symptoms associated with fluid overload
Increase exercise tolerance
Prolong life
Treatment
Correct underlying disease (e.g., coronary artery disease, hypertension, dyslipidemia, thyroid disease)
Bed rest when necessary
Sodium-restricted diet
Control symptoms with combination of drugs

- Smoking cessation is also important.

Slide 7

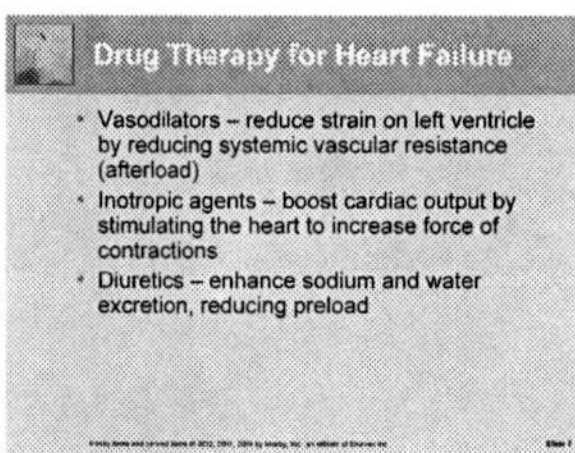
Drug Therapy for Heart Failure
Vasodilators – reduce strain on left ventricle by reducing systemic vascular resistance (afterload)
Inotropic agents – boost cardiac output by stimulating the heart to increase force of contractions
Diuretics – enhance sodium and water excretion, reducing preload

- Therapeutic outcomes: reduce systemic vascular resistance (afterload); reduce preload.

Slide 8

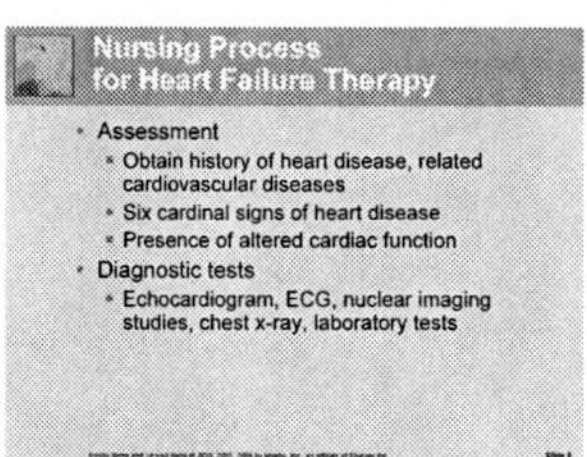
Nursing Process for Heart Failure Therapy
Assessment
Obtain history of heart disease, related cardiovascular diseases
Six cardinal signs of heart disease
Presence of altered cardiac function
Diagnostic tests
Echocardiogram, ECG, nuclear imaging studies, chest x-ray, laboratory tests

- Related diseases: hypertension, hyperlipidemia, diabetes mellitus, lung disease.
- Six cardinal signs of heart disease: dyspnea, chest pain, fatigue, edema, syncope, palpitations.

Slide 9

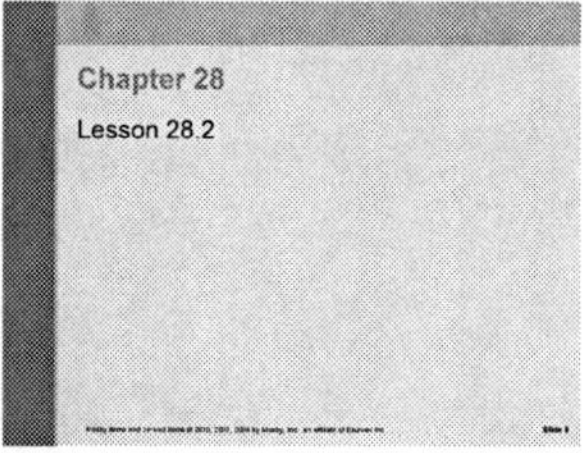
Chapter 28
Lesson 28.2

Slide 10

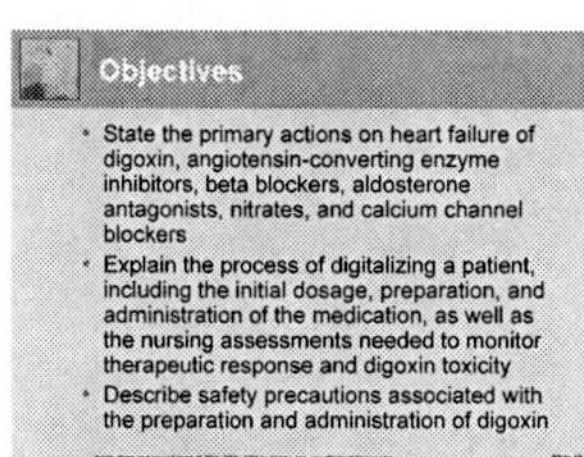
Objectives
State the primary actions on heart failure of digoxin, angiotensin-converting enzyme inhibitors, beta blockers, aldosterone antagonists, nitrates, and calcium channel blockers
Explain the process of digitalizing a patient, including the initial dosage, preparation, and administration of the medication, as well as the nursing assessments needed to monitor therapeutic response and digoxin toxicity
Describe safety precautions associated with the preparation and administration of digoxin

ELSEVIER

Slide 11

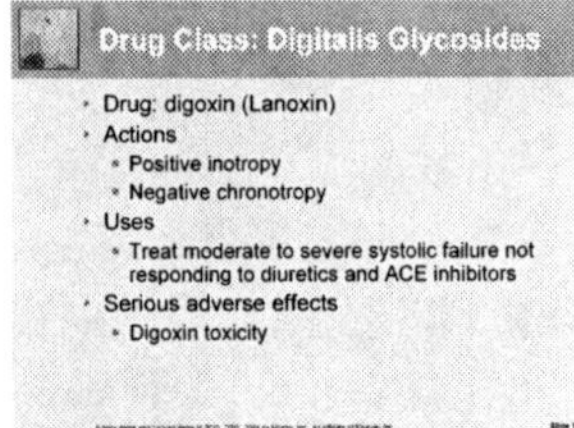
Drug Class: Digitalis Glycosides
Drug: digoxin (Lanoxin)
Actions
Positive inotropy
Negative chronotropy
Uses
Treat moderate to severe systolic failure not responding to diuretics and ACE inhibitors
Serious adverse effects
Digoxin toxicity

- Always take the apical pulse for 1 full minute before administration; do not administer when heart rate is less than 60.
- Maintenance dosing given daily.
- Digoxin toxicity related to long half-life. Digoxin immune Fab (ovine) (Digibind) is the antidote.

Slide 12

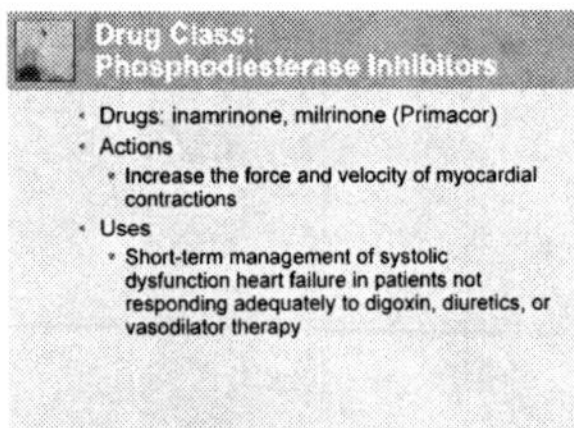
Drug Class: Phosphodiesterase Inhibitors
Drugs: inamrinone, milrinone (Primacor)
Actions
Increase the force and velocity of myocardial contractions
Uses
Short-term management of systolic dysfunction heart failure in patients not responding adequately to digoxin, diuretics, or vasodilator therapy

- Act as vasodilators, reducing preload and afterload.
- Both drugs have different common and serious adverse effects.

Slide 13

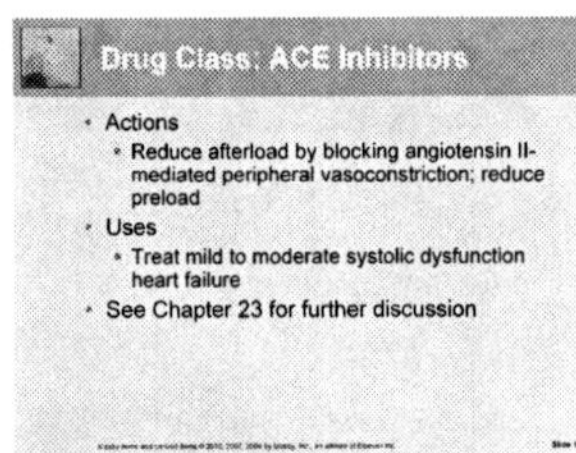
Drug Class: ACE Inhibitors
Actions
Reduce afterload by blocking angiotensin II-mediated peripheral vasoconstriction; reduce preload
Uses
Treat mild to moderate systolic dysfunction heart failure
See Chapter 23 for further discussion

- For specific drugs, see Table 23-5.
- Therapeutic outcomes: improved cardiac output with improved tissue perfusion; improved tolerance to exercise.

Slide 14

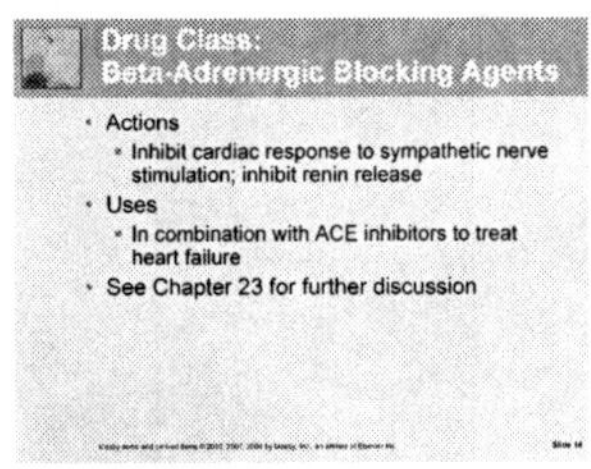
Drug Class: Beta-Adrenergic Blocking Agents
Actions
Inhibit cardiac response to sympathetic nerve stimulation; inhibit renin release
Uses
In combination with ACE inhibitors to treat heart failure
See Chapter 23 for further discussion

- For specific drugs, see Table 13-3.

Slide 15

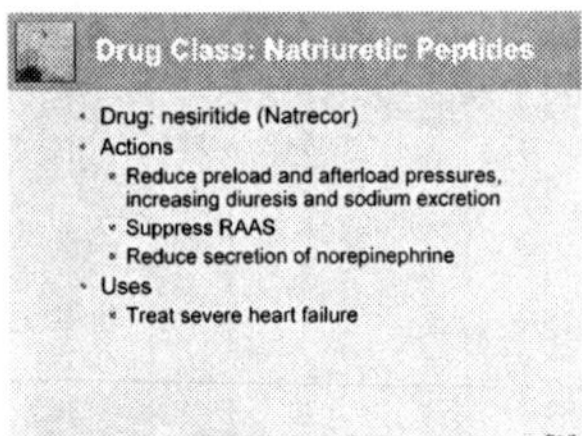
Drug Class: Natriuretic Peptides
Drug: nesiritide (Natrecor)
Actions
Reduce preload and afterload pressures, increasing diuresis and sodium excretion
Suppress RAAS
Reduce secretion of norepinephrine
Uses
Treat severe heart failure

- Natriuretic peptide is a hormone normally secreted by the cardiac ventricles in response to fluid and pressure overload.

ELSEVIER

29 Lesson Plan

Drugs Used for Diuresis

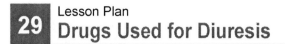

TEACHING FOCUS

This chapter introduces students to topics related to drugs used for diuresis. The student has the opportunity to become acquainted with the nursing process for drug therapy, patient education, and health promotion. The chapter also discusses the action of various classes of diuretics and the associated nursing processes.

MATERIALS AND RESOURCES

- ☐ computer and PowerPoint projector (all Lessons)
- ☐ overhead projector and transparency
- ☐ phototype serum electrolyte report
- ☐ normal laboratory value reference sheet (Lesson 29.2)

LESSON CHECKLIST

Preparations for this lesson include:

- lecture
- guest speaker: dietitian
- student performance evaluation of all entry-level skills required for comprehension and application of drug therapy used for diuresis, including:
  - carbonic anhydrase inhibitors, methylxanthines, loop diuretics, thiazide diuretics, potassium-sparing diuretics, and combination products
  - nursing processes associated with diuretic therapies
  - patient education and health promotion

KEY TERMS

aldosterone (p. 449)
electrolyte imbalance (p. 454)
hyperuricemia (p. 454)
loop of Henle (p. 453)
orthostatic hypotension (p. 454)
tubule (p. 449)

ADDITIONAL RESOURCES

PowerPoint slides: 1-19
Flashcards, Decks 1 and 2

Legend

ARQ	**PPT**	**TB**	**CTQ**	**SG**	**INRQ**
Audience Response Questions	PowerPoint Slides	Test Bank	Critical Thinking Questions	Study Guide	Interactive NCLEX Review Questions

Class Activities are indicated in ***bold italic.***

LESSON 29.1

BACKGROUND ASSESSMENT

Question: What is the purpose of diuresis? What are the different drug classes of diuretics, and what conditions are they prescribed for?

Answer: The purpose of diuresis is to increase the output of urine from the body. Diuretic treatments are typically prescribed to treat diseases or conditions, such as heart failure and renal disease, that reduce normal urine excretion. Diuretic medications act on different locations in the kidneys to enhance the excretion of

sodium. The drug classes and conditions for which they are prescribed for are the following: carbonic anhydrase inhibitor—glaucoma; loop diuretics—edema caused by heart failure, cirrhosis of the liver, or renal disease; thiazide diuretics—edema caused by heart failure, hepatic disease, pregnancy, obesity, and premenstrual syndrome; potassium-sparing diuretics—hypertension, and heart failure.

Question: What are the key components of a nursing assessment to evaluate a patient's renal function?
Answer: The nurse should first obtain a medical history, including heart disease, liver disease, renal disease, and issues related to immobility, hypertension, pregnancy, and use of corticosteroid agents. The nurse should obtain a description of current signs and symptoms, including onset, duration, and related symptoms, and current urination pattern and any recent changes noted. The nurse should ask about all current medications and dosages and patient compliance. During a physical assessment, the nurse should note the patient's skin color and temperature, the quality of the pulse, respiratory rate, lung sounds, blood pressure, and neck distension and should ask if any changes in weight have occurred. To evaluate hydration status, the nurse should check skin turgor, oral mucous membranes, and edema. To detect possible electrolyte imbalances, the nurse should assess the mental status of the patient. After obtaining laboratory data, the nurse should report findings to the health care provider.

CRITICAL THINKING QUESTION

A 65-year-old female has gained weight and noticed increased edema in her lower extremities. The health care provider diagnoses congestive heart failure and prescribes a diuretic. The patient asks the nurse why the diuretic is prescribed and what she should expect. How should the nurse answer?
Guidelines: The nurse can explain that in congestive heart failure, the pumping muscle of the heart is weakened and not able to pump as efficiently as it did before. As a result, there is excess fluid in the lungs and lower extremities. Diuretics are medicines that work on different areas of the kidneys to get rid of the excess fluid by increasing urine output. This will help improve breathing and decrease edema. The nurse can advise the patient that she can expect to be going to the bathroom more often and to measure output if the health care provider requests her to do so. Normal adverse effects may include dry mouth, dull mucous membranes, and change in skin turgor. Tell the patient that she should report confusion, gastric irritation, cramps, abdominal pain and hives, pruritus, or rash to the health care provider. The nurse should tell the patient that with the water loss there can be a loss of other nutrients, such as potassium and sodium, so it is important for her to keep regular appointments with her health care provider.

OBJECTIVES	CONTENT	TEACHING RESOURCES
Identify the action of diuretics.	■ Drug therapy with diuretics (p. 449)	PPT 4, 6 Animation: Diuretics SG Review Sheet question 5-6 (p. 189) SG Learning Activities question 1 (p. 192) Figure 29-1 (p. 450): Sites of actions of diuretics within the nephron. ▸ Discuss and review the anatomy and physiology of the kidney. ▸ Discuss drug therapy with diuretics, including action, sites of kidney action, adverse effects, and drug interactions. Class Activity ***Divide the class into groups, and assign each group one of the following classes of diuretics:*** – ***Carbonic anhydrase inhibitor*** – ***Methylxanthines*** – ***Loop***

OBJECTIVES	CONTENT	TEACHING RESOURCES
		– *Thiazide* – *Potassium-sparing* ***Ask each group to discuss the site of the action in the kidney and therapeutic outcomes of its assigned class. Have each group present its findings to the class for discussion.*** Class Activity ***Have an unlabeled diagram of a nephron, and have volunteer students identify the different sites of the nephron: glomerulus, Bowman's capsule, proximal convoluted tubule, distal convoluted tubule, and loop of Henle. Have students indicate how diuretics affect these identified areas. Review the exercise with the class.***
Describe the goal of administering diuretics to treat hypertension, heart failure, or increased intraocular pressure or before vascular surgery in the brain.	■ Drug therapy with diuretics (p. 449)	PPT 5 TB Multiple Choice question 7 SG Review Sheet question 1 (p. 189) SG Learning Activities question 17 (p. 192) Review Question for the NCLEX Examination 8 (p. 462) ▸ Discuss uses of diuretics, including the medical conditions for which diuretics are prescribed and the expected outcomes. Class Activity ***Make a chart on the board that lists the classes of diuretic drugs and corresponding medical conditions for which each is a primary treatment. These conditions should include hypertension, heart failure, increased ocular pressure, and before vascular brain surgery. For what other conditions might each drug class also be prescribed?***
Identify the effects of diuretics on blood pressure, electrolytes, and diabetic or prediabetic patients.	■ Drug therapy with diuretics (p. 449)	TB Multiple Choice question 1 INRQ 11 CTQ 2 SG Learning Activities questions 9, 24 (pp. 192-193) ▸ Discuss the effects of diuretics on blood pressure, electrolytes, and diabetic conditions. Class Activity ***Divide the class into groups, and assign each group the following conditions that diuretic therapy can affect:*** – ***Blood pressure*** – ***Electrolytes*** – ***Blood glucose***

OBJECTIVES	CONTENT	TEACHING RESOURCES
		Ask groups to explain how different classes of drugs affect each of the conditions. Groups should provide normal values for blood pressure, electrolytes, and blood glucose and also abnormal values that each type of diuretic drug class could produce. Also, consider drug interactions. Ask each group to report to the class for discussion.
Cite nursing assessments used to evaluate a patient's state of hydration.	– Nursing process for diuretic therapy (p. 449)	PPT 11-12 TB Multiple Response questions 3, 5 SG Review Sheet questions 4, 28 (pp. 189-190) SG Learning Activities questions 2, 19 (p. 192) SG Practice Question for the NCLEX Examination 1 (p. 194) Review Question for the NCLEX Examination 9 (p. 462) ▸ Discuss nursing assessments for dehydration, overhydration, and edema. Class Activity ***Lead a discussion in which students evaluate a patient's state of hydration. What are normal and abnormal findings? What observed symptoms indicate hyperkalemia, hypokalemia, hyponatremia, and hypernatremia? What observed symptoms indicate the following nursing diagnoses?*** – ***Excess fluid volume*** – ***Decreased cardiac output*** – ***Risk for deficient fluid volume*** – ***Risk for injury related to diuretic therapy*** ***Outline a nursing care plan for each nursing diagnosis, including planning, implementation, interventions, evaluation, and rationales for each element of the plan.***
Review possible underlying pathologic conditions that may contribute to the development of excess fluid volume in the body.	– Nursing process for diuretic therapy (p. 449) Review the two major diseases that diuretics are used for: heart failure and hypertension. Discuss that the primary action of most diuretics increases the flow of urine by acting on the kidneys at different sites such as the distal tubules and the loop of Henle. Review the nursing process used for diuretic therapy.	PPT 13 TB Multiple Choice question 3 TB Multiple Response questions 1, 6 INRQ 1 SG Learning Activities question 17 (p. 192) ▸ Discuss conditions that may contribute to the development of excess fluid in the body. Class Activity ***Ask students to research and make a brief report to the class about the pathologic conditions that contribute to excess fluid volume in the body. The conditions may***

OBJECTIVES	CONTENT	TEACHING RESOURCES
		include cardiovascular or pulmonary conditions, hypertension, glaucoma, liver disease, and kidney disease. Have students research the pathophysiology, common treatments, and the role of diuretics. (For students to prepare for this activity, see Homework/Assignments 1).

29.1 Homework/Assignments:
1. Ask students to research and make a brief report to the class about the pathologic conditions that contribute to excess fluid volume in the body. These conditions may include cardiovascular or pulmonary conditions, hypertension, glaucoma, liver disease, and kidney disease. Have students research the pathophysiology, common treatments, and role of diuretics.

29.1 Instructor's Notes/Student Feedback:

LESSON 29.2

CRITICAL THINKING QUESTION

A 57-year-old woman diagnosed with renal failure is discharged from the hospital after 5 days with a new prescription for a diuretic to be taken once a day. She is worried that she may develop renal failure again and asks the nurse what signs she should watch for. What should the nurse tell her?
Guidelines: The nurse should review information about the prescribed medication, its purpose, adverse effects, and any contraindications. The nurse should tell the patient to keep a record of her urination pattern and, if it changes, to notify the health care provider. Encourage her to take her new diuretic drug in the morning because it will cause her to urinate more frequently for several hours and then taper off to normal. Explain that she will be excreting electrolytes when she urinates, which can affect her blood electrolyte levels. Signs of electrolyte changes can be subtle, so the nurse should tell the patient to report any changes in her mental status, muscle cramps, tremors, or nausea immediately. The nurse should instruct her to weigh herself at the same time each morning, wearing similar clothing, and keep a record of her weight. She should notify the health care provider if she gains more than 2 pounds in 2 days.

OBJECTIVES	CONTENT	TEACHING RESOURCES
Cite nursing assessments used to evaluate renal function.	– Nursing process for diuretic therapy (p. 449)	PPT 11-12 INRQ 2-3 ▸ Discuss nursing assessments for renal function and the various renal diagnostic tests used, including blood urea nitrogen (BUN) and serum creatinine. Class Activity ***Divide the class into groups, and ask each group to make a checklist of signs and symptoms to assess when determining***

OBJECTIVES	CONTENT	TEACHING RESOURCES
		renal function. Groups should include patient history, observable signs, physical assessment, and laboratory data. Ask groups to present their findings to the class for feedback and discussion.
State which electrolytes may be altered by diuretic therapy.	– Nursing process for diuretic therapy (p. 449)	PPT 13 ARQ 4 TB Multiple Choice question 2 SG Review Sheet questions 2-3 (p. 189) SG Practice Questions for the NCLEX Examination 2, 9 (pp. 194-195) ▸ Discuss the normal laboratory values of potassium, sodium, and chloride and the signs and symptoms of electrolyte imbalance. Class Activity ***Lead a discussion in which students identify which electrolyte—potassium or sodium—causes the following imbalances: hypokalemia, hyperkalemia, hyponatremia, hypernatremia. What factors should the nurse consider in anticipating which patients are susceptible to each electrolyte imbalance?***
Review the signs and symptoms of electrolyte imbalance and normal laboratory values of potassium, sodium, and chloride.	– Nursing process for diuretic therapy (p. 449)	PPT 13 ARQ 3 TB Multiple Choice question 8 INRQ 10 SG Review Sheet question 22 (p. 190) ▸ Discuss the dietary restrictions that may be prescribed as part of diuretic therapy. Class Activity ***Based on the previous class activity, ask students to identify signs and symptoms that a patient may exhibit for each type of electrolyte imbalance. Why are these difficult to differentiate? What role do laboratory tests play? What are the normal and abnormal laboratory values? Identify the nursing interventions for patients on diuretics.***
Explain the rationale for administering diuretics cautiously to older adults and individuals with impaired renal	– Nursing process for diuretic therapy (p. 449)	TB Multiple Response question 7 CTQ 4 SG Review Sheet question 27 (p. 190) ▸ Discuss the adverse effects of diuretics that may be experienced by individuals who have

OBJECTIVES	CONTENT	TEACHING RESOURCES
function, cirrhosis of the liver, or diabetes mellitus.		particular conditions, and discuss related precautions. Class Activity ***Divide the class into small groups, and assign each group one of the following types of patients:*** – ***Older individuals*** – ***Impaired renal function*** – ***Cirrhosis of the liver*** – ***Diabetes mellitus*** ***Ask why diuretic drugs should be administered carefully. What are possible unwanted adverse effects? What drug interactions may be involved? Ask each group to make a report to the class. Discuss any significant similarities and differences of diuretic drug action for patients with different conditions. Identify appropriate nursing interventions for each group of patients.***
List adverse effects that can be anticipated whenever a diuretic is administered.	– Nursing process for diuretic therapy (p. 449)	ARQ 2 TB Multiple Choice questions 5, 11 INRQ 4, 6-7, 12 Review Question for the NCLEX Examination 10 (p. 462) Lifespan Considerations: Diuretic Therapy (p. 450) ▸ Discuss common adverse effects of diuretic therapy. Class Activity ***Lead a discussion in which students describe the adverse effects that can be expected whenever a diuretic drug is administered. What do they have in common? What types of symptoms should the nurse be alert for?*** Class Activity ***Divide students into groups of two. Have each group research adverse effects for all of the diuretic classifications. Allow time in class to compare and contrast student group findings.***
Develop objectives for patient education for patients taking loop, thiazide, and potassium-sparing diuretics.	□ Patient education and health promotion (p. 452)	PPT 14 ARQ 1 TB Multiple Choice question 10 INRQ 5, 8 Patient Self-Assessment Form: Diuretics or Urinary Antibiotics

OBJECTIVES	CONTENT	TEACHING RESOURCES
		SG Practice Question for the NCLEX Examination 7 (p. 194) ▸ Discuss patient education plans for patients taking loop, thiazide, and potassium-sparing diuretics. Class Activity ***Divide the class into pairs for nurse-patient role play. Assign each pair one of the following classes of diuretics: loop, thiazide, or potassium sparing. Ask each pair to do the following:*** ***1. Develop a patient education plan, including the purpose of the drug therapy, medications, self-assessment and monitoring, diet, and health promotion.*** ***2. Take turns role-playing the nurse explaining each element of the plan to the patient.*** ***3. Role-play helping the patient complete the Patient Self-Assessment Form.*** ***Ask volunteer pairs to present to the class for evaluation and feedback. Ask students what they learned from their own role plays and from observing the presentations.*** Class Activity ***Divide the class into groups of three. Assign each group one of the following diuretics: loop, thiazide, and potassium sparing. Have each group complete an educational plan for patient home management. Allow class time for presentation.***

29.2 Homework/Assignments:

29.2 Instructor's Notes/Student Feedback:

LESSON 29.3

CRITICAL THINKING QUESTION

A 75-year-old man whose blood pressure was 190/110 Hg mm when admitted to the hospital has generalized edema and complains of a headache. He also has been diagnosed with diabetes mellitus. He is ordered hydrochlorothiazide (HCTZ), 50 mg every day. What nursing interventions should be included in his care plan?

Guidelines: The nurse should obtain baseline vital signs, height and weight, and blood glucose level. The nurse should tell the patient that the new medication will be administered with breakfast to reduce the possibility of gastric irritation. After administration, the nurse should perform physical assessments including mental status, lung sounds, hearing changes, or other complaints. The nurse should monitor for orthostatic hypotension, gastric irritability, electrolyte imbalances, hyperuricemia, hyperglycemia, and skin irritation. The patient should be encouraged to call for assistance when getting out of bed because he may feel dizzy. The nurse should also ask him to report headache pain and to use his urinal so that urine output can be measured. A dietary consult may be ordered to review his current diet regimen, and a low-sodium diet may be ordered. The nurse should monitor daily I&O, vital signs, and weight change. Signs of hyperglycemia, cramps, tremors, nausea, and changes in mental status, muscle strength, and general appearance should also be monitored. Finally, the nurse should document and report changes to the health care provider.

OBJECTIVES	CONTENT	TEACHING RESOURCES
State the nursing assessments needed to monitor therapeutic response or the development of common or serious adverse effects from diuretic therapy.	□ Drug class: Carbonic anhydrase inhibitor (p. 453) □ Drug class: Sulfonamide-type loop diuretics (p. 453) – Nursing process for sulfonamide-type loop diuretics (p. 453) – Nursing process for ethacrynic acid (p. 455) □ Drug class: Thiazide diuretics (p. 456) □ Drug class: Potassium-sparing diuretics (p. 458) – Nursing process for amiloride (p. 458) – Nursing process for spironolactone (p. 459) – Nursing process for triamterene (p. 460) □ Drug class: Combination diuretic products (p. 460)	PPT 15-19 ARQ 5 TB Multiple Choice questions 4, 9 TB Multiple Response questions 2, 4 CTQ 1, 3 Patient Self-Assessment Form: Diuretics or Urinary Antibiotics SG Review Sheet questions 7-14, 18-21, 24-26, 29 (pp. 189-191) SG Learning Activities questions 3-8, 10, 11-16, 18, 20-21, 23 (pp. 192-193) SG Practice Questions for the NCLEX Examination 4-6, 8, 10, 12 (pp. 194-195) Review Questions for the NCLEX Examination 1-7 (pp. 461-462) Drug Table 29-1: Sulfonamide-Type Loop Diuretics (p. 454) Drug Table 29-2: Thiazide Diuretics (p. 457) Drug Table 29-3: Thiazide-Related Diuretics (p. 457)
	Review the drug acetazolamide in the drug class carbonic anhydrase inhibitors. Discuss its action and use in glaucoma.	▸ Discuss the uses, actions, and therapeutic outcomes of each class of diuretic drugs.
	Review the actions, uses, and therapeutic outcomes of the drug class thiazide diuretics.	▸ Discuss the common and serious adverse effects and drug interactions for the drug classes previously listed.

ELSEVIER

OBJECTIVES	CONTENT	TEACHING RESOURCES
		Class Activity ***Divide the class into groups, and assign each one of the following classes of diuretic drugs: sulfonamide-type loop diuretics, thiazide diuretics, or potassium-sparing diuretics. Have each group select one or two specific drugs in the class and describe the nursing assessments necessary to evaluate the therapeutic outcome. What are the expected results? What signs and symptoms should the nurse be alert for? Ask each group to make a report to the class. As a class, discuss differences and similarities between drugs or drug classes.***
Cite alterations in diet that may be prescribed concurrently with loop, thiazide, or potassium-sparing diuretic therapy.	– Nursing process for sulfonamide-type loop diuretics (p. 453) – Nursing process for thiazide diuretics (p. 456) – Nursing process for amiloride (p. 458) – Nursing process for spironolactone (p. 459) – Nursing process for triamterene (p. 460)	PPT 15-19 TB Multiple Choice question 6 SG Review Sheet questions 15-16, 23 (p. 190) SG Practice Questions for the NCLEX Examination 3, 11 (p. 194-195) Drug Table 29-4: Combination Diuretics (p. 461) ▸ Discuss the addition of potassium-rich foods and the need to administer drugs with food or milk if gastric irritation occurs. Class Activity ***Invite a dietitian who specializes in cardiac and/or renal disease to discuss diet restrictions and requirements for a patient with cardiovascular, renal disease, or both, who is taking diuretics. Ask the speaker to address fluid restrictions and measurements, sample menus for all meals, and snacks. Encourage students to ask questions and to discuss the presentation.***
Performance evaluation		Test Bank SG Learning Activities (pp. 192-193) SG Practice Questions for the NCLEX Examination (pp. 194-195) Critical Thinking Questions

29.3 Homework/Assignments:

Divide students into two groups. Assign one group to research foods high in potassium and the other group to research foods high in sodium. Have students complete research outside of class time. Allow class time for discussion of findings.

29.3 Instructor's Notes/Student Feedback:

29

Lecture Outline

Drugs Used for Diuresis

Slide 1

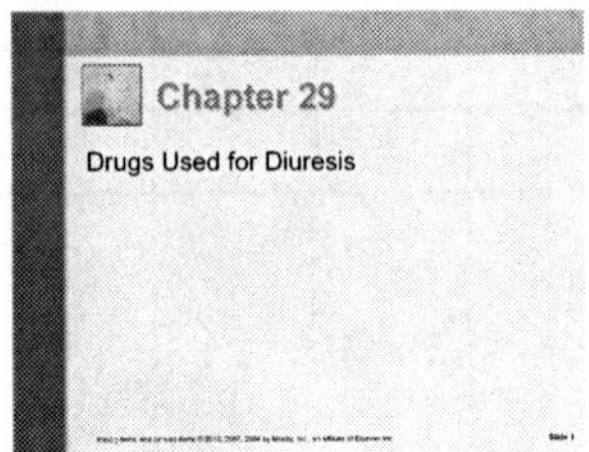
Chapter 29
Drugs Used for Diuresis

Slide 2

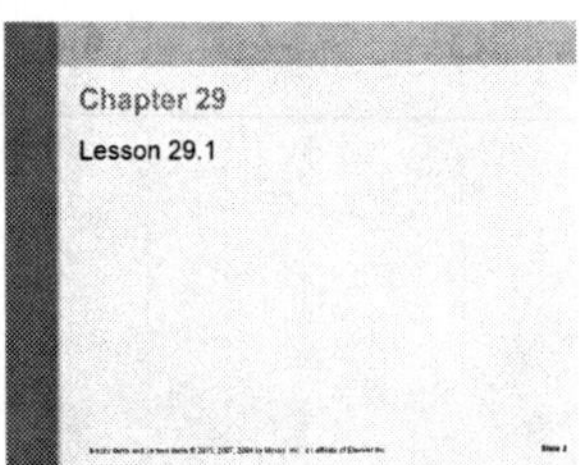
Chapter 29
Lesson 29.1

Slide 3

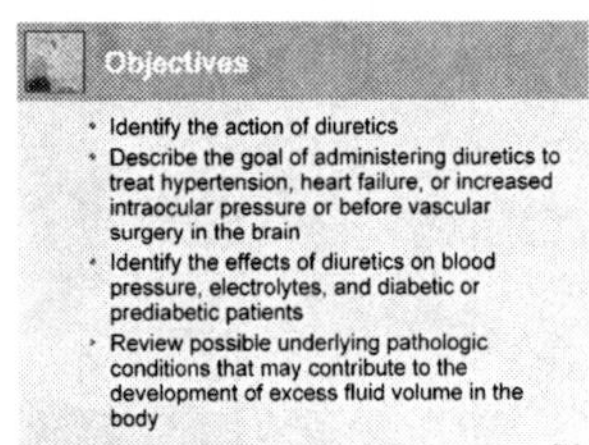
Objectives
Identify the action of diuretics
Describe the goal of administering diuretics to treat hypertension, heart failure, or increased intraocular pressure or before vascular surgery in the brain
Identify the effects of diuretics on blood pressure, electrolytes, and diabetic or prediabetic patients
Review possible underlying pathologic conditions that may contribute to the development of excess fluid volume in the body

Slide 4

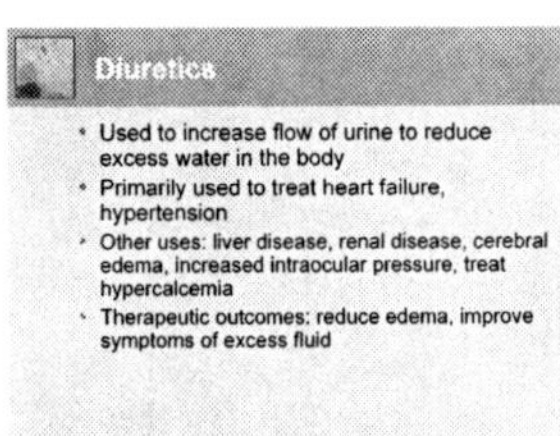
Diuretics
Used to increase flow of urine to reduce excess water in the body
Primarily used to treat heart failure, hypertension
Other uses: liver disease, renal disease, cerebral edema, increased intraocular pressure, treat hypercalcemia
Therapeutic outcomes: reduce edema, improve symptoms of excess fluid

- After lifestyle modifications, diuretics (often in addition to other antihypertensives) may be used as primary agents to treat hypertension.

Slide 5

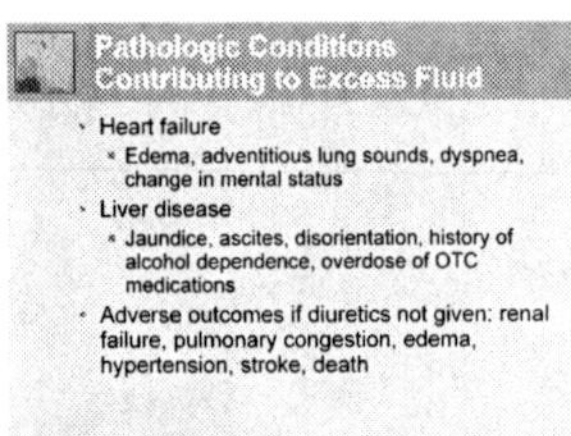
Pathologic Conditions Contributing to Excess Fluid
Heart failure
Edema, adventitious lung sounds, dyspnea, change in mental status
Liver disease
Jaundice, ascites, disorientation, history of alcohol dependence, overdose of OTC medications
Adverse outcomes if diuretics not given: renal failure, pulmonary congestion, edema, hypertension, stroke, death

ELSEVIER

Slide 6

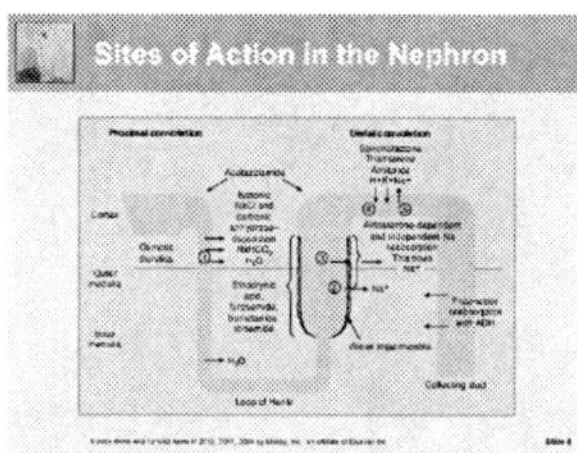
Sites of Action in the Nephron

- Diuretics act on the kidneys to decrease reabsorption of sodium, chloride, and water.
- The distal tubules is the site of action for thiazide and potassium-sparing drugs.
- The loop of Henle is the site of action for loop-diuretics.

Slide 7

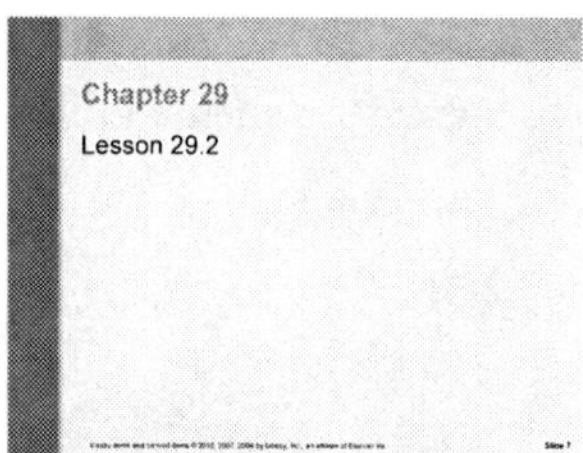
Chapter 29
Lesson 29.2

Slide 8

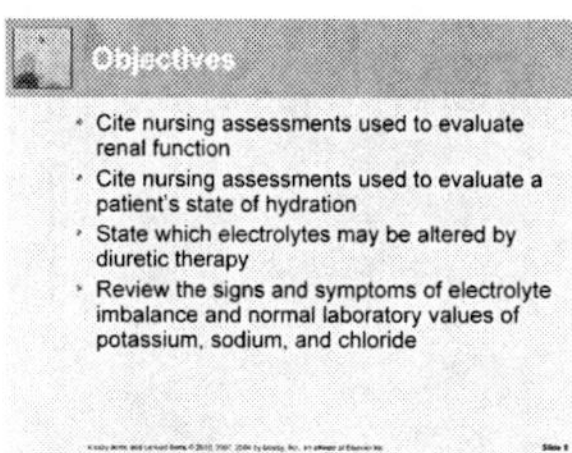
Objectives
Cite nursing assessments used to evaluate renal function
Cite nursing assessments used to evaluate a patient's state of hydration
State which electrolytes may be altered by diuretic therapy
Review the signs and symptoms of electrolyte imbalance and normal laboratory values of potassium, sodium, and chloride

---

Slide 9

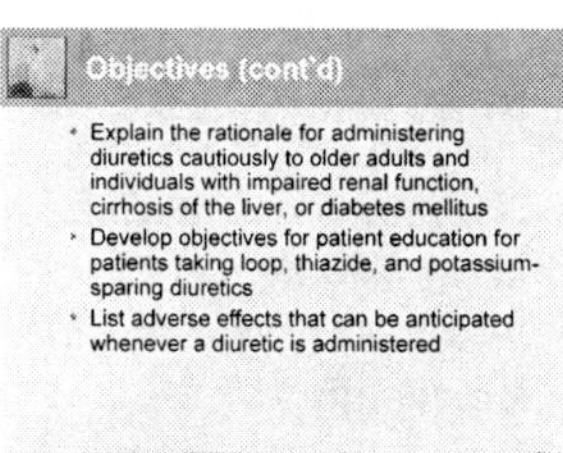
Objectives (cont'd)
Explain the rationale for administering diuretics cautiously to older adults and individuals with impaired renal function, cirrhosis of the liver, or diabetes mellitus
Develop objectives for patient education for patients taking loop, thiazide, and potassium-sparing diuretics
List adverse effects that can be anticipated whenever a diuretic is administered

---

Slide 10

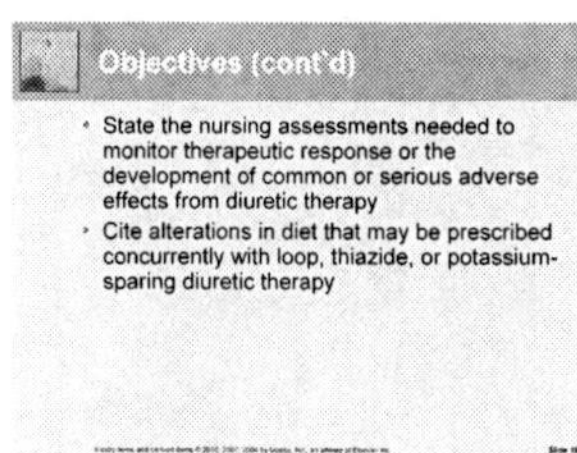
Objectives (cont'd)
State the nursing assessments needed to monitor therapeutic response or the development of common or serious adverse effects from diuretic therapy
Cite alterations in diet that may be prescribed concurrently with loop, thiazide, or potassium-sparing diuretic therapy

Slide 11

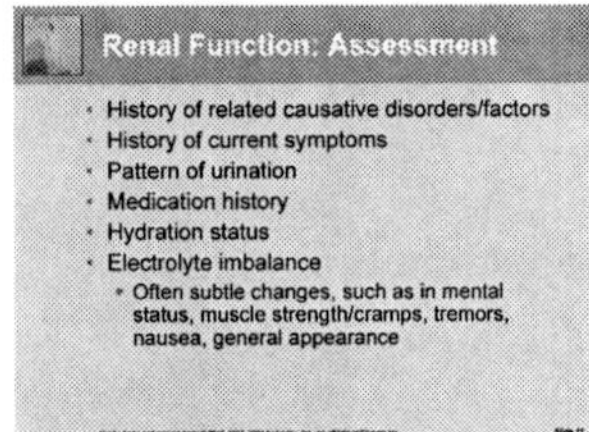
Renal Function: Assessment
History of related causative disorders/factors
History of current symptoms
Pattern of urination
Medication history
Hydration status
Electrolyte imbalance
Often subtle changes, such as in mental status, muscle strength/cramps, tremors, nausea, general appearance

---

Slide 12

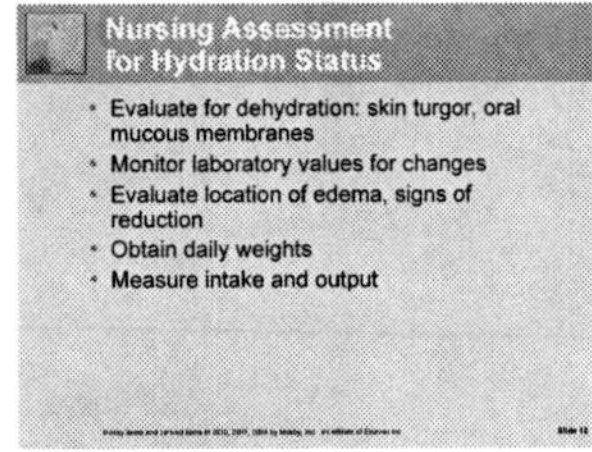
Nursing Assessment for Hydration Status
Evaluate for dehydration: skin turgor, oral mucous membranes
Monitor laboratory values for changes
Evaluate location of edema, signs of reduction
Obtain daily weights
Measure intake and output

- Common sites to check skin turgor are over the sternum, on the forehead, and on the forearm.
- Weight gain that alerts the patient or nurse to increasing edema is generally 2 lb per day.

Slide 13

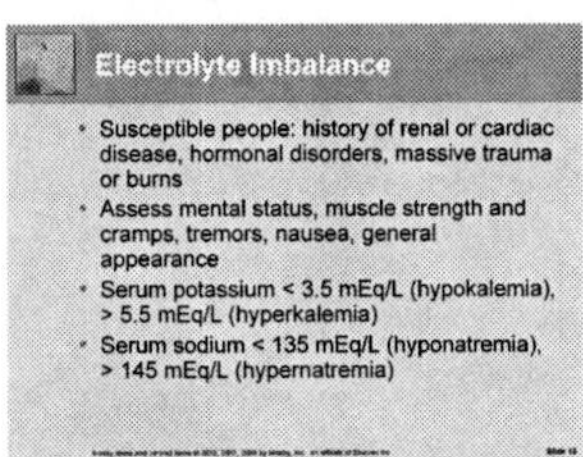
Electrolyte Imbalance
Susceptible people: history of renal or cardiac disease, hormonal disorders, massive trauma or burns
Assess mental status, muscle strength and cramps, tremors, nausea, general appearance
Serum potassium < 3.5 mEq/L (hypokalemia), > 5.5 mEq/L (hyperkalemia)
Serum sodium < 135 mEq/L (hyponatremia), > 145 mEq/L (hypernatremia)

- Potassium depletion can cause weakness of cardiovascular, respiratory, digestive, and skeletal muscles.

Slide 14

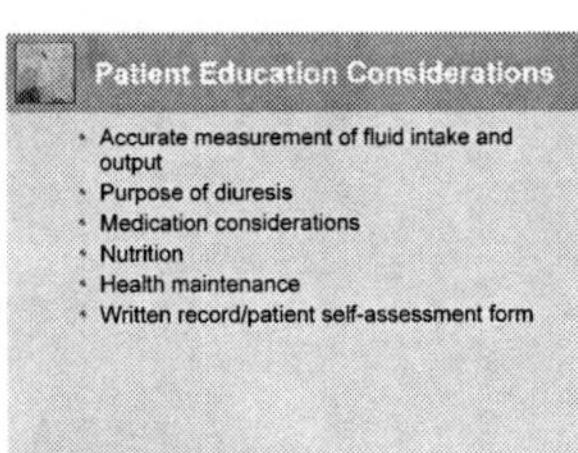
Patient Education Considerations
Accurate measurement of fluid intake and output
Purpose of diuresis
Medication considerations
Nutrition
Health maintenance
Written record/patient self-assessment form

- The prescriber orders furosemide 80 mg for a patient who had been retaining extra fluid after surgery. The nurse notes the following: BP of 142/88 (lying) and 108/60 (sitting); daily weight of 154 lb, a 1-lb drop from day before; serum potassium of 2.8 mEq/L. Should the nurse administer the furosemide? *(The nurse should report the data to the charge nurse or the physician. The patient's drop in weight is too much for 1 day; orthostatic blood pressure indicates volume depletion; potassium level shows diuresis is occurring too rapidly.)*

Slide 15

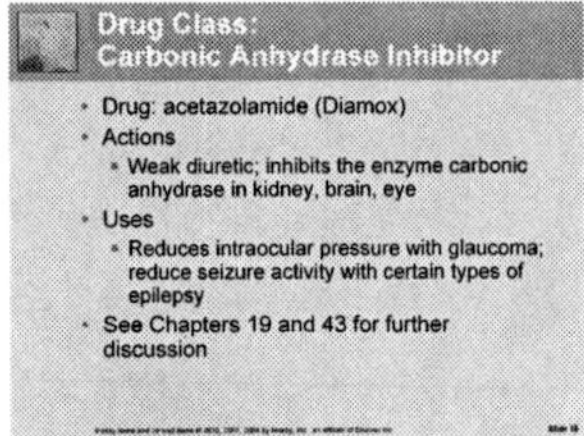
Drug Class: Carbonic Anhydrase Inhibitor
Drug: acetazolamide (Diamox)
Actions
Weak diuretic; inhibits the enzyme carbonic anhydrase in kidney, brain, eye
Uses
Reduces intraocular pressure with glaucoma; reduce seizure activity with certain types of epilepsy
See Chapters 19 and 43 for further discussion

ELSEVIER

Slide 16

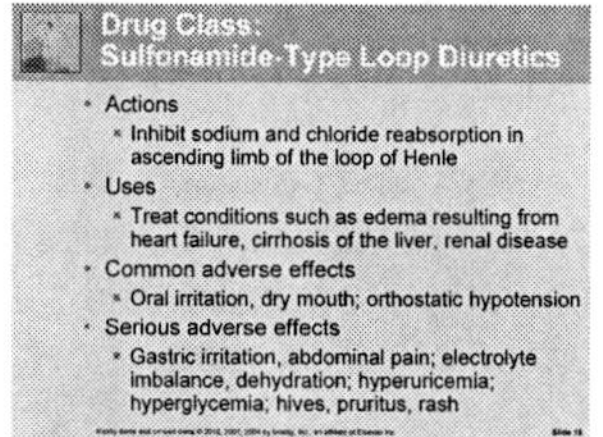
Drug Class:
Sulfonamide-Type Loop Diuretics
Actions
Inhibit sodium and chloride reabsorption in ascending limb of the loop of Henle
Uses
Treat conditions such as edema resulting from heart failure, cirrhosis of the liver, renal disease
Common adverse effects
Oral irritation, dry mouth; orthostatic hypotension
Serious adverse effects
Gastric irritation, abdominal pain; electrolyte imbalance, dehydration; hyperuricemia; hyperglycemia; hives, pruritus, rash

- Drugs: bumetanide (Bumex), furosemide (Lasix), ethacrynic acid (Edecrin), torsemide (Demadex).
- Furosemide is also used to treat hypertension.
- Ethacrynic acid is more effective than other loop diuretics in patients with significant renal failure.

Slide 17

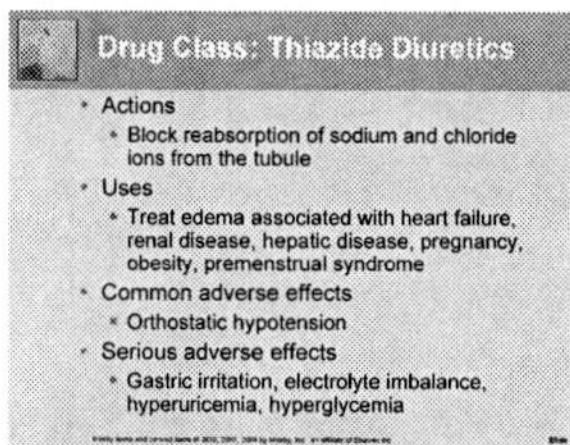
Drug Class: Thiazide Diuretics
Actions
Block reabsorption of sodium and chloride ions from the tubule
Uses
Treat edema associated with heart failure, renal disease, hepatic disease, pregnancy, obesity, premenstrual syndrome
Common adverse effects
Orthostatic hypotension
Serious adverse effects
Gastric irritation, electrolyte imbalance, hyperuricemia, hyperglycemia

- For specific drugs, see Tables 29-2 and 29-3.
- Used for more long-term management of heart failure and hypertension.
- Not strong diuretics; have a slow onset of action.

Slide 18

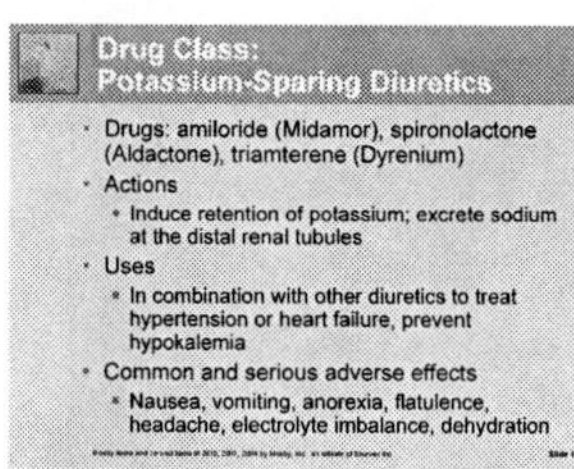
Drug Class:
Potassium-Sparing Diuretics
Drugs: amiloride (Midamor), spironolactone (Aldactone), triamterene (Dyrenium)
Actions
Induce retention of potassium; excrete sodium at the distal renal tubules
Uses
In combination with other diuretics to treat hypertension or heart failure, prevent hypokalemia
Common and serious adverse effects
Nausea, vomiting, anorexia, flatulence, headache, electrolyte imbalance, dehydration

- Instruct patients not to use salt substitutes, which are high in potassium, to prevent hyperkalemia.
- Contraindicated in patients with renal impairment because of high risk of hyperkalemia.

Slide 19

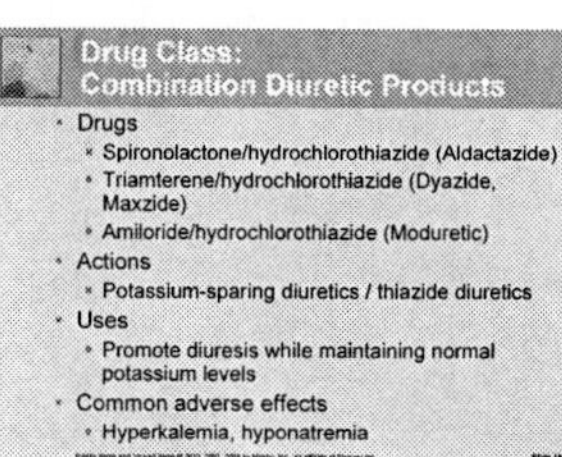
Drug Class:
Combination Diuretic Products
Drugs
Spironolactone/hydrochlorothiazide (Aldactazide)
Triamterene/hydrochlorothiazide (Dyazide, Maxzide)
Amiloride/hydrochlorothiazide (Moduretic)
Actions
Potassium-sparing diuretics / thiazide diuretics
Uses
Promote diuresis while maintaining normal potassium levels
Common adverse effects
Hyperkalemia, hyponatremia

- For specific drugs, see Table 29-4.

ELSEVIER

30 Lesson Plan

Drugs Used to Treat Upper Respiratory Disease

TEACHING FOCUS

This chapter introduces students to the upper respiratory tract anatomy and physiology and common diseases that affect the upper respiratory tract. It discusses ways to prevent the spread of these contagious diseases and methods used to treat them. Students have the opportunity to learn skills in nursing assessment and administering medication. Additionally, students have the opportunity to learn about effective methods of patient education to ensure compliance and health promotion.

MATERIALS AND RESOURCES

- ☐ computer and PowerPoint projector (all Lessons)
- ☐ nose drops, sprays, and inhalation medications (Lesson 30.2)

LESSON CHECKLIST

Preparations for this lesson include:

- lecture
- demonstration
- guest speakers: local health department representative, clinic nurse, pharmacist
- evaluation of student knowledge and skills needed to perform all entry-level nursing activities related to drugs used to treat upper respiratory disease, including:
  - causes of allergic rhinitis and nasal congestion
  - premedication and nursing assessments
  - procedures for administration of medications
  - patient education for compliance and health promotion

KEY TERMS

allergic rhinitis (p. 465)
antigen-antibody (p. 465)
antihistamines (p. 466)
anti-inflammatory agents (p. 467)
decongestants (p. 465)
histamine (p. 465)
rhinitis (p. 464)
rhinitis medicamentosa (p. 465)
rhinorrhea (p. 465)
sinusitis (p. 465)

ADDITIONAL RESOURCES

PowerPoint slides: 1-15
Flashcards, Decks 1 and 2

Legend

ARQ	**PPT**	**TB**	**CTQ**	**SG**	**INRQ**
Audience Response Questions	PowerPoint Slides	Test Bank	Critical Thinking Questions	Study Guide	Interactive NCLEX Review Questions

Class Activities are indicated in ***bold italic.***

LESSON 30.1

BACKGROUND ASSESSMENT

Question: A patient tells the nurse that she has been using phenylephrine nasal spray for several days without relief of congestion. The congestion comes back right after she uses the spray, so the patient wants to know what to do. What should the nurse suspect, and how should the nurse respond?
Answer: The patient is most likely experiencing rhinitis medicamentosa, which arises from the overuse of decongestant nasal spray. The nurse can explain that some nasal sprays can cause rhinitis medicamentosa and nasal spray addiction. These include oxymetazoline, phenylephrine, and xylometazoline. Rebound congestion may occur when the sprays are used frequently for 3 or more days. This is caused by vasoconstriction of the blood vessels and by direct irritation of the nasal membranes by the solution. The nurse also can explain that when the vasoconstrictor effects wear off, irritation causes excessive blood flow to the passages, causing swelling and engorgement to reappear. As a result, the nose feels more stuffy and congested than it did before treatment. A vicious cycle develops with increasing use of the nasal spray. The nurse should suggest that the patient gradually decrease her usage, using a saline nasal spray or antihistamines to relieve congestion.

Question: The patient reports a runny nose and itchy eyes every May. He tells the nurse that he thinks he is allergic to something and wants to know how he can determine what he is allergic to. How should the nurse reply?
Answer: The nurse can tell the patient that there are several ways to determine which substances cause an allergic response. Among the more common methods are skin tests, elimination-type tests, and the radioallergosorbent test (RAST). Skin tests are the most common and are most useful for respiratory allergies. Specific methods of skin testing may vary. The scratch test involves placement of a small amount of suspected allergy-causing substances (allergens) on the skin, usually on the forearm, upper arm, or back, and then scratching or pricking the skin so that the allergen is introduced under the skin surface. The skin is observed closely for signs of a reaction, usually swelling and redness of the site. Results are usually obtained within about 20 minutes, and several suspected allergens can be tested at the same time. A similar method involves injection of a small amount of allergen under the surface of the skin and watching for a reaction at the site. The nurse should advise the patient that he should take no antihistamines before the skin test on the day of the test to prevent false-negative results. The RAST is a laboratory test that determines the amount of specific IgE antibodies in the blood present in the case of an allergy. Other tests include immunoglobulin measurements, blood cell differential, and absolute eosinophil count (an increase in which can indicate the presence of allergy).

CRITICAL THINKING QUESTION

A mother tells the nurse that one of her children who has asthma shows signs of having a cold that has persisted for several weeks. She says that when her other children get a cold, the health care provider tells her that an antibiotic should not be prescribed because the cold is caused by a virus that does not respond to antibiotics. The health care provider says the children will get over it without treatment. The mother wants to know if she should treat the cold differently for her child who has asthma. How should the nurse respond?
Guidelines: The nurse should explain that viral respiratory illnesses, such as a cold, can trigger asthma attacks and exacerbate symptoms in patients who have asthma. The body responds to the virus by secreting chemicals that produce inflammation, inflaming airways and making them hypersensitive. Even if the viral infection subsides in a few days, the increased sensitivity of the lining of the airways can last up to 2 months, resulting in increased asthma symptoms. Infections, such as bacterial sinusitis and pneumonia, although less common than viral infections, also can trigger asthma. When mucus in the bronchial tubes is not sufficiently cleared, it becomes a potential breeding ground for bacterial infection. For this reason, the asthma attack can be triggered by a viral infection but can lead to a bacterial infection requiring an antibiotic treatment. The nurse should advise the mother to watch the child for continued symptoms, development of a cough, or trouble breathing. If any of these symptoms occurs, the mother should call the health care provider for additional treatment.

ELSEVIER

OBJECTIVES	CONTENT	TEACHING RESOURCES
Describe the function of the respiratory system.	■ Upper respiratory tract anatomy and physiology (p. 463) Review the normal anatomy and physiology of the upper respiratory tract including the nose, sinuses, pharynx, tonsils, and larynx. Discuss the function of each and how each aids in normal respirations.	PPT 5 TB Multiple Choice questions 6-7 SG Learning Activities questions 1-3 (p. 199) Figure 30-1 (p. 464): The upper respiratory tract. ▸ Discuss the respiratory function of the nose. ▸ Discuss the purpose of the sneeze reflex and what causes it.
Discuss the common upper respiratory diseases.	■ Upper respiratory tract anatomy and physiology (p. 463) ■ Common upper respiratory diseases (p. 464) ■ Treatment of upper respiratory diseases (p. 465) – Common cold (p. 465) – Allergic rhinitis (p. 466) Review the common upper respiratory diseases and their symptoms.	PPT 6-8 SG Review Sheet questions 1-2 (p. 197) SG Learning Activities questions 18-20 (p. 199) SG Practice Question for the NCLEX Examination 1 (p. 201) ▸ Discuss the respiratory system and its structures allowing with its functions. ▸ Discuss the common cold virus, rhinitis, allergic rhinitis, and sinusitis. Review the effects of histamine and the use of antihistamine drugs. Class Activity ***Have pairs of students take turns role-playing a nurse collecting data from a patient who has allergic rhinitis. The assessment should include history of illness, signs and symptoms, medical history, current medications, known allergies, and past treatments. Ask volunteer pairs to present to the class, and ask students to share what they have learned.***
State the causes of allergic rhinitis and nasal congestion.	■ Treatment of upper respiratory diseases (p. 465) – Allergic rhinitis (p. 466)	PPT 6-8 ARQ 1-2 TB Multiple Choice question 8 TB Multiple Response question 1 SG Review Sheet questions 7-9 (p. 197) ▸ Discuss what symptoms typically occur with the common cold. In addition to medications discussed in the text, what other remedies and preventive measures can be used to relieve symptoms and prevent the cold from spreading? ▸ Discuss how the allergen that causes a specific reaction can be determined and how the patient can limit exposure.

OBJECTIVES	CONTENT	TEACHING RESOURCES
		Class Activity ***Ask for volunteers to present to the class the mechanism of an allergic response as it pertains to allergic rhinitis. Ask for additional volunteers to describe the related signs and symptoms.***
Define *rhinitis medicamentosa,* and describe the patient education needed to prevent it.	■ Treatment of upper respiratory diseases (p. 465) – Rhinitis medicamentosa (p. 466) Review the drug therapy used for upper respiratory diseases with a focus on nursing implications. Discuss the nursing process and how to use it for reviewing important patient education when using drugs for symptom relief.	PPT 9-10 TB Multiple Choice questions 3-4 INRQ 2 CTQ 1 SG Review Sheet question 4 (p. 197) SG Learning Activities question 4 (p. 199) ▸ Discuss what causes the common cold and why there is no cure for it. How does the common cold differ from allergic rhinitis and rhinitis medicamentosa? ▸ Discuss why a patient might overuse decongestants, thus causing rhinitis medicamentosa. Class Activity ***Have students create patient education materials for display in a health care provider's office or clinic about rhinitis medicamentosa. The materials should explain the causes, signs and symptoms, and ways to prevent and treat the condition. Have students provide feedback on accuracy, completeness, and effectiveness of one another's work.***
Explain the major actions (effects) of sympathomi-metic, antihistaminic, and corticosteroid decongestants and cromolyn.	■ Drug therapy for upper respiratory diseases (p. 466) – Nursing process for upper respiratory diseases (p. 467) Review the treatment goal for the following upper respiratory diseases: common cold, allergic rhinitis, and rhinitis medicamentosa. Discuss the treatment strategies for each.	PPT 13-16 ARQ 3-4 TB Multiple Choice questions 2, 5 TB Multiple Response question 2 INRQ 5 CTQ 2 SG Learning Activities questions 5-6, 17, 20 (p. 199) SG Practice Question for the NCLEX Examination 2 (p. 201) Class Activity ***Divide the class into small groups. Assign each group one of these categories of medication:*** – ***Sympathomimetic*** – ***Antihistamines*** – ***Corticosteroid decongestants*** – ***Mast cell stabilizers (Cromolyn)***

OBJECTIVES	CONTENT	TEACHING RESOURCES
		Have each group outline the major actions of each type of medication and summarize for the class. As a class, compare and contrast the major features and benefits.
Identify essential components involved in planning patient education that will enhance adherence with the treatment regimen.	– Patient education and health promotion (p. 467)	PPT 10 ARQ 5 TB Multiple Choice question 9 TB Multiple Response questions 3, 5 INRQ 3 CTQ 5 SG Review Sheet question 13 (p. 197) SG Practice Question for the NCLEX Examination 6 (p. 201) ▶ Discuss the importance of establishing a regular medication schedule for a patient to administer medications. ▶ Discuss what points should be emphasized to improve medication compliance. *Class Activity* ***Invite a pharmacist to speak to the class about over-the-counter and prescription antihistamines. Is one category more likely than the other to be misused by people seeking relief from bothersome symptoms? Ask the speaker to address administration, adverse effects, dosage, other drug interactions, and patient education. Include special concerns related to children, adults, and older adults. Have students prepare questions in advance.***

30.1 Homework/Assignments:

30.1 Instructor's Notes/Student Feedback:

LESSON 30.2

CRITICAL THINKING QUESTION

A male patient in his mid-30s calls the clinic and says that he has had cold symptoms for 10 days. He says that he has been under a lot of stress and wants to know what to do because he has no time to take off work or come to the health care provider's office. What should the nurse advise the patient?

Guidelines: The nurse should advise the patient to see a health care provider if the symptoms do not improve in 5 days, if the symptoms worsen, or if new symptoms occur. The nurse should explain that having a cold makes him more susceptible to potentially serious bacterial infections, such as strep throat, middle ear infection, sinus infection, and pneumonia. The nurse should advise the patient to watch for chest pain, fever, difficulty breathing, bluish lips or fingernails, a cough that brings up greenish-yellow or grayish sputum, skin rash, swollen glands, or sore throat. The nurse should inquire if the patient has any other conditions, such as emphysema, chronic lung disease, or diabetes mellitus, that could make him more susceptible to secondary infections or make it harder to fight them off. In addition, if the patient has a weakened immune system, either from stress, diseases such as AIDS or leukemia, or the result of medications such as corticosteroids or chemotherapy drugs, the nurse should advise him to consult a health care provider immediately whenever he experiences cold symptoms.

OBJECTIVES	CONTENT	TEACHING RESOURCES
Explain why all decongestant products should be used cautiously by people with hypertension, hyperthyroidism, diabetes mellitus, cardiac disease, increased intraocular pressure, or prostatic disease.	□ Drug class: Sympathomimetic decongestants (p. 468) Review the drug class sympathomimetic decongestants for their action, uses, and therapeutic effects in treating nasal congestion. Discuss the drugs in terms of nasal sprays and patient precautions in conjunction with other drugs.	PPT 13 TB Multiple Response question 4 INRQ 4, 7 SG Review Sheet question 3 (p. 197) SG Practice Question for the NCLEX Examination 3 (p. 201) Review Question for the NCLEX Examination 8 (p. 474) Lifespan Considerations: Decongestants (p. 466) ▸ Discuss the advantages and disadvantages of taking a topical decongestant versus an oral decongestant. ▸ Discuss how a nasal decongestant can be misused and what the effect on the patient would be. Class Activity ***Divide the class into three groups, and assign each group two diseases from this list: hypertension, hyperthyroidism, diabetes mellitus, cardiac disease, intraocular pressure, or prostate disease. Ask the groups to identify adverse reactions that may occur in people who have the diseases if they take decongestant medications. Have groups share their findings with the class.***
State the premedication assessments and nursing assessments	– Nursing process for sympathomimetic decongestants (p. 468)	PPT 13 TB Multiple Choice question 1 SG Review Sheet questions 5, 17 (pp. 197-198)

OBJECTIVES	CONTENT	TEACHING RESOURCES
needed during therapy to monitor therapeutic response and common and serious adverse effects from using decongestant drug therapy.		Review Question for the NCLEX Examination 5 (p. 473) Drug Table 30-1: Nasal Decongestants (p. 468) ▸ Discuss the importance of taking a thorough history of the patient before administering decongestants. Class Activity ***Have students make drug cards for sympathomimetic decongestants with available drug form and dosage. Then ask students to role-play a nurse explaining to a patient what the intended effects are and any adverse effects or reactions to watch for. The patient should ask challenging questions, and the nurse should respond appropriately.***
Review the procedure for administration of medications by nose drops, sprays, and inhalation.	– Nursing process for sympathomimetic decongestants (p. 468)	CTQ 3-4 SG Review Sheet question 6 (p. 197) ▸ Discuss what drugs would enhance the toxic effects of nasal decongestants and how the nurse can determine if the patient is having problems based on these enhanced toxic effects. Class Activity ***Demonstrate how to administer nose drops, sprays, and inhalation medications. Are techniques different for self-administration than for administering to another person? How do techniques differ for children and adults or older adults who are unable to administer the medication for themselves?***
State the premedication assessments and nursing assessments needed during therapy to monitor therapeutic response and common and serious adverse effects from using decongestant drug therapy.	□ Drug class: Antihistamines (p. 469) – Nursing process for antihistamines (p. 469) Review the drug class antihistamines and their actions, uses, and therapeutic effects on allergic rhinitis. Discuss premedication assessments as well as common and serious adverse effects.	PPT 14 TB Multiple Response question 2 INRQ 1, 8, 10 CTQ 6 SG Review Sheet questions 10-12 (p. 197) SG Learning Activities questions 10-11, 14-15, 21 (pp. 199-200) SG Practice Questions for the NCLEX Examination 4, 9 (pp. 201-202) Review Questions for the NCLEX Examination 1-3, 6, 10 (pp. 473-474) Drug Table 30-2: Antihistamines (p. 470) ▸ Discuss the nature of antihistamines and how they act to relieve allergic rhinitis or conjunctivitis.

OBJECTIVES	CONTENT	TEACHING RESOURCES
		▸ Discuss the most common adverse effects of taking antihistamines and how a patient can minimize their impact. ▸ Discuss the effect of CNS depressants on a patient taking antihistamines. ▸ Discuss what to do if a patient develops a tolerance to the antihistamine being administered. ▸ Discuss the importance of assessing a patient's work environment before administering antihistamines. Class Activity ***Have two students role-play a nurse educating a patient taking Allegra. Have the class assist the "nurse" in determining what is important to discuss with the "patient." Review with the class therapeutic outcomes and common and serious adverse effects for antihistamines.***

30.2 Homework/Assignments:

30.2 Instructor's Notes/Student Feedback:

LESSON 30.3

CRITICAL THINKING QUESTION

An adult patient is prescribed an intranasal corticosteroid for his allergic rhinitis. He tells the nurse that his brother takes steroids for chronic obstructive pulmonary disease (COPD) and has developed thin skin, a round face, and a buffalo hump. The patient refuses to take the intranasal medication because he says stopping a runny nose is not worth the risk of serious adverse effects. How should the nurse respond?

Guidelines: The nurse should explain that although systemic steroid administration for COPD does carry serious risks and adverse effects, topical administration has far fewer problems. Nasal corticosteroids treat inflammation at the site of contact, the inner nose. Only very small amounts are absorbed into the body. The nurse also should explain that taking aerosol corticosteroids on a long-term basis, particularly at higher doses, carries a small risk of adverse effects in adults. These include an increased risk of glaucoma, cataracts, osteoporosis, and easy bruising. Individuals with certain health conditions should consult the health care provider before taking higher doses for long periods of time. The nurse should advise the patient to notify the health care provider of any changes in his skin, appearance, or susceptibility to infection.

ELSEVIER

OBJECTIVES	CONTENT	TEACHING RESOURCES
State the premedication assessments and nursing assessments needed during therapy to monitor therapeutic response and common and serious adverse effects from using decongestant drug therapy.	□ Drug class: Respiratory anti-inflammatory agents (p. 471) – Intranasal corticosteroids (p. 471) – Nursing process for intranasal corticosteroid therapy (p. 471) Review the drugs intranasal corticosteroids and cromolyn sodium in the drug class anti-inflammatory agents. Discuss the actions, uses, and therapeutic outcomes for these drugs. Review the common and serious adverse effects.	PPT 15 TB Multiple Response question 6 Animation: Corticosteroids SG Review Sheet question 16 (p. 198) SG Learning Activities questions 7-9, 16, (p. 199) SG Practice Question for the NCLEX Examination 8 (p. 202) Review Questions for the NCLEX Examination 4, 9 (pp. 473-474) Drug Table 30-3: Intranasal Corticosteroids (p. 472) ▸ Discuss when a patient would use intranasal corticosteroids and what their effect would be. ▸ Discuss why a patient should blow his or her nose thoroughly before administering intranasal corticosteroids. ▸ Discuss the importance of explaining that the effects of intranasal corticosteroids are not immediate and how a patient should be counseled on that aspect of the medication. ▸ Discuss the concept and implementation of maintenance therapy with respect to intranasal corticosteroids. Class Activity ***Have students create drug cards for corticosteroids, including adverse effects, available dosage, and form. Have them teach each other in pairs about the adverse effects and appropriate dosage of corticosteroids. How are the adverse effects of intranasal corticosteroids similar to or different from those of systemic corticosteroids?***
State the premedication assessments and nursing assessments needed during therapy to monitor therapeutic response and common and serious adverse effects from	– Nursing process for cromolyn sodium (p. 472)	PPT 16 INRQ 6, 9 SG Review Sheet questions 14-15 (p. 198) SG Practice Questions for the NCLEX Examination 5, 7 (pp. 201-202) Review Question for the NCLEX Examination 7 (p. 473) ▸ Discuss how cromolyn is administered differently from other medications for upper respiratory diseases.

OBJECTIVES	CONTENT	TEACHING RESOURCES
using decongestant drug therapy.		▸ Discuss the importance of trying cromolyn for a short period before continuing therapy. ▸ Discuss how to instruct a patient to prepare himself or herself before taking cromolyn. ▸ Discuss why a coughing adverse effect is risky when using cromolyn and what the nurse should do if this adverse effect occurs in the patient. Class Activity ***Have two students role-play a nurse educating a patient taking Flonase (nasal spray). Have the class assist the "nurse" in determining what is important to discuss with the "patient." Review with the class therapeutic outcomes and common and serious adverse effects for respiratory anti-inflammatory agents.***
Performance evaluation		Test Bank SG Learning Activities (pp. 199-200) SG Practice Questions for the NCLEX Examination (pp. 201-202) Critical Thinking Questions

30.3 Homework/Assignments:

30.3 Instructor's Notes/Student Feedback:

30 Lecture Outline

Drugs Used to Treat Upper Respiratory Disease

Slide 1

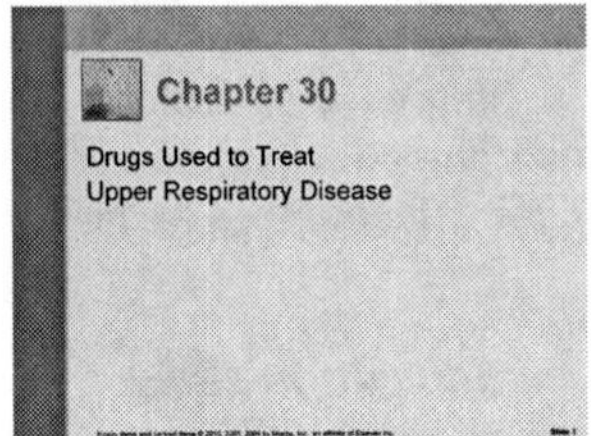
Chapter 30
Drugs Used to Treat
Upper Respiratory Disease

Slide 2

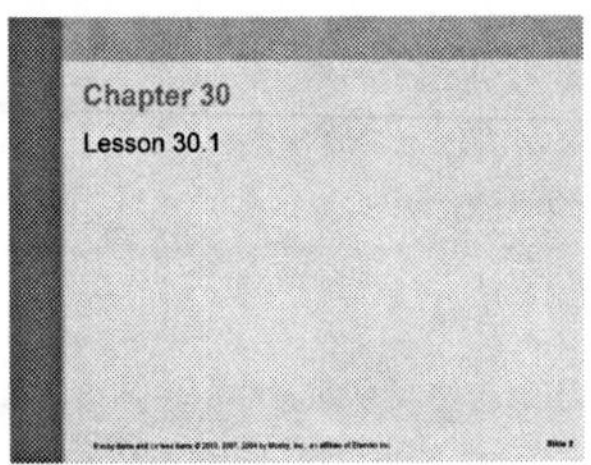
Chapter 30
Lesson 30.1

Slide 3

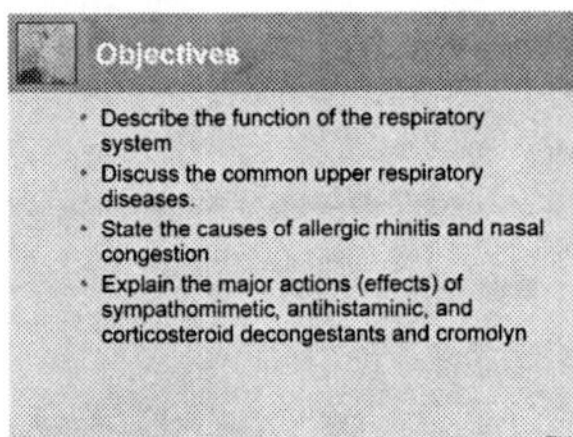
Objectives
Describe the function of the respiratory system
Discuss the common upper respiratory diseases.
State the causes of allergic rhinitis and nasal congestion
Explain the major actions (effects) of sympathomimetic, antihistaminic, and corticosteroid decongestants and cromolyn

Slide 4

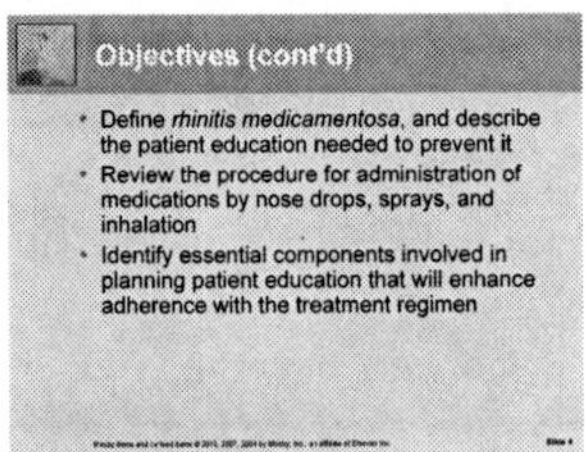
Objectives (cont'd)
Define rhinitis medicamentosa, and describe the patient education needed to prevent it
Review the procedure for administration of medications by nose drops, sprays, and inhalation
Identify essential components involved in planning patient education that will enhance adherence with the treatment regimen

Slide 5

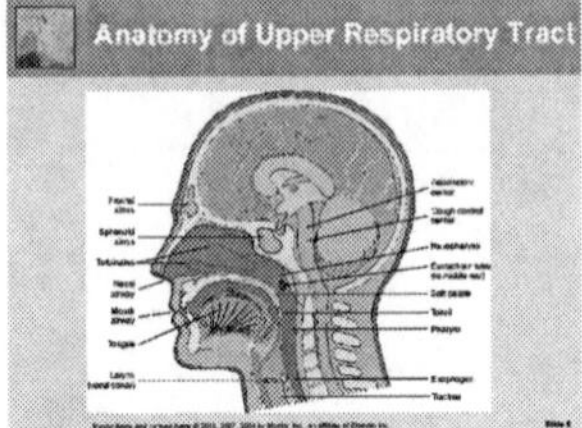
Anatomy of Upper Respiratory Tract

Slide 6

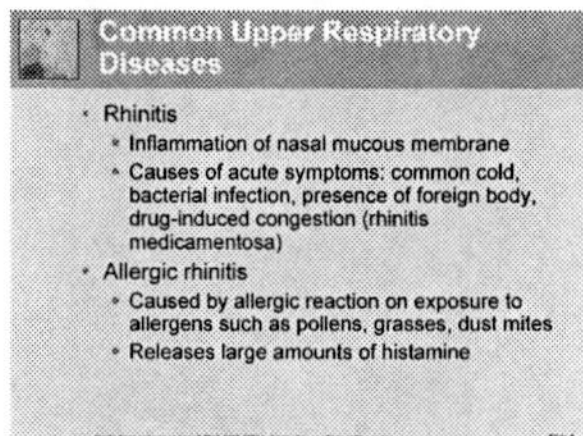
Common Upper Respiratory Diseases
Rhinitis
Inflammation of nasal mucous membrane
Causes of acute symptoms: common cold, bacterial infection, presence of foreign body, drug-induced congestion (rhinitis medicamentosa)
Allergic rhinitis
Caused by allergic reaction on exposure to allergens such as pollens, grasses, dust mites
Releases large amounts of histamine

- Rhinitis may be acute or chronic based on duration of symptoms.

Slide 7

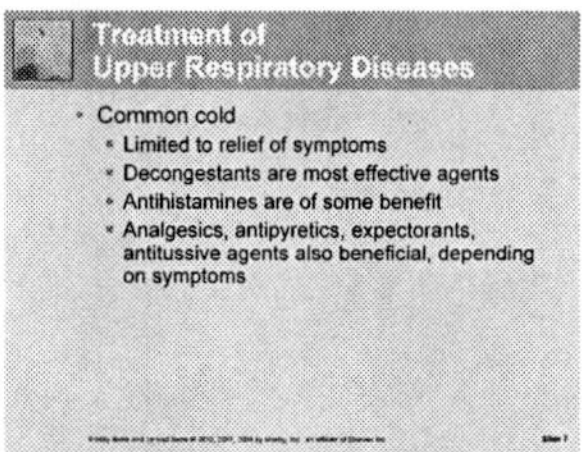
Treatment of Upper Respiratory Diseases
Common cold
Limited to relief of symptoms
Decongestants are most effective agents
Antihistamines are of some benefit
Analgesics, antipyretics, expectorants, antitussive agents also beneficial, depending on symptoms

- Conventional treatments: disinfect the environment, wash hands, obtain rest, and drink plenty of fluids.
- Usual viral course is 6 to 10 days.

Slide 8

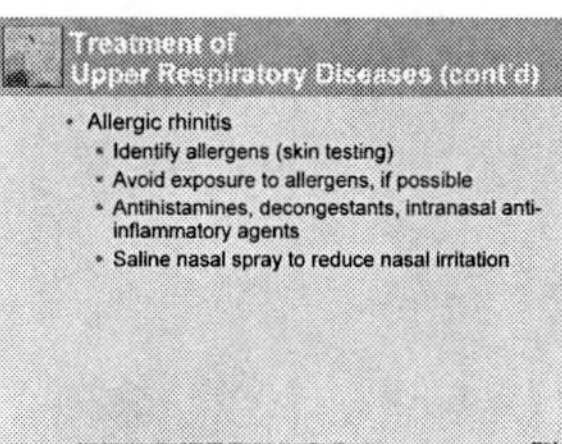
Treatment of Upper Respiratory Diseases (cont'd)
Allergic rhinitis
Identify allergens (skin testing)
Avoid exposure to allergens, if possible
Antihistamines, decongestants, intranasal anti-inflammatory agents
Saline nasal spray to reduce nasal irritation

- Immunotherapy may be indicated for partially controlled symptoms, need for high doses of corticosteroids, or with complications of asthma or sinusitis.

Slide 9

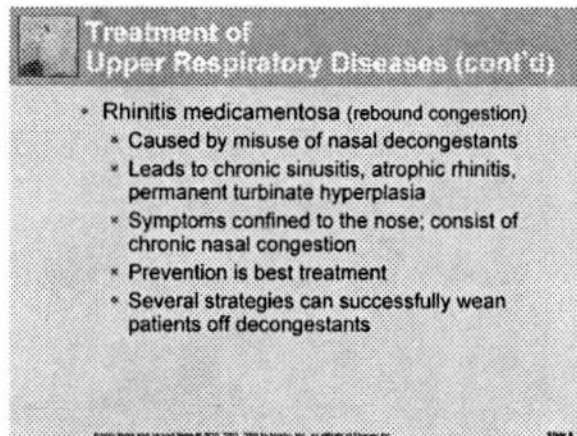
Treatment of Upper Respiratory Diseases (cont'd)
Rhinitis medicamentosa (rebound congestion)
Caused by misuse of nasal decongestants
Leads to chronic sinusitis, atrophic rhinitis, permanent turbinate hyperplasia
Symptoms confined to the nose; consist of chronic nasal congestion
Prevention is best treatment
Several strategies can successfully wean patients off decongestants

Slide 10

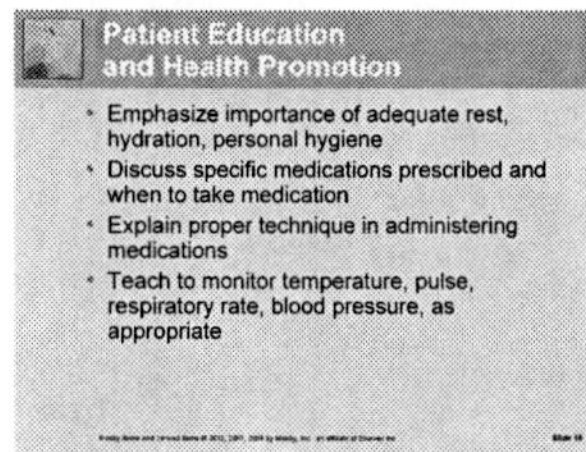
Patient Education and Health Promotion
Emphasize importance of adequate rest, hydration, personal hygiene
Discuss specific medications prescribed and when to take medication
Explain proper technique in administering medications
Teach to monitor temperature, pulse, respiratory rate, blood pressure, as appropriate

- Proper temperature and humidity soothe irritated nasopharyngeal mucosa.
- Discontinue smoking or using alcohol.

Slide 11

Chapter 30
Lesson 30.2

Slide 12

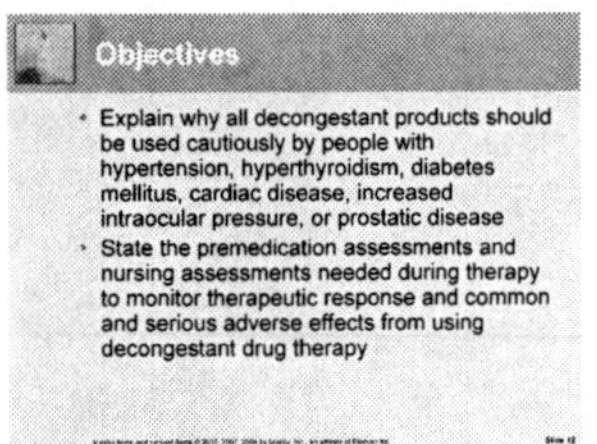
Objectives
Explain why all decongestant products should be used cautiously by people with hypertension, hyperthyroidism, diabetes mellitus, cardiac disease, increased intraocular pressure, or prostatic disease
State the premedication assessments and nursing assessments needed during therapy to monitor therapeutic response and common and serious adverse effects from using decongestant drug therapy

Slide 13

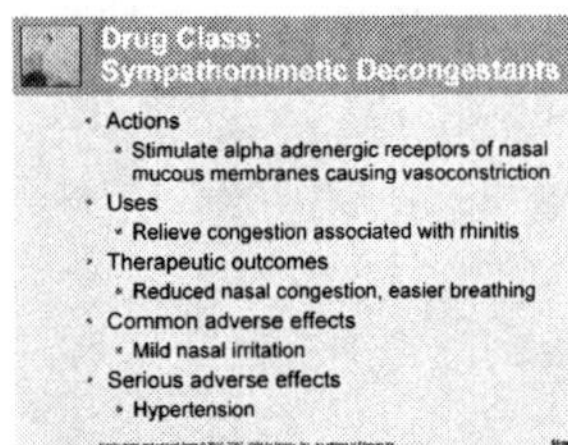
Drug Class: Sympathomimetic Decongestants
Actions
Stimulate alpha adrenergic receptors of nasal mucous membranes causing vasoconstriction
Uses
Relieve congestion associated with rhinitis
Therapeutic outcomes
Reduced nasal congestion, easier breathing
Common adverse effects
Mild nasal irritation
Serious adverse effects
Hypertension

- For specific drugs, see Table 30-1.
- Often used in conjunction with antihistamines to treat allergic rhinitis.
- Administered orally or topically as nasal spray; if used improperly, it can lead to rebound swelling.

Slide 14

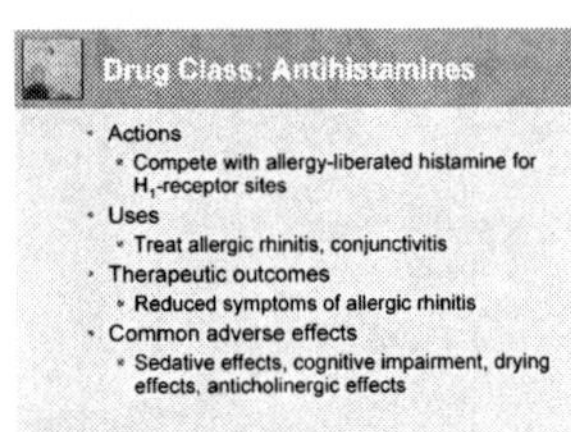
Drug Class: Antihistamines
Actions
Compete with allergy-liberated histamine for H1-receptor sites
Uses
Treat allergic rhinitis, conjunctivitis
Therapeutic outcomes
Reduced symptoms of allergic rhinitis
Common adverse effects
Sedative effects, cognitive impairment, drying effects, anticholinergic effects

- For specific drugs, see Table 30-2.
- Each drug differs in frequency and adverse effects.
- For best results, take on a scheduled basis and use before symptoms are expected to occur. Antihistamines will not stop nasal congestion.

Slide 15

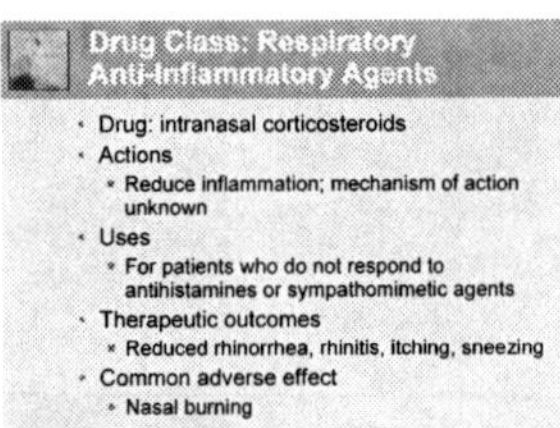
Drug Class: Respiratory Anti-Inflammatory Agents
Drug: intranasal corticosteroids
Actions
Reduce inflammation; mechanism of action unknown
Uses
For patients who do not respond to antihistamines or sympathomimetic agents
Therapeutic outcomes
Reduced rhinorrhea, rhinitis, itching, sneezing
Common adverse effect
Nasal burning

- For specific drugs, see Table 30-3.
- Use only for short term acute seasonal allergies.

Slide 16

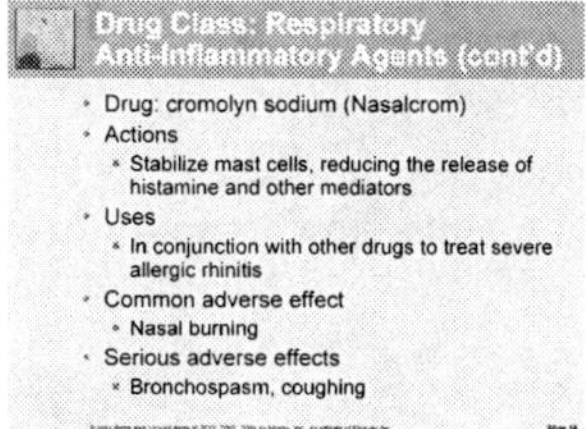
Drug Class: Respiratory Anti-Inflammatory Agents (cont'd)
Drug: cromolyn sodium (Nasalcrom)
Actions
Stabilize mast cells, reducing the release of histamine and other mediators
Uses
In conjunction with other drugs to treat severe allergic rhinitis
Common adverse effect
Nasal burning
Serious adverse effects
Bronchospasm, coughing

- Nonprescription.
- Usefulness is often limited because of the need for frequent dosing.
- May be most beneficial when used as a prophylactic treatment before an anticipated allergen exposure or in patients whose medical conditions do not allow the use of other medications (e.g., pregnancy).

31 Lesson Plan
Drugs Used to Treat Lower Respiratory Disease

TEACHING FOCUS

This chapter introduces the student to common lower respiratory diseases and how they are treated. The student will have the opportunity to learn about premedication and nursing assessments, how to administer medications, and how to provide patient education to encourage compliance.

MATERIALS AND RESOURCES

- ☐ computer and PowerPoint projector (all Lessons)
- ☐ materials for administering medications (Lesson 31.2)

LESSON CHECKLIST

Preparations for this lesson include:

- lecture
- guest speaker: respiratory therapist
- evaluation of student knowledge and skills needed to perform all entry-level nursing activities related to drugs used to treat lower respiratory disease, including:
  - causes of emphysema, chronic bronchitis, and asthma
  - educating patients taking drugs used to treat lower respiratory diseases
  - evaluation of medication effectiveness and adverse effects
  - premedication and nursing assessments
  - procedures for administration of medications

KEY TERMS

anti-inflammatory agents (p. 481)
antitussives (p. 481)
arterial blood gases (ABGs) (p. 477)
asthma (p. 478)
bronchitis (p. 478)
bronchodilation (p. 481)
bronchodilators (p. 481)
bronchospasm (p. 477)
chronic airflow limitation disease (CALD) (p. 477)
chronic obstructive pulmonary disease (COPD) (p. 477)
cough (p. 478)
diffusion (p. 476)
emphysema (p. 478)
expectorants (p. 481)
goblet cells (p. 476)
immunomodulators (p. 482)
mucolytic agents (p. 481)
obstructive airway diseases (p. 477)
oxygen saturation (p. 477)
perfusion (p. 476)
restrictive airway diseases (p. 477)
spirometry (p. 477)
ventilation (p. 476)

ADDITIONAL RESOURCES

PowerPoint slides: 1-28
Flashcards, Decks 1 and 2

Legend

ARQ	**PPT**	**TB**	**CTQ**	**SG**	**INRQ**
Audience Response Questions	PowerPoint Slides	Test Bank	Critical Thinking Questions	Study Guide	Interactive NCLEX Review Questions

Class Activities are indicated in ***bold italic.***

LESSON 31.1

BACKGROUND ASSESSMENT

Question: What is the difference between ventilation and perfusion?
Answer: Ventilation is the inhalation of air into the lungs and the exhalation of carbon dioxide from the lungs. During this process, oxygen is transported into the lungs as the chest expands. Carbon dioxide is forced out of the lungs as the chest muscles relax. Perfusion is the movement of oxygen across alveolar-capillary membranes into the bloodstream.

Question: What is a bronchodilator, and how does it work?
Answer: Bronchodilators are medications that work by relaxing the smooth muscles that line the airways. Certain conditions, such as asthma, cause airways to constrict, obstructing the amount of oxygen that can enter the lungs. Relaxing the smooth muscles makes the airways larger, allowing air to pass through the lungs more easily. Bronchodilators also are used to relieve breathing problems associated with emphysema, chronic bronchitis, and other lung diseases.

CRITICAL THINKING QUESTION

A patient newly diagnosed with COPD states, "My health care provider prescribed medications called corticosteroids. He said that they come in pill form and as an inhaler. I am used to taking pills and asked for the pill form, but he said the inhaler is better for me. Why is that?" What should the nurse say?
Guidelines: The health care provider makes the decision about which form of drug is best for the patient based on the disease stage. In acute stages of a respiratory disease or condition, an immediate or fast-acting medication, such as an oral steroid, is needed to bring the condition under control. In chronic respiratory conditions, prevention is key and can be accomplished through maintenance doses of inhaled medications, which are delivered directly to the site. Although oral (or systemic) steroids are appropriate treatments in acute or severe respiratory conditions, the potential for adverse effects is high. Therefore, it is important to consider other forms of administration, such as inhalers, for chronic use.

OBJECTIVES	CONTENT	TEACHING RESOURCES
Identify the structures of the lower respiratory tract and their functions.	■ Lower respiratory tract anatomy and physiology (p. 475) Review the anatomy of the lower respiratory tract and the purpose of goblet cells and serous glands.	PPT 5 ARQ 1 TB Multiple Choice questions 9-10 Figure 31-1 (p. 476): The respiratory tract and the alveoli. Class Activity ***Display Figure 31-1 (p. 476) without the names of the organs. Have students identify the following: pharynx, larynx, trachea, right and left mainstem bronchi, bronchioles, alveolar duct, and alveolar sacs. Have students discuss the physiology and function of the lungs. Review the exercise with the class.***
Describe the physiology of respirations.	■ Lower respiratory tract anatomy and physiology (p. 475) Discuss the difference between perfusion and diffusion in relation to ventilation. Review the respiratory tract's protective mechanisms—coughing,	PPT 5 SG Review Sheet question 1 (p. 203) SG Learning Activities questions 1, 6, 27 (pp. 207-208) Figure 31-2 (p. 476): Factors restricting the airway.

OBJECTIVES	CONTENT	TEACHING RESOURCES
	production of mucus, and ciliary hair function.	▸ Discuss the importance of the mucous fluids in the lower respiratory system and how they are produced. Class Activity ***Lead a discussion regarding the physiology and function of the lungs, focused on ventilation and perfusion. Review the exercise with the class.***
Compare the physiologic responses of the respiratory system to emphysema, chronic bronchitis, and asthma.	■ Common lower respiratory diseases (p. 477)	PPT 6 ARQ 2 Animation: Asthma SG Review Sheet questions 2, 5-8, 20 (pp. 203-204) SG Learning Activities questions 2-3, 9, 28-29, 33 (pp. 207-208) Table 31-2: Terminology Used with Spirometry (p. 478) Figure 31-3 (p. 479): Management of asthma in adults. Table 31-3: Classification, Characteristics, and Therapies for COPD (p. 480) ▸ Discuss the rise in incidence of asthma and what environmental or lifestyle factors might be contributing to that rise. Class Activity ***Divide the class into groups, and assign each group one of the following lower respiratory diseases:*** – ***Chronic bronchitis*** – ***Asthma*** – ***Emphysema*** ***Have each group outline the cause of its disease and make a chart about the pathophysiology. Have volunteer groups present to the class for questions and feedback. Ask the class how the diseases are similar and how they are different.***
Identify components of blood gases.	■ Common lower respiratory diseases (p. 477) Review pulmonary function tests and the components of blood gases.	PPT 7 TB Multiple Response question 2 SG Review Sheet questions 3-4, 15 (pp. 203-204) SG Learning Activities questions 8, 10 (p. 207) Table 31-1: Laboratory Tests Used to Assess Respiratory Function (p. 477)

OBJECTIVES	CONTENT	TEACHING RESOURCES
		▸ Discuss the concept of blood gases, their importance in the blood, and how they can be assessed to determine respiratory disease. ▸ Discuss what common laboratory and/or diagnostic studies would be used in assessing a patient for respiratory disease. Class Activity ***Ask volunteers to describe ABGs. How are they obtained? What information do they provide?***
Distinguish the mechanisms of action of expectorants, antitussives, and mucolytic agents.	■ Treatment of lower respiratory diseases (p. 480) ■ Drug therapy for lower respiratory diseases (p. 481) Review the treatment goals for each of the following disorders: cough, asthma, bronchitis, and emphysema. Discuss the guidelines for diagnosis and management of asthma including long-term control and quick relief medications.	PPT 14 ARQ 3-4 TB Multiple Choice question 1 INRQ 5 SG Review Sheet questions 9-11 (pp. 203-204) SG Learning Activities questions 4-5 (p. 207) ▸ Discuss what environmental factors might be adjusted to treat a cough. ▸ Discuss the importance of bronchodilators in the treatment of COPD. Class Activity ***Divide the class into small groups, and assign each group one of the following classes of drugs:*** – ***Expectorants*** – ***Antitussive agents*** – ***Mucolytic agents*** ***Ask each group to complete a drug card phototype that describes the mechanism of action, use, dosage, administration, adverse effects, and patient education. Are they used in conjunction with other drugs or treatment remedies? Allow class time for group presentation and discussion to differentiate the mechanisms of action for each drug.***

31.1 Homework/Assignments:

31.1 Instructor's Notes/Student Feedback:

LESSON 31.2

CRITICAL THINKING QUESTION

An adult patient who has asthma tells the nurse, "My health care provider told me to use my maintenance inhaler every day and also to take a rescue inhaler when I get an asthma attack. Why do I need to bother with the maintenance inhaler? Can't I just take the rescue inhalers when I feel sick?" How should the nurse respond?

Guidelines: The nurse should explain that there are two main types of medications to control asthma. (1) Maintenance medications include anti-inflammatories and long-lasting bronchodilators, which are often taken together to prevent attacks. Bronchodilators work by relaxing the muscles around the airway tubes to keep symptoms under control, especially at night, and last up to 12 hours. The nurse should emphasize that the patient should take the maintenance medication whether or not he experiences any symptoms. (2) The second type of asthma control medications are fast-acting bronchodilators that start working within 15 minutes and last about 4 hours. Rescue inhalers should only be used during an attack, when quick relief is needed. Current treatment guidelines indicate that a rescue inhaler should not be used more than twice a week. More frequent usage indicates that the asthma is not being controlled adequately and that a change in treatment plan should be considered. The nurse should encourage the patient to monitor the frequency and severity of attacks and immediately report any changes to the health care provider.

OBJECTIVES	CONTENT	TEACHING RESOURCES
Cite nursing assessments used to evaluate the respiratory status of a patient.	– Nursing process for lower respiratory diseases (p. 482)	PPT 8 TB Multiple Response questions 1, 3-4 SG Review Sheet question 14 (p. 204) SG Learning Activities questions 31-32 (p. 208) ▸ Discuss the critical elements of taking a patient history in assessing the patient for respiratory disease. Class Activity ***Lead the class in a discussion in which students describe the elements in a nursing assessment (data collection) to evaluate the respiratory status of a patient. What signs and symptoms might the nurse expect to find during inspection? During auscultation? What pulmonary function test might be used in diagnosis and testing the progression of a pulmonary condition?***
Review the procedures for administration of medication by inhalation.	– Nursing process for lower respiratory diseases (p. 482)	PPT 9 ARQ 5 TB Multiple Choice question 15 SG Review Sheet question 18 (p. 204) ▸ Discuss the importance of reducing anxiety in a patient as part of the implementation of therapies for respiratory disease. ▸ Discuss the proper procedure for administering inhaled medications. Demonstrate the correct way to hold inhalers and to teach the patient when to inhale, using a spacer.

OBJECTIVES	CONTENT	TEACHING RESOURCES
		Class Activity ***Invite a respiratory therapist to demonstrate and explain how to administer medications used to treat lower respiratory diseases. What patient education is appropriate? What are special considerations for children and older adults? Ask the speaker to address key factors in the appropriate use of inhalers and spacers, oxygen therapy, and in theophylline therapy. Have students prepare questions in advance.***
Implement patient education for patients receiving drug therapy for lower respiratory disease.	– Patient education and health promotion (p. 484)	PPT 10 TB Multiple Choice questions 13-14 TB Multiple Response question 5 INRQ 3-4 CTQ 4 Patient Self-Assessment Form: Respiratory Agents SG Review questions 16-18, 19, 21, 26-27, 35 (pp. 204-205) SG Practice Questions for the NCLEX Examination 6, 9 (pp. 209-210) Figure 31-4 (p. 485): Use of a spacer. ▸ Discuss how to instruct a patient in using a peak flow meter and why it is important for a person with respiratory disease. ▸ Discuss options that are available if a child or older adult cannot self-administer aerosol therapy medication. Class Activity ***Divide the class into small groups, and have each group outline a teaching plan for patients receiving a medication the group selects from each of the drug classes listed below. The groups should choose a disease or condition for which the drug is used.*** – ***Expectorants*** – ***Antitussives*** – ***Mucolytics*** ***The plan should incorporate associated factors, such as exercise, nutrition, environmental influences, and infection prevention. Ask volunteer groups to present their plan to the class for evaluation of teaching effectiveness. Then have pairs of students role-play a nurse teaching a patient key points in drug***

OBJECTIVES	CONTENT	TEACHING RESOURCES
		administration and other therapeutic measures to help manage the condition. Ask students to share what they have learned.
State the nursing assessments needed to monitor therapeutic response and the development of adverse effects from expectorant, antitussive, and mucolytic therapy.	□ Drug class: Expectorants (p. 486) – Nursing process for guaifenesin (p. 486) Review the drug guaifenesin from the drug class expectorants. Discuss its actions, uses, and therapeutic outcomes as well as common adverse effects.	PPT 15 TB Multiple Choice question 2 SG Review Sheet questions 22, 28 (pp. 204-205) SG Learning Activities question 11, 22 (pp. 207-208) ▸ Discuss the actions of expectorants and what common uses they might have. ▸ Discuss why a patient should be using a humidifier when taking an expectorant. Class Activity ***Based on the following scenarios, have students determine if the medication ordered is appropriate for the condition. Are there any special considerations in taking the drug?*** – ***After taking a prescribed expectorant, a patient who has emphysema starts to cough up copious amounts of mucus.*** – ***A 6-month-old infant is ordered saline solution for congestion.*** – ***Guaifenesin is ordered for a patient who has a dry cough. After 2 weeks, he now coughs up greenish mucus.***

31.2 Homework/Assignments:

31.2 Instructor's Notes/Student Feedback:

LESSON 31.3

CRITICAL THINKING QUESTION

A patient with COPD tells the nurse, "I take all of my medications as prescribed and they help. Is there anything else I can do to keep the condition under control?" What can the nurse advise?

Guidelines: The nurse can explain to the patient that a well-balanced diet is important for good nutrition and to maintain appropriate body weight. Too much weight can increase oxygen demands and make breathing problems worse. If the patient experiences shortness of breath, the patient can try eating small amounts of food throughout the day, instead of less frequent large meals. The patient should be encouraged to drink 8 to 10 glasses of water a day to help liquefy secretions. The nurse should remind the patient to avoid people who have respiratory infections because catching a cold or the flu can lead to serious complications and a long recovery time for people who have COPD. In addition, the nurse can suggest that moderate physical activity alternated with adequate rest periods helps maintain respiratory performance.

OBJECTIVES	CONTENT	TEACHING RESOURCES
State the nursing assessments needed to monitor therapeutic response and the development of adverse effects from expectorant, antitussive, and mucolytic therapy.	– Nursing process for potassium iodide (p. 487) – Nursing process for saline therapy (p. 487) □ Drug class: Antitussive agents (p. 487) – Nursing process for antitussive therapy (p. 488) □ Drug class: Mucolytic agents (p. 488) – Nursing process for acetylcysteine therapy (p. 489) Review the drug potassium iodide and its actions, uses, and therapeutic outcomes. Review common and serious adverse effects along with drug interactions for potassium iodide. Review the drug class saline solutions and its actions, uses, and therapeutic outcomes as inhalation therapy.	PPT 16-19 TB Multiple Choice question 3 TB Multiple Response question 6 INRQ 5-6, 10-12 CTQ 2-3 SG Review Sheet questions 23-25, 29-34, 36 (pp. 204-205) SG Learning Activities questions 12-13, 17-18, 30 (pp. 207-208) SG Practice Questions for the NCLEX Examination 1-3, 10, 15 (pp. 209-210) Review Questions for the NCLEX Examination 1, 6-7 (pp. 499-500) Drug Table 31-4: Antitussive Agents (p. 488) ▸ Discuss the effects of a saline solution on a patient with lower respiratory disease and how it would act in the patient. Class Activity ***Divide the class into several groups, and assign each group either the drug class antitussives or mucolytic agents (acetylcysteine). Ask the groups which assessments are appropriate to monitor the therapeutic effects of their assigned drug class. What findings would the nurse note if the outcome is as intended? What signs or symptoms indicate that the drug is not working as planned? Groups should also consider adverse effects and reactions, and interactions with other drugs. Have groups present their findings to the class. Then have the class compare and contrast the findings.***

ELSEVIER

OBJECTIVES	CONTENT	TEACHING RESOURCES
State the nursing assessments needed to monitor therapeutic response and the development of adverse effects from sympathomimetic bronchodilator therapy.	□ Drug class: Beta-adrenergic bronchodilating agents (p. 489) – Nursing process for beta-adrenergic bronchodilators (p. 490)	PPT 20 TB Multiple Choice questions 4, 8, 12 CTQ 1, 3 SG Review Sheet questions 12, 34, 37, 40 (pp. 204-206) SG Learning Activities questions 16, 19-20, (pp. 207-208) SG Practice Questions for the NCLEX Examination 4-5, 11 (pp. 209-210) Review Questions for the NCLEX Examination 2, 8 (p. 500) Drug Table 31-5: Bronchodilators (p. 491) ▸ Discuss why there are many adverse effects associated with the use of a beta-adrenergic bronchodilator and what can be done to minimize them. Class Activity ***Ask the class to evaluate the scenarios below and determine if the patients' symptoms are an adverse effect of the medication and, if so, why?*** – ***A patient who has bronchitis and associated wheezing takes propranolol and is not getting relief from his albuterol inhaler.*** – ***A patient who takes amitriptyline and has been taking pirbuterol says his heart is racing and skipping beats.*** – ***A patient who took terbutaline tablets with coffee at breakfast says that he feels nauseous.*** Class Activity ***Ask students to develop a teaching brochure and other educational materials for patients who have COPD. The materials should cover the following topics:*** – ***Treatment compliance*** – ***Smoking cessation*** – ***Avoiding irritants*** – ***Physical activity*** – ***Preventing infections*** – ***Nutrition and hydration*** ***Ask students to present their materials to the class for feedback. What elements are most effective?***
State the nursing assessments needed to monitor	□ Drug class: Anticholinergic bronchodilating agents (p. 490)	PPT 21 TB Multiple Choice questions 5, 11

OBJECTIVES	CONTENT	TEACHING RESOURCES
therapeutic response and the development of adverse effects from anticholinergic bronchodilator therapy.	– Nursing process for ipratropium (p. 492) – Nursing process for tiotropium (p. 493) Review the drugs ipratropium and tiotropium from the drug class anticholinergic bronchodilating agents. Discuss their actions, uses, and therapeutic outcomes as well as their common and serious adverse effects.	TB Multiple Response question 7 CTQ 3 SG Review Sheet questions 34, 38-39 (pp. 205-206) SG Learning Activities questions 21, 34 (p. 208) Review Question for the NCLEX Examination 9 (p. 500) ▸ Discuss the importance of teaching the patient how to inhale medication and what common misconceptions a patient might have about administering such medications. Class Activity ***Divide the class in half to compare and contrast sympathomimetic and anticholinergic bronchodilators. How does the drug act to produce a therapeutic response? What adverse effects can be expected, and are there any contraindications to use? Ask students what it means if a patient is using an increased amount of bronchodilators in a day. What nursing assessments and possible interventions are appropriate for the nurse to provide?***

31.3 Homework/Assignments:

31.3 Instructor's Notes/Student Feedback:

LESSON 31.4

CRITICAL THINKING QUESTION

A patient who has chronic bronchitis says, "I have been in and out of the hospital for 3 years. What are we trying to accomplish with all these exhausting procedures and so many medications? Taking oxygen everywhere is a nuisance. My doctor says my condition is not curable anyway." How can the nurse explain the treatment goals of managing chronic bronchitis?

Guidelines: The nurse can explain to the patient that in addition to medication, pulmonary rehabilitation programs aim to help patients who have chronic respiratory conditions. Interdisciplinary approaches using occupational and respiratory therapies can improve airway function and allow greater mobility. Common strategies involve aerobic exercise, such as walking or bicycling, starting slowly and progressing to longer durations. Oxygen supplementation can be used, and breathing instruction can help patients reduce exhaustion caused by a rapid respiratory rate. The nurse can explain that correcting decreased oxygen improves survival and quality of life. Oxygen is often used at night to improve sleep quality and decrease the frequency of nocturnal arrhythmias. The nurse can help the patient find ways to make the portable oxygen tank more convenient. The nurse also should stress that the patient avoid exposure to inhaled irritants, such as dust, gases, sulfur dioxide, and even aerosolized hair and deodorant products. The nurse can offer to put the patient and family in contact with community support services and educate family members about how they can support the treatment procedures to ensure compliance.

OBJECTIVES	CONTENT	TEACHING RESOURCES
State the nursing assessments needed to monitor therapeutic response and the development of adverse effects from xanthine derivative therapy.	□ Drug class: Xanthine derivative bronchodilating agents (p. 493) – Nursing process for xanthine derivative bronchodilators (p. 493) Review the drug class xanthine derivative bronchodilating agents. Discuss their actions, uses, therapeutic outcomes, common and serious adverse effects, and drug interactions.	PPT 22 TB Multiple Choice question 6 CTQ 3 SG Review Sheet questions 34, 41-44 (pp. 205-206) SG Practice Questions for the NCLEX Examination 13-14 (p. 210) Review Questions for the NCLEX Examination 3, 5 (p. 500) ▸ Discuss why a xanthine derivative might be more effective on a patient with chronic asthma. Class Activity ***Divide the students in several groups. Have students make drug cards with examples of drugs from the following classes: expectorants, mucolytics, beta-adrenergic bronchodilators, sympathomimetic bronchodilators, anticholinergic bronchodilators, xanthine derivative bronchodilators, anti-inflammatory agents, corticosteroids, antileukotriene agents, and immunomodulators. Have the students outline indications, therapeutic outcomes, and adverse effects for each class. Have the students make a table of agents available for patients with respiratory disorders.***
State the nursing assessments needed to monitor therapeutic response and the development of adverse effects from corticosteroid inhalant therapy.	□ Drug class: Respiratory anti-inflammatory agents (p. 494) – Nursing process for corticosteroids (p. 494) □ Drug class: Antileukotriene agents (p. 496) – Nursing process for montelukast (p. 496) – Nursing process for zafirlukast (p. 497)	PPT 23-26 TB Multiple Choice questions 7, 16 INRQ 1-2, 7-9 CTQ 3 SG Review Sheet questions 13, 34, 45-47 (pp. 204-206) SG Learning Activities questions 7, 14-15, 22-26, 35 (pp. 207-208)

OBJECTIVES	CONTENT	TEACHING RESOURCES
	□ Drug class: Immunomodulator agent (p. 497) – Nursing process for omalizumab (p. 497) □ Drug class: Miscellaneous anti-inflammatory agents (p. 498) – Nursing process for cromolyn sodium (p. 498)	SG Practice Questions for the NCLEX Examination 7-8, 12 (p. 210) Review Questions for the NCLEX Examination 4, 10-11 (p. 500) Drug Table 31-6: Inhalant Corticosteroids (p. 495) Class Activity ***Divide the class into groups, and assign each group one of the clinical situations below. What are realistic treatment goals for each patient? What medications would likely be prescribed?*** – ***Patient with chronic bronchitis who uses a wheelchair*** – ***Patient with COPD who uses oxygen 24 hours a day*** – ***Patient with chronic bronchitis who is admitted to the hospital with flu*** – ***Pediatric patient with asthma who has asthma attacks once a month*** – ***Adult asthma patient who uses an emergency inhaler every week*** ***Ask the groups to share their conclusions with the class. As a class, compare and contrast the treatment goals. What is the nurse's role in assessment and monitoring, and what nursing interventions are appropriate?*** Class Activity ***Divide the class into groups of two, and have each group develop an educational plan for a patient who will be on home corticosteroid inhalant therapy. Allow class time for group presentation and discussion.*** Class Activity ***Divide the class into four groups. Assign each group one of these drug classes: corticosteroids, antileukotrienes, immunomodulators, or miscellaneous anti-inflammatories. Have each group select a specific drug in its category and present to the class the drug's use, action, special considerations, common adverse effects, and contraindications.***
Performance evaluation		Test Bank SG Learning Activities (pp. 207-208) SG Practice Questions for the NCLEX Examination (pp. 209-210) Critical Thinking Questions

31.4 Homework/Assignments:

31.4 Instructor's Notes/Student Feedback:

Lecture Outline

31 Drugs Used to Treat Lower Respiratory Disease

Slide 1

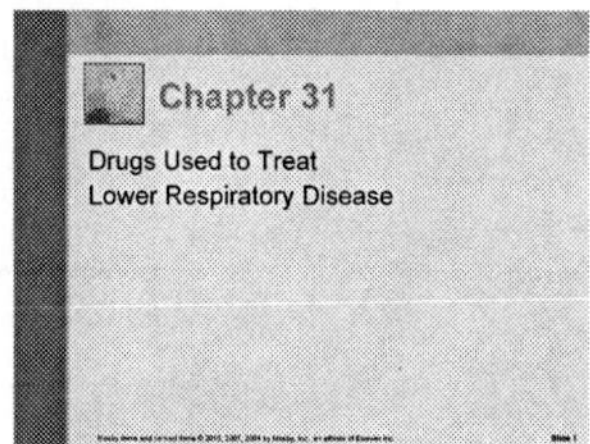
Chapter 31
Drugs Used to Treat
Lower Respiratory Disease

Slide 2

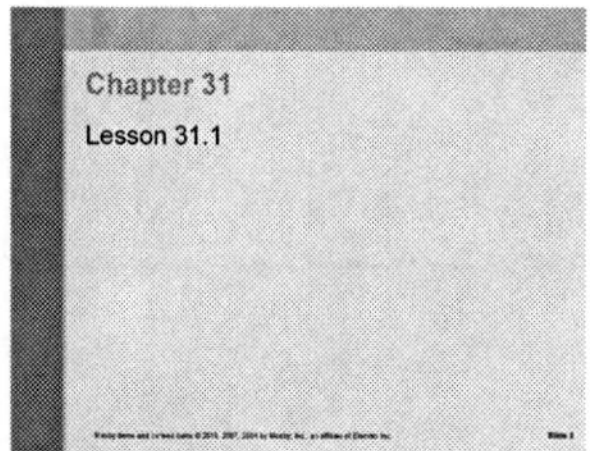
Chapter 31
Lesson 31.1

Slide 3

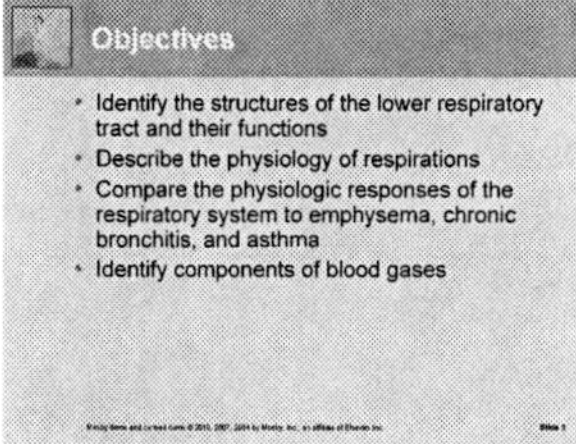
Objectives
Identify the structures of the lower respiratory tract and their functions
Describe the physiology of respirations
Compare the physiologic responses of the respiratory system to emphysema, chronic bronchitis, and asthma
Identify components of blood gases

Slide 4

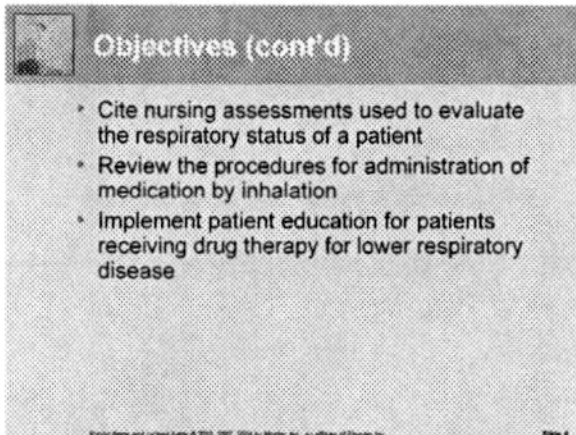
Objectives (cont'd)
Cite nursing assessments used to evaluate the respiratory status of a patient
Review the procedures for administration of medication by inhalation
Implement patient education for patients receiving drug therapy for lower respiratory disease

Slide 5

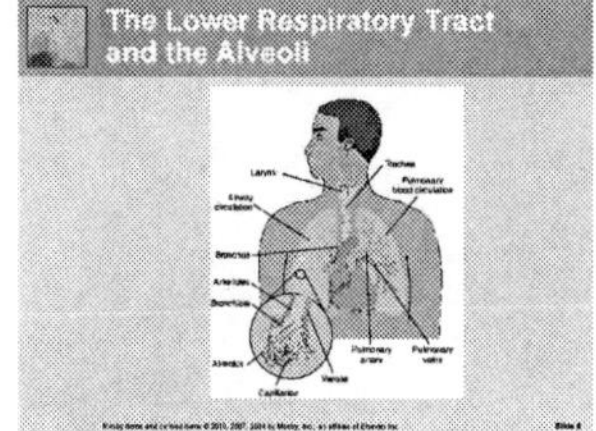
The Lower Respiratory Tract and the Alveoli

Slide 6

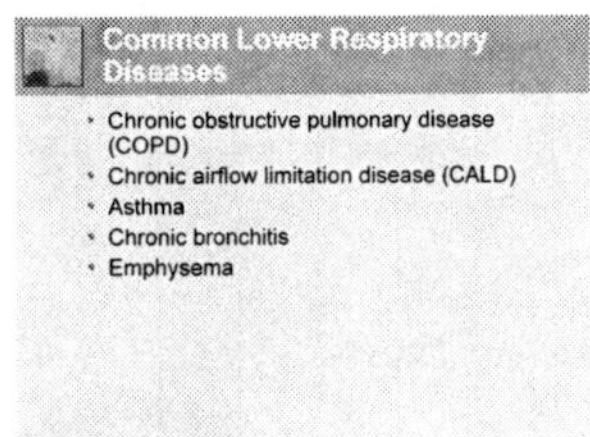
Common Lower Respiratory Diseases
Chronic obstructive pulmonary disease (COPD)
Chronic airflow limitation disease (CALD)
Asthma
Chronic bronchitis
Emphysema

- Respiratory diseases are divided into two types: obstructive and restrictive.
- Obstructive airway diseases are asthma and acute bronchitis.
- Restrictive airway diseases are chronic bronchitis and emphysema.

Slide 7

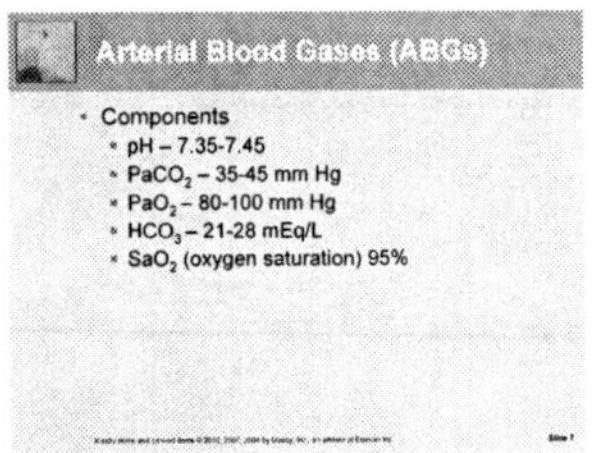
Arterial Blood Gases (ABGs)
Components
pH – 7.35-7.45
PaCO2 – 35-45 mm Hg
PaO2 – 80-100 mm Hg
HCO3 – 21-28 mEq/L
SaO2 (oxygen saturation) 95%

Slide 8

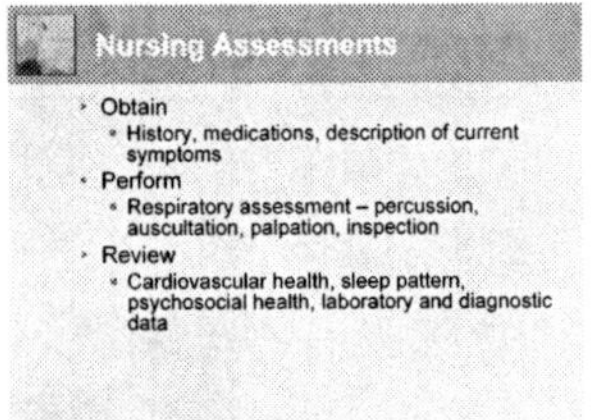
Nursing Assessments
Obtain
History, medications, description of current symptoms
Perform
Respiratory assessment – percussion, auscultation, palpation, inspection
Review
Cardiovascular health, sleep pattern, psychosocial health, laboratory and diagnostic data

---

Slide 9

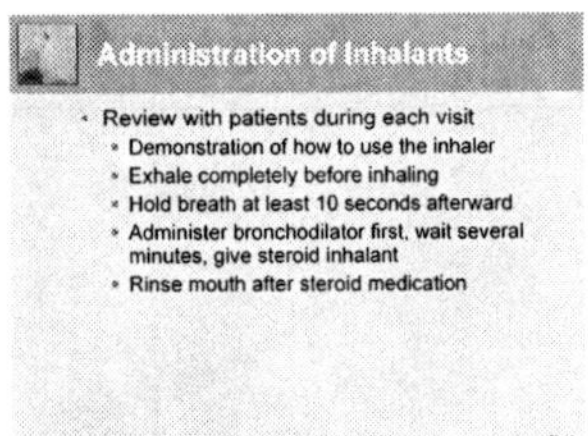
Administration of Inhalants
Review with patients during each visit
Demonstration of how to use the inhaler
Exhale completely before inhaling
Hold breath at least 10 seconds afterward
Administer bronchodilator first, wait several minutes, give steroid inhalant
Rinse mouth after steroid medication

Slide 10

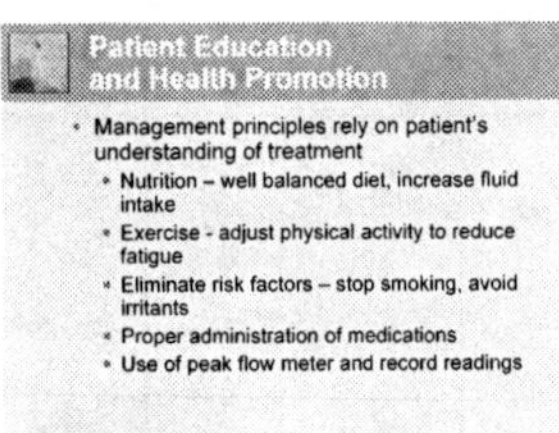
Patient Education and Health Promotion
Management principles rely on patient's understanding of treatment
Nutrition – well balanced diet, increase fluid intake
Exercise - adjust physical activity to reduce fatigue
Eliminate risk factors – stop smoking, avoid irritants
Proper administration of medications
Use of peak flow meter and record readings

- Describe ways to prevent infections.

Slide 11

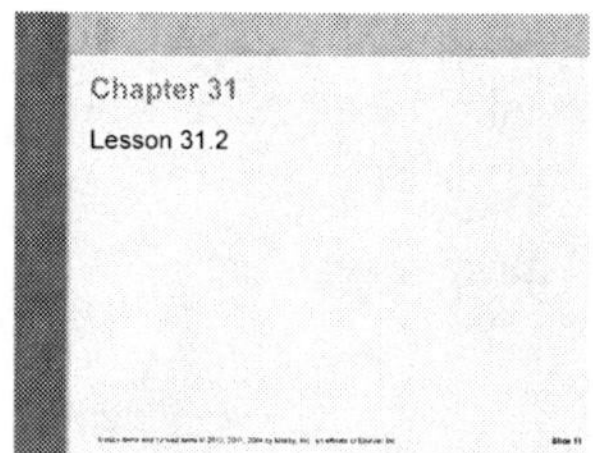
Chapter 31
Lesson 31.2

Slide 12

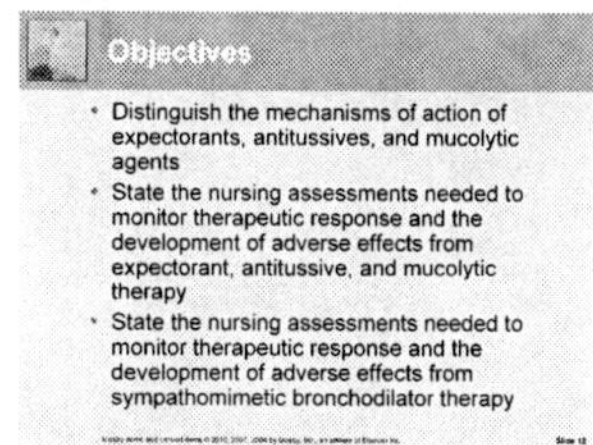
Objectives
Distinguish the mechanisms of action of expectorants, antitussives, and mucolytic agents
State the nursing assessments needed to monitor therapeutic response and the development of adverse effects from expectorant, antitussive, and mucolytic therapy
State the nursing assessments needed to monitor therapeutic response and the development of adverse effects from sympathomimetic bronchodilator therapy

Slide 13

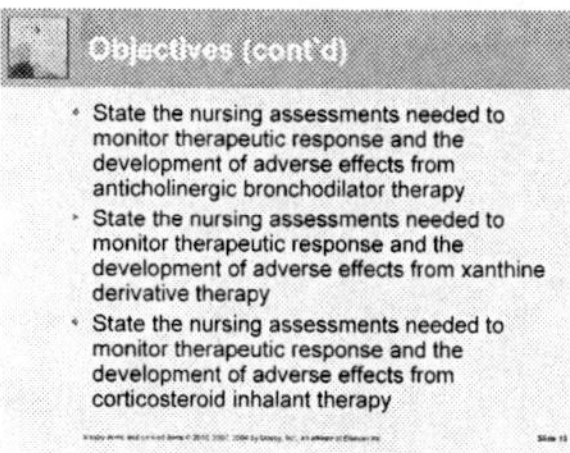
Objectives (cont'd)
State the nursing assessments needed to monitor therapeutic response and the development of adverse effects from anticholinergic bronchodilator therapy
State the nursing assessments needed to monitor therapeutic response and the development of adverse effects from xanthine derivative therapy
State the nursing assessments needed to monitor therapeutic response and the development of adverse effects from corticosteroid inhalant therapy

Slide 14

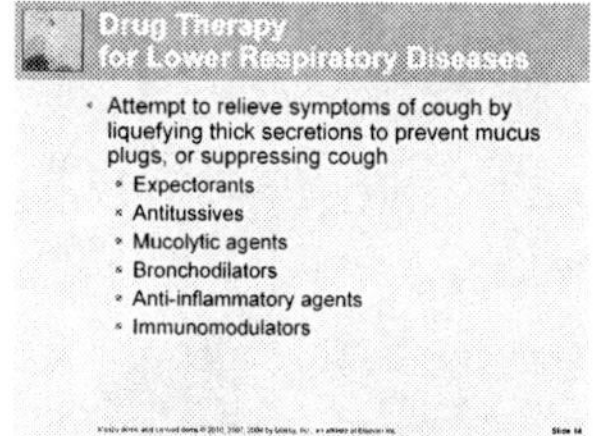
Drug Therapy for Lower Respiratory Diseases
Attempt to relieve symptoms of cough by liquefying thick secretions to prevent mucus plugs, or suppressing cough
Expectorants
Antitussives
Mucolytic agents
Bronchodilators
Anti-inflammatory agents
Immunomodulators

Slide 15

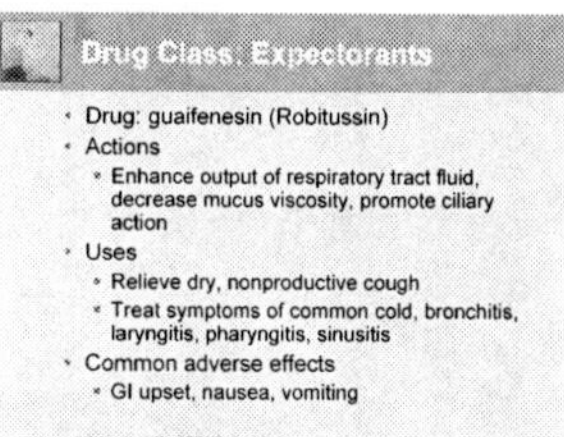
Drug Class: Expectorants
Drug: guaifenesin (Robitussin)
Actions
Enhance output of respiratory tract fluid, decrease mucus viscosity, promote ciliary action
Uses
Relieve dry, nonproductive cough
Treat symptoms of common cold, bronchitis, laryngitis, pharyngitis, sinusitis
Common adverse effects
GI upset, nausea, vomiting

- Used in combination with other agents to aid in making a nonproductive cough more productive.

Mosby items and derived items © 2010, 2007, 2004, by Mosby, Inc., an affiliate of Elsevier Inc.

Slide 16

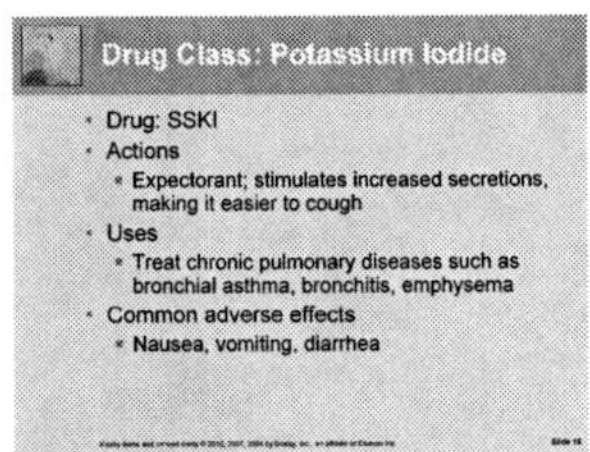
Drug Class: Potassium Iodide
Drug: SSKI
Actions
Expectorant; stimulates increased secretions, making it easier to cough
Uses
Treat chronic pulmonary diseases such as bronchial asthma, bronchitis, emphysema
Common adverse effects
Nausea, vomiting, diarrhea

- Patients should notify the prescriber if taking any other medications containing potassium.
- Concurrent use of humidification in patients taking expectorants helps to decrease the viscosity of secretions.
- Long-term use may result in goiter; thyroid function tests are important.

Slide 17

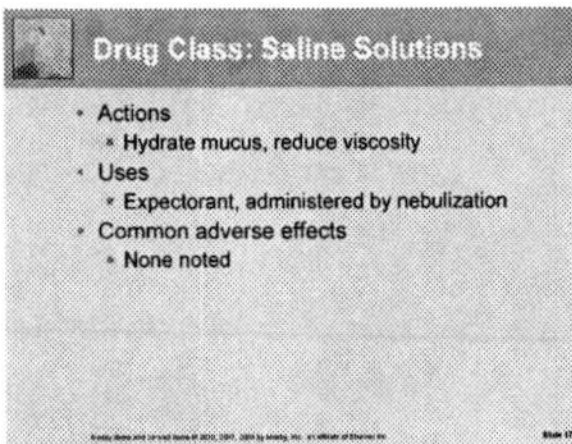
Drug Class: Saline Solutions
Actions
Hydrate mucus, reduce viscosity
Uses
Expectorant, administered by nebulization
Common adverse effects
None noted

- Commonly given to pediatric patients who cannot take antihistamines or cough suppressants.
- Therapeutic outcome: moisturized mucous membranes for less irritation from dryness.

Slide 18

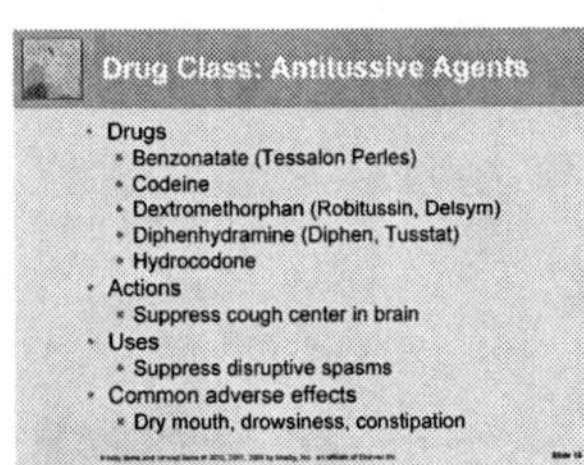
Drug Class: Antitussive Agents
Drugs
Benzonatate (Tessalon Perles)
Codeine
Dextromethorphan (Robitussin, Delsym)
Diphenhydramine (Diphen, Tusstat)
Hydrocodone
Actions
Suppress cough center in brain
Uses
Suppress disruptive spasms
Common adverse effects
Dry mouth, drowsiness, constipation

- Should be used for nonproductive cough only.

Slide 19

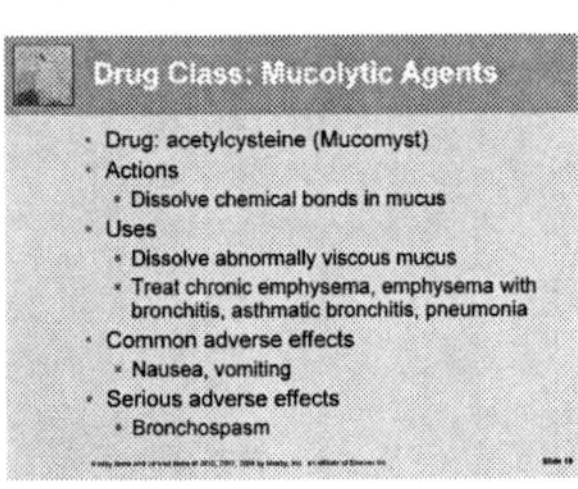
Drug Class: Mucolytic Agents
Drug: acetylcysteine (Mucomyst)
Actions
Dissolve chemical bonds in mucus
Uses
Dissolve abnormally viscous mucus
Treat chronic emphysema, emphysema with bronchitis, asthmatic bronchitis, pneumonia
Common adverse effects
Nausea, vomiting
Serious adverse effects
Bronchospasm

- Can also be used to treat Tylenol toxicity.
- Concurrent use of a bronchodilator may be necessary to prevent bronchospasm.
- Therapeutic outcome: improved airway flow.

Slide 20

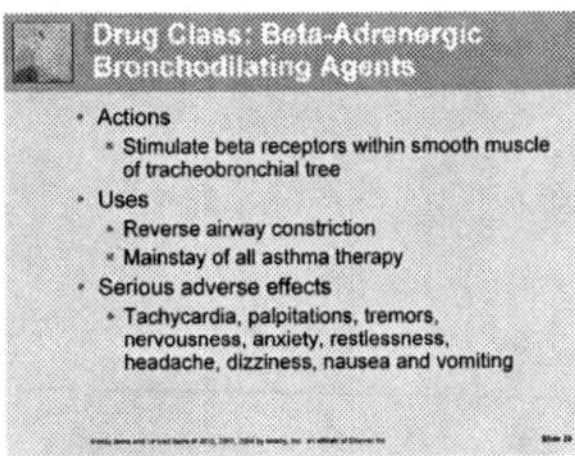
Drug Class: Beta-Adrenergic Bronchodilating Agents
Actions
Stimulate beta receptors within smooth muscle of tracheobronchial tree
Uses
Reverse airway constriction
Mainstay of all asthma therapy
Serious adverse effects
Tachycardia, palpitations, tremors, nervousness, anxiety, restlessness, headache, dizziness, nausea and vomiting

- For specific drugs, see Table 31-5.
- Used in conditions of chronic and acute asthma, bronchitis, emphysema.
- Therapeutic outcome: easier breathing with reduced wheezing.

Slide 21

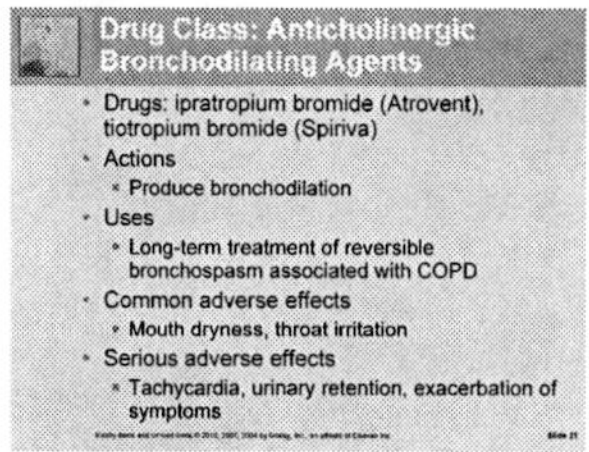
Drug Class: Anticholinergic Bronchodilating Agents
Drugs: ipratropium bromide (Atrovent), tiotropium bromide (Spiriva)
Actions
Produce bronchodilation
Uses
Long-term treatment of reversible bronchospasm associated with COPD
Common adverse effects
Mouth dryness, throat irritation
Serious adverse effects
Tachycardia, urinary retention, exacerbation of symptoms

- Used in combination with beta adrenergic bronchodilators.
- Best used for prophylaxis and maintenance and not for acute attacks.
- Tiotropium longer in duration of action than ipratropium.

Slide 22

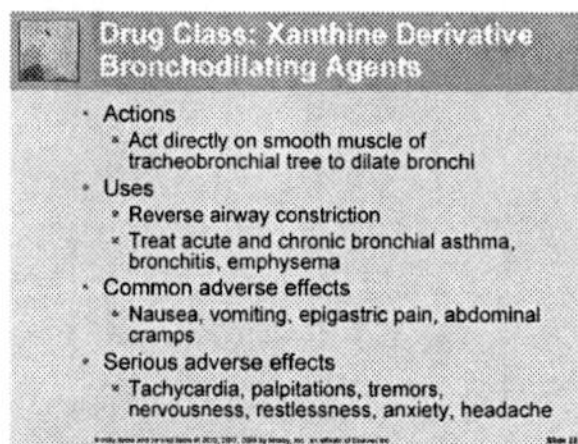
Drug Class: Xanthine Derivative Bronchodilating Agents
Actions
Act directly on smooth muscle of tracheobronchial tree to dilate bronchi
Uses
Reverse airway constriction
Treat acute and chronic bronchial asthma, bronchitis, emphysema
Common adverse effects
Nausea, vomiting, epigastric pain, abdominal cramps
Serious adverse effects
Tachycardia, palpitations, tremors, nervousness, restlessness, anxiety, headache

- For specific drugs, see Table 31-5.

Slide 23

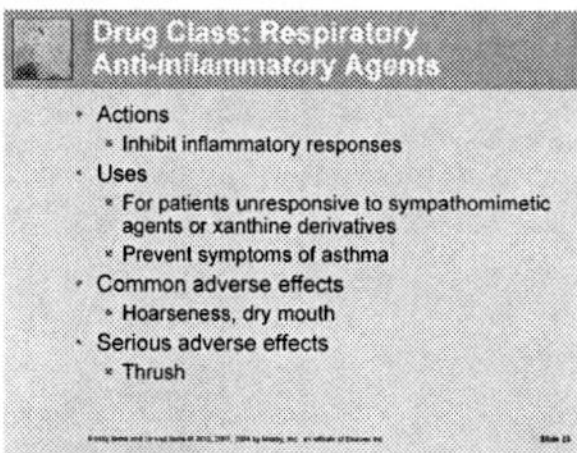
Drug Class: Respiratory Anti-inflammatory Agents
Actions
Inhibit inflammatory responses
Uses
For patients unresponsive to sympathomimetic agents or xanthine derivatives
Prevent symptoms of asthma
Common adverse effects
Hoarseness, dry mouth
Serious adverse effects
Thrush

- For specific drugs, see Table 31-6.
- Aerosols enhance effects of beta-adrenergic bronchodilators and have a direct effect on smooth muscle relaxation.
- Oral hygiene following inhalation is recommended and can prevent fungal infections.

Slide 24

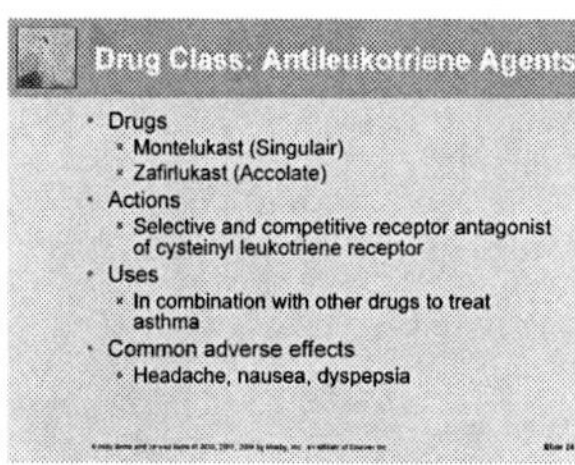
Drug Class: Antileukotriene Agents
Drugs
Montelukast (Singulair)
Zafirlukast (Accolate)
Actions
Selective and competitive receptor antagonist of cysteinyl leukotriene receptor
Uses
In combination with other drugs to treat asthma
Common adverse effects
Headache, nausea, dyspepsia

- Not bronchodilators; given orally. Should not be used to treat acute episodes of asthma.
- The cysteinyl leukotriene receptor is the one that leukotriene D4 and E4 stimulates to trigger asthma symptoms.

Slide 25

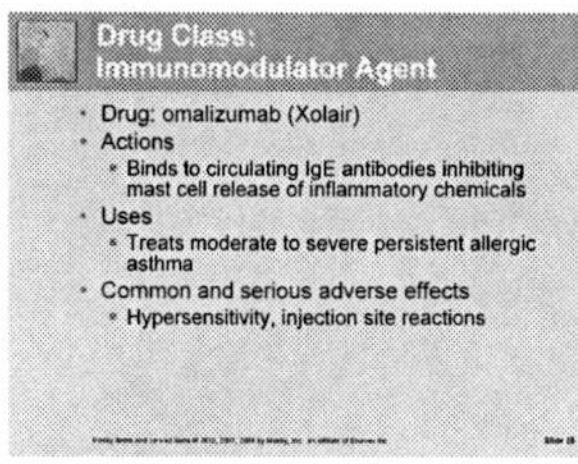
Drug Class: Immunomodulator Agent
Drug: omalizumab (Xolair)
Actions
Binds to circulating IgE antibodies inhibiting mast cell release of inflammatory chemicals
Uses
Treats moderate to severe persistent allergic asthma
Common and serious adverse effects
Hypersensitivity, injection site reactions

- Administered as a subcutaneous injection given every 2 or 4 weeks.
- Patients must have a minimum 12-year history of asthma and a positive skin test to airborne allergens and symptoms that are not adequately controlled with inhaled corticosteroids.

Slide 26

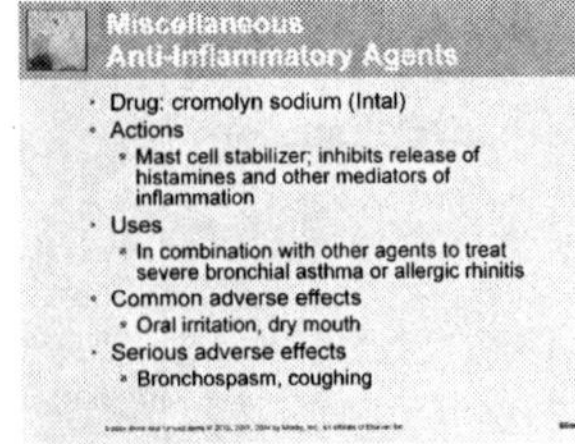
Miscellaneous
Anti-Inflammatory Agents
Drug: cromolyn sodium (Intal)
Actions
Mast cell stabilizer; inhibits release of histamines and other mediators of inflammation
Uses
In combination with other agents to treat severe bronchial asthma or allergic rhinitis
Common adverse effects
Oral irritation, dry mouth
Serious adverse effects
Bronchospasm, coughing

- Used for prophylactic management of bronchospasms and asthma.
- Also used just before exposure to conditions or substances that cause bronchospasm (wheezing or difficulty in breathing).
- Will not help an asthma or bronchospasm attack that has already started.

ELSEVIER

32 Lesson Plan
Drugs Used to Treat Oral Disorders

TEACHING FOCUS

In this chapter, the student is introduced to oral disorders affecting adult and pediatric patients. The student also has the opportunity to learn about drug therapy regimens used to treat oral disorders, including cold sores, canker sores, plaque, xerostomia, and candidal infections of soft tissues of the tongue, cheeks, and gums.

MATERIALS AND RESOURCES

☐ computer and PowerPoint projector (Lesson 32.1)

LESSON CHECKLIST

Preparations for this lesson include:

- lecture
- student performance evaluation of all entry-level skills required for student comprehension and application of patient care, including:
  - knowledge of oral disorders
  - patient teaching plans
  - drug therapy for oral disorders

KEY TERMS

candidiasis (p. 502)
canker sores (p. 501)
cold sores (fever blisters) (p. 501)
dental caries (p. 502)
dentifrices (p. 506)
gingivitis (p. 502)
halitosis (p. 502)
mouthwashes (p. 506)
mucositis (p. 502)
plaque (p. 502)
tartar (p. 502)
xerostomia (p. 504)

ADDITIONAL RESOURCES

PowerPoint slides: 1-11
Flashcards, Decks 1 and 2

Legend

ARQ	**PPT**	**TB**	**CTQ**	**SG**	**INRQ**
Audience Response Questions	PowerPoint Slides	Test Bank	Critical Thinking Questions	Study Guide	Interactive NCLEX Review Questions

Class Activities are indicated in ***bold italic.***

LESSON 32.1

BACKGROUND ASSESSMENT

Question: What are common disorders affecting the mouth? Briefly describe the causes of each.
Answer: Common disorders affecting the mouth are cold sores on the lip, canker sores, and candidal infections of soft tissues of the tongue, cheeks, and gums; disorders affecting the gums and teeth include plaque and calculus. Cold sores (fever blisters) are caused by the herpes simplex type 1 virus. Canker sores are thought to be a hypersensitivity to antigenic components of *Streptococcus sanguis*, but the exact cause is unknown. Candidiasis is a fungal infection caused by *Candida albicans*, the most common organism

associated with oral infections. Mucositis is a general term used to describe a painful inflammation of the mucous membranes of the mouth. It is commonly associated with chemotherapy and radiation therapy. Halitosis is a general term used to describe foul mouth odor. It can be caused by eating certain foods or may indicate an underlying pathologic condition.

Question: What are the primary goals of treatment for mouth disorders? List some common drugs related to the primary treatment goal.
Answer: The goals of treatment are to control discomfort, allow healing, prevent spread to others, and prevent complications. Topical analgesics and oral analgesics are commonly used to control pain. Secondary infections can be treated with topical antibiotic ointments, such as Neosporin or Mycitracin. Aphthasol is a topical anti-inflammatory agent that helps to promote healing.

CRITICAL THINKING QUESTION

A 13-year-old girl asks the community clinic nurse if she will get sores on her mouth after kissing her boyfriend, who told the girl he had cold sores. She tells the nurse that she has never had a cold sore. Upon examination, the nurse notes no abnormal findings. How should the nurse respond to the girl's question?
Guidelines: The nurse should first calm the patient's fears by explaining that most people who have recurring outbreaks of mouth lesions are infected before age 5. If this patient had been infected at a very young age, she most likely would have had an outbreak several years before now. Once a person contracts herpes simplex type 1 virus, it remains in the person's system, and there is no known cure. Lesions appear intermittently, between latent periods, and may be exacerbated by stress or illness. Obtaining a past medical history is important in patient education, and the nurse should emphasize prevention. The nurse should inform the patient that the herpes virus is easily transmitted, so protection is necessary. If she were to become infected, symptoms would include itching, burning, and numbness in the area where the lesion develops. There could be some glandular enlargement, and the actual sore would develop over 2 to 3 days. The nurse should tell the girl that liquid in the vesicles of the lesion contains live virus that is highly contagious if transferred to others by direct contact, such as kissing. Secondary bacterial infections also may occur that can be treated with antibiotics.

OBJECTIVES	CONTENT	TEACHING RESOURCES
Discuss common mouth disorders.	■ Mouth disorders (p. 501) Review the following mouth disorders and their symptoms: cold sores, canker sores, candidiasis, and mucositis. Discuss plaque formation, halitosis, and xerostomia. Review ways to prevent or control these conditions.	PPT 4-5 Review Questions for the NCLEX Examination 5, 7 (pp. 507-508) ▸ Discuss the difference between cold sores and canker sores. ▸ Discuss the signs and symptoms of cold sores. Class Activity ***Divide the class into six groups, and assign each group one of the common mouth disorders: cold sores, canker sores, mucositis, plaque, halitosis, and xerostomia. Ask each group to make a brief presentation to the class about the presentation of each condition.***
Cite the treatment alternatives and associated nursing assessments to monitor	■ Drug therapy for mouth disorders (p. 503) – Cold sores (p. 503) – Canker sores (p. 503) – Mucositis (p. 503) – Plaque (p. 504)	PPT 5-9 ARQ 1-2, 5 TB Multiple Choice questions 1-4, 6-9 TB Multiple Response questions 3-5

OBJECTIVES	CONTENT	TEACHING RESOURCES
response to drug therapy for common oral disorders.	– Halitosis (p. 504) – Xerostomia (p. 504) Review the treatment goals for mouth disorders as providing comfort, allowing healing, and preventing the spread of the disease.	INRQ 1, 6, 10 SG Review Sheet questions 1-2, 4, 8 (pp. 211-212) SG Learning Activities questions 1-7, 9-10 (p. 213) SG Practice Questions for the NCLEX Examination 1, 3, 5, 7-8 (p. 214) Review Questions for the NCLEX Examination 2-3, 6, 9 (pp. 507-508) Table 32-1: World Health Organization Oral Mucositis Scale (p. 502) Lifespan Considerations: Salivary Flow (p. 503) ▸ Discuss treatment options for cold sores and how these options are effective for cold sore treatment. ▸ Discuss the best treatment option a patient can use to combat halitosis. Class Activity ***Divide the class into six groups, and assign each group one of the common mouth disorders: cold sores, canker sores, mucositis, plaque, halitosis, and xerostomia. Ask each group to make a brief presentation to the class treatment about the remedies commonly used. What are treatment goals, and how is effectiveness assessed? What are some similarities and differences between the mouth disorders and associated treatments? Have each group make a presentation to the class for feedback and discussion.***
Identify important nursing assessments and interventions associated with the drug therapy and treatment of diseases of the mouth.	– Nursing process for oral health therapy (p. 504) – Patient education and health promotion (p. 505) Discuss baseline data to collect for comparison to determine drug effectiveness.	ARQ 4 TB Multiple Choice questions 5, 10 TB Multiple Response questions 1-2 INRQ 2-3, 5, 7, 8 CTQ 2 SG Review Sheet questions 3, 5, 7 (pp. 211-212) SG Learning Activities questions 8, 11-12 (p. 213) SG Practice Questions for the NCLEX Examination 2, 4, 6 (p. 214) ▸ Discuss situations in which a nurse may inspect a patient's dental history in a health care provider's office setting.

OBJECTIVES	CONTENT	TEACHING RESOURCES
		▸ Discuss approaches a nurse can use to create an effective teaching plan for a patient who has oral conditions and is undergoing chemotherapy. ▸ Discuss approaches that a nurse can suggest to prevent the spread of a cold sore. Class Activity ***Have two students demonstrate how to inspect the oral cavity, with one student playing the nurse and the other the patient. Have the class assist the "nurse" with what to look for and questions to ask to determine oral hygiene habits. Review the exercise with the class.***
Identify baseline data the nurse should collect on a continual basis for comparing and evaluating drug effectiveness.	– Nursing process for oral health therapy (p. 504) – Patient education and health promotion (p. 505) □ Drug class: Dentifrices (p. 506) □ Drug class: Mouthwashes (p. 506)	PPT 10-11 ARQ 3 INRQ 4, 9 CTQ 1 SG Review Sheet questions 6-7 (pp. 211-212) Review Questions for the NCLEX Examination 1, 4, 8 (pp. 507-508) ▸ Discuss the importance of dentifrices in the role of dental hygiene. What are the differences among various brands? Class Activity ***Bring to class different mouthwashes. Have students take turns reading the labels and identifying the active ingredients. Have students explain what these ingredients do and discuss the differences among each brand of mouthwash. Review the exercise with the class.***
Performance evaluation		Test Bank SG Learning Activities (p. 213) SG Practice Questions for the NCLEX Examination (p. 214) Critical Thinking Questions

32.1 Homework/Assignments::

32.1 Instructor's Notes/Student Feedback:

32 Lecture Outline

Drugs Used to Treat Oral Disorders

Slide 1

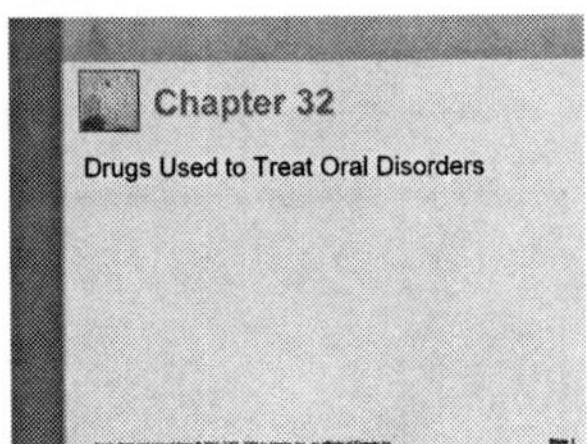

Chapter 32
Drugs Used to Treat Oral Disorders

Slide 2

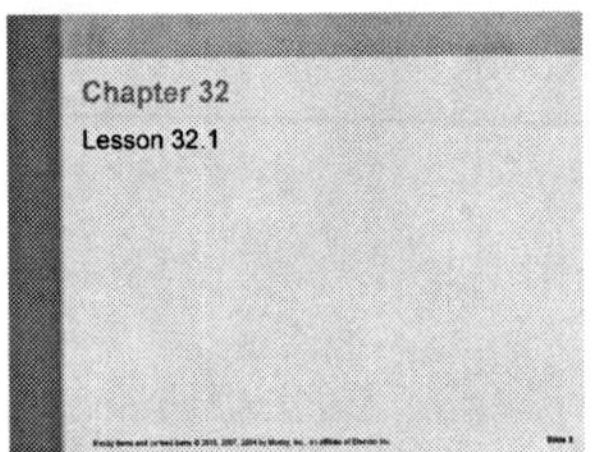

Chapter 32
Lesson 32.1

Slide 3

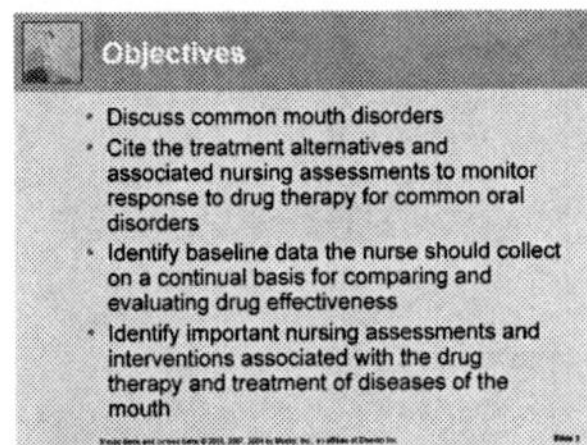

Objectives
Discuss common mouth disorders
Cite the treatment alternatives and associated nursing assessments to monitor response to drug therapy for common oral disorders
Identify baseline data the nurse should collect on a continual basis for comparing and evaluating drug effectiveness
Identify important nursing assessments and interventions associated with the drug therapy and treatment of diseases of the mouth

Slide 4

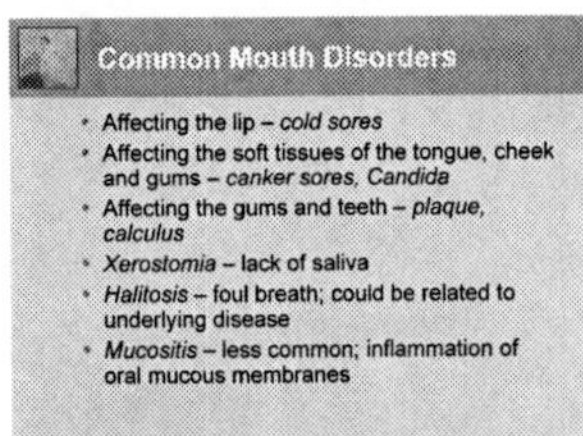

Common Mouth Disorders
Affecting the lip – cold sores
Affecting the soft tissues of the tongue, cheek and gums – canker sores, Candida
Affecting the gums and teeth – plaque, calculus
Xerostomia – lack of saliva
Halitosis – foul breath; could be related to underlying disease
Mucositis – less common; inflammation of oral mucous membranes

Slide 5

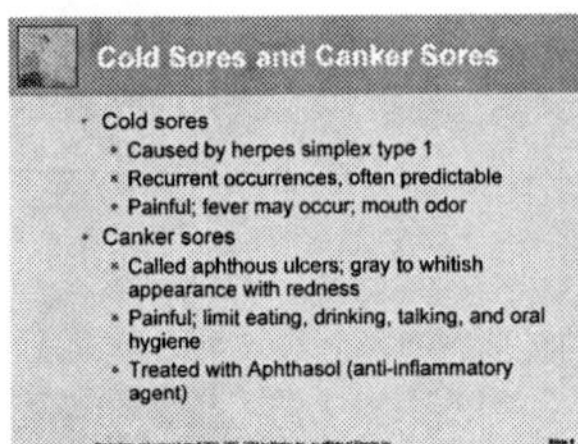

Cold Sores and Canker Sores
Cold sores
Caused by herpes simplex type 1
Recurrent occurrences, often predictable
Painful; fever may occur; mouth odor
Canker sores
Called aphthous ulcers; gray to whitish appearance with redness
Painful; limit eating, drinking, talking, and oral hygiene
Treated with Aphthasol (anti-inflammatory agent)

- Goals of treatment: control discomfort, allow healing, prevent spread to others, prevent complications.
- There is no cure for cold sores; only symptom management.
- Chemotherapy and radiation can trigger canker sores.

ELSEVIER

Slide 6

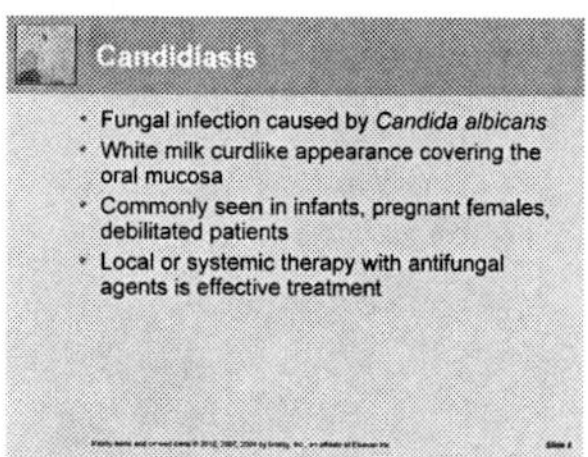
Candidiasis
Fungal infection caused by Candida albicans
White milk curdlike appearance covering the oral mucosa
Commonly seen in infants, pregnant females, debilitated patients
Local or systemic therapy with antifungal agents is effective treatment

- Common with repeated antibiotic use and other medications.
- Also seen in patients with diabetes mellitus, malnutrition, malignancies, and radiation therapy.

Slide 7

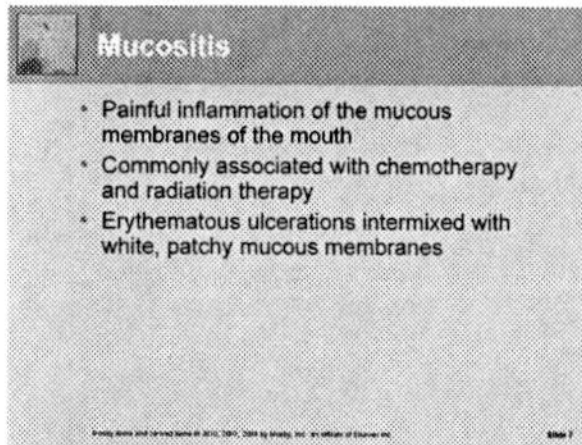
Mucositis
Painful inflammation of the mucous membranes of the mouth
Commonly associated with chemotherapy and radiation therapy
Erythematous ulcerations intermixed with white, patchy mucous membranes

- Develops 5 to 7 days after chemotherapy or radiation treatment.
- Candidal infections are often present.
- Can be severely debilitating.
- The WHO Mucositis Scale is used to standardize evaluation of mucositis.

Slide 8

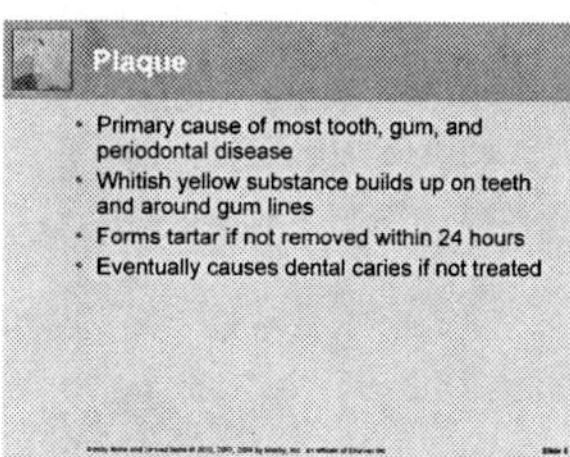
Plaque
Primary cause of most tooth, gum, and periodontal disease
Whitish yellow substance builds up on teeth and around gum lines
Forms tartar if not removed within 24 hours
Eventually causes dental caries if not treated

- Forms a sticky meshwork that traps bacteria and food particles. Bacteria secrete acids that eat into the enamel of teeth, causing dental caries.

Slide 9

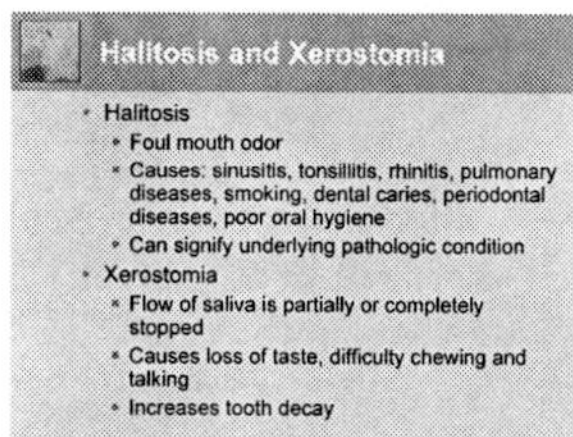
Halitosis and Xerostomia
Halitosis
Foul mouth odor
Causes: sinusitis, tonsillitis, rhinitis, pulmonary diseases, smoking, dental caries, periodontal diseases, poor oral hygiene
Can signify underlying pathologic condition
Xerostomia
Flow of saliva is partially or completely stopped
Causes loss of taste, difficulty chewing and talking
Increases tooth decay

Slide 10

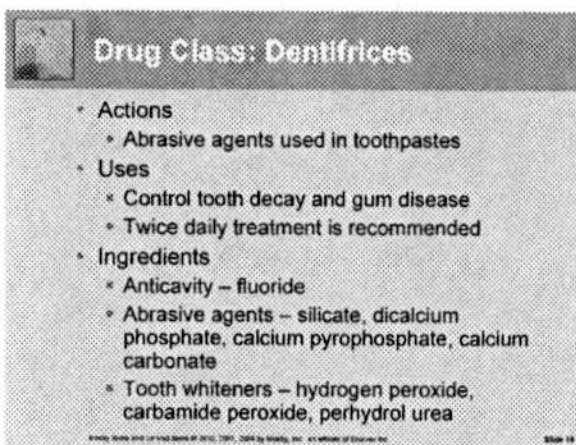
Drug Class: Dentifrices
Actions
Abrasive agents used in toothpastes
Uses
Control tooth decay and gum disease
Twice daily treatment is recommended
Ingredients
Anticavity – fluoride
Abrasive agents – silicate, dicalcium phosphate, calcium pyrophosphate, calcium carbonate
Tooth whiteners – hydrogen peroxide, carbamide peroxide, perhydrol urea

- Therapeutic outcomes: reduction of plaque formation and cavities; pleasant, refreshing taste.

Slide 11

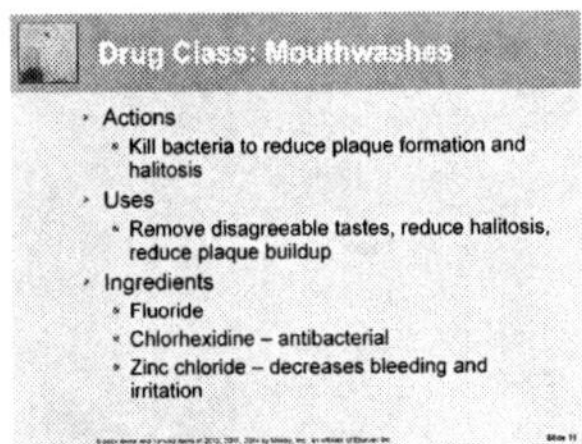
Drug Class: Mouthwashes
Actions
Kill bacteria to reduce plaque formation and halitosis
Uses
Remove disagreeable tastes, reduce halitosis, reduce plaque buildup
Ingredients
Fluoride
Chlorhexidine – antibacterial
Zinc chloride – decreases bleeding and irritation

- Used for patients who have undergone oral surgery or facial trauma.
- Therapeutic outcomes: temporary reduction in bleeding or irritation, relief of discomfort, refreshing taste, improvement of halitosis.

Lesson Plan

33 Drugs Used to Treat Gastroesophageal Reflux and Peptic Ulcer Diseases

TEACHING FOCUS

In this chapter, the student will be introduced to a review of gastrointestinal (GI) physiology and the causes of gastroesophageal reflux disease (GERD) and peptic ulcer disease (PUD). Additionally, the student will have the opportunity to learn the types of drug and treatment options available for patients with GI disorders.

MATERIALS AND RESOURCES

- ☐ computer and PowerPoint projector (all Lessons)
- ☐ drug reference handbook (all Lessons)

LESSON CHECKLIST

Preparations for this lesson include:

- lecture
- demonstration
- guest speakers: pharmacist, nutritionist
- evaluation of student knowledge and skills needed to perform all entry-level activities related to drugs used to treat GERD and PUD, including:
  - assessing knowledge of GI physiology
  - identifying the classifications of drugs used to treat GI disorders
  - evaluating the patient's condition and implementing proper safety precautions, such as wearing latex gloves before the administration of drugs to the patient
  - assessing knowledge of proper routes for drug administration
  - evaluating the patient after the administration of drugs for GI disorders

KEY TERMS

gastroesophageal reflux disease (GERD) (p. 509)
heartburn (p. 509)
Helicobacter pylori (p. 510)
hydrochloric acid (p. 509)
parietal cells (p. 509)
peptic ulcer disease (PUD) (p. 510)

ADDITIONAL RESOURCES

PowerPoint slides: 1-13
Flashcards, Decks 1 and 2

Legend

ARQ	PPT	TB	CTQ	SG	INRQ
Audience Response Questions	PowerPoint Slides	Test Bank	Critical Thinking Questions	Study Guide	Interactive NCLEX Review Questions

Class Activities are indicated in ***bold italic.***

LESSON 33.1

BACKGROUND ASSESSMENT

Question: What is the mechanism of action of antacids? What serious adverse effects can result from long-term antacid use?
Answer: Antacids lower the acidity of gastric secretions by buffering the hydrochloric acid to a lower hydrogen ion concentration. Antacids are commonly used for heartburn, excessive eating, drinking, or PUD—but all antacids are not alike. They should be used carefully to prevent adverse reactions. Serious complications are mainly associated with the inhibition of absorption of necessary medications, such as digoxin, antibiotics, and iron products. Long-term use of antacids may also mask symptoms of underlying disorders.

Question: What are the common medications and treatments for GERD and PUD?
Answer: GERD is commonly referred to as heartburn, acid indigestion, or sour stomach. It is a very common stomach disorder in the United States. GERD is the reflux of gastric secretions, primarily pepsin and hydrochloric acid, into the esophagus. Causes of GERD are a weakened lower esophageal sphincter, delayed gastric emptying, hiatal hernia, overeating, and obesity. Treatments for GERD include lifestyle changes related to symptom management and antacids, coating agents, H2 antagonists, antispasmodics, and prokinetic agents. PUD includes several stomach disorders that result from an imbalance between acidic stomach contents and the body's normal defense barriers, causing ulcerations in the GI tract. The most common illnesses include gastric and duodenal ulcers. Pain most often occurs when the stomach is empty and is relieved by food or antacids. Treatment is similar to that for GERD. The treatment goals are to relieve symptoms, promote healing, and prevent recurrence.

CRITICAL THINKING QUESTION

A 50-year-old male patient comes to the emergency department reporting chest pain, indigestion, and diaphoresis. He states that the symptoms appeared an hour ago, and he has never experienced them previously. How should the emergency department nurse respond?
Guidelines: Any signs and symptoms that appear cardiac in nature should be treated as such until a cardiac cause is ruled out. The nurse should put the patient in a cardiac room, attach him to a cardiac monitor, and obtain an ECG. There should be team involvement at this time to obtain a detailed history, assess vital signs, and begin diagnostic tests. If the patient is ruled out as having cardiac symptoms, then evaluation and care should be directed toward the GI system. The signs and symptoms of distress in these two organ systems are very similar.

OBJECTIVES	CONTENT	TEACHING RESOURCES
Describe the physiology of the stomach.	■ Physiology of the stomach (p. 509) Review the three primary functions of the stomach. Discuss the three types of secretory cells in the stomach: chief, parietal, and mucous cells. Review the role of pepsinogen, hydrochloric acid, intrinsic factor, and prostaglandins in digestion.	PPT 4 SG Learning Activities questions 1, 4, 15-16, 22 (pp. 218-219) ▸ Discuss the anatomy and physiology of the GI tract, focusing on GERD and PUD.
Cite common stomach disorders that require drug therapy.	■ Common stomach disorders (p. 509) Review the common stomach disorders: gastroesophageal reflux disease (GERD), peptic ulcer	PPT 5 ARQ 1-2 TB Multiple Response question 3 SG Review Sheet questions 1-3 (p. 215)

OBJECTIVES	CONTENT	TEACHING RESOURCES
	disease (PUD), and *Helicobacter pylori*. Discuss the difference between GERD and PUD.	SG Learning Activities question 2 (p. 218) Clinical Landmine (p. 510) ▸ Discuss the similarities and differences between the treatment options for GERD and PUD. Class Activity ***Divide the class into two groups, and assign one group GERD and the other PUD. Have each group identify the cause, signs and symptoms, diagnostic tests, medications, treatment options, patient teaching, and nursing interventions for the assigned disease. After an appropriate interval, have students list their findings on the board and identify similarities and differences.***
Identify factors that prevent breakdown of the body's normal defense barriers, resulting in ulcer formation.	■ Goals of treatment (p. 510) Review the goals of treatment for GERD and PUD, which include relief of symptoms, healing of tissue injury, and preventing recurrence.	TB Multiple Choice questions 5, 7-8 TB Multiple Response question 1 SG Learning Activities questions 2, 6, 17, 22, 23 (pp. 218-219) Class Activity ***As a class, discuss the body's natural mechanisms for protecting the stomach walls from injury. Include a description of the three types of secretory cells that line portions of the stomach and the role of prostaglandins.*** Class Activity ***Outside of class time, ask students to visit their local grocery store and pharmacy to find an over-the-counter drug used to treat PUD. Allow class time for discussion of their findings.***
Develop health teaching for an individual with stomach disorders that incorporates pharmacologic and nonpharma-cologic treatment.	■ Drug therapy (p. 511) – Nursing process for agents used for stomach disorders (p. 511) – Patient education and health promotion (p. 512) Review the changes in lifestyle such as smoking cessation, weight reduction, avoiding alcohol, and eating smaller meals that are stressed during teaching, as well as pharmacologic measures.	PPT 6 ARQ 4-5 TB Multiple Choice questions 6, 9, 11 TB Multiple Response question 5 INRQ 1, 4, 9, 14 CTQ 1 SG Review Sheet questions 4-5, 13 (pp. 215-216) SG Practice Questions for the NCLEX Examination 1, 4, 8 (pp. 220-221) Review Question for the NCLEX Examination 3 (p. 522) Lifespan Considerations: Antacids (p. 513) ▸ Discuss the effect of stress on the GI diseases GERD and PUD.

OBJECTIVES	CONTENT	TEACHING RESOURCES
		▸ Discuss the signs and symptoms of GI disorders seen in older patients and young adult patients. Class Activity ***Divide the class into two groups. Assign one group GERD and the other PUD. Have each group develop a one-page patient education newsletter for all patient ages describing the prevalence, causes, medications, and treatment options—pharmacologic and nonpharmacologic—for the assigned disease. Discuss the newsletter as a class to develop a complete education tool.*** Class Activity ***Invite a pharmacist or nutritionist to discuss pharmacologic and nonpharmacologic treatment options for GERD and PUD. Encourage class participation.*** Class Activity ***Following the nutritionist's presentation, assign students to groups of three. Allow groups to choose PUD or GERD. Have each group devise a nutritional plan and education for the patient with PUD or GERD.***

33.1 Homework/Assignments:

33.1 Instructor's Notes/Student Feedback:

LESSON 33.2

CRITICAL THINKING QUESTION

A 75-year-old woman is hospitalized as a result of a recent change in her mental status. She is in fairly good health other than a history of gastric ulcers for 10 years. During this time, she has been taking cimetidine, 400 mg twice daily. Her family was concerned when she began to complain of dizziness, headaches, and confusion with disorientation and hallucinations. What should the nurse take into consideration when assessing this patient? What laboratory tests are likely to be ordered? What is the long-term goal for this patient?

Guidelines: In the assessment of this patient, a detailed medical history should be obtained, with an emphasis on a past similar occurrence. Cimetidine may be the cause of her changed mental status because

these adverse effects can occur in older adults. However, given her advanced age, many other illnesses cannot be ruled out. Laboratory tests, including complete blood count (CBC), chemistry panels, arterial blood gases (ABGs), electrolyte profile, and electrocardiography should be completed. Safety measures should be instituted immediately to ensure the patient's safety. The adverse effects from cimetidine begin to dissipate over 3 to 4 days of discontinuation, but perhaps more slowly in an older adult. The nurse should educate the patient and family on patient safety, continued monitoring, and any new medications prescribed to treat the gastric ulcers.

OBJECTIVES	CONTENT	TEACHING RESOURCES
State the drug classifications and actions used to treat stomach disorders.	□ Drug class: Antacids (p. 512) – Nursing process for antacid therapy (p. 513) □ Drug class: Histamine-2 receptor antagonists (p. 514) – Nursing process for H2 antagonists (p. 515) □ Drug class: Gastrointestinal prostaglandins (p. 516) – Nursing process for misoprostol therapy (p. 516) □ Drug class: Proton pump inhibitors (p. 517) – Nursing process for proton pump inhibitor therapy (p. 517) □ Drug class: Coating agents (p. 518) – Nursing process for sucralfate therapy (p. 518) □ Drug class: Prokinetic agents (p. 519) – Nursing process for metoclopramide therapy (p. 519) □ Drug class: Antispasmodic agents (p. 520) – Nursing process for antispasmodic therapy (p. 520)	PPT 7-13 ARQ 3 TB Multiple Choice questions 1-4, 10 TB Multiple Response questions 2, 4 INRQ 2-3, 5, 7, 10-13, 15 CTQ 2-4 Patient Self-Assessment Form: Agents Affecting the Digestive System SG Review Sheet questions 6-12, 14-25 (pp. 215-217) SG Learning Activities questions 3, 5, 7-14, 18-20, 21, 24 (pp. 218-219) SG Practice Questions for the NCLEX Examination 2-3, 5-7, 9-12 (pp. 220-221) Review Questions for the NCLEX Examination 1-2, 4-9 (p. 522) Table 33-1: Ingredients of Commonly Used Antacids (p. 514) Drug Table 33-2: Histamine (H2) Receptor Antagonists (p. 515) Drug Table 33-3: Proton Pump Inhibitors (p. 518) Drug Table 33-4: Antispasmodic Agents (p. 521) ▸ Discuss the role of antacids in the treatment of GERD. Class Activity ***List some of the popular over-the-counter medications used in the treatment of GERD and PUD. Discuss the mechanism of action of these medications.*** Class Activity ***Divide the class into small groups, and ask each group to identify prescription medications used in the treatment of GERD and PUD. Then ask the groups to write a drug guide index card for each of these medications.***

ELSEVIER

OBJECTIVES	CONTENT	TEACHING RESOURCES
		Class Activity ***As a class, discuss the uses and therapeutic outcomes for prescription medications used in the treatment of GERD and PUD. Discuss the reasons why one medication might be selected over another medication.***
Performance evaluation		Test Bank SG Learning Activities (pp. 218-219) SG Practice Questions for the NCLEX Examination (pp. 220-221) Critical Thinking Questions

33.2 Homework/Assignments:

33.2 Instructor's Notes/Student Feedback:

Lecture Outline

33 Drugs Used to Treat Gastroesophageal Reflux and Peptic Ulcer Diseases

Slide 1

Chapter 33
Drugs Used to Treat Gastroesophageal Reflux and Peptic Ulcer Diseases

Slide 2

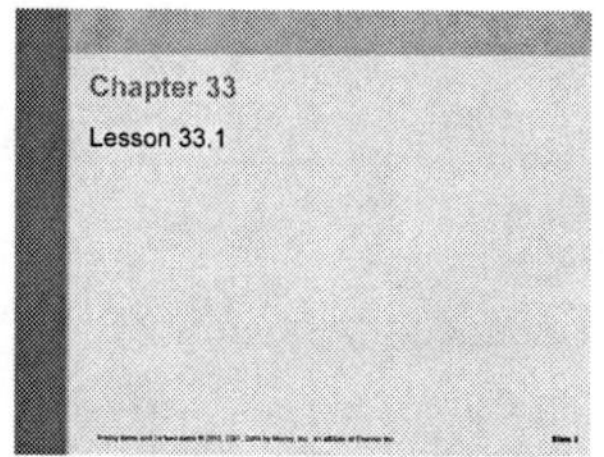
Chapter 33
Lesson 33.1

Slide 3

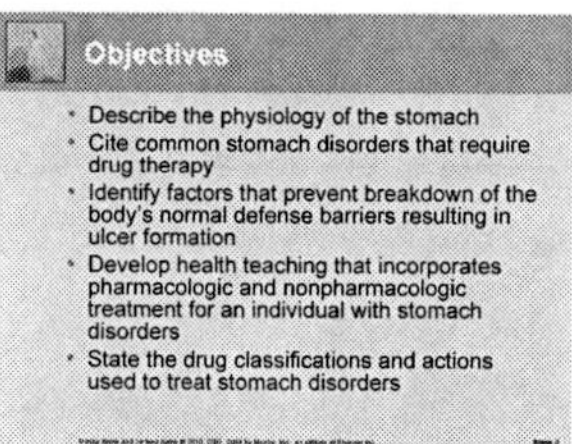
Objectives
Describe the physiology of the stomach
Cite common stomach disorders that require drug therapy
Identify factors that prevent breakdown of the body's normal defense barriers resulting in ulcer formation
Develop health teaching that incorporates pharmacologic and nonpharmacologic treatment for an individual with stomach disorders
State the drug classifications and actions used to treat stomach disorders

Slide 4

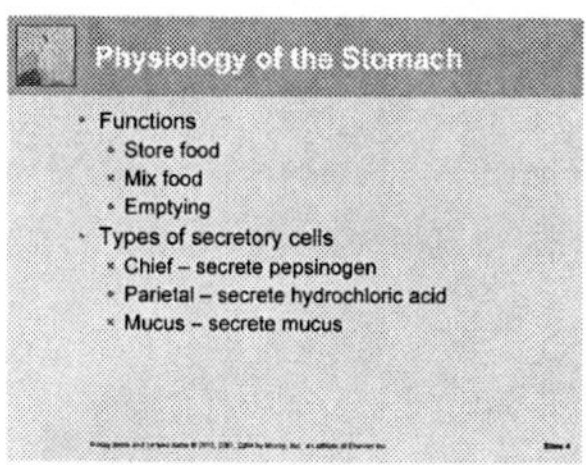
Physiology of the Stomach
Functions
Store food
Mix food
Emptying
Types of secretory cells
Chief – secrete pepsinogen
Parietal – secrete hydrochloric acid
Mucus – secrete mucus

- Hydrochloric acid is needed for optimal pH of stomach.
- Parietal cells also secrete intrinsic factor needed for absorption of vitamin B12.
- Mucus protects the stomach wall from injury to stomach acids and enzymes.

Slide 5

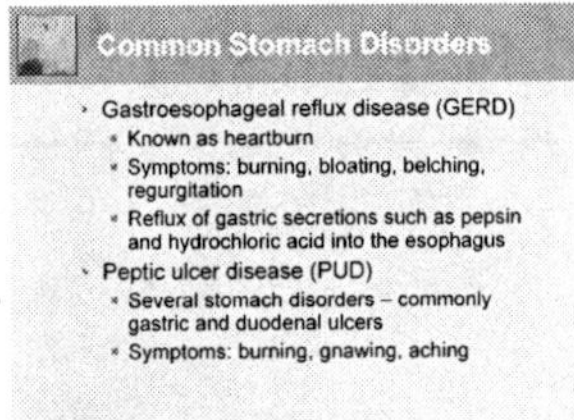
Common Stomach Disorders
Gastroesophageal reflux disease (GERD)
Known as heartburn
Symptoms: burning, bloating, belching, regurgitation
Reflux of gastric secretions such as pepsin and hydrochloric acid into the esophagus
Peptic ulcer disease (PUD)
Several stomach disorders – commonly gastric and duodenal ulcers
Symptoms: burning, gnawing, aching

- GERD is referred to as acid indigestion; PUD is commonly referred to as heartburn or sour stomach.
- Always treat signs and symptoms of heartburn as cardiac disease until it is ruled out! Symptoms may resemble conditions such as ischemic heart disease, scleroderma, and gastric cancer.

Slide 6

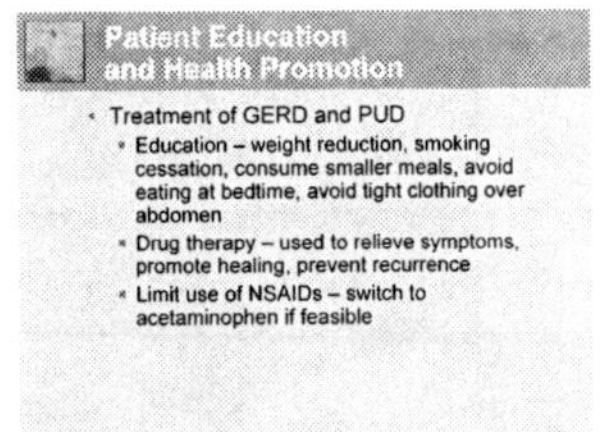
Patient Education and Health Promotion
Treatment of GERD and PUD
Education – weight reduction, smoking cessation, consume smaller meals, avoid eating at bedtime, avoid tight clothing over abdomen
Drug therapy – used to relieve symptoms, promote healing, prevent recurrence
Limit use of NSAIDs – switch to acetaminophen if feasible

Slide 7

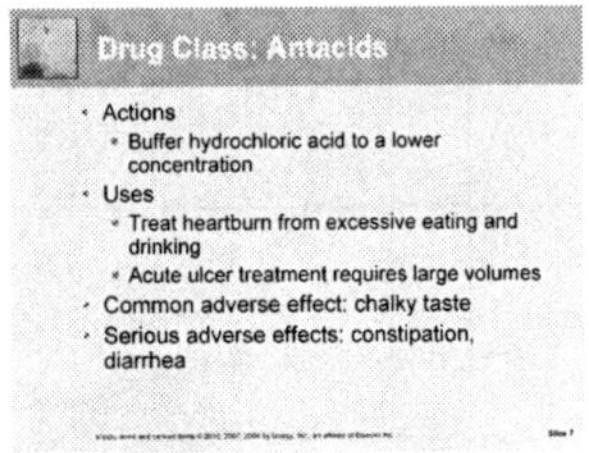
Drug Class: Antacids
Actions
Buffer hydrochloric acid to a lower concentration
Uses
Treat heartburn from excessive eating and drinking
Acute ulcer treatment requires large volumes
Common adverse effect: chalky taste
Serious adverse effects: constipation, diarrhea

- For specific drugs, see Table 33-1.
- Therapeutic outcomes: relief of discomfort, reduced frequency of heartburn, healing of irritated tissues.

Slide 8

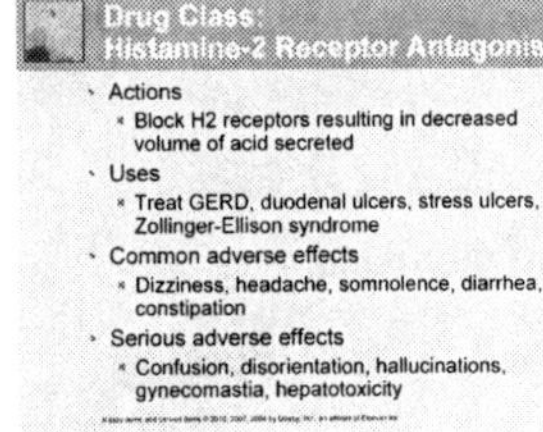
Drug Class: Histamine-2 Receptor Antagonists
Actions
Block H2 receptors resulting in decreased volume of acid secreted
Uses
Treat GERD, duodenal ulcers, stress ulcers, Zollinger-Ellison syndrome
Common adverse effects
Dizziness, headache, somnolence, diarrhea, constipation
Serious adverse effects
Confusion, disorientation, hallucinations, gynecomastia, hepatotoxicity

- For specific drugs, see Table 33-2.

Slide 9

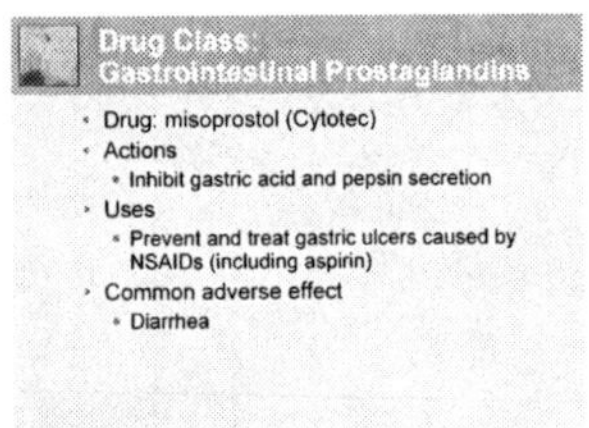
Drug Class: Gastrointestinal Prostaglandins
Drug: misoprostol (Cytotec)
Actions
Inhibit gastric acid and pepsin secretion
Uses
Prevent and treat gastric ulcers caused by NSAIDs (including aspirin)
Common adverse effect
Diarrhea

- Contraindicated for use in pregnancy because of the effect of inducing uterine contractions.

Slide 10

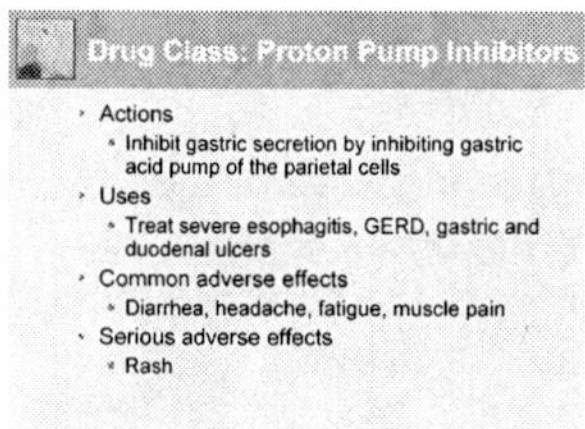
Drug Class: Proton Pump Inhibitors
Actions
Inhibit gastric secretion by inhibiting gastric acid pump of the parietal cells
Uses
Treat severe esophagitis, GERD, gastric and duodenal ulcers
Common adverse effects
Diarrhea, headache, fatigue, muscle pain
Serious adverse effects
Rash

- For specific drugs, see Table 33-3.
- Be alert to drug interactions.

Slide 11

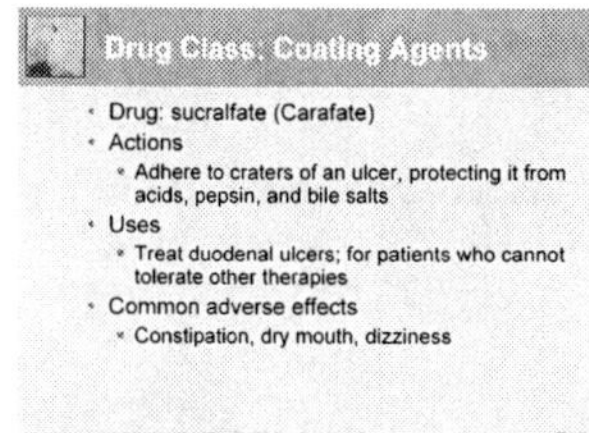
Drug Class: Coating Agents
Drug: sucralfate (Carafate)
Actions
Adhere to craters of an ulcer, protecting it from acids, pepsin, and bile salts
Uses
Treat duodenal ulcers; for patients who cannot tolerate other therapies
Common adverse effects
Constipation, dry mouth, dizziness

Slide 12

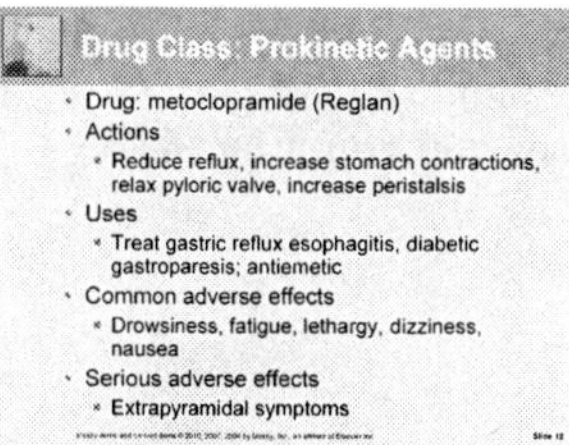
Drug Class: Prokinetic Agents
Drug: metoclopramide (Reglan)
Actions
Reduce reflux, increase stomach contractions, relax pyloric valve, increase peristalsis
Uses
Treat gastric reflux esophagitis, diabetic gastroparesis; antiemetic
Common adverse effects
Drowsiness, fatigue, lethargy, dizziness, nausea
Serious adverse effects
Extrapyramidal symptoms

- Be alert for drug interactions.

Slide 13

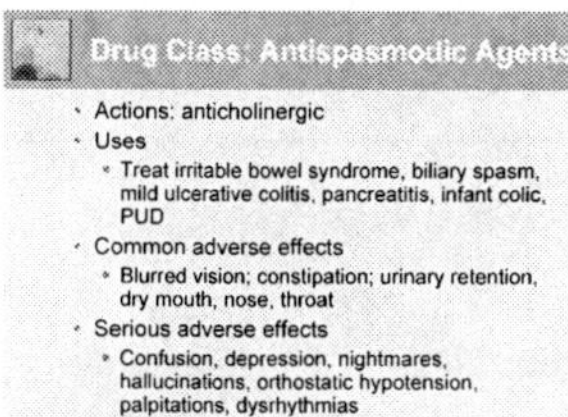
Drug Class: Antispasmodic Agents
Actions: anticholinergic
Uses
Treat irritable bowel syndrome, biliary spasm, mild ulcerative colitis, pancreatitis, infant colic, PUD
Common adverse effects
Blurred vision; constipation; urinary retention, dry mouth, nose, throat
Serious adverse effects
Confusion, depression, nightmares, hallucinations, orthostatic hypotension, palpitations, dysrhythmias

- For specific drugs, see Table 33-4.

ELSEVIER

34 Lesson Plan
Drugs Used to Treat Nausea and Vomiting

TEACHING FOCUS

This chapter examines some common underlying causes of nausea and vomiting. Students have the opportunity to learn about the six different classes of antiemetic drugs, how they act on the system, and when it is appropriate to use them. In addition, students have the opportunity to apply the nursing process to an individual's specific diagnosis, with emphasis on the proper scheduling of some antiemetic agents.

MATERIALS AND RESOURCES

☐ computer and PowerPoint projector (all Lessons)

LESSON CHECKLIST

Preparations for this lesson include:

- lecture
- evaluation of student knowledge and skills needed to perform all entry-level activities related to the causes and treatment for nausea and vomiting, including:
  - underlying causes of nausea and vomiting
  - seven therapeutic classes of antiemetics
  - actions and uses for the differing antiemetics
  - assessment and monitoring after administration of appropriate antiemetic

KEY TERMS

anticipatory nausea and vomiting (p. 525)
chemotherapy-induced nausea and vomiting (CINV) (p. 525)
delayed emesis (p. 526)
emesis (p. 523)
hyperemesis gravidarum (p. 525)
nausea (p. 523)
postoperative nausea and vomiting (PONV) (p. 524)
psychogenic vomiting (p. 525)
radiation-induced nausea and vomiting (RINV) (p. 526)
regurgitation (p. 523)
retching (p. 523)
vomiting (p. 523)

ADDITIONAL RESOURCES

PowerPoint slides: 1-18
Flashcards, Decks 1 and 2

Legend

ARQ	**PPT**	**TB**	**CTQ**	**SG**	**INRQ**
Audience Response Questions	PowerPoint Slides	Test Bank	Critical Thinking Questions	Study Guide	Interactive NCLEX Review Questions

Class Activities are indicated in ***bold italic.***

LESSON 34.1

BACKGROUND ASSESSMENT

Question: What are the common causes of nausea and vomiting?
Answer: Nausea and vomiting can accompany almost any illness. The most common causes are infection, gastrointestinal disorders, stomach irritation, overeating, motion sickness, drug therapy, surgical procedures, emotional disturbances, pregnancy, pain, unpleasant sights or odors, and chemotherapy.

Question: What guidelines can the nurse provide to prevent, minimize, or treat nausea and vomiting?
Answer: The nurse can encourage the person to try to identify the cause and take medication before an anticipated episode to prevent its occurrence. During episodes of vomiting, the individual should not eat, drink, or take oral medications because this could make the condition worse. The person should drink fluids once the vomiting stops to prevent dehydration. Provide suggestions for supplementing dietary needs for patients who experience nausea during chemotherapy treatments. Also, caution individuals not to drive or operate power equipment if they are taking antiemetic or antinausea medications, which can cause sedation or fatigue.

CRITICAL THINKING QUESTION

A male patient who has had knee surgery states that he is feeling nauseated and reports that he has not passed gas or heard bowel sounds. What class of agents would be ordered if the patient does not have bowel sounds or pass gas soon? How should the nurse monitor the patient's hydration status?
Guidelines: A dopamine antagonist, such as metoclopramide, will probably be prescribed. This medication may be ordered around the clock until the patient's condition changes because lack of bowel sounds may indicate decreased gastric motility. He may need to have a nasogastric (NG) tube inserted to extract fluids collecting in his stomach. He also may require IV fluids for hydration. An NPO (nothing by mouth) status will be enforced until either bowel sounds are present or the NG tube is removed. The nurse should measure the collected fluids at the end of each shift and the urine output. The patient's first diet will consist of clear liquids, advance to full liquids, and then to a bland or regular diet. The patient requires close monitoring until the condition resolves.

OBJECTIVES	CONTENT	TEACHING RESOURCES
Compare the purposes of using antiemetic products.	■ Nausea and vomiting (p. 523) ■ Common causes of nausea and vomiting (p. 524) – Postoperative nausea and vomiting (p. 524) – Motion sickness (p. 524) – Nausea and vomiting in pregnancy (p. 524) – Psychogenic vomiting (p. 525) – Chemotherapy-induced nausea and vomiting (p. 525) – Radiation-induced nausea and vomiting (p. 526) Review the definition for nausea and vomiting, and differentiate nausea and vomiting from retching and regurgitation. Discuss the vomiting center and factors that stimulate the center as well as other symptoms that occur during vomiting. Review the six different types of nausea and vomiting: postoperative nausea and vomiting (PONV), motion sickness, nausea and vomiting in pregnancy, psychogenic vomiting, chemotherapy-induced	PPT 4-6 ARQ 1-3 TB Multiple Choice questions 2, 4, 7 TB Multiple Response questions 1-2 INRQ 1-2, 10 CTQ 1 SG Review Sheet question 11 (p. 224) SG Learning Activities questions 1-3, 6, 16-19 (pp. 225-226) SG Practice Questions for the NCLEX Examination 5, 7 (p. 227) Review Questions for the NCLEX Examination 6-7, 9 (p. 539) Box 34-1: Causes of Nausea and Vomiting (p. 524) Table 34-1: Potential of Emesis With Intravenous Antineoplastic Agents (p. 525) ▸ Discuss Table 34-1. What different reactions might a patient undergoing cancer chemotherapy possibly expect? How would the patient be treated? ▸ Discuss possible causes for nausea and vomiting. What treatments other than drug therapy might be relevant in some cases?

ELSEVIER

OBJECTIVES	CONTENT	TEACHING RESOURCES
	nausea and vomiting (CINV), and radiation-induced nausea and vomiting (RINV). Discuss the three types of chemotherapy-induced nausea and vomiting: anticipatory nausea and vomiting, acute CINV, and delayed emesis.	▸ Discuss the meaning of hyperemesis gravidarum. How is it treated? Class Activity ***Divide the class into three groups. Have each group identify and list three potential reasons for PONV that antiemetics are used to treat. What are four other causes of nausea and vomiting? Ask students to identify which of the gaseous anesthetics has a greater incidence of causing nausea and vomiting. Have students share their findings with the class.***
State the therapeutic classes of antiemetics.	■ Drug therapy for selected causes of nausea and vomiting (p. 526) – Postoperative nausea and vomiting (p. 526) – Motion sickness (p. 526) – Nausea and vomiting in pregnancy (p. 526) – Psychogenic vomiting (p. 527) – Anticipatory nausea and vomiting (p. 527) – Chemotherapy-induced nausea and vomiting (p. 527) – Delayed emesis (p. 527) – Radiation-induced nausea and vomiting (p. 527) Review the drug therapies appropriate for the six types of nausea and vomiting as well as the three types of CINV. Discuss nonpharmacologic therapy that could help a patient suffering from nausea and vomiting secondary to treatment therapies.	PPT 7 TB Multiple Choice questions 5, 9 INRQ 5-7 CTQ 4 SG Review Sheet questions 1-2, 4, 7-8 (p. 223) SG Learning Activities questions 4-5 (p. 225) Figure 34-1 (p. 524): Sites of action of antiemetic medicines. Drug Table 34-2: Antiemetic Agents (pp. 531-535) ▸ Discuss why it is important to control nausea and vomiting. Name the seven classes of agents used as antiemetics. Class Activity ***Divide the class into groups, and assign each group one of the scenarios below. Ask each group to identify the cause of nausea and vomiting and potential treatments indicated for its occurrence.*** ***1. An 18-year-old college freshman has had nausea and vomiting for 6 months; all diagnostic test results are negative.*** ***2. A postoperative patient complains of severe nausea in the recovery room.*** ***3. A patient who receives weekly chemotherapy becomes nauseated and starts to vomit as soon as she enters the treatment room.*** ***4. A chemotherapy patient is receiving a treatment that has a high emetic potential.*** ***Have groups present their scenarios, medication treatments, and their rationales to the class for discussion.*** Class Activity ***Write the following medications and physical conditions on the board. Ask***

ELSEVIER

OBJECTIVES	CONTENT	TEACHING RESOURCES
		students to match each drug with the appropriate condition. ***Medications:*** ***1. Diphenhydramine*** ***2. Metoclopramide*** ***3. Prochlorperazine*** ***4. Lorazepam*** ***5. Palonosetron*** ***Conditions:*** ***a. Hyperemesis gravidarum*** ***b. Psychogenic vomiting*** ***c. Morning sickness*** ***d. Motion sickness*** ***e. Chemotherapy***
Discuss scheduling of antiemetics for maximum benefit.	– Nursing process for nausea and vomiting (p. 527) – Patient education and health promotion (p. 529)	PPT 8-11 TB Multiple Choice questions 1, 8 TB Multiple Response question 3-4 INRQ 3-4, 8-9 CTQ 3 SG Review Sheet question 9 (p. 223) SG Learning Activities question 20 (p. 226) SG Practice Question for the NCLEX Examination 3 (p. 227) Review Questions for the NCLEX Examination 3-4 (p. 539) ▸ Discuss the best time to administer an antiemetic. How does this differ when treating delayed emesis? ▸ Discuss the importance of maintaining hydration. How do you monitor hydration status and what special steps, if any, should you take for an infant? Class Activity ***Discuss types of situations in which it is important to schedule antiemetics so that the patient will obtain maximum benefit. Ask students the following: When is the best time to administer antiemetics for delayed emesis? For moderate emetogenic agents?*** Class Activity ***Divide the class into groups, and have them outline a nursing care plan for the following clinical situation. Have groups share their care plans with the class for discussion and feedback.***

OBJECTIVES	CONTENT	TEACHING RESOURCES
		A 68-year-old postoperative patient who had a partial colectomy is admitted to the medical-surgical unit. She has an NG tube in place and is reporting severe nausea.

34.1 Homework/Assignments:

34.1 Instructor's Notes/Student Feedback:

LESSON 34.2

CRITICAL THINKING QUESTION

A woman who occasionally experiences motion sickness in the car is going on her first cruise. She is afraid that she might experience motion sickness on the cruise ship and has obtained a prescription for promethazine. What can the nurse tell her about this drug?

Guidelines: The nurse can explain that promethazine is an antihistamine and is commonly prescribed for motion sickness. A variety of antihistamine drugs are available that are usually ordered according to the duration of motion. Usually, it is more effective to begin taking these medications before the onset of nausea, rather than after nausea has occurred. Promethazine is a short-acting drug with fewer adverse effects than others in its class. The nurse also should advise the patient that antihistamines can cause sedation.

OBJECTIVES	CONTENT	TEACHING RESOURCES
Compare the purposes of using antiemetic products.	□ Drug class: Dopamine antagonists (p. 529) – Nursing process for dopamine antagonists (p. 530) □ Drug class: Serotonin antagonists (p. 530) – Nursing process for serotonin antagonists (p. 530) □ Drug class: Anticholinergic agents (p. 536) – Nursing process for anticholinergic agents (p. 536) □ Drug class: Corticosteroids (p. 536)	PPT 12-18 ARQ 4-5 TB Multiple Choice questions 3, 6, 10 CTQ 2 Animation: Dopamine Release SG Review Sheet questions 3, 5-6, 10, 12 (pp. 223-224) SG Learning Activities questions 7-15, 21-24 (pp. 225-226) SG Practice Questions for the NCLEX Examination 1-2, 6, 8-10 (pp. 227-228) Review Questions for the NCLEX Examination 1-2, 5, 8 (p. 539) Drug Table 34-2: Antiemetic agents (pp. 531-535)

OBJECTIVES	CONTENT	TEACHING RESOURCES
	– Nursing process for corticosteroids (p. 536) ☐ Drug class: Benzodiazepines (p. 537) – Nursing process for benzodiazepines (p. 537) ☐ Drug class: Cannabinoids (p. 537) – Nursing process for cannabinoids (p. 537) ☐ Drug class: Neurokinin-1 receptor antagonists (p. 538) – Nursing process for neurokinin-1 receptor antagonists (p. 538) Review the following drug classes: dopamine antagonists (phenothiazines, butyrophenones, and metoclopramide); serotonin antagonists; anticholinergic agents, corticosteroids, benzodiazepines, cannabinoids, and neurokinin-1 receptor antagonists. Discuss their actions, uses, and therapeutic effects in treating nausea and vomiting.	▸ Discuss new drug therapy for treatment of emesis associated with chemotherapy. How do they work in controlling nausea and vomiting associated with cancer treatments? ▸ Discuss the possible causes of motion sickness, and explain the different drug therapies for long and short travel periods. ▸ Discuss what precautions you should give a patient when administering cannabinoids. What adverse effects might the patient experience? Class Activity ***Divide the class into groups, and assign each group two drug classes. Ask each group to summarize on the board the action, use, outcome, and specific indication for its assigned drug class. Have groups present their information to the class.*** Class Activity ***Based on the previous activity, have the class compare and contrast the actions of each of the drug classes. What is similar? What is different?***
Performance evaluation		Test Bank SG Learning Activities (pp. 225-226) SG Practice Questions for the NCLEX Examination (pp. 227-228) Critical Thinking Questions

34.2 Homework/Assignments:

34.2 Instructor's Notes/Student Feedback:

Drugs Used to Treat Nausea and Vomiting

Slide 1

Chapter 34
Drugs Used to Treat
Nausea and Vomiting

Slide 2

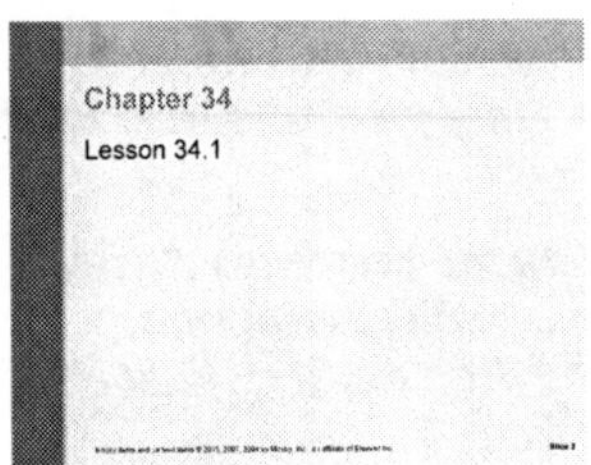
Chapter 34
Lesson 34.1

Slide 3

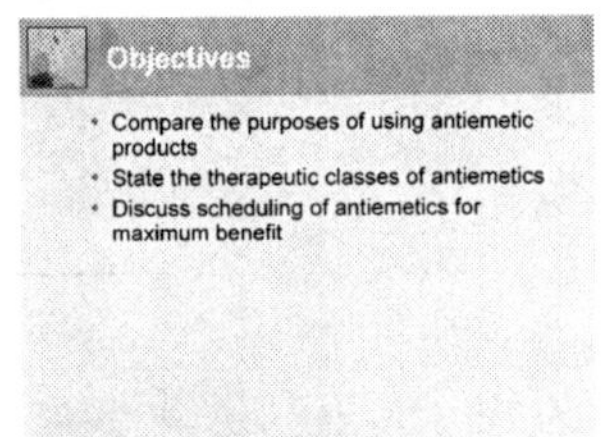
Objectives
Compare the purposes of using antiemetic products
State the therapeutic classes of antiemetics
Discuss scheduling of antiemetics for maximum benefit

Slide 4

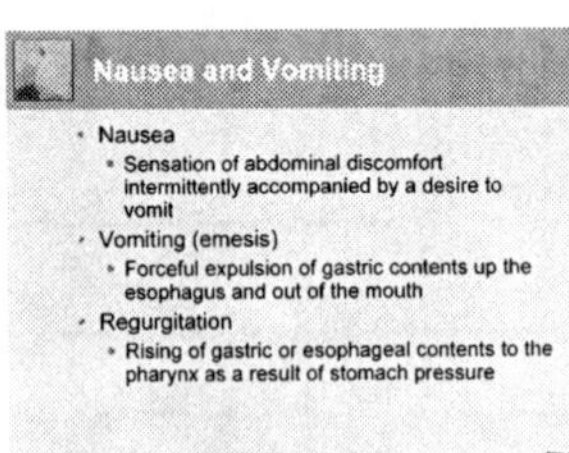
Nausea and Vomiting
Nausea
Sensation of abdominal discomfort intermittently accompanied by a desire to vomit
Vomiting (emesis)
Forceful expulsion of gastric contents up the esophagus and out of the mouth
Regurgitation
Rising of gastric or esophageal contents to the pharynx as a result of stomach pressure

- Nausea and vomiting accompanies almost any illness; wide variety of causes.
- Retching – involuntary, labored, spasmodic contractions of the abdominal and respiratory muscles without the expulsion of gastric contents; also called dry heaves.
- The cerebral cortex is the area of the brain that stimulates or suppresses vomiting.
- Regurgitation should not be confused with vomiting.

Slide 5

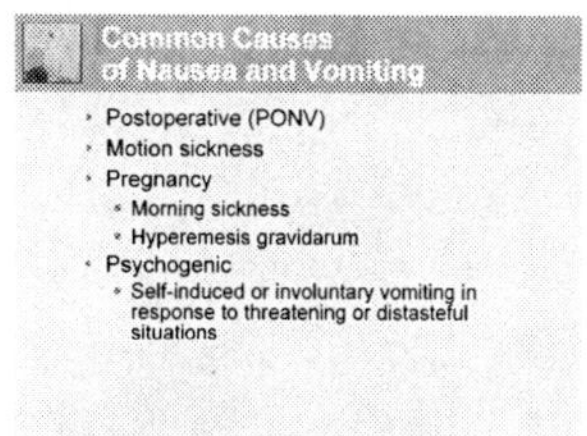
Common Causes of Nausea and Vomiting
Postoperative (PONV)
Motion sickness
Pregnancy
Morning sickness
Hyperemesis gravidarum
Psychogenic
Self-induced or involuntary vomiting in response to threatening or distasteful situations

- Surgical procedures involving general anesthesia have a higher incidence of PONV.
- Morning sickness varies in frequency throughout the day and does not cause severe effects. Hyperemesis gravidarum is greater in frequency and can lead to starvation, dehydration, acidosis.

Slide 6

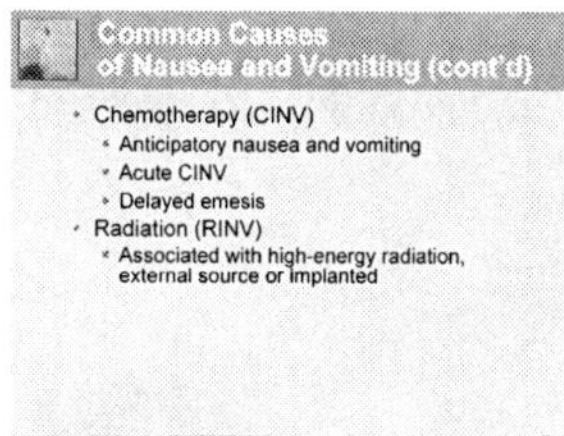
Common Causes of Nausea and Vomiting (cont'd)
Chemotherapy (CINV)
Anticipatory nausea and vomiting
Acute CINV
Delayed emesis
Radiation (RINV)
Associated with high-energy radiation, external source or implanted

- CINV is dependent on the type of medications a patient is receiving, the anticipation of illness, stress, and previous response.
- Anticipatory nausea and vomiting is triggered by sights and smells associated with treatment.
- Acute CINV is stimulated directly by chemotherapy 1 to 6 hours after treatment.
- Delayed emesis occurs 24 to 120 hours after treatment.

Slide 7

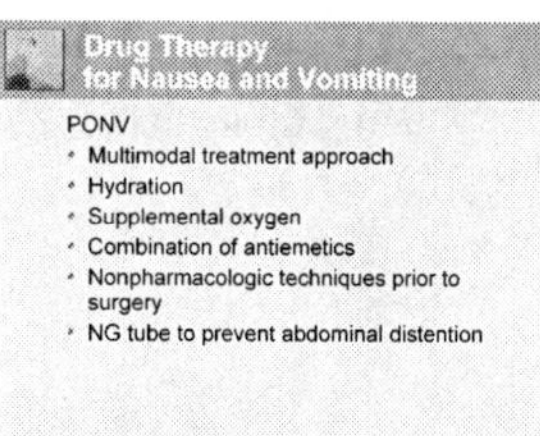
Drug Therapy for Nausea and Vomiting
PONV
Multimodal treatment approach
Hydration
Supplemental oxygen
Combination of antiemetics
Nonpharmacologic techniques prior to surgery
NG tube to prevent abdominal distention

- Multimodal treatment approach is recommended because of the variety of receptor types associated with PONV.
- Antiemetics: droperidol, dexamethasone, serotonin antagonists.
- Nonpharmacologic techniques: acupuncture, acupressure, TENS units.

Slide 8

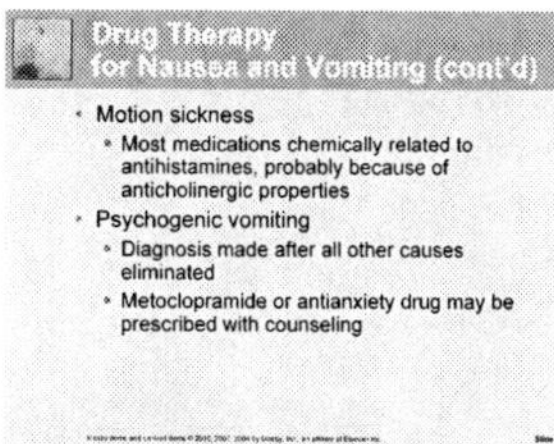
Drug Therapy for Nausea and Vomiting (cont'd)
Motion sickness
Most medications chemically related to antihistamines, probably because of anticholinergic properties
Psychogenic vomiting
Diagnosis made after all other causes eliminated
Metoclopramide or antianxiety drug may be prescribed with counseling

- Causes of motion sickness include riding in a car, boat, carnival rides.
- Motion sickness is caused by stimulation of the labyrinth system of the ear.

Slide 9

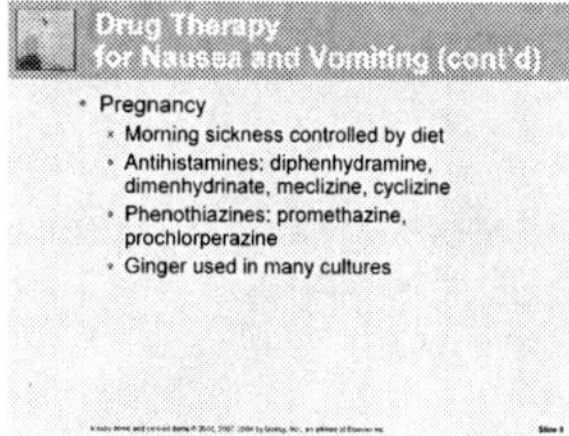
Drug Therapy for Nausea and Vomiting (cont'd)
Pregnancy
Morning sickness controlled by diet
Antihistamines: diphenhydramine, dimenhydrinate, meclizine, cyclizine
Phenothiazines: promethazine, prochlorperazine
Ginger used in many cultures

- Recommend bland foods like crackers, bread, etc., that do not stimulate acidity.
- Drug therapy can be used for nausea and vomiting associated with pregnancy when diet does not work.
- Metoclopramide (Reglan) effective in treating hyperemesis gravidarum.

ELSEVIER

Slide 10

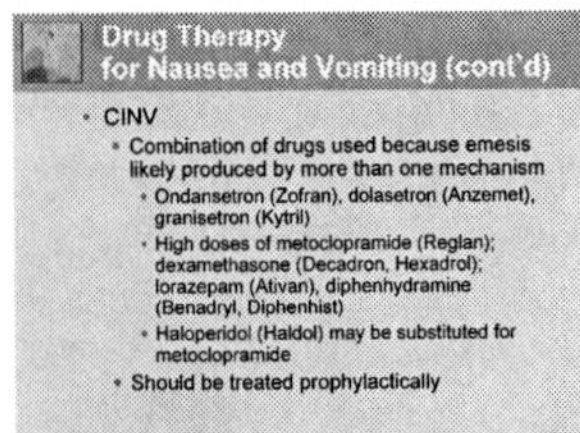

Drug Therapy for Nausea and Vomiting (cont'd)
CINV
Combination of drugs used because emesis likely produced by more than one mechanism
Ondansetron (Zofran), dolasetron (Anzemet), granisetron (Kytril)
High doses of metoclopramide (Reglan); dexamethasone (Decadron, Hexadrol); lorazepam (Ativan), diphenhydramine (Benadryl, Diphenhist)
Haloperidol (Haldol) may be substituted for metoclopramide
Should be treated prophylactically

- Administer 30 to 60 minutes before chemotherapy.
- Continue therapy 1 to 2 days after treatment, until the drugs have been metabolized out of the body.

Slide 11

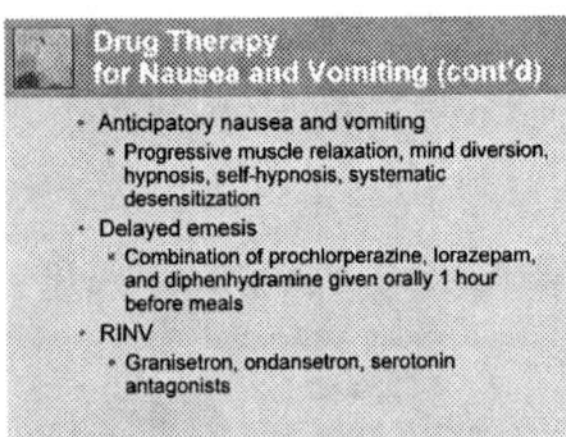

Drug Therapy for Nausea and Vomiting (cont'd)
Anticipatory nausea and vomiting
Progressive muscle relaxation, mind diversion, hypnosis, self-hypnosis, systematic desensitization
Delayed emesis
Combination of prochlorperazine, lorazepam, and diphenhydramine given orally 1 hour before meals
RINV
Granisetron, ondansetron, serotonin antagonists

- Anticipatory nausea and vomiting is associated with a negative attitude toward result of treatment.
- Rescue medications used to treat RINV include prochlorperazine and metoclopramide.

Slide 12

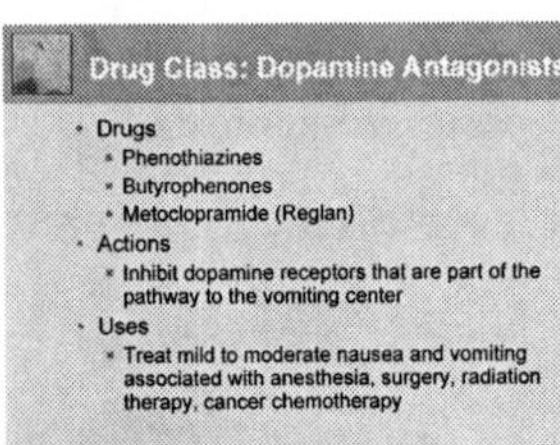

Drug Class: Dopamine Antagonists
Drugs
Phenothiazines
Butyrophenones
Metoclopramide (Reglan)
Actions
Inhibit dopamine receptors that are part of the pathway to the vomiting center
Uses
Treat mild to moderate nausea and vomiting associated with anesthesia, surgery, radiation therapy, cancer chemotherapy

- For specific drugs, see Table 34-2.
- Because these drugs inhibit dopamine receptors, watch for extrapyramidal symptoms of dystonia, parkinsonism, and tardive dyskinesia.

Slide 13

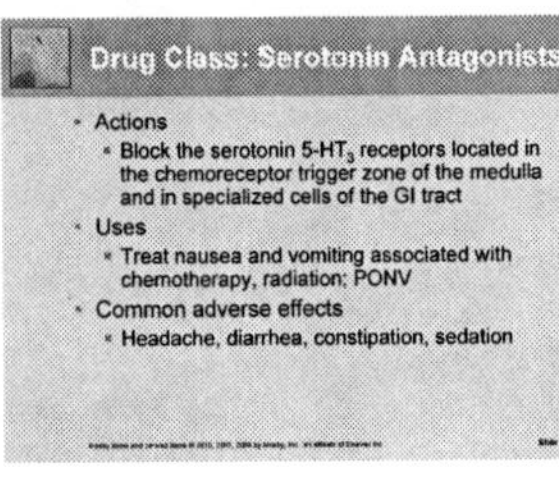

Drug Class: Serotonin Antagonists
Actions
Block the serotonin 5-HT$_3$ receptors located in the chemoreceptor trigger zone of the medulla and in specialized cells of the GI tract
Uses
Treat nausea and vomiting associated with chemotherapy, radiation; PONV
Common adverse effects
Headache, diarrhea, constipation, sedation

- For specific drugs, see Table 34-2.
- Extrapyramidal adverse effects usually do not occur with serotonin antagonists.

Slide 14

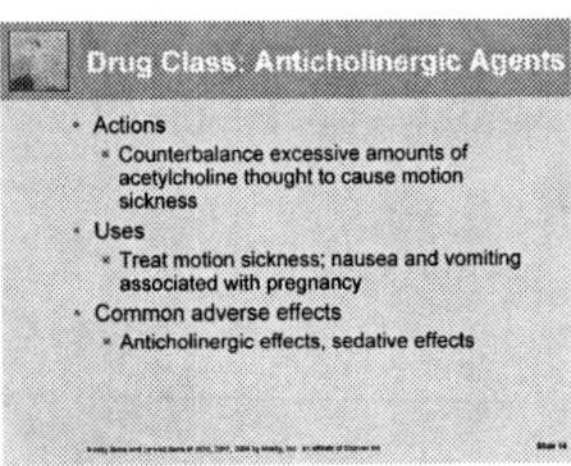

Drug Class: Anticholinergic Agents
Actions
Counterbalance excessive amounts of acetylcholine thought to cause motion sickness
Uses
Treat motion sickness; nausea and vomiting associated with pregnancy
Common adverse effects
Anticholinergic effects, sedative effects

- For specific drugs, see Table 34-2.
- Can be purchased over the counter (e.g., Dramamine, Benadryl).
- Not effective in treating CINV.
- Scopolamine is the drug of choice for short periods of motion sickness; antihistamines are preferred for longer periods.

ELSEVIER

Slide 15

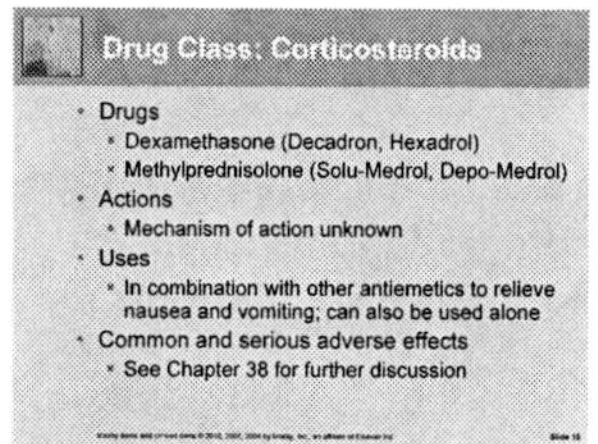
Drug Class: Corticosteroids
Drugs
Dexamethasone (Decadron, Hexadrol)
Methylprednisolone (Solu-Medrol, Depo-Medrol)
Actions
Mechanism of action unknown
Uses
In combination with other antiemetics to relieve nausea and vomiting; can also be used alone
Common and serious adverse effects
See Chapter 38 for further discussion

- Corticosteroids have few adverse effects; because fewer doses are administered, complications associated with long-term therapy do not arise.
- Elevated mood, increased appetite, and a sense of well-being also are associated actions and may help with acceptance and control of emesis.

Slide 16

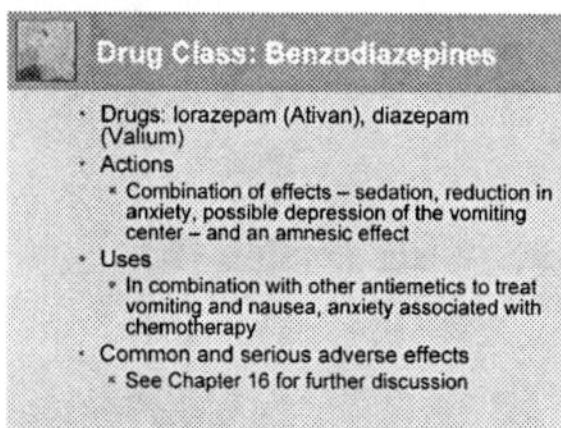
Drug Class: Benzodiazepines
Drugs: lorazepam (Ativan), diazepam (Valium)
Actions
Combination of effects – sedation, reduction in anxiety, possible depression of the vomiting center – and an amnesic effect
Uses
In combination with other antiemetics to treat vomiting and nausea, anxiety associated with chemotherapy
Common and serious adverse effects
See Chapter 16 for further discussion

- Used in combination with metoclopramide, dexamethasone, and serotonin antagonists.

Slide 17

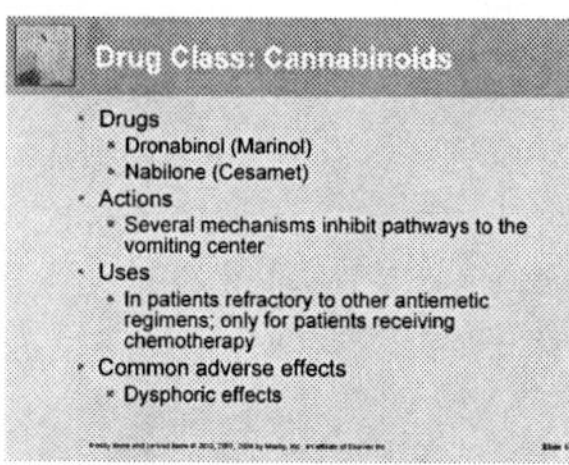
Drug Class: Cannabinoids
Drugs
Dronabinol (Marinol)
Nabilone (Cesamet)
Actions
Several mechanisms inhibit pathways to the vomiting center
Uses
In patients refractory to other antiemetic regimens; only for patients receiving chemotherapy
Common adverse effects
Dysphoric effects

- Cannabinoids are synthetic analogs of tetrahydrocannabinol (THC), the active ingredient in marijuana.

Slide 18

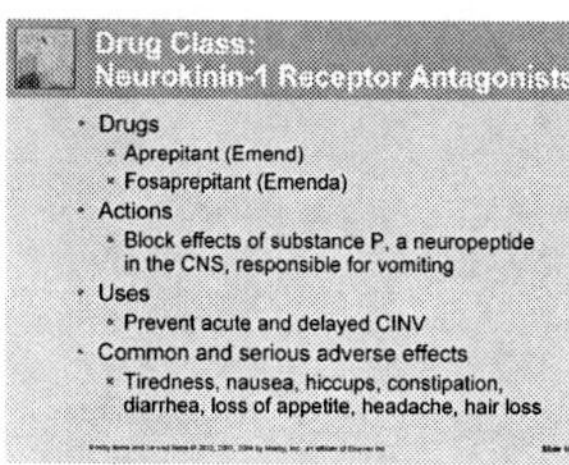
Drug Class:
Neurokinin-1 Receptor Antagonists
Drugs
Aprepitant (Emend)
Fosaprepitant (Emenda)
Actions
Block effects of substance P, a neuropeptide in the CNS, responsible for vomiting
Uses
Prevent acute and delayed CINV
Common and serious adverse effects
Tiredness, nausea, hiccups, constipation, diarrhea, loss of appetite, headache, hair loss

- May be used in combination with a corticosteroid and a 5-HT3 receptor antagonist for control of CINV.
- Aprepitant is taken only for a maximum of 3 days; adverse effects are short lived.

ELSEVIER

35 Lesson Plan
Drugs Used to Treat Constipation and Diarrhea

TEACHING FOCUS

This chapter examines some common causes of constipation and diarrhea. Students have the opportunity to learn how laxatives and antidiarrheal agents act on the system and when it is appropriate to use them. In addition, students apply the nursing process and assess patients for electrolyte imbalance and monitor for dehydration.

MATERIALS AND RESOURCES

- ☐ computer and PowerPoint projector (all Lessons)

LESSON CHECKLIST

Preparations for this lesson include:

- lecture
- guest speaker: nurse specialist
- evaluation of student knowledge and skills needed to perform all entry-level activities related to the causes and treatment for constipation and diarrhea, including:
  - identifying the underlying causes of constipation and diarrhea
  - naming the nine possible causes of diarrhea
  - understanding the actions and uses for the differing laxatives and antidiarrheal agents
  - monitoring for acute symptoms and dehydration
  - using the nursing process to assess patients and administer prescribed medications

KEY TERMS

constipation (p. 540)
diarrhea (p. 540)
laxatives (p. 543)

ADDITIONAL RESOURCES

PowerPoint slides: 1-18
Flashcards, Decks 1 and 2

Legend

ARQ	PPT	TB	CTQ	SG	INRQ
Audience Response Questions	PowerPoint Slides	Test Bank	Critical Thinking Questions	Study Guide	Interactive NCLEX Review Questions

Class Activities are indicated in ***bold italic.***

LESSON 35.1

BACKGROUND ASSESSMENT

Question: What is one factor that can cause both constipation and diarrhea?
Answer: A person's diet can cause either constipation or diarrhea. A diet that has too little residue or too little fluid can create constipation. A diet that is very spicy or has a lot of fatty food may cause diarrhea. The key to normal bowel functioning is a healthy, balanced diet.

ELSEVIER

Question: What important information should the nurse obtain in an assessment of a patient who is reporting constipation or diarrhea?
Answer: The nurse should assess for the duration of the condition and the number of stools that have occurred. He or she should ask about the amount, consistency, color, odor, and presence of abnormal components, such as undigested food, and any additional signs or symptoms that accompany the condition. If possible, the nurse should obtain a sample of the stool. The nurse should try to identify the potential cause of the condition by taking a thorough history. This would include the patient's age, history of previous gastrointestinal (GI) problems, such as irritable bowel syndrome or inflammatory bowel disease, food intake, potential exposure to contaminated food, recent travel outside of the United States, use of laxatives, immobility, medications, or other medical conditions.

CRITICAL THINKING QUESTION

A 30-year-old patient has been admitted for management of severe diarrhea. He reports having 12 to 18 stools per day. What nursing interventions should the nurse provide for him?
Guidelines: The nurse will need to monitor the patient's hydration status with either oral or parenteral solutions as ordered by the health care provider because diarrhea causes dehydration. The health care provider may order a stool culture to rule out an infectious cause of the diarrhea. Fluids such as weak tea, water, or clear soup are suggested. The patient should avoid food and fluids that may further irritate the GI system. The nurse should assess for bowel sounds in all four quadrants and report characteristics of bowel sounds to the health care provider. The nurse should monitor the patient's weight daily and electrolyte values. The patient should increase the frequency and length of rest periods and decrease activity because the latter will stimulate peristalsis. The nurse should provide antidiarrheal agents as needed and monitor and document their results. Finally, the nurse should instruct the patient on how to cleanse the perianal area with mild soap and water after each bowel movement and apply a protective ointment, such as zinc oxide or Vaseline.

OBJECTIVES	CONTENT	TEACHING RESOURCES
State the underlying causes of constipation.	■ Constipation (p. 540) Review the definition and common causes of constipation: improper diet, lack of exercise, failure to respond to defecation impulses, muscular weakness of colon, hypothyroidism, anemia, tumors of the bowel, and drug therapy.	PPT 4-5 ARQ 1 TB Multiple Response question 1 SG Learning Activities questions 1, 4, 17-18 (pp. 231-232) ▸ Discuss possible causes of constipation. When should action be taken to relieve a patient of symptoms of constipation? Class Activity ***Divide the class into small groups. Have each group create educational materials on the causes of constipation and when action could be taken to help relieve the person of the symptoms. Then have the groups present their materials to the class.***
Explain the meaning of "normal" bowel habits.	■ Constipation (p. 540)	PPT 4 TB Multiple Choice question 1 SG Learning Activities questions 19-20 (p. 232) ▸ Discuss what one should look for in "normal" bowel habits. Is it necessary to have a bowel movement every day? Class Activity ***Ask volunteers to define normal bowel habits.***

OBJECTIVES	CONTENT	TEACHING RESOURCES
Cite nine causes of diarrhea.	■ Diarrhea (p. 540) □ Intestinal infections (p. 541) □ Spicy or fatty foods (p. 541) □ Enzyme deficiencies (p. 541) □ Excessive use of laxatives (p. 541) □ Drug therapy (p. 541) □ Emotional stress (p. 541) □ Hyperthyroidism (p. 541) □ Inflammatory bowel disease (p. 541) □ Surgical bypass (p. 541) Review the definition and the nine common causes of diarrhea.	PPT 6-7 TB Multiple Choice question 8 SG Learning Activities questions 2-3, 21 (pp. 231-232) ▸ Discuss the factors that may cause diarrhea. Under what conditions should a patient seek the advice of a health care professional? Class Activity ***Divide the class into three groups, and assign each group three of the nine causes of diarrhea. Have the groups discuss how each of the conditions can cause diarrhea and when it would be necessary for a patient to seek care from a health care provider. Then have the groups present their findings to the class.***
Describe medical conditions for which laxatives should *not* be used.	■ Treatment of altered elimination (p. 541) □ Constipation (p. 541) □ Diarrhea (p. 541)	PPT 8 TB Multiple Choice questions 3, 9 INRQ 6-7, 10 CTQ 2 SG Review Sheet question 6 (p. 230) Review Question for the NCLEX Examination 8 (p. 549) ▸ Discuss when a patient seeking relief from constipation should seek the advice of a health care professional. ▸ Discuss what happens when a patient overuses a laxative. What type of laxative should not be used on a daily basis? Class Activity ***Divide the class into small groups, and have each group identify, list, and provide rationales for medical conditions for which laxatives should not be used. Then have the groups present their findings to the class.***
Identify electrolytes that should be monitored whenever prolonged or severe diarrhea is present.	– Nursing process for constipation and diarrhea (p. 541) – Patient education and health promotion (p. 543)	PPT 10 Review Question for the NCLEX Examination 9 (p. 549) ▸ Discuss when a patient requires electrolyte replacement. ▸ Discuss the use of polyethylene glycol electrolyte solution. Class Activity ***Divide the class into small groups. Have each group identify which***

OBJECTIVES	CONTENT	TEACHING RESOURCES
		laboratory values of the electrolytes should be monitored for malabsorption, dehydration, fluid, and electrolyte and acid-base imbalances. Instruct each group to include normal and abnormal values. Then have the groups present their lists to the class.
Describe nursing assessments needed to evaluate the patient's state of hydration when suffering from either constipation or dehydration.	– Nursing process for constipation and diarrhea (p. 541) Review the treatment options for both constipation and diarrhea, which include gathering information from the patient about diet, exercise, and known disease processes. Review the laboratory tests that monitor for hydration status.	PPT 10 TB Multiple Choice question 7 TB Multiple Response question 2 SG Review Sheet question 5 (p. 230) ▸ Discuss what signs to monitor in the treatment of diarrhea. What precautions would you give a patient to prevent dehydration in the early stages of diarrhea? Class Activity ***Divide the class into two groups. Assign one group constipation and the other dehydration. Have each group create an appropriate care plan for the assigned topic, including assessment, planning, implementation, and evaluation. Have the groups share their plans with the class.*** Class Activity ***Divide the class into groups, with two students in each group. Assign half of the groups constipation and the other half diarrhea. Have each group prepare a discharge education plan for its assigned condition. Allow class time for presentation.***

35.1 Homework/Assignments:

35.1 Instructor's Notes/Student Feedback:

LESSON 35.2

CRITICAL THINKING QUESTION

A 45-year-old patient with cancer, who takes large amounts of narcotics for pain, lives at home and spends most of her day in a recliner chair. Upon assessment, she states that she feels bloated and has been incontinent of small amounts of liquid stool two to three times a day. What would the nurse recommend to promote normal bowel function?

Guidelines: The patient's symptoms indicate fecal impaction. This has probably been caused by the continuing use of narcotics. To treat the impacted stool, administration of a lubricant laxative would allow a smooth passage of the fecal contents. The nurse can also suggest that the patient use a bulk-forming laxative; these are recommended for individuals who require a laxative on a regular basis to manage elimination. The nurse should encourage the patient to increase fluids, include fiber within her diet, and increase activity if possible. A patient who has a depressed immune system secondary to chemotherapy should avoid fresh fruits and vegetables because of an increased risk for infection and the likelihood of increased bacterial counts associated with these food items.

OBJECTIVES	CONTENT	TEACHING RESOURCES
Identify the indications for use, method of action, and onset of action for stimulant laxatives, saline laxatives, lubricant or emollient laxatives, bulk-forming laxatives, and fecal softeners.	□ Drug class: Laxatives (p. 543) – Nursing process for laxative therapy (p. 545) Review the drug class laxatives and its subclassifications: stimulant laxatives, saline laxatives, lubricant laxatives, bulk-producing laxatives, and fecal softeners. Discuss the actions, uses, and therapeutic outcomes of each type, as well as common and serious adverse effects and any drug interactions.	PPT 13-17 ARQ 2-4 TB Multiple Choice questions 2, 4, 6, 10, 11-13 TB Multiple Response question 3 INRQ 1, 8-9 CTQ 1, 3 SG Review Sheet questions 1-3, 7-9 (pp. 229-230) SG Learning Activities questions 5, 13-16 (p. 231) SG Practice Questions for the NCLEX Examination 1-3, 6-7 (p. 233) Review Questions for the NCLEX Examination 5-6 (p. 549) Drug Table 35-1: Laxatives (p. 546) ▸ Discuss Table 35-1. Compare how different laxatives act on the intestines and appropriate uses for each. Class Activity ***Write the names of the following commercial medications on the board, and have students identify the appropriate drug class.*** – ***Metamucil*** – ***Peri-Colace*** – ***Ex-Lax*** – ***Go-LYTELY*** – ***MiraLax*** – ***Phillips's Milk of Magnesia***

OBJECTIVES	CONTENT	TEACHING RESOURCES
		Class Activity ***Have each student write a condition or situation (such as preoperative bowel preparation) that requires a laxative. Collect the written notes, and have the students take turns selecting one of the conditions. Have the students identify the appropriate laxative for the condition.***
State the differences between locally acting and systemically acting antidiarrheal agents.	□ Drug class: Antidiarrheal agents (p. 545) – Nursing process for antidiarrheal agents (p. 547) Review the drug class antidiarrheals and the two broad categories of this class, locally acting agents and systemically acting agents. Discuss the actions, uses, and therapeutic outcomes of each type, as well as common and serious adverse effects and any drug interactions.	PPT 18-19 ARQ 5 TB Multiple Choice question 5 INRQ 4-5, 11-12 CTQ 4 SG Review Sheet questions 4-5 (pp. 229-230) SG Learning Activities questions 7-12 (p. 231) SG Practice Questions for the NCLEX Examination 4-5, 8-10 (pp. 233-234) Review Questions for the NCLEX Examination 1-4, 7 (pp. 548-549) Drug Table 35-2: Antidiarrheal Agents (pp. 547-548) ▸ Discuss the differences between systemic acting agents and those that act locally. When is it appropriate to use each? Class Activity ***Invite a clinical nurse specialist to discuss conditions that cause diarrhea, treatments, and the differences between the locally and systemically acting antidiarrheal agents.*** Class Activity ***Facilitate a class discussion on when antidiarrheal agents should be avoided (e.g., active GI infection).***
Cite conditions that generally respond favorably to antidiarrheal agents.	□ Drug class: Antidiarrheal agents (p. 545) – Nursing process for antidiarrheal agents (p. 547) Review the drug class antidiarrheals and the two broad categories of this class, locally acting agents and systemically acting agents. Discuss the actions, uses, and therapeutic outcomes of each type, as well as common and serious adverse effects and any drug interactions.	PPT 18 ▸ Discuss Drug Table 35-2. What are the actions and uses for different antidiarrheal agents? Class Activity ***Have two students role-play the nurse educating the patient who is taking Imodium for diarrhea. Have the class assist the nurse in explaining how the drug works to relieve diarrhea and the need to limit the use of antidiarrheal agents. Review the exercise with the class.***

OBJECTIVES	CONTENT	TEACHING RESOURCES
Review medications studied to date, and prepare a list of those that may cause diarrhea.	– Nursing process for antidiarrheal agents (p. 547)	▶ Discuss what advice you might give a patient taking antibiotics. Under what conditions should a patient take an antidiarrheal agent? Class Activity ***Lead a discussion about medications that cause diarrhea, such as antibiotics, and when the antidiarrheal agent should be taken. Discuss the use of adding daily yogurt to the diet to prevent*** **Clostridium difficile** ***for the patient on antibiotics who develops diarrhea.***
Performance evaluation		Test Bank SG Learning Activities (pp. 231-232) SG Practice Questions for the NCLEX Examination (pp. 233-234) Critical Thinking Questions

35.2 Homework/Assignments:

35.2 Instructor's Notes/Student Feedback:

35 Lecture Outline

Drugs Used to Treat Constipation and Diarrhea

Slide 1

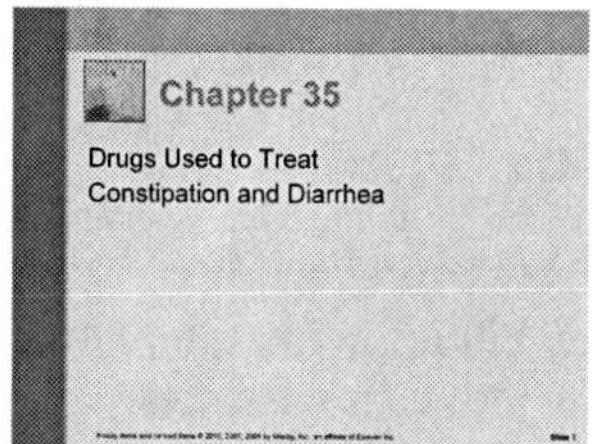
Chapter 35
Drugs Used to Treat
Constipation and Diarrhea

Slide 2

Chapter 35
Lesson 35.1

Slide 3

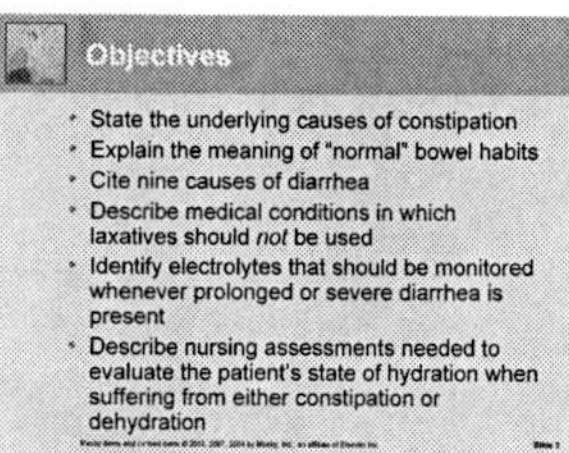
Objectives
State the underlying causes of constipation
Explain the meaning of "normal" bowel habits
Cite nine causes of diarrhea
Describe medical conditions in which laxatives should not be used
Identify electrolytes that should be monitored whenever prolonged or severe diarrhea is present
Describe nursing assessments needed to evaluate the patient's state of hydration when suffering from either constipation or dehydration

Slide 4

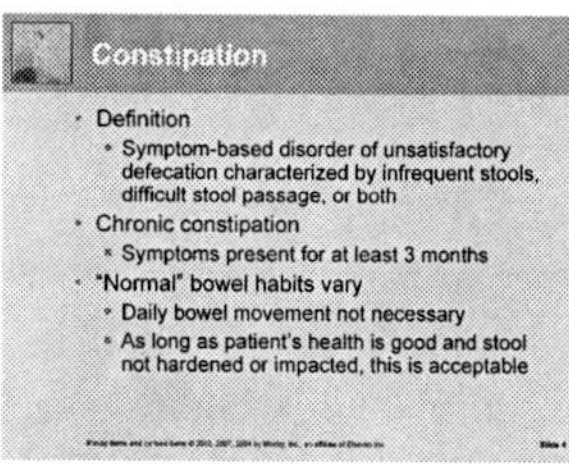
Constipation
Definition
Symptom-based disorder of unsatisfactory defecation characterized by infrequent stools, difficult stool passage, or both
Chronic constipation
Symptoms present for at least 3 months
"Normal" bowel habits vary
Daily bowel movement not necessary
As long as patient's health is good and stool not hardened or impacted, this is acceptable

- Occasional constipation is not detrimental to a person's health, but may cause general discomfort, abdominal fullness, anorexia, or anxiety.

Slide 5

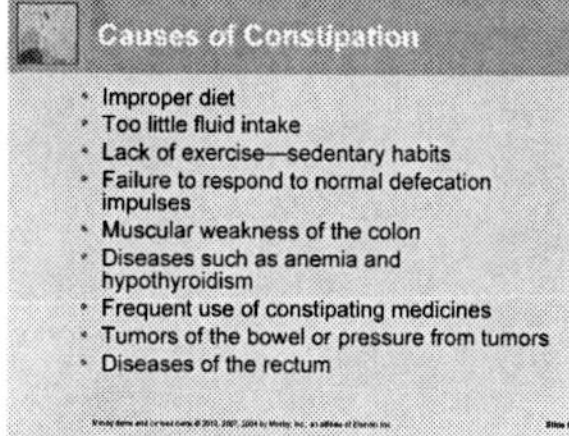
Causes of Constipation
Improper diet
Too little fluid intake
Lack of exercise—sedentary habits
Failure to respond to normal defecation impulses
Muscular weakness of the colon
Diseases such as anemia and hypothyroidism
Frequent use of constipating medicines
Tumors of the bowel or pressure from tumors
Diseases of the rectum

- Diets that have too little residue (lacking fruits and vegetables or high in constipating foods) and too little fluid may result in constipation.
- Examples of medications causing constipation: morphine, codeine, anticholinergic agents.

Slide 6

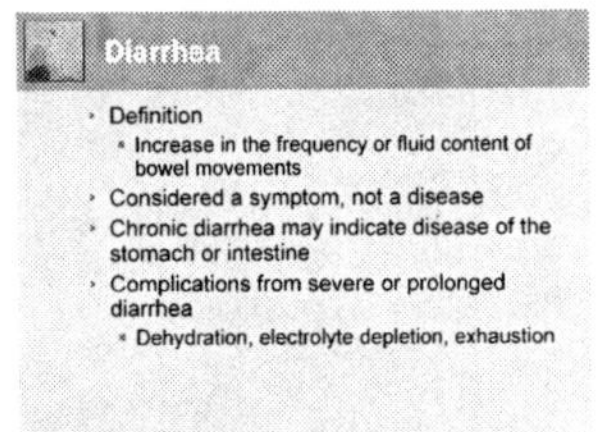
Diarrhea
Definition
Increase in the frequency or fluid content of bowel movements
Considered a symptom, not a disease
Chronic diarrhea may indicate disease of the stomach or intestine
Complications from severe or prolonged diarrhea
Dehydration, electrolyte depletion, exhaustion

Slide 7

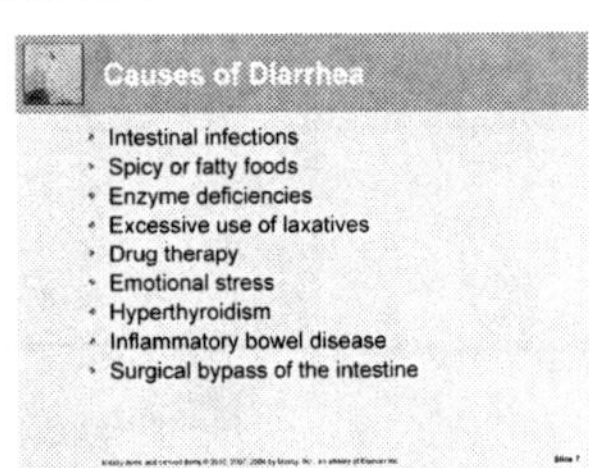
Causes of Diarrhea
Intestinal infections
Spicy or fatty foods
Enzyme deficiencies
Excessive use of laxatives
Drug therapy
Emotional stress
Hyperthyroidism
Inflammatory bowel disease
Surgical bypass of the intestine

- Antibiotics may cause diarrhea because they kill off normal flora in the bowel. Antacids containing magnesium may also cause diarrhea.
- Inflammatory bowel diseases include diverticulitis, ulcerative colitis, gastroenteritis, Crohn's disease.

Slide 8

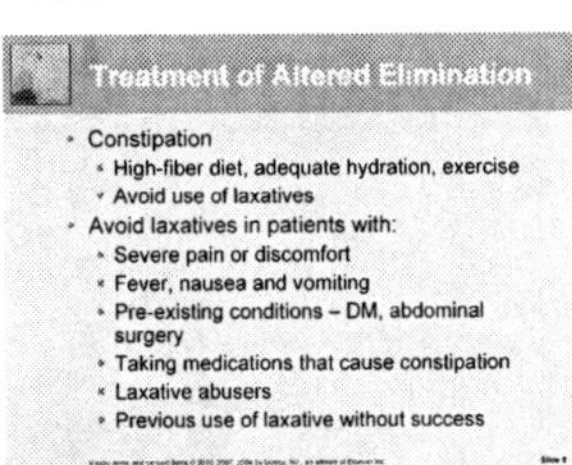
Treatment of Altered Elimination
Constipation
High-fiber diet, adequate hydration, exercise
Avoid use of laxatives
Avoid laxatives in patients with:
Severe pain or discomfort
Fever, nausea and vomiting
Pre-existing conditions – DM, abdominal surgery
Taking medications that cause constipation
Laxative abusers
Previous use of laxative without success

- Prescribed medications that cause constipation: iron, aluminum antacids, antispasmodics, muscle relaxants.
- Do not administer laxatives to patients with undiagnosed abdominal pain, or inflammation of the GI tract.

Slide 9

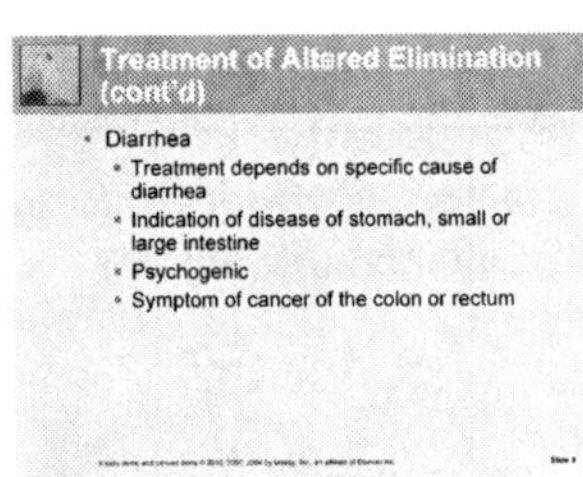
Treatment of Altered Elimination (cont'd)
Diarrhea
Treatment depends on specific cause of diarrhea
Indication of disease of stomach, small or large intestine
Psychogenic
Symptom of cancer of the colon or rectum

- Diarrhea can be chronic, mild, or severe.

Slide 10

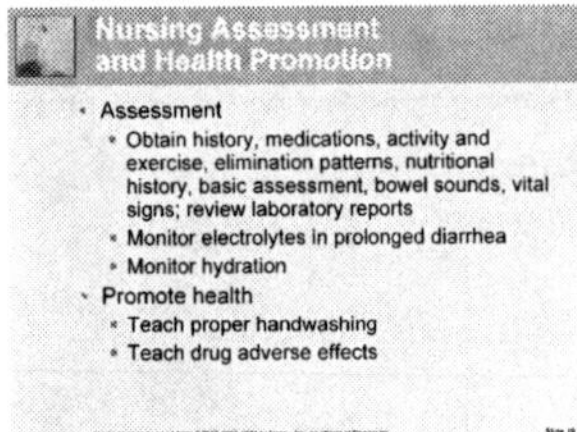
Nursing Assessment and Health Promotion
Assessment
Obtain history, medications, activity and exercise, elimination patterns, nutritional history, basic assessment, bowel sounds, vital signs; review laboratory reports
Monitor electrolytes in prolonged diarrhea
Monitor hydration
Promote health
Teach proper handwashing
Teach drug adverse effects

- Monitor hydration by evaluating volume of intake, urine output, skin turgor, moisturization of mucous membranes, and daily weight.

ELSEVIER

Slide 11

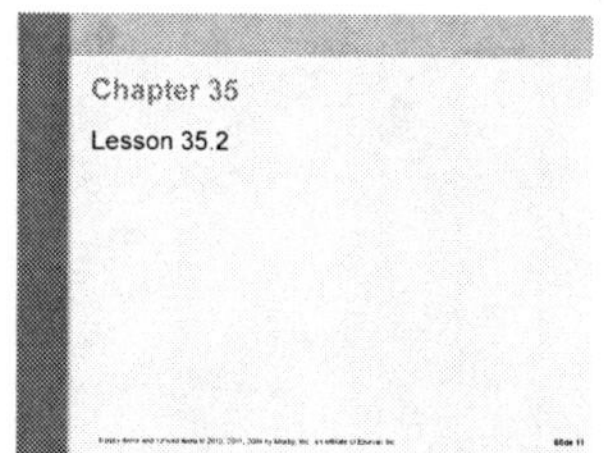
Chapter 35
Lesson 35.2

Slide 12

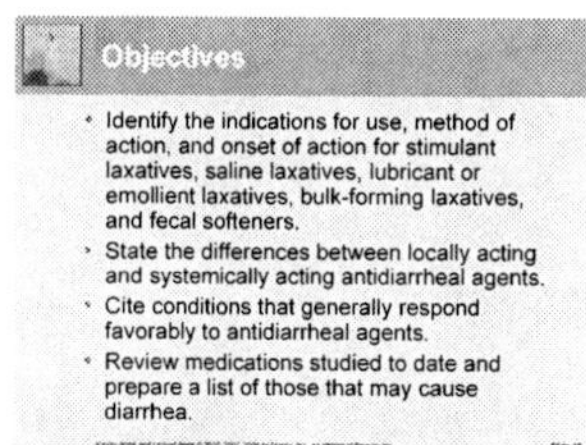
Objectives
Identify the indications for use, method of action, and onset of action for stimulant laxatives, saline laxatives, lubricant or emollient laxatives, bulk-forming laxatives, and fecal softeners.
State the differences between locally acting and systemically acting antidiarrheal agents.
Cite conditions that generally respond favorably to antidiarrheal agents.
Review medications studied to date and prepare a list of those that may cause diarrhea.

Slide 13

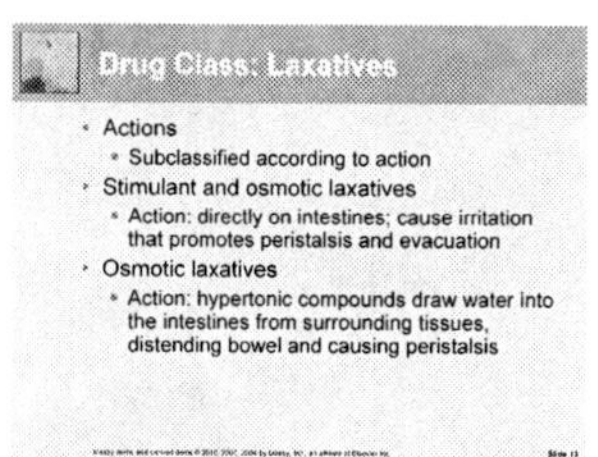
Drug Class: Laxatives
Actions
Subclassified according to action
Stimulant and osmotic laxatives
Action: directly on intestines; cause irritation that promotes peristalsis and evacuation
Osmotic laxatives
Action: hypertonic compounds draw water into the intestines from surrounding tissues, distending bowel and causing peristalsis

- Common adverse effects: excessive bowel stimulation, diarrhea.
- Serious adverse effects: abdominal tenderness, pain, bleeding, vomiting, diarrhea, increasing abdominal girth.

Slide 14

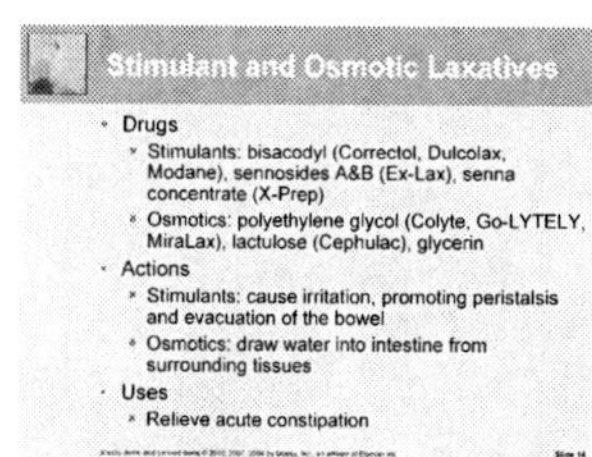
Stimulant and Osmotic Laxatives
Drugs
Stimulants: bisacodyl (Correctol, Dulcolax, Modane), sennosides A&B (Ex-Lax), senna concentrate (X-Prep)
Osmotics: polyethylene glycol (Colyte, Go-LYTELY, MiraLax), lactulose (Cephulac), glycerin
Actions
Stimulants: cause irritation, promoting peristalsis and evacuation of the bowel
Osmotics: draw water into intestine from surrounding tissues
Uses
Relieve acute constipation

- Lactulose and polyethylene glycol are effective in relieving chronic constipation.
- Larger doses of polyethylene glycol are routinely used as bowel preparations before radiologic examination of abdominal organs.

Slide 15

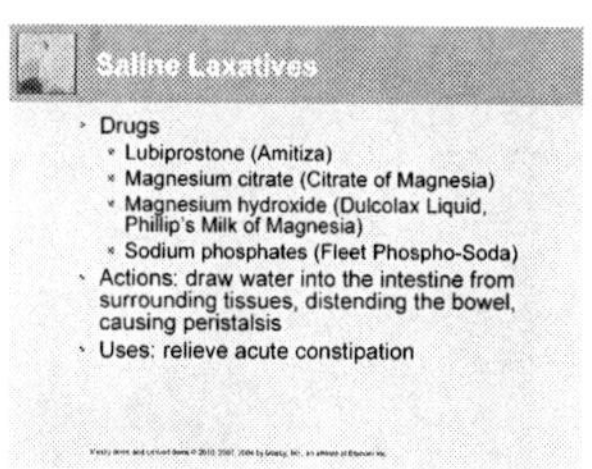
Saline Laxatives
Drugs
Lubiprostone (Amitiza)
Magnesium citrate (Citrate of Magnesia)
Magnesium hydroxide (Dulcolax Liquid, Phillip's Milk of Magnesia)
Sodium phosphates (Fleet Phospho-Soda)
Actions: draw water into the intestine from surrounding tissues, distending the bowel, causing peristalsis
Uses: relieve acute constipation

- Usually act within 1 to 3 hours and up to 6 hours for sodium phosphates.
- Continuous use may alter electrolyte balance and cause dehydration.

ELSEVIER

Slide 16

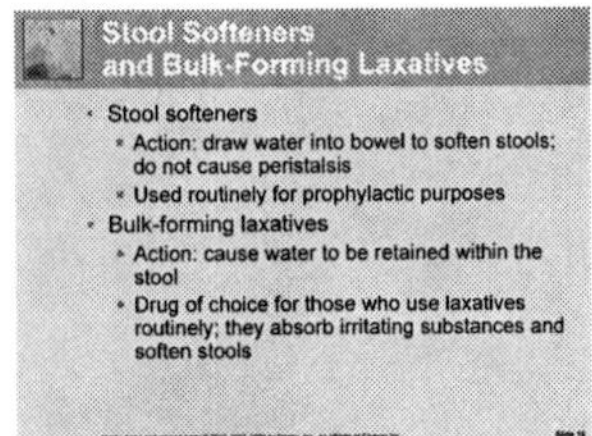
Stool Softeners
and Bulk-Forming Laxatives
Stool softeners
Action: draw water into bowel to soften stools; do not cause peristalsis
Used routinely for prophylactic purposes
Bulk-forming laxatives
Action: cause water to be retained within the stool
Drug of choice for those who use laxatives routinely; they absorb irritating substances and soften stools

- For specific drugs, see Table 35-1.

Slide 17

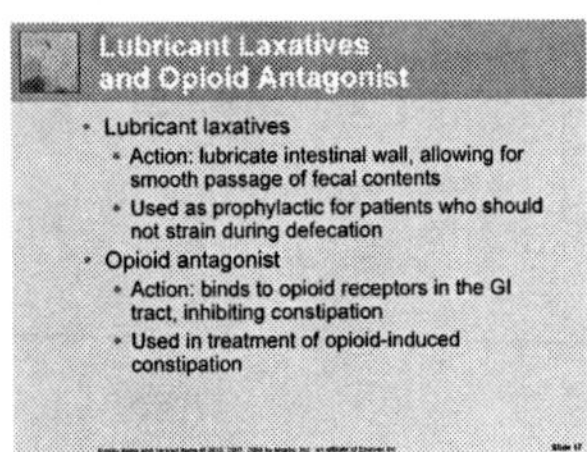
Lubricant Laxatives
and Opioid Antagonist
Lubricant laxatives
Action: lubricate intestinal wall, allowing for smooth passage of fecal contents
Used as prophylactic for patients who should not strain during defecation
Opioid antagonist
Action: binds to opioid receptors in the GI tract, inhibiting constipation
Used in treatment of opioid-induced constipation

- For specific drugs, see Table 35-1.

Slide 18

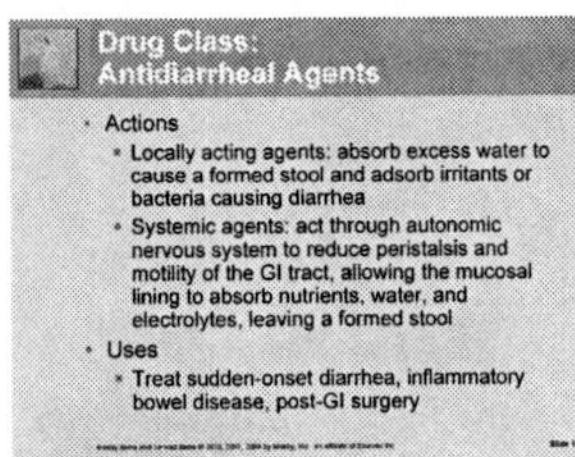
Drug Class:
Antidiarrheal Agents
Actions
Locally acting agents: absorb excess water to cause a formed stool and adsorb irritants or bacteria causing diarrhea
Systemic agents: act through autonomic nervous system to reduce peristalsis and motility of the GI tract, allowing the mucosal lining to absorb nutrients, water, and electrolytes, leaving a formed stool
Uses
Treat sudden-onset diarrhea, inflammatory bowel disease, post-GI surgery

- For specific drugs, see Table 35-2.

Slide 19

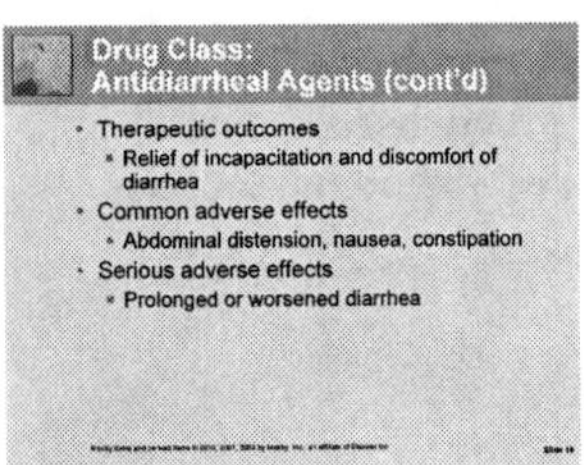
Drug Class:
Antidiarrheal Agents (cont'd)
Therapeutic outcomes
Relief of incapacitation and discomfort of diarrhea
Common adverse effects
Abdominal distension, nausea, constipation
Serious adverse effects
Prolonged or worsened diarrhea

- Many OTC antidiarrheal medications are available.

ELSEVIER

36 Lesson Plan

Drugs Used to Treat Diabetes Mellitus

TEACHING FOCUS

This chapter focuses on the treatment of diabetes mellitus. Following an introduction to the classification and various types of diabetes, drug therapy is introduced, and care of the patient and assessment parameters are described. Students are given detailed patient education and health promotion information for dealing with the various aspects of the disease. The important issues of correctly identifying hypoglycemic and hyperglycemic episodes in a timely manner are addressed, in addition to various types of insulin and administration regimens. The use of oral hypoglycemic agents, antidiabetic agents, and antihypoglycemic agents are also presented as they are used in the treatment of type 2 diabetes mellitus.

MATERIALS AND RESOURCES

- □ computer and PowerPoint projector (all Lessons)
- □ dry erase board (Lesson 36.1)

LESSON CHECKLIST

Preparations for this lesson include:

- lecture
- evaluation of student knowledge and skills needed to perform all entry-level activities related to the drugs used to treat diabetes mellitus, including:
  - the types of diabetes mellitus and their treatments
  - drug therapy for diabetes mellitus
  - the nursing process and patient education programs for diabetes mellitus
  - types of insulin and its use in the treatment of diabetes
  - oral hypoglycemic agents, antidiabetic agents, and antihypoglycemic agents

KEY TERMS

diabetes mellitus (p. 550)
gestational diabetes mellitus (p. 551)
hyperglycemia (p. 550)
hypoglycemia (p. 553)
impaired fasting glucose (IFG) (p. 552)
impaired glucose tolerance (IGT) (p. 552)
intensive therapy (p. 554)
macrovascular complications (p. 552)
microvascular complications (p. 552)
neuropathies (p. 553)
paresthesia (p. 553)
prediabetes (p. 552)
type 1 diabetes mellitus (p. 551)
type 2 diabetes mellitus (p. 552)

ADDITIONAL RESOURCES

PowerPoint slides: 1-26
Flashcards, Decks 1 and 2

Legend

ARQ	**PPT**	**TB**	**CTQ**	**SG**	**INRQ**
Audience Response Questions	PowerPoint Slides	Test Bank	Critical Thinking Questions	Study Guide	Interactive NCLEX Review Questions

Class Activities are indicated in ***bold italic.***

ELSEVIER

LESSON 36.1

BACKGROUND ASSESSMENT

Question: What are the four types of diabetes mellitus?
Answer: Diabetes mellitus is a group of diseases characterized by hyperglycemia resulting from defects in insulin secretion, insulin action, or both. There are four types of diabetes mellitus. Type 1 diabetes mellitus often occurs in children and is lifelong. It used to be known as insulin-dependent diabetes mellitus (IDDM). It occurs when the pancreas does not secrete any insulin. Patients with type 1 diabetes require exogenous insulin for life. In type 2 diabetes mellitus, the pancreas still maintains some capability to produce and secrete insulin, but insulin secretion is reduced, and the cells are resistant to the remaining circulating insulin. These patients are usually treated with oral hypoglycemic agents but may also require some exogenous insulin. Type 2 diabetes mellitus is the most common form. A third type of diabetes mellitus occurs in patients who have other diseases that include a diabetic component, such as Cushing's syndrome. Their symptoms last only during the crisis and are treated in various ways, depending on the condition. Gestational diabetes is found in some women during pregnancy and usually resolves itself about 6 weeks postpartum.

Question: What are common adverse effects seen with the use of oral hypoglycemic agents? What is hepatotoxicity, and why is it considered serious?
Answer: Many of the commonly used oral hypoglycemic agents have similar adverse effects, such as nausea, vomiting, headaches, and hypoglycemia. These adverse effects tend to disappear after the patient becomes accustomed to the medication. Toxicity of the liver, also known as hepatotoxicity, can be caused by an accumulation of multiple drugs. The symptoms are anorexia, nausea, jaundice, hepatomegaly, splenomegaly, and abnormal liver function tests. These adverse effects can lead to serious problems, such as liver failure. Patients on long-term oral hypoglycemic agents require frequent liver monitoring.

CRITICAL THINKING QUESTION

A 60-year-old man was recently diagnosed with type 2 diabetes mellitus. During a visit to the patient's home, the home care nurse sees the patient eating a large, unhealthy breakfast. When asked about his eating habits, the patient says that he is not very good about keeping his records up to date and that he is just happy that he will never have to give himself insulin shots. What type of patient teaching should be done here, and how could the nurse encourage patient compliance?
Guidelines: This patient is exhibiting noncompliant behaviors by ignoring the dietary guidelines established to control his disease and by failing to record his monitoring parameters. The nurse should reinforce patient teaching regarding diet, exercise, and other lifestyle changes and recommend that the patient find a way to keep records of his blood glucose level that would fit into his daily activities. The nurse should further explore the patient's noncompliance and try to determine possible reasons, such as depression. The nurse should also educate and inform the patient that when oral hypoglycemics are used to treat type 2 diabetes mellitus, a diabetic diet must be followed. If a diet is not adhered to and oral medications do not control the disease, insulin may be needed to control blood glucose. The nurse should also report this patient's noncompliance to both the charge nurse and the health care provider, and he or she should document it properly.

OBJECTIVES	CONTENT	TEACHING RESOURCES
State the current definition of diabetes mellitus.	■ Diabetes mellitus (p. 550) Review the definition of diabetes mellitus.	PPT 6 SG Review Sheet questions 1, 7-8 (pp. 235-236) SG Learning Activities questions 2, 17 (p. 241) ▸ Discuss the characteristics of diabetes mellitus. Class Activity ***Lead a class discussion about diabetes mellitus, and have students outline the pathologic conditions of the disease and identify its signs and symptoms. Record student responses on the board for comparison.***

OBJECTIVES	CONTENT	TEACHING RESOURCES
Identify normal fasting glucose levels.	■ Diabetes mellitus (p. 550) Review the categories for fasting plasma glucose that may indicate impaired glucose tolerance (IGT) or impaired fasting glucose (IFG).	PPT 9 SG Review Sheet question 6 (p. 236) Review Question for the NCLEX Examination 8 (p. 583) ▸ Discuss the parameters of normal blood sugars, preprandial and postprandial. ▸ Discuss how a health care provider determines if a patient has diabetes mellitus. Class Activity ***Have students identify factors that would increase or decrease blood sugars and explain why.***
Identify the extent of the disease within the United States.	■ Diabetes mellitus (p. 550) Review the prevalence of diabetes in the population according to the Centers for Disease Control and Prevention (CDC).	PPT 6 ARQ 1 ▸ Discuss the risk factors for diabetes mellitus. Is there any way to prevent the disease from occurring? Class Activity ***Divide the class into groups. Have each group create a concept map that illustrates the prevalence of diabetes in the United States based on gender, age, ethnicity, and other factors. Have each group share its findings with the class.*** Class Activity ***Divide the class into small groups. Have each group discuss the reasons for the high incidence of undiagnosed diabetes mellitus in the United States, and identify three ways in which that number could be reduced. Have each group share its findings with the class for discussion.*** Class Activity ***Discuss nursing interventions to combat the increase in type 2 diabetes mellitus in school-age children in the United States.***
Describe the current classification system for diabetes mellitus.	■ Diabetes mellitus (p. 550) Discuss the subclasses of diabetes (type 1 and type 2), the various diseases that have a diabetic component, and gestational diabetes.	PPT 7-8 TB Multiple Response questions 1, 5 SG Review Sheet questions 4-5, 14 (pp. 235-236) SG Learning Activities questions 1, 18-20 (pp. 241-242) Box 36-1: Classification of Diabetes Mellitus by Pathologic Cause (p. 551) Table 36-2: Criteria for Diagnosis of Diabetes Mellitus (p. 552) ▸ Discuss the classification system for diabetes mellitus.

OBJECTIVES	CONTENT	TEACHING RESOURCES
		Class Activity ***Divide the class into small groups, and assign each group one of the following types of diabetes mellitus: type 1, type 2, gestational diabetes, and diabetes resulting from another disorder, such as pheochromocytoma. Have each group outline the pathologic conditions, symptoms, and treatments of its assigned condition and present its findings to the class for discussion. Record key characteristics from each group for comparison.***
Differentiate between the symptoms of type 1 and type 2 diabetes mellitus.	■ Diabetes mellitus (p. 550) Review the treatment goal for type 1 and type 2 diabetes, and discuss how type 1 patients will always need insulin to control their blood glucose.	PPT 7 TB Multiple Response questions 2, 4 SG Review Sheet questions 2-3 (p. 235) SG Learning Activities questions 18-20 (pp. 241-242) Table 36-1: Features of Type 1 and Type 2 Diabetes Mellitus (p. 552) ▸ Discuss the symptoms of type 1 and type 2 diabetes mellitus. ▸ Discuss and list the various manifestations of neuropathies. Class Activity ***Present the following characteristics to the class, and have students identify which type of diabetes mellitus each characteristic indicates:*** – ***Pancreas produces some insulin*** – ***Requires exogenous insulin*** – ***Symptoms progress rapidly*** – ***Usually occurs later in life*** – ***Can be controlled by diet alone*** – ***Patients sometimes go into remission***
Identify the objectives of dietary control of diabetes mellitus.	■ Treatment of diabetes mellitus (p. 553) Review the treatment goal for diabetic patients to prevent ketoacidosis and symptoms resulting from hyperglycemia. Discuss the importance of dietary management for control of diabetes, especially for those with type 2. The goal with diet is to prevent postprandial hyperglycemia and hypoglycemia.	PPT 10 ARQ 2 TB Multiple Response question 3 SG Review Sheet question 10 (p. 236) Review Question for the NCLEX Examination 9 (p. 583) Table 36-3: Treatment Goals for Diabetes and Comorbid Diseases (p. 554) ▸ Discuss the objectives of dietary control of diabetes mellitus and the particular challenges associated with dietary control. ▸ Discuss practical measures that patients can take to ensure that they receive proper nutrition.

ELSEVIER

OBJECTIVES	CONTENT	TEACHING RESOURCES
		▸ Discuss dietary treatment of diabetes using medical nutrition therapy (MNT). Class Activity ***Divide the class into groups. Have each group create a menu plan that outlines a full day's meals and snacks for a diabetic patient. Be sure that students incorporate real-world eating, including how to make good restaurant and menu choices. Have each group share its menu with the class. Then lead a class discussion about the special dietary needs of diabetics.***
Define *intensive therapy.*	■ Treatment of diabetes mellitus (p. 553) Discuss intensive therapy and its application to diabetic patients.	PPT 11 SG Review Sheet question 11 (p. 236) ▸ Discuss the term *intensive therapy* and what it includes—self-monitoring of blood glucose four or more times a day, MNT, exercise, and three or more insulin injections or insulin pump uses. Class Activity ***Divide the class in half. Have one half explain the symptoms and treatment of hyperglycemia and the other half explain the symptoms and treatment of hypoglycemia. Discuss dietary goals for management of patients with diabetes. Review the exercise with the class.***
Identify the major nursing considerations associated with the management of the patient with diabetes (e.g., nutritional evaluation, dietary prescription, activity and exercise, and psychological considerations).	■ Drug therapy for diabetes mellitus (p. 554) – Nursing process for patients with diabetes mellitus (p. 555)	PPT 10, 13 TB Multiple Choice question 7 Patient Self-Assessment Form: Antidiabetic Agents SG Review Sheet question 15 (p. 236) Lifespan Considerations: Insulin (p. 562) ▸ Discuss under what circumstances insulin is likely to be used as therapy and when oral hypoglycemic agents are more likely to be used. ▸ Discuss psychosocial aspects of the diabetes diagnosis. ▸ Discuss what further investigations are necessary if the diabetic patient exhibits hypertension. Class Activity ***Lead a class discussion about management of diabetes mellitus. Ask students to identify nursing considerations for the various aspects of the disease's management, including diet, exercise, medication, and blood and urine testing. Record student responses on the board for comparison.***

OBJECTIVES	CONTENT	TEACHING RESOURCES
		Class Activity ***Divide the class into groups, and have each group discuss the role of weight reduction or management in the treatment of diabetes. Then have each group identify three nursing interventions to promote weight loss or management in a diabetic patient. Have students identify common difficulties and pitfalls in diabetes management and how the nurse can address these difficulties. Have groups share their findings with the class for discussion.***
Differentiate among the signs, symptoms, and management of hypoglycemia and hyperglycemia.	– Nursing process for patients with diabetes mellitus (p. 555) Discuss the signs and symptoms of hypoglycemia and hyperglycemia.	PPT 11 INRQ 19 CTQ 4 TB Multiple Choice question 2 SG Review Sheet questions 16, 43-45 (pp. 236, 239) Review Question for the NCLEX Examination 5 (p. 583) ▶ Discuss the treatments for hyperglycemia and hypoglycemia. Class Activity ***Present the following signs and symptoms to the class, and have students identify which ones indicate hypoglycemia and which indicate hyperglycemia:*** – ***Tremors*** – ***Hunger*** – ***Nausea and vomiting*** – ***Clammy skin*** – ***Fruity breath*** – ***Rapid pulse*** – ***Abdominal pain*** ***Have students discuss the rationale for each symptom to enhance their understanding of why the specific symptom presents.*** Class Activity ***Divide the class into groups. Assign each group either hypoglycemia or hyperglycemia, and have students create a concept map for the pathologic conditions, signs and symptoms, treatments, complications, and management for their assigned topic. Then have groups present their findings to the class.***
Develop a health teaching plan for people taking any type of insulin or oral hypoglycemic agent.	– Patient education and health promotion (p. 559)	PPT 11 ARQ 3 TB Multiple Choice questions 4, 10-11 INRQ 1, 4, 21-23 CTQ 1, 3

OBJECTIVES	CONTENT	TEACHING RESOURCES
		SG Learning Activities questions 22-23 (p. 242) SG Practice Questions for the NCLEX Examination 2, 9 (pp. 243-244) Figure 36-3 (p. 565): Diabetes health care plan. ▸ Discuss how you would teach the patient and family members how to recognize hypoglycemia and hyperglycemia. ▸ Discuss how you would design a teaching plan for self-monitoring blood glucose. ▸ Discuss several commonly used schedules of insulin dosing. Why are rapid-acting and short-acting insulins combined? Class Activity ***Lead a class discussion about treatment of diabetes. Ask students to compare and contrast the patient teaching necessary for the use of insulin and oral hypoglycemic agents. Record student responses on the board for comparison.*** Class Activity ***Divide the class into groups. Have each group outline the patient teaching necessary for a patient who has just been diagnosed with type 1 or type 2 diabetes mellitus. For example, how are injection sites chosen, how often should urine be tested for ketones, and what are the dietary exclusions? Have groups share their findings with the class.***
Identify the symptoms of the major complications of diabetes.	■ Complications of diabetes mellitus (p. 552) Review the microvascular, macrovascular, and neuropathic complications of diabetes. Discuss how to delay or prevent these complications with control of blood glucose with drug therapy and treatment of comorbid diseases as they occur.	PPT 12 SG Review Sheet questions 9, 19-22, 47 (pp. 236-237, 239) ▸ Discuss how "minor" symptoms of diabetes can develop into major complications. ▸ Discuss the need for diabetic self-management. Class Activity ***Divide the class into groups, and have each group discuss the progression of minor diabetic symptoms into major complications and the relationship to controlled blood sugars.***
Discuss the difference between microvascular and macrovascular complications.	■ Complications of diabetes mellitus (p. 552)	PPT 12 Figure 36-1 (p. 553): Complications of diabetes mellitus. ▸ Discuss the definitions of microvascular and macrovascular. ▸ Discuss the different body symptoms that are affected by diabetes mellitus.

ELSEVIER

OBJECTIVES	CONTENT	TEACHING RESOURCES
		Class Activity ***Distribute a list of pathologic changes associated with diabetes mellitus, and have students determine if the change is microvascular or macrovascular. List the changes under the appropriate headings on a dry erase board.***
Discuss the contributing factors, nursing assessments, and nursing interventions needed for patients exhibiting complications associated with diabetes mellitus.	– Nursing process for patients with diabetes mellitus (p. 554)	PPT 13 ▸ Discuss how patients are assessed for peripheral vascular disease. Class Activity ***List complications that are associated with diabetes on the board: cardiovascular disease, peripheral vascular disease, visual alterations, renal disease, infection, neuropathies, impotence, and hypertension. Have students volunteer to review each one in terms of what type of complications they are. Review the exercise with the class.***

36.1 Homework/Assignments:

36.1 Instructor's Notes/Student Feedback:

LESSON 36.2

CRITICAL THINKING QUESTION

A 13-year-old girl was recently diagnosed with type 1 diabetes mellitus and has been hospitalized for the past 5 days to stabilize her blood glucose levels. She asks the nurse about insulin shots and expresses concern about gaining weight because of all the extra meals she will need to start eating. How should the nurse begin to educate this patient?

Guidelines: Type 1 diabetes mellitus requires lifelong exogenous insulin. Because hospital stays are limited, there is a great deal of teaching to be done in a short time to ensure safe discharge of the patient. Body image is very important to preadolescent and adolescent girls. The nurse needs to explain that the extra meals are required to prevent hypoglycemia and to help her grow and develop normally. Many children diagnosed with type 1 are small for their age and usually undergo a growth spurt once their diabetes is controlled. Frequent blood glucose monitoring is also crucial early in the disease until the patient is well controlled. Because this patient is old enough to administer her own insulin, the nurse should teach her how to administer insulin injections. When teaching the patient about insulin injections, the nurse should reassure

the patient by explaining that although she is frustrated now, the injections will get easier. The nurse should refer the patient and her family to a support group and to community resources to help her cope with type 1 diabetes mellitus.

OBJECTIVES	CONTENT	TEACHING RESOURCES
Discuss the action and use of insulin as opposed to oral hypoglycemic and antihyperglyce-mic agents to control diabetes mellitus.	□ Drug class: insulins (p. 564) – Nursing process for insulin (p. 568) Review the four types of insulin: rapid acting, short acting, intermediate acting, and long acting. Discuss the onset, peak, and duration of each type of insulin. Review the importance of teaching patients to monitor their blood glucose levels when they are taking insulin.	PPT 16-17 INRQ 2-3, 15-17, 20 Animation: Drugs for Type 1 Diabetes: Insulin Animation: Drugs for Type 2 Diabetes: Oral Hypoglycemic Drugs SG Review Sheet questions 23-41, 46, 48-49 (pp. 237-239) SG Learning Activities questions 3-4, 7-8, 21-23 (pp. 241-242) SG Practice Questions for the NCLEX Examination 1, 3, 10-13 (pp. 243-244) Review Questions for the NCLEX Examination 1-4, 6, 10 (pp. 582-583) Drug Table 36-5: Commercially Available Forms of Insulin (p. 567) Table 36-6: Compatibility of Insulin Combinations (p. 568) ▸ Discuss the allergenicity of insulin. What are the signs of allergic reaction to insulin? ▸ Discuss the production of insulin in the body. ▸ Discuss the different types of insulin. ▸ Discuss the factors that determine how often insulin must be administered. Class Activity ***Divide the class into groups, and assign each group one type of insulin. Have students identify the onset, peak, and duration of each type of insulin, and record findings on the board for comparison.***
Identify the mechanism of action of the different oral antidiabetic agents.	□ Drug class: Biguanide oral antidiabetic agent (p. 569) – Nursing process for metformin (p. 570) □ Drug class: Sulfonylurea oral hypoglycemic agents (p. 570) – Nursing process for sulfonylurea oral hypoglycemic agents (p. 571) □ Drug class: Meglitinide oral hypoglycemic agents (p. 572)	PPT 18-21 INRQ 5-7, 11-14, 18 SG Review Sheet questions 12, 50-55 (pp. 236, 240) SG Learning Activities questions 6, 9-10, 12, 15-16 (p. 241) SG Practice Questions for the NCLEX Examination 4-7, 14 (pp. 243-244) Review Questions for the NCLEX Examination 7, 11 (p. 583)

OBJECTIVES	CONTENT	TEACHING RESOURCES
	– Nursing process for meglitinide therapy (p. 573) □ Drug class: Thiazolidinedione oral antidiabetic agents (p. 574) – Nursing process for thiazolidinedione therapy (p. 574) Review the oral antidiabetic agents used in type 2 diabetes. Discuss the difference between the antidiabetic agents that stimulate the pancreas to secrete insulin and those that increase the body's sensitivity to insulin and decrease the liver's production of glucose.	Figure 36-2 (p. 555): Sites and mechanisms of action of antidiabetic agents. Table 36-4: Summary of Physiologic Effects of Antidiabetic Agents (p. 556) Drug Table 36-7: Oral Hypoglycemic Agents (p. 571) Drug Table 36-8: Meglitinide Oral Hypoglycemic Agents (p. 574) Drug Table 36-9: Thiazolidinedione Oral Hypoglycemic Agents (p. 575) ▸ Discuss common drug interactions and their complications. Class Activity ***Divide the class into groups, and assign each group one of the following drugs used to treat diabetes: biguanide, sulfonylurea, meglitinide, thiazolidinedione, and alpha-glucosidase inhibitor agents. Have each group outline the actions, uses, adverse effects, and nursing interventions for its assigned drug and present its findings to the class. Record student findings on the board for comparison.***
Discuss the action and use of insulin as opposed to oral hypoglycemic and antihyperglyce-mic agents to control diabetes mellitus.	□ Drug class: Alpha-glucosidase inhibitor agents (p. 575) – Nursing process for acarbose (p. 576) – Nursing process for miglitol (p. 577) □ Drug class: Amylinomimetic agent (p. 578) – Nursing process for pramlintide (p. 578) □ Incretin-based antidiabetic therapy (p. 579) □ Drug class: Incretin mimetic agent (p. 580) – Nursing process for exenatide (p. 580) □ Drug class: Dipeptidyl peptidase-4 inhibitor (p. 581) – Nursing process for sitagliptin (p. 581) □ Drug class: Antihypoglycemic agents (p. 582) – Nursing process for glucagon (p. 582)	PPT 22-26 INRQ 8-10 SG Review Sheet questions 12-13, 56-59 (pp. 236, 240) SG Learning Activities questions 5, 11, 13-14, 24-25 (pp. 241-242) SG Practice Question for the NCLEX Examination 8 (p. 244) ▸ Discuss the mode of action of antihyperglycemic agents, such as acarbose, pramlintide, exenatide, and sitagliptin. ▸ Discuss hepatotoxicity adverse effects of acarbose therapy and how it should be monitored. Class Activity ***Lead a class discussion about drugs used to treat diabetes. Ask students to compare and contrast oral hypoglycemic agents and antihyperglycemic agents. Record students' responses on the board for comparison.*** Class Activity ***Have students identify the indications for use of oral hypoglycemic agents, antihyperglycemics, and antihypoglycemics. What adverse effects and drug interactions should the nurse be aware of, and how should each drug be monitored?***

ELSEVIER

OBJECTIVES	CONTENT	TEACHING RESOURCES
Performance evaluation		Test Bank SG Learning Activities (pp. 241-242) SG Practice Questions for the NCLEX Examination (pp. 243-244) Critical Thinking Questions

36.2 Homework/Assignments:

36.2 Instructor's Notes/Student Feedback:

Lecture Outline

Drugs Used to Treat Diabetes Mellitus

Slide 1

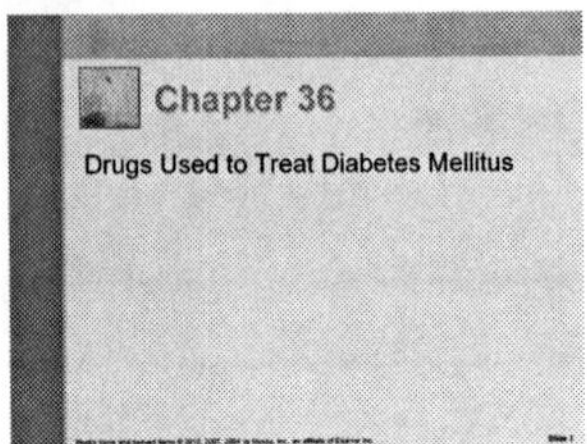
Chapter 36
Drugs Used to Treat Diabetes Mellitus

Slide 2

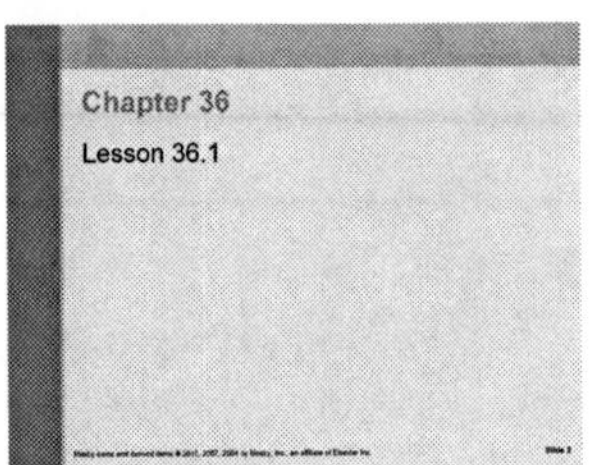
Chapter 36
Lesson 36.1

Slide 3

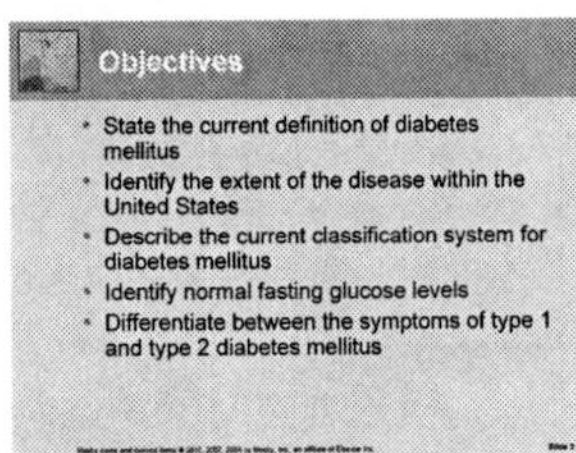
Objectives
State the current definition of diabetes mellitus
Identify the extent of the disease within the United States
Describe the current classification system for diabetes mellitus
Identify normal fasting glucose levels
Differentiate between the symptoms of type 1 and type 2 diabetes mellitus

Slide 4

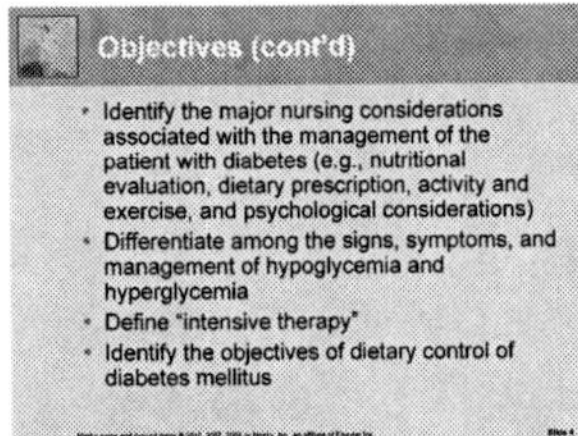
Objectives (cont'd)
Identify the major nursing considerations associated with the management of the patient with diabetes (e.g., nutritional evaluation, dietary prescription, activity and exercise, and psychological considerations)
Differentiate among the signs, symptoms, and management of hypoglycemia and hyperglycemia
Define "intensive therapy"
Identify the objectives of dietary control of diabetes mellitus

Slide 5

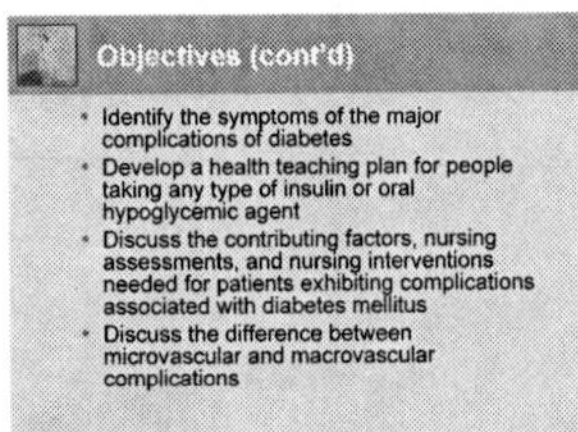
Objectives (cont'd)
Identify the symptoms of the major complications of diabetes
Develop a health teaching plan for people taking any type of insulin or oral hypoglycemic agent
Discuss the contributing factors, nursing assessments, and nursing interventions needed for patients exhibiting complications associated with diabetes mellitus
Discuss the difference between microvascular and macrovascular complications

ELSEVIER

Slide 6

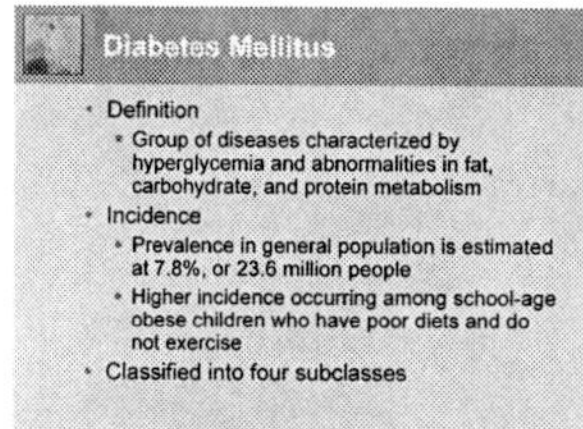
Diabetes Mellitus
Definition
Group of diseases characterized by hyperglycemia and abnormalities in fat, carbohydrate, and protein metabolism
Incidence
Prevalence in general population is estimated at 7.8%, or 23.6 million people
Higher incidence occurring among school-age obese children who have poor diets and do not exercise
Classified into four subclasses

- Leads to microvascular, macrovascular, and neuropathic complications.
- Risk of heart disease and stroke is 2 to 4 times greater in patients with diabetes compared with those without.
- Incidence is higher in African Americans, Hispanics, American Indians, Native Alaskans, and women.

Slide 7

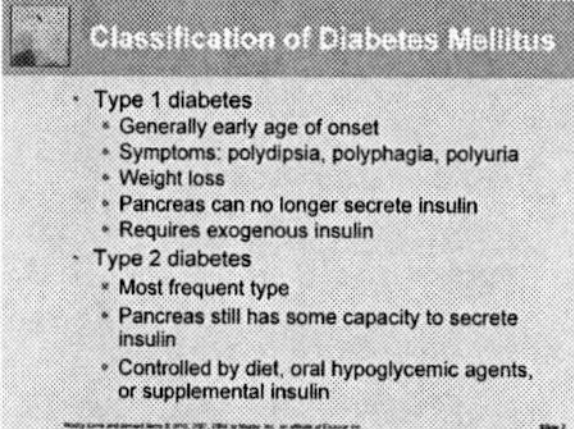
Classification of Diabetes Mellitus
Type 1 diabetes
Generally early age of onset
Symptoms: polydipsia, polyphagia, polyuria
Weight loss
Pancreas can no longer secrete insulin
Requires exogenous insulin
Type 2 diabetes
Most frequent type
Pancreas still has some capacity to secrete insulin
Controlled by diet, oral hypoglycemic agents, or supplemental insulin

- Type 1 DM usually occurs among school-age children who may "blank" out or pass out at school; requires lifelong exogenous insulin.
- Type 2 DM represents 90% of the diabetic population. Metabolic syndrome is common among these patients.

Slide 8

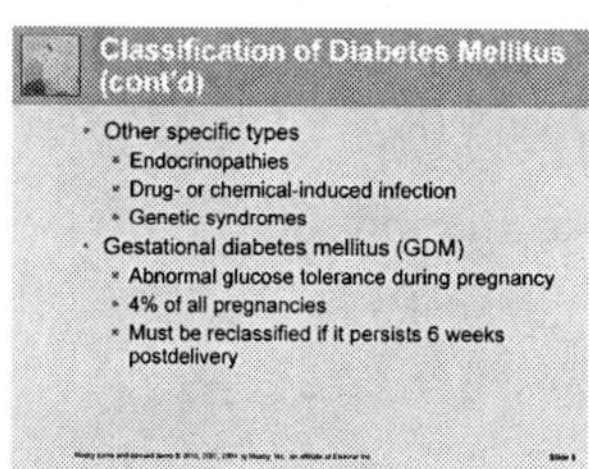
Classification of Diabetes Mellitus (cont'd)
Other specific types
Endocrinopathies
Drug- or chemical-induced infection
Genetic syndromes
Gestational diabetes mellitus (GDM)
Abnormal glucose tolerance during pregnancy
4% of all pregnancies
Must be reclassified if it persists 6 weeks postdelivery

- Other types of diabetes are usually temporary and may be treated with insulin or oral hypoglycemic agents.
- Treatment for GDM is strictly regulated by the obstetrician for medication, activity, and diet management.

Slide 9

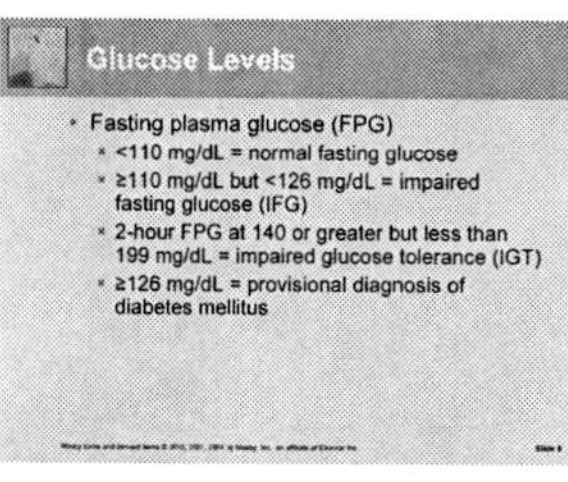
Glucose Levels
Fasting plasma glucose (FPG)
<110 mg/dL = normal fasting glucose
≥110 mg/dL but <126 mg/dL = impaired fasting glucose (IFG)
2-hour FPG at 140 or greater but less than 199 mg/dL = impaired glucose tolerance (IGT)
≥126 mg/dL = provisional diagnosis of diabetes mellitus

- Patients with IGT are often euglycemic (normal blood sugar) and develop hyperglycemia when challenged with an oral glucose tolerance test.
- Prediabetes is now recognized as the intermediate stage between normal glucose homoeostasis and diabetes.

Slide 10

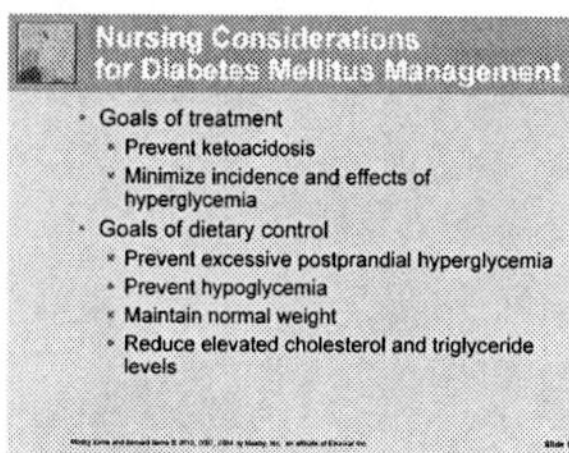
Nursing Considerations for Diabetes Mellitus Management
Goals of treatment
Prevent ketoacidosis
Minimize incidence and effects of hyperglycemia
Goals of dietary control
Prevent excessive postprandial hyperglycemia
Prevent hypoglycemia
Maintain normal weight
Reduce elevated cholesterol and triglyceride levels

- Diabetes mellitus is a lifelong disease that requires constant monitoring and evaluation.

Slide 11

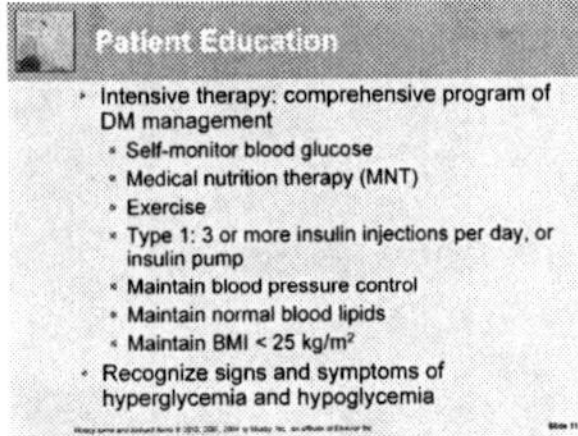
Patient Education
Intensive therapy: comprehensive program of DM management
Self-monitor blood glucose
Medical nutrition therapy (MNT)
Exercise
Type 1: 3 or more insulin injections per day, or insulin pump
Maintain blood pressure control
Maintain normal blood lipids
Maintain BMI < 25 kg/m²
Recognize signs and symptoms of hyperglycemia and hypoglycemia

- Patients need constant and continual education.
- Also recommend smoking cessation, and be aware of psychological adjustment.

Slide 12

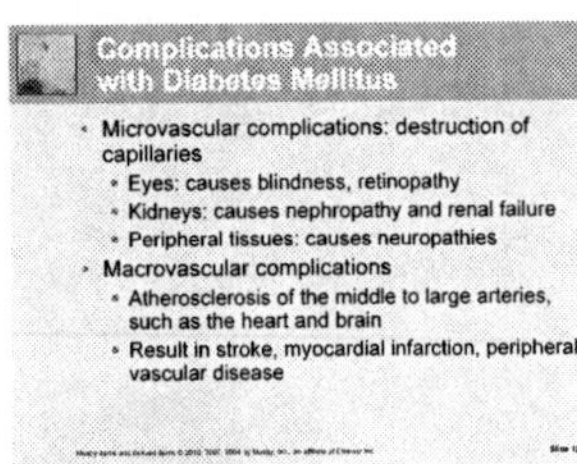
Complications Associated with Diabetes Mellitus
Microvascular complications: destruction of capillaries
Eyes: causes blindness, retinopathy
Kidneys: causes nephropathy and renal failure
Peripheral tissues: causes neuropathies
Macrovascular complications
Atherosclerosis of the middle to large arteries, such as the heart and brain
Result in stroke, myocardial infarction, peripheral vascular disease

- Can lead to comorbid diseases (Figure 36-1).
- Diabetic patients are also more susceptible to infection.

Slide 13

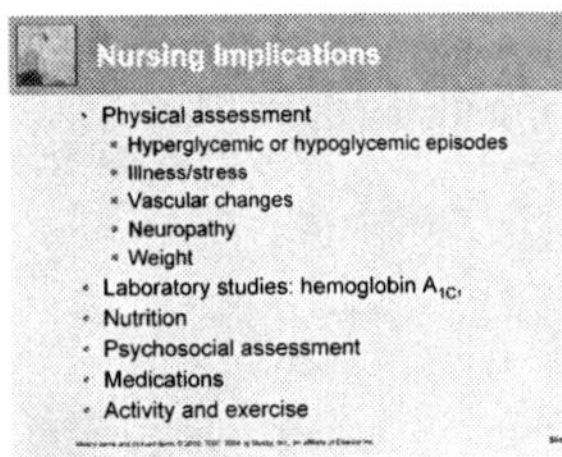
Nursing Implications
Physical assessment
Hyperglycemic or hypoglycemic episodes
Illness/stress
Vascular changes
Neuropathy
Weight
Laboratory studies: hemoglobin A1C
Nutrition
Psychosocial assessment
Medications
Activity and exercise

- Illness and stress may bring about both hypoglycemic and hyperglycemic episodes.
- To detect vascular changes, check vision frequently.
- Neuropathy—importance of foot care—check for infection.

Slide 14

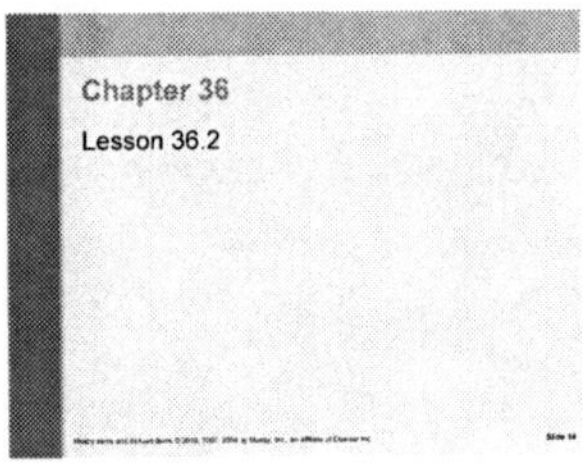
Chapter 36
Lesson 36.2

Slide 15

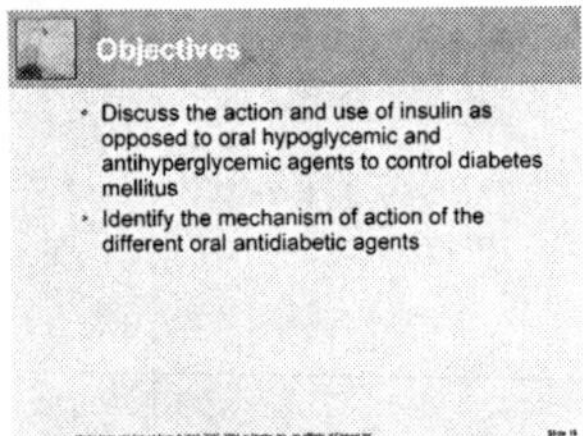
Objectives
Discuss the action and use of insulin as opposed to oral hypoglycemic and antihyperglycemic agents to control diabetes mellitus
Identify the mechanism of action of the different oral antidiabetic agents

ELSEVIER

Slide 16

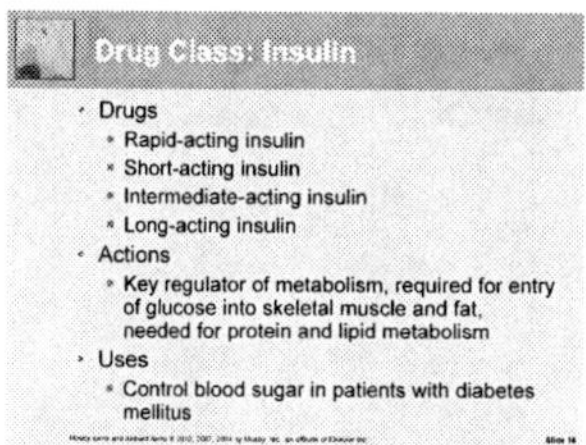
Drug Class: Insulin
Drugs
Rapid-acting insulin
Short-acting insulin
Intermediate-acting insulin
Long-acting insulin
Actions
Key regulator of metabolism, required for entry of glucose into skeletal muscle and fat, needed for protein and lipid metabolism
Uses
Control blood sugar in patients with diabetes mellitus

- For specific drugs, see Table 36-5.
- Common and serious adverse effects: hyperglycemia, hypoglycemia, allergic reactions, lipodystrophies.

Slide 17

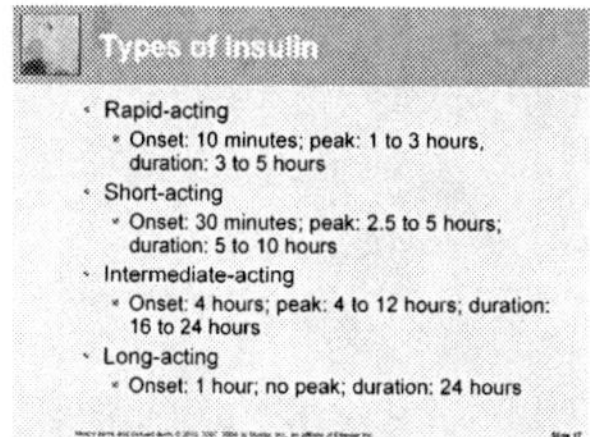
Types of Insulin
Rapid-acting
Onset: 10 minutes; peak: 1 to 3 hours, duration: 3 to 5 hours
Short-acting
Onset: 30 minutes; peak: 2.5 to 5 hours; duration: 5 to 10 hours
Intermediate-acting
Onset: 4 hours; peak: 4 to 12 hours; duration: 16 to 24 hours
Long-acting
Onset: 1 hour; no peak; duration: 24 hours

- For specific drugs, see Table 36-5.

Slide 18

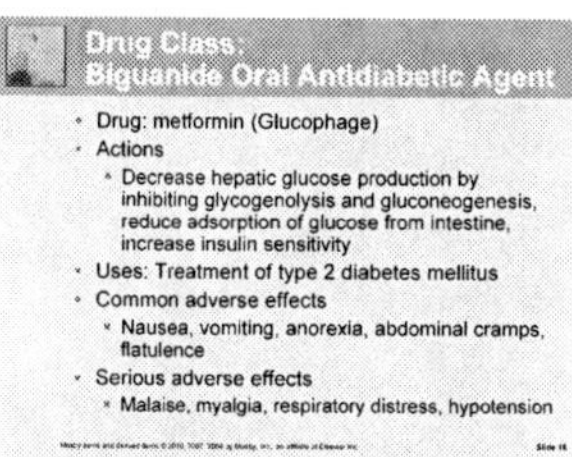
Drug Class: Biguanide Oral Antidiabetic Agent
Drug: metformin (Glucophage)
Actions
Decrease hepatic glucose production by inhibiting glycogenolysis and gluconeogenesis, reduce adsorption of glucose from intestine, increase insulin sensitivity
Uses: Treatment of type 2 diabetes mellitus
Common adverse effects
Nausea, vomiting, anorexia, abdominal cramps, flatulence
Serious adverse effects
Malaise, myalgia, respiratory distress, hypotension

- Used when diet and exercise alone are not effective.
- Benefits of metformin: will not cause hypoglycemia, does not cause weight gain, affects triglycerides to a modest degree.

Slide 19

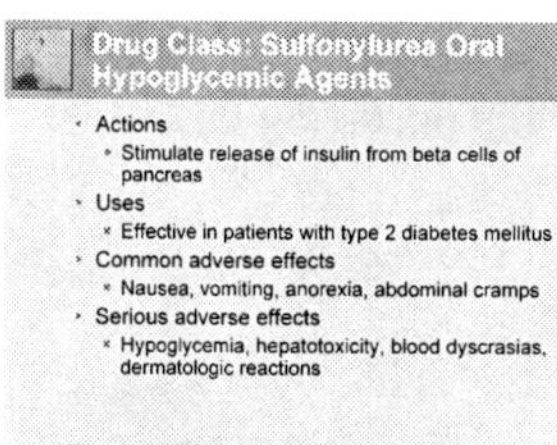
Drug Class: Sulfonylurea Oral Hypoglycemic Agents
Actions
Stimulate release of insulin from beta cells of pancreas
Uses
Effective in patients with type 2 diabetes mellitus
Common adverse effects
Nausea, vomiting, anorexia, abdominal cramps
Serious adverse effects
Hypoglycemia, hepatotoxicity, blood dyscrasias, dermatologic reactions

- For specific drugs, see Table 36-7.
- Many drug interactions are possible; carefully review the medications patients are taking concurrently with these hypoglycemic agents.

Slide 20

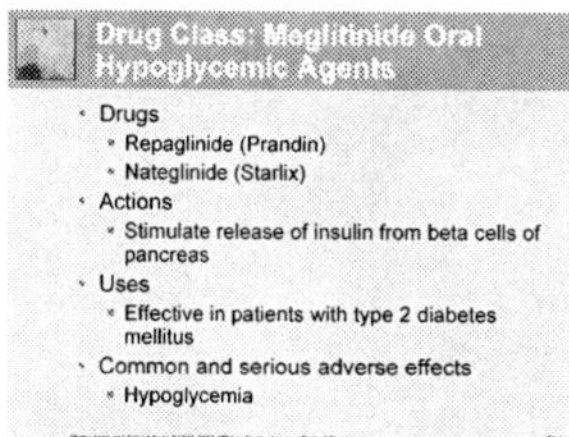
Drug Class: Meglitinide Oral Hypoglycemic Agents
Drugs
Repaglinide (Prandin)
Nateglinide (Starlix)
Actions
Stimulate release of insulin from beta cells of pancreas
Uses
Effective in patients with type 2 diabetes mellitus
Common and serious adverse effects
Hypoglycemia

Slide 21

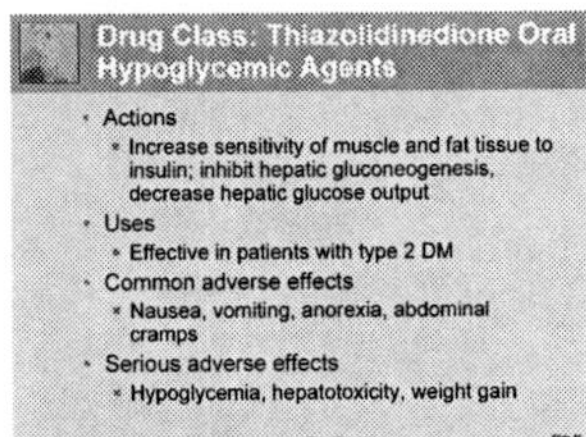
Drug Class: Thiazolidinedione Oral Hypoglycemic Agents
Actions
Increase sensitivity of muscle and fat tissue to insulin; inhibit hepatic gluconeogenesis, decrease hepatic glucose output
Uses
Effective in patients with type 2 DM
Common adverse effects
Nausea, vomiting, anorexia, abdominal cramps
Serious adverse effects
Hypoglycemia, hepatotoxicity, weight gain

- For specific drugs, see Table 36-9.
- These drugs do not stimulate the release of insulin from the beta cells of the pancreas. Insulin must be present for drugs to work.

Slide 22

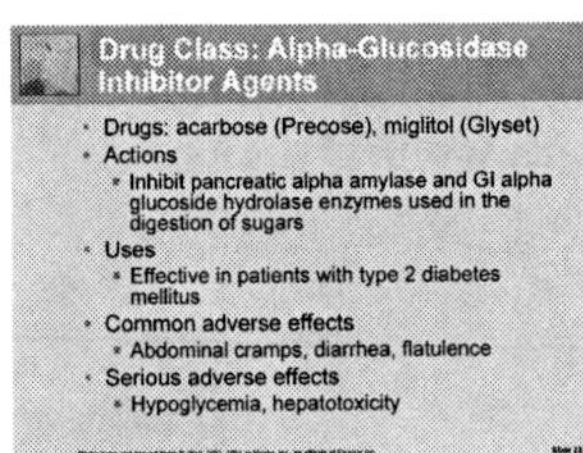
Drug Class: Alpha-Glucosidase Inhibitor Agents
Drugs: acarbose (Precose), miglitol (Glyset)
Actions
Inhibit pancreatic alpha amylase and GI alpha glucoside hydrolase enzymes used in the digestion of sugars
Uses
Effective in patients with type 2 diabetes mellitus
Common adverse effects
Abdominal cramps, diarrhea, flatulence
Serious adverse effects
Hypoglycemia, hepatotoxicity

- Acarbose will not cause hypoglycemia.

Slide 23

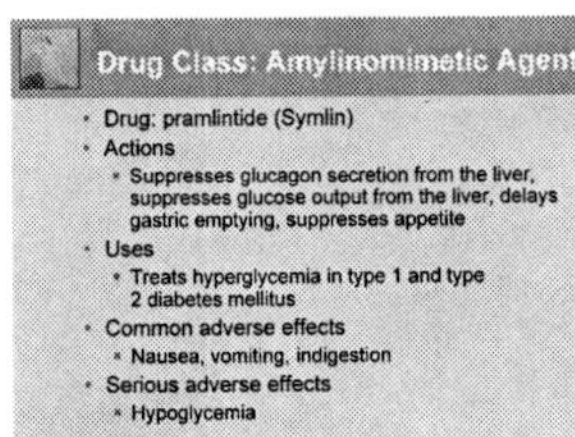
Drug Class: Amylinomimetic Agent
Drug: pramlintide (Symlin)
Actions
Suppresses glucagon secretion from the liver, suppresses glucose output from the liver, delays gastric emptying, suppresses appetite
Uses
Treats hyperglycemia in type 1 and type 2 diabetes mellitus
Common adverse effects
Nausea, vomiting, indigestion
Serious adverse effects
Hypoglycemia

- Given subcutaneously.
- Pramlintide is a synthetic analog of amylin, a protein secreted by the pancreas with insulin in response to food intake.

Slide 24

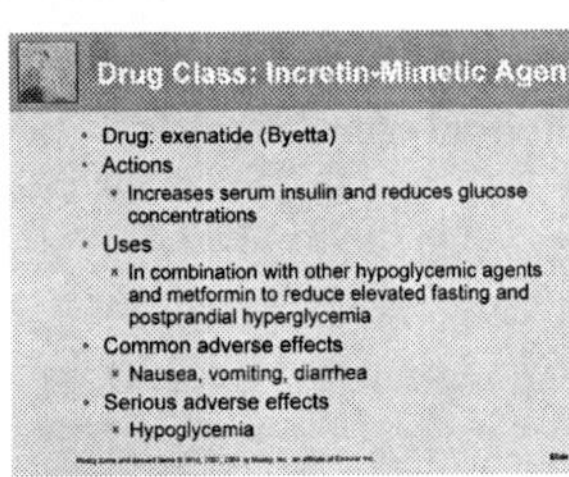
Drug Class: Incretin-Mimetic Agent
Drug: exenatide (Byetta)
Actions
Increases serum insulin and reduces glucose concentrations
Uses
In combination with other hypoglycemic agents and metformin to reduce elevated fasting and postprandial hyperglycemia
Common adverse effects
Nausea, vomiting, diarrhea
Serious adverse effects
Hypoglycemia

- Incretin peptides are proteins released from the ileum and colon in response to ingestion of carbohydrates and fats.
- Exenatide is a synthetic version of the naturally occurring GLP-1 hormone.

Slide 25

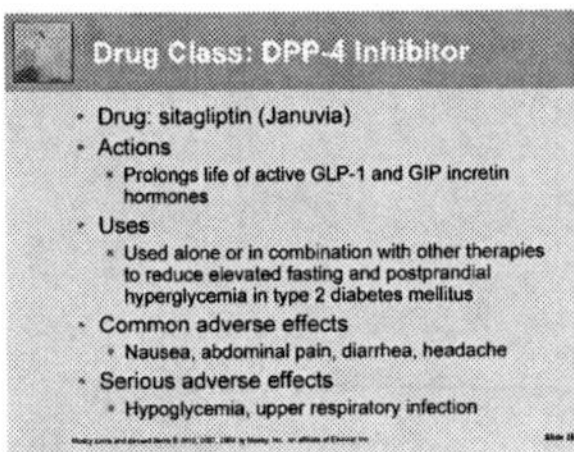
Drug Class: DPP-4 Inhibitor
Drug: sitagliptin (Januvia)
Actions
Prolongs life of active GLP-1 and GIP incretin hormones
Uses
Used alone or in combination with other therapies to reduce elevated fasting and postprandial hyperglycemia in type 2 diabetes mellitus
Common adverse effects
Nausea, abdominal pain, diarrhea, headache
Serious adverse effects
Hypoglycemia, upper respiratory infection

- The enzyme DPP-4 quickly metabolizes GIP and GLP-1; sitagliptin, a DPP-4 inhibitor, slows this effect.
- Drug interactions are of concern with sitagliptin.

ELSEVIER

Slide 26

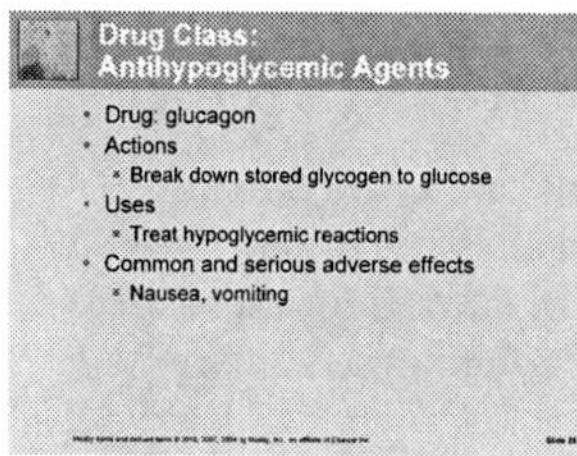
Drug Class:
Antihypoglycemic Agents
Drug: glucagon
Actions
Break down stored glycogen to glucose
Uses
Treat hypoglycemic reactions
Common and serious adverse effects
Nausea, vomiting

- Glucagon is dependent on the presence of glycogen for action. In cases of starvation, adrenal insufficiency, or chronic hypoglycemia, it will not work.
- Glucagon also aids in converting amino acids to glucose (gluconeogenesis).
- Can be administered subcutaneously, IM, or IV.

37 Lesson Plan
Drugs Used to Treat Thyroid Disease

TEACHING FOCUS

This chapter focuses on the drug therapy used to treat thyroid disorders. The signs and symptoms of hyperthyroidism and hypothyroidism are discussed, along with the treatments for these disorders. Students have the opportunity to learn how to assess the patient for such disorders and to monitor the patient who is on therapy for a thyroid disorder. Special attention is given to the nursing process for the implementation of radioactive iodine therapy.

MATERIALS AND RESOURCES

- ☐ computer and PowerPoint projector (all Lessons)

LESSON CHECKLIST

Preparations for this lesson include:

- lecture
- evaluation of student knowledge and skills needed to perform all entry-level activities related to drugs used to treat thyroid disease, including:
  - the anatomy and physiology of the thyroid gland
  - treatments and drug therapy for thyroid disease
  - nursing assessments of the patient with thyroid disease
  - thyroid replacement hormones and antithyroid medications

KEY TERMS

cretinism (p. 584)
hyperthyroidism (p. 585)
hypothyroidism (p. 584)
iodine-131 (p. 589)
myxedema (p. 584)
thyroid-stimulating hormone (p. 584)
thyrotoxicosis (p. 585)
thyroxine (T_4) (p. 584)
triiodothyronine (T_3) (p. 584)

ADDITIONAL RESOURCES

PowerPoint slides: 1-11
Flashcards, Decks 1 and 2

Legend

ARQ	PPT	TB	CTQ	SG	INRQ
Audience Response Questions	PowerPoint Slides	Test Bank	Critical Thinking Questions	Study Guide	Interactive NCLEX Review Questions

Class Activities are indicated in ***bold italic.***

LESSON 37.1

BACKGROUND ASSESSMENT

Question: What is the difference between hypothyroidism and hyperthyroidism? What are the signs and symptoms of each?

Answer: Hypothyroidism occurs when inadequate amounts of thyroid hormone are produced. There are two types of hypothyroidism, myxedema and cretinism. Myxedema occurs during adult life and begins with mild and vague symptoms. Cretinism is congenital hypothyroidism; this type is rare today. Signs and symptoms

of hypothyroidism include slowness in motion and speech, decreased appetite, weight gain, constipation, intolerance to cold, and dry puffy skin. Hyperthyroidism occurs when excess amounts of thyroid hormone are produced. Its signs and symptoms are rapid pulse, cardiac enlargement, palpitations, arrhythmias, agitation, tremors, weight loss, intolerance to heat, and warm, flushed skin.

Question: What is the primary goal of thyroid replacement therapy? List the more common forms of thyroid hormone replacements, and briefly describe their functions.
Answer: The primary goal of thyroid replacement therapy is to return the patient to a normal thyroid (euthyroid) state. Several forms of thyroid hormone replacement are available from both natural and synthetic sources. Levothyroxine provides physiologic replacement of both T_3 and T_4 hormones. Liothyronine is a synthetic form of the natural thyroid hormone T_3; it is usually used when prompt thyroid hormone replacement is necessary. Liotrix is a synthetic mixture of levothyroxine and liothyronine. Thyroid USP is derived from pig, beef, and sheep thyroid glands. It is the oldest available form and the least expensive, but because of its lack of purity and stability, it is generally not the drug of choice.

CRITICAL THINKING QUESTION

What lifestyle changes and patient teaching are necessary for a patient diagnosed with myxedema?
Guidelines: Hypothyroidism is common among adults. The condition requires lifelong treatment, but with the proper lifestyle adjustments and medications it is usually well controlled. The lifestyle adjustments include maintaining a warm home environment, adopting a low-calorie diet with increased amounts of roughage, and drinking plenty of water. It is also important that patients understand the necessity of complying with the lifelong medications and treatments. As patients return to preillness thyroid function, other adjustments will need to be made. These include changing caloric requirements, increasing levels of exercise and physical activity, and adapting the home environment to fit the needs of the illness.

OBJECTIVES	CONTENT	TEACHING RESOURCES
Describe the function of the thyroid gland.	■ Thyroid gland (p. 584) Review the location and description of the thyroid gland. Discuss the regulation of the thyroid by the hypothalamus and anterior pituitary gland. Review the thyroid hormones triiodothyronine (T_3) and thyroxine (T_4), and explain the function of these hormones.	PPT 5 SG Review Sheet questions 1-2 (p. 245) SG Learning Activities questions 3, 10-11 (p. 247) Class Activity ***Using an unlabeled diagram of the thyroid gland, have students identify the location and explain how the gland is regulated by the hypothalamus. Have students review the functions of the thyroid hormones T_3 and T_4. Review the exercise with the class.*** Class Activity ***Divide the class into groups. Have each group outline the role of the hypothalamus and the anterior pituitary gland in the release of thyroid hormones and discuss the role of thyroid hormones in the body. Then have each group share its findings with the class.***
Describe the signs, symptoms, treatment, and nursing interventions associated with hypothyroidism and hyperthyroidism.	■ Thyroid diseases (p. 584) Review hypothyroidism and hyperthyroidism in terms of the signs and symptoms of each disease. Discuss the terms *myxedema*, *cretinism*, and *thyrotoxicosis*.	PPT 6 ARQ 1, 4 TB Multiple Choice questions 3, 8 TB Multiple Response questions 1, 4-5 SG Review Sheet questions 3-6, 10, 13-14 (p. 245) SG Learning Activities questions 1-2, 4-5, 9, 12-14, 17-19 (p. 247)

OBJECTIVES	CONTENT	TEACHING RESOURCES
		SG Practice Questions for the NCLEX Examination 1, 6 (p. 248) Review Question for the NCLEX Examination 7 (p. 591) ▸ Discuss the nursing interventions associated with hypothyroidism and hyperthyroidism. Class Activity ***Present the following signs and symptoms to the class, and have students determine which pertain to hypothyroidism and which pertain to hyperthyroidism:*** – ***Lethargy*** – ***Decreased appetite*** – ***Rapid pulse*** – ***Decreased blood pressure*** – ***Insomnia*** – ***Tremors*** – ***Dry, coarse skin*** – ***Heat intolerance*** – ***Rapid speech*** – ***Increased susceptibility to infection***
State the three types of treatment for hyperthyroidism.	■ Treatment of thyroid diseases (p. 585) Review the treatment goals of therapy for hyperthyroidism (to suppress the production of thyroid hormones) and for hypothyroidism (to replace thyroid hormones). Discuss the three types of treatments used for hyperthyroidism.	PPT 7 TB Multiple Choice question 1 SG Review Sheet question 15 (p. 246) ▸ Discuss the advantages and disadvantages of each of the treatments of hyperthyroidism. Class Activity ***Divide the class into groups, and assign each group one of the following treatments of hyperthyroidism: subtotal thyroidectomy, iodine-131, or antithyroid medication. Have each group outline the goals and process of its assigned treatment, explain under which conditions it is used, and identify three appropriate nursing interventions. Then have each group present its findings to the class.*** Class Activity ***Divide students into groups of three. Have each group develop a teaching plan for home medication management for the patient taking thyroid replacement therapy. Allow class time for discussion. Plans should include adverse effects, laboratory monitoring, diet, and exercise.***
Identify the two classes of drugs used to treat thyroid disease.	■ Drug therapy for thyroid diseases (p. 585) Review the thyroid replacement hormones levothyroxine,	INRQ 3-4 SG Review Sheet questions 11-13 (p. 245) SG Learning Activities question 11 (p. 247)

ELSEVIER

OBJECTIVES	CONTENT	TEACHING RESOURCES
	liothyronine, liotrix, and thyroid USP. Discuss the actions, use, and therapeutic outcomes of each drug. Review common and serious adverse effects as well as known drug interactions for thyroid replacement hormones.	Drug Table 37-1: Thyroid Hormones (p. 588) ▸ Discuss the two basic classes of drugs used to treat thyroid disorders in terms of their modes of action. Class Activity ***Lead a class discussion about the classes of drugs used to treat thyroid disease. Have students identify the different drugs prescribed, which condition they are used to treat, and what their adverse effects are.*** Class Activity ***Divide the class into four groups. Assign each group one of the following: premedication assessment, planning and implementation, evaluation, or drug interactions. Have each group develop a patient-family teaching plan for their designated category for patients taking drugs for thyroid disorders.***
Explain the nutritional requirements and activity restrictions needed for an individual with hyperthyroidism.	– Nursing process for thyroid disorders (p. 585) – Patient education and health promotion (p. 587) Review the nursing process used for patients with thyroid disorders in terms of focused assessments and laboratory studies to monitor. Discuss patient education needed for patients being treated for hyperthyroidism and hypothyroidism.	PPT 8 SG Review Sheet questions 7-9 (p. 245) SG Learning Activities questions 15-16 (p. 247) SG Practice Questions for the NCLEX Examination 4-5 (p. 248) Review Question for the NCLEX Examination 6 (p. 591) ▸ Discuss the gastrointestinal symptoms that a patient with hyperthyroidism might exhibit. Class Activity ***Divide the class into groups, and have each group develop a diet and exercise plan for a patient with either hyperthyroidism or hypothyroidism. Then have each group present its plan to the class for discussion.***

37.1 Homework/Assignments:

37.1 Instructor's Notes/Student Feedback:

LESSON 37.2

CRITICAL THINKING QUESTION

A 60-year-old woman is being treated with radioactive iodine for hyperthyroidism. After the room has been properly prepared, the patient accidentally knocks the medication over onto the nurse's gloved hand, the bedding, and the floor. How should the nurse react to the spill?

Guidelines: Patient safety takes priority. Before doing anything else, the nurse should assess the patient to see if any medication has spilled on her skin. Next, the nurse should call in another nurse to notify a supervisor of the situation. The soiled linen should then be removed and promptly disposed of in the container designated for radioactive waste disposal. The nurse should continue to wear the latex gloves during this time. Because another nurse was notified, properly trained personnel should already be taking the steps to begin the cleanup for a radioactive spill. The accidental contamination incident needs to be reported to the charge nurse, and the appropriate policy and procedure need to be followed. The nurse also needs to fill out an incident report and order another dose of medication for the patient.

OBJECTIVES	CONTENT	TEACHING RESOURCES
State the drug of choice for hypothyroidism.	□ Drug class: Thyroid replacement hormones (p. 588) – Nursing process for thyroid hormone replacement therapy (p. 588) Review the thyroid replacement hormones levothyroxine, liothyronine, liotrix, and thyroid USP. Discuss the actions, use, and therapeutic outcomes of each drug. Review common and serious adverse effects as well as known drug interactions for thyroid replacement hormones.	PPT 9 TB Multiple Choice questions 6-7 TB Multiple Response question 3 INRQ 8-9 CTQ 1, 4 Patient Self-Assessment Form: Thyroid Medications SG Practice Question for the NCLEX Examination 9 (p. 249) Review Questions for the NCLEX Examination 1-2 (p. 591) ▸ Discuss the different thyroid replacement hormones used to treat hypothyroidism. Class Activity ***Ask a volunteer student to draw four columns on the board with the following headings: levothyroxine, liothyronine, liotrix, and thyroid USP. Have students list actions and uses of each drug option available to treat hypothyroidism. How does the health care provider select one drug over the others for treatment?***
Cite the actions of antithyroid medications on the formation and release of the hormones produced by the thyroid gland.	□ Drug class: Antithyroid medicines (p. 589) Review the radioactive iodine iodine-131 used for the treatment of hyperthyroidism, discussing actions, uses, and therapeutic outcomes. Review the drugs propylthiouracil and methimazole from the drug class antithyroid	PPT 10-11 TB Multiple Choice question 2 INRQ 1-2, 5 Patient Self-Assessment Form: Antithyroid Medications SG Review Sheet question 17 (p. 246) SG Practice Question for the NCLEX Examination 8 (p. 248)

OBJECTIVES	CONTENT	TEACHING RESOURCES
	agents, discussing actions, uses, and therapeutic outcomes. Review common and serious adverse effects as well as known drug interactions with these antithyroid medications.	▸ Discuss the goals of antithyroid medication. Class Activity ***Lead a class discussion about radioactive iodine. Ask students to explain how radioactive iodine works to decrease the release of thyroid hormones. Write student responses on the board for comparison.*** Class Activity ***Have the class outline the actions of the two antithyroid medications, identify their indications, and list any special considerations for each drug. Record student responses on the board for comparison.***
Identify the types of conditions that respond favorably to the use of radioactive iodine-131.	– Nursing process for radioactive iodine (p. 589)	PPT 10-11 ARQ 3 TB Multiple Choice questions 4-5 INRQ 10-11 CTQ 4 SG Practice Questions for the NCLEX Examination 3, 10 (pp. 248-249) Review Questions for the NCLEX Examination 8-9 (p. 592) ▸ Discuss how radioactive iodine is administered. Class Activity ***Divide the class into groups. Have each group outline the safety precautions that should be exercised when using radioactive iodine and identify appropriate nursing interventions and patient teaching. How can both the nurse and the patient be protected from excessive exposure? Then have groups share their findings with the class for discussion.*** Class Activity ***Lead a class discussion about iodine-131. Have students identify which patients are likely candidates for radioactive iodine therapy (and why), and discuss adverse effects of the therapy. Write student comments on the board for comparison.*** Class Activity ***Discuss the pros and cons for each of the following caregivers in delegating patient care: a pregnant nurse, a newly graduated nurse, a nurse with oncology experience.***

OBJECTIVES	CONTENT	TEACHING RESOURCES
Cite the action of propylthiouracil on the synthesis of triiodothyronine and thyroxine.	– Nursing process for propylthiouracil and methimazole (p. 590)	PPT 11 ARQ 2 TB Multiple Choice question 9 CTQ 2-4 SG Review Sheet questions 16, 18-19 (p. 246) Review Question for the NCLEX Examination 5 (p. 591) ▸ Discuss the mode of action of propylthiouracil and why there may be a delay before the onset of action. Class Activity ***Divide the class into groups. Have each group outline the action of propylthiouracil on the synthesis of T_3 and T_4, and discuss how it differs from iodine-131 What are the indications for long-term use? Have groups share their findings with the class for discussion.***
Explain the effects of hyperthyroidism on doses of warfarin and digoxin and on those taking oral hypoglycemic agents.	– Nursing process for propylthiouracil and methimazole (p. 590) – Drug interactions (p. 591)	PPT 11 ARQ 5 TB Multiple Choice question 2 INRQ 7 CTQ 3 SG Review Sheet question 20 (p. 246) SG Practice Questions for the NCLEX Examination 2, 7 (p. 248) Review Questions for the NCLEX Examination 4, 10 (pp. 591-592) ▸ Discuss why hyperthyroid patients receiving warfarin therapy and antithyroid treatment should be carefully monitored. ▸ Discuss why a gradual reduction in digoxin will be necessary in hyperthyroid patients receiving antithyroid replacement therapy. Class Activity ***Lead a class discussion about the adverse effects of antithyroid therapy. Have students identify adverse effects, what signs should be monitored, and how antithyroid therapy affects the dosages of other medications. Record students responses on the board for comparison.***

ELSEVIER

OBJECTIVES	CONTENT	TEACHING RESOURCES
Performance evaluation		Test Bank SG Learning Activities (p. 247) SG Practice Questions for the NCLEX Examination (pp. 248-249) Critical Thinking Questions

37.2 Homework/Assignments:

37.2 Instructor's Notes/Student Feedback:

37

Lecture Outline

Drugs Used to Treat Thyroid Disease

Slide 1

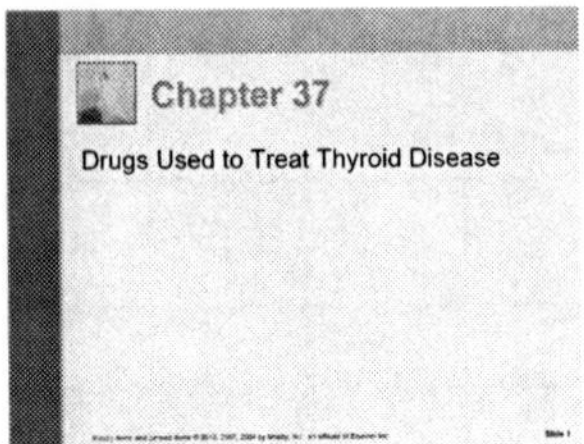
Chapter 37
Drugs Used to Treat Thyroid Disease

Slide 2

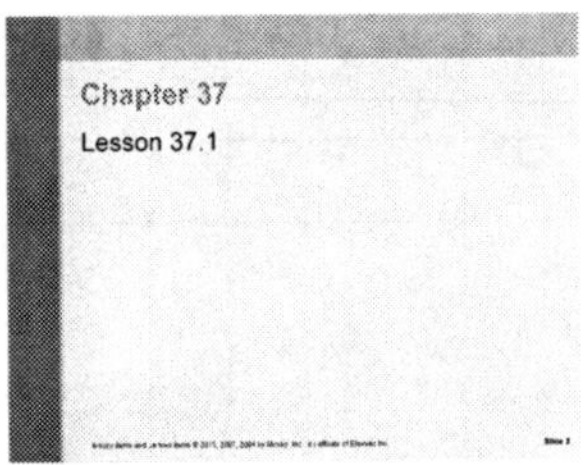
Chapter 37
Lesson 37.1

Slide 3

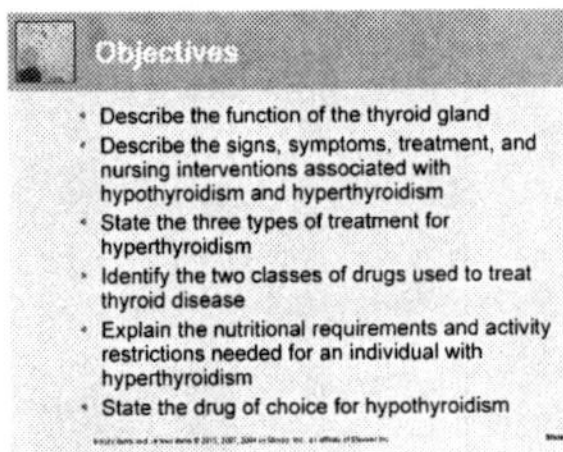
Objectives
Describe the function of the thyroid gland
Describe the signs, symptoms, treatment, and nursing interventions associated with hypothyroidism and hyperthyroidism
State the three types of treatment for hyperthyroidism
Identify the two classes of drugs used to treat thyroid disease
Explain the nutritional requirements and activity restrictions needed for an individual with hyperthyroidism
State the drug of choice for hypothyroidism

Slide 4

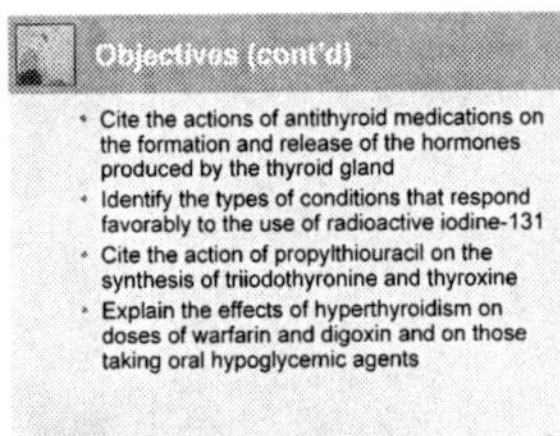
Objectives (cont'd)
Cite the actions of antithyroid medications on the formation and release of the hormones produced by the thyroid gland
Identify the types of conditions that respond favorably to the use of radioactive iodine-131
Cite the action of propylthiouracil on the synthesis of triiodothyronine and thyroxine
Explain the effects of hyperthyroidism on doses of warfarin and digoxin and on those taking oral hypoglycemic agents

Slide 5

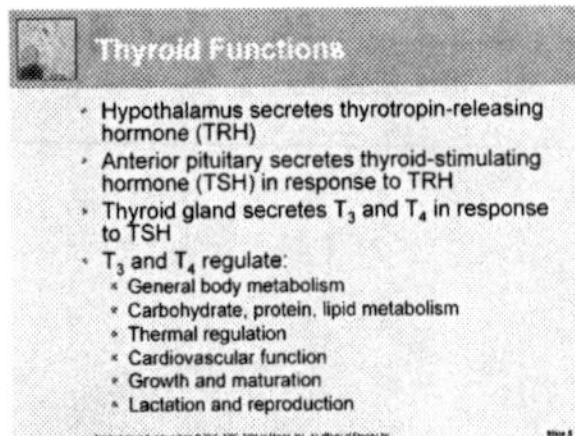
Thyroid Functions
Hypothalamus secretes thyrotropin-releasing hormone (TRH)
Anterior pituitary secretes thyroid-stimulating hormone (TSH) in response to TRH
Thyroid gland secretes T3 and T4 in response to TSH
T3 and T4 regulate:
General body metabolism
Carbohydrate, protein, lipid metabolism
Thermal regulation
Cardiovascular function
Growth and maturation
Lactation and reproduction

- Thyroid function is regulated by the hypothalamus and the anterior pituitary gland.
- Synthesis of thyroid hormones depends on sufficient iodine intake through food and water.

ELSEVIER

Slide 6

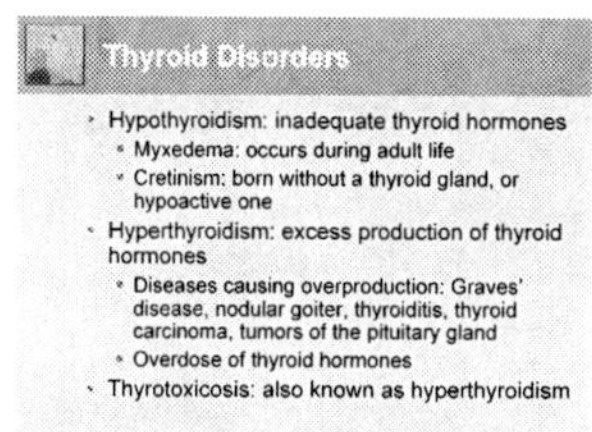
Thyroid Disorders
Hypothyroidism: inadequate thyroid hormones
Myxedema: occurs during adult life
Cretinism: born without a thyroid gland, or hypoactive one
Hyperthyroidism: excess production of thyroid hormones
Diseases causing overproduction: Graves' disease, nodular goiter, thyroiditis, thyroid carcinoma, tumors of the pituitary gland
Overdose of thyroid hormones
Thyrotoxicosis: also known as hyperthyroidism

Slide 7

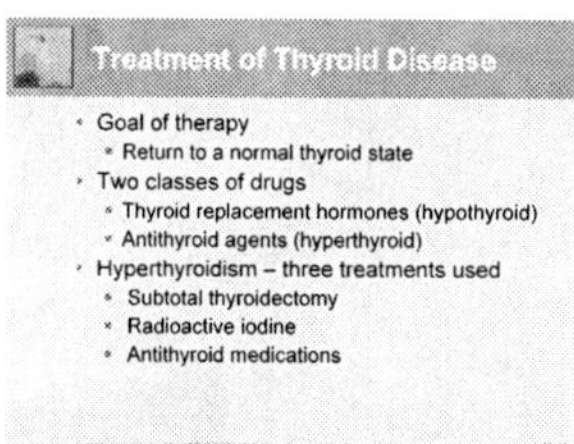
Treatment of Thyroid Disease
Goal of therapy
Return to a normal thyroid state
Two classes of drugs
Thyroid replacement hormones (hypothyroid)
Antithyroid agents (hyperthyroid)
Hyperthyroidism – three treatments used
Subtotal thyroidectomy
Radioactive iodine
Antithyroid medications

- May be 1 to 3 weeks after drug initiation that the drug's effects are noticed.

Slide 8

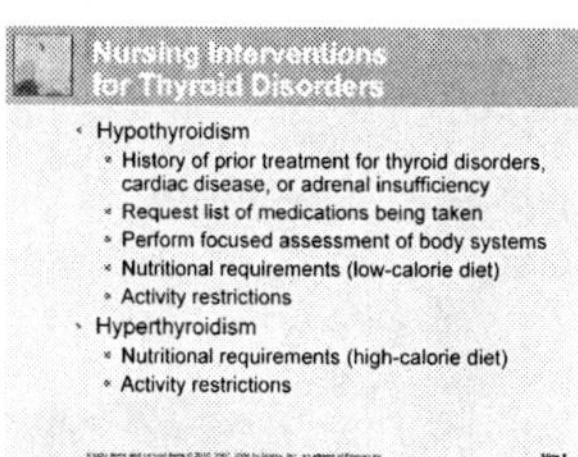
Nursing Interventions for Thyroid Disorders
Hypothyroidism
History of prior treatment for thyroid disorders, cardiac disease, or adrenal insufficiency
Request list of medications being taken
Perform focused assessment of body systems
Nutritional requirements (low-calorie diet)
Activity restrictions
Hyperthyroidism
Nutritional requirements (high-calorie diet)
Activity restrictions

- Not all systems may be affected. Nursing care, diagnosis, and treatment focuses on affected systems.
- Encourage moderate exercise as tolerated, focusing on safety during ambulation if muscle weakness, wasting, or discomfort is present.

Slide 9

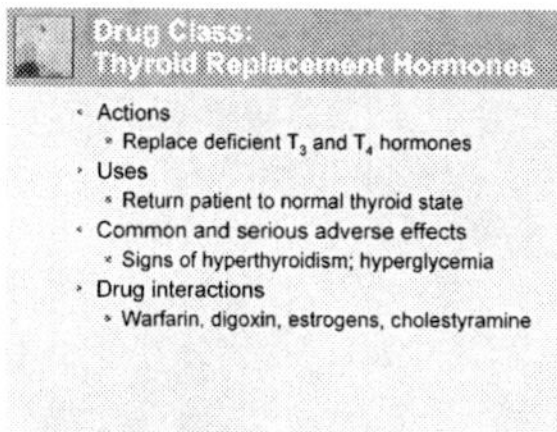
Drug Class: Thyroid Replacement Hormones
Actions
Replace deficient T3 and T4 hormones
Uses
Return patient to normal thyroid state
Common and serious adverse effects
Signs of hyperthyroidism; hyperglycemia
Drug interactions
Warfarin, digoxin, estrogens, cholestyramine

- For specific drugs, see Table 37-1.
- Levothyroxine is the most commonly used medication.
- Patients taking oral hypoglycemic agents or insulin may require adjustment.

Slide 10

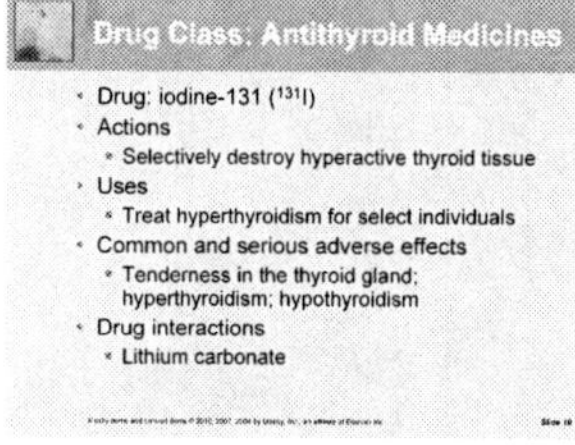
Drug Class: Antithyroid Medicines
Drug: iodine-131 (131I)
Actions
Selectively destroy hyperactive thyroid tissue
Uses
Treat hyperthyroidism for select individuals
Common and serious adverse effects
Tenderness in the thyroid gland; hyperthyroidism; hypothyroidism
Drug interactions
Lithium carbonate

- Used primarily for certain patients who may not be candidates for more aggressive treatment.
- Iodine-131 is a radioactive isotope of iodine that is absorbed into the thyroid gland in high concentrations.
- 3 to 6 months for full benefit to be seen.
- Extremely dangerous; wear latex gloves, watch for personnel who have allergies, follow hospital policy for spills.

ELSEVIER

Slide 11

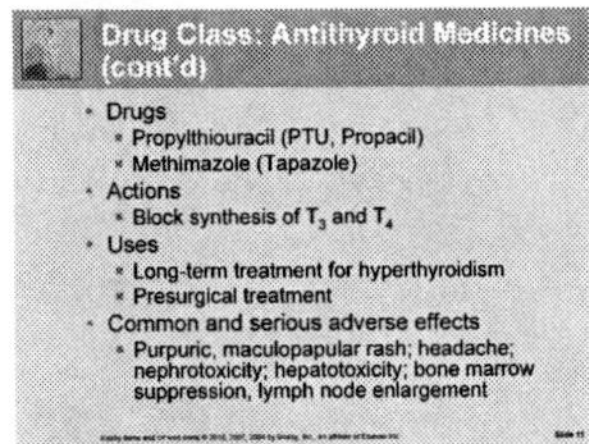
Drug Class: Antithyroid Medicines (cont'd)
Drugs
Propylthiouracil (PTU, Propacil)
Methimazole (Tapazole)
Actions
Block synthesis of T3 and T4
Uses
Long-term treatment for hyperthyroidism
Presurgical treatment
Common and serious adverse effects
Purpuric, maculopapular rash; headache; nephrotoxicity; hepatotoxicity; bone marrow suppression, lymph node enlargement

- Will not destroy T_3 and T_4 already produced; few days to 3 weeks before symptoms improve.
- Drug interactions: warfarin dosage may have to be increased; digoxin dosage may have to be decreased.

38 Lesson Plan

Corticosteroids

TEACHING FOCUS

In this chapter, students are introduced to topics related to corticosteroids. Students become acquainted with the action and use of corticosteroids and the nursing process for corticosteroid therapy. Mineralocorticoids and glucocorticoids are also discussed.

MATERIALS AND RESOURCES

☐ computer and PowerPoint projector (all Lessons)

LESSON CHECKLIST

Preparations for this lesson include:

- lecture
- evaluation of student knowledge and skills needed to perform all entry-level activities related to corticosteroid therapy, including:
  - functions of the adrenal gland and actions of mineralocorticoids and glucocorticoids in the body
  - baseline assessments needed for patients receiving corticosteroids
  - clinical uses of mineralocorticoids and glucocorticoids
  - adverse effects associated with mineralocorticoids and glucocorticoids
  - the nursing processes for corticosteroid therapy, including assessment, nursing diagnoses, planning, and implementation

KEY TERMS

corticosteroids (p. 593)
cortisol (p. 597)
glucocorticoids (p. 593)
mineralocorticoids (p. 593)

ADDITIONAL RESOURCES

PowerPoint slides: 1-12
Flashcards, Decks 1 and 2

Legend

ARQ	PPT	TB	CTQ	SG	INRQ
Audience Response Questions	PowerPoint Slides	Test Bank	Critical Thinking Questions	Study Guide	Interactive NCLEX Review Questions

Class Activities are indicated in ***bold italic.***

LESSON 38.1

BACKGROUND ASSESSMENT

Question: What assessment criteria does the nurse observe to determine if the patient is dehydrated?
Answer: To determine whether a patient is dehydrated, the nurse should look for the following signs: poor skin turgor, sticky oral mucous membranes, shrunken or deeply furrowed tongue, crusted lips, weight loss, deteriorating vital signs, soft or sunken eyeballs, weak pedal pulses, delayed capillary filling, excessive thirst, high urine specific gravity or no urine output, and possible mental confusion.

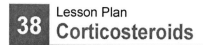

ELSEVIER

Question: Why is it important to assess the mental status of patients taking corticosteroids, and how does the nurse assess for changes in mental status?
Answer: Patients receiving higher doses of corticosteroids are susceptible to psychotic behavioral changes. The most susceptible patient is one with a history of mental dysfunction. The nurse needs to perform a baseline assessment of the patient's ability to respond rationally to the environment and the diagnosis of underlying diseases. The nurse should check for orientation to date, time, and place and assess for level of confusion, restlessness, or irritability. The nurse should also make regularly scheduled mental status evaluations and compare the findings. For anxiety, the nurse should determine what degree of apprehension is present and if any stressful events precipitated the anxiety.

CRITICAL THINKING QUESTION

A patient who has been prescribed steroids for a respiratory disorder tells the nurse that he is feeling much better after a week of therapy and is going to stop taking this medication. What information should the nurse give this patient about abruptly stopping steroid therapy? What adverse reactions might he experience?
Guidelines: The nurse should tell the patient that steroids, in the form of cortisol, are normally secreted by the adrenal glands. When a patient takes steroids, it suppresses the production of the patient's own steroids. Therefore, this drug has to be discontinued gradually to ensure that the adrenal glands are able to start secreting steroids appropriately as the drug dosage is reduced. The nurse should tell the patient that if he stops abruptly, he will experience the following signs and symptoms: fever, weakness, anorexia, nausea, orthostasis, hypotension, faintness, and dyspnea. His blood glucose level may drop, and he may have joint and muscle pain. In addition, his disease may worsen without the prescribed drug therapy.

OBJECTIVES	CONTENT	TEACHING RESOURCES
Review the functions of the adrenal gland.	■ Corticosteroids (p. 593) Review the hormones secreted by the adrenal cortex, mineralocorticoids and glucocorticoids. Discuss their functions in regulating metabolism and electrolytes.	PPT 5 SG Review Sheet questions 1, 3, 14 (pp. 251-252) SG Learning Activities questions 1-2, 4, 15, 22 (p. 253) ▸ Discuss the different hormones secreted by the adrenal gland. Class Activity ***As a class, discuss the structure and functions of the adrenal glands. Then divide the class into small groups, and have each group discuss how the corticosteroids regulate biologic activity.***
State the normal actions of mineralo-corticoids and glucocorticoids in the body.	■ Corticosteroids (p. 593) Review the nursing process used for patients on corticosteroids in terms of focused assessments and laboratory studies to be monitored. Review how to assess for hydration status and the need to carefully monitor nutrition.	PPT 5 TB Multiple Response question 2 CTQ 2 Animation: Corticosteroids SG Review Sheet questions 4, 12, 16-17 (pp. 251-252) SG Learning Activities questions 3, 5, 11-12 (p. 253) ▸ Discuss the characteristics of mineralocorticoids and glucocorticoids.

OBJECTIVES	CONTENT	TEACHING RESOURCES
		Class Activity ***List the following on the board: fluid and electrolyte balance, fat metabolism, treatment of Addison's disease, carbohydrate metabolism, anti-inflammatory activity, protein metabolism, and immunosuppressant activity. Have students pair up, and call on each pair to place mineralocorticoids or glucocorticoids under each heading. Review the exercise with the class.***
Cite the disease states caused by hypersecretion or hyposecretion of the adrenal gland.	■ Corticosteroids (p. 593)	SG Review Sheet question 11 (p. 252) ▸ Discuss the conditions that can be treated with corticosteroids. Class Activity ***Have students research how hyposecretion or hypersecretion can cause the following conditions:*** – ***Cushing's syndrome*** – ***Addison's disease*** – ***Hypopituitarism*** ***Select several students to report their findings to the class and lead a class discussion. (For students to prepare for this activity, see Homework/Assignments 1.)***
Identify the baseline assessments needed for a patient receiving corticosteroids.	– Nursing process for corticosteroid therapy (p. 593)	PPT 6 TB Multiple Choice question 1 TB Multiple Response questions 3-4 INRQ 1, 7 CTQ 3 SG Review Sheet questions 6, 10, 15 (pp. 251-252) SG Practice Questions for the NCLEX Examination 1, 4-5 (p. 254) Review Questions for the NCLEX Examination 3, 5-6 (p. 600) ▸ Discuss the nursing process for corticosteroid therapy. ▸ Discuss the behavioral changes associated with corticosteroid therapy. Class Activity ***Divide the class into small groups, and assign each group one or two of the following baseline assessment factors:*** – ***Medication history*** – ***Central nervous system*** – ***Physical assessment***

OBJECTIVES	CONTENT	TEACHING RESOURCES
		– ***Status of hydration*** – ***Laboratory tests*** – ***Nutrition*** ***Have the groups discuss which baseline assessments need to be taken in each area. Then have the groups report to the class and explain the importance of the individual assessments.***

38.1 Homework/Assignments:
1. Have students research how hyposecretion or hypersecretion can cause the following conditions: Cushing's syndrome, Addison's disease, and hypopituitarism.

38.1 Instructor's Notes/Student Feedback:

LESSON 38.2

CRITICAL THINKING QUESTION

The patient is taking furosemide (Lasix) and prednisone. What adverse effects should the nurse be alert for with the interaction of these two drugs?

Guidelines: The nurse should be aware that furosemide is a diuretic that enhances fluid and electrolyte excretion. Furosemide produces potassium loss, and corticosteroids may also enhance the loss of potassium. Symptoms the nurse should look for are changes in mental status, decrease in muscle strength, muscle cramps, tremors, nausea, drowsiness, anxiety, and lethargy.

OBJECTIVES	CONTENT	TEACHING RESOURCES
Develop measurable objectives for patient education for people taking corticosteroids.	– Patient education and health promotion (p. 596) Review patient education focused on health promotion for patients on corticosteroids.	PPT 12 ARQ 2 TB Multiple Choice questions 6-7 TB Multiple Response questions 1, 6 INRQ 2, 4, 11 CTQ 1 Patient Self-Assessment Form: Corticosteroids SG Review Sheet questions 9, 13 (p. 252) SG Learning Activities questions 19-20 (p. 253)

ELSEVIER

OBJECTIVES	CONTENT	TEACHING RESOURCES
		SG Practice Question for the NCLEX Examination 7 (p. 254) ▸ Discuss the symptoms that patients should report to the health care provider when taking corticosteroids. ▸ Discuss coping mechanisms for patients experiencing stress related to corticosteroid therapy. Class Activity ***Divide the class into five groups. Assign each group one of the following nursing diagnoses related to steroid therapy: activity intolerance, excess fluid volume, acute or chronic pain, ineffective tissue perfusion, and risk for injury. Have each group develop patient teaching guidelines for the diagnosis. Then have each group present its guidelines to the class.***
Prepare a list of the clinical uses of mineralo-corticoids and glucocorticoids.	■ Drug therapy with corticosteroids (p. 597) □ Drug class: Mineralocorticoids (p. 597) – Nursing process for fludrocortisone (p. 597) □ Drug class: Glucocorticoids (p. 597) – Nursing process for glucocorticoids (p. 597)	PPT 7-9 ARQ 5 TB Multiple Choice questions 3, 5 TB Multiple Response question 5 Patient Self-Assessment Form: Corticosteroids SG Review Sheet question 2 (p. 251) SG Learning Activities questions 6-10 (p. 253) SG Practice Questions for the NCLEX Examination 3, 8-10 (pp. 254-255) Review Questions for the NCLEX Examination 1-2, 4 (p. 600) Drug Table 38-1: Corticosteroid Preparations (p. 598) ▸ Discuss the clinical uses of mineralocorticoids and glucocorticoids. ▸ Discuss issues related to the premedication assessment, planning, and implementation of fludrocortisone therapy. Class Activity ***Divide the class into two groups. Assign one group the topic of mineralocorticoids and the other the topic of glucocorticoids. Have each group create a list of clinical uses of mineralocorticoids and glucocorticoids.***

OBJECTIVES	CONTENT	TEACHING RESOURCES
Discuss the potential adverse effects associated with the use of corticosteroids, and give examples of specific patient education needed for the patient taking these agents.	– Nursing process for glucocorticoids (p. 597)	PPT 10-11 ARQ 1, 3-4 TB Multiple Choice questions 2, 4, 8-10 INRQ 3, 5-6, 8-10 SG Review Sheet questions 5, 7-8 (p. 251) SG Learning Activities questions 13-14, 16-18 (p. 253) SG Practice Questions for the NCLEX Examination 2, 6, 11 (pp. 254-255) Review Questions for the NCLEX Examination 7-9 (p. 600) ▸ Discuss risks of infection associated with glucocorticoids. Class Activity ***Lead the class in a game in which you allow students to describe a particular adverse effect related to steroid use. Have students respond with the name of a steroid in the form of a question.***
Performance evaluation		Test Bank SG Learning Activities (p. 253) SG Practice Questions for the NCLEX Examination (pp. 254-255) Critical Thinking Questions

38.2 Homework/Assignments:

38.2 Instructor's Notes/Student Feedback:

38 Lecture Outline
Corticosteroids

Slide 1

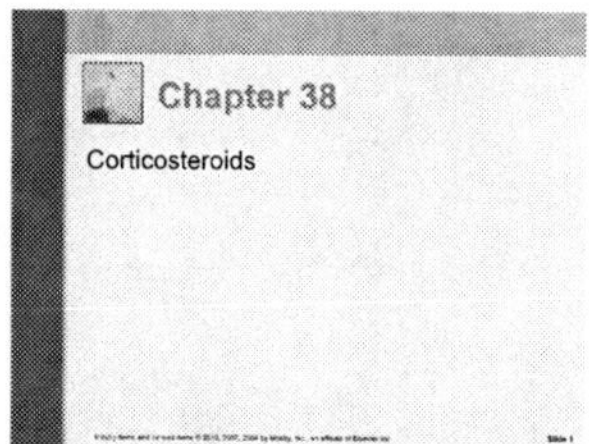
Chapter 38
Corticosteroids

Slide 2

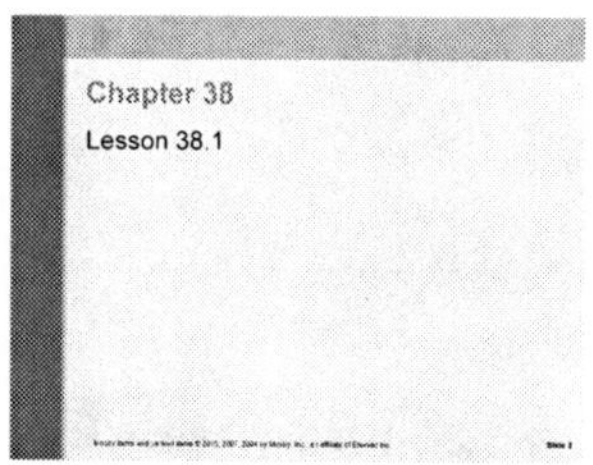
Chapter 38
Lesson 38.1

Slide 3

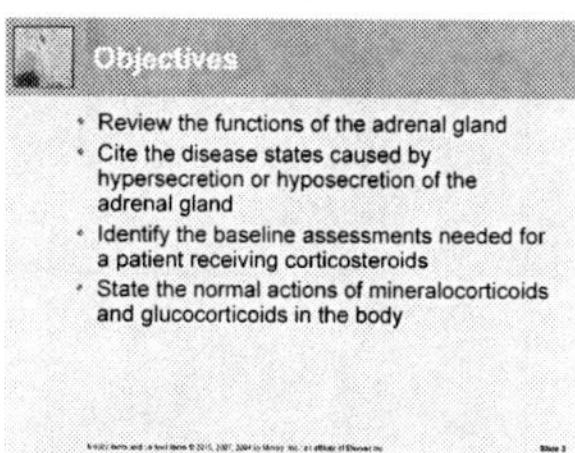
Objectives
Review the functions of the adrenal gland
Cite the disease states caused by hypersecretion or hyposecretion of the adrenal gland
Identify the baseline assessments needed for a patient receiving corticosteroids
State the normal actions of mineralocorticoids and glucocorticoids in the body

Slide 4

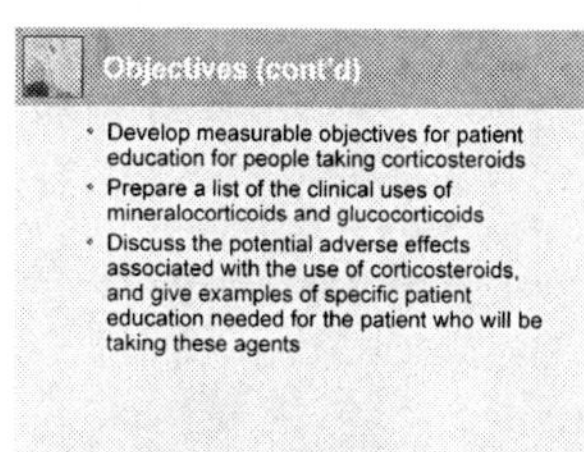
Objectives (cont'd)
Develop measurable objectives for patient education for people taking corticosteroids
Prepare a list of the clinical uses of mineralocorticoids and glucocorticoids
Discuss the potential adverse effects associated with the use of corticosteroids, and give examples of specific patient education needed for the patient who will be taking these agents

Slide 5

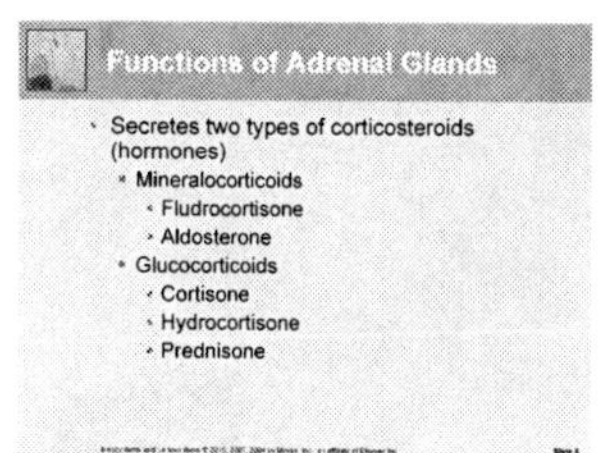
Functions of Adrenal Glands
Secretes two types of corticosteroids (hormones)
Mineralocorticoids
Fludrocortisone
Aldosterone
Glucocorticoids
Cortisone
Hydrocortisone
Prednisone

- Adrenal glands are located on the top of each kidney; they also regulate sex hormones.
- Mineralocorticoids and glucocorticoids have different functions and adverse effects.
- Diseases associated with adrenal glands are Addison's disease, pheochromocytoma, and hyperpituitarism.

Slide 6

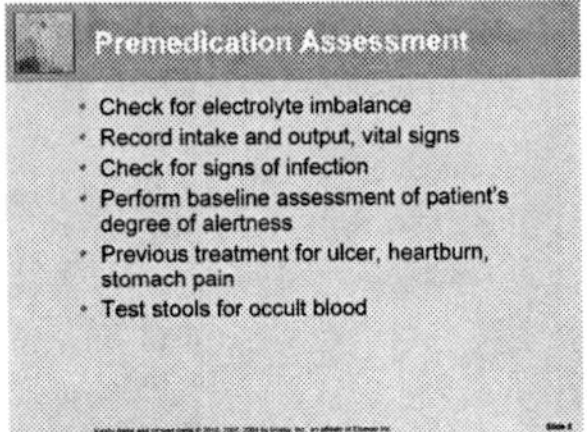
Premedication Assessment
Check for electrolyte imbalance
Record intake and output, vital signs
Check for signs of infection
Perform baseline assessment of patient's degree of alertness
Previous treatment for ulcer, heartburn, stomach pain
Test stools for occult blood

- Lab values to check for electrolyte imbalance: K+, Ca+, Na+, Cl-.
- Signs of infection to look for in a patient taking steroids: general malaise, sore throat, low-grade fever.

Slide 7

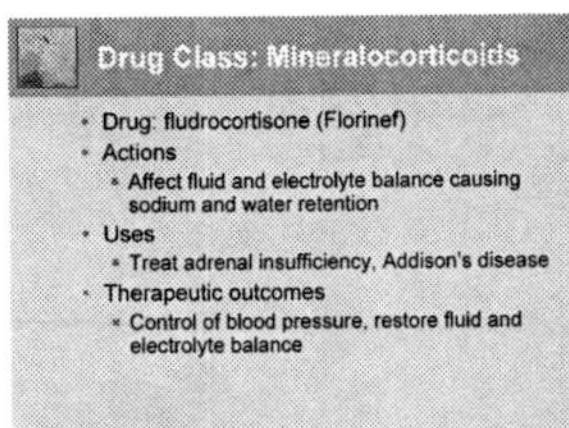
Drug Class: Mineralocorticoids
Drug: fludrocortisone (Florinef)
Actions
Affect fluid and electrolyte balance causing sodium and water retention
Uses
Treat adrenal insufficiency, Addison's disease
Therapeutic outcomes
Control of blood pressure, restore fluid and electrolyte balance

- Used in combination with glucocorticoids.
- Fludrocortisone is the only drug that has true mineralocorticoid effects.

Slide 8

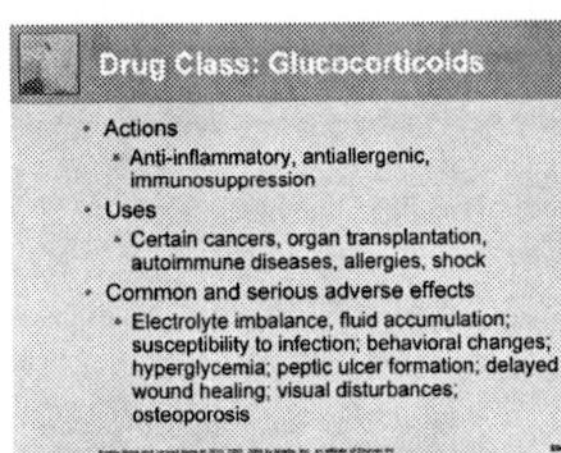
Drug Class: Glucocorticoids
Actions
Anti-inflammatory, antiallergenic, immunosuppression
Uses
Certain cancers, organ transplantation, autoimmune diseases, allergies, shock
Common and serious adverse effects
Electrolyte imbalance, fluid accumulation; susceptibility to infection; behavioral changes; hyperglycemia; peptic ulcer formation; delayed wound healing; visual disturbances; osteoporosis

- For specific drugs, see Table 38-1.
- All corticosteroids (glucocorticoids and mineralocorticoids) share varying degrees of mineralocorticoid and glucocorticoid effects.
- Alternate-day therapy may be used to treat chronic conditions.

Slide 9

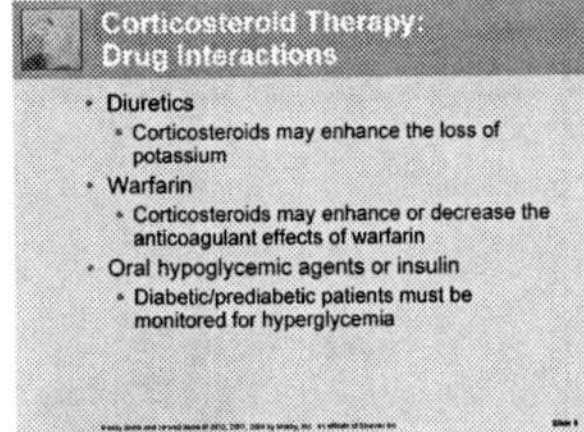
Corticosteroid Therapy: Drug Interactions
Diuretics
Corticosteroids may enhance the loss of potassium
Warfarin
Corticosteroids may enhance or decrease the anticoagulant effects of warfarin
Oral hypoglycemic agents or insulin
Diabetic/prediabetic patients must be monitored for hyperglycemia

Slide 10

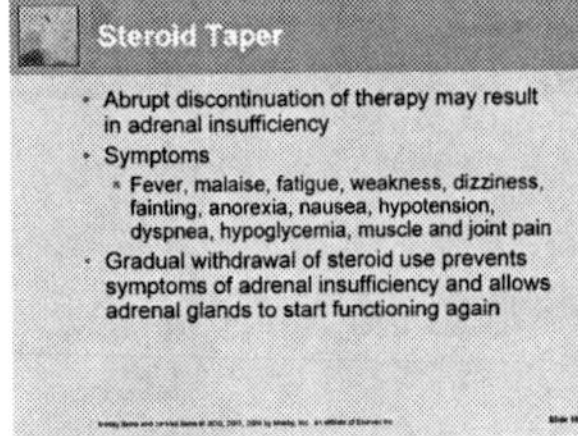
Steroid Taper
Abrupt discontinuation of therapy may result in adrenal insufficiency
Symptoms
Fever, malaise, fatigue, weakness, dizziness, fainting, anorexia, nausea, hypotension, dyspnea, hypoglycemia, muscle and joint pain
Gradual withdrawal of steroid use prevents symptoms of adrenal insufficiency and allows adrenal glands to start functioning again

Slide 11

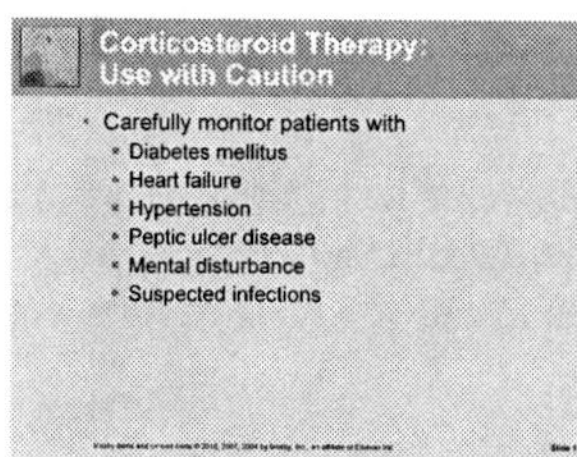
Corticosteroid Therapy: Use with Caution
Carefully monitor patients with
Diabetes mellitus
Heart failure
Hypertension
Peptic ulcer disease
Mental disturbance
Suspected infections

- Corticosteroids may:
  - Cause hyperglycemia in diabetic patients.
  - Mask symptoms of infection.
  - Induce hypertension.
  - Induce psychotic behavioral changes in patient with a history of mental instability.

Slide 12

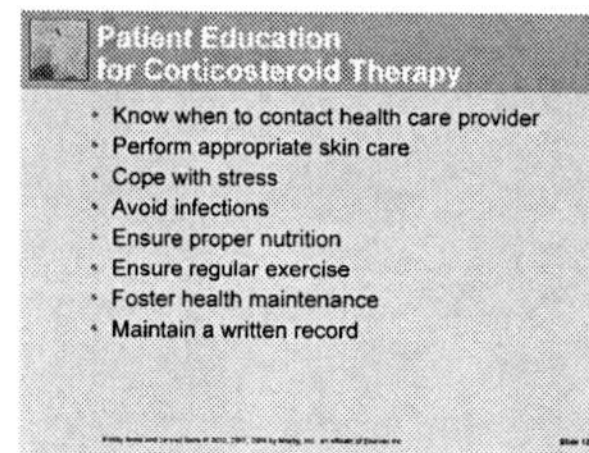
Patient Education for Corticosteroid Therapy
Know when to contact health care provider
Perform appropriate skin care
Cope with stress
Avoid infections
Ensure proper nutrition
Ensure regular exercise
Foster health maintenance
Maintain a written record

ELSEVIER

39 Lesson Plan

Gonadal Hormones

TEACHING FOCUS

In this chapter, students are introduced to topics related to gonadal hormones. Students have the opportunity to learn about gonads and gonadal hormones, including the actions, uses, and therapeutic outcomes of estrogens, progestins, and androgens. Students also have the opportunity to learn about the nursing process for gonadal hormones.

MATERIALS AND RESOURCES

- ☐ computer and PowerPoint projector (all Lessons)

LESSON CHECKLIST

Preparations for this lesson include:

- lecture
- evaluation of student knowledge and skills needed to perform all entry-level activities related to gonadal hormones, including:
  - production and drug therapy
  - the nursing process
  - the actions, uses, and therapeutic outcomes associated with estrogens, progestins, and androgens
  - premedication assessment, planning, implementation, evaluation, and adverse effects of estrogens, progestins, and androgens

KEY TERMS

androgens (p. 601)
estrogen (p. 601)
gonads (p. 601)
ovaries (p. 601)
progesterone (p. 601)
testosterone (p. 601)

ADDITIONAL RESOURCES

PowerPoint slides: 1-10
Flashcards, Decks 1 and 2

Legend

ARQ	**PPT**	**TB**	**CTQ**	**SG**	**INRQ**
Audience Response Questions	PowerPoint Slides	Test Bank	Critical Thinking Questions	Study Guide	Interactive NCLEX Review Questions

Class Activities are indicated in ***bold italic.***

LESSON 39.1

BACKGROUND ASSESSMENT

Question: Androgens are used to treat breast cancer in postmenopausal women with certain cell types of cancer. What adverse effects should the nurse explore with the female patient who is taking androgens?
Answer: The nurse should inform the patient that adverse effects might include deepening of the voice, hoarseness, growth of facial hair, clitoral enlargement, and menstrual irregularities. Such adverse effects could lead to a change in the patient's self-image and self-esteem.

Question: The nurse is evaluating a diabetic patient who has been prescribed an androgen. Considering these two factors, what observations are important for the nurse to note?
Answer: Diabetic patients taking androgens and insulin or hypoglycemic drugs may develop hypoglycemia. The nurse should observe her patient for headache, weakness, decreased coordination, general apprehension, diaphoresis, hunger, and blurred or double vision. If such symptoms occur, the dosage of the hypoglycemic drugs or insulin may need to be reduced.

CRITICAL THINKING QUESTION

A patient with breast cancer has been taking androgens. One of the drug's adverse effects could be hypercalcemia. What symptoms should the nurse observe for? Identify the nursing interventions that could prevent this adverse effect.
Guidelines: The nurse should monitor the patient for nausea, vomiting, constipation, poor muscle tone, and lethargy. The nurse should inform the patient about the importance of forcing fluids to minimize the possibility of renal calculi. The patient should drink 8 to 12 8-ounce glasses of water daily. The nurse should also advise the patient that performing weight-bearing and active and passive exercises to the degree tolerated by the patient will help minimize loss of calcium from the bones. Also, the nurse should keep track of the patient's bowel movement status daily to help detect constipation.

OBJECTIVES	CONTENT	TEACHING RESOURCES
Describe the gonads.	■ The gonads and gonadal hormones (p. 601) Review the reproductive glands of males and females, the testes and the ovaries. Discuss the function of the male sex hormone testosterone. Review the hormones estrogen and progesterone and their function as female sex hormones.	PPT 5 SG Review Sheet questions 1-3 (p. 257) SG Learning Activities questions 1, 3-4 (p. 259) ▸ Discuss the male and female gonads and gonadal hormones.
Describe the body changes that can be anticipated with the administration of androgens, estrogens, or progesterone.	■ The gonads and gonadal hormones (p. 601)	PPT 5 ARQ 5 TB Multiple Choice question 8 INRQ 5, 7, 9 SG Review Sheet question 4 (p. 257) SG Learning Activities questions 2, 5, 11 (p. 259) SG Practice Questions for the NCLEX Examination 1-2, 8 (p. 260) Lifespan Considerations: Diabetes Mellitus (p. 602)

OBJECTIVES	CONTENT	TEACHING RESOURCES
		▸ Discuss the body changes associated with the production of testosterone, androgens, estrogen, and progesterone. Class Activity ***Divide the class into three groups, and assign each group one of the gonadal hormones. Have each group create patient teaching materials on the actions and therapeutic uses of the hormones. Then have each group present its materials to the class.***
Compare the adverse effects seen with the use of estrogen hormones with those seen with a combination of estrogen and progesterone.	– Nursing process for gonadal hormones (p. 601) – Patient education and health promotion (p. 602) Review the treatment goals and therapeutic outcomes for using gonadal hormones for the following: birth control, hormonal balance, prevention of osteoporosis, treatment of severe acne in females, and palliative treatment of prostate and breast cancer.	PPT 6 INRQ 1, 3-4, 12 ▸ Discuss the adverse effects of estrogen and estrogen and progesterone therapy. ▸ Discuss the elements of assessment, including reproductive history, medication history, smoking history, and physical examination. ▸ Discuss the implications of prolonged self-administration of gonadal hormones. ▸ Discuss the effect of gonadal hormones on patients with diabetes mellitus. Class Activity ***Have pairs of students work together to create a teaching plan for estrogen and progesterone therapy.*** Class Activity ***Divide the class into two groups. Assign one group estrogen hormones and the other group progesterone hormones. Have each group research its assigned hormone for uses and adverse effects. Allow class time for student presentation and discussion.***
State the uses of estrogens and progestins.	■ Drug therapy with gonadal hormones (p. 602) □ Drug class: Estrogens (p. 602) – Nursing process for estrogen therapy (p. 603) □ Drug class: Progestins (p. 605) – Nursing process for progestins (p. 605) Review the drug class estrogens and their actions, uses, and therapeutic outcomes. Discuss common and serious adverse effects while on estrogens and known drug interactions.	PPT 7-9 ARQ 2-4 TB Multiple Choice question 1 TB Multiple Response questions 1, 3 SG Review Sheet question 9 (p. 257) SG Learning Activities questions 6-7, 9, 12, 14-15 (p. 259) SG Practice Question for the NCLEX Examination 6 (p. 260) Review Questions for the NCLEX Examination 2, 5-6 (p. 608) Drug Table 39-1: Estrogens (pp. 604-605)

OBJECTIVES	CONTENT	TEACHING RESOURCES
		Clinical Landmine: Use of Gonadal Hormones During Pregnancy (p. 603) Drug Table 39-2: Progestins (p. 606) ▸ Discuss the actions, uses, and therapeutic outcomes of estrogens and progestins. Class Activity ***Give students a list of the therapeutic outcomes expected from estrogen and progestin. Then have students research the hormones to learn how they achieve each of their outcomes. Select several students to present their findings to the class. (For students to prepare for this activity, see Homework/ Assignments 1.)***
Differentiate between the common adverse effects and those requiring consultation with the physician that occur with the administration of estrogen or progesterone.	■ Drug therapy with gonadal hormones (p. 602) □ Drug class: Estrogens (p. 602) – Nursing process for estrogen therapy (p. 603) □ Drug class: Progestins (p. 605) – Nursing process for progestins (p. 605) Review the drug class progestins and their actions, uses, and therapeutic outcomes. Discuss common and serious adverse effects while on progestins and known drug interactions.	PPT 7-9 ARQ 1 TB Multiple Choice questions 4-6, 9 TB Multiple Response questions 2, 4-5 INRQ 2, 6, 8 CTQ 2 SG Review Sheet questions 7-8, 11, 13 (pp. 257-258) SG Practice Questions for the NCLEX Examination 4-5, 7, 9-10 (p. 260) Review Question for the NCLEX Examination 8 (p. 609) ▸ Discuss the effects of gonadal hormone therapy on a pregnant patient. ▸ Discuss the adverse effects of estrogen and progestin therapy. Class Activity ***Divide the class into small groups. Have the students come up with a written plan of monitoring parameters of the potential adverse effects of hormone therapy that the patient can use at home.*** Class Activity ***Divide the class into two groups. Assign one group estrogen and the other group progesterone. Have each group research adverse effects warranting health care provider notification. Allow class time for student discussion.***

OBJECTIVES	CONTENT	TEACHING RESOURCES
Identify the rationale for administering androgens to women who have certain types of breast cancer.	□ Drug class: Androgens (p. 605) – Nursing process for androgens (p. 606) Review the drug class androgens and their actions, uses, and therapeutic outcomes. Discuss common and serious adverse effects while on androgens and known drug interactions.	PPT 10 CTQ 1-2 TB Multiple Choice questions 2-3, 7 INRQ 10 SG Review Sheet questions 5, 10-13 (pp. 257-258) SG Learning Activities questions 3, 8, 10, 13 (p. 259) SG Practice Questions for the NCLEX Examination 1-3, 8 (p. 260) Review Questions for the NCLEX Examination 1, 3-4 7, 9 (pp. 608-609) Lifespan Considerations: Androgens (p. 608) Drug Table 39-3: Androgens (p. 607) ▸ Discuss how androgen therapy affects long bone development. Class Activity ***As a class, discuss the uses and adverse effects of androgen therapy in postmenopausal women with breast cancer.*** Class Activity ***Divide the class into groups with three students per group. Assign each group one of the categories within the adverse effects to androgens. Have each group research appropriate mechanisms for the nurse to use to monitor these adverse effects (e.g., noting electrolyte laboratory values, voice changes, hirsutism). Facilitate class discussion on the use of androgens in the male pediatric patient and necessary evaluation of the child during drug therapy.***
Performance evaluation		Test Bank SG Learning Activities (p. 259) SG Practice Questions for the NCLEX Examination (p. 260) Critical Thinking Questions

39.1 Homework/Assignments:
1. Give the students a list of the therapeutic outcomes expected from estrogen and progestin, and have the students research the hormones to learn how they achieve each of the outcomes.

39.1 Instructor's Notes/Student Feedback:

39 Lecture Outline

Gonadal Hormones

Slide 1

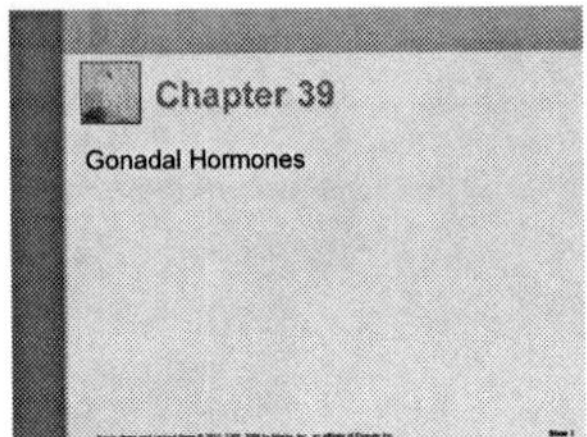
Chapter 39
Gonadal Hormones

Slide 2

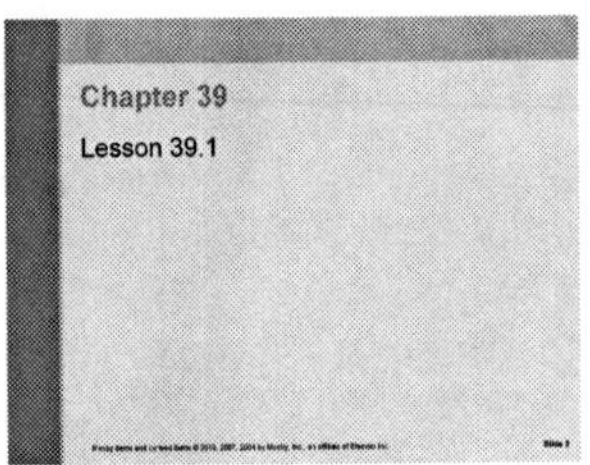
Chapter 39
Lesson 39.1

Slide 3

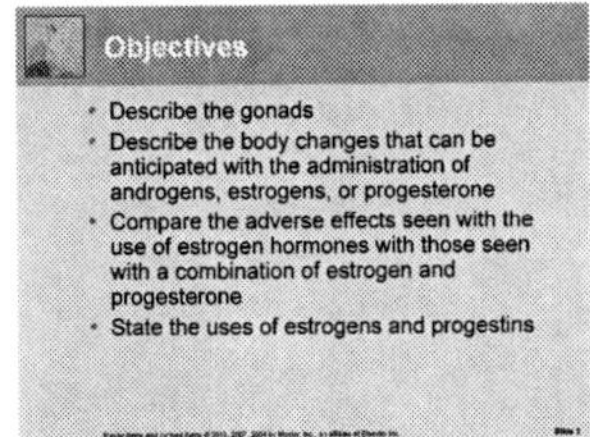
Objectives
Describe the gonads
Describe the body changes that can be anticipated with the administration of androgens, estrogens, or progesterone
Compare the adverse effects seen with the use of estrogen hormones with those seen with a combination of estrogen and progesterone
State the uses of estrogens and progestins

Slide 4

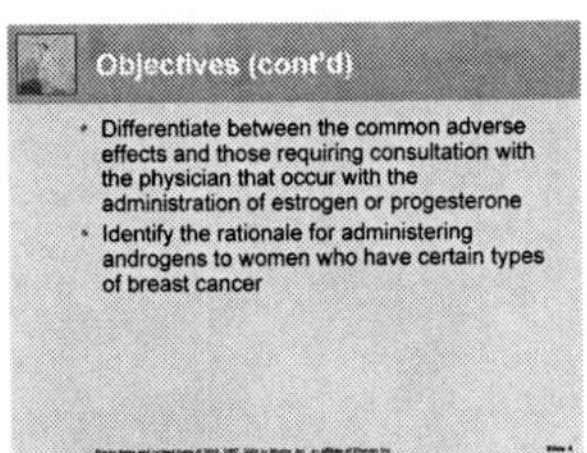
Objectives (cont'd)
Differentiate between the common adverse effects and those requiring consultation with the physician that occur with the administration of estrogen or progesterone
Identify the rationale for administering androgens to women who have certain types of breast cancer

Slide 5

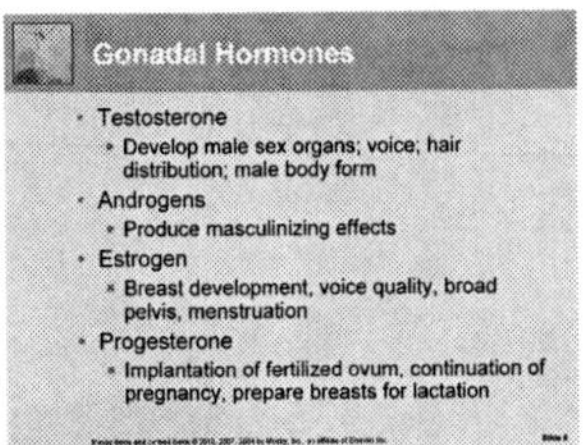
Gonadal Hormones
Testosterone
Develop male sex organs; voice; hair distribution; male body form
Androgens
Produce masculinizing effects
Estrogen
Breast development, voice quality, broad pelvis, menstruation
Progesterone
Implantation of fertilized ovum, continuation of pregnancy, prepare breasts for lactation

- Gonads are the reproductive glands.
- Testosterone is produced by the testes in males.
- Estrogen and progesterone are produced by the ovaries in females.
- Androgens are produced by the adrenal gland.

Slide 6

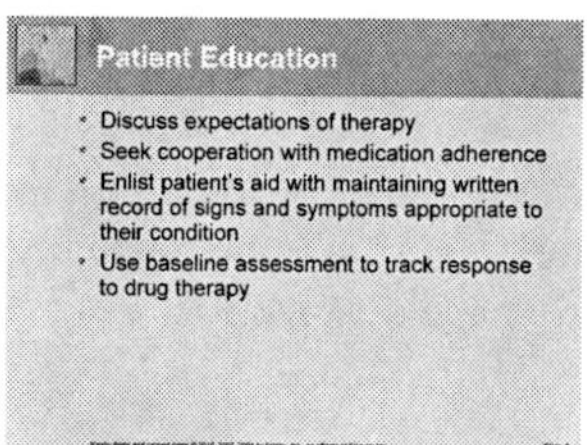
Patient Education
Discuss expectations of therapy
Seek cooperation with medication adherence
Enlist patient's aid with maintaining written record of signs and symptoms appropriate to their condition
Use baseline assessment to track response to drug therapy

Slide 7

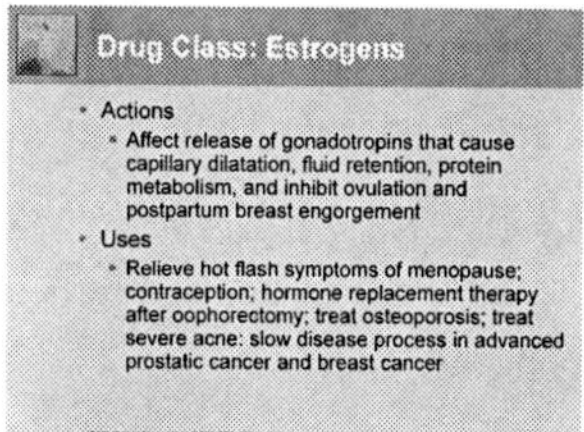
Drug Class: Estrogens
Actions
Affect release of gonadotropins that cause capillary dilatation, fluid retention, protein metabolism, and inhibit ovulation and postpartum breast engorgement
Uses
Relieve hot flash symptoms of menopause; contraception; hormone replacement therapy after oophorectomy; treat osteoporosis; treat severe acne: slow disease process in advanced prostatic cancer and breast cancer

- For specific drugs, see Table 39-1.

Slide 8

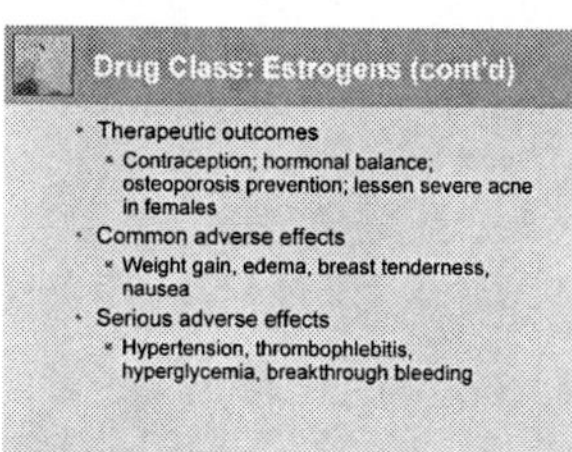
Drug Class: Estrogens (cont'd)
Therapeutic outcomes
Contraception; hormonal balance; osteoporosis prevention; lessen severe acne in females
Common adverse effects
Weight gain, edema, breast tenderness, nausea
Serious adverse effects
Hypertension, thrombophlebitis, hyperglycemia, breakthrough bleeding

- Drug interactions: may diminish the anticoagulant effects of warfarin; may inhibit the metabolism of phenytoin resulting in phenytoin toxicity; increase in thyroid hormone dosage may be required if hypothyroidism results.

Slide 9

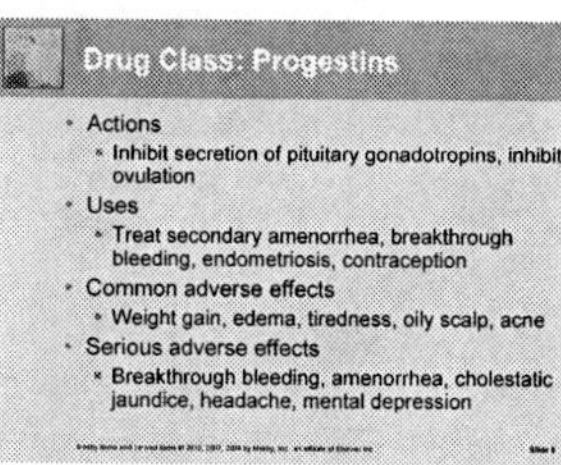
Drug Class: Progestins
Actions
Inhibit secretion of pituitary gonadotropins, inhibit ovulation
Uses
Treat secondary amenorrhea, breakthrough bleeding, endometriosis, contraception
Common adverse effects
Weight gain, edema, tiredness, oily scalp, acne
Serious adverse effects
Breakthrough bleeding, amenorrhea, cholestatic jaundice, headache, mental depression

- For specific drugs, see Table 39-2.
- Contraindicated in pregnancy because of the possibility of birth defects.

Slide 10

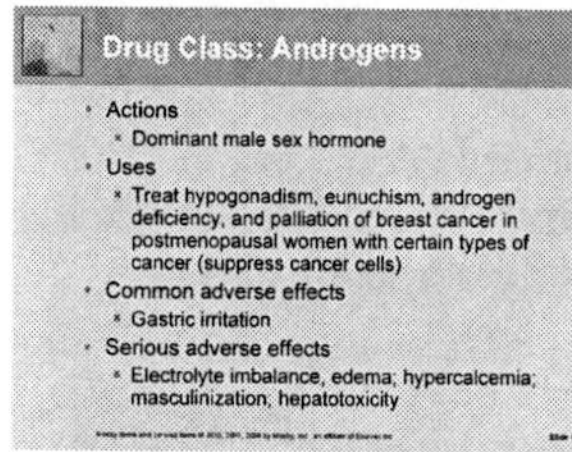
Drug Class: Androgens
Actions
Dominant male sex hormone
Uses
Treat hypogonadism, eunuchism, androgen deficiency, and palliation of breast cancer in postmenopausal women with certain types of cancer (suppress cancer cells)
Common adverse effects
Gastric irritation
Serious adverse effects
Electrolyte imbalance, edema; hypercalcemia; masculinization; hepatotoxicity

- For specific drugs, see Table 39-3.
- Male children must have periodic x-rays of long bones to ensure that bone elongation is not hindered by therapy.

40 Lesson Plan
Drugs Used in Obstetrics

TEACHING FOCUS

In this chapter, the student will have an opportunity to learn about drug therapy in pregnancy, including the assessment and nursing interventions for the pregnant patient from the first trimester through the postpartum period. The immediate nursing care of the newborn following delivery will be discussed as well.

MATERIALS AND RESOURCES

- ☐ computer and PowerPoint projector (all Lessons)

LESSON CHECKLIST

Preparations for this lesson include:

- guest speakers: labor and delivery nurse
- evaluation of student knowledge and skills needed to perform all entry-level activities related to drugs used in obstetrics, including:
  - nursing process for obstetrics
  - uterine relaxants and stimulants
  - other agents, including clomiphene, magnesium sulfate, and Rh_o(D) immune globulin
  - neonatal ophthalmic solutions

KEY TERMS

augmentation (p. 619)
dysfunctional labor (p. 619)
lochia (p. 614)
precipitous labor and delivery (p. 619)
pregnancy-induced hypertension (PIH) (p. 612)

ADDITIONAL RESOURCES

PowerPoint slides: 1-24
Flashcards, Decks 1 and 2

Legend

ARQ	**PPT**	**TB**	**CTQ**	**SG**	**INRQ**
Audience Response Questions	PowerPoint Slides	Test Bank	Critical Thinking Questions	Study Guide	Interactive NCLEX Review Questions

Class Activities are indicated in ***bold italic.***

LESSON 40.1

BACKGROUND ASSESSMENT

Question: What are the four primary clinical indications for the use of uterine stimulants?
Answer: They are (1) induction or augmentation of labor, (2) control of postpartum atony and hemorrhage, (3) control of postsurgical hemorrhage (as in cesarean birth), and (4) induction of therapeutic abortion.

Question: What is included in the premedication assessment for administration of oxytocin?
Answer: Never leave a patient receiving an oxytocin infusion unattended, and make sure that the IV site is functional before adding oxytocin. Always use an infusion pump. Monitor vital signs, especially blood pressure and pulse. Obtain baseline assessment data of mother's hydration status. Monitor I&O throughout drug therapy. Monitor the characteristics of uterine contractions, along with fetal heart rate and rhythm. Watch for fetal distress. Perform reflex testing, and check amount and characteristics of vaginal discharge.

ELSEVIER

CRITICAL THINKING QUESTION

You are taking care of a patient who just delivered a baby. She has not had any prenatal classes and comments to you that she is looking forward to breast-feeding her baby, but does not know much about it. What is important for this patient to know about breast-feeding right after delivery?

Guidelines: You can help the patient relax by letting her know that the breasts do not secrete milk for the first few days, but secrete a thin yellowish fluid called colostrum. After 3 to 4 days, breast milk is available. When the breasts become engorged, the patient may be uncomfortable; the patient can relieve her discomfort by nursing the infant more frequently, such as every 90 minutes, hand-expressing milk, or massaging her breasts. Relief can also be obtained by taking a warm shower or applying warm, moist heat. Consult with the health care provider if discomfort is not relieved before the patient takes any over-the-counter drugs.

OBJECTIVES	CONTENT	TEACHING RESOURCES
Describe nursing assessments and nursing interventions needed for the pregnant patient during the first, second, and third trimesters of pregnancy.	■ Obstetrics (p. 610) – Nursing process for obstetrics (p. 610) Review the assessment data that must be obtained from a pregnant woman, including vital signs, weight gain during pregnancy, medications, and nutrition evaluation.	PPT 5 TB Multiple Response question 1 SG Review Sheet question 1 (p. 261) ▸ Discuss the assessment of the pregnant woman during the first, second, and third trimesters. ▸ Discuss the assessment of the pregnant patient at risk during the first, second, and third trimesters. Class Activity ***Divide the class into three groups, one for each of the trimesters of a normal pregnancy. Half of each group will research nursing assessments, and half will research nursing interventions. Have one person from each group present the findings to the class. (For students to prepare for this activity, see Homework/Assignment #1.)***
Identify appropriate nursing assessments, nursing interventions, and treatment options used for the following obstetric complications: infection, hyperemesis gravidarum, miscarriage, abortion, preterm labor, premature rupture of membranes, gestational diabetes, and pregnancy-	– Nursing process for obstetrics (p. 610) Review complications of pregnancy: preterm labor, premature rupture of membranes, pregnancy-induced hypertension, hyperemesis gravidarum, and gestational diabetes. Discuss the use of drug therapy for these complications.	PPT 6 TB Multiple Choice question 10 TB Multiple Response question 2 SG Review Sheet questions 2-4, 7 (pp. 261-262) SG Learning Activities question 1 (p. 268) Review Questions for the NCLEX Examination 8-9 (p. 631) Figure 40-1 (p. 613): Alternatives to the treatment of preterm labor. ▸ Discuss the assessment of the pregnant patient at risk. ▸ Discuss the nursing assessment and intervention for preterm labor, premature rupture of membranes, gestational diabetes mellitus, and PIH. Class Activity ***Divide the class into six groups, one for each obstetric complication listed in the***

ELSEVIER

OBJECTIVES	CONTENT	TEACHING RESOURCES
induced hypertension.		***learning objective. Have each group identify appropriate nursing assessments, nursing interventions, and treatment options for each complication. Have each group present its findings to the class.***
State the purpose of administering glucocorticoids to certain women in preterm labor.	– Nursing process for obstetrics (p. 610)	TB Multiple Choice question 2 SG Review Sheet question 8 (p. 263) ▸ Discuss the reason for administering glucocorticoids to women in preterm labor. ▸ Discuss when glucocorticoids are recommended. Class Activity ***Give students 20 minutes to write down the purpose of administering glucocorticoids in preterm labor and to identify the parameters to be followed. Have students volunteer to present what they wrote and lead a class discussion.***
State the methods and time parameters of each approach to the termination of a pregnancy.	– Nursing process for obstetrics (p. 610) Discuss abortion and miscarriage in all three trimesters.	PPT 7 SG Review Sheet question 5, 22 (pp. 261, 264) ▸ Discuss the methods of terminating a pregnancy during the various stages of pregnancy. ▸ Discuss and identify the nursing interventions when a patient is terminating a pregnancy. Class Activity ***Divide the class into three groups. Assign each group an approach to the termination of a pregnancy. Have each group research the methods and time parameters, and have one student from each group present to the class. (For students to prepare for this activity, see Homework/Assignment #2.)***
Summarize the care needs of the pregnant woman during labor and delivery and the immediate postpartum period including the patient education needed before discharge to promote safe self-care and care of the newborn.	– Patient education and health promotion (p. 618)	PPT 8-9 Patient Self-Assessment Form: Prenatal Care Patient Self-Assessment Form: Postpartum Care SG Review Sheet questions 9, 11, 13, 15 (p. 263) SG Learning Activities questions 2, 4, 7 (p. 268) Table 40-1: Apgar Scoring System (p. 614) Table 40-2: Gestational Age (p. 614) Class Activity ***Divide the class into two groups. Have one group present care needs during labor and delivery and the other group present***

ELSEVIER

OBJECTIVES	CONTENT	TEACHING RESOURCES
		care needs for the immediate postpartum period. Have one student from each group present its findings to the class. Class Activity ***Invite a labor and delivery nurse to the class to discuss patient care for a woman in labor and postpartum care for the new mother and infant.***

40.1 Homework/Assignments:
1. Divide the class into three groups, one for each of the trimesters of a normal pregnancy. Half of each group will research nursing assessments and half will research nursing interventions. 2. Divide the class into three groups. Assign each group an approach to pregnancy, and have each group research the methods and time parameters of each approach to the termination of a pregnancy.

40.1 Instructor's Notes/Student Feedback:

LESSON 40.2

CRITICAL THINKING QUESTION

The nurse is caring for a patient who is 1 hour postpartum after a normal vaginal delivery. She is receiving oxytocin to control uterine atony and postpartum hemorrhage. What does the nurse need to know about postpartum hemorrhage?

Guidelines: Postpartum hemorrhage occurs with a blood loss of 500 mL or more, creating hemodynamic instability. It is a potentially life-threatening complication. Postpartum atony and hemorrhage may occur up to 24 hours after a normal vaginal delivery of the fetus and placenta. The uterus remains flaccid and "boggy"; there may be retained fragments of placenta, or vaginal lacerations could be the cause of postpartum hemorrhage. Oxytocin is routinely administered IV after delivery of the placenta to cause uterine contractions and decrease blood loss. The fundus height needs to be checked every 5 minutes, and vaginal bleeding needs to be checked every 30 minutes. Intake and output vital signs must be monitored every 15 to 30 minutes, as ordered, and recorded. The health care provider must be immediately notified of any changes.

OBJECTIVES	CONTENT	TEACHING RESOURCES
Describe specific nursing concerns and appropriate nursing actions when uterine stimulants are administered for induction of labor,	■ Drug therapy in pregnancy (p. 619) □ Drug class: Uterine stimulants (p. 619) – Nursing process for dinoprostone (p. 620) – Nursing process for misoprostol (p. 621)	PPT 14-18 TB Multiple Choice question 12 INRQ 1-2, 12 CTQ 5-6 SG Review Sheet questions 10, 18-19, 21 (pp. 263-264) SG Learning Activities questions 6, 10 (p. 268)

OBJECTIVES	CONTENT	TEACHING RESOURCES
augmentation of labor, and postpartum atony and hemorrhage.	– Nursing process for ergonovine and methylergonovine (p. 622) – Nursing process for oxytocin (p. 622) Review the drugs dinoprostone, misoprostol, ergonovine and methylergonovine, and oxytocin from the drug class uterine stimulants. Discuss the actions, uses, and therapeutic outcomes of each. Review common and serious adverse effects and any known drug interactions, as well as oxytocin precautions.	SG Practice Questions for the NCLEX Examination 1-5, 11 (pp. 269-270) Review Questions for the NCLEX Examination 1, 3 (p. 631) ▸ Discuss the nursing procedures and concerns when administering uterine stimulants for the induction of labor. ▸ Discuss the nursing procedures and concerns when administering cervical ripening agents before the induction of labor. ▸ Discuss the nursing procedures and concerns when administering uterine stimulants for augmentation of labor. Class Activity ***Divide the class into four groups. Assign each group one of the four reasons why uterine stimulants are used. Have the students research and discuss the nursing concerns and actions for each reason. Have each group present its findings to the class. (For students to prepare for this activity, see Homework/ Assignment #2.)***
Compare the effects of uterine stimulants and uterine relaxants on a pregnant woman's uterus.	■ Drug therapy in pregnancy (p. 619) □ Drug class: Uterine stimulants (p. 619) □ Drug class: Uterine relaxants (p. 624) Review the drugs magnesium sulfate and terbutaline sulfate, their actions, uses, and therapeutic outcomes from the drug class uterine relaxants.	ARQ 2 SG Review Sheet questions 24, 28 (pp. 264-265) ▸ Discuss the effects of uterine stimulants and uterine relaxants on a pregnant woman's uterus. Class Activity ***Divide the class into two groups, one for stimulants and one for relaxants. Have each group prepare a quiz on its topic. Have the opposite group take the quiz in a set amount of time. Reconvene the class, and discuss the results.***
State the actions, primary uses, nursing assessments, and monitoring parameters for uterine stimulants, uterine relaxants, clomiphene citrate, magnesium sulfate, and $Rh_o(D)$ immune globulin.	■ Drug therapy in pregnancy (p. 619) □ Drug class: Uterine stimulants (p. 619) – Nursing process for dinoprostone (p. 620) – Nursing process for misoprostol (p. 621) – Nursing process for ergonovine and methylergonovine (p. 622) – Nursing process for oxytocin (p. 622)	PPT 19-22 ARQ 1, 3-4 TB Multiple Choice questions 1, 4-6, 11 INRQ 3-5, 14 CTQ 4 SG Review Sheet questions 16-17, 20, 25-27, 34-37 (pp. 263-265) SG Learning Activities questions 5, 11-14, 16-17, 20-25 (p. 268) SG Practice Questions for the NCLEX Examination 13-15 (p. 270)

OBJECTIVES	CONTENT	TEACHING RESOURCES
	□ Drug class: Uterine relaxants (p. 624) – Nursing process for magnesium sulfate (p. 624) – Nursing process for terbutaline (p. 626) □ Drug class: Other agents (p. 627) – Nursing process for clomiphene (p. 628) – Nursing process for $Rh_o(D)$ immune globulin (human) (p. 629) Discuss the common and serious adverse effects as well as any known drug interactions, and magnesium toxicity.	Review Questions for the NCLEX Examination 2, 4, 7 (p. 631) Clinical Landmine: Oxytocin Infusion (p. 623) Clinical Landmine: Magnesium Toxicity (p. 625) ▸ Discuss the actions, uses, dosages, route of administration, and therapeutic outcomes for uterine relaxants. ▸ Discuss the actions, uses, dosages, route of administration, and therapeutic outcomes for cervical ripening agents. ▸ Discuss the actions, uses, dosages, route of administration, and therapeutic outcomes for uterine stimulants ▸ Discuss the actions, uses, dosages, route of administration, and therapeutic outcomes for clomiphene citrate. ▸ Discuss the actions, uses, dosages, route of administration, and therapeutic outcomes for magnesium sulfate. ▸ Discuss the actions, uses, dosages, route of administration, and therapeutic outcomes for $Rh_o(D)$ immune globulin. Class Activity ***Divide the class into five groups, one for each drug class. Have each group research the actions, dosages, route of administration, primary uses, nursing assessments, and monitoring parameters for each class of drugs. Have a representative from each group present the group's findings to the class. (For students to prepare for this activity, see Homework/Assignment #1.)***

40.2 Homework/Assignments:

1. Divide the class into five groups, one for each drug class. Have each group research the actions, primary uses, dosages, route of administration, nursing assessments, and monitoring parameters for each class of drugs.
2. Divide the class into four groups. Assign each group one of the four reasons why uterine stimulants are used. Have the students research and discuss the nursing concerns and actions for each reason.

40.2 Instructor's Notes/Student Feedback:

LESSON 40.3

CRITICAL THINKING QUESTION

A patient is admitted to the labor-delivery unit for premature labor. The health care provider orders call for the infusion of terbutaline. What should you know about this drug and its effects on pulse and blood pressure?

Guidelines: Terbutaline is a bronchodilator that relaxes smooth muscles, arresting premature labor. When it is used for premature labor, hypotension can occur initially after the loading dose and at the start of the infusion. Therefore, the blood pressure and heart rate must be monitored. Obtain baseline vital signs, and repeat every 5 minutes thereafter until the patient is stable. Continuous fetal monitoring should occur. The infusion should be stopped if a heart rate of more than 120 beats/min is not decreased with fluid increase or rolling the patient on her left side. Terbutaline should not be used in women with known heart conditions.

OBJECTIVES	CONTENT	TEACHING RESOURCES
Cite the effects of adrenergic agents on beta-1 and beta-2 receptors, and then identify the relationship of these actions to the serious adverse effects when adrenergic agents are used to inhibit preterm labor.	– Nursing process for magnesium sulfate (p. 624) – Nursing process for terbutaline (p. 626)	PPT 19-20 SG Review Sheet questions 29-31 (p. 265) SG Learning Activities question 18 (p. 268) Box 40-1: Guidelines for Use of Terbutaline with Premature Labor (p. 626) ▸ Discuss the various types of uterine relaxants, including when each is used and potential adverse effects. Class Activity ***Divide the class into two groups. Have one group research the effects of the adrenergic agents and one group research the adverse effects. Each group will present the findings to the class and discuss the relationship between the two. (For students to prepare for this activity, see Homework/ Assignment #1.)***
Describe specific assessments needed before and during the use of terbutaline or magnesium sulfate.	– Nursing process for magnesium sulfate (p. 624) – Nursing process for terbutaline (p. 626)	PPT 19-20 INRQ 6-7 CTQ 2-3 SG Review Sheet questions 32-33, 38-45 (p. 266) SG Learning Activities question 8 (p. 268) SG Practice Questions for the NCLEX Examination 6, 12 (pp. 269-270) ▸ Discuss the nursing assessments required when administering terbutaline. ▸ Discuss the nursing assessments required when administering magnesium sulfate. Class Activity ***Divide the class into small groups, assigning each group one of the following uterine relaxants: terbutaline or***

OBJECTIVES	CONTENT	TEACHING RESOURCES
		magnesium sulfate. Ask them to identify the nursing assessment before and during the administration of the drug. Have each group present its results to the class. Have the class critique the results for any missed points.
Identify emergency supplies that should be available during magnesium sulfate therapy.	– Nursing process for magnesium sulfate (p. 624)	PPT 19 TB Multiple Choice questions 3, 9 SG Review Sheet question 46 (p. 267) SG Practice Question for the NCLEX Examination 7 (p. 269) Review Question for the NCLEX Examination 5 (p. 631) Clinical Landmine: Magnesium Toxicity (p. 625) ▸ Discuss magnesium toxicity and the antidote for magnesium toxicity. *Class Activity* ***As a class, discuss magnesium toxicity, including symptoms, monitoring and assessment, and treatment.***
Identify the action, specific dosage, administration precautions, and proper timing of the administration of $Rh_o(D)$ immune globulin and rubella vaccine.	– Nursing process for $Rh_o(D)$ immune globulin (human) (p. 629)	PPT 22 ARQ 5 TB Multiple Choice question 7 TB Multiple Response question 3 INRQ 8 CTQ 1 SG Review Sheet questions 6, 47-49 (pp. 261, 267) SG Learning Activities questions 3, 9 (p. 268) SG Practice Question for the NCLEX Examination 8 (p. 270) ▸ Discuss the nursing process for administering $Rh_o(D)$ immune globulin, including all situations in which it is required. ▸ Discuss the nursing process for the administration of the rubella vaccine. *Class Activity* ***Divide the class into four groups. Have each group develop patient teaching materials on the actions, specific dosage, administration precautions, and time for both immune globulin and rubella vaccines. Have each group present its materials to the class.***

OBJECTIVES	CONTENT	TEACHING RESOURCES
Summarize the immediate nursing care needs of the newborn following delivery.	□ Drug class: Other agents (p. 627) – Nursing process for erythromycin ophthalmic ointment (p. 629) – Nursing process for phytonadione (p. 630) Review assessment and care of the newborn. Review the drug erythromycin ophthalmic ointment used to prevent ophthalmia neonatorum, and phytonadione used to prevent vitamin K deficiency bleeding of the newborn. Discuss the action, use, and therapeutic outcome of each drug, and review common and serious adverse effects as well as administration precautions.	PPT 23-24 TB Multiple Choice question 8 INRQ 9-11 SG Review Sheet questions 12, 14, 16, 50-56 (pp. 263, 267) SG Learning Activities questions 15, 19 (p. 268) SG Practice Questions for the NCLEX Examination 9-10 (p. 270) Review Question for the NCLEX Examination 6 (p. 631) ▸ Discuss the purpose and administration of erythromycin ophthalmic ointment and phytonadione in newborns. *Class Activity* ***Invite a labor and delivery nurse to discuss and demonstrate the care of the newborn immediately following delivery. Include documentation of the administration of ophthalmic ointment and phytonadione.***
Performance evaluation		Test Bank SG Learning Activities (p. 268) SG Practice Questions for the NCLEX Examination (pp. 269-270) Critical Thinking Questions

40.3 Homework/Assignments:

1. Divide the class into two groups. Have one group research the effects of the adrenergic agents and one group research the adverse effects.

40.3 Instructor's Notes/Student Feedback:

40 Lecture Outline
Drugs Used in Obstetrics

Slide 1

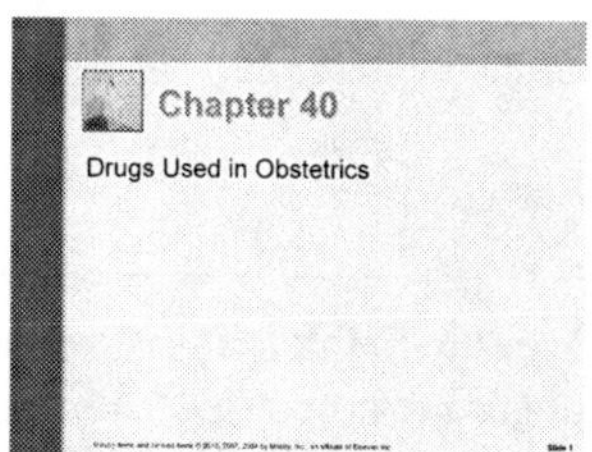
Chapter 40
Drugs Used in Obstetrics

Slide 2

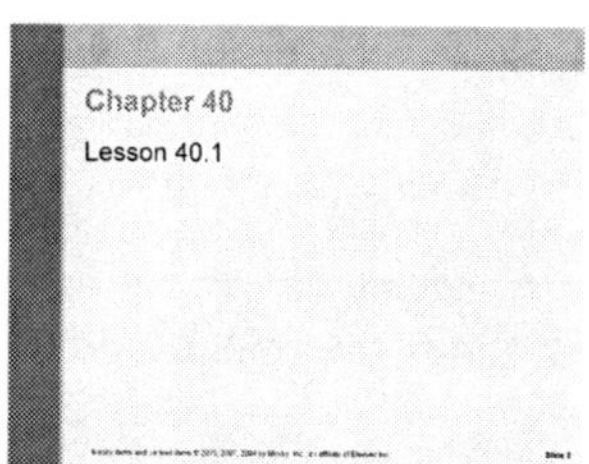
Chapter 40
Lesson 40.1

Slide 3

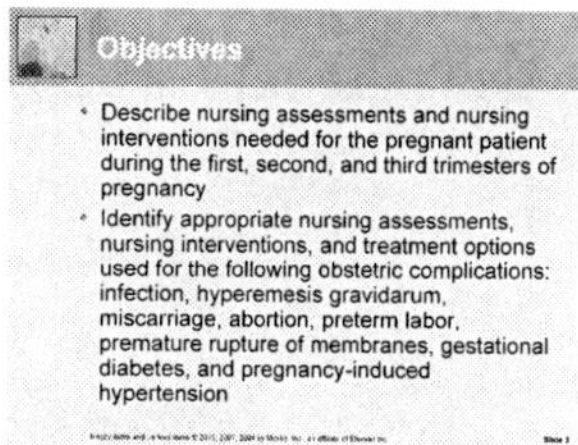
Objectives
Describe nursing assessments and nursing interventions needed for the pregnant patient during the first, second, and third trimesters of pregnancy
Identify appropriate nursing assessments, nursing interventions, and treatment options used for the following obstetric complications: infection, hyperemesis gravidarum, miscarriage, abortion, preterm labor, premature rupture of membranes, gestational diabetes, and pregnancy-induced hypertension

Slide 4

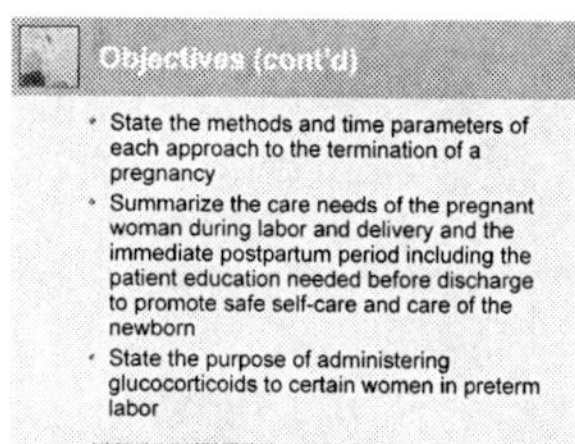
Objectives (cont'd)
State the methods and time parameters of each approach to the termination of a pregnancy
Summarize the care needs of the pregnant woman during labor and delivery and the immediate postpartum period including the patient education needed before discharge to promote safe self-care and care of the newborn
State the purpose of administering glucocorticoids to certain women in preterm labor

Slide 5

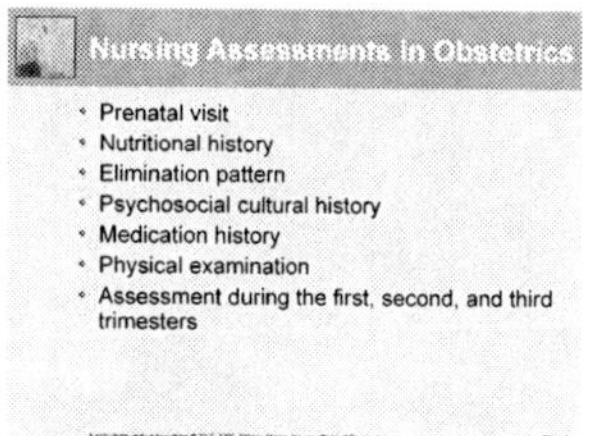
Nursing Assessments in Obstetrics
Prenatal visit
Nutritional history
Elimination pattern
Psychosocial cultural history
Medication history
Physical examination
Assessment during the first, second, and third trimesters

- Encourage patients to voice concerns about the physiologic changes of pregnancy.
- Be aware of cultural and family influences.
- Assess if the woman is accepting of the pregnancy.
- During subsequent assessments, look for signs of potential complications and preterm labor.

ELSEVIER

Slide 6

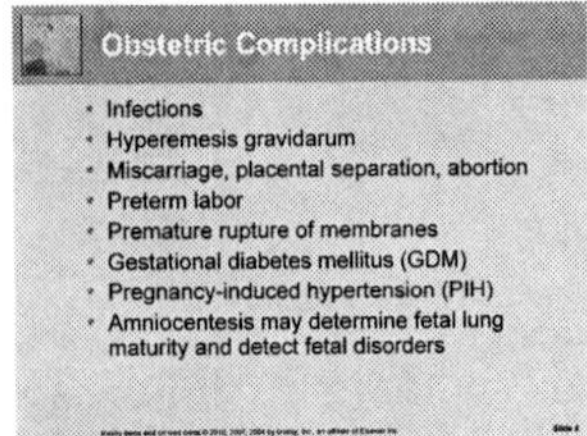
Obstetric Complications
Infections
Hyperemesis gravidarum
Miscarriage, placental separation, abortion
Preterm labor
Premature rupture of membranes
Gestational diabetes mellitus (GDM)
Pregnancy-induced hypertension (PIH)
Amniocentesis may determine fetal lung maturity and detect fetal disorders

- Most common infection is urinary tract infection.
- PIH includes pre-eclampsia and eclampsia.

Slide 7

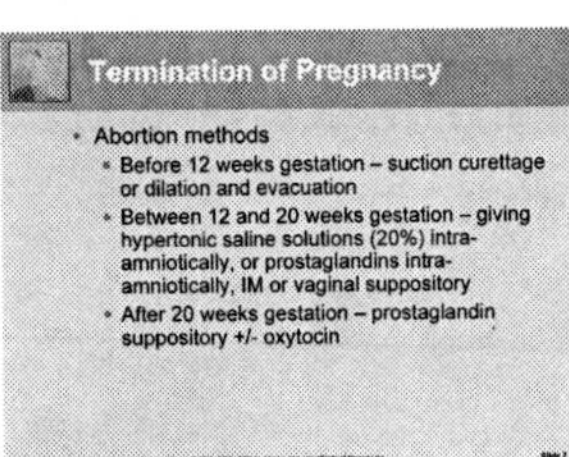
Termination of Pregnancy
Abortion methods
Before 12 weeks gestation – suction curettage or dilation and evacuation
Between 12 and 20 weeks gestation – giving hypertonic saline solutions (20%) intra-amniotically, or prostaglandins intra-amniotically, IM or vaginal suppository
After 20 weeks gestation – prostaglandin suppository +/- oxytocin

- Encourage talking about the feelings associated with the termination of a pregnancy; feelings of grief, sadness, or anger are common.
- Be alert to depression that may develop over the next few weeks.

Slide 8

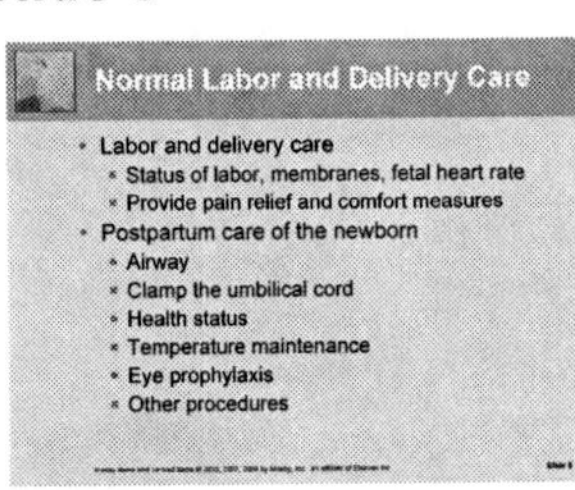
Normal Labor and Delivery Care
Labor and delivery care
Status of labor, membranes, fetal heart rate
Provide pain relief and comfort measures
Postpartum care of the newborn
Airway
Clamp the umbilical cord
Health status
Temperature maintenance
Eye prophylaxis
Other procedures

- Apgar scoring assesses the newborn's health status at 1 minute and 5 minutes after delivery.
- Always carry out interventions between contractions so the patient can use any prepared childbirth techniques.

Slide 9

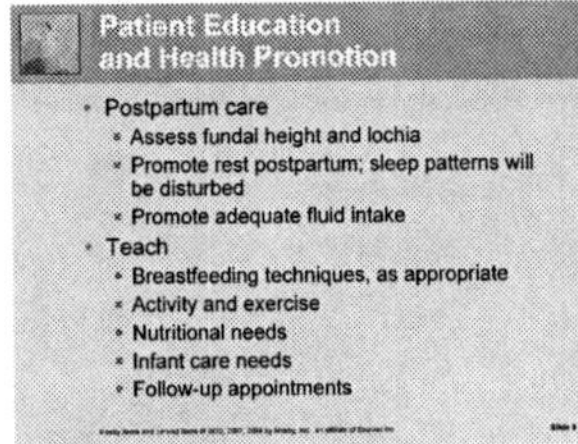
Patient Education and Health Promotion
Postpartum care
Assess fundal height and lochia
Promote rest postpartum; sleep patterns will be disturbed
Promote adequate fluid intake
Teach
Breastfeeding techniques, as appropriate
Activity and exercise
Nutritional needs
Infant care needs
Follow-up appointments

Slide 10

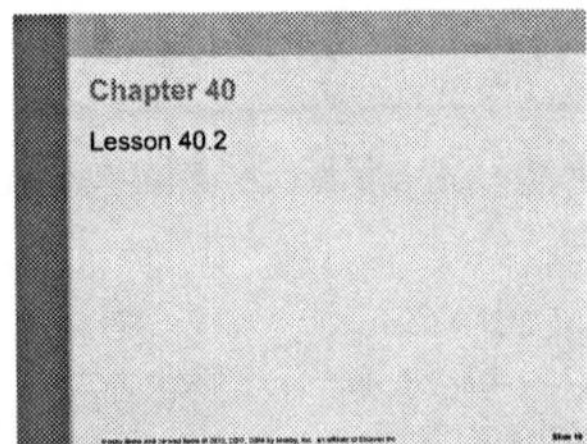
Chapter 40
Lesson 40.2

Slide 11

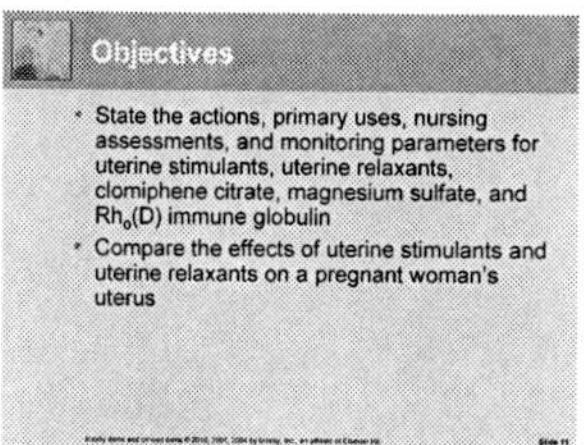
Objectives
State the actions, primary uses, nursing assessments, and monitoring parameters for uterine stimulants, uterine relaxants, clomiphene citrate, magnesium sulfate, and Rh_0(D) immune globulin
Compare the effects of uterine stimulants and uterine relaxants on a pregnant woman's uterus

Slide 12

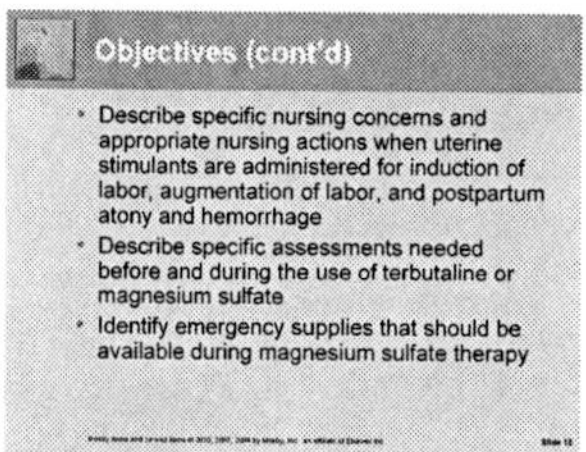
Objectives (cont'd)
Describe specific nursing concerns and appropriate nursing actions when uterine stimulants are administered for induction of labor, augmentation of labor, and postpartum atony and hemorrhage
Describe specific assessments needed before and during the use of terbutaline or magnesium sulfate
Identify emergency supplies that should be available during magnesium sulfate therapy

Slide 13

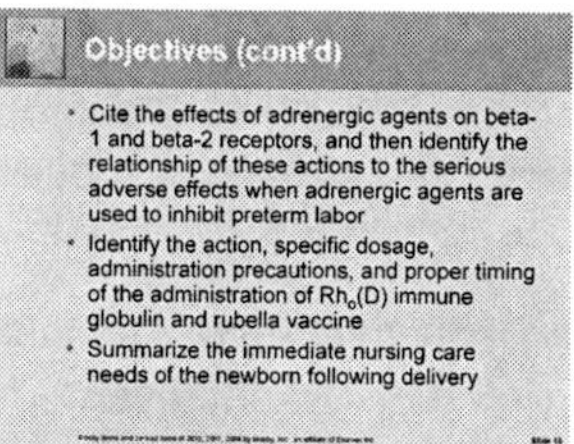
Objectives (cont'd)
Cite the effects of adrenergic agents on beta-1 and beta-2 receptors, and then identify the relationship of these actions to the serious adverse effects when adrenergic agents are used to inhibit preterm labor
Identify the action, specific dosage, administration precautions, and proper timing of the administration of Rh_0(D) immune globulin and rubella vaccine
Summarize the immediate nursing care needs of the newborn following delivery

Slide 14

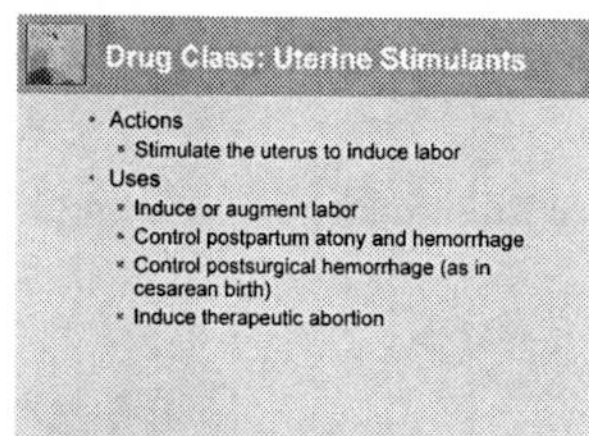
Drug Class: Uterine Stimulants
Actions
Stimulate the uterus to induce labor
Uses
Induce or augment labor
Control postpartum atony and hemorrhage
Control postsurgical hemorrhage (as in cesarean birth)
Induce therapeutic abortion

Slide 15

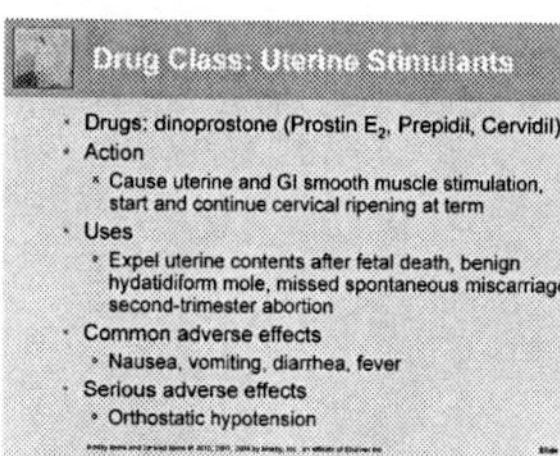
Drug Class: Uterine Stimulants
Drugs: dinoprostone (Prostin E_2, Prepidil, Cervidil)
Action
Cause uterine and GI smooth muscle stimulation, start and continue cervical ripening at term
Uses
Expel uterine contents after fetal death, benign hydatidiform mole, missed spontaneous miscarriage, second-trimester abortion
Common adverse effects
Nausea, vomiting, diarrhea, fever
Serious adverse effects
Orthostatic hypotension

- Available as vaginal suppository or gel applied to the cervix.
- Occasionally used in conjunction with oxytocin.
- Antiemetics and antidiarrheals are ordered PRN.

ELSEVIER

Slide 16

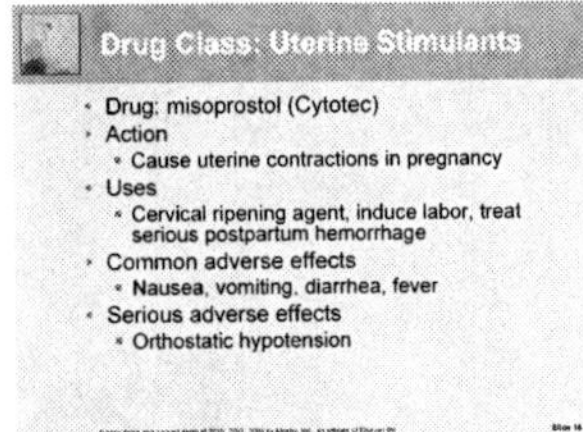
Drug Class: Uterine Stimulants
Drug: misoprostol (Cytotec)
Action
Cause uterine contractions in pregnancy
Uses
Cervical ripening agent, induce labor, treat serious postpartum hemorrhage
Common adverse effects
Nausea, vomiting, diarrhea, fever
Serious adverse effects
Orthostatic hypotension

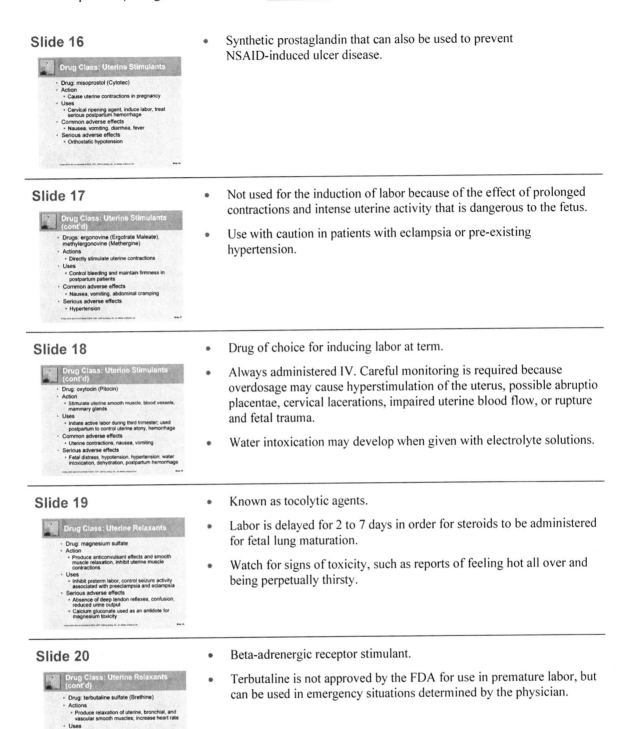

- Synthetic prostaglandin that can also be used to prevent NSAID-induced ulcer disease.

Slide 17

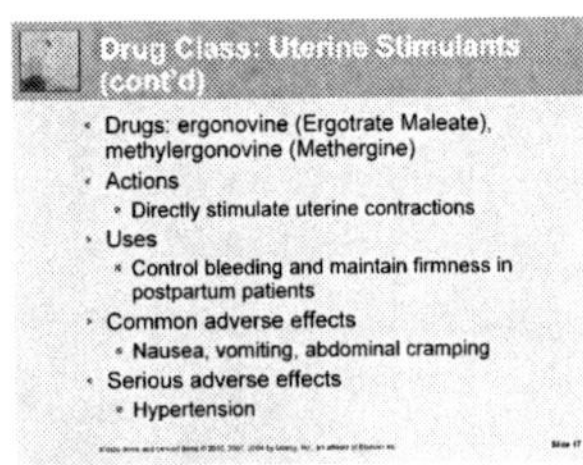
Drug Class: Uterine Stimulants (cont'd)
Drugs: ergonovine (Ergotrate Maleate), methylergonovine (Methergine)
Actions
Directly stimulate uterine contractions
Uses
Control bleeding and maintain firmness in postpartum patients
Common adverse effects
Nausea, vomiting, abdominal cramping
Serious adverse effects
Hypertension

- Not used for the induction of labor because of the effect of prolonged contractions and intense uterine activity that is dangerous to the fetus.
- Use with caution in patients with eclampsia or pre-existing hypertension.

Slide 18

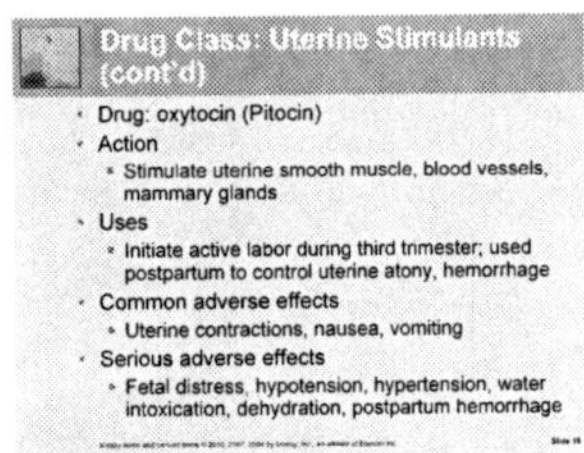
Drug Class: Uterine Stimulants (cont'd)
Drug: oxytocin (Pitocin)
Action
Stimulate uterine smooth muscle, blood vessels, mammary glands
Uses
Initiate active labor during third trimester; used postpartum to control uterine atony, hemorrhage
Common adverse effects
Uterine contractions, nausea, vomiting
Serious adverse effects
Fetal distress, hypotension, hypertension, water intoxication, dehydration, postpartum hemorrhage

- Drug of choice for inducing labor at term.
- Always administered IV. Careful monitoring is required because overdosage may cause hyperstimulation of the uterus, possible abruptio placentae, cervical lacerations, impaired uterine blood flow, or rupture and fetal trauma.
- Water intoxication may develop when given with electrolyte solutions.

Slide 19

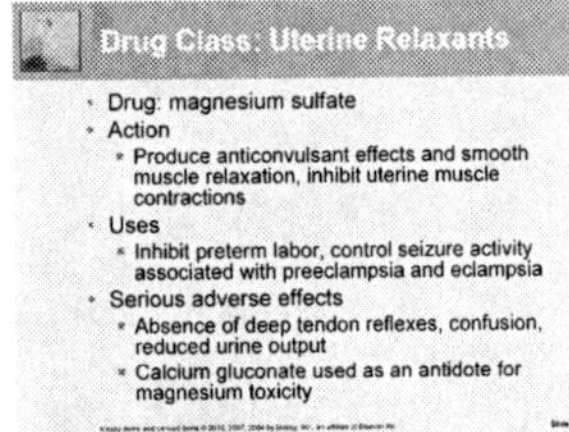
Drug Class: Uterine Relaxants
Drug: magnesium sulfate
Action
Produce anticonvulsant effects and smooth muscle relaxation, inhibit uterine muscle contractions
Uses
Inhibit preterm labor, control seizure activity associated with preeclampsia and eclampsia
Serious adverse effects
Absence of deep tendon reflexes, confusion, reduced urine output
Calcium gluconate used as an antidote for magnesium toxicity

- Known as tocolytic agents.
- Labor is delayed for 2 to 7 days in order for steroids to be administered for fetal lung maturation.
- Watch for signs of toxicity, such as reports of feeling hot all over and being perpetually thirsty.

Slide 20

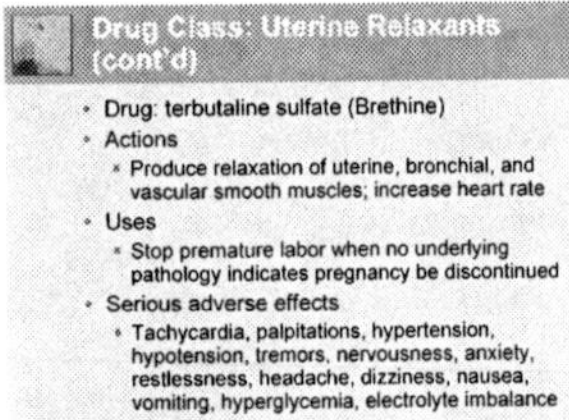
Drug Class: Uterine Relaxants (cont'd)
Drug: terbutaline sulfate (Brethine)
Actions
Produce relaxation of uterine, bronchial, and vascular smooth muscles; increase heart rate
Uses
Stop premature labor when no underlying pathology indicates pregnancy be discontinued
Serious adverse effects
Tachycardia, palpitations, hypertension, hypotension, tremors, nervousness, anxiety, restlessness, headache, dizziness, nausea, vomiting, hyperglycemia, electrolyte imbalance

- Beta-adrenergic receptor stimulant.
- Terbutaline is not approved by the FDA for use in premature labor, but can be used in emergency situations determined by the physician.

ELSEVIER

Slide 21

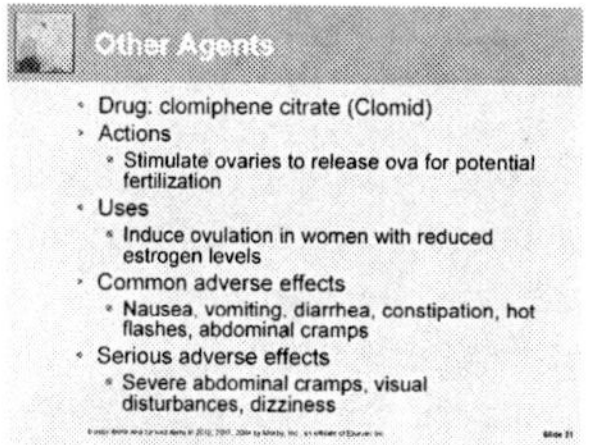
Other Agents
Drug: clomiphene citrate (Clomid)
Actions
Stimulate ovaries to release ova for potential fertilization
Uses
Induce ovulation in women with reduced estrogen levels
Common adverse effects
Nausea, vomiting, diarrhea, constipation, hot flashes, abdominal cramps
Serious adverse effects
Severe abdominal cramps, visual disturbances, dizziness

- Patients must have a complete physical examination to rule out other pathologic causes for lack of ovulation before initiating clomiphene therapy.
- Treatment raises the possibility of multiple fetuses.
- Intercourse timing is important to the therapy's success.

Slide 22

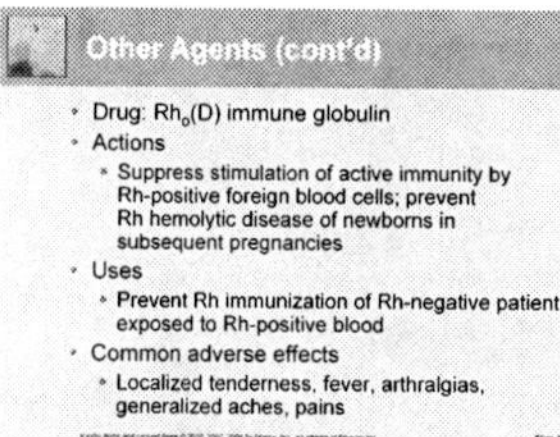
Other Agents (cont'd)
Drug: $Rh_o(D)$ immune globulin
Actions
Suppress stimulation of active immunity by Rh-positive foreign blood cells; prevent Rh hemolytic disease of newborns in subsequent pregnancies
Uses
Prevent Rh immunization of Rh-negative patient exposed to Rh-positive blood
Common adverse effects
Localized tenderness, fever, arthralgias, generalized aches, pains

- Brand names: RhoGAM, HyperRHO, WinRho, Rhophylac, MICRhoGAM.
- Also used to treat idiopathic thrombocytopenia purpura (ITP), diminished platelet count related to spontaneous destruction of platelets.
- Administered IM or IV, depending on which type of immune globulin used.
- Serious adverse effects: urticaria, tachycardia, hypotension.

Slide 23

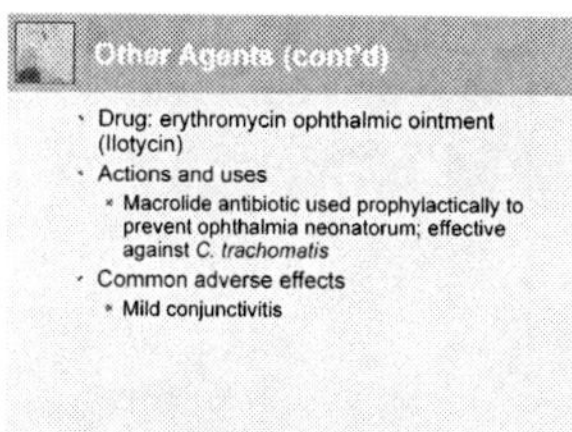
Other Agents (cont'd)
Drug: erythromycin ophthalmic ointment (Ilotycin)
Actions and uses
Macrolide antibiotic used prophylactically to prevent ophthalmia neonatorum; effective against *C. trachomatis*
Common adverse effects
Mild conjunctivitis

- A new tube of the medication should be started for each infant.
- Wash hands before administration to prevent bacterial contamination.
- DO NOT irrigate eyes after administration.

Slide 24

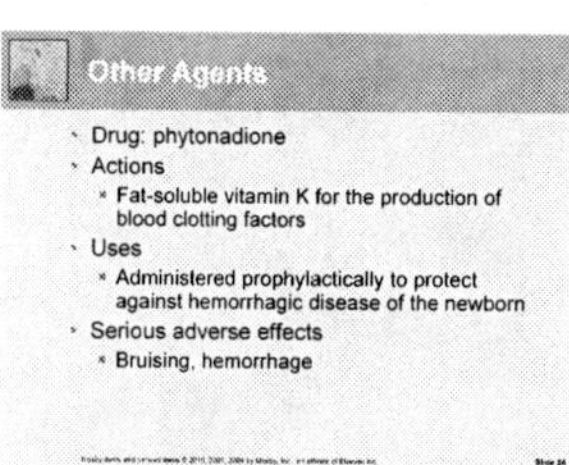
Other Agents
Drug: phytonadione
Actions
Fat-soluble vitamin K for the production of blood clotting factors
Uses
Administered prophylactically to protect against hemorrhagic disease of the newborn
Serious adverse effects
Bruising, hemorrhage

- Newborns are often deficient in vitamin K and clotting factors (referred to as vitamin K bleeding deficiency).
- There is no assessment required premedication.
- NEVER administer IV; ordered to be given IM.

41 Lesson Plan

Drugs Used in Men's and Women's Health

TEACHING FOCUS

In this chapter, students have an opportunity to understand vaginitis and the drug therapy for leukorrhea and genital infections. The nursing process for men's and women's health will be discussed, including patient education and health promotion. Students will have an opportunity to learn about drug therapy for contraception, including oral contraceptives, transdermal contraceptives, and intravaginal hormonal contraceptives. Drug therapy for benign prostatic hyperplasia (BPH) will be discussed, including alpha-1 adrenergic blocking agents and antiandrogen agents. Drug therapy for erectile dysfunction will also be discussed, including phosphodiesterase inhibitors.

MATERIALS AND RESOURCES

- ☐ computer PowerPoint projector (all Lessons)
- ☐ diagram of the female reproductive system (Lesson 41.1)
- ☐ drug reference book (all Lessons)
- ☐ female mannequin (Lesson 41.3)
- ☐ transdermal contraceptive device and an intravaginal contraceptive device (Lesson 41.3)

LESSON CHECKLIST

Preparations for this lesson include:

- lecture
- guest speaker: pharmacist
- evaluation of student knowledge and skills needed to perform all entry-level activities related to drugs used in men's and women's health, including understanding:
  - vaginitis
  - drug therapy for leukorrhea and genital infections
  - the nursing process for men's and women's health
  - patient education and health promotion
  - drug therapy for contraception
  - the drug class: oral contraceptives
  - the nursing process for oral contraceptives
  - the drug class: transdermal contraceptives
  - the nursing process for transdermal contraceptives
  - the drug class: intravaginal hormonal contraceptives
  - the nursing process for intravaginal hormonal contraceptives
  - drug therapy for BPH
  - the drug class: alpha-1 adrenergic blocking agents
  - the nursing process for tamsulosin
  - the drug class: antiandrogen agents
  - the nursing process for finasteride
  - drug therapy for erectile dysfunction
  - the drug class: alpha-1 phosphodiesterase inhibitors
  - the nursing process for sildenafil

KEY TERMS

dysmenorrhea (p. 638)
leukorrhea (p. 632)
sexually transmitted diseases (p. 632)

ADDITIONAL RESOURCES

PowerPoint slides: 1-20
Flashcards, Decks 1 and 2

Legend

ARQ	**PPT**	**TB**	**CTQ**	**SG**	**INRQ**
Audience Response Questions	PowerPoint Slides	Test Bank	Critical Thinking Questions	Study Guide	Interactive NCLEX Review Questions

Class Activities are indicated in ***bold italic.***

LESSON 41.1

BACKGROUND ASSESSMENT

Question: How do estrogens and progestins induce contraception?
Answer: Estrogens and progestins induce contraception by inhibiting ovulation. Estrogens block pituitary release of follicle-stimulating hormone (FSH), preventing the ovaries from developing a follicle from which the ovum is released. Progestins stop the release of luteinizing hormone (LH) from the pituitary gland. LH is the hormone that induces the release of an ovum from a follicle. Hormones also alter cervical mucus, which inhibits the migration of sperm, and change the endometrial wall, which impairs the fertilized ovum from implanting itself in it.

Question: What is vaginitis?
Answer: Vaginitis is a very common diagnosis for adult women and is a condition of the vagina characterized by burning, itching, swelling, infection, and abnormal discharge. Normal discharge is clear or milky and does not have an odor. Any change in the amount, color, or smell or any of the above signs or symptoms is usually a sign of imbalance of the healthy vaginal bacteria. It can also be caused by a virus. The most common organisms causing vaginitis are *Candida albicans*, *Trichomonas vaginalis*, and *Gardnerella vaginalis*. It can also develop as a secondary infection from the administration of certain antibiotics.

CRITICAL THINKING QUESTION

A 30-year-old woman has had vaginitis several times in the past 6 months. She is currently not sexually active and has negative test results for sexually transmitted diseases. She underwent dental work recently, and she must take antibiotics before dental visits because of a heart murmur. What suggestions might a nurse make about the prevention and treatment of further episodes of vaginitis?
Guidelines: The patient's episodes of vaginitis are probably triggered by antibiotic use and are secondary infections caused by the fungus *C. albicans*. The nurse should advise the patient to use an over-the-counter antifungal cream, ointment, or suppository during or following antibiotic use. The nurse should discuss hygiene tips with the patient, such as proper cleansing of the genital area, wiping from front to back after voiding and defecating, and avoiding synthetic underwear, deodorants, douches, and scented toilet paper and soaps. If, after following these steps, symptoms do not abate or worsen, the patient should be instructed to see a health care professional.

OBJECTIVES	CONTENT	TEACHING RESOURCES
Identify common organisms known to cause leukorrhea.	■ Vaginitis (p. 632) Review the term *vaginitis*—an abnormal vaginal discharge—and its underlying causes, such as infectious and noninfectious reasons. Discuss the common organisms that cause vaginitis, including sexually transmitted diseases.	PPT 5 TB Multiple Choice question 1 SG Review Sheet questions 1-3 (p. 271) SG Learning Activities question 1 (p. 274) Table 41-1: Causes of Vaginal Discharge (p. 633) ▸ Discuss the most common organisms causing the infectious type of leukorrhea including *C. albicans*, *T. vaginalis*, and *G. vaginalis*. ▸ Discuss the physiologic and noninfectious causes of leukorrhea. Class Activity ***Have two students role-play the nurse educating a patient who has reported vaginitis. Have the class assist the "nurse" with explaining to the "patient" common causes of vaginitis and treatment options. Review the exercise with the class.***
Cite the generic and brand names of products used to treat *Candida albicans*, *Trichomonas vaginalis*, and *Gardnerella vaginalis*.	■ Vaginitis (p. 632) ■ Drug therapy for leukorrhea and genital infections (p. 632)	PPT 5 Review Questions for the NCLEX Examination 1-2 (p. 654) Drug Table 41-2: Causative Organisms and Products Used to Treat Genital Infections (p. 634) ▸ Discuss the drugs used to treat *C. albicans*, *T. vaginalis*, and *G. vaginalis*, discussing both the generic and brand names. ▸ Discuss the pros and cons of some of the popular drugs used to treat these organisms. Be sure to include Flagyl and Diflucan. Class Activity ***Divide the class into four groups, and assign each group two products used to treat* C. albicans, T. vaginalis, *and* G. vaginalis. *Have the students look up the products in a drug reference book. Have one student from each group go to a pharmacy and request information regarding that group's two products. Have each group compare the information from the pharmacy (which is given to patients) with the information in the drug reference book, and report the findings to the class. (For students to prepare for this activity, see Homework/Assignment 1.)***
Discuss specific interviewing techniques that can be used to	– Nursing process for men's and women's health (p. 632)	PPT 6-7 TB Multiple Response question 3

OBJECTIVES	CONTENT	TEACHING RESOURCES
obtain a history of sexual activity.		SG Review Sheet questions 4-5 (p. 271) ▸ Discuss the role of a nurse in obtaining a history of sexual activity from patients. ▸ Discuss the psychosocial considerations when asking patients about their sexual history. Class Activity ***Prepare slips of paper describing patients in different age-groups: adolescents, young adults, middle-aged adults, and older adults. Divide the class into four groups, and give each group one of the slips. Have each group write a sexual history questionnaire for its assigned age-group. Then have members of each group role-play a nurse interviewing a patient using the questionnaire for the class. Have the class critique the interviews.***
Review specific techniques for administering vaginal medications.	– Patient education and health promotion (p. 636)	PPT 8 TB Multiple Response question 1 SG Review Sheet question 8 (p. 271) ▸ Discuss the proper way to apply medications topically or intravaginally using ointments, troches, or suppositories. ▸ Discuss 1-day, 3-day, and 7-day vaginal medications. Class Activity ***Using a diagram of the female reproductive system, have students describe the proper way to apply vaginal medications.***
Develop a plan for teaching self-care to women and men with sexually transmitted diseases. Include personal hygiene measures, medication administration, methods of pain relief, and prevention of spread of infection or reinfection.	– Patient education and health promotion (p. 636)	PPT 8-9 CTQ 2 SG Review Sheet questions 6-7, 9 (p. 271) SG Learning Activities questions 11-12 (p. 274) Box 41-1: Sexually Transmitted Diseases (p. 633) Clinical Landmine: Limitations of Condoms in Preventing STDs (p. 636) ▸ Discuss the health self-care instructions for women with sexually transmitted diseases. ▸ Discuss the health self-care instructions for men with sexually transmitted diseases. Class Activity ***Divide the class into four groups. Assign each group one of the following: personal hygiene, medication administration, pain relief, or prevention of spread of infection. Have each group create a self-care***

OBJECTIVES	CONTENT	TEACHING RESOURCES
		teaching plan and then perform role plays of a nurse teaching a patient. Then have each group present its plan to the class. Lead the class in combining them into one complete self-care teaching plan.

41.1 Homework/Assignments:
1. Divide the class into four groups. Assign each group two products used to treat *C. albicans*, *T. vaginalis*, and *G. vaginalis*. Have the students look up the products in the drug reference book. Have one student from each group go to a pharmacy and request information regarding that group's two products. Have each group compare the information from the pharmacy, which is given to patients, with the information in the drug reference book, and report the findings to the class.

41.1 Instructor's Notes/Student Feedback:

LESSON 41.2

CRITICAL THINKING QUESTION

A nurse is giving instructions to a 19-year-old woman who has just been given a prescription for combination oral contraceptives. What will the nurse instruct her about missing any pills?

Guidelines: If the patient misses one pill, she should take it as soon as she remembers it, and then take the next pill at the regularly scheduled time. If two pills are missed, the patient should take two pills as soon as she remembers and two the next day. When two pills are missed, spotting may occur. Until the present pack of pills is finished, another form of birth control should be used. If the patient misses three or more pills, another form of birth control must be used immediately. A new pack of pills should be started the next Sunday, even if the patient is menstruating. After missing three or more pills, another form of birth control should be used through the next month. The patient probably will not get pregnant after missing one pill, but she should still use another form of birth control. With missing two or more pills, there is a real possibility of becoming pregnant. If there are any questions, the patient should call her health care provider.

OBJECTIVES	CONTENT	TEACHING RESOURCES
Compare the active ingredients in the two types of oral contraceptive agents.	■ Drug therapy for contraception (p. 637) □ Drug class: Oral contraceptives (p. 637) – Nursing process for oral contraceptives (p. 638) Review the most common forms of artificial birth control used today. Discuss the age range for women who can safely use oral contraception.	PPT 13-14 TB Multiple Choice question 2 CTQ 4 SG Review Sheet question 10 (p. 271) Review Question for the NCLEX Examination 8 (p. 654) Drug Table 41-3: Monophasic Oral Contraceptives (pp. 639-640) Drug Table 41-4: Biphasic Oral Contraceptives (p. 641)

ELSEVIER

OBJECTIVES	CONTENT	TEACHING RESOURCES
	Review the drug class oral contraceptives, their actions, uses, and therapeutic outcomes. Discuss oral contraceptives in terms of common and serious adverse effects, as well as drug interactions. Review patient education important to cover when a woman forgets to take a pill.	Drug Table 41-5: Triphasic and Progestin-Only Oral Contraceptives (pp. 642-643) ▸ Discuss the active ingredients of the combination pill and compare with Seasonale. ▸ Discuss the active ingredients of the minipill. Class Activity ***Divide the class into three groups. Using a drug reference book, have one group research the combination pill, the second group research Seasonale, and the third group research the minipill. Make sure each group knows the active ingredients in its assigned pill. Then have each group explain to the class what it has just learned, stating a central concept in just a few sentences.***
Differentiate between the actions and the benefits of the combination pill and the minipill.	□ Drug class: Oral contraceptives (p. 637) – Nursing process for oral contraceptives (p. 638)	PPT 14 ARQ 1 TB Multiple Choice questions 3, 9 SG Review Sheet question 11 (p. 271) SG Learning Activities question 15 (p. 274) Review Question for the NCLEX Examination 3 (p. 654) ▸ Discuss the actions and benefits of the combination pill. ▸ Discuss the actions and benefits of the minipill. Class Activity ***Divide the class into two groups. Using Internet resources, have half the class research the pill and the other half the minipill. Then stage a debate in class regarding the benefits and risks of each. Have students take notes during the debate and write a one-page summary. (For students to prepare for this activity, see Homework/Assignment #1.)***
Describe the major adverse effects and contraindications to the use of oral contraceptive agents.	□ Drug class: Oral contraceptives (p. 637) – Nursing process for oral contraceptives (p. 638)	TB Multiple Choice question 4 INRQ 5, 8 SG Review Sheet questions 12-13, 16 (p. 272) SG Learning Activities questions 2-3, 13 (p. 274) Review Question for the NCLEX Examination 7 (p. 654) Herbal Interactions: St. John's Wort (p. 644)

OBJECTIVES	CONTENT	TEACHING RESOURCES
		▸ Discuss the major adverse effects and contraindications of the combination pill. ▸ Discuss the advantages of Seasonale. ▸ Discuss the major adverse effects and contraindications of the minipill. Class Activity ***Assign an adverse effect or contraindication of oral contraceptives to each student. Have the students research a published article that highlights their assigned contraindication or adverse effect, summarize the article, and present their findings to the class.***
Develop specific patient education plans to be used to teach a patient to initiate oral contraceptive therapy with the combination pill and the minipill.	– Nursing process for oral contraceptives (p. 638)	PPT 13-14 ARQ 2 TB Multiple Response questions 2, 4 INRQ 4 CTQ 1 SG Review Sheet questions 14-15 (p. 272) SG Learning Activities question 14 (p. 274) SG Practice Question for the NCLEX Examination 5 (p. 276) ▸ Discuss the nursing process to teach a patient to use the combination pill. ▸ Discuss the nursing process to teach a patient to use the minipill. Class Activity ***Have each student develop an education plan for patient teaching—half the class for the combination pill and half for the minipill. Have selected students present their plans in class for discussion.***

41.2 Homework/Assignments:

1. Divide the class into two groups. Using the Internet, have half the class research the pill and the other half the minipill. Have a debate in class regarding the benefits and risks of each. Have students take notes during the debate and write a one-page summary.

41.2 Instructor's Notes/Student Feedback:

LESSON 41.3

CRITICAL THINKING QUESTION

A patient has been diagnosed with BPH. During the assessment, he comments that he does not want to get prostate cancer from BPH, and he hopes the medicine that the health care provider prescribes will keep him from getting it. How should the nurse respond?

Guidelines: BPH, or enlarged prostate, is common in males older than 50 years. The condition affects more than half of men in their 60s and almost 90% in their 70s. As part of the male reproductive system, the prostate gland, secretes a fluid that is discharged with sperm. The gland lies just below the neck of the bladder and surrounds the proximal urethra. Many men will need treatment because problems with urination often accompany BPH. BPH is much more common than prostate cancer, but an enlarged prostate can be caused by prostate cancer. The signs and symptoms of both are often the same. One drug that could be prescribed is tamsulosin, which is used to reduce mild to moderate manifestations of urinary obstruction. It does not reduce prostate size. The other drug, finasteride, is used to treat symptoms associated with BPH, reduce the risks associated with urine retention, and minimize the need for surgery. The patient should be encouraged to ask questions. Make sure that he understands the difference between BPH and prostate cancer.

OBJECTIVES	CONTENT	TEACHING RESOURCES
Identify the patient teaching necessary with the administration of the transdermal contraceptive and the intravaginal hormonal contraceptive.	□ Drug class: Transdermal contraceptives (p. 644) – Nursing process for transdermal contraceptives (p. 644) □ Drug class: Intravaginal hormonal contraceptive (p. 646) – Nursing process for intravaginal hormonal contraceptive (p. 646) Review the drug class transdermal contraceptives, their actions, uses, and therapeutic outcomes. Discuss the drugs in terms of common and serious adverse effects, as well as drug interactions. Review the instructions given to women who forget to change the patch. Review the drug class intravaginal hormonal contraceptives, their actions, uses, and therapeutic outcomes. Discuss the drugs in terms of common and serious adverse effects, as well as drug interactions. Review patient education given to women on the proper use of the ring and what to do if a woman forgets to change the ring.	PPT 15-16 ARQ 3 INRQ 1, 6, 9 SG Review Sheet questions 17-21 (p. 272) SG Practice Questions for the NCLEX Examination 1, 8 (pp. 275-276) Review Questions for the NCLEX Examination 5, 6 (p. 654) ▸ Discuss the nursing process to teach a patient to use transdermal contraception. ▸ Discuss the nursing process to teach a patient to use the intravaginal hormonal contraceptive. Class Activity ***Using a female mannequin, demonstrate to the class how to apply a transdermal contraceptive device and how to insert an intravaginal contraceptive device. Then have the students take turns practicing the medication administration using a mannequin.***

OBJECTIVES	CONTENT	TEACHING RESOURCES
Describe pharmacologic treatments of benign prostatic hyperplasia.	■ Drug therapy for benign prostatic hyperplasia (p. 648) □ Drug class: Alpha-1 adrenergic blocking agents (p. 648) – Nursing process for alpha-1 blocking agents (p. 649) □ Drug class: Antiandrogen agents (p. 649) – Nursing process for dutasteride (p. 650) – Nursing process for finasteride (p. 651) Review the normal function and secretions of the prostate gland. Discuss the condition benign prostatic hyperplasia (BPH).	PPT 17-19 ARQ 4 TB Multiple Choice questions 5, 7 TB Multiple Response question 5 INRQ 3, 7 10 SG Review Sheet questions 22-25 (pp. 272-273) SG Learning Activities questions 4, 8-9 (p. 274) SG Practice Questions for the NCLEX Examination 4, 9 (pp. 275-276) Review Question for the NCLEX Examination 9 (p. 654) Table 41-6: Symptoms of Benign Prostatic Hyperplasia (p. 648) Drug Table 41-7: Alpha-1 Blocking Agents (p. 649) ▸ Discuss alpha-1 adrenergic blocking agents in the treatment of BPH. ▸ Discuss antiandrogen agents in the treatment of BPH. Class Activity ***Divide the class into two groups, one for tamsulosin and one for finasteride. Have each group research its assigned drug in a drug reference book and write a one-page paper that summarizes its actions, expected outcomes, and nursing interventions. Have the groups present their findings to the class.*** Class Activity ***List on the board the following: prostatic antibacterial factor (PAF), acid phosphatase, and prostate-specific antigen (PSA). Have students volunteer to explain what each term refers to in relation to the normal functioning of the prostate gland. Review the exercise with the class.***
Describe the pharmacologic treatment of erectile dysfunction.	■ Drug therapy for erectile dysfunction (p. 651) □ Drug class: Phosphodiesterase inhibitors (p. 651) – Nursing process for phosphodiesterase inhibitors (p. 652) Review the condition erectile dysfunction (ED) and common causes of the condition	PPT 20 ARQ 5 TB Multiple Choice questions 6, 8 INRQ 2 CTQ 3 SG Review Sheet questions 26-28 (p. 273) SG Learning Activities questions 5, 7-8, 16 (p. 274)

ELSEVIER

OBJECTIVES	CONTENT	TEACHING RESOURCES
	(psychological, physiologic, and medications), as well as treatment options for ED. Review the drug class phosphodiesterase inhibitors, their actions, uses (for ED and pulmonary arterial hypertension), and therapeutic outcomes. Discuss the drugs in terms of common and serious adverse effects, as well as drug interactions.	SG Practice Questions for the NCLEX Examination 6-7, 10 (p. 276) Review Question for the NCLEX Examination 4 (p. 654) Table 41-8: Drugs that May Cause Erectile Dysfunction (p. 652) Drug Table 41-9: Phosphodiesterase Inhibitors Used for Erectile Dysfunction (p. 653) ▸ Discuss phosphodiesterase inhibitors in the treatment of erectile dysfunction. ▸ Discuss the adverse effects of sildenafil and drug interactions. Class Activity ***Invite a pharmacist to class to discuss the pharmacologic treatment of erectile dysfunction, including sildenafil and recently released drug treatments. Have students prepare a list of questions in advance.*** Class Activity ***Have two students role-play the nurse educating a patient taking sildenafil from the drug class phosphodiesterase inhibitors for ED. Have the class assist the "nurse" in determining what is important to discuss with the "patient." Discuss therapeutic outcomes and common and serious adverse effects, as well as drug interactions for phosphodiesterase inhibitors. Review the exercise with the class.***
Performance evaluation		Test Bank SG Learning Activities (p. 274) SG Practice Questions for the NCLEX Examination (pp. 275-276) Critical Thinking Questions

41.3 Homework/Assignments:

41.3 Instructor's Notes/Student Feedback:

41 Lecture Outline

Drugs Used in Men's and Women's Health

Slide 1

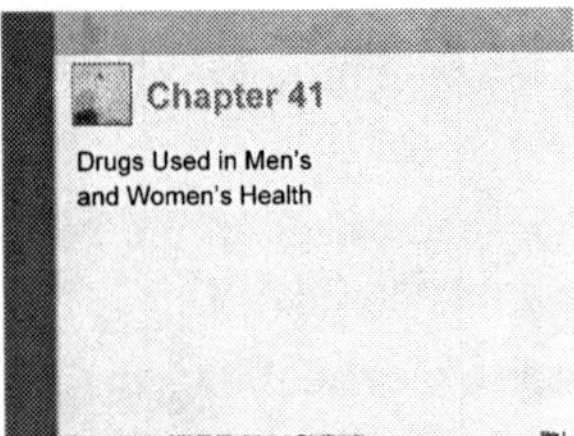
Chapter 41
Drugs Used in Men's and Women's Health

Slide 2

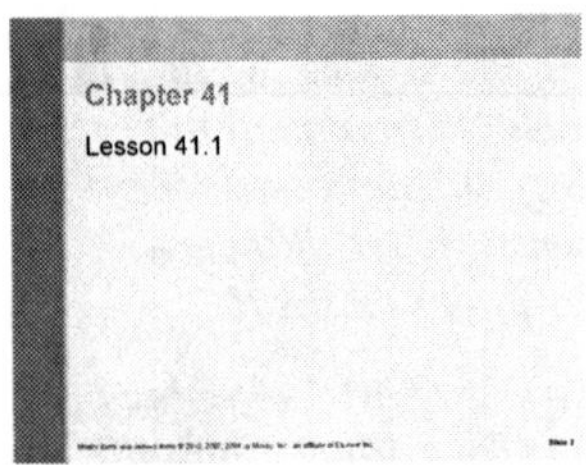
Chapter 41
Lesson 41.1

Slide 3

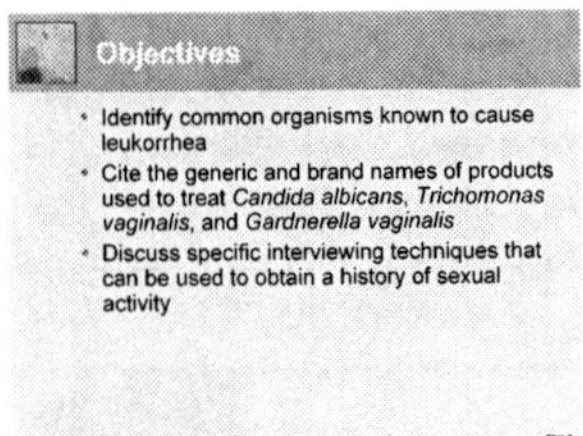
Objectives
Identify common organisms known to cause leukorrhea
Cite the generic and brand names of products used to treat Candida albicans, Trichomonas vaginalis, and Gardnerella vaginalis
Discuss specific interviewing techniques that can be used to obtain a history of sexual activity

Slide 4

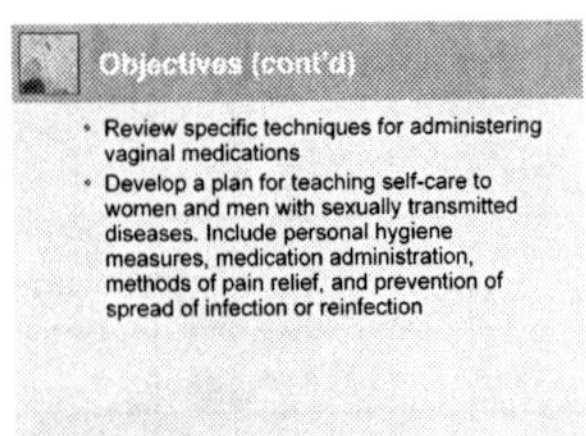
Objectives (cont'd)
Review specific techniques for administering vaginal medications
Develop a plan for teaching self-care to women and men with sexually transmitted diseases. Include personal hygiene measures, medication administration, methods of pain relief, and prevention of spread of infection or reinfection

Slide 5

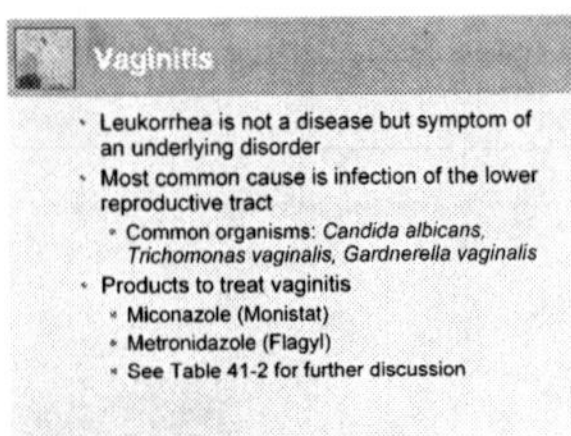
Vaginitis
Leukorrhea is not a disease but symptom of an underlying disorder
Most common cause is infection of the lower reproductive tract
Common organisms: Candida albicans, Trichomonas vaginalis, Gardnerella vaginalis
Products to treat vaginitis
Miconazole (Monistat)
Metronidazole (Flagyl)
See Table 41-2 for further discussion

- For specific drugs, see Table 41-2.
- Secretions from the vagina usually represent a normal physiologic process.
- Secondary infection may develop after the use of broad-spectrum antibiotics.

Slide 6

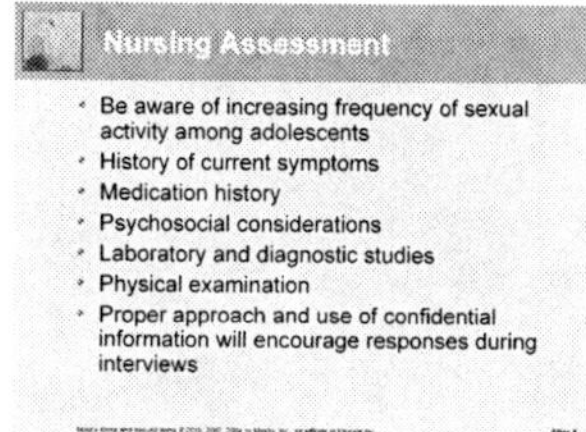
Nursing Assessment
Be aware of increasing frequency of sexual activity among adolescents
History of current symptoms
Medication history
Psychosocial considerations
Laboratory and diagnostic studies
Physical examination
Proper approach and use of confidential information will encourage responses during interviews

- Advocate safe sex and abstinence for adolescents.
- Be aware of state laws related to providing care for minors as relates to STDs and contraception.

Slide 7

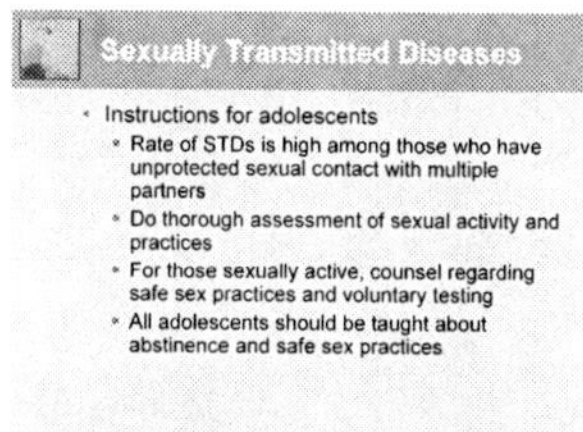
Sexually Transmitted Diseases
Instructions for adolescents
Rate of STDs is high among those who have unprotected sexual contact with multiple partners
Do thorough assessment of sexual activity and practices
For those sexually active, counsel regarding safe sex practices and voluntary testing
All adolescents should be taught about abstinence and safe sex practices

- STDs can exist without exhibiting symptoms.
- Must parental consent be obtained before teens receive medical care for STDs? *(No)*
- Must parental consent be obtained before teens receive testing and counseling for HIV? *(Varies from state to state)*

Slide 8

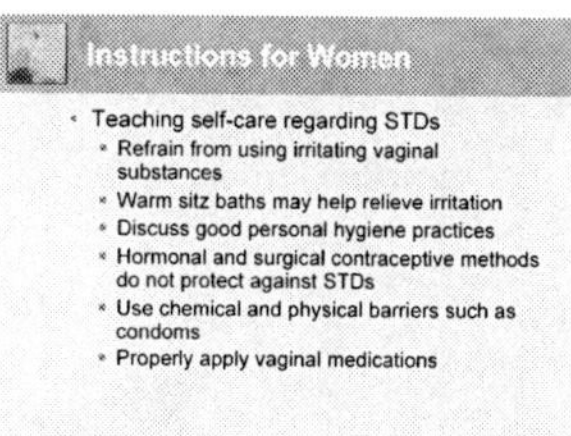
Instructions for Women
Teaching self-care regarding STDs
Refrain from using irritating vaginal substances
Warm sitz baths may help relieve irritation
Discuss good personal hygiene practices
Hormonal and surgical contraceptive methods do not protect against STDs
Use chemical and physical barriers such as condoms
Properly apply vaginal medications

- Keep cultural and religious beliefs of patients in mind.

Slide 9

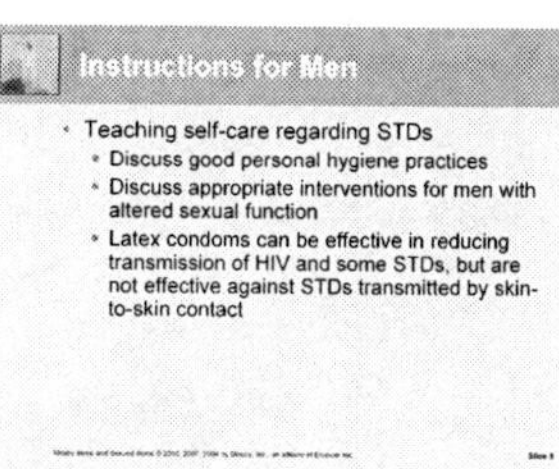
Instructions for Men
Teaching self-care regarding STDs
Discuss good personal hygiene practices
Discuss appropriate interventions for men with altered sexual function
Latex condoms can be effective in reducing transmission of HIV and some STDs, but are not effective against STDs transmitted by skin-to-skin contact

- Abstain from sex when any infections are present.
- Encourage patients diagnosed with an STD to persuade partners to be examined and tested promptly.

Slide 10

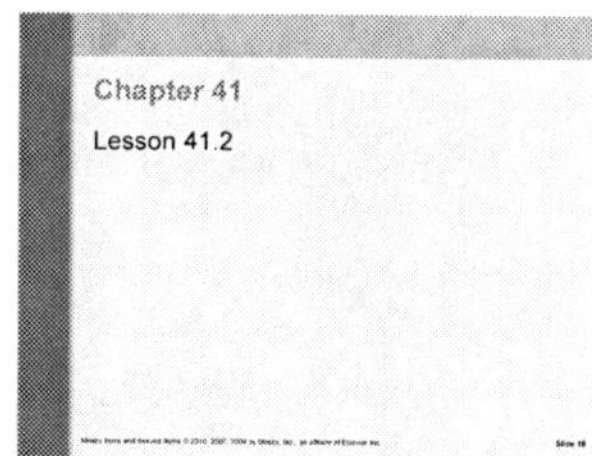
Chapter 41
Lesson 41.2

ELSEVIER

Slide 11

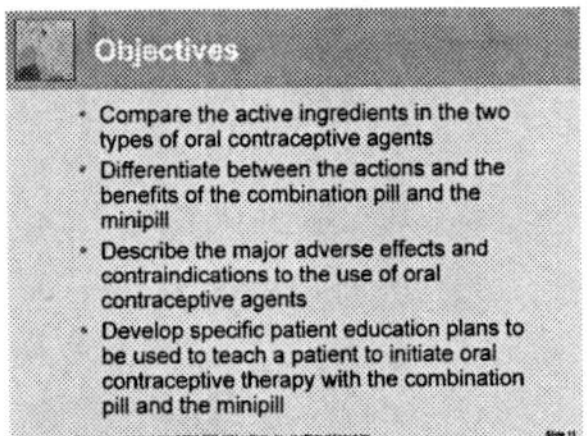
Objectives
Compare the active ingredients in the two types of oral contraceptive agents
Differentiate between the actions and the benefits of the combination pill and the minipill
Describe the major adverse effects and contraindications to the use of oral contraceptive agents
Develop specific patient education plans to be used to teach a patient to initiate oral contraceptive therapy with the combination pill and the minipill

Slide 12

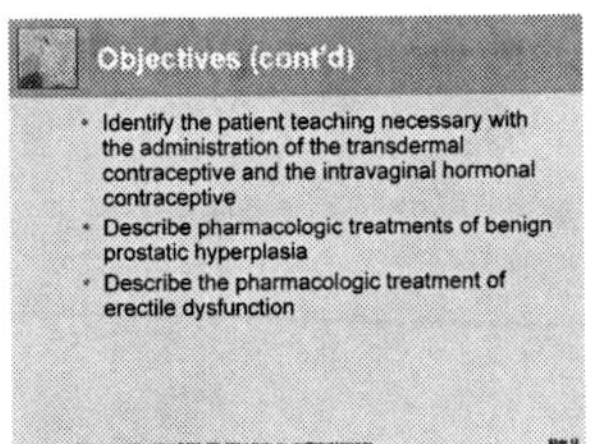
Objectives (cont'd)
Identify the patient teaching necessary with the administration of the transdermal contraceptive and the intravaginal hormonal contraceptive
Describe pharmacologic treatments of benign prostatic hyperplasia
Describe the pharmacologic treatment of erectile dysfunction

Slide 13

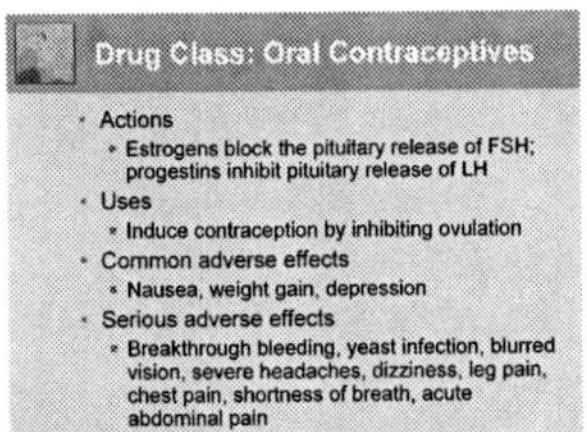
Drug Class: Oral Contraceptives
Actions
Estrogens block the pituitary release of FSH; progestins inhibit pituitary release of LH
Uses
Induce contraception by inhibiting ovulation
Common adverse effects
Nausea, weight gain, depression
Serious adverse effects
Breakthrough bleeding, yeast infection, blurred vision, severe headaches, dizziness, leg pain, chest pain, shortness of breath, acute abdominal pain

Slide 14

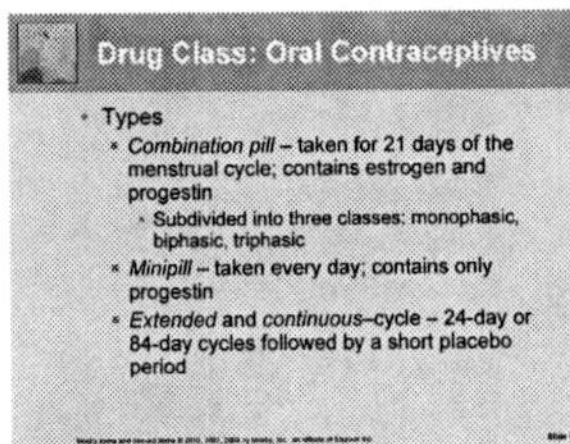
Drug Class: Oral Contraceptives
Types
Combination pill – taken for 21 days of the menstrual cycle; contains estrogen and progestin
Subdivided into three classes: monophasic, biphasic, triphasic
Minipill – taken every day; contains only progestin
Extended and continuous-cycle – 24-day or 84-day cycles followed by a short placebo period

- For specific drugs, see Tables 41-3, 41-4, and 41-5.
- Ensure a complete physical exam before starting oral contraceptives.

Slide 15

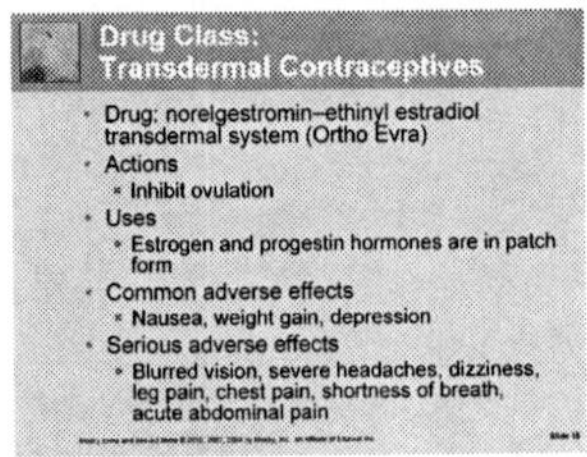
Drug Class: Transdermal Contraceptives
Drug: norelgestromin–ethinyl estradiol transdermal system (Ortho Evra)
Actions
Inhibit ovulation
Uses
Estrogen and progestin hormones are in patch form
Common adverse effects
Nausea, weight gain, depression
Serious adverse effects
Blurred vision, severe headaches, dizziness, leg pain, chest pain, shortness of breath, acute abdominal pain

- Apply weekly for 3 weeks. During the fourth week, no patch is worn and menses should begin.
- The FDA warned that increased estrogen exposure of the patch (compared to the minipill) may increase the risk of blood clots.

Slide 16

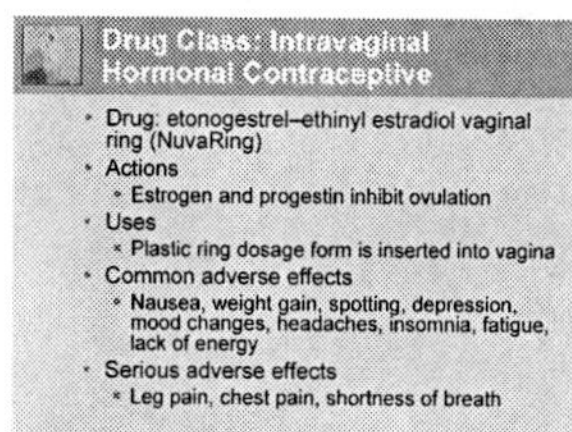
Drug Class: Intravaginal Hormonal Contraceptive
Drug: etonogestrel–ethinyl estradiol vaginal ring (NuvaRing)
Actions
Estrogen and progestin inhibit ovulation
Uses
Plastic ring dosage form is inserted into vagina
Common adverse effects
Nausea, weight gain, spotting, depression, mood changes, headaches, insomnia, fatigue, lack of energy
Serious adverse effects
Leg pain, chest pain, shortness of breath

- Inserted into the vagina for 3 weeks; removed for a 1-week period and menses should begin.

Slide 17

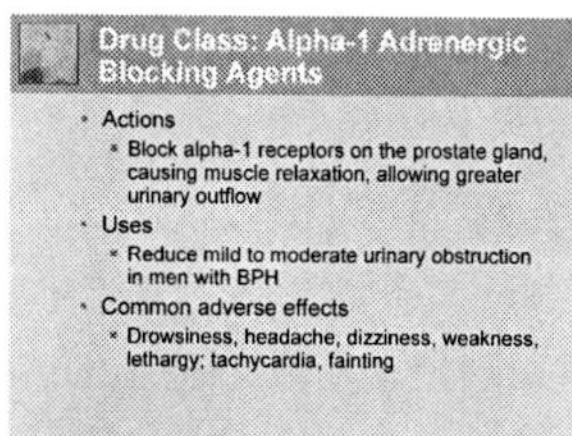
Drug Class: Alpha-1 Adrenergic Blocking Agents
Actions
Block alpha-1 receptors on the prostate gland, causing muscle relaxation, allowing greater urinary outflow
Uses
Reduce mild to moderate urinary obstruction in men with BPH
Common adverse effects
Drowsiness, headache, dizziness, weakness, lethargy; tachycardia, fainting

- For specific drugs, see Table 41-7.
- BPH does not cause prostate cancer but can be a symptom.
- BPH is much more common than prostate cancer.
- Alpha-1 blocking agents do not reduce prostate size or inhibit testosterone synthesis.

Slide 18

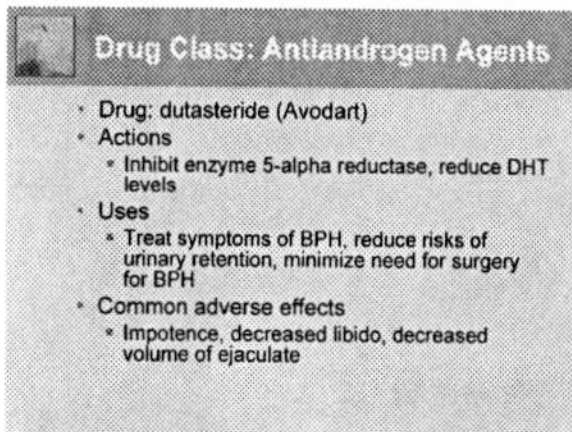
Drug Class: Antiandrogen Agents
Drug: dutasteride (Avodart)
Actions
Inhibit enzyme 5-alpha reductase, reduce DHT levels
Uses
Treat symptoms of BPH, reduce risks of urinary retention, minimize need for surgery for BPH
Common adverse effects
Impotence, decreased libido, decreased volume of ejaculate

Slide 19

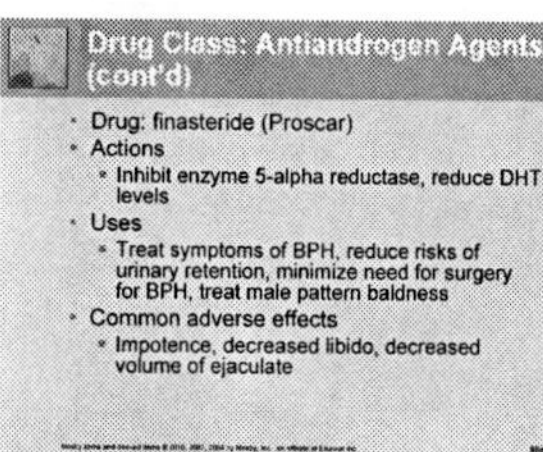
Drug Class: Antiandrogen Agents (cont'd)
Drug: finasteride (Proscar)
Actions
Inhibit enzyme 5-alpha reductase, reduce DHT levels
Uses
Treat symptoms of BPH, reduce risks of urinary retention, minimize need for surgery for BPH, treat male pattern baldness
Common adverse effects
Impotence, decreased libido, decreased volume of ejaculate

- Elevated DHT levels induce male pattern baldness.
- Finasteride causes a decrease in serum PSA levels by about 50% in patients with BPH.
- Always investigate sustained increased PSA levels while the patient is receiving finasteride.

Slide 20

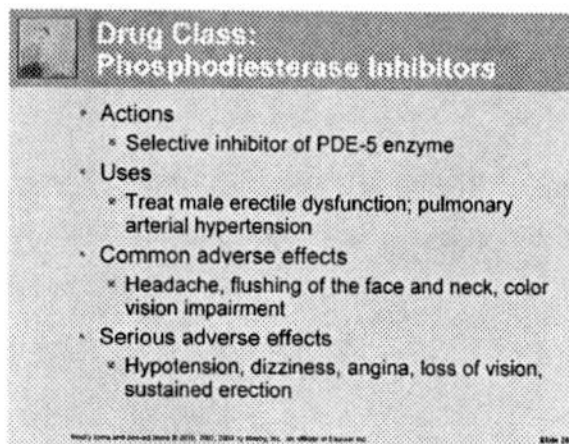
Drug Class: Phosphodiesterase Inhibitors
Actions
Selective inhibitor of PDE-5 enzyme
Uses
Treat male erectile dysfunction; pulmonary arterial hypertension
Common adverse effects
Headache, flushing of the face and neck, color vision impairment
Serious adverse effects
Hypotension, dizziness, angina, loss of vision, sustained erection

- For specific drugs, see Table 41-9.
- Nitrates are contraindicated because they can potentially cause hypotension and dysrhythmias.
- Erection is highly variable; sexual stimulation is required for an erection.
- Not an aphrodisiac; does not increase sexual desire or stimulation.

42 Lesson Plan

Drugs Used to Treat Disorders of the Urinary System

TEACHING FOCUS

In this chapter, the student will be introduced to conditions affecting the urinary systems—more specifically, urinary tract infections. Additionally, the student will have the opportunity to learn the types of drugs used to treat these disorders and patient teaching to prevent further urinary tract infections.

MATERIALS AND RESOURCES

- ☐ computer and PowerPoint projector (all Lessons)
- ☐ diagram of the anatomy of the urinary system (male and female) (Lesson 42.1)
- ☐ examples of patient urinalysis reports with and without urinary tract infections (Lesson42.3)
- ☐ drug reference book (all Lessons)

LESSON CHECKLIST

Preparations for this lesson include:

- lecture
- demonstration
- evaluation of student knowledge and skills needed to perform all entry-level activities related to treatment of urinary disorders, including:
  - assessing for knowledge of conditions relating to the urinary system
  - evaluating proper skills for care and treatment of patients diagnosed with urinary tract infections
  - assessing for the proper development of teaching plans for patients diagnosed with urinary tract infections

KEY TERMS

acidification (p. 658)
cystitis (p. 655)
frequency (p. 662)
incontinence (p. 662)
nocturia (p. 663)
overactive bladder (OAB) syndrome (p. 663)
prostatitis (p. 655)
pyelonephritis (p. 655)
urethritis (p. 655)
urge incontinence (p. 663)
urgency (p. 662)
urinary antispasmodic agents (p. 663)

ADDITIONAL RESOURCES

PowerPoint slides: 1-19
Flashcards, Decks 1 and 2

Legend

ARQ	**PPT**	**TB**	**CTQ**	**SG**	**INRQ**
Audience Response Questions	PowerPoint Slides	Test Bank	Critical Thinking Questions	Study Guide	Interactive NCLEX Review Questions

Class Activities are indicated in ***bold italic.***

LESSON 42.1

BACKGROUND ASSESSMENT

Question: What are some important nursing assessments and interventions associated with drug therapy for the treatment of diseases of the urinary system?
Answer: It is important that the nurse always assess voiding characteristics, such as frequency, amount, and color, regardless of the drug prescribed. Common interventions include increased fluid intake, evaluation of adverse effects, and administration of medication. For patients who are taking various medications, it is important to note adverse reactions and possible drug interactions.

Question: Identify the importance of a nursing assessment for the patient with signs and symptoms of a urinary tract infection. What tests are used to determine urinary tract infections?
Answer: The information the nurse gains through assessment of the patient's clinical signs and symptoms is very important for detection and initiation of proper care. A thorough medical history, including any history of urinary tract infections or current symptoms, is essential. Older patients might exhibit changes in mental status with urinary tract infections. Other patients will show signs and symptoms, such as burning, frequency of urination, fever and chills, and general malaise. The best determinant for urinary tract infections is a urinalysis and urine culture obtained by sterile midstream urination. A urinalysis is a physical, chemical, and microscopic examination of the urine. Other tests that can determine urinary tract infections include a complete blood count, cystoscopy, and kidney function test.

CRITICAL THINKING QUESTION

An 85-year-old female patient was transferred from a nursing home with new onset of neurologic changes of confusion. She has an indwelling Foley catheter for incontinence. Her urine is yellow, with some sediment. She has a history of atrial fibrillation that is well controlled and a history of peptic ulcer disease (PUD). What nursing assessment should be the first one performed? Which tests are likely to be ordered by the health care provider? What will be included in the discharge teaching plan regarding medications and other treatments?
Guidelines: The first assessment should be to obtain a complete history. As a result of the patient's confusion, the nurse will need to contact the patient's family and the nursing home staff to obtain a more detailed history. The patient should have baseline vital signs taken, especially temperature, and should be assessed for signs and symptoms of chills, malaise, and dehydration. Because the patient has a Foley catheter, a sterile specimen should be obtained and sent for urinalysis and culture. If the result of the urinalysis is positive for a urinary tract infection, the Foley catheter should be removed because it can be the source of the infection. The patient will likely be started on antibiotics during the wait for the culture report identifying the organism and drug sensitivity. In terms of nursing interventions, it will be necessary to administer fluids and keep an accurate record of the I&O. The patient will be using diapers for incontinence, so skin care is essential. As part of the discharge plan, the nurse should relay to the nursing home staff the need for continued monitoring of signs and symptoms of urinary tract infection, medication orders, drug interactions, continued hydration, I&O, monitoring of mental status, skin care, and repeat urine culture after antibiotics are completed.

OBJECTIVES	CONTENT	TEACHING RESOURCES
Develop a health teaching plan for an individual who has repeated urinary tract infections.	■ Urinary tract infections (p. 655) – Nursing process for urinary system disease (p. 656) – Patient education and health promotion (p. 658) Review the different types of urinary tract infections: pyelonephritis, cystitis, prostatitis, and urethritis. Discuss the common organisms associated with urinary	PPT 4-5 CTQ 1 SG Review Sheet questions 1-4, 6, 8 (p. 277) SG Learning Activities questions 5, 14-15, 18 (p. 280) SG Practice Question for the NCLEX Examination 6 (p. 281) Lifespan Considerations: Urinary Tract Infections (p. 656)

OBJECTIVES	CONTENT	TEACHING RESOURCES
	tract infections. Review the nursing process in terms of how to manage patients with urinary tract infections.	▸ Discuss a diagram of the urinary tract system for males and females. ▸ Discuss why an indwelling urinary catheter is removed when a patient is diagnosed with a urinary tract infection. ▸ Discuss the rationale for identifying the bacterial organism causing a urinary tract infection. How is this information obtained? Discuss common bacteria found in the urinary tract. Class Activity ***Divide the class into three groups, and assign each group one of the following scenarios:*** ***– A 23-year-old woman who is sexually active*** ***– A 50-year-old woman who is 2 weeks postsurgery after bladder repair because of urinary incontinence*** ***– A sexually active 63-year-old man with a history of urinary tract infections and prostatitis*** ***Have students identify a patient teaching plan to prevent urinary tract infections.***
Analyze Table 42-1 and identify specific portions of a urinalysis report that would indicate proteinuria, dehydration, infection, or renal disease.	– Nursing process for urinary system disease (p. 656) – Patient education and health promotion (p. 658)	SG Review Sheet question 5 (p. 277) SG Learning Activities question 1 (p. 280) Table 42-1: Urinalysis (p. 657) ▸ Discuss the importance of and the method of collecting urine samples properly. Class Activity ***Divide the class into small groups, and have them list the tests that are conducted for a urinalysis. Students should provide the range of normal values for each test and indicate what abnormally high or low levels might indicate.*** Class Activity ***Lead a discussion of Table 42-1. Then distribute urinalysis reports to the class to review and determine whether there is an infection or not.***

42.1 Homework/Assignments:

42.1 Instructor's Notes/Student Feedback:

LESSON 42.2

CRITICAL THINKING QUESTION

A 50-year-old man comes to the emergency department with complaints of burning and pain on urination and states that he has frequent episodes of nocturia. The health care provider orders a routine urinalysis to rule out urinary tract infection. Aside from a urinary tract infection, what other possible causes might account for the patient's signs and symptoms? What other signs and symptoms would be seen on assessment? What should the nurse recommend after discharge from the emergency room?

Guidelines: If a urinalysis is normal, it is important to look at other diseases or infections that could cause the patient to experience these symptoms. Considering the patient's age and a complaint of nocturia, it is most likely that the patient has prostatitis. After being medicated for pain, the patient should be instructed to follow up immediately with his attending health care provider for a complete physical examination, including checking his prostate gland and medication adverse effects.

OBJECTIVES	CONTENT	TEACHING RESOURCES
Identify essential components involved in planning patient education that will enhance compliance with the treatment regimen.	– Patient education and health promotion (p. 658) Discuss patient education and health promotion measures important to review for comfort and prevention of recurrence of infection.	PPT 6 INRQ 5 Patient Self-Assessment Form: Urinary Antibiotics ▸ Discuss important items to address in a teaching plan for a patient diagnosed with a urinary tract infection. List these on the board. ▸ Discuss the nurse's role in educating women to prevent future occurrences of a urinary tract infection. ▸ Discuss how and why phenazopyridine hydrochloride turns urine a reddish-orange color. Class Activity ***Have student pairs take turns role-playing a nurse providing education to a patient. Have the nurse identify specific steps the patient can take to implement care. The***

OBJECTIVES	CONTENT	TEACHING RESOURCES
		nurse should consider outcomes that demonstrate compliance and identify approaches to enhance patient compliance.
Explain the major action and effects of drugs used to treat disorders of the urinary tract.	■ Drug therapy for urinary tract infections (p. 658) □ Urinary antimicrobial agents (p. 658) Review the drug therapy used for treatment of urinary tract infections. Discuss the actions and uses of antimicrobial agents as well as the need to know whether the infection is acute, chronic, complicated, or uncomplicated.	PPT 11 INRQ 2-4 CTQ 2 Animation: Antibiotics SG Review Sheet questions 9, 11-12, 25-28, 31-32 (pp. 277-279) SG Learning Activities questions 2, 3, 6, 8, 16, 17, 19, 20 (p. 280) ▸ Name and discuss the action, uses, dosage, and administration of antimicrobial agents to treat urinary tract infections. Write this information on the board. Class Activity ***List the drugs used to treat urinary tract infections. Ask students to describe the actions and major adverse effects of each drug. What assessments should the nurse perform for a patient taking the drug?*** Class Activity ***Divide the class into four groups, and assign each group one of the following antimicrobial agents:*** – ***Fosfomycin*** – ***Norfloxacin*** – ***Methenamine mandelate*** – ***Nitrofurantoin*** ***Have each group prepare a chart that outlines the information discussed and other pertinent information for its assigned antimicrobial agent and present its findings to the class.***

42.2 Homework/Assignments:

42.2 Instructor's Notes/Student Feedback:

LESSON 42.3

CRITICAL THINKING QUESTION

A 17-year-old girl is diagnosed with cystitis and a urinary tract infection. The nurse recommends that the patient increase fluid intake along with taking her prescribed Pyridium. What type of patient teaching should the nurse provide regarding Pyridium?

Guidelines: The nurse should first talk with the patient and her parents regarding the causes of urinary tract infections and the greater occurrence in females than males. The nurse should explain to the patient and parents that Pyridium is an agent used to produce a local anesthetic effect on the mucosa of the ureters and bladder, which relieves some of the burning, pain, urinary frequency, and urgency. It acts within 30 to 45 minutes after taking it. The nurse should alert the patient not to be alarmed if she notices a reddish-orange color to her urine; this is a usual effect of Pyridium. In addition, the health care provider will prescribe another medication to treat the infection.

OBJECTIVES	CONTENT	TEACHING RESOURCES
Prepare a chart of antimicrobial agents used to treat urinary tract infections. Give the drug names, the organisms treated, and special considerations (e.g., the need for acidic urine, changes in urine color, and effect on urine tests).	■ Drug therapy for urinary tract infections (p. 658) □ Urinary antimicrobial agents (p. 658)	SG Review Sheet questions 7, 10, 12-24 (pp. 277-278) SG Learning Activities questions 4, 6-7, 9, 11, 13 (p. 280) ▸ Discuss and identify the brand names for the following medications: cinoxacin, fosfomycin, norfloxacin, methenamine mandelate, nitrofurantoin, and nalidixic acid. ▸ Discuss why fluid intake is important for a patient diagnosed with a urinary tract infection. Class Activity ***Ask students to list both generic and brand names of each drug and the recommended adult doses. What factors affect selection of a specific drug? What factors affect the duration of treatment?*** Class Activity ***Develop an input-output sheet for a patient on urinary tract infection medications (for the duration of the course of medications). Why is it important for the patient taking antimicrobial agents to have adequate fluid intake? What is the minimum urinary output that should be targeted?***
Identify baseline data that the nurse should collect on a continuous basis for comparison and evaluation of drug effectiveness.	□ Drug class: Fosfomycin antibiotics (p. 659) – Nursing process for fosfomycin (p. 659) □ Drug class: Quinolone antibiotics (p. 659) – Nursing process for quinolones (p. 660) Review the drug fosfomycin from the drug class fosfomycin antibiotics. Discuss the action, use,	PPT 11-13 CTQ 2 SG Review Sheet question 10 (p. 277) ▸ Discuss the importance of the nurse's role in assessing the patient diagnosed with a urinary tract infection, including recording characteristics of the urine, such as the frequency, amount, color, and odor of urine, and whether the patient experiences urgency, burning, or pain during urination.

OBJECTIVES	CONTENT	TEACHING RESOURCES
	and therapeutic outcome of this drug as a single-dose treatment for urinary tract infections caused by *Escherichia coli*. Review common and serious adverse effects as well as the known drug interactions. Review the drug class quinolone antibiotics, their actions, uses, and therapeutic outcomes for use in treatment of urinary tract infections. Discuss the common and serious adverse effects as well as known drug interactions.	Class Activity ***Have student pairs take turns performing a premedication assessment for a patient with a urinary tract disorder.***
Identify important nursing assessments and interventions associated with the drug therapy and treatment of diseases of the urinary system.	□ Drug class: Fosfomycin antibiotics (p. 659) – Nursing process for fosfomycin (p. 659) □ Drug class: Quinolone antibiotics (p. 659) – Nursing process for quinolones (p. 660) □ Drug class: Other urinary antibacterial agents (p. 661) – Nursing process for methenamine mandelate (p. 661) – Nursing process for nitrofurantoin (p. 662)	PPT 12-15 INRQ 7 SG Review Sheet questions 7, 15, 18-23, 29 (pp. 277-279) SG Learning Activities questions 4, 6-7, 9, 15 (p. 280) SG Practice Questions for the NCLEX Examination 1, 2, 9 (pp. 281-282) Review Questions for the NCLEX Examination 2-6 (pp. 666-667) Drug Table 42-2: Quinolone Urinary Antibiotics (p. 660) ▸ Discuss the rationale that corroborates that cinoxacin and nalidixic acid are ineffective to treat *Pseudomonas* species. Class Activity ***Ask students to list all adverse reactions for the antimicrobial agents presented. Discuss appropriate nursing assessments for patients taking these agents.***
Identify the symptoms, treatment, and medication used for overactive bladder syndrome.	■ Drug therapy for overactive bladder syndrome (p. 662) □ Drug class: Anticholinergic agents for overactive bladder syndrome (p. 663) – Nursing process for urinary anticholinergic agents (p. 663) ■ Miscellaneous urinary agents (p. 665) – Nursing process for bethanechol (p. 665)	PPT 16-19 INRQ 6, 8-12 SG Review Sheet questions 30-32 (p. 279) SG Learning Activities questions 2, 8, 10-14 (p. 280) SG Practice Question for the NCLEX Examination 3-5, 7, 8, 10-12 (pp. 281-282) Review Questions for the NCLEX Examination 1, 7-10 (pp. 666-667)

OBJECTIVES	CONTENT	TEACHING RESOURCES
	– Nursing process for neostigmine (p. 665) – Nursing process for phenazopyridine (p. 666) Review what is meant by the term *overactive bladder syndrome* (OAB). Define the following terms: frequency, urgency, incontinence, urge incontinence, and nocturia. Discuss the difference between OAB wet and OAB dry. Review first-line pharmacologic treatment for OAB.	▸ Explain the symptoms and pharmacologic treatment of overactive bladder syndrome. ▸ Discuss and name the actions, uses, organisms treated, dosage, and administration of drugs used to treat overactive bladder syndrome. Class Activity ***Have students list interventions that would assist a patient who has overactive bladder syndrome.***
Performance evaluation		Test Bank SG Learning Activities (p. 280) SG Practice Questions for the NCLEX Examination (pp. 281-282) Critical Thinking Questions

42.3 Homework/Assignments:

42.3 Instructor's Notes/Student Feedback:

42

Lecture Outline

Drugs Used to Treat Disorders of the Urinary System

Slide 1

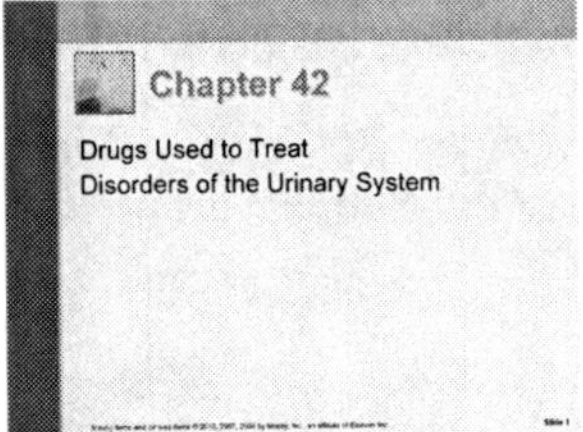
Chapter 42
Drugs Used to Treat
Disorders of the Urinary System

Slide 2

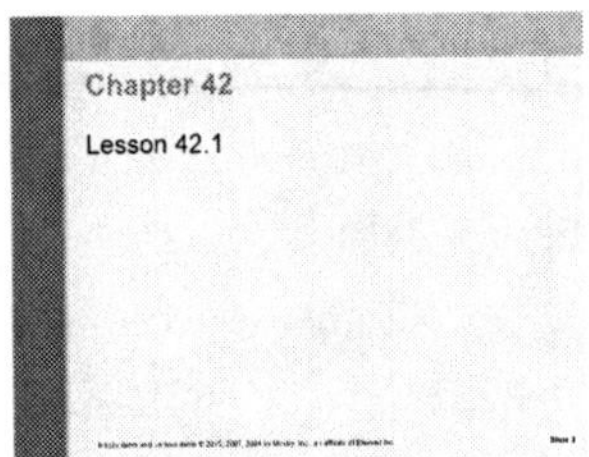
Chapter 42
Lesson 42.1

Slide 3

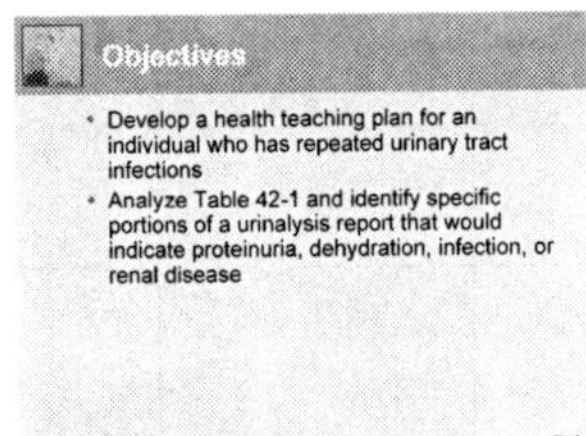
Objectives
Develop a health teaching plan for an individual who has repeated urinary tract infections
Analyze Table 42-1 and identify specific portions of a urinalysis report that would indicate proteinuria, dehydration, infection, or renal disease

Slide 4

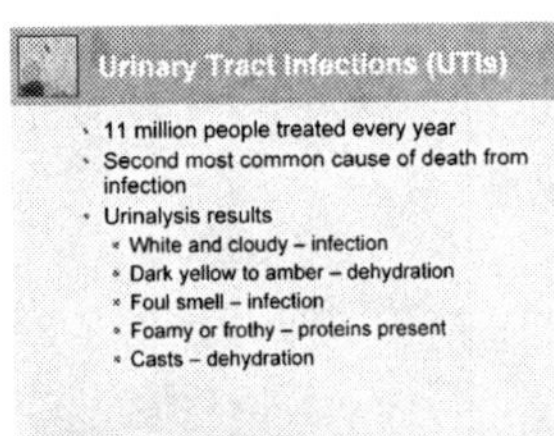
Urinary Tract Infections (UTIs)
11 million people treated every year
Second most common cause of death from infection
Urinalysis results
White and cloudy – infection
Dark yellow to amber – dehydration
Foul smell – infection
Foamy or frothy – proteins present
Casts – dehydration

- Women are 10 times more likely to get UTIs than men.
- First sign of UTI in older adult is confusion.

Slide 5

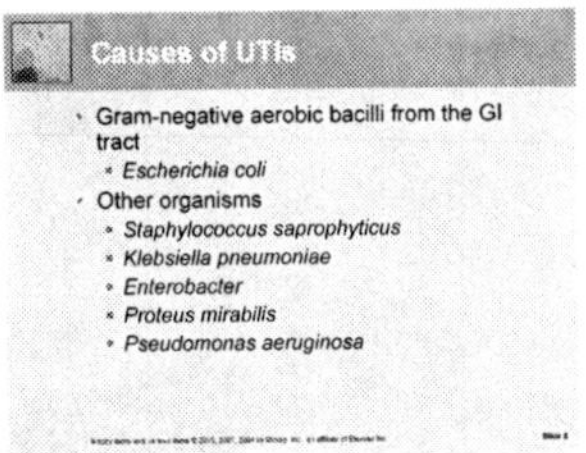
Causes of UTIs
Gram-negative aerobic bacilli from the GI tract
Escherichia coli
Other organisms
Staphylococcus saprophyticus
Klebsiella pneumoniae
Enterobacter
Proteus mirabilis
Pseudomonas aeruginosa

- *E. coli* accounts for 80% of urinary tract infections.

Slide 6

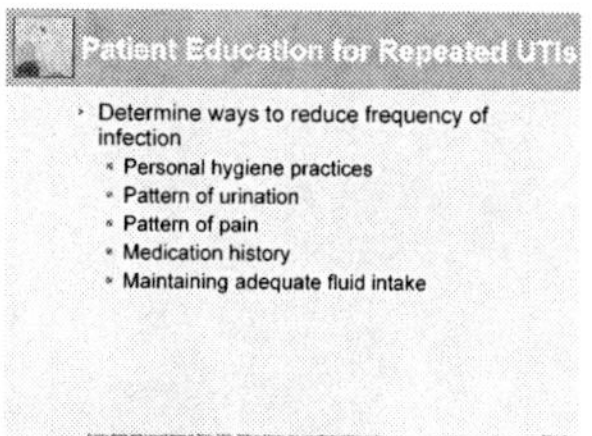
Patient Education for Repeated UTIs
Determine ways to reduce frequency of infection
Personal hygiene practices
Pattern of urination
Pattern of pain
Medication history
Maintaining adequate fluid intake

Slide 7

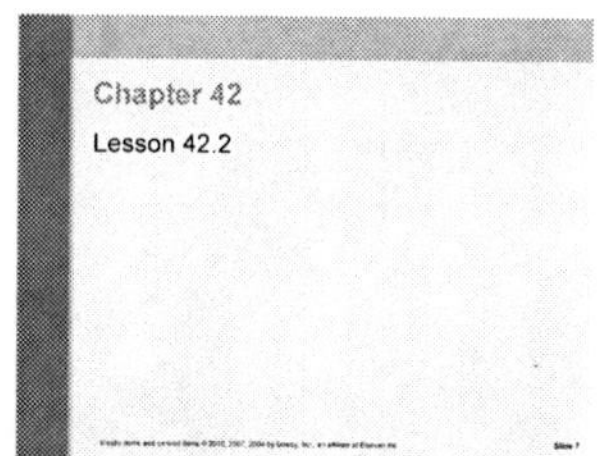
Chapter 42
Lesson 42.2

Slide 8

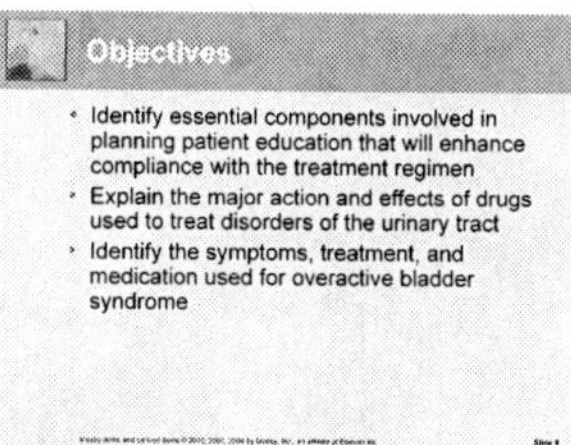
Objectives
Identify essential components involved in planning patient education that will enhance compliance with the treatment regimen
Explain the major action and effects of drugs used to treat disorders of the urinary tract
Identify the symptoms, treatment, and medication used for overactive bladder syndrome

---

Slide 9

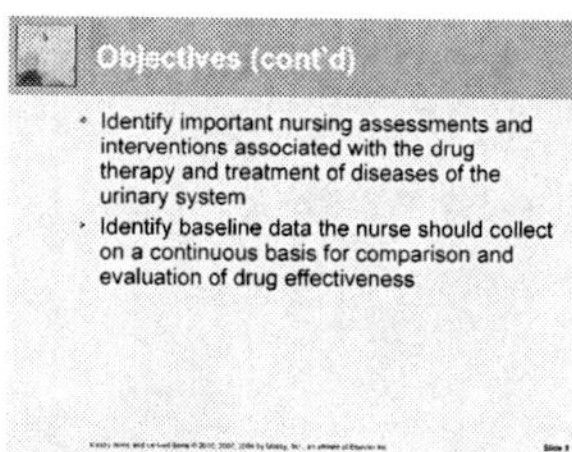
Objectives (cont'd)
Identify important nursing assessments and interventions associated with the drug therapy and treatment of diseases of the urinary system
Identify baseline data the nurse should collect on a continuous basis for comparison and evaluation of drug effectiveness

---

Slide 10

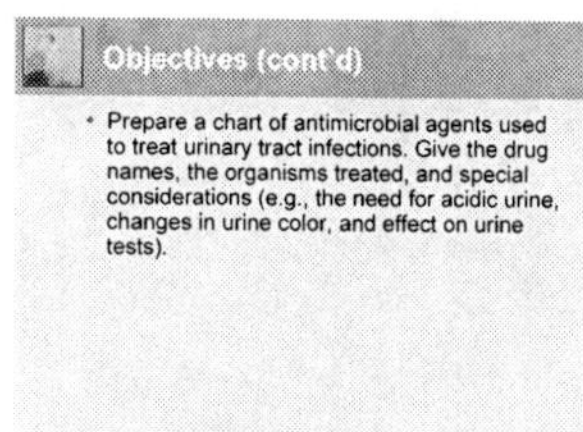
Objectives (cont'd)
Prepare a chart of antimicrobial agents used to treat urinary tract infections. Give the drug names, the organisms treated, and special considerations (e.g., the need for acidic urine, changes in urine color, and effect on urine tests).

Slide 11

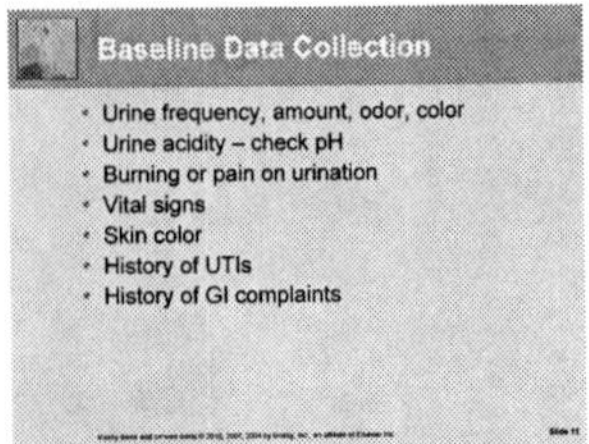
Baseline Data Collection
Urine frequency, amount, odor, color
Urine acidity – check pH
Burning or pain on urination
Vital signs
Skin color
History of UTIs
History of GI complaints

- An increased acidity of urine decreases the incidence of infective organism growth.

Slide 12

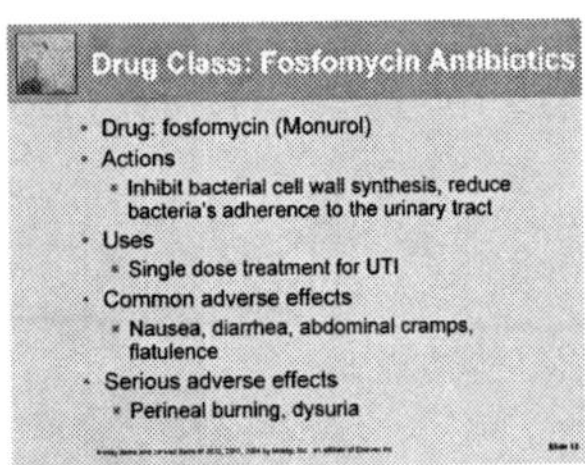
Drug Class: Fosfomycin Antibiotics
Drug: fosfomycin (Monurol)
Actions
Inhibit bacterial cell wall synthesis, reduce bacteria's adherence to the urinary tract
Uses
Single dose treatment for UTI
Common adverse effects
Nausea, diarrhea, abdominal cramps, flatulence
Serious adverse effects
Perineal burning, dysuria

- Also treats uncomplicated acute cystitis in women caused by *E. coli* and *Enterococcus faecalis*.

Slide 13

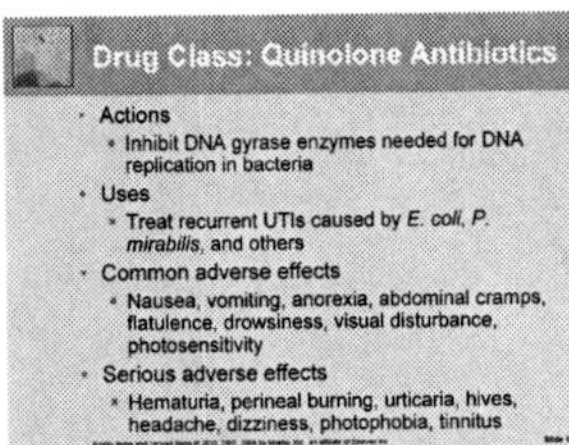
Drug Class: Quinolone Antibiotics
Actions
Inhibit DNA gyrase enzymes needed for DNA replication in bacteria
Uses
Treat recurrent UTIs caused by E. coli, P. mirabilis, and others
Common adverse effects
Nausea, vomiting, anorexia, abdominal cramps, flatulence, drowsiness, visual disturbance, photosensitivity
Serious adverse effects
Hematuria, perineal burning, urticaria, hives, headache, dizziness, photophobia, tinnitus

- For specific drugs, see Table 42-2.
- Quinolone antibiotics are not effective against the *Pseudomonas* species.

Slide 14

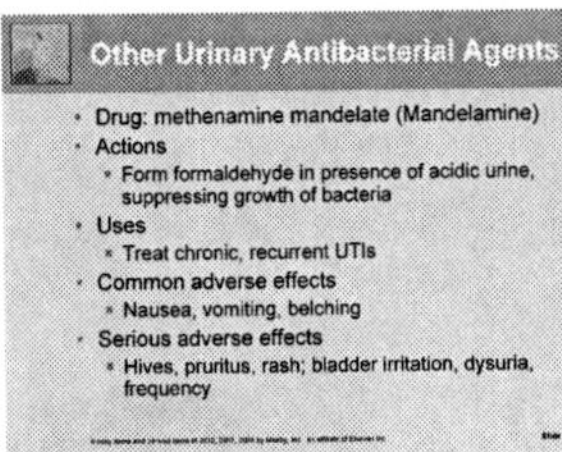
Other Urinary Antibacterial Agents
Drug: methenamine mandelate (Mandelamine)
Actions
Form formaldehyde in presence of acidic urine, suppressing growth of bacteria
Uses
Treat chronic, recurrent UTIs
Common adverse effects
Nausea, vomiting, belching
Serious adverse effects
Hives, pruritus, rash; bladder irritation, dysuria, frequency

- Do not crush tablet; this will allow formaldehyde to form in the stomach, causing nausea and belching.
- Vitamin C also may be given to help acidify urine.
- Test urine pH at regular intervals; keep pH at < 5.5.

Slide 15

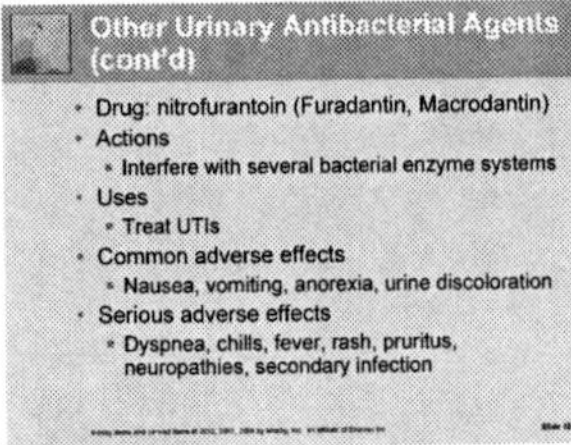
Other Urinary Antibacterial Agents (cont'd)
Drug: nitrofurantoin (Furadantin, Macrodantin)
Actions
Interfere with several bacterial enzyme systems
Uses
Treat UTIs
Common adverse effects
Nausea, vomiting, anorexia, urine discoloration
Serious adverse effects
Dyspnea, chills, fever, rash, pruritus, neuropathies, secondary infection

- Effective against gram-positive and gram-negative organisms such as *Streptococcus faecalis*, *E. coli,* and *Proteus* species.
- Must be in the bladder in sufficient concentrations to be therapeutic.
- Urine may turn rust brown to yellow.

Slide 16

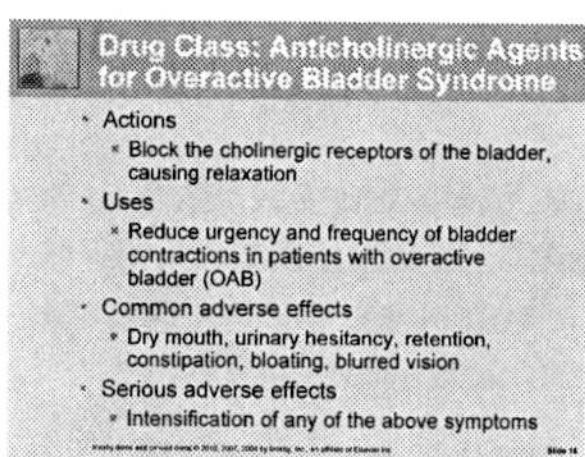
Drug Class: Anticholinergic Agents for Overactive Bladder Syndrome
Actions
Block the cholinergic receptors of the bladder, causing relaxation
Uses
Reduce urgency and frequency of bladder contractions in patients with overactive bladder (OAB)
Common adverse effects
Dry mouth, urinary hesitancy, retention, constipation, bloating, blurred vision
Serious adverse effects
Intensification of any of the above symptoms

- For specific drugs, see Table 42-3.
- OAB has three primary symptoms: frequency, urgency, urinary incontinence.

Slide 17

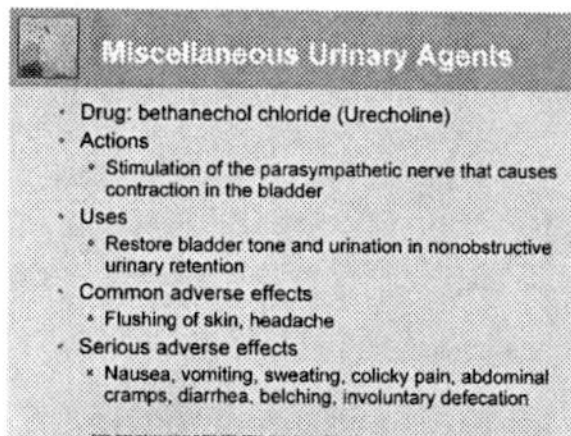
Miscellaneous Urinary Agents
Drug: bethanechol chloride (Urecholine)
Actions
Stimulation of the parasympathetic nerve that causes contraction in the bladder
Uses
Restore bladder tone and urination in nonobstructive urinary retention
Common adverse effects
Flushing of skin, headache
Serious adverse effects
Nausea, vomiting, sweating, colicky pain, abdominal cramps, diarrhea, belching, involuntary defecation

- Other actions include stimulation of gastric motility, increased gastric tone, and restoration of peristalsis.

Slide 18

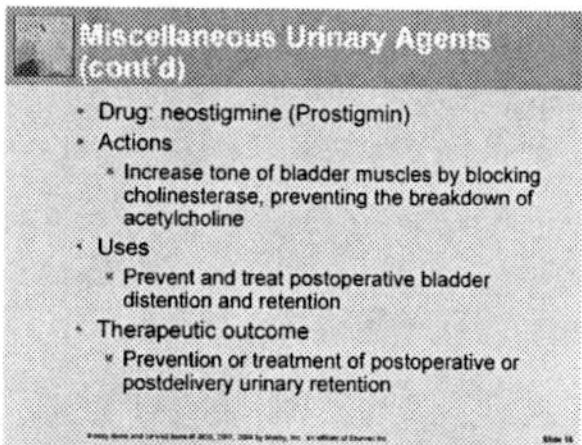
Miscellaneous Urinary Agents (cont'd)
Drug: neostigmine (Prostigmin)
Actions
Increase tone of bladder muscles by blocking cholinesterase, preventing the breakdown of acetylcholine
Uses
Prevent and treat postoperative bladder distention and retention
Therapeutic outcome
Prevention or treatment of postoperative or postdelivery urinary retention

---

Slide 19

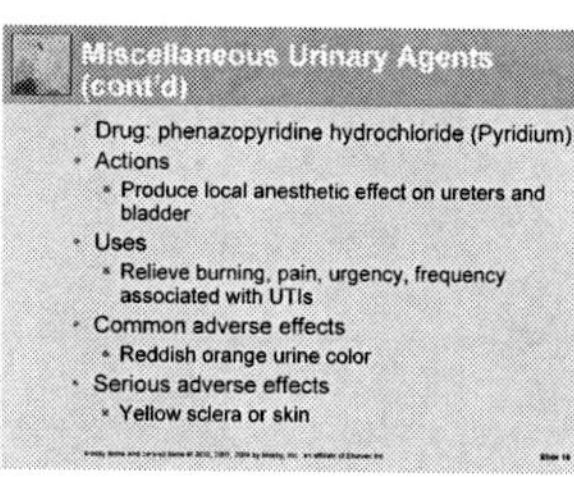
Miscellaneous Urinary Agents (cont'd)
Drug: phenazopyridine hydrochloride (Pyridium)
Actions
Produce local anesthetic effect on ureters and bladder
Uses
Relieve burning, pain, urgency, frequency associated with UTIs
Common adverse effects
Reddish orange urine color
Serious adverse effects
Yellow sclera or skin

- Also used to reduce bladder spasms, which relieves the resulting urinary retention.
- Used in urologic surgery.

ELSEVIER

43 Lesson Plan
Drugs Used to Treat Glaucoma and Other Eye Disorders

TEACHING FOCUS

In this chapter, students are introduced to the anatomy and physiology of the eye, including the eyeball and its three layers: the cornea, the iris, and the lens. Students also have the opportunity to learn the disorders of the eye, including glaucoma and the major types of glaucoma. Additionally, students have the opportunity to learn the procedures used to assess patients who have a potential for or have been diagnosed with eye disorders.

MATERIALS AND RESOURCES

- ☐ computer and PowerPoint projector (all Lessons)
- ☐ drawing of the cross section of the eye (Lesson 43.1)
- ☐ guest speaker: ophthalmologist

LESSON CHECKLIST

Preparations for this lesson include:

- lecture
- demonstration
- evaluation of student knowledge and skills needed to perform all entry-level activities related to the pathophysiology of eye disorders, including:
  - anatomy and physiology of the eye
  - comprehension of drugs used to manage and treat eye disorders

KEY TERMS

closed-angle glaucoma (p. 670)
cornea (p. 668)
cycloplegia (p. 669)
dilator muscle (p. 668)
intraocular pressure (p. 670)
iris (p. 668)
lacrimal canaliculi (p. 669)
lens (p. 668)
miosis (p. 668)
mydriasis (p. 668)
near point (p. 668)
open-angle glaucoma (p. 670)
sclera (p. 668)
sphincter muscle (p. 668)
zonular fibers (p. 668)

ADDITIONAL RESOURCES

PowerPoint slides: 1-21
Flashcards, Decks 1 and 2

Legend

ARQ	PPT	TB	CTQ	SG	INRQ
Audience Response Questions	PowerPoint Slides	Test Bank	Critical Thinking Questions	Study Guide	Interactive NCLEX Review Questions

Class Activities are indicated in ***bold italic.***

LESSON 43.1

BACKGROUND ASSESSMENT

Question: What are the major organs of the eye?
Answer: The cornea is the outermost sheath of the anterior eyeball. It is transparent so that light can enter the eye. The sclera is the eye's white portion. It is continuous with the cornea and is nontransparent. The iris is the diaphragm that surrounds the pupil and gives the eye its blue, green, hazel, brown, or gray color. The lens is a transparent gelatinous mass of fibers encased in an elastic capsule situated behind the iris. Its function is to ensure that the image on the retina is in sharp focus.

Question: Distinguish the difference between glaucoma and open-angle glaucoma.
Answer: Glaucoma is an eye disease caused by abnormally elevated intraocular pressure (IOP), which may result from excessive production of the aqueous humor or from diminished ocular fluid outflow. Increased pressure, if not treated, can lead to permanent blindness. Closed-angle glaucoma occurs when there is a sudden increase in IOP caused by a mechanical obstruction of the trabecular network in the iridocorneal angle. Symptoms appear gradually, but especially when the pupil is dilated, such as with the use of mydriatic agents for eye examinations. Open-angle glaucoma develops over the years as pathologic changes prevent the outflow of aqueous humor. IOP builds up and, if not treated, can cause permanent blindness.

CRITICAL THINKING QUESTION

A patient comes to the emergency department (ED) complaining of sudden headache, blurred vision, eye pain, and halos seen around white lights. He denies previous treatment of this problem. He states that he hit his head yesterday while fixing a bathroom sink. The nurse triages the patient and sends him immediately to the ED for further evaluation by the health care provider. What type of assessment should the nurse perform on this patient? Why does the nurse evaluate this patient's complaint as a true emergency?
Guidelines: The nurse should perform a thorough assessment of the patient's current complaint, or the reason the patient came to the ED. The nurse should note that the patient hit his head and is complaining of ocular signs and symptoms. Because the patient may have acute angle-closure glaucoma related to a head trauma, he requires immediate care to decrease IOP and to prevent blindness from occurring.

OBJECTIVES	CONTENT	TEACHING RESOURCES
Describe the anatomy and physiology of the eye.	■ Anatomy and physiology of the eye (p. 668) Review the normal anatomy and physiology of the eye. Identify the following eye structures: cornea, sclera, iris, sphincter muscle, lens, zonular fibers, lacrimal canaliculi, and dilator muscle. Define the following terms: *miosis*, *mydriasis*, *accommodation*, *near point*, and *cycloplegia*. Review the three layers of the eye.	PPT 4-5 SG Review Sheet questions 1-2 (p. 283) SG Learning Activities questions 1-2, 17-18 (p. 289) Figure 43-1 (p. 669): Cross section of the eye. Figure 43-2 (p. 669): Effect of light or ophthalmic agents on the iris of the eye. ▸ Discuss how the iris promotes eye color. ▸ Discuss the dilation and constriction of the pupil. ▸ Discuss the role of eyelashes when a foreign body invades the eye. Class Activity ***Hand out an unlabeled diagram of the eye showing its structures, including the cornea, sclera, iris, sphincter muscle, lens, zonular fibers, lacrimal canaliculi, and dilator muscle. Have students pair up and together fill in the blank lines to identify the eye structures.***

OBJECTIVES	CONTENT	TEACHING RESOURCES
		Discuss the terms **miosis, mydriasis, accommodation, near point,** ***and*** **cycloplegia** *in relation to the eye structures and functions. Review the exercise with the class.*
Describe the normal flow of aqueous humor in the eye.	■ Anatomy and physiology of the eye (p. 668) Review what glaucoma is and the three major types—primary, secondary, and congenital—as well as closed-angle glaucoma and open-angle glaucoma. Discuss the flow of aqueous humor and increased intraocular pressure (IOP).	PPT 6 ARQ 1 TB Multiple Choice questions 1-3 TB Multiple Response question 1 SG Review Sheet question 3 (p. 283) Figure 43-3 (p. 670): Anterior and posterior chambers of the eye. Figure 43-4 (p. 670): The flow of the aqueous humor.
Identify the changes in normal flow of aqueous humor caused by open-angle and closed-angle glaucoma.	■ Glaucoma (p. 670) ■ Drug therapy for glaucoma (p. 671) Review the principal treatment for patients with open-angle glaucoma and the types of drugs used to control IOP. Discuss the nursing process in relation to glaucoma patients, which includes an eye examination and the topics to teach after eye surgery. Review ways to foster health maintenance and verify the patient's ability to self-administer medications.	PPT 6-7 INRQ 2 SG Review Sheet questions 4-6, 7-10 (pp. 283-284) SG Learning Activities questions 3-5 (p. 289) Figure 43-5 (p. 671): Obstruction to the flow of aqueous fluid, causing closed-angle glaucoma. Class Activity *List on the board the following terms:* **primary glaucoma, secondary glaucoma, congenital glaucoma, closed-angle glaucoma,** ***and*** **open-angle glaucoma.** *Have students volunteer to explain each condition and the associated safety measures to teach patients. Review the exercise with the class.*

43.1 Homework/Assignments:

43.1 Instructor's Notes/Student Feedback:

LESSON 43.2

CRITICAL THINKING QUESTION

A patient with acute angle-closure glaucoma is prescribed IV mannitol, an analgesic, and an antiemetic. What should the nurse caring for the patient look for after the mannitol is administered? Why did the health care provider order an analgesic and antiemetic? What type of environment should the nurse set up for this patient?

Guidelines: Mannitol is used for the emergency treatment to decrease IOP and prevent blindness in acute angle-closure glaucoma. Mannitol is considered an osmotic diuretic and will cause immediate diuresis. The nurse should explain to the patient the action of the drug and the need to place a Foley catheter to monitor the urine output adequately. The analgesic was ordered to help reduce the eye pain, and the antiemetic is to prevent nausea and vomiting, which is common with this type of eye injury. The nurse should provide a quiet, dark environment for this patient to help relieve additional strain to the eyes.

OBJECTIVES	CONTENT	TEACHING RESOURCES
Explain the baseline data that should be gathered when an eye disorder exists.	– Nursing process for glaucoma and other eye disorders (p. 671)	TB Multiple Response questions 2, 4 INRQ 7 CTQ 1 SG Review Sheet questions 13, 43 (pp. 285, 288) SG Learning Activities questions 6-8 (p. 289) ▸ Discuss how the nurse can promote safety when caring for patients diagnosed with eye disorders. ▸ Discuss why the nurse should watch for eyelid closure when assessing a patient. Class Activity ***Divide the class into small groups, and have each group plan an assessment (data collection) of a patient with glaucoma. Have each group present its assessment plan to the class for discussion. Then lead a class discussion about the signs and symptoms of glaucoma and appropriate nursing interventions.***
Develop teaching plans for a person with an eye infection and a person receiving glaucoma medication.	– Patient education and health promotion (p. 672) □ Drug class: Osmotic agents (p. 673) – Nursing process for osmotic agents (p. 674) □ Drug class: Carbonic anhydrase inhibitors (p. 675) – Nursing process for carbonic anhydrase inhibitors (p. 675) □ Drug class: Cholinergic agents (p. 676)	PPT 11-18 ARQ 3-4 TB Multiple Choice questions 4-5, 7 TB Multiple Response questions 5-7 INRQ 1, 3, 7-8, 10 CTQ 1 Patient Self-Assessment Form: Eye Medications SG Review Sheet questions 11-12, 14-26, 28 (pp. 284-286)

OBJECTIVES	CONTENT	TEACHING RESOURCES
	– Nursing process for cholinergic agents (p. 676) □ Drug class: Cholinesterase inhibitors (p. 678) – Nursing process for cholinesterase inhibitors (p. 678) □ Drug class: Adrenergic agents (p. 678) – Nursing process for adrenergic agents (p. 679) □ Drug class: Beta-adrenergic blocking agents (p. 680) – Nursing process for beta-adrenergic blocking agents (p. 680) □ Drug class: Prostaglandin agonists (p. 680) – Nursing process for prostaglandin agonists (p. 680)	SG Learning Activities questions 6-8, 12-14, 19-20, 22 (pp. 289-290) SG Practice Questions for the NCLEX Examination 1-4, 6-7, 9, 11 (pp. 291-292) Review Questions for the NCLEX Examination 1-3, 5, 8 (p. 687) Lifespan Considerations: Diminished Visual Acuity (p. 673) Drug Table 43-1: Osmotic Agents (p. 674) Drug Table 43-2: Carbonic Anhydrase Inhibitors (p. 675) Drug Table 43-3: Cholinergic Agents (p. 677) Drug Table 43-4: Adrenergic Agents (p. 679) Drug Table 43-5: Beta-Adrenergic Blocking Agents (p. 681) Drug Table 43-6: Prostaglandin Agonists (p. 681) ▸ Discuss the reasons why a patient diagnosed with glaucoma has to seek lifelong treatment. ▸ Discuss why personal hygiene is important to the prevention of an infection. Class Activity ***Divide the class into small groups, and have each group develop a chart listing three types of drugs used to treat eye infection along with the adverse effects and drug interactions. Have each group present its chart to the class.***
Review the correct procedure for instilling eye drops or eye ointments.	■ General considerations for topical ophthalmic drug therapy (p. 669) ■ Other ophthalmic agents (p. 681) □ Drug class: Anticholinergic agents (p. 681) – Nursing process for anticholinergic agents (p. 682) □ Drug class: Antifungal agents (p. 683) – Nursing process for natamycin (p. 683) □ Drug class: Antiviral agents (p. 683)	PPT 11, 19-21 ARQ 2, 5 TB Multiple Response question 3 INRQ 6, 9, 11 CTQ 2 SG Review Sheet questions 27, 29-42 (pp. 286-288) SG Learning Activities questions 5, 9-11, 15-16, 21 (pp. 289-290) SG Practice Questions for the NCLEX Examination 5, 8, 10 (pp. 291-292)

ELSEVIER

OBJECTIVES	CONTENT	TEACHING RESOURCES
	– Nursing process for antiviral agents (p. 683) □ Drug class: Antibacterial agents (p. 684) □ Drug class: Corticosteroids (p. 685) □ Drug class: Ophthalmic anti-inflammatory agents (p. 685) □ Drug class: Antihistamines (p. 685) □ Drug class: Antiallergic agents (p. 686) □ Drug class: Diagnostic agent (p. 686) □ Drug class: Artificial tear solutions (p. 686) □ Drug class: Ophthalmic irrigants (p. 686) □ Drug class: Vascular endothelial growth factor antagonist (p. 686) Review techniques to use for instillation of eye drops and the proper administration of topical application of ophthalmic drugs, generally in the form of eye drops or ointments. Discuss the precautions to take such as compressing the lacrimal sac to prevent systemic absorption and how to prevent eye infections from expired drugs.	Review Questions for the NCLEX Examination 4, 6-7 (p. 687) Drug Table 43-7: Anticholinergic Agents (p. 682) Drug Table 43-8: Antiviral Agents (p. 684) Drug Table 43-9: Ophthalmic Antibiotics (p. 684) Table 43-10: Corticosteroids (p. 685) Table 43-11: Ophthalmic Antihistamines (p. 685) ▸ Discuss cerebral dehydration and how to reduce it once diagnosed in a patient with an eye disorder. ▸ Discuss the condition intraocular hypertension potentially arising in patients who are diagnosed with an eye disorder. Class Activity ***Divide the class into small groups, and have each group develop a teaching plan to illustrate the procedure for instilling eye drops.*** Class Activity ***Invite an ophthalmologist as a guest speaker to discuss eye examinations, disorders of the eye, and treatment. Have students prepare related questions before the presentation.*** Class Activity ***Have two students role-play an experienced nurse instructing a novice nurse about the infusion of Ureaphil for treatment of acute narrow-angle glaucoma. Have the class assist the experienced nurse in determining what needs to be reviewed for the management of this infusion. Review the exercise with the class.***
Performance evaluation		Test Bank SG Learning Activities (pp. 289-290) SG Practice Questions for the NCLEX Examination (pp. 291-292) Critical Thinking Questions

43.2 Homework/Assignments:

43.2 Instructor's Notes/Student Feedback:

43 Lecture Outline
Drugs Used to Treat Glaucoma and Other Eye Disorders

Slide 1

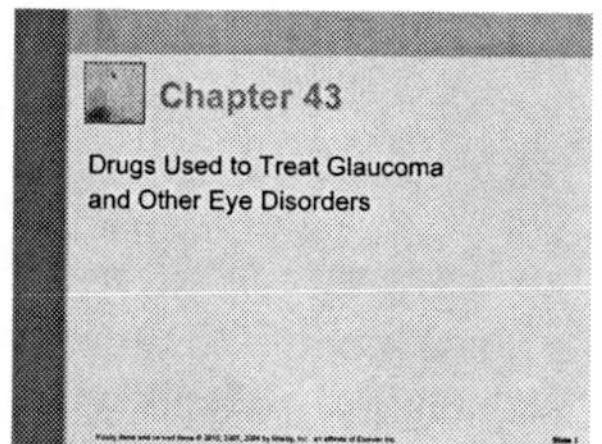
Chapter 43
Drugs Used to Treat Glaucoma and Other Eye Disorders

Slide 2

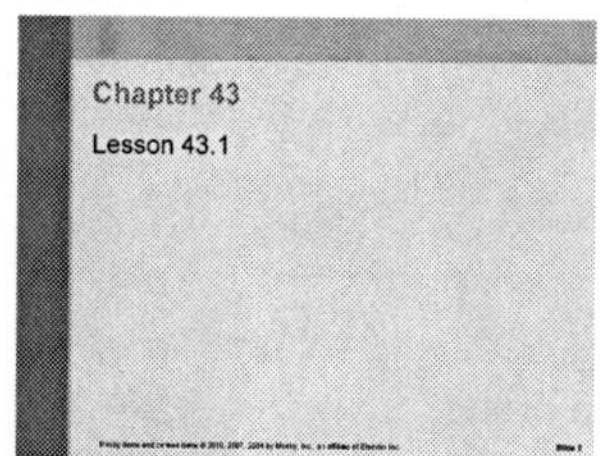
Chapter 43
Lesson 43.1

Slide 3

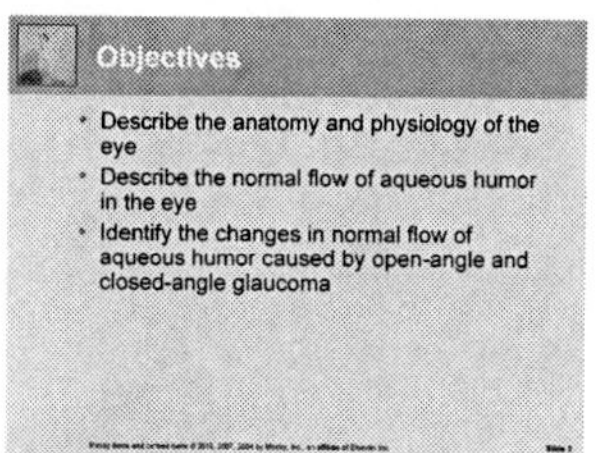
Objectives
Describe the anatomy and physiology of the eye
Describe the normal flow of aqueous humor in the eye
Identify the changes in normal flow of aqueous humor caused by open-angle and closed-angle glaucoma

---

Slide 4

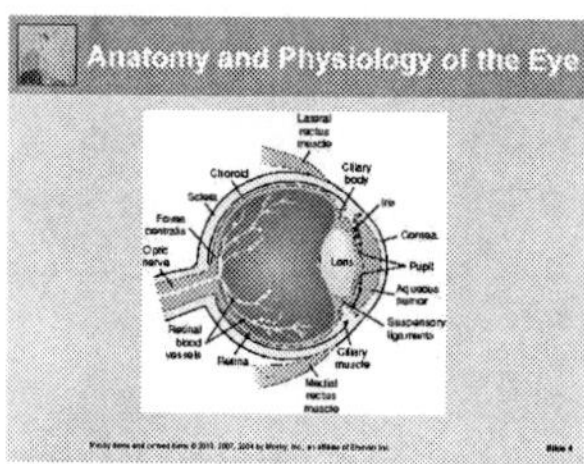
Anatomy and Physiology of the Eye

- The eyeball has three layers:
  - Corneoscleral coat—protective coat
  - Choroid—nutritive middle vascular layer
  - Retina—light-sensitive inner layer

Slide 5

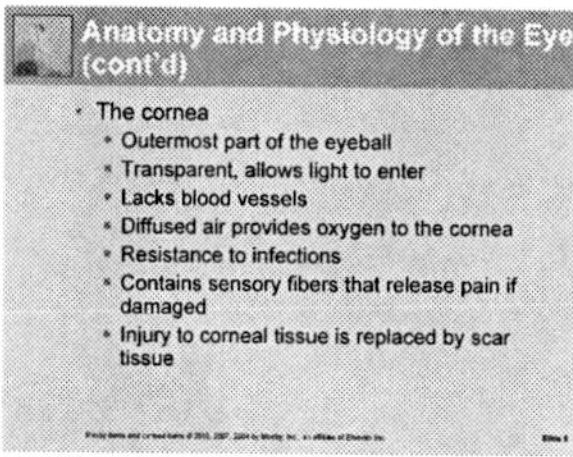
Anatomy and Physiology of the Eye (cont'd)
The cornea
Outermost part of the eyeball
Transparent, allows light to enter
Lacks blood vessels
Diffused air provides oxygen to the cornea
Resistance to infections
Contains sensory fibers that release pain if damaged
Injury to corneal tissue is replaced by scar tissue

- The eye receives nutrition from the aqueous humor.
- Corneal abrasions are highly susceptible to infection.

Slide 6

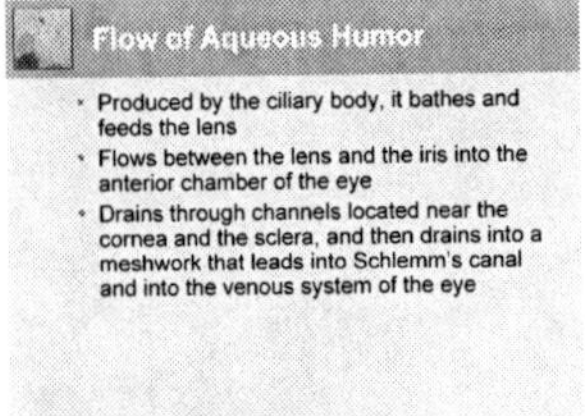
Flow of Aqueous Humor
Produced by the ciliary body, it bathes and feeds the lens
Flows between the lens and the iris into the anterior chamber of the eye
Drains through channels located near the cornea and the sclera, and then drains into a meshwork that leads into Schlemm's canal and into the venous system of the eye

- Abnormalities of the drainage system can lead to glaucoma.
- Open-angle and closed-angle glaucoma—increased or decreased flow exists.

Slide 7

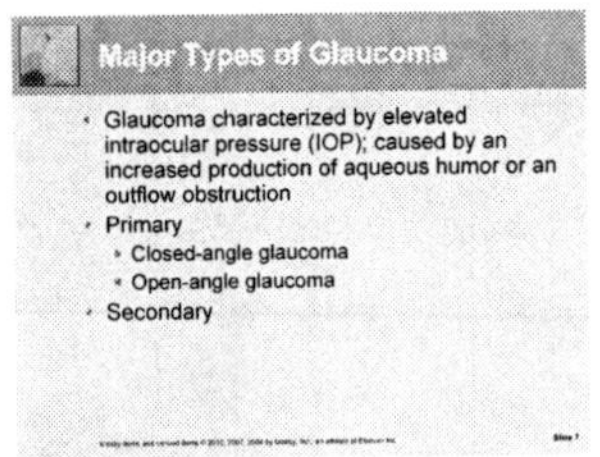
Major Types of Glaucoma
Glaucoma characterized by elevated intraocular pressure (IOP); caused by an increased production of aqueous humor or an outflow obstruction
Primary
Closed-angle glaucoma
Open-angle glaucoma
Secondary

- Closed-angle—occurs when there is a sudden increase in IOP caused by a mechanical obstruction in the iridocorneal angle in patients with narrow anterior chamber angles.
- Open angle—develops slowly over the years as pathologic changes occur.
- Secondary—results from previous eye injury or disease, or cataract surgery.

Slide 8

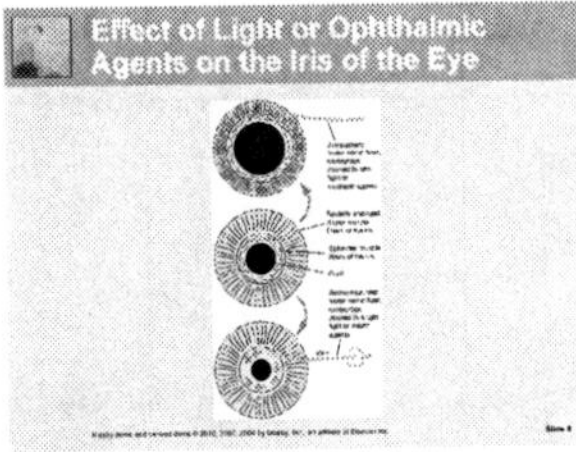
Effect of Light or Ophthalmic Agents on the Iris of the Eye

- Mydriasis is the contraction of the dilator muscle and relaxation of the sphincter muscle, which causes the pupil to dilate.

Slide 9

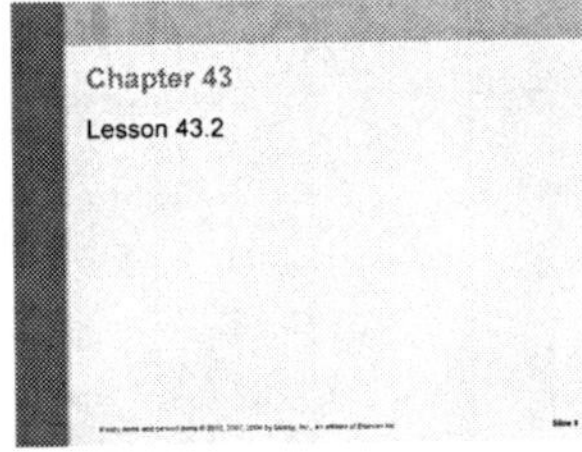
Chapter 43
Lesson 43.2

Slide 10

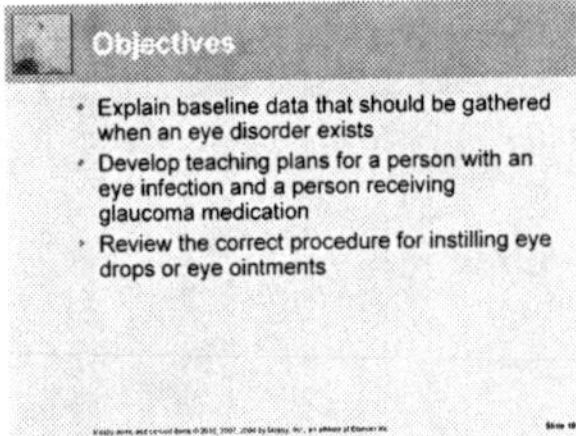
Objectives
Explain baseline data that should be gathered when an eye disorder exists
Develop teaching plans for a person with an eye infection and a person receiving glaucoma medication
Review the correct procedure for instilling eye drops or eye ointments

Slide 11

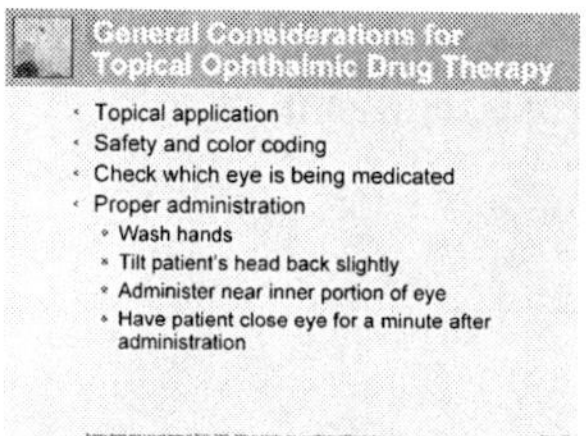
General Considerations for Topical Ophthalmic Drug Therapy
Topical application
Safety and color coding
Check which eye is being medicated
Proper administration
Wash hands
Tilt patient's head back slightly
Administer near inner portion of eye
Have patient close eye for a minute after administration

- If more than one drug is to be administered at about the same time, separate the administration of the different medicines by at least 5 minutes.
- Minimize systemic absorption of ophthalmic drops by compressing the lacrimal sac for 3 to 5 minutes after instillation.

Slide 12

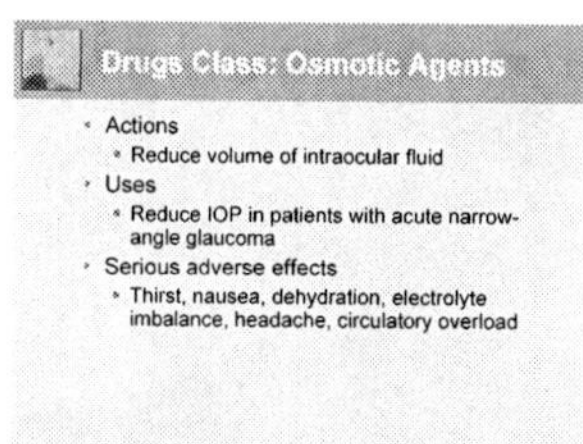
Drugs Class: Osmotic Agents
Actions
Reduce volume of intraocular fluid
Uses
Reduce IOP in patients with acute narrow-angle glaucoma
Serious adverse effects
Thirst, nausea, dehydration, electrolyte imbalance, headache, circulatory overload

- For specific drugs, see Table 43-1.
- Can be given IV, orally, or topically.
- Mannitol used for reduction of IOP.

Slide 13

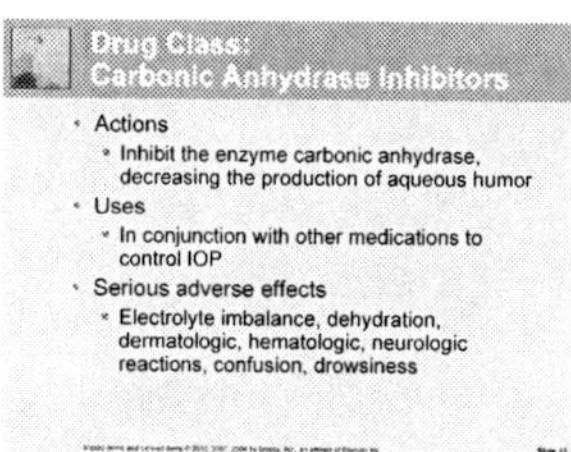
Drug Class: Carbonic Anhydrase Inhibitors
Actions
Inhibit the enzyme carbonic anhydrase, decreasing the production of aqueous humor
Uses
In conjunction with other medications to control IOP
Serious adverse effects
Electrolyte imbalance, dehydration, dermatologic, hematologic, neurologic reactions, confusion, drowsiness

- For specific drugs, see Table 43-2.

Slide 14

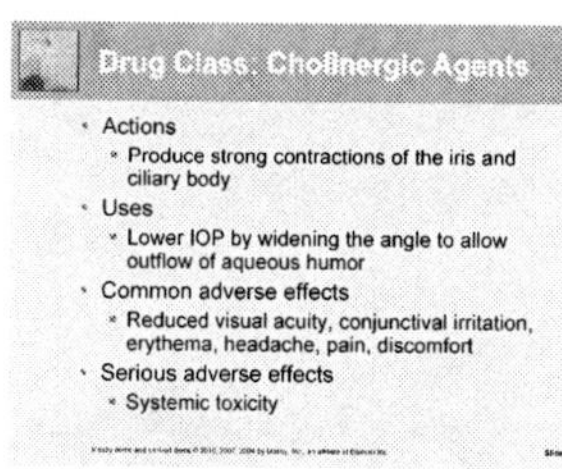
Drug Class: Cholinergic Agents
Actions
Produce strong contractions of the iris and ciliary body
Uses
Lower IOP by widening the angle to allow outflow of aqueous humor
Common adverse effects
Reduced visual acuity, conjunctival irritation, erythema, headache, pain, discomfort
Serious adverse effects
Systemic toxicity

- For specific drugs, see Table 43-3.
- Other uses include counteracting the effects of mydriatic and cycloplegic agents after surgery or eye examinations.

Slide 15

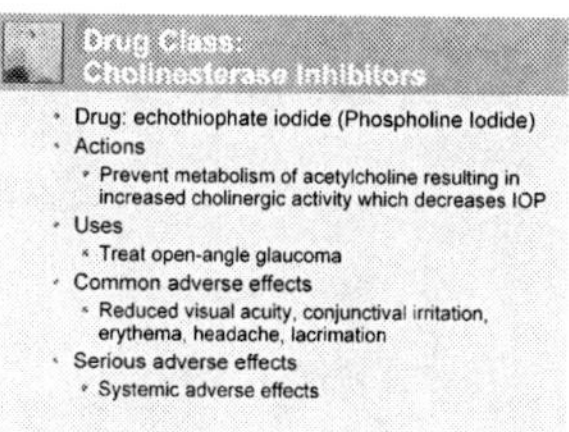
Drug Class: Cholinesterase Inhibitors
Drug: echothiophate iodide (Phospholine Iodide)
Actions
Prevent metabolism of acetylcholine resulting in increased cholinergic activity which decreases IOP
Uses
Treat open-angle glaucoma
Common adverse effects
Reduced visual acuity, conjunctival irritation, erythema, headache, lacrimation
Serious adverse effects
Systemic adverse effects

- Reserved for use in patients who do not respond to cholinergic agents.

ELSEVIER

Slide 16

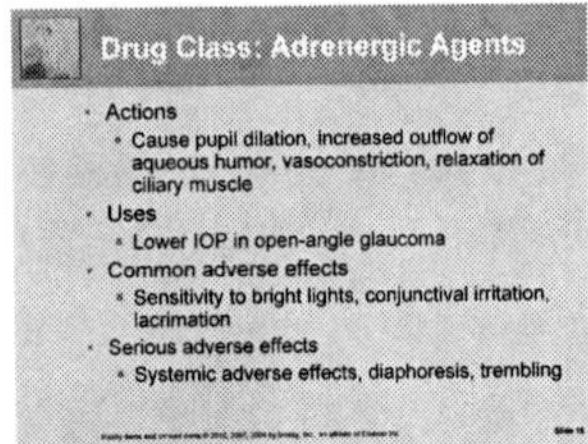
Drug Class: Adrenergic Agents
Actions
Cause pupil dilation, increased outflow of aqueous humor, vasoconstriction, relaxation of ciliary muscle
Uses
Lower IOP in open-angle glaucoma
Common adverse effects
Sensitivity to bright lights, conjunctival irritation, lacrimation
Serious adverse effects
Systemic adverse effects, diaphoresis, trembling

- For specific drugs, see Table 43-4.
- Use with caution in patients with hypertension, diabetes mellitus, hyperthyroidism, heart disease, arteriosclerosis, and asthma.

Slide 17

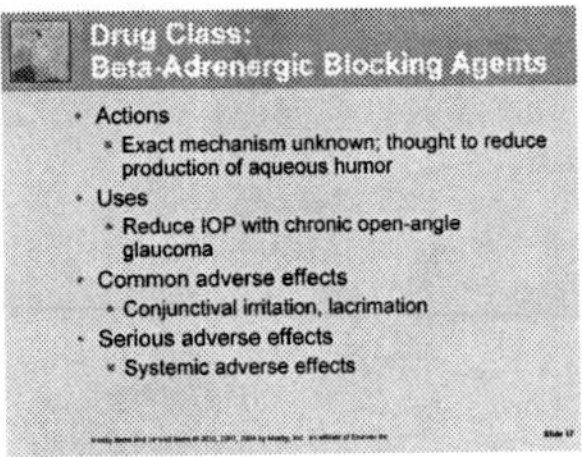
Drug Class:
Beta-Adrenergic Blocking Agents
Actions
Exact mechanism unknown; thought to reduce production of aqueous humor
Uses
Reduce IOP with chronic open-angle glaucoma
Common adverse effects
Conjunctival irritation, lacrimation
Serious adverse effects
Systemic adverse effects

- For specific drugs, see Table 43-5.
- There is no blurred vision or night blindness effects from these drugs.

Slide 18

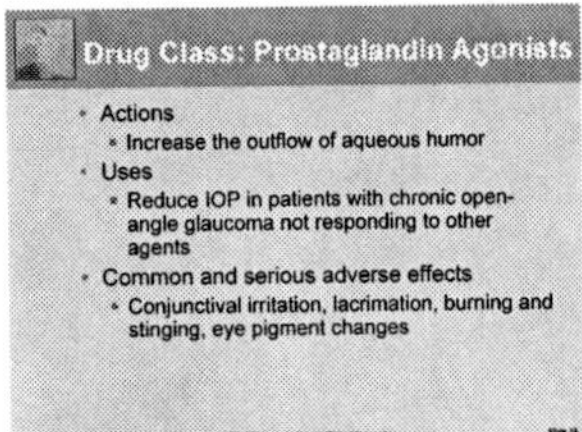
Drug Class: Prostaglandin Agonists
Actions
Increase the outflow of aqueous humor
Uses
Reduce IOP in patients with chronic open-angle glaucoma not responding to other agents
Common and serious adverse effects
Conjunctival irritation, lacrimation, burning and stinging, eye pigment changes

- For specific drugs, see Table 43-6.

Slide 19

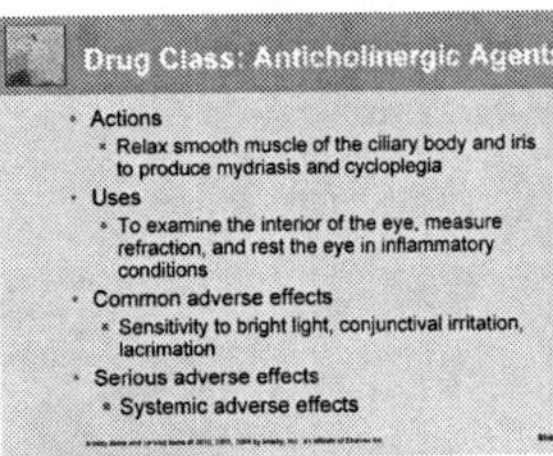
Drug Class: Anticholinergic Agents
Actions
Relax smooth muscle of the ciliary body and iris to produce mydriasis and cycloplegia
Uses
To examine the interior of the eye, measure refraction, and rest the eye in inflammatory conditions
Common adverse effects
Sensitivity to bright light, conjunctival irritation, lacrimation
Serious adverse effects
Systemic adverse effects

- For specific drugs, see Table 43-7.
- These agents will cause in increase in IOP.

Slide 20

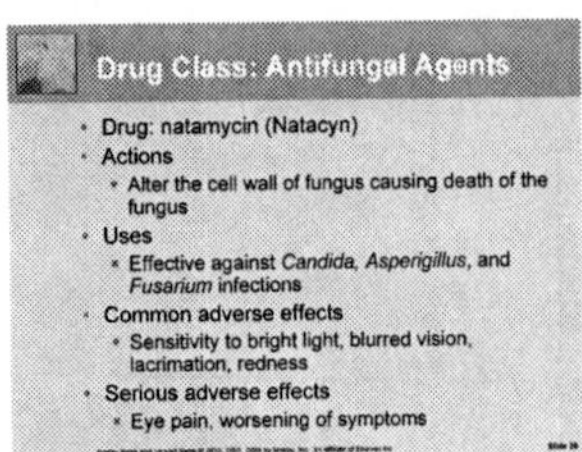
Drug Class: Antifungal Agents
Drug: natamycin (Natacyn)
Actions
Alter the cell wall of fungus causing death of the fungus
Uses
Effective against Candida, Aspergillus, and Fusarium infections
Common adverse effects
Sensitivity to bright light, blurred vision, lacrimation, redness
Serious adverse effects
Eye pain, worsening of symptoms

Slide 21

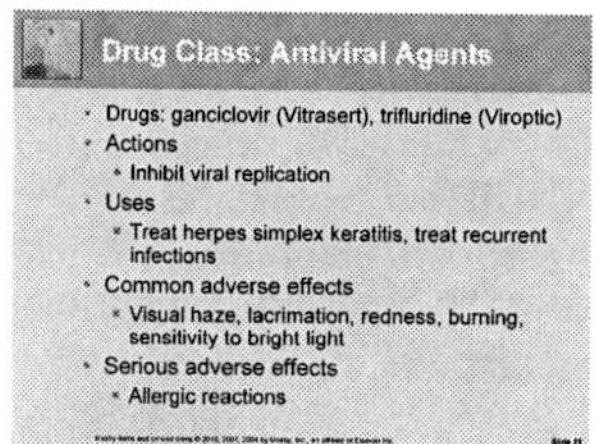
Drug Class: Antiviral Agents
Drugs: ganciclovir (Vitrasert), trifluridine (Viroptic)
Actions
Inhibit viral replication
Uses
Treat herpes simplex keratitis, treat recurrent infections
Common adverse effects
Visual haze, lacrimation, redness, burning, sensitivity to bright light
Serious adverse effects
Allergic reactions

44 Lesson Plan
Drugs Used for Cancer Treatment

TEACHING FOCUS

In this chapter, students have the opportunity to learn about drugs affecting neoplasms. The actions and uses of the five classes of antineoplastic agents are discussed, along with the goals and therapeutic outcomes of chemotherapy. Students have an opportunity to apply the nursing process and develop a patient education plan to monitor common adverse effects and the progression or regression of the disease.

MATERIALS AND RESOURCES

- ☐ computer and PowerPoint projector (all Lessons)

LESSON CHECKLIST

Preparations for this lesson include:

- lecture
- evaluation of student knowledge and skills needed to perform all entry-level nursing activities related to understanding the goals of chemotherapy and antineoplastic treatment, including:
  - citing the rationale for giving chemotherapeutic drugs on a precise time schedule
  - distinguishing between targeted anticancer agents, chemoprotective agents, and bone marrow stimulants in treating cancer
  - describing nursing assessments and necessary interventions for adverse effects
  - developing patient education objectives for a patient receiving chemotherapy
  - explaining the normal cycle for cell replication and describing the effects of cell cycle–specific and cell cycle–nonspecific drugs within this process

KEY TERMS

cancer (p. 688)
cell cycle–nonspecific (p. 689)
cell cycle–specific (p. 689)
chemoprotective agents (p. 697)
combination therapy (p. 697)
metastases (p. 688)
palliation (p. 697)
targeted anticancer agents (p. 697)

ADDITIONAL RESOURCES

PowerPoint slides: 1-20
Flashcards, Decks 1 and 2

Legend

ARQ	**PPT**	**TB**	**CTQ**	**SG**	**INRQ**
Audience Response Questions	PowerPoint Slides	Test Bank	Critical Thinking Questions	Study Guide	Interactive NCLEX Review Questions

Class Activities are indicated in ***bold italic.***

LESSON 44.1

BACKGROUND ASSESSMENT

Question: What are the goals of chemotherapy?
Answer: Chemotherapy destroys cancer cells that rapidly divide in an uncontrolled manner. The goals of chemotherapy are either curative or palliative, depending on the type and stage of the cancer cells. Curative chemotherapy aims to eliminate all tumor cells in the patient's body; it can be used in combination with

other treatments, such as surgery or radiation, to remove or shrink the tumor, thereby making adjuvant therapies more successful or less traumatic. Curative chemotherapy can also be administered to destroy potential stray cancer cells that may remain following treatment with surgery or radiation. Palliative chemotherapy is administered to provide relief from symptoms caused by cancer at an advanced stage. The goal of palliative treatment is not to rid the patient of the cancer cells but to control the growth, which decreases the number of potential symptoms.

Question: What is the nurse's key role in the treatment of patients with cancer?
Answer: A diagnosis of cancer evokes considerable fear and anxiety in the patient and the patient's family. The nurse, who is often the primary contact among the patient, the health care provider, and other members of the health care team, helps the patient adapt to the diagnosis and treatment plan. Nurses are often the first to observe and report adverse effects of medications or complications of therapy. The nurse also provides health care teaching to patients and family members; this helps achieve the best outcomes for the treatment plan and promotes the best quality of life for the involved patient.

CRITICAL THINKING QUESTION

A 60-year-old woman has been diagnosed with small cell lung cancer. What patient education should the nurse provide regarding adverse effects associated with cisplatin chemotherapy?
Guidelines: The nurse should start by explaining that chemotherapy works by killing the rapidly dividing cells of cancer. Because other body organs (hair, skin, gastrointestinal tract, and bone marrow) also possess normal rapidly dividing cells, chemotherapy can affect these systems too. The result can be adverse effects, such as fatigue, nausea, vomiting, and a decrease in the immune system. The nurse should explain that medications are used to prevent and treat adverse effects. In addition, because the immune system is decreased, measures should be taken to prevent infection during chemotherapy, such as avoiding crowds, proper hand washing, and limiting fresh fruits and vegetables, which can carry microorganisms. The patient should also be educated to report potential signs of infection, including fever, chills, body aches, or sore throat. The nurse should make the patient aware that because loss of appetite and fatigue are common, the patient should eat small, high-calorie meals frequently throughout the day to maintain balanced nutrition, which is important to recovery. Frequent rest periods are recommended to decrease energy consumption and combat fatigue. The nurse should also educate the patient to increase fluid intake, which is important in flushing out the metabolites of cisplatin to prevent kidney impairment. The nurse should mention that blood tests will be performed to monitor kidney function and blood counts. The patient should be made aware that additional adverse effects of cisplatin are a metallic taste in the mouth and ringing in the ears. These effects are temporary and should resolve with discontinuation of the medication. Finally, the nurse should provide the patient with written instructions and allow ample time for questions and concerns.

OBJECTIVES	CONTENT	TEACHING RESOURCES
Discuss the incidence of cancer.	■ Cancer and the use of antineoplastic agents (p. 688) Review the definition for cancer as a disorder of cellular growth, and identify the different types of cancer.	Figure 44-1 (p. 689): Leading sites of new cancer cases and deaths—2008 estimates. ▸ Discuss the incidence of cancer in the population occurring to the American Cancer Society.
Explain the normal cycle for cell replication, and describe the effects of cell cycle-specific and cell cycle-nonspecific drugs within this process.	■ Cancer and the use of antineoplastic agents (p. 688) Discuss the terms *metastases*, *apoptosis*, *cell cycle–specific*, and *cell cycle–nonspecific*. Discuss the phases of cellular proliferation and how many antineoplastic agents are designed to work.	PPT 4-7 ARQ 1, 3 TB Multiple Choice questions 1-2, 5 INRQ 2 SG Review Sheet questions 1-3, 8, 13, 15-16 (pp. 293-294)

OBJECTIVES	CONTENT	TEACHING RESOURCES
		SG Learning Activities questions 3-4, 17-18, 20 (p. 296) Figure 44-2 (p. 689): The cell cycle. ▸ Discuss the difference between cell cycle–specific and cell cycle–nonspecific drugs. ▸ Discuss the generation time of a normal cell. When is a cell considered G_0? What is the difference between the G_0 and G_1 phases? Class Activity ***Using the diagram of the cell cycle with the phases unlabeled, have volunteer students describe the phases of cellular proliferation and how knowledge of these phases has been used to design antineoplastic agents. Review the exercise with the class.*** Class Activity ***Ask students to define the differences between cell cycle–specific and cell cycle–nonspecific chemotherapy, including the concepts of schedule and dose dependency.***
Cite the rationale for giving chemotherapeutic drugs on a precise time schedule.	■ Cancer and the use of antineoplastic agents (p. 688)	PPT 7 TB Multiple Choice questions 3-4 CTQ 1 SG Review Sheet question 14 (p. 294) Review Questions for the NCLEX Examination 7, 9 (p. 707) ▸ Discuss what you would need to know about a drug's action to schedule the administration and dosage properly. ▸ Discuss what it means when a medication is said to be dose dependent. Class Activity ***Using the diagram created in the previous class activity depicting the normal cycle of cell replication, have students explain how knowledge of neoplastic cellular kinetics and cell cycle stages relate to chemotherapy administration. How does delivery of cell cycle–specific drugs at specific intervals maximize cytotoxicity?***
Cite the goals of chemotherapy.	■ Cancer and the use of antineoplastic agents (p. 688) Review the goals of drug therapy for cancer. Discuss the terms *palliation* and *combination therapy*.	PPT 12 INRQ 4 Animation: Cancer Treatment: Chemotherapy Animation: Cancer Treatment: Radiation Therapy

OBJECTIVES	CONTENT	TEACHING RESOURCES
		SG Review Sheet question 10 (p. 294) SG Learning Activities questions 1, 16 (p. 296) Review Question for the NCLEX Examination 8 (p. 707) ▸ Discuss the goals of chemotherapy. When might a patient receive prophylactic chemotherapy? ▸ Discuss what is meant by palliation. Class Activity ***List on the board the following terms:* palliation therapy, combination therapy, monoclonal antibodies, tyrosine, kinase inhibitors, proteasome inhibitors, chemoprotective agents, *and* bone marrow stimulants. *Divide the class into five groups, and have each group discuss the goals of therapy for cancer patients using one of the following terms:* palliation therapy, combination therapy, targeted anticancer agents, chemoprotective agents, *and* bone marrow stimulants. *Review the exercise with the class.***
Describe the role of targeted anticancer agents in treating cancer.	■ Drug therapy for cancer (p. 689) Review the types of targeted anticancer agents: monoclonal antibodies, tyrosine, kinase inhibitors, and proteasome inhibitors.	PPT 18-19 CTQ 6 SG Review Sheet questions 5, 17 (pp. 293-294) SG Learning Activities question 15 (p. 296) Drug Table 44-2: Targeted anticancer agents (pp. 698-699) ▸ Discuss and compare the different actions of the targeted anticancer agents in Table 44-2. Class Activity ***Have students list each targeted anticancer agent and the cancers for which they are indicated.***
Describe the role of chemoprotective agents in treating cancer.	■ Drug therapy for cancer (p. 689) Review what chemoprotective agents are used for. Discuss the application of the nursing process for patients on chemotherapy.	PPT 18-19 TB Multiple Choice question 10 CTQ 6 SG Review Sheet questions 6, 18 (pp. 293, 295) SG Learning Activities question 2 (p. 296) Review Question for the NCLEX Examination 6 (p. 707) Drug Table 44-3: Chemoprotective Agents (p. 700)

OBJECTIVES	CONTENT	TEACHING RESOURCES
		▸ Discuss the role of targeted anticancer agents and chemoprotective agents in treating cancer. How do they differ? Class Activity ***Divide the class into two groups. Have group 1 characterize targeted anticancer agents and their role in cancer treatment. Have group 2 characterize chemoprotective agents and their role in cancer treatment.*** Class Activity ***Ask students to identify whether the following drugs are targeted anticancer agents or chemoprotective agents:*** – ***Mesna (Mesnex)*** – ***Filgrastim (Neupogen)*** – ***Rituximab (Rituxan)*** – ***Dexrazoxane (Zinecard)*** – ***Amifostine (Ethyol)*** – ***Epoetin alfa (Procrit)***
Describe the role of bone marrow stimulants in treating cancer.	■ Drug therapy for cancer (p. 689) Review what bone marrow stimulants are used for. Discuss the application of the nursing process for patients on chemotherapy.	PPT 18-19 ARQ 2 TB Multiple Choice questions 9, 11 INRQ 8-9 CTQ 6 SG Review Sheet question 7 (p. 293) SG Learning Activities questions 10-11 (p. 296) SG Practice Questions for the NCLEX Examination 6, 8 (p. 298) Review Question for the NCLEX Examination 5 (p. 707) Drug Table 44-4: Bone Marrow Stimulants (p. 700) ▸ Discuss the role of bone marrow stimulants in treating cancer. How do they differ from targeted anticancer agents? Class Activity ***Have the class list the trade and generic names of the bone marrow stimulants in Table 44-4. Then ask the class to explain the drugs' effects, and list the blood cell types affected.*** Class Activity ***Divide the class into small groups, and assign each group one of the following systems: gastrointestinal, integumentary, and immune or bone marrow cells. Have each group describe the effects of chemotherapy on the body system, and identify associated nursing assessments and interventions.***

ELSEVIER

OBJECTIVES	CONTENT	TEACHING RESOURCES
		Class Activity ***Have students list examples of antiemetic drugs, dosages, and time of administration. Next, have students identify what complications may occur from untreated nausea and vomiting.*** Class Activity ***Ask students to call out common medications used to treat cancer pain and their adverse effects. How are those adverse effects managed with lifestyle changes and medication?***
Develop patient education objectives for a patient receiving chemotherapy.	– Nursing process for chemotherapy (p. 697) – Patient education and health promotion (p. 703)	PPT 20 ARQ 4 TB Multiple Choice question 12 TB Multiple Response question 4 INRQ 3 Patient Self-Assessment Form: Antineoplastic Agents SG Review Sheet questions 19, 21-22 (p. 295) SG Learning Activities question 19 (p. 296) SG Practice Questions for the NCLEX Examination 3-5 (p. 297) Review Question for the NCLEX Examination 4 (p. 707) ▸ Discuss how you would prepare a patient for neutropenia. ▸ Discuss the nonmedical issues that might need to be addressed in a patient education plan. Why is it important to involve family members? Class Activity ***Divide the class into pairs, and have them take turns role-playing a nurse providing patient education to a patient anticipating chemotherapy treatment. Students should review teaching tools and how to complete self-assessment forms before the role play.*** Class Activity ***Divide the class into three groups, and assign each group one of the following patient scenarios:*** – ***A 68-year-old man with lymphoma is ordered cyclophosphamide (Cytoxan).*** – ***A 58-year-old woman with lung cancer is prescribed ifosfamide (Ifex).*** – ***An 80-year-old man with colon cancer is ordered carmustine (BCNU).*** ***Have each group devise a care plan.***

44.1 Homework/Assignments:

44.1 Instructor's Notes/Student Feedback:

LESSON 44.2

CRITICAL THINKING QUESTION

A 52-year-old patient has been diagnosed with advanced ovarian cancer. Why do her drug orders include amifostine (Ethyol) in addition to her cisplatin chemotherapy regimen?

Guidelines: Amifostine (Ethyol) is a chemoprotective agent that is ordered to reduce the renal toxicity associated with repeated administration of cisplatin. Administration of this chemoprotective agent does not enhance the efficacy of cisplatin in destroying the cancer cells, but rather protects against the toxic adverse effects of cisplatin. Amifostine is considered a "prodrug" that increases the amount of free thiol in normal tissue cells when it is metabolized. Increased free thiol is then available to bind with the toxic metabolites of cisplatin, thereby reducing the renal toxicity associated with cisplatin administration. Blood tests to monitor the patient's kidney function and adequate oral and intravenous fluids are also indicated.

OBJECTIVES	CONTENT	TEACHING RESOURCES
State which types of chemotherapeutic agents are cell cycle–specific and those that are cell cycle–nonspecific.	□ Drug class: Alkylating agents (p. 705) – Nursing process for alkylating agents (p. 705) Review the drug class alkylating agents used to eradicate malignant cells. Discuss the actions, uses, and therapeutic outcomes of alkylating agents. Review the premedication assessments needed for patients receiving these agents.	PPT 13 TB Multiple Response questions 1-2 CTQ 4 SG Review Sheet questions 4, 12, 27 (pp. 293-295) SG Learning Activities questions 6, 8, 12 (p. 296) SG Practice Questions for the NCLEX Examination 9, 11-12 (p. 298) Review Questions for the NCLEX Examination 1-2 (p. 707) Drug Table 44-1: Cancer Chemotherapeutic Agents (pp. 690-696) ▸ Discuss the actions of alkylating agents. What happens if a patient develops resistance? Class Activity ***Ask students to identify each of the following as cell cycle–specific or cell cycle–nonspecific agents:***

OBJECTIVES	CONTENT	TEACHING RESOURCES
		– *Chlorambucil (Leukeran)* – *Cytarabine (Cytosar)* – *Cyclophosphamide (Cytoxan)* – *Fluorouracil (5-FU)* – *Mechlorethamine (nitrogen mustard)* – *Mercaptopurine (Purinethol)* Class Activity ***Have students define the mechanism of action for alkylating agents, providing examples of this drug class and specifying the types of cancer treated with these agents.***
State which types of chemotherapeutic agents are cell cycle–specific and those that are cell cycle–nonspecific.	□ Drug class: Antimetabolites (p. 705) – Nursing process for antimetabolites (p. 705) Review the drug class antimetabolites used to inhibit key enzymes and kill cells during the S phase of maturation. Discuss the actions, uses, and therapeutic outcomes of antimetabolites. Review the premedication assessments needed for patients receiving these agents.	PPT 14 SG Review Sheet questions 4, 12, 27 (pp. 293-295) SG Learning Activities question 13 (p. 296) SG Practice Question for the NCLEX Examination 10 (p. 298) ▸ Discuss the phase of the cell maturation cycle for which antimetabolites are cycle specific. Class Activity ***Have students define the mechanism of action for antimetabolites, provide examples of this drug class, and specify the types of cancer treated with these agents. Next, have students identify baseline data that would be important to a premedication assessment for this drug.***
State which types of chemotherapeutic agents are cell cycle–specific and those that are cell cycle–nonspecific.	□ Drug class: Natural products (p. 705) – Nursing process for natural products (p. 705) Review the drug class natural products used as cell cycle–specific agents. Discuss the actions, uses, and therapeutic outcomes for natural products. Review the premedication assessments needed for patients receiving these agents.	PPT 15 INRQ 10 SG Review Sheet questions 4, 12, 27 (pp. 293-295) SG Learning Activities question 5 (p. 296) ▸ Discuss which cancers react positively to natural products. Class Activity ***Have students define the mechanism of action for natural products, provide examples of this drug class, and specify the types of cancer treated with these agents.*** Class Activity ***Have two students role-play a nurse instructing a patient receiving paclitaxel (Taxol) for ovarian cancer. Have the class assist the nurse in determining the pertinent patient information to impart and the adverse effects to report. Review the exercise with the class.***

OBJECTIVES	CONTENT	TEACHING RESOURCES
State which types of chemotherapeutic agents are cell cycle–specific and those that are cell cycle–nonspecific.	□ Drug class: Antineoplastic antibiotics (p. 705) – Nursing process for antineoplastic antibiotics (p. 706) Review the drug class antineoplastic antibiotics used to inhibit DNA or RNA synthesis. Discuss the actions, uses, and therapeutic outcomes of antineoplastic antibiotics. Review premedication assessments needed for patients receiving these agents.	PPT 16 INRQ 7, 11 Patient Self-Assessment Form: Antineoplastic Agents SG Review Sheet questions 4, 12, 27 (pp. 293-295) SG Learning Activities question 9 (p. 296) SG Practice Question for the NCLEX Examination 7 (p. 298) Review Question for the NCLEX Examination 3 (p. 707) ▸ Discuss how antineoplastic antibiotics act on DNA. What adverse effects might one expect from antineoplastic antibiotics? Class Activity ***Have students define the mechanism of action for antineoplastic antibiotics, provide examples of this drug class, and specify the types of cancer treated with these agents. What are two systems that should be particularly evaluated in the medication preassessment?***
State which types of chemotherapeutic agents are cell cycle–specific and those that are cell cycle–nonspecific.	□ Drug class: Hormones (p. 706) – Nursing process for hormones (p. 706) Review the drug class hormones, which includes corticosteroids, estrogens, and androgens as a chemotherapy agent. Discuss the actions, uses, and therapeutic outcomes of hormones. Review the premedication assessments needed for patients receiving these agents.	PPT 17 TB Multiple Choice question 6 SG Review Sheet questions 4, 12, 27 (pp. 293-295) SG Learning Activities question 14 (p. 296) ▸ Discuss how corticosteroids may be used in palliative therapy. ▸ Discuss what types of malignancies might be treated with hormones. What is the treatment for postmenopausal women with metastatic breast cancer? Class Activity ***Have students define the mechanism of action for hormonal agents, provide examples of this drug class, and specify the types of cancer treated with these agents.*** Class Activity ***Call out specific chemotherapy agents, and ask the students to identify the specific drug class to which they belong.***

OBJECTIVES	CONTENT	TEACHING RESOURCES
Performance evaluation		Test Bank SG Learning Activities (p. 296) SG Practice Questions for NCLEX Examination (pp. 297-298) Critical Thinking Questions

44.2 Homework/Assignments:

44.2 Instructor's Notes/Student Feedback:

44 Lecture Outline

Drugs Used for Cancer Treatment

Slide 1

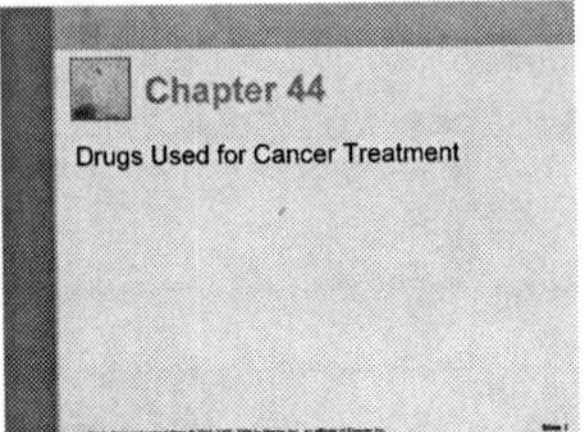
Chapter 44
Drugs Used for Cancer Treatment

Slide 2

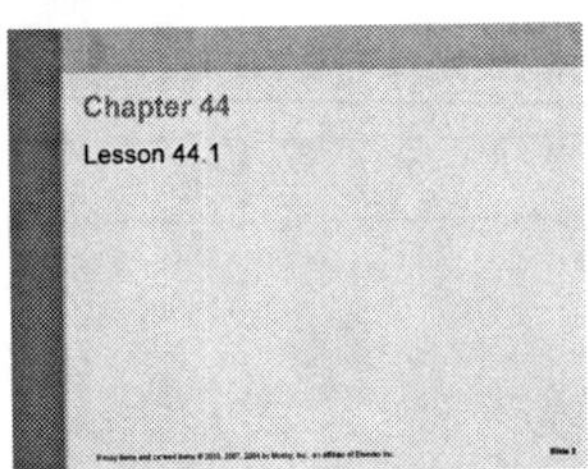
Chapter 44
Lesson 44.1

Slide 3

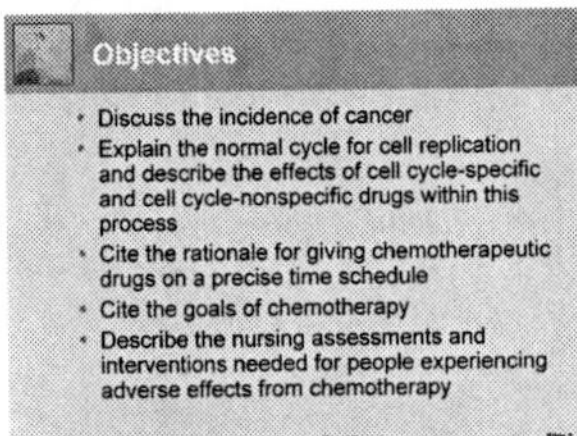
Objectives
Discuss the incidence of cancer
Explain the normal cycle for cell replication and describe the effects of cell cycle-specific and cell cycle-nonspecific drugs within this process
Cite the rationale for giving chemotherapeutic drugs on a precise time schedule
Cite the goals of chemotherapy
Describe the nursing assessments and interventions needed for people experiencing adverse effects from chemotherapy

Slide 4

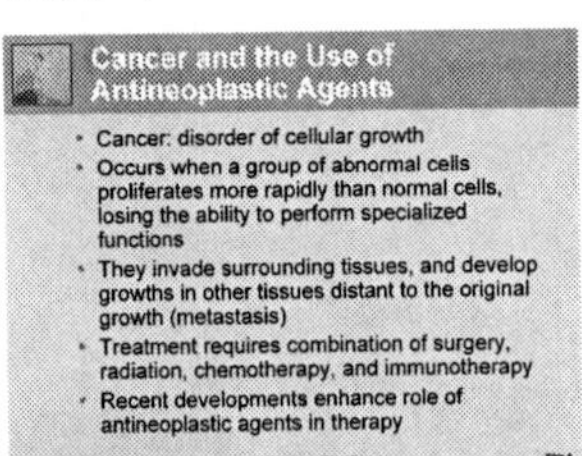
Cancer and the Use of Antineoplastic Agents
Cancer: disorder of cellular growth
Occurs when a group of abnormal cells proliferates more rapidly than normal cells, losing the ability to perform specialized functions
They invade surrounding tissues, and develop growths in other tissues distant to the original growth (metastasis)
Treatment requires combination of surgery, radiation, chemotherapy, and immunotherapy
Recent developments enhance role of antineoplastic agents in therapy

- Many types of cancer cells lose the ability to die properly as part of their normal life cycle.

Slide 5

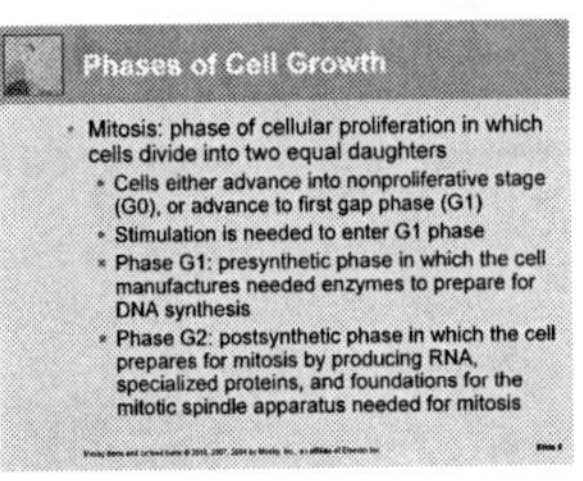
Phases of Cell Growth
Mitosis: phase of cellular proliferation in which cells divide into two equal daughters
Cells either advance into nonproliferative stage (G0), or advance to first gap phase (G1)
Stimulation is needed to enter G1 phase
Phase G1: presynthetic phase in which the cell manufactures needed enzymes to prepare for DNA synthesis
Phase G2: postsynthetic phase in which the cell prepares for mitosis by producing RNA, specialized proteins, and foundations for the mitotic spindle apparatus needed for mitosis

- G0 is the largest variable in the cell cycle. During this resting phase, the cell is not actively replicating.
- Draw a diagram depicting the life cycle of a cell.

Slide 6

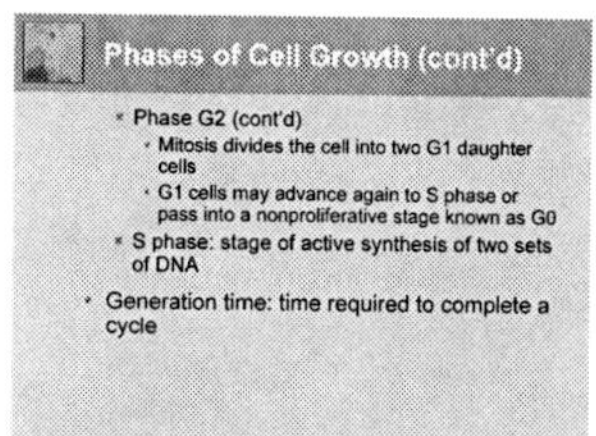
Phases of Cell Growth (cont'd)
Phase G2 (cont'd)
Mitosis divides the cell into two G1 daughter cells
G1 cells may advance again to S phase or pass into a nonproliferative stage known as G0
S phase: stage of active synthesis of two sets of DNA
Generation time: time required to complete a cycle

Slide 7

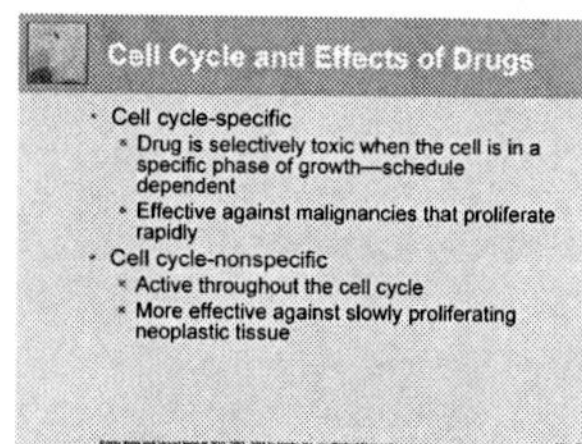
Cell Cycle and Effects of Drugs
Cell cycle-specific
Drug is selectively toxic when the cell is in a specific phase of growth—schedule dependent
Effective against malignancies that proliferate rapidly
Cell cycle-nonspecific
Active throughout the cell cycle
More effective against slowly proliferating neoplastic tissue

- It is important to correlate the dosage schedule with the known cellular kinetics of that type of neoplasm.
- Drugs usually administered when the cell is most susceptible to the cytotoxic effects of the agent for a greater "kill rate."
- Provide examples of specific drugs that are cell cycle–specific and cell cycle–nonspecific.

Slide 8

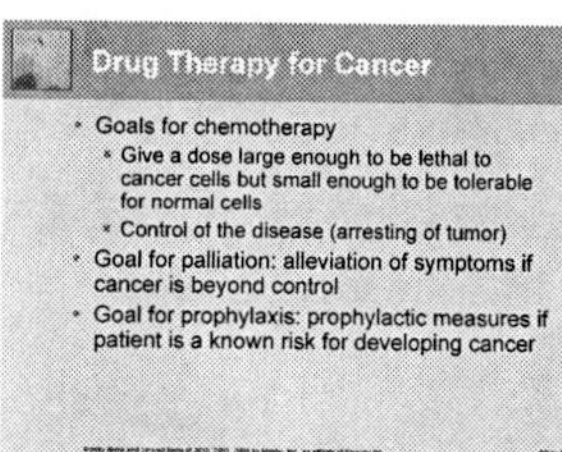
Drug Therapy for Cancer
Goals for chemotherapy
Give a dose large enough to be lethal to cancer cells but small enough to be tolerable for normal cells
Control of the disease (arresting of tumor)
Goal for palliation: alleviation of symptoms if cancer is beyond control
Goal for prophylaxis: prophylactic measures if patient is a known risk for developing cancer

- Combination therapy is superior in therapeutic effect than using a single agent alone.

Slide 9

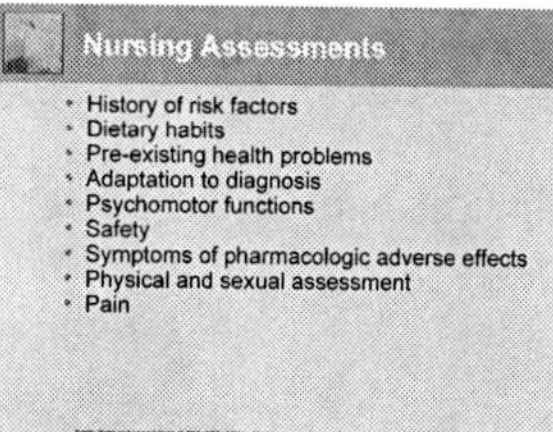
Nursing Assessments
History of risk factors
Dietary habits
Pre-existing health problems
Adaptation to diagnosis
Psychomotor functions
Safety
Symptoms of pharmacologic adverse effects
Physical and sexual assessment
Pain

Slide 10

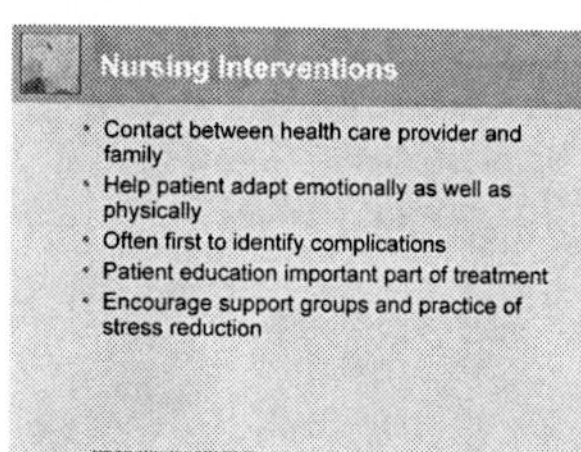
Nursing Interventions
Contact between health care provider and family
Help patient adapt emotionally as well as physically
Often first to identify complications
Patient education important part of treatment
Encourage support groups and practice of stress reduction

ELSEVIER

Slide 11

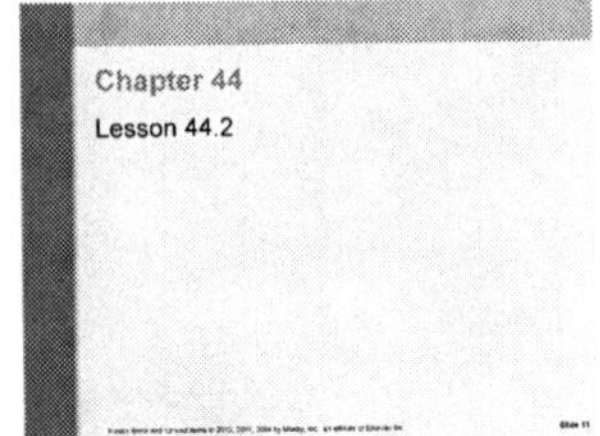
Chapter 44
Lesson 44.2

Slide 12

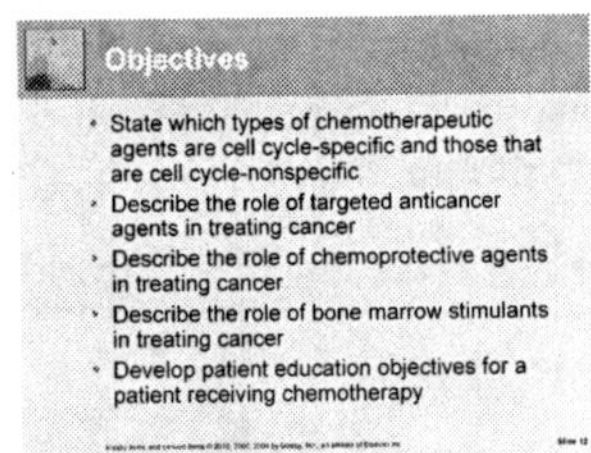
Objectives
State which types of chemotherapeutic agents are cell cycle-specific and those that are cell cycle-nonspecific
Describe the role of targeted anticancer agents in treating cancer
Describe the role of chemoprotective agents in treating cancer
Describe the role of bone marrow stimulants in treating cancer
Develop patient education objectives for a patient receiving chemotherapy

Slide 13

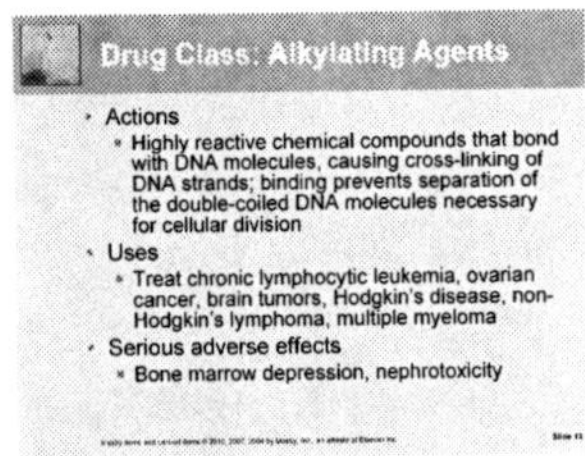
Drug Class: Alkylating Agents
Actions
Highly reactive chemical compounds that bond with DNA molecules, causing cross-linking of DNA strands; binding prevents separation of the double-coiled DNA molecules necessary for cellular division
Uses
Treat chronic lymphocytic leukemia, ovarian cancer, brain tumors, Hodgkin's disease, non-Hodgkin's lymphoma, multiple myeloma
Serious adverse effects
Bone marrow depression, nephrotoxicity

- For specific drugs, see Table 44-1.
- These agents are cell cycle–nonspecific, capable of combining with cellular components at any phase of the cell cycle.
- Common adverse effects: GI symptoms, anorexia, nausea, vomiting.

Slide 14

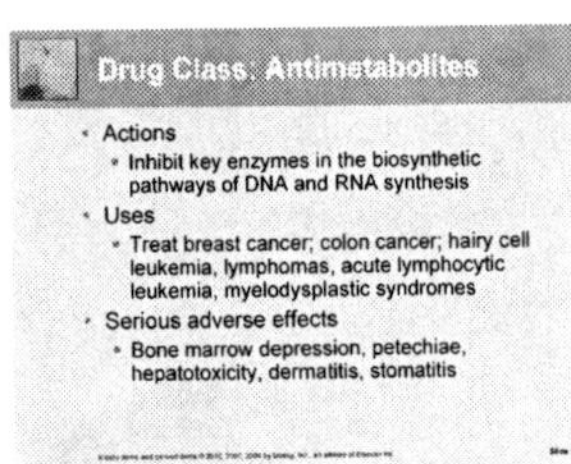
Drug Class: Antimetabolites
Actions
Inhibit key enzymes in the biosynthetic pathways of DNA and RNA synthesis
Uses
Treat breast cancer; colon cancer; hairy cell leukemia, lymphomas, acute lymphocytic leukemia, myelodysplastic syndromes
Serious adverse effects
Bone marrow depression, petechiae, hepatotoxicity, dermatitis, stomatitis

- For specific drugs, see Table 44-1.
- Antimetabolites are cell–specific, killing cells during the S phase of cell maturation.
- Common adverse effects: GI symptoms, anorexia, nausea, vomiting.

Slide 15

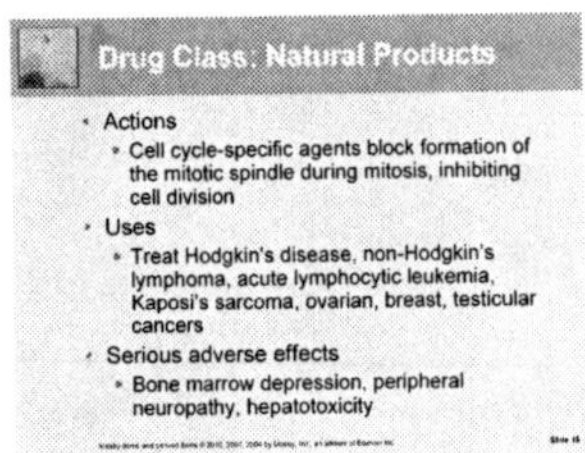
Drug Class: Natural Products
Actions
Cell cycle-specific agents block formation of the mitotic spindle during mitosis, inhibiting cell division
Uses
Treat Hodgkin's disease, non-Hodgkin's lymphoma, acute lymphocytic leukemia, Kaposi's sarcoma, ovarian, breast, testicular cancers
Serious adverse effects
Bone marrow depression, peripheral neuropathy, hepatotoxicity

- For specific drugs, see Table 44-1
- The vinca alkaloids vincristine and vinblastine are natural derivatives of the periwinkle plant.
- Common adverse effects: nausea, vomiting, diarrhea.

ELSEVIER

Slide 16

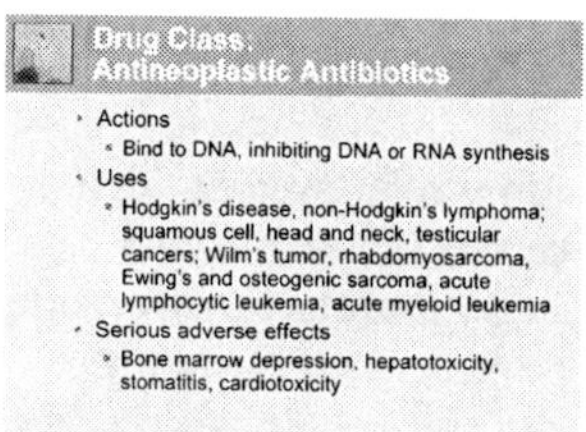
Drug Class: Antineoplastic Antibiotics
Actions
Bind to DNA, inhibiting DNA or RNA synthesis
Uses
Hodgkin's disease, non-Hodgkin's lymphoma; squamous cell, head and neck, testicular cancers; Wilm's tumor, rhabdomyosarcoma, Ewing's and osteogenic sarcoma, acute lymphocytic leukemia, acute myeloid leukemia
Serious adverse effects
Bone marrow depression, hepatotoxicity, stomatitis, cardiotoxicity

- For specific drugs, see Table 44-1.
- Common adverse effects: nausea, vomiting, red urine, diarrhea, chills.

Slide 17

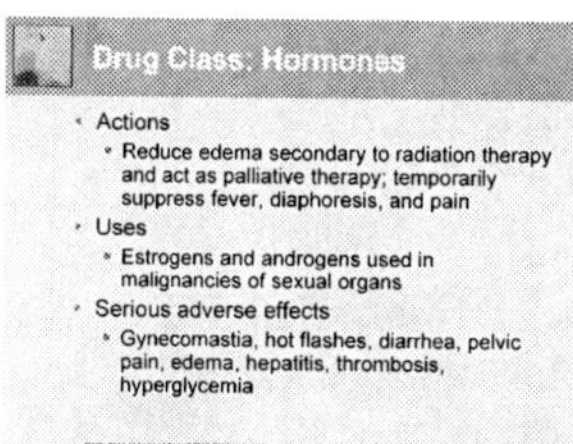
Drug Class: Hormones
Actions
Reduce edema secondary to radiation therapy and act as palliative therapy; temporarily suppress fever, diaphoresis, and pain
Uses
Estrogens and androgens used in malignancies of sexual organs
Serious adverse effects
Gynecomastia, hot flashes, diarrhea, pelvic pain, edema, hepatitis, thrombosis, hyperglycemia

- For specific drugs, see Table 44-1.
- Edema is associated with radiation therapy because it is the inflammatory response to cellular death.

Slide 18

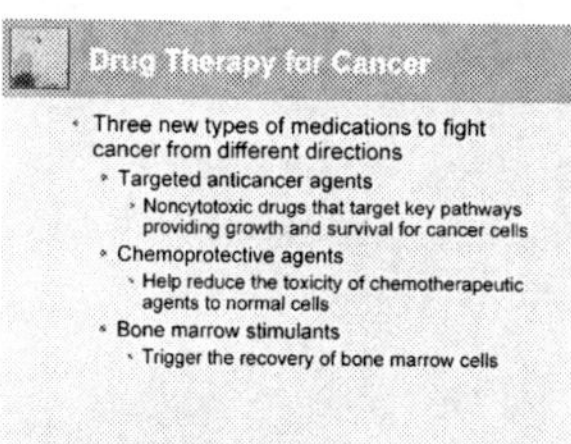
Drug Therapy for Cancer
Three new types of medications to fight cancer from different directions
Targeted anticancer agents
Noncytotoxic drugs that target key pathways providing growth and survival for cancer cells
Chemoprotective agents
Help reduce the toxicity of chemotherapeutic agents to normal cells
Bone marrow stimulants
Trigger the recovery of bone marrow cells

- For specific drugs, see Tables 44-2, 44-3, and 44-4.
- Targeted anticancer agents evolved from research indicating cell membrane receptors control cell proliferation, cell migration, angiogenesis, and cell death, which is integral to the growth and spread of cancer.

Slide 19

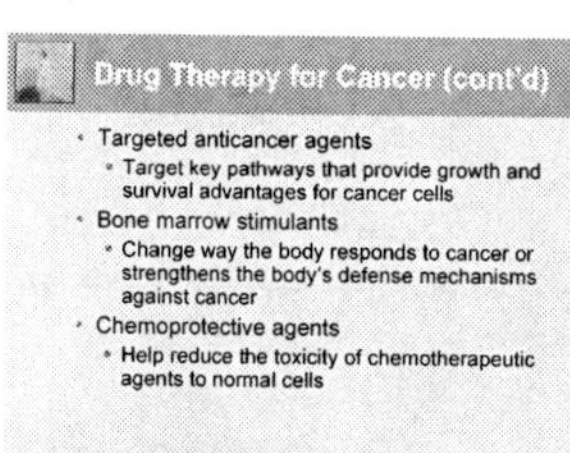
Drug Therapy for Cancer (cont'd)
Targeted anticancer agents
Target key pathways that provide growth and survival advantages for cancer cells
Bone marrow stimulants
Change way the body responds to cancer or strengthens the body's defense mechanisms against cancer
Chemoprotective agents
Help reduce the toxicity of chemotherapeutic agents to normal cells

- For specific drugs, see Tables 44-2, 44-3, and 44-4.
- Bone marrow stimulants assist with early recovery of the immune response and prevent infections from becoming pathologic.
- Blood counts must be assessed closely to determine the degree of bone marrow suppression.

Slide 20

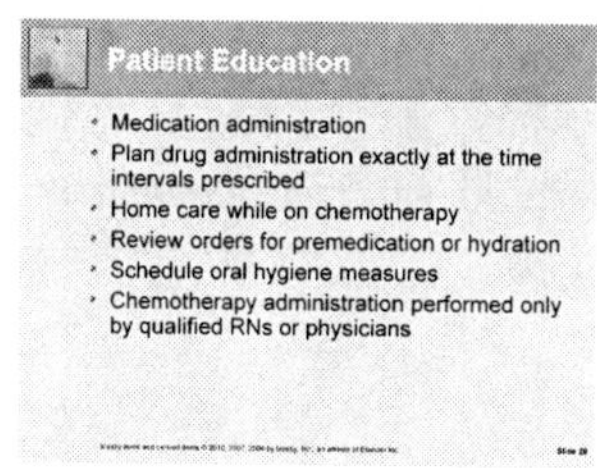
Patient Education
Medication administration
Plan drug administration exactly at the time intervals prescribed
Home care while on chemotherapy
Review orders for premedication or hydration
Schedule oral hygiene measures
Chemotherapy administration performed only by qualified RNs or physicians

- Emphasize the prevention of complications through maintenance of nutrition and hydration and commitment of hygiene practices.
- Explain how to minimize the chance of infection when neutropenia is present.
- Encourage seeking pain relief.
- Home care includes washing soiled linens separately, washing twice, flushing the toilet after use two or three times.

45 Lesson Plan
Drugs Used to Treat the Muscular System

TEACHING FOCUS

In this chapter, students have the opportunity to learn about drug therapy for the muscular system, including centrally acting skeletal muscle relaxants, direct-acting skeletal muscle relaxants, and neuromuscular blocking agents. In addition to discussing the actions and uses of drugs administered for muscle disorders, this chapter examines adverse effects and discusses what precautions need to be taken when assessing, monitoring, and administering muscle relaxants and neuromuscular blocking agents.

MATERIALS AND RESOURCES

- ☐ computer and PowerPoint projector (all Lessons)
- ☐ sample patient chart (Lesson 45.2)

LESSON CHECKLIST

Preparations for this lesson include:

- lecture
- evaluation of student knowledge and skills needed to perform all entry-level activities related to understanding the actions and uses of muscle relaxants and neuromuscular blocking agents, including:
  - listing assessment data needed to evaluate a patient with skeletal muscle disorder
  - stating nursing assessments needed to monitor therapeutic response and possible adverse effects from skeletal muscle relaxant therapy
  - describing the effect of centrally acting skeletal muscle relaxants on the nervous system and safety precautions before and during their use
  - developing patient education objectives for a patient receiving skeletal muscle therapy
  - describing the four uses of neuromuscular blocking agents and their physiologic effects
  - stating what to look for on a patient's chart when using neuromuscular blocking agents

KEY TERMS

cerebral palsy (p. 708)
hypercapnia (p. 709)
multiple sclerosis (p. 708)
muscle spasms (p. 711)
neuromuscular blocking agents (p. 714)
spasticity (p. 711)

ADDITIONAL RESOURCES

PowerPoint slides: 1-14
Flashcards, Decks 1 and 2

Legend

ARQ	PPT	TB	CTQ	SG	INRQ
Audience Response Questions	PowerPoint Slides	Test Bank	Critical Thinking Questions	Study Guide	Interactive NCLEX Review Questions

Class Activities are indicated in ***bold italic.***

LESSON 45.1

BACKGROUND ASSESSMENT

Question: What is the effect of centrally acting skeletal muscle relaxants on the body, and what safety precautions are related to their use?
Answer: Centrally acting skeletal muscle relaxants relieve acute muscle spasms by depressing the central nervous system. All centrally acting muscle relaxants produce some level of sedation and require safety precautions, such as avoiding driving and operating power equipment. Safety precautions should be observed if the patient experiences dizziness or weakness. Patients should also be instructed to avoid other central nervous system depressants, such as alcohol, anticonvulsants, antihypertensives, potassium supplements, and tranquilizers, because they can cause drug interactions with centrally acting muscle relaxants.

Question: What nursing assessments are indicated when caring for a patient who has received neuromuscular blocking agents?
Answer: Neuromuscular blocking agents relax muscles but do not affect pain, memory, or consciousness. A baseline reading of vital signs and mental and respiratory status should be obtained before neuromuscular blocking agents are administered. Following administration, close observation of vital signs and respiratory function should continue because drug adverse effects may occur as late as 48 hours after drug administration. The nurse should assess for cough reflex, ability to swallow secretions, signs of hypoxia and hypercapnia, and muscle strength. A pulse oximeter should be used to confirm clinical observations. The nurse should continue to assess for pain and any changes in mental status and should confirm that respiratory support equipment is available in the immediate patient care area.

CRITICAL THINKING QUESTION

A 56-year-old early retiree pulled a muscle during a golf tournament and now has back spasms causing him severe pain. His health care provider has ordered cyclobenzaprine (Flexeril) 10 mg three times daily. What education should the nurse provide to the patient and his wife regarding management of his muscle spasms?
Guidelines: The nurse should instruct the patient and his wife about the medication that his health care provider has ordered, including dosage, administration schedule, and common adverse effects. Because cyclobenzaprine causes some sedative effects, the nurse should caution the patient to avoid driving, drinking alcohol, or operating power equipment and assess allergies and present medications. The nurse should also provide information on the nonsteroidal anti-inflammatory analgesics prescribed to reduce the patient's pain and swelling, and the nurse should instruct the patient to take the medications on a regular, around-the-clock schedule to achieve adequate pain relief. Cold packs for the first 24 hours (at which time they are switched to heat packs) are helpful during the initial period following an injury to help reduce swelling. Bed rest may also be indicated.

OBJECTIVES	CONTENT	TEACHING RESOURCES
Prepare a list of assessment data needed to evaluate a patient with a skeletal muscle disorder.	■ Muscle relaxants and neuromuscular blocking agents (p. 708) – Nursing process for skeletal muscle relaxants and neuromuscular blocking agents (p. 708) Review the nursing process used for patients who are receiving skeletal muscle relaxants and neuromuscular blocking agents. Discuss the musculoskeletal disorders that impair an	PPT 6-7 TB Multiple Choice question 6 TB Multiple Response question 2 INRQ 1-2 SG Review Sheet questions 1-6 (p. 299) SG Learning Activities questions 10, 12-13 (p. 302) SG Practice Question for the NCLEX Examination 7 (p. 304)

OBJECTIVES	CONTENT	TEACHING RESOURCES
	individual's ability to perform activities of daily living (ADLs). Review the assessments necessary to cover for patients receiving skeletal muscle relaxants and neuromuscular blocking agents, including respiratory depression.	▸ Discuss the nursing assessments needed to evaluate a patient with a skeletal muscle disorder. What medications should you specifically ask about when taking a medication history? ▸ Discuss the specific instructions that a nurse would give a patient immediately after an injury that produced swelling. Class Activity ***Instruct students to create an assessment form for use in evaluating a patient with a skeletal muscle disorder.*** Class Activity ***Have students work in pairs. Using the assessment (data collection) tool they created for the previous class activity, have students role-play the assessment process for a patient with a skeletal muscle disorder. After a reasonable time interval, have the students switch roles.***
State the nursing assessments needed to monitor the therapeutic response and the development of common and serious adverse effects from skeletal muscle relaxant therapy.	– Nursing process for skeletal muscle relaxants and neuromuscular blocking agents (p. 708) Review the drug therapy used for muscle disorders, including centrally acting skeletal muscle relaxants, direct-acting skeletal muscle relaxants, and neuromuscular blocking agents. Discuss the patient education needed for the use of these drugs.	PPT 8 TB Multiple Response question 3 INRQ 3, 7-8, 11 SG Learning Activities question 14 (p. 302) ▸ Discuss what special precautions a nurse would need to take to protect the airways of patients who are paralyzed or have less control over swallowing, coughing, and deep breathing. Class Activity ***As a class, discuss common adverse effects and related nursing assessments and interventions for skeletal muscle relaxant therapy. Suggestion: Assign specific medications to compare and contrast the similarities and differences.*** Class Activity ***Divide the class in half. Assign half of the class skeletal muscle relaxants and the other half neuromuscular blocking agents. In each subgroup, have students pair with a partner. Have student groups review the nursing evaluation for the patient taking skeletal muscle relaxants or neuromuscular blocking agents. Allow time for subgroup presentation and discussion.***
List steps required to treat respiratory depression.	– Nursing process for skeletal muscle relaxants and neuromuscular blocking agents (p. 708)	PPT 8 TB Multiple Choice question 8 SG Review Sheet questions 14-15 (p. 300) SG Learning Activities question 11 (p. 302)

OBJECTIVES	CONTENT	TEACHING RESOURCES
		▸ Discuss the early signs of respiratory depression. What changes as distress progresses? Class Activity ***Compose a case study for a patient taking neuromuscular blocking agents who has gone into respiratory depression. Have students work in pairs, and have them determine signs of respiratory depression and nursing actions relevant to the case study.***
Develop a health teaching plan for patients with skeletal muscle relaxant therapy.	– Patient education and health promotion (p. 710) Review the drug class direct-acting skeletal muscle relaxants. Discuss the actions, uses, and therapeutic outcomes for these drugs. Review the common and serious adverse effects with direct-acting skeletal muscle relaxants, as well as known drug interactions.	PPT 9 ARQ 5 Patient Self-Assessment Form: Muscle Relaxants ▸ Discuss what you would include in a health teaching plan for a patient. What must the patient understand about medication, activity levels, and pain relief methods? ▸ Discuss what safety precautions a nurse would include when developing a health teaching plan. Class Activity ***Ask each student to develop a checklist for in-home use with patients to monitor adverse effects and therapeutic effects of treatment.***
Describe the effect of centrally acting skeletal muscle relaxants on the central nervous system and the safety precautions required during their use.	■ Drug therapy for muscle disorders (p. 711) □ Drug class: Centrally acting skeletal muscle relaxants (p. 711) – Nursing process for centrally acting skeletal muscle relaxants (p. 711) – Nursing process for baclofen (p. 713) □ Drug class: Direct-acting skeletal muscle relaxant (p. 713) – Nursing process for dantrolene (p. 713) Review the drug class centrally acting skeletal muscle relaxants and baclofen. Discuss the actions, uses, and therapeutic outcomes for these drugs. Review the common and serious adverse effects with centrally acting skeletal muscle relaxants and baclofen, as well as known drug interactions.	PPT 10-12 ARQ 2-3 TB Multiple Choice questions 2-3, 7 INRQ 4-5, 9-10 CTQ 1, 4-5 SG Review Sheet questions 7-13, 16-17 (pp. 299-300) SG Learning Activities questions 8-9 (p. 302) SG Practice Questions for the NCLEX Examination 1-2, 8, 10-11 (pp. 303-304) Review Questions for the NCLEX Examination 1, 3-4, 8-9 (p. 716) Drug Table 45-1: Centrally Acting Muscle Relaxants (p. 712) ▸ Discuss the special precautions that a nurse would need to take when a patient receives different muscle relaxants. ▸ Discuss the uses of baclofen. What adverse effects might a nurse expect? Which drugs interact with baclofen, and how?

OBJECTIVES	CONTENT	TEACHING RESOURCES
		Class Activity ***Have each student research a drug monograph for a centrally acting skeletal muscle relaxant, and write a description of its mechanism of action. (For students to prepare for this activity, see Homework/Assignments 1.)*** Class Activity ***Have students read the drug monographs for baclofen and dantrolene and compare and contrast their characteristics, including their mechanism of action, uses, and therapeutic outcomes.***

45.1 Homework/Assignments:

1. Have each student research a drug monograph for a centrally acting skeletal muscle relaxant and write a description of its mechanism of action.

45.1 Instructor's Notes/Student Feedback:

LESSON 45.2

CRITICAL THINKING QUESTION

A female patient is scheduled to begin electroconvulsive therapy for severe depression. What patient education should be included in the nurse's preparation of the patient regarding the neuromuscular blocking agent that will be administered during the therapy?

Guidelines: Explain to the patient that electroconvulsive therapy delivers a safe amount of electricity to induce a medically controlled seizure. General anesthetic is used during the procedure, so the patient should not eat or drink before the therapy to prevent aspiration of stomach contents. During the procedure, an anesthetist or anesthesiologist will administer the anesthetic, and the patient will be closely monitored during and after the therapy for any adverse effects. The nurse should ensure that respiratory equipment and antidotes are available in the patient care area. The nurse should inform the patient that adverse effects from the therapy can include confusion, headache, and mild muscle soreness or stiffness. The nurse should assess any allergies and medications that the patient is currently taking, including over-the-counter or herbal supplements, to identify possible drug interactions. The patient will also be assessed for other medical disorders, such as liver, kidney, or neurologic diseases, that might complicate the use of neuromuscular blocking agents. The nurse should explain to the patient that the nursing staff will assess the patient's vital signs before and after the procedure and will assist her in ambulating following the therapy. The nurse should allow the patient to ask questions to demonstrate that she understands the treatment.

OBJECTIVES	CONTENT	TEACHING RESOURCES
Describe the physiologic effects of neuromuscular blocking agents.	□ Drug class: Neuromuscular blocking agents (p. 714) Review the drug class neuromuscular blocking agents. Discuss the actions, uses, and therapeutic outcomes for these drugs. Review the common and serious adverse effects with neuromuscular blocking agents, as well as known drug interactions.	PPT 13-14 ARQ 4 TB Multiple Response question 9 SG Review Sheet questions 18, 20 (p. 300) SG Learning Activities questions 1, 5-7 (p. 302) SG Practice Questions for the NCLEX Examination 4, 6, 12 (pp. 303-304) Review Question for the NCLEX Examination 6 (p. 716) Drug Table 45-2: Neuromuscular Blocking Agents (p. 715) ▸ Discuss the physiologic effects of neuromuscular blocking agents (see Drug Table 45-2). ▸ Discuss why it is important to administer analgesics on schedule to a patient on a respirator. Class Activity ***Ask students to write a description of how neuromuscular blocking agents work. Have volunteers read their descriptions, and have other students provide feedback or corrections.*** Class Activity ***As a class, compare and contrast the different mechanisms of action for the drug classes presented in this chapter.***
State where information on the use of these agents is found in the patient's chart.	– Nursing process for neuromuscular blocking agents (p. 714)	SG Review Sheet question 23 (p. 301) ▸ Discuss why it is important to check the anesthetist's record for surgical patients. Class Activity ***Bring a sample patient chart to class, and demonstrate where the information would be recorded. If an electronic medical record is used in the health facility, describe where to find this information in the computerized chart. Describe a patient who has received a specific dose of a particular neuromuscular blocking agent, and ask students to describe how it should be charted.***
Identify the effect of neuromuscular blocking agents on consciousness,	□ Drug class: Neuromuscular blocking agents (p. 714) – Nursing process for neuromuscular blocking agents (p. 714)	PPT 13 ARQ 1 TB Multiple Choice question 4

OBJECTIVES	CONTENT	TEACHING RESOURCES
memory, and the pain threshold.		SG Review Sheet question 19 (p. 300) ▸ Discuss the effect of neuromuscular blocking agents on consciousness, memory, and the pain threshold. Class Activity ***Divide the class into three groups: pain, consciousness, and respiratory function. Have each group describe the effects of neuromuscular blocking agents on its assigned topic and the nursing assessments (data collection) required for a patient receiving neuromuscular blocking agents.***
Cite four uses of neuromuscular blocking agents.	□ Drug class: Neuromuscular blocking agents (p. 714) – Nursing process for neuromuscular blocking agents (p. 714)	TB Multiple Choice question 5 TB Multiple Response question 4 SG Review Sheet questions 18, 24 (pp. 300-301) Review Questions for the NCLEX Examination 2, 10 (p. 716) Drug Table 45-2: Neuromuscular Blocking Agents (p. 715) ▸ Discuss the four uses of neuromuscular blocking agents. Class Activity ***Ask each student to list four uses of neuromuscular blocking agents. Then ask students to describe a premedication assessment and rationale for patients who might receive one of these agents.***
List the equipment that should be available in the immediate patient care area when neuromuscular blocking agents are to be administered.	– Nursing process for neuromuscular blocking agents (p. 714)	TB Multiple Choice question 1 SG Review Sheet question 26 (p. 301) SG Learning Activities question 3 (p. 302) SG Practice Question for the NCLEX Examination 3 (p. 303) ▸ Discuss what equipment you should have available for emergencies when administering neuromuscular blocking agents. ▸ Discuss which antidotes can be used in the event of an overdose of neuromuscular blocking agents. Class Activity ***Have each student identify and describe the actions and possible adverse effects of antidotes to neuromuscular blocking agents. Ask students to describe the proper***

OBJECTIVES	CONTENT	TEACHING RESOURCES
		treatment for overdose of a neuromuscular blocking agent, and have them provide appropriate nursing interventions.
Describe essential components of patient assessment used for patients receiving neuromuscular blocking agents.	□ Drug class: Neuromuscular blocking agents (p. 714) – Nursing process for neuromuscular blocking agents (p. 714)	TB Multiple Choice questions 10-11 CTQ 2-4 SG Review Sheet questions 20-22, 25 (pp. 300-301) SG Learning Activities question 2 (p. 302) SG Practice Questions for the NCLEX Examination 5, 9 (pp. 303-304) Review Questions for the NCLEX Examination 5, 7 (p. 716) ▸ Discuss what the nurse should check on a patient's chart before administering neuromuscular blocking agents. ▸ Discuss which elements of a health history assessment (data collection) are important when assessing a patient who is receiving neuromuscular blocking agents. Class Activity ***Ask students to list medications that potentiate the effects of neuromuscular blocking agents. Why do they interact with neuromuscular agents?***
Describe disease conditions that may affect a patient's ability to tolerate the use of neuromuscular blocking agents.	– Nursing process for neuromuscular blocking agents (p. 714)	TB Multiple Response question 1 ▸ Discuss which disorders might affect a patient's ability to tolerate neuromuscular blocking agents. ▸ Discuss what adjustments in the administration of neuromuscular blocking agents might be made for neonatal or older adult patients. Class Activity ***Ask students to list disease conditions that affect a patient's ability to tolerate neuromuscular blocking agents and to describe why premedication assessment is important.***
Performance evaluation		Test Bank SG Learning Activities (p. 302) SG Practice Questions for the NCLEX Examination (pp. 303-304) Critical Thinking Questions

45.2 Homework/Assignments:

45.2 Instructor's Notes/Student Feedback:

45 Lecture Outline

Drugs Used to Treat the Muscular System

Slide 1

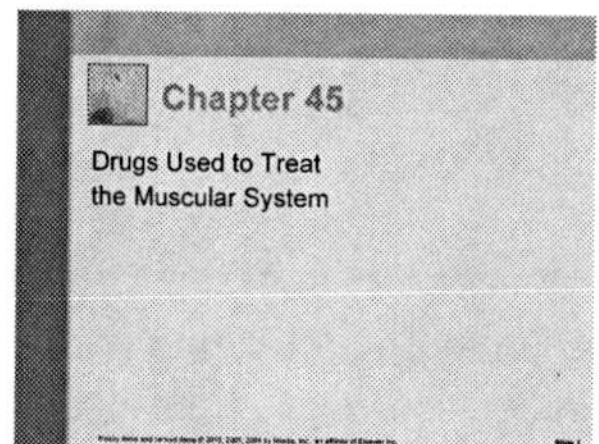
Chapter 45
Drugs Used to Treat
the Muscular System

Slide 2

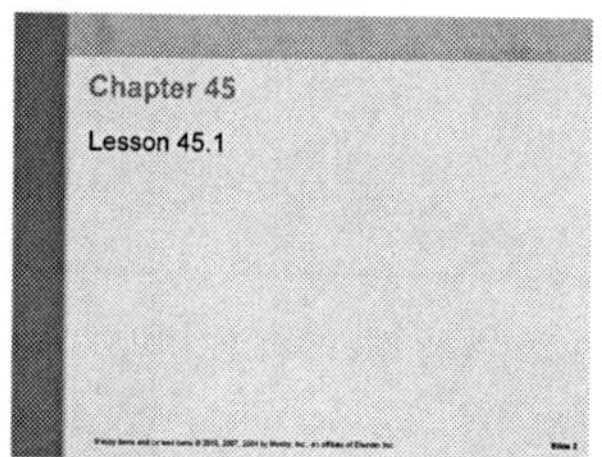
Chapter 45
Lesson 45.1

Slide 3

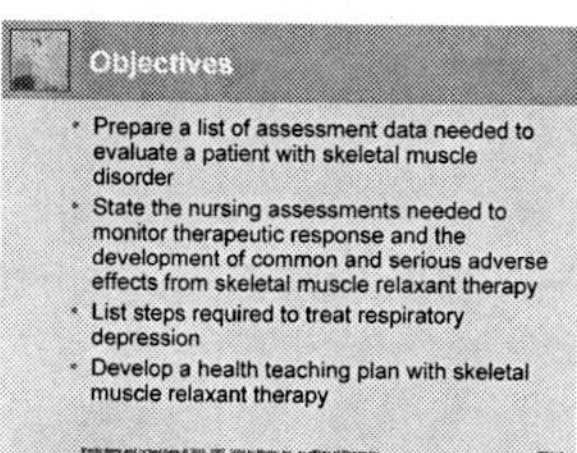
Objectives
Prepare a list of assessment data needed to evaluate a patient with skeletal muscle disorder
State the nursing assessments needed to monitor therapeutic response and the development of common and serious adverse effects from skeletal muscle relaxant therapy
List steps required to treat respiratory depression
Develop a health teaching plan with skeletal muscle relaxant therapy

Slide 4

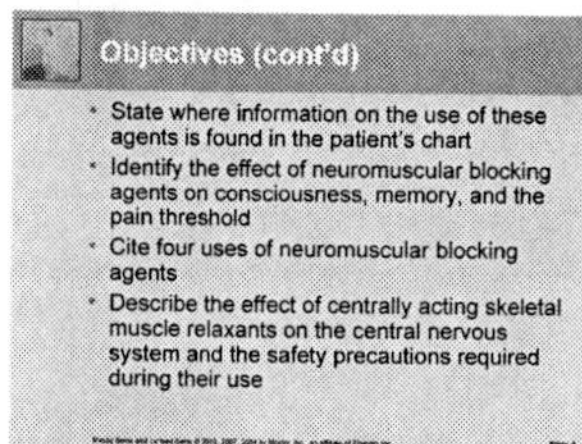
Objectives (cont'd)
State where information on the use of these agents is found in the patient's chart
Identify the effect of neuromuscular blocking agents on consciousness, memory, and the pain threshold
Cite four uses of neuromuscular blocking agents
Describe the effect of centrally acting skeletal muscle relaxants on the central nervous system and the safety precautions required during their use

Slide 5

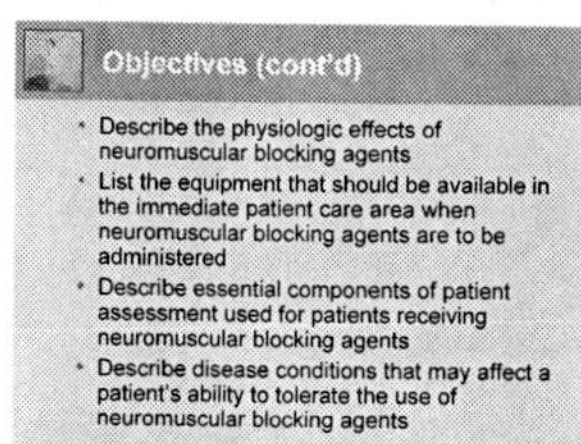
Objectives (cont'd)
Describe the physiologic effects of neuromuscular blocking agents
List the equipment that should be available in the immediate patient care area when neuromuscular blocking agents are to be administered
Describe essential components of patient assessment used for patients receiving neuromuscular blocking agents
Describe disease conditions that may affect a patient's ability to tolerate the use of neuromuscular blocking agents

Slide 6

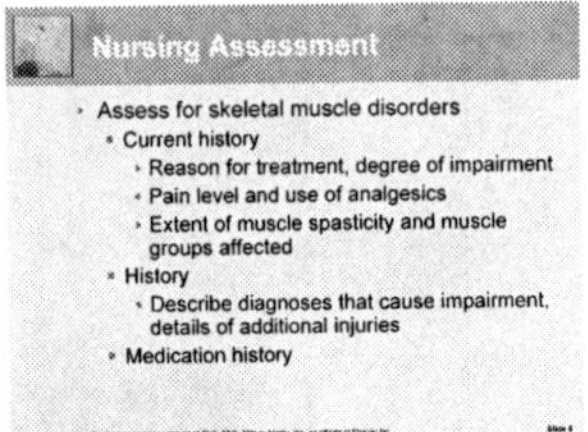
Nursing Assessment
Assess for skeletal muscle disorders
Current history
Reason for treatment, degree of impairment
Pain level and use of analgesics
Extent of muscle spasticity and muscle groups affected
History
Describe diagnoses that cause impairment, details of additional injuries
Medication history

- Skeletal muscle disorders include cerebral palsy, multiple sclerosis, muscular dystrophy, spinal cord injury, osteoarthritis, rickets, poliomyelitis, scoliosis, and stroke.
- Activities or occupations at higher risk include those requiring lifting of heavy objects, resulting in dislocations, sprains, fractures, joint replacements.

Slide 7

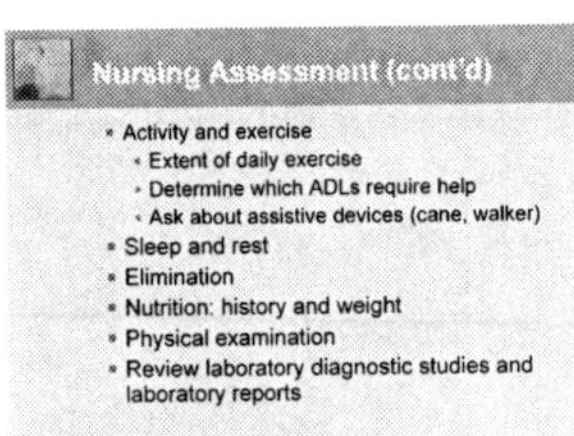
Nursing Assessment (cont'd)
Activity and exercise
Extent of daily exercise
Determine which ADLs require help
Ask about assistive devices (cane, walker)
Sleep and rest
Elimination
Nutrition: history and weight
Physical examination
Review laboratory diagnostic studies and laboratory reports

- Nonpharmacologic treatments may be used, including a heating pad, massage therapy, acupuncture, and cupping.

Slide 8

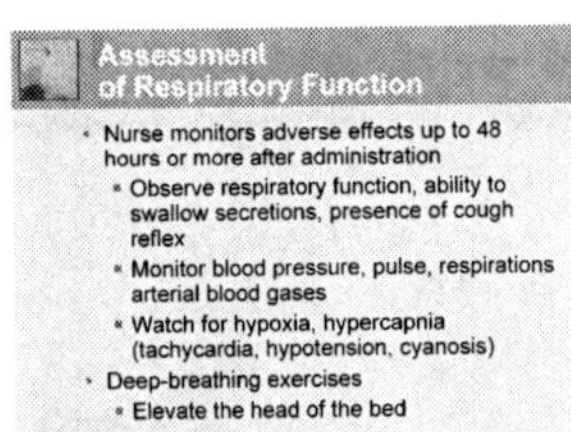
Assessment of Respiratory Function
Nurse monitors adverse effects up to 48 hours or more after administration
Observe respiratory function, ability to swallow secretions, presence of cough reflex
Monitor blood pressure, pulse, respirations arterial blood gases
Watch for hypoxia, hypercapnia (tachycardia, hypotension, cyanosis)
Deep-breathing exercises
Elevate the head of the bed

- Secretions are increased with the use of neuromuscular blocking agents.
- Equipment to have on hand with use of neuromuscular blocking agents: suction, oxygen, ventilators (mechanical), and resuscitation equipment.

Slide 9

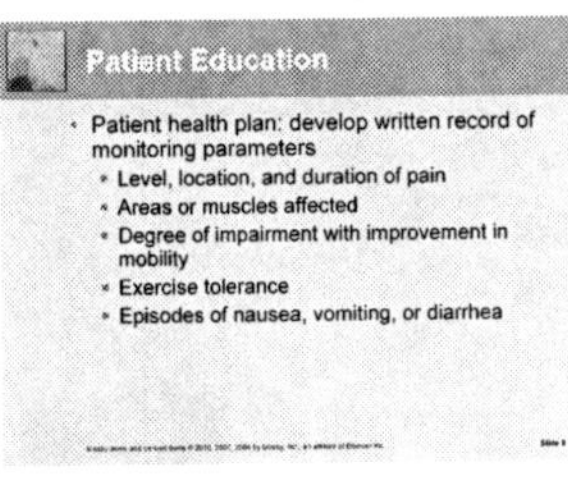
Patient Education
Patient health plan: develop written record of monitoring parameters
Level, location, and duration of pain
Areas or muscles affected
Degree of impairment with improvement in mobility
Exercise tolerance
Episodes of nausea, vomiting, or diarrhea

- Neuromuscular blocking agents DO NOT relieve pain.

Slide 10

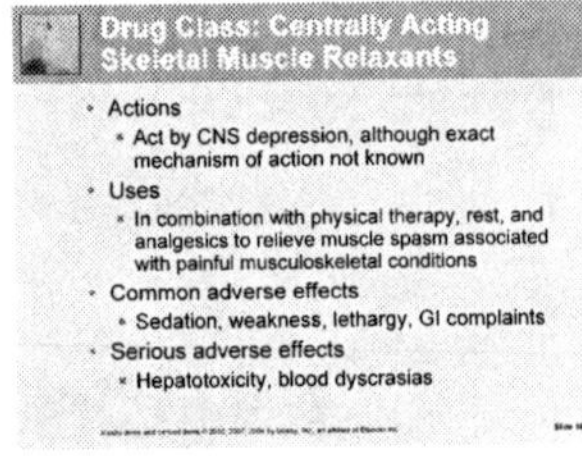
Drug Class: Centrally Acting Skeletal Muscle Relaxants
Actions
Act by CNS depression, although exact mechanism of action not known
Uses
In combination with physical therapy, rest, and analgesics to relieve muscle spasm associated with painful musculoskeletal conditions
Common adverse effects
Sedation, weakness, lethargy, GI complaints
Serious adverse effects
Hepatotoxicity, blood dyscrasias

- For specific drugs, see Table 45-1.
- Should not be used for muscle spasticity associated with spinal cord or cerebral disease; may cause further impairment.
- Benefits come from sedative effects rather than actual muscle relaxation.

Slide 11

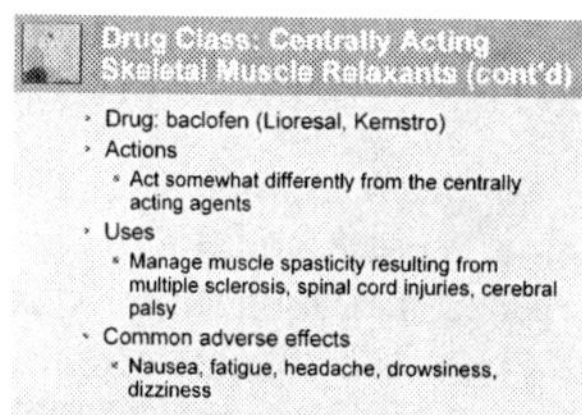
Drug Class: Centrally Acting Skeletal Muscle Relaxants (cont'd)
Drug: baclofen (Lioresal, Kemstro)
Actions
Act somewhat differently from the centrally acting agents
Uses
Manage muscle spasticity resulting from multiple sclerosis, spinal cord injuries, cerebral palsy
Common adverse effects
Nausea, fatigue, headache, drowsiness, dizziness

- Intrathecal pump infusion is used in the management of cerebral palsy.

Slide 12

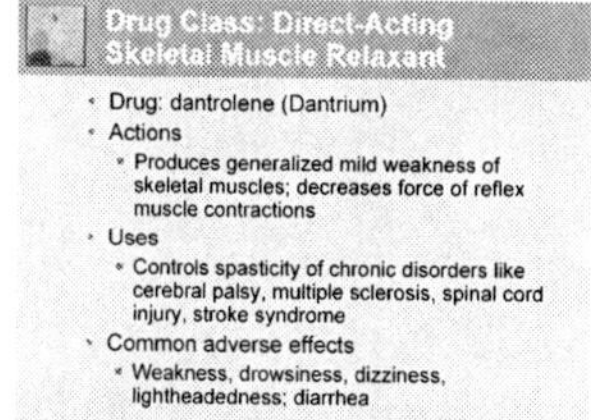
Drug Class: Direct-Acting Skeletal Muscle Relaxant
Drug: dantrolene (Dantrium)
Actions
Produces generalized mild weakness of skeletal muscles; decreases force of reflex muscle contractions
Uses
Controls spasticity of chronic disorders like cerebral palsy, multiple sclerosis, spinal cord injury, stroke syndrome
Common adverse effects
Weakness, drowsiness, dizziness, lightheadedness; diarrhea

- Other actions: hyperreflexia, clonus, muscle stiffness, involuntary muscle movements, spasticity.
- Also used to treat neuroleptic malignant syndrome associated with use of antipsychotic agents.
- Serious adverse effects: photosensitivity, hepatotoxicity.

Slide 13

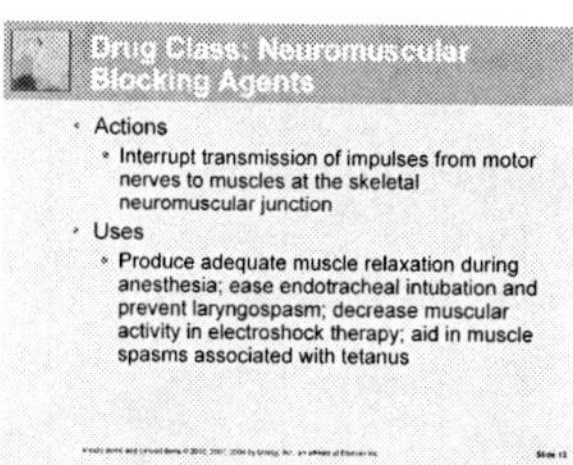
Drug Class: Neuromuscular Blocking Agents
Actions
Interrupt transmission of impulses from motor nerves to muscles at the skeletal neuromuscular junction
Uses
Produce adequate muscle relaxation during anesthesia; ease endotracheal intubation and prevent laryngospasm; decrease muscular activity in electroshock therapy; aid in muscle spasms associated with tetanus

- For specific drugs, see Table 45-2.
- These agents have no effect on consciousness, memory, or pain threshold; analgesics and sedatives must also be administered because the patient may be in extreme pain and unable to speak.
- Administered only by qualified anesthetist or anesthesiologist.
- Watch closely for signs of respiratory failure.

Slide 14

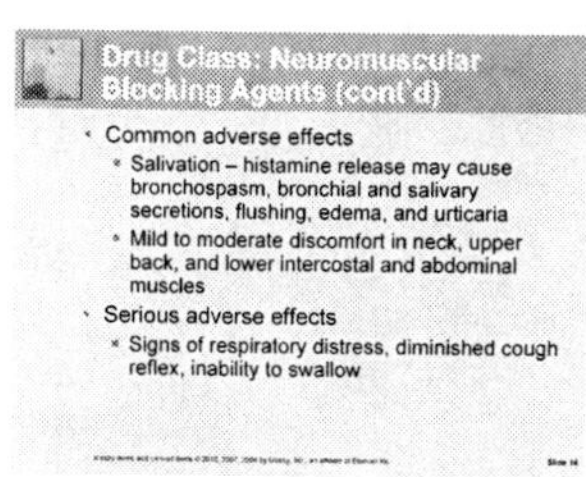
Drug Class: Neuromuscular Blocking Agents (cont'd)
Common adverse effects
Salivation – histamine release may cause bronchospasm, bronchial and salivary secretions, flushing, edema, and urticaria
Mild to moderate discomfort in neck, upper back, and lower intercostal and abdominal muscles
Serious adverse effects
Signs of respiratory distress, diminished cough reflex, inability to swallow

- Drug interactions: aminoglycoside antibiotics, beta-adrenergic blocking agents, and diuretics enhance therapeutic and toxic effects.
- Treatment of overdose: artificial respirations and antidotes to reverse the effects.

46 Lesson Plan
Antimicrobial Agents

TEACHING FOCUS

In this chapter, students are introduced to various antimicrobial agents. Drug monographs include information on the modes of action of the agent, the various conditions for which it is used, and the expected therapeutic outcome. A generalized nursing process for antimicrobial therapy is discussed, including patient assessment before and during therapy, physical examination, laboratory tests, and possible adverse effects. Students have the opportunity to examine patient education issues related to antimicrobial therapy and the underlying conditions that necessitate it. Special attention is given to proper assessment for allergic reaction and treatment of allergic drug reactions.

MATERIALS AND RESOURCES

☐ computer and PowerPoint projector (all Lessons)

LESSON CHECKLIST

Preparations for this lesson include:

- lecture
- guest speaker: nurse
- evaluation of student knowledge and skills needed to perform all entry-level nursing activities related to antimicrobial agents, including:
  - the antimicrobial drug classes
  - representative drugs from each class and important information about each drug
  - the mode of action of the various antimicrobials
  - how to assess for likelihood of allergic reaction
  - how to respond to allergic drug reactions and other adverse effects of antimicrobial therapy
  - the nursing process for antimicrobial therapy
  - how to develop a patient education plan for patients on various types of antimicrobial therapy

KEY TERMS

antibiotics (p. 717)
gram-negative microorganisms (p. 726)
gram-positive microorganisms (p. 726)
hypoprothrombinemia (p. 726)
nephrotoxicity (p. 719)
ototoxicity (p. 719)
pathogenic (p. 717)
penicillinase-resistant penicillins (p. 733)
prophylactic antibiotics (p. 718)
thrombophlebitis (p. 727)

ADDITIONAL RESOURCES

PowerPoint slides: 1-48
Flashcards, Decks 1 and 2
Animation: Vaccination

Legend

ARQ	**PPT**	**TB**	**CTQ**	**SG**	**INRQ**
Audience Response Questions	PowerPoint Slides	Test Bank	Critical Thinking Questions	Study Guide	Interactive NCLEX Review Questions

Class Activities are indicated in ***bold italic.***

LESSON 46.1

BACKGROUND ASSESSMENT

Question: What are the major actions of antimicrobial agents? What criteria are used in the selection of antimicrobial agents?
Answer: Antimicrobial agents are chemicals that eliminate living microorganisms that are pathogenic to the patient. They can be of chemical origin or derived from other living organisms. Those derived from other living organisms are called antibiotics. Most antibiotics used today are harvested from large colonies of microorganisms, which are then purified and chemically modified into semisynthetic antimicrobial agents. The selection of the antimicrobial agent must be based on the sensitivity of the pathogen and the possible toxicity to the patient. If possible, infecting organisms should first be isolated and identified. Culture and sensitivity tests should be completed. The antimicrobial therapy is then started based on the sensitivity results and the clinical judgment of the health care provider.

Question: What are three major nursing diagnoses related to antimicrobial therapy?
Answer: It is important that nurses consider the entire patient when administering and monitoring antimicrobial therapy. The nurse needs to be knowledgeable about the drugs, including physiologic parameters for monitoring expected therapeutic activity and adverse effects. The nursing process should include assessment, planning, and implementation, followed by patient education and health promotion. Nursing diagnoses related to antimicrobial therapy include actual infection related to deficient fluid volume, and risk for injury.

CRITICAL THINKING QUESTION

A man is admitted to the hospital for IV antibiotic therapy related to osteomyelitis. The nurse begins the admission process by taking a detailed past history. The nurse asks the patient about his current symptoms and complaints, previous infections, and response to antibiotic therapy. When the nurse asks the patient about any history of sexually transmitted diseases, the patient responds, "That's none of your business." How should the nurse respond? Why is it important to obtain a past history regarding sexually transmitted diseases?
Guidelines: It is common for patients to exhibit reluctance when discussing past medical history related to sex. The reluctance might be related to the patient's culture, sexual orientation, religion, or disposition. The nurse should explain that she or he understands that this can be an uncomfortable issue to discuss and that the patient is correct in saying that it is none of the nurse's business. However, to give the best treatment to the patient, especially when administering antibiotic therapy, these are facts the health care team needs to know. The nurse should explain to the patient that all information remains confidential and then show the patient the Health Insurance Portability and Accountability Act (HIPAA) form regarding confidentiality. If the patient understands this information, he then may be more willing to discuss his situation. If he still refuses to give information, the nurse needs to document his refusal and notify the charge nurse and health care provider.

OBJECTIVES	CONTENT	TEACHING RESOURCES
Explain the major actions and effects of drugs used to treat infectious diseases.	■ Antimicrobial agents (p. 717) Review the definition of antimicrobial agents and how they are manufactured. Discuss the nursing process as it relates to antimicrobial therapy with special attention to adverse effects such as allergies, secondary infections, and organ toxicity.	PPT 6 ARQ 1 Animation: Antibiotics Animation: Antivirals Animation: IV Antibiotic Therapy for Streptococcal Infection SG Learning Activities questions 1, 11, 13, 15-18 (p. 315) Review Question for the NCLEX Examination 12 (p. 779)

OBJECTIVES	CONTENT	TEACHING RESOURCES
		▸ Discuss the possible origins of antimicrobial agents. ▸ Discuss how antimicrobial agents are classified. Class Activity ***Divide the class into small groups, and have each group draw a concept map showing the actions and effects of a drug related to an infectious disease. Then have each group share its concept map with the class.***
Identify criteria used to select an effective antimicrobial agent.	■ Antimicrobial agents (p. 717)	TB Multiple Choice question 4 SG Review Sheet question 1 (p. 305) SG Learning Activities question 37 (p. 316) ▸ Discuss factors that are used to select an appropriate antimicrobial agent. Class Activity ***Divide the class into five groups, and have each group take one component of the nursing process. Review with the class how to apply the nursing process in terms of infection management. Discuss with the class important teaching points to cover when educating patients about ways to prevent adverse effects when they are avoidable. Review the exercise with the class.***
Identify baseline data the nurse should collect on a continual basis for comparison and evaluation of antimicrobial drug effectiveness.	– Nursing process for antimicrobial therapy (p. 718)	PPT 7-8 TB Multiple Response question 2 SG Review Sheet question 5 (p. 306) ▸ Discuss which baseline data should be assessed on a continual basis for evaluation of the effectiveness of antimicrobial therapy. Class Activity ***Invite a nurse to speak to the class about how he or she collects data to evaluate the effectiveness of antimicrobial drugs. Have the students prepare specific questions for the nurse in advance.***
Describe the nursing assessments and interventions for the common adverse effects associated with antimicrobial agents: allergic reaction, direct	– Nursing process for antimicrobial therapy (p. 718)	PPT 7-8 TB Multiple Choice questions 1, 6-7, 11-12 TB Multiple Response questions 1 INRQ 1-2, 8 CTQ 3-5 SG Review Sheet questions 2, 7-8, 17, 73-74 (pp. 305-307, 312)

OBJECTIVES	CONTENT	TEACHING RESOURCES
tissue damage (e.g., nephrotoxicity, ototoxicity, hepatotoxicity), secondary infection, and other considerations, such as photosensitivity, peripheral neuropathy, and neuromuscular blockage.		SG Learning Activities questions 2-5, 14, 19-22, 38, 41, 43, 46, 49 (pp. 315-317) Review Questions for the NCLEX Examination 1, 3-4, 10 (pp. 778-779) ▸ Discuss common signs of allergic reaction to an antimicrobial. Which patients are more likely to exhibit allergic drug reactions? ▸ Discuss the symptoms of hepatotoxicity. When can they be expected to occur? Class Activity ***List on the board the following infections: urinary tract infections, meningitis, wound infections, and life-threatening septicemias. Have students volunteer to identify whether these infections are considered opportunistic or nosocomial, or community-acquired or secondary infections. Discuss common organisms that cause these infections. Review the exercise with the class.***
Identify significant data in a patient history that could alert the medical team that a patient is more likely to experience an allergic reaction.	– Nursing process for antimicrobial therapy (p. 718)	SG Review Sheet question 6 (p. 306) SG Learning Activities question 45 (p. 317) ▸ Discuss what questions to ask that will help determine if the patient is more likely to experience an allergic drug reaction. Class Activity ***Divide the class into groups, and have each group identify three items in a patient history that could alert the medical team to a possible allergic reaction. Have each group share its findings with the class for discussion.***
Describe basic principles of patient care that can be implemented to enhance an individual's therapeutic response during an infection.	– Patient education and health promotion (p. 721) Review common microorganisms that cause urinary tract infections, meningitis, wound infections, and life-threatening septicemias. Discuss drug therapy used to treat nosocomial gram-negative infections and those used before surgery to reduce the organisms in the intestinal tract.	Patient Self-Assessment Form: Antibiotics SG Review Sheet questions 4, 10 (p. 306) SG Learning Activities questions 23-26, 42, 51 (pp. 316-317) ▸ Discuss how a patient who is receiving antibiotics for an infection should be advised to take care of himself or herself during drug therapy. ▸ Discuss how to advise the patient with a communicable infection to prevent transmitting the infection to others. Class Activity ***Lead a class discussion on the basic principles of patient care for a patient with an infection.***

46.1 Homework/Assignments:

46.1 Instructor's Notes/Student Feedback:

LESSON 46.2

CRITICAL THINKING QUESTION

While making patient rounds, the nurse notices that a patient's right arm is swollen, red, and painful to the touch at the IV site. The nurse knows from the report that the patient needs an IV for a cefaclor (Ceclor) infusion to treat her urinary tract infection. What should the nurse do in this situation?

Guidelines: The nurse should inform the charge nurse of the assessment findings. The IV should be removed and reinserted into a large vein because cefaclor is known to cause phlebitis. The nurse needs to apply cool compresses to the infiltrated site and elevate the affected arm to decrease swelling and help alleviate the pain. The site should be checked at least twice per shift for complications, such as signs and symptoms of infection. Documentation of findings and treatment need to be recorded and, if required by hospital policy, an incident report should be completed.

OBJECTIVES	CONTENT	TEACHING RESOURCES
Develop a plan for implementing patient education for patients receiving aminoglycosides, carbapenems, cephalosporins, glycylcyclines, ketolides, penicillins, quinolones, streptogramins, sulfonamides, tetracyclines, antifungal agents, and antiviral agents.	■ Drug therapy for infectious disease (p. 722) □ Drug class: Aminoglycosides (p. 722) – Nursing process for aminoglycosides (p. 723) □ Drug class: Carbapenems (p. 724) – Nursing process for carbapenems (p. 724) □ Drug class: Cephalosporins (p. 726) – Nursing process for cephalosporins (p. 726) □ Drug class: Glycylcyclines (p. 728) – Nursing process for tigecycline therapy (p. 728) □ Drug class: Ketolides (p. 729) – Nursing process for telithromycin therapy (p. 729)	PPT 12-17 TB Multiple Choice questions 3, 10 TB Multiple Response question 3 INRQ 4-7 SG Review Sheet questions 11-16, 18-20, 23-26, 28-31, 104 (pp. 306-309, 314) SG Learning Activities questions 9, 30-36, 43, 48, 52 (pp. 315-317) SG Practice Questions for the NCLEX Examination 1-5, 15-17 (pp. 318-320) Review Questions for the NCLEX Examination 7-9 (p. 779) Drug Table 46-1: Aminoglycosides (p. 723) Drug Table 46-2: Carbapenems (p. 725) Drug Table 46-3: Cephalosporins (p. 727) Drug Table 46-4: Macrolides (p. 731)

OBJECTIVES	CONTENT	TEACHING RESOURCES
	□ Drug class: Macrolides (p. 730) – Nursing process for macrolides (p. 730) Review the drug class aminoglycosides as agents used to treat gram-negative infections. Discuss the actions, uses, and therapeutic outcomes for aminoglycosides, as well as common and serious adverse effects and known drug interactions. Review the drug class carbapenems as agents used to treat lower respiratory tract and intra-abdominal infections, as well as gram-negative or gram-positive septicemias. Discuss the actions, uses, and therapeutic outcomes for carbapenems, as well as common and serious adverse effects and known drug interactions. Review the drug class cephalosporins as agents used to treat gram-positive infections as well as gram-negative bacteria. Discuss the actions, uses, and therapeutic outcomes for cephalosporins as well as common and serious adverse effects and known drug interactions. Review the drug tigecycline from the drug class glycylcyclines as an agent used as a broad-spectrum antibiotic effective against resistant bacterial infections. Discuss the actions, uses, and therapeutic outcomes for glycylcyclines as well as common and serious adverse effects and known drug interactions. Review the drug telithromycin from the drug class ketolides as an agent used to treat resistant lung infections. Discuss the actions,	▸ Discuss which microorganisms aminoglycosides are effective against. ▸ Discuss under which conditions carbapenems are commonly used. ▸ Discuss the action of glycyclines and how they differ from tetracyclines. ▸ Discuss when ketolides are used. Class Activity ***Divide the class into groups, and have each group outline the actions of aminoglycosides on the body and explain their uses. Then have groups share their findings with the class for discussion.***

OBJECTIVES	CONTENT	TEACHING RESOURCES
	uses, and therapeutic outcomes for ketolides, as well as common and serious adverse effects and known drug interactions. Review the drug class macrolides as agents used to treat gram-negative and gram-positive infections, depending on which agent is more effective. Discuss the actions, uses, and therapeutic outcomes for macrolides, as well as common and serious adverse effects and known drug interactions.	
Differentiate between gram-negative and gram-positive microorganisms and between anaerobic and aerobic properties of microorganisms.	□ Drug class: Cephalosporins (p. 726) – Nursing process for cephalosporins (p. 726) □ Drug class: Glycylcyclines (p. 728) – Nursing process for tigecycline therapy (p. 728) □ Drug class: Ketolides (p. 729) – Nursing process for telithromycin therapy (p. 729) □ Drug class: Macrolides (p. 730) – Nursing process for macrolides (p. 730)	PPT 14-17 Animation: Anthrax Infection Animation: Smallpox Animation: Tuberculosis Infection SG Review Sheet questions 3, 19, 21-22, 27 (pp. 305, 307-308) SG Learning Activities question 8 (p. 315) Drug Table 46-3: Cephalosporins (p. 727) Drug Table 46-4: Macrolides (p. 731) ▸ Discuss the possibility of cross-hypersensitivity to other classes of antibiotics. ▸ Discuss the advantages of macrolides over other classes of drugs. ▸ Discuss which type of infections cephalosporins are commonly used for. ▸ Discuss which microorganisms cephalosporins are most likely to be effective against. Class Activity ***Have students volunteer the different characteristics of gram-negative and gram-positive bacteria and aerobic and anaerobic bacteria. Be sure that the students discuss common sources of each type of infection and related treatments. Record student responses on the board in a table format.***
Develop a plan for implementing patient education for patients	□ Drug class: Oxazolidinones (p. 731) – Nursing process for linezolid (p. 732)	PPT 19-23, 24-26 ARQ 2 TB Multiple Choice question 2, 5, 8

OBJECTIVES	CONTENT	TEACHING RESOURCES
receiving aminoglycosides, carbapenems, cephalosporins, glycylcyclines, ketolides, penicillins, quinolones, streptogramins, sulfonamides, tetracyclines, antifungal agents, and antiviral agents.	□ Drug class: Penicillins (p. 733) – Nursing process for penicillins (p. 733) □ Drug class: Quinolones (p. 735) – Nursing process for quinolones (p. 736) □ Drug class: Streptogramins (p. 738) – Nursing process for streptogramins (p. 738) □ Drug class: Sulfonamides (p. 738) – Nursing process for sulfonamides (p. 739) □ Drug class: Tetracyclines (p. 740) – Nursing process for tetracyclines (p. 740) □ Drug class: Antitubercular agents (p. 741) – Nursing process for ethambutol (p. 741) – Nursing process for isoniazid (p. 742) – Nursing process for rifampin (p. 743) Review the drug class penicillins as agents used to treat pneumonias, urinary tract infections, syphilis, and as prophylaxis before surgery or dental procedures. Discuss the actions, uses, and therapeutic outcomes for penicillins, as well as common and serious adverse effects and known drug interactions. Review how bacteria have developed resistance to penicillins and the subsequent development of penicillinase-resistant penicillins. Review the drug class quinolones as well as the fluoroquinolones used to treat a wide range of gram-negative and gram-positive infections. Discuss the actions,	CTQ 2 SG Review Sheet questions 32-52, 104 (pp. 309-311, 314) SG Learning Activities questions 6-7, 9-10, 12, 28-29, 39-40, 44, 47, 53 (pp. 315-317) SG Practice Questions for the NCLEX Examination 6-11 (pp. 319-320) Review Questions for the NCLEX Examination 2, 11 (pp. 778-779) Drug Table 46-5: Penicillins (p. 734) Drug Table 46-6: Quinolones (p. 737) Drug Table 46-7: Sulfonamides (p. 739) Drug Table 46-8: Tetracyclines (p. 740) ▸ Discuss the advantages of penicillinase-resistant penicillins. ▸ Discuss which type of infections the various quinolones are commonly used for. ▸ Discuss the mode of action of streptogramins. ▸ Discuss the mode of action of sulfonamides. ▸ Discuss the use of tetracyclines in children and lactating mothers. *Class Activity* ***Divide the class into groups, and assign each group one of the following antimicrobial drugs: aminoglycosides, carbapenems, cephalosporins, macrolides, or quinolones. Have each group diagram its drug's actions on the body and describe its uses and adverse effects. Then have each group make a brief presentation to the class.***

OBJECTIVES	CONTENT	TEACHING RESOURCES
	uses, and therapeutic outcomes for quinolones, as well as common and serious adverse effects and known drug interactions. Review the drug quinupristin-dalfopristin from the drug class streptogramins as an agent used against vancomycin-resistant infections. Discuss the actions, uses, and therapeutic outcomes for quinupristin-dalfopristin, as well as common and serious adverse effects and the many known drug interactions. Review the drug class sulfonamides as agents used to treat otitis media and urinary tract infections. Discuss the actions, uses, therapeutic outcomes, and increasing resistance to sulfonamides, as well as common and serious adverse effects and known drug interactions. Review the drug class tetracyclines as agents used to treat common infections for patients allergic to penicillins. Discuss the actions, uses, and therapeutic outcomes for tetracyclines, as well as common and serious adverse effects and known drug interactions. Review the drugs ethambutol, isoniazid, and rifampin from the drug class antitubercular agents as drugs used to treat tuberculosis infections. Discuss the actions, uses, and therapeutic outcomes for antitubercular agents, as well as common and serious adverse effects and known drug interactions.	

ELSEVIER

46.2 Homework/Assignments:

46.2 Instructor's Notes/Student Feedback:

LESSON 46.3

CRITICAL THINKING QUESTION

A 45-year-old man is admitted into the hospital with complaints of increased temperature, cough with sputum production, and night sweats. He has a history of human immunodeficiency virus (HIV) infection. The health care provider orders a sputum test and chest x-ray to check for tuberculosis (TB). Why does the health care provider suspect TB? What is the nursing priority in this case? What is the recommended treatment for TB?

Guidelines: The health care provider ordered sputum cultures to check for TB because HIV-positive patients are more susceptible to TB infection caused by their compromised immune systems. A nursing priority is to put the patient in an isolation room and to initiate respiratory precautions for TB to protect the patient, staff, and visitors. All hospital staff members who were in contact with the patient should be tested for TB in addition to family members or others in contact with the patient. Patients with TB are placed on a combination of antitubercular agents that they will need to take for at least 6 months. Isolation precautions should last for approximately 7 to 10 days after treatment is initiated. The nurse should focus on teaching the patient and family about TB and prevention of its transmission.

OBJECTIVES	CONTENT	TEACHING RESOURCES
Identify criteria used to select an effective antimicrobial agent.	□ Drug class: Antitubercular agents (p. 741) – Nursing process for ethambutol (p. 741) – Nursing process for isoniazid (p. 742) – Nursing process for rifampin (p. 743) □ Drug class: Miscellaneous antibiotics (p. 744) – Nursing process for aztreonam (p. 744) – Nursing process for chloramphenicol (p. 745) – Nursing process for clindamycin (p. 745) – Nursing process for daptomycin therapy (p. 746)	PPT 24-26, 27-28 ARQ 3-4 INRQ 10 SG Review Sheet questions 52-72, 104 (pp. 311-312, 314) SG Learning Activities question 50 (p. 317) SG Practice Question for the NCLEX Examination 12 (p. 320) Review Question for the NCLEX Examination 5 (p. 778) ▸ Discuss the interaction of rifampin with oral contraceptives. ▸ Discuss the adverse hematologic effects of therapy with chloramphenicol.

OBJECTIVES	CONTENT	TEACHING RESOURCES
	– Nursing process for metronidazole (p. 747) – Nursing process for spectinomycin (p. 748) – Nursing process for tinidazole (p. 749) – Nursing process for vancomycin (p. 750) Review the following miscellaneous antibiotics: aztreonam, chloramphenicol, clindamycin, daptomycin, metronidazole, spectinomycin, tinidazole, and vancomycin. Discuss each one in terms of the action, use, and therapeutic outcome of the drug. Review each drug for particular common and serious adverse effects, as well as any known drug interactions.	▸ Describe the unique action of daptomycin. Class Activity ***As a class, discuss TB treatment. Why is TB treated with a combination drug therapy?*** Class Activity ***Have two students role-play the nurse instructing a patient taking aztreonam for treatment of a urinary tract infection caused by* Neisseria gonorrhoeae. *Have the class assist the nurse in determining the pertinent patient information to discuss and the common and adverse effects, as well as known drug interactions. Review the exercise with the class.***
Review parenteral administration techniques and the procedure for vaginal insertion of drugs.	□ Drug class: Topical antifungal agents (p. 751)	PPT 29 SG Review Sheet question 9 (p. 306) SG Learning Activities question 27 (p. 316) SG Practice Question for the NCLEX Examination 13 (p. 320) Drug Table 46-9: Topical Antifungal Agents (pp. 752-753) ▸ Discuss how you would advise a patient with a vaginal fungal infection to administer the medication and prevent reinfection. Class Activity ***Divide the class into groups, and have each group list five common antifungal agents and explain their uses. Then have each group share its findings with the class for discussion and comparison.***
Develop a plan for implementing patient education for patients receiving aminoglycosides, carbapenems, cephalosporins, glycyclines, ketolides, penicillins, quinolones,	– Nursing process for topical antifungals (p. 751) □ Drug class: Systemic antifungal agents (p. 751) – Nursing process for amphotericin B (p. 753) – Nursing process for fluconazole (p. 754) – Nursing process for flucytosine (p. 755)	PPT 29-36, 37-48 ARQ 5 TB Multiple Choice question 9 INRQ 3, 9 SG Review Sheet questions 75-104 (pp. 312-314) SG Practice Question for the NCLEX Examination 14 (p. 320)

OBJECTIVES	CONTENT	TEACHING RESOURCES
streptogramins, sulfonamides, tetracyclines, antifungal agents, and antiviral agents.	– Nursing process for griseofulvin (p. 756) – Nursing process for itraconazole (p. 757) – Nursing process for ketoconazole (p. 758) – Nursing process for terbinafine therapy (p. 759) □ Drug class: Antiviral agents (p. 759) – Nursing process for abacavir (p. 759) – Nursing process for acyclovir (p. 760) – Nursing process for atazanavir (p. 761) – Nursing process for didanosine (p. 763) – Nursing process for efavirenz (p. 764) – Nursing process for emtricitabine (p. 765) – Nursing process for enfuvirtide (p. 766) – Nursing process for etravirine (p. 767) – Nursing process for famciclovir (p. 767) – Nursing process for fosamprenavir (p. 768) – Nursing process for lamivudine (p. 769) – Nursing process for maraviroc (p. 770) – Nursing process for oseltamivir (p. 772) – Nursing process for raltegravir (p. 772) – Nursing process for ribavirin (p. 773) – Nursing process for stavudine (p. 774) – Nursing process for tenofovir (p. 775) – Nursing process for valacyclovir (p. 776) – Nursing process for zanamivir (p. 776)	Review Question for the NCLEX Examination 13 (p. 779) Drug Table 46-10: Recommended Doses for Maraviroc (p. 771) ▸ Discuss which infections are commonly treated with systemic antifungal agents. ▸ Discuss the specific indications for amphotericin B. ▸ Discuss the time frame within which treatment with oseltamivir should occur to be successful. ▸ Discuss signs of hepatotoxicity that may develop in patients taking antiviral drugs. ▸ Discuss which drugs are more likely to cause central nervous system (CNS) symptoms that should be reported. Class Activity ***Divide the class into groups, and have each group outline the baseline assessments to be done for a patient with meningitis who has been prescribed amphotericin B. Then have groups share their findings with the class*** Class Activity ***Have two students role-play the nurse instructing a patient taking abacavir (Ziagen) for treatment of HIV-1 infection. Have the class assist the nurse in determining the pertinent patient information to discuss and the common and serious adverse effects, as well as known drug interactions. Review the exercise with the class.***

OBJECTIVES	CONTENT	TEACHING RESOURCES
	– Nursing process for zidovudine (p. 777) Review the drug class systemic antifungal agents as drugs used to treat systemic fungal infections. Discuss the actions, uses, and therapeutic outcomes for systemic antifungal agents, as well as common and serious adverse effects and known drug interactions. Review the drug class antiviral agents as drugs used to treat viral infections including HIV. Discuss the actions, uses, and therapeutic outcomes for antiviral agents, as well as common and serious adverse effects and known drug interactions.	
Performance evaluation		Test Bank SG Learning Activities (pp. 315-317) SG Practice Questions for the NCLEX Examination (pp. 318-320) Critical Thinking Questions

46.3 Homework/Assignments:

46.3 Instructor's Notes/Student Feedback:

46 Lecture Outline
Antimicrobial Agents

Slide 1

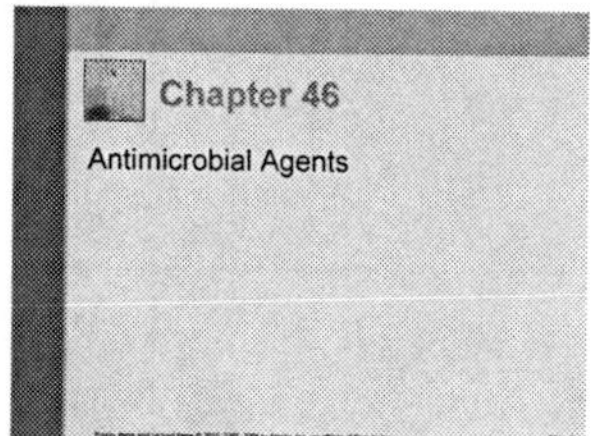
Chapter 46
Antimicrobial Agents

Slide 2

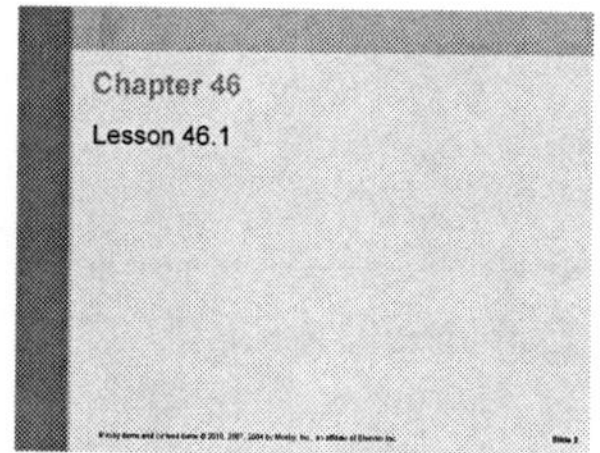
Chapter 46
Lesson 46.1

Slide 3

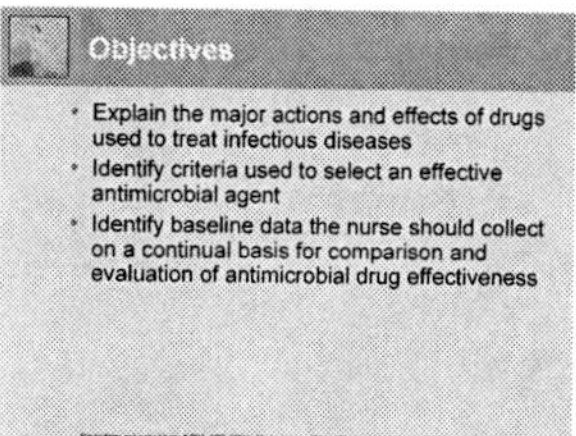
Objectives
Explain the major actions and effects of drugs used to treat infectious diseases
Identify criteria used to select an effective antimicrobial agent
Identify baseline data the nurse should collect on a continual basis for comparison and evaluation of antimicrobial drug effectiveness

Slide 4

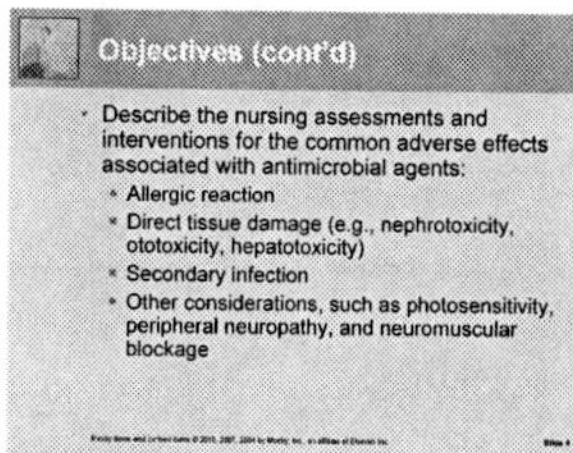
Objectives (cont'd)
Describe the nursing assessments and interventions for the common adverse effects associated with antimicrobial agents:
Allergic reaction
Direct tissue damage (e.g., nephrotoxicity, ototoxicity, hepatotoxicity)
Secondary infection
Other considerations, such as photosensitivity, peripheral neuropathy, and neuromuscular blockage

Slide 5

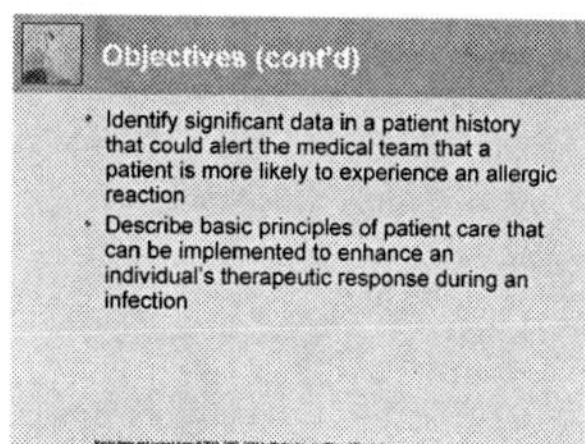
Objectives (cont'd)
Identify significant data in a patient history that could alert the medical team that a patient is more likely to experience an allergic reaction
Describe basic principles of patient care that can be implemented to enhance an individual's therapeutic response during an infection

Slide 6

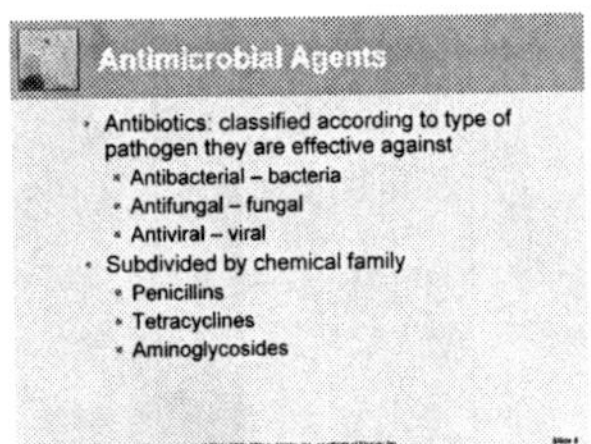
Antimicrobial Agents
Antibiotics: classified according to type of pathogen they are effective against
Antibacterial – bacteria
Antifungal – fungal
Antiviral – viral
Subdivided by chemical family
Penicillins
Tetracyclines
Aminoglycosides

- Culture and sensitivity tests determine the causative pathogen.
- Other considerations for use: toxicity potential to the patient, clinical judgment, previous infection treatments and reactions to antibiotics.

Slide 7

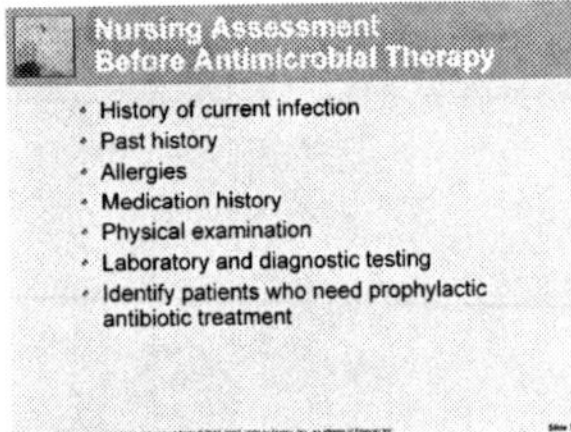
Nursing Assessment Before Antimicrobial Therapy
History of current infection
Past history
Allergies
Medication history
Physical examination
Laboratory and diagnostic testing
Identify patients who need prophylactic antibiotic treatment

- Laboratory test values indicating infection: CBC, ESR, BUN, AST, ALT, GGT, C-reactive protein, electrolytes.
- American Heart Association recommends prophylactic antibiotics for patients with certain cardiac conditions.

Slide 8

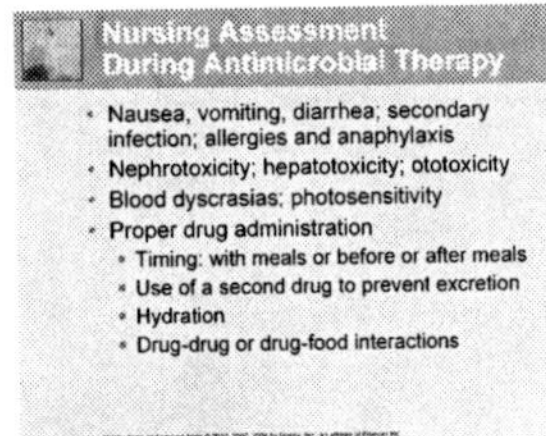
Nursing Assessment During Antimicrobial Therapy
Nausea, vomiting, diarrhea; secondary infection; allergies and anaphylaxis
Nephrotoxicity; hepatotoxicity; ototoxicity
Blood dyscrasias; photosensitivity
Proper drug administration
Timing: with meals or before or after meals
Use of a second drug to prevent excretion
Hydration
Drug-drug or drug-food interactions

- Nephrotoxicity is evidenced by increasing BUN and creatinine, decreased urine output.
- Ototoxicity is damage to the eighth cranial nerve, primarily by aminoglycosides – hearing loss, dizziness, tinnitus.
- Photosensitivity occurs with certain antibiotics.

Slide 9

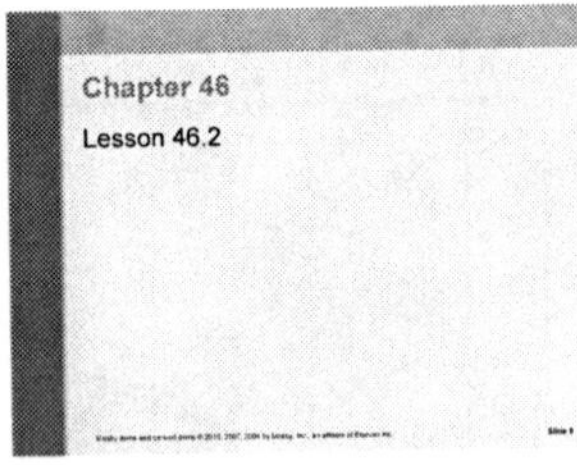
Chapter 46
Lesson 46.2

Slide 10

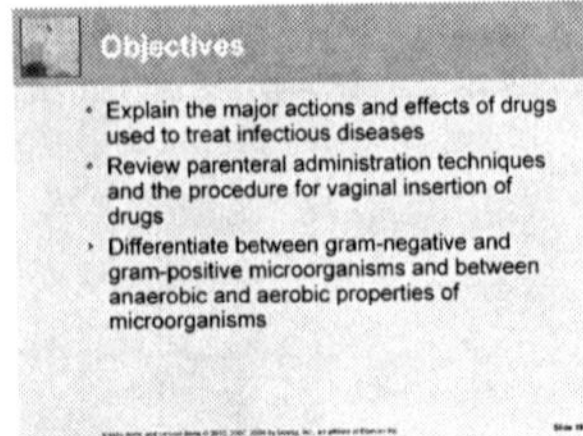
Objectives
Explain the major actions and effects of drugs used to treat infectious diseases
Review parenteral administration techniques and the procedure for vaginal insertion of drugs
Differentiate between gram-negative and gram-positive microorganisms and between anaerobic and aerobic properties of microorganisms

ELSEVIER

Slide 11

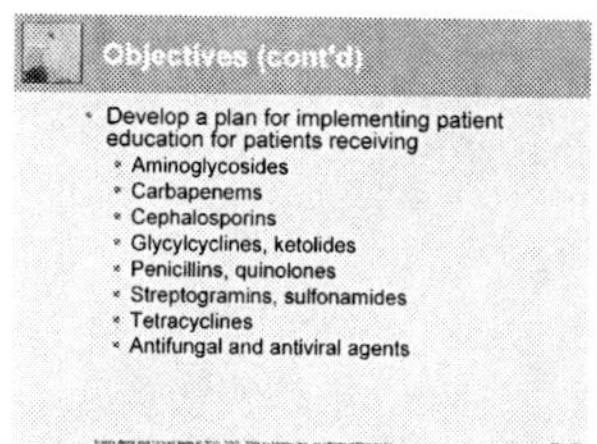
Objectives (cont'd)
Develop a plan for implementing patient education for patients receiving
Aminoglycosides
Carbapenems
Cephalosporins
Glycylcyclines, ketolides
Penicillins, quinolones
Streptogramins, sulfonamides
Tetracyclines
Antifungal and antiviral agents

Slide 12

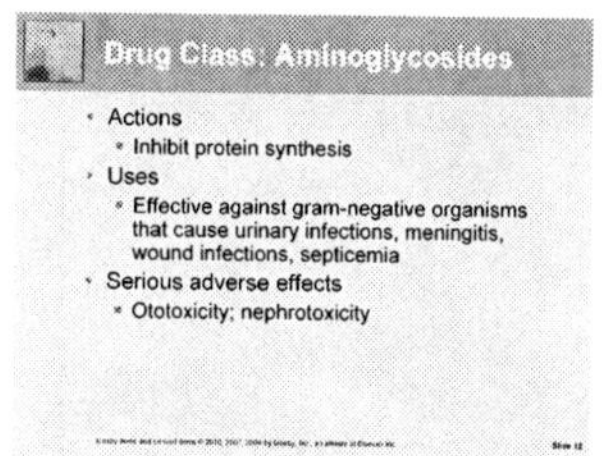
Drug Class: Aminoglycosides
Actions
Inhibit protein synthesis
Uses
Effective against gram-negative organisms that cause urinary infections, meningitis, wound infections, septicemia
Serious adverse effects
Ototoxicity; nephrotoxicity

- For specific drugs, see Table 46-1.
- Aminoglycosides stop organisms from multiplying and spreading.

Slide 13

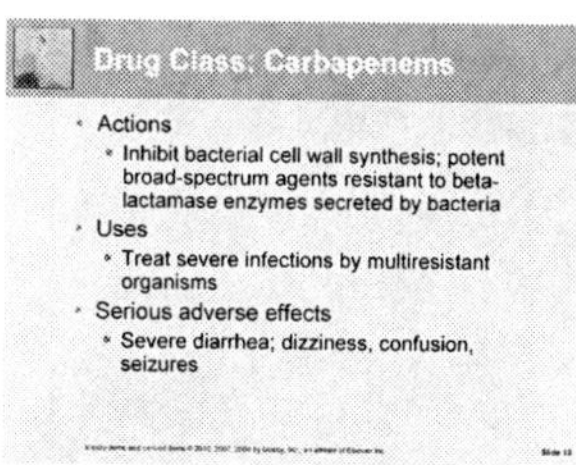
Drug Class: Carbapenems
Actions
Inhibit bacterial cell wall synthesis; potent broad-spectrum agents resistant to beta-lactamase enzymes secreted by bacteria
Uses
Treat severe infections by multiresistant organisms
Serious adverse effects
Severe diarrhea; dizziness, confusion, seizures

- For specific drugs, see Table 46-2.
- Effective against intra-abdominal infections and pelvic sepsis.
- Cilastatin is given with imipenem (Primaxin) to prevent the inactivation of imipenem by a renal enzyme. Cilastatin is not an antibiotic.

Slide 14

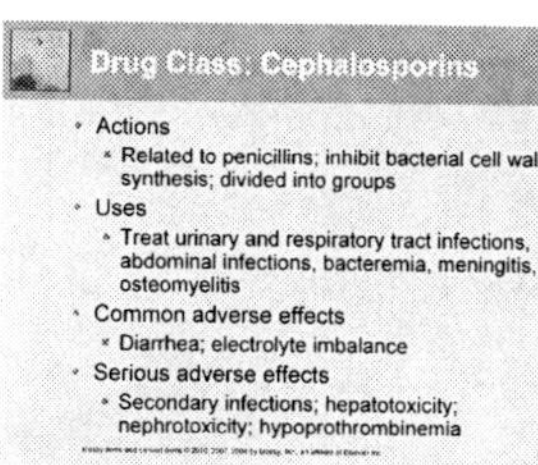
Drug Class: Cephalosporins
Actions
Related to penicillins; inhibit bacterial cell wall synthesis; divided into groups
Uses
Treat urinary and respiratory tract infections, abdominal infections, bacteremia, meningitis, osteomyelitis
Common adverse effects
Diarrhea; electrolyte imbalance
Serious adverse effects
Secondary infections; hepatotoxicity; nephrotoxicity; hypoprothrombinemia

- For specific drugs, see Table 46-3.
- First generation agents are effective against gram-positive microorganisms.
- Second and third generation agents have increased activity against gram-negative organisms.
- Fourth generation agents are broad spectrum.

Slide 15

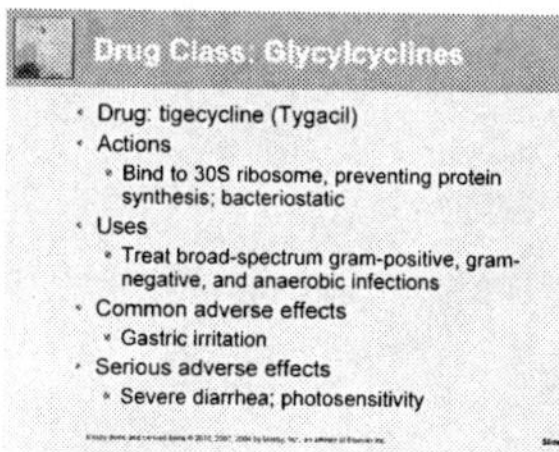
Drug Class: Glycylcyclines
Drug: tigecycline (Tygacil)
Actions
Bind to 30S ribosome, preventing protein synthesis; bacteriostatic
Uses
Treat broad-spectrum gram-positive, gram-negative, and anaerobic infections
Common adverse effects
Gastric irritation
Serious adverse effects
Severe diarrhea; photosensitivity

- New family of antibiotics; tigecycline first drug.
- Used in complicated skin infections (MRSA, MSSA), intra-abdominal infections.
- Do not administer to those younger than age 18 because of the interference with tooth development.

ELSEVIER

Slide 16

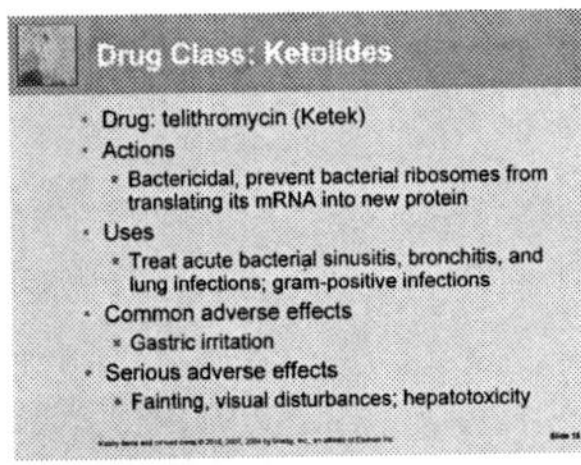
Drug Class: Ketolides
Drug: telithromycin (Ketek)
Actions
Bactericidal, prevent bacterial ribosomes from translating its mRNA into new protein
Uses
Treat acute bacterial sinusitis, bronchitis, and lung infections; gram-positive infections
Common adverse effects
Gastric irritation
Serious adverse effects
Fainting, visual disturbances; hepatotoxicity

- Telithromycin is first drug of this class.
- Chemically similar to macrolides.
- Contraindicated in patients with myasthenia gravis.

Slide 17

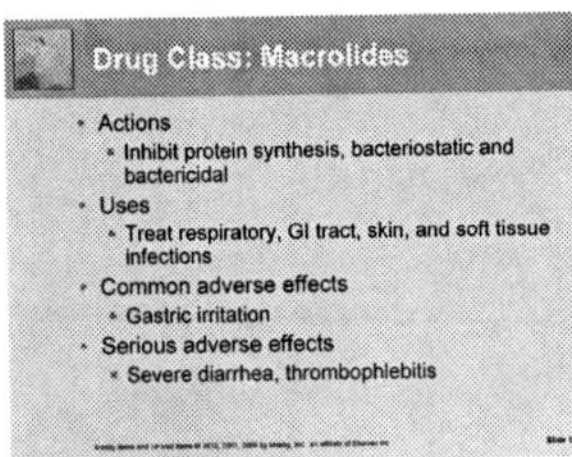
Drug Class: Macrolides
Actions
Inhibit protein synthesis, bacteriostatic and bactericidal
Uses
Treat respiratory, GI tract, skin, and soft tissue infections
Common adverse effects
Gastric irritation
Serious adverse effects
Severe diarrhea, thrombophlebitis

- For specific drugs, see Table 46-4.
- Macrolides are usually the second choice when penicillins, cephalosporins, and tetracyclines are contraindicated.

Slide 18

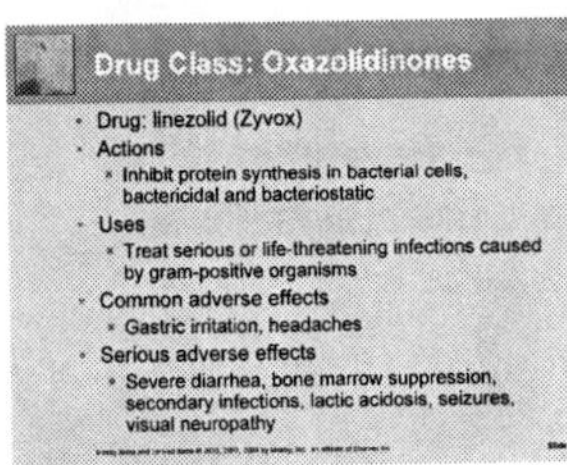
Drug Class: Oxazolidinones
Drug: linezolid (Zyvox)
Actions
Inhibit protein synthesis in bacterial cells, bactericidal and bacteriostatic
Uses
Treat serious or life-threatening infections caused by gram-positive organisms
Common adverse effects
Gastric irritation, headaches
Serious adverse effects
Severe diarrhea, bone marrow suppression, secondary infections, lactic acidosis, seizures, visual neuropathy

- New class of antimicrobial agents; linezolid is first drug.
- May be used for vancomycin-resistant *E. faecium* (VRE), MRSA, and MSSA; effective against gram-positive organisms only.

Slide 19

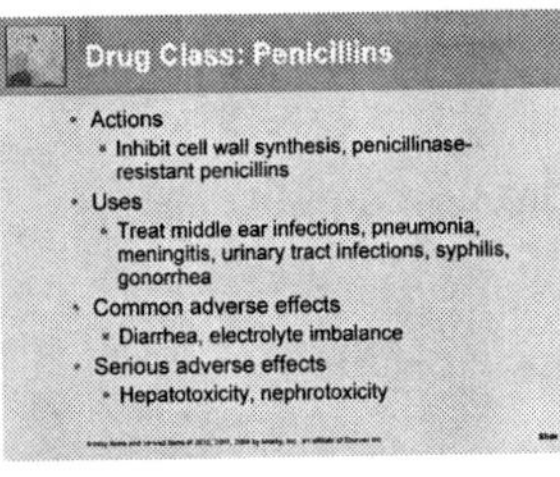
Drug Class: Penicillins
Actions
Inhibit cell wall synthesis, penicillinase-resistant penicillins
Uses
Treat middle ear infections, pneumonia, meningitis, urinary tract infections, syphilis, gonorrhea
Common adverse effects
Diarrhea, electrolyte imbalance
Serious adverse effects
Hepatotoxicity, nephrotoxicity

- For specific drugs, see Table 46-5.
- Penicillinase is the enzyme that bacteria produce to destroy the antibacterial activity of penicillin.

Slide 20

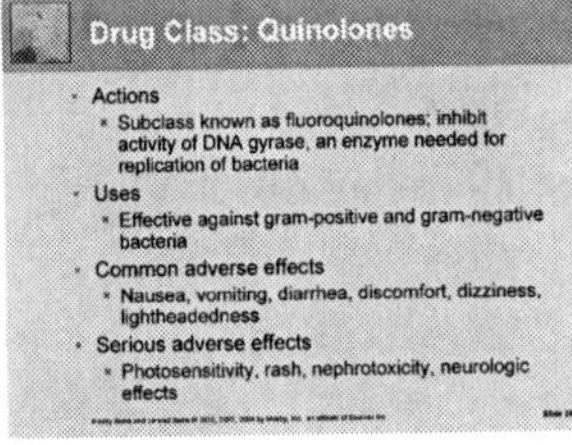
Drug Class: Quinolones
Actions
Subclass known as fluoroquinolones; inhibit activity of DNA gyrase, an enzyme needed for replication of bacteria
Uses
Effective against gram-positive and gram-negative bacteria
Common adverse effects
Nausea, vomiting, diarrhea, discomfort, dizziness, lightheadedness
Serious adverse effects
Photosensitivity, rash, nephrotoxicity, neurologic effects

- For specific drugs, see Table 46-6.

ELSEVIER

Slide 21

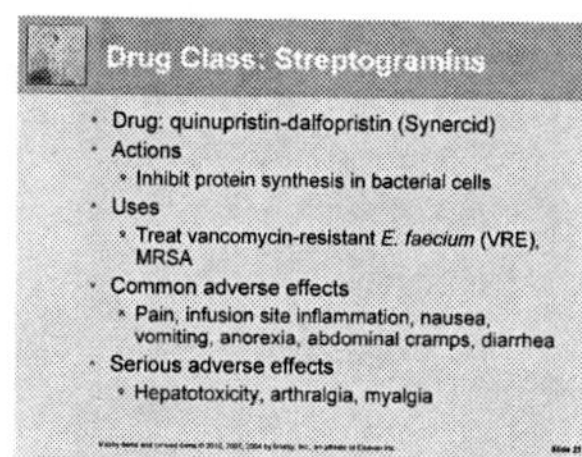
Drug Class: Streptogramins
Drug: quinupristin-dalfopristin (Synercid)
Actions
Inhibit protein synthesis in bacterial cells
Uses
Treat vancomycin-resistant E. faecium (VRE), MRSA
Common adverse effects
Pain, infusion site inflammation, nausea, vomiting, anorexia, abdominal cramps, diarrhea
Serious adverse effects
Hepatotoxicity, arthralgia, myalgia

- New class developed from pristamycin.
- Important for treatment with vancomycin-resistant bacteria; reserved for cases in which other antibiotics are not effective.

Slide 22

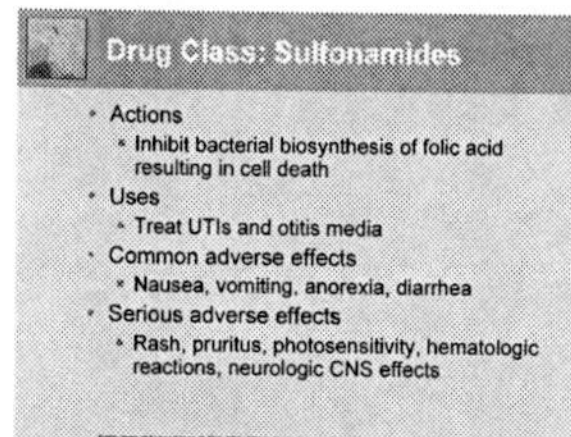
Drug Class: Sulfonamides
Actions
Inhibit bacterial biosynthesis of folic acid resulting in cell death
Uses
Treat UTIs and otitis media
Common adverse effects
Nausea, vomiting, anorexia, diarrhea
Serious adverse effects
Rash, pruritus, photosensitivity, hematologic reactions, neurologic CNS effects

- For specific drugs, see Table 46-7.
- Sulfonamides work fast, usually after one or two doses.
- Used prophylactically in patients susceptible to streptococcal infection or rheumatic fever when penicillin is contraindicated.

Slide 23

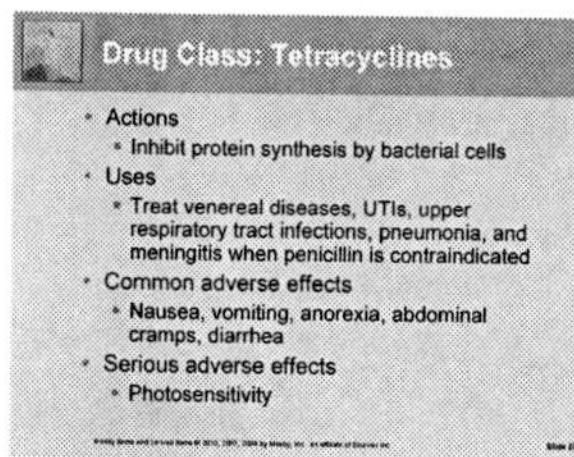
Drug Class: Tetracyclines
Actions
Inhibit protein synthesis by bacterial cells
Uses
Treat venereal diseases, UTIs, upper respiratory tract infections, pneumonia, and meningitis when penicillin is contraindicated
Common adverse effects
Nausea, vomiting, anorexia, abdominal cramps, diarrhea
Serious adverse effects
Photosensitivity

- For specific drugs, see Table 46-8.
- Can stain teeth; not recommended for children younger than age 8 or pregnant women.

Slide 24

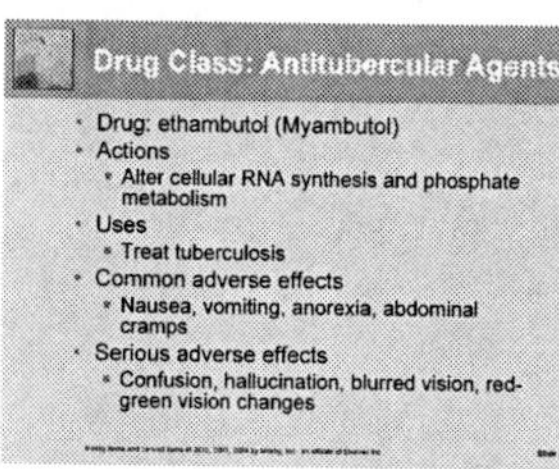
Drug Class: Antitubercular Agents
Drug: ethambutol (Myambutol)
Actions
Alter cellular RNA synthesis and phosphate metabolism
Uses
Treat tuberculosis
Common adverse effects
Nausea, vomiting, anorexia, abdominal cramps
Serious adverse effects
Confusion, hallucination, blurred vision, red-green vision changes

- All three medications (ethambutol, isoniazid, rifampin) must be used in combination to prevent resistant organisms.
- Major problems with toxicity can occur.
- Treatment can last 6 months.

Slide 25

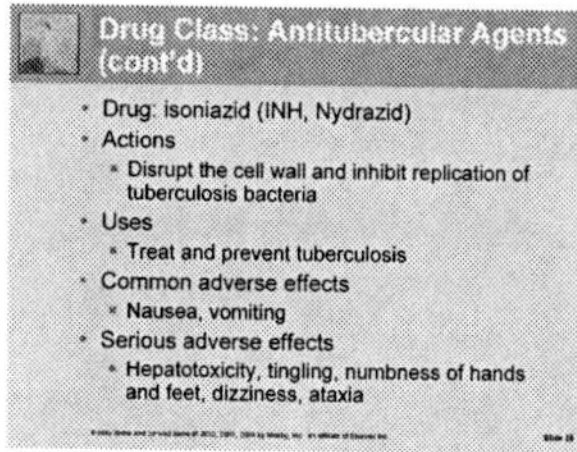
Drug Class: Antitubercular Agents (cont'd)
Drug: isoniazid (INH, Nydrazid)
Actions
Disrupt the cell wall and inhibit replication of tuberculosis bacteria
Uses
Treat and prevent tuberculosis
Common adverse effects
Nausea, vomiting
Serious adverse effects
Hepatotoxicity, tingling, numbness of hands and feet, dizziness, ataxia

- Adverse effects are dose related; concurrent use of pyridoxine usually prevents symptoms.

Slide 26

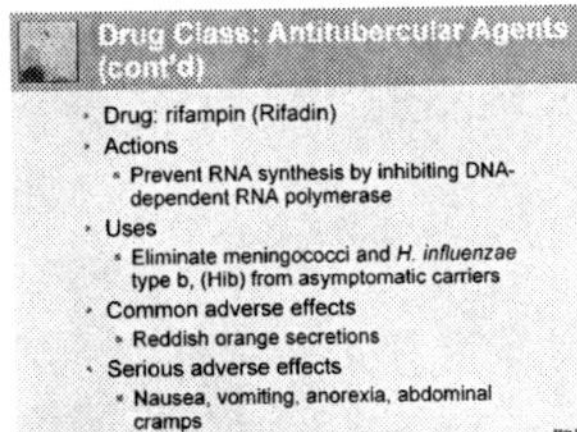
Drug Class: Antitubercular Agents (cont'd)
Drug: rifampin (Rifadin)
Actions
Prevent RNA synthesis by inhibiting DNA-dependent RNA polymerase
Uses
Eliminate meningococci and H. influenzae type b, (Hib) from asymptomatic carriers
Common adverse effects
Reddish orange secretions
Serious adverse effects
Nausea, vomiting, anorexia, abdominal cramps

- Also used in combination with other agents to treat tuberculosis.

Slide 27

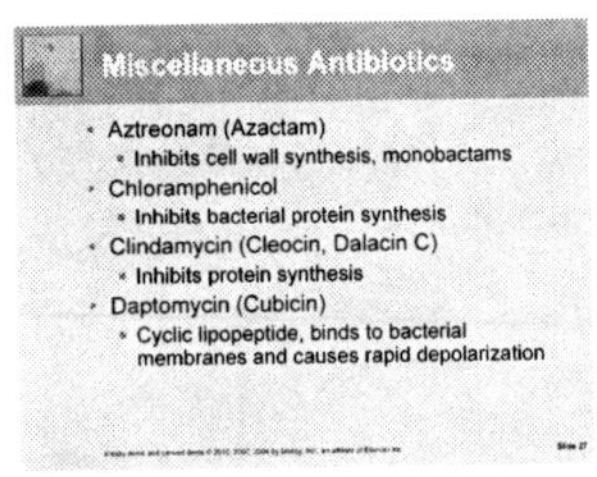
Miscellaneous Antibiotics
Aztreonam (Azactam)
Inhibits cell wall synthesis, monobactams
Chloramphenicol
Inhibits bacterial protein synthesis
Clindamycin (Cleocin, Dalacin C)
Inhibits protein synthesis
Daptomycin (Cubicin)
Cyclic lipopeptide, binds to bacterial membranes and causes rapid depolarization

- Chloramphenicol may have hematologic effects.
- Daptomycin is used only for cases of vancomycin resistance; may also cause skeletal muscle weakness and pain.

Slide 28

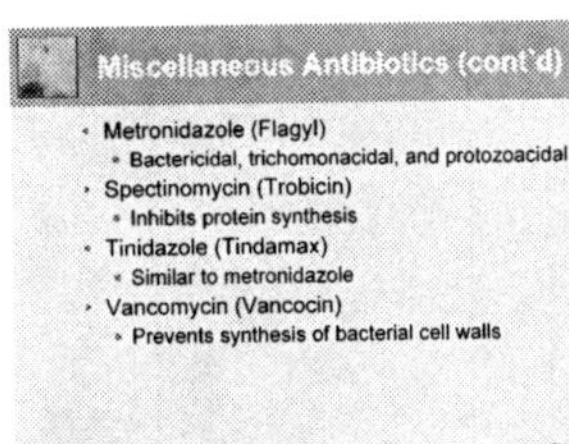
Miscellaneous Antibiotics (cont'd)
Metronidazole (Flagyl)
Bactericidal, trichomonacidal, and protozoacidal
Spectinomycin (Trobicin)
Inhibits protein synthesis
Tinidazole (Tindamax)
Similar to metronidazole
Vancomycin (Vancocin)
Prevents synthesis of bacterial cell walls

- Metronidazole has bactericidal, trichomonacidal, and protozoacidal activity.
- Vancomycin is effective against gram-positive organisms.

Slide 29

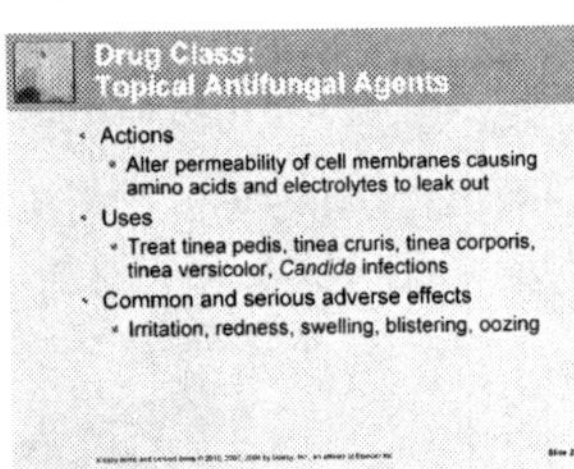
Drug Class: Topical Antifungal Agents
Actions
Alter permeability of cell membranes causing amino acids and electrolytes to leak out
Uses
Treat tinea pedis, tinea cruris, tinea corporis, tinea versicolor, Candida infections
Common and serious adverse effects
Irritation, redness, swelling, blistering, oozing

- For specific drugs, see Table 46-9.
- Watch for secondary skin rashes.

Slide 30

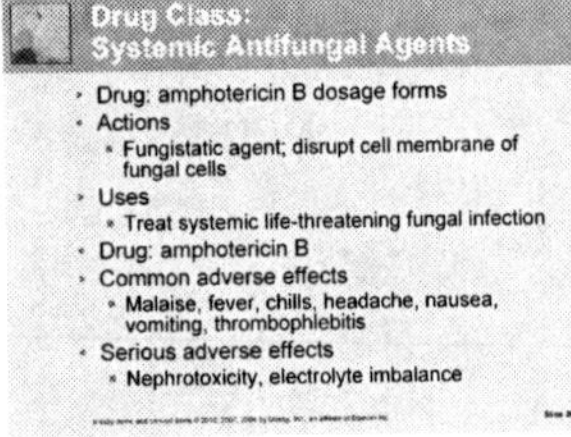
Drug Class: Systemic Antifungal Agents
Drug: amphotericin B dosage forms
Actions
Fungistatic agent; disrupt cell membrane of fungal cells
Uses
Treat systemic life-threatening fungal infection
Drug: amphotericin B
Common adverse effects
Malaise, fever, chills, headache, nausea, vomiting, thrombophlebitis
Serious adverse effects
Nephrotoxicity, electrolyte imbalance

- Dosage forms: amphotericin B with or without sodium desoxycholate (Fungizone IV), amphotericin B cholesteryl sulfate complex (Amphotec), amphotericin B lipid complex (Abelcet), amphotericin B liposomal (AmBisome).
- Should not be used for noninvasive fungal infections such as thrush, vaginal candidiasis, esophageal candidiasis.

ELSEVIER

Slide 31

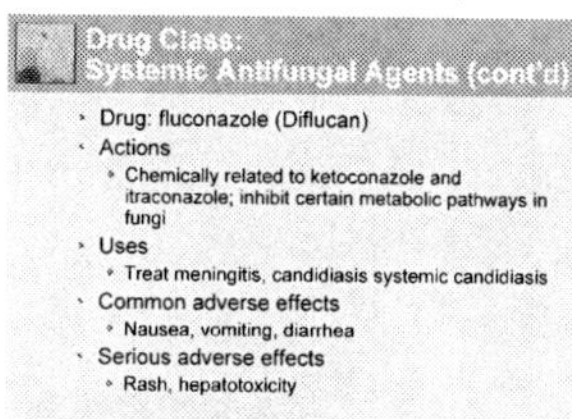
Drug Class:
Systemic Antifungal Agents (cont'd)
Drug: fluconazole (Diflucan)
Actions
Chemically related to ketoconazole and itraconazole; inhibit certain metabolic pathways in fungi
Uses
Treat meningitis, candidiasis systemic candidiasis
Common adverse effects
Nausea, vomiting, diarrhea
Serious adverse effects
Rash, hepatotoxicity

- Administered via IV and oral routes.

Slide 32

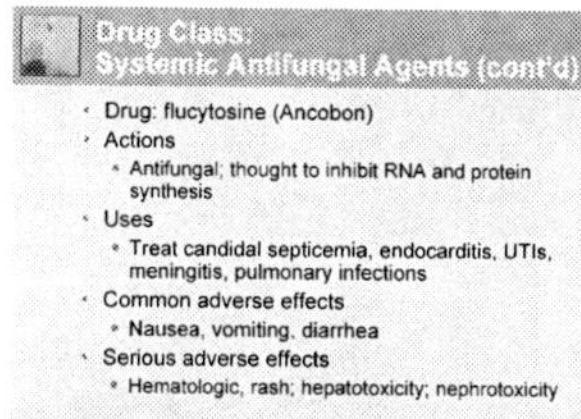
Drug Class:
Systemic Antifungal Agents (cont'd)
Drug: flucytosine (Ancobon)
Actions
Antifungal; thought to inhibit RNA and protein synthesis
Uses
Treat candidal septicemia, endocarditis, UTIs, meningitis, pulmonary infections
Common adverse effects
Nausea, vomiting, diarrhea
Serious adverse effects
Hematologic, rash; hepatotoxicity; nephrotoxicity

Slide 33

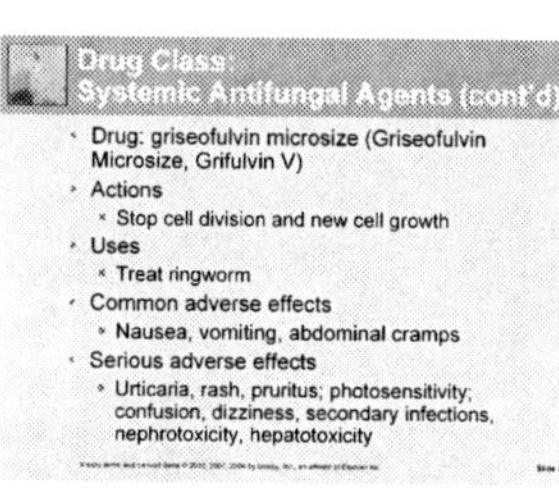
Drug Class:
Systemic Antifungal Agents (cont'd)
Drug: griseofulvin microsize (Griseofulvin Microsize, Grifulvin V)
Actions
Stop cell division and new cell growth
Uses
Treat ringworm
Common adverse effects
Nausea, vomiting, abdominal cramps
Serious adverse effects
Urticaria, rash, pruritus; photosensitivity; confusion, dizziness, secondary infections, nephrotoxicity, hepatotoxicity

- Available orally only.
- Treatment often required for several months.

Slide 34

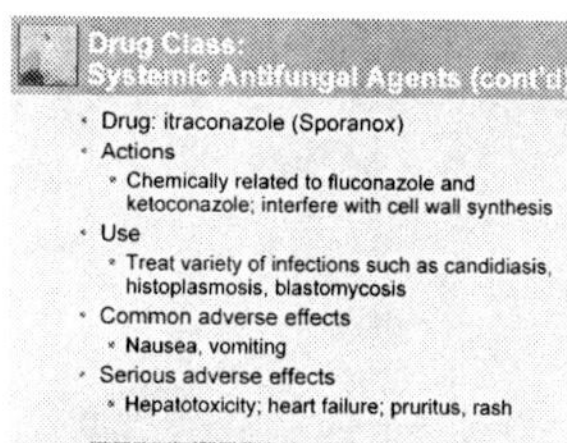
Drug Class:
Systemic Antifungal Agents (cont'd)
Drug: itraconazole (Sporanox)
Actions
Chemically related to fluconazole and ketoconazole; interfere with cell wall synthesis
Use
Treat variety of infections such as candidiasis, histoplasmosis, blastomycosis
Common adverse effects
Nausea, vomiting
Serious adverse effects
Hepatotoxicity; heart failure; pruritus, rash

- Do not administer to patients with a history of heart failure; has negative inotropic properties.
- Has many drug interactions because it is a potent inhibitor of metabolizing enzymes in the liver.

Slide 35

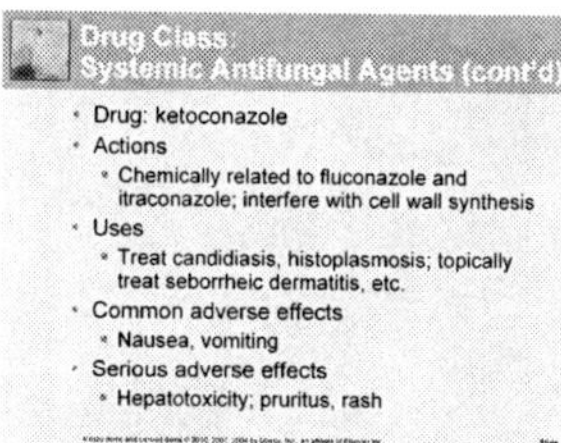
Drug Class:
Systemic Antifungal Agents (cont'd)
Drug: ketoconazole
Actions
Chemically related to fluconazole and itraconazole; interfere with cell wall synthesis
Uses
Treat candidiasis, histoplasmosis; topically treat seborrheic dermatitis, etc.
Common adverse effects
Nausea, vomiting
Serious adverse effects
Hepatotoxicity; pruritus, rash

Slide 36

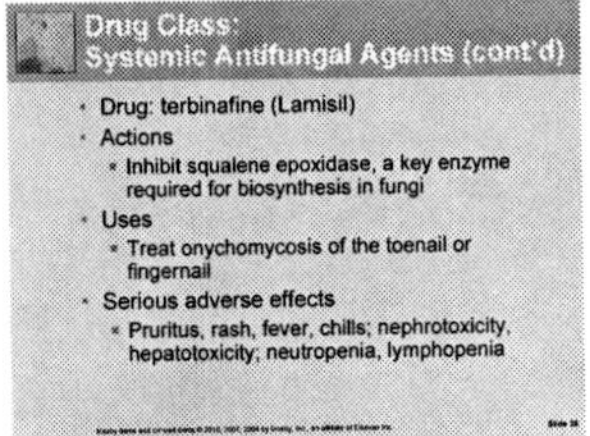
Drug Class:
Systemic Antifungal Agents (cont'd)
Drug: terbinafine (Lamisil)
Actions
Inhibit squalene epoxidase, a key enzyme required for biosynthesis in fungi
Uses
Treat onychomycosis of the toenail or fingernail
Serious adverse effects
Pruritus, rash, fever, chills; nephrotoxicity, hepatotoxicity; neutropenia, lymphopenia

Slide 37

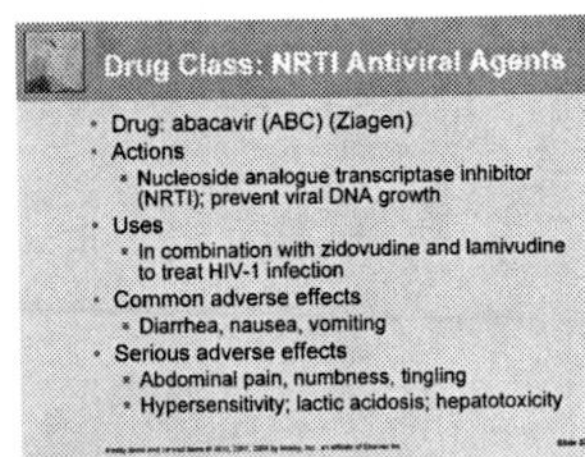
Drug Class: NRTI Antiviral Agents
Drug: abacavir (ABC) (Ziagen)
Actions
Nucleoside analogue transcriptase inhibitor (NRTI); prevent viral DNA growth
Uses
In combination with zidovudine and lamivudine to treat HIV-1 infection
Common adverse effects
Diarrhea, nausea, vomiting
Serious adverse effects
Abdominal pain, numbness, tingling
Hypersensitivity; lactic acidosis; hepatotoxicity

- First guanosine NRTI.
- Effectiveness with HIV depends on the stage. Antiviral agents usually slow progress in stages 1 and 2, but have little or no effect on stages 3 and 4.

Slide 38

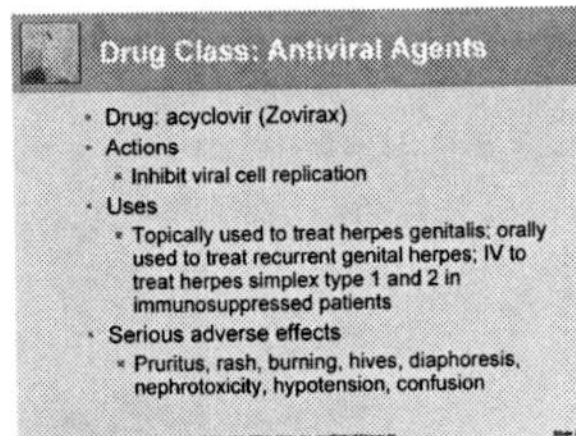
Drug Class: Antiviral Agents
Drug: acyclovir (Zovirax)
Actions
Inhibit viral cell replication
Uses
Topically used to treat herpes genitalis; orally used to treat recurrent genital herpes; IV to treat herpes simplex type 1 and 2 in immunosuppressed patients
Serious adverse effects
Pruritus, rash, burning, hives, diaphoresis, nephrotoxicity, hypotension, confusion

- Valacyclovir is a prodrug of acyclovir.

Slide 39

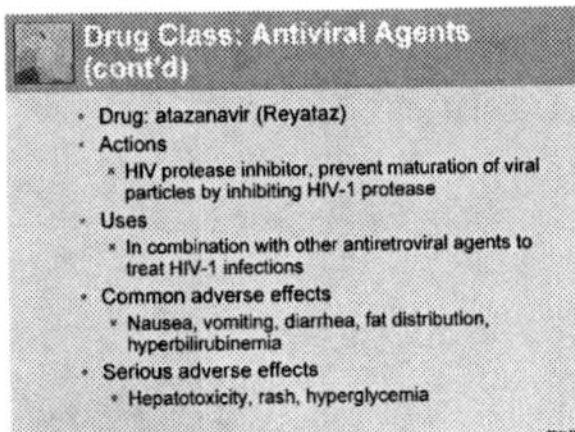
Drug Class: Antiviral Agents (cont'd)
Drug: atazanavir (Reyataz)
Actions
HIV protease inhibitor, prevent maturation of viral particles by inhibiting HIV-1 protease
Uses
In combination with other antiretroviral agents to treat HIV-1 infections
Common adverse effects
Nausea, vomiting, diarrhea, fat distribution, hyperbilirubinemia
Serious adverse effects
Hepatotoxicity, rash, hyperglycemia

Slide 40

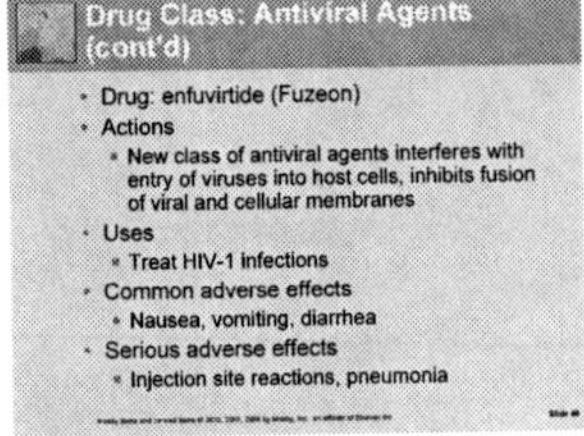
Drug Class: Antiviral Agents (cont'd)
Drug: enfuvirtide (Fuzeon)
Actions
New class of antiviral agents interferes with entry of viruses into host cells, inhibits fusion of viral and cellular membranes
Uses
Treat HIV-1 infections
Common adverse effects
Nausea, vomiting, diarrhea
Serious adverse effects
Injection site reactions, pneumonia

Slide 41

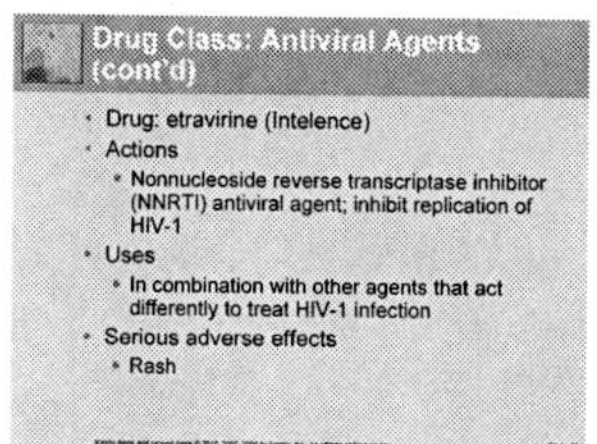
Drug Class: Antiviral Agents (cont'd)
Drug: etravirine (Intelence)
Actions
Nonnucleoside reverse transcriptase inhibitor (NNRTI) antiviral agent; inhibit replication of HIV-1
Uses
In combination with other agents that act differently to treat HIV-1 infection
Serious adverse effects
Rash

Slide 42

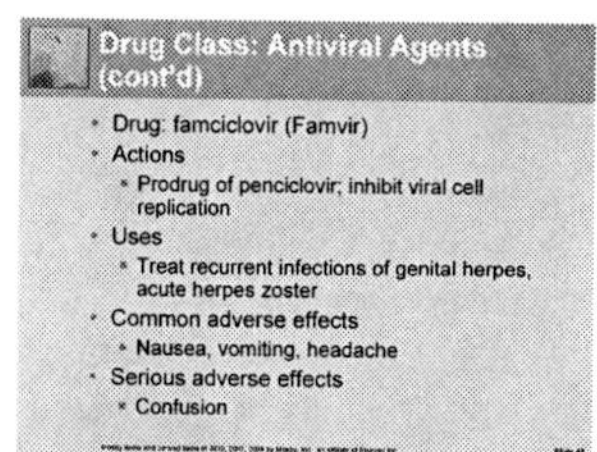
Drug Class: Antiviral Agents (cont'd)
Drug: famciclovir (Famvir)
Actions
Prodrug of penciclovir; inhibit viral cell replication
Uses
Treat recurrent infections of genital herpes, acute herpes zoster
Common adverse effects
Nausea, vomiting, headache
Serious adverse effects
Confusion

Slide 43

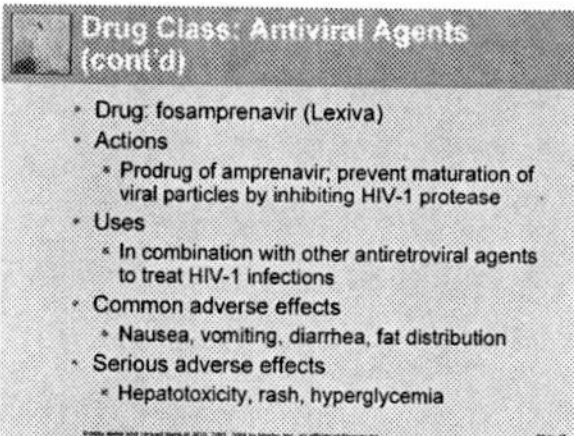
Drug Class: Antiviral Agents (cont'd)
Drug: fosamprenavir (Lexiva)
Actions
Prodrug of amprenavir; prevent maturation of viral particles by inhibiting HIV-1 protease
Uses
In combination with other antiretroviral agents to treat HIV-1 infections
Common adverse effects
Nausea, vomiting, diarrhea, fat distribution
Serious adverse effects
Hepatotoxicity, rash, hyperglycemia

- Be alert to multiple drug interactions.

Slide 44

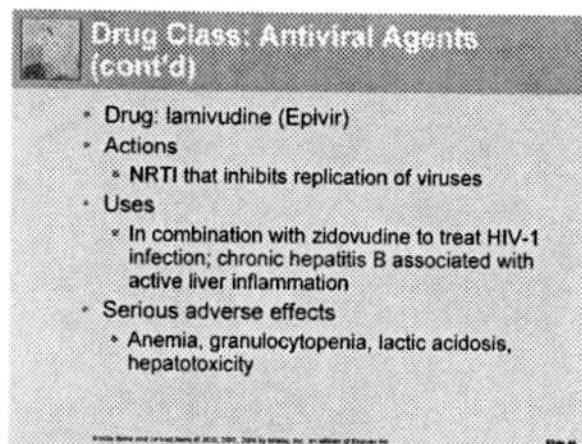
Drug Class: Antiviral Agents (cont'd)
Drug: lamivudine (Epivir)
Actions
NRTI that inhibits replication of viruses
Uses
In combination with zidovudine to treat HIV-1 infection; chronic hepatitis B associated with active liver inflammation
Serious adverse effects
Anemia, granulocytopenia, lactic acidosis, hepatotoxicity

Slide 45

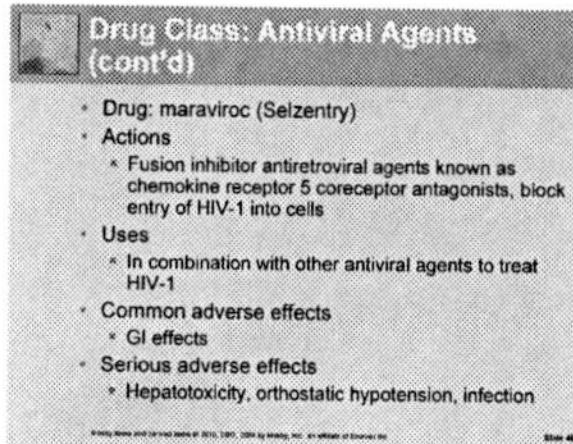
Drug Class: Antiviral Agents (cont'd)
Drug: maraviroc (Selzentry)
Actions
Fusion inhibitor antiretroviral agents known as chemokine receptor 5 coreceptor antagonists, block entry of HIV-1 into cells
Uses
In combination with other antiviral agents to treat HIV-1
Common adverse effects
GI effects
Serious adverse effects
Hepatotoxicity, orthostatic hypotension, infection

- First member of the new category chemokine receptor 5 coreceptor antagonists.

Slide 46

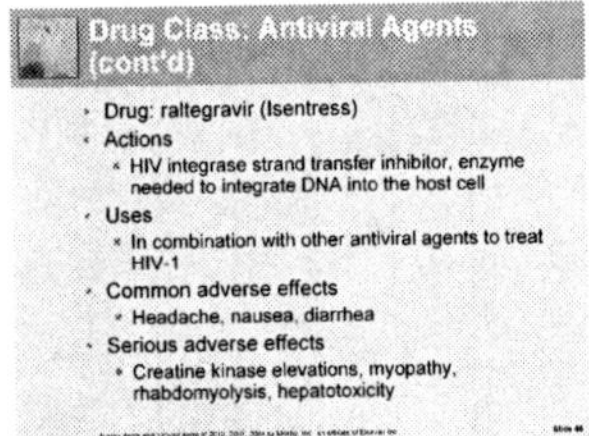
Drug Class: Antiviral Agents (cont'd)
Drug: raltegravir (Isentress)
Actions
HIV integrase strand transfer inhibitor, enzyme needed to integrate DNA into the host cell
Uses
In combination with other antiviral agents to treat HIV-1
Common adverse effects
Headache, nausea, diarrhea
Serious adverse effects
Creatine kinase elevations, myopathy, rhabdomyolysis, hepatotoxicity

---

Slide 47

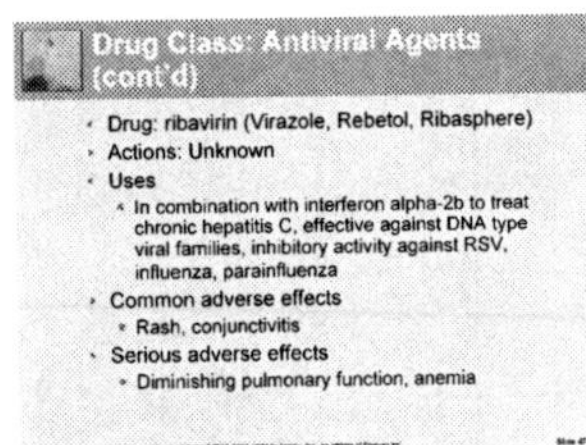
Drug Class: Antiviral Agents (cont'd)
Drug: ribavirin (Virazole, Rebetol, Ribasphere)
Actions: Unknown
Uses
In combination with interferon alpha-2b to treat chronic hepatitis C, effective against DNA type viral families, inhibitory activity against RSV, influenza, parainfluenza
Common adverse effects
Rash, conjunctivitis
Serious adverse effects
Diminishing pulmonary function, anemia

- Virazole is in aerosol form; Rebetol is in oral capsule and suspension form; Ribasphere is in oral tablets and capsules.

Slide 48

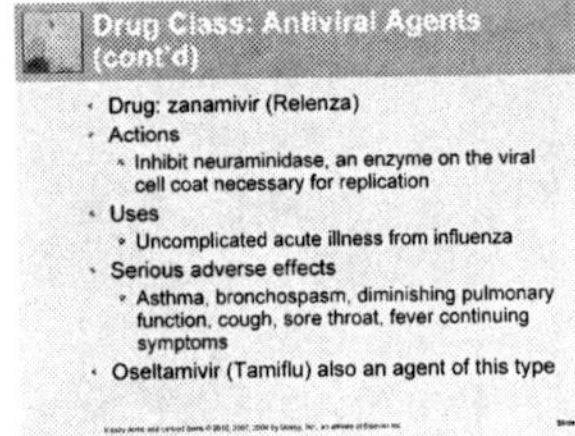
Drug Class: Antiviral Agents (cont'd)
Drug: zanamivir (Relenza)
Actions
Inhibit neuraminidase, an enzyme on the viral cell coat necessary for replication
Uses
Uncomplicated acute illness from influenza
Serious adverse effects
Asthma, bronchospasm, diminishing pulmonary function, cough, sore throat, fever continuing symptoms
Oseltamivir (Tamiflu) also an agent of this type

47 Lesson Plan Nutrition

TEACHING FOCUS

This chapter focuses on nutritional concepts, such as recommended dietary allowances (RDAs) and dietary reference intakes (DRIs). Students will have the opportunity to learn the categories of macronutrients, their importance to health maintenance, and food sources of nutrients. Vitamins and minerals and their significance to body functioning are also presented. The role proper nutrition plays in the healing process, postsurgery, and other stressful events is also emphasized. In addition, students will have the opportunity to become acquainted with the indications and assessment for enteral and parenteral feeding and their proper implementation.

MATERIALS AND RESOURCES

- ☐ computer and PowerPoint projector (all Lessons)
- ☐ food guide pyramids (Lesson 47.1)

LESSON CHECKLIST

Preparations for this lesson include:

- lecture
- guest speaker: home care nurse
- evaluation of student knowledge and skills required to perform all entry-level nursing activities related to nutrition, including:
  - interpreting DRIs, RDAs, and food guide pyramids
  - identifying the function of macronutrients, minerals, and vitamins in the body
  - assessing nutritional status, requirements, and deficiencies
  - macronutrients
  - nutritional requirements and deficiencies
  - recognizing malnutrition states
  - administering enteral and parenteral nutrition

KEY TERMS

adequate intake (AI) (p. 784)
carbohydrates (p. 790)
Dietary Reference Intakes (DRIs) (p. 784)
disaccharides (p. 790)
enteral nutrition (p. 794)
essential fatty acids (p. 790)
Estimated Average Requirement (EAR) (p. 784)
Estimated Energy Requirement (EER) (p. 790)
fats (p. 790)
fiber (p. 790)
gluconeogenesis (p. 791)
kilocalories (p. 784)
kwashiorkor (p. 794)
lipids (p. 790)
macronutrients (p. 781)
marasmus (p. 794)
minerals (p. 791)
mixed kwashiorkor-marasmus (p. 794)
monosaccharides (p. 790)
parenteral nutrition (p. 794)
peripheral parenteral nutrition (PPN) (p. 794)
physical exercise (p. 793)
polysaccharides (p. 790)
proteins (p. 791)
Recommended Dietary Allowances (RDAs) (p. 784)
Tolerable Upper Intake Level (UL) (p. 784)
total parenteral nutrition (TPN) (p. 794)
tube feedings (p. 794)
vitamins (p. 791)
water (p. 791)

ADDITIONAL RESOURCES

PowerPoint slides: 1-22
Flashcards, Decks 1 and 2

Legend

ARQ	**PPT**	**TB**	**CTQ**	**SG**	**INRQ**
Audience Response Questions	PowerPoint Slides	Test Bank	Critical Thinking Questions	Study Guide	Interactive NCLEX Review Questions

Class Activities are indicated in ***bold italic.***

LESSON 47.1

BACKGROUND ASSESSMENT

Question: What are the differences between DRIs and RDAs? What are the definitions of AI, EAR, and UL?
Answer: DRIs provide quantitative estimates of nutrient intakes to be used for the assessment and planning of diets for healthy people. The RDA table is a component of the DRIs and lists the average daily dietary intake level sufficient to meet the nutrient requirements of nearly all healthy individuals in a group. (Groups are based on gender, age, and whether an individual is pregnant or lactating.) RDAs are not intended to meet the nutritional needs of ill patients and do not account for nutritional value that may be lost in cooking. AI is a value based on observed or experimentally determined approximations of nutrient intake by a group of healthy people. EAR is a nutrient intake value that is estimated to meet the requirements of half of the healthy individuals in a group. Finally, UL is defined as the highest level of daily nutrient intake that is likely to pose no risk of adverse health effects to almost all those in the general population.

Question: What is the definition of a vitamin? Can you name some fat-soluble and water-soluble vitamins?
Answer: Vitamins are a specific set of chemical molecules that regulate human metabolism and are necessary to maintain health. To be classified as a vitamin, a chemical must be ingested because the human body does not make sufficient quantities to maintain health, and the lack of a vitamin in the diet produces a specific vitamin deficiency disease. Fat-soluble vitamins are vitamins A, D, E, and K. Water-soluble vitamins include vitamin C, niacin, riboflavin, thiamine, and others.

CRITICAL THINKING QUESTION

A nursing student has an assignment from her nutrition class to create a diet plan for a vegetarian patient. What types of nutritional needs should the nurse consider for this patient? What nutritional supplements should this patient be instructed about?
Guidelines: When educating vegetarian patients about nutrition, it is necessary to stress that these exchanges are essential to their well-being. Vegetarians lack many of the necessary proteins and fats found in animal meat, and it is imperative that these proteins and fats be replaced with other foods. For example, soy products are an excellent source of protein for vegetarian patients, and nuts are a good source of fats. Vegetarians will also need to take supplemental vitamins and minerals to replace essential nutrients found only in animal-based foods. Also it is recommended that these patients have regular blood tests to ensure that they have adequate amounts of iron to prevent anemia.

ELSEVIER

OBJECTIVES	CONTENT	TEACHING RESOURCES
Differentiate between information found in the Dietary Reference Intake tables and the Recommended Dietary Allowances table.	■ Principles of nutrition (p. 780) ■ Dietary Reference Intakes (p. 784) Review the components of nutrition—macronutrients such as fats, carbohydrates, fiber, and proteins. Discuss the revised food pyramid (MyPyramid) and recommended 2005 Dietary Guidelines. Review the definitions of the four values that make up the Dietary Reference Intakes (DRIs): Estimated Average Requirements (EARs), Recommended Dietary Allowances (RDAs), Adequate Intakes (AIs), and Tolerable Upper Intake Levels (ULs). Discuss the types of carbohydrates—monosaccharides, disaccharides, and polysaccharides. Review fiber, lipids and essential fatty acids, proteins, vitamins, and minerals and their importance in nutrition. Discuss gluconeogenesis and the need to balance nutritional intake.	PPT 5-8 ARQ 1 TB Multiple Choice question 8 SG Review Sheet questions 1-7 (pp. 321-322) Review Questions for the NCLEX Examination 5, 7 (p. 803) Figure 47-1 (p. 782): Sample MyPyramid. Figure 47-3 (p. 783): An alternative food guide pyramid. Table 47-2: Dietary Reference Intakes: Macronutrients (pp. 785-788) Table 47-3: Dietary Reference Intakes (DRIs): Recommended Levels for Individual Intake (p. 789) ▸ Discuss the factors on which the RDAs are based (e.g., gender, age). ▸ Discuss the significance of the UL. Class Activity *Have several menus made up based on proper nutrition, poor nutrition, and at least one component of proper nutrition missing. Have students pair up. Using a scale from 1 to 5, have each pair indicate which diet menu would be the healthiest based on proper nutrition and calorie proportion. Have each pair compete for the greatest number of correct responses. Review the exercise with the class.* Class Activity *Divide the class into two groups. Request the first group to research individualized dietary guidelines by accessing MyPyramid at* **http://www.mypyramid.gov** *and complete a report. Assign the second group to a research project on ways for healthy eating as cited in* **www.oldwayspt.org** *and complete a report of their findings. Allow class time for presentations and discussion.*
Compare and contrast the Estimated Energy Requirement for a healthy male and female of similar height, weight, and level of activity.	□ Macronutrients (p. 784)	PPT 8 TB Multiple Choice question 3 Table 47-4: Calculation of Estimated Energy Requirements (EER) (p. 790) ▸ Discuss some factors that would lead to an increase in an individual's metabolic needs.

OBJECTIVES	CONTENT	TEACHING RESOURCES
		Class Activity ***Have students calculate their individual EER. Compare their results. Discuss the factors that affect the calculations.***
Identify the function of macronutrients in the body.	□ Macronutrients (p. 784)	PPT 9-11 ARQ 2 TB Multiple Choice questions 5, 9 TB Multiple Response questions 1, 4-5 SG Review Sheet questions 8-11 (p. 322) SG Learning Activities questions 1-2, 6, 15-16 (p. 324) Review Question for the NCLEX Examination 4 (p. 803) Table 47-2: Dietary Reference Intakes: Macronutrients (pp. 785-788) Table 47-1: Dietary Fat Sources (p. 782) Figure 47-2 (p. 783): Plant oils and saturated, monounsaturated, and polyunsaturated fatty acids. Lifespan Considerations: Food for Thought (p. 791) ▸ Discuss the major function of carbohydrates in the diet. ▸ Discuss and differentiate between monounsaturated, polyunsaturated, saturated, and trans fats. Which are considered to be cardioprotective, and which are thought to promote atherosclerosis? Class Activity ***Write down the different types of fats on the board. Ask students to identify sources for each one. Stress which fats should be minimized in a patient's diet and which common foods contain these types of fats.***
Research good dietary sources of fiber.	□ Macronutrients (p. 784)	PPT 10 TB Multiple Choice question 1 TB Multiple Response question 3 Review Question for the NCLEX Examination 3 (p. 803) ▸ Discuss the differences between dietary fiber and functional fiber. ▸ Discuss nutritional sources rich in fiber.

OBJECTIVES	CONTENT	TEACHING RESOURCES
		Class Activity ***Ask students which foods they would recommend to a patient with high cholesterol. Discuss how fiber can help reduce blood cholesterol concentrations.*** Class Activity ***Have students complete a nutritional intake diary for 1 week. Have them identify individualized fiber content to determine if this was adequate or not. Ask that they include dietary fiber recommendations with their diary.***
Differentiate between fat-soluble and water-soluble vitamins.	□ Vitamins (p. 791)	PPT 12 TB Multiple Choice question 4 INRQ 7-9 SG Review Sheet questions 12, 28 (pp. 322-323) SG Learning Activities questions 5, 8-10, 19 (p. 324) Table 47-5: Vitamins (p. 792) ▸ Discuss some examples of fat-soluble vitamins and water-soluble vitamins, and name some dietary examples of each. ▸ Discuss what makes a vitamin fat soluble versus water soluble. Class Activity ***Have each student research at the library a particular vitamin deficiency, such as scurvy or anemia. Have students create a fact sheet on the deficiency, including common causes, results, and preventive measures using dietary changes and supplements. (For students to prepare for this activity, see Homework/Assignment #1.)***
List five functions of minerals in the body.	□ Minerals (p. 791) □ Water (p. 791)	PPT 12 ARQ 5 TB Multiple Choice question 6 SG Review Sheet question 13 (p. 322) Table 47-6: Essential Minerals (p. 793) ▸ Discuss why minerals are essential to the health of the body. ▸ Discuss several kinds of minerals, their function in the body, and good dietary sources. Class Activity ***Divide the class into small groups. Have each group research a particular***

OBJECTIVES	CONTENT	TEACHING RESOURCES
		diet of its choosing and determine if the selected diet places an individual at risk for mineral deficiency. Have groups report their findings in class. (For students to prepare for this activity, see Homework/Assignment #2.)
Identify the exercise guidelines currently recommended for people with different daily patterns of physical activity (sedentary, low active, active, and very active).	■ Physical activity (p. 793) Review the need to incorporate daily activities into a healthy lifestyle, and discuss reasons for the increase in obesity in our society. Discuss the four different levels of physical activity and the recommendations from the National Academy of Sciences.	PPT 13 TB Multiple Choice question 2 ▸ Discuss why calorie reduction alone may be insufficient for weight loss. ▸ Discuss factors that influence a person's activity level and eating habits and what can be done to improve them. Class Activity ***Have students list the risks and complications associated with obesity. Make a chart on the board.*** Class Activity ***List on the board the levels of physical activity: sedentary, low active, active, and very active. Have volunteer students explain what each one means and give an example of a person who fits these different levels. Review the exercise with the class.*** Class Activity ***Divide the class into five groups. Assign each group one of the following life spans: infancy, school-aged (6 to 10); adolescence; middle adult (age 40), and geriatric (65 and over). Have each group research age-related physical activity recommendations. Allow class time for presentation.***

47.1 Homework/Assignments:

1. Have each student research at the library a particular vitamin deficiency, such as scurvy or anemia. Have students create a fact sheet on each deficiency, including common causes, results, and preventive measures using dietary changes and supplements.
2. Divide the class into small groups. Have each group research a particular diet of its choosing and determine whether the selected diet places an individual at risk for mineral deficiency. Have students report their findings in class.

47.1 Instructor's Notes/Student Feedback:

LESSON 47.2

CRITICAL THINKING QUESTION

A 55-year-old female patient is receiving TPN after minor surgery related to ulcerative colitis. The patient does not have an ileostomy or colostomy and can produce regular bowel movements. What daily assessments should the nurse complete to ensure that TPN is adequate and no problems or potential problems exist for the patient?

Guidelines: Until the patient heals and her gastrointestinal system resumes normal nutrient absorption, the patient will receive TPN for approximately 7 to 10 days. During this time, the nurse needs to ensure that the patient is maintaining a healthy weight by recording daily weights in addition to intake and output (I&O). Because TPN includes both insulin and glucose, the nurse must watch for adverse reactions to either of these additives. Therefore the nurse should check blood glucose levels twice daily, or as ordered, to detect hyperglycemia or hypoglycemia. The nurse also needs to remember that this patient will remain NPO until the health care provider starts to gradually reduce the TPN.

OBJECTIVES	CONTENT	TEACHING RESOURCES
Describe physical changes associated with a malnourished state.	■ Malnutrition (p. 794) □ Therapy for malnutrition (p. 794) – Nursing process for nutritional support (p. 795) Review the three types of malnutrition: marasmus, kwashiorkor, and mixed kwashiorkor-marasmus. Discuss the ways nutrition is provided for when disease states and various physical conditions prevent normal oral intake, such as parenteral nutrition and enteral nutrition. Review the actions, uses, and therapeutic outcomes for each type of alternative nutrition.	PPT 17 SG Review Sheet questions 14, 18 (p. 322) SG Learning Activities questions 3, 7 (p. 324) SG Practice Question for the NCLEX Examination 6 (p. 326) ▸ Discuss the physical changes associated with marasmus. ▸ Discuss the physical changes associated with kwashiorkor. Class Activity ***Divide the class into three groups, and assign each group one of the three types of malnutrition. Have the groups discuss dietary recommendations for their assigned type of malnutrition and then present their findings to the class.*** Class Activity ***Divide the class into three groups. Have one group be prepared to discuss the three types of malnutrition. Have another group be prepared to discuss parenteral nutrition, and have the third group be prepared to discuss enteral nutrition. Include in the presentation the typical types of patients involved with each. Have on hand examples of tubes used for parenteral and enteric nutrition. Review the exercise with the class.***
Describe nutritional assessments essential before the administration of tube feedings and parenteral nutrition.	■ Malnutrition (p. 794) □ Therapy for malnutrition (p. 794) – Nursing process for nutritional support (p. 795)	PPT 19 ARQ 3 TB Multiple Response question 2 INRQ 3, 6 CTQ 1, 4, 6

OBJECTIVES	CONTENT	TEACHING RESOURCES
		SG Review Sheet questions 16-17, 25-27 (pp. 322-323) SG Learning Activities questions 4, 18 (p. 324) SG Practice Questions for the NCLEX Examination 1-2, 4-5, 7 (pp. 325-326) Clinical Landmine (p. 794) ▸ Discuss why nutritional assessments are essential before administration of enteral or parenteral nutrition. Class Activity ***Have students list and discuss some of the possible reasons a patient may need nutritional support.***
Cite common laboratory and diagnostic tests used to monitor a patient's nutritional status.	■ Malnutrition (p. 794) □ Therapy for malnutrition (p. 794) – Nursing process for nutritional support (p. 795)	PPT 18 CTQ 6 SG Review Sheet question 15 (p. 322) ▸ Discuss the various tests that are used to diagnose and monitor a patient's nutritional status and instances in which a health care provider might prescribe each one. Class Activity ***Ask for student volunteers to come to the board and list a test performed for nutritional assessment. Supply the range of normal values for each test listed. Then lead the class in a discussion about the various tests, and ask the students if they are surprised by the results. Why or why not?***
Discuss nursing assessments and interventions required during the administration of enteral nutrition.	– Patient education and health promotion (p. 797) □ Enteral nutrition (p. 798) – Nursing process for enteral nutrition (p. 798)	PPT 19 ARQ 4 TB Multiple Choice question 7 INRQ 1-2, 5 CTQ 2, 5 Patient Self-Assessment Form: Nutritional Therapy SG Review Sheet questions 19-24 (p. 322) SG Learning Activities questions 11-14, 17, 20 (p. 324) SG Practice Questions for the NCLEX Examination 8-10 (p. 326) Review Questions for the NCLEX Examination 1-2, 8-10 (p. 803)

OBJECTIVES	CONTENT	TEACHING RESOURCES
		Table 47-7 Enteral Formulas (p. 799) Clinical Landmine (p. 797) Herbal Interactions (p. 800) ▸ Discuss the nursing assessments that are required during administration of enteral nutrition. ▸ Discuss common potential food-drug interactions. Class Activity ***Divide the class into small groups. Have the groups identify possible adverse effects that some patients might experience from glucose and insulin. Also have the groups discuss measures that could be taken to prevent hyperglycemia. Then ask a volunteer from each group to share the group's findings with the class.***
Discuss home care needs of a patient being discharged on any form of enteral or parenteral nutrition.	– Patient education and health promotion (p. 797) – Enteral nutrition (p. 798) – Nursing process for enteral nutrition (p. 798) □ Parenteral nutrition (p. 801) – Nursing process for parenteral nutrition (p. 801)	PPT 19-22 CTQ 3 ▸ Discuss important nursing assessments related to monitoring of enteral therapy. ▸ Discuss how you would instruct a patient being discharged on enteral or parenteral nutrition. ▸ Discuss how you would formulate written instructions for patients and their caregivers in the event of aspiration or tube replacement. Class Activity ***Invite a home care nurse to discuss the policies and procedures involved in caring for a patient receiving enteral or parenteral nutrition at home.***
Performance evaluation		Test Bank SG Learning Activities (p. 324) SG Practice Questions for the NCLEX Examination (pp. 325-326) Critical Thinking Questions

47.2 Homework/Assignments:

47.2 Instructor's Notes/Student Feedback:

47 Lecture Outline
Nutrition

Slide 1

Chapter 47
Nutrition

Slide 2

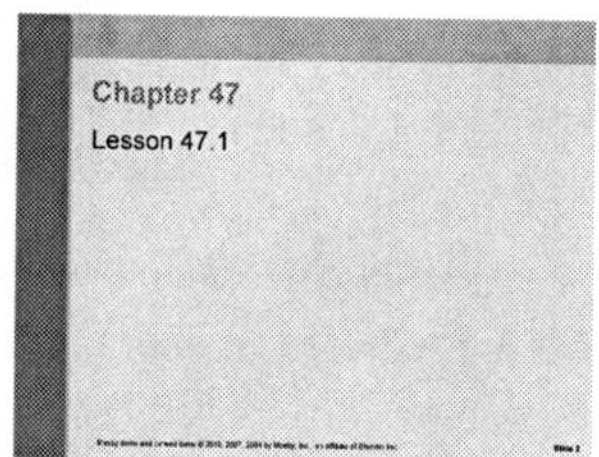
Chapter 47
Lesson 47.1

Slide 3

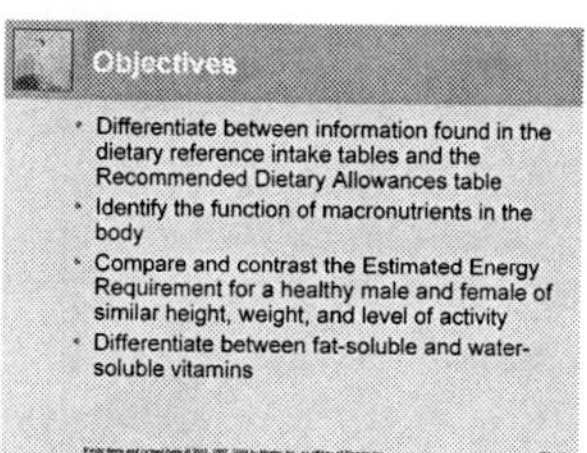
Objectives
Differentiate between information found in the dietary reference intake tables and the Recommended Dietary Allowances table
Identify the function of macronutrients in the body
Compare and contrast the Estimated Energy Requirement for a healthy male and female of similar height, weight, and level of activity
Differentiate between fat-soluble and water-soluble vitamins

Slide 4

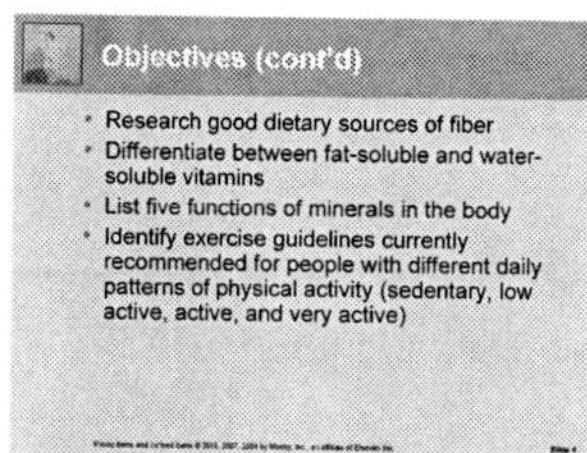
Objectives (cont'd)
Research good dietary sources of fiber
Differentiate between fat-soluble and water-soluble vitamins
List five functions of minerals in the body
Identify exercise guidelines currently recommended for people with different daily patterns of physical activity (sedentary, low active, active, and very active)

Slide 5

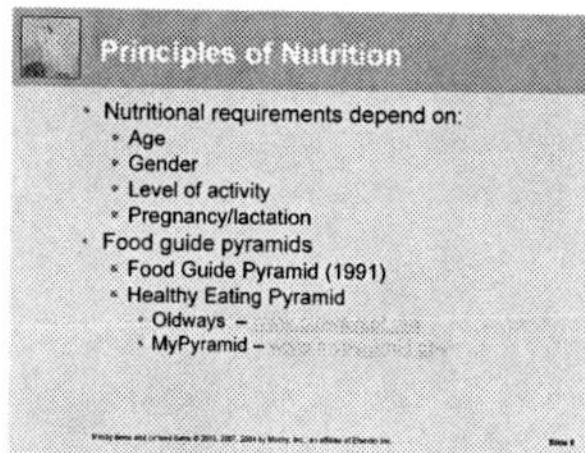
Principles of Nutrition
Nutritional requirements depend on:
Age
Gender
Level of activity
Pregnancy/lactation
Food guide pyramids
Food Guide Pyramid (1991)
Healthy Eating Pyramid
Oldways –
MyPyramid –

- Essential nutritional assessment: history of nutritional deficit and patient dietary practices, laboratory tests, physical changes.

ELSEVIER

Slide 6

Dietary Reference Intakes
MyPyramid

- USDA retired the old Food Guide Pyramid and replaced it with MyPyramid, a new symbol, and interactive website (www.mypyramid.gov).

Slide 7

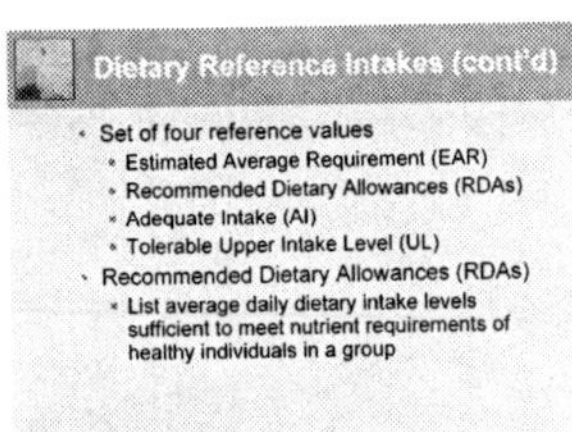
Dietary Reference Intakes (cont'd)
Set of four reference values
Estimated Average Requirement (EAR)
Recommended Dietary Allowances (RDAs)
Adequate Intake (AI)
Tolerable Upper Intake Level (UL)
Recommended Dietary Allowances (RDAs)
List average daily dietary intake levels sufficient to meet nutrient requirements of healthy individuals in a group

- RDA does not meet the nutritional needs of ill patients. It is based on the EAR plus 2 standard deviations.

Slide 8

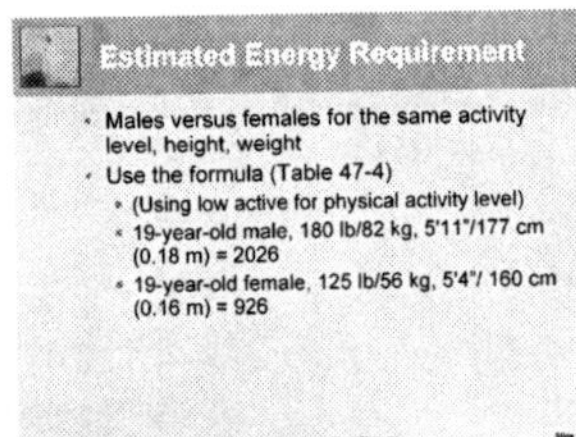
Estimated Energy Requirement
Males versus females for the same activity level, height, weight
Use the formula (Table 47-4)
(Using low active for physical activity level)
19-year-old male, 180 lb/82 kg, 5'11"/177 cm (0.18 m) = 2026
19-year-old female, 125 lb/56 kg, 5'4"/ 160 cm (0.16 m) = 926

- EER is the average dietary energy intake that is predicted to maintain energy.

Slide 9

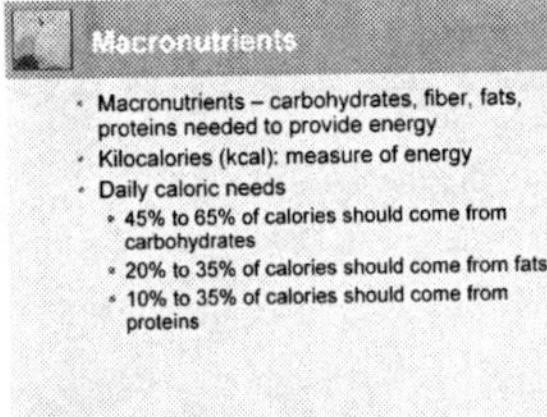
Macronutrients
Macronutrients – carbohydrates, fiber, fats, proteins needed to provide energy
Kilocalories (kcal): measure of energy
Daily caloric needs
45% to 65% of calories should come from carbohydrates
20% to 35% of calories should come from fats
10% to 35% of calories should come from proteins

- Reasons for increased metabolic needs: increased activity, surgery, trauma, burns, infection.

Slide 10

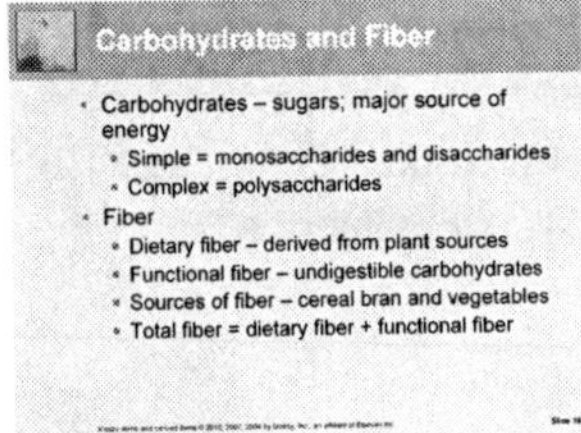
Carbohydrates and Fiber
Carbohydrates – sugars; major source of energy
Simple = monosaccharides and disaccharides
Complex = polysaccharides
Fiber
Dietary fiber – derived from plant sources
Functional fiber – undigestible carbohydrates
Sources of fiber – cereal bran and vegetables
Total fiber = dietary fiber + functional fiber

- Examples of monosaccharides: glucose, fructose, and galactose.
- Common table sugar is known as sucrose.

Slide 11

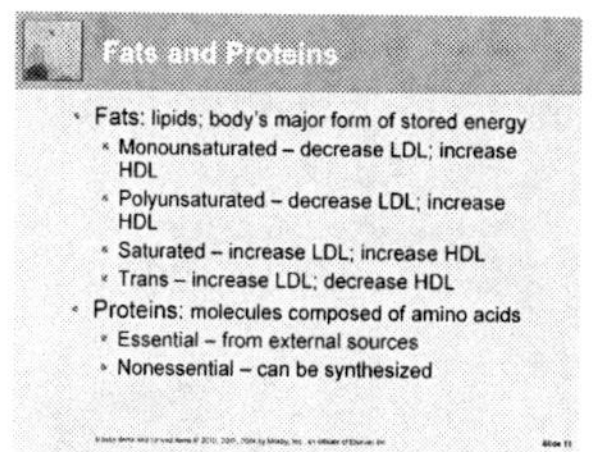
Fats and Proteins
Fats: lipids; body's major form of stored energy
Monounsaturated – decrease LDL; increase HDL
Polyunsaturated – decrease LDL; increase HDL
Saturated – increase LDL; increase HDL
Trans – increase LDL; decrease HDL
Proteins: molecules composed of amino acids
Essential – from external sources
Nonessential – can be synthesized

- Olive oil is a monounsaturated fat. Sources of polyunsaturated fats include nuts, seeds, and soybeans.
- Saturated fats come from red meats, butter, and high-fat dairy products.
- Some sources of trans fats are commercially fried foods, stick margarine, processed ready-to-eat foods, snack foods.
- Consumption of saturated fats and trans fats leads to heart disease.

Slide 12

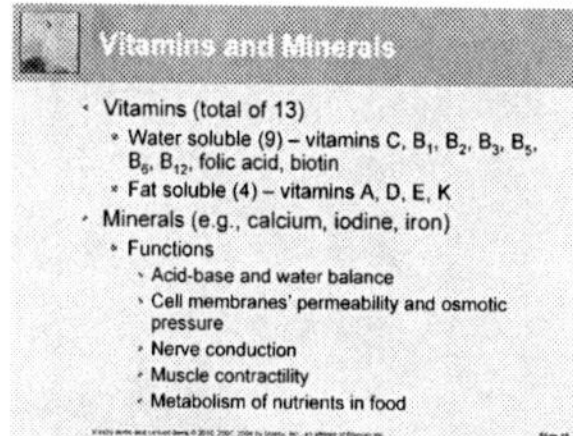
Vitamins and Minerals
Vitamins (total of 13)
Water soluble (9) – vitamins C, B1, B2, B3, B5, B6, B12, folic acid, biotin
Fat soluble (4) – vitamins A, D, E, K
Minerals (e.g., calcium, iodine, iron)
Functions
Acid-base and water balance
Cell membranes' permeability and osmotic pressure
Nerve conduction
Muscle contractility
Metabolism of nutrients in food

- Vitamin deficiencies – beriberi is a thiamine (B_1) deficiency; scurvy is a vitamin C deficiency.
- Minerals are inorganic chemicals in nature, components of enzymes, hormones, and bone and tooth structure.

Slide 13

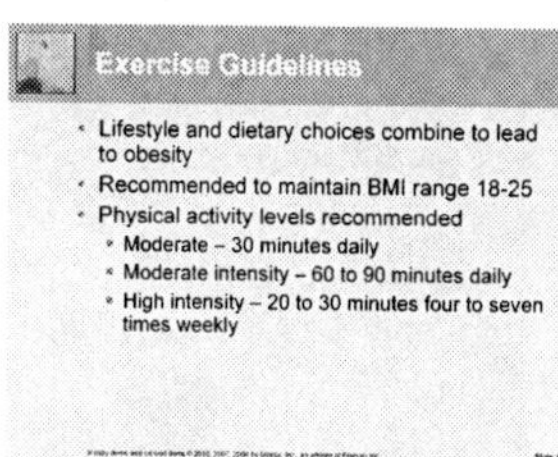
Exercise Guidelines
Lifestyle and dietary choices combine to lead to obesity
Recommended to maintain BMI range 18-25
Physical activity levels recommended
Moderate – 30 minutes daily
Moderate intensity – 60 to 90 minutes daily
High intensity – 20 to 30 minutes four to seven times weekly

- Obesity leads to type 2 diabetes, cardiovascular disease, and premature death.

Slide 14

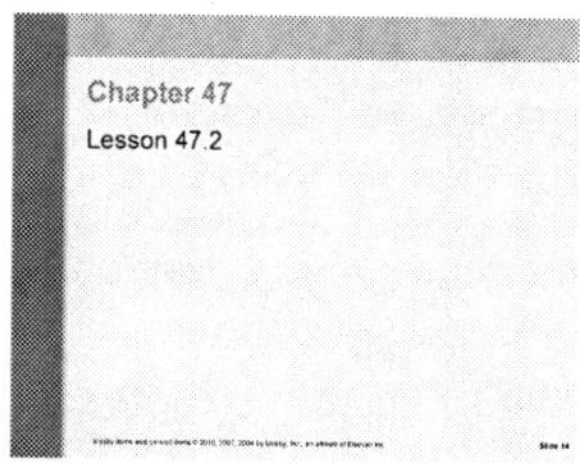
Chapter 47
Lesson 47.2

Slide 15

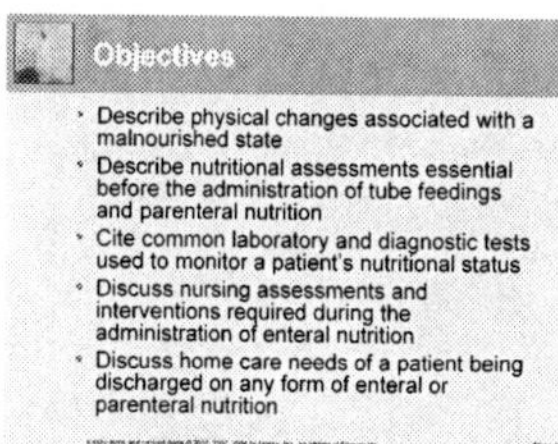
Objectives
Describe physical changes associated with a malnourished state
Describe nutritional assessments essential before the administration of tube feedings and parenteral nutrition
Cite common laboratory and diagnostic tests used to monitor a patient's nutritional status
Discuss nursing assessments and interventions required during the administration of enteral nutrition
Discuss home care needs of a patient being discharged on any form of enteral or parenteral nutrition

ELSEVIER

Slide 16

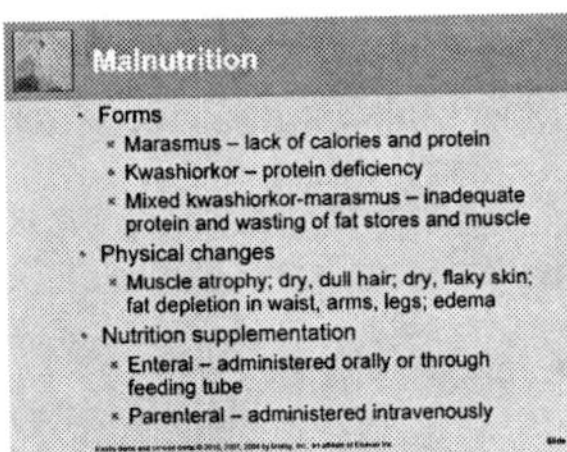
Malnutrition
Forms
Marasmus – lack of calories and protein
Kwashiorkor – protein deficiency
Mixed kwashiorkor-marasmus – inadequate protein and wasting of fat stores and muscle
Physical changes
Muscle atrophy; dry, dull hair; dry, flaky skin; fat depletion in waist, arms, legs; edema
Nutrition supplementation
Enteral – administered orally or through feeding tube
Parenteral – administered intravenously

- Patients with chronic disease are more likely to be malnourished and have nutrition deficits.
- Marasmus is the most common form of malnutrition in hospitalized patients who suffer from chronic disease.
- Patients with kwashiorkor are difficult to recognize because they appear well nourished.

Slide 17

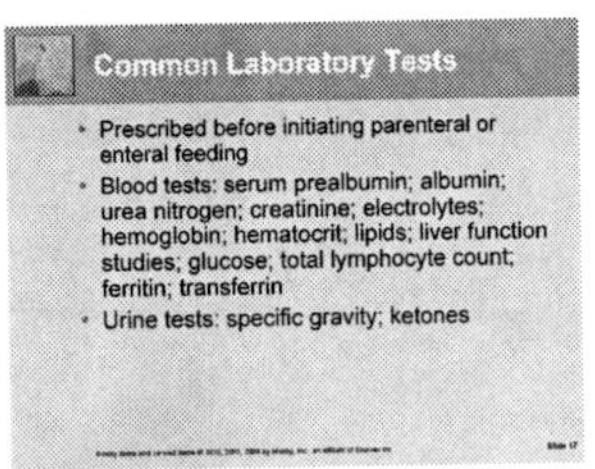
Common Laboratory Tests
Prescribed before initiating parenteral or enteral feeding
Blood tests: serum prealbumin; albumin; urea nitrogen; creatinine; electrolytes; hemoglobin; hematocrit; lipids; liver function studies; glucose; total lymphocyte count; ferritin; transferrin
Urine tests: specific gravity; ketones

Slide 18

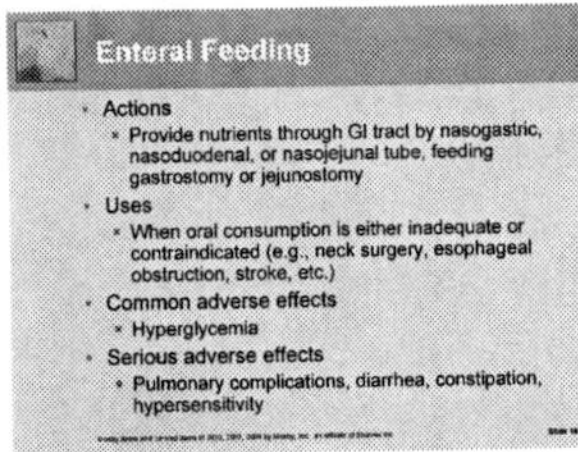
Enteral Feeding
Actions
Provide nutrients through GI tract by nasogastric, nasoduodenal, or nasojejunal tube, feeding gastrostomy or jejunostomy
Uses
When oral consumption is either inadequate or contraindicated (e.g., neck surgery, esophageal obstruction, stroke, etc.)
Common adverse effects
Hyperglycemia
Serious adverse effects
Pulmonary complications, diarrhea, constipation, hypersensitivity

- Record accurate intake and output measurements.
- Ensure that sterile administration techniques are followed.
- Check for fluid overload.

Slide 19

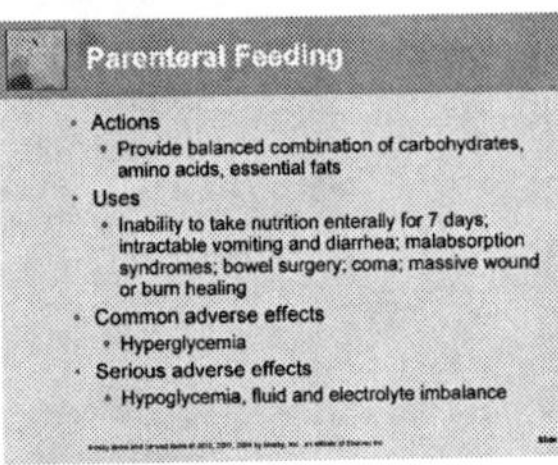
Parenteral Feeding
Actions
Provide balanced combination of carbohydrates, amino acids, essential fats
Uses
Inability to take nutrition enterally for 7 days; intractable vomiting and diarrhea; malabsorption syndromes; bowel surgery; coma; massive wound or burn healing
Common adverse effects
Hyperglycemia
Serious adverse effects
Hypoglycemia, fluid and electrolyte imbalance

- Peripheral parenteral nutrition (PPN) is used for patients requiring nutritional support for a limited time of 3 to 4 weeks.
- Total parenteral nutrition (TPN) can be given long or short term, depending on indication.
- Be aware that hepatotoxicity or allergy to the formula may develop.

Slide 20

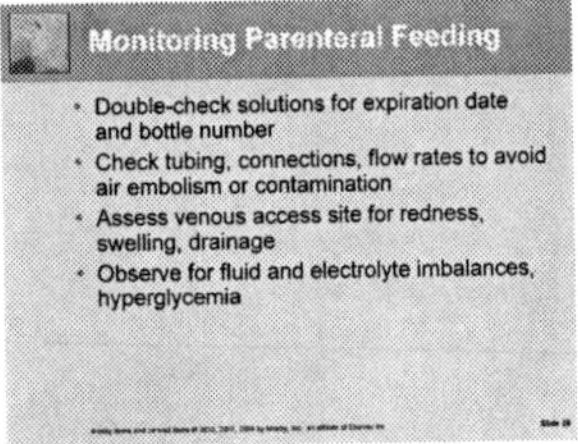
Monitoring Parenteral Feeding
Double-check solutions for expiration date and bottle number
Check tubing, connections, flow rates to avoid air embolism or contamination
Assess venous access site for redness, swelling, drainage
Observe for fluid and electrolyte imbalances, hyperglycemia

- Discard TPN solution that remains after 24 hours.

ELSEVIER

Slide 21

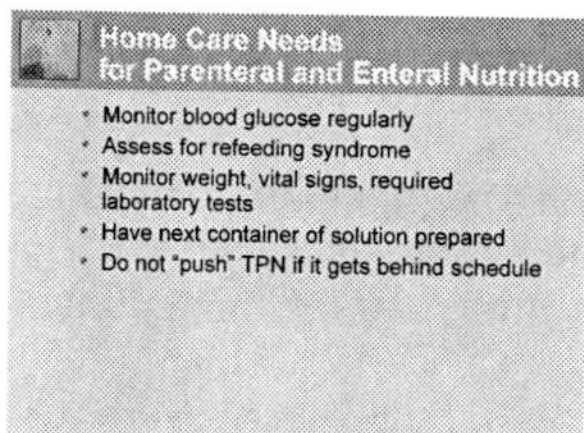
Home Care Needs for Parenteral and Enteral Nutrition
Monitor blood glucose regularly
Assess for refeeding syndrome
Monitor weight, vital signs, required laboratory tests
Have next container of solution prepared
Do not "push" TPN if it gets behind schedule

- TPN must be tapered and never completely disconnected.

48 Lesson Plan
Herbal and Dietary Supplement Therapy

TEACHING FOCUS

In this chapter, the student will be introduced to topics related to herbal and dietary supplement therapy. Students will have the opportunity to become acquainted with various herbal medicines and dietary supplements. The nursing process for herbal and dietary supplement therapy, including assessment, nursing diagnoses, planning, and implementation will be discussed.

MATERIALS AND RESOURCES

- ☐ computer and PowerPoint projector (all Lessons)
- ☐ photos or advertisements of various herbal and dietary supplement products (Lesson 48.1)

LESSON CHECKLIST

Preparations for this lesson include:

- lecture
- evaluation of student knowledge and skills needed to perform all entry-level nursing activities related to herbal and dietary supplement therapy, including:
  - understanding the nursing process for herbal and diet supplement therapy
  - describing the actions, uses, and adverse effects of various herbal therapies
  - describing the actions, uses, and adverse effects of various dietary supplements
  - understanding the relationship between herbal and dietary supplement use and cultural and/or ethnic beliefs

KEY TERMS

botanicals (p. 806)
dietary supplements (p. 804)
herbal medicines (p. 806)
phytomedicine (p. 806)
phytotherapy (p. 806)

ADDITIONAL RESOURCES

PowerPoint slides: 1-14
Flashcards, Decks 1 and 2

Legend

ARQ	PPT	TB	CTQ	SG	INRQ
Audience Response Questions	PowerPoint Slides	Test Bank	Critical Thinking Questions	Study Guide	Interactive NCLEX Review Questions

Class Activities are indicated in ***bold italic.***

LESSON 48.1

BACKGROUND ASSESSMENT

Question: What does the Dietary Supplement Health and Education Act of 1994 legislate for dietary supplements?
Answer: The legal classification of dietary supplements, considered a food category, includes almost all herbal medicines, vitamins, minerals, amino acids, and other supplemental chemicals used for health. It allows manufacturers to include information on the label and in their advertising that explains how their products affect the human body. Those labels and advertisements must contain a statement that the product

ELSEVIER

has not been evaluated by the U.S. Food and Drug Administration (FDA) for treating, curing, or preventing any illness. However, unlicensed individuals can make claims about the ingredients of these supplements. Dietary supplements are not required to be safe and effective.

Question: How should the nurse collect data about herbal and diet therapy?
Answer: The patient's reasons for using dietary supplements should be discussed, in addition to a list of which supplements the patient is taking. The nurse should ask the patient whether the symptoms for which the supplement is being taken increased, decreased, or remained unchanged. Is the patient's health care provider aware that the patient is taking supplements? The nurse should determine whether the products were recommended to the patient and by whom and for what purpose. The list of dietary supplements should also include any prescription or over-the-counter medication being taken and should indicate whether any of the dietary supplements are being taken in place of a prescribed medication. In addition, the patient's cultural, ethnic, and religious beliefs should be discussed.

CRITICAL THINKING QUESTION

A 45-year-old female patient reports that she was running and experienced heart palpitations. During the patient assessment, she states that she has been trying to lose weight. In addition to exercising and watching her diet, she is taking ma-huang to speed rate of weight loss for a few weeks. What should the nurse tell her?
Guidelines: Ma-huang, or ephedra, naturally occurs in plant form. Ephedrine, its active ingredient, is a central nervous system stimulant and is regulated as a drug when chemically synthesized. The Chinese herb has been promoted to increase weight loss and energy. It has also been presented as an aphrodisiac and sports performance enhancer. On December 30, 2003, the FDA issued a consumer alert on the safety of dietary supplements that contain ephedra and advised consumers to stop buying and using these products. The FDA states that dietary supplements containing ephedra alkaloids present an unreasonable risk of illness or injury. Ephedra elevates the blood pressure and heart rate, causing palpitations, in addition to nervousness, headache, dizziness, and insomnia. There have been reported deaths with its overuse.

OBJECTIVES	CONTENT	TEACHING RESOURCES
Describe the possible impact of the use of herbal and dietary supplement products on cultural/ethnic beliefs.	■ Herbal medicines, dietary supplements, and rational therapy (p. 804) – Nursing process for herbal and diet supplement therapy (p. 805) – Patient education and health promotion (p. 806) Review herbal medicine, dietary supplements, and their resurgence in popularity of alternative therapies. Discuss the classification of herbal therapy as a dietary supplement and not as medication. Review patient education and waysof fostering health through the understanding of herbal therapies.	PPT 4-10 TB Multiple Choice question 3 Appendix H: Template for Developing a Written Record for Patients to Monitor Their Own Therapy SG Review Sheet questions 1-5 (pp. 327-328) SG Learning Activities questions 1, 13-15 (p. 332) Figure 48-1 (p. 805): Certification marks. Box 48-1: Factors to Consider When Recommending Herbal Medicines and Other Dietary Supplements (p. 805) ▸ Discuss herbal medicines, dietary supplements, rational therapy, and legislation intending to address the safety and efficacy of herbal and dietary supplements. ▸ Discuss the lack of standard manufacturing processes used in the production of herbal and dietary supplements.

OBJECTIVES	CONTENT	TEACHING RESOURCES
		▸ Discuss labeling and its indication regarding manufacturing practices but not safety and/or effectiveness. ▸ Discuss the role of the health care professional as it relates to counseling regarding herbal and dietary supplements. ▸ Discuss factors to consider when recommending herbal medicines and other dietary supplements. ▸ Discuss topics to consider during the assessment process, including patients' reasons for interest or use, lists of symptoms, and sources of recommendation. ▸ Discuss how cultural and ethnic beliefs may affect an individual's decision to use herbal or dietary supplements. ▸ Discuss steps to take regarding health care provider notification and charting for individuals who take herbal or dietary supplements. ▸ Discuss the importance of discussing expectations of therapy, monitoring of symptoms, interactions with prescribed medications, and maintenance of a patient self-assessment form. Class Activity ***Divide the class into small groups, and ask each to develop a list of guidelines for advising patients taking herbal supplements. Refer to Box 48-1 (p. 805).***
Summarize the primary actions, uses, and interactions of the herbal and dietary supplement products cited.	■ Herbal therapy (p. 806) □ Common name: Aloe (p. 806) □ Common name: Black cohosh (p. 807) □ Common name: Chamomile (p. 807) □ Common name: Echinacea (p. 808) □ Common name: Ephedra (p. 808) □ Common name: Feverfew (p. 809) □ Common name: Garlic (p. 809) Review herbal medications as natural substances usually derived from plant sources. Discuss the	PPT 11-12 ARQ 1 TB Multiple choice questions 1, 4-5. 9 TB Multiple Response questions 1, 4 INRQ 1, 3-4 CTQ 1-5 SG Review Sheet questions 6-18 (pp. 328-329) SG Learning Activities questions 9-11, 18-22 (pp. 332-333) SG Practice questions for the NCLEX Examination 1-2, 6-8 (pp. 334-335) Herbal Interactions: Black Cohosh (p. 807) Herbal Interactions: Echinacea (p. 808)

OBJECTIVES	CONTENT	TEACHING RESOURCES
	parts of plants that these herbs can come from—roots, seeds, and/or leaves. Review the effects of having these herbs not regulated like medications.	Herbal Interactions: Ephedra (p. 809) Herbal Interactions: Feverfew (p. 809) Herbal Interactions: Garlic (p. 810)
	Review aloe as an herbal therapy used to treat skin irritations, such as burns and psoriasis. Discuss the need to monitor blood sugars closely in diabetic patients.	▸ Discuss aloe, including its actions, uses, and adverse effects. Note its interactions with diabetic therapy. ▸ Discuss black cohosh, including its actions, uses, and adverse effects. Note its interactions with hormone replacement therapy and antihypertensive therapy. Emphasize that it should not be confused with blue cohosh.
	Review black cohosh as an herbal therapy used to treat premenstrual syndrome (PMS), dysmenorrhea, and menopause. Discuss the difference between black cohosh and blue cohosh.	▸ Discuss chamomile, including its actions, uses, and adverse effects. ▸ Discuss echinacea, including its actions, uses, and adverse effects. Note its interactions with immunosuppressive therapy.
	Review chamomile as an herbal therapy used for its anti-inflammatory and antibacterial properties. Discuss rare allergic adverse effects.	▸ Discuss ephedra, including its actions, uses, and adverse effects. Note its interactions with beta-adrenergic blocking agents, MAOIs, antihypertensive therapy, methyldopa, and reserpine. ▸ Discuss feverfew, including its actions, uses, and adverse effects. Note its interactions with nonsteroidal anti-inflammatory drugs (NSAIDs) and anticoagulants.
	Review echinacea as an herbal therapy used to prevent colds. Discuss other uses for echinacea and the need to educate patients with an autoimmune disease not to take it.	▸ Discuss garlic, including its actions, uses, and adverse effects. Note its interactions with anticoagulants. Class Activity ***Present photos or advertisements of various herbal and dietary supplement products that are discussed in the chapter. Discuss each product, including the actions, uses, and interactions of the supplement.***
	Review ephedra as an herbal therapy used as a weight loss product and energy booster because it acts as a central nervous system stimulant. Discuss the adverse effects associated with the use of ephedra.	
	Review feverfew as an herbal therapy used to treat migraine headaches and rheumatoid arthritis. Discuss common effects with feverfew.	

OBJECTIVES	CONTENT	TEACHING RESOURCES
	Review garlic as an herbal therapy used to lower serum cholesterol. Discuss common effects and garlic's antiplatelet effects.	

48.1 Homework/Assignments:

48.1 Instructor's Notes/Student Feedback:

LESSON 48.2

CRITICAL THINKING QUESTION

During a patient assessment, the patient says that she has been depressed during the past few weeks and wants to take an herbal product to help her depression. The patient says that she has heard of St. John's wort and wants to know whether the nurse thinks it would help her depression. How should the nurse respond?

Guidelines: St. John's wort has been used in Europe for years to treat depression. Americans have also learned that it is effective, and its adverse effects are rare. Hypericin and other ingredients contribute to the herb's therapeutic effect, although the hypericin content has no relation to the herb's antidepressant effect. Available in powder, tablet, capsule, and liquid form, St. John's wort boosts serotonin levels, prolonging the effect of serotonin, dopamine, and norepinephrine. The herb also helps promote sound sleep. The adverse effects of St. John's wort may cause photosensitivity; patients should stop taking the drug if they experience pruritus and edema. Individuals should always consult with a health care provider before taking the herb, especially if they are taking other dietary supplements or prescription drugs.

OBJECTIVES	CONTENT	TEACHING RESOURCES
Summarize the primary actions, uses, and interactions of the herbal and dietary supplement products cited.	□ Common name: Ginger (p. 810) □ Common name: Ginkgo (p. 810) □ Common name: Ginseng (p. 811) □ Common name: Goldenseal (p. 812) □ Common name: Green tea (p. 812) □ Common name: Saw palmetto (p. 813)	PPT 12-14 ARQ 2-5 TB Multiple Choice questions 2, 6-8, 10 TB Multiple Response questions 2-5 INRQ 2, 5-10 CTQ 5 SG Review Sheet questions 6, 19-38 (pp. 328-331)

OBJECTIVES	CONTENT	TEACHING RESOURCES
	□ Common name: St. John's wort (p. 813) □ Common name: Valerian (p. 814) ■ Other dietary supplements (p. 814) □ Common name: Coenzyme Q_{10} (p. 814) □ Common name: Creatine (p. 815) □ Common name: Gamma-hydroxybutyrate (GHB) (p. 815) □ Common name: Lycopene (p. 816) □ Common name: Melatonin (p. 816) □ Common name: Policosanol (p. 817) □ Common name: Omega-3 fatty acids (p. 817) □ Common name: S-adenosylmethionine (SAM-e) (p. 818) Review ginger as an herbal therapy used to treat nausea and gastric upset. Discuss ginger's antiplatelet effects. Review ginkgo as an herbal therapy used as a memory aid. Discuss other uses for ginkgo and its properties. Review ginkgo's antiplatelet effect and known drug interactions. Review ginseng as an herbal therapy used to strengthen general vitality. Discuss known effects and studies that are inconsistent about its effects. Review goldenseal as a topical herbal therapy used for its weak antibacterial properties in treating canker sores. Discuss the common misconceptions about goldenseal and why not to take it orally.	SG Learning Activities questions 2-8, 12, 16-17, 23-25 (pp. 332-333) SG Practice questions for the NCLEX Examination 3-6 (pp. 334-335) Review questions for the NCLEX Examination 1-7 (pp. 819-820) Herbal Interactions: Ginger (p. 810) Herbal Interactions: Ginkgo (p. 811) Herbal Interactions: Ginseng (p. 812) Herbal Interactions: Green tea (p. 812) Herbal Interactions: St. John's wort (p. 814) Herbal Interactions: Coenzyme Q_{10} (p. 815) Herbal Interactions: Gamma-hydroxybutyrate (GHB) (p. 816) Herbal Interactions: Melatonin (p. 817) Herbal Interactions: S-Adenosylmethionine (p. 819) Table 48-1: American Heart Association Recommended Daily Intake of Omega-3 Fatty Acids (p. 818) ▸ Discuss ginger, including its actions, uses, and adverse effects. Note its interactions with anticoagulants. ▸ Discuss ginkgo, including its actions, uses, and adverse effects. Note its interactions with anticoagulants. ▸ Discuss ginseng, including its actions, uses, and adverse effects. Note its interactions with anticoagulants and insulin. ▸ Discuss goldenseal, including its actions, uses, and adverse effects. ▸ Discuss green tea, including its actions, uses, and adverse effects. Note its interactions with many drugs, including monoamine oxidase inhibitors (MAOIs), beta agonists, and warfarin. ▸ Discuss saw palmetto, including its actions, uses, and adverse effects. Note its interaction with finasteride. ▸ Discuss St. John's wort, including its actions, uses, and adverse effects. Note its interactions with serotonin stimulants. ▸ Discuss valerian, including its actions, uses, and adverse effects. Note its interactions with medications with sedative properties.

ELSEVIER

OBJECTIVES	CONTENT	TEACHING RESOURCES
	Review green tea as an herbal therapy used to lower lipid levels. Discuss the effects of green tea due to its caffeine content. Review known drug interactions. Review saw palmetto as an herbal therapy used to treat symptoms of BPH. Discuss known drug interactions and rare adverse effects. Review St. John's wort as an herbal therapy used to treat depression. Discuss serotonin syndrome and how to avoid it. Review common effects and drug interactions. Review valerian as an herbal therapy used as a sleep aid. Discuss confusion that may arise between valerian and valium. Review coenzyme Q_{10} as a dietary supplement used to treat chronic heart failure. Discuss the various uses of coenzyme Q_{10}. Review creatine as a dietary supplement used as a performance enhancing substance. Discuss common effects from creatine use. Review GHB as a dietary supplement used as a sedative. Discuss its use as a date rape drug and the adverse effects from GHB. Review lycopene as a dietary supplement used to reduce the risk of prostate cancer and lower cholesterol levels. Discuss other uses for lycopene and foods in which it is commonly found (e.g., tomatoes and tomato products). Review melatonin as a dietary supplement used to treat insomnia and jet lag. Discuss effects and paradoxical reactions to melatonin.	▸ Discuss coenzyme Q_{10}, including its actions, uses, and adverse effects. Note its interactions with antilipemic agents, beta-adrenergic blocking agents, insulin and oral hypoglycemic agents, and warfarin. ▸ Discuss creatine, including its actions, uses, and adverse effects. ▸ Discuss GHB, including its actions, uses, and adverse effects. Note its interactions with numerous drugs, including antihistamines, analgesics, and antidepressants. ▸ Discuss lycopene, including its actions and uses. ▸ Discuss melatonin, including its actions, uses, and adverse effects. Note its interactions with CNS depressants. ▸ Discuss the actions and uses of policosanol. ▸ Discuss SAM-e, including its actions, uses, and adverse effects. Note its interactions with antidepressants and levodopa. Class Activity ***Divide the class into pairs, and assign each pair a dietary supplement. Have students take turns role-playing a nurse teaching a patient about the actions, uses, and interactions of the dietary supplement.***

ELSEVIER

OBJECTIVES	CONTENT	TEACHING RESOURCES
	Review policosanol as a dietary supplement used to treat dyslipidemia and claudication. Discuss known drug interactions. Review omega-3 fatty acids for their cardioprotective effects. Review SAM-e as a dietary supplement used to treat depression, osteoarthritis, and fibromyalgia.	
Performance evaluation		Test Bank SG Learning Activities (pp. 332-333) SG Practice questions for the NCLEX Examination (pp. 334-335) Critical Thinking questions

48.2 Homework/Assignments:

48.2 Instructor's Notes/Student Feedback:

48 Lecture Outline
Herbal and Dietary Supplement Therapy

Slide 1

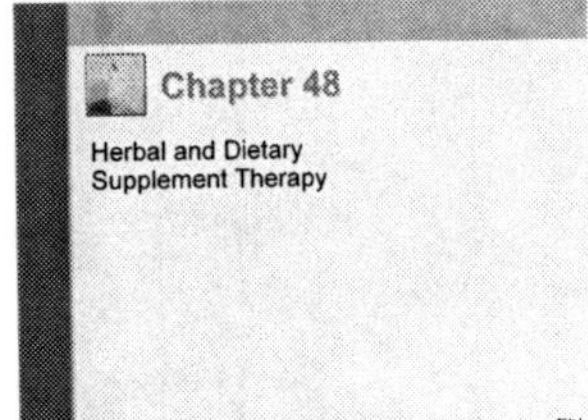
Chapter 48
Herbal and Dietary Supplement Therapy

Slide 2

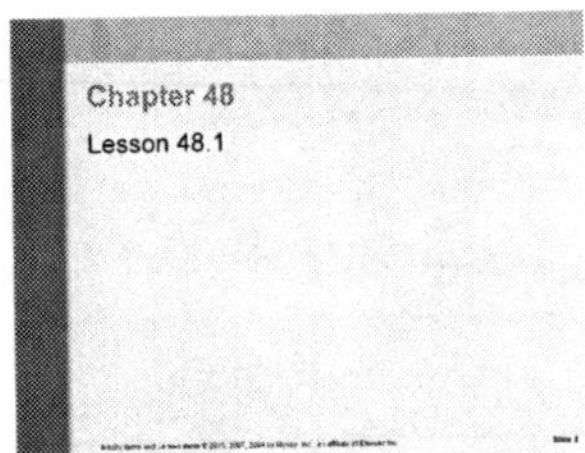
Chapter 48
Lesson 48.1

Slide 3

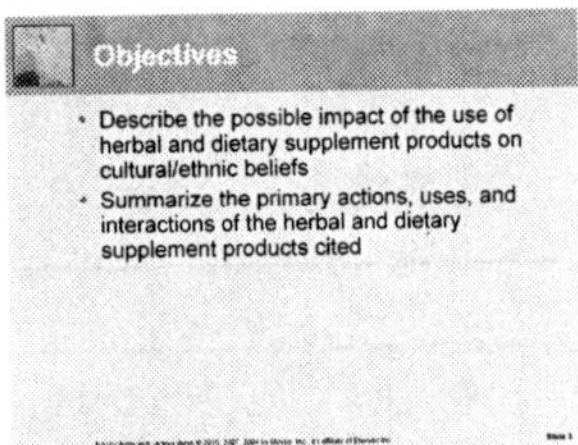
Objectives
Describe the possible impact of the use of herbal and dietary supplement products on cultural/ethnic beliefs
Summarize the primary actions, uses, and interactions of the herbal and dietary supplement products cited

- Self-care and alternative therapies are very popular.
- There are more than 250 herbal medicines.

Slide 4

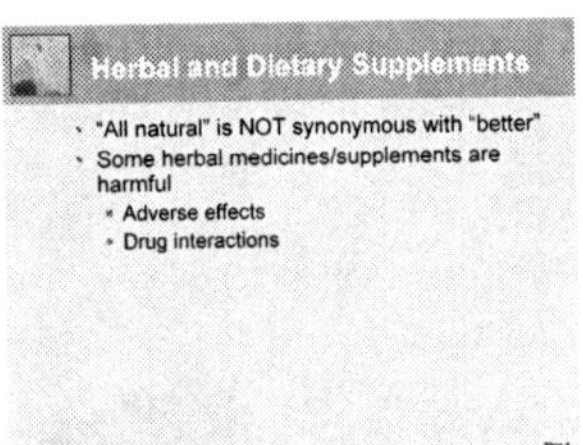
Herbal and Dietary Supplements
"All natural" is NOT synonymous with "better"
Some herbal medicines/supplements are harmful
Adverse effects
Drug interactions

- Most have been used for centuries.

Slide 5

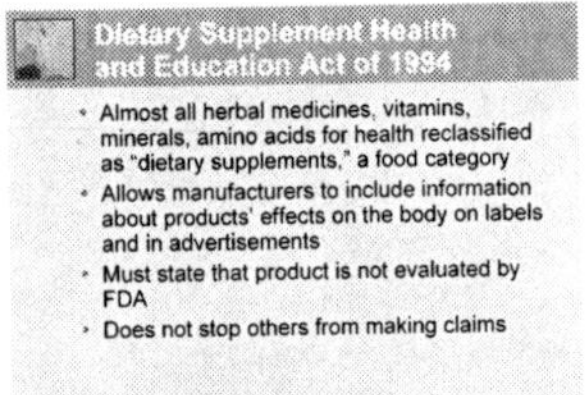
Dietary Supplement Health and Education Act of 1994
Almost all herbal medicines, vitamins, minerals, amino acids for health reclassified as "dietary supplements," a food category
Allows manufacturers to include information about products' effects on the body on labels and in advertisements
Must state that product is not evaluated by FDA
Does not stop others from making claims

- Intent of DSHEA was to ensure that safe and appropriately labeled products remain available to consumers who want to use them.
- Anyone can make claims of therapeutic value; most claims are unproven.

Slide 6

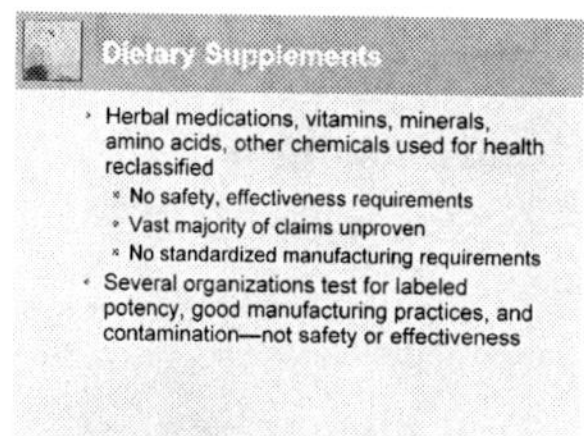
Dietary Supplements
Herbal medications, vitamins, minerals, amino acids, other chemicals used for health reclassified
No safety, effectiveness requirements
Vast majority of claims unproven
No standardized manufacturing requirements
Several organizations test for labeled potency, good manufacturing practices, and contamination—not safety or effectiveness

- National Sanitation Foundation (NSF) International began testing dietary supplements in 2003.

Slide 7

Label Certification
ConsumerLab.com
NSF
Contents Tested
USP
A
B
C

- **A,** From ConsumerLab.com; **B,** from NSF International; **C,** from U.S. Pharmacopeia.

Slide 8

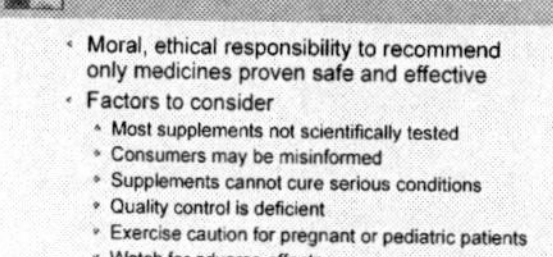
Role of Health Care Professional
Moral, ethical responsibility to recommend only medicines proven safe and effective
Factors to consider
Most supplements not scientifically tested
Consumers may be misinformed
Supplements cannot cure serious conditions
Quality control is deficient
Exercise caution for pregnant or pediatric patients
Watch for adverse effects
Examine label carefully

- Be aware of a medicine's legal versus popular use.
- Reliable resources specific to dietary supplements are widely available, as are peer-reviewed journal articles.
- Knowledge should be based on current scientific information.

Slide 9

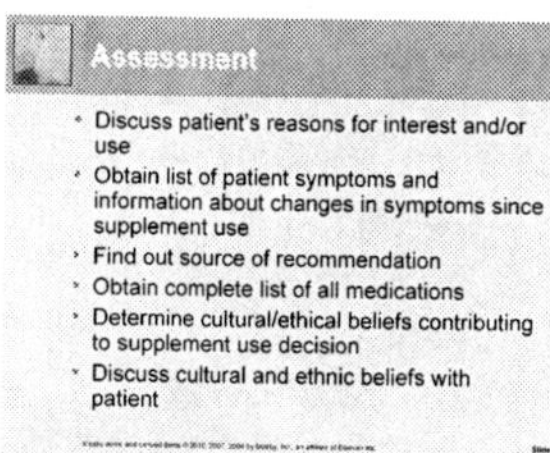
Assessment
Discuss patient's reasons for interest and/or use
Obtain list of patient symptoms and information about changes in symptoms since supplement use
Find out source of recommendation
Obtain complete list of all medications
Determine cultural/ethical beliefs contributing to supplement use decision
Discuss cultural and ethnic beliefs with patient

- Dietary supplements are affected by religious beliefs also (e.g., many Muslims prefer alcohol-free products).

Slide 10

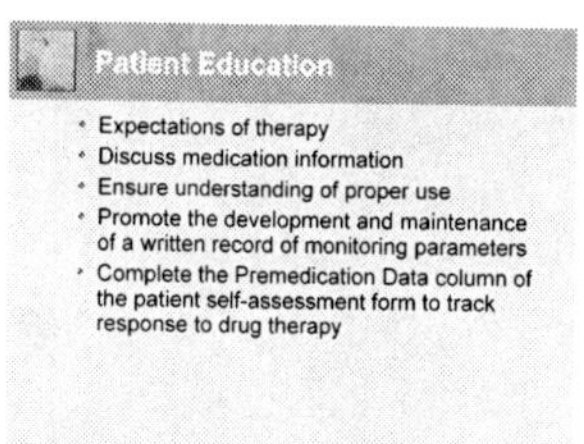
Patient Education
Expectations of therapy
Discuss medication information
Ensure understanding of proper use
Promote the development and maintenance of a written record of monitoring parameters
Complete the Premedication Data column of the patient self-assessment form to track response to drug therapy

- Enhanced compliance is based on belief in the prescribed regimen.
- Disclosure of taking dietary supplements before surgical procedures is extremely important.

ELSEVIER

Slide 11

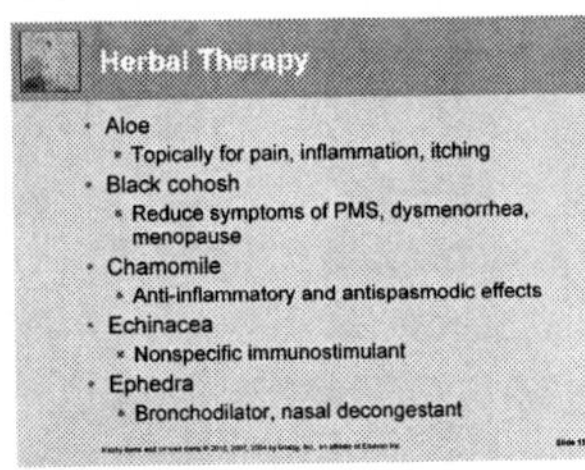
Herbal Therapy
Aloe
Topically for pain, inflammation, itching
Black cohosh
Reduce symptoms of PMS, dysmenorrhea, menopause
Chamomile
Anti-inflammatory and antispasmodic effects
Echinacea
Nonspecific immunostimulant
Ephedra
Bronchodilator, nasal decongestant

- Aloe may have hypoglycemic effects.
- Echinacea may interfere with immunosuppressive therapy.
- Ephedra is contraindicated in patients with heart conditions, hypertension, diabetes, and thyroid disease.

Slide 12

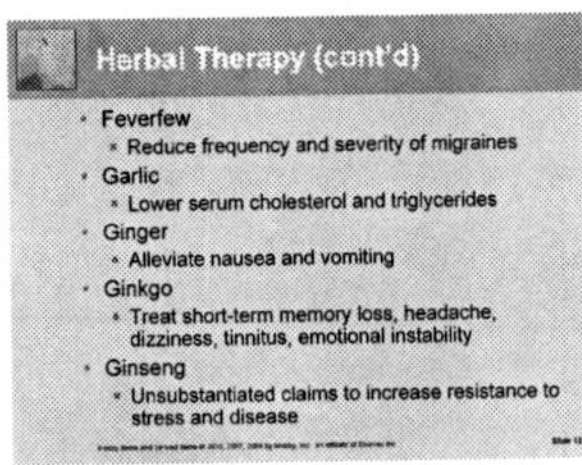
Herbal Therapy (cont'd)
Feverfew
Reduce frequency and severity of migraines
Garlic
Lower serum cholesterol and triglycerides
Ginger
Alleviate nausea and vomiting
Ginkgo
Treat short-term memory loss, headache, dizziness, tinnitus, emotional instability
Ginseng
Unsubstantiated claims to increase resistance to stress and disease

- Feverfew, garlic, ginger, and ginkgo reduce platelet aggregation. Ginseng may affect platelet aggregation and blood coagulation.
- Ginkgo is often used by geriatric patients.

Slide 13

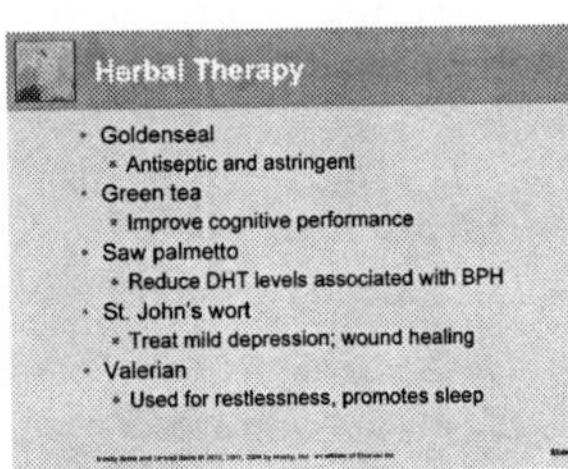
Herbal Therapy
Goldenseal
Antiseptic and astringent
Green tea
Improve cognitive performance
Saw palmetto
Reduce DHT levels associated with BPH
St. John's wort
Treat mild depression; wound healing
Valerian
Used for restlessness, promotes sleep

- Goldenseal may have weak antibacterial properties and may stimulate the immune system to help fight a cold.
- Watch for serotonin syndrome with St. John's wort.
- Do not confuse valerian with valium.

Slide 14

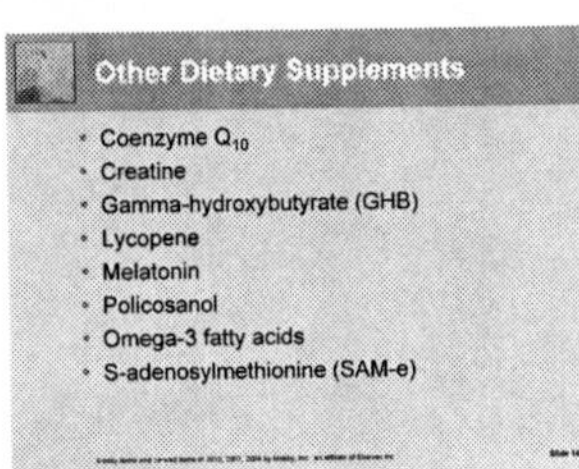
Other Dietary Supplements
Coenzyme Q10
Creatine
Gamma-hydroxybutyrate (GHB)
Lycopene
Melatonin
Policosanol
Omega-3 fatty acids
S-adenosylmethionine (SAM-e)

- Creatine is used as a performance enhancing substance.
- GHB ("rave drug") can cause death, and was banned by the FDA in 1990.

49 Lesson Plan
Substance Abuse

TEACHING FOCUS

In this chapter, the student will be introduced to topics related to substance abuse. The student will become acquainted with definitions of substance abuse, the substances that are commonly abused, theories on why substances are abused, signs of impairment, screening, health professionals and substance abuse, and principles of treatment. The student will have the opportunity to put this information into context by participating in classroom activities and discussions.

MATERIALS AND RESOURCES

☐ computer and PowerPoint projector (all Lessons)

LESSON CHECKLIST

Preparations for this lesson include:

- lecture
- guest speaker: licensed practical nurse
- evaluation of student knowledge and skills needed to perform all entry-level activities related to the principles underlying substance abuse, including:
  - exploring models that influence the assessment and treatment of substance abuse
  - describing the different types of screening tools used to assess alcohol and substance abuse
  - citing the responsibilities of professionals who suspect substance abuse by a colleague
  - explaining the primary long-term goals in the treatment of substance abuse
  - studying the withdrawal symptoms and approaches to treatment and relapse prevention for major substances that are commonly abused

KEY TERMS

addiction (p. 821)
dependence (p. 821)
illicit substance (p. 821)
impairment (p. 821)
intoxication (p. 830)
substance abuse (p. 821)

ADDITIONAL RESOURCES

PowerPoint slides: 1-18
Flashcards, Decks 1 and 2

Legend

ARQ	**PPT**	**TB**	**CTQ**	**SG**	**INRQ**
Audience Response Questions	PowerPoint Slides	Test Bank	Critical Thinking Questions	Study Guide	Interactive NCLEX Review Questions

Class Activities are indicated in ***bold italic.***

LESSON 49.1

BACKGROUND ASSESSMENT

Question: What are the three major theories of substance abuse?

Answer: The biologic model basically states that substance abuse is hereditary, which means that a person is predisposed to it. Some genes have been shown to be associated with alcoholism and other types of substance abuse. Researchers believe that these genetic failures block feelings of well-being and result in

anxiety, anger, low self-esteem, and other negative feelings and make a person crave the substance to suppress the bad feelings. Psychological theories state that alcoholics seek satisfaction through oral behaviors, such as drinking, because they are fixated at the oral stage of development. Behavior theories see addictive behavior as bad habits that can be changed. Cognitive theories say that addiction is based on a distorted way of thinking about substance abuse. Sociocultural factors play a role in the choice of drugs: which ones to use, how much to use, and treatment. Attitudes, values, nationality, religion, gender, family background, and social environment all play a role in substance abuse.

Question: What should a nurse do if he or she suspects that a colleague is impaired?
Answer: The nurse should make a confidential report to his or her supervisor, one who is familiar with the institution's policies on substance abuse. The institution will initiate an investigation and observe and document the person's behavior to build a record to support the suspicion. Examples of inappropriate actions need to be well documented because an accurate record can also help the individual realize the problem and voluntarily submit to treatment. When considering whether to report a colleague, the nurse should understand that it is not unfair or disloyal because the nurse is protecting patients, that the unreported colleague could die as a result of not being reported, that the colleague could still retain his or her license and not lose a career, and that the nurse could be named in a lawsuit if he or she does not report it—in some states, reporting is mandatory.

CRITICAL THINKING QUESTION

A 36-year-old patient who was found unconscious and was taken to the emergency department has been on the nursing unit for 24 hours, and laboratory results show that he was intoxicated. The patient has a history of alcohol abuse. What should the nurse be aware of while taking care of him?
Guidelines: Intoxication is defined as the ingestion of ethanol to the point of clinically significant maladaptive behavioral or psychological changes accompanied by slurred speech, incoordination, unsteady gait, and impairment in attention or memory. A physical dependence develops if a person drinks to excess over long periods of time; a decrease in the blood alcohol level over 4 to 12 hours can cause symptoms of alcohol withdrawal. The symptoms can begin a few hours after the drinking has stopped and can continue for 10 days. Acute withdrawal delirium (delirium tremens, the DTs) is an acute toxic state. Some of the signs and symptoms include anxiety, uncontrollable fear, tremor, irritability, agitation, insomnia, and incontinence. Hallucinations are common. Blood pressure and pulse are all usually elevated, and the patient has dilated pupils. This is a life-threatening state.

OBJECTIVES	CONTENT	TEACHING RESOURCES
Differentiate among the key terms associated with substance abuse.	■ Definitions of substance abuse (p. 821) ■ Substances of abuse (p. 821) Review the definition of substance abuse as defined by the *Diagnostic and Statistical Manual of Mental Disorders* (DSM-IV-TR). Discuss the six categories of substances that are abused: stimulants, depressants, narcotics, cannabis, hallucinogens, and inhalants. Review the definitions of the following terms: impairment, dependence, addiction, and illicit substance. Discuss the statistical significance of the number of people with substance abuse.	PPT 4, 10 ARQ 1 INRQ 1 SG Review Sheet questions 1, 10 (p. 337) SG Learning Activities questions 1-7, 9-13 (p. 339) Box 49-1: Substances of Abuse (p. 822) Box 49-2: Substances Whose Adverse Effects May Induce Substance Abuse (p. 822) ▸ Discuss substances of abuse. List substances that are commonly abused. ▸ Discuss substances whose adverse effects may induce substance abuse. Class Activity ***As a class, discuss symptoms associated with substance abuse. Use the board to match substances and symptoms.***

ELSEVIER

OBJECTIVES	CONTENT	TEACHING RESOURCES
		Class Activity ***Divide the class into small groups, and have each group develop educational materials for high school students on one of the following topics:*** – ***Substance-related disorders*** – ***Substance abuse*** – ***Impairment*** – ***Dependence and/or addiction*** – ***Illicit substances*** ***Have each group present its materials to the class.***
Explore biologic, psychological, and sociocultural models that influence the assessment and treatment of substance abuse.	■ Theories on why substances are abused (p. 822) Review the major theories on substance abuse: biologic model (genes and hereditary condition), psychological theories (psychoanalytic theory, behavior or learned theory, cognitive theory, and family system theory), and sociocultural factors (attitudes, values, and norms). Discuss how each theory has led to treatment alternatives.	PPT 5 TB Multiple Choice question 3 TB Multiple Response questions 1, 4 INRQ 2, 5-6, 8 SG Review Sheet question 2 (p. 337) SG Learning Activities questions 14-15 (p. 339) Review Question for the NCLEX Examination 4 (p. 841) ▸ Discuss the biologic, psychological, and sociocultural models. Offer a case example of a substance abuser, and discuss how the individual's substance abuse would be explained by proponents of each model. Class Activity ***Divide the class into three groups. Assign a model of substance abuse to each group, and have the groups discuss the model and the hypotheses of the model. What combination of factors may make a person more susceptible to drug abuse and interfere with recovery? Then have each group present its findings to the class.***
Describe the different types of screening tools used to assess alcohol and substance abuse.	■ Signs of impairment (p. 827) ■ Screening for alcohol and substance abuse (p. 827) Review the signs of impairment as a cluster of symptoms that are manifested as both physical and mental changes, as well as the behavioral and social effects. Review the four categories of screening instruments: comprehensive drug abuse screening and assessment, brief	PPT 6-7 TB Multiple Choice questions 1, 5 INRQ 3-4 SG Review Sheet questions 3-4, 22 (pp. 337-338) SG Learning Activities questions 8, 16 (p. 339) Table 49-2: Screening Instruments for Substance Abuse (p. 828) Box 49-3: CAGE Questionnaire (p. 828) ▸ Discuss signs of impairment. Note that substance abuse is often signaled by a cluster of signs, and list possible signs that may manifest.

ELSEVIER

OBJECTIVES	CONTENT	TEACHING RESOURCES
	drug abuse screening, alcohol abuse screening, and drug and alcohol abuse screening for adolescents. Discuss how each instrument is used and when to use the CAGE Questionnaire.	▸ Discuss the four categories of screening instruments. ▸ Discuss screening for alcohol and substance abuse. Offer examples of different instruments, including DAST and CAGE. Class Activity ***Have the students investigate treatment programs in their community and the types of screening tool that facility uses. Have the students report their findings to the class. (For students to prepare for this activity, see Homework/Assignment 1.)***
Cite the responsibilities of professionals who suspect substance abuse by a colleague.	■ Health professionals and substance abuse (p. 827) □ Legal considerations of substance abuse and dependence (p. 829) □ Educating health professionals about substance abuse (p. 829) Review the expectations of health care professionals when they suspect their coworkers of abuse. Discuss behavioral changes and performance deterioration that may occur. Review legal considerations and laws that protect people from discrimination on the basis of past drug addiction.	PPT 8-9 ARQ 2 TB Multiple Choice question 4 TB Multiple Response question 2 SG Review Sheet questions 5-6 (p. 337) Review Question for the NCLEX Examination 10 (p. 841) Drug Table 49-1: Substances of Abuse (pp. 823-826) ▸ Discuss factors that may contribute to substance abuse among health professionals. ▸ Discuss signs of substance abuse among health professionals. Class Activity ***As a class, discuss health professionals and substance abuse—specifically, the proper steps that a nurse should take if he or she suspects a colleague of substance abuse. Discuss the legal protections for the health professional who makes a conscious effort to be treated for addiction.***

49.1 Homework/Assignments:

1. Have students investigate treatment programs in their community and the types of screening tools that facility uses.

49.1 Instructor's Notes/Student Feedback:

LESSON 49.2

CRITICAL THINKING QUESTION

A colleague tells a fellow nurse that she has been discovered abusing morphine. She is wondering about the legal considerations of substance abuse. What should the nurse tell her?

Guidelines: All states have laws pertaining to the reporting of substance abuse by health care workers. In some states, the suspected impairment is reported to the professional's licensing or disciplinary board; in others, it is referred to the professional society's impairment committee. In this case, as long as the professional is participating in the rehabilitation program, the committee may not report it to the licensing board. As long as the health professional is making an effort to get treated, re-establishing a career with legal protection is a viable option. Also, the 1992 Americans with Disabilities Act (ADA) considers someone who is dependent on drugs, no longer using, and getting treatment, to be protected by the ADA from discrimination on the basis of past drug addiction. However, if a person is still using and it impairs job performance or conduct, that person can be disciplined, discharged, or denied employment and is not considered to have a disability under the ADA.

OBJECTIVES	CONTENT	TEACHING RESOURCES
Explain the primary long-term goals in the treatment of substance abuse.	■ Principles of treatment for substance abuse (p. 829) Review the long-term goals in the treatment of substance abuse. Discuss the principles used in the treatment of substance abuse.	PPT 13 TB Multiple Response question 3 CTQ 1 SG Review Sheet questions 7-8 (p. 337) SG Learning Activities question 17 (p. 339) SG Practice Questions for the NCLEX Examination 3, 5 (p. 340) Figure 49-1 (p. 830): The twelve steps of Alcoholics Anonymous. ▸ Discuss principles of treatment for substance abuse. List diagnostic criteria for the assessment of substance abuse defined in the DSM-IV-TR. ▸ Discuss principles of treatment for substance abuse. List organizations that help abusers, such as Alcoholics Anonymous, Narcotics Anonymous, and Women for Sobriety. Discuss some of the principles of the 12-step programs. Class Activity ***There are three long-term goals offered by the American Psychological Association (APA) for the treatment of substance abuse. Divide the class into three groups, and assign one goal to each group. Have each group discuss the goal and present its findings to the class.***
Study the withdrawal symptoms and approaches to treatment and relapse prevention for major	□ Alcohol (p. 830) □ Opioids (p. 832) □ Amphetamine-type stimulants (p. 834) □ Cocaine (p. 835) – Nursing process for substance abuse (p. 836)	PPT 14-18 ARQ 3-5 TB Multiple Choice questions 2, 6, 8-9 TB Multiple Response question 5 INRQ 7, 9-10

OBJECTIVES	CONTENT	TEACHING RESOURCES
substances that are commonly abused.	– Patient education and health promotion (p. 839) Review alcohol intoxication, withdrawal, treatment, and relapse prevention. Discuss opioid intoxication, withdrawal, treatment, and relapse prevention. Discuss amphetamine-type stimulant intoxication, withdrawal, and treatment. Discuss cocaine intoxication, withdrawal, and treatment. Review the nursing process as it applies to substance abuse. Review patient education and health promotion strategies.	CTQ 2-3 Animation: Opiate Intoxication SG Review Sheet questions 9, 11-21, 23 (pp. 337-338) SG Learning Activities question 18 (p. 339) SG Practice Questions for the NCLEX Examination 1-2, 4, 6-8 (p. 340) Review Questions for the NCLEX Examination 1-3, 5-9 (p. 841) Figure 49-2 (p. 831): Alcohol withdrawal syndrome. Table 49-3: Determination of Glasgow Coma Score (p. 837) Figure 49-3 (p. 839): A model for change in substance use disorders. ▸ Discuss the physiologic changes associated with alcohol use. Define and discuss the indications of alcohol intoxication. ▸ Discuss the symptoms of alcohol withdrawal, treatment strategies, and relapse prevention. Note the medications approved for use in helping promote abstinence. ▸ Discuss the physiologic changes associated with opioid use. Define and discuss the indications of opioid intoxication. ▸ Discuss the symptoms of opioid withdrawal, treatment strategies, and relapse prevention. Note the medications approved for use in helping promote abstinence. ▸ Discuss the physiologic changes associated with cocaine use. Define and discuss the indications of cocaine intoxication. ▸ Discuss the symptoms of cocaine withdrawal and treatment strategies. ▸ Discuss the nursing process for substance abuse. Review items important for assessment, planning, and implementation. Discuss important communication strategies and behaviors for nurses working with substance abusers. ▸ Discuss a model for change in substance use disorders. Describe how this model for change can be incorporated into the different steps of the nursing process for substance abuse.

OBJECTIVES	CONTENT	TEACHING RESOURCES
		Class Activity ***Divide the class into small groups, and assign each group a substance of abuse. Have each group develop patient education and health promotion materials related to the assigned substance, including symptoms of intoxication and withdrawal, treatment options, and relapse prevention. Have each group present its materials to the class.***
Performance evaluation		Test Bank SG Learning Activities (p. 339) SG Practice Questions for the NCLEX Examination (p. 340) Critical Thinking Questions

49.2 Homework/Assignments:

49.2 Instructor's Notes/Student Feedback:

49 Lecture Outline
Substance Abuse

Slide 1

Chapter 49
Substance Abuse

Slide 2

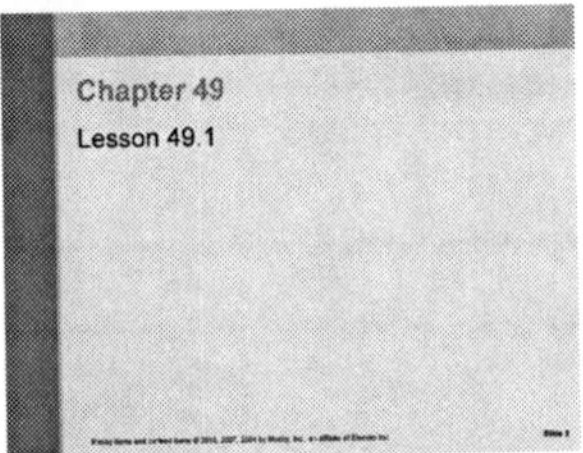
Chapter 49
Lesson 49.1

Slide 3

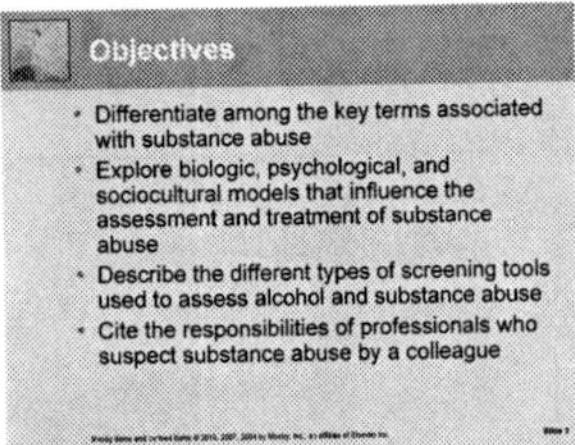
Objectives
• Differentiate among the key terms associated with substance abuse
• Explore biologic, psychological, and sociocultural models that influence the assessment and treatment of substance abuse
• Describe the different types of screening tools used to assess alcohol and substance abuse
• Cite the responsibilities of professionals who suspect substance abuse by a colleague

Slide 4

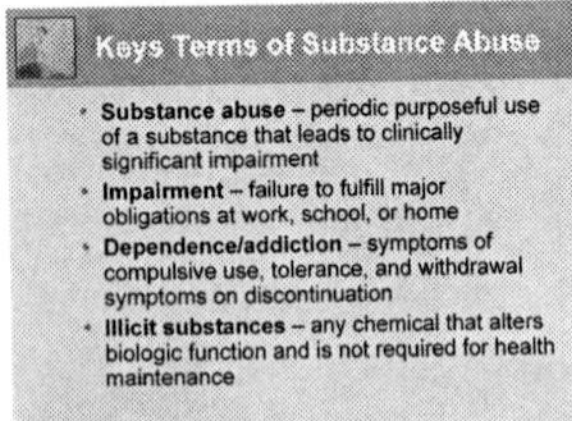
Keys Terms of Substance Abuse
• Substance abuse – periodic purposeful use of a substance that leads to clinically significant impairment
• Impairment – failure to fulfill major obligations at work, school, or home
• Dependence/addiction – symptoms of compulsive use, tolerance, and withdrawal symptoms on discontinuation
• Illicit substances – any chemical that alters biologic function and is not required for health maintenance

- Substance abuse has increased from 14.5 million cases in the United States in 2000, to 22.3 million in 2007. These cases include abuse of alcohol, illicit drugs, or both.
- Risk factors include a history of depression, history of other substance abuse, family history, peer pressure, and low socioeconomic status.

Slide 5

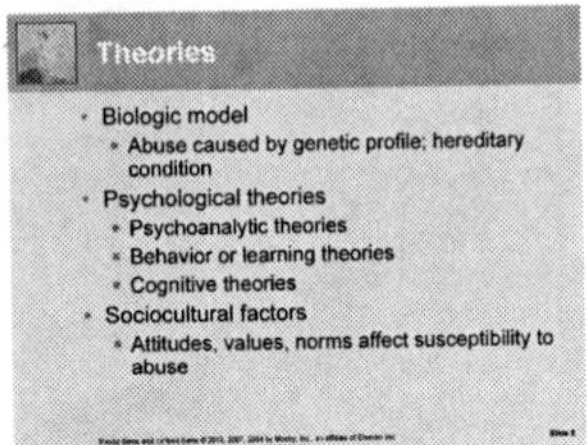
Theories
• Biologic model
• Abuse caused by genetic profile; hereditary condition
• Psychological theories
• Psychoanalytic theories
• Behavior or learning theories
• Cognitive theories
• Sociocultural factors
• Attitudes, values, norms affect susceptibility to abuse

- Genetic aberrations may block feelings of well-being; genes may play a role in alteration of metabolic enzyme systems.

ELSEVIER

Slide 6

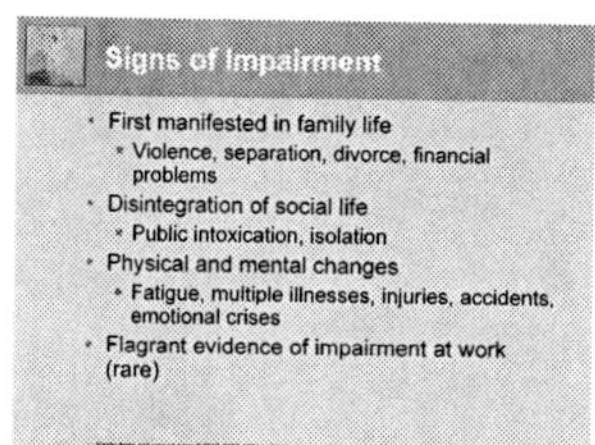
Signs of Impairment
First manifested in family life
Violence, separation, divorce, financial problems
Disintegration of social life
Public intoxication, isolation
Physical and mental changes
Fatigue, multiple illnesses, injuries, accidents, emotional crises
Flagrant evidence of impairment at work (rare)

Slide 7

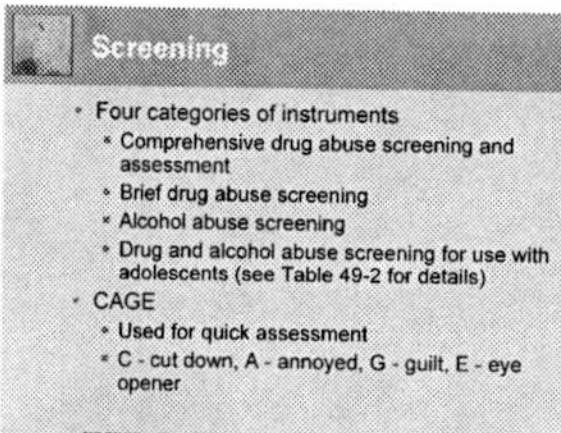
Screening
Four categories of instruments
Comprehensive drug abuse screening and assessment
Brief drug abuse screening
Alcohol abuse screening
Drug and alcohol abuse screening for use with adolescents (see Table 49-2 for details)
CAGE
Used for quick assessment
C - cut down, A - annoyed, G - guilt, E - eye opener

- Crucial that the proper instruments be used with specific patients. A disadvantage is the time it takes to administer the assessment.
- CAGE screening asks four questions that provide the interviewer a quick alcohol abuse assessment.

Slide 8

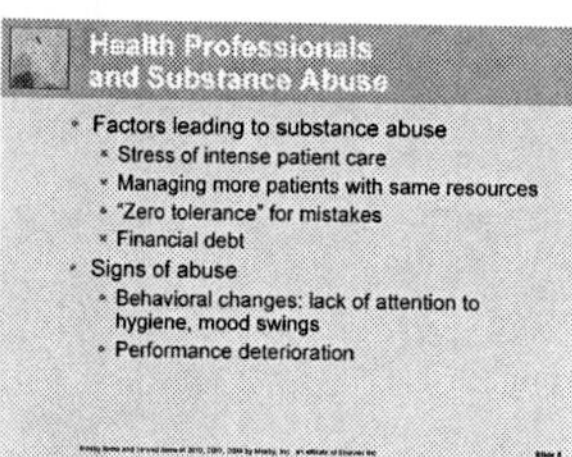
Health Professionals and Substance Abuse
Factors leading to substance abuse
Stress of intense patient care
Managing more patients with same resources
"Zero tolerance" for mistakes
Financial debt
Signs of abuse
Behavioral changes: lack of attention to hygiene, mood swings
Performance deterioration

- Prevalence of abuse by health professionals is not precisely known; probably similar to that of general population.
- More prescription drug abuse common because of ease of access.
- Drug screening does not violate one's constitutional rights to privacy as ruled by the Supreme Court.

Slide 9

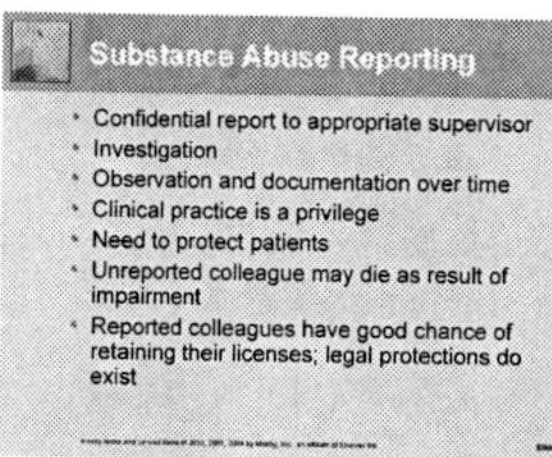
Substance Abuse Reporting
Confidential report to appropriate supervisor
Investigation
Observation and documentation over time
Clinical practice is a privilege
Need to protect patients
Unreported colleague may die as result of impairment
Reported colleagues have good chance of retaining their licenses; legal protections do exist

- Refer to policies of the institution. All states have laws pertaining to reporting the impairment of health care workers.
- In some states, reporting to a licensing authority is mandatory.
- Failure to report may cause a nurse to be named in a malpractice lawsuit.

Slide 10

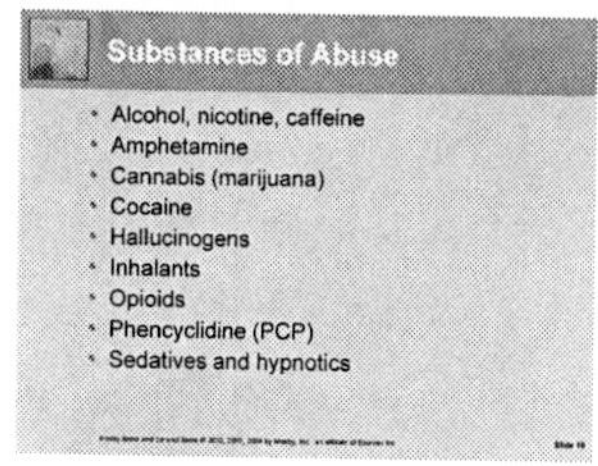
Substances of Abuse
Alcohol, nicotine, caffeine
Amphetamine
Cannabis (marijuana)
Cocaine
Hallucinogens
Inhalants
Opioids
Phencyclidine (PCP)
Sedatives and hypnotics

- Frequently abused substances cause a "high" that leads to repeated use and subsequent addiction to the substance.

ELSEVIER

Slide 11

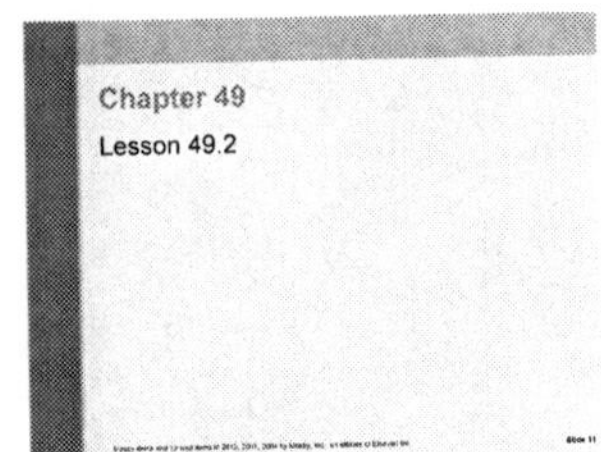
Chapter 49
Lesson 49.2

Slide 12

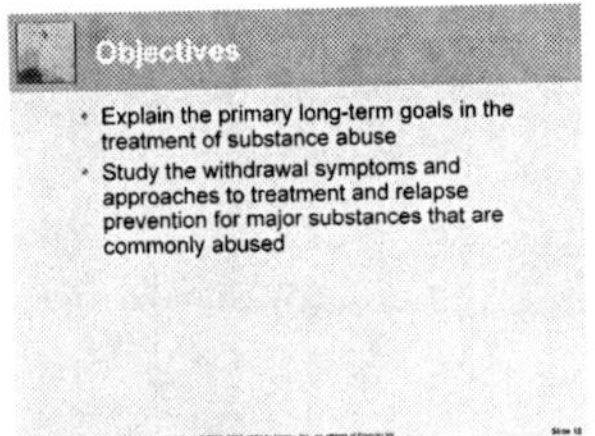
Objectives
Explain the primary long-term goals in the treatment of substance abuse
Study the withdrawal symptoms and approaches to treatment and relapse prevention for major substances that are commonly abused

Slide 13

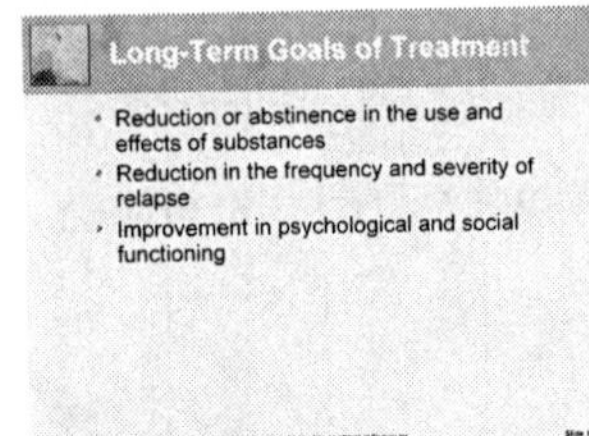
Long-Term Goals of Treatment
Reduction or abstinence in the use and effects of substances
Reduction in the frequency and severity of relapse
Improvement in psychological and social functioning

- Treatment requires lifelong effort with a combination of psychological support and drug therapy.
- Long-term recovery is affected by negative consequences of abuse, as well as social and community support.

Slide 14

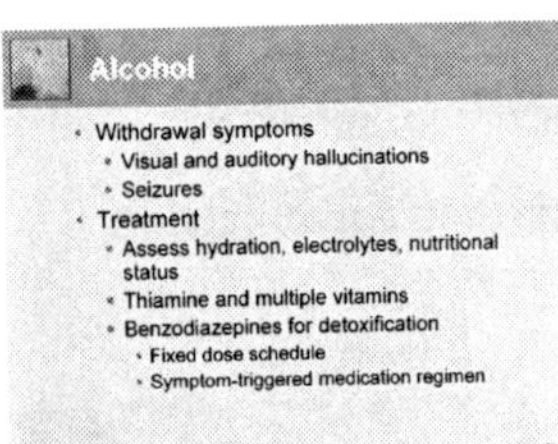
Alcohol
Withdrawal symptoms
Visual and auditory hallucinations
Seizures
Treatment
Assess hydration, electrolytes, nutritional status
Thiamine and multiple vitamins
Benzodiazepines for detoxification
Fixed dose schedule
Symptom-triggered medication regimen

- Alcohol abuse found in all socioeconomic levels. Denial of the problem is a common characteristic.

Slide 15

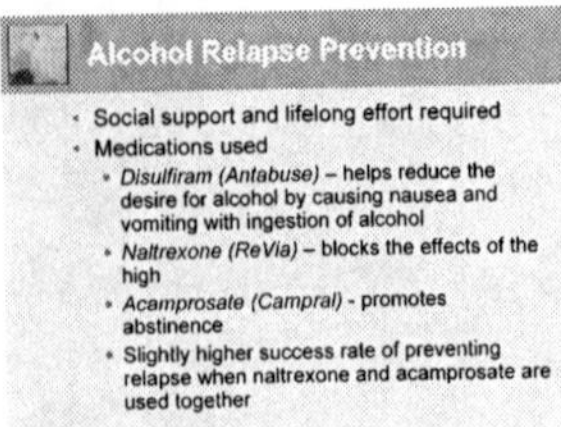
Alcohol Relapse Prevention
Social support and lifelong effort required
Medications used
Disulfiram (Antabuse) – helps reduce the desire for alcohol by causing nausea and vomiting with ingestion of alcohol
Naltrexone (ReVia) – blocks the effects of the high
Acamprosate (Campral) - promotes abstinence
Slightly higher success rate of preventing relapse when naltrexone and acamprosate are used together

- Treatment includes total abstinence.
- Supportive counseling, support for family.

ELSEVIER

Slide 16

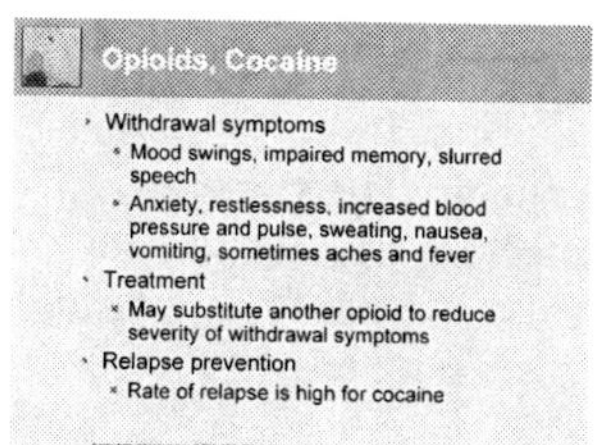
Opioids, Cocaine
Withdrawal symptoms
Mood swings, impaired memory, slurred speech
Anxiety, restlessness, increased blood pressure and pulse, sweating, nausea, vomiting, sometimes aches and fever
Treatment
May substitute another opioid to reduce severity of withdrawal symptoms
Relapse prevention
Rate of relapse is high for cocaine

- Withdrawal from opioids very uncomfortable, but not life-threatening.
- No medicines are approved to treat cocaine dependence; two areas under investigation for treatment include vaccines and maintenance drugs.

Slide 17

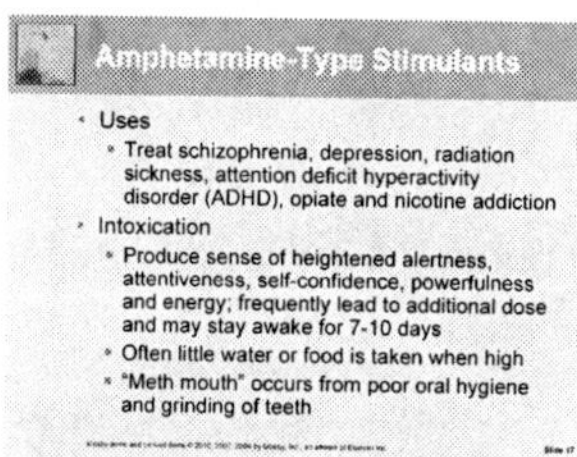
Amphetamine-Type Stimulants
Uses
Treat schizophrenia, depression, radiation sickness, attention deficit hyperactivity disorder (ADHD), opiate and nicotine addiction
Intoxication
Produce sense of heightened alertness, attentiveness, self-confidence, powerfulness and energy; frequently lead to additional dose and may stay awake for 7-10 days
Often little water or food is taken when high
"Meth mouth" occurs from poor oral hygiene and grinding of teeth

- Methamphetamine is the second most abused illicit substance after marijuana.
- Rehydration is often necessary for these patients who have not had water or food while on a high.
- Withdrawal from methamphetamine is more prolonged than cocaine, and patients must be monitored for suicidal ideation.

Slide 18

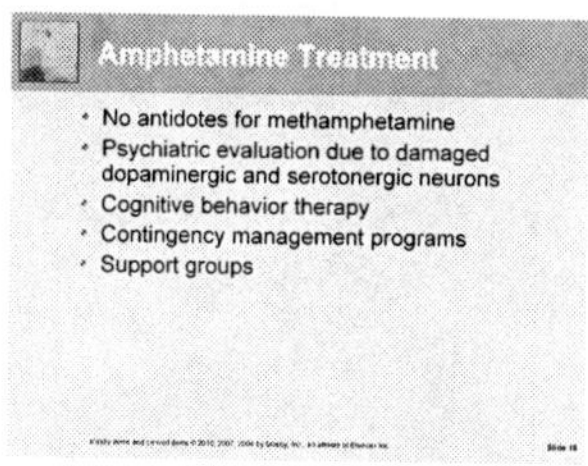
Amphetamine Treatment
No antidotes for methamphetamine
Psychiatric evaluation due to damaged dopaminergic and serotonergic neurons
Cognitive behavior therapy
Contingency management programs
Support groups

ELSEVIER

Lesson Plan

50 Miscellaneous Agents

TEACHING FOCUS

In this chapter, the student will be introduced to topics related to miscellaneous agents. The student will become acquainted with the actions, uses, therapeutic outcomes, and nursing processes associated with allopurinol, colchicine, disulfiram, lactulose, probenecid, and tacrine. The student will have the opportunity to put this information into context by participating in classroom activities and discussions.

MATERIALS AND RESOURCES

- ☐ computer and PowerPoint projector (all Lessons)

LESSON CHECKLIST

Preparations for this lesson include:

- lecture
- guest speaker: licensed practical nurse
- evaluation of student knowledge and skills needed to perform all entry-level nursing activities related to principles underlying miscellaneous agents, including:
- acamprosate
  - allopurinol
  - colchicine
- disulfiram
- donepezil
- lactulose
- memantine
  - probenecid
  - tacrine

ADDITIONAL RESOURCES

PowerPoint slides: 1-12
Flashcards, Decks 1 and 2

Legend

ARQ	PPT	TB	CTQ	SG	INRQ
Audience Response Questions	PowerPoint Slides	Test Bank	Critical Thinking Questions	Study Guide	Interactive NCLEX Review Questions

Class Activities are indicated in ***bold italic.***

LESSON 50.1

BACKGROUND ASSESSMENT

Question: What should nurses know about disulfiram?
Answer: It is used for patients who want to stay sober and are in an alcoholic treatment program. It should be used only in conjunction with other rehabilitation therapy. Patients must not drink or apply alcohol in any form during treatment with disulfiram and must be fully informed of the consequences of drinking alcohol while taking this therapy. This includes dietary sources and over-the-counter products. Even small amounts of alcohol can cause a reaction. The intensity of the reaction can be different for each individual, but it is generally proportional to the amount of disulfiram and alcohol ingested. Disulfiram is slowly absorbed from

the gastrointestinal tract and is slowly eliminated from the body. The drug is not a cure for alcoholism. It is not known whether disulfiram can cause fetal harm when administered during pregnancy.

Question: What should a nurse know about tacrine (Cognex) before administering it?
Answer: It is used to treat Alzheimer's disease, but will not cure it. It improves cognitive ability in some patients with the disease. Tacrine can cause liver problems, and regular blood tests must be done. Studies on effects in pregnancy have not been done in humans or animals, and it is not known if it passes through to breast milk. It is important to know whether the patient is smoking tobacco and what other medications the patient is taking, especially cimetidine (Tagamet), inflammation or pain medications, neuromuscular blocking agents, and theophylline. The following medical problems may affect the use of tacrine: asthma, heart problems, liver disease, Parkinson's disease, stomach ulcers, urinary tract blockage, brain disease, seizures, and head injury. The drug is best taken on an empty stomach and works best when taken at regular intervals. Adverse effects include dizziness and unsteadiness.

CRITICAL THINKING QUESTION

A 65-year-old patient has been ordered disulfiram as part of an alcohol rehabilitation program. After reading his history and physical, the nurse notes that the patient is also taking warfarin (Coumadin) and phenytoin (Dilantin). What is the significance of these drugs?
Guidelines: The nurse should note that the patient is taking warfarin for a previous diagnosis of cerebrovascular accident (CVA) and phenytoin for seizures. Because disulfiram could enhance the anticoagulant effect of warfarin, the nurse must observe the patient for petechiae, ecchymoses, nosebleeds, bleeding gums, dark tarry stools, and bright red or coffee ground emesis. The health care provider must be notified, and the dosage of warfarin may have to be adjusted. The prothrombin time (PT) and international normalized ratio (INR) should also be monitored. Disulfiram slows the metabolism of phenytoin. Patients must be monitored for signs of phenytoin toxicity. Serum blood levels of phenytoin must be monitored, and dosage may have to be adjusted. The health care provider must be notified.

OBJECTIVES	CONTENT	TEACHING RESOURCES
Describe the actions, uses, therapeutic outcomes, and nursing process associated with acamprosate and allopurinol.	■ Miscellaneous agents (p. 842) □ Acamprosate (p. 842) – Nursing process for acamprosate (p. 842) □ Allopurinol (p. 843) – Nursing process for allopurinol (p. 843) Review miscellaneous agents as those drugs that do not fall under any classification, have unknown mechanisms of action, or are the only drug of their type. Review acamprosate (Campral) as an agent used in alcohol rehabilitation programs. Discuss the actions, uses, and therapeutic outcomes, as well as common and serious adverse effects for acamprosate. Review allopurinol (Zyloprim) as an antigout medication. Discuss the	PPT 4-5 ARQ 5 TB Multiple Choice questions 1, 8-9 INRQ 2-3 SG Review Sheet questions 1-4 (p. 341) SG Learning Activities questions 9-10, 16, 18 (p. 343) Review Questions for the NCLEX Examination 2-3, 7 (p. 850) ▸ Discuss the nursing process for acamprosate and allopurinol. Discuss important items to cover during the premedication assessment. Note common and serious adverse effects and drug interactions. Class Activity ***Divide the class into four groups, and assign each group one of the following related to allopurinol: actions, uses, outcomes, or nursing process. Have the groups discuss their topics and present their findings to the class. Does this drug treat or prevent a gout attack?***

OBJECTIVES	CONTENT	TEACHING RESOURCES
	actions, uses, and therapeutic outcomes, as well as common and serious adverse effects for allopurinol. Review known drug interactions.	Class Activity ***List on the board the following miscellaneous agents: acamprosate, allopurinol, colchicine, disulfiram, donepezil, lactulose, memantine, probenecid, and tacrine. Have students match each drug to one of the following categories: alcohol rehabilitation, Alzheimer's, ammonia reducer, and uric acid reducer. Review the exercise with the class.***
Describe the actions, uses, therapeutic outcomes, and nursing process associated with colchicine.	□ Colchicine (p. 844) – Nursing process for colchicine (p. 844) Review colchicine as an antigout medication. Discuss the actions, uses, and therapeutic outcomes, as well as common and serious adverse effects for colchicine.	PPT 6 ARQ 3 TB Multiple Choice questions 4, 11 TB Multiple Response question 1 INRQ 1 SG Review Sheet questions 5-7 (p. 341) SG Learning Activities question 5 (p. 343) SG Practice Questions for the NCLEX Examination 6, 8 (pp. 344-345) ▸ Discuss colchicine. Explain its actions, uses, and therapeutic outcomes. Class Activity ***Divide the class into four groups, and have each group discuss the nursing process for colchicines, including important items to cover during the premedication assessment, adverse effects, and drug interactions. Then have each group present its findings to the class. Does this drug treat or prevent a gout attack?***
Describe the actions, uses, therapeutic outcomes, and nursing process associated with disulfiram and donepezil.	□ Disulfiram (p. 844) – Nursing process for disulfiram (p. 845) □ Donepezil (p. 846) – Nursing process for donepezil (p. 846) Review disulfiram (Antabuse) as an agent used in alcohol rehabilitation programs. Discuss the actions, uses, and therapeutic outcomes, as well as common and serious adverse effects for disulfiram. Review known drug interactions.	PPT 7-8 ARQ 1 TB Multiple Choice questions 5-6 TB Multiple Response question 2 INRQ 4, 9 SG Review Sheet questions 8-11 (pp. 341-342) SG Learning Activities questions 8, 11, 17 (p. 343) SG Practice Questions for the NCLEX Examination 5, 7, 9 (pp. 344-345) Review Questions for the NCLEX Examination 4-5 (p. 850)

OBJECTIVES	CONTENT	TEACHING RESOURCES
	Review donepezil (Aricept) as an agent used to treat Alzheimer's disease. Discuss the actions, uses, and therapeutic outcomes, as well as common and serious adverse effects for donepezil. Review known drug interactions.	▸ Discuss the need for cautious use of disulfiram in patients with conditions such as diabetes mellitus, hypothyroidism, epilepsy, cerebral damage, chronic or acute nephritis, hepatic cirrhosis, or hepatic failure. ▸ Discuss the nursing process for disulfiram, especially the symptoms of hepatotoxicity. ▸ Discuss the nursing process for donepezil. Class Activity ***Divide the class into four groups, and assign each group one of the following related to disulfiram: actions, uses, outcomes, or nursing process. Have each group discuss its topic, and then present its findings to the class.*** Class Activity ***Outside of class time, have students review items they commonly use for hygiene, noting the presence of alcohol in the products. Discuss the findings in class.*** Class Activity ***Divide students into pairs, and have each pair complete a patient-caregiver education plan for donepezil. Education should include the following considerations: administration, common and serious adverse effects, and drug interactions. Allow class time for discussion.***
Describe the actions, uses, therapeutic outcomes, and nursing process associated with lactulose and memantine.	□ Lactulose (p. 847) – Nursing process for lactulose (p. 847) □ Memantine (p. 847) – Nursing process for memantine (p. 848) Review lactulose (Cephulac) as an agent used to decrease ammonia levels. Discuss the actions, uses, and therapeutic outcomes, as well as common and serious adverse effects for lactulose. Review known drug interactions. Review memantine (Namenda) as an agent used to treat Alzheimer's disease. Discuss the actions, uses, and therapeutic outcomes, as well as common and serious adverse effects for memantine. Review known drug interactions.	PPT 9-10 ARQ 2 TB Multiple Choice questions 2, 10, 12 TB Multiple Response question 4 INRQ 5-6 SG Review Sheet questions 12-15 (p. 342) SG Learning Activities questions 2, 7, 12, 15 (p. 343) SG Practice Questions for the NCLEX Examination 3-4, 10 (pp. 344-345) Review Questions for the NCLEX Examination 1, 6 (p. 850) ▸ Discuss the need for cautious use of lactulose in patients with diabetes mellitus. ▸ Discuss the important items related to lactulose during the premedication assessment, noting common and serious adverse effects and drug interactions.

OBJECTIVES	CONTENT	TEACHING RESOURCES
		▸ Discuss the nursing process for lactulose. Note the signs of electrolyte and fluid imbalance. ▸ Discuss the nursing process and clinical indications for memantine. Class Activity ***Divide the class into student pairs, and have them take turns teaching each other about actions, uses, outcomes, and nursing process related to lactulose.*** Class Activity ***Have students research Alzheimer's disease, including clinical symptoms, treatment, and caregiver considerations. Allow class time for student presentation.***
Describe the actions, uses, therapeutic outcomes, and nursing process associated with probenecid.	□ Probenecid (p. 848) – Nursing process for probenecid (p. 848) Review probenecid as an antigout agent. Discuss the actions, uses, and therapeutic outcomes, as well as common and serious adverse effects for probenecid. Review known drug interactions.	PPT 11 ARQ 4 TB Multiple Choice question 3 INRQ 7 SG Review Sheet questions 16-17 (p. 342) SG Learning Activities question 14 (p. 343) SG Practice Question for the NCLEX Examination 2 (p. 344) Review Question for the NCLEX Examination 8 (p. 850) ▸ Discuss the actions, uses, and therapeutic outcomes related to probenecid. ▸ Discuss the nursing process for probenecid. Discuss important items to cover during the premedication assessment. Note common and serious adverse effects and drug interactions. Class Activity ***Divide the class into small groups. Have each group design a nursing care plan for a patient prescribed probenecid for chronic gouty arthritis. Then have each group present its plan to the class for feedback.***
Describe the actions, uses, therapeutic outcomes, and nursing process associated with tacrine.	□ Tacrine (p. 849) – Nursing process for tacrine (p. 849) Review tacrine (Cognex) as an agent used to treat Alzheimer's disease. Discuss the actions, uses, and therapeutic outcomes, as well as common and serious adverse	PPT 12 TB Multiple Choice questions 7, 13 TB Multiple Response question 3 INRQ 8 SG Review Sheet questions 18-19 (p. 342) SG Learning Activities questions 1, 3-4, 6, 13 (p. 343)

OBJECTIVES	CONTENT	TEACHING RESOURCES
	effects for tacrine. Review known drug interactions.	SG Practice Question for the NCLEX Examination 1 (p. 344) ▸ Discuss the important items to cover during the premedication assessment for a patient with Alzheimer's disease. Note the common and serious adverse effects and drug interactions. Class Activity ***Have two students role-play the nurse instructing a family member of a patient receiving tacrine for Alzheimer's. Have the class assist the "nurse" with what needs to be reviewed for patient teaching. Review the exercise with the class.***
Performance evaluation		Test Bank SG Learning Activities (p. 343) SG Practice Questions for the NCLEX Examination (pp. 344-345)

50.1 Homework/Assignments:

50.1 Instructor's Notes/Student Feedback:

50 Lecture Outline
Miscellaneous Agents

Slide 1

Chapter 50
Miscellaneous Agents

Slide 2

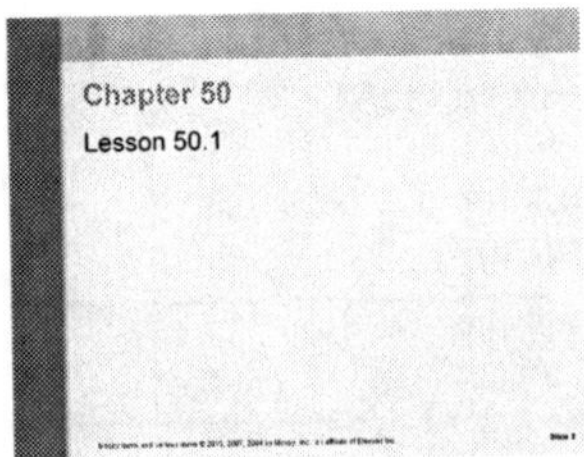
Chapter 50
Lesson 50.1

Slide 3

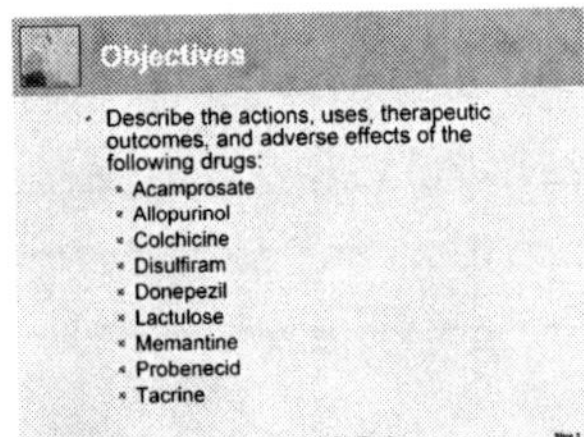
Objectives
Describe the actions, uses, therapeutic outcomes, and adverse effects of the following drugs:
Acamprosate
Allopurinol
Colchicine
Disulfiram
Donepezil
Lactulose
Memantine
Probenecid
Tacrine

Slide 4

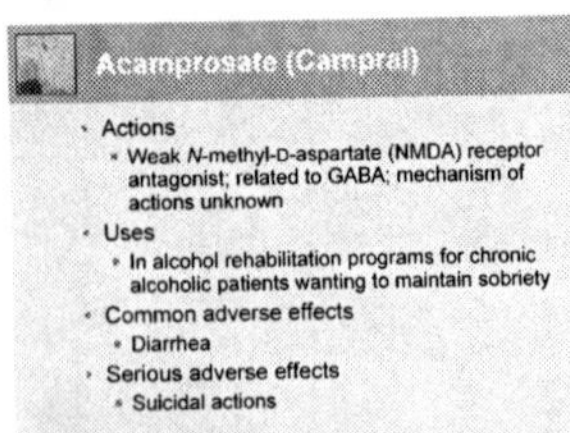
Acamprosate (Campral)
Actions
Weak N-methyl-D-aspartate (NMDA) receptor antagonist; related to GABA; mechanism of actions unknown
Uses
In alcohol rehabilitation programs for chronic alcoholic patients wanting to maintain sobriety
Common adverse effects
Diarrhea
Serious adverse effects
Suicidal actions

- Should be used only in conjunction with other rehabilitative therapy; it does not treat withdrawal symptoms.
- No clinically significant drug interactions have been reported.

Slide 5

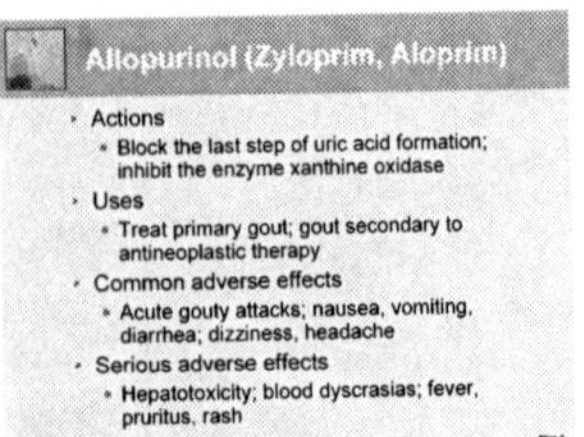
Allopurinol (Zyloprim, Aloprim)
Actions
Block the last step of uric acid formation; inhibit the enzyme xanthine oxidase
Uses
Treat primary gout; gout secondary to antineoplastic therapy
Common adverse effects
Acute gouty attacks; nausea, vomiting, diarrhea; dizziness, headache
Serious adverse effects
Hepatotoxicity; blood dyscrasias; fever, pruritus, rash

- Not effective in treating acute attacks of gouty arthritis.

ELSEVIER

Slide 6

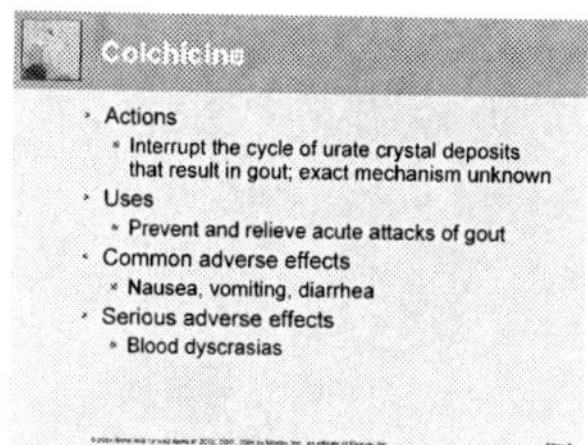
Colchicine
Actions
Interrupt the cycle of urate crystal deposits that result in gout; exact mechanism unknown
Uses
Prevent and relieve acute attacks of gout
Common adverse effects
Nausea, vomiting, diarrhea
Serious adverse effects
Blood dyscrasias

- Does not affect the amount of uric acid in blood or urine.
- Never administer IM or subcutaneously. Watch for extravasation if given IV.
- Discontinue medication if GI symptoms develop.

Slide 7

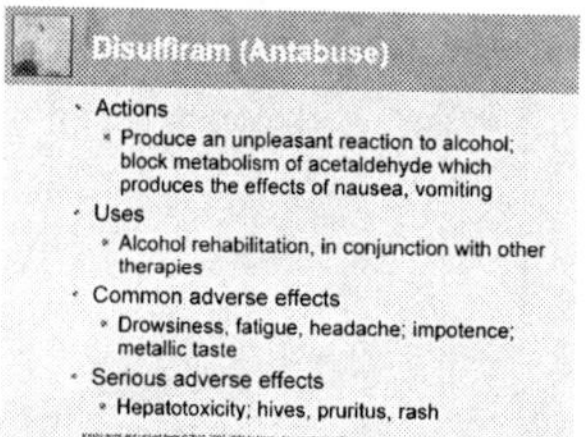
Disulfiram (Antabuse)
Actions
Produce an unpleasant reaction to alcohol; block metabolism of acetaldehyde which produces the effects of nausea, vomiting
Uses
Alcohol rehabilitation, in conjunction with other therapies
Common adverse effects
Drowsiness, fatigue, headache; impotence; metallic taste
Serious adverse effects
Hepatotoxicity; hives, pruritus, rash

- Warn patients to not drink alcohol or apply alcohol in any form. To administer, patient must have abstained from alcohol for at least 12 hours.
- Encourage patient not to discontinue therapy.
- Never give to a patient who is intoxicated.

Slide 8

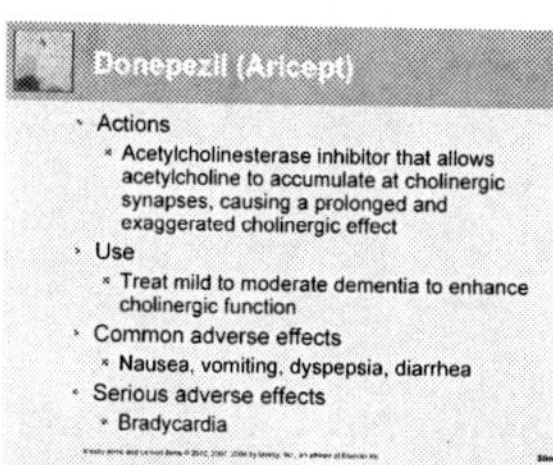
Donepezil (Aricept)
Actions
Acetylcholinesterase inhibitor that allows acetylcholine to accumulate at cholinergic synapses, causing a prolonged and exaggerated cholinergic effect
Use
Treat mild to moderate dementia to enhance cholinergic function
Common adverse effects
Nausea, vomiting, dyspepsia, diarrhea
Serious adverse effects
Bradycardia

- Drug's function diminishes with ongoing loss of cholinergic neurons.
- Does not prevent or slow the neurodegeneration of Alzheimer's disease.

Slide 9

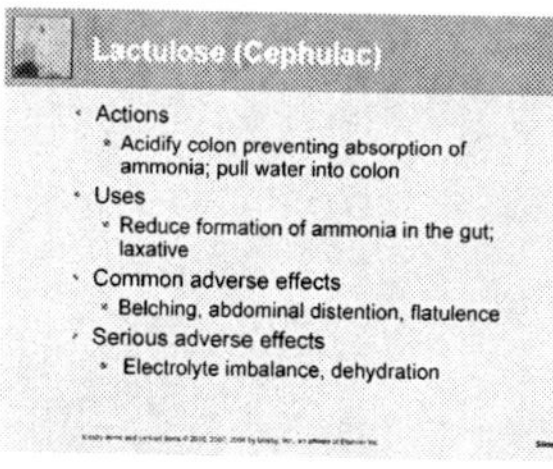
Lactulose (Cephulac)
Actions
Acidify colon preventing absorption of ammonia; pull water into colon
Uses
Reduce formation of ammonia in the gut; laxative
Common adverse effects
Belching, abdominal distention, flatulence
Serious adverse effects
Electrolyte imbalance, dehydration

- Use with caution in patients with diabetes.
- Hypokalemia is most likely to occur.

Slide 10

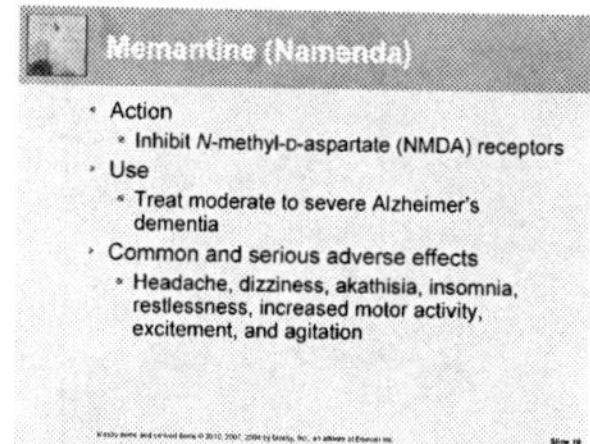
Memantine (Namenda)
Action
Inhibit N-methyl-D-aspartate (NMDA) receptors
Use
Treat moderate to severe Alzheimer's dementia
Common and serious adverse effects
Headache, dizziness, akathisia, insomnia, restlessness, increased motor activity, excitement, and agitation

- Patients show improvement in cognitive function and behavioral symptoms and a slower decline in activities of daily living, but memantine does not prevent or slow the neurodegeneration of Alzheimer's disease.

ELSEVIER

Slide 11

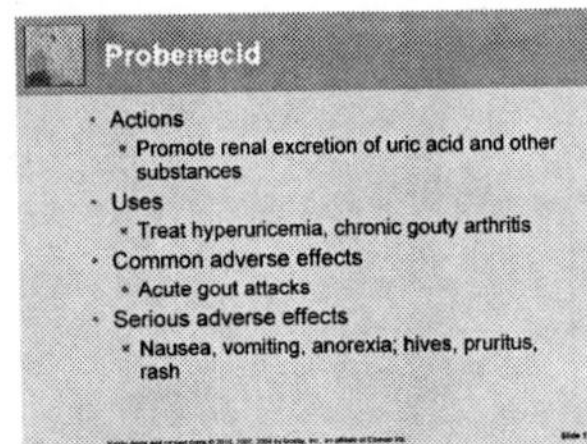
Probenecid
Actions
Promote renal excretion of uric acid and other substances
Uses
Treat hyperuricemia, chronic gouty arthritis
Common adverse effects
Acute gout attacks
Serious adverse effects
Nausea, vomiting, anorexia; hives, pruritus, rash

- Not effective in acute gouty attacks.
- Patient should be encouraged to continue therapy even though gout attacks may increase for first few months of therapy.

Slide 12

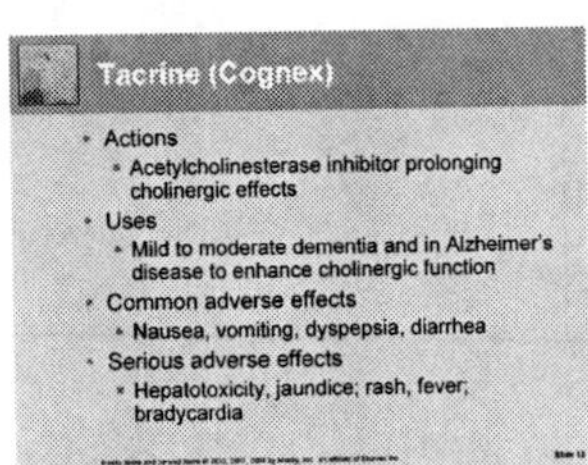
Tacrine (Cognex)
Actions
Acetylcholinesterase inhibitor prolonging cholinergic effects
Uses
Mild to moderate dementia and in Alzheimer's disease to enhance cholinergic function
Common adverse effects
Nausea, vomiting, dyspepsia, diarrhea
Serious adverse effects
Hepatotoxicity, jaundice; rash, fever; bradycardia

- May have to reduce dose with GI adverse effects.
- Routine laboratory tests are extremely important.